CHRISTOLOGY

OF

THE OLD TESTAMENT

CHRISTOLOGY

OF

THE OLD TESTAMENT

and a

Commentary on the Messianic Predictions

BY

E. W. HENGSTENBERG, D.D.

Foreword by

WALTER C. KAISER, JR.

KREGEL PUBLICATIONS
GRAND RAPIDS, MICHIGAN 49501

Library of Congress Catalog Card Number 77-129739
ISBN 0-8254-2812-2

First American edition . . . 1970
This reprint edition is an abridgment by
Thomas Kerchever Arnold of the transla-
tion from the German of Dr. Reuel Keith.
Reproduced from the *Francis and John
Rivington* edition, London, 1847.

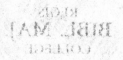

CONTENTS

GENERAL INTRODUCTION

THE MESSIANIC PROPHECIES OF
ISAIAH

CONTENTS

THE PROPHET
AMOS

THE PROPHET
MICAH

THE PROPHET
HAGGAI

THE PROPHET
MALACHI

THE PROPHET
JEREMIAH

THE PROPHET
EZEKIEL

FOREWORD

One century has now elapsed since the death of one of the greatest defenders of orthodoxy: Ernst Wilhelm Hengstenberg (1802-1869). This man, more than many others of his day or ours epitomized that wonderful combination of an earnest Christian experience and thorough Biblical scholarship. Included in his preserved last words were "No orthodoxy without pietism, no piety without orthodoxy."

Thus this German Lutheran Biblical scholar and editor unwittingly summarized his own life and works. After he was born in Fröndenberg where his ancestors had lived and left major marks on the political and ecclesiastical annals from the fourteenth century downwards, E. W. Hengstenberg was at first severely limited by lameness and poor health in general. Although he was not permitted to read until he was seven years old, once he began he avidly poured over his books daily from five or six o'clock each morning until eight o'clock in the evening with only a three hour intermission.

Evidence of the classical education his father gave him began to appear as he reached his seventeenth birthday when he sold a translation of the Latin author Aurelius Victor to a publisher who was unaware that their translator was only a teenager. Before he reached his twentieth birthday, he had also completed a translation of Aristotle's *Metaphysics*.

Even before he came to personal faith in Jesus Christ, his instincts, desires, and judgments were being shaped by the subjects he studied and the books he read. His proclivity for the Old Testament and Semitic philology were demonstrated in the dissertation which he submitted for the Doctor of Laws degree. It was a Latin translation and notes of the Arabic author Amrulkeisi Moallakah. Likewise, his leanings towards orthodoxy were also marked by his candid response to a new work which was sweeping Germany and already marking a new era: Schleiermacher's *Glaubenslehre*. While appreciating the depth of insight in Schleiermacher, he nevertheless did not become infected by the shallowness of its argument, for he said, "I shall not remain what I am; if indeed I did so, I should never be a theologian; but to that man I shall never betake myself."

On the basis of his work in semitic languages at Bonn, he was recommended to a teaching post in Eastern languages at Bâsle Missionary College. There he experienced his conversion and "found the pearl of great price" which he had not found while "seeking goodly pearls" at Bonn.

In the meantime, he had obtained a Doctor of Divinity degree at Tübingen and at the age of 26 he was named ordinary Professor of Theology at the University of Berlin. Just one year before this honor was bestowed upon him, he became the founder in 1827, and for 42 succeeding years, the editor and chief contributer of the *Evangelische Kirchen-Zeitung*, a bi-weekly journal issued on behalf of Lutheran orthodoxy. This paper relentlessly pursued all forms of Rationalism and heresy but fearlessly asserted the neglected truths of orthodoxy to a modern age.

The real impact of Hengstenberg, however, comes from his writings and the most important, influential and ablest work he produced was *The Christology of the Old Testament*. In this work, the reader will see Hengstenberg as the expositor, philologist, and devout Christian who finds in the Old Testament what those disciples on the road to Emmaus missed because they were so foolish and "slow of heart" (Lk. 24:25-27). Christ is identified as the center of the Old Testament revelation and herein lies the majesty and greatness of this work. Nearly everyone will be delighted with the abundance of material already encompassed in this work which exhibits an excellent control of the tools of philology and exegesis. Its very survival and present usefulness is a strong testimony to its intrinsic worth.

The Christology of The Old Testament began to appear in 1828, the same year Hengstenberg attained full professorship at the University of Berlin and was completed in 1835. A second edition appeared in 1854-1857. The present abridged edition preserves every important passage in the four volume set except the Angel of the Lord discussion and the important II Samuel 7 text. Indeed in almost every instance, up to one-half of the original discussion of every important passage has been captured in this brilliant abridgement by T. K. Arnold.

Hengstenberg's other literary attainments may now be briefly surveyed. Several learned essays were collected and published in 1831-39 under the modest German title: *Contributions Toward the Introduction to the Old Testament*. These essays were separated and published in English during 1847 and 1848 under the titles *Dissertations on the Genuineness of the Pentateuch* and *Dissertations on the Genuineness of Daniel and the Integrity of Zechariah.* His now famous and much appreciated *Commentary on the Psalms* first appeared in 1842-1845 and a second edition in 1849-1852 (English edition 1844-1848).

The work Hengstenberg hoped would be his best turned out to be the one that earned him the most grief because of his exposition of Mary Magdalene's conversion and the statement "for she loved much." That work was entitled *The Gospel of John Expounded* (1861-1863). The English translation appeared in 1865.

Also to his credit are *The Prophecies of Ezekiel Expounded* (1867-1868), *A Commentary on Ecclesiastes with Treatises on Song of Solomon, Isaiah,* etc. (English 1869), *Baalam and His Prophecies* (1842), *Commentary on Revelation* and the posthumous publications of *The Book of Job*, and *The History of the Kingdom of God in the Old Testament*.

What a legacy for Hengstenberg to bequeath to succeeding generations and how excellent is the magnification of the One whom he found to be the central person in that Old Testament! May his spiritual descendants follow in his train to the Glory of our Great God and Savior Jesus Christ.

June, 1970

Walter C. Kaiser, Jr.
M.A., Ph.D. Candidate
Assoc. Prof. of Old Testament
Trinity Evangelical Divinity School

PREFACE

I HAVE long been persuaded that the manner in which the so-called *study* of Sacred Prophecy is conducted in England is not only a disgrace to the Clergy, but a grievous injury to the Church; threatening to substitute a wild, superficial, sentimental theology in the place of that sober and severe, that deep and earnest, but lowly wisdom which the formularies of the Church embody, and which, I am sure, the true doctrine of the Cross involves. The loosest reasoning, nay, the mere semblance of the forms of reasoning; the slightest analogy, the most fortuitous coincidences . . . though each rival system can boast of as many and as curious, . . . are now thought sufficient foundations for huge structures, all sure to deceive many by their fair fronts and symmetrical arrangements, and equally sure to fall in a few years for ever.

It appeared to me, when I first became acquainted with Dr. Hengstenberg's Christology, that it was admirably suited to be a *corrective* of our perverse method of dealing with the Prophetical portions of the Word of God. Here we have the pattern of an investigation founded upon distinct principles; of the most scrupulous, laborious, and minute examination of the very letter of the text, combined with an honest endeavour to make the analogy of scripture an important rule of interpretation, and with an anxiety to learn from the text, thus carefully considered, the meaning that it really conveys. The reverential and pious spirit of its author appears on every page ; and I, for my own part, am convinced of the *general* soundness of his principles of prophetic interpretation, which are nearly those of our countryman, John Smith, the friend of Bishop Patrick and Cudworth, as explained in his " Select Discourses," to which Dr. Hengstenberg acknowledges his obligations.

I would earnestly recommend to the reader the important chapter (" On the Nature of Prophecy ") in which these principles are laid down, and the consequences that flow from them carefully deduced : for if this is the *right key* to prophetic interpretation, it is certain that *no other can* unlock its mysteries . . . at least so fully as to open the way for us to an *adequate* (it may be *necessarily* an *imperfect*) understanding of them all.

In the study of the work an English reader will *occasionally* be reminded of the unhappy state of things in Germany, where simple traditional faith can no longer be calculated upon by any author who writes upon sacred subjects for the educated classes. He will here and there be pained by laboured proofs of what it is distressing to see treated as a doubtful point ; but discussions of this kind occur chiefly in the earlier portions of the work : in the later ones, the author himself appears to move with greater confidence, and to assume a less apologetic tone. He has, moreover, seen reason to reject some of his former doubts as unfounded ; especially those which led him, in the present work, to deny the reference of Balaam's prophecy to the Messiah. In an express work upon the History of Balaam, he holds that, though the reference to victories over the Moabites and children of ' Seth' (= *tumult*) proves the Messianic reference to be not *primary* and *absolute*, yet the actual subjugation of the Moabites, for instance, by David, and other victories obtained by kings of Israel over heathen nations, could only be *types* and *preludes* at best of *the* full realization of the *idea* under THE KING OF ISRAEL, whose dominion was to be, not *temporary*, but *eternal :* that what Balaam prophesies of the Israelitish monarchy is too glorious to be confined to any effects that weak man can realize.

With respect to my own share in the present volume, it has merely consisted in an abridgement and occasional correction of the American translation. The original work is the *substance* of Academical Lectures : it consists of three octavo volumes, and, in the present state of Hebrew knowledge in England, could not hope, in its original form, for any considerable number of readers. My endeavour has been to adapt it even for such earnest inquirers as are unacquainted with the language of the Old Testament, but yet to retain enough of the grammatical and philological discussions to excite the Hebrew scholar's desire to possess the original work, and to convince all who read it that the results arrived at are founded upon a minute and careful examination of the original text.

The translation was made in America by Dr. Reuel Keith, and may be obtained, without difficulty, through Messrs. Wiley and Putnam, the American booksellers (Paternoster-row).

The work must have been a very difficult one to translate, and the English as well as the American theological student ought to feel grateful to Dr. Keith for his performance of so laborious a task. Undoubtedly he might, in a second edition, make his version considerably *more idiomatic*, and *here and there* correct a misunderstanding of his author's meaning : but upon the whole he has at least produced a faithful translation. I do not, indeed, pretend to have compared it throughout with the original, but have always had the German work by me to refer to, whenever any obscurity in the version might lead me to suspect an incorrectness.

One fault Dr. Keith has been led into by the over literal translation of the *present tense*, where it is used, by a German idiom, for the *future*. I am sorry that I did not observe this till a great part of the work was printed off; for, as this use is comparatively rare with us, but *extremely common* in German, the literal translation becomes in English an incorrect representation of the original. I must beg the reader to bear this in mind, when he is surprised by the present tense in cases where the English version has the future. I am also sorry that I have not departed from Dr. Keith's practice of using the modern form of the third person singular in the present tense, instead of the older form in *th*.

In conclusion, let me express an earnest wish, that the present work may have the effect, which I think it ought to have, in encouraging amongst us deeper and truer views of the structure and interpretation of Sacred Prophecy.

T. K. A.

CHAPTER I

PRELIMINARY OBSERVATIONS

1. THOUGH man retained, after the fall, some feeble remains of the Divine image, consisting in an obscure consciousness of his original happy condition, and an earnest desire to regain it; yet this was insufficient of itself to effect the great end of his being, a reunion with his Maker. It was of value only as it made him capable of receiving aid from above; it rendered his return to God possible, but could not be its efficient cause. The need of a Divine interposition for the restoration of fallen man, who was no more able of himself to regain his lost communion with God than to establish this communion at first, is evident from experience and observation, which show that he is averse to good, inclined to evil, and incapable of fulfilling by his own strength the demands of the holiness and justice of God. But with respect to the way in which God should interpose, we could determine nothing without experience. As no speculative reason could have decided before the establishment of the Divine Institutions for man's salvation, that they must be precisely what they are; so neither can it now, after their introduction, prove by *a priori* arguments, that the method adopted was alone possible, necessary, and founded in the nature of God. Rather we learn its necessity from the fact of its having been adopted; for God does nothing which is unnecessary, and has not its foundation in his own nature. We learn it from Scripture, which represents the method revealed as necessary, and the only one that was possible. And we learn it in part from our own experience; since the more fully we appropriate to ourselves the means of salvation which God has provided, the more deeply do we feel, not from human reason, but from the witness of the Spirit, that these means, and these only, are efficacious to heal the diseases of our souls.

2. Why the sending of that Divine Redeemer and Restorer, which had been purposed from eternity, did not immediately succeed the fall;—why four thousand years must first elapse, and in the mean time diseased humanity seek in vain to heal itself, in the absence of the divine Physician, who alone could give relief; is a

1

question too profound for human wisdom, which in this life is but fragmentary, and even when it has humbled itself under the mighty hand of God, receives from Him only so much light as it needs for sanctification. From the lateness of his advent we can with certainty conclude no more than this; that, to accomplish what it has accomplished already, and will accomplish hereafter, it could not have happened earlier by a single moment. We can however, with great probability, assign the reason existing in the human race for this delay, if we consider the nature and condition of fallen man, and God's dispensations towards him, from the time of his apostasy to the coming of the Redeemer. We perceive that God could not send his Son into the world till the way was sufficiently prepared for his advent. The design of this preparation could be no other, than to produce, among an important portion of the human race, such a state of things as is requisite in order to the acceptance of the divine aid when proffered. For although man, when he returns to God, has nothing positively good to present to Him, but must receive all from Him; yet he must have a *capacity of receiving* before he can receive. The method by which God *prepared* the heathen nations for this capacity of receiving his grace, was very different from that by which He *elicited* it amongst the Jews.

3. The heathen were in general left to themselves. God suffered the disease which had poisoned their whole nature, to put forth all its power, that when the Physician should appear, they might not deceive themselves respecting their true condition. The fundamental evil of fallen man is pride—the feeling that he possesses powers and advantages, which, even before his apostasy, he enjoyed only in consequence of his fellowship with God. Pride, however, is never more effectually made to feel its weakness, and look beyond itself for aid, than when left to make a trial of its own strength. At the time of the Messiah's advent this trial had been fully made by the most distinguished people of the heathen world. They had already wearied themselves long enough in their own ways, and had learnt by degrees that they could lead to nothing firm and sure. Their religions, the offspring of human invention, had outlived their influence; and the illusion which once blinded the eyes of their votaries, had passed away. In vain were the efforts to restore their ancient authority by new embellishments. It is only the true religion, that carries within itself the principle of a perpetual renovation. The self-made systems of the philosophers had run their course: one had supplanted another, until at last, from their very multiplicity, men had become distrustful of their truth, and of all human science, and longed, though often perhaps unconsciously, for higher certainty. They had seen the instability of all human greatness and glory; that the bloom of nations as well as of individuals faded away; and that even what was most exalted and seemed established for thousands of years, was hastening to its overthrow: they had seen Greece and Rome torn to pieces by assailants from within and from without. Hence arose in the minds of men, an earnest, though indistinct desire to obtain some sure resting-place, some haven of security amidst the storms of time;

something not subject to the constant alternation of growth and decay to fasten themselves to; to be able to labour for objects, which did not contain within themselves the germ of their own destruction. And in a moral point of view also, how easily would history dissipate the proud dreams of the natural man, did he not entirely avoid its light. The attractive garb, which vice had assumed in former times, was laid aside; and it now appeared in its native and hideous deformity. Pretended virtues also were stript of their disguise[1]. And thus an undefinable anxiety was awakened, to be rescued by a higher hand from the power of natural corruption, to be delivered from the enormous coil of the reigning wickedness. This longing after something stable in theory and practice, after redemption from sin and evil, was both brought to distinct consciousness and fully satisfied by the preaching of the gospel of Jesus Christ.

4. We have already said, that a different method was adopted to prepare the Jews for the Redeemer's advent. Among them the preparation was made by a direct influence. It was in the first place the *conditio sine quá non* of the appearing of the messenger, that the knowledge of Him who sent him should not be entirely lost, at least among those in whose country He should manifest Himself at the appointed time. This, however, required an immediate divine interposition; so prone is man, when left to himself, to the senseless worship of idols. God therefore separated from his kindred Abraham, the father of that people among whom the Saviour was to appear; allured him to his service by blessings and promises; and by condescending to his weakness raised him by degrees to Himself. He afterwards pursued the same course, not only towards the immediate descendants of the patriarch, but towards the whole people who derived their origin from him; to whom, besides his general relation to all mankind, He sustained the peculiar relation of their King. He established all their institutions, and made Himself their centre; seeking, in a manner suited to affect their senses, to bind them to Himself, and ensure their fidelity by the law of visible retribution, manifest in all the events of their history; according to which, faithful devotion to his service was rewarded by prosperity, revolt and perfidy punished by adversity. He strengthened their faith by a visible sign of his appearance, and by many wonderful works; He made known to them his will, exhorted, warned, and threatened them by sending continually new ambassadors clothed with his own authority and power. Further, the promulgation of the *Law* was, in the strictest sense, a preparation for the coming of the Redeemer. The moral law is, indeed, imprinted on the heart even of fallen man, and ennobles his corrupt nature. But then he possesses no living principle to bring his sinful inclinations under subjection to this law. The law is dead, while his sinful propensities are full of life. The conflict between conscience and the love of sin is insupportable; and finding it impossible by his own power to secure to himself true peace of mind by the subjugation of the latter, he seeks a false and unsub-

[1] " Certatur ingenti quodam nequitiæ certamine."—Seneca, de Ira. 2. 8.

stantial peace by suppressing the voice of the former. To effect this purpose, he brings down to his own low standard the attributes of God, and the demands of his holy law. But that it might not be in the power of the Hebrews to pursue this course, God gave them an outward revelation of his law. The opposition between the will of God and the will of man was now too obvious to be concealed; and as mere semblance of peace could no longer be maintained, it became necessary that true peace should be sought. ' By the law is the knowledge of sin;' and where this knowledge truly exists, there also is the desire to be freed from sin; or in other words, the felt need of redemption.

5. But though God, in his wisdom and holiness, had purposed that many centuries should elapse between the fall and the redemption of man, yet immediately after the former, and at subsequent periods, He was pleased to declare that great salvation and deliverance from the consequences of the first transgression, which should be accomplished in future times.

6. The knowledge of this original revelation was not entirely lost even among heathen nations. As, on the one hand, the doctrine of a happy primeval condition of mankind was diffused through all antiquity, so that even Voltaire himself[1] is obliged to confess, "that the fall of degenerate man is the foundation of theology among nearly all ancient nations," so, on the other, we meet with hopes more or less definite of a time of restoration[2]. This is particularly the case with the doctrine of the Persians on this subject, whose religion is in general distinguished from that of other nations of antiquity by more worthy conceptions of God, and loftier representations of a future life. The Persians expected that the present course of the world, in which a conflict is carried on between the kingdoms of Ormuzd and Ahriman (producing that strange mixture of physical and moral good and evil which we witness), would be succeeded by a time of restoration, in which Ahriman was to be entirely destroyed; when men should be purified from sin, and enjoy a perfectly happy and peaceful life on the glorified earth. An important passage on this subject is found in Plutarch[3]: "Ormuzd, born of the purest light, and Ahriman, the offspring of darkness, fight against each other. But a predestinated time will come, when Ahriman, after having filled the earth with famine and pestilence, shall thereby be entirely destroyed and extirpated. Then shall the earth be smooth and level; all men shall be happy, speak but one language, and be united in the same mode of life and the same political condition. But Theopompus says, that, according to the doctrine of the Magi, these two gods are alternately to triumph and to be subdued, each for three thousand years, and that during the next three thousand years they will mutually contend, and the one will make war upon the other and

---

[1] In his Philosophy of History.

[2] It is true that several of the Fathers, and especially Clement of Alexandria, have considerably exaggerated this fact, from a mistaken desire to render the Christian religion acceptable to the heathen.

[3] De Iside et Osiride, c. 47.

destroy what he had accomplished. But finally, the god of the lower world, Ahriman, shall be entirely vanquished. Men will then be happy ; they will need no more nourishment, and cast no more shadows[1]." We find in the Zend books and the Bundehesch a similar representation of the happiness of mankind after the renovation of the earth, which is to take place when the world shall have existed twelve thousand years. " Then there will be no night, no cold nor hot wind, no corruption, no fear of death, no evil caused by Dews[2] ; and then the fiend, the ambitious prince, shall exalt him no more[3]." If, however, there existed only such passages as these, it might appear probable that this expectation was of human origin ; but we see it in other instances connected with the appearance of a person of more than human power and dignity[4]. We introduce here, in the first place, a passage from the Schahristani[5]. " Zoroaster relates in the book of Zendavesta, that in the last time a man shall appear named Oschanderbega, that is, Man of the World. He will adorn the world with religion and righteousness. During his time Peetiarch also will appear, and greatly injure the interests of his kingdom for twenty years. Afterwards Osiderbega will manifest himself to the inhabitants of the world, promote righteousness, destroy iniquity, and restore the ancient order of things. Kings shall obey him, and all his undertakings shall prosper. He will give the victory to true religion. In his times, rest and peace shall prevail, all dissensions cease, and all grievancy be done away." Here, therefore, we find two persons united in the restoration, Oschanderbega and Osiderbega.

7. Similar to this is the statement which Tavernier received from a Persian priest, mentioned in his Travels[6]. According to this statement the restoration is to be effected by three miraculously begotten persons, the last of whom, Sennoïethotius, will be the most illustrious, and will convert all. Under him the General Resurrection and the Judgment will take place. Then the kingdom of darkness shall be entirely subverted, the hills shall be made low, &c.—We find also a threefold person even in the Zendavesta and Bundehesch. The three prophets were named Oschederbami, Oschedermah, and Sosiosch, and their origin is derived in a wonderful manner immediately from Zoroaster. In the last times,

---

[1] See the Commentary on this passage by Anquetil du Perron, in Kleuker's Zendavesta, Anh. 1. p. 127—144.

[2] Evil Spirits. [3] Anq. du Perron, l. c. p. 138.

[4] We do not here appeal to the doubtful testimony of Abulfaradsch, who (in his Historia Dynastiarum, p. 54,) asserts that Zoroaster taught, that in the last times a virgin should miraculously conceive, and at the birth of her child a star should appear in the day-time with the sign of the virgin in the centre, and at its appearance the disciples should go to worship the child and offer him their gifts. It is the Word which established the heavens.—It is easy to see that this relation is not strictly true. It may, however, be shown by other and unexceptionable testimony, that it is not a mere fabrication, but rests on historical grounds.

[5] See Hyde : De Relig. Vet. Pers. p. 388, ed. 2.

[6] See Reisebeschreibung, 4. 8. t. 1. p. 181 of the Germ. Trans., and also in the Appendix to Hyde, l. c.

after the earth shall have been afflicted with evil of every kind, plague, pestilence, hail, famine, and war, Oschederbami and Oschedermah first appear with great and supernatural powers, and effect the conversion of a large portion of mankind. At last Sosiosch, the greatest of the three, makes his appearance. Under him follows the Resurrection. He will judge the living and the dead, give new glory to the earth, and remove from a world of sorrows the germ of evil [1]. "Paris and all her plots shall be defeated by him whose origin is the fountain, by the victorious hero Sosiosch, who shall be born of the water of Kanse; by Oschederbami and Oschedermah, who shall come forth from the ground [2]." " After that Sosiosch will restore the dead to life, by that which comes forth from a bull and a white *hom*. Sosiosch will give all men this liquor to drink; they shall be great and incorruptible as long as being endures. All the dead as they had died, great or small, shall drink thereof and live again. And finally, at the command of the righteous judge Ormuzd, Sosiosch will, from an elevated place, render to all men what their deeds deserve. The dwelling of the pure will be the splendid Gorotmann. Ormuzd himself will take their bodies to his presence on high [3]." If we leave out of view the division of that among three persons which belongs only to one (analogous to which is the notion of two Messiahs among the later Jews and the Samaritans), we shall not fail to perceive the coincidence of this expectation with the prophecies of the Old Testament, and the fulfilment; and shall not be disposed to ascribe it to any mere human origin.—Among the Greeks such expectations were far more rare, indefinite, and general. It is, however, erroneous to assert, as has been done, that they were strangers to these hopes, and possessed only the tradition of an *ancient* golden age [4]. Hesiod expected the *return* of a better time :

> " O would that I, ere this fifth age began,
> Had died, or were *hereafter to be born* [5] !
> For this the iron age :—
> But as the former ages of mankind
> Jove has destroyed, *so this shall he destroy.*"

Among the Platonic and Stoic philosophers this expectation afterwards gave rise to the doctrine concerning the ' Great Year' of the world, or that period when, with the same position of the stars and planets in the heavens, all things will return to their original condition, and to the same course of events [6]. More definite expectations seem to have existed among the Romans, but upon a close examination it becomes exceedingly doubtful whether they were derived from an original revelation. No evidence of this is afforded by the two well known passages, viz. that of Suetonius: " There had prevailed throughout the whole eastern world an old and constant opinion, that

---

[1] Zendav. Vendidad, 19. 2. 375.　　　　[2] Bundehesch, 31, Th. 3. p. 111.
[3] See Kleuker's Zendavesta, Th. 3. p. 30; Angh. Th. 1. p. 281, seq.
[4] Tholuck, l. c. p. 274.　　　[5] ἢ ἔπειτα γενέσθαι. Works and Days, 171.
[6] See Heyne's Virgil, t. 1. p. 96, ed. a. 1800.

a people were at that time to go forth from Judæa, and obtain supreme power;" and that of Tacitus, " Many persons entertained the persuasion, that it was contained in the old books of the priests; that at that very time the East should grow strong[1]." It is true that Kaiser[2] has recently asserted, that the notions of the Messiah, which, according to these passages, were current among the Romans, were derived from the East and from the Sibylline books; appealing, in support of his opinion, with regard to the first, to the expression, " an old and constant opinion throughout the whole East," and with regard to the second, to the expression, " that it was contained in the old books of the priests." But still the Jewish origin of these ideas, which is obvious, and confirmed by Josephus[3], is not by any means excluded by these expressions. With respect to the first, the dispersion of the Jews after the Babylonish exile must have made their religious opinions in general, and especially their hopes respecting the Messiah, known beyond the boundaries of Judæa, and have secured for them an unobserved entrance; and as to the second, it is well known, that it was not the Christians, but before them the Jews, who first put into the mouths of the Sibyls expectations of a Messiah, in spurious predictions after the true Sibylline prophecies were lost.

8. An appeal is also made in favour of the existence of the Messianic predictions in the Sibylline books of the Romans to another apparently important testimony, the Fourth Eclogue of Virgil, composed in honour of the consul Pollio. In this poem Virgil announces that

> " Now the last age of the Cumæan song
> Is come[4]"—

declaring that during the consulship of Pollio, with the birth of the expected child, the golden age will return. But, (1) it is nevertheless very uncertain whether Virgil really alluded to a prediction of the Cumæan Sibyl. Boecler, Fabricius, and Eckhard have suggested, that he refers to the poem of Hesiod, who was born at Cumæ, and whose poem therefore might as well be called Cumæan, as Ascræan, from the place of his later abode. Perhaps the poet may have intentionally employed the former name, to indicate, that, like a Sibyl, Hesiod had prophesied of future times.—This supposition, that Virgil alludes to Hesiod, is confirmed by the close resemblance of their imagery, the former describing the golden age to come, and the latter that which was past; and this may the more readily be allowed, since Hesiod, as we have seen, expected this period to return.

9. (2) But granting that Virgil referred to the Cumæan Sibyl, he could not have had in view the ancient and genuine Sibylline predictions. These had long before been burnt with the Capitol. The

---

[1] " Percrebuerat oriente toto vetus et constans opinio esse in fatis, ut eo tempore Judæâ profecti rerum potirentur." Vita Vespasiani, c. 4. " Pluribus persuasio inerat, antiquis sacerdotum literis contineri, eo ipso tempore fore ut valesceret oriens." Tac. Hist. 5. 13.

[2] Psalmen, p. 335. [3] De B. Jud. 7. 5. 4.

[4] " Ultima Cumæi venit jam carminis ætas."

writings which, in the time of Virgil, passed under the name of Sibylline prophecies, were in a great measure spurious. True it might easily have happened, that the Jewish expectations of a future restitution should have been clothed in the Roman costume, and ascribed to the Sibyl. But even this supposition is unnecessary, since in the Eclogue of Virgil there is no expectation indulged beyond the return of the golden age; the same which we find among the Greeks.

10. But now when we turn to the Hebrews, an entirely different prospect is presented. We could not have expected to find among the Heathen nations any thing more than vague and distorted anticipations of a happier future. *Their* hopes were circumscribed by the revelations on this subject which were early imparted to mankind; and which were necessarily indefinite and general, in consequence of the character and condition of those who received them. Moreover, these revelations must have been greatly corrupted in the course of time, since they were opposed to the sentiments of the Heathen, who were left to themselves and had no participation in the further revelations from above. Among the Hebrews, on the contrary, these hopes, instead of standing by themselves, appear in the most intimate connexion with the whole system of the theocracy. The early predictions were secured from every species of corruption by being committed to writing. Frequent new revelations kept the expectation of the people alive, and rendered it continually more and more definite. And thus the doctrine of a coming Redeemer, even when partially misunderstood, became the soul and centre of all theocratic expectations; and the more so, since (as the people of the old covenant were left in as much darkness respecting the time of his first coming as Christians are respecting that of his second) their hopes were not weakened by the great distance to which the time of the fulfilment was removed. Since, therefore, the disclosures respecting the coming of a Redeemer, made to the Hebrews, alone have the seal of Divine authority; since they alone have come to us pure and free from all human additions, we are very properly accustomed to give to them exclusively the name of Messianic predictions.

We now proceed to consider the various purposes which these predictions promoted in the theocracy; a task which is the more necessary, because it is often brought as an *a priori* objection against the existence of real prophecies of the Messiah in the Old Testament, that the prediction of events so remote must be useless, and therefore unworthy of God.

11. (1) If their views had been limited to the present, the covenant people would have been in danger of becoming extremely contracted and selfish. This state of mind could not fail to be attended with most injurious consequences. It would lead them to unworthy and degrading thoughts of God; limiting either his omnipotence or his love; and to the most pernicious ideas of their own excellence, since the preference of them to the heathen, were it to be permanent, would hardly be regarded as founded on any thing else than superior natural qualifications, which rendered them, above all other people,

worthy of the favour of God. It was therefore highly necessary, that the means should be perceived to be no more than means, and that the view should be directed beyond the preparatory arrangements to the great end to be attained. Hence it was announced, even before the establishment of the theocracy, and afterwards continually kept in view, that the special relation of God to Israel was only temporary; and that in future times a great Deliverer should appear, in whose kingdom all the nations of the earth, Heathen as well as Jews, should be embraced. The necessity of this is manifest from the fact, that, notwithstanding such plain predictions, the greater part of the Jews, blinded by their worldliness, gave themselves up to the most destructive belief in God's special regard for their own nation. How difficult would it have been, even for the truly pious, without these predictions, to preserve themselves from the prevailing errour!

12. (2) The promise of the Messiah was a means of retaining the people in their allegiance to the Lord, in times of calamity. On Him, as the great restorer and enlarger of the theocracy, the prophets grounded their consoling declarations. Thus, for example, Isaiah[1] shows the unreasonableness of the fear that the state would be entirely destroyed by the Assyrians, from the fact, that the people from whom the Messiah was to spring *could not* be thus destroyed; and Jeremiah[2], and Ezekiel[3] present to the view of the despairing people their future illustrious king. Although the prophets often refer for consolation to nearer and joyful events of less importance, yet they never fail to return to this as the greatest of blessings, and the pledge of all the others. This design of the predictions of the Messiah, which respected the whole people, could be accomplished, even when they were erroneously apprehended from misunderstanding the imagery in which they were clothed. And thus even those who, through their own fault, indulged for the most part worldly expectations of the Messiah, would be preserved in outward allegiance. Nor was this of small importance, since the continuation of the external theocracy was indispensable to the manifestation of Christ. The kernel was preserved by means of the shell.

13. (3) The prediction of the Messiah was a means of promoting genuine piety and true devotion to God. The Prophets distinguish between the pious and the ungodly. They proclaim, that the Messiah will bestow rich blessings upon the former, but by his righteous punishment destroy the latter. What could have presented to the pious a stronger motive for perseverance, and to the wicked for conversion, than the lively representation of these rewards and punishments[4]?

14. (4) In the Old Testament, moreover, the Gospel, which proclaims forgiveness of sins through the mercy of God, accompanies the Law. How must those, in whom the Law had accomplished its end, have been consoled by the hope of pardon, when He, who *was to take* upon Himself their sins, as He *has taken* ours, set before them the con-

[1] Isa. 7. 14.   [2] Jer. 23. 6.   [3] Ezek. 34. 23.
[4] Compare Isa. 2—4. Mal. 3. 19, &c.

dition of their salvation in predictions like those recorded in the fifty-third chapter of Isaiah.

15. (5) But the chief object of prophecy was so to prepare the way for Christ, that, when He should come, He might be identified by a comparison of the prediction with its fulfilment. How necessary this was, is shown by the fact that, notwithstanding this preparation, the greater portion of the people misapprehended the Messiah. This however, was the case only with those whose worldly views prevented an impartial comparison of the prediction with its fulfilment. Had He not been particularly described before his coming, it would have been extremely difficult for even the spiritually-minded to identify Him. The importance of the Messianic predictions in this respect is manifest from the testimony of Christ and his Apostles. Christ, indeed, declares, that a disposition of mind which qualifies to receive the outward proofs of his divine mission, is indispensable to the knowledge of Himself [1], and ascribes the unbelief of the Jews to the want of this disposition [2]. But He also represents the evidence from prophecy as perfectly sufficient in itself; and reproves the Jews because they did not acknowledge it as such [3]. He was pointed out by God Himself, through John the Baptist, as the *promised* Messiah [4]. He declared Himself to be such [5]. And lest the coincidence between the prediction and its fulfilment might be thought fortuitous, He repeatedly says, 'The prophecy must needs have been fulfilled [6].' In Matthew 5. 17, He gives, as an end of his being sent, the fulfilment of the prophecies. How important for the establishment of his claims He regarded the agreement between the prophecy and its fulfilment, we learn from the fact, that at his last entrance into Jerusalem He so ordered all the circumstances, as to make them harmonize with the predictions concerning Him [7]. That Jesus was the Christ, constituted an important part of what the Apostles announced, not only to the Jews, but also to the Heathen [8].

16. The importance of these predictions, under the old dispensation, cannot then be doubted. The question may however arise, whether they are *still* important to the Christian Church [9].

17. (1) A previous question here arises, whether genuine prophecies of the Messiah really exist in the Old Testament. Schleiermacher, denying this, finds there only indistinct longings, expressions of the feeling of the need of redemption, such as we meet with among the Heathen; and asserts that the contrary opinion cannot be satisfactorily maintained. This assertion will be sufficiently refuted in the sequel. We only remark here, that with its truth or falsehood the authority of Christ and his Apostles must stand or fall. That *they* believed the Scripture to contain genuine predictions, is evident from the passages in their writings already referred to, as well as from a great number of others to be hereafter quoted in the proper place.

---

[1] John 7. 17.   [2] John 5 44.   [3] John 5. 39—47.
[4] John i. 19—41.   [5] John 4. 25, 26. Matt. 26. 63, 64. 11. 3, &c.
[6] Luke 24. 25. 44, &c., Matt. 26. 54.   [7] Matt. 21. 1. John 12. 12.
[8] Acts 10. 43. 1 Cor. 15. 3. 2 Cor. 1. 20.
[9] This has recently been denied by Schleiermacher, Dogm. 1. p. 116.

18. (2) The authority of Christ and his Apostles is equally subverted by the assertion, that an accurate and particular agreement between the event and the prophecy is of no importance. If this be the case, why is the coincidence of the prophecy with its fulfilment shown in the minutest circumstances of the life of Christ? Wherefore did He, when risen from the dead, explain to his Apostles those passages in the Old Testament which treated of his life, his sufferings, and his death? Wherefore did He so order every thing in his last visit to Jerusalem, that the prophecies and their accomplishment should accurately coincide? If it was important for *that* age to show this agreement, it is no less so for *ours*, since the Apostles pursued this course with the Heathen as well as Jews. The majority of the people of Christian countries are in the same condition as the Jews at the appearance of Christ: they know Him not, and have yet to become acquainted with Him for the first time. This result, it is true, can no more be effected in their case, than in that of the Jews, by the Messianic predictions alone; nor indeed can all the external proofs of the truth of Christianity combined, however conclusive in themselves, produce conviction, so long as the mind is not susceptible of the impression they are designed to make. But where the mind is open to receive this evidence, the fulfilment of prophecy exerts the happiest influence. This is too clearly proved by history to be denied. In how many instances have men been first drawn to the Saviour by reading the fifty-third chapter of Isaiah! How many disciples have been strengthened in the beginning of their course by this and similar predictions!

19. (3) Nor are these prophecies of value to those only who are just commencing the Christian life : they are no less beneficial to more advanced believers. No man's faith is so strong and constant, that he may despise the means of strengthening it, vouchsafed by God Himself; and the Christian will be the less inclined to do this, the more intimately and spiritually he has become united to the Redeemer. The further he has advanced, the more earnestly does he desire to comprehend the divine institutions for his salvation in all their relations, and to follow the plan which the wisdom of God saw fit to devise. Here nothing is unimportant. The smallest trace has meaning, because it is connected with the whole. All is mutual ; as the completion sheds light on the preparation, so does the preparation illustrate the completion.

20. Finally, when Schleiermacher further objects, that we cannot rest our strong faith in Christianity on Judaism, since our confidence in that is unquestionably far weaker ; Steudel has already well replied, that we do not rely on the predictions considered in themselves, but on the evidence which results from comparing them with the fulfilment. Besides, the notion of a weaker faith in the Old, and a stronger one in the New Testament, cannot be admitted by him whose conviction is consistent ; for whoever truly believes Christ and the Apostles, must acknowledge the divine authority of the Old Testament, to which they give such clear and definite testimony.

21. If now we trace the progress of the Messianic prediction in

general among the Hebrews, we shall see that the reign of David forms an important era in its history. It is true, indeed, that this prophecy is not the work of men, but the inspiration of that Spirit, who, under the Old Testament, glorified the Redeemer who was to come, as among us He glorifies Him now that He has come. But as we shall hereafter see, the representations of prophecy were necessarily figurative. The Messiah, therefore, could not be fully exhibited, until history had given to the Prophets materials, from which their metaphorical representations could be formed. The earlier theocracy supplied no sufficient groundwork for a complete delineation of Him. His character and offices, therefore, first appear fully unfolded in the time of David, to whom the Messiah was promised as a descendant. As the visible theocracy then furnished the materials for the representation of the Messiah's kingdom, so the typical head of the former served as the model of all that should be said for the glory of his antitype, the head of the latter.

Chapter II

History of the Messianic Prediction among the Hebrews.

1. Messianic Predictions in the Pentateuch
a. In Genesis

22. If we leave out of view the revelations, which, during the period of history comprised in Genesis, may have been imparted, in moments of high and divine excitement, to individual believers for their own benefit[1], and examine the prophecies of the Messiah as recorded in this book, we shall perceive them continually increasing in precision and clearness.

23. The promise of the Messiah, given immediately after the fall, as it is the first, so is it also the most indefinite. Opposed to the fearful threatening stands the consoling promise, that the reign of sin and its consequent evils should not last for ever ; that the posterity of the woman should one day gain the victory over their dreaded conqueror. Here except the victory itself all is left undetermined : we are not informed how it is to be achieved ; nor even whether by some peculiarly gifted race, or by a single individual, among the descendants of the woman.

24. After the destruction of a sinful world, when Noah with his three sons alone remained, the *general* promise was so far circumscribed, that deliverance was to be accomplished through the posterity of Shem.

25. The prediction became still more definite, when God began to prepare the way for this salvation by separating a single individual,

---

[1] See John 8. 56.

Abraham, from the corrupt mass, to make him the depository of his revelations, and by afterwards specifying which of his descendants should inherit this honour with all its attendant blessings, to the exclusion of all the rest, according to his own free purpose. From among the descendants of Shem, God selected, first, the family of Abraham, next that of Isaac, and lastly that of Jacob, as the one from which the promised salvation should proceed. But even these annunciations, though more distinct than those of an earlier period, are still very indefinite, when compared with those which were subsequently given, and with the fulfilment. In them the blessing, indeed, was foretold, but not its author. It remained still uncertain, whether it was by means of a single individual, or of a whole race, descended from the patriarch, that salvation should be extended to the remaining people of the earth. Moreover, the method by which this blessing should be imparted, was not clearly revealed.

26. A part of this obscurity was removed by the last Messianic prediction of Genesis 49. 10. After what had taken place already, it was indeed to be expected that it would not be left undetermined, which of the twelve sons of Jacob should be the source of salvation to the whole world; and that, when the patriarch, just before his death, delivered over to his sons, in the spirit of prophecy, the promises imparted to himself and his forefathers, he would not omit that which was more important than all the rest. Here, however, not only does the Messianic prediction receive its usual limitation, by the selection of Judah as the one to whom the promise belonged, but becomes unexpectedly much more definite and clear than before. Here, for the first time, the *Person* of the Messiah comes before us, and the nature of his kingdom is defined ; for he is represented as a *peaceful* Prince, who should unite under his mild sceptre all the nations of the earth.

27. We proceed now from these preparatory remarks to an exposition of the particular passages.

The Protevangelium, OR THE FIRST ANNUNCIATION OF THE GOSPEL

28. As the mission of the Messiah was rendered necessary by the fall, so the first obscure intimation of Him was given immediately after that event. It is found in the sentence denounced against the tempter[1], which cannot be rightly understood, till we have ascertained who the tempter was.

29. It is in the first place beyond all doubt, that a real serpent was engaged in the temptation ; and, consequently, the opinion of those must be rejected, who regard the serpent as merely a symbolical designation of the evil Spirit. This opinion would make it necessary, in order to be consistent, that we should adopt the allegorical mode of interpretation throughout the whole narrative. For we are not at liberty, in the same historical relation, to adopt at one time the alle-

[1] Gen. 3. 14, 15.

gorical or symbolical, and at another the simple and literal method. Now against the allegorical interpretation of the whole there are many objections,—as : the connexion with what follows, in which the history is continued of the same human pair, who are here represented as acting ; the accurate geographical description of Paradise ; the fact, that the condition of mankind, threatened in this narrative as a punishment, actually exists ; the absence of every indication, from which it might be inferred that the author designed to write an allegory and not a history ; the passages in the New Testament, where the account of the fall is referred to as a real history [1] ; the embarrassment, uncertainty, and capriciousness of the allegorical interpreters, when they attempt to exhibit the truth intended to be conveyed, which, if the author had designed his composition for an allegory, must have been so obvious as to be easily discovered.

30. The presence of a real serpent is proved, moreover, not only by the remark [2], ' Now the serpent was more subtil than any beast of the field,' but by the punishment denounced, which must necessarily refer, in the first instance, to the serpent. These last reasons may also serve to refute the idea of others, that Satan assumed merely the *semblance* of a serpent.

31. But if it is certain that what Eve saw was a real serpent, it is no less so that he was not the principal tempter, but only an instrument, employed by an evil Spirit with which she was unacquainted. In favour of this we advance the following reasons : (1) Although the writer intentionally related the history as it had been handed down to their descendants from the parents of mankind, who could judge of things only as they appeared to the eye ; and has employed no word to point out the invisible author of the temptation ; yet that he designed to lead his reflecting reader to the knowledge of him, is manifest from the whole character of the narrative ; while, at the same time, he had his own sufficient reasons for confining the great mass of the people to the outward appearance, and not explaining its cause, the knowledge of which might so readily give rise to that destructive superstition, which was so widely spread among the other nations of the East. What deserves peculiar regard is, that the serpent speaks and exhibits, in general, all the marks of a rational being. This need not have appeared surprising to Eve. She was so little acquainted with the nature of animals, their characteristic difference from men, and the powers with which God had endowed them, that the speaking of the serpent could have awakened in her mind at most only an obscure suspicion of the agency of some higher and invisible power. But what reflecting reader of later times would not be led to the knowledge of this invisible cause, as soon as he connected the certainty, that here was something beyond the power of an ordinary serpent, with the probability that he who was known from other sources to be the author of all evil, performed an active part at its first entrance into the world ? True, indeed, Le Clerc, Eichhorn, Döderlein, Dathe, Less, and especially Gabler, have sought to show, after Abarbanel,

---

[1] 2 Cor. 11. 3. 1 Tim. 2. 13, 14. Rom. 5 12.   [2] Gen. 3. 1.

that the account of the conversation of Eve with the serpent must be explained by a well-known Orientalism, according to which, even inanimate external objects, that give rise to thought, are personified and introduced as speaking. The serpent, they urge, by his eating the fruit with impunity, awakened many thoughts in the mind of Eve ; and suggested a doubt with respect to the prohibition : which rising doubt, with the accompanying desire, was expressed, in accordance with the genius of the Orientals, in the form of a dialogue between the serpent and Eve.—This opinion is liable to these objections : it ascribes to a simple historical relation what can have place only in poetry ; it rests entirely upon caprice, since, against all the rules of sound exposition, it understands one part of the narrative literally, and allegorizes the other ; it is sustained by no analogous place in the writings of the Old Testament, since even with respect to the history of Baalam there is no good reason for rejecting the literal interpretation, which even Herder has defended ; it rests upon no other foundation, than the alleged absurdity of supposing a literal conversation to have taken place between the serpent and Eve,—a foundation which of itself gives way, the moment the agency of an evil Spirit is supposed [1]. Besides, there are many other things which suggest the idea of an invisible author of the temptation, concealed under the visible one,—the declaration, chap. 3. 1, so remarkably suited to awaken attention, and the curse itself, which plainly relates in a higher sense to an invisible tempter, as it does in a lower to the visible agent which he employed.

32. (2) We draw another argument from the *tradition* of the fall of our first parents, preserved in the sacred books of the Persians. According to the Zendavesta [2], the parents of the human race, Meschia and Meschianeh, were created by God pure and good, and destined for happiness on condition of humility, obedience to the requirements of the law, and purity in their thoughts, words, and deeds. But betrayed by the cruel ' Ahriman, who from the beginning sought only to deceive,' they fell from God, and forfeited their happiness by eating fruit. According to the same book [3], Ahriman springs from heaven to earth in the form of a serpent ; and another distinguished evil spirit is called the serpent Dhu [4].

33. (3) Among the Jews, also, there is a tradition, that Satan was concerned in the temptation of our first parents. " By the envy of the *devil*," says the book of Wisdom [5], "came death into the world." In later Jewish writings, Sammael, the head of the evil spirits, because he tempted Eve in the form of a serpent, is called *old serpent*[6], or simply *serpent*[7].

34. (4) But what gives indubitable certainty to the agency of Satan

---

[1] Storr has well observed, " Hæc opinio a natura rerum priscæque vetustatis simplicitate sic abhorret, ut tam artificiose affectatum tumorem narrationi vetustæ tribuere nequeamus, nisi indubiis auctoritatibus coacti, quas vero penitus desideramus."

[2] Th. 3. p. 84, 85.   [3] Ibid. 3. p. 62.

[4] Pt. 2. p. 217.   See Rhode, die heil. Sage d. Zendvolkes, p. 392.

[5] Wisdom 2. 42.   [6] נחש הקדמני   [7] נחש

in this transaction, is the testimony of the New Testament. In Revel. 12. 9, the leader of the evil spirits is named 'the great dragon, that old serpent, called the devil and Satan[1].' Paul, indeed, when he says, 'as the serpent beguiled Eve through his subtilty[2],' after the example of the narrative itself, suffers the unseen cause of the temptation to remain concealed, and speaks only of that which was visible ; but that the former was not unknown to him is evident from Rom. 16. 20. 'and the God of peace shall *bruise Satan* under your feet shortly[3],' where the allusion to Gen. 3. 15 is not to be mistaken. Finally we must maintain, with the generality of both the ancient and modern interpreters, that when Christ Himself called Satan ' *a murderer* from the beginning,' He referred to his having brought death into the world by sin[4], even though the opinion, first advanced by Cyril of Alexandria, that the Saviour rather alluded to the murder committed by Cain, has found an acute defender in Nitzsch, and is also preferred by Lücke. Our reasons are the following : that the phrase, ' from the beginning[5],' must be taken in its strictest sense, is shown by the parallel passages already referred to in the Apocalypse, as well as in the Jewish writings ; and that Christ, when He called Satan 'a murderer[6],' had in view the fall of our first parents, is shown by the passage quoted from Wisdom 2. 24, as well as that to which Tholuck has appealed in the Sohar Chadasch, where the ungodly are called "the children of the old serpent, who has slain Adam and all his descendants."—Besides, how could Jesus expect his words to be understood by his hearers, except as referring to the moral, and, indirectly, even physical murder, which Satan commenced with the parents of mankind, since his agency in the fall was the prevailing belief of the people ; while the notion that he tempted Cain, to which there is no allusion in the Mosaic narrative, cannot be supposed to have been so generally received, that Christ would have alluded to it in such vague and indefinite terms? True it is alleged, that also in 1 John 3. 12[7], the murder committed by Cain is referred to Satan ; but there this reference is not only plainly pointed out, but the reason of it is manifest in what goes before. Finally, that Christ alluded to the fall is confirmed by the fact, that the murder committed by Satan is placed in the nearest connexion with his lying disposition, as manifested in the seduction of our first parents. The force of these arguments will not surely be destroyed by the single consideration which has been urged in favour of the reference to the deed of Cain, viz. that Christ had just before charged the Jews with a murderous disposition in the *strict and literal* sense, and with hatred of the truth, and therefore called them the children of the devil ; and that consequently, in order to justify this language, Satan must be represented as a *literal* murderer. It is here erro-

---

[1] ὁ δράκων ὁ μέγας, ὁ ὄφις ὁ ἀρχαῖος (נחש קדמני) ὁ καλούμενος διάβολος. Likewise 20. 2.

[2] ὡς ὁ ὄφις Εὖαν ἐξηπάτησεν ἐν τῇ πανουργίᾳ, 2 Cor. 11. 3.

[3] ὁ δὲ θεὸς τῆς εἰρήνης συντρίψει τὸν σατανᾶν ὑπὸ τοὺς πόδας ὑμῶν ἐν τάχει.

[4] John 8. 44.   [5] ἀπ' ἀρχῆς.   [6] ἀνθρωποκτόνος.

[7] " Not as Cain, who *was of that wicked one*, and slew his brother."

neously taken for granted, that in the temptation of our first parents, he was a murderer only in a *spiritual* sense. He was so in the simplest and most literal sense of the term, since the transgression, caused by him, involved the loss of immortality [1]. Hence the assertion, that allusion to the fall would have been a mere playing upon words, is seen to be groundless.

35. (5) To these particular testimonies from the New Testament, we lastly add another of considerable weight, lately brought forward again by Hahn, drawn from the parallel between the history of the first and second Adam [2]. That Christ must be tempted by the prince of this world, in order that, by his persevering resistance, He might despoil him of his dominion over it, shows that Adam also was assailed by the same tempter, and by being overcome laid the foundation of this dominion.

36. But before we proceed to make use of the results we have gained, we must first examine the grounds on which the agency of Satan, in the fall of man, has been controverted [3]. The principal objections that have been urged, the insufficiency of which may be seen from what has already been advanced, are the following :

37. (1) " The author calls the serpent, in reference to the history of the fall, and the deception which he practised upon Eve, the most subtile of all the beasts of the field. Had he been thinking of a supernatural cause, he would not have made this assertion, since the devil could just as well have employed the most stupid animal." To this we reply, that the author related the circumstances as they appeared to our first parents ; and, ignorant as they were of the invisible cause, they must have ascribed a high degree of cunning to the serpent from the part which he acted. Moses states this fact with the design of leading his more intelligent readers to a right solution of the problem.

38. (2) " The devil could not speak by means of a serpent, since the serpent has no organs of speech." We answer here with Calvin, " If it seems incredible that beasts have spoken at the command of God, whence has man speech, except because God has formed his tongue ? The Gospel proclaims, that, to illustrate the glory of Christ, articulate sounds were formed in the air without a tongue ; an assertion which is less probable to carnal reason, than that speech should be elicited from the mouth of the brute creation. What, therefore, will the petulance of ungodly men find here that it can justly attack [4] ?" That

---

[1] Compare with the relation in Genesis, Wisdom 2. 24 ; Rom. 5. 12.

[2] Compare Rom. 5. 14, &c., 1 Cor. 15. 45.

[3] These have been most ful'y stated by Eichhorn (Urgeschichte, Th. 3. p. 114. seq.) and Gabler (Th. 2. p. 137, seq.) These critics have been followed by Dathe on the Pentateuch, Kuinoel (Mess. Weiss. p. 2.) Jahn (Vaticinia Messiana, p. 216. 222, and Nachträge zu seinen theol. Werken, p. 148), and lastly, Baumgarten-Crusius (Grundzüge der bibl. Dogm. p. 348.)

[4] "Si incredibile videtur locutas esse Deo jubente bestias, unde homini sermo, nisi quia ejus linguam Deus formavit ? Editas sine linguâ in aëre fuisse voces ad illustrandam Christi gloriam, Evangelium prædicat ; minus hoc rationi carnis probabile, quam ex brutorum animalium ore elici sermonem. Quid igitur hic impiorum petulantia insectatione dignum inveniet ?"

speech should appear to proceed from the mouth of a serpent, is just as conceivable as the influence of the soul on the body, and many other things of the kind.

39. (3) " How can it be reconciled with the goodness and wisdom of God, that a powerful Spirit should have been permitted to tempt the parents of mankind to apostasy ? God must have foreseen the fall which would be the consequence of this permission : and did He, nevertheless, permit this diabolical deception ? Who can justify this proceeding ?" Where we are assured on sufficient grounds, that any thing has been done by God, we are not to let our confidence be over-thrown by the inability of our short-sighted reason to justify his pro-ceedings. ' Canst thou draw out Leviathan with a hook ?' But in this instance we are not obliged to appeal solely to the infinite dis-tance between God and man, for we can give at least a probable jus-tification of this dispensation of Providence. This would indeed be impossible, if we held the opinion of the old divines, which *so* mag-nifies the divine image, as to ascribe to Adam the *actual exercise* of the highest wisdom and holiness. But this opinion is contrary to the Mosaic relation. The assertion, that man was made in the image of God, implies rather that he possessed the *capacity* of wisdom and holiness, and was free from that moral depravity, which we bring with us into the world as an inheritance derived from him. The narrative moreover shows, that his condition was analogous to that of child-hood. This low condition of unconscious innocence was to be changed into one of intelligent piety and devotion to God ; and to effect this change probation was necessary. For this purpose God gave the command, and at the same time permitted the temptation to transgress. Had man endured the trial, he would have been carried forward, without the necessity of a painful course of discipline, from one degree of improvement to another. The foresight of man's dis-obedience could not move God to guard him from temptation. It was better for man, if he would not persevere in goodness, to be brought to perfection by suffering the effects of his sin, than to remain in his former imperfect condition. We must not consider the fall apart from the redemption. God, who foresaw the fall, had already purposed, by a method of salvation of his own appointment, not only to remove its consequences, but also thereby to bring man to that perfection, which he would indeed have attained by firmly resisting the tempter, but did not possess at his creation, and could not have acquired without a trial.

40. (4) " The curse is directed only against an irrational creature." Nothing being known of any other author of the temptation than the serpent, the curse was indeed necessarily directed in the first instance against it ; the object being, to produce in man an abhorrence of sin by the punishment of the only author of sin then known to him. But this does not exclude a *double reference* of the curse; and we are justified in supposing such a double reference, the moment it is known that Satan was engaged in the temptation.

41. (5) " It cannot have been the opinion of the writer, that an evil Spirit was concerned in the fall of man, since in the whole of the Old

Testament until the period of the Babylonian exile, there is to be found no trace of such a Spirit. The idea of Satan was borrowed from the Chaldeans; and it was after their example that the Jews made him play the part of a tempter with our first parents." That the doctrine concerning Satan prevailed among the Jews *before* the Babylonian exile is evident, in the first place, from the very ancient book of Job, which very few critics venture to assign to so late a period as the exile. It is true, that Baumgarten-Crusius [1] has lately endeavoured to prove that the Satan of the book of Job is not the Satan of the later books of the Old Testament, but rather a good and pure Angel, who sustained only the office of a complainant, informer, or attorney-general. In proof of this he alleges, that the writer numbers him among the sons of God, and that the odiousness of his office ought not to be transferred to his person. But not to mention that the new derivation given to the word Satan [2] cannot be justified on grammatical principles, this hypothesis has nothing in its favour. When the writer makes Satan appear before the throne of God, he employs a poetic fiction. He no more intended this for a real transaction, than he actually believed it necessary for Jehovah, whose infinite power and wisdom he has so gloriously exhibited, to deliver up a man to Satan to be proved, before He could ascertain the genuineness of his virtue. When it is said that Satan appeared in the midst of the Angels before God, we cannot infer, as some have done, that the writer regarded him as one of the *good* Angels: even here he is true to his own nature, of craft, hatred, and envy. Nor is it by any means true, that the existence of evil Spirits is *not* taught in the Pentateuch. The opinion of those who think Satan to be intended by Azazel, to whom the goat [3] is sent away into the wilderness, is the only one that agrees with the context. Baumgarten-Crusius has indeed objected, after the example of Deyling, that the bringing of an offering to an evil Spirit would not only be inconsistent with the import of this particular ceremony of atonement, but in opposition to the whole system of the Mosaic religion. There is, however, no ground for the supposition, that one of the goats was brought as a *sacrifice* to Azazel. So far as it was regarded in this light, it was consecrated, as well as the other, to Jehovah [4]. Its being sent forth was only a symbolical transaction. By this act the kingdom of darkness and its prince were renounced; and symbolically the sins to which he had tempted, and by which he had sought to enslave either the people or individuals, were sent back to him again; and the truth was expressed, that he to whom God grants forgiveness is freed from the power of evil [5].—It is very true, that Moses

[1] After Herder, Eichhorn, Ilgen, and Jahn.   [2] שטן
[3] Lev. 16. 8.   [4] Compare verse 10.

[5] The contrast between ליהוה and לעזאל verse 8, as well as the tradition of the later Jews, that Azazel is a name of Sammaël, speaks in favour of this explanation. See passages quoted by Spencer, Rosenmüller, and Winer. The passage in Deut. 32. 17, is less explicit. The word שדים which there occurs, is rendered by the Seventy δαιμόνια, and by the Vulgate *dæmonia;* and in favour of the opinion, that it signifies invisible wicked spirits, we have also the Syriac, [ܐ], *evil demon.*

says but little concerning the kingdom of darkness, and speaks with a degree of obscurity, which only the more intelligent could penetrate ; but for this he had, as we have already seen, his own sufficient reasons.   He observed a similar conduct with respect to other doctrines also, for example, that of immortality, of which he gave only brief hints, intelligible to those alone, to whom the knowledge of it would be beneficial.   Against the supposition that the Hebrews derived the doctrine concerning Satan from Chaldea, we may urge, not only the passage referred to, but also the fact, that the Ahriman of the Persians, and the Satan of the Hebrews, are entirely different beings.   The Ahriman of the Persians is the fundamental principle of evil, coeternal with that of good, and if not entirely equal with it in power, at least so nearly equal as to carry on against it a long and arduous warfare   The Satan of the Hebrews is, on the contrary, entirely subject to Jehovah: without His permission he dare not injure any one, or tempt any one to evil.

42. Thus, it has been sufficiently shown, (1) that a real serpent was present at the temptation, and (2) that it was the mere instrument of the actual seducer, Satan.   Hence arises the necessity of giving a double meaning to the curse denounced against the tempter.   It must refer, in the first place, to the instrument, for otherwise it would have been entirely unintelligible to the first human pair, and without an immediate aim : but in its chief import it must relate to the real tempter ; since he alone had properly done, what deserved the punishment and curse.—Let us now, upon these principles, proceed to interpret the passage.   ' Because thou hast done this, thou art cursed above all cattle, and above every beast of the field : upon thy belly shalt thou go, and dust shalt thou eat all the days of thy life[1].'

43. So far as these words relate to the serpent, there are two opinions respecting their meaning.   Some suppose, that after the fall a change took place in the nature of the serpent: others, that he retained the same nature as before ; but after the fall, that which before was his nature became his curse.   The former opinion accords far better with the context, and, but for the influence of doctrinal views, no man would ever have thought of another interpretation.   The difficulty, however, which led to the second exposition is of no real importance. It is in itself probable, and consistent with his usual mode of proceeding, that Satan should have chosen a pleasing and attractive instrument of temptation.   Since, in the view of the author, the fall not only deranged the whole constitution of man, but extended its baleful and accursed influence through the whole system of nature[2] ; since, before the fall, the whole world of animals bore the image of the innocence and peacefulness of man, and the law of mutual destruction had not yet begun to operate among them[3] ; what possi-

---

[1] Verse 14.   [2] Gen. 3. 17.

[3] Gen. 1. 30.—That the whole animal world cannot possibly have come from the Creator's hand in its present condition, has been strikingly shown by Krummacher.   But he has also, in opposition to the Holy Scriptures, derived the *imperfect* and *evil* from the want of control over matter in the creation, and has therefore maintained a dualism.

ble difficulty is there in supposing, that the instrument of the temptation was itself made to suffer, in a peculiar degree, the consequences
of the first transgression ?

44. These words, then, doom the serpent to exhibit the loathsome-
ness of sin by means of that disgusting form which, as well as every
thing evil and hateful, was the consequence of the first transgression.
He must, as it were, serve as a visible representative of the kingdom
of darkness, and Satan its head, who had employed him as his instrument. But here we meet with the objection, that it was absurd to
inflict a curse upon the serpent, since the poor animal was not to
blame for being abused by a higher power [1]. In reply to this, we
may well be satisfied with what Calvin has long since said : " If it
seems absurd to any body, that an irrational animal is punished for
another's fraud, it is obvious to answer, that there was good reason
for cursing the serpent, when it, which had been created for the good
of man, was turned to his destruction. By this act of vengeance
God wished to prove, how high a value he sets on the salvation of
man : as if a father should curse the sword with which his son was
slain." The punishment of the serpent is neither more nor less
unjust, than the suffering condition into which the fall has brought
the whole creation [2]; than the Mosaic direction, that a beast which
had been abused, should be burnt with the guilty author of the crime ;
or than the bringing of animals to the altar to be slain as sin-
offerings.

45. If now we refer this verse to the spiritual author of the temptation, omitting what belongs only to the instrument, it declares : Extreme contempt, shame, and humiliation shall overtake thee. " This
enemy of mankind" (says Calmet) " crawls as it were on his belly
through the shame and disgrace to which he is reduced."

46. Satan believed that he should enlarge his kingdom and his
power by the seduction of man ; but God, who viewed the fall in
connexion with redemption, saw this transaction in a far different
light. The eating of dust or ashes occurs also elsewhere as the
symbol of the deepest humiliation and grief.

47. Verse 15. ' And I will put enmity between thee and the
woman, and between thy seed and her seed : he shall strike thy head,
and thou shalt strike his heel [3].'

48. As it respects the serpent, the meaning is, ' Thy posterity shall
inflict upon that of the woman curable wounds, but hers upon thine
incurable.' The serpent is killed when its head is crushed, while
injuries on other parts of the body are not fatal ; its bite is nowhere so harmless as on the heel.

49. Such was the only meaning which our first parents at least
attached to the divine threatening. But, imperfectly as it was under-

---

[1] Gabler.   [2] Comp. Rom. 8. 20, &c.

[3] We give to the verb שׁוּף with Gabler, Jahn, and others, the meaning *to
strike*. It has in its favour not only that it is here equally appropriate in both
members, but also that it suits the only two other places where it occurs besides
Job 9. 17, and Ps. 139. 11. Every other interpretation requires more meanings than are to be given to the word.

stood, it must have inspired them with abhorrence of sin, as well as with strong consolation. They regarded the serpent as the sole author of that misery, the full burden of which they felt. How consoling then must have been the assurance, that he by whom they had been overcome, who had seemed the more to be dreaded from their ignorance of the presence of an invisible and higher power, should not perpetually enjoy his triumph, but suffer defeat and overthrow from their posterity! Far more consoling must have been this assurance to them, or at least to their descendants, when, by becoming acquainted with the natural powers of the serpent, they were led to distinguish between the visible and the invisible cause of their temptation.

50. Our own experience bears testimony to the truth of the divine threat, that enmity should henceforth exist between the serpent and the human race. Abhorrence of the serpent is natural to man.

51. As it respects the chief import of the threatening, its relation to Satan, the greater part of the earlier Christian interpreters think, that the Messiah is directly pointed out by the seed of the woman who should bruise the serpent's head. But to this it may be objected that it does violence to the language, to understand, by the seed of the woman, any particular *individual;* and the more so since we are compelled to understand by the seed of the serpent, a *plurality*, the spiritual children of Satan, the head and members of the kingdom of darkness, called in the New Testament ' serpents,' ' the offspring of vipers,' and ' children of the devil.' To avoid this difficulty, we must understand her posterity in general. According to this explanation the sense is as follows : ' True; thou hast now inflicted on the woman a severe wound, and thy associates shall continue to assault her posterity. But with all thy malice, thou and thy associates shall be able to inflict on mankind only curable wounds; while, on the contrary, the posterity of the woman shall one day triumph over thee, and make thee feel all thy weakness.'

52. According to this interpretation, the passage justly bears the name of the Protevangelium, which has been given it by the Church. But still the future triumph of the kingdom of light over the kingdom of darkness is announced only in general forms. The *person* of the Redeemer, who is the leader in the conflict [1], and supplies his people with all their strength to maintain it, is not here revealed. More however we should not expect in the very beginning of the human race. A gradual progress and development are as observable in the kingdom of grace, as in the kingdom of nature. The prediction contains much that coincides with the tradition of the other nations of Asia, who possessed only the original revelation, which was comparatively obscure; whilst among the Hebrews new revelations were continually shedding fresh light, and rendering more and more complete the glorious image of the Redeemer.

53. Let us now briefly examine the objections, which have been

---

[1] That St. Paul so understood the passage, appears from his allusion to it, Rom. 16. 20, where the promise is regarded as relating to Christians as a body.

brought against the existence of the Protevangelium in this passage, at least so far as they concern the interpretation we have given.

54. (1) " Why do Christ and the Apostles, who refer so many passages of the Old Testament to Jesus, make no use of this ? It must have been of all others the most important and the most worthy of their attention. Why then do we not find so much as an allusion to it ?" The answer is easy. The writers of the New Testament did not distinctly refer this prophecy to Jesus, because it is not sufficiently definite, since it contains no direct reference to the *person* of the Messiah. It was natural, that the writers of the New Testament should quote the many more obvious passages. It is not however true, that the New Testament contains *no* allusion to this passage. See the place already referred to in the Epistle to the Romans. But that Christ and his Apostles here found the Protevangelium, in our sense of the term, is plainly proved by those passages in the New Testament, from which we have shown, that they believed *Satan* to have been concerned in the apostasy [1].

55. (2) " By the seed of the serpent, neither bad men nor fallen angels can well be intended, for in what sense can these be called the *posterity* of the devil ? Bad men are at once excluded by the consideration that they *belong to* the descendants of Eve, and consequently cannot be *put in opposition* to them." We remark, in reply, that nothing is more common in the Scripture, than for the natural relation between father and son to be transferred to spiritual relations. In this very book men of a godly disposition are called *the sons of God*. The scholars of the prophets bear the name of their *sons ;* and that it is no uncommon thing to transfer this spiritual relation to Satan, is shown by the appellation of the ungodly in the New Testament, to which we have referred [2]. In the passage also of the Sohar already quoted, they are named the ' children of the old serpent.' With respect to the second part of the objection, it by no means shows that ungodly men cannot belong to the seed of the serpent, although the import of this term is not limited to them, but embraces all the subjects of Satan.

56. (3) " Such an annunciation of the gospel would have been entirely unintelligible to our first parents, for they felt no need of a Redeemer, and had no idea of the design of his appointment." This assertion is contradicted by the narrative. That Adam and Eve, after eating the forbidden fruit, were seized with a deep sense of guilt, is evinced by the shame they felt, the common offspring of those sinful desires and of conscience, as well as by their tormenting fear of God, with whom they had hitherto enjoyed affectionate communion. This feeling of guilt must have been greatly increased, when the curse, which God had denounced against the earth, began to be executed, and man was driven out from paradise. Nature, before in subjection, but now risen up in rebellion against him ; his frail body, which from the moment of the fall had begun to die ; and especially the dis-

[1] For whoever believes this cannot help seeing in our passage a promised victory over *Satan*. [2] See 51.

quietude of his own breast, all reminded him of his guilt. But the conviction of his guilt must have made him feel his need of a redemption, and thus have prepared him to welcome the promise of a future victory over the kingdom of darkness. Nor was this promise important to Adam and Eve alone, but to all their posterity. The expectations of a future and glorious redemption, which are found to have existed among heathen nations, are but the echoes of this and similar predictions imparted to the ancient fathers of the human race.

Genesis 9:26, 27

English Bible	*Hengstenberg*
57. Blessed be the Lord God of Shem—	Praised be Jehovah, the God of Shem—
God shall enlarge Japheth, and he shall dwell in the tents of Shem.	May God enlarge Japheth, may he dwell in the tents of Shem.

58. This passage contains the blessing of Noah upon his two sons, Shem and Japheth. Even the twenty-sixth verse, "Praised be Jehovah the God of Shem," intimates the preservation of the true religion among the descendants of Shem. The patriarch, whose expressions are not to be regarded as mere wishes of his own, but as predictions also, beholds a degree of prosperity destined for his son Shem, so great, that instead of announcing it to him in direct terms, he is moved to break forth in praise to God, by whom it was to be conferred.

59. The nature of this prosperity was indicated in two ways. (1.) God is not called by the name Elohim, expressive of his general relation to the world, but by the name Jehovah, which refers to his revelation and to his institutions for man's redemption. (2.) Jehovah is styled the ' God of Shem.' It is thus intimated that God would sustain to the posterity of Shem a relation entirely peculiar, favouring them with revelations of his will, and making them partakers of his temporal and spiritual blessings.

60. The twenty-seventh verse goes still further. Its immediate object indeed is only to pronounce the blessing of Japheth; but at the same time it includes a far greater blessing destined for Shem, and thus completes the declaration respecting him in the foregoing verse. " May God enlarge [1] Japheth; may he dwell in the tents of Shem."

[1] We agree with those interpreters who give to the verb פתה the meaning *to be broad;* which indeed occurs but once in the Hebrew, Prov. 20. 19, but is the prevailing one in Chaldee. For this interpretation we have not only the authority of most of the ancient versions (the 70 render πλατύναι ὁ Θεὸς τῷ ᾿Ιάφεθ. The Vulg. *dilatet Deus Japheth*); but it is confirmed also by the consideration that verbs of a similar import are elsewhere construed with ל. See chap. 26. 22. The usual meaning in Hebrew is to *persuade*, or *enable one to do any thing.*

But as this passage has received various interpretations, we must justify that, which we have now given.

61. With respect to the import of this blessing, there is a difference of opinion. Many interpreters[1] understand the passage literally, or at least regard the literal meaning as the principal one. It is here foretold, they say, that the posterity of Japheth should one day gain possession of the country belonging to the posterity of Shem, and reduce them to subjection. They compare the passage with the prediction of Balaam[2], according to which the Chittim, a people descended from Japheth, should oppress Ashur and Eber; and find it fulfilled in the conquest of Palestine by the Greeks and Romans. But this interpretation is certainly inadmissible. Bochart himself remarks that the blessings of Japheth should be regarded only in a manner supplementary to the blessing of Shem. How then can we suppose that Noah, to favour Japheth, should here by predicting evil diminish the value of the splendid promises made to Shem, who was plainly to be exalted above both his brothers?

62. We must then adopt the figurative interpretation, according to which, by the dwelling of Japheth in the tents of Shem, it is to be intimated, that the true religion was to be preserved among the posterity of Shem, and imparted by them to the descendants of Japheth, who were to be received among the true worshippers of God[3].

63. The figurative mode of expression found in this passage has its parallel in various places of Scripture. In Zechariah ' the tents of Judah[4],' and in Malachi ' the tents of Jacob[5] ' are the designation of the theocracy. In St. Luke reception ' into everlasting habitations[6]' is reception into the everlasting kingdom of God. This interpretation is also confirmed by a comparison with the promises to Abraham, Isaac, and Jacob. As it is there foretold, that through the descendants of the Patriarchs all nations should be blessed, so here it is predicted, that the institutions to be established among the posterity of Shem, should afterwards be extended to the posterity of Japheth. The only objection to this interpretation advanced by Mercer and others, that many of *Ham's* descendants have participated in the salvation that originated with the posterity of Shem, is refuted by the remark, that here, the object being to punish Ham for his crime, only the future adversity, and not the prosperity of his descendants was foretold; while, on the contrary, only prosperity was announced to Shem and Japheth, higher to the former, inferior to the latter.

---

[1] Bochart, Calmet, Le Clerc, and others.   [2] Num. 24. 24.

[3] " Hoc prorsus, hoc prænuntiabatur cum diceretur : Latificet Deus Japheth et habitet in tentoriis Sem, id est, in ecclesiis, quas filii prophetarum apostoli construxerunt."—Augustin.

[4] Zech. 12. 7.   [5] Mat. 2. 12.   [6] Luke 16. 9.

Promises to the Patriarchs

64. The first promise which here comes under consideration was made to Abraham before he emigrated from his native land to Canaan. Gen. 12. 3, it is said : ' In thee shall all the families of the earth be blessed.' The same promise is repeated, Gen. 18. 18, only instead of 'families[1],' we read 'nations[2].' Chap. 22. 18, this promise is repeated to Abraham as a reward for his ready compliance with the command to offer up his son Isaac.   There the indefinite expression 'through thee[3],' is explained by 'through thy seed[4].' Chap. 26. 4, the same promise is confirmed to Isaac. Chap. 28. 14, it is delivered to Jacob.   In the former two places, it is ' through thee,' in the two latter ' through thy seed ;' but here it is instead, ' through thee and thy seed,' which is equivalent to ' through thee,' *that is*, ' thy seed[5].'

65. The undeniable meaning of these promises made to the Patriarchs is, that through their posterity salvation should be conferred upon all the nations of the earth.   The nature of this blessing, however, is not accurately defined.   But even the Patriarchs themselves must have inferred from sure indications, that temporal blessings could have been intended only so far as they are the necessary consequences of spiritual blessings, and as true religion never fails to improve the outward condition of man.   They could not have supposed, that the promise referred to mere *temporal blessings*, because they could have perceived no method by which such blessings could be conferred upon the heathen through their posterity.   Further, how could they think, that *all* the nations of the earth were to obtain temporal *blessings* through them, when it had been foretold, that their posterity would be the source of temporal *calamities* to not a few of the heathen nations, by reducing them to subjection[6]?   Finally, since the object of the blessings, partly given and partly promised to the Patriarchs and their descendants, was to promote the knowledge and practice of the true religion, and since they were imparted on this very condition[7], the Patriarchs must have expected their posterity to be the source of blessings to the heathen only by introducing them to the privileges of this religion.

66. Thus much they could easily have inferred from the language of this promise ; but as to the mode in which this blessing was to be extended to the heathen, it gave no information ; and to a further development of *this* mystery, another more particular revelation from God was necessary.   That this was vouchsafed to Abraham, although no where expressly mentioned in his history, is not only probable from the near relation in which he stood to God[8], but is rendered

---

[1] מִשְׁפָּחוֹת   [2] גּוֹיִם   [3] בְּךָ,   [4] בְזַרְעֲךָ

[5] The Vav being exegetical.   For Hengstenberg's arguments against those who limit the promise in various ways, see the original work.

[6] See Gen. 15 16, &c.   [7] Ibid. 17. 1. 18. 17—19. 22. 16—18. 26. 5.

[8] Gen. 18. 17.

certain by the testimony of our Lord Himself[1], where he affirms
that Abraham had been favoured with a prophetic view of his future
manifestation.

67. The prediction we have been examining is often quoted in the
New Testament, and its fulfilment assigned to the time of the Messiah[2]. A difficulty occurs in the last place, from the circumstance
that St. Paul lays a peculiar stress upon the singular ' seed[3],' which is so
often used in a collective sense ; and seems desirous of showing from
it, that Christ alone could have been intended by the seed of Abraham,
through whom the heathen should be blessed. But this difficulty is
removed by the remark, that he by no means asserts the *necessity*
of this interpretation (which, from his knowledge of Hebrew *could
not* be, and from Romans 4. 13, *was not* the case), but only its
possibility. The fulfilment showed, that the heathen were not to be
blessed by the descendants of Abraham in general, but by one of
them in particular; and St. Paul draws our attention to the fact that the
Lord, who, when He made the promise, had its fulfilment, which He
Himself was to accomplish, already in view, intentionally selected an
expression, which, besides the more comprehensive meaning that
would naturally be given it by the patriarchs, admitted also the
more restricted one which was established by the accomplishment.
Who can reasonably deny, that such may have been the motive for
choosing this expression? We have a case analogous to this in the
Protevangelium ; and the old interpreters have erred in regarding
them both as necessarily referring directly and solely to the person
of the Messiah[4].

Genesis 49:10

68. We here premise that we decidedly hold the genuineness of
Jacob's blessing contained in chap. 49. The chief objection that
has been urged against it, seems to be the doctrinal and *therefore inadmissible one*, that the passage cannot be genuine, because it contains
manifest references to future events, the knowledge of which Jacob
could have had no natural means of possessing. That it does indeed
contain such references cannot be denied. Though with respect to
some of the predictions of Jacob, human causes may be pointed out,
which might have given him an anticipation of the future, (several
distinct references arbitrarily assumed by the opposers of its genuineness must, however, be rejected,) still it contains many predictions
too definite, and too strikingly confirmed by history to be ascribed to
natural causes. Unless we are prepared to deny the historical truth
of the whole book of Genesis, thus involving ourselves in inextrica-

---

[1] " Your father Abraham rejoiced to see my day, and he saw it and was
glad." John 8. 56.
[2] Acts 3. 25, 26. Rom. 4. 13—16. Gal. 3. 8. 16.
[3] זֶרַע.   [4] See also on Deut. 18. and on 2 Sam. 7.

ble difficulties, and also disregarding the authority of the New Testament, we must acknowledge that Jacob also, as well as Isaac his father, and Abraham, received immediate revelations from God. Why then may not this have been the case in the present instance? especially as it is so easy to assign an end which is worthy of God in this last revelation of his purposes to Jacob.—The remaining objections are manifestly sought in order to conceal the fact, that the opinion of their authors rests entirely on doctrinal grounds.   When it is asserted, that a strain of poetry so lofty, animated, and rich in imagery could not have proceeded from a superannuated old man on the brink of the grave, it is not even necessary to refer to the help of God, which freed the soul of the patriarch from the depressing influence of the body.   It may suffice to remark, on the one hand, that the discourse does *not* possess the high poetical character, still less the artistical *completeness*, ascribed to it ; and on the other, that we must not judge of it by the present condition of society, when, with the predominance of the understanding, poetry has become a work of art ; but we must transport ourselves back to the remotest antiquity, when, from the predominance of the imagination and fancy, poetry was a thing of nature, and the objects that presented themselves to the mind, were already clothed in poetical expression and imagery. Much light is thrown on this subject by the history of the old Arabian poetry.   The poets of that country, before the time of Mohammed, often recited long poems extempore.   The poet Lebid, who reached the great age of 157 years, composed a poem while dying : and the poet Hareth, when he recited extempore his Moallakah, which is still extant, was already 135 years old.

69. Of just as little consequence is the alleged difficulty of conceiving how the blessing promised by Jacob could have been handed down *verbatim* to Moses.   Here also the history of the Arabian poetry furnishes the best refutation.   The art of writing was introduced among the Arabians but a short time before Mohammed[1].   Till then their longest poems, some consisting of more than a hundred verses, were preserved by mere oral tradition ; and those which still remain bear internal evidence of the fidelity with which they were handed down.   It has been often remarked, that before the invention of writing, the power of memory was much greater than at present.

70. As it would therefore have been an easy task for the descendants of Jacob, to retain the comparatively brief expressions of the founder of the race ; so must the importance attached to them have furnished a powerful motive, to transmit them with the greatest fidelity from generation to generation.   Such was the length of human life, that the tradition would have to pass through but few hands in descending to Moses : and who can assure us, after all, that Moses did not find this passage already committed to writing?

71. We should digress too far from our purpose, were we to give any thing more than some brief hints of the positive arguments for the genuineness of this portion of Scripture.—All is natural, and too

---

[1] See De Sacy, l. c. p. 306. 348.   Amrulkeisi Moall. ed Hengstenberg, p. 3.

exactly in harmony with the circumstances of Jacob, to have been the
work of a later author.   See especially verse 18, where the patriarch breaks forth in an ejaculation, and prays to God that his happy
dissolution may soon take place.— A *later* writer would have put
into the mouth of Jacob far more of the events which had already
happened ; and have introduced something exactly suited to the existing condition of each tribe.   How little characteristic, for example,
is what is said of Asher, Naphtali, Gad, and Benjamin ! But that
Jacob should have given such mere hints is sufficiently probable ;
for his weakness compelled him to be brief, and he could express
only what was given to him.—Had the writer lived after Moses, he
could never have spoken of the distribution of the Levites in such
terms, as are here employed for the purpose of humbling their
ancestor ; and least of all could he have done this, had he been contemporary with David, when the lot of the children of Levi, so
commended by Moses, was an extremely distinguished one.

72. If then it is evident, that we have here before us the words of the
dying Jacob, instead of being surprised, we naturally expect to find
in them an allusion to the times of the Messiah.   The promises
which were first made to his fathers, and were afterwards delivered to
Jacob himself, embraced two objects—first, a numerous posterity,
and their settlement in the land of Canaan ; and secondly, the blessings which, through them, should be conferred upon all nations.
How then can it well be supposed, that Jacob, when delivering over
these promises to his *sons*, should stop short at their *first* object ?—
that, beholding them in spirit already in possession of the promised
land, he should describe the dwelling-places they should receive,
and many circumstances of their history, but neglect to mention the
second object, which was incomparably the more important, and had
been equally often repeated ?   Is it not far more likely that, as before
among the sons of Abraham and Isaac, so here also among the sons
of Jacob, *the individual* should be pointed out, who, according to the
will of God, was to be the inheritor of this promise, which was continually assuming a more definite form ?

73. The probability of the supposition is not a little strengthened
by the singular unanimity of tradition in its favour.   The unanimity
of the older Jewish writers, in regarding the Messiah [1] as the *subject* of
this prophecy, much as they differed about its import, shows how firm
and sure, and of course how ancient was the tradition they followed.
The Samaritans also explained the passage of the Messiah.   Some of
them did, indeed, hold the doctrine of *two* Messiahs (one who had
already appeared, and another who was yet to come), and, referring

---

[1] Thus it was interpreted by the Chaldaic paraphrases; the Targum of Onkelos, of Jerusalem, and of Jonathan; the Talmud, the Sohar, and the old book
Bereshith Rabba, and even by several of the more modern commentators, as
Jarchi, though they were tempted by that strong prejudice to which others
yielded to give the passage which holds so important a place in the controversy
with Christians another interpretation.

the passage solely to the former, denied its relation to the true
Messiah; but this proves nothing, since the notion of two Messiahs
was of modern origin among the Samaritans, as well as among the
Jews; and in all probability the reference to the true Messiah (which
was never entirely given up) was at the earlier period generally
adopted.

74. Finally, in the Christian Church, the Messianic interpretation
has from the earliest times (as we find it mentioned even by Justin
Martyr) been generally approved. Grotius himself is here obliged
to find the Messiah; and Le Clerc appears as the only critic of his
time who opposes this interpretation. This remarkable unanimity
justifies us in adopting the principle, that the reference to the Messiah
must not be rejected, unless it is proved to be erroneous by other
and better arguments: until then, it deserves the preference over all
other interpretations, even allowing them to be in other respects
equally well founded.

75. We examine first, the justness of the Messianic interpretation.
Every thing depends upon the meaning which we give to the word
Shiloh [1]. The interpretation of this word, which is liable to no objection,
and has every thing in its favour, is that of *pacifier*, or *peacemaker*.
Jahn, indeed, objects that nouns of this form do not denote the *doer
of an action* : but allowing this to be the fact, we need only suppose
that originally it had the abstract meaning *rest* (which is favoured by
the use of Shiloh as the name of a place); but that here, however, as
in numberless other cases, the abstract is used for the concrete [2]. No
name is more consonant to the other Messianic expectations of the
Hebrews, than that of *peacemaker*; which, according to the more
comprehensive meaning given by the Hebrews to words which signify
rest and *peace*, includes also the notion of one who brings salvation [3].
Not only is peace said to be in general characteristic of the times of
the Messiah [4], but He Himself bears the name *Prince of Peace* [5], of

---

[1] The interpretations rejected by Hengstenberg are—(1.) שִׁילֹה, compounded
of the noun שִׁיל ('*child*,' a meaning that cannot be established and the suffix ה for יּ
"Until his, *i. e.* Judah's, son or descendant, the Messias, shall come." (2.) The word
is erroneously pointed. It should be שֶׁלֹה compounded of the pref. שׁ f. אֲשֶׁר and
suf. ה for יּ. The language is elliptical; "until he comes to whom it is, or
belongs," that is, the dominion, or the sceptre. (3.) From the verb שׁלה *qui-
evit.*—With respect to the form of the noun, it is fully sustained by analogy.
Thus כִּדוֹר *tumult of war*, from כָּדַר *to be troubled*, כָּשׁוֹר from כָּשַׁר, שִׁיחוֹר from
שְׁחַר, שָׁלֹה from יִשְׁלָה, קִישׁוֹר from יָקֹשׁר, צִינֹק from יִצנק.

[2] Thus the word שָׁלוֹם *peace*, of similar import, is not only, in general, used in a
concrete sense, he who is *prosperous, peaceful, secure*, but also (precisely in the
same way as שִׁילֹה) as *nomen agentis*, and as a designation of the Messiah, Micah
5. 4. וְזֶה הָיָה שָׁלוֹם, *and this man shall be peace*, *i. e.* the author of peace, see
Ephes. 2. 14.

[3] See שׁלה *e. g.* Ps. 122. 7.
[4] Ps. 72. Zech. 9. 10. Jer. 23. 6. Isa. 11. &c.
[5] Isa. 9. 5, שַׂר הַשָּׁלוֹם

the same import as the word Shiloh most probably given in reference to that name in the passage before us [1].

76. Having thus settled the meaning of the word Shiloh, we proceed to give the translation of the whole verse.—

"The sceptre [2] shall not depart from Judah, nor the lawgiver [3] from between his feet [4] [*i. e.* from Him], until the Peacemaker comes, and Him shall the nations obey [5]."

77. The meaning of this language, according to most of the interpreters, is, that the tribe of Judah should not cease to subsist as a

---

[1] See also the similar appellation in Micah 5. 4.

[2] שֵׁבֶט, *staff, sceptre*, one of the insignia of dominion, which, however, was borne not merely by kings, but also by generals, and other high officers. The old translators reject the trope, and render—*ruler*, or *dominion*.

[3] מְחֹקֵק, *lawgiver, commander, ruler;* the 70, ἡγούμενος. Many interpreters: *the staff of command*, which will agree with שֵׁבֶט in the parallelism. Moreover מִבֵּין רַגְלָיו, *out of the place between his feet*, might then easily admit of a literal sense. But this interpretation is without proof.

[4] After the 70, Jerome, Onkelos, the Targ. Hieros. and Jonathan, many interpreters (as Jahn, Rosenm. and others) take מִבֵּין רַגְלָיו as *euphemismum generationis*, and as standing elliptically for אֲשֶׁר יָצָא מִבֵּין רַגְלָיו. They appeal especially to Deut. xxviii. 57 (the after-birth, הַיּוֹצֵאת מִבֵּין רַגְלֶיהָ). This passage, as Gesenius also remarks, is not conclusive. They appeal also to the somewhat similar forms of expression which often occur: "de femore or de visceribus alicujus exire," for *to be begotten*. But in all the places where these forms occur, the verb יָצָא is inserted, see for example Gen. 35. 11. Exod. 1. 4. 2 Sam. 7. 12, and we would not here assume so harsh an ellipsis, unless no other suitable interpretation could be found. This interpretation, moreover, destroys the parallelism which seems to require that מִבֵּין רַגְלָיו should answer to מִחֹקְקָה. This difficulty vanishes when we assume, with some interpreters, that the figure of *a lion*, which occurs in v. 9, is here carried forward—" Exprimuntur mores ac habitus leonis, dum incubat praedae suae, quam accubando *inter pedes suos* ita servat ac tenet, ut nemo eam ipsi facile eripiat." But another interpretation established by Ernesti (Opus philol. crit. p. 173, seq.) has yet more to recommend it. According to this מִבֵּין רַגְלָיו is synonymous with the simple מִמֶּנּוּ. As the Hebrews not unfrequently place the special in all cases instead of the general, so do they often employ the members of the body for the whole man. Thus especially is יָד *the hand*, often used. In the Arabic *between the hands*, is often put for *with*, in the Alcor. Sur. 60. 12, *between her hands and feet*, stands for: *in herself, with herself*. In Greek we find the corresponding forms ἐκ τῶν ποδῶν ἀποχωρεῖν and ἐκ ποδῶν ἀπέρχεσθαι, for *to go away*. In Latin also, *pes* occurs redundant in the same manner. Thus Cic. pro rege Deïot. 1. § 2, uses the expression, *servum abducere a legatorum pedibus*, for *a legatis*.

[5] The noun יְקָהָה is to be derived from the verb יָקַה, which does not, it is true, occur again in Hebrew; its meaning, however, is ascertained by means of the corresponding Arabic وَقَهَ *to obey*. The noun in Prov. 30. 17, as well as here, has the meaning, *obedience*. Some interpreters, after the example of the 70 (αὐτὸς προσδοκία τῶν ἐθνῶν). The Syr. and Jerome erroneously translate: *expectation*. That by עַמִּים we are not to understand, as Hug supposes, the tribes, but the heathen nations, is evident, since this prophecy refers back to the former ones, according to which all nations were to be blessed in the seed of Abraham, Isaac, and Jacob.—See Isa. 11. 10, &c.

people, and have a government of their own, until the Messiah came ;
that then, however, it should lose its dominion; which, they say,
was fulfilled soon after the coming of Christ, by the destruction of
Jerusalem.

78. We however believe the following to be its true meaning : Judah
shall not cease to exist as a tribe, nor lose its superiority, until it
shall be exalted to higher honour and glory through the great
Redeemer who shall spring from it, and whom not only the Jews,
but all the nations of the earth shall obey.

79. This exposition of the passage is, in the first place, liable to no
philological difficulty. For *till* not unfrequently means *up to* and *afterwards*[1].—The objection of Deyling, that " the patriarch speaks of a
temporal sceptre, whereas the sceptre and kingdom appointed to the
Messiah in this world is *spiritual* and *mystical*," is unfounded.   The
kingdom of the Messiah, in the Old Testament, is not placed in opposition to the theocracy, but appears as a continuation of it [2].   As,
according to Isaiah [3], the Prince of Peace sits upon the throne of
David, and prolongs the duration of David's kingdom for ever ; and
in Amos [4], the fallen tabernacle of David is to be rebuilt by Him ; so
here the Redeemer, who shall spring from Judah, appears as the
Enlarger of his dominion, hitherto limited to a single people, over all
nations.

80. What especially determines us to prefer the above explanation
to the other, which is generally received, is, that the future termination of the dominion of his tribe, which, according to the latter
explanation, is here foretold, does not at all accord with the joyful
nature of the remaining part of this address to Judah.   Besides, it
would seem too early to announce already the future rejection of
Judah ; and such an interpretation could not be admitted, unless no
other could on good ground be established.   And, lastly, it supposes Jacob to have left the promise of the Messiah *indefinite*,
whereas the analogy of the other instances would lead us to expect,
that it would be extended and limited to *one* of his sons.

81. Let us now turn our attention to the *fulfilment* of this prophecy.   Two things are foretold.   That the tribe of Judah should
not cease to exist as a people, and have a government of its own, till
the Redeemer should appear.   And here we must bear in mind, that
the prophecy relates to its *permanent* condition before the coming of
the Messiah.   The *temporary* cessation of the national subsistence,
therefore, as for example, during the Babylonian exile—granting
that the tradition of the Jews, that they still existed as a people, and

---

[1] This usage is happily explained by Abenezra : " Non est sensus verborum
sceptrum esse recessurum cum venerit Schiloh ; sed hæc locutio similis est illi :
non deerit huic panis, donec veniat tempus, quo ei erunt agri vineæque multæ
(i. e. quando veniet tempus ejusmodi, multo minus ei panis deerit), item Gen.
28. 15.   Non deseram te, usque dum fecero, quod locutus sum tibi, quod
nempe velim te reducere in hanc terram, i. e. multo minus te reductum in terram
deseram : similiter dicitur : non auferetur sceptrum de Jehudah, donec veniat
Schiloh, i. e. nunquam auferetur sceptrum de Jehudah, multo minus, quum
venerit Schiloh."

[2] Comp. 2 Sam. 7. 12, &c.   [3] Isa. 9. 6.   [4] Amos 9. 11.

had governors of their own during that period, is not to be believed—
can as little disprove the truth of this prediction, as the period of
unbelief and apostasy, which is now passing away [1], destroys the truth
of the promise which Christ gave to his New Testament Church.   If
we take this into consideration, we shall see that history most
strikingly confirms this part of the prediction : while the ten tribes
have never had a *national* existence, since they were carried away
into captivity, the tribe of Judah returned, and continued to subsist,
till the appearance of the Messiah, *the other* tribes, with *their* institutions and privileges, having long before passed away. – If any one
is disposed, with many interpreters, to go further (for which, however, there is properly no sufficient reason), and find in this verse a
prediction, not only of the continuance of the national self-subsistence
of the tribe of Judah until the coming of the Shiloh, but also of its
superiority over the other tribes, history will supply him with the evidence of its fulfilment.   Even during the journey through the wilderness, and afterwards in the time of the Judges, this tribe maintained
a certain pre-eminence : with the elevation of the house of David it
obtained the regal dominion.   After the division of the kingdom, it
had the advantage of.possessing Jerusalem, the legal capital, and the
temple : after the return from the captivity, it gave the name to the
whole nation : and the high council which decided in temporal and
spiritual affairs, was established within its limits.   Even under the
dominion of the Romans it retained no inconsiderable power.—(2) It
was also predicted that, through the Messiah, the tribe of Judah
should extend its dominion over many nations.   The fulfilment is
shown in Matt. 1. 1—16.   It is in allusion to this prophecy that
Christ is called, in the fifth chapter of the Apocalypse, the lion of the
tribe of Judah [2].

b. Messianic Predictions in the Remaining Books of the Pentateuch

82. The contents of the last four books of the Pentateuch are such,
that prophecies of the Messiah could not occur in them so frequently
as in Genesis.   Having in that book opened the prospect into futurity, and, at the same time, prepared the way, by the law respecting
the prophets, for clear discoveries, and for proving the connexion of
the preparatory institution with the final and perfect one which was
to follow it, Moses could now the more easily content himself with the
actual preparation for the coming of the Messiah, by the firm establishment of the theocratical institutions.   It was necessary that the
people should *live themselves* into the spirit of these institutions, before
the hope of the Messiah could be rightly conceived, and exert its
proper influence ; and it was well that their views at present should
not be too far diverted from them.

---

[1] *i. e.* from Germany.
[2] On the *other* interpretations see the original work, vol. 1. p. 74 : Transl. vol. 1.
p. 61.

83. The first passage, commonly referred to the Messiah, is contained in the prophecy of Balaam.

Numbers 24:17 et seqq.

English Bible	*Hengstenberg*
84. ' I shall see him, but not now: I shall behold him, but not nigh: there shall come a Star out of Jacob, and a Sceptre shall rise out of Israel, and shall smite the corners of Moab, and destroy all the children of Sheth. And Edom shall be a possession, Seir also shall be a possession for his enemies ; and Israel shall do valiantly. Out of Jacob shall come he that shall have dominion, and shall destroy him that remaineth of the city.'	' I see him, but not now ; I behold him ; but not nigh. A star goes forth from Jacob ; a sceptre arises out of Israel. He smites the borders of Moab, and destroys all the sons of Seth, and Edom shall be a possession, Seir also shall be a possession for his enemies. Out of Jacob shall come forth a Ruler, and shall destroy the last remnant out of the city.'

85. A powerful ruler of the Israelites, who shall arise at a future time, and gain a signal triumph over their enemies, the Moabites and Idumeans, here presents himself to the spiritual eyes of the prophet. By this *Ruler*, the Jews from the earliest times have understood the Messiah, either exclusively, or else principally, with a secondary reference to David. It is evident how widely this interpretation prevailed among the Jews, from the circumstance that the famous pseudo-Messiah, who appeared in the time of Adrian, borrowed from it the surname Bar-Chochab, Son of the Star.—From the Jews, this exposition passed to the Christians. Cyril of Jerusalem defended it against Julian[1]. Either its exclusive relation to the Messiah was maintained, or it was allowed to refer indeed, in the first instance, to David ; but then both himself and his temporal victories were regarded as typical of Christ, and His spiritual triumphs, which (according to this exposition) the prophet had especially in view.

86. Considered in itself, the supposition of an *inferior* reference to David, and a *higher* one to Christ, is liable to no objection. In this case, neither David, nor Christ as an individual, but the royal race, who should hereafter arise among the people of Israel, would have been represented to the prophet as personified ; and, guided by the fulfilment, we should then have had to decide, what belonged to the one or the other member of this race. Just so the promise to David[2] relates to *the whole royal race*, and the fulfilment enables us to judge what refers to Solomon, what to other leaders of the visible

[1] See Jul. ed. Spanh. p. 263 c.   [2] 2 Sam. 7.

theocracy, and what to Christ [1]. But it is not enough that there is no *a priori* objection to this supposition; it must be established by positive arguments; and it would seem that arguments of sufficient cogency are not to be obtained.

87. (1) It has, it is true, in its favour the argument from tradition. But as this is never conclusive by itself, so here it loses nearly all its force from the fact, that the passage furnishes the Jews with a welcome support to their worldly expectations concerning the Messiah. A single ancient testimony in favour of the reference of the fifty-third chapter of Isaiah to the Messiah, is of more weight than *all* their Messianic interpretations of this passage.

88. (2) No evidence can be drawn from the New Testament. An appeal has indeed been made to the account of the star which announced the birth of the Redeemer [2]. But the two cases have nothing in common; as is evident even from the total silence of St. Matthew, who makes a point of showing the agreement between prophecy and its fulfilment. Besides Balaam did not mean a *literal* star, but used the word 'star' metaphorically, as is customary among all nations, to designate a great and illustrious ruler.

89. (3) It is equally impossible to bring forward internal evidence of its application to Christ in any sense. The prophecy is *completely fulfilled in David*. This king destroyed many of the Moabites, and made the remainder tributary. 'He smote Moab, and measured them with a line, casting them down to the ground; even with two lines measured he to put to death, and with one full line to keep alive. And so the Moabites became David's servants, and brought gifts [3].' Here the historical fulfilment is described in language that comes near, in strength at least, to the language of this prediction [4]. He also subdued the Idumeans [5], and all the neighbouring enemies of the theocracy [6].

90. But we must not pass over the internal evidences which the advocates for the reference to the Messiah have here brought forward.—Their chief argument is taken from the words, 'he shall destroy all the sons of Seth.' By the 'sons of Seth' we are to understand, it is said, the whole human race, since all men are descended from Seth the son of Adam [7]. Were this opinion correct, there would certainly be *one* feature of the prophecy which would *not* suit David. But to this Michaelis has well replied, that men might aptly enough be called after their *first* and *last* common ancestors, sons of Adam, or sons of Noah, but it would be very strange were they to be named after any of the eight patriarchs who

[1] In many other instances whole races are beheld by the prophets as individuals.
[2] Thus Origen c. Cels. l. 12. sect. 2.   [3] 2 Sam. 8. 2.
[4] So Ps. 60.8. 'Moab is my washpot: over Edom will I cast out my shoe,' &c.
[5] ' He put garrisons in Edom: throughout all Edom put he garrisons, and all they of Edom became David's servants.'—2 Sam. 9. 14.
[6] ' Of all the nations which he had subdued: of Syria, and of Moab, and of the children of Ammon, and of the Philistines, and of Amalek, and of the spoil of Hadadezer son of Rehob, king of Zobah.'—2 Sam. 8. 11, 12.
[7] So Onkelos, who translates בני אנשא.

came between. Besides, the context does not allow of this exposition. Balaam speaks first, in the seventeenth verse, of Moab ; in the
eighteenth, of Edom ; and shall he here between them abruptly make
the *whole human race* the subject of his prophecy ? The parallel,
moreover, between Edom and Seir[1], leads us to think that the sons
of Seth are nearly, if not entirely, identical with Moab ; and we
embrace the opinion of Verschuir, that ' *Seth*' is here not a proper
name, but an appellative, meaning ' *tumult*.' ' *Sons of tumult*' is an
appropriate designation, either for the Moabites alone, or for them and
the neighbouring tribes together, who were always restless and inclined
for war[2].—An appeal is also made to Balaam's exordium, which
(it is urged) would lead us to suspect something far more important.
But then it is forgotten, that in the third verse, he makes one equally
pompous, without afterwards announcing any thing more than the
temporal prosperity of Israel.—Lastly, much stress is laid on the
declaration of Balaam to the king of Moab, that he would foretell
what should happen to his people ' *in the latter days*[3].' This expression, it is thought, can be understood only of the times of the
Messiah. It is true that the *later* prophets are accustomed to use it
with this specific meaning : but it is equally certain, that, at an
earlier period, it was used indefinitely, meaning simply *the future ;
the time to come*[4].

91. There is, then, no sufficient reason for referring this prophecy
to the Messiah. On the other hand, the objections to this reference
are strong. It is indeed true, that the increase of the extent and
glory of the divine kingdom by the Messiah, is often represented
under the image, borrowed from the earthly theocracy, of the *conquest* of those who were to be received into it[5]. But then the context
always enables us to perceive that the representation is figurative.
It is not so, however, in the present case. It appears rather from
the fourteenth verse ; ' I will show thee what this people shall do to
thy people,' that it is *misfortune* and not prosperity, that Balaam
announces to the king. This difficulty would indeed vanish, were
we with other interpreters to understand the prediction as announcing not the *conversion*, but the *destruction* of Christ's enemies, as in
the second, and hundred and tenth Psalms. But this opinion is not
sufficiently sustained by the remark (which is correct in itself), that
the prophets frequently designate the enemies of the Messiah's kingdom by the name of some nation peculiarly hostile to the visible
theocracy ; since, that the mention of the Moabites is not here figurative, and as a part for the whole, is proved from the circumstance
that Balaam had the king of the Moabites before him, and declared

---

[1] Ver. 18.

[2] שת for שֵׁאת (Lam. 3. 47.) from שָׁאָה *fragorem edidit.* In Jer. 48. 45. (which
is imitated from this passage) we have, in parallelism with Moab, בְּנֵי שָׁאוֹן
filii tumultûs.

    [In Eng. Bible (margin) :
           ' And shall devour the corner of Moab,
           The crown of the head of *the children of noise*.']

[3] בְּאַחֲרִית הַיָּמִים   [4] Deut. 4. 30. Gen. 49.   [5] See Ps. 110. 3.

it to be his purpose to speak concerning the future destinies of *his* people. Further, although the Messiah in other places is exhibited as a strict judge of his enemies, yet this character is never given to Him as his *only* character, the blessings He will confer on those who submit to his authority being entirely overlooked. The person described by Balaam cannot possibly be the same, who, according to the promises made to the patriarchs, was to confer blessings upon all nations, and (according to the forty-ninth chapter of Genesis) to be the author of peace, to whom the nations were to yield a willing obedience.

Deuteronomy 18:15-18

92. 'The Lord thy God will raise up unto thee a Prophet, from the midst of thee, of thy brethren, like unto me ; unto him ye shall hearken : according to all thou desiredst of the Lord thy God in Horeb in the day of the assembly, saying, Let me not hear again the voice of the Lord my God, neither let me see this great fire any more, that I die not. And the Lord said unto me, They have well spoken that which they have spoken. I will raise them up a Prophet from among their brethren, like unto thee; and I will put my words into his mouth ; and he shall speak unto them all that I shall command him.'

93. We here, in the first place, bring together the arguments which favour the reference to Christ. (1) It is authorized by tradition. The later Jewish expositors have, indeed, as we have seen, relinquished it. But then this has arisen entirely from polemic views. It can be satisfactorily proved, that the Messianic interpretation was, throughout, the prevailing one among the older Jews[1]. Sufficient evidence of this is supplied by the New Testament. The manner in which Peter and Stephen quote this passage shows, that it was usually referred to the Messiah. They deem it superfluous to *prove* this, but consider it as universally acknowledged.—It is highly probable that Philip had this passage especially in view, when he said to Nathanael, ' We have found him, of whom *Moses in the Law* . . . . *did write*, Jesus of Nazareth[2].' In John 6. 14, the people, at the feeding of the five thousand, exclaim : " This is of a truth *that Prophet* that should come into the world." The Messianic interpretation,

[1] In evidence of this an appeal has been made sometimes to 1 Macc. 14. 41 : καὶ ὅτι οἱ Ἰουδαῖοι καὶ οἱ ἱερεῖς εὐδόκησαν τοῦ εἶναι αὐτῶν Σίμωνα ἡγούμενον καὶ ἀρχιερέα εἰς τὸν αἰῶνα, ἕως τοῦ ἀναστῆναι προφήτην πιστόν. This, however, is incorrect. For that we are not here to understand by ' the sure [*E. B.* faithful] prophet' (*i. e.* one sanctioned by miracles or fulfilled predictions), the Messiah—the prophet promised by Moses, as after Luther many of the older expositors have done, is evident from the absence of the article, and also from the adjective πιστός. The sense is rather : ' Simon and his family shall hold the highest dignity in the state, until God Himself, by a future prophet (there being none at that time), should make another appointment.'

[2] John 1. 46.

therefore, was not that of a few learned men, but of the whole people [1]. This interpretation prevailed also among the Samaritans. The woman of Samaria says, " I know that Messias cometh, which is called Christ: when he is come, he will tell us all things [2]." As the Samaritans received only the Pentateuch, the notion which is here expressed of the Messiah, as a divinely enlightened instructor, could have been derived from no other source than the passage before us. The last words agree almost verbatim with those in the eighteenth verse of the prophecy, ' and he shall speak unto them all that I shall command him.'

94. (2) The reference of the prophecy to the Messiah rests on the sure evidence of the New Testament. It is not improbable, as some have supposed, that Christ Himself referred particularly to this place [3], when He says that Moses wrote of Him; since his expression relates rather to that part of the Pentateuch, where Moses acts in his own person, than where he appears as a mere reporter; and the Jews would be more likely to acknowledge that this prophecy was fulfilled in Him, than that in the forty-ninth chapter of Genesis, which presents the Messiah in his *glory*. Further: He explained to his disciples the prophecies relating to Himself in the Pentateuch [4]. And it cannot be supposed that the very passage which was brought forward by Peter as *the most conclusive of all* [5], should not have been so represented by Christ. The manner in which the citation is made, excludes the notion, that Moses speaks of Christ only as included among the prophets, taken collectively. Peter says expressly, Moses and the later prophets have foretold ' of these days [6];' and it appears from the words ' *that* prophet [7],' that he did not understand the singular in a collective sense. That Stephen, in Acts 7. 36, also referred the passage to Christ, would not of itself be conclusive, for the authority of Stephen ought not to have exactly the same weight as that of the Apostles. But we must not overlook Matt. 17. 5, according to which a voice was heard from heaven in attestation of Christ, " This is my beloved Son, in whom I am well pleased; HEAR HIM." As the first part of this declaration is taken from the Messianic prediction in the forty-second chapter of Isaiah, so is the second part from the passage under consideration; and by this employment of its words its meaning is clearly shown.

95. (3) There is also internal evidence of its relation to the Messiah. That Moses designed to designate, principally at least, an *individual*, and not the *collective body* of the prophets, appears from this, that the Hebrew word [8] employed is always used in the singular, and with singular suffixes, whereas in the case of collective nouns, it is usual to interchange the singular and

---

[1] The appeal, as to John 1. 21 and 7. 40, is, however, groundless, since the prophet is there distinguished from Christ.

[2] John 4. 25.   [3] John 5. 46.   [4] According to Luke 24. 44.

[5] Acts 3. 22, 23.   [6] τὰς ἡμέρας ταύτας.

[7] τοῦ προφήτου ἐκείνου.—' And it shall come to pass that every soul which will not hear *that* prophet, shall be destroyed from among the people.'—Acts 3. 23.

[8] נָבִיא

plural. The force of this argument is evident from the fact, that not a few non-Messianic interpreters have been compelled by it to make some particular individual the subject. Moreover, the word does not occur elsewhere as a collective noun, nor are the prophets any where spoken of in the manner alleged. The doctrine concerning the Messiah was already current among the people. How then could they understand the promise, in which only one person was mentioned, in any other way than as referring at least chiefly to the one expected ?—Besides, even the words ' *like* unto me,' and ' *like* unto thee,' agrees *better*, to say the least, with the Messianic interpretation, than with any other. Even when (avoiding the errour of the old interpreters, who extended the *likeness* to every particular) we confine it to the point of resemblance intimated by the actual words in which the promise was conveyed, there still remains a difficulty in making the prophets *collectively* the subject of it. The point of resemblance is (according to the eighteenth verse) the office of *Mediator*. Because the Israelites are unable to endure the terrours of the Divine majesty, God will communicate with them in future times through a Mediator, as He had hitherto done through Moses. This can be true of the prophetic *order* only in a certain sense, and is properly accomplished only in Christ, who is the *one Mediator* of the New Covenant, as Moses was of the Old.

96. Doubtless, however, there are some arguments which seem to oppose the *exclusive* reference of the prophecy to Christ, as an individual. (1) The connexion. This is twofold. Moses, in the fifteenth verse, first utters the promise in his own name. Here it refers to what had gone before. He had forbidden to the people of Israel the use of all those means, by which the idolatrous nations sought to go beyond the boundaries of human knowledge. ' Thou shalt not do so,' is his language : ' for what you seek in vain by these unlawful expedients, shall be really imparted to you from God.' Not only was it entirely proper on such an occasion to remind them of the Messiah (since his manifestation, being the most perfect of God's revelations, best satisfies the desire for higher degrees of knowledge), but it would have been strange indeed, if the founder of the old dispensation, when so suitable an opportunity presented itself, neglecting to direct the attention of the people to the author of the new one, had spoken *only* of the intervening and inferior communications from God. But on the other hand, it would be equally strange, if he had taken *no notice whatever* of these intermediate communications : if, after laying down [1] the distinctive marks of the true and the false prophets, he had here referred merely to the divine revelations to be expected at a *far distant period*, and overlooked those to be vouchsafed in the mean time ; thus neglecting to employ a method peculiarly suited to prepare the way for his exhortations.—In the eighteenth verse the promise stands in a different connexion. In the fifteenth verse, Moses had delivered it in his own person. In order to give to it the higher authority, he relates in the following verses, when

[1] In chap. 13.

and in what manner he had received it from God. It was delivered
to him on Sinai, where God in the promulgation of the Law had communicated directly with the people, in order to give them a deeper impression of the holiness of the Law, to strengthen their confidence in
the mediation of Moses, and to show them the folly of desiring any
other method of Divine communication. But the people, struck with
consternation before the dreadful majesty of God, had prayed that he
would no longer speak to them directly, but through a mediator, as
he had done in times past [1]. In consequence of this request, God
said to Moses: "They have well spoken ; I will raise them up a
Prophet from among their brethren, like unto thee, and I will put
my words in his mouth; and he shall speak unto them all that I
shall command him." We cannot fail to perceive that here, if ever,
a divine revelation of the coming of Christ would be appropriate,
who, as Mediator between God and man, veiled his Godhead, and
brought the Divinity in human form near to men. Yet at the same
time we should expect some allusion to the inferior messengers of
God who were to precede him.

97. (2) But the *exclusive* reference to the Messiah as an individual, seems most inconsistent with the twentieth and two following verses. There the marks of a *false* prophet are given. If the
foregoing has no relation to the *true* prophets, it will be difficult to
perceive any just connexion of ideas in the passage.

98. How then can the two suppositions be reconciled, that Moses
had the Messiah undeniably in view, and yet that the prediction
relates also to the prophets in general ?—Most naturally in the following manner. Moses had Christ here in view, though not merely in
reference to his visible manifestation, but also to his previous invisible
influence ; as the Spirit of Christ is said by Peter to have spoken
through the prophets [2]. He does not indeed speak of the prophets as
a collective body, to which Christ also in the end incidentally belonged, as Calvin and other commentators supposed ; but the *prophetical order* appeared to him *personified in Christ*, in whom his
idea of it was completely realized. There is then here a reference to
the other prophets also, not however as individuals, but in relation
to that Spirit by which, though in an inferior degree, they were influenced, and made one with their head. They were contemplated
in Christ, because they were merely his organs. It was His Spirit
that gave them their being.

2. The Messianic Psalms

99. After the death of Jacob, Messianic prophecy received no considerable enlargement, nor any more specific determination, until the
reign of David, when, as heretofore only the *tribe* had been designated from which the Redeemer was to spring, so now the particular
family was selected. This was done in the prediction which God by

---

[1] See Exod. 20.   [2] 1 Pet. 1. 11.

the prophet Nathan delivered to David at a time when, penetrated with gratitude for victory over all his foes, and his elevation from the deepest obscurity to the highest honour, he had resolved to erect for God a permanent temple, instead of the moveable tabernacle in which He had hitherto vouchsafed to dwell[1]. Some interpreters[2] have erroneously referred this promise *exclusively* to the Messiah. It contains too many things which can relate only either to Solomon or to the other natural descendants of David, to allow of this interpretation. For example[3], the descendant of David builds a temple for God; language which, taken in connexion with the previous mention of David's desire to build a temple, can be understood only of the earthly temple to be erected by Solomon. According to the fifteenth verse, when the descendants of David should commit iniquity, God would not cast them entirely away, but visit them with gentle chastisement; here, also, the reference to a mere human and therefore sinful posterity is plain. Moreover this promise[4] is said by David himself to relate in the first instance to Solomon; and that Solomon so understood it is manifest[5]. But on the other hand, we would just as little venture, with Grotius and others, to refer it to Solomon *alone;* or with others, to Solomon and the rest of the earthly kings of the house of David. When we reflect that the promise of the great Redeemer, who should spring from the tribe of Judah, could not be unknown to David, we feel certain, that in the words, "And thy house and thy kingdom shall be established for ever before thee: thy throne shall be established for ever," he must have seen something far more than could ever be fulfilled in his son Solomon, or any of his mere human descendants, who, like every thing earthly and mortal, must one day come to an end.

100. That he certainly did so, is plain from the powerful emotion which the communication awakened in his bosom[6]. Just views of it have been taken by those who[7] give it a double reference, first to Solomon and his successors, and also to Christ. It is very frequently the case in the prophetic annunciations that whole families and races are viewed as an individual; and then, whatever belongs to their different members is ascribed to *him*[8]. So is it in the passage before us.

---

[1] 2 Sam. 7. 11—16. 'Also the Lord telleth thee that he will make thee an house. And when thy days be fulfilled, and thou shalt sleep with thy fathers, I will set up thy seed after thee, which shall proceed out of thy bowels, and I will establish his kingdom. He shall build an house for my name, and I will establish the throne of his kingdom for ever. I will be his father, and he shall be my son. If he commit iniquity, I will chasten him with the rod of men, and with the stripes of the children of men: but my mercy shall not depart away from him, as I took it from Saul, whom I put away before thee. And thine house and thy kingdom shall be established for ever before thee : thy house shall be established for ever.'

[2] As Calovius.   [3] Ver. 13.

[4] ' Behold a son shall be born to thee who shall be a man of rest, and I will give him rest from all his enemies round about; for his name shall be Solomon, and I will give peace and quietness unto Israel in his days.'   1 Chron. 22. 9.

[5] From 1 Kings 5. 5. 8. 17, &c. 2 Chron. 6. 7.

[6] 2 Sam. 7. 18.

[7] As Augustine, de Civ. Dei, 17. 8, 9.

[8] See, for example, the blessing of Jacob, Gen. 49.

Many things relate only to David's natural posterity, as the building of the temple and the mild chastisement: others exclusively to the Messiah, as the repeated assurance of the endless duration of his dominion; and, finally, others are fulfilled in an inferior sense in Solomon and his descendants, and in a higher one in Christ, as the promise, ' I will be his Father and he shall be my son.'

101. Thus, therefore, an important advance was made. Relying upon this prediction, the prophets not only announced the derivation of Messiah from David, from whose life they borrowed the lineaments with which, when ennobled and perfected, they might describe his illustrious descendant; but David also himself, and other holy men who composed the Psalms, were led by the Divine Spirit into a deeper understanding of this promise, and received further illumination respecting its object [1].

102. The Psalms which are justly regarded as prophetic of the Messiah, may be divided into two classes :

a. Psalms in which the Messiah is celebrated in His glory, and His dominion described by images drawn from the earthly theocracy

103. These Psalms have much in common, and so plainly refer to the *same* subject, that if the Messianic character of one be established, that of all the rest will follow.   When we compare these predictions with those of an earlier period, we at once discover an important difference.   Those of an earlier period had been more brief, more in the form of allusions ; but now, the foundation being provided, the prophecies could become finished descriptions.   To David the Messiah was announced as a *king*, as his successor on his throne. And thus in his own contemplation, and in that of the other holy authors of the Psalms, the earthly head of the theocracy formed the substratum of its future illustrious Renovator and Restorer.

Psalm 2

104. The name of the author of this Psalm is not given in the superscription : but tradition (ascertained by its being classed among the Psalms of David), the fact that events of his time form the ground work of its representations, its resemblance to his acknowledged

---

[1] That David in particular was excited by the Divine promise, and afterwards received further illumination from the prophetic spirit which dwelt within him, is asserted by Peter, Acts 2. 30, 31.   The latter rests moreover on the testimony of the Lord Himself, Matt. 22. 43, where he says, 'David spake ἐν πνεύματι, moved by the Holy Spirit.   That true Messianic predictions are contained in the Psalms is evident from the fact that the Lord after his resurrection proved to his disciples that all that had happened to Him had been foretold not only in the other books of the Old Testament, but also in the Psalms.

Psalms[1], and the testimony of the New Testament[2], all combine to prove it to have been composed by David.—Its contents are as follows. The holy Psalmist in prophetic vision beholds a multitude of nations with their kings in mad rebellion against God and his Anointed, their rightful sovereign[3], while he raises his eyes from the wild tumult on earth to God enthroned in the exalted rest of heaven[4], and declares that he will easily quell the powerless rebellion; he hears the voice of Jehovah proclaiming that He had established his Anointed as king[5], and that, consequently, all resistance to his authority, being likewise directed against Himself the Omnipotent, must be fruitless. Immediately after, the Psalmist[6] hears another voice, that of the Anointed, declaring that Jehovah has given to Him as his Son, whom He demonstrates to be such by powerful proofs, the people of the whole earth for his possession, with the right and the power to inflict the severest punishment upon all who should resist his lawful dominion. He now[7] addresses the kings as if they were actually present, and exhorts them, ere the fearful vengeance threatened against the despisers of the Son should burst upon their heads, to seek forgiveness by humble submission to their king, the Son of God, who is no less merciful to his friends, than terrible to his enemies.

105. This Psalm, according to the view we have taken of its contents, possesses, like many of the predictions of the prophets, a dramatic character. Different persons one after another (as, the author himself, the rebellious kings, Jehovah, his Son and Anointed) make their appearance, and speak or act without the change of person being expressly mentioned.

106. The question now arises, who is meant by ' the Anointed' and ' the Son of God?'—That the Messiah is intended, appears from all those arguments in general, by which He can be shown to be the subject of *any* passage of the Old Testament.

107. (1) The testimony of tradition. It is an undoubted fact, and unanimously admitted even by the recent opposers of its reference to Him, that the Psalm was universally regarded by the ancient Jews as foretelling the Messiah. The high priest asked Jesus, whether He were the Christ, the Son of God[8]; thus borrowing from it two appellations of the expected Redeemer; and also Nathanael said to Christ with reference to this Psalm, " Thou art the Son of God : thou art the King of Israel[9]." In the older Jewish writings also[10] there is a variety of passages in which the Messianic interpretation is given to this Psalm. Even Kimchi and Jarchi confess, that it was the prevailing one among their forefathers; and the latter very honestly gives his reason for departing from it, when he says, he preferred to explain it of David for the refutation of the heretics[11], that is, in

---

[1] Especially to the 110th.   [2] Acts 4. 25.
[3] Ver. 1—3.   [4] Ver. 4, 5.   [5] Ver. 6.
[6] Ver. 7—9.   [7] Ver. 10—12.   [8] Matt. 26. 63.
[9] In John 1. 49.   [10] As the Sohor, the Talmud, &c.
[11] להשובת המינם

order to destroy the force of the arguments drawn from it by the Christians [1]. The Christians sought to prove his eternal generation from the Father: to deprive them of this proof, the more modern Jews thought best to refer it to another subject.

108. (2) Here, if any where, plain references of the New Testament speak in favour of the Messianic interpretation. In Acts 4. 25, 26, the whole company of the Apostles quote the first verses of this Psalm, and refer them to Christ. It is true that Ammon, after Eckermann, has asserted, that they made use of these verses merely that they might offer their prayers to God in a more emphatic language by adopting the words of the Old Testament; but the incorrectness of this opinion is easily shown. The form of the quotation itself, 'who by the mouth of thy servant David hast said [2],' proves that the Apostles believed the Psalm to contain a direct prediction of Christ. It is usual on other occasions, when a Messianic prediction is quoted from the Psalms, to refer to a Divine revelation as to its source [3]. To this we may add, that the Apostles found the Messianic interpretation handed down by tradition, and confirmed it (as appears from other passages also) by their authority [4]. Paul quotes the seventh verse of this Psalm, and explains it of the resurrection of Christ [5]. That this is not a mere allusion, is evident from the fact, that the Apostle advances this and other passages as a proof, that the promise made to the fathers was fulfilled in the resurrection of Christ. In Heb. 1. 5., 5. 7. it is quoted as evidence of the exaltation of Christ above all angels; and in the fifth chapter it is said that God spake the words of this verse to *Him* [6].

109. (3) A no less striking proof in favour of this interpretation is afforded by the Psalm itself. It plainly possesses features which correspond to no earthly king, and can belong to the Messiah alone. In the first place, the king anointed appears as a being of a nature more than human. We here first appeal to the seventh verse : "Thou art my son; this day have I begotten thee." We concede to the modern critics, that from the appellation *Son of God*, abstractedly considered, no conclusion can be drawn, it being not unfrequently given to the earthly leaders of the theocracy. But then, in such instances, the appellation results from the idea, not of generation, but of representation and subordination; it is not the *natural*, but the *moral* relation of father and son which is transferred to the relation between God and his earthly representative. The name *Son of God* in such

---

[1] The words "for the refutation of the heretics" are indeed omitted in many Jewish and Christian editions, probably from fear of the censors of the press, and because this confession was found to be too candid. But Pococke, in his notes Miscel. ad Portam Mosis, p. 308, seq. ed. Lips. has restored them from a manuscript, and they are found also in an Erfurt MS.

[2] ὁ διὰ στόματος Δαβὶδ τοῦ παιδός σου εἰπών.

[3] Matt. 22. 43. Acts 2. 30, 31.   [4] Acts 13. 33.

[5] ' As it is also written in the second Psalm, Thou art my Son, this day have I begotten thee.'

[6] ' So also Christ glorified not himself to be made an High Priest, but he that said unto him, Thou art my Son, to-day have I begotten thee.'—Heb. 5. 5.

cases is entirely synonymous with that of servant of God. But that here the name of *Son of God* must be taken in a different sense, and indicate a proper sonship, is shown by the other member of the parallelism, 'This day have I begotten thee.' It has often been thought that the *eternal* generation of the Son from the Father is asserted in these words. The word *to-day*[1] has been taken as the designation of *eternity*, in which there is neither past nor future, and which may therefore most fully be expressed by the image of the present. So among the fathers, Athanasius, and Augustine, who says: " *In eternity neither is there any thing past, as if it had ceased to be, nor future, as if it were not yet; but only present, because whatever is eternal, exists always*[2]." This interpretation (which was opposed by Theodoret in ancient, and Calvin in modern times) is untenable, since the writers of the Psalms never represent eternity by the present, although this is often done by the later theologians and philosophers[3]. But equally unfounded is the explanation of many modern interpreters, who, in order to give the verse an earthly subject, translate *yalad* either to *adopt*, or to *make a son* in the sense of subordination and representation[4]. We give to it the *declarative* meaning, which is sufficiently established and correct[5]. It is not uncommon in the language of Scripture to say of a person or thing, that it *becomes*, when it is made known to be what it is[6]. In the declarative sense the word can mean nothing else than to *declare to have been begotten*. 'I have this day begotten thee,' that is, 'I have this day *declared* that thou art begotten by me.' This, then, is in all respects the same as, 'I have declared thee to be my son :' so also in Jer. 2. 27, 'Thou art my Father,' and 'thou hast begotten me,' are also used as synonymous. But this can be the case only when the literal meaning of the word *son* is retained, and not when it is used in a mere moral sense. The parallelism then requires that the words 'thou art my son,' should be taken literally. Now that kings are not called the *sons of God* in this sense, but only metaphorically, is generally acknowledged by interpreters. Not

[1] היום.

[2] " In æternitate nec præteritum quidquam est, quasi esse desierit; nec futurum, quasi nondum sit, sed præsens tantum, quia quidquid æternum est, semper est."

[3] Compare Philo de Profug. p. 458, ed. Francof.: σήμερον ἐστὶν ὁ ἀπέρατος καὶ ἀδιεξίτητος αἰών· μηνῶν γὰρ καὶ ἐνιαυτῶν, καὶ συνόλως χρόνων περίοδοι δόγματα ἀνθρώπων εἰσὶν, ἀριθμὸν ἐκτετιμηκότων, τὸ δὲ ἀψευδὲς ὄνομα αἰῶνος, ἡ σήμερον.

[4] The first of these translations is liable to this objection, that not a single instance can be found where ילד occurs in the sense supposed. Equally unsustained is the other interpretation.

[5] In this sense Paul also understood the expression, Acts 13. 33 where he explains the verse of the resurrection as the fact whereby Christ was eminently declared to be the Son of God. The declaration of Jehovah must be regarded as being made at the time when by clear proofs He had made known his Son as such: then היום may preserve its suitable interpretation.—See the examples in Glassius, Philol. s. 3. No. 15.

[6] See Rom. 1. 4, where from a disregard of this usage ὁρισθέντος has been falsely rendered *who was proved*, in which sense the verb does not occur.

a single example has been adduced, where *to beget* means to make
a son in the metaphorical sense. In 1 Cor. 4. 15 [1], the discourse
is concerning a real begetting by the communication of the Holy
Ghost, analogous to a physical one. We add to these considerations,
that in the twelfth verse the subject of the Psalm is called simply *the
son*, which indicates a sonship of a peculiar and exclusive character,
that renders any more accurate definition unnecessary ; and if we
compare Ps. 45. 7, and 110. 5 [2], there can no doubt remain, that the
language before us relates to one who is the Son of God in a *literal*
and *proper* sense. Besides, there are other traits that indicate his
superhuman character : see particularly the twelfth verse. There the
rebels are exhorted to submit with humility and reverence to their
king, because his wrath would soon be kindled, while, at the same
time, he would confer blessings upon those who put their trust in
him. If what is here said of *wrath* will not (as De Wette remarks)
agree with an *earthly* king, much less will the exhortation to seek
the *favour* of this king, and trust in his protection. The people of
Israel were at all times exhorted by the sacred writers not to trust
in feeble mortals, but to put their confidence in their mighty God and
flee to Him alone for succour [3]. The difficulty of reconciling this
passage with the non-Messianic character of the Psalm was seen
long ago by Abenezra, who sought to remove it by the supposition
of a sudden change of the subject. ' Kiss the Son, lest he, that is,
Jehovah, be angry.' But this supposition is entirely arbitrary.
Where no strong reason for an exception exists in the context, the
pronoun must refer to the noun immediately preceding. Here this
noun is *Son*, and so far from there being any reason for an exception to the rule we have mentioned, it is said of Him in the ninth
verse that He shall break the nations in pieces with an iron sceptre [4].

110. Further, the people and kings of the earth seek to cast off the
yoke of Jehovah and the king whom He had established over them [5] :
from one end of the earth to the other they are given to him by
Jehovah for his possession [6]. The utmost extravagance could not make
these declarations respecting any *earthly head* of the theocracy. On
the other hand, it is the standing description of the kingdom of the
Messiah, that it should extend to the ends of the earth and embrace
all nations within its limits [7].

111. Moreover the idea of an earthly king is inconsistent with the
fact, that rebellion against the Anointed and Son of Jehovah, is represented as rebellion against Jehovah Himself ; and the nations are

---

[1] ' In Christ Jesus I have begotten you through the Gospel.'
[2] Where the same subject receives the names אֲדֹנָי and אֱלֹהִים

[3] Compare Ps. 118. 9. 146. 13. Mic. 7. 5.   [4] Comp. also Ps. 110. 6, 7.
[5] Ver. 1—3.   [6] Ver. 8.
[7] Comp. Zech. 9. 9. Isa. 2. 2. Mic. 4. 1.—Rosenm. and De Wette have shown that
אֶפֶס does not like גְּבוּל mean *boundary*, but *extremity ;* and that the phrase אַפְסֵי
אָרֶץ is never used for the bounds of Palestine, but always in its widest signification. Equally arbitrary is the limitation of the comprehensive word גּוֹיִם either
to the surrounding tribes, or to the descendants of Israel. The parallel passages
Ps. 72. 8—11, are decisive in favour of the most extensive meaning.

exhorted to submit to Him with humility and reverence. It would have been a totally different case, had the enemies here described been those who were meditating the subversion of the theocracy; but instead of that, they have no other object in view, than to free themselves from the yoke of this king; and it is impossible to find an instance where aiming at such an object is treated as rebellion against Jehovah Himself.

112. Finally, that the non-Messianic interpretation is entirely arbitrary, is manifest from the total disagreement of its defenders respecting the subject and occasion of the Psalm, as well as from the peculiar difficulties which attend every decision on these points, except that which has been generally adopted. Before this interpretation can be in any measure probable, it must at least be shown that this Psalm may refer either to David or to Solomon. But the possibility even of this, is contested by Rosenmüller and De Wette, after the example of Hensler, with arguments which cannot be easily refuted. The opinion of those who, after the Jewish expositors, maintain that the Psalm was composed by David concerning himself, when the Philistines came up against him [1], is seen to be erroneous, not only because the hill of Zion [2] is called *holy*, an appellation which could not be given to it till after the tabernacle had been erected upon it, which was subsequent to the Philistine war; but also, because the people and kings are here spoken of as striving to release themselves from a dominion to which *they had before been subject;* whereas neither the Philistines, nor any other foreign nation was at that time subject to the Israelites [3].—Against the supposition that it refers to the contest with Ishbosheth, or to the rebellion of Absalom, there is the objection, not only that the Psalm speaks of *foreign* foes, but also that it speaks of *several* kings with their people.—As little can the Psalm, as others suppose, relate to the war mentioned in 2 Sam. 8., for David had not then to contend with people, who, having before been reduced to subjection, had risen up in rebellion against his authority. Those who, notwithstanding these reasons, assert the reference of the Psalm to David, must confess that they can point out no condition in the history of David with which it harmonizes; which, when we consider the comparative fulness of our accounts of his life, is in fact to confess that he is *not* its subject.—Still less can this Psalm relate to Solomon; for, from the remark [4] that constant peace prevailed during his reign, it is evident that there could have been no such resistance to his authority as is here described. Since then the reference of the Psalm to either David or Solomon is impossible, nothing remains for us but to adopt the Messianic interpretation. For should we concede to De Wette, as we are by no means

---

[1] 2 Sam. 5. 17.   [2] Ver. 6.

[3] The additional argument advanced by Rosenmüller and De Wette, that David was not anointed on the hill of Zion, but first at Bethlehem, and afterwards at Hebron, is not valid, because the preposition עַל can be very well rendered *over*, and then the chief seat of the theocracy, as is often the case, designates the theocracy itself.

[4] 1 Kings 4. 5. and 1 Chron. 22. 9.

disposed to do, that the expressions must not be too strictly interpreted, since a flattering court poet (!) may have indulged himself
in much extravagance ; yet even the grossest flatterer could not have
used such language of any of the later kings.   Assuredly the extravagance of the poet would not *then* have appeared in the description of the present, but only in the promises of the future.   Not only
however are the people and kings of the whole earth promised to
this king for a possession, but they are also represented as *already in
subjection* to his dominion, and on the point of freeing themselves
from it.   It rests upon the non-Messianic interpreter to show, by an
appeal to history, the existence, or at least the possibility, of this historical fact.   That this however cannot be done is evident from the
fact, that De Wette has not once ventured to offer a conjecture on
the subject.

113. These reasons for the Messianic interpretation, and against
every other, are so clear, that some of those whose doctrinal views
must have strongly biassed them against it, have been compelled to
decide in its favour, *e. g.* Eichhorn, Bertholdt, Rosenmüller (in his
second edition), &c.—It now only remains briefly to refute the objections which have been urged against this interpretation.

114. (1) " According to the doctrine of Christianity, the Messiah is
no conqueror of nations, bearing an iron sceptre ; his kingdom is not
of this world [1]."   For the refutation of this objection it is not necessary to adopt the explanation of Augustine and Theodoret, ·who
understand the ninth verse metaphorically, making it refer not to the
destruction of sinners, but of sins [2].   Although such a figurative
representation is not entirely without example, yet here it is by no
means allowed by the context.   According to this, the Psalm speaks
of severe punishment, which the Son of God will inflict upon his
foes, if they obstinately persist in their rebellion against his rightful
authority, whilst at the same time forgiveness is promised on condition of repentance and submission.   But this is by no means in
opposition to the doctrine of either the Old Testament or the New
concerning the Messiah.   In the Old Testament it is said of Him,
' He shall smite the earth with the rod of his mouth, and with the
breath of his lips shall he slay the wicked [3].'   ' He shall break in
pieces the oppressor [4].'   ' He shall judge among the heathen, and
destroy the enemies of his kingdom [5].'   In the New Testament the
same Christ, who, when He came in the form of a servant, *judged no
man*, shall hereafter appear in glory to inflict fearful vengeance on
his foes [6].   Even temporal judgements, inflicted as an earnest of the
great and final judgement of the enemies of the divine kingdom, are

---

[1] De Wette.

[2] The former gives the sense thus : " Contere in iis terrenas cupiditates et
veteris hominis lutulenta negotia et quidquid de peccatore limo contractum
atque inolitum est."   The latter says: συντρίψει αὐτοὺς ὡς σκεύη κεραμέως,
ἀναλύων καὶ ἀναπλάττων διὰ τῆς τοῦ λουτροῦ παλιγγενεσίας, καὶ τῷ πυρὶ τοῦ
πνεύματος στερεμνίους ἀπεργαζόμενος

[3] Isa. 11. 4.   [4] According to Ps. 72. 4.   [5] And Ps. 110. 6.
[6] Compare Matt. 24. and many other places.

ascribed to Christ; who thus came to the destruction of Jerusalem [1]. It is the more difficult to conceive how any one can here find a contradiction to the *Christian* conceptions of the Messiah, since the New Testament (from which these conceptions are derived) describes the punishment that Christ shall inflict upon his enemies, in the very words of this Psalm [2]. The whole objection arises from not discriminating between the first and second coming of Christ, whereby men have been led to regard as general what is peculiar to the former.

115. (2) " The Messiah is to subdue the nations hitherto unsubdued, and bring them under his sway ; but in this Psalm those who are *already his subjects* rise up in rebellion against Him. It is also difficult to show the fulfilment of this. There have indeed been nations which for a time declared themselves hostile to the doctrine of Jesus ; but where is the nation, which, having received his religion, afterwards assailed and endeavoured to extirpate it [3] ?" The first part of this objection is done away by the remark, that, in a prophetical view of coming events, every thing depends on the position which the inspired seer occupies. He places himself either in the *present*, and then extends his view over the future ; or else, in the *nearer future*, and overlooks that which is more remote. Thus, for example, Isaiah, in the fifty-third chapter, takes his stand between the passion and the glorification of Christ, so that the former appears to him as past, the latter as future. So too here, the prophet feels himself, in spirit, placed in the time when the Messiah has already appeared, and subjected many nations to his dominion. He beholds them rising up in rebellion against their rightful Lord, and predicts that their efforts shall be all in vain ; that the Father shall continually confer new glory upon the Son, and destroy those who despise Him.—Nor can it appear strange that David should predict the future rebellion of people and kings against the Messiah, even if we leave out of view his supernatural illumination. He had learnt enough of the corruption of mankind to anticipate that, when his great descendant should appear, all would not cheerfully submit to him, nor persevere in obedience to his authority.—For the most striking refutation of the second part of the objection, we refer to the history of the last century. God grant that it may not also be refuted by that of the present ! Rebellion against Christ may exist, while the Christian name is retained ; and we have one memorable example, in recent times, where even this was no longer done.

116. (3) " The whole character of the Psalm, the lively and progressive description, the vivid representation of the enemies, all lead to the conclusion that the aim of this poem was local, and the subject of it a *present* occurrence [4]." Were this argument just, it would disprove *all* predictions of the Messiah ; for, since the prophecies were given in a vision, every thing in them must necessarily have ap-

[1] Matt. 10. 23.   [2] See Apoc. 2. 27. 12. 5. 19. 15.
[3] So De Wette and Hensler.   [4] So Herder and Möller.

peared as *present;* the representations are always full of life, and
could not but frequently assume a dramatic character.

Psalm 45

117. After a brief introduction, the sacred poet celebrates the praises
of an illustrious king, who is distinguished by beauty of person,
sweetness of speech, heroism, and righteousness [1]. In his kingdom
(which is everlasting, and in which he appears with the highest
comeliness and dignity) the most remarkable joys and honours are
enjoyed by him as the reward of his distinguished merit [2]. This
splendour is heightened by his wives, the daughters of kings, among
whom one is particularly distinguished, who shines on his right hand
in gold of Ophir [3]. To her the poet [4] addresses himself, exhorting
her to devote herself, with all her affections, to her lord and king,
and sacrifice every thing else for him ; thus will she enjoy his tenderest love, and with it the highest reverence of the most flourishing
nations. He next [5] describes the splendours of the bride, when introduced to the king, with other virgins, her intimate companions.
Lastly, he again turns to the king [6], and promises him an illustrious
progeny, who, under his auspices, should rule the whole earth ; at
the same time expressing the hope that his poem might, even in
future ages, contribute to advance his glory among many nations.

118. We feel compelled to refer this Psalm to the Messiah, for the
following reasons :

119. (1) The testimony of tradition. Not only does the Chaldee
paraphrast explain the Psalm of the Messiah, but the same interpretation is found in many passages of other ancient Jewish writings [7].
Even several later Jewish expositors, as Abenezra and Kimchi, relying upon tradition, explain it in this manner. But we can trace
this tradition much further back. It is utterly inconceivable that
the collectors of the Psalms should have placed this in their collection had it been a bridal ode, intended for the marriage of an
Israelitish king, or one composed by some miserable flatterer in
honour of a Persian monarch. The weight of this objection falls
with peculiar force on those who make a *Persian king* the object of
those praises which, according to their view, are squandered away in
this Psalm. For were its subject a king of *Israel*, as David or Solomon, it might with some plausibility be said, that, in the time of
those who collected the Psalms, its true interpretation being lost, it
was adopted by them, and consecrated to the worship of God, because
they ascribed to it a mystical meaning, which, though erroneous, was
already prevalent. But if the subject is a Persian king, he must
have lived after the Jews and Persians had begun to have frequent

---

[1] Ver. 3—6.   [2] Ver. 7—9.   [3] Ver. 10.
[4] Ver. 11—13.   [5] In ver. 14—16.   [6] Ver. 17, 18.
[7] See the collection by Schöttgen l. c. p. 234.

intercourse with each other, and consequently, after the Babylonian exile. The collectors of the Psalms, therefore, must have been nearly contemporary with the author of this poem, and they are chargeable with the guilt of having knowingly received among the Psalms of praise to God, a poem which, if it refer to a mere mortal, contains, as we shall soon see, blasphemous expressions. This supposition can surely have no weight with those, who know how carefully the Jews, after they had been taught by misfortune during the captivity, avoided whatever might tend to dishonour their God; and how strong their national pride and their hatred and contempt of whatever did not belong to their own people became, precisely at this period.

120. (2) The Messianic interpretation is sustained by the authority of the New Testament. The author of the Epistle to the Hebrews [1], quotes this Psalm to prove the exaltation of Christ above the angels. This cannot be merely an *allusion*, since, according to the non-Messianic interpretation, his argument would lose all its force, and his appeal would be entirely useless.

121. (3) Not less strong is the internal evidence [2]. We will here, following the order of the Psalm, produce those characteristics which are applicable to the Messiah alone. From the superscription [3] itself we derive a twofold argument. If this Psalm were a poem upon any worldly subject, how could it have been committed to the sons of Korah, to be used in the service of God? Who can suppose that a nuptial poem, dedicated to Solomon, or an ode composed by some flatterer in praise of a Persian king, could have been sung in the public worship, and of course introduced into the sanctuary? Stark, perceiving the force of this objection, felt compelled to deny the genuineness of the superscription, but without the slightest reason [4].

122. The second and third verses contain plain indications that they are to be figuratively understood. In the former the words, ' Thou art fairer than the children of men,' are by De Wette and others referred to personal beauty, which in ancient times was highly esteemed. But, that this was employed by the poet merely as an image to represent the high *moral perfection* of the king, is evident from the declaration, ' Therefore hath God blessed thee for ever,' since mere beauty of form cannot possibly be the ground of God's blessing [5]. In the third verse, the king is summoned to gird his

---

[1] Chap. 1. 8, 9.

[2] Hengstenberg says: "still more important is the internal evidence."

[3] Ver. 1.

[4] Hengstenberg derives his second argument from the term מַשְׂכִּיל applied to this Psalm in the title; maintaining that the meaning of that word is ' *devout poem;*' a term that is very descriptive of the thirteen Psalms to which it is prefixed. See his reasons, p. 113 of the original. (89 of Am. Transl.)

[5] Theodoret: "ὁ δὲ ψαλμὸς κάλλος αὐτοῦ καλεῖ οὐ τὸ τοῦ σώματος, ἀλλὰ τῆς ἀρετῆς καὶ πάσης δικαιοσύνης, τὸ ἁμαρτίας οὐ δεξάμενον σπῖλον, τὸ πάσης κηλῖδος ἐλεύθερον.—De Wette and Rosenm., it is true, seek to evade the difficulty by translating עַל־כֵּן *because*, after the example of Calvin, instead of *therefore*. But this expedient is inadmissible (1) because this meaning of עַל־כֵּן is in general incapable of proof, and is not necessarily required in any of the places quoted by

sword upon his thigh, but at the same time the writer intimates the
metaphorical nature of the language by the explanatory phrase[1],
' *Thy glory and thy majesty.*' What earthly monarchs effect by the
sword, shall this exalted godlike king accomplish by his glory and
majesty, whereby he shall vanquish his foes without the aid of any
of the means employed by men. Altogether similar is the language of Isaiah : ' He shall slay the wicked with the *rod of his mouth*[2];'
that is, what other kings effect by instruments of punishment, he
shall effect by his bare words[3].—The characteristics also given in
the fifth verse, that the king whom the poet celebrates, goes forth for
the establishment and promotion of truth and righteousness joined
with mildness, suggest the idea of a conflict which is not to be fought
with fleshly weapons ; and they cannot be taken in their natural
import when referred to any other subject, so well as when referred
to the Messiah, of whom it is also said in Isaiah, ' That righteousness
shall be the girdle of his loins, and faithfulness the girdle of his reins[4].'
—When, in the sixth verse, the king is described as a mighty
warrior, who subdues many nations, this does not at all suit Solomon,
who was engaged in no war, but agrees well with the Messiah, who
likewise is often represented under the image of a powerful and
victorious warrior[5].—But the strongest argument for the Messianic
interpretation is found in the seventh verse. There the king is
addressed as *God.* The non-Messianic interpreters have here resorted to various expedients. Several of them take *Elohim*[6] not as
the vocative, but as the genitive. How unnatural this interpretation
is, and how plainly the mere result of necessity, appears from the
fact that no one of the ancient translators, among whom the Jewish
certainly cannot be charged with doctrinal prejudice, ever thought of
it. All translate in the vocative[7].—Still more unjustifiable is the
explanation of those, who[8] take *Elohim* in the nominative case :

De Wette; (2) because לְעוֹלָם would then be entirely unsuitable and superfluous;
(3) because עַל־כֵּן can have no other meaning, than that which it has in ver. 8 :
" thou lovest righteousness and hatest iniquity, *therefore* he hath anointed thee,"
&c.

[1] הוֹדְךָ וַהֲדָרֶךָ   [2] 11. 14.

[3] The words הוֹד and הָדָר are commonly employed in connexion, to designate
the majesty and glory of Jehovah, see Ps. 96. 6. 104. 1. 111. 3. Rosenmüller and
De Wette suppose that the sword of the king is called 'glory and majesty,' *qui est
decus tuum et splendor.* But the insipidity of this interpretation is obvious at
first sight, and that it is erroneous is still more evident from the beginning of
ver. 5. The repetition of הָדָר which there occurs, "and in this thy glory," shows
that the word is used in its full and literal import.

[4] Isa. 11. 5.   [5] Isa. 53. 12. Ps. 110. 5. and elsewhere.   [6] אֱלֹהִים

[7] The 70 : ὁ θρόνος σου ὁ θεὸς εἰς αἰῶνα αἰῶνος. Aquila : ὁ θρόνος σου θεὲ
εἰς αἰῶνα καὶ ἔτι. Symmachus : ὁ θρόνος σου ὁ θεὸς αἰώνιος καὶ ἔτι. Theodotion : ὁ θρόνος σου ὁ θεὸς εἰς τὸν αἰῶνα τοῦ αἰῶνος. The Chaldee : ' thronus
gloriæ tuæ, Domine, stabilis in sempiternum.' In favour of the vocative also is
the foregoing voc. גִּבּוֹר, ver. 4.—Interpreters who maintain that *Elohim* is the gen.
translate the passage thus : (1) ' *Thy God's throne* endures for ever and ever,' (De
Wette and Gesenius) (2) ' *Thy throne is God's throne*' (Abenezra, Paulus, Ewald).
For the reasons against these versions see the original, p. 117. (p. 91.)

[8] After R. Saadias Haggaon, as cited by Kimchi.

' Thy throne is God for ever and ever;' *i. e.* He will for ever sustain thy throne. This has not even the semblance of support in the usage of the language ; and it is manifest from the parallel passages [1] that *for ever and ever* must be an attribute of the kingdom, and not of God. The demonstration that *Elohim* cannot be understood otherwise than as the vocative, sufficiently refutes one class of our opponents.—Not a few among them acknowledge this, but assert that the name *Elohim* may be given to judges, kings, &c. But against this interpretation there are the following objections. (1) We will not, with Winer and others, deny that *Elohim* is *ever* used for the magistracy among men [2]. No where, however, is *any single magistrate* called *Elohim*, but always only the *magistracy* as representing the tribunal of God. Since therefore even a theocratic *conqueror* was never so called, certainly much less could the name be given to a king at the celebration of his nuptials; and least of all to a Persian king, who could not even be called 'son of God,' since this title belonged exclusively to the leader of the theocracy. (2) To understand *king* by *Elohim* in this place, is attended with the greatest difficulty, since in the Psalms for the sons of Korah, this is the prevailing and almost exclusive name for the *Deity* instead of Jehovah. If now we moreover consider that the second and the hundred and tenth Psalms ascribe to the Messiah names, attributes, and actions, which belong exclusively to God, we shall feel the less hesitation to take *Elohim* here in its full and natural meaning, and acknowledge the Messiah as the subject of the Psalm.—The promise of the eternal duration of his throne in the same verse leads us also to the Messiah. Allowing that *for ever and ever* may in itself be capable of a *limited* meaning, yet that such is not the case here is evident from the context, the connexion with *Elohim*, and a comparison with the parallel passages [3].—In the eighth verse the subject of the Psalm is again called *God*. True, De Wette takes ' *Elohim*' as the nominative to the verb; and the repetition, ' thy God,' is to intimate (he says) that God is especially gracious to the king : but as it has been shown that *Elohim* in the foregoing verse is the *vocative* and object of address, so here too no other interpretation is admissible.—An important argument for the necessity of the figurative interpretation is furnished by the eleventh verse : ' Hearken, O daughter, and consider, and incline thine ear.' How unsuitable the appellation *daughter* would be in an address to an earthly queen, is manifest from the efforts of several non-Messianic interpreters to exchange it for another. Thus Mendelssohn translates : ' *Princess*, hearken, give me thine ear.' Its offensiveness and incompatibility with the manners of the East, has been fully shown by Döderlein [4]. Teachers employ the epithet *son* when addressing their pupils [5]; but a poet would have found but

---

[1] In 2 Sam. 7. 13. and Ps. 89. 29.

[2] See Exod. 21. 6. 22. 7, 8. also Ps. 82. 1.

[3] 2 Sam. 7. and Ps. 89., cited in our remarks on Ps. 2. and especially with Ps. 72, where verse 5, we find as synonymous עִם שֶׁמֶשׁ and לִפְנֵי יָרֵחַ

[4] Theol. Bibl. 1. p. 193.   [5] Ps. 34. 12. Prov. 1. 8. " my son," &c.

little favour, had he been disposed to treat a daughter of Pharaoh or a Persian princess as his pupil. But if we follow the Messianic interpretation, all incongruity disappears. It is a frequent custom of the Hebrew poets and prophets to personify lands, nations, and cities, as young women or matrons[1]. To seek no further for examples, even in the thirteenth verse the ' *Daughters* of Tyre' stands for Tyre. So too here the Psalmist personifies the covenant people, representing them as a bride, who shall be brought in costly array to the illustrious king, who will take her as his beloved, on condition that she renounces for him all that she had loved before. This figurative representation need the less surprise us, since the same image is so often employed, in both the Old and New Testaments, to represent the relation of God or of Christ to his people. Thus, throughout the whole of the Song of Solomon, God appears as the lover, and the people of Israel as the beloved or bride. Isaiah predicted[2], ' Thy maker shall then be thy *husband :* his name is Jehovah of hosts. And thy Redeemer the Holy One of Israel : the God of the whole earth shall he be called.' In chapter 62. 5. he says, ' For as a young man marrieth a virgin, so shall thy sons marry thee, and as a bridegroom rejoiceth over the bride, so shall thy God rejoice over thee.' And in chapter 50. 1. the decree of rejection, which God pronounced against the people of Israel, is styled a *bill of divorcement*[3]. In the New Testament also Christ calls Himself a *bridegroom*[4]. John regards himself as only the friend of the bridegroom, and points out Christ as the bridegroom who should possess the bride[5].—The necessity of the metaphorical interpretation may also be shown by the fifteenth verse. There it is said, ' she shall be brought unto the king in raiment of needle-work, the virgins her companions that follow her shall be brought unto thee.' These virgins are the same who in the tenth verse are called *kings' daughters.* This of itself proves, that we must not suppose, with some interpreters, they are merely conductors and attendants of the bride. Moreover, the words ' her companions,' and ' they shall be brought unto thee,' show, that these virgins also, no less than the bride, are to be united with the king in love. Here then an insuperable difficulty arises in the way of those who regard this psalm as a nuptial ode ; since it was not the custom to take more than one wife at the same time[6]. But the Messianic interpretation entirely removes this difficulty. The companions of the queen, who, though inferior in rank, are still to be united with the king, are then *the heathen nations*, over whom the people of Israel, as the ancient covenant people of God, enjoy indeed a certain outward pre-eminence, but who, according to the

[1] See Isa. 4. 4. ' Daughters of Zion,' for the cities of Judah, and 23. 12. ' Daughters of Zion,' for Zion.
[2] Isaiah 54. 5.   [3] Comp. further Jer. 3. 1. Hos. 1—3. Ezek. 16. 23.
[4] Matt. 9. 15.   [5] John 3. 29. See also Rom. 7. 4. Eph. 5. 27. 1 Cor. 11.
[6] That the Psalm, unless it be referred to the Messiah, can be taken for nothing else than a song of praise to a king, on occasion of his marriage, appears from the exhortation, verse 11, which can properly relate only to a bride, and not to a wife of the king. The same is true also of the promise verse 17.

standing prediction of the prophets and the authors of the Psalms, were to have an equal share in the blessing of the Messiah's kingdom [1]. A metaphorical representation altogether similar is found in Cant. 6. 7, 8. ' There are threescore queens, and fourscore concubines, and virgins without number, but my dove is but one.' Here therefore we are taught in the usual figurative language, what in other Messianic Psalms is simply expressed [2] ; ' That the Messias shall take for his possession all the people of the earth [3] ;' ' That he shall reign from sea to sea, and from the Euphrates to the ends of the earth,' etc.—In the seventeenth verse it is said, the king will make his sons princes in all the earth. That the words ' over all the earth [4]' can have only the meaning we have given, and cannot be translated ' in all the land,' De Wette himself confesses. He says, also, that it is only by the extravagance of flattery, that such language could be addressed to a Persian king. But besides the arguments already adduced against the supposition that the subject is a Persian king, we may add the close resemblance between this Psalm and the seventy-second, which De Wette himself explains of a king of Israel. The Messianic interpretation gives a sense as natural, as it is suitable. The poet derives his figurative representation from the circumstances of the time in which he lived. Solomon had divided Palestine into twelve departments [5], and it would seem that David had already established his sons as regents under himself; as was also done by Rehoboam [6]. And as the earthly heads of the theocracy divided their kingdom, which was confined to the bounds of Palestine, among their sons, so shall the Messiah divide among his offspring his far wider dominion, which extends over the whole earth. It follows, however, from the character of the union from which they spring, that these are not natural, but spiritual children [7].—Finally, the prediction in the eighteenth verse, that many nations shall praise him, is, to say the least, more applicable to the Messiah, than to any earthly king.

123. Having thus brought forward the positive proofs for the Messianic character of the Psalm, it now remains to remove the objections which have been urged against it, at least so far as they have not been refuted by what has already been advanced [8]. We take them principally from Paulus.

124. (1) " True there are frequently metaphorical representations in the Hebrew writers ; but it is not the practice of a good writer to carry out the allegory so far." But, in answer to this, we have a sufficient

[1] Thus of old the Chaldee paraphrase and Kimchi.

[2] Ps. 2. 8.   [3] Ps. 72. 8.   [4] בְּכָל־הָאָרֶץ

[5] See 1 Kings 4. 7. and 2 Sam. 8. 18.   [6] 2 Chron. 11. 23.

[7] This metaphorical representation can moreover be sustained by analogous examples. See Isa. 53. 10.

[8] Of this character is the general charge, so often repeated by several non-Messianic interpreters, of capricious allegorizing. But this objection is valid only when the interpreter fails to show (either from internal or external evidence) that the literal meaning cannot be the true one, and that the author designed to represent spiritual objects by sensible images.

number of examples, even though we should not choose to appeal to the splendid example of the 'Song of Songs.' We need only compare the allegorical representations of the fall of Babylon [1] (where Babylon is personified and described as a rich delicate lady, who is now bereaved of her husband, and overwhelmed in the deepest misery), and the similar representations, extended to the minutest particulars, in the sixteenth and twenty-third chapters of Ezekiel, and the figurative description continued through the three first chapters of Hosea,—and we shall be obliged to confess, that the author of this Psalm has confined himself within very narrow limits.

125. (2) "The Psalmist, who could borrow his colouring from all the royal splendour of a Jewish monarch, in order to describe his Messiah, has nevertheless chosen very unskilfully, and given him a costume which does not belong to him. The kingdom of the Jewish Messiah can indeed be presented to him as a bride clothed in all the splendour of the East, and attended by maidens and companions; but then he has but *one* bride, *one* spouse, the people of Israel."—One can scarcely conceive what is meant by this objection. Is it meant to be asserted that the sacred poets and prophets of the Old Testament regarded their Messiah as destined for the Jews alone? This has already been sufficiently refuted by the passages quoted from the Psalm. But if it was expected that the kingdom of the Messiah should embrace the heathen as well as the Jews, since it is conceded that the *Jewish people* can be personified as his bride, what reason can be given, why the *heathen nations* should not be represented in the same manner; especially as the circumstances of an Oriental court, where many wives of inferior rank stand by the side of one peculiarly distinguished, gives so much occasion to carry out the allegory to such an extent? In ascribing to the people of Israel an outward distinction of this kind, the author wisely followed the mode of representing the Messiah's kingdom which prevails throughout the Old Testament; where the Jewish people are always regarded as the original stock, and the heathen nations, who were only to be engrafted upon it, sustain a relation somewhat subordinate; a view of the subject afterwards confirmed by Christ and his apostles [2].

126. (3) "Figures such as 'so shall the king greatly desire thy beauty [3]' are improper, and not usual with the sacred writers." If so, we must allow it to be equally objectionable, when Isaiah compares the delight of God in his people with that of a bridegroom in his bride; or when Paul styles the Church a bride, not having spot, or wrinkle, or any such thing, and, therefore, enjoying the perfect love of her exalted bridegroom. To say nothing of other passages, is not *spiritual beauty* represented in *these* passages, as well as in that before us, by the figure of *personal beauty?*

127. (4) "How shall this bride of the Messiah forget her own people? Why she is herself this people personified." But precisely because the representation is figurative, and the covenant people appears personified as a bride, must the thought, that, after their

---

[1] Isa. 47.   [2] Rom. 11.   [3] Verse 12.

union with this exalted king, they should render to him their exclusive love, and renounce every previous inclination, not directed to
him, be expressed in a manner consistent, not with the thing described,
but with this figurative representation; with the relation, that is,
between a bride and a bridegroom. The passage in Gen. 2. 24.
'Therefore shall a man leave his father and mother,' supplied the
Psalmist with a beautiful groundwork; he seems also to have had
in view Gen. 21. 1: 'And the Lord spake to Abraham, Get thee out
of thy country, and from thy kindred and thy father's house [1].'

128. (5) "How came *Tyre* alone to be mentioned, instead of all
the heathen nations?" The Messianic interpretation does not require
us to suppose this; but that Tyre, as the richest city of the ancient
world, is here by synecdoche put for the richest nations, is, in
itself, liable to no objection, and is moreover confirmed by the
addition 'the richest of the people [2]' i. e. the richest among all nations.
Nothing, moreover, is more common in the Old Testament than for
a passage to be *individualized*, if I may say so, by the mention of a
single name, while the writer has in view the whole, and not pre-
eminently that particular part. There is a parallel passage in Psalm
72. 10: 'The kings of *Tarshish* and of the isles shall bring presents;
the kings of *Sheba* and *Seba* shall offer gifts.' Further, Isaiah 60.
6: 'All they from *Sheba* shall come; they shall bring gold and incense, and declare the praise of the Lord.' As in both these places,
Tarshish, Sheba, and *Seba*; so here, *Tyre* is used to designate the
richest of the heathen nations.

129. The Messianic interpretation therefore is sufficiently justified.
We only remark further, that we must be on our guard against that
caprice, which would require something literal corresponding to each
single line, which often serves only to complete the picture. Thus
in the eighth and ninth verses, we must look for nothing more than
the thought, that God will confer upon the Messiah the highest exaltation and glory, which is represented by imagery borrowed from
the splendour of an eastern court. So also the description of the
royal bride [3] means only, that the richest blessings and greatest glory
shall be conferred upon the covenant people, if, with sincere love,
they devote themselves to their Lord and King.

Psalm 72

130. ARGUMENT. This Psalm, like the forty-fifth, celebrates an exalted and illustrious king, who is distinguished for righteousness, and with benevolent concern takes under his care the miserable and the oppressed [4]. Under his
reign universal peace will prevail; and in consequence of the righteousness

---

[1] The Chaldee explains it well on the whole, though the figure is too literally
understood: "et obliviscere opera mala impiorum populi tui, et idolorum, quæ
coluisti in domo patris tui Abrahami."

[2] עֲשִׁירֵי־עָם   [3] Verse 13—15.   [4] Verse 1. 2. 4. 12—15.

introduced by him, a rich abundance of blessings be poured forth [1]. These blessings are not, like those conferred by distinguished earthly kings, to endure only for a time, and then be interrupted by his death; but, like himself, they are eternal; and consequently the gratitude and reverence of hissubj ects towards him will be eternal also [2]. His kingdom is by no means confined to the limits of Palestine, but is co-extensive with the whole earth. All nations, even the most powerful, the most uncivilized, and the most remote, shall reverently obey him, not indeed as being subdued by the power of his arms, but freely choosing his service under the influence of his righteousness alone [3]. Through him will be fulfilled the great promise made to Abraham, that in his seed all the nations of the earth should be blessed.

131. Let us examine the reasons which make it necessary to refer this Psalm to the Messiah [4].

132. (1) The clear testimony of tradition. The Chaldee paraphrasts render the first verse, ' *O God, give the knowledge of thy judgements to Messiah the King: and thy justice to the son of King David* [5].' Schöttgen has collected numerous passages to this effect from the older Jewish writers, and Jarchi remarks expressly, that the ancients explained the whole Psalm of the Messiah.

133. (2) The proof from parallel passages is here peculiarly strong. On the one hand, the Psalm itself contains the most distinct reference to an older Messianic prediction, the words of which it employs; on the other, in a later prediction, the Messiah's kingdom is described in words taken from *it*. We cannot (for example) in the seventeenth verse, ' and men shall be blessed in him, all nations shall call him blessed,' mistake the allusion to the promise made to Abraham (which is here *interpreted*), that *in him should all the families of the earth be blessed* [6]. And in Zechariah [7] the extension of the Messiah's kingdom is described in words taken from the eighth verse of this Psalm : ' and his dominion shall be from sea to sea, and from the river even to the ends of the earth [8].'

134. (3) There is nothing in the Psalm unsuitable to the Messiah (provided we distinguish the figures from that which they represent), and many of its features can belong to *no other* subject. We will go through the whole Psalm with reference to this point. De Wette finds even in the first verse an objection to the Messianic interpretation. The prayer that God would give righteousness to the king is (he argues) inconsistent with it, because the Messiah is regarded as the most righteous. We remark, in reply, that the dis-

---

[1] Ver. 3. 6, 7. 16.   [2] Ver. 5. 7. 17.   [3] Ver. 8—11.

[4] We take ל in its usual acceptation, and regard Solomon as the author of the Psalm, after the example of the Chaldee interpreters in former, and Kaiser in recent times. As David in Ps. 2. and 110. makes the *disturbed* and *warlike* condition of his own kingdom the groundwork of his representation of that of the Messiah, so does Solomon employ the *peaceful, flourishing*, and *happy* condition of his kingdom to represent that of his great descendant.

[5] " Deus, scientiam judiciorum tuorum da regi Messiæ, et justitiam tuam filio Davidis regis."

[6] Thus of old, Theodoret: ἐνταῦθα τῆς περὶ τὸν ᾿Αβραὰμ καὶ τὸν ᾿Ισαὰκ καὶ τὸν ᾿Ιακὼβ ἐπαγγελίας ἐμνημόνευσε.

[7] Zech. 9. 10.

[8] To this we may add its close resemblance to other Messianic predictions, namely, besides Psalms 2. 45. 110. with Isa. 9. and 11.

course is not here concerning righteousness in general, but righteousness as God possesses it, and employs it in the government of
the world, and as it was needed by the king in the administration of
his kingdom[1]. The weakness of the objection is manifest from the
eleventh chapter of Isaiah (where the Messiah before he enters upon
his kingly office, and begins his reign, is endowed by God with all
the requisite qualifications), and from the first verse of the forty-
second chapter, where he first receives the Spirit of God, and then
establishes righteousness among the heathen[2]. The fulfilment also
shows that Christ, although with regard to his *divine* nature He combined in Himself all perfections, yet as to his *human* nature, was
endowed by the Holy Ghost with the requisite qualifications for dis-
charging the duties of his office.—The appellation *king* is justified
not only by other passages in the Psalms[3], but also by Jer. 33. 17 :
' David shall never want a man to *sit upon the throne* of the house of
Israel,'—and Exod. 37. 24 : ' and David my servant shall be *king*
over them.'—The title *king's son* belongs to the Messiah as son of
David, and is of similar import with the metaphorical title elsewhere
used[4], *sprout of David*.—The traits of character given in the second
and fourth verses, rectitude in governing and peculiar concern for
oppressed innocence (one of the most illustrious virtues of a ruler),
are of very frequent occurrence in the prediction of the Messiah :
' But with righteousness shall he judge the poor, and reprove with
equity for the meek of the earth[5].'—Peace also, which, according to
the third verse, shall reign throughout his kingdom, in consequence
of the prevalence of righteousness, is not unfrequently given as a
characteristic sign of the times of the Messiah. ' Of the increase of
his government and his peace there shall be no end[6].' In Isaiah 11.
9, the *knowledge of the Lord* (as *righteousness*, in the passage before
us) is given as the cause of that peace which distinguishes the kingdom of the Messiah.—The fifth verse furnishes a strong proof in
favour of our interpretation : ' They shall fear thee as long as the
sun and the moon endure, throughout all generations.' The evidence
of this passage would indeed be greatly weakened, were we to suppose[7] that the object of this address is *God*. But, as Michaelis justly
remarks, none but the grossest flatterer *could* have made such a
declaration of Solomon, since no king, who does not himself reign
eternally, can cause his people to fear God so long as the sun and
moon endure. There are, however, sufficient reasons to suppose,
with most interpreters[8], that the author here directly addresses the
king, of whom he had spoken before in the third person[9]. Grotius,

[1] The imperative חֵן however, as is evident from what follows, is not used in
the optative sense, but is to be taken as the future ; see Ps. 110. 2.
[2] Comp. 49. 2. 61. 1.
[3] ' Yet have I set my *king* upon my holy hill of Zion,' Ps. 2. 6.   See also 45. 8.
[4] צֶמַח דָוִיד   [5] Isa. 11. 4.   [6] Isa. 9. 6.
[7] With Calvin, Döderlein, Michaelis, and Dathe.
[8] And at last De Wette.
[9] This opinion is favoured by a comparison with the seventh verse, where the
expression, ' as long as the moon endureth,' as well as the corresponding word

in order to show that such language may be spoken of a man, compares the passage in Ovid : " cum *sole* et *lunâ* semper Aratus erit." But there, it is living for ever in the *memory of others* which is spoken of ; here, on the contrary, reverence is to be paid to one who *himself lives*, as appears from the verse itself, and a comparison with the seventh and seventeenth verses.   But as eternity of dominion can be ascribed to no earthly king, so does it constitute one of the essential characteristics of the Messiah.   In Isaiah 9. 5, He is styled the *Father of eternity*, and according to the sixth verse, He shall establish his kingdom *from henceforth even for ever*.—In the sixth verse, the image of a rain, which falls soft and lovely upon a new mown meadow, covering it with fresh green, while, if drought prevail, the sun burns it, the roots and every thing withers, is very expressive of the Messiah [1].   David, in his last Psalm [2], when he speaks with deep emotions of the promise made to himself respecting the Messiah, employs the same image to describe the blessings of his reign, in a passage which obviously refers to the Messiah ; for David extols his great descendant, not as the sovereign of any one people, but as the Lord of the human race [3].—In the seventh verse, we again have the characteristic marks of the Messiah's reign, righteousness, peace, and endless duration.—In the eighth verse, the kingdom of this illustrious monarch extends over the whole world.   ' He reigns from sea to sea, and from the Euphrates to the extremity of the earth.'   There is here a very remarkable reference to the passage where the boundaries of the earthly theocracy are given : ' And I will set thy bounds from the Red Sea even unto the sea of the Philistines (the *Mediterranean*), and from the desert unto the Euphrates [4] ;' ' from the wilderness to Lebanon, and from the Euphrates to the Mediterranean sea [5].'   The author of the Psalm takes two of the boundaries here given ; and then instead of the corresponding ones, subjoins others which are far wider, and coincide with the ends of the earth [6]. —The ninth to the eleventh verses afford a strong proof of the correctness of the Messianic interpretation.   Here, in the first place,

---

לְעוֹלָם in the twelfth verse, must relate to the king and not to God; and by 2 Sam. 7. 15. which lies at the foundation of this as well as of all other Messianic predictions in the Psalms, where the phrase עַד עוֹלָם is likewise spoken of David's posterity. Comp. also Ps. 89. 37, 38. and 45. 7.

[1] Calvin : " hoc præcipue in Christo videmus impleri, qui arcanam gratiam stillando facit ecclesiam suam pullulare."

[2] 2 Sam. 23. 5.   [3] מוֹשֵׁל בָּאָדָם   [4] Exod. 23. 31.   [5] Deut. 11. 24.

[6] Some interpreters would make "from sea to sea," mean nothing more than "from the Red Sea to the Mediterranean," and אַפְסֵי אֶרֶץ not *the ends of the earth*, but merely *the extremities of Palestine*. But there is no example to justify us in giving the alleged restricted meaning to the expression "from sea to sea," unless it were limited by an additional epithet, as in the passage of the Pentateuch to which we have referred.   Nor does אַפְסֵי אֶרֶץ ever mean the *bounds of Palestine*, but always those of the *whole earth*.   Moreover, according to what follows, not only Palestine, but the whole earth, with all lands and rulers, shall be subject to this king.   Now extension over the whole earth is a usual characteristic of the Messiah's kingdom.   See, besides Ps. 2. 8. 22. 28. Zech. 9. 10., among other places, Micah 5. 4.: ' He shall be great even unto the ends of the earth.'

merely as a part for the whole, several far distant nations, some of them rude and uncivilized, others rich and powerful, are named, who shall submit themselves to the king, and do homage to him with presents. Next, lest it might be supposed that none but the people mentioned by way of example, were to obey him, it is said, ' All nations shall fall down before him, all kings shall serve him.' The non-Messianic interpreters seek to show the fulfilment from the tenth chapter of the first book of Kings, according to which the Queen of Sheba, and others also, brought costly presents to Solomon [1]. But though we would not wish to deny that this writer, in his figurative representation, had these transactions in view, we must, nevertheless, assert, that they are by no means a fulfilment of the prophetic language of the Psalm. What is said is *far too great for Solomon*, since several people are named, with whom he had no connexion ; and every limitation is afterwards removed by the word '*all.*' The gifts, moreover, which are here spoken of, are not, as Dereser has erroneously supposed, those of *friendship*, such as men brought to Solomon ; but they are the signs of *obedience, subjection*, and *reverence*. Over all these nations this king shall reign, and they shall serve Him with the deepest humility. Every difficulty is removed by the reference to the Messiah. The bringing of gifts is, then, merely a metaphorical representation of homage and reverence, just as in the fifteenth verse, the admiring gratitude of the delivered towards his deliverer is represented by the figure of bringing gold from Sheba.—The representation in the twelfth verse, &c. of the method by which the king whose praises are celebrated, has gained so wide a dominion, suits no earthly king, but agrees well with the Messiah. He has not, like worldly conquerors, triumphed by the power of his arms ; but by his illustrious attributes, by his righteousness and love, he has won the hearts of men, and made them yield a willing submission to his sway.—With respect to the fifteenth verse, we must first establish the true interpretation. We translate : ' *that he may live, and give to him of the gold of Sheba* [*Sabæa*], *and pray for him continually, and bless him daily.*' We take ' *the poor* man,' as the subject [2] throughout, and understand ' to live,' as it frequently means elsewhere, to be sustained in life [3]. The bringing of the gold of Sheba, which was regarded as the most precious [4], represents the cordial and devoted gratitude of the ransomed towards their deliverer. An incongruity arises, if we overlook the figurative character of the expression, since the poor man has no gold, whereby he can show his gratitude to the king who delivers him. The expression, ' and pray for him' (borrowed from the intercession of faithful subjects for their beloved king, and therefore in a manner figurative), so far agrees with the Messiah, as the gratitude and love of his people

[1] Ver. 25.   [2] *i. e.* the nominative to the verb.
[3] De Wette and others translate : " *He (the king) lives, and they give him of the gold of Sabæa.*' For Hengstenberg's arguments against this interpretation, see the original work.
[4] ' All they from Sheba shall come: they shall bring gold and incense.' Is. 60. 6.

are expressed in prayers for the advancement of his glory, and the continual increase of his kingdom.

135. We translate the sixteenth verse: ' *Though there were only a handful* [1] *of corn in the land, yet even on the summit of the hills its fruit will rustle like Lebanon* [2];' *i. e.* though, before the reign of this king, there was such a scarcity, that only a handful of grain remained for seed, yet this little will be so blessed, that even in the most barren places, as on the summits of the hills, the harvest, moved by the wind, rustles like the trees of the lofty Lebanon. Thus the superabundant blessings of the Messiah's kingdom are characterised by a most expressive image. In the second part of the verse, '*and out of the city men blossom as grass of the earth* [3],' the great populousness of the new kingdom of God, to be founded by the Messiah, is described by a metaphor signifying large population, taken from the condition of the earthly theocracy under Solomon : ' *Judah and Israel were many, as the sand which is by the sea in multitude* [4].'—In the seventeenth verse, we translate with Luther : ' *His name shall be continued among his posterity as long as the sun endures* [5].' If *this* prediction is fulfilled in its highest sense only in the Messiah, much more is that which is contained in the second part of the verse : ' *And men shall regard themselves as blessed through him, all nations shall praise him.*' While the remembrance of a distinguished leader of the earthly theocracy lives only within the narrow bounds of Palestine, endless praise and glory shall be ascribed to this exalted king, for his never ceasing benefits, by all the people of the whole earth.

---

[1] פִּסַּת *minutum* (*frumenti*) or a handful. The masc. פַּס occurs Gen. 37. 3. 23. and 2 Sam. 13. 18, 19. in the sense of *particula, pars minuta.* In the Chaldee portion of Daniel it is found with the additional word יְדָא in the sense of *vola manûs,* chap. 5. 5.

[2] E. T. ' There shall be a handful of corn upon the earth upon the top of the mountains ; the fruit thereof shall shall like Lebanon :' &c.

[3] Either out of *Jerusalem,* under whose image the theocracy, of which it was then the seat, presented itself (a sense which is rendered probable by the parallel passages soon to be cited), or out of every city in subjection to the great king ; out of *the cities.*

[4] 1 Kings 4. 20. Similar is the description of the times of the Messiah, Zech. 2. 8 : ' *Jerusalem shall be inhabited as towns without walls, for the multitude of men and cattle therein,*' with which comp. the fifteenth verse : ' *and many nations shall be joined to the Lord in that day, and shall be my people.*' Also Is. 49. 20 : ' *The children, which thou shalt have after thou hast lost the other, shall say again in thine ears, The place is too strait for me ; give place to me that I may dwell.*'

[5] לִפְנֵי שֶׁמֶשׁ יִנּוֹן שְׁמוֹ

Psalm 110[1]

136. ARGUMENT.—An illustrious king is celebrated in this Psalm, whom God has exalted to sit with Him on his throne, and to whom He has promised a wide extension of his kingdom and the dominion over numerous enemies, notwithstanding all their efforts to resist[2]. He is surrounded by a host of warriors, who freely and joyfully devote themselves to his service, and, clothed in sacred garments, go forth to battle[3]. Nor does he enjoy merely the *regal* dignity; but, according to an unchangeable Divine decree, he shall unite with it the priesthood, as Melchisedec had done before, and that, not merely a short and transitory, but an everlasting priesthood[4].—Those who refuse submission to his decree, however great may be their power, shall be ' stricken through in the day of his wrath[5].'—He is ever engaged with untiring zeal in promoting the enlargement of his kingdom[6].

137. The grounds of the Messianic interpretation are here as strong, as in any prediction of the Old Testament; so that this Psalm greatly confirms the interpretation we have given of the three preceding ones. For it is manifest, and ought never to have been overlooked, that when the Messianic character of one of the Psalms of this class is established, so also is that of all the others. Especially is the resemblance between this and the second Psalm self-evident. The arguments for the Messianic interpretation are the following.

138. (1) The testimony of tradition. The prevalence of this interpretation in the time of Christ is evident, as is generally allowed, from Matt. 22. 41—46[7]. Christ takes it for granted that the Psalm relates to the Messiah, nor did it occur to the Pharisees to question this fact, in order to escape from the difficulty in which they found themselves involved, though their interest must have led them to do so, had there been any diversity of opinion on the subject. It is true, that soon *after* the coming of Christ, when the Christians derived from this Psalm one of the strongest proofs of the Deity of the Messiah, the polemic prejudices of the Jews prevailed over their previous attachment to tradition. Justin Martyr[8] and Tertullian[9] mention the explanation which makes *Hezekiah* the subject as common among them; and Chrysostom found them to entertain a great diversity of opinions. It was supposed to relate to *Abraham*—to *Zerubbabel*—to the *Jewish people*. But still the weight of the internal evidence and the authority of tradition induced many of the older Jews to adhere to the Messianic interpretation[10].

139. (2) The evidence from the New Testament is scarcely more

---

[1] The style of this Psalm, like that of the second, is somewhat dramatic. In the first verse the author addresses his hearers; in the second to the fourth verses the king; and in the fifth to the seventh verses Jehovah.

[2] Ver. 1. 2.   [3] Ver. 3.   [4] Ver. 4.

[5] Ver. 5. 6.   [6] Ver. 7.

[7] ' How then doth *David in spirit call him Lord*, saying, The Lord said unto my Lord, Sit thou on my right hand till I make thine enemies thy footstool?' Ver. 43, 44.

[8] In the dialogue c. Tryph. p. 86. Würzb.   [9] Adv. Marc. 5. 9.

[10] Wetstein on Matt. 22. 44.

conclusive in any instance than in the present; so that all those interpreters, who do not entirely reject the authority of Christ and the
Apostles, though not inclined, in other respects, to acknowledge the
Messianic interpretation, are yet compelled to adopt it here. Christ
Himself declares [1] that David composed the Psalm [2] under the influence of the prophetic inspiration, when futurity was disclosed to his
view by the Spirit of God ; and assuming its unquestionable reference to the Messiah, he proved from it the erroneousness of the
representation of Him (at that time very current among the Jews)
which did not recognise His superhuman dignity and Godhead [3].—
This Psalm is also quoted and explained as referring to Christ by
Peter [4], in his discourse immediately after the effusion of the Holy
Spirit [5].   There are also many allusions to it besides these [6].

140. (3) Let us now see, how far the result obtained from external
testimony is confirmed by internal evidence. In the first place, the
Messianic interpretation is confirmed by the *superscription*, which
ascribes the composition of the Psalm to *David*. For, if *David* was
its author, neither *himself*, nor any other person but the Messiah, *can*
be its subject. For *what man* could David consistently call *his
Lord* [7] ?—The reference to the Messiah is also proved by the words
in the first verse, ' Sit thou on my right hand.' This expression is
figurative. Worldly kings place on their right hand, not merely
those whom they wish in a special manner to honour, as Solomon did
Bathsheba [8] ; but those likewise whom they associate with themselves in the government. Thus Salome, expecting that Christ was
to found an earthly kingdom [9], prayed for her two sons, James and
John, that He would allow them to sit, the one *on his right hand*,
and the other *on his left* [10]. Sitting on the right hand of God is not,
however, expressive of *complete Divine majesty*. And, according to
the Messianic interpretation, the expression relates, as it does throughout the New Testament, not to the *Divine nature* of Christ (in which
He is *equal* in dignity with the Father), but to his *human nature*, in
which He has obtained a participation in the Divine government as

---

[1] Matt. 22. 44. comp. with Mark 12. 36. and Luke 20. 42.
[2] ἐν πνεύματι, or, according to Mark, ἐν πνεύματι ἁγίῳ.
[3] Hengstenberg properly considers the foolish notion of Stolz, Borhek, and
Paulus, that our Saviour represented the Messianic interpretation of the passage
inadmissible, as unworthy of any formal refutation.
[4] Acts 2. 35. 36.   [5] See 1 Cor. 15. 25, &c. Heb. 7. 17.
[6] See Eph. 1. 20. Acts 5. 31, and all those passages where Christ is represented
as sitting at the right hand of God.
[7] Εἰ Δαβὶδ ὁ βασιλεὺς καὶ εὐσεβὴς βασιλεὺς, ὁ καὶ προφητικῆς χάριτος
ἠξιωμένος, κύριον ἑαυτοῦ καλεῖ τὸν δεσπότην Χριστὸν, οὐκ ἄρα μόνον ἄνθρωπος κατὰ τὴν Ἰουδαίων ἄνοιαν, ἀλλὰ καὶ Θεὸς, ὡς τοῦ Δαβὶδ δημιουργός τε καὶ
κύριος.—*Theodoret.* So Lactantius: ' Qui propheta quum rex esset, quem ap-
pellare dominum suum posset, qui sederet ad dextram Dei, nisi Christum filium
Dei, qui est Rex regum et Dominus dominorum ?'
[8] 1 Kings 19.   [9] Matt. 20. 21.
[10] Passages from the Greek writers likewise in which a participation in the
government is signified by sitting on the right hand, may be found collected by
Knapp (De Christo ad dextram Dei sedente, in his Opusc.).

a reward for the work of redemption [1]. But still this language implies a *participation* in the Divine glory and dominion : it is never
spoken of earthly kings, who reign indeed as the servants of God and
by his authority, but are not, on that account, co-regents with him.

141. In the third verse the non-Messianic interpreters find themselves involved in great embarrassment by the expression, *in holy
ornaments* [2]. De Wette attempts two ways of escape. The first
makes the supposition, that the warriors appear clothed in sacred
garments, on account of the religious ceremonies, the sacrifices, &c.
which preceded their warlike expedition. But not only he himself
confesses there can no proof be brought of such a practice, but it is
highly improbable that it existed. For, since the sacred dress was
peculiar to the priests, even granting [3] that religious ceremonies may
have preceded the going forth to war, we cannot suppose that, during
their performance, the host of warriors were clothed in sacred garments. Still more improbable is the second supposition of De Wette,
viz. that arming for war is intended. But the difficulty is entirely
done away by the Messianic interpretation. The expression is then
designed to mark the difference between *this* conflict and *earthly* wars.
As the leader is at the same time *king* and *priest*, so shall the people
whom he conducts to war, be an *army of priests*, arrayed in *sacred
garments*, and not in the *blood-stained clothing of the warrior*, which
(according to Isaiah 9. 4.) shall be consumed in the flames together
with all the instruments of war, at the appearing of the Messiah,
whose kingdom does not, like the former theocracy, stand in need of
human weapons. The fifth verse furnishes a strong proof in favour
of this interpretation. There God confirms it by an oath, that this
King shall be also a Priest for ever after the order of Melchisedec [4],
who united in his own person the regal and the priestly dignity [5]. In
this declaration a total change in the previous condition of things is
implied. For, according to the Mosaic constitution, the priesthood
was exclusively confined to the family of Levi, during the existence
of the old covenant ; and how carefully God watched over the preservation of this arrangement, was shown in earlier times by the fate
of the company of Korah, Dathan, and Abiram, and afterwards by
that of King Uzziah [6], who was smitten with an incurable leprosy
while intruding upon the priestly office by burning incense in the
Temple [7]. The declaration of Jehovah is introduced with such so-

---

[1] Chrysostom therefore errs when he says : εἶδες τὸ ὁμότιμον; ὅπου γὰρ
θρόνος, βασιλείας σύμβολον· ὅπου θρόνος εἷς, τῆς αὐτῆς βασιλείας ἰσοτιμία.
The truth, on the other hand, was seen by Theodoret: ὡς γὰρ θεὸς ὁ υἱὸς
αἰώνιον ἔχει τὸν θρόνον, ἀλλ' ἔλαβεν ὡς ἄνθρωπος, ὅπερ εἶχεν ὡς θεός·—ὡ ς
ἄνθρωπος τοίνυν ἀκούει· κάθου ἐκ δεξιῶν μου· ὡς γὰρ θεὸς αἰώνιον ἔχει τὸ
κράτος.

[2] בְּהַדְרֵי קֹדֶשׁ   [3] What cannot be proved from 1 Sam. 7.

[4] That Melchisedec was a priest, in the proper and full sense of the term, is
proved by the fact, that Abraham acknowledged his superiority, although he
himself performed the functions of a *household* priest.

[5] According to Gen. 14. 18.   [6] According to 2 Chron. 26. 16.

[7] Theodoret: εἰ τοίνυν ἐκ Δαβὶδ ὁ Χριστὸς κατὰ σάρκα, ὁ δὲ Δαβὶδ ἐξ Ἰούδα·

lemnity—('He hath sworn,' strengthened by the addition of ' and will not repent')—as leads us to expect something very uncommon, and widely different from the existing state of things. The comparison with Melchisedec also, who was a priest in the full sense of the term, shows that a *real* and *perfect priesthood*, and an order of things the reverse of that which then existed, are intended. In this comparison, the priesthood promised to the king is manifestly contrasted with that of Aaron. As in the seventy-second Psalm, so also here, the Messianic interpretation is confirmed by the prophet Zechariah; who, plainly referring to this Psalm, announces that the Messiah should '*be a* priest *upon his* throne[1],' should unite, that is, the regal and the priestly dignity in his own person, which he represents as an occurrence altogether novel and extraordinary.

142. In the fifth verse the king receives the name *Adonai*[2], which is peculiar to God alone, being never ascribed to any created being. The non-Messianic interpreters have attempted to escape from this difficulty in three different ways; either they have asserted, without the semblance of proof, that *Adonai* may be used in speaking of men[3],—or they have capriciously · changed the text[4],—or lastly, they have supposed that not *Jehovah*, but the *king* is addressed, which is the opinion of De Wette. The '*Lord on thy right hand*,' will then mean, '*the Lord is thy support*.' But this opinion is erroneous. For (1), although it cannot be denied that the expression, to be at the right hand of any one, may import the same as to sustain him; yet this sense is here inadmissible, because it is not to be supposed that the Psalmist would in so brief a space employ the same expression in both a literal and a figurative sense; saying, in the beginning of his Psalm, that the king is on the right hand of Jehovah, and here, that Jehovah is on the right hand of the king. (2) But few surely will be disposed with Dereser to refer the seventh verse also, '*He shall drink of the brook in the way, therefore shall he lift up the head*' to Jehovah[5]. That this reference is inadmissible was seen by De Wette, who supposes 'a very natural and customary change of person.' But however *customary* the change of persons may be, it will surely not readily appear to any one to be *natural* in the present instance. For it is obviously one and the same warrior, who, in the *fifth* and *sixth* verses, with resistless power overthrows the people and their kings, and in the *seventh* verse is engaged in eager pursuit of the remnant of the host of his enemies,

τήνδε κατὰ τὴν τάξιν Μελχισεδὲκ ἀρχιερωσύνην ἔλαβεν ὁ Χριστὸς, πέπαυται μὲν ἡ Λευιτικὴ ἱερωσύνη, εἰς δὲ τὴν Ἰούδα φυλὴν ἡ τῆς μείζονος ἱερωσύνης εὐλογία μετέβη.

[1] Chap. 6. 12.

[2] As in Ps. 45. 7, 8. the king is called אֱלֹהִים in Mal. 3. 1. הָאָדוֹן and Isa. 9. 5. אֵל

[3] As Rosenmüller, 1st Edit.   [4] Reading אֲדֹנִי or, אָדֹן instead of אֲדֹנָי

[5] Calvin has well remarked on this verse: "Similitudo est a strenuis et robustis ducibus sumta, qui dum festinant ad hostes persequendos, non indulgent delitiis, sed ad potum contenti sunt obviis quibusque fluminibus, et quidem in transcursu, ut stantes sitim e flumine restinguant. Nam et hoc modo Gideon cordatos et bellicosos milites expertus est, quia ignavos esse colligens, qui bibendi causâ se curvabant, domum remisit."

suffering nothing to stay his course. Still De Wette has laboured to adduce reasons against supposing Jehovah to be the object of address. He says (1), " It is incongruous that Jehovah should be here addressed and not the king, to whom the discourse had before been directed." But when the dramatic character, which this Psalm has in common with the second Psalm, is considered, it is not easy to perceive wherein this incongruity consists. The opinion that the king is addressed in Psalm 72. 5, is defended by De Wette himself, although he is not elsewhere addressed in the whole Psalm, but is always spoken of in the third person, and a direct address to Jehovah immediately precedes! The change of the person addressed is so frequent, that it is useless to bring forward examples. (2) " Besides, the king enthroned on the right hand of Jehovah (*i. e.* in a state of *rest*) cannot be conceived as engaging in war." This objection is founded on a misunderstanding of the words, ' *Sit thou on my right hand until I make thy foes thy footstool.*' The sense is, although numerous and powerful enemies rise up against thee, they cannot prevent me from making thee a partaker of my dominion, until thou shalt have entirely subdued them by the power which I will impart. That sitting on the right hand does not imply a state of *inaction* is evident from the eighth verse, where the king appears at the head of a countless host, and where De Wette himself translates : ' *Thy people willingly follow thee to battle,*' and on the seventh verse (which he agrees with us in referring to the king), in direct contradiction to his own interpretation, he remarks : " The poet in a lively manner places himself on the scene of *conflict, where his king appears as a triumphant warrior.*" (3) " The expression, ' *in the day of his wrath,*' agrees better with Jehovah."—This is indeed the case if we make the Psalm refer to an *earthly* king ; but not if its subject is Jehovah's exalted co-regent, the Messiah, of whom it is said also, in Psalm 2. 9, that ' *He will break his enemies with a rod of iron, and dash them in pieces like a potter's vessel,*' and in the twelfth verse, that ' *his wrath shall soon be kindled; but blessed are all they that put their trust in him.*'

143. Relying upon the strength of these reasons, the Christian Church has always firmly held the Messianic interpretation [1].

144. It might be expected, that those who reject this interpretation would justify their disregard of the authority of Christ and his Apostles, as well as of the internal proofs, by at least the *semblance* of reason ; but here, as in so many other instances, we must content ourselves with a bare " stat pro ratione voluntas." They only remark, in passing, that the image which is presented in this Psalm, of a warlike king destroying his foes, contains few features that can agree with Christ. But here we reply, (1) That we must carefully distinguish the *figure* from that which it represents, and not disregard the fact, that the features which form the portrait of this great

---

[1] Chrysostom says that those who reject it are καθάπερ οἱ μεθύοντες καὶ μηδὲν σύμφωνον φθεγγόμενοι, μᾶλλον δὲ καθάπερ οἱ ἐν σκότῳ βαδίζοντες καὶ προσαράσσοντες ἀλλήλους.

and more than human king, are taken, as usual, from an earthly head
of the theocracy.   Thus the expression, ' *God shall send forth the
rod of thy strength out of Zion*,' means in simple language : God
under thy reign will greatly enlarge the boundaries of the theocracy,
hitherto confined to Palestine[1].   So in the third verse, the spiritual
triumph which Christ gains over the world by his friends and servants, is represented, as is often the case, under the image of a victory
in war.   The king appears at the head of a host as numerous as
splendid[2], entirely and cheerfully devoted to his service[3] ; at the
same time however the figurative character of the representation is
suggested by the expression ' in sacred ornaments.'   In the fifth, and
two following verses, the punishment which the king inflicts upon
his enemies is represented by the figure of the fearful ruin, which an
earthly conqueror brings upon his vanquished foes[4].   (2) It is however true, that this king, even after the description is divested of its
metaphorical character, appears as a severe judge and avenger of his
enemies.   But here is nothing inconsistent with the fulfilment, when
we consider the point of view taken by the Psalmist.   It is not the
Messiah in his *humiliation*, that here, as well as in all the other
Psalms of this class, presents himself ; but the Messiah in his *glory*.
The author here, as in the second Psalm, takes his station in that
period of time when the Messiah, after having finished his work, has
been exalted by God to a participation in his government, and endowed with power to subdue his enemies[5].

145. As to the date of the Psalm, Palm and Muntinghe have, not
without reason, assigned it to about the same time as the second.
This idea is favoured by their great resemblance.   In both Psalms
numerous enemies, who rise up against the king, are easily vanquished and destroyed.   In both, we hear Jehovah assuring the king
of dominion and victory over his enemies.   The supposition of
Pareau, that the union of the priestly and regal dignity in the person

---

[1] Comp. Is. 2. 3. Mic. 4. 2. ' From Zion shall go forth the law, and the
word of Jehovah from Jerusalem.' Ps. 72. 8.   So the third verse.

[2] Both are included in the words, ' *Out of the womb of the early dawn shall be to
thee the dew of thy youth*,' i. e. thy war-host shall be like the dew, the son of the
morning.   Thereby the increase of the people of Christ, which is as great as un-
perceived and sudden, and at the same time their amiableness and freshness are
designated.

[3] The noun נְדָבֹת often occurs in the sense : *voluntariæ oblationes*. Comp. e. g.
Exod. 35. 29. and indeed not merely in the proper, but also in the spiritual
sense, as Ps. 119. 108.   This sense is here also more suitable than the one
usually assigned to the word : ' willingnesses,' as *abstractum pro concreto*, for ' willing.' The people present themselves as a free-will offering to their divine king.

[4] Comp. the similar representation in Isaiah 63.

[5] That what Christ says of Himself in reference to his lowly condition must
not be transferred to Him in his state of exaltation, we have already seen on
Ps. 2.   Comp. also Luke 19. 27.   Calvin strikingly observes : " Si quis roget :
ubi igitur ille clementiæ et mansuetudinis spiritus, quo præditum fore alibi
docet scriptura ? respondeo sicuti erga oves mansuetus est pastor, lupis autem
et furibus asper et formidabilis, ita Christum suaviter et placide fovere, qui se
ejus custodiæ committunt, sed qui obstinatâ malitiâ excutiunt ejus jugum, sen-
suros quam terribili potentia instructus sit."

of the Messiah was made clear to David, at the bringing up of the ark of the covenant [1], where he himself performed, in a measure, sacerdotal functions, is inconsistent with the fact, that he had not yet received the Divine promise which proved the groundwork of all his Messianic hopes and prophecies.

b. Psalms in which the suffering Messiah is described

146. FROM the Psalms already examined, we learn to know the Messiah as a *divine and glorious King*, whom all the nations of the earth shall obey, and also as a *Priest* of a far higher and more illustrious order than the priests of the first covenant; who was, consequently, to make an atonement for the sins of his people; for this was the peculiar duty of the sacerdotal order. But the Psalms we have hitherto considered, are silent both concerning the method, by which, *as a king*, he should gain his widely extended dominion, and, *as a priest*, accomplish the work of expiation. Their authors contemplate him as *already exalted to glory*.—But in another class of Psalms, those previous *sufferings* of the Messiah, by which the atonement was made, and which were rewarded by his subsequent glorification, constitute the chief object of prophetic vision. This ought not to awaken surprise, as we shall hereafter more fully show, in the chapter concerning the idea of the suffering Messiah in the Old Testament. Even in the second and hundred and tenth Psalms, innumerable enemies array themselves against the Messiah. David himself and all other true believers of the Old Testament, had so deeply experienced the corruption and wickedness of men, that they could have expected nothing else, than that the sufferings of their own lives should have their counterpart in the life of the Messiah; they were therefore sufficiently prepared for the Divine revelation on this subject, with which they were favoured.

147. To this class belong especially Psalms 16, 22, 40. It is a peculiarity of these Psalms, that the subject of them is himself introduced as speaking; whereas the subject of the foregoing Psalms is usually spoken of in the third person [2]. The interpreters who refer these Psalms to the Messiah are divided into two classes.

148. (1) The larger number suppose, that the Psalmist made the condition and the sentiments of the suffering Messiah his own, that he might introduce *him* as speaking, or rather speak himself in *his* person. In itself, this notion is not objectionable. Nothing is more frequent in poetry of all kinds, than for persons to be thus introduced; and in prophetic poetry this is the more natural, because the nature of the prophetic vision, in which every thing appears as *present*, necessarily gives to the representation a dramatic character. Thus, for example, in the second Psalm, the poet at one time speaks in his own person, at another in that of Jehovah, and lastly in the

[1] Related in 2 Sam. 6. 12—19. [2] Comp. however, Ps. 2.

person of his exalted king ; and this too without particularly designating, who it is that speaks. So also in the hundred and tenth
Psalm Jehovah appears as the speaker. Thus the prophets in perpetual alternation, speak, now in their own person, and now in the
person of Jehovah. They represent in their symbolical transactions
at one time Jehovah, at another the Jewish people, and then again
some other subject [1].

149. (2) After Calvin and Grotius, other expositors [2] suppose that
there is in these Psalms a sort of *double sense ;* that the subject of
them, in the *literal* and *lower* sense, is in each case the author himself ; and that, when thus interpreted, every thing that is said presents a natural and consistent meaning. Nevertheless the Holy
Spirit so influenced the minds of the writers, that they uttered many
things, applicable to themselves only in a metaphorical sense, but
which were *literally* and *completely* fulfilled in the history of the
Messiah. In support of this method of interpretation, they appeal
to the typical character of the Old Testament in general (the persons
and events of which obscurely represented and prefigured the Church
of the New Testament), and especially to the circumstance that
David, in his sufferings and his exaltation, was a type of the Messiah.
They remark that in common life a man often utters expressions,
which he did not at the moment fully comprehend, but which subsequently appear to him of the greatest importance.

150. It is easy to perceive the causes which gave rise to this
method of interpretation. There are in the Psalms of this class,
besides those special descriptions which are fulfilled only in the
history of Christ, general representations, which seem better to suit
a pious and suffering Israelite, than the Messiah [3]. This has persuaded several interpreters to give up, as untenable, the opinion that
the Messiah speaks in them *throughout* and *exclusively.* But, on the
other hand, they had too much regard for truth, to deny the special
references to the Messiah which they contain ; and too much reverence
for the testimony of the New Testament to resolve with the rationalists entirely to reject the Messianic interpretation. They sought
therefore to find a middle course.

[1] A remarkable illustration of this fact is found in the forty-ninth chapter of
Isaiah. As the prophet in the forty-second chapter had in his own person
directed the discourse to the Messiah, as if present, so here he speaks in the
person of the Messiah to the Gentiles.

[2] As Dathe and Steudel.

[3] Thus Ps. 16. 3, 4. the speaker numbers himself with the pious worshippers of
God on earth with whom he contrasts the ungodly. And the whole representation verse 1—8. contains scarcely a single circumstance which is *peculiar* to
the history of the Messiah, unless, indeed, as many interpreters have done, we
supply by a forced interpretation what is wanting in the text. So in Ps. 22. 5, 6.
the speaker appeals to the example of his forefathers, whose prayers God had
heard when they were in distress, and grounds upon it his supplication for similar deliverance. In Ps. 40. 14—18. the description is so general, that these verses
occur again in the seventieth Psalm, a Psalm of complaint and supplication
suited to *any* suffering servant of God. And, in general, we find in the Psalms
of prayer and complaint, which have no relation to the Messiah, passages that
agree almost verbally with those in the Psalms of this class.

151. It is scarcely necessary to remark, that this mode of exposition must be rejected, as soon as the difficulty in which it obviously originated, is in some other way removed. Now this is done (such at least is my own belief) by the two following considerations. (1) Christ in his state of humiliation was entirely like us in every thing, except sin ; like us, He placed his confidence in God, He lamented, complained, prayed. Much therefore which is said of Him, must be capable of a *more general* application. (2) It has been unjustly taken for granted, that, if we regard the Messiah as the speaker, we must suppose the authors of the Psalms to have been deprived of all agency and consciousness. Whether the Messiah be introduced as *himself* speaking, or be spoken of in the third person, can here, however, occasion no difference ; since the sacred poets would, just as much in the one case as in the other, be hurried away beyond the sphere of their own conceptions. With respect to those Psalms in which the suffering Messiah appears as the speaker, the writers not only received in their minds a *general impression* of his severe sufferings, but *special traits* were revealed to them, which were peculiar to Him, and could be affirmed of no other person. In describing this general impression, the ideas already in their minds were employed as the groundwork. As, in their description of the glorified Messiah, an illustrious earthly king serves as the substratum : so here the image in general of a pious man in affliction presented itself to their minds, from their own experience and that of others. And, like the author of those Psalms which describe him in his glory, they gave to this image those special features, which suit only the Messiah. Thus all is made clear, and we need not either (with the older interpreters, who overlooked the human features in these Psalms) find special references to the Messiah when none exist ; or, with recent interpreters, deny such references, when they are known to exist, both by internal evidence, and the clearest declarations of the New Testament.

152. The necessity therefore which alone could justify this second method of interpretation, does not exist. On the contrary, it is liable to several serious objections. (1) One of the most weighty is, that in these Psalms special traits occur, which cannot *in any sense* be applicable to David, or to any other pious sufferer of the Old Testament. This mode of explanation therefore is attended with *the same* difficulties, as that which the rationalists have adopted [1]. (2) To this it must be added, that it cannot be reconciled with the manner in which these Psalms are regarded in the New Testament, which, *without any intimation of a double sense*, explains them simply of the Messiah. It even expressly *denies* the reference of the sixteenth Psalm to any other object. (3) The sixteenth Psalm, as well as the fortieth, plainly shows how little this mode of interpretation is applicable to *all* the Psalms of this class. If we refer them to the Messiah they contain passages which can agree with him only, and in no respect with a saint of the Old Testament under suffering ; as his resurrection

---

[1] See on Ps. 22.

in the former, and his sacrificial death in the latter; if, on the contrary, we adopt the views of the rationalists, who make the former speak only of deliverance from great danger, and the latter of willing obedience to the commands of God, the sense is completed in David or any other pious man in affliction, and the reasons for a higher reference to the Messiah disappear.

Psalm 16

153. ARGUMENT.—The contents of this Psalm are as follows. The speaker commences with a prayer to God for his aid, founded on the assurance that He is his God, and his highest good [1]. He delights in the society of the faithful worshippers of Jehovah, while he avoids all companionship with those unhappy men, who seek their happiness from other sources and not from God [2]. He felicitates himself on account of his intimate relation to God, which is better than all the good things of earth, and expresses his gratitude for being made a partaker of this blessedness [3]. Confiding in his relation to God, he need never be disheartened; on the contrary, even now, in the near prospect of death, he is consoled and joyful from the conviction that the Lord will not leave him for ever in its power, but conduct him through it to a new life of happiness and glory [4].

154. To the end of the eighth verse, the Psalm is of a general character; those who affirm and those who deny its reference to the Messiah are in the main agreed as to its meaning. A difference of interpretation, however, arises at the ninth verse. According to the Messianic interpretation, the Messiah here expresses the hope of his resurrection and glorification. The meaning of the tenth verse will then be: '*Thou wilt not abandon my soul to Sheol, nor suffer thy holy one to see corruption* [5].'

155. The reasons for referring the Psalm to the Messiah are the following. (1) By far the most important proof is that which is derived from the New Testament. But no where is the testimony more complete than in the present instance; so that the Divine illumination of the Apostles and even of Christ Himself depends upon the Messianic character of this Psalm: since He promised them this illumination, and in their interpretation of those passages of the Old Testament which related to Him, they followed his guidance. Peter, in his discourse immediately after the out-pouring of the Holy Spirit, explains the Psalm of Christ, and indeed of Him only, in such a manner that he controverts its reference to David, and assigns

---

[1] Ver. 1, 2.   [2] Ver. 3, 4.   [3] Ver. 7.   [4] Ver. 8—11.

[5] עָזַב with לְ, *to abandon*, שַׁחַת *corruption*. The rationalist interpreters, on the contrary, understand the ninth and tenth verses as referring to nothing more than the hope expressed by David, or some other pious man, that God would bestow upon him rich blessings even in the present life. They translate the tenth verse, '*Thou dost not deliver over my soul to the realm of shades, nor suffer thy darling to see the pit.*' שַׁחַת in the sense of *pit*.

the reasons why he *could not* here have spoken of himself[1]. Paul also[2], not only refers it to Christ, but *opposes the opinion* that it was written concerning David. That the Apostles do not here speak in the way of accommodation is evident (not to mention that such an accommodation is as utterly unworthy of the Apostles as incapable of proof) even from the fact that they find it necessary to vindicate the reference to the Messiah, and oppose the reference to David, whence it follows that the former was unusual, and the latter prevalent among those whom they addressed. The assertion of De Wette[3], that the Apostles designed to declare nothing more, than that the *full, entire, deep* truth of the Psalmist's hope was first fulfilled and verified in Christ, fails to redeem their authority, because, according to the interpretation of the rationalists, nothing remains which has not been *completely fulfilled* in the history of the Psalmist, and of course the Apostles could have had no reason to oppose the correct and literal explanation, which refers the Psalm to David. Michaelis has justly remarked[4], "if what Le Clerc and others allege respecting the literal sense of this Psalm be correct, Peter would have deserved to be told : 'with all thine apparent candour, thou art a deceiver, seeking to delude the ignorant multitude. Thou pretendest, that the Psalm speaks of a resurrection from the dead, and is incapable of any other interpretation ; whereas it relates, if literally understood, merely to a deliverance from great danger of this life, to which David, its author, was more than once exposed.' "—Again, several defenders of the Messianic interpretation have, not without reason, assumed that, in addition to the testimony of the Apostles, we have also that of Christ Himself. For as Christ[5], after His resurrection explained to His disciples the predictions concerning Himself in the Old Testament, we should surely expect that a passage to which they give a degree of importance so entirely peculiar, and of which they speak with a conviction so strong and free from doubt, would be one of those which He had interpreted. And as, according to the latter passage, His resurrection also was predicted in the prophecies of the Old Testament, where could He more naturally have pointed it out to them than in the Psalm before us ? (2.) Even, therefore, if we believed the contents of the Psalm to present many difficulties in the way of the Messianic interpretation, still, with the modesty which becomes a Christian expositor, we ought rather to accuse our own ignorance, than impute an errour to the authors of the New Testament. This, however, is by no means the case. The Messianic interpretation needs no peculiar and forced explanation, in opposition to the laws of the language. On the contrary, although we concede that the older interpreters, particularly Michaelis, have brought forward many reasons for the reference to the Messiah, which will not bear examination ; and acknowledge also, that the method can be philologically justified, by which recent interpreters have set

---

[1] Acts·2. 25—31.   [2] Acts 13. 35—37.
[3] In direct contradiction to what he had just before remarked in reply to Eckermann.
[4] L. c. p. 3.   [5] According to Luke 24. 27. and 44. 46.

aside the references to Christ, which His Church has always found in this Psalm; we must, nevertheless, assert, that every impartial critic must regard the Messianic interpretation of the three last verses, as the easiest and most natural, and that it would be universally adopted, were it not for the influence of doctrinal views. And in fact it appears, that in ancient times no one ever supposed that these verses could contain any thing else, than the hope of a proper resurrection. Paul and Peter presuppose this as an established truth; and they speak with a confidence, which shows that they could not have expected from any of their hearers the objection, that the Psalm spoke merely of deliverance from great danger. That it was believed that the words, ' *my flesh shall rest securely*,' could not be explained to mean any thing but *incorruptibility*, is shown by the Jewish fable founded upon it, that the body of David did not putrefy[1].

156. It must, indeed, be conceded, that the true import of this Messianic prediction was difficult to be understood before its fulfilment. This is manifest from the fact, that as early as the time of Christ, it was pretty generally explained of David. But still it was surely by no means impossible, for an attentive student of the prophecies to understand it correctly. Whoever had learnt from the fifty-third chapter of Isaiah to know the servant of God, who after having died for us, should be exalted to the highest glory and enjoy a never ending life; or from the twenty-second Psalm had become familiar with the thought of a Messiah, who should pass through suffering to glory, and, at the same time, had perceived that the speaker in a Psalm was not necessarily and in all cases its *subject*— might easily come to the conclusion, that not David, but the Messiah, in the expectation of whose advent the whole spiritual life of the people centred, here appears as the speaker, and foretells his own resurrection. And even granting that *no one* under the Old Testament attained to this knowledge, it is yet so obvious to us (who can institute a far more extensive comparison of the prophecies illustrated by the fulfilment), that, even without the evidence of the New Testament, we must have regarded the Messianic interpretation as at least the most probable. That the Psalm, according to the Messianic interpretation, contains things beyond the mere human knowledge of the Psalmist, need the less prejudice us against it, since Peter[2] expressly remarks, that David *as a prophet* (i. e. by *Divine revelation*) here foresaw the resurrection of Christ.

157. We must now proceed to refute the objections which have been brought against the reference of the Psalm to the Messiah.

158. (1) "The third verse, where the speaker expresses his longing after the pious worshippers of God, who dwelt in the land, i. e. in Palestine, does not suit the Messiah, but David, who, fleeing from

---

[1] See Lightfoot on Acts 2. 29. and the remarkable passage from Jalkut Schimoni, fol. 95. ed. Franc. by Michaelis l. c. p. 12. Kimchi also cites as the current explanation of these words, "post mortem sibi non esse dominaturum vermem," and interprets the tenth and eleventh verses, not of deliverance from danger, but of a happy resurrection.

[2] Acts 2. 30.

the presence of Saul, was compelled to take up his abode among the heathenish Philistines [1]." We here, in the first place, offer an explanation of this difficult verse. After many had despaired of interpreting the received text, and tried a variety of conjectural emendations, its genuineness has been acknowledged by the recent interpreters. We interpret it: '*joining myself*[2] *to the holy ones who are on the earth, and the excellent, all my delight is in them.*' Jahn's objection is drawn from the words '*which are on the earth*[3],' which he translates '*which are in the land,*' (i. e. *Palestine*) : but the words ' *the holy ones who are on the earth,*' or ' *the holy ones of the earth,*' is a pleonastical [4] phrase for ' *the holy ones,*' ' *the holy.*' If, however, a peculiar stress *must* be laid on the words, we should interpret them as intended to distinguish ' *the holy ones on the earth*' from the *angels,* to whom the title of ' *the holy ones*[5]' peculiarly belongs, almost as a proper name.

159. (2) "The fourth verse also favours the reference of the Psalm to David. The abhorrence of idolatry, there expressed, does not suit the Messiah, whose chief enemies were not idolaters, but Jews; it agrees well however with David, who, during his residence among the heathenish Philistines, probably experienced strong temptation to idolatry, and, at any rate, suffered much from its adherents [6]." But granting that idolatry is in reality the *special subject* of this verse, as these interpreters suppose, it would nevertheless furnish no proof against the Messianic interpretation. For in any event it cannot, as Knapp assumes, be inferred from the contents of the verse, that the speaker had been tempted to idolatry, nor as Jahn supposes, that idolaters were his enemies. The speaker would rather merely declare in the fourth verse his entire separation from idolaters, as he does in the third verse his fellowship with the pious worshippers of God. The idolaters would then be mentioned as *species pro genere,* for all the despisers of the true God, these being the chief despisers of Him, at the time of the composition of the Psalm; in accordance with the custom of putting a part for the whole, of which there are examples without number. It is, however, in the highest degree probable, that the supposition that idolatry is particularly mentioned, depends entirely on a false interpretation : and that the passage should be rendered not '*many are the idols of those who hasten after other (gods)*[7] ;' but ' *many are the pains of those*

[1] Thus Jahn, Vatic. Mess. II. p. 251.

[2] We take ל in its usual signification *to—to the saints,* i. e. *associating with them, belonging to them.* Calvin: "Sanctis me adjungam socium,—nempe quod se applicabit ad pios Dei cultores et illorum socius erit vel comes, sicuti omnes Dei filios fraternæ conjunctionis nexu inter se devinctos esse oportet, ut eodem affectu et studio patrem suum colant."

[3] אֲשֶׁר בָּאָרֶץ הֵמָּה

[4] אֶרֶץ is used pleonastically in other instances, as for example in Ps. 76. 10. עַנְוֵי אֶרֶץ where it occurs in a manner entirely similar.

[5] קְדוֹשִׁים. See Ps. 89. 8. Job 5. 1. &c.

[6] Thus Knapp and Jahn.

[7] יִרְבּוּ עַצְּבוֹתָם אַחֵר מָהָרוּ The noun עַצֶּבוֹת has never, like its cognate עֲצַבִּים the

who hasten elsewhere[1].' That *elsewhere* is the same as, '*after other gods*' (which De Wette asserts) is an arbitrary supposition. It signifies any departure whatever from God, any confidence, either in our own strength, or that of other created beings, or of idols.—Nor can it any more be proved from the words, '*I will not pour out their drink offerings of blood,*' that idolaters are spoken of in this sense. The best interpreters agree, that these words must not be literally understood, and made to refer to the common practice among the heathen of using blood instead of wine in their libations, or of mingling wine with blood, but that they are rather to be taken in a figurative sense. '*Drink offerings of blood*'—that is, those which God as much abhors *as if* they consisted of blood instead of wine, which was what He had prescribed. But God so regards not merely the offerings of idolaters, but those also of the outward members of the theocracy, which are presented from mere selfish motives, and without that true theocratic disposition, which was necessary to render the sacrifice acceptable[2]. The sense therefore is: '*I detest the sacrifices of the wicked, which are displeasing to God.*' Consequently there is no trace of any *special reference to idolatry.*

160. (3) "The plural 'thy holy ones[3]' in the tenth verse is opposed to the Messianic interpretation. It is true that the marginal reading has, instead of this, the singular 'thy holy one[4]', and in favour of this reading there are very numerous and important critical authorities. But the reading of the text is the *more difficult*, and *therefore* to be preferred. [Because no transcriber who found the *easier* reading in his copy, would have changed it into the harder one.] According to this, however, the subject of discourse cannot be the resurrection, which is peculiar to the Messiah, but merely a deliverance from dangers, which the Psalmist claims for all the pious in general as well as for himself[5]." But the marginal reading is certainly the true one. In favour of the singular we have not only the greatest number of manuscripts and the best[6], but still earlier testimony. It is confirmed by all the old translations,—it is confirmed by the Apostles Peter and Paul; who, when they prove the resurrection of Christ from this Psalm, with the strongest conviction that their proof could not be invalidated, make it manifest that in their time the reading *thy holy ones*, by which their whole interpretation could so easily be refuted, did not exist :—and this is confirmed by the silence of the Jews. These reasons are so striking, that even the skil-

---

meaning *idols;* but always that of *pains.* אַחֵר never stands alone for *other gods,* but only where Jehovah appears as the speaker, and contrasts Himself with them, as in Isaiah 42. 8.

[1] Storr, Rosenmüller, and De Wette. אַחֵר as accus. of the neut. (in answer to the question *whither*) in the sense *aliorsum,* elsewhere.

[2] See Isa. 63. 3 : ' He that (with such a wrong disposition) offereth an oblation is as one who offereth swine's blood.' Prov. 21. 22. ' The sacrifice of the wicked is an abomination.'

[3] חֲסִידֶיךָ   [4] חֲסִידְךָ

[5] Thus Rosenmüller and De Wette.   [6] 156 Codd. Ken. 80. Codd. de Rossi.

ful defenders of the reading ' *thy holy ones* [1]' undertake its defence
only on the supposition that the *plural* here stands for the *singular*,
and they declare that the idea of its being a proper plural is altogether inadmissible. The argument which is urged in favour of
the plural, that the more difficult reading is to be preferred here,
as well as every where else, is only specious; for it is absurd to
extend this rule of criticism so far, as to disregard the whole weight
of external evidence. Besides, the authority of this rule depends
entirely on the circumstance, that the origin of the easier reading can
be more readily explained than that of the more difficult one [2]. But
here the case is exactly the opposite. The plural must have been
extremely welcome to the Jews, because it furnished them with the
best means of refuting the Messianic interpretation of the Psalm, by
which they were embarrassed even by the Apostles [3]. If now the
plural may at first have found its way into the text by accident,
which could so easily happen, or [4] may have been *substituted* for the
reading of the text from polemic zeal against the Christians, in either
case it was natural for later transcribers to prefer a reading, which so
greatly favoured the opinions of the Jews; and that nevertheless this
was done only by comparatively few, must be ascribed to the over-
whelming preponderance of external arguments [5].

[1] חֲסִידֶיךָ

[2] [i. e. *generally*, the easier reading is a *conjectural emendation* of the harder
one; whereas it is most improbable, that any transcriber, finding the easier reading, would have changed it into the more difficult one. How then did the more
difficult one find its way into the text? The answer *generally* must be, because
the transcriber *found it in his copy*: i. e. it is the true reading.]

[3] That this reading was used for such a purpose is shown by the Perusch
Tillim of Jacob de Mercado, Amsterd. 1653: " Scriptum חֲסִידֶיךָ plene duobus
Jod ut complectatur etiam *sanctos alios* præter *eum*. Per חֲסִידֶיךָ igitur dicere
voluit, etiam ego horum comprehendor numero et ero sicut unus ex illis." See
other passages in Aurivillius, de vera Lectione voc. חֲסִידֶיךָ in dissert. ed.
Michaelis, p. 136.

[4] As Aurivillius thinks.

[5] Other philological objections are answered by our author thus: (4.) " The
construction of the verb עָזַב with the preposition לְ designates the *terminus ad
quem*. If the Messianic interpretation were the true one, instead of לִשְׁאוֹל we
should have בִּשְׁאוֹל." (Hufnagel.) But the verb עָזַב with לְ, אֶל and עַל signifies, *to
give up to another;* whether to be received or retained, the connexion must in
every case decide. Michaelis has justly remarked, that Sheol is here personified,
and represented as an insatiable animal, which will not surrender the prey,
which it has once overpowered. See Prov. 30. 16. Ps. 49. 15. Is. 5. 14.

(5.) " The noun שַׁחַת never signifies *corruption,* as it must according to this interpretation, but always *grave*. And this meaning of the word is here also sustained by the parallelism." Thus Rosenmüller, Jahn, De Wette. It is indeed
true that the noun שַׁחַת commonly derived from שׁוּחַ *to subside* (as נַחַת from נוּחַ)
means *a pit, a grave*. But that another שַׁחַת derived from שָׁחַת *corrupit, perdidit,*
with the meaning *corruptio, putredo,* was in use in the living language, appears
from the testimony of the old translators, who (with the exception of the Chaldee,
the latest among them), not only with Peter and Paul, render the word *corruption* in this passage, but also in others, where the connexion requires it to be
translated *pit*. Nay, it is even capable of proof, that the word occurs in this

161. (6) " This Psalm coincides so entirely in style, expressions, and sentiments, with the fifty-sixth, fifty-seventh, and fifty-ninth Psalms (which have the same appellation, *Michtam*, in the super-scription, and appear from external and internal evidence to relate to David's exile during the persecution of Saul), that it must necessarily refer, like them, to David and to the same circumstances of his life [1]." Even De Wette remarks, that he is unable to find this alleged resemblance; and surely every one will agree with him after a careful comparison. It is by no means so great, as that which it bears to other supplicatory Psalms; its resemblance to them, however, according to our introductory remarks, can be no objection to its reference to the Messiah.

162. (7) " This interpretation is in opposition to all the notions of the Jews respecting the Messiah. They expected Him to be a hero, a conqueror, a mighty king; a suffering Messiah was unknown to them [2]." In answer to this objection, we would refer to the chapter concerning the suffering Messiah in the Old Testament.

163. (8) " The Jews by no means expected a *resurrection* of the Messiah, as appears from a passage of Maimonides, quoted by Pococke [3]." Thus Rosenmüller. But if this assertion were correct, still it would furnish no proof; for we can by no means infer with certainty, that a doctrine is *not contained* in the Old Testament, because the Jews, who were not favoured with the light afforded by the fulfilment, and were moreover blinded by manifold prejudices, did not find it there. The assertion, however, is entirely erroneous. The unimportant testimony of the philosopher Maimonides is more than overbalanced by the passages which Schöttgen [4] has adduced from the Sohar, the Talmud, and Jalkut Shimoni [5].

Psalm 22

164. ARGUMENT.—This Psalm consists of two parts, ver. 1—22 and 23—32. A worshipper of God in extreme distress presents before Him his anxious complaint. He reminds him, that, since He had always delivered his pious forefathers from their affliction, He would appear to act inconsistently should He on the contrary abandon him to his unparalleled sufferings, to the contempt of the whole people, to the bitter mockery and scorn of his enemies [6].—He prays that God, who had watched over him with such tender love from the commencement of his being, would not now forsake him [7].—But the feeling of

---

sense in the Hebrew text. Allowing it to be doubtful in other passages to which an appeal has been made, it undoubtedly occurs in Job 17. 14, where שַׁחַת *corruption*, stands in the parallelism with רִמָּה *worm*. Ps. 55. 24, the meaning *corruption* is at least the most probable. As to parallelism, that is certainly not destroyed by the Messianic interpretation. For the expression ' *thou wilt not give up my soul to Sheol*,' is the same in other words as ' *thou wilt not suffer thy Holy One to see corruption*,' with only the difference, perhaps, that according to the contrast which already occurs in the foregoing verse, the former, as Dathe rightly remarks, relates to the *soul*, the latter to the *body*.

[1] Thus Rosenmüller.   [2] Ruperti.   [3] Porta Mosis, p. 159, 60. ed. Ox.
[4] De Messia, p. 565 seq.   [5] See Heinrichs on Acts 11. 24.
[6] Ver. 1—8.   [7] Ver. 10—12.

misery is still too strong to be overcome; he is not yet consoled by the inward assurance that his prayer is heard. Again therefore does he give utterance to his emotions, and bewail his still increasing wretchedness. He is encompassed by numerous bloodthirsty foes. The most dreadful sufferings have consumed all his strength; intense thirst torments him; they have pierced his hands and his feet; every member is made to feel its peculiar anguish. His enemies feast their eyes with malicious joy upon the spectacle which he presents. They part his garments among them, and cast lots upon his vesture [1].— This repetition of his complaint is then followed [2] by a repetition of his prayer, now accompanied by the assurance of a favourable hearing.

165. In the second part, the speaker declares the method in which he will manifest his thankfulness for the promised deliverance, and also the consequences which shall flow from it. When freed from his distress, he will highly extol the goodness of God, and exhort the believing Israelites to praise Him, and put their trust in Him [3]. And what is of still higher importance, he will celebrate a sacrificial feast in honour of his Lord in accordance with his vow. This sacrificial feast shall be of a kind altogether unusual. Not merely the poor shall be partakers of it; but those also who enjoy the greatest abundance, shall be invited along with the most needy. It shall not be too simple for the latter, and the former shall not be excluded from it by their wretchedness. And not only shall the believing Israelites in great numbers come to this feast, but the heathen likewise, from one end of the earth to the other, after they shall be converted to God in consequence of the deliverance of his devout worshipper; who is henceforth to be acknowledged as Lord and King in all the world. The nourishment which this feast will supply, is not merely transient and corporeal, calling for nothing more than momentary gratitude. It is spiritual and everlasting [4]. Nor are the consequences of this memorable transaction to be limited to the present time. The heathen, who consecrate themselves to Jehovah, are henceforth to be numbered for ever among his people, hitherto limited to Israel alone [5]; and the mercy of God in the deliverance of his servant shall be celebrated with joyful thanksgiving from generation to generation [6].

166. Interpreters have taken three different views of this Psalm. —(1) The modern Jews and the rationalists. These are unanimous only in their opposition to the Messianic interpretation: in all other respects the greatest difference prevails among them. Many of them, proceeding upon the supposition that David is named as the author in the superscription, make him also the subject. But they differ widely, when they attempt to fix on the period in the life of David to which the Psalm relates. Some refer it to the time of Saul's persecution; others, to that of David's flight from Absalom, and others still to that of the Syrian war. On the other hand, some interpreters of this class confess, that *no* corresponding condition can be found in the life of David, and seek for another subject in Jewish history [7]. And lastly, others seeing the difficulties

[1] Ver. 13—19.   [2] Ver. 20—22.   [3] Ver. 23—25.   [4] Ver. 26—30.

[5] We explain the second member from the thirty-first verse with Dathe and Jahn: '*Deo erunt ut nova generatio ascripti*,' i. e. '*in catalogum membrorum novæ ecclesiæ referentur.*' The verb סָפַר in the sense denied by Rosenmüller: *numerare*, Ps. 40. 6. Job 38. 37. The forced interpretation, 'it shall be related by the Lord in future generations,' owes its origin solely to the effort to set aside a Messianic feature. The translation of לַאדֹנָי by, *by the Lord*, is as harsh as that of לַדּוֹר by, *in future generations*, and is unauthorized.

[6] Ver. 31, 32.

[7] So Jahn (*Vatic. Mess.* 2. p. 267), who regards Hezekiah as the subject.

which attend the reference of it to any individual subject besides the Messiah, resort to a supposed personification [1].

167. (2) A second class suppose, that it contains many things which must be referred only to David, and others which are peculiar to Christ. They seek to reconcile this, by the supposition that David himself was the sufferer, and composed the Psalm about the time of Saul's persecution, or Absalom's rebellion; but that, under the guidance of the Holy Spirit, he uttered many things which are applicable to him only in an inferior, or metaphorical sense, but are literally and completely fulfilled in the history of the Messiah [2].

168. (3) And lastly, by far the greatest number of interpreters acknowledge the Messiah as the exclusive subject of the Psalm. This interpretation was followed by a portion of the older Jews, and has always been the prevailing one in the Christian Church.

169. We feel compelled by the weight of evidence to decide in favour of the last interpretation. The principal arguments are the following:—

170. (1) It is sustained by the testimony of tradition. It is true that De Wette asserts [3] that the Psalm was *never* understood by the Jews of the suffering Messiah [4]. But this groundless assertion is sufficiently refuted by the clear testimony drawn from the Jewish writers by Jo. H. Michaelis [5] and Schöttgen [6]. These passages are the more conclusive, because the Jews must have been extremely *desirous* to find out some other mode of explaining the Psalm, both on account of their opposition to the notion of a suffering Messiah in general, and of the embarrassment in which they were involved by its close agreement, according to the Messianic interpretation, with the history of Jesus Christ. Hence we cannot explain why this interpretation was not entirely and universally rejected, in any other way than by supposing, that the *doctrinal interest* of the Jews was counteracted by the *authority of tradition*.

171. (2) We urge, in the next place, the testimony of the New Testament. That Christ [7] uttered the first words of this Psalm on the cross, would not of itself be conclusive, because He might have used them merely in the way of accommodation. It is, however, a fact well worthy of attention.—But, on the other hand, nothing can

---

[1] So Kimchi and Jarchi (who make the subject of the Psalm the suffering of the Jewish people in their present dispersion), and De Wette (who seems inclined to the opinion that it describes the sufferings in the Babylonian exile).

[2] Thus Calvin, Melanchthon, Musculus, Rüdinger, Grotius, Venema, Dathe, Seiler, Kuinoel and others,

[3] P. 238.

[4] Jahn endeavours in vain to prove from Matt. 27. 43, that in the time of Christ, the Psalm was not understood of the Messiah. It cannot even be inferred from that passage (though it is probable for other reasons), that the *Jews who mocked Jesus* (and who surely did not belong to the better portion, who were capable of receiving the idea of a suffering Messiah) did not adopt the Messianic interpretation.

[5] Comm. in Ps. p. 138.   [6] De Messiâ, p. 232, &c.

[7] According to Matt. 27. 46. Mark 15. 34.

be more unnatural than the supposition, that the quotations in
John 19. 24 [1] and Heb. 2. 11, 12 [2], are mere allusions.

172. (3) But by far the most conclusive evidence is that drawn
from internal sources.—Numerous traits are here combined, which
either singly, or at all events in this combination, are not to be found
in the history of David, or of any other person than the Messiah.
And here, before we proceed to particulars, we must premise a
general remark. The opposers of the Messianic interpretation, as
Hufnagel and Rosenmüller, have made the task easy for themselves,
by considering the features appropriate to the Messiah separately,
and not in their mutual connexion. But it is this latter consideration which is of peculiar force ; for nothing but doctrinal prejudice
can suppose that *all the circumstances* which have so literally con-
curred in the history of Jesus, can be met with, *in the same combination*, in the life of any other person. It is on this account that those
facts become significant, which, as the piercing of the hands and
feet, are not *in themselves* peculiar to Christ, and may be often
repeated.—Let us here present, in one view, the principal characteristics of the Messiah. In the eighth verse it is said : ' *All that see
me laugh me to scorn, they shoot out the lip*, they shake the head.'
In St. Matthew we read : '*And they that passed by reviled him,
wagging* [or *shaking*] *their heads* [3].' In the ninth verse, the scoffers
are introduced, saying : ' *He trusted on the Lord, that he would
deliver him : let him deliver him, seeing he delighted in him.*' In
Matthew they say : ' *He trusted in God ; let him deliver him now,
if he will have him* [4].' Both passages so literally correspond, that the
resemblance cannot possibly be regarded as the result of accident.
Michaelis has very properly remarked : " They quoted from this
Psalm (as people are accustomed to do, who are much conversant with
the Bible), because its language harmonized with their sentiments,
without being aware of its character, and how unhappily for themselves they were fulfilling its predictions." But even were we to
suppose that the revilers of Christ used these words independently of
the Psalm, still the coincidence would not be at all the less remarkable. It is also manifest that, from among the many words that
were uttered, Matthew selected these especially, for the purpose of
pointing out the agreement between the prophecy and its fulfilment.
Nor is there any doubt that, in bringing forward the remaining
circumstances in which this agreement consists, he designed to lead
his reader to the conviction, that in the sufferings of Christ, the most
remarkable predictions of the Old Testament respecting the Messiah's
sufferings, were completely fulfilled. And hence the opinion of

---

[1] 'They said therefore among themselves, Let us not rend it, but cast lots for
it whose it shall be : that the scripture might be fulfilled, which saith, They
parted my raiment among them, and for my vesture they did cast lots.'

[2] '——for which cause he is not ashamed to call them brethren, saying, I will
declare thy name unto my brethren ; in the midst of the church will I sing
praise unto thee.'

[3] κινοῦντες τὰς κεφαλὰς αὐτῶν.   [4] Matt. 27. 43.

those, who maintain that the distinct citations from this Psalm are mere allusions, appears still more erroneous.—In the fifteenth and sixteenth verses we read : ' *I am poured out like water, and all my bones are out of joint ; my heart is like wax : it is melted in the midst of my bowels. My strength is dried up like a potsherd ; and my tongue cleaveth to my jaws ; and thou hast brought me into the dust of death.*' These words were literally fulfilled in the inexpressible anguish attending the crucifixion of Christ[1]. The exact fulfilment of the circumstance, ' *My tongue cleaveth to my jaws,*' which indicates extreme thirst[2], is expressly mentioned by John[3] : ' *Jesus . . . that the scripture might be fulfilled, said,* I thirst.'—But one of the most remarkable traits is that in the seventeenth verse, where the translation, ' *They have pierced through*[4] *my hands and my feet,*' is the only one sustained by philological and sufficient arguments. These words, however, can refer neither to David, nor to any other sufferer except the Messiah ; since, as Gesenius remarks[5], " Men pierced indeed *the body* of their enemy, but not his *hands and feet.*" They rather refer to Christ, who, as a consequence of the punishment of the cross, endured this suffering.

173. But here we meet with yet another difficulty. After it had been, from the earliest time, received by the Church as an unquestionable fact, that, when Christ was crucified, not merely his hands, but also his feet were pierced through with nails, an attempt has been made, after the example of Dathe, by Paulus, to prove that this was *not* the case. He has been followed by Rosenmüller, Kuinöl, Fritsche, and many others, no one of whom has thought of examining his proofs, though they are easily refuted, and clearly manifest the

---

[1] Hufnagel, Diss. in h. Ps.: "Acerbissimos dolores his verbis graviter describit, summosque cruciatus ita hominem afficere docet, ac si ipsa corporis compages firmis nexibus superstructa iis omnino destituatur."

[2] Lam. 4. 4.

[3] John 19. 28. So also in the nineteenth verse : "I can number my bones," which Jahn rightly explains : "in singulis meis ossibus tremorem singularem sentio, ut ea dinumerare possim."

[4] We take, with Pococke, Gesenius, and De Wette, the form כָּאֲרִי as the irregular plural for כָּאֲרִים. This form will then be the plural participle of כּוּר. Although this participle is properly כָּר, yet the *scriptio plena* is not in other instances without example : thus Hos. 10. 14. קָאם v. Ez. 28. 24, 26. שָׁאמִים (despisers). There is every thing in favour of giving the verb כּוּר (which is not again found in Hebrew) the sense *to pierce through.* This interpretation is sustained (1) by the Hebrew usage. כּוּר is then synonymous with the verb כָּרָה *to bore through,* which often occurs. Such a permutation of the verbs עו and לה is very common. Thus דום and דמה *to be silent,* דוך and דחה *to bruise,* בז and בזה *to despise,* and many others. (2) The testimony of the Seventy, who translate ὤρυξαν χεῖράς μου καὶ πόδας μου as well as the Syriac version, which has ܟܒܠ *perforarunt, transfixerunt,* and the Vulgate, *foderunt.* This coincidence of the three most important direct translations deserves great regard. (3) And lastly the comparison with the Arabic is decisive. There the agreement of כּוּר with כָּרָה which we have assumed, really exists.

[5] See p. 1340.

existence of doctrinal prejudice, and the desire of setting aside a Messianic prediction [1], that has clearly been fulfilled. We cannot here enter into a full examination, but shall endeavour to offer such remarks as may suffice to refute it. We observe, in the first place, that *not a single reason* can be adduced, for the opinion that the feet were not nailed; since the passages in which the feet are said to have been *bound with cords* plainly prove nothing; for the hands also were *bound*, yet they were afterwards *nailed*. On the contrary, it can be proved by the surest historical testimony, that the nailing of the feet actually took place. An important proof is found in Plautus [2]. There a slave, who expected the worst consequences from the return of his master, exclaims, "Ego dabo ei talentum primus qui in crucem excucurrerit, Sed eâ lege, ut *offigantur* bis *pedes*, bis brachia [3]." Paulus seeks to evade the force of this passage on two grounds. He remarks, (1) "It is manifest here from the tenour of this discourse, that the slave expected something *uncommonly* severe and cruel, and of course that *offigi pedes* was not usual in the punishment of the cross." But all that is extraordinary here, is manifestly what is implied in the word *bis;* usually the hands and feet were nailed but *once;* the slave dreaded a *double* nailing. The *offigi pedes* stands moreover in the same relation as the *offigi brachia*, and can be regarded as extraordinary no more than that. (2) "The text is uncertain. More correctly may be read with Pareus, ut *obfringantur bis pedes, bis brachia*, and then the subject of discourse will be the *breaking* of the arms and legs, as in the case of malefactors." But this reading is absurd, since the breaking of the legs *shortened* and *alleviated* the punishment, instead of *aggravating* it. It is to be rejected on other grounds also: the reading *offigantur* is confirmed by manuscripts, and nothing but doctrinal prejudice can reject it, against all critical authority.—The second important passage is taken from Tertullian [4], "Si adhuc quæris dominicæ crucis prædicationem, satis jam potest tibi facere vigesimus primus Psalmus, totam Christi continens passionem, canentis jam tunc gloriam suam : foderunt, inquit, manus meas et pedes, *quæ propria* (al. edd. *proprie*) *est atrocia crucis*." The testimony of this writer is of the highest authority, because he lived at a time when crucifixion, which was first abolished under the Christian emperors, was still practised ; and he here declares, that the *nailing* of the *feet*, as well as of the *hands,* belonged to the *peculiar severity of this punishment*. Paulus has here also invented a way of escape. He remarks : "Tertullian means to assert that the crucifixion of Jesus was attended with uncommon cruelty." But this extremely forced interpretation cannot be admitted, because in that case instead of '*is*' we should have had '*was;*'

---

[1] There is also the further difficulty, that if the feet of Christ were pierced, it cannot be explained from *natural causes*, how at his resurrection he could leave the grave and walk about.

[2] Mostellaria, act. 2. sc. 1. v. 13.

[3] The word *offigantur* stands here in the sense of *affigantur*, which is the reading in several editions, as the Bipont, and that of Gronovius.

[4] Adv. Marcionem 3. 19.

and because the words "*which is the peculiar severity of the cross,*" relate not merely to the piercing of the feet, but likewise to that of the hands; so that even the piercing of the hands must also be regarded, according to Paulus, as a degree of cruelty *peculiar* to the crucifixion of Christ.

174. It is then sufficiently evident, that in the punishment of the cross, not merely the hands, but also the feet were pierced through. This is established also by the fact, that the Fathers, in the numerous instances where they refer to the piercing of Christ's feet, never so much as intimate that this was any thing uncommon, but always speak of it as the inevitable attendant of crucifixion. But even if it were not capable of proof, as it clearly is, that the nailing of the feet was customary in the punishment of the cross, we should still have evidence that it was done at the crucifixion of Christ, though it might have been unusual. We will not here appeal to the testimony of the Fathers, among whom Justin says: "As they crucified Him, they pierced through his hands and feet by driving in nails:" since it may be objected with some plausibility, as it has been by Paulus, that the reference of this Psalm to his crucifixion gave rise to the notion that the feet of Christ were nailed. We rely only on the passage in Luke 24. 39: '*Behold my hands and my* feet, *that it is I myself*[1].' The way in which Paulus endeavours to evade this testimony is indeed ingenious, but not on that account the less unsatisfactory. He supposes that Christ showed to his disciples his hands and his feet, not as those parts of his body in which the marks of the crucifixion were visible, but as those, which, being naked, would give them an opportunity of seeing that He possessed flesh and bones. In opposition to this we have not only the corresponding passage in John 20. 27. where Christ convinced Thomas of the identity of his person by showing the *wounds* in his hands and side, but the expression itself shows that the disciples were first to *identify his person*[2] by seeing the *wounds in his hands and feet*, and *then* convince themselves, by the sense of touch, that his body was *real*, and not a *mere apparition.*—Paulus also objects, that Christ is said in John to have shown only his hands and side, but not his feet. But with equal propriety it might be inferred from Luke 24. 39, where He shows only his hands and feet that the wounds in his *side* never existed. The truth is that Christ pointed as He pleased, sometimes to these marks of his identity, sometimes to those. To have appealed to them *all* on every occasion, would have been superfluous.—Another way of evading the force of this passage has been chosen by Kuinöl and others. They suppose, indeed, that Christ pointed out his hands and feet as the parts in which the marks of his crucifixion were visible, but contend, that these marks in the feet were not made by *nails*, but by the *cords* with which they had been bound. But then it would be impossible to conceive, why He did not much oftener appeal to the far stronger evidence of the wound in his side, since

---

[1] ἴδετε τὰς χεῖράς μου καὶ τοὺς πόδας μου, ὅτι αὐτὸς ἐγώ εἰμι.
[2] ὅτι αὐτὸς ἐγώ εἰμι.

some remaining traces of the cords on his feet, could not surely prove the identity of his person.

175. Thus it has been fully shown, that notwithstanding all the objections and difficulties that have been invented and urged, the reference of the seventeenth verse to the death of Christ on the cross, stands sufficiently confirmed. The strange objection advanced by Hufnagel, and repeated by Rosenmüller, that had the author intended to predict the sufferings of Christ on the cross, he must have given a far more accurate and detailed description, is scarcely deserving of refutation : for, in the first place, there are traits which, to say the least, do not so fully agree with the sufferings of any other person, as with those of the Messiah—see the fifteenth, sixteenth, and eighteenth verses—and in the second it is unreasonable to require, that *prophecy* should be as clear and circumstantial as *history*.

176. We now proceed with our purpose of noticing those traits which point out Christ as the subject of the Psalm. In the eighteenth verse is said, 'They part my garments among them, and cast lots upon my vesture.' In John 19. 23, 24 : 'Then the soldiers, when they had crucified Jesus, took his garments, and made four parts, to every soldier a part; and also his coat : now the coat was without seam, woven from the top throughout. They said therefore among themselves, Let us not rend it, but cast lots for it, whose it shall be : that the Scripture might be fulfilled, which saith, They parted my raiment among them, and for my vesture they did cast lots. These things therefore the soldiers did.' Rosenmüller and Jahn [1] suppose that these words of the Psalm indicate merely the *purpose*, as if he had said, 'They are already so sure of my destruction, that they determine how they will divide my clothes among themselves.' This opinion manifestly owes its origin to the difficulty of finding in the life of David any thing corresponding to the language of the verse, when taken in its natural and obvious meaning. But if it could be admitted, when we consider the verse by itself, yet it *must* be seen to be erroneous, when we connect this trait with many others which were literally fulfilled in the history of Christ.

177. We now come to the second part of this Psalm. In the portion from the twenty-sixth verse to the thirtieth, the Messianic interpretation finds a strong support. The representation here is figurative. It was customary for the Jews in great distress to make vows, which chiefly related to the bringing of thank-offerings [2]. Only the fat pieces of these offerings were burnt upon the altar; the rest, after the portion designed for the priest had been cut off, was consumed in sacrificial meals, to which the offerers invited the stranger, the widow, the orphan, and the poor, and made them partakers of their prosperity and joy. So here the blessings, which should flow to others from the deliverance of the sufferer, are represented under the image of a great sacrificial feast [3] to be prepared by him, of which

[1] Vat. Mess. 2. p. 260.   [2] Comp. Ps. 61. 9. 116. 14—18.
[3] In the New Testament also, the blessings of the Messiah's reign are very often represented under the image of a feast, Matt. 8. 11. 22. 2. Luke 13. 29. 14. 16. Rev. 19. 9.

not merely the pious Israelites should partake, but all the heathen likewise from one end of the earth to the other, who are now to be converted to the true God.   Here the reference to the Messiah is obvious.   In the Old Testament the hope of a general conversion of the heathen is always connected with the time of the Messiah, and constitutes one of its distinctive marks.   Altogether similar to the passage before us is Isaiah 42, 49, 53, where the prophet describes the distinguished servant of God as one who should convert and bless the heathen.   An exact parallel to the words [1]: ' *For the kingdom shall then be the Lord's : and he shall reign among the nations,*' is found in the Messianic predictions of the prophets.   Obadiah [2] says, ' *And the kingdom shall be the Lord's.*'   Zechariah [3], ' *And the Lord shall be king over :ll the earth ; in that day there shall be one Lord and his name one.*'—The twenty-eighth verse brings to remembrance the promises made to the patriarch, and announces their fulfilment. The non-Messianic interpreters are here involved in no little difficulty [4].   Several of them, as Mendelssohn and Hufnagel, seek to escape by giving to the future verbs in the twenty-sixth to the thirtieth verses, an optative sense.   But in opposition to this, Hensler has already well replied, that, admitting [5] that the speaker uttered only his *wishes*, still nothing will be gained by this, since no man could hope for what is not only entirely destitute of probability, but altogether *impossible*.

178. Having thus brought forward the positive arguments for the reference of this Psalm to the Messiah, let us now see to what objections each of the non-Messianic interpretations that have been suggested is liable.   To those who make David the subject of the Psalm we reply, (1) That he was never in such distress as is here described.   In the war with the Syrians [6], to which Paulus makes the Psalm refer, he was throughout successful.—With as little propriety can we fix upon the rebellion of Absalom.   In this Psalm the sufferer appears alone, the object of universal scorn, forsaken of every helper [7], given up to the violence of blood-thirsty enemies, and at the point of death ; there David was in the midst of a brave and numerous host, and in no danger of his life.   Nor in the persecution of Saul did the danger and distress of David rise to such a height [8]. (2) To this it must be added, that, while this description of suffering contains much which does not suit David, there is, on the other hand, among so many particulars, nothing which gives intimation of

[1] In ver. 29.   [2] Obad. 21.   [3] Zech. 14. 9.

[4] This also is plain enough from other attempts. Thus Paulus, e. g., translates אֶמְסֵי אֶרֶץ *border lands*, wholly against the *usus loquendi*. Jahn subjoins to the words: ' *all nations shall fall down before thee,*' the limitation ' *nempe quæ audient hanc gloriosam liberationem,*' which is refuted by the parallelism alone, ' *all the ends of the earth.*'   De Wette explains the twenty-ninth verse unnaturally, and in opposition to the parallel passages cited, ' *for all nations ought to pray to Jehovah, since he is King of the World.*'

[5] Though contradicted by the whole tenour of the discourse and the perfect אָכְלוּ in the thirtieth verse.

[6] 2 Sam. 10.   [7] Ver. 12.

[8] See a further examination of this point in Jahn, l. c. p. 266.

the event, or the time to which this lamentation of David belongs.
" In other Psalms, which are *less circumstantial* than this, we can
often tell whether they were composed in the flight before Saul or in
that before Absalom, and can readily decide with precision concerning
them.   But this Psalm, abounding as it does in particulars, does not
afford us a single trace to lead us to the words in the history of
David's misfortunes to which it relates." Michaelis.   (3) David's
sufferings were inflicted upon him by his own countrymen : the remembrance of his deliverance, therefore, must also be confined to the
bounds of Palestine.   How then could he possibly hope that his
deliverance in the time of Saul's persecution, or Absalom's rebellion,
could make an impression on the heathen ?   How could he expect it
to produce a result, which all the previous miraculous manifestations
of God in the history of the whole nation, though made before the
eyes of the heathen, had failed to effect?

179. The hypothesis of Jahn, which makes Hezekiah the subject
of the Psalm, has neither more nor less in its favour than a hundred
others, which may be easily suggested, if we are willing to rest satisfied with certain general resemblances, overlooking the rest, or
evading them by a forced interpretation. It is refuted by the superscription itself, which can be rejected only by caprice, and which
ascribes the Psalm to David as its author.   Jahn erroneously supposes, that, according to this hypothesis, the portion of the Psalm, from
the twenty-sixth verse, &c. will have its suitable meaning ; since[1] the
Divine aid vouchsafed to Hezekiah made such an impression on the
nations, that many of them brought offerings to the Lord at Jerusalem.   But this fact by no means proves, that they were led by
Hezekiah's deliverance to regard the God of Israel as the only true
God ; they rather inferred from it, in accordance with their poly-
theistic notions, that He too was *one among many*, and that it would
therefore be well to secure his favour.   But that something far different is spoken of in this Psalm is self evident.   Here the heathen
shall be partakers with the person delivered in his prosperity and
joy ; here his deliverance shall exert a lasting influence on all the
people of the whole earth, and produce the most beneficial of all
changes ; here they shall all be united in one kingdom and one great
family under God as their only head.

180. The interpretation, which makes the Jewish people the subject, is liable to most of the objections which are urged against the
same method of explaining the fifty-third chapter of Isaiah (see
our remarks on that passage).   It is even more untenable in the
present instance, because the distinctive marks of an individual are
more numerous, and we no where find the smallest trace to justify
the idea of a personification.   On the contrary, the mother of the
sufferer is mentioned, a tongue, jaws, hands and feet, bones and garments, are ascribed to him ; nay, in the seventh verse, he is distinguished from the ungodly, and in the twenty-third verse from his
brethren.   But the most conclusive objection against this interpretation is, that the subject of the Psalm is an *innocent* sufferer, whose

[1] According to 2 Chron. 32. 23.

sufferings are to promote the welfare of his own people, as well as
that of the heathen; whereas, on the contrary, the sufferings of the
Jewish people were never undeserved, but, according to the theocratical law of a visible retribution, were always the consequences of
forsaking God, and were represented as such by the prophets and
sacred poets.

181. The opinion that the Psalm relates in a lower sense to David,
and in a higher to Christ, rests on two suppositions: (1) That it
can be shown to be entirely fulfilled in a lower sense in the history
of David; and, (2) that it contains much that cannot refer to
Christ.—That the former supposition is erroneous, has been already
sufficiently shown. That the latter is equally so will be proved in
the refutation of the objections against the Messianic interpretation,
to which we now proceed.

182. (1) " What seems most inconsistent is, that it is not *suffering* itself, but the *deliverance from suffering*, that is here represented
as the means of promoting the worship of the true God. Now, it
was by *the sufferings* which He voluntarily underwent that Christ
founded the kingdom of God: consequently by this his chief peculiar
work of redemption is rather mistaken than taught by the Psalmist.
Of what use then to Christians is the Messianic interpretation of a
Psalm, in which the Christian notion of the Messiah is not to be
found?"— Thus De Wette. But even in the New Testament we meet
with the very same mode of representation. Though Christ accomplished our redemption, not by his resurrection, but by his humiliation, not by his glorification, but by his death; yet notwithstanding
in numerous passages, his resurrection and glorification are given as
the causes of man's salvation, because without these the *import* of his
humiliation and death would have remained concealed. In the fifty-
third chapter of Isaiah, the persons speaking conclude from the deep
humiliation of the Messiah, that He is smitten of God on account of
his own sins; and it is only when they see Him exalted to glory,
that they come to the knowledge of his being wounded for *their*
transgressions. So also the subject of this Psalm, as long as his
sufferings last, is the scorn of men and despised by the people[1]: but
it is with his *deliverance* that that influence of his on mankind, which
is so full of blessings, commences as a consequence of his sufferings.
Whether the Psalmist saw with entire clearness the efficacy of the
Messiah's sufferings in advancing the work of salvation, we may
leave undetermined; it is sufficient that the Psalm contains nothing
in opposition to the Christian notion of the Messiah.

183. (2) " The lamentations of this sufferer are unworthy of the
Messiah. Christ did not, like him, pray to God for longer life, nor
that God would preserve him from the hands of his enemies; but
in the plan of his life He took in *death* as an essential part[2]." Here
every thing depends on forming in our minds that image of Christ
which the New Testament presents, and not an *arbitrary one* of our
own invention. Then shall we find those complaints not unworthy

---

[1] Ver. 8.   [2] Thus Hufnagel and Schulze.

of Him. In ' the days of his flesh he offered up prayers and supplications with strong crying and tears, unto him that was able to
save him from death[1].' In Gethsemane He said to his disciples,
just before his crucifixion, ' My soul is exceeding sorrowful even
unto death,' and prayed to his Father, ' If it be possible let this cup
pass from me[2].' Nor is this all. Christ Himself, when burdened
with the sins of the whole world, uttered on the cross the first words
of this very Psalm, which express the strongest feelings of complaint[3].
As to the prayer for deliverance from the power of his enemies and
from death, this can occasion no difficulty, since Christ as man
actually offered this very prayer to God, and it was completely answered in his resurrection from the grave.

184. (3) " The sufferer hopes for such a deliverance as his forefathers had experienced[1]. This agrees well with any ordinary Israelite
in affliction, but not with Christ[5]." This objection has been already
answered in the introduction to the Psalms of this class[6].

185. (4) " Jesus could not have been predicted as praying for
deliverance from the sword[7]." But here, as in Zech. 13. 7, the
sword is a figurative designation of a violent death. To insist on the
literal interpretation, would be to require that the parallel expressions, ' the *power of the dog*,' ' the *lion's mouth*,' and ' the *horns of the
unicorn*,' be interpreted in the same manner.

186. (5) " Jesus never made vows for the preservation of his life,
as the subject of this Psalm does[8]." But if this single feature of
the representation is to be taken *literally*, so must the *whole*. Then
must we adopt the supposition, that the sufferer obliged himself to
prepare a literal feast, of which all the inhabitants of the earth, Jews
and heathen, rich and poor, might partake, and thereby come to the
knowledge and worship of the true God.

187. (6) " The sufferer in the Psalm is not yet in the power of
his enemies, but only in imminent danger[9]." This supposition is
not justified by the passages quoted. In the twelfth verse, ' Be not
far from me ; for trouble is *near ;*' *near*, as Abenezra long since remarked, is intentionally contrasted with *far*, and we cannot hence
infer that the speaker was then merely in *expectation* of distress. In
the remaining verses the sufferer is represented as surrounded by
bloodthirsty enemies. This does not, it is true, determine whether
he were already in their power, or in fear that he should be. But
from other passages it is manifest that the former was the case. For
He whose hands and feet are pierced through[10], and whose clothes

[1] Heb. 5. 7.   [2] Matt. 26. 36. Mark 14. 32.
[3] The cause of this deep distress and these complaints is strikingly given by
Calvin : " Certe susceptâ nostrâ personâ nostroque reatu necesse habuit ad Dei
tribunal se instar peccatoris sistere. Hinc horror ille et pavor, qui ad depre-
candam mortem eum coegit ; non quia tam acerbum illi foret e vitâ migrare, sed
quia ante oculos erat Dei maledictio, quæ peccatoribus incumbit. Quodsi primo
conflictu elicitæ fuerunt sanguinis guttæ, ut opus fuerit consolatore angelo,
Luc. 22. 43. non mirum est si in ultimo agone confessus est tantum dolorem."
[4] Ver. 5, 6.   [5] Thus Dathe, De Wette.   [6] Comp. Rom. 9. 5.
[7] Paulus, De Wette.   [8] Paulus, De Wette.
[9] Ver 12, 13. 21, 22. De Wette, Dathe.   [10] Ver. 17.

are divided [1], must surely be *already in the power* of his enemies. But suppose it proved by the passage referred to, that He was not yet in the power of his enemies, it would then only be necessary to give to the Psalm a wider scope, so as to make it include the sufferings of Christ both *before* and *during* his crucifixion.

188. (7.) " His lamentation continues for a longer time than Jesus endured the agonies of death upon the cross [2]." But the crucifixion was not the *commencement*, but only the *climax*, of the sufferings of Christ. The passage already cited from the epistle to the Hebrews [3] is entirely parallel.

189. We know of no other objections which have been urged against the Messianic interpretation of this Psalm. In conclusion, we adopt the words of Theodoret : " *I mourn over the fatuity of the Jews, because, though perpetually reading the divine oracles, they see not the truth which shineth therein; but assert that this Psalm was spoken of David.—For we do not see any of these things fulfilled in the case of David, or any of David's descendants. The Lord Christ is the only one ; he who was of David according to the flesh, God the Word who was made man, he who took from David the form of a servant. For he filled the whole earth and sea with the knowledge of God, and persuaded those who had long been wandering and offering worship to idols, to worship the God Who is, instead of things that are not [4].*"

Psalm 40 [5]

190. ARGUMENT.—The Messiah, who is here [6] introduced as speaking, in the first place anticipates the time, when, having finished his work and endured his sufferings, He will have been glorified by Jehovah. He renders him thanks-

---

[1] Ver. 19.   [2] Ver. 3. Dathe, Paulus, De Wette.   [3] Heb. 5. 7.

[4] Ἐγὼ δὲ τὴν Ἰουδαίων ἐμβροντησίαν θρηνῶ, ὅτι τοῖς θείοις λογίοις διηνεκῶς ἐντυγχάνοντες, τὴν ἐν τούτοις διαλάμπουσαν οὐ συνορῶσιν ἀλήθειαν, ἀλλ' εἰς τὸν Δαβὶδ εἰρῆσθαι τὸν ψαλμὸν ἀποφαίνονται.—Τούτων γὰρ οὐδὲν ἐπὶ τοῦ Δαβὶδ ὁρῶμεν γεγενημένον, οὐδὲ ἐπί τινος τῶν ἐκ Δαβίδ. Μόνος δὲ ὁ Δεσπότης Χριστὸς, ὁ ἐκ Δαβὶδ κατὰ σάρκα, ὁ ἐνανθρωπήσας Θεὸς λόγος, ὁ ἐκ Δαβὶδ λαβὼν τὴν τοῦ δούλου μορφήν. Πᾶσαν γὰρ γῆν καὶ θάλασσαν τῆς θεογνωσίας ἐπλήρωσε, καὶ πέπεικε τοὺς πάλαι πλανωμένους, καὶ τοῖς εἰδώλοις προσφέροντας τὴν προσκύνησιν, ἀντὶ τῶν οὐκ ὄντων, τὸν ὄντα προσκυνῆσαι θεόν.

[5] The contents of this Psalm, according to the non-Messianic interpretation, are these. David, or some other suffering Israelite, thanks the Lord for a deliverance which has been granted him, ver. 1—6. He promises, from gratitude to God, to honour him, not by occasional sacrifices, but by devoting himself to his service, and by complying with the moral requisites of the law, which would be far more acceptable in his sight, ver. 7—9. He promises, moreover, zealously to proclaim the aid which Jehovah had vouchsafed to him, and thus to glorify his name, ver. 10, 11. But although the sufferer has happily escaped from one calamity, he is still surrounded by far greater sufferings and dangers. He therefore renews, ver. 12—18. his supplication to his Lord, and prays that he would deliver him from the manifold evils which his sins have brought upon him, and put his enemies to shame ; thus giving all true worshippers, as well as himself, occasion to rejoice and confirm their faith.

[6] As in Isaiah 49. Ps. 16. and 22.

giving and praise for his deliverance [1]. He praises God for the wonderful mercies in general which He bestows upon men, and since it is impossible to mention all his benefits, He extols only the greatest of all, the redemption ac-complished by Himself. Since no legal sacrifices of whatever kind could please and satisfy God, the Messiah having been taught by Him their ineffi-cacy and made obedient to his will, presents Himself as the true sacrifice of whom Moses had already written in the sacred books, resolved with joyful zeal to fulfil the will of God [2]. He again [3] praises the righteousness, faithfulness, and love of God, which He had experienced in his deliverance. As the speaker in the eleven first verses, had placed Himself in the *future*, and contemplated his sufferings as already endured, so in the twelfth verse He returns to the *present*. Oppressed by the thought of the severe distress which He must un-dergo in making expiation for sin, He prays to God for his merciful support.

191. The non-Messianic interpreters translate the eighth verse, ' *in the volume of the book* (the Pentateuch) it is *prescribed to me,*' *namely, what I have to do.* According to the Messianic interpreta-tion, the sense is as follows : ' *In the volume of the book it is written of me ;*' both *directly* in the prophecies of the Messiah, and *indirectly* in all that is said of sacrifices and offerings, as these prefigured Christ [4].

192. There can be no doubt, that those who acknowledge the Divine authority of the Epistle to the Hebrews, must decide in favour of the Messianic interpretation. The Psalm is there [5] quoted and explained of the vicarious sacrifice of Christ, in such a way as entirely to exclude the idea of a mere accommodation [6]. The only objections which have been urged against the Messianic interpretation are not conclusive. (1) De Wette remarks, that the reference of the Psalm to the Messiah in the Epistle to the Hebrews, is grounded on the erroneous interpretation of the seventh verse by the Seventy. But it can be shown that the Seventy have here given the *sense*, though not a *literal translation* of the Hebrew text. Unless we are to sup-pose their translation entirely unmeaning, the words, ' *a body hast thou prepared me* [7],' can only mean ' *Thou requirest nothing outward, but myself for sacrifice, and that I will freely offer to thee* [8].' The corresponding Hebrew is of the same import : ' *Thou hast bored mine ears.*' To bore the ears is a figurative expression for the imparting

---

[1] Ver. 1—5.   [2] Ver. 6—9.   [3] Ver. 10, 11.

[4] Comp. John 5. 39. 46.   [5] Chap. 10. 5, &c.

[6] Several interpreters have indeed sought, though with little success, to find a middle path. Those who, as Calvin and Muntinghe, refer the Psalm in a lower sense to David and in a higher one to Christ, fail in their purpose of sustaining the authority of the Epistle to the Hebrews. For granting the correctness of the explanation given in this Epistle of ver. 7—9, the Psalm, as we have already seen, cannot in a lower sense be referred to David, for he could not represent himself as the *true* offering in opposition to those which were *typical*, nor say, that it was written of *him* in the Pentateuch. We can no more concur with Venema, Seiler, and Dathe, who assert that in ver. 1—6 and 12—18, David speaks; but in ver. 7—11, or, as Kaiser thinks, ver. 7, 8, the Messiah ; for the supposition of this unnatural change of persons has nothing to support it.

[7] σῶμα δὲ κατηρτίσω μοι.

[8] The use of σῶμα need not surprise us here, since Paul, Rom. 12. 1, exhorts Christians to present their bodies (τὰ σώματα) a living sacrifice, holy and accep-table to God.

of certain precepts, and rendering others willing to follow them [1]. This is shown, not only by the corresponding expression [2] which occurs in Isa. 50. 5, in the sense, to *give a command and make one willing to execute it;* but also by the *practice* of boring the ears as a sign of obedience, which, as it were, embodies the expression. Thus, according to Exod. 21. 5, 6, the right ear of the servant who chose to remain with his master was bored. So also the Turkish monks are accustomed to bore their ears, as a sign of their attention to the Divine revelation and their obedience to the Divine commands [3]. The same custom exists also among the Persians and the Tartars [4]. Among the Turks, those who transgress any precept of their religion, are nailed by the ears, that they may learn to esteem and obey it [5]. ' *Thou hast bored mine ears,*' is then the same as ' *Thou hast taught me that it is not the bringing of outward offerings, but the offering of myself that is well pleasing to thee, and hast made me willing to act in conformity with thy instructions.*' The Seventy completely expressed this sentiment. They only changed the phraseology, as the metaphor was not in use among the Greeks : nor does the author of the Epistle to the Hebrews use the phrase, ' *a body hast thou prepared me,*' in any other sense than that which, according to the context, belongs to the Hebrew words, if the Psalm relates to the Messiah.

193. (2) Dathe objects, that it seems incongruous that the Messiah in the former part should speak of his sufferings as *already endured,* and thank God for his deliverance, while in the latter, on the contrary, He prays for the Divine support in distress. But this is not a decisive objection, since all depends on the station in which the sacred poet places the Messiah, whom he introduces as speaking. There is nothing against the supposition, that he first contemplates him after he had endured his sufferings and finished his work, and *then* in his state of humiliation. In a similar manner in the fifty-third chapter of Isaiah, the passion of the Messiah appears at one time as *already past,* at another *as still future.*

194. (3) Hensler urges particularly the words, ' *Mine iniquities have taken hold upon me* [6].' This objection is certainly very plausible. It does not, however, decide the question, for the passage should be translated, ' *The punishment of my iniquities has got hold of me* [7].' But that in a Psalm, which treats of the vicarious satisfaction of the Messiah, and when this is contrasted with the offering of

---

[1] Vitringa: " Aperta auris est mens prompta et prona, tum ad recipiendas, intelligendas ac discernendas doctrinas, quæ cui instillantur, tum ad obsequium mandati, quod per aures ad animum fertur."

[2] פָּתַח אֹזֶן

[3] Comp. Iken, Dissertt. p 226. Septem Castrensis Mon. de Turc. morib. c. 13: " Illi qui inaures portant in auribus, significant se obedientes esse in spiritu, propter raptuum frequentiam." Another author : " Il y en a aussi, qui porte quelque chose à l'oreille, pour marquer leur obéissance et leur soumission à l'esprit, qui les transporte dans des ravissemens."

[4] Ib. p. 227.   [5] Ibid. p. 231.   [6] Ver. 13.

[7] The parallelism with רָעוֹת shows that עֲוֹנֹתַי is not here to be translated, *mine iniquities,* but the *punishment of mine iniquities*—a sense in which it often occurs, and which is given by Abenezra and Rosenmüller.

victims which suffered the punishment properly due to sinners, the sufferings inflicted upon him for sins not his own, might be called the *punishment of his sins*, is evident from the similar expressions in the fifty-third chapter of Isaiah : ' *He hath borne our griefs and carried our sorrows ;* ' ' *He was wounded for our transgressions; he was bruised for our iniquities ; the chastisement of our peace was upon him.*' ' *The Lord hath laid upon him the iniquity of us all.*' This objection would be entirely removed, were we to suppose with Pareau, that the Psalm originally consisted of but twelve verses, the remainder having been afterwards added. This opinion is favoured by the entirely different character of the latter portion of the Psalm ; the fact that it occurs again as the Seventieth Psalm, and that we have other examples of such additions. Still, however, we hesitate to adopt it.

3. Predictions of the Messiah in the Prophets

195. We have already seen, that the predictions of the Messiah in the Psalms were much more definite than those of an earlier date. Several points of high importance, as his deity, his sufferings, and his eternal priesthood, were here first disclosed ; others, as the extension of the blessings of his salvation to the heathen, and his triumph over all his enemies, were rendered more definite and clear. The authors of the Psalms were succeeded by the Prophets in the work of predicting the Messiah. Were the word Prophet to be taken in its broader meaning, as a designation of all those to whom extraordinary divine revelations were made (as in the Old Testament itself the patriarchs and several composers of Psalms are in this sense called Prophets or Seers), then indeed the Psalms which relate to the Messiah might be classed with the Messianic predictions of the Prophets. Here, however, we use the word in its more ordinary and restricted signification, to designate those who possessed not merely the *donum*, but also the *munus propheticum;* men sent to the covenant people immediately from God, appointed to guard his rights, and in his name to teach, counsel, exhort, rebuke, and reveal the future. We here offer, in the first place, some general remarks respecting the predictions of the Messiah by these ambassadors of God.

196. (1) Though prophecy began to flourish in the time of Samuel, we possess none of the predictions of that early period. Our earliest written prophecies belong to the reigns of Uzziah, Jotham, Ahaz, and Hezekiah. We cannot with certainty determine how far the predictions of the older Prophets, which have not come down to us, made important disclosures respecting the Redeemer. There are, however, reasons which make it probable that it was not until this later period, that the prediction of the Messiah became the grand subject of all the annunciations of the Prophets. In them it does not stand unconnected with passing events ; nor in the case of

those who are called to act in public, does it proceed merely from their own necessities; but has almost always a distinct reference to the condition of the people, and is designed to aid the Prophets in exerting a present influence upon them. The more the state declined, and the more powerful the enemies which rose up against it and threatened its destruction, the more did the desponding people, if they were to be preserved in allegiance to the Lord, need the assurance of the future glory of the theocracy, and its preeminence over the heathen nations. The more corruption prevailed, the more necessity there was to alarm the ungodly, and comfort the pious, by pointing to the time when the Messiah should make a separation between them, and impart to the latter all the blessings of his kingdom. It was therefore in this later period that the revelation of the Messiah was first entrusted principally to the Prophets; as hitherto, when it had no reference to the condition of public affairs, it had been committed more especially to the holy Psalmists.

197. (2) Neither the authors of the Messianic Psalms, nor the Prophets, give at any one time a full description of the Messiah; they rather confine themselves to certain features of his character. And here a difference of some importance is found between them. The writers of the Messianic Psalms (in accordance with the *subjective* nature of this species of poetry), generally take such views of him, as were suggested by *their own* lives, circumstances, and experience. Thus David represents the Messiah as a sufferer, surrounded by powerful enemies, and at last, after a severe conflict, attaining to victory and glory. Solomon beholds him, as the sovereign of a vast, peaceful, and prosperous kingdom; and sees the most distant nations paying their reverential homage by bringing him presents. But the Prophets, on the contrary, were not governed in their representations of the Messiah so much by *their own* experience and circumstances, as by *the necessities of those to whom they spake*, and the effect which they wished to produce on their minds. Hence it has happened that in their writings he is presented to us on the whole more in his state of exaltation, than as suffering and making expiation for us. To influence the great body of the people was a principal object in revealing his future advent to the Prophets; and the great body of the people was not prepared for the doctrine of a *suffering* and *atoning* Messiah.—How much the Messianic predictions of the Prophets were modified by the necessities of the times, is especially evident from a comparison of the first part of Isaiah and Zechariah, with the second. The first part of Isaiah consists of a number of separate pieces, which were made public at the time they were composed. Here the appearance of the Messiah in his humiliation is barely alluded to; while on the contrary he is *constantly exhibited* in his glory, with a view to encourage the people under their outward calamities. The second part, on the other hand, which forms one connected whole, was probably not made known to the public; it was designed rather for posterity than the existing generation; and not so much for the people at large, as for the pious individuals among them. Here therefore the Prophet might ex-

hibit the character of the Messiah in its full extent; and give prominence to those important features, which in the first part were
kept more in the back ground. And thus we find in the second
part, the idea of the *teaching*, *suffering*, and *atoning* Messiah every
where prevalent.—So also in the Prophet Zechariah. In the first
part, the discourses all relate to existing circumstances. It was
here the main object of the Prophet to tranquillize and console the
minds of the people, who were disquieted and cast down by a comparison of the present depressed condition of the theocracy with its
former prosperity and splendour. In this part, therefore, we behold
the Messiah only in his glory, and prepared to raise the now fallen
theocracy to great honour, and extend its sway over the heathen
nations. Whatever might damp this joyful hope is kept out of view.
In the second part, on the contrary, which was probably not published, the Prophet is more at liberty. Here he announces the
appearing of the Messiah in an humble condition, describes his
death, the rejection of the greater part of the people, their restoration
after having been purified by severe chastisement. With these considerations before us, we shall not be surprised, if we meet with the
Messiah only in his exalted state in those Prophets whose predictions
were delivered as a whole in public, and related to the existing condition of the people (as was the case with Ezekiel, Jeremiah, Micah,
Hosea, and Amos); and we shall not be disposed to regard as
essential a discrepancy, which is owing entirely to a difference of
circumstances. To each prophet such a revelation of the future was
made, as accorded with the times in which he lived.

198. (3) We cannot perceive in the Messianic predictions of the
Prophets, as we do in the Pentateuch, a *gradual advancement* in
clearness and precision. Isaiah sees the Messiah as distinctly as
Malachi, and his prophecies, and those of Micah, contain more special
characteristics of him, than are to be found in Jeremiah and Ezekiel.
This is explained by the circumstance, that each Prophet always received his predictions directly from above, adapted to his own capacity (which may have been greater in the case of the earlier, than the
later Prophets), and also to the necessities and the comprehension of
those for whose benefit they were intended. But still the Messianic
prediction, on the whole, continued to be more and more fully developed. Special traits were revealed to individuals along with
such as were common to all. Some particulars (as for example
that the Messiah should honour the second temple with his presence), could, from the nature of the case, be made known only to
the later Prophets.—We shall here present a brief summary of the
predictions of the Messiah by the Prophets, following the chronological order.

a. Prophets under Uzziah, Jotham, Ahaz, and Hezekiah, from 811-699 B.C.

199. (1) HOSEA[1]. The coming of the Messiah stands in contrast with the threatening that the people should be carried away captive by the Assyrians. This calamity shall be followed by a time of mercy and blessing. The Israelites shall return to Jehovah, and to the great and godlike descendant of David. Jehovah will then grant them forgiveness of sins, and again bestow upon them his ancient love. When they are thus reconciled to God, strife shall cease, and they shall be blest with peace and prosperity.

200. (2) AMOS. The threatening relates to the carrying away of the Israelites and Jews into captivity, and their dispersion into all lands; the prediction of prosperity[2], both to the return from captivity, and to the introduction of the Messiah's reign. A great king shall arise from the fallen family of David, and restore it to its ancient splendour. Through him the theocracy shall be extended over the heathen, who had heretofore been enemies, or strangers to it. Rich blessings shall be granted; even the inanimate creation shall assume new glory. The only special characteristic, is the appearing of the Messiah, when the family of David had fallen into obscurity.

201. (3) ISAIAH. Of all the Prophets he is the richest in specific predictions of the Messiah[3]. His view of the Messiah is for the most part connected with the prospect of deliverance from the Assyrians, and also from the Babylonian exile. But still he is so full of the hope of the Redeemer, that he often makes a transition to it from other subjects. See, for example, the prophecy against Egypt[4], and that against Tyre[5]. In both instances the Prophet concludes the representation of the calamities which were soon to fall upon these countries, with the prediction of their future prosperity when blest with true religion. It is characteristic of Isaiah, on the one hand, that he discriminates so severely between the pious and the ungodly part of the nation, repeatedly excluding the latter from all the blessings expected in future time,—and on the other, that he dwells with such delight on the future enlargement of the theocracy by the accession of the heathen. His predictions plainly show, that he clearly perceived the connexion of the preparatory arrangements of Divine providence, with the great end to be accomplished, and that the former never usurped the place of the latter in his estimation.—The Messianic predictions of Isaiah may be divided into two classes : those in which the glorified Messiah filled the whole vision of the Prophet, and those in which he beheld him in his lowly condition, although at the same time he saw the glorious

---

[1] Principal passages: chap. 2. 1—3. 16—25. 3. 5. 14. 2, &c.
[2] Chap. 9.
[3] The principal passages are chap. 2. 4. 7. 14. 9. 11. 32. 42. 49. 50. 52. 13. &c. 53. 55. 1—5 59. 20, 21. 61. Besides, there are many representations of the times of the Messiah, where he is not personally introduced.
[4] Chap. 19.   [5] Chap. 23.

result of his humiliation. To the former class belong all that are found in the first part, and the fifty-fifth and fifty-ninth chapters in the second part, besides many general descriptions of the Messiah's kingdom. The contents of these prophecies are as follows; after the people shall have been severely punished by the hand of God, and long involved in the darkness of sin and in its attendant calamities, the great Restorer shall be born of a virgin; he shall be truly God, and at the same time a descendant of the family of David, which before his advent will have fallen into obscurity. This king, who shall be great, wise, and righteous, and filled with the Spirit of God, shall dispel the darkness of those who receive him, free them from the Divine displeasure to which they stand exposed, and make them happy. The region of Galilee shall especially experience his blessings. The theocracy, hitherto confined to a single people, shall become co-extensive with the globe itself. Its holy members shall be blessed with perfect inward and outward peace; even external nature, being freed from evil after the destruction of sin which caused it, shall be restored to its original condition.—The latter class consists of the remaining predictions of the second part. Here Isaiah represents the Messiah as an illustrious prophet and teacher, who, endowed by God with rich gifts, humbles himself and comes in meekness and lowliness to seek those who are lost. He announces the severe sufferings, the scorn and contempt of the people which await him, as well as his subsequent exaltation by the hand of God, and the extension of his religion over the people of the earth, who shall humbly submit to his authority. The fifty-third chapter differs in one respect from the remaining portions of this class; his vicarious satisfaction is here brought distinctly forward, as the *end to be accomplished* by the Messiah's sufferings. The special characteristics are: besides the descent of the Messiah from David, his Deity, his atonement, his death, his birth of a virgin [1], at a time when the royal family of David had already sunk into total obscurity [2], his being endowed with the fulness of the Divine Spirit [3], the peculiar blessing conferred on the region of Galilee [4], the opposition and unbelief of the covenant people [5], his burial with a rich man [6].

203. (4) MICAH [7]. The promise is connected with the threatening of an entire desolation of Jerusalem by the Chaldeans. In the little town of Bethlehem, where the family of David originated, an illustrious Ruler shall be born, whose origin is eternal, and his majesty and his glory divine. He shall make the theocracy glorious, and extend it over the heathen from one end of the earth to the other. The subjects of the Divine kingdom shall dwell in peace and prosperity under his reign. All that was opposed to the revealed will of God in former times shall be done away, and all enemies of the theocracy be destroyed. The chief features of his prophecy are the divine and human nature of the Messiah, and, what is peculiar to this Prophet, his birth in Bethlehem.

[1] Chap. 7. 14.   [2] 11. 1. 53. 2.   [3] 11. 2. 42. 1.
[4] 8. 23.   [5] Chap. 49.   [6] 53. 9.
[7] The principal passages are chap. 4. 1—8. 5. 7. 7, &c.

204. (5) JOEL, who probably belongs to this period. Object of the threatening—the desolation of the land by the Chaldeans. Messianic passage the third chapter. No representation of the Messiah as a person. As a characteristic mark of the times of the Messiah, the description of which is connected with that of the deliverance from captivity, the outpouring of the Holy Spirit upon all men without distinction is particularly set forth. With this is connected the description of the heavy punishment, which shall be inflicted upon all the enemies of the kingdom of God.

b. Prophets shortly before and during the Babylonish Captivity

205. (1) ZEPHANIAH. Object of the threatening : the carrying away of all the inhabitants of the kingdom of Judah, and the desolation of the land by the Chaldeans. The predicted salvation [1] relates at the same time to the deliverance from captivity, and the times of the Messiah. The covenant people shall become as righteous and pure from all former defilement as prosperous and happy. The heathen also (as the Prophet had already declared [2]) after having been severely chastised, shall embrace the true religion, and give themselves with one accord to the service of God.

206. (2) JEREMIAH. The return from the Babylonian exile, and the times of the Messiah are not always accurately distinguished by this prophet [3]. After severe sufferings of the people, Jehovah will raise up a great descendant of David, through whom they shall obtain remission of their sins, and be delivered and blest. By and through him the old and imperfect covenant shall be succeeded by a new and better one. What the law, as an outward institution, could not accomplish under the former dispensation, God shall effect under the new one by writing his law in the hearts of his people. Chief characteristics :—the cessation of the Levitical worship [4], the extirpation of sin, the writing of the law on the hearts of the people, and the establishment of a new covenant [5].

207. (3) EZEKIEL [6]. Object of the threatening ; the Babylonish exile; the Messianic prediction connected with the promise of deliverance from captivity. From the fallen family of David, deprived of its dominion on account of the crimes of the people, and after the Israelites shall have returned from exile, an exalted king shall arise, by the wonderful interposition of Jehovah, in whose sovereignty and protection the nations of the earth shall put their trust, and learn to know the true God as the supreme disposer of all things. Jehovah will then cleanse the people of Israel from sin, and give them a new heart and a new spirit ; He will take away the stony heart out of their flesh, and give them a heart of flesh, and free them from impurity. The theocracy shall be far more illustrious than ever before.

[1] Chap. 3. 9—20.   [2] Chap. 2. 11.
[3] The chief passages are chap. 3. 16—18. 23. 1—8. 31 31, &c. 33. 14—26.
[4] Chap. 3. 16.   [5] 31. 31, &c. 23. 6. 33. 16.
[6] Principal passages, chap. 11. 17, &c. 17. 22—24. 21. 29—32. 34. 22—30. 36. 25, &c. 37. 21—28. chap. 40—48.

The Spirit of God shall go forth from it like a living stream, and quicken into life a world dead in sin.　The characteristic representation of the agency of the Holy Spirit under the new dispensation is worthy of special notice.

208. (4) DANIEL [1].　After the overthrow of the four great kingdoms of the world, the Messiah shall establish his kingdom, which shall extend over all people and endure for ever.　The deliverance from exile shall not synchronize with the times of the Messiah; Jerusalem shall first be built again, but in troublous times ; then, at a future period, the Messiah's kingdom shall come, and with it the fulfilment of the prophecies, the forgiving of sins, and the giving of the Holy Ghost.　The Messiah shall indeed suffer a violent death ; but his death shall be avenged by a severe judgement upon a faithless people, by the ruin of the state and the sanctuary.　But on the other hand, he will renew the covenant with those who acknowledge his dignity.　Chief traits :—the union of the Divine and human natures in the Messiah, indicated by his appearing at the same time in the clouds of heaven, and in the form of a man [2] ; the specification of the *time* which should elapse before his coming; the clear distinction between the deliverance from captivity and the times of the Messiah ; the characteristic designation of the nature of the New Testament economy; the Messiah's violent death; the destruction of Jerusalem.

c. Prophets after the Captivity

209. It is peculiar to these Prophets, that in them the intimate connexion disappears between the prospect of deliverance from the exile and that of the redemption by the Messiah, which we find in most of the earlier Prophets ; and thus the latter becomes more plain and definite.

210. (1) HAGGAI [3].　In him the Messianic prediction is suited to the occasion on which it was uttered.　He aims to console those who had seen the glory of the former temple.　After a great political revolution shall have taken place, the glory of the second temple shall surpass that of the first.　All the heathen nations shall seek admission into the theocracy.　Chief trait :—the commencement of the Messianic times during the existence of the second temple.

211. (2) ZECHARIAH.　His predictions of the Messiah, next to those of Isaiah, are the most marked and definite [4].　The predictions of the first part, in accordance with their design to console those who were distrest at beholding the small beginning of the new state, are of a more general character, and leave many weighty points untouched.　The Messiah shall unite the priestly and the regal dignity. Through him the sins of the land shall be blotted out, rich blessings be introduced, and the theocracy immeasurably enlarged, and ex-

[1] Principal places, chap. 2. 44. 7. 13. 14. 26. 27. 9. 25—27.
[2] Chap. 7. 13.　　　　　　　　　[3] Chap. 2. 6—9.
[4] Chief places : chap. 2. 3. 8—10. 6. 9—15. 8. 18, &c. 9. 9. 10 11—14.

tended over the heathen nations. The features scattered over the second part form, when collected, the following image : Jehovah at some future period shall interpose once more in favour of His poor people in a remarkable manner. He will cause the great and promised king of Israel, who is united with Himself by oneness of nature, to appear in humiliation and obscurity. But, deceived by their corrupt leaders, the greater portion of the people shall despise the mild guidance of this good Shepherd ; they shall even pierce him through. His flock, though scattered at first, shall be collected and guarded by Jehovah, and his death shall be followed by a Divine judgement, which shall sweep away by far the greatest portion of the Jewish people. The kingdom of this illustrious messenger of God shall be extended over all nations. The small remnant of the Jews, after being purified by manifold sufferings, shall finally be reconciled to Jehovah. He will pour out His spirit upon them in after times. This shall move them to devote themselves to him whom they had pierced, with the deepest grief for their sins. Then shall they obtain the pardon of their transgressions. Every thing shall be put away which under the former theocracy was contrary to the revealed will of God. Finally the enemies of the theocracy shall once more assault it with united strength, and greatly afflict it. But the Lord will defend His people, confer new glory upon His Church, and annihilate its obstinate enemies. Chief traits :—the mysterious oneness of the Messiah with Jehovah [1], the union of the regal dignity with that of the high priest [2]; the entrance of the Messiah into Jerusalem upon an ass [3] ; his being betrayed for thirty pieces of silver [4]; his death [5] ; the unbelief of the greater portion of the Jews ; their rejection and punishment [6] ; their final restoration [7].

212. (3) MALACHI [8]. The Messiah, who is a partaker of the Divine nature, will not appear, as the Jews expected, to inflict vengeance on the heathen, but to institute a strict examination among the covenant people themselves. His appearance shall bring destruction to the ungodly, but blessings to the righteous. He will send a Prophet like Elias before his coming. Should the end of his advent not be attained, the inevitable ruin of the land must be the consequence. The Lord will then collect for Himself true worshippers from among all the heathen. The Messianic prediction in Malachi is intended not to console, but to threaten and chastise : and thus the prominence given to certain points, and the passing over of others is explained. Chief traits :—the Divine nature of the Messiah is exhibited by this Prophet, with peculiar clearness ; his coming while the second temple remains ; the punishment to be inflicted by him on the Jewish people. Entirely peculiar to Malachi is the sending of a forerunner of the Messiah.

---

[1] Chap. 13. 7.   [2] Chap. 3. 8—10. 6. 9—15.   [3] Chap. 9. 9.
[4] Chap. 11. 12.   [5] Chap. 12. 10. 13. 7.   [6] Chap. 11. 13. 8.
[7] Chap. 12. 10, &c. 13. 9.   [8] Chap. 1. 11. 2. 17. 3. 6. 13—24.

CHAPTER III

THE NATURE OF PROPHECY

213. OUR first inquiry relates to the *condition of the Prophets* immediately before, and during the act of prophesying. Since the controversies with the Montanists, it has been the prevailing opinion of the Church, that the essential difference between the Prophets of God and the heathen diviners, consists in the fact, that the latter spoke in an *ecstasy*, but the former in the *full possession of reason and consciousness;* and consequently with a clear knowledge of what they uttered[1].

214. This view of the subject arises from the correct feeling, that there must be an essential difference between the condition into which the true Prophets were brought by the Spirit of God, and that of the false Prophets, who were not subjected to its influence. Still a close examination of the passages of the Scriptures relating to the state of the former, shows that the nature of this difference has been misconceived; and that the true Prophets, also, were in a state *essentially unlike their ordinary condition;* a state of *ecstasy*, in which the use of their rational powers was suspended, their own agency ceased, and they became completely passive under an overpowering influence of the Spirit of God; so that, as Philo says, the Prophets were interpreters, whose organs God employed to impart His revelation[2]. Even the preparation usually made for it, shows the state of the Prophets to have been an extraordinary one. They made use of music to lull their passions to repose, and inflame their love for that which was divine[3]. Then they were seized by the Spirit of God, and that in so powerful a manner, that their own agency was suppressed. This is evident from the expressions '*the hand of God*, or *the Spirit of God came upon him*, or *fell upon him*[4].' The irresistible nature of this seizure is indicated in Jeremiah[5], by the words '*Lord, thou hast persuaded me, and I have suffered myself to be persuaded; thou hast been too strong for me, and hast prevailed.*' To the same purpose is the language of the New Testament: '*for holy men of God spake, being borne along*

---

[1] According to Eusebius, Miltiades wrote a book: περὶ τοῦ μὴ δεῖν προφήτην ἐν ἐκστάσει λαλεῖν (Hist. Eccl. 5. 17.) Jerome expresses, "Neque vero, ut Montanus cum insanis feminis somniat, prophetæ in ecstasi loquuti sunt, ut nescirent quid loquerentur, et cum alios erudirent, ipsi ignorarent quid dicerent." Chrysostom: τοῦτο γὰρ μάντεως ἴδιον, τὸ ἐξεστηκέναι, τὸ ἀνάγκην ὑπομένειν, τὸ ὠθεῖσθαι, τὸ ἕλκεσθαι, τὸ σύρεσθαι, ὥσπερ μαινόμενον. Ὁ δὲ προφήτης οὐχ οὕτως, ἀλλὰ μετὰ διανοίας νηφούσης καὶ σωφρονούσης καταστάσεως, καὶ εἰδὼς ἃ φθέγγεται, φησὶν ἅπαντα· ὥστε καὶ πρὸ τῆς ἐκβάσεως κἀντεῦθεν γνώριζε τὸν μάντιν καὶ τὸν προφήτην. Later theologians have generally followed the Fathers of the Church.

[2] E. g. de Præm et Pœn. p. 711, ed. Hoesch. ἑρμηνεὺς γάρ ἐστιν ὁ προφήτης, ἔνδοθεν ὑπηχοῦντος τὰ λεκτέα τοῦ θεοῦ.

[3] See 2 Kings 3. 15. 1 Sam. 10. Cornelius a Lapide remarks, on the first chapter of Ezekiel, that the Prophets took their station by the side of the river, that in the stillness and delightful scenery around them, they might, through the soft murmur of the water, be refreshed, enlivened, and prepared for the Divine ecstasies.

[4] Ezek. 1. 3. 1 Sam. 19. 20, and 2 Kings 3. 15. 2 Chron. 15. 1.   [5] 20. 7.

by the Holy Ghost[1]' [which the English Bible translates incorrectly, "as they were moved by the Holy Ghost"]. The suppression of their own agency, terrour before the Divine Majesty, and the extraordinary nature of God's revelations, were attended with great perturbation and agony of spirit. When Abraham[2] had a vision, it is said, '*Behold horrour and great darkness fell upon him.*' When the Spirit seized Balaam, he falls to the ground[3]. Daniel[4], after beholding a vision, is entirely deprived of his strength, and sinks down with faintness[5], being sick 'certain days' in consequence of his struggle. The inward conflict was at times so great, that the Prophets tore off their clothes[6], as it is said of Saul in the first book of Samuel, that he also, no less than the other Prophets, has stript off his clothes, fallen to the ground, and prophesied. That the Prophets were in an extraordinary state is evident from their having been declared *insane* by unbelievers. Thus the servants of the court[7] say to Jehu, after a prophet had been with him, 'Wherefore came *this mad fellow*[8] unto thee?' See a passage perfectly similar, Jer. 29. 26. That there were external indications that this state was altogether of an unusual character, appears also from the relation in the tenth chapter of the first book of Samuel. It is said to Saul, in the sixth verse, '*The Spirit of the Lord shall come upon thee, and thou shalt prophesy with them,*' and in the eleventh verse, as he prophesies with the Prophets, all who had known him before exclaim with surprise, '*What has happened to the son of Kish? Is Saul also among the Prophets?*' There must, therefore, have been something more observable in Saul, than merely his joining with the disciples of the Prophets in their songs.

215. There is, then, no reason to doubt, that the Hebrew Prophets as well as the heathen Seers, were in an *ecstasy*. The LXX, Gen. 15. 12, employ this very expression. We find in the New Testament terms which are at least equivalent. Christ and the Apostles often declare, that the prophets spake 'in the Spirit;' and John, in like manner, Rev. 1. 10, and 4. 2, designates his ecstasy by the words '*I was in the Spirit*[9].'

216. Since, then, we have found that the Fathers did not accurately distinguish between true and false prophecy, the question arises in what *did* the difference between them consist? Tertullian long ago made a distinction between *ecstasy*[10] and *phrenzy*[11], attributing the latter to the false Prophets. This was correct. The true Prophets were

---

[1] Ὑπὸ πνεύματος ἁγίου φερόμενοι ἐλάλησαν ἅγιοι θεοῦ ἄνθρωποι, 2 Pet. 1. 21.—Knapp compares the expressions of profane writers: κατέχεσθαι ἐκ θεοῦ, *corripi deo, deum pati.*—Crusius justly regards the fact, that the condition of the Prophets, while uttering their prophecies, was extraordinary, and not the usual, permanent one, as the occasion of their so frequently repeating the formula, 'Thus saith the Lord;' while the Apostles, whose divine illumination was permanent, and connected with their own consciousness, use it but seldom, and only when they wish to distinguish their own advice from the commandments of the Lord, 1 Cor. 7. 10.

[2] Gen. 15. 12.
[3] Num. 24. 4.   Ezekiel likewise, 1. 28, and John, Rev. 1. 17.
[4] 10. 8—10.   [5] Chap. 8. 27.   [6] 1 Sam. 17. 24.   [7] 2 Kings 9. 11.
[8] מְשֻׁגָּע.   [9] Ἐγενόμην ἐν πνεύματι.   [10] Ἔκστασις.
[11] Mανία, *furor.*

certainly elevated to a loftier region. The action of the inferior principles of the soul, as well as its consciousness and self-possession, was suspended ; the capacity for contemplating the things of God was emancipated from its earthly fetters, and thus prepared, like a pure mirror, to receive the impressions of Divine truth. The unusual condition of the body which accompanied this ecstasy, was caused by the struggle of the Prophet, resisting the Spirit of God, which, with the triumph of the latter, *terminated in repose.*—The ecstasy of the heathen Seers, on the contrary, consisted, it is true, in the suppression of reason and consciousness, but then this was owing to the inferior faculties of the soul being excited to opposition against the higher. This conflict did not tend to *repose*, but the more the excitement increased, the higher the tone to which the feelings were roused, the more violent the storm of passion, the more complete was the inspiration supposed to be[1]. In the end, a variety of narcotic means were employed[2]. The state of the Prophets was *supernatural ;* that of the heathen diviners was *unnatural,* a momentary insanity[3].

217. From the fact that the Prophets, when uttering their predictions, were *not* in possession of reason and consciousness, but *in an ecstasy*, we deduce an important consequence. *They received all Divine revelations by an immediate perception.* While, in the case of the Apostles, the illumination of the Holy Spirit equally pervaded all the powers of the soul, by no means excluding the operation of the understanding ; in that of the Prophets the impressions were all made on the internal sense ; which, reflection and the external senses being at rest, received the revelations of the Spirit of God.

218. The evidence of this is indeed already included in that which established the reality of the prophetic ecstasy. It is however susceptible of independent proof. We make our first appeal to the important passage, Num. 12. 5—8. There the distinction is pointed out between the Divine revelation made to Moses, and that made to

---

[1] " This *pseudo-prophetical* spirit being not able to rise up above this low and dark region of sense or matter, or to soar aloft into a clear Heaven of vision, endeavoured alway, as much as might be, to strengthen itself in the *Imaginative* part : and therefore the wizards and false Prophets of old and later times have been wont alway to heighten their phansies and imaginations by all means possible." John Smith (of Prophesie : Select Discourses, p. 186, ed. 1673).—Hengstenberg calls this " *a very valuable treatise.*"

[2] V. Dale.

[3] As the derivation of the Greek μάντις from μαίνω indicates.—The Pythia is represented as insane by the Scholiasts in the Plutus of Aristophanes, and by Lucan, l. 5.

> —— " Bacchatur demens aliena per antrum
> Colla ferens, vittasque Deî, Phœbæaque serta
> Erectis discussa comis, per inania templi
> Ancipiti cervice rotat, spargitque vaganti
> Obstantes tripodas, magnoque exæstuat igne
> Iratum te, Phœbe, ferens."

So the Cassandra of Lycophron. According to Lucian, the seers foamed at the mouth, their eyes rolled, their hair flew about, their whole appearance was ferocious, and their motions those of a madman.

the Prophets. The appointment of Moses to be the founder and lawgiver of a dispensation required perfect and intelligible proof. The Divine revelations were therefore imparted to him internally and externally, in *plain* and *literal terms*[1]. On the contrary, they were always imparted to the Prophets in *visions*[2] or in *dreams*, and of course, while reflection and outward sensation were suspended[3], a method which sufficiently answered the design of their office. We are led to the same result by the appellation ' *Seers* ' frequently given to the Prophets[4].

219. In these appellations the word *see* is used in a wider sense for *every mode of immediate perception;* as it sometimes is in other cases, as for example, Ex. 20. 18. The passage in Num. 24. 3, 4. deserves particular attention. Balaam there calls himself ' the man whose eye is opened, who *sees the visions* of the Almighty, whose eyes are opened, when he falls to the ground.'

220. Of the same description are the numerous passages in which the Prophets assert, that they see and hear things imperceptible by the senses. ' I *see* him,' says Balaam, ' the illustrious king of Israel, but not now ; I *behold* him, but not nigh[5].' Isaiah *sees* the Lord sitting upon a lofty throne surrounded by seraphim. Micaiah[6] *sees* the Lord sitting upon his throne, and all the host of heaven standing by him on his right hand and left. Ezekiel[7] *sees* a field covered with dry bones of the dead, which were re-animated by the breath of the Lord. The immediate connexion between the ecstasy and the activity of the internal sense is plain from the first chapter of Ezekiel. It is said in the third verse, ' The hand of the Lord was upon him there ;' and directly after, in the fourth verse, ' and *I saw,* and behold it came.' Habakkuk[8] placed himself upon the watch, to *see* what the Lord would say to him. Daniel *hears* a loud voice on the banks of the Ulai[9]. Finally, this view of the mode in which Divine revelations were made to the Prophets, is sustained by all those facts, which, as we are about to show, have necessarily resulted from it.

221. This characteristic of prophecy has not been entirely un-known to the great body of interpreters. But they have usually confined it to those portions of the prophecies, in which it is par-

---

[1] Οὐ δι' αἰνιγμάτων, as Philo has expressed it.   [2] בְּמַרְאָה.

[3] In coincidence with this passage, the older Jewish interpreters determined the distinction between the Divine revelation made to Moses, and that made to the Prophets—"They supposed the *imaginative* power to be set forth as a *stage* upon which certain *visa* and *simulacra* were represented to their understandings, just, indeed, as they are to us in our common dreams; to see the intelligible mysteries in them, and so in these types and shadows, which were symbols of some spiritual things, to behold the antitypes themselves. But in case the *imaginative* faculty be not thus set forth as the *scene* of all prophetical illumination, but that the expression of things nakedly, without any *schemes* or *pictures*, be made immediately upon the understanding itself, then is it reckoned to be the *gradus Mosaicus*, wherein God speaks as it were *face to face*."—J. Smith, p. 172.

[4] רֹאִים and חֹזִים : so their predictions חִזָּיוֹן—מַחֲזֶה—חָזוֹן—חֲזוּת—חָזוּת— חֲזָה—חָזָה—חָזָה—מַרְאָה and מַרְאֶה.   [5] Num. 24. 17.   [6] 1 Kings 22. 19.
[7] Chap. 37.   [8] Chap. 2. 1.   [9] See Ezekiel 17. 12. 40. 3, 4.
Zech. 1. 14. Apoc. 4. 1. 21. 10. Amos 7. 13.

ticularly obvious, as in the sixth chapter of Isaiah, the first chapter of Ezekiel, the first part of Zechariah, and the second part of Daniel, which have therefore been exclusively denominated *visions*[1]. But as there is no real difference between these predictions and the rest, our arguments are equally applicable to all; and there is ample evidence that all possess sufficient characteristics of a *vision*, if the facts are correctly apprehended.

222. We now proceed to unfold the peculiar properties which result from this nature of prophecy.—(1) *We have no right to expect, that the Prophets will always describe the events of which they speak in all their connexions and relations.* " The Prophet," says Herder, " was not a preacher according to our notions, still less an expositor of a doctrinal topic." Such a connected and comprehensive mode of representing a subject, can be expected only of one who teaches in the possession of his understanding and consciousness. The Prophets uttered on every occasion merely what was communicated to the internal perception; and that only *was* communicated, which was suited to the existing condition of things. This is especially the case with the Messianic predictions, to which our present discussion has particular reference. The Prophets never, at any *one* time, present the *whole compass* of the doctrine concerning the Messiah. In one place they are concerned chiefly with his *person;* in another they are exclusively employed in describing the *nature of his kingdom.* Often the Messiah in his *glory* is the object of their contemplation. Malachi leaves the first appearing of Christ in a state of humiliation unnoticed, and does not mention the interval between his forerunner and the destruction of Jerusalem. Frequently the minutest circumstances are noticed, while those of far more importance are omitted. Often the most joyful events of the future are alone exhibited; at another time the prospect is chiefly filled with those of a gloomy character. Thus Jeremiah[2], for example, connects the conversion of the first-fruits of the Jews with their general conversion expected in future times, and omits to mention the intermediate *rejection* of the greater part[3]. On the contrary, Malachi and Daniel exhibit chiefly the opposite side of the picture, the rejection of the people, the desolation of the land and of the city. The Prophets often overlook all the obstacles which oppose the progress of the Messiah's kingdom, and therefore exhibit in one view its feeble commencement and its glorious completion. To this peculiarity of prophecy Paul seems to refer, when he says, ' *for we know in part, and we prophesy in part*[4].' We infer from it, that *all individual predictions* must be regarded merely as *fragments*, and that we possess a complete picture only when we have *collected* and *combined* the several features.

---

[1] The explanation, which usually follows the visions, belongs to the ecstasy as much as does the vision itself. Maimonides illustrates this by a comparison with a person dreaming, who in imagination, as if he were awake, relates his dream to another, and explains its meaning.

[2] Chap. **23.** 5, 6.   [3] So also Ezekiel **34.** 22—30. **37.** 21—28.

[4] 1 Cor. **13.**

This may be more easily accomplished, since history shows us in what order they must be arranged.

223. In recent times, as the general nature of prophecy has been misunderstood, so also has this quality which results from it. The attempt has been made to show from it, that the Prophets differed from each other in regard to the idea of a Messiah; and this has been urged as a proof, that this idea was of human origin. Where Joel, for example, describes only the nature of the Messiah's kingdom, and not the Messiah himself, it is inferred, that his expectations were not connected with a *person*. Since Jeremiah speaks only of the Messiah in *glory*, he can have had no idea of a *suffering* Messiah.— The incorrectness of this mode of considering the subject, may be easily shown even from the views of our opponents. It would prove not only that the Prophets contradicted one another, but likewise *themselves*. Thus for example, Isaiah, in the second chapter, as also Joel, without mentioning the Messiah himself, gives a description of his times. On the other hand, in the prophecy connected with this [1], and delivered at the same time, the Messiah is named. So also in the second part of his prophecies many Messianic representations of a general character are found, in connexion with those which relate to the Messiah as a *person* [2]. Jeremiah [3] in his thirty-first chapter speaks only of the nature of the Messiah's kingdom, while in the twenty-third chapter and other places his *person* is the subject of discourse. Isaiah in many passages describes only the *glorified* Messiah; but in the fifty-third chapter he draws a portrait of the Messiah in his *humiliation*, which he represents as the cause of his *subsequent exaltation to glory*.

224. As then we should not determine the doctrine of Plato, for instance, from any *single* passage, but from the *whole* of his works, it is plain, that, in order to understand a Prophet's representations of the Messiah, we must combine into a *single* image the various features occurring in different places. If this be granted, it is likewise obvious that we are not to infer, that because particular Prophets have left unnoticed large portions of the great picture, they were therefore unacquainted with them. Were more of the predictions of Joel extant, they would probably supply each other's deficiencies, as in the case of Isaiah. Had Jeremiah prophesied under the same circumstances as Isaiah in his second part, he would not have omitted to describe the *suffering* Messiah. It appears moreover at once that this view is erroneous, from its requiring us to suppose that the later Prophets were ignorant of all former predictions, nay even of the popular belief of the whole nation.

225. This errour of recent critics arises from viewing the Prophets too much as mere *doctrinal teachers*, and consequently expecting them to bring forward in each place the *whole compass of their doctrine*. Did we regard them as *Jews*, which they really were, we should not be surprised to find, that they communicated only what they *saw*, without intermingling what they had previously learnt in

---

[1] Chap. 4.   [2] Chap. 53, &c.   [3] Ver. 31, &c.

the ordinary way, from the revelations made to other men of God, and from the general belief of the people. The plausible objection to the view we have taken, which may be drawn from the alleged use of earlier predictions by subsequent Prophets, will be answered when we come to the second chapter of Isaiah.

226. (2) The medium through which the Prophets received their revelations being the internal sense, every thing necessarily appeared to them in the *present* time.—This explains many individual peculiarities. (1) It is not then surprising, that the Prophets should speak of events and persons which belong even to the most *distant future*, as if actually *present*, or even point to them. Thus, for example, Isaiah says, 'Unto us a Child *is born;* unto us a Son *is given*[1].' In another passage he points to the Messiah, '*Behold* my servant whom I uphold, mine elect in whom my soul delighteth[2].' And in the forty-fifth chapter[3] Cyrus appears, and is addressed. Often a demonstrative pronoun is used instead of a noun. The misapprehension of this peculiarity of the prophetic writings has led some interpreters to think, that here and in other places, the discourse related to persons and events *actually present;* a mistake which has rendered their interpretations entirely false. (2) The want of precision in the use of the tenses by the Prophets is explained by the same consideration. As they contemplated objects not in *time*, but in *space*, no accurate *determination of time* ought to be expected from them. They often employ either the *first aorist* or the *preterite* when speaking of the *most distant future*[4]. (3) From the same cause must the distance of time generally have been *unknown to the Prophet*, without a special revelation. They were not so much *chronological historians* as *describers of pictures*. When for example they *saw the Messiah standing before them*, by what means could they know how long a time should elapse before his advent[5]? Hence when they speak of the times of the Messiah their language is altogether indefinite[6]. Nay they even say expressly that the time is not known to them, but only to God[7]. Thus is explained the characteristic peculiarity of the prophecies, without the knowledge of which a large portion of them must be entirely misunderstood, viz.

[1] Chap. 9. 5.   [2] Chap. 42. 1.   [3] Ver. 1—8.

[4] On such places we usually find the remark, that the Prophet employed the preterite to indicate the *certainty of the fact.* The truth however was seen by Iken on Isa. 53. "Fundamentum talis styli dispositionis ex modo, quo prophetis futura revelabantur repetendum potius censeo. Non semper illud fiebat expressis verbis. Toti interdum corripiebantur spiritu; facultas mentis, cujus ope res nobis representamus, in iis acuebatur, ita ut recondita futuri temporis fata in imagine quasi ipsis exhibita non aliter contemplarentur, *ac si oculis ea cernerent.* Hinc non potuerunt non præsenti aut præterito tempore uti, cum naturalis dicendi ordo id flagitaret," &c.

[5] B. Crusius very justly observes: "Prophetæ divinâ luce, quâ illuminantur, ad futura plerumque prospexerunt, quemadmodum fit, quando cœlum stelliferum intuemur. Videmus enim supra nos sidera; quanto a nobis intervallo absint, nec non quæ propius, quæ remotius distent, non item animadvertimus."

[6] Thus the common phrase בְּאַחֲרִית הַיָּמִים, which properly means only, *in future times.*

[7] So Zech. 14. 7: 'it shall be one day, *which shall be known to the Lord,*' &c.

that events which are separated by great distance of time from each
other appear as *continuous*. The Prophets in vision could contemplate objects only in *juxtaposition*, not in *succession*.—Let us illustrate this by some examples. The city of Babylon received its first
shock when it was taken by the Persians; but yet more than a
thousand years elapsed before its utter downfall and total extinction.
Nevertheless Jeremiah [1] connects the *capture* and its *final destruction*,
without mentioning that there was any interval between. In the
predictions relating to the theocracy, where either blessings or
judgements are foretold, those that are nearer and less important
are connected in the representation with those which are more distant and of greater moment, in such a manner that the vast space
of time which intervenes is not intimated. Here the combination
always depends on the internal relation of the nearer and the more
distant events. So Isaiah [2], omitting all the intermediate occurrences,
makes the redemption by the Messiah *immediately* follow the deliverance of Israel from the Assyrians. In the same manner Isaiah,
Micah, Hosea, Amos, Ezekiel, and Jeremiah very often connect the
restoration from exile with the *redemption through the Messiah*,
although no Prophet represents *him* as the leader of the returning
captives. With Zechariah, who lived after the exile, the scene had
already changed. He connects the more spiritual redemption of the
Jews with their nearer *temporal* deliverance, partly under Alexander,
and partly in the time of the Maccabees. Even in the description
of the Messiah's kingdom its gradual development is unnoticed, and
its beginning and glorious end are placed in immediate connexion.
So Zechariah [3] describes the splendid completion of the Messiah's
kingdom, immediately after having represented Him in a state of
humiliation. Joel [4] does not distinguish between the *first effusion of
the Spirit* on the day of Pentecost, and that which the Church is
always to enjoy. Sometimes events, instead of being placed in juxtaposition, are blended together, just as in a distant prospect objects
flow into one another and appear mingled, when in reality they are
far apart. This remark throws much light, especially on the second
part of Isaiah. There the deliverance from exile, and the deliverance through Christ, very often appear in juxtaposition; but in
many representations they are presented to the eye of the Prophet
combined; sometimes the one, and sometimes the other being the
more prominent. In like manner all the judgements of the future
are frequently brought together in one view—the fore ground and
the back ground are blended [5]. Ignorance of these properties of the
prophetic representations has been the cause of much misapprehension. Prophecies intimately connected have been torn asunder by
critics, because it was not perceived that the Prophets frequently
place events in *immediate succession*, which are *connected with each
other by some internal relation*, although they are *far apart* in point

---

[1] Chap. 50, 51.   [2] Chap. 11.   [3] Chap. 9. 9, 10.   [4] Chap. 3.
[5] "Quemadmodum simili fallaciâ opticâ longissime distans turris domûs
propinquæ tecto incumbere, aut lunæ discus montibus nemoribusque contiguus
videtur." Velthusen, l. c. p. 89.

of *time*[1]. Others avail themselves of this juxtaposition and blending together of the most distant events to disprove the Divine
origin of the prophecies; but very unjustly, because it does not
imply that the Prophet's views were *false*, but only *limited*. Had a
prophet foretold that Christ would appear after a definite number of
years, and the event did not correspond with the prediction, it could
not have proceeded from God ; but when, in accordance with the
general nature of a vision, he *refrains from all determination of time*
(to which he makes no pretension), we can no more object to the
Divine origin of prophecy on this ground, than we can because each
individual prophet did not foresee *every event* of future time. Others,
who acknowledge the Divine origin of prophecy, taking it for granted
that each representation must necessarily relate to the *same time*, or
the *same objects*, endeavour to remove by a forced interpretation,
whatever does not accord with the principle on which they proceed[2].
Or, they suffer themselves to be led (by this and another peculiarity
of the prophetic style hereafter to be developed, arising from the prevalence of *imagery* in the visions of the Prophets) to the unnatural
assumption of a *double sense*, thus opening a wide field to the indulgence of caprice.

227. That the Prophets were conscious of this characteristic of their
predictions, appears from their comparing themselves so often with
watchmen, who from some lofty tower overlook the surrounding
region, and give notice of the approach of friends or foes[3]. How
essential this property is to the nature of prophecy, appears from its
characterising even the predictions of Christ ; and it is in a great
measure owing to ignorance of it, that they have so often been falsely
interpreted. Even to *Him* the events of the future presented themselves as in a large picture, and therefore in *space*, not in *time*. In
describing its separate parts, as the destruction of Jerusalem, and the
day of judgement, the designations of time which He employs[4] relates
to the succession of the objects, as they appeared to Him in prophetic
vision, and not as they were actually to take place. On this subject
the passage in 1 Pet. 1. 10—12 is replete with instruction[5]. There
the Apostle asserts that true and divine revelations of the future,
namely, concerning the suffering of the Lord and the glory that
should follow, were imparted to the prophets by the Spirit of Christ.
Nevertheless they *sought in vain to discover the time* when the events
they predicted should take place, and in this respect they were far
behind those who lived at the time of the fulfilment of their predictions.

228. It now remains to answer the question, how we can ascertain
the chronological order of events predicted in this manner. The

---

[1] See our remarks on Isaiah 11.
[2] Jahn especially has frequently fallen into this errour.
[3] Comp. with 2 Sam. 13. 34. 18. 24—27. 2 Kings 9. 17—20, the passages in
Micah 7. 4. Jer. 6. 17. Ezek. 3. 17. 33. 1—9.
[4] As *immediately* ($\varepsilon\dot{v}\theta\dot{\varepsilon}\omega\varsigma$), Matt. 24. 29.
[5] 1 Pet. 1. 11. " Searching what, or *what manner of time*, the Spirit of Christ
which was in them did signify, when it testified beforehand the sufferings of
Christ, and the glory that should follow."

means of doing this (some of which were possessed by the prophets and their contemporaries, and others are peculiar to those who were to come after them), were the following.

229. (1) The Prophets were often divinely instructed respecting the order of time in which the events were to happen. Thus it was revealed to Jeremiah in an extraordinary manner, that the Babylonian exile would continue seventy years. Thus in Joel 3. 1, the time of the Messiah is plainly represented [1] as commencing after the deliverance from exile; Isaiah [2] distinguishes two courses of time, one *before* and the other *after* the Messiah; and Daniel gives the time that should elapse between the deliverance from captivity and the commencement of the Messiah's kingdom ; but yet (which deserves especial attention) in *so obscure* a manner, that his contemporaries could learn nothing further from his prophecy, than that the former event should *precede the latter*, the more definite knowledge being reserved for those who lived after the fulfilment.—So also Christ, in the gospel of Matthew, after having, throughout the whole of the foregoing representation, spoken of the two future analogous events, without noticing their distance from each other in time, distinguishes between them in the twenty-fourth chapter [3], where the contrast between ' *all these things* [4] ' and ' *of that day* [5],' should be well considered ; and says that the former, the destruction of Jerusalem, shall take place before the eyes of the present generation ; the latter, the day of judgement, in some remote and unknown period.   Aided by such designations of time, we may, even in those prophetic representations where they are wanting, convert without serious difficulty the *juxtaposition* of events into a *succession*, though the *exact distance between them* may remain undetermined.

230. (2) The succession of events which are blended together, may be easily ascertained by a comparison with other passages in which they occur separately. Thus in the second part of Isaiah, it is only necessary to select the passages in which the deliverance by Cyrus, and that by Christ, was presented separately to the mental vision of the prophet, and compare them with those in which the two events are *intermingled*, and the separation of them will not be a difficult task.

231. (3) The Prophets sometimes indicate the mode in which events are to take place, not taking their station, as is usually done, in the *actual present* (and thence overlooking the future), but in the *nearer future* (as if it were the present), thence overlooking the *more distant future*. Thus Isaiah, in the second part of his prophecies, generally places himself in the Babylonian exile ; in the fifty-third chapter, between the *sufferings* and the *glorification* of the Messiah, because the former were to be represented as the conditional ground of the latter.   His sufferings are expressed in the *past* tense, his exaltation in the *future*.

232. (4) But by far the surest means was the *fulfilment*.—Even

---

1 By the phrase אַחֲרֵי כֵן.   2 8. 23.   3 Ver. 34. 36.
4 Πάντα ταῦτα.   5 Τῆς ἡμέρας ἐκείνης.

before the Messiah's appearance, this afforded considerable aid in respect to the predictions concerning Him. The deliverance from exile and the redemption by Christ are very often placed in juxtaposition, or blended together. Now when the former *had taken place*, it was easy to distinguish what related to each respectively. And thus we find the prediction of the Messiah becomes more pure and distinct in the Prophets after the exile. But this means was rendered still more efficacious by the coming of Christ. We have already seen that the appearance of Christ in a *state of humiliation*, and the final *glorification* of his kingdom, are not in point of time separated from each other by the Prophets. But *after the first event had taken place*, this separation could be easily made. So also Christ's own predictions necessarily became much more distinct after the first event to which they related (the destruction of Jerusalem) had taken place.

233. (3) If all disclosures of the future were made to the Prophets in mental vision, it must have been by *figurative representations ;* since only *images*, and not *abstract notions*, could in this way be perceived. But the images in which the future was presented to the mind of the Prophets, must have been taken from objects and relations with which they were familiar. For on the one hand, God does not operate as if by magic on the minds of those to whom He communicates Himself, but in a manner adapted to their peculiar capacities and knowledge ; and on the other, the prophecies would not have answered their purpose, had they consisted of *unknown images*, for they must have been totally unintelligible.

234. If we apply this rule to the Messianic predictions, it necessarily results from the nature of prophecy, that the kingdom of the Messiah should be represented by metaphors taken from the Mosaic dispensation ; and that the *facts* as well as the *persons* of the former, should receive the names of those of the latter, which were connected with them by an internal resemblance.—This mode of representation is founded in the fact, that the Mosaic economy was ordered with *distinct reference to the Christian dispensation*, and *prefigures* it. As it respects the three offices of *prophet, high priest*, and *king*, this was long ago noticed by Eusebius in a full discussion of the subject [1].

235. We will now illustrate these remarks by examples.—In their representations of the Messiah the existing theocracy furnished the Prophets with a threefold groundwork, to which they might superadd, in each instance, the difference between the original and the type. The Messiah appeared to them as an exalted king, and all the traits peculiar to him they combined in the image of an illustrious leader of the earthly theocracy, whose glory was only a faint reflection of the glory of his great successor [2]. And as the Messiah was most completely represented by David, he is called expressly by *his* name [3]. He appeared to them also as a *prophet* endowed with all the fulness of the Holy Ghost, who, completely realizing the *ideal* of

---

[1] Hist. Eccles. l. 3.   [2] Compare Mic. 5. Isa 11. Jer. 23.
[3] See Hos. 3. 5. Jer. 30. 9. Ez. 34. 23.

the prophetic office, should teach, admonish, and rebuke, not merely within the narrow limits of Palestine, like the Prophets by whom he had been prefigured, but among all the people of the earth [1]. And lastly, he appeared to them as a *high priest*, who should actually procure that forgiveness of sins, which was only symbolically represented by the high priests of the old covenant [2].   And as the Messiah was regarded as the *most exalted prophet, high priest, and king*, so his kingdom appeared, not as separate and different from the theocracy, but its fullest completion.   Frequently Jerusalem or Zion, as the existing seat of the theocracy, served to designate it.   Thus Joel [3] expresses the thought, that only the members of the theocracy should escape in the heavy judgement which impended, by the words ' in *Zion* and in *Jerusalem* shall be deliverance.'   Isaiah, Micah, and Ezekiel, contemplate the future triumph of the theocracy over all the religions of the heathen, as an exaltation of the mountain on which the temple stood, above the hills ; and the future conversion of the heathen appeared to the two former, as their flowing to the hill of Zion ; and to Jeremiah [4] as a vast enlargement of Jerusalem.—The same mode of representation extends to all the individual traits. The universality of the influence of the Holy Spirit in the times of the Messiah, appears to Joel as a general extension of the three forms of Divine revelation existing under the old covenant. Zechariah expresses the idea that all nations shall worship the true God, by predicting their participation in the *feast of tabernacles*.   The perfect love and faithfulness of the people towards their God, appear to Hosea [5], Micah [6], and Zechariah [7], as the putting away of whatever, under the former theocracy at any time, or especially in the days of the prophet, disturbed the relation to God ; for example, the service of Baal, or idolatry in general; seeking help from Assyria and Egypt; and false prophecy.   When the glory and felicity of the Messianic times are exhibited, the prosperous condition of the theocracy under David and Solomon becomes the basis of the redemption [8].   The general truth, that peace and love should prevail among the people, when they had found reconciliation with God, was received by the Prophets under the image of the termination of the most deplorable dispensation that occurred during the theocracy, the separation of the kingdoms of Israel and Judah [9].   The enemies of the Messiah's kingdom were not only designated by the general name of the enemies of the theocracy [10]; but they not unfrequently bore precisely the name of some one people then peculiarly hostile or powerful, which appeared in the vision of the Prophets, as the representative of all the rest : as Moab [11], Edom [12], Magog.—These examples,

---

[1] Comp. Is. 42. 49. and other passages.   [2] Ps. 110. Zech. 6. Isa. 53.
[3] 3. 5.   [4] 23. 8.   [5] Chap. 2. and 14.
[6] Chap. 5.   [7] Chap. 13.
[8] Comp. e. g. Hos. 2. 20. Jer. 23. 6. Mic. 4. 1. and Zech. 3. 10. with 1 Kings 4. 24.
[9] Comp. Hos. 2. 2. Isa. 11. 13.   [10] בּוֹיִם.
[11] Isa. 63. and Amos 9. 12.   [12] Ezekiel 38.

which might be greatly increased, will be sufficient to illustrate our
view of the subject.

236. This peculiarity of prophecy has been in many ways overlooked or misunderstood. Two opposite errours may especially be
noticed. The first is that of the carnal Jewish interpreters, whose
example the majority of the rationalists have followed, though influenced indeed by other motives. These either entirely fail to perceive the metaphorical character of the prophecies ; or, without any
governing principle of hermeneutics, adhere to the literal interpretation, wherever it will serve to confirm their preconceived opinions.
The leading interest of the Jews is positive, that of the modern
critics negative. Those orthodox interpreters also, who insist upon
a strictly literal interpretation of that portion of the prophecies which
has not yet been fulfilled, are in some degree involved in the same
errour. This mode of interpretation is finding more supporters
every day in England ; and even in Germany has a considerable
number of defenders, especially in Würtemberg.—The second mistake is that of those who deprive the prophecies of all substance
and meaning, by giving undue prominence to their figurative character. This mode of interpretation is adopted by not a few of
the rationalists ; and while those who followed the foregoing
method, were influenced by the desire to point out a contradiction
between the Old Testament and the New, it is the prevailing
motive with these, by generalizing as much as possible, to do away
the coincidence between the prophecy, rightly understood, and its
fulfilment. It is not unusual to see the very same interpreter
following either mode of explanation, as suits his convenience. This
errour is also partially committed by those orthodox interpreters who
in all that *transcends* the appearance of Christ in a state of *humiliation*, seek, often through unbelief, to get rid of the *substantial
reality*, that lies at its foundation ; explaining all that the Prophets
reveal concerning the *future glory* of the kingdom of God in such a
manner, as to render it a mere shell without a kernel.

237. Would we avoid these different paths of errour, we must
(after having proved the figurative character of prophecy in general,
as necessarily resulting from its nature) establish sure rules by which
to distinguish between the image and the fact it represents.

238. (1) Where a comparison can be made with the fulfilment, this
affords the surest guide in making the distinction. But here caution is
necessary, since the prophets, as we have before shown, often represent
events as *successive*, which are *separated from each other by a long
period of time :* for instance, the obscure beginning of the Messiah's
kingdom, and its glorious termination. It must therefore be accurately ascertained beforehand, whether a prediction has been in
general, and to what extent, already fulfilled. In this respect the
declarations of the New Testament concerning the future development of the kingdom of God, will be of the greatest service. The
Apocalypse particularly is important, inasmuch as it again takes up
the yet unfulfilled portion of the prophecies of the Old Testament,
and represents their accomplishment as still future. In relation,

however, to that part of the prophecies, which (partly by a simple comparison of the prediction with history, and partly by the declarations of Christ and his Apostles) can be shown to have been already fulfilled, we may with perfect propriety avail ourselves of history, in order to distinguish between what is figurative and what is literal. We must however make a clear distinction between these two questions : ' In what sense did the *Prophets* understand these predictions ? ' and 'what meaning did *God* intend them to convey ? ' These questions are shown to be different, as soon as it has been proved that the Prophets spoke in an ecstasy. We cannot in the ways proposed find the answer to the first, nor is it of much importance to us. Since the Prophets were only organs of the Holy Spirit, we may not inquire whether, during their ecstasy and the suppression of reason and consciousness, they understood correctly, or incorrectly ; and they afterwards stood in the same relation to their predictions as their hearers or readers, so that *their* views of them cannot be decisive of their true import. But the second question may be answered by the fulfilment. The same God, who opened the prospect of futurity to the Prophets, effected also the accomplishment of their predictions. The rule of interpretation, which requires us always to seek the sense intended by the author, is thus preserved inviolate. The difference between us and our opponents lies rather in the answer to the question, ' Who is to be considered as the real *author* of the prophecies.' *They* look only at the human instruments ; *we* elevate our thoughts to the Divine Author. —Several interpreters[1], endeavouring to find a middle course, adopt the notion of a double sense of prophecy ; the one, that which the Prophets conceived, the other, that which God designed. This assumption, which is entirely untenable, arises from neglecting to discriminate between the *objective* meaning of a prophecy and its *subjective* meaning or meanings. In every composition, the former can be but *one*, the latter may be *as various as its readers are numerous*. It is only with the former that we are concerned ; and we are fully justified in seeking it by a comparison with the fulfilment, as soon as we have become convinced that prophecy is from God, whether by a comparison of the prophecy with history, *or* by the testimony of the New Testament, or by the evidences by which the Prophets demonstrated their Divine mission to their contemporaries. Whilst our opponents are unable (as they always must be) to show that this conviction of ours is unfounded, they ought not to question our right to call history to our aid in determining the sense of prophecy. History, moreover, not only makes us divest the prophecies of their metaphorical and theocratic dress ; but also often serves as a guide where, without its aid and confined to the prophecy alone, we might be inclined to extend that which is figurative too far. Thus in the twenty-second Psalm, for example, we should perhaps regard the parting of the garments, the piercing of the hands and feet, &c., as the mere *filling up of the picture*, if these particular circumstances

---

[1] As Seiler and Jahn.

were not repeated in the history of Christ ; in the ninth chapter of Zechariah, the Messiah's riding upon an ass might have been thought a mere figurative description of his humble condition, his meekness, and pacific character, if history did not make it necessary to refer it to a transaction which symbolically represented these qualities : and without its light, the reward of thirty pieces of silver, in the eleventh chapter of Zechariah, would have suggested only in general the idea of the little success which attended the efforts of the Messiah among the Jews. And so in many other instances.

239. Other marks, by which to distinguish between the figurative and the literal, are contained in the prophecies themselves. Of these the Prophets and their contemporaries *might* have availed themselves ; although it must often have been difficult for them to make the distinction, for want of the surest guide—the fulfilment. These marks we have yet to exhibit.

240. (2) Those descriptions are obviously figurative, in which there is a distinct reference to earlier occurrences in the history of the Israelites. Here we are always to select only the general, fundamental idea which connects the future with the past event. Thus when it is said, Isa. 11. 15, 16, the Lord in effecting a new deliverance for the Israelites will dry up the Arabian Gulf, and divide the Nile into seven streams, so that we may pass over dry-shod ; the fact here foretold is only *the redemption of the covenant people*, which is presented to the prophet under the *image* of the former deliverance from Egyptian bondage [1]. When Hosea, in reference to the deliverance of the Israelites, says [2], ' God will lead them into the desert, there he will speak kindly with them, then he will conduct them into the land of Canaan, and first indeed into the fruitful valley of Achor, it is generally acknowledged that the Prophet designs to express by this representation (taken from the earlier history of the Israelites) nothing further than the thought, that God would first deliver them from misery, and then comfort and abundantly bless them [3].

241. (3) In numerous other places we are compelled to have recourse to a metaphorical sense, or make the prophets directly contradict themselves. Should we, for example, as several cabbalists have done, understand those passages literally, in which the Messiah is called expressly *King David*, and give to them the meaning : *David will arise from the dead, and take possession of the kingdom*, we should make them *contradict* others, in which he is designated as the *sprout* or *son of David*. Should Jer. 33. 18, be taken in the literal sense, as predicting the continuation of the Levitical priesthood, and the sacrificial service, this passage contradicts chap. 31. 31, which declares that in the time of the Messiah all are to stand in an immediate relation to God, and chap. 3. 16, according to which the Levitical worship shall cease ; not to mention the passages in the remaining prophets, and other arguments to be brought forward in their place in proof of its figurative meaning. This argument is especially valid against those who give a literal construction to those

---

[1] So also Zech. 10. 11.　　[2] Chap. 2. 14, 15.　　[3] See Isa. 4. 5. 12. 3.

passages which speak of the wars and victories of the theocracy in the time of the Messiah. The Prophets in many places give especial prominence to the fact, that the kingdom of the Messiah is to be a kingdom of peace, and all the heathen under a Divine influence are voluntarily to become its subjects. If now the same Prophets, who describe the kingdom of the Messiah as entirely peaceful, nevertheless speak of wars and triumphs of the theocracy [1], in the one case or the other their expressions *must necessarily be figurative.* In any such case, the figure must always be sought on the side where an occasion for it can be shown, by considering the images usually employed by the Prophets.

242. (4) Other passages contain in themselves the evidence that they are not to be otherwise than figuratively interpreted. Thus, even independently of the distinct testimony of Christ, and of history, we need not with the older Jews and some recent critics, as Bauer and Baumgarten-Crusius, understand by the Prophet Elijah whose appearance Malachi announces, the *real* Elijah, but *another prophet who should be like him.* Such a figurative representation being sustained by the most certain analogies; for example, by the metaphorical use of the name *David,* which is generally acknowledged. Thus the literal interpretation of Isa. 53. 12 appears at once to be inadmissible, because a *worldly* triumph is not to be won by the deepest humiliation, and *worldly* rulers do not impart forgiveness of sins and justification to their subjects. At first sight there seems to be much in favour of understanding the last eight chapters of Ezekiel literally, but still they contain many passages which are not capable throughout of any other than a figurative sense, and which therefore give us a clue to the right interpretation of the whole. This rule applies, especially, to the passage, chap. 47. 1—12. A great stream of water, of unfathomable depth, shall issue from the temple. This stream shall restore the waters of the Dead Sea, and diffuse life wherever it flows. Only the pools and the miry places, which do not receive its waters, remain unhealed. Who that has even a slight acquaintance with the figurative language of the Old Testament, can fail to perceive in this passage a representation of the influence of the Holy Spirit under the Christian dispensation [2]? That Edom, in the thirty-fourth and sixty-third chapters of Isaiah, is only a metaphorical designation of the enemies of the theocracy, is indisputably evident from the context, as the threatened judgement is represented as extending to *all the people of the earth.*

243. (5) In discriminating between the imagery and what it was designed to represent, we must have regard to the general character of each individual prophet. It is plain that, although all the Prophets behold the truth in images, yet with some of them, these images have far more reality, and the figurative dress is far more transparent than with others; just as in this respect a considerable difference is observable in each particular prophet, according as his

---

[1] Comp. Isa. chap. 2. with chap. 9. &c.
[2] The same may be said of the similar figurative representation, Zech. 14. 10.

own agency was more suppressed at *one* time than *another*. If, for example, a passage like that in Ezekiel 40—48 were found in *Isaiah*, there would be far stronger reason than at present for giving it an interpretation as literal as possible.

244. (6) In many instances the attention is *expressly directed* to the figurative character of a description, and an intimation given of the reality which lies at the foundation. Thus in Zech. 10. 11, the metaphorical representation suggested by the deliverance from Egypt, ' they shall go through the *sea*,' the Prophet himself explains by adding the word ' *affliction*.' The wars in Ps. 110. 3, cannot be of this world, because the Psalmist sends forth the warriors in *sacred garments*. Ps. 45. 3, cannot be understood of *beauty of person*, since the beauty there celebrated is the ground of God's blessing.

245. (7) In the case of predictions yet unfulfilled, this discrimination is always to be made in accordance with the analogy of the faith. Since the same Spirit spoke by the Prophets and by the writers of the New Testament, there can be no contradiction between them [1]. This principle requires us to reject that explanation of the prophecies relating to events still future, which, by understanding them in a literal sense, makes them foretell the *future pre-eminence of the Jewish people*, the *rebuilding of the temple*, and the *restoration of the Levitical service*. But then this rule must be applied with caution, and be preceded by a careful examination of the system of doctrine contained in the New Testament. It has manifestly been *misapplied* in various ways. For instance, by those who, entirely mistaking the reality which lies at the foundation of the figure, wish to interpret spiritually all prophecies which relate to the prosperous external condition of the kingdom of God, under the pretext that the kingdom of Christ is spiritual ; a pretext founded on overlooking the distinction between the kingdom of grace and the kingdom of glory, which latter, according to the New Testament, as well as the Old, is to be established on earth.

246. (8) As the Prophets and their contemporaries were not always able, by those marks which were given, to distinguish between the figure and the reality, so neither have *we* always the means of doing it with certainty, in the case of those prophecies which are yet to be fulfilled. It is necessary here not to go beyond the evidence in our decisions. As, with respect to that part of the prophecies which has been already fulfilled, history has taught us to distinguish, against appearances, between the figure and the reality, so must we wait for its light, before we can decide respecting much that yet remains to be accomplished.

247. (IV.) A necessary result of the condition of the Prophets, while delivering their predictions, as we have represented it, is their *obscurity*, considered in themselves, and before their fulfilment ; which, nevertheless, is to be considered as only comparative. This obscurity is the result of the three properties already mentioned. (1) Clear views of *only certain portions* of the vast future were usually granted to the Prophets. Their prophecies must be joined together, and the

---

[1] As Theodoret has aptly shown in his remarks on Ezekiel 48.

fragments combined so as to form a whole, if prophecy and its fulfilment are to correspond.   This is not difficult for *us*, since history
teaches where each particular feature must be arranged; nor were
those who lived *before the fulfilment* entirely destitute (as we have
already seen) of the means of making this combination.   It must,
however, have been far more difficult for them, and the Prophets
themselves may often have erred in this respect.   That, for example, it
was difficult for those who were without the light afforded by the fulfilment, to reconcile those passages which speak of a Messiah in *glory*,
with those in which a Messiah in *humiliation* is foretold, is evident
from the fact, that the Jews invented for that purpose the fiction of
two Messiahs.   (2) Still more was this obscurity produced by the
circumstance, that the Prophets contemplated the future *in space*,
not in *time;* and that, therefore, near and distant events, which
resembled each other, were often contemplated by them as connected, or blended together.   It is true that here also, even before
the fulfilment, a combination of various marks might afford much
light; but then it must have been very difficult always to discover
these marks, and it was easy to err.   If, for example, the Prophets
themselves (after their ecstasy was over), or their contemporaries,
or their immediate successors, studied the predictions in which the
deliverance from the Babylonian exile and the redemption by
Christ appear as *continuous*, they might easily fall upon the
opinion, that both events were actually to take place in connexion.
How easily this opinion could arise, we see from Malachi 2. 17.
From this passage it is evident that the idea had become firmly
established among the Jews in the exile, that they should be delivered and exalted to great prosperity by the Messiah, and that the
worldly-minded part of the people murmured at the disappointment
of this hope.   The intimate connexion of the feeble commencement,
and the glorious end of the Messiah's kingdom in the prophetic
representations, caused even John the Baptist and the Apostles to
expect, that the appearance of Christ must be immediately followed
by the erection of his visible kingdom.   (3) But a still greater
cause of this obscurity was the *figurative character* of the prophecies.
We have seen indeed that, independently of the fulfilment, marks for
distinguishing between the figure and the reality are not wanting.   But
still it must have been very difficult, and often impossible, to carry out
this distinction into particulars.   The Prophets and the other members of the old covenant stood in the same relation to the prophecies
of that period, as we do to those which relate to the future development of the kingdom of God, viz., to those of the Apocalypse.   We
perceive their figurative character, and yet it is often impossible to
decide what is real, and what was designed merely to complete the
picture. Still greater misapprehension must be caused by the figurative character of the prophecies, when the inherent difficulty is
increased, by their being interpreted by those whose carnal disposition led them to *desire* to find expressed in them certain hopes,
which they fondly cherished.   The carnal national pride of the
Jews caused them to despise all the means of correct information
which they already enjoyed; and so, by understanding the theocratic

images literally, they collected from the prophecies their worldly conceptions of the Messiah and his kingdom.

248. That this comparative obscurity of their predictions was not unknown to the prophets themselves, appears from many of their own declarations. Isaiah, Jeremiah, and Ezekiel often assert that their predictions are unintelligible to the worldly-minded portion of the people, and would not be understood by them till they were fulfilled to their injury[1]. Daniel and Zechariah declare, in several places, that they do not understand the meaning of their visions, and at a later period are taught their import for the first time. Hence the meaning of those visions[2] which were followed by no explanation, must have remained obscure to the Prophet himself. Chap. 12. 4. 9, Daniel is commanded to seal up a vision which was entirely unintelligible to him until the last time, or the time of the fulfilment, when many should come and fully understand it. But this peculiarity of prophecy is described with peculiar distinctness in the remarkable passage of 2 Pet. 1. 19—21, which affords a confirmation of our whole view of the subject[3]. Peter, in the preceding verses, had appealed in proof of the truth of Christianity to historical facts, confirmed by sufficient testimony. He next, in the passage before us, appeals as a second proof to the whole compass of the Messianic predictions of the Old Testament, which had now become clear and certain by the fulfilment, whereas, before its shining light fell upon them, they resembled a faintly burning taper, which could but imperfectly illuminate the surrounding darkness. He then assigns the cause, *why* prophecy does not acquire its full light (and with that the usefulness of which it is capable) till after the fulfilment. The Prophets themselves had not a clear knowledge of the import of their predictions[4], because they did not speak of themselves, nor even in the possession of reason and consciousness, but in an ecstasy,

---

[1] See Isa. 6. 9—13. 29. 10, &c. Jer. 23. 20. 30. 24. Ezekiel 33. 33.

[2] Ezekiel 40—48.

[3] See on this the excellent treatise of Knapp, the first of his Opuscula.

[4] We take ἐπίλυσις with Knapp in the ordinary and established sense, *interpretation*. Steudel objects against this, that Peter could not justly found the proof, that the Prophets did not understand the meaning of their own communications, upon the fact of their being given by Divine inspiration. But in saying this, the term φερόμενοι seems to have escaped his notice. Peter grounds his proof, not upon Divine inspiration in general, but upon the *ecstasy* of the Prophets, in which consciousness and the self-controul of their mental powers were suspended. Steudel as well as Ullmann, and indeed Œcumenius, wish to understand ἐπίλυσις as meaning *prophecy itself;* and they appeal to a passage in Philo, where the Prophets are called θεοῦ ἑρμηνεῖς. But, supposing it to be proved that this word *might* bear such a sense in some cases, yet it could not in this for the following reasons: first, because 'interpretation' here must necessarily be referred back to προφητεία γραφῆς; secondly, on account of the parallel passage in the first Epistle, where likewise he is speaking of the obscurity which attended prophecy even to the Prophets themselves; and finally, because a confirmation of the principal idea καὶ ἔχομεν βεβαιότερον τὸν προφητικὸν λόγον, as it is furnished in ver. 20, 21, by the first mode of explanation, is far more in place, than such a confirmation of the subordinate idea ᾧ καλῶς ποιεῖτε προσέχοντες, as would stand in the same verses, according to the second explanation.

and as the instruments of the Holy Ghost, '*being borne along by the Holy Ghost*[1].' This passage is important for us in two respects. (1) It confirms our right (which we have already shown to be well founded, but which is denied by our opponents) to dispel the darkness of the predictions of the Messiah by the light of their fulfilment. In harmony with this is the passage already quoted, 1 Pet. 1. 10—12, where it is said to have been revealed to the Prophets themselves, that the perfect knowledge of what they foretold concerning the mysterious advent of the Messiah, belonged to the time of the fulfilment; and that the chief import of prophecy did not relate to *them* and *their contemporaries*, but to *those who were to come after*. (2) The reason of the obscurity of the prophecies, and the consequent need of the light of history is ascribed to the fact, that the Prophets spake in an ecstasy, and thus the ground of our whole representation is strengthened.

249. Recent interpreters, by despising the comparison of the fulfilment with the prediction, go back to the position of those who lived before the fulfilment; and from the darkness which, through their own fault, continues to rest upon the prophecies, they draw an argument against their Divine origin. Thus, for example, Ammon declares: "The simple sentences expressed in cool historical prose: Israel has no king to expect, but a teacher; this teacher will be born at Bethlehem in the reign of Herod: He will sacrifice his life for the truth of his religion, under Tiberius; through the destruction of Jerusalem, and the utter ruin of the Jewish state, He will propagate his doctrine in all parts of the world;—these few sentences would not only bear the character of true predictions, but, could their genuineness be shown, they would be incomparably more valuable than all the oracles of the Old Testament put together." Now without being permitted to fathom the depth of the Divine counsels, we are able to prove these requisitions unwarrantable, and inconsistent with the design of prophecy; and can justify the method in which God has been pleased to reveal his purposes. (1) It is contrary to the nature of God to *force men to believe*. He *conceals Himself* in His works and in His providence, in order that He may be found only by those who seek Him. And thus, on the one hand, He made the prophecies so plain, that those who did not voluntarily deceive themselves, might understand all that was essential and important; and on the other, He left them so obscure, that those who disliked the truth should not be compelled to see it. We might with the same justice require God to perform daily miracles, to convince the despisers of His name of their folly, as desire greater clearness in the prophecies. (2) Had they possessed the clearness of history, their accomplishment would have been impossible. Had God, for example, caused the sentences just quoted to be written down; had the life of Christ, his rejection by the Jews, and its mournful consequence, the destruction of Jerusalem, been in every respect described as completely and as intelligibly, even for the

[1] ὑπὸ πνεύματος ἁγίου φερόμενοι.

carnally minded, as in the New Testament, the purpose of redemption, which required the death of Christ, could not have been accomplished. By the present character of the Messianic prophecies, on the contrary, the end of leading the pious to the manifested Messiah, was completely attained, without thereby defeating a higher and far more important plan. (3) Besides, the obscurity spread over certain portions of prophecy rendered them far more beneficial to believers, than they otherwise could have been. If, for example, the believers who lived many centuries before Christ's appearance had known that it would be so long delayed, how much would their love have been cooled, and their hope enfeebled? How could the expectation of the Messiah have become the central point of their whole religious life? Had the primitive Christians foreseen that the second coming of Christ would be deferred at least eighteen hundred years, how much feebler would have been the influence of this doctrine, than when they expected his advent every hour, and were directed to watch, because He would come as a thief in the night, in such an hour as they did not expect. (4) We have already had frequent occasion to remark, that a large part of the Messianic predictions was designed to exert an *immediate influence* upon the mass of the people, and retain them, even though it were only in profession, faithful to the Lord. This object could not have been attained had they possessed the clearness of history. It was, however, well accomplished by so ordering the prophecies, that even their misapprehension, through the fault of those to whom they were given, was attended with beneficial results. The rude and carnal people took possession of the covering, and believed they had found the substance itself ; and contributed to preserve the outward conditions required in order that the true contents of prophecy might be realized. (5) Should it be asked what end could be answered by that portion of prophecy which was obscure *in itself*, and not merely from a carnal disposition, we suggest that the Prophets, as appears from the passages already quoted from the New Testament, uttered their predictions, not merely for their contemporaries, but for posterity. For the former the perspicuous part was owing sufficient. We conclude with the words of the excellent Pascal [1], which indeed refer to the whole of revelation, but admit of special application to the prophecies : " Il y a assez de lumière pour ceux, qui ne désirent que de voir, et assez d'obscurité pour ceux, qui ont une disposition contraire.—Il y assez d'obscurité pour aveugler les reprouvez, et assez de clarté pour les condamner et les rendre inexcusables.—Le dessein de Dieu est plus de perfectionner la volonté, que l'esprit. Or la clarté parfaite ne serviroit qu'à l'esprit, et nuiroit à la volonté. S'il n'y avoit point d'obscurité, l'homme ne sentiroit pas sa corruption.   S'il n'y avoit point de lumière, l'homme n'espereroit point de remède.—Tout tourne en bien pour les élûs jusqu'aux obscuritez de l'écriture ; car ils les honorent à cause des clartez divines, qu'ils y voyent: et tout tourne en mal aux reprouvez jusqu'aux clartez; car ils les blasphêment à cause des obscuritez qu'ils n'entendent pas."

[1] Pensées sur la Religion. Amst. 1734, p. 95.

250. (V.) The *dramatic* character of the prophecies is another result of the condition of the Prophets while delivering them. Both persons and events presented themselves to their mental vision ; this is as it were the theatre on which the former appeared, speaking and acting [1]. Hence we can explain the frequent change of the speakers, some-times, as Isa. 14. 3, 4, with previous notice, often without, and we are justified in supposing that the Messiah in particular is in many places introduced as speaking [2].

251. (VI.) Lastly, from the condition of the Prophets, the opinion is proved to be correct, that the symbolical transactions which they described, were for the most part not real but only passed in vision, an opinion which (as Maimonides long since perceived [3]) the nature of them obliges us to adopt. For since the sphere of the prophets, so long as they were in ecstasy, was not the *external*, but the *internal world*, every action performed by them in this state must of necessity be *internal* also. The cases where these symbolical actions can be shown to have really been performed, are to be regarded as exceptions, in which the Prophets departed from their proper sphere [4].

THE MESSIANIC PROPHECIES
OF ISAIAH

Introductory Remarks

252. The superscription [5] places the Prophet Isaiah under the reign of the kings, Uzziah, Jotham, Ahaz, and Hezekiah ; and the correctness of this testimony can be shown with certainty from other sources. That the Prophet first came forward under king Uzziah, is evident from the superscription of the sixth chapter, which con-tains a representation of the vision by which Isaiah, in the year that Uzziah died, received his call to the prophetic office. None of the oracles found in our collection are assigned by a definite super-

---

[1] Comp. Is. 15 and 63, and Ps. 2.

[2] Comp. our remarks on Ps. 2. 16. 22. Isa. 42. 49.

[3] Comp. l. c. chap. 46. He says justly : " Absit ut Deus prophetas suos stultis vel ebriis similes reddat eosque stultorum aut furiosorum actiones facere jubeat."

[4] Comp. Jo. Smith, p. 315. *" The prophetical scene or stage upon which all appa-ritions were made to the Prophet, was his imagination :* and there all those things which God would have revealed unto him were acted over *symbolically*, as in a *masque*, in which divers persons are brought in, amongst which the Prophet himself bears a part: and therefore he, according to the exigency of this dramatical *apparatus*, must, as the other actors, perform his part, sometimes by speaking and reciting things done, propounding questions, sometimes by acting that part which in the *Drama* he was appointed to act by some others; and so not only by speaking, but by gestures and actions, come in in his due place among the rest."—See the further discussion on Hosea 1—3.

[5] Chap. 1. 1.

scription to the reign of Jotham, though weighty reasons compel us to
believe, that the prophecies from the second chapter to the fifth were
composed under him : several of the existing prophecies, from the
seventh chapter onward, belong to the reign of Ahaz ; and that he was
actively employed under Hezekiah, we learn from chapters thirty-six
to thirty-nine. We have certain accounts of his agency only until the
fifteenth year of this king, at the commencement of which the embassy of the king of Babylon came to Jerusalem [1]. He *must* therefore have exercised his office at least forty-seven years, from 759 to
713 before Christ, viz. one year under Uzziah, sixteen under Jotham,
sixteen under Ahaz, and fourteen under Hezekiah. It is however
more than probable that Isaiah lived much longer. From the statement [2] that he wrote the life of king Hezekiah, it appears that he
survived him. The account of the Talmud and the Church Fathers,
that he died a violent death under Manasseh, the successor of Hezekiah, conducts us still further. This saying, which is alluded to
even in the epistle to the Hebrews [3] (where a comparison with the
tradition shows that ' *were sawn asunder* ' must be referred to Isaiah),
has indeed been greatly corrupted by false additions ; but it has
been too widely spread, is related by writers too diverse from each
other, and is moreover in itself too probable, to have no foundation
in fact [4]. Even in the Talmud, the original tradition, which asserts
only that Isaiah was slain by Manasseh, may be distinguished from
the later embellishments. The silence of the historical books
respecting so important an occurrence has indeed been urged, but
considering the briefness of the narrative it is sufficient that [5] it is
related that ' Manasseh shed much innocent blood in Jerusalem.'
The innocent persons who were murdered, were doubtless those
who abhorred the idolatry introduced by Manasseh, and therefore
especially the Prophets ; Isaiah may have been one of them, without
being mentioned by name, particularly as, on account of his advanced
age, he had probably at that time in a great measure relinquished his
public duties [6]. The supposition that Isaiah was still alive during
part of Manasseh's reign, is favoured also by the character of the
second part of his prophecies. This contains many things (particularly the lamentations over gross idolatry, sacrifice of children, and evil
rulers) which do not suit either the times of the captivity or the reign
of the pious Hezekiah, but correspond well with that of Manasseh.

253. Nor does this supposition ascribe to Isaiah an extraordinary
old age. Allowing him to have been twenty years old, when he
entered upon his office [7], at the death of Hezekiah he would be

[1] See chap. 39.   [2] 2 Chron. 32. 32.   [3] Chap. 11. 37.
[4] Justinus Martyr, Dialog. c. Tryphone, p. 349, ed. Col. ὃν πρίονι ξυλίνῳ
ἐπρίσατε. Tertullianus de Patientiâ, c. 14. His patientiæ viribus secatur
Esaias. Lactantius, l. 4. c. 11. Esaias, quem ipsi Judæi serrâ consectum
crudelissime necaverunt. Ambros. in Luc. c. 20. Esaias, cujus facilius com-
pagem corporis serrâ divisit, quam fidem inclinavit. Augustin. de Civ. Dei,
l. 18. c. 24. Hieron. on Jes. c. 1. 10. c. 20. 27.
[5] 2 Kings 21. 16.   [6] See the introduction to chap. 40—66.
[7] That an earlier call to the prophetic office was not uncommon appears from
Jer. 1. 6.

about eighty-two; and there is no reason to suppose he may not
have lived seven or eight years longer under Manasseh. Indeed
the priest Jehoiada [1] reached the age of one hundred and thirty [2]. As
Isaiah led the abstemious ascetic life of the Prophets, we may suppose that the powers of his body and mind even in old age remained
unimpaired.

254. Isaiah was therefore contemporary with Hosea and Micah.
Of the circumstances of his life, little is known to us. He appears
to have had his permanent residence at Jerusalem. Of his agency
under Jotham, we know only what may be learned from the prophecy, chapters two to five. Probably he lived at that period in
greater seclusion on account of his youth. Under the ungodly Ahaz,
he came forth in the full power of an ambassador of God, but his
counsel and his warning were derided. Hezekiah, a worthy head of
the theocracy, was the first who acknowledged him and followed his
counsels; under the ungodly Manasseh he probably retired and
lived in the happier future, but still without entirely resigning, in
the comfortless present, his office as a reprover [3], until at last he
sealed with his death the truth for which he had lived.

255. Great respect was paid to him after his death. The historical
books, in general so very sparing in their accounts of those Prophets whose writings we possess, are comparatively full in their
notices of him; Jeremiah imitated him, and marks are found in
other prophets of the diligent reading of his productions. But at a
later period, the fulfilment of his prophecies of far distant events
(as the conquests of Cyrus, the return from captivity, the overthrow of the Babylonish monarchy) procured for the Prophet
a still higher reputation than those already fulfilled in his lifetime,
respecting the overthrow of the Syrians and the Israelites, the invasion by the Assyrians, the deliverance accomplished by the help
of God, and the extension of life for fifteen years vouchsafed to
Hezekiah, &c. Josephus relates [4] that it was by reading the prophecy of Isaiah relating to himself, that Cyrus was moved to the
acknowledgement of the God of Israel, the deliverance of the Jews,
and the rebuilding of the temple [5]. Jesus, the son of Sirach, says
of him [6]: "*Esay the Prophet, who was great and faithful in his
vision.—He saw by an excellent spirit what should come to pass at
the last, and he comforted them that mourned in Sion. He showed*

---

[1] According to 2 Chron. 24. 15.

[2] The tradition of the great age of Isaiah has been preserved among the
oriental Christians, who attribute to him an age of one hundred and twenty
years.

[3] See chap. 56—58.   [4] Antiq. Jud. 11. 1. § 12.

[5] Jahn draws attention to the circumstance, that this relation is only the
commentary on Ezra 1. 2, where Cyrus, in his edict in favour of the Jews, says:
'Jehovah the God of heaven has given me all the kingdoms of the earth, and
commanded me to build him a house at Jerusalem in Judea.' These words
plainly presuppose that Cyrus was acquainted with the prophecies, chap. 44. 28,
and chap. 45.

[6] Chap. 48. 22—25.

what should come to pass for ever, and secret things or ever they came." Philo and Josephus speak of him with equal reverence. He must, however, have attained the highest degree of authority, when the most splendid portion of his predictions was fulfilled by the appearing of Christ, and the establishment of his kingdom. The whole New Testament is interwoven, sometimes with direct quotations, and sometimes with thoughts and expressions undesignedly borrowed from his prophecies; rarely is the cardinal doctrine of Christianity, the doctrine of the vicarious satisfaction, delivered by the Apostles, without a manifest allusion to Isaiah. The writings of the Fathers are full of his praise [1].

256. Isaiah, like all the prophets, had a twofold calling; to exert an influence on the *present*, and to reveal the *future*. With respect to the former, called to be a minister of the old covenant, he pointed to its foundation, the Law, and required, above every thing else, that it should be maintained [2]. But called also to be a minister of the spirit, not of the letter, under the old covenant, his zeal was awakened against those who sought the substance in the observance of the outward form, who in their regard for that which was suited to the old covenant, and to the pupilage of mankind, forgot what was common both to the old and the new [3]. The fundamental idea which pervades his prophecies is, that the glory belongs to God alone, shame and humiliation to man; that all confidence must be placed in the Creator and not in the creature; that all help in temporal and spiritual concerns, comes from Him alone; that every inclination, every effort, which is directed towards perishing objects, instead of Him, is sinful. Hence the frequent annunciation of the ruin of all that is proud and lofty—hence his hostility against idolatry, as well as vice in general, which constantly appears to him as ingratitude to God, as treason against Him—hence his resistance to those who, when the state was oppressed by foreign enemies, expected aid from alliances with powerful and neighbouring nations. All help comes from God; He will not abandon His *faithful* covenant people; the *unfaithful* will only be plunged in still deeper distress by all their alliances and preparations for war. He constantly seeks to impress upon the minds of the people the fundamental law of the theocracy proclaimed by its author, the reciprocal relation between faithfulness towards God and prosperity; between unfaithfulness and adversity; and shows that the people should blame themselves and not God, in all their calamities; and that He, being full of mercy, is

[1] Jerome says: "Sic exponam Esaiam, ut illum non solum prophetam, sed Evangelistam et Apostolum doceam;" and in another passage, "Non prophetiam mihi videtur texere Esaias, sed evangelium;" and Augustin also remarks, de Civ. Dei, l. 18, c. 29, that in the opinion of several, his numerous predictions of Christ and the Church entitled him to the name of an evangelist rather than a prophet. When Augustin, after his conversion, inquired of Ambrose, which of the sacred books he should chiefly read, Ambrose recommended Isaiah: "quod præ ceteris evangelii vocationisque gentium sit prænuntiator apertior." Cf. Aug. Conf. 9. 5.
[2] Chap. 8. 16. 20. 30. 9. 10.
[3] Comp. e. g. chap. 1. 11, &c. 29. 13. 58. 1. &c.

ready to pardon their sins, and deliver them from their distress, if they will only return to Him.

257. In exerting an influence on the present times, the Prophet was sustained and aided by the second part of his office, that of disclosing the future, which nevertheless was designed to accomplish other and far more important objects. The predicted destruction of the kingdom of Israel, the desolation of Judah by Sennacherib, the Babylonish captivity, and the total desolation of the land, must have served, by exemplifying the law of a visible retribution, to make his censures and admonitions the more impressive; while the prediction of the deliverance from the Assyrians, and the return from the exile, must have consoled the pious, and encouraged them to be faithful. The predictions against foreign nations showed the Israelites the omnipotence of their God, and the feebleness of all that was human, and powerfully dissuaded them from trusting in the help of man; at the same time they clearly exhibited to them the retributive justice of God, which decided the fate, even of those nations to whom He had not revealed Himself, and much more, that of his covenant people. But with Isaiah, the substance of the prophecies, in a stricter sense, is the annunciation of the Messiah. A sprout of David, according to his human nature, but at the same time God from eternity, born of a virgin, at a period when the royal family of David had fallen into the deepest obscurity, will live, suffer, and die, to abolish the sins of mankind:—after his glorification, his kingdom will be founded on earth, and extended over all the heathen nations, till the earth shall be full of the knowledge and the worship of the Lord, through the Spirit, which will be poured out upon all flesh. And as Isaiah, when acting upon his contemporaries, insisted on faith in general, despair of our own strength, and confidence in the power of God; so in his Messianic predictions, he appears as a herald of faith in its stricter sense.

258. The style of Isaiah is, in general, characterized by simplicity and sublimity; in the use of imagery, he holds an intermediate place between the poverty of Jeremiah and the exuberance of Ezekiel. In other respects, the style is suited to the subject, and changes with it. In his denunciations and threatenings, he is earnest and vehement; in his consolations and instructions, mild and insinuating; in the strictly prophetic passages, full of impetuosity and fire. He so lives in the events he describes, that the future becomes to him as the past and the present[1].

---

[1] The arrangement of the collection is as follows:—The whole may be divided into two parts, the first of which embraces chaps. 1—39. Chaps. 1—12 of this part contain prophecies against Judah and Jerusalem; these stand in the correct chronological order, except that chap. 6, which contains the consecration of the Prophet, and belongs to the year in which king Uzziah died, should have been placed first. Chaps. 2—5 belong to the reign of Jotham; all the rest, as far as chap. 10. 4, to the time of Ahaz; the following, to the end of chap. 12, to that of Hezekiah. Chaps. 13—23 contain a series of prophecies respecting foreign nations, interrupted only by chap. 22. Chaps. 24—35 consist chiefly of predictions concerning Judah, which probably all belong to the reign of Hezekiah. Then follow chaps. 36—39. an historical appendix, containing

Isaiah 2-4

259. These chapters form one connected discourse, which may however be divided into three parts.

260. Chap. 2. 2—4, the Prophet describes the happy times of the Messiah, when the theocracy then limited to a single people, and greatly harassed and despised, should be extended over all mankind, true religion be propagated from Jerusalem; and, after the submission of all nations to the authority of God, all dissension and strife should cease.

261. The second part of the discourse [1] consists of admonitions, description of the prevailing corruptions, and threatening of the divine chastisement. As the Prophet had previously described the times of the Messiah in order to prepare the people for his admonition, so now, in order to arouse the ungodly from their security, and quicken the zeal of the pious, he discloses a different scene;— the divine chastisements, whereby, so far from the whole people having a part in the Messiah's kingdom, a large portion of them should be destroyed. This section is introduced by the exhortation to the people, contained in the fifth verse, to walk in the light of Jehovah, i. e. to make themselves worthy to share in this blessedness, by genuine piety. The Prophet next describes, alternately, the reigning depravity, and the Divine judgements thereby occasioned. The representation is in a great measure general; and as it is merely the application of the fundamental principles of the theocracy, that punishment necessarily follows sin, that all that is proud will be humbled, and all that is lofty abased by the Lord, it may, for the most part, with equal propriety be referred to *all* the various judgements inflicted upon the Jews, the carrying away into captivity, the capture of the city by the Romans, &c.; nay in the highest and fullest sense, the threatening will be accomplished by the last general divine judgement, to be inflicted upon those who place their trust in the creature and not in the Lord. But as is usual in the representations of the Divine judgements, there are here also some special features, which make it necessary to regard the Prophet as threatening, not only the judgements of God in general, but especially the Babylonish exile. Of this sort, e. g., is the predicted carrying away of all the nobles and handicraftsmen, chap. 3. 3, which was strikingly and literally fulfilled, when king Jehoiakim was carried away by Nebuchadnezzar [2]; and the annunciation [3] that boys and children—i. e. inexperienced and unskilful rulers—should receive the government of the state.

accounts of the agency of Isaiah, during the same period. The second part, chaps. 40—66, was probably composed in the time of Manasseh, and constitutes one connected whole.

[1] Chap. 2. 5. 4. 1.   [2] 2 Kings 24. 14.   [3] Ver. 9.

262. Chap. 4. 2—6, forms the third part of the discourse. That he might not too much discourage the pious, and at the same time might give his admonition the more effect with the ungodly, the Prophet, before he concludes, takes another survey of that happier future, with the description of which he had commenced. After the Divine chastisement, those who shall either have continued faithful to their God, or have again returned to Him, shall be exalted to happiness and glory, through a Redeemer, who shall be both God and man. The whole Church of God, which had heretofore consisted of a mixture of righteous and wicked, shall then be holy. As of old, the people of Israel in their Exodus from Egypt were led by a visible symbol of the Divine presence, so will the new Church of God enjoy his gracious presence, and be defended by it from every danger.

263. The time when the prophecy was composed, can be ascertained with considerable certainty. The state is represented as being in a flourishing and warlike condition, and the luxury which had followed wealth is especially rebuked [1]. Such was the condition of the state, according to the accounts of the historical books, in the time of Uzziah and Jotham. But the prophecy can scarcely have been composed under Uzziah, because Isaiah entered on his office in the year that Uzziah died; and also because it is probable, that in the second chapter Isaiah had before him the prophecy of Micah, who came forward first under Jotham. Nor is there any more reason to assign it to the time of Ahaz. Under him a great apostasy was followed by heavy calamities. At the very beginning of his reign, the land was invaded by the Assyrians and Ephraimites, who had already in the time of Jotham combined against Judah, and had been waiting only for the death of this king; the devastation they produced was so great, that the soil could not be cultivated for a long time afterwards, and the people were obliged to live solely on the produce of their herds [2]. Afterwards the king became tributary to the Assyrians. We are, then, compelled to assign the composition of the prophecy to the time of Jotham [3].—Our purpose requires us here to examine only the first and third part of the prophecy.

---

[1] See chap. 2. 7, and the whole latter part of chap. 3.

[2] Chap. 7. 15, 16.

[3] The mention, chap. 3. 12, of the rule of children and women, forms no objection, since by נְשִׁים not precisely the kings are meant, but in general, the leaders of the people; nor the mention of idolatry, since that continued under Jotham, although he himself was devoted to the service of God.

264. *And it shall come to pass in the last time, that the mountain of the house of Jehovah shall be firmly established on the top of the mountains, exalted above the hills, and all nations shall stream to it. And many nations shall go and say, Come, let us repair to the mountain of Jehovah, and to the house of the God of Jacob, that he may teach us his ways, and we may walk in his paths. For from Zion shall go forth the law, and the word of Jehovah from Jerusalem. Then will Jehovah be a judge between the people, and rebuke many nations; they shall beat their swords into ploughshares, and their spears into pruninghooks; no people shall lift up the sword against another; they shall learn war no more.*

265. This section, with some unimportant changes, is found also in the Prophet Micah[1]. As to the manner in which this fact is to be explained, there is a difference of opinion amongst commentators. Some assume that Micah made use of Isaiah, others that Isaiah made use of Micah: others, again, that *both prophets* availed themselves of some well-known earlier prophecy. Of these the most probable opinion is that Isaiah made use of Micah: for (1) The prediction in Isaiah is disconnected with what goes before, and yet begins with the copulative Vav; in Micah, on the contrary, it stands in connexion with what precedes and follows. If the passage were as disconnected in Micah, as in Isaiah, then, indeed, we might suppose that both had taken a more ancient oracle, and prefixed it to their prophecies, as a sort of text, or motto. This, however, is not the case. (2) In the discourses of the Prophets, the promise usually follows the threatening: this order is observed by Micah; in Isaiah, on the contrary, the promise contained in this passage precedes the threatening, and another promise follows. This of itself renders it probable that Isaiah first described the view of futurity, which was disclosed to him, in the words of a prophecy, which perhaps at that time had attracted special attention, in order that afterwards, when following the usual course, he should return to the promise, he might give it in his own words.—The older theologians supposed in such cases that the passages were communicated alike to both the sacred writers by the Holy Spirit. The truth here lies between this view of the subject, and that adopted in recent times. The *same vision* was granted to Micah and Isaiah; the *substance* could not have been borrowed, since all was disclosed to the Prophets in vision, and therefore immediately. But one *may* have borrowed from the other, when clothing in words that which was given to him in vision. In the case before us, Isaiah, who uttered his predictions after Micah,

---

[1] Chap. 4. 1—3.

may have remembered a prophecy of that prophet, and availed himself in a great measure of its words, because they seemed to him
best suited to express the views he had received. In accordance
with this are the sentiments of Abarbanel.

266. The phrase here translated ' *in the last time* [1] ' originally signifies any period of future time, whether nearer or more distant [2].
Commonly however the prophets used it in a stricter sense, of the
time of the Messiah, because the *definite time* was unknown to them [3].
By ' *the mountain of the Lord's house* ' is to be understood, either
the hill Moriah alone upon which the Temple was built, or the whole
mountain of Zion, of which Moriah was considered as a part;
whence it is so often said, in Scripture, even after the ark of the
covenant had been brought from Zion to Moriah, that God dwells
in Zion.   The poetical representations may be either [4] as if other
great mountains, Sinai, Lebanon, and Bashan, should run together,
and place themselves one upon another beneath it, elevating it upon
their snowy summit, so that it could be seen to the ends of the
earth ; or it may be supposed that the expression ' *it shall be established on the top of the mountains*,' implies that it will be so exalted,
as to be far above all other mountains, the loftiest of which shall
appear to serve, as it were, for its foundation.   Here therefore it is
said, that the small and inconsiderable temple-mountain shall hereafter be exalted and remain above all the mountains of the earth.
The question now arises, in what sense is this to be taken [5].   That
the elevation of the mountain is *moral* and not *physical*, is acknowledged by all judicious interpreters.   But it may still be asked,
whether we are to look for the figure in the *exaltation alone*, or in
the *mountain* also.   The latter explanation is adopted by those
among the Fathers, as Jerome, Augustin, and Tertullian, who understand by the mountain Christ.   It is manifest, however, that this
interpretation is arbitrary, not resulting from any necessary relation
between the figure and the reality.—No less arbitrary is the explanation of several other Christian interpreters, who think that the
Church of Christ is particularly designated by the *mountain of the
Lord's house*.   Those come nearer the truth, who understand the
theocracy to be intended by it, by a metonymy of the *place* for the
thing placed there.   The sense will then be : *the theocracy, before
limited to a single people, shall hereafter be enlarged, and extended over all nations ; the religion of the Israelites, which had its
chief seat on mount Zion, shall gain the victory over all false
religions.*   Thus Michaelis and others.—But the following verse,

---

[1] אַחֲרִית הַיָּמִים
[2] In this sense it occurs Gen. 49. 1. Dan. 2. 28.
[3] 1 Pet. 1. 11.
[4] According to Michaelis.
[5] *Some* among the Jews understood it entirely according to the letter, and
supposed, that in the days of the Messiah, God would bring down Mount Tabor,
and Carmel, and place Jerusalem upon their summit.

where Zion and Jerusalem *must* be taken literally, renders it more probable, that here also the figure is to be confined to the *exaltation*, and the mountain is to be taken literally. But in what way then shall the mountain of the Lord's house become more illustrious than all the other mountains of the earth? Because upon it, or at Jerusalem, the glory of the Lord shall be more clearly revealed, than in any other place: indeed from thence shall the true religion, to be founded by the Messiah, be extended over the whole world.—A parallel passage is found in Ezekiel [1]: ' *In the visions of God brought He me into the land of Israel, and placed me* on a very high mountain: *upon it was as a built city.*' Here also the Prophet beholds the comparatively insignificant hill of Zion exalted in the time of the Messiah. The passage is also illustrated by the sixteenth and seventeenth verses of the sixty-eighth Psalm, where the neighbouring loftier mountains are represented as envious of the preference given to mount Zion by Jehovah, in choosing it as his dwelling-place. Jarchi strikingly remarks, that the predicted elevation of the mountain of the Lord's house above all mountains, at the same time expresses the superiority of the revelation of the Divine glory, about to be made upon it, over all its manifestations before the coming of the Messiah: ' *The sign which shall be given on that mountain shall be greater than the signs that were given on Sinai, on Carmel, or on Tabor.*'—' *And all nations shall stream to it [2].*' The reception of the heathen into the theocracy, glorified by the appearance of the Messiah, is here figuratively represented, as if they were all journeying to mount Zion, then exalted above all mountains, and serving them as it were for a banner. Then particularly shall be fulfilled the promise, constantly repeated even in Genesis, that the religion of Abraham should at a future period be extended to all the heathen nations.

267. The representation in the third verse is metaphorical. All the Israelites were obliged to appear annually before the Lord in his temple, to show their reverence for him, and be instructed in his ways. The image is taken from these pilgrimages to Jerusalem. At that time, not merely one single people, but all the nations of the earth shall go up to the seat of the true God: all nations, that is, shall return to the worship of the true God, and embrace his revealed religion, which shall be preached from Jerusalem to all mankind. The nations who receive the annunciation of the true religion made from Jerusalem, are figuratively represented as proceeding thither to be instructed in its truths. To indicate the zeal with which the nations should press to the mountain of Jehovah, the Prophet represents them as *exhorting* and *urging* each other onward: ' *Come, let us repair,*' &c. Altogether similar is the prophecy of Zechariah [3]: ' *The inhabitants of one city shall go to another and say, Let*

---

[1] Chap. 40. 2.

[2] The verb נָהַר, *to flow*, then, *to stream to*. The preterite is determined to be the future by the preceding future. In the use of the tenses the Prophets are very inaccurate, since they beheld all in the present.

[3] Chap. 8. 21, 22.

us go to pray before the Lord, and to seek the Lord of Hosts, we will also go with you,' &c. The heathen will first obtain the knowledge of religion, and then live in accordance with its dictates. " The teacher (as Kimchi well remarks) is the king Messiah." The true religion shall be extended to the heathen, particularly through the Messiah, according to the constant predictions of the Prophets. The last words, ' *for from Zion shall go forth the law, and the word of the Lord from Jerusalem,*' are not spoken by the people exhorting one another, but by the Prophet. In them he gives the reason why the nations journey with such zeal to *Jerusalem.* According to several interpreters, Zion and Jerusalem are here an image of the theocracy. The sense would then be, the people shall seek access to the theocracy, because in it only is the true revelation of God to be found. But it is much better to understand Zion and Jerusalem literally. At Jerusalem the glorious revelation of God by the Messiah shall take place ; from thence shall the knowledge of it be extended to all the heathen nations ; therefore are all their eyes directed thither [1]. What the Prophet here says literally, Ezekiel expresses in figurative language [2], representing the extension of the true religion from Jerusalem over the whole earth, under the image of a river, which springs up in the temple, and then flows forth [3].

268. In the first two members of the fourth verse, the subject is not expressed; but there can be no doubt that Jehovah is meant, who should accomplish, through the Messiah, what is here attributed to him. According to Calvin and Vitringa, ' *he will judge among the nations*' is equivalent to he *will reign, will have his throne among them.* But though the verbs which signify *to judge,* in the Shemitish languages have for the most part the secondary meaning *to reign,* because, in ancient times, both functions were usually combined in one person ; yet this cannot be the case in the instance before us ; because from what follows, ' *and they shall beat their swords,*' &c. (which indicates the effect of this judging), it appears that the word is to be limited to the settling of disputes prevailing among them [4]. The sense then is : *the nations which have hitherto selfishly followed each one its own interest, and allowed themselves in manifold acts of injustice towards each other, shall then acknowledge Jehovah as their common judge. His spirit and word shall convince the aggressor of his misconduct* (as the umpire shows to each of the contending parties his injustice), *settle every controversy,*

---

[1] Theodoret. οὗτος ὁ εὐαγγελικὸς λόγος ἀπὸ τῆς Ἰερουσαλὴμ οἷον ἀπό τινος πηγῆς ἀρξάμενος πᾶσαν τὴν οἰκουμένην διέδραμε, τοῖς μετὰ πίστεως προσιοῦσι τὴν ἀρδείαν προσφέρων.

[2] Chap. 47. 1, &c.

[3] See also Zech. 14. 8. The word תּוֹרָה properly *law*, stands here for religion in general, entirely synonymous with דְּבַר יְהוָֹה, *the word of Jehovah.* In like manner מִשְׁפָּט chap. 42. 1—4, and νόμος in the New Testament, Rom. 3. 27.

[4] Which meaning also is required even by the construction of the verb with בֵּין· שׁפט with בֵּין *to judge between,* to act the part of an umpire between two contending parties. The verb הוֹכִיחַ *to show, to prove,* then with לְ *to convince any one of a fault, to instruct, to rebuke.* See Gesenius, s. v.

and produce general quietness and peace[1]. The Divine doctrine and the Divine life shall prevail among all people, and unite them in the bonds of love and harmony[2].—It now remains to make some remarks on the whole prophecy.

269. (1) Even Theodoret had occasion to refute those who referred it to the condition of the Jews after their return from the Babylonish captivity[3]. In this prophecy, the characteristic marks are given, which, in the Messianic predictions of all the Prophets, and especially in those of Isaiah, are attributed to the time of the Messiah: first, the extension of the religion of Jehovah over the whole earth[4]: then, universal peace[5].

270. (2) The prophecy belongs to that class, in which the *person* of the Messiah is not described, but only the *nature of his kingdom*. We have before shown, in the general introduction, that it cannot be inferred from this, that the hopes of the Prophet were not connected with a *personal Messiah*. Gesenius ascribes to him the idea that the conversion of the heathen was to be effected by the *prophets*. But this is contradicted by the following reasons. (1) The notion that the Prophets were to be the mediators of the new covenant, which should embrace the heathen also, is found neither in Isaiah nor in any other Prophet[6]. (2) Not only do precisely the same traits that are found in this portion, occur in the other *personal* Messianic predictions of Isaiah, but the Messiah appears as a person, even in the prophecy, chap. 4, which is a continuation and completion of the same discourse, of which the passage before us forms a part[7]. (3) According to Gesenius's own opinion, this portion is a fragment from the larger prediction of Micah[8]. But in that, there is first a passing allusion to the person of the Messiah[9], and afterwards he is *fully* described in his *person* and his *office*[10]. Isaiah,

---

[1] The images under which this peace is then exhibited, are not unusual in heathen poets. Martial, 14. 34.

" Pax me certa ducis placidos curvavit in usus:
     Agricolæ nunc sum, militis ante fui."

On the contrary, Joel 4. 10. Virg. Georg. 1. 506. Ovid. Fast. 1. 697, the change from peace to war is represented under the image of a conversion of the instruments of agriculture into swords and spears.

[2] אֵת an instrument of agriculture, which cannot be certainly determined; that it differed from מַחֲרֵשָׁה *a plough*, appears from 1 Sam. 13. 20, 21.

[3] Among recent interpreters, this reference is approved by Dathe, Hensler, and Vogel, while Grotius refers it entirely to the time when the city was delivered from the siege of Rezin and Pekah. But how untenable this view is, appears from its requiring the third verse to be referred to the peace, which should be granted to the Jews by the Persians and other nations; since that verse does not speak concerning the friendly conduct of the heathen nations towards the Jews, but that which God should cause these nations to show towards one another.

[4] See e. g. chap. 9. 6. 11. 10. 19. 18, &c. 42. 49. 53. 60. Ps. 22. 28.

[5] See e. g. chap. 9. 4. 11. 6—9. Ps. 72. 3. Zech. 9. 10.

[6] See the refutation of this hypothesis at chap. 53.

[7] Gesenius himself says, 1. s. 224, " Isaiah is accustomed to connect the hope of the better times with a king."

[8] Chap. 4. 5.   [9] Chap. 4. 5.   [10] Chap. 5. 1, &c.

therefore, could expect nothing else, than that his hearers and readers would connect the hopes here expressed with the same subject, with which they had been connected in the well-known prediction of Micah. Precisely for this reason it was superfluous to point out the person of the Messiah, as every one would of himself refer the prophecy to him.

271. (3) The Jews urge against the fulfilment of this prophecy in Christ, that the peace here predicted did not follow the introduction of Christianity, but on the contrary many and bloody wars have since been waged. This objection has caused much difficulty to Christian interpreters, because they erroneously supposed that we must look for the complete fulfilment in an early period of the Christian dispensation. Several of the Fathers (Theodoret, Cyril, Eusebius, Chrysostom) refer the prophecy to the external peace which prevailed in the Roman empire at the introduction of the Christian religion. But this is a very unfortunate hypothesis, since the peace here described is not to be the result of external causes, but an effect of the reception of the true religion. The view of those is nearer the truth, who think that the Prophet represents, not so much what would *actually happen*, as what the Gospel *would be suited to effect*, and *would effect*, in all those who should embrace it by a true faith [1]. But this explanation is also unsatisfactory. It is the uniform doctrine of the Prophets, that, after every opposing enemy of the kingdom of God shall have been subdued, it will be exalted to a glorified condition, in which the peace, whereby its members had been inwardly blessed, shall also outwardly prevail in the whole conduct of the people, nay even in the irrational part of the creation ; and all discord, which originated with the fall of man, and all destruction shall cease [2]. To this period this prediction also in its highest sense refers. It has already been fulfilled, in so far as every member of the Messianic kingdom has acquired a peaceful disposition, and Christianity has influenced the conduct of whole nations, and softened their former cruelty into comparative mildness. The Prophet here, as usual, overlooks the gradual development of the Messiah's kingdom, and embraces its commencement and its termination in the same description. This is true also in reference to the predicted conversion of all the heathen nations. Its fulfilment has already *commenced ;* its *completion* will follow in future times. It must however be observed, that the spiritual eye of the Prophet is here attracted to *the one prominent* side of the picture ; *the other* therefore remains unnoticed in his description. It is the uniform doctrine of the Prophets, and of the New Testament, that a large portion of

---

[1] Thus the author of the *Dialogus cum Tryphone*, in a beautiful passage, from which we must here quote : οἵτινες ἀπὸ τοῦ νόμου καὶ τοῦ λόγου τοῦ ἐπελθόντος ἀπὸ Ἱερουσαλὴμ διὰ τῶν τοῦ Ἰησοῦ ἀποστόλων τὴν θεοσέβειαν ἐπιγνόντες ἐπὶ τὸν θεὸν Ἰακὼβ καὶ θεὸν Ἰσραὴλ κατεφύγομεν καὶ οἱ πολέμου καὶ ἀλληλοφονίας καὶ πάσης κακίας μεμεστωμένοι, ἀπὸ πάσης τῆς γῆς τὰ πολεμικὰ ὄργανα ἕκαστος τὰς μαχαίρας εἰς ἄροτρα καὶ τὰς σιβύνας εἰς γεωργικὰ μετεβάλομεν, καὶ γεωργοῦμεν εὐσέβειαν, δικαιοσύνην, φιλανθρωπίαν, πίστιν, ἐλπίδα, κ. τ. λ.

[2] See e. g. chap. 11. 6, 7.

mankind will persist in rejecting salvation, and consequently be destroyed by a Divine judgement before the kingdom of God shall be glorified. We can therefore infer from this prophecy only, that the saving power of the Gospel shall hereafter be extended to a much greater portion of mankind, than it has hitherto been.

272. (4) Michaelis and Palm, after the example of the Jews, refer this prophecy to a time when Jehovah will establish his residence at Zion ; and thence extend his reign over all nations united in one theocracy. This view originates here, as well as in other places, from not perceiving the figurative character of the prophetic discourse ; the inconsistency of such an erroneous literal explanation, is manifest from the fact, that its defenders themselves are obliged to understand the *exaltation of the mountain of the Lord's house* figuratively.

ISAIAH 4. 2, SEQ.

273. The Prophet having in the preceding part sought to give effect to his admonition by announcing the Divine judgement which threatened obstinate sinners, now endeavours to accomplish the same purpose, by describing the happiness which those who remained faithful should enjoy, after the destruction of the wicked[1].

274. Verse 2. ' *Then will the sprout of Jehovah serve for decoration and for honour, the fruit of the land for exaltation and for ornament, to the escaped of Israel*[2].' As the Messianic represen-- tation, in this passage as well as the foregoing one, embraces the beginning and the end of the Messiah's kingdom, so the determination of time by no means implies that the Divine judgements threatened against the covenant people in the preceding part, will be inflicted before the commencement of the times of the Messiah. To the Prophet, who beheld all in *vision* and therefore as *present*, the judgements in the foregoing portion were presented as combined in one picture ; here, on the contrary, he beholds in the same manner the blessings of the Messiah's reign ; the ' *then* ' properly relates, not so much to the succession of events in reality, as in the vision of the Prophet. We must not so much regard the *determination of time*, as the *main thought* (which runs through all the Messianic predictions of Isaiah, and has been confirmed by history), that *not all* the members of the visible theocracy, but only the *pious part of them* would share in the blessings of the Messiah's kingdom[3].

---

[1] Chrysostom : ἐπειδὴ σφόδρα κατέσεισε τὴν διάνοιαν αὐτῶν τῇ τῶν λυ- πηρῶν ἀπειλῇ καὶ τὴν συμφορὰν ἱκανῶς ἐτραγῴδησε καὶ μακρὸν ἀπέτεινε λό- γον τὰ φόβερα διηγούμενος, μεταβάλλει λοιπὸν ἐπὶ τὰ χρηστότερα. Τοῦτο γὰρ ἰατρείας ἀρίστης τρόπος μὴ καίειν μηδὲ τέμνειν μόνον, ἀλλὰ καὶ τὰς ἐκεῖθεν γινομένας ὀδύνας προσηνέσι παραμυθεῖσθαι φαρμάκοις.

[2] *Then*, i. e. after the judgments.

[3] After Grotius, Dathe, Vogel, Michaelis, Koppe, and Augusti, Gesenius understands by it the *new increase of the people* after their defeats. He explains

275. (1) By '*the Sprout of Jehovah*' must be understood the Messiah; who is often represented in Scripture under the image of a *sprout* or *shoot*[1]. That *Branch* or *Sprout of Jehovah* is synonymous with *Son of Jehovah*, appears from the following reasons. (1) *Jehovah* generally stands in contrast with the *Sprout of David*. If this means a *son* of David, so also must *Sprout of Jehovah* designate a *son* of Jehovah in the proper sense. (2) *Sprout of Jehovah* in this passage stands in opposition to *fruit of the land*[2]. As now *the fruit of the land* (= *Judea*) designates him who was to be born in Judah, or *spring from the house of Judah*, so also *Branch of Jehovah* can refer only to his origin. (3) The only objection which has been brought against this explanation is, that in the time of Isaiah there could have been no knowledge of the Divine and human nature of the Messiah. But this assertion is already sufficiently refuted by the prophecy of Micah, which Isaiah had before him when he composed this prophetical discourse. There[3], in a manner altogether similar, the *temporal birth* of the Messiah at Bethlehem (= *fruit of the land*), and his *everlasting procession from the Father* (= *Branch of Jehovah*), are placed in intimate connexion. If we refer to Isaiah himself, not only are the temporal birth of the Messiah[4] and his Divine dignity (contained in the name *Immanuel*) contrasted, but we find precisely the same antithesis as in the passage before us[5], '*unto us a child is born*' (= *fruit of the land*); '*unto us a Son of God*[6] is given*' (= *Branch of Jehovah*[7]).—' *The escaped of Israel*,' is a designation of the pious portion of the people, who, spared in the threatened judgements of God, shall now participate in the blessings of the Messiah's reign. The sense of this verse then is, *While the people shall be visited with a severe Divine punishment, a small remnant shall remain faithful to Jehovah, whom a Divine Redeemer shall bless, make happy, and glorify.*

276. Verse 3. '*And he that remains in Zion, and is left in Jerusalem, shall be called holy; every one who is written among the living in Jerusalem*[8].' In respect to the words *in Zion* and *in Jerusalem*, the idea of *place* is not to be urged. *Zion* and *Jerusalem*, as the seat of the theocracy, stand here for the *covenant people*, who, in the

it thus : "Then again will the Sprout of Jehovah be splendid and glorious, and the fruit of the land excellent and beautiful for the delivered of Israel.—Fruit of the land is taken in a literal sense, and understood to mean the produce of the land." For the objections to this see Hengstenberg, p. 34, vol. 1. pt. 2 :—p. 300 Am. Translation.

[1] Chap. 11. 1. 10. 53. 2, and in reference to the same image, ver. 8, '*he was cut off.*' Rev. 5. 5, '*root of David.*' Jer. 23. 5. 33. 15. Zech. 3. 8. 6. 12, the man whose name is *the* BRANCH.

[2] Vitringa and others translate the words, *fruit of the earth*, and understand by them the Messiah according to his human nature.

[3] Chap. 5. 1.   [4] Chap. 7. 14.   [5] Chap. 9. 6.

[6] So Hengstenberg.

[7] The Seventy who translate ἐπιλάμψει ὁ Θεὸς, and the Syriac interpreters, *erit ortus domini*, have understood the word צמח of the *rising* of the sun, although it never has this meaning, but is used only of the *springing forth* of plants.

[8] The collectives הַפִּשְׁאָר and הַנּוֹתָר are synonymous with פְּלֵיטַת יִשְׂרָאֵל in the preceding verse.

vision of the Prophet, cannot be separated from their place of residence. That *local limitation* was not the purpose of the Prophet, appears from the following verse, where, in connexion with Jerusalem, the other cities are mentioned, and the idea of the covenant people in a comprehensive sense is thus expressed. According to the usual idiom of Isaiah, ' *shall be called,*' stands for ' *shall be.*' ' *Holy*' must be taken in its full import[1]: it points out an *essential difference* between the kingdom of the Messiah, and the former theocracy : whilst in the theocracy the pious and the ungodly were mingled together; in the new kingdom of God, after the great separation between the righteous and the wicked, those only shall have a part, who represent in their lives the holiness of its Head, and thus fulfil the requisition, ' *Be ye holy, for I am holy.*' This is the constant doctrine of the Prophets. In the ninth verse of the eleventh chapter, ' *They shall not sin nor destroy on all my holy mountain, for the land is full of the knowledge of the Lord, as the water covers the bottom of the sea.*' The ground of this holiness is stated in the fifty-third chapter; the eminent servant and Son of God (who, as is said in the second verse, shall be for decoration and for ornament to the members of his kingdom) will cleanse and justify by his vicarious sufferings the human race sunk in sin. Jeremiah and Ezekiel predict, that in the times of the Messiah God will give a new heart of flesh in place of the heart of stone.—In the last words, ' *every one that is written among the living in Jerusalem,*' the figure is taken from the custom of *enrolling the names of the citizens in a list.* In the ninth verse of the thirteenth chapter of Ezekiel, ' *they shall not be* written in the catalogue of the house of Israel,' is identical with the parallel phrase, ' *they shall not remain in the assembly of my people.*' Such a book is here, and in other passages of Scripture, figuratively attributed also to Jehovah. To *enter the name* of any one in this book is to appoint him to *life ;* to *blot out the name* of any one, is to appoint him to *death.* In the thirty-second verse of the thirty-second chapter of Exodus, Moses, after the Israelites had sinned by worshipping the golden calf, prays, ' *Now forgive their sin ; if not,* blot me also out of Thy book, which Thou hast written,' *i. e.* ' *slay* me[2].' In the first instance then, those who are written among the living, are no other than the *escaped,* those *who were left in Zion, and remained in Jerusalem,* of the preceding verse. And the sense of the verse is : ' *the faithful servants of Jehovah, who shall be spared during the heavy judgements to be inflicted by Him, shall constitute a select and holy company.*'—' *Life* ' is here used in a pregnant sense, = *happiness.* The ungodly shall indeed all perish by the Divine judgements, but the godly shall be preserved, and participate in the blessedness of the Messiah's reign[3].

---

[1] Koppe translates the word (קָדוֹשׁ) ' *inviolable ;*' Michaelis translates it ' *holy,*' but limits it to the renunciation of idolatry.

[2] See Psalm 69. 29. 139. 16.

[3] In this pregnant sense: to appoint to *true life,* to *happiness,* to a *participation in all the privileges* of the Messiah's kingdom, the expression occurs, among other places, Dan. 12. 1. Apoc. 3. 5. 13. 8. 20. 15. 22. 19. Phil. 4. 3. Luke 10. 20. So

277. Verse 4. This happy condition of the chosen will be introduced, ' *when Jehovah has washed away the filth of the daughters of
Zion, and removed the blood-guiltiness of Jerusalem from the midst of
her, by the spirit which will judge and burn*[1].' The Prophet here
returns to the punishments which shall overtake the ungodly, while
the pious partake in the blessings of the Messiah's kingdom.
Daughters of Zion, and *of Jerusalem*, according to Gesenius, is a
poetical enunciation for all the *inhabitants* of Jerusalem. But this
explanation is inadmissible. (1) Because not the *sons of Jerusalem*,
but *Jerusalem itself* is contrasted with the *daughters of Zion*; but
there is surely no reason to understand by *Jerusalem* only its *male
inhabitants*. (2) The figure is also entirely unsuitable. It cannot
be said of the *sinful inhabitants* who were devoted to destruction,
that their sins should be *washed away*; this expression would be
proper, only upon the supposition, that Jehovah still designed to
grant them forgiveness and mercy. It may however well be said of
the *city*[2], that Jehovah *purifies it from sin* when he *destroys the
sinners*. We must therefore, with Rosenmüller and others, understand by daughters of Zion, the remaining cities of Judea. It is a
usual figure with the orientals, to regard the capital as the mother,
and the other cities as her daughters[3]. The same image lies at the
foundation in the ninth verse of the fortieth chapter, where Zion, as
the *mother*, is called upon to announce to the remaining cities of Judah,
as her *daughters*, the joyful tidings of redemption.—Sins are here
represented under the image, common among all nations, of physical
impurities. *Blood*[4], or *blood-guiltiness*, includes also robbery, oppression, and in general all aggravated crimes. The washing away of
sin from Jerusalem and the remaining cities, or, without a figure,
the putting an end to sins, is effected by ' the *Spirit of judgement and
the Spirit of burning*;' *i. e.* by a judging and burning Spirit. The
Spirit of God is the Divine power by which He operates upon and
fills the creation; the source of physical and moral life, which pene-
trates the dead mass, and gives it form and expression; the bond of
union between the Creator and the creatures He has made[5]. It is
this Spirit by whom God upholds and rules the world. In the
sixteenth verse of the second chapter of the second book of Kings
the disciples of the Prophet believed Him to have taken away Elisha.
Hence the judgement upon the ungodly is here also represented as
executed by Him[6].

of old the Chaldee paraphrast: " all those appointed to eternal life shall see
the consolation of Jerusalem, *i. e.* the Messiah."

[1] Several fathers explain the verse of a purification of the better portion of the
people. So Theodoret: κάθαρσιν δὲ τὴν διὰ λουτροῦ παλιγγενεσίας προλέγει.
But this explanation is obviously unnatural.

[2] To which also מְקִרְבָּהּ leads us.

[3] See Jos. 17. 16. 1 Chron. 18. 1. It is a strange remark of Gesenius, that
this is indeed a geographical, but not a poetical expression, since manifestly it
can only have passed over from the language of poetry into that of geography.

[4] ·דמים.   [5] Gen. 1. 2. Psalm 104. 30. Job 33. 4.

[6] בָּעֵר is the Infin. Nominasc. in Piel. Of the two senses of the verb in Piel,
to burn and *to take away*, several interpreters here prefer the latter; but the

278. Verse 5. '*And Jehovah creates over the whole place of mount Zion, and over her assemblies, a cloud by day and a column of smoke, and the splendour of a flaming fire by night. For around all that is glorious there is a covering.*' The figure is here taken from the journey of the Israelites through the desert. During that journey they were guided, and at the same time protected, by a visible symbol of God's gracious presence, a Shekinah as the Jews call it. By night it resembled a pillar of smoke, which allowed the fiery splendour enclosed in the midst of it to shine through [1]; by day it assumed more the form of a cloud, as it was then more spread out [2]. This phenomenon was: (1) *A sign of the Divine presence* suited to the necessities of an unrefined people, which afterwards settled over the ark of the covenant in the holy of holies [3]. It was Jehovah's seat, whence his commands and answers to the inquiries of the Israelites were issued. Its varied aspect, now pleasing, now terrific, revealed the corresponding intentions of God towards his people [4]. The ungodly were consumed by fire, which fell from this cloud [5]. (2) It served the Israelites for *guidance, defence,* and *protection.* It pointed out the direction which they should take in their journey through the desolate wilderness [6]. During the passage through the Red Sea, it stood between them and their foes, and prevented them from coming near each other. Lightning darted down from it upon their enemies, and threw them into confusion [7]. By day, when it spread itself out, it afforded them protection from the heat of the sun [8]. A similar favour shall, after the coming of the Messiah, be vouchsafed to his purified and holy Church. The figure includes two things, the *Divine presence,* and the *Divine protection;* both have *to a certain extent* been experienced by the Church, since the coming of the Redeemer: as God in Christ was really present with men, and since his glorification has been and is present with his Church, filling it with his Spirit, so also does He defend it from every danger: but at the completion of the Messiah's kingdom the prediction will be *perfectly fulfilled,* in a way which can now only be conjectured [9]. The assemblies meant are *festival assemblies,*

---

former, which also occurs chap. 40. 16 and 44. 15, and which the Seventy adopt, πνεύματι καύσεως, gives a far better meaning. The image is taken from a *fire, in which impure metal is melted;* and as the fire separates the dross, so would the Divine spirit of judgement separate the ungodly. See Ezek. 22. 21. ' *Yea I will gather you and* blow upon you the fire of my wrath, and ye shall be melted therein,' or the figure may be from *stubble,* which is consumed by fire, Mal. 3. 19. In a manner altogether similar it is said, Matt. 3. 11, that Christ would baptize the ungodly with fire.

[1] עָשָׁן וְנֹגַהּ אֵשׁ לֶהָבָה.　　　　　　　[2] עָנָן.
[3] Ex. 40. 34, &c. 1 Kings 8. 10.　　　　　　[4] Ex. 16. 10.
[5] Lev. 10. Num. 16.　　　[6] Ex. 13. 21.　　　[7] Ex. 14. 19—24.
[8] Num. 10. 34. Ps. 105. 39.

[9] Parallel is chap. 60. 1, where it is said כְּבוֹד יְהֹוָה, his gracious presence shall arise upon the Church. See 19. 20. Zech. 2. 10. Theodoret says: ἡνίκα τὸν Ἰσραὴλ ὁ θεὸς ἠλευθέρωσε τῆς τῶν Αἰγυπτίων δουλείας, ἦγεν αὐτὸν νεφέλης ἐπικειμένης καὶ νύκτωρ μὲν δαδουχούσης καὶ τοῦ φωτὸς χωρηγούσης τὴν χρείαν, μεθ᾽ ἡμέραν δὲ σκηνὴν καὶ ὄροφον μιμουμένης καὶ τῆς ἡλιακῆς

assemblies for the praise of God [1]. Whereas heretofore the symbol of the Divine presence dwelt in the holy of holies [2], which no man except the high-priest, and he only once a year, might enter ; in the time of the Messiah, *the immediate presence of God will be experienced in every assembly of his saints* [3] ; ' *for around all that is glorious there is a covering.*' The reason is here given, *why* God would cause his mercy to rule over the glorified church. As men are accustomed carefully to wrap up and guard costly articles, lest they should be injured, so when the Church of God is adorned with illustrious virtues, He surrounds it with his mercy, and guards it from every danger [4].

279. Ver. 6. ' *And there shall be a tabernacle for a shade by day from the heat, and for a protection and for a refuge from storm and rain.*' The simple meaning is, God guards his Church from every danger. Affliction and trouble can no more injure it, than the heat and rain can injure him who is under the covering of a thick tent. That which affords this protection to the Church will be the gracious presence of Jehovah, mentioned in the foregoing verse.

280. We have now only to add a few general remarks.—(1) The opinion of those who [5] think the prophecy was fulfilled in the latter half of Hezekiah's reign, refutes itself. By the ' *sprout of Jehovah*' can be intended neither the Jewish people, planted by God, nor king Hezekiah, but only the Messiah. The errour into which these interpreters have fallen is the more manifest, since they themselves adopt the Messianic interpretation of the twentieth chapter, which obviously must refer to the same times.

281. (2.) The comparison of the prophecy of the Messiah, in the second chapter, with this, shows very clearly, how necessary it is to consider the individual Messianic prophecies only as *fragments*, which supply each other's deficiencies, since commonly only partial views of the object were exhibited to the spiritual eye of the Prophet. As an important deficiency in the representation in the second chapter is supplied by this, in the mention of a *personal* Messiah ; so on the contrary a deficiency in *this* is supplied by the predicted *participation of the heathen* in the blessings of the Messiah's kingdom, which is found in *that.*

ἀκτῖνος τὸ λυποῦν ἀπειργούσης. Τούτων ἀπολαύσειν νοητῶς μετὰ τὴν τοῦ σωτῆρος ἡμῶν ἐπιφάνειαν τοὺς εἰς αὐτὸν πεπιστευκότας ἡ προφητεία προλέγει καὶ διὰ τῆς νεφέλης ταύτης ἀπαλλαγήσεσθαι τοῦ ὑετοῦ σκληρότητος καὶ καύματος καταφλέγοντος.

[1] Others render מקראים *places of assembling;* but the word never has this meaning.
[2] 1 Kings 8.   [3] Ver. 3.
[4] חֻפָּה a noun, *covering, case;* not, as Gesenius takes it, the preterite in Pual. See the original work.
[5] As Michaelis and Palm.

Isaiah 7

282. The remarkable prophecy contained in this chapter is preceded by an historical introduction. Rezin, king of Damascene Syria, and Pekah, king of Israel, had even during the reign of Jotham combined against the kingdom of Judah ; and, about the beginning of the reign of Ahaz, they invaded the land with a formidable army [1]. The unbelieving king Ahaz was greatly alarmed ; instead of putting his trust in Jehovah, he believed he could obtain deliverance only by an alliance with the Assyrians, and resolved to send an embassy to them with presents. Such an alliance threatened the theocracy with the greatest danger, partly because every sin against the theocracy, according to its law of visible retribution, must be expiated by a visible Divine judgement ; and such a sin would here be committed, since the confidence, which belonged to God alone, would be withdrawn from Him, and reposed in men ; and partly because, in a political point of view, an alliance with a warlike power greatly superior, and intent only on its own aggrandizement, was much more dangerous to the Jewish state, than even the present war. The Prophet Isaiah, called by his office to guard the Divine rights, and to avert the danger which must spring from their violation, by warnings, admonitions, threatenings, and promises, is sent to Ahaz to inspire him with courage and confidence in God, just as he is employed before the city in making the necessary arrangements to cut off the advancing hostile army from its supplies of water. The Prophet first seeks to work upon the mind of the king, who was probably surrounded by his nobles, and a multitude of the common people, by taking with him his son [2], whose symbolical name, which contained a prediction of the *future destinies* of the nation, indicated that the king's fear that the state would be utterly destroyed, was unfounded. The king being thus prepared, the Prophet next endeavours to make upon him a deeper impression, by the distinct prophecy relating to the present condition of the state, that his enemies would not only entirely fail in their plan of dividing the kingdom of Judah between them, but also that the kingdom of Ephraim was itself near that ruin, which it designed for others ; and would at last, within sixty-five years, entirely lose its national existence [3]. Ahaz makes no reply, but his whole deportment shows that he is unimpressed by the discourse of the Prophet, and determined to persevere in his resolution, not to look to God for deliverance, but to the Assyrians. The Prophet, commissioned by Jehovah, now offers to confirm the certainty of his declaration by a *miraculous sign*, to be determined by the king, without any restriction, that there may be no suspicion of imposture. But the unbelieving Ahaz

---

[1] See 2 Kings 16. 1—6.
[2] *Shear-Jashub,* which had the *double* meaning of '*the remnant will return*', and '*the remnant will repent.*' See on verse 3.
[3] Verses 1—9.

dreads communications from heaven ; he has already chosen his own mode of deliverance, and, preferring to rely on human aid alone, declines the offer of the Lord with a courteous reply, which is even borrowed from the Law[1]: ' *I will not ask, neither will I tempt the Lord.*' A sign is then *forced* upon him, because, as king of Judah, he *must* see and hear for the whole people, how true and faithful the Lord is. The future appearing of the Messiah was at that time the *general belief* of the people ; but fear, which always renders men inconsistent, caused them to forget this faith, and expect the total subversion of the state. The Prophet now gives this wonderful event, as a sign, that the apprehensions of the king and the people are groundless. So certainly, he declares, as the Messiah shall hereafter be born of a virgin among the covenant people, so *impossible is it that the people, among whom,* according to former promises, *he is to be born, and the family from which he is to descend, can be brought to ruin.* The Prophet does still more ; he fixes the period at which the land shall be entirely freed from its enemies. The overthrow of the two hostile kingdoms shall follow in the same space of time as will elapse between the birth of the Messiah (whom in *vision* he beholds as *present*) and his arriving at an age to distinguish good from evil ; consequently in about *three years*[2]. The Prophet had thus far directed all his efforts to convince Ahaz, and the people, that on the side from which they expected danger there was nothing to be feared : he now, however, while the Spirit of God disclosed to him the prospect of futurity, announces that the danger would come from that very quarter to which the unbelieving Ahaz looked for deliverance, namely, from the Assyrians, who would invade the land, and lay it waste[3]. It appears[4] that the Prophet's discourse made no impression upon Ahaz. He sent an embassy with large presents to the king of Assyria. Damascus also[5], the capital of Syria, was taken by the king of Assyria, Tiglath Pilezer, after Ahaz had suffered a terrible overthrow from Rezin and Pekah[6]. The land of Israel was laid waste, and a great part of its inhabitants were carried away into captivity[7]. And thus the prediction of the Prophet, respecting the destruction of the two allied kings, was fulfilled exactly at the appointed time. But the deliverance, which *would have been wrought* for Ahaz without further sacrifices, had he believed the Prophet and followed his counsels, must be purchased at a heavy price. He was obliged, even at that time, to suffer severe distresses from the Assyrians[8] ; and the dependence on Assyria, into which he was brought, formed the first link in that chain of misfortunes which, partly by the Assyrians, partly by their successors, the Babylonians, fell upon the kingdom of Judah. And thus also was the second part of the Prophet's prediction fulfilled.

283. The relation of these occurrences in the book of Kings[9], is brief.. The author of the books of the Chronicles had access to more

---

[1] Deut. 47. 16.   [2] Ver. 10—16.   [3] Ver. 17—25.

[4] From 2 Kings 16. 7.   [5] 2 Chron. 28. 5.

[6] 2 Kings 16. 9.   [7] 2 Kings 15. 29.

[8] See 2 Chron. 28. 1—20.   [9] 2 Kings 16.

accurate sources of information, and gives a fuller account. He particularly mentions the great overthrow which Ahaz, as a punishment of his unbelief, suffered from Rezin and Pekah ; although they were not able to take Jerusalem, but were obliged to return without accomplishing their object, carrying with them, however, a great multitude of captives, whom, in consequence of the admonition of the Prophet Oded, the Israelites afterwards liberated. Many interpreters have incorrectly supposed, that the two relations refer to different expeditions. The greater fulness of the account in the Chronicles does not justify this supposition, and the events follow each other in a perfectly natural order [1].

284. Verse 3. ' *Then said the Lord unto Isaiah : Go forth now to meet Ahaz, thou and Shearjashub thy son, at the end of the conduit of the upper pool, in the highway of the fullers' field.*' We must here first explain the geography. Among the fountains of Jerusalem the principal was the Gihon or Siloah, without the city, on the southwest side of Zion. The water of this sweet and copious fountain was conducted by water-courses into several pools and reservoirs. Two of these pools were called the *upper* and the *lower*, probably because the one received its water from the other. From the upper pool there was an aqueduct [2], probably to another pool, from which the king's garden was watered. Near this aqueduct was the public *highway* [3] : this was called the way of the washers', or fullers' field, because it led to a field in which the fullers were accustomed to cleanse and dry their fulled cloth. On the one side of this highway was the aqueduct, on the other the fullers' field. The fullers had chosen this place because it lay near the aqueduct. The interpreters here inquire, what could have brought Ahaz to this spot ? The most probable answer is, that he went there to see whether, by obstructing the fountain or changing its course, he could not deprive his enemies of water. This must have done them essential injury, since water is exceedingly scarce in the neighbourhood of Jerusalem. The correctness of this answer is evident from the thirty-second chapter of the second book of Chronicles [4], where Hezekiah employs the same measure against Sennacherib ; and from the eighteenth chapter of the second book of Kings [5], where Rabshakeh takes possession of this place.—But what induced the Prophet to seek the king precisely in this spot ? Probably the great multitude of people who were accustomed to assemble there. Besides the king himself might have gone forth attended by many of his counsellors. It was important that the Prophet should execute his commission in the presence of many witnesses.—For what purpose did he take with him his son Shearjashub? This could not have been accidental, for

---

[1] See the clear representation of this subject by Lightfoot, Opp. t. 1. p. 111, 2. ed. 1687. For Hengstenberg's arguments against this, see the original work (vol. 1. pt. 2, p. 48, G. vol. 1. p. 316, A.). He allows, however, " that this portion cannot have been composed by the Prophet *at the same time* with the rest. That it was written at a somewhat later period appears from its giving the result, ver. 1.

[2] תַּעֲלָה   [3] מְסִלָּה   [4] Ver. 1—4.   [5] Ver. 17.

then he would not have mentioned a circumstance in itself so unimportant. The reason must lie in the etymology of the name, since the child performs no part on the occasion. The Prophet was accustomed to give his sons *symbolical names, which had relation to the destinies of the people*[1]. According to Gesenius, the name Shearjashub imports nothing further than *the remnant will repent.* But then no reason could be given for his being taken thither. There is rather a *double sense* intended by the name Shearjashub[2]: 'the remnant will *return,*' and 'the remnant will *repent*[3].' This name referred to the prediction often uttered by the Prophet, that in consequence of a Divine chastisement the people should be carried into exile, but that a *part of them* would *repent* and then *return.* King Ahaz and his people feared nothing less than the total ruin of the state. Isaiah took his son with him, 'as the living evidence of the preservation of the Jewish people amidst the most terrible desolation of the greatest part of them.' After he had thus sought to free their minds from the extreme of fear, he endeavoured to raise them to joyful hopes, by a direct prophetic annunciation, which showed that the future carrying away of the people, which was denounced against them, was not in the least to be apprehended from the present invasion.

285. Verse 4. '*And say unto him*[4], mind (or, beware) *and be quiet*[5] *:*' as much as to say, *do but,* or *do above all things, be quiet*[6]. *Beware now* serves to render a command or prohibition more emphatic. So in the fourth verse of the thirteenth chapter of Judges, '*Beware and drink no wine.*' Ahaz is admonished to trust in God, who would maintain the cause of his people, and not to show his unbelief by seeking foreign alliances[7].—'*Fear not, and let not thy heart be faint,*' despond not '*before* (or *on account of*) *the ends of these two smoking firebrands,*' ["*for the fierce anger of Rezin with Syria and of the son of Remaliah.*" E. T.] The enemies of the king considered in themselves were powerful enough. They are therefore here called firebrands. But the extinction of their power and glory was near. The Prophet is even on the point of announcing their approaching destruction by the Assyrians. He therefore calls them *ends of firebrands,* which no longer blaze, but only glimmer[8].—It is by way of contempt that the king of Israel is not called by his own name. The Hebrews and Arabians, when

---

[1] See chap. 8.
[2] According to the different meanings of the verb שׁוּב *to return,* and *to repent.*
[3] This double sense also occurs in the passage, chap. 10. 21, 22.
[4] The preterite must often be translated as Imp. when an imperative has preceded.
[5] הִשָּׁמֵר וְהַשְׁקֵט.
[6] *Vulg.* "*vide ut sileas.*"
[7] Calvin : Jubet quietâ et tranquillâ esse mente, ut et exterius contineat sese et intus pacato sit animo. Illi enim sunt fidei effectus. Impietas nunquam est quieta; ubi vero fides est, illic tranquillus est mentis status, nec trepidatur ultra modum.
[8] Chrysostom : δαλοὺς ξύλου καλεῖ τοὺς βασιλέας, ὁμοῦ μὲν αὐτῶν τὸ σφοδρὸν, ὁμοῦ δὲ τὸ εὐχείρωτον ἐνδεικνύμενος. καὶ γὰρ τὸ καπνιζομένων διὰ τοῦτο προσέθεικε, τουτέστιν ἐγγὺς ὄντων τοῦ σβεσθῆναι λοιπόν.

they wish to speak reproachfully of any one, omit his proper name, and call him merely the son of this or that, especially when his father was but little known and respected. So Saul names David in contempt the *son of Jesse* [1].

286. Verses 5, 6. [*Because Syria, Ephraim, and the son of Remaliah have taken evil counsel against thee, saying, Let us go up against Judah, and vex* [2] *it, and let us make a breach therein for us, and set a king in the midst of it,* even *the son of Tabeal.* E. T.] Of the son of Tabeal, whom the confederate kings wished to make regent, we know nothing further, nor is it important that we should. But is there not an incongruity in the assertion, that the kings wished to divide the land between themselves, and yet still set a king over it? Either the former statement is to be limited: the kings wished to cut off such portions of the country as were most convenient to each of them, and then to place a king over the remainder; or they wished *virtually* to divide the whole between themselves, by setting up a king who should be subject and tributary to both.

287. Verse 7. Thou hast no occasion to fear on account of these pernicious designs of thy foes. '*For thus saith the Lord God; it shall not stand, neither shall it come to pass.*'

288. Verses 8, 9. The sense of these verses is as follows. The revolution which these two kings contemplate, shall not be effected. No changes shall take place. The kingdoms of Damascus and Israel shall not be enlarged by the acquisition of the kingdom of Judah; and Jerusalem shall not become the seat of a Syrian or Israelitish prince. We will, for the present, leave unnoticed the latter part of the eighth verse, which is controverted. '*For the head of Syria shall still be Damascus, and the head of Damascus Rezin, and the head of Ephraim Samaria, and the head of Samaria the son of Remaliah.*' The expression, each one shall remain what he is, must be limited to his receiving no enlargement. The kings shall not now succeed in their purpose of enlarging their dominions, and hereafter they shall lose what they at present possess. The Prophet subjoins, '*If ye believe not, ye continue not* [3].' You have no occasion, says the Prophet, to fear. God has resolved to aid you, and defeat the designs of your enemies; no portion of your land shall be taken from you. Nevertheless, in order that you may

---

[1] 1 Sam. 20. 27. 31.

[2] The verb קוץ properly signifies *to experience disgust,* in Hiph. *to cause disgust,* and then, since disgust and anxiety are related feelings, *to make anxious* and *drive to extremity* Schultens has shown, that in the Arabic writers, *tædio afficere urbem,* is used precisely of *besieging* and *distressing* a city. The suffix in נְקִיצֶנָּה relates to Judah, and not, as some interpreters suppose, to Jerusalem understood, as is evident from the following וְנַבְקִיעֶנָּה, which can be referred only to Judah.

[3] The verb אמן ' *to be firm,*' in Niph. ' *to be fortified; to have security,*' in Hiph. ' *to make firm, to declare* or *believe a thing to be firm.* Symm. ἐὰν μὴ πιστεύσητε, οὐ διαμενεῖτε. Theodot. ἐὰν μὴ πιστεύσητε, οὐδ᾽ οὐ μὴ πιστευθείητε, on which Theodoret remarks: τῆς γὰρ πίστεως ἡ σωτηρία καρπός. A parallel passage is 2 Chron. 20. 20, when Jehoshaphat says to the distressed people, הַאֲמִינוּ בַּיהוָה אֱלֹהֵיכֶם וְתֵאָמֵנוּ, ' Believe in the Lord your God; so shall ye be secure.'

obtain deliverance from God, you must believe his promise made
through me, and place your confidence, not in the help of man, the
aid of the Assyrians, but in God alone. Unless you do this, you
shall never prosper. The faith, which the Prophet here requires,
despair of their own strength, and confidence in the Divine power,
and laying hold of the promise of God, is essentially the same with
Christian faith, which is only a modification of it[1].—We come now
to the addition : ' *Within threescore and five years shall Ephraim
be destroyed, that it be no more a people*[2].' This passage presents
difficulties. Hence several interpreters have supposed it to be *corrupted*, others[3] have denied its *genuineness*. The reasons of the
latter are the following : (1) " The number sixty-five does not suit ;
for the kingdom of Ephraim suffered the first overthrow from Tiglath-
pilesar, soon after the present invasion[4], the other in from about nineteen to twenty-one years afterwards, from Shalmaneser in the sixth
year of Hezekiah, when the ten tribes were carried away[5]." Jerome
and the Jewish commentators long ago perceived this difficulty, and
made various efforts to remove it. The explanation which has been
most approved, is that of Archbishop Usher. The kingdom of the
ten tribes was indeed *greatly reduced* by Shalmaneser, but still not
deprived of all its inhabitants. That Israelites still remained in the
land is clearly manifest from several passages[6]. The *entire extinction*
of the state and people of Israel did not take place till Esarhaddon
put new colonists from Babylon, Cuth, and other regions in possession of the country, who expelled the ancient inhabitants[7]. This
happened *exactly sixty-five years after it had been predicted by
Isaiah.* After that period the ten tribes, which had in all probability heretofore lived under their own laws, and unmingled with
any other people, never again constituted a state of themselves.
The objections of Gesenius to this explanation are unimportant.
Thus, when he says, it cannot be imagined why the Prophet should
have mentioned that remote calamity, instead of the nearer and far
heavier one ; how much might in this manner be objected against
the Prophet! He *had already announced the nearer calamity* by
calling the two kings ends of smoking firebrands, and he returns to
it again : but he here suddenly casts a look at the final catastrophe
of the hostile land, and thus combines in one view the *commencement*
and the *termination* of its misfortunes. ' Thou hast no occasion to
fear before the king of Israel. In a short time, from *two* to *three*
years[8], the misfortunes of the kingdom of Ephraim shall commence

---

[1] The erroneous interpretation of Grotius is insipid: " an ideo non creditis,
quia non confirmamini sc. signo aliquo conspicuo?" That of Plüschke is unnatural, who makes these words the commencement of the following verse: If
ye will not believe without a sensible proof, then ask, Jehovah proceeds to say to
Ahaz, a sign from thy God.

[2] יֵחַת fut. Niph. from the verb חתת. מֵעָם that is מִהְיוֹת עָם. Similar is 1 Sam.
15. 23. ' He has rejected thee מִמֶּלֶךְ from the king,' that is, ' so that thou art not
king.'

[3] As Plüschke, Gesenius.   [4] 2 Kings 15. 29, 30.
[5] 2 Kings 17. 3, 4.   [6] 2 Chron. 34. 6, 7. 33. 2 Kings 23. 19, 20.
[7] Comp. 2 Kings 17. 24 with Ezra 4. 2. 10.   [8] See ver. 16.

with the desolation of the land, and its condition shall be continually growing worse and worse, until at last, after sixty-five years, it shall be entirely destroyed [1].' It is easy to perceive the design of this distinct annunciation. It must serve to console Ahaz, if he possessed the slightest faith. For although there was not in this later ruin of the kingdom of Israel, any more than in the significant name of Shearjashub, a proper assurance of deliverance from the present danger, yet must its definite prediction serve to lessen his fear of his enemies, whom he regarded as invincible, and also strengthen his confidence in Jehovah, by whose providence all things must be controuled, since he could cause the events of futurity to be foretold with such precision. The prophecy had moreover the general aim of all definite predictions; it was intended to prove that God, the Head of the theocracy, was almighty and infinite in knowledge, and to confirm the Divine mission of the Prophet.—Those, who are not satisfied with this solution of the chronological difficulty, and reject the passage as spurious, involve themselves in another far greater. For granting the designation of time to be *false*, how could it be supposed that any one who was disposed to interpolate, *would introduce it?* His object could have been no other than to produce authority for the prophet by attributing to him a prediction which had been plainly fulfilled. That the expedient here adopted by Gesenius is unnatural, is so very obvious as to require no further pointing out.

289. (2) " The passage contradicts the sixteenth verse of the chapter, where the depopulation of both hostile lands is represented as soon to take place." But this proves nothing, since the entire extinction of the people as a people, foretold in this verse, is something very different from the mere laying waste of the country.

290. (3) " The use of such definite numbers is contrary to the analogy of all other predictions." This objection is refuted even by the sixteenth verse, the genuineness of which is not contested. There also the time of the overthrow is *accurately*, though *not numerically* defined. It is, indeed, true, that as a general rule, the relations of time and space are kept in the back-ground in the prophetic vision. But this rule is not without exceptions. The Prophets were sometimes instructed as to the distance of time by a special Divine revelation. Isaiah himself, in the twentieth chapter, foretells, by means of a symbolical action, that *after three years*, the Egyptians and Ethiopians should be conquered by the Assyrians. In the fifteenth verse of the twenty-third chapter he declares that Tyre, seventy years after its fall, should revive and flourish anew. In the fifth verse of the thirty-eighth chapter he announces to Hezekiah, when dangerously ill, that God would add yet fifteen years to his life. The seventy years which, according to Jeremiah, should elapse before the

---

[1] Chrysostom: ἵνα γὰρ μὴ ἀκούων ὁ βασιλεὺς ὅτι μετὰ ἑξήκοντα πέντε ἔτη ἀπολοῦνται λέγῃ πρὸς ἑαυτὸν, τί οὖν; ἐὰν νῦν ἡμᾶς λαβόντες τότε ἀπολοῦνται, τί τὸ ὄφελος ἡμῖν ; θάρρει φησὶ καὶ περὶ τῶν παρόντων. ἁλώσονται γὰρ τότε παντελῶς· νῦν μέντοι πλέον οὐδὲν τῶν οἰκείων ἕξουσι, ἀλλ᾽ ἔσται ἡ κεφαλὴ Ἐφραΐμ, κ. τ. λ.

termination of the captivity, Gesenius regards as a round number.
But as, according to the passages in Jeremiah, the eleventh and
twelfth verses of the twenty-fifth chapter, and tenth and following
verses of the twenty-ninth chapter, no one could doubt that the
captivity would last seventy years, so a comparison of the ninth
chapter of Daniel and the twenty-first verse of the thirty-sixth chapter
of the second book of Chronicles shows that the number was then
understood as a definite determination of time, and that the captivity
actually continued so long. And lastly we appeal to the numbers
in Daniel. Even those who deny the genuineness of this book,
cannot assert that it is contrary to the analogy of all the prophetic
oracles to give definite numbers.

291. (4) " The words stand in an unsuitable place, and interrupt
the necessary succession of the four members." Were this objection
entirely correct, it would nevertheless prove nothing more than the
necessity of supposing, with several interpreters, a slight transposi-
tion, and of inserting these words after, ' *the head of Samaria is the
son of Remaliah* [1].' At any rate a difficulty which consists in a mere
matter of taste, is insufficient to prove the spuriousness or genuineness of a passage. But this difficulty is only apparent. The discourse of the Prophets is not always governed by logical rules, but
follows the change of objects as they appear in vision. Before the
Prophet proceeds with the sentence he had begun, and says that the
king has at present as little to fear from Israel as from Syria, his
view is suddenly directed to the final result of the calamity impending over the kingdom of Israel, and he cannot refrain from immediately announcing it, in order to animate the courage of the king,
and prepare him the better to receive the prediction of the nearer
deliverance. Had these words been subsequently interpolated, they
would certainly not have been placed where they now stand, but at
the end of the tenth verse, where they seem to belong.

292. But while the objections against their genuineness are thus
insufficient, it is sustained by the authority of all the manuscripts, and
old translations, as well as by every thing in general that is opposed
to the supposition that glosses have been incorporated with the text
of Isaiah.

293. Verse 10. ' *Moreover the Lord spake again unto Ahaz,
saying,*' i. e. the Prophet spake in Jehovah's name and as commissioned by Him.

294. Verse 11. On hearing this discourse Ahaz was entirely
silent; but his whole deportment gave the Prophet to understand
that it had produced no impression. He therefore says to him:
' *Ask for thyself a sign from Jehovah thy God ; ask it from the depth or
from the height* [2].' Had Ahaz been a true theocratic prince, possessing
the spirit of David, even though we should suppose it possible for
his confidence in the invisible head of the theocracy to have been

---

[1] Ver. 10.
[2] Theodoret: ἐπειδὴ οὖν ἀπιστεῖς τοῖς εἰρημένοις καὶ ψεῦδος νομίζεις τὴν
ἐμὴν ὑπόσχεσιν, ἐγὼ βεβαιώσω θαυματουργίᾳ τοὺς λόγους. Αἴτησον τοίνυν
ὑπὲρ βούλῃ σημεῖον, εἴτε οὐράνιον εἴτε ἐπίγειον.

shaken before, yet he must at least have believed the word of God by the Prophet, even though not assured of its truth by an outward sign. But as such a firm confidence was not to be expected from him, God condescended to his weakness of faith ; the Prophet proposed to demonstrate the truth of his prediction by a miraculous event, to be named by Ahaz, from which he might at the same time perceive the omnipotence of God, and the Divine mission of the Prophet. The word *sign* [1] signifies in general *a thing*, or *an event*, or *an action*, which shall serve as an assurance that something future shall come to pass. (1) In some cases this assurance consisted only in this, that with a *nearer event* God caused a *more remote one* to be foretold, which presupposed the former as having taken place. Thus, as a sign that the deliverance from Egypt should certainly be effected, God gives to Moses [2] the assurance, that *after that event* the people would sacrifice to him on mount Sinai. In this case the sign contains in itself nothing miraculous, but still it is suited to strengthen faith, inasmuch as it shows the certainty of the Divine purpose ; proves that the promise does not depend on the conduct of those to whom it was imparted, but is unconditional ; and finally demonstrates, in general, that the whole of futurity lies open before God. (2) In other cases the assurance given by the sign consists in this, that the bare word is connected with something external, and thereby fitted to make a stronger impression on the senses. Here also there is nothing miraculous. We have an instance of this, e. g. when Isaiah [3] calls his two sons, to whom he had given symbolical names significant of the future destinies of the Jewish people, *signs and wonders*, i. e. striking or remarkable signs. See also the third verse of the twentieth chapter of Isaiah, where as a sign of the misfortunes, which in three years would come upon Egypt and Ethiopia, the Prophet goes naked and barefoot for that space of time. (3) In another class of signs, an event, *natural* indeed in itself, but yet *one not to be foreseen by human sagacity*, is predicted, the occurrence of which at an earlier period then furnishes the proof, that the prediction of a still more distant event will also be fulfilled. In this case, it is not the sign itself, but *the prediction of it*, which constitutes the miracle and the evidence. Thus Samuel [4] gives to Saul several signs, that God has destined him to be the king of Israel, e. g. he would meet two men in a place accurately designated, who would inform him that the lost asses were found ; further on he would meet with three men, the first of whom would be carrying three kids, the next three loaves of bread, and the third a sack of wine, &c. In the thirty-fourth verse of the second chapter of the first book of Samuel the sudden death of his two sons is given to Eli as a sign, that all the calamities threatened against his family should certainly be inflicted [5]. (4) In other cases the assurance was given by the immediate performance of a miraculous action, which, transcending the ordinary laws of nature, silenced every doubt, either of the Divine mission of the Prophet, or of the

---

[1] אוֹת, σημεῖον.   [2] Ex. 3. 12.   [3] Chap. 8. 18.
[4] 1 Sam. 10.   [5] See also Jer. 44. 30.

omnipotence of God, and every suspicion of fraud. Thus e. g. Isaiah [1]
caused the shadow on the sun-dial of Ahaz to go back ten degrees,
as a sign of the fifteen years yet to be added to the life of Hezekiah. Of this kind also were the signs which were granted to
Gideon [2], and also, in many respects, the plagues of Egypt. Now it
is impossible that, in the present instance, the sign can belong to
any other than the last-mentioned class. For if the Prophet had
been unable or unwilling to give a proper miraculous sign, where is
the fitness of the answer of Ahaz? How can the Prophet [3] bring
against him the charge of offending, not merely men, but also God ?
Surely the confidence with which the Prophet here offers a miracle
to the king, must embarrass the opposers of revelation. Plüschke
knows of nothing better to oppose to the fact, than the *a priori*
objection, that it is unworthy of God to produce a miraculous
natural phenomenon for a limited human purpose, an objection
which can have no weight with any one who regards this occurrence,
not as standing alone, but as connected with the whole system of the
theocracy [4].—Isaiah leaves to Ahaz not merely the determination of
the place where the sign should be exhibited, but also that of the
sign itself. Rightly Le Clerc : ' *Ask that any thing should be done
either on earth or in the heavens, and it shall be done for thee.*'
Theodoret makes the appropriate remark, that both kinds of miracles,
which God here proposed to the choice of Ahaz, he performed for his
pious son Hezekiah, since *in the heavens* He produced a phenomenon,
which caused the retrocession of the shadow on the sun-dial of
Ahaz, and *on earth*, in a wonderful manner destroyed the Assyrians,
and restored the king to health. Jerome remarks, that, among the
plagues of Egypt, the lice, frogs, &c., were *signs on earth*, while the
hail, the fire, and the three days' darkness were *signs in heaven*.

295. Verse 12. ' *But Ahaz said, I will ask no sign, and will not
tempt Jehovah.*' Ahaz declines the proposal ; as it was the weakness
of his faith which had caused the offer, so it was his unbelief
which led him to reject it. Ahaz gives as a reason, that he would
not tempt the Lord, appealing to the passage in the tenth verse of
the sixth chapter of Deuteronomy. To *tempt* God is the same as to
put him to the proof ; since unbelief requires that He should exhibit
his omnipotence in a visible way, and does not rest satisfied with
the former demonstrations of his mercy, and with his word. But
Ahaz would not have tempted God by asking for a sign, since one
had been offered him by the Prophet in the name of God. His
answer may be regarded, either as one of bitter scorn, as if he had
said, I will not put thy God to the proof in which He will be found
wanting ; I will not embarrass thee, by taking thee at thy word ; or
as the language of a hypocrite, who assumes the mask of reverence
for God and his command [5]. The latter is the more correct explanation. For (1) it does not appear from the accounts of Ahaz, that
he had despised the God of Israel, *as having no existence ;* but rather

---

[1] Chap. 38. 8.   [2] Judges 6.   [3] Ver. 13.

[4] הַעֲמֵק שְׁאָלָה properly *make low, ask* (for, *obtain by asking*) *for thyself a miracle
to take place on earth.*

[5] Thus Chrysostom and Calvin.

that, like most of the idolatrous Israelites, he regarded him indeed as *a* God, but only as *one* among *many*, and not perhaps the most powerful, and therefore believed he must seek the favour of the others likewise. (2) Even if we suppose the unbelief of Ahaz to have been *total*, it is highly improbable that he should, in the present condition of the state, have been so imprudent as publicly to insult the religion of the people, and thus rouse one part of them against himself, and discourage another. Had he been a thorough unbeliever, and set aside all regard for the people, Isaiah would hardly have escaped punishment for the reply in the thirteenth verse; nor would Ahaz have answered the previous declaration of the Prophet, merely by a cautious silence. But here the question arises, why did Ahaz decline the offer of the Prophet; why did he not rather ask from him a miracle which he could not perform, if he were a false prophet, and which, if it should really take place, must put an end to all his anxieties? He may have had various reasons for his conduct. Had the Prophet failed in the performance of his promise, not merely the piously disposed portion of the people, but the great mass of those also who still maintained a certain external conformity to the religion of their fathers, would have been entirely disheartened. Had the Prophet on the other hand really performed the miracle, it would not have benefited Ahaz. In his unbelief, he looked only upon what was human, as certain, and upon all that was of God, as uncertain. He believed that he needed no other aid than that of the Assyrians. Total unbelief darkens the understanding. Had the plainest miracle been wrought, though it might have impressed him at first, he would soon have doubted respecting it, against the testimony of his senses, and against all reason. To this must be added another ground, which lies in the religious notions of those times, and which was first particularly pointed out by Michaelis. According to the heathen notions on the subject of religion, every nation had its own gods. Those of one people were more, and those of another less powerful[1]. If then Isaiah had performed a miracle, Ahaz might have believed him to have been sent indeed by the God of his country, who might have had the *best disposition*, but *not the power* to defend him. He held it, therefore, in any event, to be the best course, not to comply with the offers of the Prophet, and quietly to prosecute the measures once resolved on, thinking perhaps that Isaiah would be deceived by the piously sounding expression. The Prophet, however, thoroughly understood the king. Soft and mild before, he now became at once, when the honour of God was concerned, zealous and vehement.

296. Verse 13. ' *And the Prophet said : Hear ye now, O house of David, is it too little for you to provoke men, that you must also provoke my God ?* ' We are here naturally led to inquire, to what the antithesis between God and men can refer[2]. The true inter-

---

[1] Isaiah 10. 10, 11. 36. 18—20. 37. 10—13.

[2] According to some, this is the sense: ' *Since it is a sin to grieve men by undeserved suspicion, how much more highly does he offend who refuses to trust in God,*

pretation seems to be the following.   When Ahaz before refused to believe the bare prediction of the Prophet, his transgression was more excusable, as Isaiah had not given an outward proof of his Divine mission ; so that Ahaz in a measure sinned only against men, against the Prophet, by unjustly suspecting him of falsely pretending to a revelation from God.   Therefore Isaiah remained mild and calm.   But when Ahaz rejected the offered sign, the case was changed.   God Himself was insulted by this rejection of his offer, through unbelief [1].—Of verses fourteen to sixteen we give, in the first place, that explanation which appears to us to be the true one, and afterwards those which differ from ours, with the reasons for and against them.

297.   Verse 14. Ahaz had refused the proffered sign, and the Prophet was compelled to relinquish the hope of raising him to confidence in Jehovah.   But he must have been desirous that the deliverance should not be regarded, when it came, as the work of chance, but ascribed to the mercy of the Supreme Ruler of the theocracy ; and that the confidence of the pious in HIM should be confirmed.   He therefore gives a sign, even against the will of Ahaz, whereby the confidence of every true member of the theocracy, in the prediction already given concerning the deliverance from the confederated kings, must be strengthened.   I behold, he declares, the wonderful event of futurity, the birth of a Divine Redeemer of a virgin.   How can ye who expect him, fear so inconsistently, that the state will go to ruin ?   Kocher : " Ideo dabit Dominus ipse vobis signum h. e. etiam nolentibus dabit, sed non impiis, quibus convincendis aliud sensusque feriens et conveniebat, et oblatum, sed per malitiam contumaciamque contemtum rejectumque erat.   Ergo piis dabit—stabit Deus promissis, implebit fidem, itaque et Davidis domus perstabit, neque de ea triumphaturus hostis, nedum eam destructurus est."   ' *Therefore behold Jehovah himself will give you a sign : behold the virgin has conceived and bears a son, and she calls his name Immanuel* [2].'   By ' *the* virgin ' is meant *the particular*

---

in whose name I speak.'   But the Prophet would then have said nothing which he might not have said before ; since Ahaz put no faith in the bare prediction, and yet the address of the Prophet must especially refer to the rejection of the proffered miraculous sign.   According to others (Vitringa, Rosenmüller, Plüschke) the sense is this: ' *Thou despisest not me, not men, but God ;* ' but according to this explanation also the antithesis is not quite clear.

[1] בֵּית דָוִד *House of David*, as a collective, takes the plural.   There must have been in attendance upon the king other princes of the *House of David*, who were partakers with him in the guilt of unbelief.   The appellation seems to have been chosen by design, to taunt them (as Calvin observes) with having degenerated from the piety of David.   הַמְעַט מִכֶּם, not *Is it a small thing to you ?* but *Is it too small*, or *too little for you.* מִן is comparative.   See Ges. Lehrg. p. 690.   The verb הִלְאָה means properly *to weary*, then *to make impatient, to reduce to extremity ;* here spoken of God after the manner of men.   The Prophet says emphatically *my God*, the God whose true servant I am, and in whom ye hypocrites have no longer any portion.

[2] The particle הִנֵּה is used demonstratively, and often indeed, when the Prophets pointed to objects which they beheld, not by an external, but internal perception.

virgin, who was present to the inward perception of the Prophet, the virgin *there ;* unless we should choose to explain it with others, *the virgin whom ye know*[1]. After the example of the Jews, recent interpreters choose to assert that the word translated *virgin*[2] means only a *young woman.* Their reasons, which may be easily refuted, are as follows : (1) "The etymology shows that the idea intended to be conveyed, is not that of pure virginity, nor of the married or unmarried state." Here, as well as throughout this whole inquiry, the notion of a *pure virgin,* and that of an *unmarried woman,* are blended together. The former is not indeed required by the etymology of the word, but the latter certainly is[3]. (2) "For a *pure virgin* the Hebrews had another name[4], and even that is used by Joel[5] for a *young married woman.* Now it is highly improbable, that they should have had two entirely synonymous expressions for the same thing." This objection also is removed, if we only separate the ideas, which have been confounded, of a *pure virgin*[6] and of a *young unmarried woman*[7]. In the passage quoted from Joel, it is extremely doubtful whether a *young widow* laments the death of her husband, or a *virgin* that of her betrothed. Even in the former case the passage would prove nothing. For we are not here permitted, without consulting the usage of the language, to draw a conclusion from a single word of similar import[8]. (3) "The usage of the language also is against the meaning *pure virgin.* If this meaning is not necessarily excluded in the twenty-sixth verse of the sixty-eighth Psalm and the eighth verse of the sixth chapter of Canticles, it cannot possibly be the true one in the nineteenth verse of the thirtieth chapter of Proverbs." This objection, also, entirely fails of its object. We concede that in the cited passage of Proverbs, according to the most probable interpretation, the idea of a pure virgin is not expressed. But what is gained by this, since we do not cla⁞m for the word the sense of *unspotted purity,* but only that of the *unmarried state ?* The usage of the language most decidedly favours the latter meaning. It is undeniably the meaning in all the six places where the word occurs, besides this in Isaiah[9]. In

---

[1] Chrysostom says: οὐκ εἶπεν ἰδοὺ παρθένος, ἀλλ᾽ ἰδοὺ ἡ παρθένος, καὶ μετὰ ἀξιώματος προφήτῃ πρέποντος τὸ ἰδού. Μόνον γὰρ οὐκ ὁρῶντος ἦν τὰ γινόμενα καὶ φανταζομένου καὶ πολλὴν ἔχοντος ὑπὲρ τῶν εἰρημένων πληροφορίαν. τῶν γὰρ ἡμετέρων ὀφθαλμῶν ἐκεῖνοι σαφέστερον τὰ μὴ ὁρώμενα ἔβλεπον.

[2] עלמה.

[3] For עלמה derived from עלם *to grow up, to become marriageable,* can mean nothing else than *puella nubilis,* a marriageable young woman. Jerome well remarks, and in accordance with the etymology, that עלמה does not mean a virgin in general, but a virgin in early youth.

[4] בתולה.   [5] Chap. 1. 8.

[6] Designated by בתולה.   [7] Designated by עלמה.

[8] Thus in German poetry, perhaps in a single instance, *Jungfrau* could be used for *junge Frau,* but it would occur to no poet to use *Dirne* or *Fräulein,* when speaking of a married woman.

[9] Viz. Gen. 24. 3. Ex. 2. 8. Ps. 68. 26. Cant. 1. 3. 6. 8. Prov. 30. 19.

Arabic and Syriac also, the corresponding words are never used in reference to married women [1]. (4) " The Jewish translators and interpreters assert that the word means a *young married woman* [2]." This however can prove nothing. They thus translated from polemic zeal against the Christians, in order to wrest from them a proof passage [3]. This, then, is the result of our investigation : the word [4] signifies *a young unmarried woman*, without having, *in itself,* any direct reference to unspotted chastity, which however, in this connexion, is of course implied [5].—We are not to suppose that the child should actually receive the name Immanuel as a *proper name,* since, according to the usage of the Prophets, and especially of Isaiah, that is often ascribed to a person or thing as a name, which belongs to him in an emir.ent degree, as an attribute [6]. The name *Immanuel* may be understood in different ways. Several interpreters, as Jerome [7], find in it nothing more than the *Divine aid* and *protection.* According to others, on the contrary, the name must relate to the assumption of our nature by God in the person of the Messiah, i. e. *God become man* [8]. The two interpretations are consistent with each other : indeed the Prophet himself seems to have intended a *double sense* in the name. The name *God with us,* is indeed in the *lower sense* only a designation of the *Divine aid,* which should be granted through the Messiah ; but, in the *higher sense,* it refers to *God's becoming man in his person,* by which He was first truly "*with us* [9]." This then is the import of the words, ' She will call his name *God with us ;* consequently, he *will be fully entitled to* this name, since

---

[1] Jerome remarks : " Lingua quoque Punica proprie virgo עלמה appellatur."

[2] Aquila, Symm., Theod. translate νεᾶνις.

[3] The Seventy, who had no such motive, rendered עלמה by παρθένος.

[4] עלמה.

[5] The form הָרָה is not, as Rosenmüller supposes, a participle of the verb הור, which does not occur, but the feminine of the verbal adjective הָרֶה *pregnant.* We may translate either, *the virgin is pregnant,* or *the virgin becomes pregnant and brings forth a son.* The participle יֹלֶדֶת, standing for the present, as well as הנה, shows that the event, which was to take place in future times, was present to the Prophet.—The form קָרָאת may be 3d fem. for קָרְאָה, as in Jer. 44. 23. But still there is no objection to regard it as 2d fem., *thou namest* ; as an apostrophe to the virgin, and then it becomes entirely regular. It was not unusual among the Hebrews for the *mothers* to give the names to the children. Gen. 4. 1. 25. 19. 37. 29. 32. There is, therefore, no good reason to suppose, with many of the older interpreters, that by attributing to the mother the giving of the name, it is indicated that the child should have no human father. *She will name* is moreover, in reference to the manner of that age, the same as *they shall name,* or *he shall be named.* Thus Matt. καλέσουσι, Jerome *vocabitur.*

[6] See chap. 9. 5. 61. 6. 62. 4.   [7] Referring to Ps. 46. 8. 12. 89. 25.

[8] Thus Theodoret: δηλοῖ δὲ τὸ ὄνομα τὸν μεθ᾽ ἡμῶν θεόν, τὸν ἐνανθρωπή-σαντα θεόν, τὸν τὴν ἀνθρωπείαν φύσιν ἀνειληφότα θεόν. So likewise Irenæus, Tertullian, Chrysostom, Lactantius, Calvin, Rosenmüller, and many others.

[9] Chrysostom well observes: τότε γὰρ μάλιστα μεθ᾽ ἡμῶν ὁ θεὸς γέγονεν ἐπὶ τῆς γῆς γῆς ὀφθεὶς καὶ τοῖς ἀνθρώποις συναναστρεφόμενος, καὶ τὴν πολλὴν ἐπιδεικνύμενος περὶ ἡμᾶς κηδεμονίαν.

in him and through him God will be with us.' That this higher meaning really belongs to the passage, plainly appears from the parallel passage, chap. 9. 5, where the Messiah is called *the mighty God*[1], and where this *eternal' existence* and *Divine glory* are contrasted with his *temporal birth*.

298. According then to the explanation now given, it is foretold in this verse, that the Messiah should hereafter be born of a virgin among the covenant people, and reveal God by a visible manifestation. Traces of the belief in the birth of the great Redeemer of a *virgin*—not to mention the obscure intimations in the prediction concerning the seed of the woman, who should bruise the serpent's head,—are found in the second verse of the fifth chapter of Micah: '*he will give them up, till she who shall bear hath borne.*' Nay more, traces of this belief are found among nearly all nations, and in all the ancient religions, especially those of Asia[2].—The arguments, for the correctness of the interpretation we have given, besides those hereafter to be adduced in opposition to that of the Jews and the recent interpreters, are chiefly the following.

299. (1) Were there no other evidence, the passage in the twenty-second verse of the first chapter of Matthew would alone be sufficient proof. Matthew, after having related the miraculous conception of Christ, says : '*Now all this was done, that it might be fulfilled which was spoken of the Lord by the prophet, saying*[3],' &c. According to the Evangelist, therefore, the prophecy can be referred only to Mary, the mother of Jesus. That Matthew by no means intended to speak in the way of accommodation, but has thus explained it in the strictest sense, is conceded almost unanimously by the recent interpreters. It was one design of the events of the evangelical history, to place in a clear light the faithfulness and omniscience of God, by means of the exact accomplishment of the predictions of the Old Testament. See the fifty-fourth verse of the twenty-sixth chapter of Matthew, where Christ, in order to show the necessity of his death, says : '*But how then shall the Scriptures be fulfilled, that thus it must be*[4] *?*' It is true, that in order to invalidate this argument, an appeal has been made to the fact, that Matthew on other occasions quotes passages of the Old Testament, where there is not a fulfilment of prophecy, but only a resemblance. Thus, e. g. in the fifteenth verse of the second chapter; where a passage of Hosea, which certainly relates only to the people of Israel, is referred to Christ. But the difference in the forms of quotation is to be well considered. In the fifteenth verse of the second chapter we have barely ἵνα πληρωθῇ, which, as we have already seen in the general Introduction, does not of itself justify the assumption that the Prophet designed to give the proper explanation of the quoted passages ; but here Matthew shows by the preceding '*all this was done*,' that he intends

[1] אֵל גִּבּוֹר.

[2] Huet., Rosenmüller, Gesenius (on the passage).

[3] Τοῦτο δὲ ὅλον γέγονεν, ἵνα πληρωθῇ τὸ ῥηθὲν ὑπὸ τοῦ κυρίου διὰ τοῦ προφήτου, κ. τ. λ.

[4] Πῶς οὖν πληρωθῶσιν αἱ γραφαί ; ὅτι οὕτω δεῖ γενέσθαι.

to *give an interpretation*, not merely to *make an allusion*. Further, in the passage in the fifteenth verse of the second chapter, the comparison is obvious; *as* under the Old Testament, the Church of God in its members was called out of Egypt, *so* was it under the New Testament in its head; here, on the contrary, if we reject the Messianic explanation, the likeness also disappears. For what point of connexion is there between the two occurrences; the wife of the Prophet, according to the course of nature, conceives, and brings forth a son, who serves as a sign and symbol of the deliverance; and Mary, a pure virgin, miraculously conceives the Messiah, who accomplishes this deliverance? The *point of comparison* must surely lie in the conception *by a virgin, who still remained such* [1].

300. (2) That the Messianic interpretation was the prevailing one among the Prophet's contemporaries, and therefore the true one, is evinced by the parallel passage in the second verse of the fifth chapter of Micah, already quoted. Micah there first predicts, in the first verse, the birth at Bethlehem of him, who shall be ruler in Israel, whose goings forth have been from of old, from everlasting. He then proceeds to announce the impending calamities of the people; '*in the mean time shall he give them up until she who shall bear hath borne* [2].' The expression '*who shall bear*,' presupposes the miraculous birth of the Messiah, and evidently refers to a definite prediction which had gone before. "She is not indeed expressly called a virgin, but that she is so is self-evident, since she shall bear the hero of Divine origin (from everlasting), and consequently *not begotten by a mortal*. Each of these predictions throws light upon the other; Micah discloses the Divine origin of the person predicted, Isaiah the wonderful manner of his birth [3]." There is also a striking similarity in other respects between the two prophecies. According to both, severe sufferings shall precede the birth of the child [4], which shall terminate with his appearing; in both, the Divine dignity is placed in contrast with the temporal birth.

301. (3) The Messianic prediction, in the fifth verse of the ninth chapter, so strikingly resembles this, as to oblige us to assume, that the subject of both is the same. '*Behold a virgin has conceived, and brings forth a son;*' '*unto us a child is born, a son is given.*' '*They shall call his name Immanuel*,' Deus in terrâ; he shall '*be called Wonderful, Counsellor, Mighty God, Father of Eternity, Prince of peace.*'

302. The Messianic interpretation has been the prevailing one in the Christian Church in all ages. It was followed by all the Fathers and other Christian expositors till the middle of the eighteenth century; some of them, however, held that besides its higher refer-

---

[1] Appositely Rosenmüller in Gabler's Journal, l. c. "Such a mere fanciful application is in itself improbable, since it would here be without an aim, where that which was wonderful and Divine in the event related, was both demonstrated and heightened, by the very circumstance of its being predicted by a Prophet."

[2] In E. T. '*until the time that she which travaileth hath brought forth.*'

[3] Rosenmüller, l. c.   [4] Isa. 7. 17.

ence to the Messiah, it related in a lower sense to an event in the time of the Prophet [1].—The principal objections which, after the example of the Jews, Isenbiehl, Gesenius, and others, have brought against this interpretation, are the following.

303. (1) "It was the main object to give to the unbelieving Ahaz a sign, which would be *immediately accomplished*, and which lay as it were before his eyes. How could this be effected by the promise of the miraculous birth of the Messiah, which occurred many centuries afterwards? How could Ahaz receive a promise *to be fulfilled at a later period*, as a pledge of an event *previously to take place?*" It is of the highest importance here to observe, that although the Prophet directed his discourse in the first instance to Ahaz and his house, as the representatives of the people, yet the sign was intended, not so much for him, as for the people in general, and especially for the pious portion of them [2]. They feared at that time the total ruin of the state, as appears from the Prophet's taking along with him his son Shearjashub, as well as from the purpose of the enemy to effect it, sufficiently manifest in the sixth verse. The Prophet reminded the people of their firm faith in the coming of the Messiah, pointing out the inconsistency between this faith and their fear of the entire subversion of the state. Since the king, he declares, has despised the miracle offered to him by me, God reminds you, through me, of that great event of the future (which is well known, though now forgotten by you), the wonderful birth of the Messiah. Let this be to you a sign of deliverance [3]. As that predicted event will *certainly* come to pass, so is it *equally certain* that before it *has* come to pass the state cannot be destroyed.—And as to the objection, that the promise of the Messiah could be no assurance of safety, since he was not to appear till many centuries later, were it just, it would apply with equal force to *all* the predictions of the Messiah. Yet not Isaiah only, but even Jeremiah and Ezekiel consoled the people, when they were carried away into exile, by predicting the future restoration of the theocracy to a far more glorious condition through the Messiah, *whose appearance was nevertheless many centuries distant.* Indeed the time of his coming was not accurately known to the Prophets themselves: when they spoke of him, they beheld him *present* [4]; and though they did not presume definitely to fix the time of his appearing, which God had withheld from them in order that the prediction might have the more effect, yet they could scarcely have supposed that it would be so long deferred. And even

---

[1] Among the modern interpreters, it has been defended by Lowth, Koppe, Kocher, Dereser, Rosenmüller (ed. II.), Kleuker, and Meyer.

[2] Chrysostom : καί φησι τὸ σημεῖον οὐχὶ τῷ ῞Αχαζ δίδοσθαι λοιπὸν, ἀλλὰ τῷ κοινῷ τῶν Ἰουδαίων δήμῳ. Παρὰ μὲν γὰρ τὴν ἀρχὴν πρὸς αὐτὸν τὸν λόγον ἀπέτεινεν, ἐπειδὴ δὲ ἀνάξιον ἐκεῖνος ἑαυτὸν ἀπέφηνε, τῷ κοινῷ τοῦ λαοῦ διαλέγεται.

[3] Thus Theodoret: ἐπειδὴ ἐδεδίεσαν τῶν πολεμίων προσβολὴν καταλύσειν ἀπειλούντων τὴν Δαβιτικὴν βασιλείαν, ἀναγκαίως διδάσκει, ὡς ἀδυνάτοις ἐπιχειροῦσι. Δεῖ γάρ φησι φυλαχθῆναι τὸ Δαβιτικὸν γένος, ἕως ἂν ἔλθῃ ὃ ἀπόκειται, Gen. 49.

[4] See Chap. 9. 5: "unto us a child is given, a son is born."

if they *had* known the long time which must elapse before his coming, yet still the promise of the Messiah would *always* have been to the Jews a sure pledge that their state could not be utterly ruined.—We now proceed briefly to reply to some objections of Isenbiehl against this method of removing the first-mentioned doubt. " The Prophet (he says) here proposes truths to be remembered by the people, which needed *confirmation*. The sign was the ground of their conviction, and therefore must have been *clear* and *plain*." This objection is set aside by the well established fact, that the future birth of the Messiah, and the redemption of the people through him, were at that time *the general belief*. It appears from the manner in which the contemporaries of the Prophet, Hosea[1] and Micah[2], predict the Messiah, that they also supposed him to be known to the people. This being the case, the truth predicted must have been clear and intelligible to them. " If the Messiah is here the subject of discourse, then *nothing new* is said to the house of David; consequently we have here neither a prediction, nor a sign, but only a rhetorical motive." It is true that what is here said is new, only so far as what was old was *delivered anew* by God to the Prophet, and *confirmed anew* by Divine authority. *Every* prediction of the Messiah was at the same time *both old and new*. Every immediate disclosure respecting future things is a prophecy, whether they may have been known before, or not. According to the remarks already made, a *sign* is *any thing that seems to confirm the belief that a future event will actually take place*. Now the promise of the Messiah, not merely recalled to mind, but confirmed anew by Divine authority, was perfectly suited to the purpose, at least in regard to that part of the people, who held the Prophet to be an ambassador of God, and to them particularly was his discourse directed.—" The ground of consolation suits all other circumstances equally well, and is too general. The Messiah could be borne of the family of Ahaz, without the preservation of the Jewish state in its existing condition, and the continuance of Ahaz on the throne. The Babylonish exile occurred, and yet the Messiah was *not born*. Isaiah then would have employed a sophistical argument." The ground of consolation contained in this verse is indeed general. As the Prophet, by taking with him his son Shearjashub (= *the remnant shall return*), had endeavoured, before he announced deliverance from the present calamity, to remove the fear of the total ruin of the state, though its inhabitants might indeed suffer a temporary captivity, so here also he prepared the mind for the prediction in the sixteenth verse of the fifteenth chapter, of a speedy deliverance from the present danger, by first showing, that the apprehension of the *entire ruin* of the kingdom was groundless : a people to whom, though at a remote period a Divine Redeemer was to be sent, must even at present be under the peculiar care of God's providence.

304. (2) " The biblical idea of a *sign* every where else, is entirely disregarded by this interpretation. It makes it refer to a more dis-

---

[1] Chap. 3. 5.   [2] Chap. 5.

tant event; but, according to the usage of the language elsewhere, a *sign* is a second predicted event, whose *earlier fulfiment* then becomes a certain pledge of the fulfilment of the former, on which it properly depends." We will not here repeat what we have said before concerning the import of a *sign*. This objection is at once sufficiently refuted by the single passage in the twelfth verse of the third chapter of Exodus, in which, as well as in that before us, a *later* occurrence is made *the sign* of an *earlier* one. "*God said, I will be with thee, and this shall be to thee the sign that I have sent thee;* when thou hast led my people out of Egypt, ye shall sacrifice to God on this mountain," that is, you may infer the certainty of the deliverance of the people to be effected through you, from the circumstance that, *after* the happy accomplishment of the Exodus from Egypt, you shall present offerings to me upon this mountain. See further the thirtieth verse of the thirty-seventh chapter of Isaiah: ' *And this shall be a sign to thee*' (of deliverance from the Assyrians), ' *eat this year that which groweth of itself; the next year, what springs up again wild; the third year sow and reap, plant vineyards, and eat the fruit thereof,*' i. e. ye shall *as surely* be delivered from the Assyrians *as* ye shall, &c. Moreover the future event, on which, in this case, the certainty of a present result was grounded, was *regarded as so certain by the people* (which was by no means the case in the two instances cited), that an appeal to it must have been no less convincing, than the present performance of a miracle.

305. (2) "The representations of misfortune which follow, in the seventeenth verse, &c., do not correspond with so magnificent a prediction." This objection is no doubt the weakest of all. Every one who has but a superficial acquaintance with the prophetic writings, knows that they every where predict that the coming of the Messiah shall be preceded by severe Divine judgements and afflictions of the people. It is only necessary to compare the fourth, ninth, and eleventh chapters, and the fifth chapter of Micah, where the description of the Divine judgements precedes, and the second chapter, where, as in the present instance, the prediction of deliverance by the Messiah is given before the denunciation of the judgements which should precede it.

306. (4) " The relation in the eighth chapter so nearly resembles this, that if the Messianic interpretation is there plainly untenable, we are tempted to believe that it must be here also. The name and the birth of a child there, as well as here, serve as a sign of deliverance from Syrian domination. If we must there understand by the mother of the afflicted child, the wife of the Prophet, and by the child one of his sons, so also must this same interpretation be correct here." This passage, far from proving the point intended, serves rather to refute the notion that Immanuel was one of the Prophet's sons. For it is not probable, that the Prophet would have given *two* of his sons symbolical names which related to *one and the same event;* on the contrary, it is entirely suitable to the Messianic interpretation, that a visible sign should have been added to the invisible one, which consisted solely of the promise. Meyer observes: "the

oral, indefinite sign, was not sufficient; it should also be connected with and receive its visible seal, from a matter of fact." The relation differs also in many respects widely from that before us, and certainly has not the same resemblance to it, as the sixth verse of the ninth chapter; here the mother of the child is called a *virgin*, there the *prophetess* [1]; here we have the bare *annunciation* of the birth of a child, there a full account, in which we are told that the Prophet received direction from Jehovah to give his child a name significant of the speedy ruin of Israel and Syria. He further made a record of the transaction, and took credible witnesses, who after the fulfilment should testify to the day on which it was composed, and thereby confirm it; he moreover went in unto the prophetess and she conceived and bore a son; and lastly, in the passage before us, it is the mother who names the child; in that, the father.

307. (5) "The eighteenth verse of the eighth chapter, where the Prophet says that his sons are for signs and wonders in Israel, is in favour of the explanation, that his child was the son of the Prophet and not the Messiah." There would yet remain Shearjashub and Maher-shalal-hash-baz, whom the Prophet seems to have before him in the above-mentioned passage.

308. Ver. 15, 16. '*Milk and honey shall he eat until he knows to reject the evil and choose the good.—Nevertheless, before the child shall know to reject the evil and choose the good, the land shall be forsaken, before whose two kings thou fearest.*' The explanation of these two verses caused the older interpreters much difficulty. The majority supposed that in ver. 15 the true humanity of the Redeemer who should be born, is announced. The name Immanuel indicates (they say) the *Divine*, the eating of milk and honey the *human* nature of the Messiah. Milk and honey were the common food of young children. The sense of the verse would then be: He shall be *brought up and gradually come to maturity, like other children* [2]. But this forced explanation is liable to this objection, besides several others, that it is here entirely out of place to announce the true *humanity* of the Messiah, since it was already implied in the prediction that he should be born of a virgin; and that, in an unnatural manner it interrupts the connexion between the fourteenth and sixteenth verses. These interpreters, for the most part, assume a change of the subject in the sixteenth verse [3]. But this cannot be admitted; since one and the same characteristic, the ability to distinguish be-

[1] נְבִיאָה

[2] Thus Jerome: "Dicam et aliud mirabilius: ne eum putes in phantasmate nasciturum, cibis utetur infantiæ, butyrum comedet et lac." Calvin: "ne existimemus ipsum hic quoddam spectrum imaginari, signa humanitatis declarat, quibus demonstrat Christum revera carnem nostram induisse." In like manner, Irenæus, Chrysostom, Basil, and lastly Kleuker and Rosenmüller, the latter of whom regards this verse as a parenthesis.

[3] By נַעַר Immanuel is not to be understood, but in the opinion of some (as Kleuker), Shearjashub, who accompanied the Prophet; while according to others, no particular child is designated by the word, but it is said in general terms, the desolation of the hostile land shall take place in a shorter time than that, which elapses between the birth of a child and the developement of his moral powers. Thus Calvin.

tween good and evil, is ascribed to the subject in both verses. The
sudden transition is moreover altogether abrupt and unnatural.
Others [1] refer the sixteenth verse also to the Messiah, and resort
to a *jamdudum ;* before the Messiah comes to years of discretion, the
land shall have been *long* forsaken : an interpretation so manifestly
unnatural, that it need not be refuted. How then is it possible to
make these two verses harmonize with the preceding ? How can
the Prophet make the development of the powers of a child, who
should be born seven hundred years later, synchronize with the
deliverance of the land from its enemies, which took place in a little
time after his prediction [2] ? The view of Vitringa, Lowth, and
Koppe, comes nearest the truth. According to them, the Prophet
employs the period *between the birth of the Messiah, and the development of his faculties,* as a measure of time for the complete deliverance of the land from its enemies. It is of the utmost importance
to observe, that the fifteenth and sixteenth verses were spoken by
the Prophet in the same *ecstasy,* in which he beheld the Messiah
(in the fourteenth verse) as present. His vision here, as in all other
cases, has no concern with time [3]. The child appearing before his prophetic eye as already born, he borrows from him his measure of
time. What he means to say, is, that within the space of *about
three years,* the two hostile kingdoms will be overthrown. This
he expresses by saying, that the same space of time would elapse
before that event as between the birth of the child, which he then
beheld as present, and his coming to the age of discretion.—Having
made these general remarks, we now proceed to an explanation
of particulars. It is asked, in the first place, what we are to
understand by eating milk [4] and honey. Several interpreters take
this as a designation of *wealth* and *abundance :* but they have confounded the two very different modes of expression, viz. to *eat*
milk and honey, and to *flow with* milk and honey ; and the twenty-
second verse plainly shows, that the eating of milk and honey
must be regarded as a consequence of a general devastation of the
country. The fields being laid waste, those who remained must
lead a nomadic life, being sustained by wild honey, and the produce

[1] As J. D. Michaelis.

[2] Rosenmüller has remarked, that the Prophet really supposed the Messiah
would be born in his time. But this expedient, at least as he understood it, is
inadmissible. It is true, that the time of the Messiah's appearance was concealed from the Prophets; but it was for this very reason, that they *refrained from
any positive determination of it.* We can however show from sure grounds, that
the Prophet did not expect the Messiah to appear so soon. For the sufferings
to be inflicted by the Assyrians, foretold in the seventeenth verse, &c., must
plainly follow the deliverance from the Israelites and Syrians, and precede the
appearing of the Messiah. And thus is it also in the remaining passages. It
is true, that in the vision of the Prophet the Messiah always appears as present ;
but at the same time he every where announces that before his coming heavy
divine judgements and severe afflictions should overwhelm the people. According to the eleventh chapter, the royal family of David shall then be fallen
into entire obscurity, and a great part of the people be scattered throughout all
lands.

[3] As in the fifth verse of the ninth chapter.

[4] חמאה not butter, but thick and curdled milk.

of their herds, which would now be more numerous than before, in consequence of the great abundance of pasturage. The phrase, ' to know to choose the good and refuse the evil,' signifies the first commencement of moral consciousness in the child, at the age of from two to three years [1]. The sense of the verse therefore is : *the existing generation, represented by this child, whose birth was viewed by the Prophet as present, would not for some years to come obtain the quiet possession of the country, but would be obliged to live on the produce of their herds, which would find abundant pasturage in the devastated land.* Then, in the sixteenth verse, follows the prediction, that nevertheless before the close of this period, the ruin of the two hostile kings, and the desolation of their lands (by the Assyrians) would ensue. So that afterwards, the products of the country which would in the mean time be cultivated, could again be quietly enjoyed [2].—The land will be *forsaken*, that is, it will be laid waste, and deprived of its inhabitants [3].

309. The prophet had thus far predicted only joyful events. He had foretold the deliverance of the land from both the hostile kings ; and as a pledge for the fulfilment of his prophecy, he had appealed to a still more joyful event to be expected in future times. He now pauses for a while, as appears from the absence of a connecting word between the sixteenth and seventeenth verses. His vision is filled with mournful images : new foes, the Assyrians and Egyptians, inundate the land, and convert it into a desert.

310. Gesenius chooses to think that this prophecy of the desolation of Judea by the Assyrians and Egyptians was *never fulfilled*, and is to be regarded as merely a prophetic threatening. His argument is, that the distress brought upon the Jews by Tiglath-pileser in the reign of Ahaz [4], was too inconsiderable to be regarded as the fulfilment of this prediction : and *after* the reign of that monarch we *must not*, he says, seek for its fulfilment, since it is expressly said : ' Jehovah will bring upon *thee.*' But to this objection it may be justly replied, that Ahaz is not here mentioned as an *individual*, but as sustaining the royal dignity, in contradistinction to *the people.* ' Upon *thee*, and upon thy people,' is equivalent to ' *upon the people, and their king.*' Thus, even when Divine judgements, which are not to be inflicted for centuries, are threatened, it is always said, ' Jehovah will bring upon *you*,' &c., although none of the sinners present would live till the prediction should be fulfilled. And this is entirely consistent with the peculiarity of the prophetic vision, already often referred to, that every thing appeared to the Prophets as *present.* Transgression, and its punishment, were exhibited to their spiritual vision, without their perceiving in general the distance of time between them. And when the punishment had several

[1] Deut. 1. 39. Jonah 4. 11.

[2] כִּי in the sense of *yet*, as chap. 8. 23. קוץ with מִפְּנֵי, to *be distressed*, to *fear before any one.*

[3] אֶרֶץ embraces here, at the same time, the land of Israel, and Syria, as is evident from the following words : *before whose two kings thou fearest.*

[4] In respect to which comp. 2 Chron. 28. 20, &c.

gradations, these were left unnoticed, because its commencement and completion were blended in one picture. For an example, we refer to the fifty-first verse of the fiftieth chapter of Jeremiah, where the capture of Babylon by Cyrus, and its final and total ruin, are combined in one description. So here the prediction of the approaching calamity to be caused by the Assyrians, embraces the whole chain of misfortunes, which began with Tiglath-pileser, and ended with Nebuchadnezzar [1]. It was the Assyrians, from whom the Jews thenceforth suffered most. The wretchedness also is included, which Sennacherib under Hezekiah, and Esarhaddon under Manasseh, brought upon the land.

311. The prophet intimates that the calamity to be inflicted by the Egyptians would not be so great, since he does not mention it in the seventeenth verse, but speaks solely of the Assyrians [2]. Eichhorn justly remarks : " The Prophet loses sight of the Egyptians so quickly, because, being already deprived of half their power, they only seldom, and as it were in passing, came into view." As Palestine lay between Egypt and Assyria, it could not but suffer in every war in which both powers were engaged. In this respect also the fulfilment of the prophecy was *gradual*. It was the most completely accomplished, when Pharaoh-Necho, king of Egypt, on the occasion of a war with the Babylonians, conquered the land of Judea, and made it tributary after king Josiah had fallen in battle [3].

312. The figure which the Prophet employs to represent the invading foes is taken, as Eichhorn rightly observes, from the nature of their respective countries. Egypt, especially at the mouths of the Nile, abounds in vermin and insects. Hence the host of the Egyptians appeared to the Prophet, as an enormous swarm of flies. " From the marshes of the Euphrates, he sees the Assyrians advance in swarms of wasps and hornets."

313. Having finished our explanation of the chapter, we must now devote a few moments' attention to those explanations of verses fourteen to sixteen, which differ in essential points from that which has been given. They may be divided into two classes.—(I.) Several interpreters do not indeed deny the reference to the Messiah, but they suppose the Prophet had in view, *in the first instance*, an occurrence of his own time. They believe there is here a *double sense*. The Prophet, they tell us, in speaking of a child of his time, was led by Divine Providence to use expressions which are far better suited to Christ, and are applicable to this child only in a very inferior sense [4].

---

[1] The king of Babylon is expressly called, 2 Kings 23. 29, the king of Assyria, and the best Greek writers also take Assyria in a wider sense.

[2] Upon which Gesenius unjustly grounds his assertion that the words אֶת מֶלֶךְ אַשּׁוּר are to be taken as a gloss. The difficulty, that the words אֶת מֶלֶךְ אַשּׁוּר cannot be taken as epexegetical of יָמִים is removed by the remark, that before the last member is again to be supplied, ' Jehovah will bring, or cause to come upon thee, the king of Assyria.'

[3] 2 Chron. 35. 20. 2 Kings 23. 29.

[4] Thus it was interpreted in the time of Jerome, by an anonymous writer, whom he censures, on account of it: " Quidam de nostris *judaizans* Esaiam prophetam duos filios habuisse contendit, Jaschub et Emmanuel. Et Emmanuel

This interpretation was defended, among others, by Grotius, Richard Simon, and Le Clerc. But it was plainly owing to the seeming difficulties of the strict Messianic explanation : it arose partly from inability to remove them, and partly from a desire to sustain, at least in some degree, the authority of the evangelist Matthew. It has already been shown, that if the prophecy was *properly fulfilled* in the time of Ahaz, no reason whatever can be found, in the text of the Prophet, for a higher reference to the Messiah, since all resemblance thus disappears. The Messianic and non-Messianic interpretation *totally differ as to the meaning of the words.* According to the former, *Almah* is a virgin, *who remains one even after her conception ;* according to the latter, a virgin *who does not remain such ;* the former regards Immanuel as *Deus in terrá,* the latter merely as a *symbol* of the Divine assistance. If therefore we adopt the former, there can be *no reference to the time of the Prophet ;* if the latter, it *exhausts the sense,* and nothing remains to show that we have here a type of the Messiah. Dathe, who perceived these difficulties, but still could not resolve to follow the strict Messianic interpretation, has resorted to a very peculiar expedient. He supposes that Isaiah speaks literally of a virgin of his time, who as a true virgin (modo miraculoso) should bear a son in confirmation of his prediction. Then indeed there would be a resemblance to the birth of Christ ; but surely no one would join with him in its purchase at such a price. To a certain extent Lowth, Koppe, and Meyer belong to this class of interpreters. According to them, the Prophet does not indeed speak of a *particular* child, who should be born in his time, but still he connects the destinies of his country with the name and destinies of a child, whose conception he represents to himself at this moment as possible. "The meaning which would most readily occur to Ahaz (says Meyer) was this : when a maiden now marries, becomes pregnant, and bears a son, she may call his name *God with us,* since God *will* then *be with us.*" Nevertheless the prediction has, they allow, an ultimate reference to Christ. " The prophecy," says Lowth, " is introduced in so solemn a manner ; the sign is so marked, as a sign selected and given by God Himself, after Ahaz had rejected the offer of any sign of his own choosing, out of the whole compass of nature ; the terms of the prophecy are so peculiar, and the name of the child so expressive, containing in them much more than the circumstances of the birth of a common child required, or even admitted ; that we may easily suppose that, in minds prepared by the general expectation of a great Deliverer to spring from the house of David, they raised hopes far beyond what the present occasion suggested ; especially when it was found, that in the subsequent prophecy, delivered immediately afterwards, this child, called Immanuel, is treated as the Lord and Prince of the land of Judah.

de prophetissâ uxore ejus esse generatum, in typum Domini salvatoris, ut prior filius Jaschub, quod interpretatur relictus sive convertens, Judaicum populum significet, qui relictus est et postea reversus, secundus autem i. e. Emmanuel et nobiscum Deus, gentium vocationem postquam verbum caro factum est et habitavit in nobis."

Who could this be, other than the Heir of the throne of David? Under which character, a great and even a Divine person had been promised." We have quoted this passage at length because it states in a very admirable way the various grounds of the Messianic interpretation. As for the rest, none of the defenders of this hypothesis has shown the *necessity* of the inconvenient supposition of a double sense; and the difficulties of the exclusively Messianic interpretation, which seem to have induced them to resort to this expedient, have already been removed [1].

314. (II.) The non-Messianic interpretation remained for a long time the peculiar property of the Jews, until an attempt was made by John Ernst Faber to introduce it into the Christian Church. The Catholic commentator Isenbiehl followed him, in consequence of which he was thrown into prison. He had borrowed its principal points from the prelections of Michaelis, who also rejected the Messianic interpretation, on account of the difficulties attending it; difficulties which he could not remove, from ignorance of the prophetic vision, in which, from deficiency of imagination, he was unable to place himself. Since that time the non-Messianic interpretation has been quite the predominant one. These interpreters, again, disagree among themselves respecting the *Almah*, who was to bear Immanuel.

315. (1) The more ancient Jews make the *Almah*, the wife of Ahaz, and *Immanuel*, king Hezekiah. This interpretation prevailed among them even in the time of Justin [2]. But Jerome easily refuted it, by showing that Hezekiah must have been, at the time, *at least nine years old*. Kimchi and Abarbanel resorted to the supposition of a *second* wife of Ahaz, and Kelle among the moderns *agrees* with them.

316. (2) According to others, the *Almah* was a virgin not to be accurately determined by us, who was present in the place where Isaiah and the king held their conference, and to whom Isaiah pointed with his finger. As surely, declares the Prophet, as that shall soon happen, which I now predict of this virgin, so surely shall that also be fulfilled which I have before predicted respecting the issue of the war [3]. But not to mention other objections, it seems not exactly suitable and proper for the Prophet, in presence of the king and the people, to predict to a virgin her pregnancy.

317. (3) Others regard *Almah* not as an *actual*, but only as an *ideal virgin*. We will give this view in the language of Michaelis. " By the time when one who is yet a virgin can bring forth (in nine months), all will be happily changed, and the present impending danger so completely passed away, that if you yourself were to name the child, you would call him Immanuel." But according to this interpretation we see not wherein the *sign* would consist, since a mere poetic image cannot serve as a confirmatory sign.

---

[1] This hypothesis also is, in fact, subject to the difficulties which, as we have seen, attend that of Grotius and others; and an explanation which understands the אות in a literal sense cannot, as we shall hereafter see, be justified.

[2] Comp. Dial. c. Tryphone, vol. ii. p. 180, ed Wirceb.

[3] Thus Isenbiehl, Bauer, Cube, and Steudel.

318. (4) Others again conjecture the *Almah* to be the Prophet's wife[1]. According to him the sense is as follows : "The Prophet's *wife*, or *betrothed virgin*, shall conceive and bear a son, who shall be called ' God with us,' (in about nine months the people shall be already delivered); until the child shall know good from evil (a period of some years) men shall eat milk and honey (the land, that is, being uncultivated, they shall live upon the produce of their flocks, and the spontaneous productions of nature); but then the land of the two kings shall be laid waste." The sign was to be gradually developed, and contained two distinct purposes, the deliverance of Judea within nine months, and the ruin of the hostile kingdoms within about three years. The chief objections to this view, besides the arguments already advanced for the Messianic interpretation, are the following; which are likewise applicable, in part, to the three other hypotheses to which we have referred.

319. (a) Since the word *Almah* designates only a *virgin*, and never a *young married woman*, it is impossible that the wife of the Prophet, the mother of Shear-jashub, who was already sufficiently old to accompany his father, could be thereby intended. Gesenius declares himself inclined to the supposition, that the former wife of the Prophet was dead, and that he had afterwards betrothed another virgin. But this is a mere fiction[2]. Besides, we cannot perceive how the Prophet could expect to be understood, if he chose to designate his betrothed by the general expression, ' *the virgin*.' We must then, at least, suppose with Plüschke, that he took her with him, and pointed to her with his finger; but of this there is no trace in the narrative, nor would it have been proper, and in accordance with oriental manners.

320. (b) That a son of the Prophet, or any person whatever except the Messiah, is here referred to, is excluded by the circumstance, that the eighth verse of the eighth chapter is called the *land of Immanuel*, which is of itself a sufficient refutation of the third hypothesis. Grotius, Plüschke, and Gesenius resort to the supposition that *aretz* may here signify *native land*. The word, it is true, can sometimes have this meaning *from the context;* but these interpreters are not able to inform us, for what purpose the Prophet should have here directed his discourse particularly to his son Immanuel.

321. (c) We have already shown that the word *sign*[3] does not always signify a *miraculous event*. But the word[4] must still be used in this sense here so far, as to designate something by which the people and king would really be assured of the coming deliverance. Such a sign, as we have already seen, the predicted birth of the Messiah in future times really was. But the Prophet would have exposed himself to ridicule, if he had introduced, with such solemnity and such lofty expressions, an event so natural as the birth of his own son. It might indeed be said, the birth of his son pre-

---

[1] Thus Abenezra, Jarchi, Faber, Plüschke.
[2] Chap. 8. 3, the wife of the Prophet is called simply הנביאה.
[3] אות.   [4] As is shown by לכן.

dicted by the Prophet might give the Israelites a pledge for the remainder of the prophecy: inasmuch as the Prophet could not foresee by human sagacity, whether the Lord would give him a son or a daughter. But then the solemnity of his whole manner, which requires something of greater moment, remains inexplicable, and the opponents cannot avail themselves even of this expedient, since they must then allow the Prophet to have been something more than a mere politician. Plüschke supposes him to have ventured on a bold conjecture. But then it might easily have happened to him, as in the well known case at Worms [1]; and if his conjecture had failed, there would have been an end of all his reputation.

322. (d) Gesenius, making the sign refer to *two* events, instead of one according to the Messianic interpretation, supposes that a period of about three years was to elapse between the deliverance from the enemies, which was to take place in nine months, and the renewed cultivation of the land. But no reason can be perceived why the people may not have returned to the cultivation of their fields, as soon as their enemies had withdrawn. Of the thirtieth verse of the thirty-seventh chapter, Gesenius himself explains the words, " *Eat this year, what grows of itself; the next year, what springs up again wild : the third year sow and reap, plant vineyards, and eat the fruit thereof,*" as follows : " two years the land has now been laid waste by enemies, so that it has been neither sown, nor reaped ; but in this third year, being freed from your enemies, ye shall again sow and reap;" and gives as a reason why the imperatives, sow, reap, plant, must not be referred to the future, that Sennacherib, according to the thirty-sixth and thirty-seventh verses, immediately after withdrew, and then there was nothing to hinder the cultivation of the land.

323. (e) According to the interpretation of Gesenius, the space of about three years intervenes between the deliverance of Judea and the desolation of the two hostile kingdoms. But this cannot be, since it was precisely the irruption of the Assyrians into Syria which brought deliverance to Judea [2].

Isaiah 9:1-7

324. The prophecy from the first verse of the eighth chapter to the sixth verse in the ninth, forms one connected whole; it corresponds in many respects with that contained in the seventh chapter; the occasion of both is the same, the invasion of Judea by the confederated kings of Israel and Syria ; the contents and object are quite similar ; in both we have the prediction of the speedy deliverance from the Syrians and Ethiopians, and their overthrow by the As-

---

[1] Comp. Eisenmenger Entd. Judenth. ii. p. 664, seq.   [2] 2 Kings 16. 9.

syrians, and of the calamities which the Assyrians should afterwards
bring upon the land, the reference to a wonderful Divine child, who
should establish a kingdom of peace, and whose future appearance
furnishes a certain pledge for the preservation of the state in every
danger.   There is even an allusion here, in the ninth and tenth
verses, to the name given to this child in the fourteenth verse of the
seventh chapter.   But notwithstanding all these points of resemblance, the prediction now before us is not entirely contemporary
with the foregoing, as several interpreters have erroneously supposed.
It rather appears, from the difference between the fifteenth and
sixteenth verses of the seventh chapter, and the fourth verse of the
eighth, in the determination of the time which should elapse before
the ruin of the two confederate kings, that this prophecy must have
been spoken from a year to a year and a half later.

325. The course of the prophecy is as follows. The Prophet[1]
represents the speedy destruction of the two hostile kings by a symbolical transaction, with a view to make the bare word spoken in the
seventh chapter an object of sense, and thus deepen its impression.
The Prophet was commanded by Jehovah to write on a tablet or
parchment-roll, in large characters, that every one could read, the
words *Maher-shalal-hash-baz*, ' *the spoil hastens, the plunder quickly
comes*,' i. e. the time when the Assyrians shall lay waste the dominions of the two hostile kings is already near.   He was then to
cause the prophecy, like a judicial document, to be confirmed by the
authority of credible and respectable witnesses, in order that after the
fulfilment he might exhibit it to the unbelieving multitude, and
remove from himself every suspicion of a *prophesying after the event*.
The Prophet complies with the Divine command, and takes for witness the high priest Uriah[2] and Zechariah. He then receives from
Jehovah the further command to name *a son*, who was born to him
at that time, *Maher-shalal-hash-baz ;* since before this child could
speak the name of father and mother, the two hostile lands should be
laid waste by the Assyrians[3].   With respect to the fulfilment, enough
has been said in our remarks on the seventh chapter. By the *spoil of
Samaria*[4] is not to be understood the spoil which should be carried
away from *the city*, but from *the province* of Samaria.   So also in
other passages[5], the land is called by the name of the capital.   This
remark refutes the assertion of Gesenius, that the prediction, as far
as it related to the kingdom of the ten tribes, was not fulfilled until
about eighteen years after the time fixed by the Prophet.

---

[1] Ver. 1—4.   [2] 2 Kings 16. 10
[3] Some interpreters, as e. g. Calvin, suppose, that the symbolical action here
mentioned was not performed outwardly, but only in the internal contemplation
of the Prophet.   At all events, it can be shown that this was the case with *most*
of the symbolical actions of the Prophets.   They were then committed to writing
by the Prophets, and were of the same utility to the people, as if they had been
actually performed.   Thus the symbolical action in Hosea, chap. 1—3, which is
quite similar to this, certainly took place only in the mind of the Prophet.   But
that the one which is here related nevertheless really took place, seems evident
from ver. 18.
[4] Ver. 4.   [5] 2 Kings 17. 26. 23. 19. Jer. 31. 5.

326. In the verses five to eight there follows a prediction of the calamity, which as a punishment from God, should be brought upon Judah, as well as Israel, by the Assyrians, from whom Ahaz and the ungodly portion of the people expected nothing but deliverance. The enemies shall overspread the whole land. The Prophet here, however, by addressing Immanuel, the future great restorer of the theocracy, and calling the land *his* land, shows that the visible theocracy, whose concerns he already directed, could not be brought to ruin, nor the land in which he should, at a future time, be born, remain desolate [1].

[1] The question naturally occurs, what is to be understood by העם הזה ver. 6. Some interpreters understand by these words merely the kingdom of *the ten tribes*, others the *kingdom of Judah*, and lastly, others suppose the discourse to be addressed at the same time to *both*, and the Divine punishment to be threatened against both in the following verses. The latter opinion, in all probability, is the true one. The section cannot relate to the Jews alone; for it could not be brought as an accusation against them, that they took pleasure in Rezin. Several interpreters (Michaelis, Paulus, v. d. Palm, Gesenius) have indeed supposed, that a party had been formed among the Jews, who despised the royal family of David, and favoured the enemies of their country. But of this there is no evidence whatever, and even were it so, how could the Prophet charge the offence of some few individuals upon the people, and represent it as the ground of their punishment? But the supposition, that a great part of the people, weary of the existing government, would have readily submitted to the hostile kings, is inconsistent with chap. 7. 2, where it is expressly asserted, that Ahaz with his whole people was greatly terrified. In chap. 7, moreover, the invasion of the Assyrians is not by any means, as would then have been the case, represented as a punishment for rebellion against the royal house of David, but for the want of a theocratic disposition, manifested by the king and his people in seeking aid from the Assyrians. Further, that there is a joint reference to Israel appears also from ver. 14, where the two houses of Israel are spoken of, and lastly the prediction of prosperity, ver. 23, which relates directly and chiefly to one part of the kingdom of the ten tribes, shows that the corresponding threatening must in like manner relate to the same kingdom. It is otherwise impossible to see what could have induced the Prophet to announce prosperity to these regions. But it would be equally erroneous to refer the discourse, with the author of the Exeg. Handb. and others, to the Israelites alone. It is evident that the address must have been chiefly directed to the Jews, even from the fact, that ver. 11 and 12, the apostate portion of the Jews, the untheocratic multitude, are twice called *this people*, and still more so from the circumstance, that according to ver. 8 the punishment was to fall upon the Jews also, who must consequently have borne a part in the crime mentioned in this verse. We must therefore conclude with Vitringa and Lowth, that the verse refers to both Jews and Israelites. The offence in the first member, the despising of the waters of Siloah, can be referred at the same time to both. The interpreters, for the most part, understand by the soft flowing waters of Siloah, the royal house of David, reigning within narrow limits, and already on the decline; but without good reason. Contempt of the royal house of David, in itself considered, was no crime; and the Prophet here, as in chap. 7, reproaches the people for having put their trust in human aid, instead of the power of God. Were the Prophet speaking merely of despising the royal house of David, his reproach would not affect Ahaz, upon whom it ought however chiefly to fall. Rather by the soft flowing waters of Siloah, which, though neither abundant, nor splendid, were a great blessing to the inhabitants of Jerusalem, in contradistinction from the roaring waters of the Euphrates, which laid waste the adjacent country by overflowing its banks, we are to understand the kingdom of God among the Jewish people in so far as it was manifested in the kingdom of the house of David, which, though outwardly humble and without splendour, would yet afford the people

327. He says this still more plainly in the ninth and tenth verses. He here addresses the nations hostile to the theocracy—in the first instance the Assyrians [1], and announces that their efforts to destroy the covenant people were in vain, since the great deliverance which Jehovah would hereafter accomplish through Immanuel, whose name is alluded to, was a pledge even of his present help. God must *even now*, in an inferior sense, be with a people, with whom He *would be hereafter* in the truest sense.

328. The Prophet might now have announced, as he usually does elsewhere, immediately after the inferior deliverance the higher one by the Messiah ; just as, in the second part, he commonly connects the prediction of the deliverance from the captivity with that of the times of the Messiah. In order however to awaken the ungodly from their false security, and inflame the zeal of the pious, he here suspends the prediction of salvation, and gives [2] the *subjective* conditions, on which it is to be imparted, predicting at the same time the fearful calamity which will fall upon that portion of the people who fail to fulfil them. The deliverance, says the Prophet, which I announce to you, depends not on human conjecture, but on a Divine revelation ; still God has, at the same time, taught me the conditions which you must perform, before it can be obtained.

329. The Prophet here employs [3] peculiar imagery ; or rather the revelation respecting what must be done by the people is conveyed to him in a peculiar form. The Prophet has a conference with God in a vision [4]. In this interview *he himself* represents the *better part of the people* who were ready to receive the word of Jehovah, in contradistinction to those [5], of whatever rank, who rejected his authority. For this reason Jehovah speaks to him in the plural. He admonishes him to repose his confidence in Him alone, and not, like the unbelieving part of the nation, to sin against Him by distrustful fears of human power and earthly foes. As He would be to the unbelieving apostate portion of the people in both kingdoms, a

more support, security, and blessings than the most powerful foreign kingdoms, if they did not through unbelief sin against its king and make themselves unworthy of his protection. The fountain of Siloah is here appropriately used as an image of the theocracy; for it issued forth at the foot of the holy hill of Zion, which was the seat of the theocracy ; just as the Euphrates is employed as an image of the kingdom of Assyria, since it is the chief river of that country. Now Ahaz and the untheocratic portion of the people had become guilty of contemning the theocracy, inasmuch as looking only at the appearance of things, instead of raising themselves above this by faith, they had sought help from the Assyrians. The Israelites had committed the same offence, by combining with its enemies against the theocracy, which they hoped easily to overthrow. The crime mentioned in the second member, of taking pleasure in Rezin and the son of Remaliah, was peculiar to the Israelites. Instead of trusting in Jehovah alone, the Israelitish people were proud of their own might and that of Rezin their ally. The inundation by the Assyrians, which the Prophet foretold, came upon the kingdom of the ten tribes under Tiglathpileser and Shalmaneser, and upon Judah under Sennacherib.

[1] Not the Syrians, as several interpreters suppose. For the connexion of this verse with ver. 23 shows that the Prophet here had in view the common enemies of both houses of Israel, ver. 14.

[2] Ver. 11—22.   [3] Ver. 11—15.   [4] בַּחֲזַקֵת יַד יְהֹוָה.   [5] הָעָם הַזֶּה.

severe judge, and bring upon them a heavy destruction, so would He
be the faithful helper and Redeemer of the believing and obedient[1].
After Jehovah has thus addressed the better portion of the people in
the person of the Prophet, He directs His discourse[2] particularly to
him, commanding him to exhort His disciples, (*i. e.* those who rely
solely on His word and His revelation,) His faithful worshippers[3], to
perseverance in the revealed religion and to the observance of His
law[4].

330. With the sixteenth verse the admonition, thus clothed in the
form of an address of Jehovah to the Prophet, is concluded; the
latter then addresses himself to the people, and especially to those
who feared God. He declares to them his firm confidence, founded
on the Divine promise, that though Jehovah would now cause the
people to feel his heavy displeasure, yet He would not suffer them to
be destroyed. He appeals to the names of himself and his sons,
which were prophetic of salvation, *Isaiah*, 'the salvation of God,'
Shear-jashub, 'a remnant shall return,' and *Maher-shalal-hash-baz*,
which might serve the people[5] for types of future events[6], impressing
upon them, in a sensible manner, the truth, that Jehovah could not
forget His people, and suffer them to perish. He exhorts them to
rely on God alone, and not, in an unlawful manner, to seek from
other sources a knowledge of the future. He requires in general a
firm adherence to the revealed will of God, and concludes with a
lively description of the affliction which would come upon the
people, if they did not perform the conditions of the covenant, and
submit themselves entirely to the authority of the supreme Lawgiver. This threatening was fulfilled, whenever the people were
visited by the purifying chastisement of God; but was especially carried into execution, when Jerusalem was destroyed by the Romans.

331. The Prophet having thus excluded the ungodly part of

---

[1] This passage is several times cited in the N. T. Luke 2. 34. 1 Pet. 2. 7.
Rom. 9. 32, 33. It is also referred to the Messiah by the Jews; comp. Julkut
on h. l. fol. 43. c. Raym. Martini, Pug. Fid. p. 343. ed. Carpzov. It may justly
be called *Messianic*, inasmuch as the truth of this declaration will be especially
manifest at the time of Christ's appearance.

[2] Ver. 16.   [3] See chap. 54. 13.

[4] The expression in this verse is metaphorical. Writings of importance
were *bound up together*, *sealed*, and *preserved in a case*. The Divine revelation is accordingly represented as such a writing to be bound together and
sealed; the hearts of believers, upon which it should be impressed, being the
case, in which the writing thus bound and sealed is deposited. Gesenius prefers
to understand by תְּעוּדָה and תּוֹרָה the consoling prediction ver. 1; he takes ' *bind
and seal,*' literally. The Prophet, he supposes, receives command to bind up and
seal the prophecy until its fulfilment. But were this interpretation adopted, the
verse would greatly interrupt the connexion; besides it cannot be proved on
philological grounds, that by תְּעוּדָה and תּוֹרָה a single consoling prophecy would
be designated, and that such is *not* the import of the words in this place appears
from ver. 20, where, according to the explanation of Gesenius they are used to
signify *the law*. How it could be asserted, that their sense is different in the
two places, is hard to be conceived. The interpretation of בְּלִמֻּדָי *by, with consultation of my disciples*, is also unnatural. Aquila expresses the true sense of the
passage: ἐνδησον μαρτύριον, σφράγισον νόμον ἐν τοῖς διδακτοῖς μου.

[5] For אֹתוֹת and מוֹפְתִים.   [6] Isaiah 20. 3. Zech. 3. 8.

the people from the salvation, and admonished those who feared God to render themselves fit to receive it, continues[1] the prediction of salvation, interrupted at the tenth verse of the eighth chapter. The inferior deliverance is followed by the higher one, which he represents, as usual, by images taken from the earthly theocracy. After severe sufferings, the people shall experience a time of prosperity. The blessings of this period shall be chiefly enjoyed by the province of Galilee—the region of Israel, hitherto the most deeply sunk in misery and ignorance. The covenant people, from among whom, according to the preceding threatening, the ungodly have been excluded, will experience a wonderful deliverance, and be blessed with joy and peace. All the blessings will be conferred through a miraculous child, whom the Prophet[2] had named Immanuel, and to whom, in the eighth and tenth verses, he had again referred. At once man and God, born and eternal, a descendant of David and the Son of God, mighty in counsel and in action, the Restorer of peace to mankind at war among themselves, he will extend, without limit, his eternal dominion, not by force like earthly conquerors, but by righteousness.

332. Ch. 9. 1. '*For darkness shall not be upon the land, upon which there is distress; as the former time has dishonoured the land of Zebulun, and the land of Naphtali, so shall the time to come honour it, the region on the border of the sea, by the side of the Jordan, Galilee of the Gentiles*[3].'—The tribes of Zebulun and Naphtali dwelt by the sea of Gennesareth, the tribe of Zebulun having it for its eastern border, that of Naphtali for its southern. Hence the region of the two tribes was called '*the way of the sea*,' or '*the country along the sea*.' Both tribes had, at the same time, the Jordan for a boundary. Hence their district is called '*the land by the side of the Jordan*[4].' According to several interpreters, by '*Galilee of the Gentiles*' is meant only one particular part of what

---

[1] Ver. 1.   [2] Chap. 7. 14.

[3] The verbs הֵקַל properly, *to make light*, then, *contemptible, to cover with disgrace*, and הִכְבִּיד, *to make heavy*, then metaphorically, *to honour*, a sense properly peculiar to Piel, in which however Hiph. also occurs Jer. 30. 19. [The E. T. translates the former '*to afflict lightly*,' the latter '*to afflict more grievously*.'] Other interpreters, appealing to the circumstance, that there is no analogous case where כ is used precisely for כַּאֲשֶׁר, translate: '*as Jehovah in former times has made contemptible the land of Zebulun, and the land of Naphtali, so will he make it honourable in the time to come*.' The particle כ is then not used by way of comparison, but to determine the time, as is often the case. As subject, Jehovah is to be supplied, or we may with Augusti take both verbs impersonally: 'he has made contemptible,' for 'one has made contemptible,' *i. e.* 'it has been made contemptible.' Before הָאִחֲרוֹן then כעת is to be supplied. It can however be taken also in the accusative, as an answer to the question, *when*. That the passage posseses more poetical beauty, according to the former explanation, cannot be questioned. Also כ in several places has the sense of כַּאֲשֶׁר, if we only supply the ellipsis.

[4] It is true this appellation commonly signifies, 'the land *beyond* Jordan,' or 'the region of Perea;' but here this cannot be the meaning, since these words are explanatory of the land of Zebulun and Naphtali. But all Galilee was on

afterwards formed the province of Galilee. But in this passage, which is the only one where the appellation occurs, there is nothing which favours this limitation. The province was called Galilee of the *Gentiles*, because its inhabitants were even then intermingled with the Gentiles.—But in how far was this region, which was chiefly held by the tribes of Zebulun and Naphtali, made *contemptible?* The assertion seems to relate partly to its outward calamities, partly to the moral degradation of its inhabitants. (1) The district of these two tribes constituted the border-land towards the heathen nations; the Galileans were therefore always first exposed to the assaults of enemies. Thus under king Asa they experienced a severe overthrow from Benhadad, king of Syria [1]. In the time of Isaiah it was they especially, who suffered in the Assyrian invasion under Tiglath-pileser [2]. Although this event could not yet have taken place, since Isaiah [3] represents the invasion of the land of Israel by the Assyrians as still *future*, and the Jews were still harassed by the Israelites and Syrians, he may nevertheless have referred to it, since he *foresaw* that the predicted invasion of the Assyrians would first fall upon the region of Galilee. (2) The Galileans not only dwelt in the *vicinity* of the heathen, but a multitude of the latter had always remained in the country [4] from the time of their first taking possession of it. Solomon gave Hiram, king of Tyre, twenty cities in Galilee [5]. The Phenicians, with whom they held commercial intercourse, and with whom they dwelt intermingled, were among the most corrupt of all the heathen nations. That the reproach of Galilee consisted especially in this mingling of its inhabitants with heathens, who exerted the most baneful influence upon them, Isaiah himself seems to indicate by the appellation, 'Galilee of the Gentiles,' which has erroneously been regarded as a geographical name [6]. To this must be added its great distance from Jerusalem, where the power of religion was chiefly concentrated, notwithstanding the corruption of a portion of its inhabitants. Consequently, the pure knowledge of religion was in a great measure lost among the Galileans, and ignorance and superstition occupied its place. Hence arose the general contempt in which they were held in the time of Christ [7].—But wherein consisted the honour, or the glory, which in future times should be conferred upon this despised people? The evangelist Matthew gives us the answer. He says [8] that the prophecy was fulfilled, when Christ fixed his residence

---

this side the Jordan. We must therefore take עֵבֶר in the sense, *side*, which it often has. See Gesen. s. v. It here stands in the Accus. *adverbiascens.* The name גְּלִיל הַגּוֹיִם, is properly ' the *circle* of the Gentiles.'

[1] 1 Kings 15. 20.   [2] 2 Kings 15. 29.   [3] Ver. 4 and 5—7.
[4] Judges 1. 30—35.   [5] 1 Kings 9. 12.

[6] Thus Theodoret: Γαλιλαίαν δὲ τῶν ἐθνῶν καλεῖ ὡς καὶ ἀλλοφύλων συνοικούντων τοῖς Ἰουδαίοις. διὰ τοῦτο καὶ ἐν σκότει πορευομένους καὶ ἐν σκιᾷ θανάτου καὶ χώρᾳ οἰκοῦντας ὀνομάζει τοὺς τῆς χώρας ἐκείνης οἰκήτορας καὶ τοῦ θείου φωτὸς ὑπισχνεῖται τὴν αἴγλην.

[7] John 1. 47. 7. 52. Matt. 26. 69.   [8] Chap. 4. 13.

at Capernaum in Galilee, within the borders of Zebulun and Naphtali. Christ passed the greatest part of the time of His public ministry in Galilee; there lay Capernaum, His ordinary place of abode; in Galilee were most of His disciples; there He performed many miracles; there the preaching of the gospel met with much success; and even the name of Galileans was transferred to the Christians in the first centuries[1]. It is evident that this honour was not to be conferred upon Galilee at an earlier period, partly because the Galileans, as Michaelis has shown, then enjoyed no special prosperity, and partly because, according to the fifth verse of the ninth chapter, the Galileans, as well as the rest of the covenant people, were not to obtain this salvation until the appearing of the great King, who had been promised. Altogether similar is the passage in the first verse of the fifth chapter of Micah, which is properly compared with this by Gesenius. As ,there, the birth of the Messiah shall confer honour upon the *hitherto obscure* Bethlehem, so here shall Galilee, *hitherto held in contempt*, upon which the Jews cast the reproach that no prophet arose there, be raised to honour and rendered illustrious by the manifestation of the Messiah. This passage gave rise to the opinion of the Jews, that the Messiah would appear in Galilee.

333. Verse 2. ' *The people that sit in darkness see a great light; upon them who sit in the land of the shadow of death, a light arises*[2].'—The people are the Galileans, the inhabitants of the region mentioned in the foregoing verse; for there is no reason to suppose a change of the subject; still however it appears, that here as well as afterwards, there is at the same time a reference to the rest of the Jewish people. The land appears to the inward vision of the Prophet enveloped in thick darkness, which is suddenly penetrated by a clear light, as the darkness of night by a flash of lightning. Light and darkness supply the orientals with a twofold metaphor, being employed to express physical good and evil, prosperity and adversity; and also moral good and evil, righteousness and truth, sin and errour. In the former sense, they occur e. g. in the eighteenth verse of the eighteenth chapter of Job, where it is said of the ungodly: ' He shall be driven from light into darkness,' and in the seventeenth verse of the twenty-first chapter. In the latter sense, the Messiah[3] is called the *light of the heathen*, he who removes the spiritual darkness of sin and errour, as the sun disperses natural darkness[4]. In the latter sense also it is said[5], ' Behold *darkness* covers the earth, and *gross darkness* the people,' and the extension of true religion among the heathen through the Messiah, is

[1] Theodoret strikingly observes: ἡ Γαλιλαία γὰρ τῶν ἱερῶν ἀποστόλων ἦν πατρίς· ἐν ἐκείνῃ τὰ πλεῖστα τῶν θαυμάτων ὁ δεσπότης εἰργάσατο· ἐκεῖ τὸν λεπρὸν ἐκάθηρεν· ἐκεῖ τῷ ἑκατοντάρχῳ τὸν οἰκέτην ἀπέδωκεν ὑγιᾶ· ἐκεῖ τὸν τῆς Πέτρου πενθερᾶς κατέσβεσε πυρετόν· ἐκεῖ τὴν Ἰαείρου θυγατέρα τὸν βίον ὑπεξελθοῦσαν ἐπανήγαγε πρὸς ζωήν· ἐκεῖ τὰ τῆς θαλάσσης ἐστόρεσε κύματα· ἐκεῖ τοὺς ἄρτους ἐπήγασε· ἐκεῖ τὸ ὕδωρ εἰς οἶνον μετέβαλε.
[2] הָעָם   [3] Chap. 42. 6. 49. 6.   [4] John 1. 9. 8. 12.   [5] Chap. 60. 2.

represented as a coming to the great Light which has risen upon the
covenant people. According to Malachi [1], in the time of the Messiah
the Sun of righteousness shall arise upon the pious.—The question now
occurs, in which sense the figure is here to be understood. The recent
interpreters, for the most part, stop at the former, that of prosperity
and adversity ; but erroneously. As the disgrace, in the foregoing
verse, signifies not merely physical evil, but at the same time, and
indeed chiefly, sin and errour, so also must the corresponding darkness
be taken in an equally comprehensive sense. Both meanings of the
metaphor, therefore, are here to be combined. The people, physically
and spiritually miserable, shall be enlightened, sanctified, and blessed
by the coming of the Messiah. The same double sense occurs also
in the splendid passage in the first verse of the sixtieth chapter,
‘ Arise, shine, for thy *light* is come, and the glory of the Lord is
risen upon thee [2].”

334. Verse 3. The glory of the time of the Messiah is present to the
Prophet ; he beholds the covenant people increased in numbers, freed
from all suffering, and filled with joy ; in a transport he turns to
Jehovah and celebrates what He has done for his people. ‘ *Thou
increasest the people, to whom before thou gavest little joy ; they joy
before thee, according to the joy in harvest, and as men rejoice when
they divide the spoil.*’ Several interpreters [3] suppose that the Prophet here, and in the two following verses, speaks in the first
instance of prosperity near at hand, of the rapid increase of the
Israelites after their return from the Babylonish exile, in which the
inhabitants of Galilee also must have participated,—as may be inferred
from the accounts of Josephus respecting the great population of
that province in his time. Vitringa directs our attention to the fact,
that the Jewish people, after the exile, not only filled Judea, but also
spread themselves into Egypt, Syria, Mesopotamia, Asia Minor,
Greece, and Italy. But although the Prophets frequently blend in
this manner an inferior and a higher deliverance, (as *e. g.* in the second
part of Isaiah, where the blessings immediately after the exile, and
the blessings of the Messiah’s time, are often not carefully separated),
yet there appears to be here no sufficient ground for the supposition
of a double reference ; all perfectly agrees with the time of the
Messiah, if we do not mistake the figurative character of the prediction, and at the same time bear in mind, that here, as in most of
the prophecies of the Messiah, the feeble beginning of his kingdom
is closely connected with its glorious completion. The extension of
the theocracy, by the reception of the heathen, often appeared to the
Prophets under the image of a great increase of the people [4]. There
is however no reason to reject the first explanation, which gives a

[1] Chap. 4. 2.

[2] The preterites רָאוּ and נָגַהּ are explained by the circumstance, that events
really future appeared to the inward vision of the Prophet as already passed.

[3] As Calvin, Vitringa, Le Clerc.

[4] See chap. 2. 2—4. 54. 1, &c. 66. 8, &c. Ezek. 37. 26, and other places. The
words לֹא הִגְדַּלְתָּ הַשִּׂמְחָה are to be translated, *whose joy thou didst not before enlarge.*
This is a Litotes for, *upon whom thou hast heretofore inflicted heavy sufferings.*

meaning so appropriate.—The Prophet, in what follows, expresses first the nature of this joy and then its greatness under two images. The joy on account of the blessings received, is a *joy before God*, a *holy joy*. The expression is taken from the sacrificial feasts in the courts before the temple, at which the partakers *rejoiced before the Lord*[1]. Joy in harvest, and in dividing the spoil, is employed else- where, as well as here, as a metaphorical designation of *the highest joy*. The time of harvest in Palestine, especially when the harvest was abundant, was one of great rejoicing. The reapers sang songs, and those who passed by gave them a benediction, in which they wished them prosperity. The joy of an abundant harvest must have been the greater, because, according to the theocratic law of a visible retribution, it served as a proof of the Divine mercy; while on the contrary a failure of the crops was a manifestation of the Divine displeasure[2].

335. Verse 4. '*For his heavy yoke, the staff which smote his neck, the rod of his driver, thou hast broken as in the day of Midian.*' In this verse the reason of the people's joy is given. Jehovah has accomplished for them merely by His own power, without human means, a glorious deliverance and redemption. This deliverance of the theocracy from all its enemies, which has only commenced, and the completion of which is still to be expected, is here represented under the image of a deliverance from powerful oppressors; such as were the Assyrians at an earlier, and the Babylonians at a later period. But that it must not be regarded as a mere temporal deliverance, is evident from verses four to six, according to which its author shall be the Messiah, the Prince of peace; his kingdom, a kingdom of peace, extended over the whole earth, and that not, as the kingdoms of the world, by force, but by justice and righteousness. —The great deliverance to be hereafter accomplished by Jehovah, is finally compared with a deliverance, which He formerly vouchsafed to the covenant people, the deliverance of the Israelites under Gideon from the dominion of the Midianites[3]. The *day of Midian* is the day which has been rendered memorable by the overthrow of the Midianites. In Arabic, *day* often stands elliptically for *day of battle*.—The question now arises in what consists the *tertium compa- rationis* of the earlier and the later redemption. Herder thinks that it consists in the sameness of the place. He says, " The images are taken from the times of Midian, and of the victories of the judges. As it was in the northern part of the land, that the great deliverance was effected, as it was in the dark forests of Naphtali and Zebulun that the light of freedom arose upon the whole land; so also now shall the light of freedom here arise." This is indeed a beautiful point of comparison, but still it must not be regarded as the only one. It was characteristic of the deliverance from the Midianites, that it was not effected by human power, but by the most evident

---

[1] לִפְנֵי יְהוָֹה, Deut. 12 7. 14. 26.

[2] On the division of the spoil, see Jahn II. 2. § 246.

[3] Judges 7. 19, &c.

interposition of God. So also shall Jehovah accomplish the far greater redemption to be effected by the Messiah of whom Gideon was a type, not by human means, not by the force of arms, but in a miraculous manner; and thus establish the kingdom of peace on earth [1].

336. Verse 5. In this verse the idea is further unfolded, that the great redemption shall be accomplished, not by earthly weapons, but in a miraculous manner by the power of God. ' *For every war-shoe put on at the noise of battle, every garment dipt in blood shall be burnt, shall be the food of fire,*' literally : ' for with respect to every war-shoe of those who put them on in the noise of battle, and every garment of war stained with blood, it shall be for burning, for the consumption of fire.' The great future redemption will be like the deliverance under Gideon ; because far from being accomplished by force of arms, with it all contention and war will cease. Most interpreters suppose, that the image here employed, is taken from the custom among several nations, of burning the weapons and bloody garments after a battle [2]. But it by no means appears from the passages cited in its favour, that this practice prevailed among the Hebrews [3] ; besides the allusion here would be entirely unsuit-able, since the subject of discourse [4] is not a peace *which follows a conflict,* but a peace which shall be introduced by Jehovah *without a conflict.* Gesenius therefore justly regards the figurative expression as a general designation of the commencement of that peace which shall never end. The sense : ' all the preparations for war shall then be burnt, as being of no further use.' This explanation is in harmony with the numerous parallel passages, in which peace is represented as a characteristic mark of the time of the Messiah, when even in nature itself, contention, war, and destruction, shall cease [5]. *From the commencement* of the Messiah's kingdom this peace has existed in the disposition of its members ; *at the end* of this kingdom it will also outwardly prevail, and the fulfilment of this and similar pro-phecies has therefore but just commenced [6].

337. Verse 6. ' *For unto us a child is born, unto us a son is given, and the government shall be upon his shoulders, and his name shall*

---

[1] Thus Calvin.　　　　[2] See Virg. Æn. 8. 561, 562. Lowth on the passage.
[3] Psalm 46. 10. Ezek. 39. 9.　　　[4] As is shown by the particle כִּי.
[5] See e. g. chap. 11. 6, 7. Psalm 72. Micah 5. 9—13. Zech. 9. 9, 10.
[6] The ἅπ. λεγ. סְאוֹן often misinterpreted, is explained by a comparison of the Syr. Chald. Eth. and signifies a soldier's shoe, or half boot, which formed a part of his armour, Jahn, Archäol. 2. 2. p. 412. The verb סָאַן is a denominative, and signifies *to draw on such a war-shoe.* רַעַשׁ *disquiet, noise,* stands here for the tumult of battle. Rosenmüller translates בְּרַעַשׁ *cum strepitu,* and refers it to the rattling of the war-shoes, which however does not appear altogether appropriate. שִׂמְלָה *garment* receives here from the connexion the special meaning, *war-garment.* Shoe and garment stand as *species pro genere,* for all warlike preparation. מְגוֹלָלָה part. Po. from גָּלַל properly *rolled about.* The וּ in וְהָיְתָה is the Vav apodotic. The foregoing nouns stand in the nominative absolute.

be called Wonderful, Counsellor, Mighty God, Father of eternity, Prince of Peace.' The Prophet has hitherto spoken only of the salvation, which should be extended from Galilee over the rest of the land ; the author of this salvation here first appears before him in all his exaltation and glory.—We shall first give the explanation of this and the following verse, and afterwards examine the hypo-- thesis, which makes Hezekiah, instead of the Messiah, their subject. For the present, we take it for granted, that the Messianic interpre- tation is the true one.—The Prophet [1] beholds the great Redeemer as *already born.* If any one chooses to infer from thence that the subject of the prophecy must, at that time, have been actually born, he must also, on account of the preterites, in the first and following verses, assume, what no interpreter has done, that the predicted prosperity had already been conferred upon the Israelites. *Son* here seems to possess peculiar emphasis. We may either explain it with Vitringa : Unto us a son is given, namely a son of Him who has given him, or we may suppose with Herder, that *ben*, here emphatic[2], signifies a *son of God.—' On his shoulder the government shall be.'* In this prophecy the Messiah presents himself to the Prophet in glory, and not, as in other prophecies, in the form of a servant. The figurative expression here, as well as in the twenty-second verse of the twenty-second chapter, is not taken from the idea, that the government was regarded as a *burden*, but rather from the cir- cumstance, that the insignia of dominion, the mantle with which kings and other great men were clothed when they appeared in public, was worn upon the shoulders. The regal dignity was not considered as a burden, but as an ornament of which the king was the bearer[3].—With respect to the following names it is in general to be observed, that the recent interpreters, viewing them with too little regard to their mutual connexion, have not reflected that, though the reference of *some* of them to a human subject were *possible*, yet this is excluded by the connexion in which they stand with the rest. The first name[4] properly signifies as an abstract, *miracle*, and is especially employed to denote the wonderful works by which God glorified Himself in the history of the Israelites. Here it stands, as the abstract for the concrete, as a stronger expression for *miraculous*. It imports that the great king, in his being and in his works, will be exalted above the ordinary course of nature ; that his whole mani- festation will be a miracle. This meaning of the word is confirmed by the parallel passage in the eighteenth verse of the thirteenth chapter of Judges, where the angel, who announces the birth of Samson, says : ' Wherefore askest thou after my name ; it is *Wonder-*

---

[1] As in chap. 7. 14.   [2] As רב in Psalm 2. 12.
[3] Pliny : "cum abunde expertus pater, quam bene humeris tuis sederet im- perium." The passage Cic. pro Flacco, c. 38 : "de salute omnium nostrum, de fortunis civitatis, de summa reipublicæ taceo ? quam vos universam in hoc judicio vestris humeris, vestris inquam humeris, judices, sustinetis," which is commonly quoted in favour of the first mentioned opinion, is not to the purpose, since dominion is not here the subject of discourse.
[4] פֶּלֶא

ful[1],' *i. e.* my whole nature is miraculous, full of mystery, and therefore cannot be designated by any human name. Plüschke, except
that he refers the name too exclusively to miraculous works, and not
to the supernatural character of his being, justly remarks : " he
shall be called Wonderful on account of the great events which will
take place in the beginning of his reign, and during its continuance,
resembling those mighty works of God, which Israel had seen and
experienced in former times, when, *e. g.* they were led out of Egypt,
through the sea, through the wilderness, and through the Jordan[2]."
The second name[3] is a designation of *wisdom* and *intelligence*.
Supernatural wisdom and Divine power, as the two chief virtues of a
Ruler, shall adorn the great king.—The third name[4] is *the mighty
God.* Gesenius: *the mighty hero.* El[5] has indeed this meaning
also; but that this is not its sense in the passage before us, is
evident both from the twenty-first verse of the tenth chapter, where
the two words likewise occur in the sense, ' *mighty God,*' and from
the following name, which also ascribes a Divine attribute to the
king. We have already seen[6] that the doctrine of the true deity
of the Messiah was already known under the old covenant, and also
that the name Immanuel signifies, *God become man.* When Gesenius reminds us, in case the meaning *God* is here adopted, of the
custom of the Orientals to ascribe Divine attributes to kings, he
entirely overlooks the difference between the Hebrews and all idolatrous nations. The name Son of God, in the Old Testament sense
of representation and subordination, justly belonged to the theocratic
kings as well as to other magistrates. But had Isaiah called an
earthly king God, or given him Divine predicates, he would have
acted in direct opposition to his duty to defend the rights of God
from every encroachment, and have rendered himself unworthy of
the dignity of a Prophet[7]. The fourth name is [8]literally,
Father of eternity. This allows of a twofold explanation. Either,
we may suppose[9], that Father of eternity is the same as Eternal

[1] פֶּלֶא

[2] According to Jahn and Gesenius, the word here means nothing more than
remarkable, distinguished, extraordinary. But as פֶּלֶא is the standing expression
for *miracle*, see *e. g.* Ex. 15. 11. Ps. 77. 12. 15. 78. 12. Dan. 12. 6, so here especially, where it stands in connexion with other names of so high import, are we,
least of all, justified in taking the word in an unusual sense.

[3] יוֹעֵץ   [4] אֵל גִּבּוֹר   [5] אֵל

[6] In the chapter " On the Divinity of the Messiah in the Old Testament,"
which, in this abridgement, will conclude the work.

[7] Plüschke endeavours in another way to set aside the deity of the king : " In
my opinion," he says, " this name is altogether symbolical. The Messiah shall
be called strength of God, or strong God, Divine hero, in order by this name to
remind the people of the strength of God." But this explanation is refuted by
the very connexion in which גבור אל stands with יעץ. As the latter must signify
the wisdom of the king, so must the former, according to the parallel passage,
chap. 2. 2, signify his strength. In opposition to the accents, several interpreters would separate the two words אל and גבור from each other. Thus of old,
Aquila : ἰσχυρὸς, δυνατὸς, and Jahn *deus, fortis.*

[8] אֲבִי עַד

[9] According to a frequent usage of the Status Constructus.

Father, when the meaning would be, that the Messiah will not, as must be the case with an earthly king, however excellent, leave his people destitute after a short reign, but rule over them, and bless them for ever.   Or we may explain it by the usage of the Arabic, in which he who *possesses* a thing, is called *the father* of it, *e. g.* the father of mercy, the merciful.   We have the more reason to suppose this usage adopted here, since in respect to proper names especially it very often occurs in Hebrew.   Thus e. g. *Father of strength*[1], strong; *Father of knowledge*[2], intelligent; *Father of glory*[3], glorious; *Father of goodness*[4], good; *Father of compassion*[5], compassionate; *Father of peace*[6], peaceful.   According to all these analogies, ' *Father of eternity* ' is the same as *eternal*.   According to both explanations, the latter of which is much to be preferred, a Divine attribute is here ascribed to the Messiah.   For although the longest duration of which a thing is in its nature capable, is some-times expressed in Hebrew by the idea of eternity, yet this limita-tion must always be shown by the context; thus e. g. ' he shall be thy servant *for ever*[7],' for ' *as long as he lives.*'   Here, on the con-trary, not only is there no intimation in the context of such a restric-tion, but the connexion of this appellation with the others, compels us to take it in its most comprehensive sense.   The *eternal reign* of the Messiah, in contrast with the *temporal reign* of the human rulers of the theocracy, is made especially prominent also in the seventy-second Psalm, which bears throughout a strong resemblance to this pro-phecy.   That there the word *eternal*, in the seventeenth verse, is to be taken in the stricter sense, is evident from the additional phrase, ' *as long as the sun endureth*[8].'   The fifth name is ' *Prince of Peace*[9], In this name there is plainly an allusion to the name Solomon, *the peaceful*, which is perhaps directly given to the Messiah in the seventy-second Psalm.   As under the reign of Solomon, the theo-cracy enjoyed an *outward* and temporary peace, so under that of his great successor and antitype, it shall enjoy a *real* and *everlasting* peace.   In like manner also in the blessing of Jacob, the Messiah is called *Shiloh*[10], *peacemaker.*

338.   Verse 7.   ' *Without end will the dominion, without end will the peace increase on the throne of David and in his kingdom, that he may establish and sustain it by justice and righteousness, from hence-forth to eternity.   The zeal of Jehovah the Almighty will do this*[11].'

[1] אֲבִי אֵל   [2] אֲבִי דָע   [3] אֲבִי הוֹד   [4] אֲבִי טוֹב

[5] אֲבִי נֵצַם   [6] אֲבִי שָׁלוֹם   [7] Deut. 15. 17.

[8] Paulus and Jahn interpret, ' *Father of his age ;*' but this is entirely arbitrary, since עַד never occurs in this sense.   The explanation of Herder, besides being ungrammatical, is extremely forced, ' *my Father to eternity ;*' that is, he will thus address Jehovah.   It would then, at least, have read אֲבִי.   Contrary to the analogy of the other names, Plüschke, ' *everlasting Father,*' to remind them that God is the *everlasting Father of his people.*

[9] שַׂר שָׁלוֹם   [10] שִׁילֹה

[11] The word מַרְבָּה, *increase*, is a noun after the form of מַשְׁקֶה and מַרְאֶה, properly a participial form.   In the middle of it is a ם final, which was at first, in all pro-bability, accidental, but was afterwards supposed to contain great mysteries.

On the ' *throne of David and over his kingdom, that he may establish it,*' *&c.* is a concise mode of saying, This increase of power shall proceed from the Messiah, who, sitting upon the throne of David, shall extend it over his kingdom, the theocracy, which he shall be constantly intent upon sustaining by justice and righteousness. The sense is, through the great descendant of David, the Messiah, the theocracy shall for ever be increasing in extent, and after all opposition shall be subdued, its members shall be blessed with perfect inward and outward peace. But this dominion, unlike the kingdoms of the earth, shall be founded, established, and administered, not by force, but by righteousness, which shall move the hitherto hostile nations to yield to it a willing and joyful submission[1]. While the kingdoms of this world pass away, the kingdom of the Messiah will be eternal, as its King[2].—In the last words, ' *the zeal of Jehovah will effect this;*' we may either, with Herder, understand by it the *zeal of God for His honour*, which moved Him to fulfil His promise to the covenant people of a future great descendant of David, and at the same time also to vindicate His honour in opposition to the idols; or the *zeal of love*, a sense in which it often occurs[3]. The raising up of so illustrious a king, the establishment of his everlasting kingdom, the subduing all opposition to it, is a work of the love of God, which moves Him to have compassion on His people, who for their own works had deserved an entirely different fate.

339. We have here, in conclusion, still to add some general remarks, as to the subject of the fifth and sixth verses. The older interpreters unanimously acknowledge the Messiah as such; this also was the view entertained by the Jews in ancient times. The later Jewish critics, on the contrary, were offended, by the Messiah's being here described as God, contrary to their system of doctrine. On doctrinal grounds, therefore, they relinquished the received interpretation, and sought to make the passage agree with Hezekiah, but for this end were obliged to resort to the grossest perversions[4]. Grotius was the first among Christian commentators to relinquish the Messianic interpretation. Le Clerc himself acknowledges, that these predicates agree with Hezekiah only *sensu admodum diluto*.

340. It is inconceivable how any one, except from doctrinal prejudice, should regard king Hezekiah as the subject of this prediction. Against him, and in favour of the Messiah, the following are the most important arguments.

341. (1) The testimony of the New Testament. Gesenius indeed asserts that there is the less occasion to adopt the Messianic interpretation, since the New Testament gives no evidence in its favour; but he is here in errour. For if, as we have seen, the two first verses

---

[1] See the parallel passage, Psalm 72. 12, where the voluntary submission of the heathen nations, is also represented as the effect of the righteousness, mildness, and compassion of the great king.

[2] Comp. Psalm 72. 17.   [3] E. g. Cant. 8. 6.

[4] Among them R. Lipmann, however, allows the Messianic interpretation to be in a manner valid. Perceiving that the prophecy cannot relate exclusively to Hezekiah, he extends it to all his successors of the line of David, *including the Messiah*, by whom it shall be most completely fulfilled.

of this chapter must, according to the testimony of the New Testament and internal evidence, be explained of the honour and the blessings which should be conferred on despised Galilee by the Messiah, it cannot well be perceived how the author of this honour and these blessings, described in the fifth and sixth verses, can be any other than he.

342. (2) It is decisive against Hezekiah, that the discourse is not here concerning prosperity destined merely for the kingdom of Judah, but concerning a glorification chiefly of the province of Galilee, which belonged to the kingdom of the ten tribes, and over which Hezekiah neither had, nor could have any influence.

343. (3) The attributes here ascribed to the great king afford a strong argument against Hezekiah, and every earthly ruler. Herder well observes, " Could the Prophet more plainly show to whom he refers? Surely it is not to Hezekiah or Hezekiah's son, as if he were writing a birthday ode ; he speaks of a king, who himself bears all the names and blessings of the house of David, and introduces the promised golden age." If we consider the prophecy only as a human conjecture, how could the Prophet, to whom such political sagacity is ascribed on other occasions, and by which it is thought his fulfilled predictions may be explained, expect Hezekiah, who was then about ten years of age, and who came forward under such unfavourable circumstances, to realize the hopes which he had expressed concerning the future ruler, to extend his kingdom without limit, and found an everlasting dominion? How could he ascribe *Divine attributes to Hezekiah, a feeble mortal,* and thus insult the majesty of God, whose servant he was? It would have been only senseless flattery, which must have appeared to Hezekiah himself as satire, for Isaiah to utter such language ; but his character, as it is established by history, secures him against every suspicion of this sort. Even among the idolatrous heathen, the practice of ascribing divine names and predicates to kings, did not originate till a later and corrupt age ; and in what light this practice was viewed by the Jews, let the example of Josephus show [1], who regards the death of Agrippa as a punishment for not disapproving the conduct of the people, who cried out to him as a god.

344. (4) In favour of the Messiah is the similarity of this prophecy with other Messianic passages, viz. with the Psalms before quoted, especially the seventy-second Psalm, and with the remaining Messianic predictions in the first part of Isaiah. The same characteristics are here ascribed to the Messiah, which constantly occur in the prophecies respecting him, *perpetual peace* under his reign, its *vast extension,* his *everlasting dominion, &c.*

345. (5) Against Hezekiah is the parallel passage in the fourteenth verse of the seventh chapter. We have before spoken of the similarity of these two places, and shown that both must belong to one and the same subject. If then, as is generally confessed, Hezekiah cannot be the subject of the former, neither can he be of the latter.

[1] Arch. 19. 8th, 2nd.

346. Against the supposition, whereby Gesenius has endeavoured to *combine* the Messianic interpretation with that which makes Hezekiah the subject, we may urge, that no analogous example can be produced, where a Prophet had connected his hopes of the Messiah with a definite person, by whom they were not realized. Allowing the exact distance of time which separated them from the Messiah to have been unknown to the Prophets, so that they might have believed (as the Apostles did concerning the *second coming* of Christ), that His manifestation *might* take place even in their time, still no proof can be found in any passage, that, going beyond what was communicated to them from above, they predicted that it actually *would*. But it is the more improbable that the Prophet should have placed his Messianic hopes on Hezekiah, since, according to the fourteenth verse of the seventh chapter, and according to the passage before us, the Messiah was to be a higher, and more than human being, which it would have been difficult indeed for the Prophet to suppose of Hezekiah. Moreover, the view of Gesenius being assumed as correct, we must in like manner refer all the Messianic predictions of the Prophet to Hezekiah, and thereby involve ourselves in many absurdities.

347. The objections which have been brought against the Messianic interpretation, disappear of themselves before a correct insight into the nature of the prophetic vision. The most common of these objections is, that the whole connexion requires a *present* and not a *future* subject, and that we must therefore refer the whole to a prince of the royal family, already born ; but Lowth long ago justly remarked in reply, that it is the constant practice of the Prophets to place temporal deliverances in connexion with spiritual ones. As Isaiah, in the second part of his prophecies, always connects the deliverance from the captivity with the deliverance by the Messiah, passing over from the former to the latter ; and as towards the close of the tenth chapter he describes the overthrow of the Assyrians, and then in the eleventh chapter abruptly speaks of the Messiah's kingdom ; so here he suddenly directs his view to the higher benefit, after having described the inferior one[1]. Every deliverance in the nearer future, suggested at the same time to the Prophets that great deliverance in the more distant future, which was the occasion of the former, and the pledge of its accomplishment. The distance of time does not thereby come into consideration, because it is neither known, nor regarded by the Prophets, who behold all events of futurity combined in one picture.—Another objection against the Messianic interpretation, that here political expectations lie at the foundation, and the discourse is not concerning a moral kingdom, arises, partly from a literal and false understanding of the prophecy, and the disregard of its metaphorical character, and partly from ignorance of the nature of the kingdom of Christ, of which Christ is king and sovereign in the most proper sense, since by His humiliation, and the redemption thereby accomplished, He has obtained the right to exercise dominion.

[1] Chap. 8, 9, and 10.

Isaiah 11 & 12

348. This section constitutes a part of a larger whole, which begins with the fifth verse of the tenth chapter. The contents of this whole portion are as follows; the Prophet had before repeatedly described the calamity which the Assyrians, an instrument in the hand of the Lord, should bring first upon Israel, and then upon Judah. The foregoing portion [1], which, though not contemporaneous with this, was certainly not placed in connexion with it without design, was probably composed after the Syrians, confederated with the Israelites, had already been overthrown by the Assyrians. In it the Prophet had threatened the Israelites with the devastation of their country, and the final and total annihilation of their state, which were impending on account of their transgressions. This threatening had already been fulfilled in the period which had elapsed between this prophecy and the foregoing. The king Tiglath-pileser, after the conquest of Syria, had invaded the kingdom of the ten tribes, and carried away a part of its inhabitants into captivity; Salmanezer at a later period had taken Samaria, and almost put an end to the kingdom of the ten tribes, since only a few of its citizens were left in the land. Judah also, under Ahaz, had already suffered much from the Assyrians, from whom that help had been foolishly sought, which Isaiah had in vain exhorted the people to seek from God alone. But they had reason to apprehend still greater calamities from the same quarter. Under these circumstances the Prophet came forward and delivered the present discourse, the object of which is to animate the drooping courage of the people, and inspire them with firm confidence in God, who might, indeed, inflict heavy judgements upon them, (since, according to the law of visible retribution which prevailed in the theocracy, sin and apostasy must not remain unpunished), but who would never suffer them to be utterly destroyed, because their destination to receive the Messiah among themselves had not yet been fulfilled.

349. The whole discourse is of a joyful character; the Prophet had no more occasion to threaten, since his former threatening had now become a reality, and all was dismay before the approaching invasion of the king of Assyria. A two-fold deliverance of the covenant people was presented in vision to the Prophet; the latter and greater, as it pre-supposed the former, served to confirm it.

350. The first [2] portion is chiefly directed against the king of Assyria. This king, unconscious of his destination to be an instrument in the hand of God for the punishment of His rebellious people, had attributed all His victories to himself; he believed he might, with ease, entirely subdue the covenant people, and audaciously derided the Almighty God of Israel as a powerless being, who could not help His people. He shall therefore suffer a terrible over-

---

[1] Chap. 9. 7. 10. 4.   [2] Chap. 10. 5—35.

throw¹. True, he shall succeed in penetrating to Jerusalem, but
while he prepares to capture the city, he shall be overtaken by the
vengeance of Jehovah². —How strikingly this prediction was fulfilled is well known³.

351. The second portion⁴ is closely connected with the fore-
going⁵. In the last verse of the tenth chapter the Assyrians had
been compared to a magnificent forest, which should be cut down by
the hand of Jehovah; here, on the contrary, the house of David
appears as a tree which had been felled, from whose roots a small
shoot would spring forth, and, insignificant at first, grow up to a
stately tree. This portion is chiefly occupied with the description of
the illustrious attributes of the great Restorer and King, and the
nature of his kingdom⁶.

352. The contents are as follows. From the house of David,
fallen into total obscurity, a Ruler shall hereafter arise, who, though
lowly and obscure at first, will attain to great glory. The Spirit of
God, who shall dwell constantly with him, will furnish him with all
those endowments which the discharge of his official duties require.
By the aid of this Spirit he will easily discriminate between the
pious and the ungodly; he will search the heart, and therefore will
not, like worldly kings, be deceived by the outward appearance.
While he becomes the patron of oppressed innocence, and maintains
the rights of those who cannot procure justice for themselves, he will
destroy the ungodly, not like earthly kings by outward punishment,
but by the bare word of his mouth; instead of worldly splendour,
righteousness and faithfulness shall be his highest ornament⁷.
When the Prophet has thus described the person of the great
Restorer, he proceeds to speak of the character of his kingdom.
Under his reign, even in the irrational part of the creation, all discord and destruction, introduced by sin, shall cease; sin and crime
shall be known no more; his dominion will not be confined to the
ancient covenant people; the heathen, before devoted to their idols,
shall reverently turn to him⁸. While the Prophet in the first part of
the chapter has spoken rather of the Messiah in general and his
kingdom⁹, he now announces, by a figure taken from the theocracy,
what he will accomplish especially for the covenant people, for whom
indeed the prediction was in the first instance designed. The restoration of the Jews (dispersed, as the Prophet foresees, in the time of
the Messiah's appearing, into widely different lands), as it has in
part already taken place and shall be completed before the end of
the world, is represented under the image of their being led back to
the holy land, at that time the seat of the kingdom of God, succes-

¹ Ver. 5. 27.   ² Ver. 28. 34.
³ See chap. 37.   ⁴ Chap. 11 and 12.
⁵ This is evident from its commencing with Vav copulative.
⁶ Reinhard and others are disposed to derive from this a proof against its
connexion with the foregoing; but unjustly, since it is the custom of the Prophets to connect with the representation of the inferior and nearer deliverance,
that of the greater and more distant.
⁷ Ver. 1—5.   ⁸ Ver. 6—10.   ⁹ Ver. 11—16.

sively connected with it in the vision of the Prophet. The harmony
and love, which will unite the covenant people with each other in
the time of the Messiah, are represented under the image of the
extinction of the most fatal dissension of former times—the enmity
between Ephraim and Judah ; the prosperity which the people shall
enjoy, under the figure of the conquest of hostile neighbours, taken
from the prosperous reign of David ; and the removal of all hindrances
to their prosperity under the figure, furnished by the history of the
redemption from Egypt, of the drying up of the Red Sea and the
river Euphrates. In the twelfth chapter follows a song of thanksgiving, which the Prophet puts into the mouth of the redeemed [1].

353. The Messianic interpretation of this prophecy has the authority of the New Testament. Not only are *appellations* taken from
it ascribed to the Messiah, as ' *root of David* ' in the Apocalypse ;
but St. Paul *quotes* it to prove the calling of the heathen, and in
another place employs the words of it, and ascribes what is said in it
to the Messiah [2].

354. Verse 1. The Prophet announces, in the commencement [3],
that the fate of the royal house of David should be totally different
from that of the Assyrians, which he had just foretold. The
Assyrians were abased, when they were most highly exalted, the
royal house of David shall be exalted, when sunk the lowest.
" *And a rod goes forth from the stem of Jesse ; a shoot from his root
bears fruit.*' The image of a sprout for a descendant is very common [4]. Hensler endeavours to prove that the word translated ' *stem* [5] '
does not mean a trunk of a tree that has been cut down, *truncus*,
but only the trunk of a tree in general, *stipes*. But this is in oppo-

---

[1] Several recent critics have doubted the genuineness of a part or the whole of
chap. 11 and 12. On the contrary, it has been defended by Beckhaus, Jahn,
Bertholdt, Gesenius. The only tolerably plausible objection to the genuineness
of these chapters is, that the Prophet, ver. 1. speaks of the royal family of
David, as sunk into entire obscurity, and of the Jews, as well as of the Israelites,
ver. 11, &c. as though they had already been carried away captive into the most
distant lands. This objection loses all force, as soon as we apply to it the
remark, which will be proved to be just in the introduction to the second part,
that the Prophets frequently transfer themselves into the future, which then
became to them, in vision, the present. And thus the Prophet here describes
the condition of things, not in his own time, but in the time when the great promised Redeemer should appear.

[2] Apoc. 5. 5. 22. 16. Rom. 15. 12. 2 Thess. 2. 8. Theodoret speaks of the
infatuation of those (very few) who interpreted it of Zerubbabel : more (whom
Hengstenberg combats at length in the original work) have interpreted it of
Hezekiah. Among Christian commentators Grotius was the first to adopt this
interpretation.

[3] As in most prophecies of the Messiah, so also in the one before us, no
regard is paid to the gradual development of His kingdom. The fulfilment,
therefore, has only commenced, and will be completed in the future, when, after
the fulness of the Gentiles shall have been brought into the kingdom of God,
and apostate Israel converted, the consequences of the fall, even in external
nature, shall be done away.

[4] See chap. 4. 2, and the examples from profane writers by Reinhard on this
passage.

[5] נֵצֶר

sition (1) to the etymology[1]: (2) to the Hebrew usage[2]: (3) to
the connexion[3]. It is said in the second member, *a sprout from
his roots* shall bear fruit. Unless we choose to explain this
altogether unsuitably of a *wild shoot*, which springs up from the
roots of a *tree that is still standing*, we must understand by the
word : *a trunk which had been cut down to its roots.*—The
question now arises, why the Messiah is here represented as the
sprout of *Jesse*, when in other places He is called the sprout of
David[4]. The Prophet hereby wished to indicate, that the family of
David would then have so much declined, that it would be more
appropriately designated after its humbler, than its royal ancestor[5].
The expression : ' *a shoot from his roots will bear fruit,*' is as much
as to say, ' *a shoot sprung from his roots will grow up to a stately and
fruitful tree.*' By this image it is foretold, that the Messiah, before
he should attain to glory, would be obscure and lowly. A parallel
passage is found in Ezekiel[6], where the Messiah is compared to a
tender twig, which, planted by Jehovah on a high mountain, puts
forth boughs, and bears fruit, so that all the fowls dwell beneath it.
It is scarcely necessary to mention, that figure and reality are
blended together in the verse. It would be paraphrased thus : ' *as
a tree, which had been cut down, sends forth a young shoot from its
roots, which, insignificant at first, soon increases to a stately and fruitful tree, so also a king will arise from the family of David, buried in
neglect and obscurity, who, inferior and unnoticed at first, will afterwards attain to great glory*[7].'

355. Verse 2. ' *Upon Him rests the spirit of Jehovah, the spirit of
wisdom and insight, the spirit of counsel and strength, the spirit of
knowledge, and of the fear of Jehovah.*' The sense : He will possess
in abundant measure the Spirit of God, and as particular manifestations of it, the qualifications mentioned. ' *The Spirit of Jehovah, the spirit of wisdom,*' is the same as ' *the Spirit of Jehovah who*

---

[1] The word is derived from גוע equal to גדע *to cut off*, or *cut down*.

[2] The word occurs besides only in Job 14. 8 and Isa. 40. 24. In the latter
place some interpreters indeed wish to give it the meaning *trunk* in general;
but entirely without reason. See Rosenmüller on the passage.

[3] It is also opposed to the dialects. In the Talmud, and in Syriac, the word
signifies *truncus*. In Arabic the root جِذَع has the meaning *secuit*. After
all these proofs, it is of little consequence, that the Arabic جِذْع sometimes stands for *trunk* in a wider sense. Also Aquila, Symmachus, and Theodotion translate κορμὸς, *truncus*.

[4] See Micah 5. 1. Vitringa gives as the reason, that the Messiah should be
born at Bethlehem, which was the dwelling place of Jesse, but not of David.

[5] Calvin : " Davidem ipsum non nominat, sed potius Isai. Adeo enim im-
minuta erat illius familiæ dignitas, ut rusticana potius et ignobilis quam regia
videretur."

[6] Chap. 17. 22, 23.

[7] Interpreters, from not observing this mingling of figure and reality, have
been led to many erroneous explanations ; thus e. g. Vitringa asks : Who the
roots of the house of David can be ? and understands by them the most distinguished of his descendants; and J. H. Michaelis explains יִפְרֶה by *spirituali
sobole augebitur, &c.*

imparts wisdom,' &c. The genitive here does not denote possession, but effect [1]. Perhaps the circumstance, that the Messiah is first said to be endowed with the Spirit of God in general terms, and that then particular gifts are mentioned by way of example, indicates that he would not, like all other servants of God, be endowed with any merely *particular* gifts [2]. Although the word *rests* [3] is elsewhere spoken of the Spirit of God, when it takes possession of the mind [4], yet here it seems to be peculiarly emphatic. The Prophets were powerfully seized by the Spirit, and then again deserted ; but His influence with the Messiah shall be uniform and permanent [5]. In respect to the particular gifts mentioned, it is to be remarked, that the Prophet does not design to specify *all* the perfections of the Messiah ; he rather mentions only some few, after he has included all the rest in the general one, the spirit of Jehovah. Thus *e. g.* righteousness is wanting here.—Further, we are not to proceed upon the principle that all here mentioned were distinguished from each other with philosophical accuracy by the Prophet. Such accurate discrimination is not to be found in general among the Hebrews, with whom that blending together of the qualifications conferred by the Spirit, and of the theoretical and practical, which took place in real life, is also plainly expressed in the language. There is indeed a certain difference between the expressions selected, yet it is not such, that one would exclude the others. On the contrary, the first attribute [6], *wisdom*, includes nearly all the rest. The meaning of wisdom, especially among the Hebrews, is very comprehensive. It is always at the same time practical and theoretical. It comprehends the knowledge of what is good and desirable, and corresponding sentiments and conduct. It also includes prudence, or the ability to select the best means for the attainment of the best ends. It is here coupled with *insight* [7], the gift of a judging and discriminating sagacity.

---

[1] So Psalm 4. 2, אֱלֹהֵי צִדְקִי, *the God of my righteousness* ; 2 Cor. 1. 3. ὁ θεὸς πάσης παρακλήσεως. Reinhard, who in his whole explanation of this verse is influenced by the mistaken hypothesis, that it exhibits the Messiah as a prophet, erroneously supposes, after the example of the Chaldee, that רוּחַ יְהוָה means specifically the prophetic spirit ; and appeals to passages like chap. 40. 1. 61. 1. But we have seen already, that the Messiah is not here exhibited a prophet, but as a king. רוּחַ יְהוָה different from רוּחַ אֱלֹהִים, inasmuch as Elohim is the general, and Jehovah the theocratic name of God, is the power with which God qualifies His instruments for the advancement of His kingdom, and exalts and consecrates their natural endowments ; which gives skill to the theocratic artificer, the view of futurity to the prophet, and wisdom and all the virtues of a ruler to the theocratic king. See 1 Sam. 16. 13.

[2] Theodoret: τῶν μὲν γὰρ προφητῶν ἕκαστος μερικήν τινα ἐδέξατο χάριν, ἐν αὐτῷ δὲ κατῴκησε πᾶν τὸ πλήρωμα τῆς θεότητος σωματικῶς, καὶ κατὰ τὸ ἀνθρώπινον δὲ πάντα εἶχε τοῦ πνεύματος τὰ χαρίσματα.

[3] רוּחַ   [4] See Num. 11. 25.

[5] What Isaiah expresses by the word נוּחַ, John expressed by the Greek μένειν, John 1. 32, 33. 14. 16, 17, probably with distinct reference to this place. Jerome : " In quo *requievit* Spiritus Domini, id est *æterna habitatione permansit*, non ut avolaret et rursum ad eum descenderet, sed juxta Joannis baptistæ testimonium, jugiter permaneret."

[6] הָכְמָה   [7] בִּינָה

There is a difference between them in regard to the objects to which they refer: inasmuch as the former designates the moral, the latter the pure theocratic virtue of knowledge. While the first and last couple of attributes are such as the king must possess as a man, the second couple are especially requisite for kings as such, in order to the successful administration of their government. *Counsel*[1] signifies the power of forming a quick and wise resolution even in the most difficult cases. *Strength*[2], the power to carry this resolution into effect; the great king shall be mighty in counsel, and in action. We are not to understand by it *bravery in war*, since the kingdom of the Messiah is the kingdom of *peace;* he needs no worldly courage or weapons against the ungodly, but he slays them, as it is said in the fourth verse, by the breath of his mouth[3]. Of the two last attributes, the *knowledge* and the *fear* of Jehovah[4], both together convey the idea of religion so far as it comprehends (1) a knowledge of God, and (2) a corresponding disposition. Both are always viewed in Scripture as connected; without the fear of God (which does not exclude love to Him, but implies it) there can be no true knowledge of Jehovah. Hence the expressions here used for a part, are employed in other places to designate the whole[5].

356. Verse 3. '*He will easily distinguish the fear of God; he will not judge after the sight of his eyes, nor punish after the hearing of his ears*[6].' The sense is, *the king whose insight and wisdom are praised* in the foregoing verse, *will possess the gift of the discerning of spirits in so high a degree, that he will distinguish at first sight the pious from the ungodly*[7].—The two following members contain a consequence of the first. Vitringa thus renders, *therefore he will not judge after the outward appearance, &c.* The sense is : since the Messiah searches the heart, he will not judge with the danger of erring, merely according to the superficial appearance, or hearsay evidence, as the best earthly kings often must, but his decision will always be correct. In like manner, in the eighth verse of the sixteenth chapter of the first book of Samuel, it is said of God, as it is here of the Messiah, ' The Lord seeth not as man seeth, for man looketh on the outward appearance, but the Lord looketh on the heart.'

357. Verse 4. A just worldly king suffers himself to be bribed by nothing external; he protects suffering innocence, and restrains by punishment the oppressions of the wicked. Thus also will the

---

[1] עֵצָה   [2] גְּבוּרָה

[3] As here, עֵצָה and גְּבוּרָה are placed in connexion, so in chap. 9. 5 the Messiah is called in reference to the first attribute, יוֹעֵץ *counsellor*, and in reference to the second אֵל גִּבּוֹר *mighty God.*

[4] After דַּעַת, יְהוָֹה is to be supplied from what follows.

[5] Psalm 19. 9. Hos. 4. 1. 6. 6.

[6] The verb רִיחַ is sometimes construed with the accusative of the thing, sometimes as here with the prep. בְּ. To *smell* (literally *smell*) is here used metaphorically, for a quick and penetrating judgment and knowledge. So in other languages, e. g. in Cicero *odorari.*

[7] See John 1. 48, 49. Luke 7. 39.

Messiah protect the poor and innocent sufferers, and destroy the ungodly. '*He judges with righteousness the lowly, procures impartial justice for the meek in the land; he smites the earth with the rod of his mouth, slays the ungodly with the breath of his lips.*' The word [1] *low, poor* [2], occurs here with the accessory idea of *innocence, humility*, and *virtue*, as is commonly the case with words that signify *poverty* and *lowliness;* while those which signify *wealth* and *power* have often the accessory idea of *wickedness* and *oppression* [3]. That the Messiah would especially interpose for the poor and wretched, is asserted also in the fourth and twelfth verses of the seventy-second Psalm, and the seventh and following verses of the eleventh chapter of Zechariah; and this feature, taken from a pious head of the theocracy, and interwoven with the portrait of the future Messiah, is found ennobled and spiritualized in the character of Christ.—In the second part of the verse *the earth* [4] is limited to the *ungodly* [5]. The ground of this designation constantly used in the N. T. '*world,*' seems to be, that the ungodly on earth are so much superior in number and power, that the little band of the pious entirely disappear before them.—The phrase *with the rod of his mouth*, which has perplexed interpreters, and even led some of them to change the text, is easily explained by the supposition of a silent antithesis. *Staff* [6] often stands, as an instrument of punishment, for *rod of correction.* Earthly kings employ against transgressors outward instruments of punishment,—the Messiah punishes by his bare word, which alone is sufficient to 'slay the wicked.' That we are not here with Reinhard and others to understand merely severity in in punishing, (rod of his mouth, equivalent to *sententiarum severitas*,) is shown by the following member, where likewise especial importance is given to the circumstance, that the Messiah should inflict punishment by his bare word. *The breath of his lips* [7], the same as bare word, bare command [8]. That which is here spoken of the Messiah is in other passages attributed to God; thus in the thirtieth verse of the fifteenth chapter of Job it is said of the ungodly, '*he shall perish by the breath of his mouth.*' The Chaldee paraphrast translates, '*and with the breath of his lips the wicked Armillus shall be slain* [9]. He understands therefore the collectiv enoun [10] as singular, and makes it refer to the Armillus [11], the monstrous and last enemy of the Jews, who wages cruel wars with them, and slays the Messiah Ben Joseph, but shall at last be slain by the bare

---

[1] דַּל

[2] As appears from the parallelism with עֲנָוִים.

[3] בְּצֶדֶק not as Reinhard supposes, *benignly*, but with righteousness, without respect of persons.

[4] אֶרֶץ

[5] By the contrast with דַּלִּים and עֲנָוִים, and by the parallelism with רָשָׁע.

[6] שֵׁבֶט   [7] רוּחַ שְׂפָתָיו

[8] Similar to רוּחַ פִּיו which elsewhere occurs, Psalm 33. 6.

[9] וּבְמִמְלַל סִפְוָתֵיהּ יְהֵי מָמִית אַרְמִילוֹס רַשִּׁיעָא

[10] רָשָׁע   [11] ἐρημόλαος s. v. a. מחריב עם *vastator populi.*

word of the Messiah Ben David[1]. Paul employs those words in
the eighth verse of the second chapter of the second of Thessa-
lonians in describing the destruction of Antichrist by the Messiah,
who, nevertheless, like the '*ungodly*' in this verse, is probably
not an individual, but *the enemies of Christ collectively*[2]. The
Apostle justly refers the expression of the Prophet to the highest
manifestation of penal justice on the part of the Messiah against the
highest manifestation of ungodliness, without thereby excluding its
reference to all other enemies of the kingdom of God, and to all
other times. As the fulfilment of the promise of the blessing which
the Messiah would confer on the poor and the meek extends through
all history, so also does the fulfilment of the threatening against the
ungodly.

358. Verse 5. '*Righteousness will be the girdle of his loins, and
faithfulness the girdle of his waist.*' A silent contrast here also
lies at the foundation. While temporal kings are clothed with worldly
magnificence, and invested with worldly ornaments, the glory of the
Messiah will be spiritual, his most beautiful ornament, righteousness and truth[3]. The representation of attributes under the image
of garments is very frequent in the Old and New Testament[4].
Righteousness[5], the most illustrious attribute of earthly kings, is
every where made particularly prominent among those of the
Messiah[6].

359. Verse 6. After describing the person of the illustrious king,
the Prophet proceeds to describe his kingdom. On the sixth, seventh,
and eighth verses the question arises, whether the representation
is to be considered throughout as metaphorical, or as in some measure
literal; in other words, whether the Prophet would represent only
metaphorically the cessation of all hostility among men, or whether
he expected in the time of the Messiah the actual cessation of all
enmity, all destruction, all that is hurtful, even in the irrational part
of the creation. The former view was adopted by most of the older
interpreters[7]. But, nevertheless, the literal interpretation, defended
by several Jewish interpreters, and which first presents itself to every
unprejudiced critic, claims an undeniable superiority, provided it
does not adhere too closely to the particular images, but merely

---

[1] Buxtorf. Lex. Chald. c. 221—224. Eisenmenger, Entdecktes Judenth. ii. 705
seq.

[2] See Koppe on this passage.

[3] Calvin: "Non apparebit instar regum purpura indutus et diademate, aut
præcinctus baltheo, sed justitia et veritas in eo apparebunt."

[4] E. g. chap. 59. 17. Job 29. 14. Psalm 131. 9, and many passages in the
epistles of Paul.

[5] צֶדֶק

[6] For example, chap. 53. 11. Jer. 23. 5. 33. 15. Psalm 45. 5. 72. 2.

[7] Thus Theodoret remarks: διὰ τῶν ἡμέρων καὶ ἀγρίων ζώων τροπικῶς τῶν
ἀνθρωπείων ἠθῶν ἐδίδαξε τὴν διαφοράν. He refers all to the union of those in
the Christian Church, who were by nature far from each other, and on terms of
mutual enmity. Jerome even regarded the opposite interpretation as a sort of
heresy. So also Calvin (*nearly*), Vitringa, Michaelis, Jahn, and others.

embraces the fundamental thought, the removal of all destruction even from the irrational creation, and its return to its original condition. The principal reasons in its favour are the following:— (1) The parallelism with the condition of the creation before the fall, as it is presented to us in Holy Scripture. Surely it cannot be without cause, that in the history of the creation such peculiar stress is laid upon the fact, that every thing created was very good. This supposes, that the irrational creation was in a condition different from the present, in which it gives us, in some measure, a true representation of the first apostasy, and in which every hateful vice has its likeness and representative in the animal kingdom. According to this history beasts of prey did not at that time possess their present ferocious nature : they acknowledged in Adam their lord and king, peacefully collected around him and received from him their names [1]. The whole animal creation bore the image of the innocence and peace of the first man, and the law of mutual destruction was yet unknown. According to the thirtieth verse of the first chapter, grass only was appointed as the food for beasts, and herbs, besides the fruits of the trees, &c. for men. The serpent had not as yet its frightful form, and man was not afraid of intercourse with it [2]. Now as sin, whose influence extended through all nature, and subjected it to a curse [3], so that it no longer testifies merely of the existence of God, but also of the existence of transgression, produced the outward dissension, war, and destruction, which exist in irrational nature ; so also we may venture to hope, that when, in the time of the Messiah, according to the expectation of the Prophet [4], the *cause* (*inward discord*) shall be removed, the *effect* also (*outward dissension*) will cease. The Prophet even appears in particular characteristics to refer distinctly to the history of the creation ; compare the seventh verse ('lions shall eat straw like the oxen,') with the thirtieth verse of the first chapter of Genesis ; and the eighth verse ('the sucking child shall play upon the hole of the asp') with the fifteenth verse of the third chapter of Genesis. (2) The comparison of other passages of Scripture, according to which likewise, after the removal of moral evil from the rational creation, the removal of the reflection of it in the irrational shall follow. See the twenty-fifth verse of the sixty-fifth chapter, and the twenty-second verse of the sixty-sixth chapter; but especially the nineteenth and following verses of the eighth chapter of Romans. (3) A comparison of the notions derived from an original tradition respecting this subject among heathen nations. Not only, as we have seen in the general introduction, is the idea in general of a future renovation of nature found among them, but even precisely the same characteristics as are here presented. We here introduce only a few of the numerous passages collected from Greek and Roman writers, by Le Clerc, Lowth, Gesenius, and others. Virgil says in his representation of the golden age [5], "Occidet et serpens, et fallax herba veneni Occidet."—"Nec magnos metuent armenta

---

[1] Gen. 2. 19, 20.   [2] See chap. 3. 1. 14.   [3] chap. 3. 17.
          [4] Ver. 9.   [5] Ecl. 4. 21, &c. 5. 60.

leones."—" Nec lupus insidias pecori."—Horace. " Nec vespertinus circumgemit ursus ovile, Nec intumescit alta viperis humus[1]."— Theocrit. Idyll. 24. 84 : ἔσται δὴ τοῦτ᾽ ἆμαρ, ὁπηνίκα νεβρὸν ἐν εὐνᾷ—καρχαρόδων σίνεσθαι ἰδὼν λύκος οὐκ ἐθελήσει.

360. Verse 6. ' *Then the wolf dwells with the lamb ; the panther lies down with the kid ; the calf and the lion and the fattened beast are together ; a little child leads them.*'

361. Verse 7. ' *The cow and bear go about in the same pasture, their young ones lie down together ; the lion shall eat straw like the ox [2].*'

362. Verse 8. ' *The sucking child plays on the den of the asp, and the weaned child thrusts his hand into the hole of the basilisk.*' The asp of the ancients was a small, but very poisonous serpent, whose bite killed without pain by an overpowering sleep [3]. The word translated ' *basilisk*' signifies the *cerastes*, one of the most poisonous of serpents.

363. Verse 9. This peace in outward nature is a consequence of the inward peace, which will prevail in the kingdom of God, after the annihilation of all that opposes His will.—' *They shall not do evil, and shall not sin on all my holy mountain ; for the land is full of the knowledge of the Lord, as the waters cover the bottom of the sea.*' *The holy mountain* [4] is the usual appellation of Mount Zion : but it here designates *the theocracy*, of which it was the seat and central point [5]. The word retains its customary meaning (see Gesenius), but in the vision of the Prophet the kingdom of God was presented under the image of its centre and seat.—In the second member, the cause is given, which has produced this great change ; it is not external force, which can restrain merely the outbreakings of sin ; but it is a consequence of the knowledge of God, diffused by the Messiah, and the fulness of the Divine life supplied through Him. The *general* outpouring of the Spirit, and the holiness resulting from it, which, under the Old Testament, was imparted only to a few, are uniformly given as a characteristic mark of the Messiah's time [6]. It is uncertain here, as in other similar passages, whether the right translation is ' *the land*' (that is, Judea alone), or ' *the whole earth.*' If the

---

[1] Horat. Epod. 16. 53.   [2] יַחְדָּו is to be supplied in the first member.

[3] The ἅπ. λεγ. מְאוּרָה receives through the connexion and the parallelism with חֻר its definite meaning. According to Gesenius it is kindred with מְאוּרָה = מְעָרָה *hole.* But it is more naturally derived from אוֹר *to give light,* whence comes מָאוֹר. According to which it would not properly be *the hole* itself, but its *entrance, pars luci exposita :* in like manner as צֹהַר *light,* Gen. 6. 16, means, openings for light, windows. The translation *eyes* by Jahn, and *feelers* by Michaelis, is as unfounded as incongruous.

[4] הַר קֹדֶשׁ

[5] This is evident from the following כִּי, which gives the reason and would otherwise be inappropriate, even if only the land of Judea were to be understood by the word אֶרֶץ. Eichhorn well observes, As far as my kingdom extends. So likewise Kuinöl. On the contrary Jahn asserts, without reason, that הַר קָדְשִׁי here means precisely the mountainous region of Palestine.

[6] See e. g. chap. 32. 17 18. 54. 13. Jer. 31. 34. Joel 3. 1.

former, the Prophet does not describe the extension of the Divine
life throughout the world, until the following verse. See the second
verse of the fourth chapter. We may best translate it by the equally
indefinite expression, *the land ;* the Prophet himself would have
found it difficult to decide which interpretation was the true one ; he
was not concerned with its local limitation, but with the fact itself,
the abundant and general effusion of the Holy Spirit.—The knowledge of God includes love for Him, and devotion to His service.

364. Verse 10. The central point of this divine life is the great
King, from whom it proceeds.—' *And it will come to pass at that
time, that the heathen shall betake themselves to the root* [1] *of Jesse,
which stands as the banner of the people, and his rest* (= *resting
place,* or *abode*) *will be glorious.*'—The verb we have translated
shall betake themselves [2] is used in two senses ; generally : to *turn* to
Jehovah, or to the idols *in order to seek protection, help,* and *counsel,
to manifest reverence* [3] ; and specially, to *ask counsel of any one,* whether Jehovah or an idol, *as an oracle* [4]. Jahn unjustly objects to the
latter meaning in this place, that it is unsuitable to speak of consulting a *root* as an *oracle :* for that the Prophet had already laid
aside the figure is manifest from the words which follow, ' *and his
rest shall be glory,*' which also relate not to the *image* of the root, but
directly to *the person* who had been represented by it. If we adopt
this meaning, the sense will be : the nations, who have heretofore
sought for responses from their idols in vain, will now look to the
Messiah alone for instruction in the things of God. Some interpreters then suppose, that here is an allusion to Solomon, whose
wisdom attracted a multitude of strangers ; others think, that as in
former times, the answer of God was given out of the holy of holies
from the place above the ark of the covenant [5], so now it shall be
sought from the Messiah. But however the expression may be
understood, at all events it implies a religious seeking of the Messiah, and ascribes to him more than human dignity [6].—The *banner*
or *ensign* meant, was a high pole with waving banners, which in
times of distress was erected on lofty hills, as a sign for the people,
or for the warriors to assemble. The Messiah is here compared with
such a standard, around which the nations should assemble, which
had heretofore been far from salvation. And thus shall be fulfilled
the prediction of the dying Jacob [7], that the nations should be obedient to the Messiah.—As of old the tabernacle and the temple were
honoured and glorified as the seat of the gracious symbol of the
Divine presence, so shall it be now with the dwelling-place of the
Messiah, of the *Deus in terra.* The image is taken from an illus-

[1] The root here signifies by synecdoche, the tree which springs up from the root.
[2] דָּרַשׁ
[3] Thus דרש את יהוה Psalm 9. 11. 14. 2. 22. 27. 34. 5. Jer. 8. 2, with לְ 2 Chron.
15. 13, with אל Job 5. 6.
[4] Thus Gen. 25. 22. Deut. 18. 11, and especially above, chap. 8. 19, הֲלֹא־עַם אֶל
אֱלֹהָיו יִדְרֹשׁ ' Shall not a people seek an explanation from their God ?'
[5] Num. 7. 89.   [6] Hos. 3. 5.   [7] Gen. 49. 10.

trious earthly king, whose residence is honoured by worldly splendour, the embassies of foreign nations, &c. We need not ask what
is here meant by the dwelling-place of the Messiah. The sense
without a figure is, *the Messiah will be honoured by all people as
their king and Lord.*

365. The Prophet having hitherto represented the blessings of the
Messiah's kingdom more in general, and with especial reference to
the heathen nations, confines himself, in the following portion, exclusively to the benefit which, through him, should be conferred
upon the Jews. An entirely similar appearance is presented by the
two closely connected predictions of the Messiah in the second and
fourth chapters, the former of which has respect especially to the
heathen, the latter exclusively to the Jews. With respect to the
interpretation of the whole portion, two principal views especially
may be distinguished. It is understood for the most part *literally* by
some, and *figuratively* by others. (1) The first view is entertained
by very different classes of interpreters; in the first place by the
Jews, who hope the Messiah will bring back their dispersed people
to Palestine, and there establish a splendid worldly kingdom ; then
by *Christian interpreters*, as Michaelis and others, who infer from
this and similar passages, that the Jews at some future time, after their
conversion to Christ, will be restored to their native land and there
form a Christocracy, as they had a theocracy before ; and lastly by
most recent [German] interpreters, as Rosenmüller, Gesenius, and
others, who find here an expectation of the Prophet, which has not
been confirmed by history, of a spendid visible restoration of the
outward theocracy by the Messiah. (2) Those who maintain the
figurative character of the whole representation suppose, that under
theocratic images, the *spiritual deliverance of the Israelites by the
Messiah*, and their *reception into His kingdom*, are here described.
Among these again there is a difference. Some regard the *complete
fulfilment* as having *already* taken place by the introduction of
Christianity [1]. Others, as Lowth, suppose that the whole prophecy
relates to that *future general conversion* of the Jews, which the New
Testament also leads us to expect.

366. We are induced to join the advocates of the second view, in
opposition to those of the first, by the following reasons. (1) The
literal interpretation cannot be consistently *carried through.* When
it is said [2] that, in the time of the Messiah, Jehovah will *dry up the
Red Sea*, and *divide the Euphrates into seven streams*, making it
so shallow that men may pass over it with shoes, no interpreter *thinks*
of understanding this otherwise than figuratively. Since then the
foregoing representation has an entirely uniform character, the charge
of capriciousness certainly falls rather upon the advocates of the
literal, than of the figurative interpretation. (2) The defenders of
the former must suppose, that the Prophet pointedly contradicts, not

---

[1] Thus Jerome, " Ut nequaquam juxta nostros Judaizantes in fine mundi,
quum intraverit plenitudo gentium, tunc omnis Israel salvus fiat: sed hæc
omnia in primo intelligamus adventu."

[2] Ver. 15, 16.

only the other prophets, but even himself also.   According to it,
the Prophet[1] would say, for instance, that the Israelites, in the time
of the Messiah, will carry on *prosperous wars* against the Philistines,
Arabians, Edomites, and Moabites, and *reduce these people to subjection.* On the contrary, according to the sixth, seventh, and eighth verses
of this very prophecy, the kingdom of the Messiah is so entirely *a
kingdom of peace,* that contention shall cease, even in the irrational
creation : according to the tenth verse, the heathen nations also shall
share in its blessings ; according to the second verse of the second
chapter, *all* the heathen nations shall flow together to mount Zion ;
in the fourth verse of the ninth chapter, it is given as a characteristic
of the Messiah's time, that with its introduction *all war and contention shall cease ;* the Messiah, in the fifth verse, bears the name of
the *Prince of Peace ;* and according to the sixth verse, through him
peace shall be extended over the whole earth, and his kingdom established by righteousness, and not by the force of arms[3].   (3) Even
granting, what cannot *here* be conceded, that the Prophet did not himself entirely see through the figurative covering in which the subjects
were presented to him in vision, we should still, since he was only
an instrument, be perfectly justified in availing ourselves of the light
which *the fulfilment* gives, in discriminating between the figure and
the reality.   Now the fulfilment shows, that *under images taken from
the outward theocracy,* the prosperity of the covenant people, after
their conversion to Christ, is here described.—With respect to the
difference between the defenders of the figurative interpretation, we
must join with Vitringa, who unites both opinions by the supposition, that the fulfilment of the prophecy *commenced* indeed by the
reception of many of the Jews dispersed among all nations of the
earth, at the first establishment of Christianity ; but will be *carried forward through all ages,* and completed at the end of the world,
and not before, *by their general conversion.*   The Prophet announces in general terms the reception of the Jews into the Messiah's
kingdom, and their participation in its blessings ; the limitation to a
particular time was certainly as far from his purpose here, as in what
he says, in the tenth verse, of the heathen[2].

367. Verse 11. Not only the heathen, but also the Jews dispersed in
all lands, shall be brought back, and received into the kingdom of God.
—' *Then will the Lord stretch out his hand the second time,*' to de-

---

[1] Ver. 14.

[2] Jahn understands only ver. 1—10 as a prediction of the Messiah ; holding
that in the portion commencing with ver. 11, the Prophet makes an abrupt transition to the deliverance from captivity, and the victories of the Maccabees. But
this assumption is occasioned entirely by the erroneous supposition that the
prophecy must be literally understood throughout. To separate the paragraph
in this way from the foregoing does not agree with בַּיּוֹם הַהוּא ver. 11, and is
altogether unnatural; still we may suppose, that these occurrences were at the
same time within the scope of the Prophet's vision, and that he borrowed his
images from them.

[3] The second time refers to the deliverance from Egypt, as appears from
ver. 16. The Prophet compares together the greatest temporal and the spiritual
redemption of the covenant people. See Micah 7. 15. Hos. 2. 15. 1 Cor. 5. 7,

*liver the remnant of his people, which shall be left, from Assyria, from
Egypt, from Pathros, from Cush, from Elam, from Shinar, from
Hamath, and from the islands of the sea.'* Pathros, as Bochart and
Jablonski have shown, is the *Thebais*, or *Upper Egypt*, which elsewhere also is distinguished from Egypt Proper[1]. *Cush* is the Arabic
and the African *Ethiopia* or *Abyssinia*, which were inhabited by the
same race of people ; the Arabic being the mother country from which
a colony emigrated into Africa. *Elam*, properly the province *Ely-
mais* in southern Media, stands also in several other places in a wider
sense ; and here, where the names of countries are in general used
indefinitely, and where accurate geographical discrimination is not to
be thought of, it signifies all *Media and Persia*. *Shinar* is properly
the name of the region around Babylon ; here, in a wider sense, it denotes all *Mesopotamia*. By *Hamath*, one of the most important cities
of Syria, all *Syria* is designated. The expression *Isles of the Sea*[2] is
very indefinite ; it signifies in the first instance all the *islands and
coasts of the Mediterranean sea ;* but then also, all that lies beyond
them, in general *all Europe*. That the Prophet mentions these particular countries, only as a part for the whole, and by way of example,
in order to show, that the Jews shall be scattered through all lands,
even the most remote, appears from the following verse, according to which they shall be collected from all the four ends of the
earth.—The question now arises, whether the dispersion of the
Hebrews here described, really existed in the time of the Prophet, or
whether, transporting himself in spirit[3] into distant times, he represents the *later* dispersion of the Jews, as it took place, when the
Israelites had already been carried captive into Assyria after the
Babylonish exile, and especially after the destruction of Jerusalem.
The latter is the opinion of by far the larger number of interpreters ;
Gesenius has endeavoured to defend the former. But his arguments
can satisfy only a few. It is important to remark, that but little is
accomplished when it is shown, that in the time of the Prophet *individual Jews* were to be found in all the countries enumerated. For
the whole description of the Prophet shows, that he presupposes a
dispersion of the whole nation, even though we were not to connect
with it the total depopulation of Palestine. It is true that the ten
tribes were already carried into captivity ; but the *kingdom of Judah*,
the members of which likewise[4] appear among the dispersed, had
not as yet suffered this calamity to any considerable extent. But the
few Jews, who, according to Joel[5] and Amos[6], had been sold as slaves
by the Philistines, and the Phenicians, and others, who possibly in
times of distress may voluntarily have fled from their own country,

---

קָנָה *to ransom*, especially used concerning Jehovah, when He delivers the covenant people from the power of their enemies, as well as מָכַר *to sell*, when He
gives them up to their power.

[1] Comp. e. g. Plin. h. n. 18. 18.—" Excellentius Thebaidis regionis frumentum
(quam Ægypti), quoniam palustris Ægyptus."

[2] אִיֵּי הַיָּם   [3] As in ver. 1.

[4] Ver. 12.   [5] Chap. 3. 11.   [6] Chap. 1. 6. 9.

of whom however there is no historical account, do not here come under consideration. Then Gesenius has entirely failed to *prove*, that, in the time of the Prophet, even *individual Jews* were to be found in all the countries enumerated. He supposes, e. g. in total contradiction to the relation in the ninth and following verses of the fourteenth chapter of the second book of Chronicles, that in the war with the Ethiopians under king Asa, the Jews were carried away prisoners to Ethiopia. It is there expressly said, that the whole hostile army was destroyed.—But why does the Prophet here, like Micah, in the sixth and seventh verses of his fourth chapter, represent *the reception of the dispersed Israelites into the kingdom of the Messiah*, under the image of their *restoration to their native land?* The answer is, that as the kingdom of God must of necessity have a *substratum* in the vision of the Prophet, because *images* only, and not *abstract ideas*, can be exhibited in vision ; so the seat of the ancient theocracy appears to him as the central point and capital of the Messiah's kingdom, whence also this kingdom takes its rise. As then, in the second chapter, he represents the *reception of the heathen nations into the kingdom of the Messiah*, as their *journeying to Mount Zion*, so here the reception of the dispersed Jews is described as a *return to their native land*. We are not here to have respect to the locality, since this belongs merely to the *form* of the vision, but to the *fundamental idea*, the sin and apostasy of the Jews (by which they lost the old theocracy and its blessings, to which the possession of the land of Canaan especially belonged), and their repentance and conversion, whereby they gain admission into the Messiah's kingdom, and participate in its blessings.

368. Verse 12. ' *And the Lord lifts up a standard to the heathen nations; and collects the exiles of Judah, and gathers together the dispersed of Israel from the four ends of the earth.*' Several of the ancient interpreters imagined, that, as in the tenth verse, so here, *the standard* for the heathen nations is *a sign* to them to assemble, that they may *themselves* enter into the kingdom of the Messiah; a comparison of the parallel passages [1] shows rather, that the purpose for which the heathen are to be collected, is that of *conducting the dispersed Jews to their native land*. The sense without a figure is: *the heathen people* (the same, who, according to the tenth verse, have already become members of the Messiah's kingdom) *shall then be actively employed, in obedience to the command of the Lord, in promoting the reception of the despised Jews into His kingdom* [2].

---

[1] Chap. 49. 22. 62. 10.

[2] After נִצָּוֹת J. H. Michaelis supplies *sheep*, Le Clerc מִשְׁפָּחוֹת *families*, Rosenmüller נְפָשׁוֹת *souls*. But Gesenius here properly applies a usage, according to which *totality* is expressed by the combination of the *masculine* and *feminine*. Thus chap. 3. 1, מַשְׁעֵן וּמַשְׁעֵנָה properly, the *male and the female* support, stands for *every kind* of support. See examples from Arabic writers in Gesenius on the passage. Thus also here, the *men of Judah*, who had been driven away, and the *dispersed women* of Israel, for *all the dispersed* of Israel and Judah.

369. Verse 13. ' *The jealousy of Ephraim ceases; and the hostile-minded of Judah are cut off; Ephraim will not envy Judah, and Judah will not be hostile to Ephraim*[1].' Between the two tribes of Judah and Ephraim, the latter of which considered as its own all the advantages, which by any means the whole tribe of Joseph might have appropriated to itself, there existed constant jealousy and collision. This hostile disposition at last fully broke forth, after the death of Solomon, when the remaining tribes, with the exception of Benjamin and Levi, were separated from Judah by Jeroboam, an Ephraimite. The new kingdom took the name of Ephraim after the most powerful tribe. From this time, peace and harmony seldom existed between the two kingdoms, until at last the Ephraimites were carried away into captivity.—Now this schism between Ephraim and Judah was the most destructive and deplorable in the whole history of the Hebrews. The Prophet therefore could choose no more suitable image to express the idea, that when the covenant people should be received into the kingdom of the Messiah, all internal jealousy and enmity among them would cease; that common love for the great Redeemer would unite them all in the bond of harmony[2].

370. Verse 14. ' *They fly then upon the shoulders of the Philistines westward; together they plunder the sons of the East: Edom and Moab are the object of their assaults: the sons of Ammon will obey them.*' The image in the first member is taken from birds of prey, and is illustrated by the parallel passage from the eighth verse of the first chapter of Habakkuk, where it is said of the Chaldeans : ' *they fly along as the eagle, who darts upon his prey.*' The *sons of the east* are, by way of eminence, the *Arabians*, who dwell to the east of the Israelites, and from whose predatory invasions they had much to suffer. —We have already seen that this verse cannot be understood literally, but must be taken in a figurative sense. The question now occurs, what is signified by the figure? Most interpreters refer it to spiritual victories, in the conversion of these people, effected by the Hebrews[3]. But although spiritual conquests are elsewhere designated by the image of war (see the twelfth verse of the fifty-third chapter), yet this explanation seems to be inadmissible here, because, according to the whole context, the Prophet speaks of the prosperity which the *Israelites themselves* should enjoy after their reception into the kingdom of the Messiah. The true interpretation is rather the following. The nations mentioned were the most dangerous enemies of the theocracy, whom God employed for the chastisement of the apostate Israelites. When the people manifested genuine dependence on Jehovah, these enemies were not the object of dread ; such a

[1] The adversaries of Judah are those *in* Judah who were hostilely disposed (against Ephraim).
[2] Parallel passages, in which the same figurative representation prevails, are, Hos. 1. 11. 2. 1. Ez. 37. 22.
[3] " Hæ enim gentes tempore, quo Jesaias prophetabat, adversariæ erant populo Judæorum et idcirco nunc dicit, quod postquam surrexerit radix Jesse, ut regnet in gentibus, tunc—dent Apostolis manus et in locis idololatriæ Christi ecclesiæ suscitentur."

splendid period was that, e. g. in the time of David. From this the
Prophet borrows an image to embody the thought, that the people
when they should have submitted to their great King, would enjoy
the Divine protection, a rich measure of the Divine mercy, and complete security. The consequences of a return to God in the time of
the Messiah, are represented under the image of the consequences of
a return to God during the former theocracy.

371. Verse 15, 16. The removal of the hindrances, which will
stand in the way of the future redemption of the Israelites, is represented under the image of the removal of those which obstructed
their former deliverance from Egypt. ‘ *Jehovah inflicts a curse upon
the tongue of the sea of Egypt ; and waves his hand against the river,
with his vehement wind, and smites it into seven brooks, that a man
may go through with shoes* [1].’ To *visit with a curse,* imports as much
as, *entirely to destroy,* since total destruction was a consequence of
the anathema.—The *tongue of the Egyptian sea* is the head of the
Arabian gulf; of which the northern extremity divides itself into
two smaller and narrower gulfs. ‘ *The tongue* ’ is the westernmost of
these : it is that through which the Hebrews formerly passed, and
which ends at Suez [2]. By *the river* [3], by way of eminence, the
Euphrates is designated; the Nile, which Vitringa, Augusti, and
others, find here, never bears simply this name ; even in the fifth
verse of the nineteenth chapter, the word is defined, by being
employed in a prophecy against Egypt [4].—*With the vehemence of
his wind,* i. e. *with his vehement wind.* The ground of the figure
is a personification of the river; Jehovah appears as a mighty
hero, who waves His hand, armed with a frightful wind, like a sword,
against the opposing stream [5]. There is here an allusion to the
twenty-first verse of the fourteenth chapter of Exodus, according
to which the Lord dried up the Arabian gulf by a strong wind.—*He
smites it to seven streams,* for, so that it is divided into seven
streams. The image is here taken from great rivers, whose waters
are conducted into a multitude of channels. Lowth appropriately
compares the account of Herod. 1. 189. Cyrus, on his march to
Babylon, lost in a rapid stream one of his sacred white horses. He
became enraged by the accident, and regarding the stream, as in the
present instance, as an enemy, threatened to reduce it so much that

---

[1] Many interpreters—Lowth, Rosenmüller, &c. suppose that the verb
הֶחֱרִים is here synonymous with הֶחֱרִיב *to dry up;* and appeal to the frequent
interchange of the vowels of the same organ. But the verb הֶחֱרִים is of too
frequent occurrence to require us here to give it another meaning, and moreover
its usual sense is far more suitable than the one assumed.

[2] Arabian geographers call this the *tongue,* and this name occurs in Hebrew
as the name of a gulf of the Red Sea, Josh. 15. 2. 5. 18. 19.

[3] הַנָּהָר

[4] The meaning of the word עָם cannot indeed be ascertained with certainty,
as the kindred dialects afford no aid; still the meaning, *vehemence,* is favoured
by the connexion, the authority of the ancient translators, and perhaps also a
comparison with the adjective אָיֹם *fearful, terrific.*

[5] Hence also the following הֵנִיף

even women could easily ford it. Accordingly he set his whole army at work, and conducted the water of the river into three hundred and sixty ditches, on both sides of it. The Prophet therefore here promises that Jehovah in future times will open a passage for the Israelites through the Red Sea and the Euphrates, in the same miraculous manner as He had done before through the Red Sea and the Jordan. The sense is simply : *no obstacle to this redemption so great, but Jehovah will remove it by His omnipotence, as in His former deliverance of His people from Egypt.*

372. Verse 16. '*And there shall be a way for the remnant of His people, who shall be left from Assyria, as there before was for Israel, when he came out of Egypt.*' After '*from Assyria,*' we must supply the remaining countries, mentioned in the eleventh verse, in which the Israelites are dispersed ; the Prophet here omits to repeat them for the sake of brevity. The entire similarity of the expression points to the former description.

373. As the hymn of thanksgiving of the redeemed people, in the twelfth chapter, is of a more general character, and like many of the Psalms applicable to any great deliverance, and contains but few individual traits, we have no occasion to explain it.

General Preliminary Remarks on Isaiah 40-66

374. The second part of Isaiah must be ranked with the most splendid and for us the most important, portions of the Scriptures of the Old Testament. No part of these writings contains so little that is local and temporary ; none shows so clearly the connexion between the preparatory and the ultimate dispensation ;—none lingers with such delight on the description of the time, when after the great separation between the ungodly and the pious part of the ancient covenant people, the latter shall be united with the heathen in one sanctified and blessed Church of the Lord ; none presents the exalted founder of the New Covenant, which is not like the old to be limited to a single people, so clearly to our view both in His humiliation and in His glory [1].

375. We have seen in the introductory remarks on Isaiah, that the Prophet probably lived for some time under the reign of Manasseh. If now we assume that he composed the second part of his prophecies in this latter period of his life, its character will be the more intelligible, and all its peculiarities will be explained.

376. (1) This supposition accounts for the difference of the representation in the first, from that in the second part. Between the last prediction of the first part and the second part, there then will be an

---

[1] With particular reference to the second part, Jerome præf. ad Iesaiam, says of Isaiah : "Non tam propheta dicendus est, quam Evangelista. Ita enim universa Christi ecclesiæque mysteria ad liquidum persecutus est, ut non putes eum de futuro vaticinari, sed de præteritis historiam texere."

interval of from fourteen to twenty years. But as the tone of the
mind changes with years, so also does the style. Although the
second part is in no respect inferior to the first in beauty of description, still the representation is more flowing, the tone milder and
softer. Instead of the compression and conciseness of the first part,
in which the author, as it were, struggles with the language, and
only briefly suggesting his images, passes on from one to another, an
agreeable copiousness succeeds ; the images are finished and painted
with the loveliest colours, even to the minutest features. While the
two parts are essentially *one*, and closely resemble each other in many
points, there is a *difference* between them, like that between Deuteronomy and the other books of the Pentateuch, or the Epistles of
John, which he probably composed at an advanced age, and his
Gospel.

377. (2) We may in this way explain the point of view assumed by
the Prophet. Isaiah, when arrived at an advanced age, probably
ceased to take an active part in the public affairs of the theocracy,
leaving this to his younger associates in the prophetical office. He
transferred himself from the present, which afforded little that was
consoling, to the future, in which and for which alone he lived,
assured that the legacy which he should leave to posterity, would
bring forth the fruits, which in his labours for the benefit of the
present generation he had so often failed to realize. He places
himself in the time clearly predicted in his former prophecies, when
Jerusalem was already captured by the Chaldeans, the land laid
waste, and the people in the distant region of Babylonia, longing
for their native home. It is in this period of time that he thinks,
feels, and acts ; to him it has become the present, from which
(though not without frequently casting a look upon the *real
present*) he beholds the future—the nearer, the remoter, the remotest future. He directs his discourse to his unhappy countrymen in exile ; he exhorts, rebukes, and consoles them, by unfolding
the prospect of a happier future.

378. (3) This supposition explains the *arrangement* of the second
part. While the first part, embracing the predictions which the Prophet
uttered during his exertions for the benefit of the present times, consists of individual prophecies, delivered at different times, and on
various occasions, and at first separately made public, but afterwards
(being distinguished from each other by superscriptions, or some
other intelligible method) combined in a single collection ; in the
second part, on the contrary, which was not called forth by external
occasions, the individual portions cannot be so easily distinguished ;
it is more as if the whole had been uttered at the same time. The
proof of the unity of the second part is furnished, even by the following representation of its contents. The objects of the prophecy are
throughout the same. Even the language and mode of representation are far more uniform than in the different portions of the first
part. If the Prophet did not, at one and the same time, receive and
commit to writing the revelations recorded in this part, yet it is certain that no long period elapsed between them, and that he did not

make known the separate discourses to the people, but chose to leave the whole as a legacy to posterity.

379. All was communicated to the Prophets in vision, and therefore *in the present;* distance of time was in general not known to them ; hence it happens, that events connected by an internal resemblance, though really far distant from each other, seem to be closely connected, or even blended together, and must be first separated by the interpreter, who, comparing the prediction with the fulfilment, can refer to the different times to which they belong, the events which had *no relation to time,* as they appeared to the Prophets. Whoever, without adopting this principle (which lies deep in the very nature of the prophetic vision, and has been further developed in the General Introduction), attempts the interpretation of the second part of the prophecies of Isaiah, will behold throughout nothing but darkness, where under its guidance the clearest light would appear.

380. These predictions relate chiefly to *two objects.* The Prophet first consoles his people by predicting *their deliverance from the Babylonish exile;* he represents this under the most agreeable images, which are often suggested by the deliverance from Egypt ; he names the monarch, who, sent by Jehovah, should punish the oppressors of His people for their insolence, and restore the latter to their native land. But he does not stop at this inferior redemption. With the prospect of deliverance from the captivity of Babylon, is connected that of *redemption from sin and errour by the Messiah.* Sometimes both objects appear intermingled with each other, sometimes one alone is exhibited with peculiar clearness. To the latter object especially does the Prophet sometimes so exclusively direct his view, that for a time, enraptured with the glory of the spiritual kingdom of God and its exalted founder, he loses sight of the less distant future. In the representation of this spiritual redemption also, the relation of events to time is disregarded. Now the Prophet beholds its author in His *humiliation* and *suffering;* now the most distant period of the Messiah's kingdom is presented to his ravished view ; in which the human race estranged from God shall be brought back to Him, and after the annihilation of all opposition to God, *outward and inward peace shall prevail, and all the evil introduced by sin shall be abolished.* Elevated above time and space, from the eminence upon which the Holy Spirit has placed him, he extends his view over the whole progressive development of the Messiah's kingdom, from its obscure commencement to its glorious completion.

Contents of Isaiah 40, 41 [1]

381. Chap. 40. 1—11, forms a kind of introduction. The Prophet begins with a command of God to His messengers, to announce to

---

[1] [The original work contains a very able defence of the genuineness of the chapters, from chap. 40 to the end.]

the unhappy people that the Divine punishment for their sins is now about to terminate, and the time of reconciliation and mercy to commence [1]. He next represents the deliverance of the people, which God would accomplish, under an image taken from the relations of earthly kings. He represents a herald, as going forth, who orders a way to be prepared in the pathless desert for Jehovah, who would march at the head of His returning people, as of old He led the Israelites on their journey out of Egypt [2]. This will as surely happen, as Jehovah has promised it, the Almighty and Omniscient, whose word stands for ever, while all created beings are frail and transitory, and therefore deserve no confidence [3]. The Prophet requires Jerusalem to announce to the remaining cities of Judea the news of Jehovah's glorious assistance [4].

382. " The deliverance from Babylon is clearly predicted, but at the same time it is employed as an image to designate a deliverance of an infinitely higher and more important character." As Isaiah scarcely ever speaks of the inferior deliverance without alluding to the higher, so is it here. It is only through the Messiah, that the prediction of the forgiveness of sins, of the restoration of the people, of the manifestation of the glory of God, will be fulfilled in its highest and most complete sense. This concurrent reference to the higher deliverance is proved, partly by the nature of prophecy itself, and partly by the most distinct testimonies of the New Testament [5]. In these passages, the third verse is referred to John the Baptist. He was called to remove the obstacles which retarded the revelation of the glory of God in the Messiah ; he occupied the first place among the heralds, who prepared the way of the great king. The wilderness, in which he should prepare this way, was the Jewish people, sunk in sin and errour.

383. Verses 12—31. The Prophet is led by the prediction of the illustrious proof of almighty power, which God will give in the deliverance of his people, to describe the Divine omnipotence, majesty, and glory. Of this he makes a twofold application. He first shows from it [6] the vanity and folly of the worship of idols, to which he was induced, partly by the circumstances of his time, and partly by the foresight of the temptations to idolatry, to which the people of Israel would be exposed in the exile, in the midst of an idolatrous people. Next he derives from it [7] an exhortation to his people to persevering confidence in this, their almighty and all-wise God, who comes, though often not till late, to assist by his power the weakness of those who trust in Him.

384. Chap. 41 relates, as well as the foregoing, chiefly to the first great object of the predictions of the second part, the deliverance of the Jews from the Babylonish exile by Cyrus [8]. The discourse is

---

[1] Ver. 1, 2.   [2] Ver. 2—5.
[3] Ver. 6—8.   [4] Ver. 9—11.
[5] Matt. 3. 3.   Mark 1. 3.   Luke 3. 4.   John 1. 23.
[6] Ver. 18—26.   [7] Ver. 27—31.
[8] The name Cyrus is in all probability an appellative, which was an honorable distinction of the Persian kings; in the same manner, as Pharaoh among

addressed first to the idolatrous nations, who should learn the vanity of their idol worship from this manifestation of the omniscience and omnipotence of God. If they could not attribute to natural causes the prediction of the appearance of Cyrus, which Jehovah by his prophets had so long foretold, as it now came to pass ; and if they could produce no similar prophecy given by their idols, then they must confess that Jehovah really sent him, whom He promised to send. They would be the more obliged to this, since their gods afforded them no help against the mighty conqueror, while the people of Israel, who were regarded by all as lost, received through him their long-promised deliverance.—Secondly, it is addressed to the

the Egyptians, or Abimelech among the Philistines. This name was universally explained by *Sun* among the Greeks (Ctesias. Plutarchus in Artaxerxe, c. 1), and indeed justly, since خور still signifies *Sun*, in modern Persian. According to the account of Strabo, Cyrus, before he ascended the throne, was called Agradatus, and according to *Shickardi Tarcih*, p. 123, in Gesen. l. c., a still later Persian king, Bahram, likewise bore the surname كور. When therefore Isaiah here predicts the deliverance through *Koresh*, his prophecy is no more definite than the predictions of the first part, chap. 13, 14, 21, in which he foretells the overthrow of the Babylonish monarchy by the Medes and Persians. That afterwards Cyrus chiefly received this name, to the exclusion of his proper name, arose from his splendid exploits ; he was called κατ' ἐξοχὴν *the great king*. It was owing to the special guidance of Divine providence that Isaiah used this name, which he might have learnt from Persian travellers, or, as Hensler supposes, from the Medes who served in Sennacherib's army. To this our opponents can make no satisfactory reply. But suppose the name Koresh were really a proper name, and no other prophecy could be produced, in which a person, who was to appear at a future period, was mentioned by name, still this would be no proof of spuriousness. For who shall prescribe to God the rule which He shall follow in making 'His revelations ? Who shall say, that He may never depart from His usual method of proceeding ? If while, as a general rule, He unfolded the future to the Prophet, without fixing the time when events were to take place, He still in particular instances accurately determined the number of years between the prophecy and its fulfilment; He surely might, with the same propriety, in a particular instance reveal the name of a future person who should exert a special influence on the affairs of His kingdom. Indeed, the mention of a name no more transcends the powers of nature than the prediction of any one particular historical circumstance, as chap. 44. 27.—But the assertion of the opponents, that no analogous case can be shown, is altogether erroneous. We have an instance, 1 Kings 13. 2. A prophet there foretells to Jeroboam, who had erected an idolatrous altar, that a son should be born to the house of David, named Josiah. He will offer upon the altar the priests of the high places, who burn incense thereon. Since king Josiah is there called by name, 300 years before his appearance, how can it seem strange to find here the name of Cyrus about 150 years before his appearance. Should our opponents choose to assert, that the name of the king Josiah, in the book of Kings, is an interpolation of a later period, the assertion would be entirely arbitrary. In this way no proof could ever be adduced against them. But then they must also give up their appeal to the name of Cyrus; for what could they say in reply, if we should declare the name of Cyrus in these two places to be the gloss of a later reviser ? Although we are far from doing this, yet it would not be greater capriciousness than that which they practise on the passage in the book of Kings, and that whereby they declare the characteristic peculiarities, which the second part has in common with the first, to have been added for the purpose of producing conformity.

Jews in exile, who are consoled by the annunciation of the approaching deliverance, and the prosperity which is to follow. Jehovah appears, in the first verse, as the speaker, and summons the idolatrous nations to enter into judgement with Him. He proves against them the righteousness of His cause, by sending the powerful king Cyrus, whom nothing can resist. Instead, however, of being thereby brought to an humble acknowledgement of their errour, and of the omnipotence of Jehovah, in deep distress they seek assistance from their idols, but in vain [1]. Jehovah then turns to the people of Israel, and consoles them by the promise of deliverance, and of the destruction of their foes [2], in connexion with the assurance, that their affliction should be followed by great prosperity [3]. (In the fourteenth and two next verses, the Prophet announces to the people, after he has before predicted a deliverance, which should be procured for them by other instruments, which God would prepare, that at some future time they should subdue even their powerful enemies. The fulfilment is to be sought in the first instance in the time of the Maccabees. They not only contended successfully against the Syrians, but also subdued the neighbouring nations, who had been most hostile to the people of Israel. The arrangement of the prophecy is agreeable to the course of time; the deliverance from the exile by Cyrus is first announced, then the victories of the covenant people themselves.—In the representation of the prosperity, which shall follow the deliverance from adversity, the times immediately after the exile are merely the foreground, and furnish but an imperfect fulfilment. The blessings here promised will be imparted, in the complete and spiritual sense, by the Messiah.)—Jehovah then again addresses the worshippers of idols, and requires them to demonstrate the omnipotence and omniscience of their idols in opposition to Him, as He shows His omnipotence and omniscience by the sending of Cyrus, and the prediction of him by His prophets.

Isaiah 42:1-9

385. The Prophet, in the two foregoing chapters, had chiefly pointed to the deliverance from the Babylonish exile; but still his spiritual eye had already, from time to time, rested on the greater event, of which that must serve as a type. He had plainly designated the instrument who should effect the first deliverance; he should be a righteous king from the distant east. The author of the spiritual deliverance, in all his sublime humility, now appears at once before his enraptured vision; He directs the sorrowing people to him, and describes him, in the first nine verses. He then

---

[1] Ver. 5—7.   [2] Ver. 8—16.   [3] Ver. 17—20.

returns to the nearer future, and describes anew the deliverance from the captivity; the contemplation of which generally prevails until the forty-ninth chapter.

386. It will be perceived from what has been said, that we can separate this section from the foregoing and following, as a distinct portion, although there is a connexion between them, which is not to be mistaken, founded on the association of the images in the vision of the Prophet.

387. The arrangement is as follows: Jehovah is introduced as speaking throughout the whole. In the first and fourth verses, He speaks of the Messiah in the third person; He points as it were to him, and recommends him to the world. As the beloved, and chosen servant of God, endowed with the fulness of the Divine Spirit, and sustained by God, he will be a helper of all those who feel themselves poor and wretched; going about, and labouring in meekness and lowliness, and as wise as he is stedfast in accomplishing the commission entrusted to him by God, he will establish the true religion among all nations of the earth, who have heretofore been estranged from God. Jehovah then [1] turns to the Messiah, and addresses him, after the Prophet, in the fifth verse, has called the attention of his hearers to his omnipotence, as the pledge for the fulfilment of so great, and apparently almost incredible a prediction. He declares to him that it is his high destination, to be realized through His almighty aid, partly to establish a new and better covenant with his ancient people, partly to enlighten the heathen nations, and in general to redeem and bring back to God the whole human race, lying in the bondage of sin and errour. In the eighth and ninth verses, Jehovah turns to those to whom the prophecy had been given, and awakens their attention to its object. It should serve after its fulfilment, like the former predictions already fulfilled, to place in a clear light before the covenant people exposed to many temptations to idolatry, and thus to preserve them in their fidelity to Him, the superiority of Jehovah, the All-wise and Almighty, over vain idols, who can give to their worshippers no disclosures respecting the future. This portion has, as the view of its contents which has been given shows, a very dramatic character, which is founded in the nature of the prophetic vision. (See the general Introduction.)

388. We have presupposed in the exhibition of its contents the Messianic interpretation of the portion to be the true one. We must now return to the position of inquirers, and bring forward and examine the different opinions that have been advanced respecting the subject of the prophecy.

389. In the interpretation of the whole prophecy every thing depends on the question, who is to be understood by the eminent *servant of Jehovah*, who is described in the first seven verses. The opinions of interpreters on this point are divided, which is nevertheless owing rather to preconceived doctrinal views, than to the nature of the case itself. From the mere appellation nothing can be deter-

[1] Ver. 6, 7.

mined. A *servant of Jehovah* is every one who acknowledges Jehovah as his Lord, every pious worshipper of God ; but then those are especially so named, who are called by Him, whether with or without their own knowledge, to execute a particular commission in His arrangements for the salvation of men [1]. A more accurate determination of the person, if his name is not mentioned, must therefore, in each instance, be derived from the attributes ascribed to him. In reference to the prophecy before us, there is here still one remark to be made. The '*servant of Jehovah*' described in this passage is manifestly the same, who is brought before us in the forty-ninth, fiftieth, fifty-third, and sixty-first chapters. This is acknowledged by the best interpreters. We must not therefore be satisfied with showing that the characteristics here given can scarcely be found in any other person, but we must add to these all that is said in the designated passages respecting the '*servant of Jehovah*.' Had this been observed, many erroneous interpretations of this passage would have been prevented.

390. As it is, five different views respecting the subject of this prophecy may be noticed. It has been supposed to be, (1) The Jewish people [2]. Against this interpretation, to say nothing of the objections to be derived from the parallel passages, we urge, *a*) that in the sixth verse the '*servant of Jehovah*' is plainly *distinguished* from the *people* [3]. How can Jehovah say of the people, that He will make them a mediator of the covenant *with* the people ? *b*) That the description of the servant of God, as one who is *meek, mild, quiet*, and *humble* [4], is in striking contrast with what the Prophet elsewhere says, respecting the character and manners of the *people* of Israel [5].

---

[1] See on chap. 53.

[2] This hypothesis is as old as the Septuagint version. They translate : Ἰακὼβ ὁ παῖς μου, ἀντιλήψομαι αὐτοῦ, Ἰσραὴλ ὁ ἐκλεκτός μου, προσεδέξατο αὐτὸν ἡ ψυχή μου. They have introduced their interpretation into the text by interpolating the words Ἰακὼβ and Ἰσραήλ. Among the Jewish interpreters, Rabbi Sal. Jarchi follows this explanation, but so modifies it, that he understands by עֶבֶד יְהֹוָה collectively : *the righteous in Israel ;* among the recent interpreters, Eckermann, Rosenmüller in the second edition of his commentary, Paulus, and Ammon ; the last two with the same modification as Jarchi.

[3] See chap. 49. 56.   [4] Ver. 2, 3.

[5] And also that neither here, nor in any of the parallel passages, is עֶבֶד יְהֹוָה joined with a plural, but always with the singular ; while in the case of the collectives elsewhere, and especially in the passages where the Jewish people are personified as an individual, the singular and the plural are interchanged. Finally, how little this interpretation is capable of being carried through, unless manifest violence be done to the words, let the example of its latest defender, Rosenmüller, show. He says, in opposition to Telge, who makes the unnatural supposition, that the Prophet speaks, now of the people, now of their king the Messiah : "in eo minus illi assentiri possum, propterea, quod talis oratio anceps et lubrica futura esset, qua bonum scriptorem uti posse, aut unquam usum fuisse vix est credibile." On the contrary, in opposition to himself, he agrees with Jarchi in the explanation of the words לְאֻמִּים יוֹצִיא מִשְׁפָּט ver. 3 : "rex eorum non diripiet pauperes, nec egenos debilesque concutiet." He com-

391. (2) Others understand by the ' *servant of Jehovah*' Cyrus [1].
They rely chiefly upon the fact, that in what precedes, and also in
what immediately follows, the subject of discourse is likewise the
deliverance to be effected by Cyrus ; which, however, after the general
remarks which have been made respecting the nature of the second
part of the predictions of Isaiah, proves nothing. They also appeal
to the fact, that Cyrus, in the first verse of the forty-fifth chapter, is
called *the anointed ;* in the twenty-eighth verse of the forty-fourth
chapter, *the shepherd* of God ; and although he elsewhere never
bears the name, ' *servant of Jehovah,*' is yet designated by all the
characteristics which constitute the idea of such a servant. But
besides the consideration that these critics themselves prove the
erroneousness of their explanation, inasmuch as they are obliged to
assume *another subject* in the parallel passages (no one has yet ventured to explain the fifty-third chapter of Cyrus), it is liable to insuperable difficulties, arising from the passage itself. Cyrus is indeed
always represented as *a king sent by God* for the deliverance of His
people, but never as a *mediator of a new covenant between God and
the Israelites,* never as the *founder of the true religion.* How do
the words, ' *I have put my Spirit upon him,*' agree with Cyrus [2] ?
How do passages, like the second and third verses, where the servant
of Jehovah is described as *quiet, mild,* and *gentle,* agree with Cyrus,
the conqueror, who shed rivers of blood ? The erroneousness of the
whole hypothesis plainly appears, when the explanation which Koppe
gives of these verses, is compared with the text. According to him,
they express nothing more than : he was the gracious ruler of the
Jews, and of all the nations formerly subject to the Babylonians, who
voluntarily submitted to his sceptre.

392. (3) According to others, the Prophet Isaiah [3] is ' *the servant
of Jehovah* [4].' But it is only necessary to look for a moment at the
explanation of Grotius, to be convinced of the violence which is
practised, to bring the reluctant text into subjection to this hypothesis.
Should we overlook the parallel passages, in the forty-ninth and following chapters, where Isaiah could not say of himself, without
ridiculous extravagance, what is attributed to the *servant of Jehovah* [5],
still even what is *here* affirmed, is too great to be referred to himself,

pares Isa. 11. 4, where it is said of the Messiah יִשְׁפֹּט בְּצֶדֶק דַּלִּים and approaches
therefore, almost involuntarily, the true interpretation, the defenders of which
are driven to no such inconsistencies.

[1] e. g. among the Jewish interpreters Saadias Gaon, among the moderns
Vogel, Koppe, Hezel, Hensler, Augusti, Bauer.

[2] It is true that Koppe supposes that in ancient poetry this is the same as, I
help him ; I give him courage and power to conquer for my people. But as
this use of רוּחַ יְהֹוָה in general is incapable of proof, so here the connexion
throughout allows it to mean only the prophetic spirit, who qualifies for establishing the true religion.

[3] Who, chap. 20. 3, is called עֶבֶד יְהֹוָה.

[4] So among the Jewish interpreters Abenezra, among the moderns Grotius,
and after him Dathe, Döderlein, and Rosenmüller, in the first edition of his
commentary.

[5] See e. g. 49. 5, 6.

without a degree of exaggeration, and a misapprehension of his calling, not to be charged upon the humble Prophet. How, for instance, could the establishment of a new covenant with the people of God, and the conversion of all the heathen nations be ascribed to Isaiah? especially as, in other places, he expects both from the Messiah ; and his whole agency was confined to the Jewish people, and never extended to the heathen nations. In order to remove this difficulty, an appeal has been made to passages, such as the tenth verse of the first chapter of Jeremiah, where the Prophets are commanded to *do* that which they were to predict. But to this Michaelis has well replied : "This is true, but in such cases it is a single expression, not continued so long as in this instance ; it is not customary so to lengthen out a figure ; and let any one only read this, and the forty-ninth chapter, and he will easily feel the difference, and be hardly able to deny that the discourse is concerning one who shall actually convert the heathen."—Some of the defenders of this explanation, perceiving the difficulty, choose that what is said should refer only in a lower and imperfect sense to Isaiah, and in a higher and perfect one to the Messiah ; but we cannot perceive any inducement to adopt such an hypothesis, which only involves us in unnecessary embarrassment, without in the least degree obviating the difficulty.

393. (4) After the example of Rosenmüller [1], who, nevertheless, has since changed his opinion, and De Wette [2], Gesenius supposes, that here, as well as in the parallel passages, the subject of the prediction is the *prophets taken collectively*. But it will be shown on the fifty-third chapter, that such a *collectivum* of the prophets exists only in the imagination of certain critics. We here only call to mind the remark already made above, that a collective body cannot be the subject, because here, as well as in the parallel passages, the '*servant of Jehovah*' is never connected with the plural, but always with the singular ; and also that this hypothesis is in opposition to the whole analogy of the prophetic writings, in which the establishment of a new covenant with the people of Israel, and the conversion of the heathen, are never attributed to the *prophetic order*, but always to the *Messiah alone*.

394. (5) A great multitude of interpreters, far more numerous than the defenders of all the hypotheses which we have mentioned, refer the prophecy to *the Messiah*. Thus of old the Chaldee paraphrast, the faithful preserver of the exegetical tradition ; so among the later Jewish interpreters, D. Kimchi, and Abarbanel, the latter of whom says of the non-Messianic interpreters, "*All these interpreters are smitten with blindness.*' That this explanation was the prevailing one among the Jews in the time of Christ (the Alexandrian Jews are here not taken into consideration, because they had less regard for tradition), appears from the thirty-second verse of the second chapter of Luke, where Simeon, with reference to the sixth verse, calls the Messiah '*a light to lighten the Gentiles* [3].' Still

---

[1] In Gabler's Neuem Theol. Journal II. p. 340.
[2] De Morte Expiatoriâ, p. 20.   [3] φῶς εἰς ἀποκάλυψιν ἐθνῶν.

more explicit are the following passages : the seventeenth verse of the third chapter of Matthew, in which the words proclaimed from heaven at the baptism of Christ [1], ' *This is my beloved Son, in whom I am well pleased,*' were taken from the first verse of this section, in order to point out that He who had then appeared, could be no other than the one foretold by the prophets many centuries before : the fifth verse of the seventeenth chapter of Matthew, where, at the glorification of Christ towards the end of His ministry, with a view to confirm the faith of the apostles, the same words resounded from heaven by which, in the beginning of His ministry, He had been commended to the covenant people : and lastly, the eighteenth verse of the twelfth chapter of Matthew, where the first, second, and third verses are cited almost verbatim, and referred to the Messiah.   Relying upon these authorities, and upon the natural sense of the passage, the Christian Church from the beginning has referred this prophecy to Christ ; and even interpreters, as Le Clerc, who elsewhere endeavour, when practicable, to set aside the Messianic interpretation, are here found among its most decided defenders.—The objections which have been brought against the Messianic interpretation are of little weight.   We borrow them from Gesenius. He says (1) "The Messiah is excluded, since the subject is not merely a teacher of the heathen, endowed with the Spirit of God, but also the Deliverer of Israel."   But this objection rests entirely on an erroneous and literal understanding of the seventh verse.   Gesenius himself explains the first part of it, *to open the blind eyes*, figuratively. He remarks, "in the intellectual sense, therefore, to teach the ignorant."   No reason can be given, why he should refer the second part to the deliverance of the people from exile, and not to the redemption of mankind from sin and errour.   The correctness of the spiritual interpretation is evident from the fact, that ' *those who sit in darkness,*' or ' *in a dark prison,*' manifestly corresponds to ' *the light of the heathen,*' in the foregoing verse.   If in the latter case we are to understand, as all confess, a *spiritual* light, then must the darkness, and the prison, which this light is to illuminate, be *spiritual* also. (2) "It is further to be observed, that this ' *servant of Jehovah*' is not predicted as a *future* person, but is spoken of as one *already present.*"   This objection arises from ignorance of the nature of the prophetic vision, of which we have treated in the general Introduction, in which *every thing* appeared as *present.*   It is to the inward, and not to the outward vision that the particle *behold* [2] relates.   That the perception of the Prophet had no regard to time, appears even from the interchange of the preterite and future tenses.   Had the Prophet been speaking of a person *externally present*, he would surely not have chiefly employed the future.

395. The Messiah was to combine in his own person, in a higher and more complete sense, the three theocratic offices of Prophet, Priest, and King.   Should we divide the predictions, according to the office which principally prevailed in the view of the Prophet,

---

[1] οὗτός ἐστιν ὁ υἱός μου ὁ ἀγαπητὸς, ἐν ᾧ εὐδόκησα.   [2] Ver. 1.

that before us would plainly belong to those, in which the Messiah appears chiefly as a Divine *Prophet*.

396. Verse 1. Jehovah speaks: He points to His Son, and represents him as the Redeemer appointed for the salvation of the world. '*Behold my servant, whom I uphold; mine elect, in whom my soul delighteth; I have put my Spirit upon him: he shall bring forth judgement amongst the Gentiles.*'—'*Servant of Jehovah*' is the name here given to the Messiah in the state of humiliation. Matthew has instead '*My Son;*' which is of equal import, if the appellation *Son of God* be taken in the Old Testament sense, of subordination and protection. Thus, e. g. the judges and kings under the theocracy could be called *sons*, as well as *servants* of God[1].—The words, '*I have put my Spirit upon him,*' contain the condition of what follows, '*He will bring judgement among the heathen.*' The Messiah shall be endowed for the execution of his commission, not with one particular power, but with all the fulness of the Spirit of God. A parallel passage is the second verse of the eleventh chapter, where it is said of the Messiah, '*And the Spirit of Jehovah rests upon him,*' and in the first verse of the sixty-first chapter, where the Messiah says of himself[2], '*the Lord God is upon me.*' Before Christ entered upon the duties of the office committed to him by God, he received the Spirit at baptism[3], and that not in a limited degree, but in all its fulness[4].—The word *judgement* means here *religion*[5]. This sense can be easily derived from its usual acceptation. The word generally signifies *right, precept, law*, but it is customary for words, which signify *law*, to be employed to designate likewise the *whole of religion*, partly because religion gives the rule by which the life must be governed, partly because under the old covenant it subsisted in the law[6]. The word undeniably occurs in this sense in the parallel passage, in the fourth verse of the fifty-first chapter: '*For a law goes forth from me, and my judgement* (i. e. *my religion*) *I will establish for a light of the Gentiles*[7].'

397. Verse 2. '*He shall not cry, nor be loud, nor cause his voice to be heard in the street.*' In this verse, the quiet, mild, and humble character of the Messiah is represented, in opposition to the hypocritical and ostentatious teachers, who sought to make for themselves a party among the people by clamour. In this sense Matthew also introduces the passage, after relating how Christ avoided outward display and contention. This disposition was symbolically represented by the sending of the dove at his baptism[8].

[1] That Matthew employed the word παῖς in the sense *son*, and not with the LXX in that of *servant*, appears from a comparison of chap. 3. 17, and 17. 5, where παῖς is exchanged with υἱός.
[2] See Luke 4. 18.   [3] Matt. 3. 16.   [4] John 3. 34.
[5] מִשְׁפָּט
[6] See on chap. 2. 3. Thus תּוֹרָה and thus νόμος in some passages of the New Testament.
[7] See Ps. 25. 9. 2 Kings 17. 26.
[8] Calvin: "Quietum fore significat, ut vulgo dicere solemus de placido homine et quieto: il ne fait pas grand bruit. Nec enim venditabat sese populo,

398. Verse 3. ' *The bruised reed he will not break, the glimmering wick he will not extinguish, he will firmly establish religion.*' The sense of the verse : *he will not seek to spread the true religion by violent measures, better suited to stifle the feeble germs of goodness, than to nourish and bring them to a happy increase ; but with meekness, tenderness, and forbearing indulgence, he will endeavour to bring all those to salvation who do not harden themselves against it.* Two things may be signified by the glimmering wick and bruised reed. According to many interpreters, they designate men in whom only feeble remains of goodness still exist, and who may be entirely alienated by harsh treatment, while they may yet be won by mildness adapting itself to their present condition. Accordingly, to break a bruised reed is the same as utterly to harden those who are already corrupted [1].—According to another interpretation, related indeed to this, the bruised reed and glimmering wick signify those who, humbled by outward affliction, and brought to a consciousness of their sins, feel themselves poor and wretched. To break a bruised reed is then the same as to make the unhappy still more wretched. The Messiah, according to this interpretation, will not by his severity drive to despair those, who, under the burden of their sins, draw near to him with a broken heart; but will encourage them by his love, mildness, and forbearance [2]. The latter interpretation is favoured by the parallel passages, ' *he binds up the broken-hearted,*' in the first verse of the sixty-first chapter ; and ' *he knows how to strengthen the weary,*' in the fourth verse of the fiftieth chapter. In order to illustrate the image here employed, Palm compares the nineteenth chapter of the first book of Kings. The old prophets, he says, were sometimes like a storm of wind, sometimes like a gentle breeze, that breaks no bruised reed, and extinguishes no glimmering wick. Of the latter class should be the eminent servant of God [3].—The last words of the verse are interpreted in very different ways. Many interpreters translate, ' *He will inculcate religion in truth,*' that is, *faithfully* or *truly*. Some, as Le Clerc, then find here a contrast with the former constitution of religion, which, considered in itself, was not perfect, but adapted to the necessities of the human race still under the dominion of sense, and moreover in many ways disfigured by human additions. Others, as Calvin, perceive an antithesis with the foregoing members of the verse. ' *He will indeed be mild and forbearing, but yet will surrender nothing of the truth.*'

quin sæpe miracula sua vulgari prohibebat, ut ejus imperium atque auctoritatem omnes longe diversam esse intelligerent ab ea, quam reges aut principes sibi conciliant, rumore de se conciliato ad captandum favorem multitudinis." After the example of Grotius, Rosenmüller erroneously says : "Sicut qui irâ exardescunt, qui solent ita altum loqui, ut vox eorum extra domum a prætereuntibus audiatur."

[1] Thus, among others, Calvin.   [2] Thus Luther.

[3] פְּשִׁתָּה, *flax,* then *a wick made of it.* כֵּהָה, *going out,* from the verb כָּהָה, *to go out, to be weak, small, dim.* The LXX λίνον καπνιζόμενον. Vulg. *linum fumigans.* Aq. Symm. Theod. λίνον ἀμαυρόν. Matthew λίνον τυφόμενον. All designations of a light, which, when it is near being extinguished, burns obscurely, and throws out smoke.

Gesenius, ' *With mildness he declares justice* [1].' It may be most naturally translated : ' *He will conduct religion to truth;*' that is, *he will cause religion to be truly and firmly established on earth.* Thus Matthew explains it, who has given an independent translation of this verse [2], *until he has conducted the true religion to victory* [3]. By the addition of ' *until,*' he indicates the connexion between the last and two first members of the verse. Precisely by his gentle and mild nature, shall the Messiah gain the victory for truth.

399. Verse 4. ' *He will not be discouraged, nor hasty, until he hath established righteousness on the earth, and the distant lands shall place their hope in his doctrine.*' The sense : *with fervent zeal, and wise discretion, he will labour for the extension of his kingdom, and not rest until he has accomplished his object, the establishment of true religion on earth* [4]. The sense of the last clause is, that *distant lands will eagerly receive his doctrine, believe in it, and ground upon it all their hopes.* It is declared in both members, that the doctrine to be propagated by the Messiah will not be confined to the narrow bounds of Palestine, but imparted to the whole heathen world, and eagerly embraced. Matthew has translated the words, ' *and in his name shall the Gentiles trust;*' so likewise the Seventy, whom he probably followed. But it is not necessary to suppose, that he and they had before them a different reading. *On his name,* is the same as, *on him.* But whoever, in the true sense, places his hope on the doctrine of the Messiah, places it on him [5].

400. Verse 5. Here commences a new discourse of Jehovah. He had before pointed to the Messiah, and spoken of him in the third person ; from the beginning of the fifth verse to the eighth, He addresses the Messiah himself, and announces to him his destination. ' *Thus saith the Lord Jehovah, who creates the heavens and stretches them out, who spreadeth abroad the earth with its productions, who giveth breath to the people that inhabit it, the breath of life to those who walk thereon.*' *Preservation* is with the Hebrews a *continual creation.* Jehovah *daily* stretches out the heavens anew.—In the words, ' *who spreadeth*

---

[1] Rosenmüller : " Justus existet judex, neminem injuria afficiet."

[2] ἕως ἂν ἐκβάλῃ εἰς νῖκος τὴν κρίσιν.

[3] κρίσις, as a verbal translation of מִשְׁפָּט in the sense of decree, law of God, positive religion; Wisdom 17. 1. LXX, Deut. 11. 1. Ex. 15. 25. 2 Chron. 35. 13.

[4] The interpretation, which we have followed in the translation, is recommended especially by Vitringa, with whom Rosenmüller agrees. It supposes the verb יָרוּץ to be the future in Kal, from רוּץ *to run,* as a regular form, and used in its customary signification. *He will not run;* that is : *his zeal for the extension of his kingdom will be combined with wise consideration and discretion; he will do nothing rashly.* Thus of old, Aquila and Theodotion, according to the account of Jerome : *non curret.* The verb is not then synonymous with יִכְהֶה, but it forms a suitable antithesis to it : he will not become disheartened, or his zeal will not abate, but neither will he act rashly. We give to the verb יָחַל the meaning, *to trust in any thing,* which it frequently has. See Ps. 31. 25. 119. 74. Gesenius s. v.

[5] אִיִּים *islands, coasts,* here as frequently, an indefinite designation of the most distant lands.

out the earth and its productions,' we have an example of the figure
called Zeugma. The verb cannot also refer to the productions, but
a verb must be understood, as : *to bring forth* [1].

401. Verse 6. '*I Jehovah have called thee in righteousness; I
will take thee by the hand, and guard thee, and make thee the mediator of the covenant with the people, for the light of the nations.*'
In righteousnes, i. e. since my righteousness, integrity, and truth,
require it [2]. It is true, that the sending of the Messiah was a pure
work of the Divine mercy, but when God has once *given* His merciful promises, His righteousness *demands* that He should *fulfil*
them. Thus by the *righteousness* of God, His *faithfulness in the fulfilment of His promises* is frequently designated [3]. The servant of
God (1) shall ratify a new covenant with the ancient covenant people ;
and (2) shall enlighten the heathen, who have heretofore been excluded from communion with the true God. The expression, ' *I
will make thee for a covenant of the people,*' is very concise [4]. The
Messiah is called ' *the covenant of the people,*' plainly with reference
to the *new covenant to be established,* because the covenant *should be
ratified through him,* and *depended on him alone.* The nature of this
new covenant to be ratified with the covenant people, may be learnt
from the thirty-first verse of the thirty-first chapter of Jeremiah.
The new covenant to be established by the Messiah, as was the old
by Moses, shall be the covenant of mercy and of the Spirit, under
which, as Ezekiel foretold, God shall write His law in the hearts of
believers, and give them hearts of flesh instead of hearts of stone. As
the servant of God is here called ' *the Covenant of the people,*' because
the covenant depended on him, and was to be established by him, so
is he immediately after called ' *the Light of the heathen,*' because
through him the heathen were to be enlightened [5]. According to
Rosenmüller : *I give thee for a covenant of the heathen people,* is the
same as : *I establish through thee a union of the heathen nations with
thee, and with one another.* According to Steudel, on the contrary,
this sense arises : *I fulfil through thee the conditions of the covenant
formerly established with the heathen.* This will then refer to the
promise made to Abraham, that through him all nations of the earth
should be blessed. But the *covenant* made with Abraham cannot
possibly be represented as made with the heathen. This is altogether contrary to the doctrine, as well as the *usus loquendi* of the
sacred writers.—The servant of God is called *a Light to the heathen,*

---

[1] After the example of Vitringa, Rosenmüller takes the verb רָקַע in the sense,
to make firm. The meaning, however, *to spread out,* is more suitable.

[2] So Vitringa.

[3] Others translate : *to practise what is right, to administer justice.* Gesenius
even : *for prosperity;* defining the meaning of the preposition בּ in the same
arbitrary manner, as that of the noun צֶדֶק which never means simply, prosperity. Rosenmüller: I have called thee in righteousness, i. e. thou mayest
surely trust, that I will fulfil my promise to protect thee.

[4] As in the parallel passage, chap. 49. 8.

[5] Similar is what is said of him by Micah 5. 4, "And he shall be peace," for,
giver of peace, and Eph. 2. 14, αὐτὸς γάρ ἐστιν ἡ εἰρήνη ἡμῶν.

not merely in reference to his *doctrine*. As sin, errour, and super-stition, in which the heathen world was sunk, are figuratively repre-sented as a *thick darkness ;* so the Messiah, who by his doctrine and his Spirit supplies the efficacious means of illumination and of sanc-tification, is described as *a great Light,* as *the Sun of Righteousness,* which was destined to dispel this darkness [1].

402. Verse 7. ' *That thou mayest open the blind eyes, bring forth from confinement those who are chained, and out of prison, those who sit in darkness.*' What is here given as the destination of the ser-vant of God, relates as well to the Jews as to the heathen. To open the eyes means, to see ; to open the eyes of any one, to make him see. But the removal of spiritual blindness by the Messiah signifies, not merely the giving of a pure system of religion through him, but especially the imparting of that inward illumination, which always appears in Scripture as necessarily connected with sanctification, and constituting, as it were, an essential part of it. This inward con-nexion of knowledge with the will, in reference to its depravity and its cure, runs through the whole of Scripture [2].

403. Verse 8. Jehovah now turns from the Messiah to the people to whom the prophecy was imparted, and gives the object of it : ' *I am the Lord, that is my name, and my glory will I not give to another, neither my praise to graven images.*' The sense : ' I am the only true God, who cannot allow that the glory due to Me should be given to others ; therefore have I delivered this prophecy.' The name Jehovah designates God as the self-existent and unchangeable, especially in reference to His promises. And as the idea of the *true* God is in-cluded in this name, it is often used to designate Him in opposi-tion to the idols [3].

404. Verse 9. ' *Behold the former things are come to pass, and new things do I declare ; before they spring forth I tell you of them.*' The *former* things are the former prophecies already fulfilled, partly those of other prophets, partly those of Isaiah himself. To them God appeals in order to awaken faith in the truth of those which will not be fulfilled for many years. By *that which is new,* is then to be un-derstood particularly the great deliverance here announced, to be effected by the servant of Jehovah, which was prefigured by the deliverance from the Babylonish exile. The words, ' *before they spring up,*' shows that the seeds of the events announced did not exist in the present, and therefore they could not have been predicted by human sagacity and calculation.

---

[1] See chap. 9. 1.
[2] The remarks of Theodoret on this verse are very appropriate : τυφλοὺς ἐνταῦθα τοὺς τὸ ὀπτικὸν τῆς διανοίας κακῶς διακειμένους καλεῖ· τοὺς δὲ αὐτοὺς καὶ τοὺς ταῖς ἁμαρτίας πεπηδημένους σειραῖς καὶ τῷ σκότει τῆς πλάνης κατεχομένους, τούτους τοῦ ζόφου τῆς ἀγνοίας ἐλευθερώσας καὶ τῆς ἁμαρτίας τὰ δεσμὰ ῥήξας, προσήγαγε τῷ τῆς ἀληθείας φωτί.
[3] See for example Ps. 96. 5.

Isaiah 49:1-9

405. As the Prophet had before plainly described Cyrus, the author of the first deliverance, and even called him by name, so here he introduces the author of the second deliverance, the Messiah, as himself speaking, and announcing his office and the design of his mission. In this prediction, as well as in the parallel passages in the forty-second and fiftieth chapters, it is the prophetic office of the Messiah which especially engages the attention of the Prophet. After all nations of the earth have been summoned to attend to a prediction which concerns them all, and not the covenant people alone, the speaker, from the first to the third verse, declares, that he has not presumptuously assumed his office, but has been solemnly chosen and called to it by Jehovah, endowed by Him with the requisite qualifications, and finally, after having been long concealed with Him, has been sent to execute His commission, with the promise that Jehovah would glorify Himself in him, as His servant and ambassador, and not forsake him.—The result appeared at first, not to correspond with this promise. It seemed as if all that the servant of God had done, were in vain; but his confidence in Jehovah is not thereby weakened [1]. How well grounded this confidence is, Jehovah shows by assigning him, as a sort of indemnity for the unbelief of the covenant people, a far greater and higher destination, that of enlightening and blessing all the heathen nations; and by exalting him from the deepest disgrace to the highest glory, and making him the mediator of a new covenant [2].

406. In favour of the Messianic interpretation, we mention, (1) the accurate agreement which exists between the prophecy, when thus explained, and its fulfilment. This requires no further evidence here, since it is already manifest from the representation which has been given of the contents. (2) The comparison of the parallel passages mentioned, which can be referred to no other subject than the Messiah; and (3) the authority of the New Testament. In the forty-seventh verse of the thirteenth chapter of Acts, Paul and Barnabas show from this passage the destination of Christ to be the Saviour of the heathen, and the propriety of their conduct in offering to them the salvation, which was despised by the Jews. In the second verse of the sixth chapter of the second Epistle to the Corinthians, the

[1] Verse 4.
[2] (1) Ver. 5—9. According to some, the *people of Israel* are here introduced as speaking. According to these interpreters, the *whole people* are here represented as *a prophet*, and the fundamental idea is, that the Israelites will in future times become the instructors of the heathen, and spread the true religion through the earth. (2) To others, the person who speaks is the Prophet himself. (3) Gesenius, clearly perceiving the unsoundness of both interpretations, chooses that the subject of the prophecy should not be the Prophet alone, but *the collective body of the prophets*, which are represented by him.—For a refutation of these opinions, see the original work.

eighth verse is quoted, and referred to the time of the Messiah. And there is an allusion to this passage in the thirtieth and two following verses of the second chapter of Luke.

407. There is here still to be noticed a difference, which exists among the Messianic interpreters. The majority regard the Messiah as the *only and constant subject of the whole portion*. Others, on the contrary, suppose a *concurrent reference to the Church*, either throughout the whole portion, or after the seventh verse ; or they entirely separate the first seven verses from the remainder, and refer the eighth and following verses to the people of Israel. The first opinion is adopted particularly by Calvin. Vitringa advocates the second. They both appeal to the sixth chapter of the second Epistle to the Corinthians. But although what is here said of the Messiah is in a great measure applicable also to the Church and its members, inasmuch as the history of the Head is repeated in that of the members, and they too are conducted to glory through reproach, contempt, and humiliation [1], yet there is no sufficient reason to suppose, that the Prophet here intended such a concurrent reference. Had he done so, this reference must have been continued through the whole, and expressions could not have occurred, which (as that in the eighth verse, ' *I make thee the mediator of the covenant of the people*,') even according to the opinion of these interpreters, must relate exclusively to the Messiah. The passage, in the second verse of the sixth chapter of the second Epistle to the Corinthians, is not conclusive in favour of this hypothesis, because it is not necessary to refer the pronoun *thee* [2] to the Church. Paul exhorts the Corinthians to embrace with true zeal the grace that was offered to them. He reminds them, that now the time has arrived, which God had foretold by the Prophet Isaiah, the time when God has heard and succoured the Messiah, i. e. has exalted him to glory after his sufferings, and has commenced the establishment of his kingdom through him. He exhorts them therefore not to suffer this time to pass by without improvement. The pronouns here, as well as the suffixes in Isaiah, refer to the Messiah [3].

408. Verse 1. ' *Listen, ye distant lands, unto me, and hearken, ye people, from far ; the Lord hath called me from the womb ; from the bowels of my mother hath he made mention of my name*.' The Prophet here contemplates the Messiah at the time when he had *already appeared in the flesh*, and experienced many proofs of the unbelief and obduracy of the Jews [4]. These, as well as the great contempt

---

[1] It is hereby sufficiently explained, how the Prophet in other passages speaks of the people partly in the same expressions he here employs in reference to the Messiah, a circumstance which Rosenmüller erroneously regards as proof, that the people are the subject of the prophecy.

[2] σοῦ and σοί.

[3] The latter opinion, that the proper Messianic prediction includes only v. 1—7, has been defended by V. d. Palm. But, not to mention other errors, it is inconsistent with בְּרִית עָם v. 8, which V. d. Palm himself, chap. 42. 6, explains of the Messiah, and which he cannot disprove of him except by an arbitrary change of the text.

[4] See ver. 5.

which he experienced from the covenant people, are represented as *having already taken place;* on the contrary, the enlightening of the heathen, which he is to effect, the reverence of kings towards him, &c., are described as still *future.* In like manner, in the fifty-third chapter, the humiliation appears to the Prophet as *past,* the exaltation as *future* [1].—The reason why the Messiah addresses *the heathen nations* is found in the sixth verse. Through him they shall obtain salvation. In the words: ' *Jehovah hath called me from my mother's womb,*' the stress is laid rather on the *calling* itself, than on the *particular time* at which it took place. The speaker gives great importance to the fact, that *he had not presumptuously assumed* his office, but had been *called* to it by God. The Messiah here mentions his Divine appointment, the gifts which God had bestowed upon him, and the protection which He had promised, in order the more to awaken the attention of the Gentiles to what he was about to announce to them.—*From my mother's womb,* when I was yet in my mother's womb, *even before my birth* [2]. Parallel are the fifth verse of the first chapter of Jeremiah, where Jehovah says that He had destined Jeremiah for a prophet *before He had formed him in the womb of his mother, and before he was born,* and the fifteenth verse of the first chapter of Galatians; ' *God, who separated me from my mother's womb, and called me by his grace;*' where also, *the being called from the mother's womb* is put in opposition to the *presumptuous intrusion* into an office not conferred by God.—The last words, ' *He hath made mention of my name from my mother's bowels,*' have been understood literally by several interpreters. They are supposed to predict the circumstance, that Mary was commanded by an angel, before the birth of the Messiah, to call him Jesus, Saviour [3], and that the same command was given to Joseph in a dream [4]. Others, on the contrary, suppose *the making mention of his name* to be synonymous with *to call.* They appeal to the second verse of the thirty-first chapter of Exodus, where Jehovah says, He has *called Bezaleel by name,* i. e. *chosen* him. Both explanations, the special and the general, may be easily combined by the supposition, that here, as well as in many other instances, expressions which admit of a general meaning, and were probably so understood by the contemporaries of the Prophet, are literally and specially fulfilled under a particular guidance of Divine providence [5].

409 Verse 2. '*And he hath made my mouth like a sharp sword, in the shadow of his hand hath he hid me, and made me a polished*

[1] See remarks on the place.

[2] Vitringa mistranslates : before the womb of his mother, and before he was in the bowels of his mother. See on the contrary, v. 5, and chap. 44. 2. 24.

[3] Luke 1. 31.

[4] Matt. 1. 21. So Jerome ; " Dominus inquit ab utero vocavit me, et de ventre matris meæ recordatus est nominis mei. Quod nunc interim audientibus videtur obscurum, postea autem cunctis gentibus notum fiet, quando Gabriel Joseph de partu dixerit virginali; Et vocabis nomen ejus Jesum ; ipse enim salvum faciet populum suum." Likewise Le Clerc, Vitringa, Michaelis, and others.

[5] See on Zech. 9. 9.

shaft; in his quiver hath he hid me.' The *mouth* stands for *speech ;* a powerful and penetrating discourse is compared to a sword, because it pierces the soul as a sharp sword does the body [1]. So in the eleventh verse of the twelfth chapter of Ecclesiastes : ' *The words of the wise are as goads, and as nails fastened by the masters of assemblies.'* In the twelfth verse of the fourth chapter of Hebrews : ' *The word of God is quick and powerful, and sharper than any two-edged sword, and piercing even to the dividing asunder of the soul and spirit, and of the joints and marrow.'* In the sixteenth verse of the first chapter of Revelation, probably with reference to this passage, the characteristic of Christ here spoken of is exhibited under the figure of a sharp *two-edged sword* proceeding from his mouth [2]. The sense is the same, when the Messiah calls himself an *arrow.* As the arrow pierces the heart of the *outward* man, so does he pierce the heart of the *inner man;* no enemies can stand before him ; they must be slain, either that they may live in a higher sense, or that they may die for ever [3]. —As the two figures of the sword and of the arrow correspond, so also must the other two have a corresponding sense. We cannot, therefore, with many interpreters, as Grotius, Gesenius, &c., refer the words, ' *He hath hid me in the shadow of his hand,'* to the protection which Jehovah extends to the Messiah ; since in the second figure the phrase, ' *He hath hid me in his quiver,'* cannot have this sense, as Le Clerc and Vitringa have shown. The image would then, at any rate, have been very unfitly chosen, since the arrow is not placed in the quiver to be *protected,* but to be *ready for use* at the time of action. Besides, in the first figure, the simile of a sword must be carried through, as well as that of an arrow in the second. The image, therefore, according to this explanation, would be unsuitable, even so far as this member alone is concerned. For the sword, as Vitringa justly remarks, is here represented, not as *sheathed,* but as *drawn;* now a *drawn sword* needs no *protection* ; it is not a thing *to be defended,* but one with which a man *defends himself.* Far more congruous therefore is the opinion of those, who, after Abenezra and Vitringa, suppose that the *shadow of the hand of God* is what here covers and hides the sword, and serves, as it were, for its sheath. The image is perhaps taken from a dirk, which a man carries concealed in his hand, and in the moment of attack suddenly draws forth. The two figures thus explained can be fitly referred neither to *the prophet,* nor to *the people of Israel.* But on the other hand, according to the Messianic interpretation, all is suitable and clear. Before his appearing the Messiah was concealed with God, like a sword

---

[1] See the striking examples of the use of the metaphor of a *sword and bow* to designate an impressive discourse, taken from the Greek writers by Lowth, on this passage, and from him by Gesenius, &c.

[2] So likewise chap. 19. 15.

[3] Theodoret: ὁμοίως καὶ ταῦτα τροπικῶς κέκληκε, βέλος μὲν αὐτὸν τὸν τιτρώσκοντα τὰς ἐρώσας αὐτοῦ ψυχὰς, ὧν ἑκάστη βοᾷ· τετρωμένη ἀγάπης ἐγώ. יָרָה חֵץ either *a chosen,* or *a polished sharp arrow.* See Jer. 51. 11. The first interpretation is followed by Jerome, Vitringa, and others ; the latter is recommended by the circumstance, that a sharp arrow corresponds better with a sharp sword.

kept in its sheath, or like an arrow lying in the quiver. When at last he came forth from his concealment, he pierced the hearts of men like a brandished sword, or an arrow shot from a bow.

410. Verse 3. ' *And said unto me : Thou art my servant, O Israel, in whom I will be glorified.*' These words occasion the non-Messianic interpreters great difficulty. The best escape from it is that of those, who suppose the person speaking to be the *people of Israel ;* but this interpretation, as we have seen, is elsewhere liable to so many objections, that it is rejected by nearly all commentators [1]. But the Messianic interpretation entirely removes this difficulty, and with it the necessity of resorting to such violent measures. It has already been shown in the general Introduction, that in the Messianic predictions, not merely are the figures borrowed from the things and persons of the old covenant, to represent those of the new ; but also the persons of the new are expressly called by the names of those of the old, when the latter were types of the former, or resembled them in their nature or names. The enemies of the new theocracy bear the names of *Edom, Moab, Ashur ;* John the Baptist, the name of *Elias ;* the Messiah himself is frequently called *David ;* and Isaiah gives him the name of *Prince of Peace*, which is of the same import with *Solomon*. And in like manner, in the passage before us, he is called also *Israel*. But it may be asked, wherein consists that resemblance of the Messiah to Israel, on account of which he here receives his name. Most Messianic interpreters here find a reference to the twenty-eighth verse of the thirty-

---

[1] The bare mention of the explanations of those, who regard *the Prophet* as the subject, is sufficient to show that they are altogether unnatural. After the example of Grotius, Dathe supplied the preposition ל before יִשְׂרָאֵל ' *it is for Israel's benefit, that I will glorify myself in thee.*' An explanation, which besides being altogether forced, is totally inadmissible on philological grounds. As little justifiable is the interpretation of Saadias, which supposes a similar ellipsis : ' *thou art my ambassador to Israel,*' and in which, moreover, the meaning of עֶבֶד is arbitrarily modified. According to Döderlein, &c. Isaiah is here called *an Israelite* in the full sense of the word, *a true descendant* of Israel. See John 1. 18. But then the word must be יִשְׂרְאֵלִי since יִשְׂרָאֵל is always either the name of the ancestor or of the people. Others (Hensler, Staüdlin), after the example of Kimchi, regard the words as an abrupt address to Israel : ' *thou art my servant, and I will glorify myself in thee, O Israel.*' But it is easy to perceive that this interpretation, which entirely destroys the parallelism, is erroneous. This sentence would then stand entirely in the wrong place. For since the speaker addresses himself to the Gentiles, nothing belongs here but what has respect to the relation of Jehovah to His servant, and tends to fix their attention upon him. What Jehovah purposes concerning the people of Israel is here out of place. Explanations like that of Koppe, which separate the sentence from the third verse, and connect it with the following, as an address of the Prophet to his people : ' *O Israel, how could I be glorified by thee, but I must lament, in vain do I labour, &c.*' refute themselves.—Gesenius confesses that the translation that has been given is the most simple. He therefore cuts the knot which he cannot untie, and, after the example of Michaelis, denies the genuineness of the word, against the authority of all the old translations and manuscripts, one only excepted, to which he himself gives no weight. He is contradicted by the circumstance, that the second member necessarily requires a word corresponding to יִתְפָּאָר׃

second chapter of Genesis ; according to which, the name Israel, 'one who contends with God,' was given by Jehovah to Jacob, after his wrestling with him.   Christ deserves this name in its highest sense, since by his vicarious life and sufferings he mightily contended with God and prevailed [1].   It cannot be objected to this interpretation, that it attributes to the Prophet a knowledge of the work of redemption, which does not belong to the Old Testament.   For the Prophet, in the fifty-third chapter, describes this work with the clearness of history.   But, nevertheless, those may be more correct who do not seek the resemblance merely in this particular point.   As the Messiah is called *David*, principally because he should be *the head of the spiritual theocracy*, as *David* was of the *earthly ;* so here he seems to bear the name of *Israel*, principally because he is to be the *father of the spiritual people of God*, as Israel was the *father of the Jewish people* [2].   Other resemblances besides, as *piety* and *devotedness to God*, the *passing through suffering to joy*, &c. may have been considered.—Those depart further from the truth, who suppose the Messiah to be called Israel, either because he represented *the whole people*, or because he is *their king* ; or else as the *seed promised to Israel*, in whom all nations of the earth should be blessed [3].

411. Verse 4. '*And I said : I have laboured in vain, for nothing and without use have I expended my strength, but my judgement is with Jehovah, and my reward is with my Lord.*'   The Messiah having, in the foregoing verses, spoken of his dignity and Divine nature, now prepares the way to make known his destination to be the light and the salvation of the heathen, to whom the whole discourse is directed.   He laments over the little fruit which he saw in the commencement of his efforts among the Jews, but consoles himself by trusting in the righteousness of God, that the faithful performance of the work entrusted to him cannot go unrewarded.

412. Verse 5. '*And now Jehovah speaks to me, who formed me from the womb to be his servant, that I should bring back to him Jacob ; but Israel would not be gathered, and I was esteemed in the eyes of Jehovah, and my God was my strength.*'   What Jehovah has spoken does not follow till the sixth verse, which, on account of the long interruption, again commences with [4] *He, I say, has spoken.* The declaration of Jehovah relates to the appointment of the Messiah

---

[1] Thus Vitringa, Lowth, and (nearly) Le Clerc.

[2] See chap. 53. 10.

[3] Gen. 28. 14, The words אֲשֶׁר בְּךָ אֲרְפָּאֵר can be translated either *by whom*, or *in whom I will glorify myself.* Christ, as John frequently says, glorifies the Father, and is glorified by Him. But in favour of the latter interpretation is the parallel passage, chap. 44. 23, כִּי גָאַל יְהֹוָה יַעֲקֹב וּבְיִשְׂרָאֵל יִתְפָּאָר · '*Jehovah redeems Jacob and glorifies himself in Israel*,' where the verb is closely connected with the object of the glorification with בְּ· It is also more agreeable to the connexion (see on ver. 1), that the glorification of the Messiah by God, rather than the glorification of God by the Messiah, should be here introduced.   For the same reason, the idea of obedience to God is not the prominent one in the appellation *my servant*, but the idea of God's love towards him, and of his protection.

[4] וַיֹּאמֶר

to be the Saviour of the Gentiles. In this verse two reasons are
given, why this was to be the destination of the Messiah ; (1) The
Jews, to whom he was first sent, refuse to be converted, and (2) the
servant of God stands so high in His favour, and so entirely enjoys
His protection, that God cannot withhold from him the full reward
which his work deserves.—The words, ' *And now Jehovah speaks*,'
&c. are of the same import as : ' and this hope, which I cherish, that
Jehovah will not suffer my work to go unrewarded, is not vain ; it is
ratified by a distinct Divine promise, which assures me, that I have
received the heathen for a possession, as an equivalent for the unbelieving Jews.' It is represented, as though the Messiah had first
received the promise, that he should convert the heathen, after his
efforts had proved fruitless among the Jews, because this promise was
then first carried into effect. The words, ' *Who formed me from my
mother's womb*,' &c. are the same as : *who appointed me before I was
born, to be his servant and instrument in the conversion of the Jews*.
In the words, ' *But Israel was not gathered*,' the metaphor is taken
from a scattered flock, which the faithful shepherd, after all his
efforts, is unable to collect.—Most interpreters following the Masorites [1] translate : ' *That I should bring back Jacob to him, and that
Israel should be gathered to him*.' But it had been said in the foregoing verse, that the Messiah had at first spent his strength *in vain*
among the Jews, and this is given as the very reason why the Gentiles in the following verse were promised to him as a possession.
The origin of the Masorite reading is easily explained by the carnal
national pride of the Jews. They could not bear the idea, that a
great part of Israel themselves should reject the Messiah, and be cast
off by him ; they therefore sought by all means to get rid of so unpleasant a truth [2].—The words, ' *God was my strength*,' are of the
same import with, ' *I was esteemed in the eyes of Jehovah ;*' as much
as to say : He could not do otherwise than make me, his servant,
great and honorable. Others erroneously : ' *since He, my God,
gave me greater power, than the conversion of the chosen Jews required ;*' or [3] ' *since my God will employ me for the signal glorification of his name*.' These words contain the reason of what follows :
since Israel, to whom I was first sent, will not be gathered, and as I
nevertheless enjoy Jehovah's peculiar protection and high esteem,
far from depriving me of my just reward, he confers upon me the
glory of being the Saviour, not of the Jews only, but of the Gentiles
also.

413. Verse 6. ' *He, I say, said : It is too little, that thou shouldst
be my servant to raise up the tribes of Jacob, and restore the preserved of Israel ; I make thee for the light of the nations, to be my
salvation to the ends of the earth*.' That is : the conversion of the
chosen Israelites alone would be a reward too small for thee. Thy
destination is a higher one. As the sun disperses the natural darkness, so shalt thou dispel the spiritual darkness, the sin and errour

---

[1] Who read יְּ instead of לֹא.
[2] This was seen long ago by Jerome.
[3] עֹז being taken in the sense, *praise, honour.*

of the heathen. *The preserved of Israel* are those who have not perished in the Divine judgements, but have been preserved by the mercy of God[1]; here especially, those, who should have been converted and delivered by the Messiah, and consequently were preserved from the judgements which fell upon the rebellious[2]. Gesenius rightly remarks, that in the last words there is, as in other Messianic predictions[3], an allusion to the promises made to the patriarchs[4]. Through thee, says Jehovah, shall the ancient promises of a future extension of salvation to all the heathen nations be fulfilled.

414. Verse 7. ' *Thus saith Jehovah, the Redeemer of Israel, his Holy One, to him who is despised by all, to him who is abhorred of the people, to the servant of the rulers, kings shall see and rise up, princes shall see, and prostrate themselves before him, for Jehovah's sake, who is true, for the sake of the Holy One of Israel, who hath chosen thee.*' The Messiah voluntarily subjects himself to human power, although by his nature, as servant of God, he is exalted above all the powers of the world, and after his glorification shall be acknowledged by them as such. Christ submitted himself to the earthly magistracy, and refrained from using His Divine power. After *they shall see*, the object is not expressed. Some improperly supply *him;* the object is rather to be supplied from the sixth verse, *they shall see the fulfilment of the Divine promise*, by which the Messiah was destined to be the Saviour of the heathen; or generally, the splendid condition to which he shall be exalted.—To *rise up*, and to *prostrate themselves*, are both signs of humble subjection. The expression : *on account of Jehovah*, &c. is much the same as : *this shall be brought to pass by Jehovah, who is faithful in the fulfilment of his promises, and will therefore fulfil those made to thee, his chosen.*

415. Verse 8. ' *Thus saith Jehovah : At a time of mercy have I heard thee, in the day of salvation helped thee ; and I will preserve thee and give thee for a covenant of the people, that thou mayest succour the land, and distribute the heritages which have been laid waste.*' Henceforth the redemption and deliverance to be accomplished by the Messiah are described, but the deliverance from the Babylonish exile also is still continually before the eye of the Prophet, and he describes the spiritual deliverance by images taken from it. How far the Prophet himself, when his *ecstasy* had ceased, was enabled to discriminate between the two deliverances, and determine the real import of the images presented to him in vision, it is not in our power to decide. He here transfers himself in the spirit to the time when the work of redemption by the Messiah had been completed. It is at this period that the address of Jehovah is to be conceived of as

---

[1] See chap. 4. 3. 10. 21. Mic. 5. 6, 7.

[2] Several interpreters translate the last member : that I may extend my salvation to the ends of the earth ; but it is better to make לִהְיוֹת dependent on נְתַתִּיךָ. As the Messiah in the foregoing member is called *the light of the heathen*, because he enlightens them, so here he is called *the salvation of the heathen*, because he brings them salvation.

[3] e. g. Psalm 72.   [4] Gen. 12. 8. 22. 18. 26. 4.

having been made [1]. Respecting [2] *covenant of the people* for *Mediator of the covenant of the people*, see on the sixth verse of the forty-second chapter. By *the people* here the natural Israel cannot be meant. We are rather to understand by it, as appears from the sixth and seventh verses, the *better portion of the covenant people*, who constitute the foundation of the theocracy, upon which the Gentiles were to be built. In the words *that thou mayest succour the land*, &c. the figure is taken from the resuscitation of ruined cities, and desolated lands, with distinct reference to the recultivation of the land of Judea after the Babylonian exile. As the Jews after the exile shall repossess their natural inheritance, which had been laid waste, so shall the Messiah renovate the renewed spiritual inheritance, and restore it to those whom he shall have delivered from spiritual bondage.

416. Verse 9. '*In that thou sayest to the prisoners, Go forth ; to those who are in darkness, Come to the light.*' The first half only of the ninth verse belongs to the prophecy of the Messiah as a person ; with the second, commences a more general representation. The figures of the first part were explained on the sixth verse of the forty-second chapter.

Isaiah 50:4-11

417. The Messiah is again introduced as speaking. He declares that he has not come forward of his own will, but has received from Jehovah both his saving doctrine and the power to preach it [3]. He has willingly undertaken the work which Jehovah has committed to him, and endured all the sufferings and all the shame and ignominy connected with it [4]. This fortitude resulted from his firm confidence in Jehovah, who, he well knew, would stand by him, and destroy his enemies [5]. He then directs his discourse to those who fear God, and exhorts them when they shall be led in the dark path of suffering, as he had been, to place their trust in Jehovah alone. But to the ungodly, who rely upon themselves for help, instead of putting their trust in Jehovah and His servant, he declares, in the eleventh verse,

---

[1] Hence the use of the præter עֲנִיתִיךָ and עֲזַרְתִּיךָ is explained.—Several interpreters take רָצוֹן in the sense of *inclination, pleasure ;* ' *at a time of pleasure,*' i. e. *at a time when it pleased me, at a chosen time.* Thus the LXX, καιρῷ δεκτῷ ; Vulgate, *tempore placito.* But this is contradicted by the parallelism בְּיוֹם יְשׁוּעָה *in the day of salvation.* We must therefore, with others, take רָצוֹן in the sense of *grace.* The meaning will then be : when the time of imparting mercy and salvation to all men (ver. 6) has arrived, I will hear thee, and help thee ; I will exalt thee to glory, and cause that through thee my salvation shall be bestowed on mankind.

[2] בְּרִית עָם   [3] Ver. 4.   [4] Ver. 5, 6.   [5] Ver. 7—9.

that they will bring upon themselves, by their inventions, destruction to be accomplished by him.

418. The Messianic interpretation is confirmed by the authority of the Saviour himself [1]. It prevailed universally in the ancient Christian Church, and Grotius, who refers the prophecy in a lower sense to Isaiah, and only in a higher one to Christ, met with general opposition. Even Le Clerc rejected this interpretation. The reference to the Messiah has been strenuously maintained by Michaelis, and, among the recent interpreters, by Palm.

419. On the other hand several (as Döderlein, Dathe, Koppe, Augusti, &c.) suppose the Prophet himself, either Isaiah or some other one living in the exile, to be the subject of the portion. Jerome cites this interpretation, as the prevailing one among the Jews in his time. Rosenmüller also adopts it, though with singular inconsistency, since he explains all the parallel passages of the Jewish people. Gesenius also here puts in the back ground the hypothesis which he adopts in the case of the other similar passages, which makes the collective body of the prophets the subject, and appears to regard the Prophet himself as the only subject, although he so strongly insists that in the forty-second, forty-ninth, fiftieth, fifty-third, and sixty-first chapters, one and the same subject must necessarily be assumed. According to Paulus, it is not the Prophet who speaks, but the better and pious portion of the people.

420. But against these interpreters, and in favour of the Messianic, there is (1.) the testimony of the New Testament. Compare the cited passage of Luke with the twenty-seventh verse of the twenty-sixth chapter of Matthew. (2.) All the characteristics of the servant of God—all that is said of his humiliation, as well as of his exaltation and the destruction of his enemies, entirely agrees with Jesus Christ; and the most minute lines of the picture are repeated in his history. We know of nothing similar in the life of Isaiah. The eleventh verse even ascribes to the servant of God the judgement of the ungodly. (3.) The parallel passages, to which we have referred, every other interpretation of which is liable to insurmountable difficulties.

421. Finally, this Messianic prophecy is distinguished from those in the forty-second and forty-ninth chapters, to which in other respects it bears a close resemblance, by the circumstance that it dwells rather upon the sufferings and uniform patience of the Messiah; while in them the glorification which followed his sufferings, and the extension of his salvation to the heathen, are exhibited. All these several features are combined in the fifty-third chapter, where the sufferings and the exaltation of the Messiah are predicted with equal clearness.

422. Verse 4. ' *The Lord Jehovah has given me an eloquent tongue, that I may know how to console the weary ; every morning he wakeneth mine ear, that I may hearken as one instructed* [2].' The *weary* are

---

[1] Luke 18. 31, 32.

[2] Theodoret: ταῦτα ἀνθρωπίνως λέγει ὁ Δεσπότης Χριστὸς, πολλὰ δὲ τοιαῦτα καὶ ἐν τοῖς ἱεροῖς εὐαγγελίοις εὑρήσομεν· Ἰησοῦς γάρ φησι προέκοπτεν ἡλικίᾳ καὶ σοφίᾳ καὶ χάριτι παρὰ Θεῷ τε καὶ ἀνθρώποις.

those who, oppressed by suffering and sin, feel fatigued and burthened, *those 'who travail and are heavy laden*[1];' the same who, in the third verse of the forty-second chapter, were represented under the figure of a bruised reed and smoking wick[2]. The figure is taken from a teacher, who, in the morning, before he commences his instruction, summons his pupils to him. After Christ had assumed the form of a servant, He always spake and acted under the influence of the Holy Spirit[3].

423. Verse 5. ' *The Lord Jehovah opened mine ear, and I was not disobedient and drew not back.*' The phrase *to open the ear* is used as well of the imparting of instruction, as also of *giving a commission*[4]; the latter is the meaning here. The Messiah receives from God a very difficult commission, the command to accomplish the redemption of mankind : he willingly undertakes it, notwithstanding all the sufferings therewith connected. The expressions are taken from a yoke of oxen, who go backward instead of forward, and will not suffer themselves to be guided.

424. Verse 6. ' *I gave my back to those who smite, and my cheeks to those who pluck ; I hid not my face before reproach and spittle.*' Although this was in part especially fulfilled in Christ[5], yet these particular traits, according to the custom of the Hebrew poets to *particularize* every thing, served in the first instance for the contemporaries of the Prophet to express the thought, that the Messiah would experience, and patiently endure, the most shameful and abusive treatment. But God so directed the event, that *even these special traits* occurred again in the history of the Messiah ; a remark which we have already made before, and shall yet have occasion many times to repeat. To pluck out the beard is the greatest of all indignities in the East[6]. Among the Romans, mischievous boys were accustomed to pull out the long beard of the philosophers with tweezers, and the phrase *vellere barbam* was employed for *to insult, to abuse.* See the passages in Le Clerc ad h. l.—' *I have not hid my face before reproach and spittle.*' To spit, even in the presence of any one, in the East, is considered as an insult[7]. But how much more to spit in one's face[8] ? Christ[9] refers this passage to himself[10].

---

[1] Matt. 11. 28.

[2] *To awaken the ear* is to prepare one to receive the revelation and instruction. The expressions, *to uncover the ear,* and *to open the ear,* and *to bore the ear,* in the sense *to reveal,* are all related.

[3] Several interpreters translate בַּלִּמּוּדִים as *disciples,* i. e. like docile disciples. It is true that לִמּוּדִים often has this meaning ; but it is not easy to suppose that the word should be used in two different senses in the very same verse. It is better therefore to translate ' *as one instructed,*' like a learned or *practised,* i. e. attentive person, and with complete insight into what is imparted.

[4] 1 Sam. 9. 15.   Ruth 4. 4.

[5] Matt. 26. 67.   Luke 18. 31.

[6] 2 Sam. 10. 4.   Lowth on chap. 7. 20.   Harmer's Observations, II. p. 61. III. p. 434, seq.

[7] See Herodotus and Xenophon in Lowth on the passage : Harmer's Observations, III. p. 376 ; Niebuhr, Beschreibung von Arabien, § 26.

[8] See Num. 12. 14.   Deut. 25. 9.   Job 7. 19. 30, 10.

[9] Luke 18. 31.   [10] See Mark 14. 65. 15. 19.

425. Verse 7. ' *But the Lord Jehovah helps me : therefore shall I not be brought into disgrace ; therefore do I make my face as a flint, and know, that I shall not be ashamed* [1].' The sense is : I know that Jehovah will conduct me through suffering to glory, and in the view of the future I endure with fortitude all that is inflicted upon me. The expressions : to harden the heart, the forehead, the face, were employed both in a good and in a bad sense,—in a good sense for *firmness in the discharge of duty, and in enduring the sufferings connected with it :* as here, and in the eighth verse of the third chapter of Exodus, it is said : ' *I make thy face hard against their face, and thy forehead hard against their forehead. I make thy forehead as hard as a diamond, which is harder than a rock. Therefore fear not before them.* '

426. Verse 8. ' *He is near, who justifies me, who will contend with me ? Let us stand forth together : let him, who will be my adversary before the tribunal, come near to me.* ' We must conceive this discourse of the servant of God as spoken in his humiliation, and during his sufferings. The image, as is frequently the case, is taken from a judicial proceeding. God Himself will soon stand forth at the same time as his powerful patron and his judge, and by deed declare him righteous, and his enemies guilty. He has therefore so little occasion to dread his foes, and fear their power, that he can confidently challenge them to engage with him in the unequal conflict.

427. Verse 9. ' *Behold the Lord Jehovah will help me ; who is he that will condemn me ? behold they shall all pass away as a garment, the moth shall consume them.* ' In the last member the figure and reality are blended together. It is as much as to say : they shall pass away, as a garment which is devoured by moths.

428. Verse 10. The servant of God concludes with a twofold address, first, in this verse, to those who fear God, then in the following to the ungodly.—' *Who is there among you that fears Jehovah, and regards the voice of his servant ? if he walks through darkness in which no light shines upon him, let him trust on Jehovah, and stay himself on his God.* ' The Messiah admonishes those who fear God, not to seek deliverance by their own power, when they find themselves in severe calamity, but, in imitation of his example, to throw themselves entirely into the arms of the faithful God, who will then illuminate *their* night, as he had done *his*.—' Who is there among you, &c.' is the same as : if there is any one among you ; but implying that the number of the pious is *small*.—Darkness without light denotes suffering, from which there appears to be no escape and no deliverance.—' *Let him trust in Jehovah, let him stay himself on his God,* ' viz., as I have done or do. Then will the same Divine assistance be granted to him.

429. Verse 11. ' *Behold, all ye, who strike a fire, furnish yourselves with blazing torches, walk in the conflagration of your fire, in the glowing fire, which you have kindled. This shall ye receive at my hand ; in sorrow shall ye lie down.* ' The figure, commenced in the

---

[1] בּוֹשׁ *to be ashamed, deceived in his hope, to be disgraced.*

foregoing verse, is carried on in this. The pious walk patiently through the darkness, until *Jehovah* kindles a light for them.   The ungodly kindle a fire *for themselves;* but the fire, that should light and warm, consumes them.   Without a figure : every one, who, refusing to hear the servants of Jehovah, and put his trust in God, seeks deliverance by *his own* plans, shall perish, although he may for a time flatter himself with the agreeable expectation of a happy issue.   Jerome, Le Clerc, Vitringa, Michaelis, Lowth, and Palm, give too narrow a meaning to a general expression, which is still daily fulfilling, when they make it refer merely to the projects of the rebellious Jews after the time of Christ, who by their insurrection against the Romans kindled a fire, which consumed their city and nation.   This was indeed *one* remarkable instance of the fulfilment of the declaration [1]. By the words, *at my hand,* &c., the Messiah appropriates to himself the judgement of the ungodly.— *To lie down* is spoken of those who are lost without deliverance ; here perhaps (in continuation of the figure of the fire) of those who are severely burnt by it.

Isaiah 52:12—53 [2]

430. We have now come to a portion which may be regarded, in many respects, as the most important of all the Scriptures of the Old Testament, and better adapted than any other to lead us to a right understanding of the whole.   The clare-obscure, which usually attends the prophetic representation, seems here to have entirely vanished.   The highest operation of the Spirit of God coincides with the most entire suppression of all conscious and voluntary agency on the part of the Prophet.   And thus, like a pure mirror, he has reflected upon us the sublime and Divine truth which was given him ;

---

[1] Schultens, Döderlein, and Paulus, render the ἄπ. λεγ. זִקּוֹת *bands ;* a meaning which does not suit the connexion. Rosenmüller and Gesenius compare זִקִּים Prov. 26. 18, which however comes from a radical זָקַק and suppose, that the word means *burning arrows*, which, shot from a slackened bow, cause a fire where they fix themselves. But this is inadmissible, since it cannot be said : walk in burning arrows, which you have set on fire. The explanation of Vitringa, Augusti, and others, is less objectionable, who give to the word the meaning *fagots :* ye, who kindle a fire, and encompass yourselves or the same with fagots, in order to make a great conflagration.   The Chaldee זִקְתָּא has the meaning *stick.* But " walk in the fagots, which ye have kindled," would still be somewhat stiff. It is most in accordance with the connexion to translate it : *torches* or *glowing fire.* Thus the LXX, φλόγα. Vulgate *flammas.* In the Syriac זִקָּא has the meaning *lightning.* To gird about torches or fire is the same as, to encompass or furnish themselves therewith.
[2] The original work contains a valuable history of the interpretations of this passage.

or rather, the Spirit of Christ in the Prophet has employed him as an instrument to reveal the sufferings he should endure after his manifestation in the flesh, and the glory that should follow [1].

431. We have already seen, in our general preparatory remarks, that the main subject of the second part of the predictions of Isaiah is the deliverance of the people of God ; and that, a twofold deliverance, from the Babylonian exile, and from sin and errour. The two are not accurately distinguished from each other. It may however be remarked in general, that from the commencement to the forty-ninth chapter, the former, and in the remaining chapters, the latter, was predominant in the view of the Prophet. Each of these deliverances shall be accomplished by a servant and messenger of Jehovah ; the first by Cyrus, the second by Christ. The Prophet had already, in a preceding part of the book, so plainly described Cyrus, that no trait remained to be added. Nor had he left the latter unnoticed : God's servant and chosen, him whom His soul loves—Israel, by whom he glorifies Himself. But the features which he had hitherto given were not sufficient to form a perfect image. He had described him as the Divine teacher and messenger, who, endowed by God with rich gifts, humbled himself, and meek and lowly came to seek that which was lost : he had represented him as a glorious King, who should found a kingdom of peace and righteousness, continually enlarge its boundaries, receive into it all the heathen nations, richly bless its members, and severely punish the despisers of his name. But still one great feature in the portrait was wanting. He had announced, that Cyrus should accomplish the temporal deliverance by his military valour, and the victories which Jehovah would grant him ; but the method in which the spiritual deliverance should be accomplished was not yet communicated to him. True, he had spoken already of the deepest humiliation of the Messiah ; he had, in the fiftieth chapter, predicted the severe sufferings, the scorn and contempt of the people which should overtake the servant of God. But he had not said, that these very sufferings should be the only efficient cause of our salvation. Here then, for the first time, he completes the picture, when he announces, that the Messiah, at the same time both priest and offering, shall expiate our sins by his blood, and present himself to God as a sacrifice for our transgressions ; that he shall bear our infirmities, and by his wounds heal ours. Three offices were instituted by God under the theocracy, those of Prophet, Priest, and King ; in a higher and more complete sense the Messiah was to combine them all in his own person.

432. The contents of the prophecy are as follows. From the thirteenth to the fifteenth verse of the fifty-second chapter, Jehovah speaks. These verses contain a brief summary of what is enlarged upon in the fifty-third chapter. The deepest possible humiliation of the servant of God shall be followed by his exaltation to the highest glory ; the nations of the earth shall be redeemed by him, and their kings shall submit to him with reverence. From the first to the tenth

[1] 1 Pet. 1. 11.

verse of the fifty-third chapter, the Prophet speaks. The first verse
is not in connexion with the rest, but contains a sort of introduction,
or exclamation of complaint. The Prophet, speaking in the name
of all who foretell the Messiah, and of all who preach him after his
appearance, announces that many will not believe their report, many
will not acknowledge, as such, this glorious manifestation of the omnipotence and mercy of God. He then, in the second verse, continues the discourse, with this difference only, that he henceforth
considers himself as one of the people, or rather as one of the better
part of the people, who misapprehended the Redeemer at first in his
humiliation, but recognized him as their Saviour and benefactor after
his glorification, and perceived that his sufferings had been endured
by him only for our salvation. This is the substance of the discourse :
the servant of Jehovah will appear in lowliness and with no outward
splendour. Sufferings more severe than man ever endured will overtake him. Freely and patiently will he endure them. Finally, he
will be taken away by a violent death. The rage of his enemies,
which is still unsatisfied, will endeavour, though in vain, even in
death, to dishonour him, the righteous and the innocent[1]. The
people, beholding his sufferings, and being ignorant of their cause,
believed them to be the deserved punishment of his own misdeeds,
but (as the speakers now perceive) erroneously. It was not his own
transgressions that were punished, but ours in him. His sufferings
were voluntarily undergone for the salvation of men, who were exposed
to destruction without them. God Himself was pleased in this way
to restore for communion with Himself those, who, having departed
from Him, were wandering in their own ways[2]. Great glory is designed for him after Jehovah has been reconciled by the sacrifice of
his life freely offered. The knowledge and love of God will be
established on earth through him, and a numerous Church collected[3].
In the eleventh and twelfth verses, Jehovah again appears as the
speaker, and confirms what had been said by the Prophet.

ISAIAH 52. 13

433. Jehovah speaks. Some interpreters suppose this verse to be
connected with the foregoing ; others, that it begins a new portion,
which has nothing in common with what preceded. The first opinion is undeniably the more correct. The Prophet, it is true, in the
foregoing section[4], had been chiefly concerned with the nearer deliverance from the Babylonian exile. But at the same time, under the
figure of the temporal deliverance, the spiritual one was concealed.
As now, in the foregoing portion, the deliverance itself, so in this its

---

[1] Ver. 2, 3. 7—9.   [2] Ver. 4—6.   [3] Ver. 10.
[4] Chap. 52. 1—12.

author appears before the spiritual eye of the Prophet. '*Behold, my servant shall reign well, he shall be high and extolled, and very exalted.*' The prophets do not proceed in the manner of historians, who follow the order of time, but they conduct us at once *in mediam rem*, and often begin with that which in strictness they should end with. An example of this we have in the case before us ; where the Prophet commences with the glorification, instead of the humiliation.—By *behold* he indicates that a new object is presented to his view. Jehovah *points*, as it were, to the Messiah, *as if he were present*, as appears from the following verse, where he is addressed. The point of time, taken by the Prophet, in his internal vision, is the period between the humiliation of the Messiah and his glorification. The latter is here, and in the following verses, generally designated by the future tense, the former by the past [1]. In the second member, the Prophet combines all the verbs of the Hebrew language, which signify elevation, and yet subjoins *very* in order most emphatically to exhibit the glorious exaltation of the Messiah.

434. Verse 14. As this verse is closely connected with the fifteenth, we here give the translation of both : '*As many were shocked at my servant,* [for] *his countenance was so disfigured, that it was no more a human countenance ; his form, that it was no longer a human form ; so will he sprinkle many Gentile nations ; kings will shut their mouths before him ; for what was never announced to them they see, and what they never heard they perceive.*' The sense is : as the humiliation of the Son of man was the greatest possible, as he was abhorred by all those who beheld him in that condition ; so will his glorification also be equally remarkable ; people and kings will submit to him with the deepest reverence [2]. With respect to the sense of the *parenthesis*, the interpreters justly observe, that the deformity of his visage and form does not refer merely to the *person* of the Messiah, but must also be understood in a metaphorical sense. According to Palm, the foundation of the figure is a sick person, who is entirely deformed by a severe disease. As his acquaintances are alarmed when they see him, so are beholders shocked at the appearance of the Messiah. " The Prophet " (says Luther) " does not speak of the form of Christ in respect to his person ; but of the political and regal form of a sovereign, who, though an earthly king, does not go forth in the

---

[1] The verb הִשְׂכִּיל has a twofold meaning, *to act wisely*, and *to be prosperous ;* in accordance with the opinion of the Hebrews, that wisdom, i. e. piety, was the cause of prosperity, but folly, i. e. ungodliness, of adversity. The old translators have nearly all adopted the former. The recent interpreters, on the contrary, after the Chaldee paraphrast, have for the most part chosen the second meaning ; appealing especially to the parallelism with the second member. But it is better to unite them both : *he will reign well ;* which indicates, at the same time, the *prosperous* and the *wise* government of his kingdom by the glorified Messiah, who appears as usual under the image of a powerful king. In this sense the verb is undeniably used in reference to the Messiah, Jer. 23. 5. Comp. besides 1 Kings 2. 3.

[2] The verb שָׁמֵם with עַל *to be astonished at any one ;* whether from *admiration* or *abhorrence*, must be determined by the connexion. In the latter sense it occurs, e. g. in Jer. 18. 16. 19. 18.

form of a king, but as the meanest of all servants, so that a more despised person than he, was never seen in the world." But most interpreters err, in making the metaphorical expression refer solely to the mean and despised condition of the Messiah, and not to his sufferings likewise [1]. " These expressions (says Palm) cannot be fully explained by a reference to the obscure poverty and degradation of our Redeemer; we must represent him to ourselves *in his sufferings*, in *most dreadful contempt and misery ;* and then we may be able to justify the strong language of the Prophet." The humiliation and the cross of Christ were to the Jews a stumbling-block [2], and to many they continue to be so still.

435. Verse 15. By *sprinkling* the heathen is meant that he will *cleanse them from sin*. The High Priest was yearly to *sprinkle blood* towards the ark of the covenant, in order to obtain forgiveness for the people [3]; the cleansed leper [4] was *sprinkled;* the unclean were *sprinkled* with consecrated water. The consequence of these sprinklings was restoration to external theocratical purity. Now it is very common in the Old Testament for *spiritual* and *inward purifications*, and *sanctification*, to be represented by images and expressions taken from the *outward* purifications and sanctifications ; and this was the more natural, since the latter, besides their main design, had the secondary one, of symbolizing that which was spiritual. So e. g. Ezekiel [5] alludes to the practice of sprinkling with consecrated water those who were to be purified : ' *And I will sprinkle clean water upon you, and ye shall be clean. From all your filthiness, and from all your idols will I cleanse you.*' David refers to the same practice [6]. ' *Cleanse me with hyssop* (see the cited passage, in the fourteenth chapter of Leviticus) *that I may be clean.*' This explanation is followed by the authors of the New Testament, when, with reference to this passage, they speak of a '*sprinkling of the blood*' of Christ [7].

436. The phrase, *to shut the mouth*, as well as the related one, *to lay the hand on the mouth*, is a designation of humble, and reverential subjection. In presence of a more honourable person, one does not venture to speak [8]. The ground of this humble submission is given in the second part of the verse. The heathen, in receiving intelligence of the wonderful exaltation of the great servant of God, and of the mystery of his redemption, will be receiving intelligence of what was never before made known to them, as it had been to the Jews [9].

---

[1] Thus of old Jerome, t. 4, p. 1, 612. ed. Vallarsi. t. 5, ed. Francof.: " Non quo formæ significet fœditatem, sed quo in humilitate venerit et paupertate."

[2] 1 Cor. 1. 3.   [3] Lev. 1. 6. 16. 18, 19.

[4] Lev. 14. 17, &c.   [5] Chap. 36, 25.

[6] Ps. 51. 9.   [7] Comp. 1 Pet. 1. 2. Heb. 12. 24.

[8] See Job 29. 9. Ps. 107. 47. Ez. 16. 63. Mic. 7. 16.

[9] Theodoret (Opp. t. 2, p. 357, ed. Hal.) : Οἱ γὰρ τὰς προφητικὰς οὐ δεξάμενοι προρρήσεις, ἀλλὰ τοῖς εἰδώλοις δουλεύοντες, ὄψονται διὰ τῶν κηρύκων τῆς ἀληθείας τοῦ κηρυττομένου τὸ κράτος καὶ γνώσονται αὐτοῦ τὴν δύναμιν. Jerome : " Principes seculi, qui non habuerunt legem et prophetas, et quibus de eo non fuerit nuntiatum, ipsi videbunt et intelligent. In quorum comparatione Judæorum duritia reprehenditur, qui videntes et audientes Jesaiæ in se vaticinium compleverunt."

Isaiah 53

437. Before the Prophet, in continuation of the thirteenth, four-teenth, and fifteenth verses of the foregoing chapter, begins the repre-sentation of the vicarious sufferings of the Messiah, he laments over the unbelief of a large portion of mankind, occasioned by his deep humiliation, and especially over that of the Jews, since the believing submission of a great part of the Gentiles had already been foretold in the preceding verse. '*Who believes our report, and the arm of Jehovah, to whom is it revealed ?*' The Prophet includes with him-self all the heralds of the Messiah. It is not necessary to sup-pose, with Jerome, Palm, and others, that he includes merely his fellow prophets, who had predicted the *future* Redeemer, since the Prophet must easily foresee that the same causes would also hinder the general success of the message concerning the *manifested* Mes-siah, and he might therefore include those who should proclaim it, to whom the verse is referred in the thirty-eighth verse of the twelfth chapter of John, and in the thirty-sixth verse of the tenth chapter of Romans.—The question does not imply an *entire negation*, but only expresses astonishment at the *small number* of believers ; or rather, the Prophet, whose spiritual eye rests upon the great multitude of the unbelievers, overlooks, for the moment, the other side, and in his grief expresses that as *general*, which is applicable only to a *large part*. The arm, as the seat of power, frequently signifies *power* itself[1]. The *arm of Jehovah* is therefore a designation of the *Divine omnipotence*[2]. This then is the sense of the second member : *Who rightly perceives the glorious manifestations of the omnipotence of God, which will be exhibited in the sending of the Messiah ?* The omnipotence of God is manifest to him, who believes the message concerning the Messiah ; for his mission itself, the miracles he wrought, his resurrection and glorification, are the greatest demon-strations of the Divine omnipotence. On the contrary, unbelief in Christ proceeds from a doubt of the omnipotence of God ; since the unbeliever will not admit the interposition of a supernatural cause.

438. Verse 2. ' *He grew up before him as a shoot, as a root-sprout out of dry ground; he had no form nor beauty that we should look upon him; no comely appearance, that we should desire him.*' This verse refers to the humble condition of the Messiah before his suffer-ings. *Before him*, i. e. *Jehovah*, that is, *observed by Jehovah: known to him*, although *unknown to the world*. The Prophet thereby incidentally points to the cause of his humiliation. The word [3] *root*, here designates [4], by Synecdoche, the *stem* or *shoot that springs from*

---

[1] Jer. 17. 5. Job 22. 8. 2 Chron. 32. 8.
[2] Chap. 59. 16. Deut. 4. 34. 5. 15. 26. 8.
[3] שֹׁרֶשׁ   [4] As in chap. 11. 10.

the root. A shoot that springs up in a dry soil is insignificant and puny. This comparison appears to allude to the origin of the Messiah from a family, which had once resembled a lofty tree in height and glory, but was now sunk in abasement. See the first verse of the eleventh chapter, where the Messiah is called a sprout from the root of Jesse. As the Messiah is here, in reference to his state of humiliation, compared to a weak and insignificant sprout, so in Exodus [1], in reference to his state of glorification, he is compared to a lofty and splendid cedar, under which all the fowls of heaven shall dwell. The Jews expected, that he should thus appear even from the very first; and because they were disappointed, they despised him. What is said of the form and the beauty of the Messiah is not so much to be referred to *his person* as to his *whole appearance* in his state of abasement. The history of its founder is repeated in the history of the Church. As in the one case, so in the other, the way to glory and joy is through humiliation and suffering.

439. Verse 3. ' *He was despised, and the most abject of all men, a man of sorrows and familiar with disease ; he was as one before whom a man covers the face ; we despised him, and esteemed him not.*' From the humble condition of the Messiah in general, the Prophet proceeds to his sufferings. He was *one known to disease,* i. q. *a confidant* of disease—one who has formed, as it were, the bond of friendship with it ; corresponding to ' *the man of sorrows.*' *Disease,* here and in the following verse, is a figurative designation of severe sufferings of body and of soul [2]. It is not without reason that Koppe and Ammon conjecture, that the image is taken particularly from the leprosy, which was not only one of the most terrible diseases, but was also, in a special manner, regarded as a Divine punishment. By this supposition, many expressions in the following verses are explained. The next words mean literally, ' *he was as a hiding of the face before him,*' i. e. as a thing or person before whom a man covers his face, because he cannot bear the disgusting sight.

440. Verse 4. In this verse the Prophet includes with himself the better portion of the people. Those who have attained to faith in the Messiah, confess in this verse that they have greatly erred in despising the servant of God on account of his humiliation and suffering.—' *But he bare our sickness, and took our pains upon himself, and we esteemed him as one afflicted of God, smitten and tormented of God.*' He, that is, from whom we turned away with horrour, because we inferred from his sufferings some great crime of his own, for the punishment of which they had been inflicted by God, bore the punishment not of his own sins, but of ours. The very thing which gave offence to us, not only belonged to the work which God had committed to him, but constituted its most important part.—In the words, *he bore,* &c., the metaphor is taken from an oppressive burden, which one removes from the shoulders of another, and places on his own.— *Our sickness, our pains,* stand for the sickness which *we should*

---

[1] Chap. 17. 23.
[2] Thus it often occurs, e. g. Is. 1. 4—6 Ez. 33. 10. Ps. 103. 3.

have suffered,—the pains which *we should have endured.* Diseases and pains are an image of the outward and inward sufferings, which the Messiah should undergo in our stead, and thereby deliver us from the punishment of our sins. Matthew, in the seventeenth verse of the eighth chapter, cites these words, after having related that Christ had delivered men from their *bodily infirmities.* Recent interpreters have hence erroneously concluded that Matthew has by no means referred the passage to the *vicarious sufferings* of Christ. But that Apostle was certainly far from intending by this *special* reference, to set aside the *principal* one. Christ was sent for the general purpose *of removing by the sacrifice of Himself the evil which sin had brought into the world.* This work He *commenced,* when He cured bodily diseases. Thereby He pointed to His chief calling; to the spiritual evils of men to be removed by Him, with the same power, through His vicarious satisfaction. That Matthew had no intention of denying the spiritual import of the passage, appears from the twenty-eighth verse of the twentieth chapter: ' *He came—to give his soul a ransom for many.*' After all the three words we must supply: *on account of his own sins.* For it was true, that the sufferings of the Messiah *were* inflicted by God; the mistake was only in reference to their *design.* To infer great guilt from great suffering was very customary with the Hebrews. It arose from a misconception of the theocratic doctrine of retribution. They erroneously extended the law of visible retribution (by which the fate of the covenant people was always determined) to individuals; not reflecting that God, according to His wise and holy purposes, can inflict suffering on the pious, even without the previous commission of sin.

441. Verse 5. ' *And he was pierced for our misdeeds and bruised for our sins; the punishment was laid on him, that we might have peace, and by his wounds we are healed.*' The Prophet here again includes himself, not merely by a rhetorical figure, but in the consciousness of his sinfulness and need of redemption. Properly: *the punishment of our peace,* i. e. the punishment whereby peace, salvation, and happiness were procured for us—our reconciliation with God effected. The word [1] stands also in other places for chastisement by *words,* but here the whole context, in which severe sufferings are the subject of discourse, as well as the parallelism, requires it to be understood of chastisement by *deed* [2]. The interpretation of a certain theological school, therefore, is wholly inadmissible, which, in order to remove from the passage the doctrine of Christ's vicarious satisfaction, translates: ' the instruction of our peace (how we can be again reconciled to God) is in him.'—As the punishment of sin and suffering are often represented under the image of a disease, so is deliverance from them under that of *healing.*

442. Verse 6. The cause is given which moved the Messiah to undergo such severe sufferings, viz. the wretchedness of mankind who

[1] מוּסָר

[2] This also appears from עָלָיו which indicates that the punishment lay as an oppressive burden upon him who made atonement.

were alienated from God, but whom God would reconcile to Himself by his sufferings. ' *We all were going astray like sheep, we turned every one to our own way; but Jehovah cast upon him the sin of us all.*' Under the figure of sheep without a shepherd, who are exposed without defence to all dangers, the Prophet represents the miserable state of mankind estranged from God, and sunk in sin and errour [1]. We were going astray like the flock, i. e. we wandered like the flock, e. g. a wandering flock, a flock which has no shepherd [2]. In general the image of *sheep without a shepherd* is frequently employed to exhibit, at one time the *moral debasement*, at another, the *wretchedness* of men estranged from God [3].—' *We turned every one, &c.*' As a lonely wanderer pursues his way in sadness, and exposed to manifold dangers, so were we proceeding through life alone, neither guided by God, nor united with our brethren by His love. Augusti says, "Each one acted and lived only for himself, not for a common object; there was no public spirit." His remarks are just, if taken in a *deeper sense.* It is only the common bond of union with God, which can unite all; without this there is only caprice, self-will, and discord. According to Kimchi and others, the punishment is here represented as an assaulting enemy; they take the word in the latter sense, and translate: *commanded it to rush against him like an enemy.* Still we may very well abide by the general meaning, *he caused to light on him.* The sense is: Jehovah caused him alone to bear the sufferings, which we should have borne as a punishment for our sins [4].—The word ' *sin* [5],' here, as is often the case, includes also the '*punishment of sin.*' The view of the Hebrews, respecting the close connexion of sin and punishment, of virtue and prosperity, is plainly stampt on the language, and the two ideas are often expressed by the same words.

443. Verse 7. The Prophet had commenced, in the second verse, the description of the sufferings of the Messiah; in the fourth, fifth, and sixth verses, he had digressed, in order to assign the causes of these severe sufferings. He now resumes the description, and sets before us in this verse the perfect meekness and patience of the great servant of God in his distress. ' *He was abused, but he suffered patiently, and opened not his mouth; as a lamb which is brought to the slaughter, and as a sheep which becomes dumb before its shearers, he opened not his mouth* [6].' In harmony with it in sense is the twenty-third verse of the second chapter of the First Epistle of Peter,

---

[1] Theodoret: Οὔτε γὰρ ἴσα πάντων τὰ πλημμελήματα, οὐδὲ εἷς ὁ τρόπος, ἀλλὰ γὰρ τὰ Αἰγυπτίων εἴδωλα καὶ ἄλλα τὰ Φοινίκων, καὶ τὰ Ἑλλήνων ἕτερα καὶ ἄλλα τῶν Σκυθῶν· ἀλλ' ὅμως, εἰ καὶ διάφοροι τῆς πλάνης οἱ τρόποι, πάντες ὁμοίως τὸν ὄντα Θεὸν καταλελοιπότες, ἐφʹκειμεν προβάτοις πλανωμένοις καὶ προκειμένοις τοῖς λύκοις.

[2] Comp. 1 Pet. 2. 25: ἦτε γὰρ ὡς πρόβατα πλανώμενα.

[3] See Ez. 34. 3. Matt. 9. 36.

[4] So Symm.: Κύριος δὲ καταντῆσαι ἐποίησεν εἰς αὐτὸν τὴν ἀνομίαν πάντων ἡμῶν. Vulg.: "posuit in eo iniquitatem omnium nostrum."

[5] עָוֹן

[6] Comp. Jer. 11. 19, "I was as a lamb that is led to the slaughter." Comp. 1 Pet. 1. 18, 19. Acts 8. 32. 35. John 1. 29.

' *Who, when he was reviled, reviled not again ; when he suffered, he threatened not ; but committed himself to him that judgeth righteously.*' Christ opened indeed his mouth, but *not* to threaten, *not* to revile, but only to promote the honour of God, to bear testimony to his love, to pray for his enemies.

444. Verse 8. The sense is : a violent death was the termination of the sufferings which he assumed on account of the sins of the people. —' *By oppression and a judicial sentence he was dragged to punishment (but who can declare his posterity ?) he was taken away out of the land of the living for the sin of my people, upon whom the punishment should have fallen.*' It is most correct with several interpreters (Döderlein, Kuinöl, &c.) to regard *oppression and judgement* here as a Hendiadys for, an *oppressive, unrighteous, judicial proceeding.* So in the twelfth verse of the nineteenth chapter of the first book of Kings, *silence and a voice,* for *a low voice :* in the eleventh verse of the twenty-ninth chapter of Jeremiah, *futurity and hope,* for *a hopeful futurity* [1].—The word we have translated, *he was dragged to punishment,* may (with Rosenmüller and others) be translated, *he was taken away :* namely, out of the living, as it is said in the second hemistich [2]. This interpretation is certainly more favoured by the parallelism than the former [3]. That the words must then signify a *violent* death is evident from the ninth verse, where it is said that the ungodly, not satisfied with his murder, attempted to abuse him even in death. To this we are led also by the expression itself. For although the verb [4] is indeed in some passages used also of a merely natural death, yet on account of the parallelism, ' *he was taken away out of the land of the living,*' it can here refer only to a violent death, or to a proceeding which had caused such a death [5].—' *Who can express his posterity ?*'—*the number of his descendants* [6] ? The Prophet,

[1] לָקַח: it occurs of a violent leading away to punishment, 1 Kings 20. 33. Prov. 24. 11; of a violent taking away in general, Ez. 22. 25. Similar words are also used in Arabic of a violent leading away to death or imprisonment.

[2] Comp. Ezek. 33. 4. 6.

[3] The older interpreters for the most part refer these words to the glorification. They take מִן not as causative, but in the sense *out of,* and translate the verb לָקַח either by : *to rescue, to deliver,* or by : *to take up, to take away,* namely to God. So the Vulg.: " de angustia et judicio sublatus est." Jerome on the passage says : " de tribulatione atque judicio ad Patrem victor ascendit." Joh. H. Michaelis : " exemtus et ad dextram majestatis assumtus est." Entirely similar is the explanation of Gesenius : from his distress death finally delivered him ; borrowed from Martini, who paraphrases : " exantlatis cruciatibus et diris animam efflavit." But this interpretation has the whole context against it.

[4] לָקַח

[5] וְאֶת דּוֹרוֹ מִי יְשׂוֹחֵחַ The interpretations rejected by Hengstenberg are :— " Who will declare the length of his life ?" i. e. who is able to determine the duration of his future life ? " Who of his contemporaries will consider it," or " considered it ? " or " that he was taken out of the land of the living, on account of the sin of my people." " Who of all his contemporaries spoke ? " there was no man among all his contemporaries who uttered a single word in his vindication.

[6] Thus the LXX: τὴν γενεὰν αὐτοῦ τίς διηγήσεται; In like manner Kimchi : " quis dicturus esset ejus generationem tam magnam fore ?"

as it were anticipating himself, points by an incidental remark from the lowest humiliation of the Messiah to his glorification. The verb [1], *to be cut off*, *to be destroyed*, *never* occurs (not even in the passages in the sixth verse of the eighty-eighth Psalm, and the fifty-fourth verse of the third chapter of the Lamentations, cited in favour of such a meaning) of a *peaceful* and *natural*, but always of a *violent* and *premature* death. The metaphorical expression seems here to be used with reference to the foregoing image of a shoot.—In the last member, Paulus, after the example of several older translators, erroneously supposes [2], that here *Jehovah* must again speak : whereas He is not introduced again as speaking till the eleventh verse. ' *On account of the sins of my people*,' is not different from, ' *on account of our sins.*' The speaker does not place himself *in opposition* to his people, but *includes himself* among them.

445. Verse 9. ' *They appointed him his grave with the wicked (but he was with a rich man after his death), although he had done nothing unrighteous, and there was no guile in his mouth.*' The sense is : not satisfied with his sufferings and his death, they sought to insult him, the innocent and the righteous one, even in death, since they wished to bury his corpse among criminals. It is then incidentally remarked, that this object was not accomplished. Christ was buried by Joseph of Arimathea, who is here called *rich* [3], as in the fifty-seventh verse of the twenty-seventh chapter of Matthew.—As the Prophet had said in the foregoing verse that the Messiah would die a violent death, like a malefactor, so he here subjoins, that they had also appointed, or, according to Iken, prepared for him a common interment with executed criminals [4].

446. Verse 10. In this verse the prediction of the glorification of the servant of God commences. The sense is : all the suffering described has been inflicted upon his servant by Jehovah, and will end with his glorification and the establishment of the Divine kingdom on earth.—' *But it pleased Jehovah to bruise him ; he has subjected him to disease (laid upon him heavy sufferings). When he has brought a sin-offering, he shall behold a posterity, he shall prolong his days, and the purpose of Jehovah shall prosper through him.*' According to Palm, this verse is connected with what precedes. He was innocent ; why then was he so tormented and afflicted ? Because

---

[1] נִגְזַר   [2] On account of the word עַמִּי   [3] עָשִׁיר

[4] The וֹ in וְאֵת is adversative : but with a rich man in his death ; *he was*, is to be supplied. בְּמֹתָיו we translate *after his death ;* a meaning already required by the parallelism with קִבְרוֹ. בְּ is taken in the sense of *afterwards*, as in Isaiah 16. 14 (in three years, for, after three years), Lev. 11. 31 (every one who touches them in their death, for, after they are dead). And thus the objection to this interpretation, that Jesus was with criminals in his death, and with a rich man in his grave, falls to the ground. After the example of several others, Gesenius interprets: "They gave him his grave with the ungodly and with a wicked wretch in his death," scil. they gave him his grave. Martini translates : " Pararunt illi sepulchrum cum scelestis, tumulum sepulchralem cum violentis, quamquam ille vim nemini intulerat et a fraude fuerat alienus." Rosenmüller translates : " He committed his interment to the ungodly and the criminals, after he was dead." These translations are powerfully refuted by our author.

it was Jehovah's will, and not because the Lord was too weak to rescue him out of the hands of his enemies. And what was the ground of this will? He should present a voluntary sin-offering, redeem mankind through his sufferings. The disease and bruising are only a figure of the severe suffering inflicted by Jehovah on the Messiah [1]. It is not indeed here expressly said, that the Messiah will be, not only the Priest who brings the sin-offering, but the sacrifice also; this however was not necessary, since it was sufficiently clear from what had preceded [2]. As, in reference to the outward theocracy, purity was regained and the transgression expiated through the typical sacrifices which the typical priests presented, while at the same time there was an allusion to the great future sacrifice; so the Prophet here announces, that through the anti-typical offering which the anti-typical and only true priest should bring (compare the fifteenth verse of the fifty-third chapter), purity as to the inward theocracy, and the forgiveness of sins should be procured. Here also, according to the usual custom of the Prophet, things of the New Testament are represented under images taken from those of the Old Testament. According to this passage, Paul affirms [3], that God has made Christ to be '*sin*[4],' i. e. a *sin-offering*, whereby we became righteous before God: so in the third verse of the eighth chapter of Romans, God, he says, has sent his own Son '*for sin*[5], that is, '*as a sin-offering:*' and Christ is called, in several passages, '*a propitiation*[6],' that is, '*a propitiatory sacrifice*' for all sins. Compare the fourteenth verse of the ninth chapter of Hebrews: '*who offered himself without spot to God*[7].' Without a figure therefore the sense is: *when he has freely given himself up to bitter suffering and a bloody death, in order, by the expiation of our sins, to procure for us forgiveness and righteousness*. In the description of the rewards which the servant of God will receive for accomplishing the work committed to him, the *inferior* must again serve *as a figure to designate the higher*. Long life and numerous descendants are regarded by the Hebrews as the highest prosperity, as a theocratic blessing and a reward of piety. In a higher and spiritual sense shall this reward be given to the Messiah [8]. These descendants [9] are none other than the many and mighty, whom God, according to the twelfth verse, has given to the Messiah for a possession, and who, according to the fifteenth verse of the fifty-second chapter, were to be freed from sin, and the eleventh verse. justified through him, the punishment of whose sins he has taken upon himself in the fifth verse, and for whom, in the twelfth verse,

---

[1] Comp. ver. 3, 4.

[2] The word אָשָׁם *guilt, transgression*, and then *sin-offering*. Comp. Jahn, Archäologie, Th. 3. § 100 and § 102.

[3] 2 Cor. 5. 21.   [4] ἁμαρτία.   [5] περὶ ἁμαρτίας.

[6] ἱλασμὸς, ἱλαστήριον.   Rom. 3. 25. 1 John 2. 2. 4. 10.

[7] ὃς ἑαυτὸν προσήνεγκεν ἄμωμον τῷ Θεῷ.

[8] The LXX (ἡ ψυχὴ ὑμῶν ὄψεται σπέρμα μακρόβιον), the Vulgate (*posteritatem videbit longævam*), and Lowth would connect the two members יַאֲרִיךְ יָמִים and יִרְאֶה זֶרַע with one another; but it is far better to take them separately.

[9] דֹּרוֹ

he intercedes with God. The natural relation between father and
son is often transferred to spiritual subjects. The prophets bore the
name of father, their disciples that of sons of the prophets. See the
twenty-fifth verse of the second chapter of the first book of Kings.
In a higher sense, believers begotten of God in a spiritual manner,
obedient to him, as dutiful children, and forming, as it were, his
family, are called the posterity of God, or of the Messiah. Thus
in the thirty-first verse of the twenty-second Psalm : ' *The seed
which shall serve him shall be reckoned to the Lord for a posterity,*'
i. e. the descendants of the Messiah shall be considered as God's
posterity, as His children.

447. Verse 11. Jehovah is again introduced as speaking.—" *Because of the labour of his soul he beholds,* [*he*] *satisfies himself;
by his knowledge shall he, the righteous one, my servant, justify
many and bear their sins* [1].' Here, as in the foregoing verse, the
suffering is given as the cause of the glorification. ' *Beholds*'
what?—In supplying the ellipsis interpreters differ[2] : but it is
best to supply, ' *the fruits and rewards of his sufferings,*' announced in the foregoing verse. The verbs *beholds* and *satisfies* are
connected in different ways. Some apply the Hebrew usage, which
places *two verbs*, where *we* apply but one with an adjective or
adverb = *he will see himself satisfied*[3]. The correct view becomes
evident from the remark, overlooked by nearly all interpreters, that
the figure of a husbandman lies at the foundation, who, cultivating
his land with labour and care, first beholds with pleasure the ripe
fruit, then gathers in the harvest and satisfies himself ; he has sown
in tears, and now reaps in joy. It hence appears that the two verbs
must be separated, and that they form a sort of climax. The *his* is
here objective. ' Through *his* knowledge,' i. e. ' through the knowledge *of him*.' This is the condition by which any one appropriates
to himself the righteousness procured by the Messiah[4]. That *justification* in the proper sense, and not *mere instruction*, is here the
subject of discourse, appears from the whole context ; the Messiah
throughout the whole portion is certainly described, not as a *teacher*,
but as a *priest*, who, in order to deliver us from sin, has presented
himself as a voluntary sin-offering. And throughout the whole
verse, the subject of discourse is not the procuring of righteousness
(this was done in the state of humiliation described in the second and
seven following verses), but only the conferring of it, of which the
acknowledgement of the servant of God had been mentioned in the
preceding clause as the *subjective condition*. The Messiah takes upon
himself the sins of every one, who, after his exaltation, fulfils this
condition, i. e. he causes his own vicarious obedience to be imputed

[1] מִן in מֵעֲמַל shows the *causa efficiens*. Rightly the Vulg.: *Pro eo, quod
laboravit anima ejus.*

[2] Some propose טוֹב *good;* others זרע

[3] Rosenmüller supplies בַּאֲשֶׁר between the verbs, which however gives a false
sense.

[4] Thus Joh. H. Michaelis, Le Clerc, Palm.

to him, and imparts to him forgiveness. '*He will bear their sins,*'
is the same, only under a different image, as '*he will justify them.*'

448. Verse 12. '*Therefore will I give him the mighty for a portion, and he shall divide the strong as a spoil, for a reward ; because
he has given up his life to death, and suffered himself to be numbered
with the transgressors. And he will take the sins of many upon himself, and make intercession for the transgressors* [1].'—'*He will divide
the strong as spoil,*' that is, among his companions ; which imports
nothing more than : he *will have them in his power,* and do with
them as he pleases* [2]. After the example of Jewish interpreters [3],
some late critics (Paulus, Gesenius, &c.) would draw from these
words a proof against the reference of the prophecy to Christ, who
certainly enjoyed no worldly triumph. But such a misapprehension
of the figurative language can hardly be explained, except by attributing it to doctrinal prejudice. According to the usual custom of the
prophets to exhibit spiritual objects by sensible images, the spiritual
victory of Christ over the nations who take his easy yoke upon
themselves, is here described under the figure of a worldly victory.
That worldly triumphs are not here the subject of discourse, appears
(1) from the manner, pointed out in the preceding verses, in which
the Messiah has attained to this exaltation. Such triumphs are not
won by the deepest humiliation, by suffering and death, voluntarily
endured for the salvation of mankind : (2) from what the Messiah,
in the state of exaltation, shall accomplish in behalf of those who
betake themselves to him. He shall sprinkle them with his blood [4],
justify them and bear their sins [5], and intercede for sinners [6] ;—
these are surely not designations of an earthly conqueror [7].
Similar figures are found in the eighth verse of the second Psalm,
where Jehovah says to the Messiah : "Ask of me, and I will
give thee the heathen for an inheritance, and the uttermost
parts of the earth for thy possession." Compare the tenth verse
of the eleventh chapter of Isaiah.—The merits of the servant of
God are then once more repeated, as a reward for which God has
granted him these great spiritual conquests. In the words, '*he has
poured out his life unto death* [8],' or *in death,* the metaphor is taken
from animals, which lost their life with their blood, on which account
blood was regarded as the seat of the soul. Compare the fourth
verse of the ninth chapter of Genesis, and the eleventh verse of the
seventeenth chapter of Leviticus. There is an allusion to the figure

---

[1] Several (Gesenius and others) translate the second member : '*he will divide
spoil with the strong.*' But we obtain a far stronger and finer sense if we regard
את not as a preposition, but as the sign of the accusative.

[2] Martini : "Victoris est de præda parta disponere ejusque optima parte sibi
vindicata, reliquæ inter socios partitionem facere." Comp. Gen. 49. 27. Ex. 15. 9.
Ps. 68. 13. Judg. 5. 30.

[3] Abarbanel, &c.   [4] Chap. 52. 13.   [5] Ver. 11.   [6] Ver. 12.

[7] The רַבִּים and עֲצוּמִים are none others than the nations and kings, chap. 52. 15,
and the generation and posterity of the Messiah, ver. 8. 10.

[8] הֶעֱרָה לַמָּוֶת נַפְשׁוֹ, properly.

of an animal sacrifice in the tenth verse.—The word [1], ' *he was num-bered*,' has here, as we have already seen in the seventh verse, the secondary meaning, *he suffered himself to be numbered*. This is demanded by the context, and the parallelism with : ' *he has poured out his life*.' The ground of the Messiah's glorification was not that he was numbered, but that ' he *voluntarily* suffered himself to be numbered' with the transgressors. The evangelist Mark adduces this passage, when he relates that Christ was fastened to the cross between two thieves, without intending by this special reference to exhaust the whole sense of the declaration [2].—Most interpreters here erroneously understand *making intercession* [3] of mere prayer. Not by simple prayer, as plainly appears from the preceding con-text, will the servant of God intercede with Him for sinners, but by presenting before Him his vicarious suffering and his merits, as a ground of their obtaining mercy and forgiveness of their sins [4].

449. We have now, *first*, to refute the objections to the Messianic interpretation ; *secondly*, to bring forward the grounds on which it rests ; and *lastly*, to show that the non-Messianic interpretation is untenable. We borrow the objections from Gesenius, who has col-lected every thing at all plausible which the earlier writers, and particularly the Jews, have alleged.

450. (1) " Though the similarity of the condition of this pious sufferer with Christ is so great, yet still there is much also which is unsuitable to him." All that Gesenius here adduces has been already refuted in the exposition ; excepting only, that according to

---

[1] נִמְנָה

[2] We must not, with many interpreters, after the example of the LXX, take יַפְגִּיעַ as referring to the state of humiliation. (So also Gesenius, in direct con-tradiction to his remark on ver. 11, that all the futures in the preceding and fol-lowing verses relate to the state of exaltation. If יַפְגִּיעַ here stands for the præter, then surely יִסְבֹּל must there stand for it also.) Rather is the aorist נָשָׂא deter-mined to be the *future* by the context, in which only the exaltation is the subject of discourse, and it corresponds with יִסְבֹּל. Compare what has been said on the foregoing verse. The verb פָּגַע has in Kal, among other significations, the meaning *to meet* ; in Hiph. therefore *to cause to meet*. To make something meet, or happen to any one (whether petitions or actions must be determined by the context), stands then for, *to intercede with him*.

[3] הִפְגִּיעַ

[4] Very happily Calvin : " Ut in veteri lege sacerdos, qui nunquam sine san-guine ingrediebatur, simul pro populo intercedebat, ita quod illic adumbratum fuit, in Christo impletum est. Primum enim sacrificium corporis sui obtulit et sanguinem fudit, ut pœnam nobis debitam persolveret. Deinde ut valeret expiatio advocati officio functus est, atque intercessit pro omnibus, qui fide hoc sacrificium amplecterentur." Comp. Rom. 8. 34 (ὃς καὶ ἐντυγχάνει ὑπὲρ ἡμῶν), Heb. 9. 24 (Christ has gone into the holy place νῦν ἐμφανισθῆναι τῷ προσώπῳ τοῦ Θεοῦ ὑπὲρ ἡμῶν), 1 John 2. 1 (παράκλητον ἔχομεν πρὸς τὸν πατέρα, Ἰησοῦν Χριστὸν δίκαιον).

the fifteenth verse of the fifty-second chapter, kings should do homage to the servant of God in person. But this stands self-refuted; for that the homage should be paid to him *in person*, is no more required than it is in the parallel passage (49. 7), that kings should *see* him *in person*, and princes worship him *in person*[1]. Who can deny, without treating all history with contempt, that kings have bowed and do still bow their knees before the glorified Christ?

451. (2) "The name *servant of God* never occurs of the Messiah." Granting this assertion to be true, still it would prove nothing. The appellation *servant of God,* in the stricter sense, designates, as we have already seen. any one who is called to the execution of a Divine purpose, and who stands to God in a relation similar to that sustained by the servants of a court[2] to earthly kings. Moses was called *servant of Jehovah*[3], and so was Joshua[4]. Every Israelitish king was a *servant of Jehovah;* David was often thus called[5]; Eliakim bears this name[6]; the Prophet calls *himself* so[7]: and in so far as they were destined to preserve the knowledge and worship of the true God, the Jewish people also bear this name in several places. It is attributed to the angels[8]. Even Nebuchadnezzar[9] is called a *servant of Jehovah,* in so far as he was an instrument in the hand of God, though without his own knowledge and will. It is merely accidental that Cyrus does not bear this title; all the attributes of a servant of God being ascribed to him. It is therefore, in every respect, inconceivable why the Messiah, the great messenger of God[10]; he who, in the assumed *form of a servant,* was obedient to God even unto death[11]; who came not to do his own will, but the will of Him who had sent him[12], should not receive this appellation, since he was strictly that which the name imports; a name which was common to *all* the ministers and instruments of God. But in addition to this, the assertion is by no means correct. The Messiah does bear the name in a passage[13] unanimously interpreted of him: "I will bring forth, saith God, my servant the Branch[14]."

452. (3) "The idea of a *suffering and atoning* Messiah is foreign to the Old Testament, and in contradiction to its prevailing representations, even admitting it to have been entertained by some about the age of Christ." This objection also has been borrowed from the Jews. What has been remarked in the general Introduction is suffi-

---

[1] I have endeavoured to give the meaning of this passage, which a literal translation of it would hardly convey.
[2] Called עֲבָדִים by the Hebrews.   [3] Num. 12. 7.
[4] Judg. 2. 8.   [5] e. g. Ps. 89. 21.
[6] Chap. 22. 20.   [7] Chap. 20. 3.
[8] Job 4. 18, where עֲבָדָיו stands in the parallelism with מַלְאָכָיו 'his messengers.'
[9] Jer. 25. 9. and 27. 6.
[10] מַלְאֲכִי Mal. 3. 1.
[11] Phil. 1. 7.   [12] John 6. 38.   [13] Zech. 3. 8.
[14] Where the Chaldee explains, מְשִׁיחָא וְיִתְגְּלֵי, *Messiam et revelabitur.* He receives it chap. 42. 1. (where the Chaldee interprets, עַבְדִי מְשִׁיחָא· הָא Kimchi: הוּא מֶלֶךְ הַמָּשִׁיחַ) chap. 49. 3. 6. chap. 50. 10: consequently in nearly all the Messianic passages in the second part.

cient for its refutation. It will have no weight so long as the authority of Christ is valid in the Church, who himself affirmed that his whole suffering had been predicted in the Old Testament, and explained to his disciples the prophecies respecting it. But even if the idea of a suffering and atoning Messiah occurred in no other passage of the Old Testament, still it would prove nothing. For we could not determine *a priori*, that God might not enlighten one particular prophet, who showed himself susceptible of such a revelation, respecting a subject which He concealed from the rest. It is certainly true, that in the Messianic predictions the *prophetic* and *regal* offices of Christ are represented more frequently than his *sacerdotal* office ; the great mass of the people, who were to be retained through these predictions in an adherence (though only an outward one) to Jehovah, could as little understand this doctrine, as the apostles could before the Spirit was given ; while for the pious, whose minds were prepared for its reception, the intimations which were given were sufficient. Besides the fiftieth chapter, we here direct the attention to the passage in the first verse of the eleventh chapter, which even Gesenius interprets of the Messiah, where his appearance in humiliation is indicated (as in the second verse of the fifty-third chapter) by the figure of a *feeble shoot that springs up from the stem of Jesse, which had been cut down.* But it is difficult to perceive wherein consists the contradiction between the doctrine of the suffering and that of the glorified Messiah. Were there, however, an apparent contradiction, it would be done away by the history of Christ. Indeed the suffering appears, even in this prophecy, as the condition of the glorification ; the glorification as its consequence and reward. The Messiah appears here also as a king, to whom all earthly kings with their people should be subject.—The whole assertion proceeds from the erroneous opinion, that each individual Messianic prophecy must contain a *full picture* of the Messiah ; whereas, on the contrary, they supply one another's deficiencies, and for the most part present us with only a partial view of Christ.

453. (4) " The Messianic interpretation regards all as future ; which the language does not allow. The suffering, contempt, and death of the servant of God are here represented throughout as past, since in the first ten verses of the fifty-third chapter all is expressed in the preterite. Only the glorification appears as future, and is expressed in the future tense. The writer therefore stands between the suffering and the glorification, and announces that he who has hitherto suffered shall now be glorified. The latter only is still future." The answer to this has already been given on the thirteenth verse of the fifty-second chapter. The Prophet does not occupy an *historical*, but a *prophetic* point of view. The prophets described events as they followed each other in prophetic vision. That which formed the condition was expressed in the present or past ; that which was the consequence in the future. Compare the general preliminary remarks on the second part of Isaiah. As the Prophet there takes his station in the Babylonish exile, and thence beholds the deliverance as future, so he here places himself between the

suffering and the glorification of the Messiah; and the former appears to him as past, the latter as yet to come. This was the only way in which he could discriminate between the condition and its consequence, and place in their proper relation the suffering and exaltation of the Messiah. *Besides, it is by no means true that the Prophet always represents the suffering as past, and speaks of it only in the preterite.* In some instances he passes involuntarily from the prophetic to the historical point of view, and employs the future, even where he speaks of the suffering [1].

454. (5) "It is perfectly evident that this servant of God is the same person who is the subject of discourse in the parallel passage. Compare the first seven verses of the forty-second chapter, the first nine verses of the forty-ninth chapter, the fourth and seven following verses of the fiftieth chapter, and the first three verses of the sixty-first chapter. In these passages there is yet a great deal more which cannot apply to Christ." We here entirely agree with our opponents, that the subject of both portions must be the same, and we must with them complain of the mischievous inconsistency of those interpreters who find the Messiah here, but another subject there. We believe, however, that on these passages we have sufficiently proved that what Gesenius adduces from them, as irreconcileable with the Messianic interpretation, either rests on a false exegesis (which is too literal, and overlooks the figurative character of the prophetic discourse), or would, if it were correct, militate still more strongly against his own exposition. How, e. g., can the introduction of the Messiah, in some of the passages referred to, as *speaking*, be an objection with one, according to whose own interpretation a person, and that moreover not an actual, but a fictitious person, the collective body of the prophets, comes forward in the very same manner as a *speaker?*

455. (6) "In what precedes, as well as in what follows, the subject of discourse is the restoration of the state after the exile. It was consequently quite impossible for those, who then read the oracle, to refer it to a Redeemer to be expected in future times." Nor was this necessary. The only point of importance was, that the Prophet and his hearers should become acquainted with the future suffering of the great servant of God, as the condition of their salvation, and embrace the coming Redeemer with the same love, with which we ought to embrace Him now He has appeared. The fact was sufficient; the *when* they needed not to know, as indeed the nature of the prophetic vision did not admit of their knowing it. Without detriment to the reality they might constantly suppose the great event would ensue immediately after the deliverance from the Babylonish exile. Indeed, had they known the long distance of time, it would have enfeebled their desire and cooled their love. "It could but little concern the reader of that day, to know what was to

---

[1] Thus ver. 7 יִפְתַּח, ver. 8 יְשׁוֹחֵחַ, ver. 10 תָּשִׂים, according to Gesenius also יַפְגִּיע, ver. 12, while on the contrary, ver. 12, he uses the præter נָשָׂא of the state of exaltation. (Comp· יִסְבֹּל ver. 11.)

happen after half a thousand years." He only can say this, who has
no regard for what is most dear to others, and constitutes the central
point of their whole life.

456. The further allegation of Gesenius, that this interpretation
forcibly separates the portion from its connexion with the whole
book ; and that to understand it as a definite prediction is against
the analogy of all biblical prophecies, which refer in vague anticipations to the immediate future, has been already sufficiently refuted,
and will here be left unnoticed. It only remains to remark a striking
contradiction, which occurs on one and the same page (vol. 3, p. 164).
It is first said, that all biblical prophecies relate only to the immediate future, and directly after, the author declares that the hope,
which he too finds expressed in the passage, of a splendid triumph
of the religion of Jehovah over the heathen at some future day, has
been realized by the prevalence of Christianity, and he therefore
does not hesitate, so far as this goes, to acknowledge in the portion
before us a Messianic prophecy which has been fulfilled.

457. We now proceed to exhibit the grounds of the Messianic
interpretation. All the arguments are here combined by which in
general any passage can be proved, upon the principles laid down in
the Introduction, to relate to the Messiah.

458. (1.) This interpretation is confirmed by the testimony of
tradition. The Jews, in more ancient times, unanimously referred
this prophecy to the Messiah. The authority of tradition, however,
in this case, is so much the more weighty, in proportion as the Messianic interpretation was at variance with the disposition of the people,
while the origin of the later non-Messianic interpretations can be
satisfactorily explained by the prevailing mode of thinking.

459. (2.) The citations of this prophecy in the New Testament serve
not only to show, that the Messianic interpretation was the prevailing one in those times (otherwise the writers would have *justified*
it, as e. g. in the case of the sixteenth Psalm, and in reference to the
Divine dignity of the Messiah, in the hundred and tenth Psalm ; the
same thing is also evident from the declaration of John the Baptist,
taken from the passage before us, "*Behold the Lamb of God, which
taketh away the sin of the world*[1]." Compare the fourth, seventh,
and eleventh verses of the fifty-third chapter), but also to furnish us
with infallible evidence of its correctness. That[2] the first verse of
the fifty-third chapter is cited in the New Testament to explain the
unbelief of the greatest part of the people, and with the formula,
'*that it might be fulfilled*,' by St. John, would not, it is true, of itself
be sufficient for proof. The passage, however, in the thirty-seventh
verse of the twenty-second chapter of Luke affords decisive evidence. Christ himself there says, the prophecies relating to Him are
about to have an end[3] ; and that therefore the declaration, "*he was*

---

[1] John 1. 29.   [2] John 12. 38. Rom. 10. 16.
[3] So only can the expression τὰ περὶ ἐμοῦ τέλος ἔχει be understood ; comp.
Matt. 26. 54, where Christ says he must suffer and die in order that the Scripture
may be fufilled.

numbered with the transgressors," must also be accomplished in Him [1].
—He therefore places the prophecy with those which treat of Himself,
and it is certainly so far Messianic as our Lord could know the
truth, and desire to speak it.   The reply of Gesenius, that Mark
does not attribute these words to Jesus, but adduces them on a later
occasion [2] in his own person, can surely prove nothing.   Why should
not Mark, in his own person, adduce a prophecy relating to Christ,
which Christ himself had previously cited?   And we make no
groundless assumption when we assert, that in those passages
where Christ says he must suffer and die, *according to the
Scriptures* [3], he had this passage chiefly in view [4].   For the opponents themselves confess, that if the doctrine of a suffering and
atoning Messiah is contained *any where* in the Old Testament,
it is in this passage.   In the twenty-eighth and seven following verses of the eighth chapter of the Acts, Philip, in reply to the
question of the treasurer from Ethiopia, as to the subject of the
prophecy, explains it of Christ, and grounds upon it all his instructions concerning Him.   The passage in the seventeenth verse of the
eighth chapter of Matthew has already been adduced in the exposition.   After De Wette, Gesenius lays peculiar stress upon the circumstance, that the passage was never referred to the atoning death
of Christ, and maintains that the citation, in the seventeenth verse of
the eighth chapter of Matthew militates against this doctrine.   In
respect to the latter point we refer to the exposition ; the former is
incorrect.   The apostle Peter (in the twenty-first and four following
verses of the second chapter of the first Epistle), when speaking of
the vicarious satisfaction of Christ, *employs verbatim the principal
passages of this prophecy.*   It was not because the apostles did not
explain this prophecy of the expiatory death of Christ, that they
so seldom cited it, when they speak on that subject, but because it
was so familiar to them and to those to whom they wrote, that direct
quotation was unnecessary, a bare allusion being sufficient.   This
appears from the numerous passages in which we meet with allusions
to the prophecy, or reminiscences of it [5].   This passage is, as it were,
the theme, which lay at the foundation of the apostolic annunciation
respecting the atoning death of Jesus.   This Gesenius himself confesses in a passage, which stands in striking contradiction to that just
quoted, l. c. p. 191.   "Most Hebrew readers, who were now so
familiar with the ideas of sacrifice and substitution, must however
have necessarily so understood it, *and it is not to be doubted, that the
apostolic representation of the expiatory death of Christ rests pre-
eminently on this ground.*"

460. (3.) There can be no question, and the best interpreters [6]
acknowledge, that the subject of these prophecies can be no other

---

[1] Comp. chap. 53. 12.   [2] Chap. 15. 28.
[3] κατὰ τὰς γραφάς.   [4] Comp. Gen. Introd.
[5] Comp. e. g. Mark 9. 12. Rom. 4. 25. 1 Cor. 15. 5. 2 Cor. 5. 21. 1 John 3. 5.
1 Pet. 1. 19.
[6] Gesenius, Palm, and others.

than that of those in the forty-second, forty-ninth, fiftieth, and sixty-first chapters. Now if these can be referred only to the Messiah, all the arguments in favour of their Messianic character, which we will not here repeat, are equally applicable to the prophecy before us, and *vice versâ*. In addition to this, the passage in the first verse of the eleventh chapter [1], which is also explained of the Messiah by Gesenius, has so striking a resemblance to the second verse of the fifty-third chapter, that both must be referred to the same subject.

461. (4.) To these external arguments we must subjoin the internal, derived from the characteristics attributed to the subject of the prediction. Though each particular feature can be shown to have been fulfilled in Christ, yet we will here confine ourselves to that which belongs to him exclusively, and can be referred to no one else without entire caprice. We mention, first of all, the doctrine that through the vicarious sufferings of the great servant of God, the people are freed from the punishment of sin, reconciled to God, and made righteous. Several have attempted, and that in different ways, to remove this doctrine from the portion. Kimchi remarks: "We must not suppose that the thing is so in fact, that Israel in exile really bears the sins and diseases of the heathen, for this would militate against the justice of God, but that the heathen will pass such a judgement upon it, when they behold the splendid redemption of Israel." It is easy to see the weakness of this argument of Kimchi's against the vicarious satisfaction. This doctrine would militate against the justice of God only where the sufferer (the opposite of this case, according to the passage) did *not* assume his sufferings *voluntarily*; and besides, such *a priori* and dogmatic objections are of no weight, since corrupt reason is not in a condition to sit in judgement on the doctrines of revelation. It is equally plain, that the method by which he proposes to get rid of the doctrine is extremely forced, and would leave nothing certain in all the Scriptures. Some more recent interpreters [2] have chosen another way. They propose to take the expressions as only figurative, and that we should not seek in them for the doctrine of a vicarious satisfaction for our sins, provided by the righteousness of God through the Messiah. According to Martini, all these expressions signify nothing more than "calamitates illas gravissimas ministro isti divino perferendas popularibus ejus utiles futuras atque salutares." But it is decisive in favour of the literal interpretation, that the Prophet speaks of this subject, not merely in one particular passage, but constantly returns to it, and always places the redemption and the suffering of the Messiah, in relation to each other, as cause and effect. Thus he says [3], "*the Messiah will deliver many heathen from their sins* [4];" "*he has taken our diseases and pains upon himself* [5];" "*he was pierced for our transgressions*," &c. [6]; "*Jehovah has cast upon him*

---

[1] וַיֵּצֵא חֹטֶר מִגֵּזַע יִשָׁי וְנֵצֶר מִשָּׁרָשָׁיו יִפְרֶה.
[2] Martini, ad h. l. De Wette, De Morte Expiatoria, p. 22, seq.
[3] Chap. 52. 15.   [4] Chap. 53. 4.   [5] Ver. 5.
[6] Ver. 6.

the sins of us all [1] *;" " he has borne the punishment which the people should have borne* [2] *;" " he has presented himself as a sin-offering to God,"* &c. To this it may still be added, that the expressions, ' *he shall sprinkle,*' in the fifteenth verse of the fifty-second chapter, and '*sin-offering,*' in the tenth verse of the fifty-third chapter, are taken from sacrifices ; and the suffering and death of the Messiah are represented as effecting an inward reconciliation with God, in the same manner as the death of the victim signified objectively, that outward purity was thereby restored, as to the external theocracy. Indeed, substitution evidently took place in the sacrifices, in respect to external theocratic purity, though by no means in reference to inward sanctification ; and this might well be done without prejudice to the Divine institution of sacrifices. Thus much is certain, *that had the Prophet wished to deliver the doctrine of the vicarious satisfaction, he could not possibly have used stronger expressions.* No passage of the New Testament on the expiatory death of Jesus is more definite in doctrine than this ; and yet the vicarious satisfaction is there taught, even in the opinion of numerous rationalist interpreters of recent times [3]; those only excepted, who (as Paulus) are so strongly biased by doctrinal interest, that they entirely sacrifice exegesis to it. But upon these, time has already passed judgement. The arguments are so striking, that even Rosenmüller, Gesenius, and others, cannot avoid confessing that the passage contains the doctrine of a vicarious satisfaction, after Alschech among the Jews has done homage to the truth.—We now proceed to consider the arguments of De Wette (l. c.) against the literal meaning. 1. He appeals to two passages where the word *ransom* [4] occurs in a figurative sense. The first is the third verse of the forty-third chapter of Isaiah, where Jehovah says He has given Egypt, Ethiopia, and Seba as a ransom for the Israelites. We must here entirely agree with De Wette, in opposition to Gesenius, who [5] finds in this passage also the doctrine of a vicarious satisfaction [6]. A satisfaction of this sort contradicts all the Old Testament ideas of the Divine justice, and, as we shall hereafter see, has no analogy in its favour. De Wette justly says : " Ad amorem Jehovæ erga populum suum demonstrandum comparat propheta Israelitarum sortem cum sorte aliorum populorum, qui dum illi captivitate liberarentur, in ditionem Persarum redacti sint, ita ut quasi dici posset hos populos in locum Israelitarum succedere et eorum libertatem suâ redimere." The second is the eighteenth verse of the twenty-first chapter of Proverbs, " the evil doer is a *ransom* for the righteous, and the ungodly for the pious." This pas-

---

[1] Ver. 8.   [2] Ver. 10.

[3] Comp. e. g. De Wette, Dogmatik, § 1. 293, seq. Bretschneider, Dogm. § 1. 154, 155.

[4] כֹּפֶר   [5] l. c. p. 190.

[6] " The Divine justice was not yet satisfied by the suffering of the people in exile, and therefore other nations are given up for them." What Gesenius remarks, p. 75, on the passage itself, is in contradiction to this. " Jehovah gives great, rich, and powerful nations, as Egypt, Ethiopia, and Seba, as a prize to the conqueror, instead of Israel, and, *as it were*, a ransom for them."

sage, as Gesenius himself acknowledges (thereby confirming the correctness of the figurative acceptation of the third verse of the forty-third chapter of Isaiah), means nothing more than this : " the sufferings which the pious have long endured are afterwards imposed upon the ungodly in their stead ; the latter must, *as it were*, redeem the former." But still both these passages fail to prove the point in question. For the existence of the doctrine of the vicarious satisfaction in this passage does not depend on a *single expression*, which certainly might be interpreted figuratively, but on *the perpetual recurrence of the same doctrine under the greatest diversity of expression* [1]. 2. "The Prophet is so free from all superstition, that he almost rejects sacrifices, and the whole outward worship of God [2]. But it is impossible to perceive what difference there should be between an expiation of sin accomplished by animals, and one accomplished by a man." The Prophet in the cited passage, like all prophets, zealously opposes the opinion that sacrifices, *ex opere operato*, procure the Divine favour and forgiveness of sins, which would be entirely contrary to their original design and import. That it does not follow from this, that he rejected the doctrine of the vicarious satisfaction, is very evident from the example of the writers of the New Testament, and indeed of the whole Christian Church, who, with similar sentiments as to sacrifices, still taught this doctrine. When De Wette places expiation by animals upon a level with expiation by a man, he falsely assumes that, in the view of the Prophet, the servant of God was a mere man. Surely, what the Prophet says of the glorified Messiah is unsuitable to a mere man ; and that he was well acquainted with the Divine nature of the Messiah appears from other Messianic passages, in which Divine names and properties are attributed to him. That a man should make satisfaction for men would certainly, as we shall see hereafter, be contrary to the doctrine of the Old Testament. The passage therefore is inappropriate here, which De Wette cites from the sixth chapter of Micah [3], where the people, inquiring how they should make atonement to Jehovah, and whether they should offer their own children as a sin-offering, are told that Jehovah does not require this, but righteousness, love, and humility. It was only in virtue of his perfect innocence and righteousness, such as were never found in any man, that the servant of God could deliver us from sin ; and on this very circumstance peculiar stress is laid [4]. When (3) De Wette maintains that the Prophet could not teach this doctrine, because it is *subversive of piety*, the promotion of which he had so much at heart, we might also prove with this *a priori* argument (which arises from want of experience, and, as it is to be hoped, is no longer held valid by the author himself), that the whole Christian Church, that a Luther, an Arndt, a Spener, have not held it. The doctrine of the vicarious

---

[1] Besides in the passages referred to, the expression כֹּפֶר occurs, and not, as in this instance אָשָׁם (compare יִדֶּה), which does not so easily admit of being understood figuratively.

[2] Comp. 86. 3.   [3] Ver. 6—8.   [4] Comp. chap. 9. 11.

satisfaction is then definitely and clearly contained in this passage. But now we find in the New Testament the same things said of Christ, as are here attributed to the subject of the prophecy. It is true that Christ, during His life, more seldom expressed Himself definitely and clearly concerning the design of His death, and His vicarious satisfaction [1]. The reason was, that the carnally-minded disciples were not prepared, before Christ's death, and the giving of the Holy Spirit which depended upon it, to understand this doctrine in its true import; it pre-eminently, therefore, belongs to the "many things" which Christ had still to say to the disciples, but which they could not yet bear. But after His death He fully instructed His disciples concerning it [2]; and the complete information which they have given us, flowed partly from His instructions, and partly from the illumination promised immediately to them, and actually granted.

462. There is, besides, the specific trait given in the ninth verse, that the servant of God should be interred with a rich man (Joseph of Arimathea). It would be superfluous further to point out the coincidence between the prophecy and its fulfilment, since it must be self-evident to every one acquainted with the evangelical history.

463. These positive arguments for the Messianic interpretation are likewise so many negative ones against every other. It would be an idle waste of time to refute the views (approved of only by their authors) of those who would refer the prophecy to any individual subject besides Christ, from king Uzziah to the Maccabees. All these interpreters have been satisfied with seizing upon some single feature, which is found again in the history of some individual. The rest they have entirely overlooked, or sought to set aside by false and unnatural interpretations. By such a mode of proceeding, one might invent innumerable expositions of the prophecy, besides those already mentioned. The refutation would consequently be useless; since it is merely accidental, whether this or that person has not proposed some individual or other, to whom the prophecy no more refers than to a hundred others. It is an objection to all these references to distinct individuals, that they make their appearance here, without exception, as a *deus ex machinâ;* no one can tell whence they come, and whither they go, or give any reason why the Prophet abruptly brings them before us.

464. There are only three interpretations which are entitled to our attention, on account of their more general prevalence and greater plausibility. The first regards as the subject the *whole Jewish people;* the second, *the pious part* of them; and the third, the *collective body of the prophets.* It is common to them all, that the subject is not an actual, but only an ideal person, a *collectivum* personified.

465. Against the first of these, we urge chiefly the following arguments :—

---

[1] See, however, Matt. 20. 28. 26. 28. John 3. 14. 6. 51—55. 12. 27, &c. Bretschneider, l. c. § 154.
[2] Luke 24. 27.

466. (1.) It is true, that the Jewish people are sometimes personified as a unity, and called *servant of Jehovah*. But such a personification extended through a whole section, without the slightest intimation that the discourse does not relate to one individual, can be confirmed by no analogous example. In the third verse the subject is termed '*he ;*' in the tenth verse a *soul* is attributed to him ; *grave* and *death* are used in reference to a subject of the singular number. Did the Prophet wish to be understood, he must have given at least some hint as to his meaning [1]. In addition to these objections, such an extended allegory, which, as we have already remarked, is without an example in the Hebrew literature, would be very inappropriate and feeble.

467. (2.) The subject of the portion has undertaken his sufferings *voluntarily ;* (according to the tenth verse the servant of God *presents himself as a sin-offering ;* in the twelfth verse he is *crowned with glory, because he has poured out his life in death*, which the usage of the language permits us to understand only of a voluntary act of self-devotion ;) *innocent* himself, he bears the sins of others [2]; his sufferings are the efficient *cause of the righteousness* of the people [3]; he suffers *quietly* and *patiently*, without allowing himself to be provoked to bitterness against the authors of his sufferings [4]. Of all these four marks not one belongs to the people of Israel. (a) They did not go *voluntarily* into the Babylonish exile, but were carried away by violence. (b) They did not *suffer innocently*, but bore in the exile the *punishment of their own sins*. This had been predicted by Moses [5] as a theocratic judgement. In this light it is represented by all the prophets. Jeremiah and Ezekiel perpetually inculcate anew, that this punishment will surely fall upon the people, on account of the prevalence of gross vice, and especially in consequence of idolatry. Isaiah himself, in the second part, admonishes the Jews that they would be driven into exile by the Divine justice, and delivered from it only by the Divine mercy [6]. And when we look at the immediate occasion of the exile, what is said of the sufferer, in the ninth verse, does not suit the Israelites : " *He had done no unrighteous deed, and there was no guile in his mouth.*" The immediate occasion of the exile, complained of by Jeremiah, was the *perjured alliance with Egypt* against Nebuchadnezzar. Rosenmüller endeavours to remove this difficulty by the remark that the Prophet does not speak in his own person, but in that of the heathen people, who

---

[1] It is totally different in the other passages, where the Prophet designates the people of Israel by the name עֶבֶד יְהֹוָה. He there guards against all uncertainty by adding the name יַעֲקֹב and יִשְׂרָאֵל comp. chap. 41. 8, 9. 44. 1, 2. 21. 45. 4. 48. 20 : moreover, in order to show that the עֶבֶד יְהֹוָה is a collective, he makes use of the plural along with the singular, when speaking of and to the Israelites. Comp. e. g. 42. 24, 25. 48. 20, 21, 43. 10—14. 44. 8. But there is nothing like this in the case before us.

[2] Ver. 4—6 and ver. 9.   [3] Ver. 11.   [4] Ver. 7.

[5] Lev. 26. 14. Deut 28. 15. 29. 19. 32. 1.

[6] Comp. e. g. 56—59, particularly the penitential confession of the people themselves in the last chapter.

would conciliate the favour of the Israelites by this flattery. But this explanation is untenable, even if we leave out of view that the Prophet would not, without further remark, put into the mouth of others a discourse, the contents of which he did not himself approve, since he could not fail to perceive that his approbation would be taken for granted by every one. For the innocence of the subject is declared, not only in the first ten verses of the fifty-third chapter, which Rosenmüller, after the example of the Jews, attributes to the heathen, but just as plainly also in the discourse of Jehovah, in the thirteenth and two following verses of the fifty-second chapter, and the eleventh and twelfth verses of the fifty-third chapter. Only if innocent himself could the sufferer deliver the heathen from sin; in the eleventh verse he is called distinctly the righteous; in the twelfth it is spoken of as meritorious, that he suffers himself to be numbered with the transgressors. (c) The suffering of the Jewish people cannot be represented as the efficient cause of the righteousness of the heathen, as vicarious in their behalf. This could not be the case, even because the Jewish people neither voluntarily assumed their sufferings, nor were they innocently involved in them; on the contrary, they suffered *through their own fault* and *against their will*. But, in general, there is, and from the nature of the case there could be, no example in the Old Testament of the sufferings of one man being regarded as vicarious for others. De Wette himself proves that the Hebrews neither held, nor could hold, the doctrine of a vicarious satisfaction made by men. As now, it has been proved that a vicarious satisfaction *is* taught in Isaiah, he cannot avoid referring the prophecy to the Messiah.—The first condition of such a satisfaction, and that which is so represented in the portion before us, is the *entire innocence* of the sufferer. Whoever is himself sinful, cannot assume the punishment of another's sins; but his suffering is either a punishment from the Divine justice, or a corrective from the Divine mercy. The doctrine of a vicarious *human* satisfaction, therefore, would be in direct contradiction to that of the Old Testament, respecting the universal sinfulness of mankind[1]. Even the prophets, the best and noblest part of the nation, often include themselves with the people when they speak of their sinfulness. Isaiah[2], when he was favoured with a view of the Divine glory, says, "Woe is me, for I am of unclean lips; I dwell in the midst of a people of unclean lips." A substitution by man is most distinctly contradicted also in the sixth and two following verses of the sixth chapter of Micah, and the eighth and two following verses of the forty-ninth Psalm. "*No brother can redeem his brother; no man can give to God a ransom for another. So precious is the ransom of their souls, that he must wait for ever, even though he should live for ever, and not see the grave.*" It is likewise contradicted by the passage in the twentieth verse of the eighteenth chapter of Ezekiel: "*The soul that sinneth it shall die; the son shall not bear the iniquity*

---

[1] Comp. Gen. 6. 5. 8. 21. Job 15. 14—16. Ps. 14. 3. 51. 7. 53. 4. Prov. 20. 9.
[2] Chap. 6.

of the father, nor the father the iniquity of the son ; but the righteous-
ness of the righteous shall be upon him, and the unrighteousness of the
unrighteous shall be upon him." Nor would it avail any thing here
also, with Kimchi, to resort to the supposition, that the Prophet only
expresses the thoughts of the heathen, without giving them his ap-
proval. For the doctrine of the vicarious satisfaction is contained in
the discourse of Jehovah, no less than in those verses in which the
heathen are introduced as speaking.

468. We must however here enter into an examination of the
passages by which Gesenius endeavours to prove, in opposition to
De Wette, that the doctrine of a vicarious satisfaction by man is
widely diffused elsewhere in the Old Testament, and deeply impressed
on the Hebrew mode of thought. These passages are the following.
" The guilt of the fathers is visited upon the children [1]." This however does not relate to *substitution*, for *substitution* does not consist
in the circumstance, that another is punished at the same time with
the guilty, but that he who has committed the sin is entirely freed
from punishment, in consequence of its being assumed by another.
This last however has a totally different object and import. It was
intended to make the sensible impression of visible rewards and
punishments yet deeper by their extension to the descendants of the
pious and the ungodly. All ancient legislators held it necessary to
sustain their laws by the same means. On this subject Cicero says [2],
" Nec vero me fugit, quam sit acerbum, parentium scelera filiorum
pœnis lui. Sed hoc præclare legibus comparatum est, ut caritas
liberorum amiciores parentes reipublicæ redderet." Now as in other
states the promulgation of this law was thought to be indispensably
necessary for attaining the object of the state, we shall find it the
more expedient in the theocracy, in proportion as its object was
higher than that of all other states. — " The punishment is inflicted
on the posterity, when it had not taken place before [3]." Nearly the
same holds good here also. The crime, which Saul had perpetrated
upon the Gibeonites, had brought a plague upon the land of the
Israelites, who had suffered it to remain unpunished. As the proper
offender could no longer be punished, and yet the punishment must
be inflicted in order to sustain the holiness of the Law with the
people, the descendants (who according to this law were also culpable) were punished, or the author of the crime was punished in them.
It is sometimes unavoidable, that a part should suffer, if the whole
is to be preserved, which could be effected in the theocracy only by
most strictly maintaining the sanctity of the Law. There was here
no substitution, even because it was not the author of the crime, but
the people who had left it unpunished, who were freed from the
penalty incurred. — " Jehovah caused David's sin in numbering the
people to be expiated by a three days' pestilence, and the death of
seven thousand people [4]." Here also there is nothing said of a
vicarious satisfaction. The punishment was not *voluntarily* under-

---

[1] Ex. 20. 6.   [2] Ep. 12 ad Brutum.
[3] 2 Sam. 21. 1—14.   [4] 2 Sam. 24. 10—25.

gone ; the people did not suffer *innocently ;* for although in this particular instance they had taken no part in the offence, still they
could not complain of the punishment as unjust, because on account
of their sinfulness in general in other respects, no punishment could
be greater than they deserved.   That David was not exempted from
punishment through the punishment of the people is evident from
his praying to God in deep distress [1], rather to punish himself and
his family.   It was here also the object of the punishment inflicted
on the people to promote the sacredness of the law, and awaken
reverence for the Divine justice among a people, who, yet rude and
carnal, must be led and kept in obedience by these outward chastisements, because they could not yet be influenced by love.—" The sin
of David with Bathsheba was expiated by the death of the child [2]."
But this passage by no means proves the point.   For Nathan had
already announced forgiveness to David [3] before he foretold the
death of the child ; its death, therefore, cannot be regarded as vicarious, and indeed the loss of the child was so distressing to David [4],
that the suffering fell rather upon him than the child.   The reason
why the child must die is given in the narrative itself, in the fourteenth verse : had David been entirely exempted from punishment,
the enemies of the Lord would have accused God of partiality, and
taken occasion therefrom to blaspheme His name.   The suffering of
David also for the loss of the child must aggravate his suffering for
the cause of it, the sin he had committed.—" Because Achan seized
upon that which was consecrated, the whole army of Joshua was
given up to the enemy [5]."   Here again we look in vain for substitution : for the transgressor himself was not saved from punishment,
through the calamity which was sent upon the people.   On the contrary, he was burnt with all his goods and his family [6].   The punishment of the people was designed to make them zealous to extirpate
from among them every crime and misdemeanour ; the individual is
strictly watched, when the whole body is made answerable for his
actions.   It was nothing more than a theocratic punishment, intended
as a warning.—Even in Isaiah [7], "sinners are punished for the sins
of their fathers, as well as their own."   That there is here no substitution, which requires, along with a voluntary assumption, an entire
freedom from guilt, is evident, even from what Jehovah says : " *I will
recompense your transgression and the transgression of your fathers
together.*"   The sense is no other than this : You, who are the more
culpable for not having been led to repentance by the long-suffering
of God, shall experience in full measure the punishment, which
indeed your forefathers, whom you are in no respect behind in wickedness, have merited.—The passage in the thirty-fifth verse of the
eleventh chapter of Daniel resembles even more closely the passage
before us : the subject of discourse is there the martyrdom of the
pious in the religious persecutions, and it is said : ' The pious will fall,
in order to purify, cleanse, and sanctify those, i. e. the rest ;' which

---

[1] Ver. 17.   [2] 2 Sam. 12. 15—18.   [3] Comp. ver. 13.
[4] Comp. ver. 22.   [5] Josh. 7. 1.
[6] Comp. ver. 15. 24.   [7] Chap. 65. 7.

can hardly be understood in any other way than as referring to their death as martyrs." But the sense of this passage is plainly no other, than that the example given by the pious, of self-denial, and a stedfastness in the faith of the fathers not to be shaken even by death, will exert a salutary influence upon the rest, and strengthen the wavering; a result confirmed by the history of all religious oppressions.—" Among the Arabians also a very frequent proverbial expression is grounded upon this idea, *let my life be thy ransom;* and several similar sayings show at least that the notion of a vicarious satisfaction was very familiar to the orientals, and hence passed over into the language itself." What these expressions have to do here, is hard to be conceived. They plainly signify nothing further than: " Thou art so dear to me, that I would willingly give up what I most love, my own life and the life of my father, if I could thereby rescue thee from impending danger."—This then is the result of our investigation : among all the passages cited by Gesenius, there is not one which conveys the idea of a vicarious satisfaction effected by man for man. Besides, this idea is excluded by the doctrinal system of the Old Testament, and least of all can a vicarious satisfaction on the part of the people of Israel be the subject of discourse, since its essential requisites, *their own innocence,* and *the voluntary assumption of the suffering,* were in their case entirely wanting.

469. (d) The fourth characteristic also of the suffering subject, entire patience and devotedness to the will of God, do not belong to the Israelitish people. How can it be said of the whole people, that they have not opened their mouth to complain, when even the noblest and best of them poured out their sadness in complaints and imprecations [1]? They must surely have been an entirely different people from the representations of the prophets, and particularly of Isaiah himself, if the Prophet could give them this praise.

470. (3.) In this interpretation it is altogether arbitrarily assumed that in the first ten verses the heathen, or the foreign nations hitherto hostile to the Jews, are introduced as speaking. The heathen are never thus introduced without some intimation of it in what precedes and follows. And even were we not to hesitate on this account, how could they, or the Prophet in their name, declare that it was the burden of their punishment, which oppressed the exiled Jews?

471. (4.) This hypothesis makes the groundless assumption, that the death and burial of the servant of God is to be referred only to his misfortunes and ruin. It is indeed true that [2] the carrying away into the exile is represented under the figure of a death, and the deliverance from it under that of a resurrection [3]; but there every thing shows that the discourse is only to be understood figuratively, while here there is not the slightest intimation of this.

472. (5.) It is contradicted by the parallel passages in which the servant of God is plainly distinguished from the people [4].

---

[1] Comp. Jer. 20. 7, seq. 15. 10—21. Ps. 137. 8, 9. Lam. 3. 64—66.
[2] Ezek. 37.   [3] Comp. also Isaiah 26, 19.
[4] Comp. chap. 42. 6 49. 5, 6. 50. 9.

473. (6.) It renders a very unnatural interpretation of several verses necessary. Thus e. g. in the first verse of the fifty-third chapter (compare the exposition), also the second verse, where, after Jarchi, Rosenmüller explains the words: " he grew up before him as a shoot and as a root out of a dry soil:" ' priusquam ad hanc magnitudinem ascenderet, gens erat perquam humilis et ascendit e terra sicut surculus.' But this were an entirely unsuitable figure, as the Israelites had certainly been prosperous in the beginning, and did not experience adversity till afterwards [1].

474. The interpretation, which makes the *pious portion of the people* the subject, need not detain us so long. It has much resemblance to the one which refers the prophecy to the collective body of the prophets, and is liable to several of the objections immediately to be adduced against that hypothesis. Of the arguments which refute the interpretation that makes the whole people the subject, those under No. 1, 2, and 4, apply also, with some slight modifications, to the present exposition. What may still be specially urged against it is the following. The speakers, in the first nine verses, represent themselves as entirely free from all suffering; they place themselves in contrast with that suffering servant of God, who has taken upon himself the suffering due to them. How could the godly portion of the people say this, when in the same captivity they participated in the unhappy lot of the ungodly? How could the suffering of the pious be vicarious for the ungodly, since they themselves suffered? That the ungodly enjoyed in the exile a comparatively better lot than the pious, is a groundless hypothesis. It is contradicted by the example of a Daniel, of Esther and Mordecai, of Ezra, and the opulent Nehemiah [2].

475. We come now to the last hypothesis to be examined; the idea of those who regard the *collective body* of the prophets as the

---

[1] Comp. Ps. 80. 9.   Ez. 19. 10—13.   Jer. 2. 21.

[2] Neh. 5. 14—19.   Another turn which has been given to the hypothesis supposes ' *servant of Jehovah* ' to designate only the nobler part of the nation carried away by Nebuchadnezzar, who made expiation seventy years for the sins of their brethren, and died, but afterwards returned in their posterity. On this occasion the author of the prophecy, one of the Jews left behind, presents and recommends them to his countrymen in Palestine, as their deliverers and sanctifiers. The principal arguments against this perfectly strange idea are the following. (1.) That only the noblest and best of the people were carried away is contradicted by Ez. 20. 28, where it is said that the rebels and apostates from Jehovah should be separated and carried away; and also by Jer. 39. 9, 10, where it is said that only a mass of the lowest people were left behind. But it was precisely among the distinguished and great, as appears from the complaints of the prophets, that the corruption was peculiarly great, and hence the punishment fell, in an especial manner, upon them. Comp. 2 Chron. 36. 14, seq. (2.) The Israelites who were left in Palestine fled to Egypt, Jer. chap. 43. 4—8. 44, 1, 2. 2 Kings 25. 56. Consequently no settled inhabitants remained in the country. Palestine became a wild land of Nomades. No where is there an intimation that the returning exiles found a part of the former inhabitants still in the land. These arguments are so conclusive, that we scarcely need to call the attention further to the fact, that this hypothesis can be carried out only by many distortions of the text, by erroneously assuming that Isaiah was not the writer, &c.

object of the prophecy, and suppose it to contain a sort of *apotheosis*
of the prophetic order. The prophets, who even before the exile
had much to suffer, were exposed during that period to still greater
contempt and derision ; to which might be added, contempt and
derision on the part of the heathen. Hence may be explained, it is
said, the apology of the prophetic order for themselves, as well as the
origin of such splendid and enthusiastic hopes as we find here and in
the parallel passages in the forty-second and following chapters.
Against this hypothesis we offer the following remarks :

476. (1.) The supposition of such a personification of the prophetic order rests upon arguments which prove nothing. This will
be evident from an examination of the passages to which its defenders appeal. The first of these is the twenty-sixth verse of
the forty-fourth chapter, where Jehovah says, " *I am he who ve-*
rifies the word of his servant, and fulfils the prophecy of his mes-
sengers." The parallel *messengers* is supposed to indicate that
servant stands collectively. But there is absolutely no reason to
think that there is here a *synonymous*, and not rather a *synthetic*
parallelism. The latter is indeed indicated by the second member
of the verse : " *who says of Jerusalem, She shall be inhabited;*
and of the cities of Judah, They shall be built again ;" where
Jerusalem and the *cities of Judah* constitute in like manner not a
synonymous but a *synthetic* parallelism. By ' *the servant of Jehovah* '
Isaiah himself is to be understood [1]. What he says of *himself* in the
first member, he says in the second in respect to *all prophets of the*
true God.—The second passage, adduced only by De Wette, and
passed over by Gesenius as not affording proof, is in the twenty-first
verse of the fifty-ninth chapter : " *And I make such a covenant with*
them, saith the Lord ; my Spirit which is with thee, and my words
which I have put in thy mouth, shall not depart from thy mouth, nor
from the mouth of thy seed and thy seed's seed, saith the Lord, from
henceforth to eternity." This is said to be equivalent to : " What you
have uttered by the inspiration of my Spirit shall be repeated by all
the prophets of later ages, who are, as it were, the sons of that prophet." Even granting this exposition to be correct, the passage
would still fail of proving a personification of the prophetic order.
But Rosenmüller has justly observed, in opposition to it, after the
example of the best interpreters : " He does not speak to the prophet
but to the Hebrew people, as is clearly proved by the words that
precede and those that follow. There is here an enallage of persons ;
the Prophet having begun in the third person plural, goes on in
the second singular, directing his discourse immediately to the
people." Compare the second verse of the thirty-second chapter.
All the promises which precede and follow relate to the whole community ; and it were a singular leap, if the Prophet first announced
a covenant to be established with this community, and then, in
assigning the object of it, should suddenly pass over to the mercies
which would be conferred, not upon the people, but the prophetic

---

[1] As in chap. 20. 3.

order[1]. But this hypothesis is not only incapable of being proved, but altogether improbable. It rests on the entirely erroneous view that the prophets formed a corporation by themselves. The difference between them and the priests consisted precisely in this, that the latter formed an exclusive order, which constantly supplied its own members; while the call to the prophetic office depended solely on the will of Jehovah, and the relation of every prophet was to Him, and not to the remaining prophets. The objection, which has been adduced against the hypothesis of the Jewish people being the subject under No. 1, applies therefore with still greater force in this case; the defenders of that hypothesis might appeal to passages where the Jews appear as an individual, but there are none where the prophets are so represented.

477. (2.) But this opinion appears most untenable, if we take the position of its defenders, and deny the genuineness of the second part. Immediately after the Babylonian exile the prophetic order ceased; Jewish tradition is unanimous in giving Haggai, Zechariah, and Malachi as the last of the prophets, and prophecy is included among the things which were wanting to the second Temple. The communication of the prophetic spirit anew is not expected till a future time. All Jewish chronologists make the cessation of the prophetic office a chronological epoch, and begin with it a new era, as is done even in the twenty-seventh verse of the ninth chapter of the first book of Maccabees, with which compare the forty-sixth verse of the fourth chapter, and the forty-first verse of the fourteenth chapter. Now, even leaving entirely out of view the true idea of a prophet, it is difficult to conceive how the Prophet could speak of a great corporation of the prophets, at a time when there were only a few of them still in existence, who, in respect to the power, the abundance, and the purity of the spirit, were far inferior to those of more ancient times. It is difficult to imagine how the Prophet could cherish the enthusiastic hope, that they, whose authority even before the exile was sunk so low among the people, would attain to such glory, spread the true religion over the whole earth, and even, as the defenders of this hypothesis maintain, live to enjoy a worldly triumph.

478. (3.) Of the arguments which have been advanced against the explanation which makes the Jewish people the subject, those under No. 2 and 4 are applicable also to this. Never do we find an example, where prophets freely submitted to suffering in the hope of thereby delivering others from sin. On the contrary, when sufferings are inflicted upon them, they always declare that heavy Divine punishment should fall upon the authors of their distress[2]. That they were very far from regarding themselves as entirely free from sin and guilt, we have already seen.

479. (4.) The servant of God can be no other than he who forms

---

[1] It is unnecessary to dwell on chap. 53. 8, since the argument drawn from לָמוֹ has already been refuted.

[2] Comp. e. g. Jer. 20. 1?.

the object of the parallel prophecies, in the forty-second and following chapters.   But in these still more occurs which can by no means
belong to the prophetic order.   Thus in the third verse of the forty-
ninth chapter, the servant of God is called Israel, a difficulty which
Gesenius knows of no other method to remove than that of declaring
the word spurious in opposition to the manuscripts and translations.

480. (5.) The Prophet regards himself, in the second and following verses, as a different person from the servant of God, and contrasts himself with him.   He includes himself among the people.
Now, how could the Prophet say, that he took part in despising the
prophetic order, that he endured his sufferings for himself, and
regarded himself as one smitten of God, &c. ?   Gesenius appeals to
the ninth and four following verses of the fifty-ninth chapter, where
the Prophet numbers himself with the people, and also calls their
sins his own.   See also the twenty-fourth verse of the forty-second
chapter.   But this is certainly a different case.   The Prophet, like
every other member of the people, had a real part in their sins [1].   But
how could he take part in the contempt, &c. of his own order ?   How
could the vicarious sufferings, in which he himself participated, be
borne for him ?

481. (6.) The sufferings of the prophets in the exile were the
same as those of the people.   That the former were by no means
chiefly oppressed by the heathen appears from the example of Jeremiah.   After the capture of the city, Nebuchadnezzar showed him
great respect, and gave him the choice of his place of residence.
Compare the eleventh and following verses of the thirty-ninth
chapter of Jeremiah.   How then could the people despise them, how
believe them to be smitten of God ?

482. (7.) The sufferings of the prophets could not be regarded as
instead of the sufferings of the ungodly part of the people ; for the
latter suffered no less than the former.

483. (8.) According to this hypothesis, the prophets indulged the
hope, that they should be the rulers of the restored and flourishing
state, and celebrate worldly triumphs.   To say nothing of the folly
of this hope, it was entirely opposed to the destination of the prophetic order.   The government in the theocracy was ever assigned
to the posterity of David by Divine appointment.   Consequently,
had the prophets laid claim to it, they would have rebelled against
God, whose rights it was their duty to defend.   The prophets were
extraordinary messengers of God, the invisible head of the theocracy,
called to teach, reprove, warn, and console ; heralds of peace and
righteousness to an apostate people.   That they remained true to
this destination is proved by the whole history of the Israelites.

484. (9.) But should we, as indeed we are obliged to do, understand figuratively what is said of the servant of God, and find in
the passage spiritual instead of worldly triumphs, still it would not
be applicable to the prophetic order.   It would be against the
analogy of all other prophecies respecting the conversion of the

[1] Comp. Dan. 9. 5, &c.

heathen, if the prophets here attributed it to themselves. No where do we find an example of the prophets mistaking their destination to operate only on the covenant people ; no where the mention of an attempt on their part to extend their agency to the heathen nations. Never do they look to themselves for the accomplishment of their high hopes in reference to the future, but always to the Messiah alone. They are so little influenced by prejudices in favour of their order, they give themselves up so entirely to the instructions of the Holy Spirit, that they even repeatedly announce, that in Messianic times the necessity for the prophetic order will entirely cease, since all will then be immediately taught of God[1].

485. (10.) It is an unnatural assumption of these interpreters, that the death and burial relate to one portion of the prophetic order, the glorification, on the contrary, to those who sinned, since it is one and the same subject, who suffers, dies, and is glorified.

486. The interpretation, therefore, which rests on the infallible testimony of the New Testament, is here also demonstrated by internal and external arguments, to be the true one in opposition to all who reject this testimony. If the *ground* which produced these devious interpretations be once removed, there will be as little necessity for a detailed refutation of them, as there is that the interpreter should still notice the perverse interpretations of the Socinians.

THE PROPHET ZECHARIAH

GENERAL PRELIMINARY OBSERVATIONS [2]

487. ZECHARIAH, like Jeremiah and Ezekiel, was of priestly descent. In the first verse of the first chapter, Berechiah is named as his father, and Iddo as his grandfather. The latter, among the exiles who returned with Joshua and Zerubbabel, filled the respectable office of overseer of a class of priests[3]. That Berechiah died early appears from the fact, that in the sixteenth verse the same Zechariah is mentioned as immediate successor of Iddo in this office, under Joiachim, successor of Joshua. Accordingly Zechariah, at least in his later years, exercised, together with the prophetic, a priestly office also. This early death and the comparative obscurity of the father explain why, in the first verse of the fifth chapter of Ezra, the descent of this prophet is referred immediately to the grandfather, according to a practice occurring elsewhere in similar cases.

---

[1] Comp. e. g. Joel, chap. 3. Isaiah 54. 13. 59. 21. 4. 3. 11. 9. Ez. 11. 19. 36. 27. Jer. 31. 33.

[2] Compare above, 211.   [3] Compare Neh. 12. 4.

488. The discourse, which opens the collection of the prophecies of Zechariah, was held[1] in the eighth month of the second year of Darius, beyond all doubt Darius the son of Hystaspes. This was, no doubt, the commencement of his course as a prophet; as appears, partly from the character of the discourse (which in its general tenour is clearly a preparatory introduction), and partly from the chronological arrangement of the collection, apparent from the superscriptions of the second and third prophecy[2], which prove that the predictions, in the ninth and five following chapters, which are without date, belong to a period subsequent to the foregoing.

489. The Prophet must have been still young when he first came forwards. For his grandfather Iddo was then in the full discharge of the duties of his office, as appears from the fact already mentioned, that Zechariah was his immediate successor. In addition to this, the Prophet, in the eighth verse of the second chapter, is expressly called a young man. As now[3], the family of the Prophet returned to Judea with the first expedition of the exiles in the first year of Cyrus, which was eighteen years previous to the second year of Darius the son of Hystaspes, Zechariah can have passed only the first years of his childhood in Babylonia, and consequently the Babylonish colouring of his prophecies was owing, not (as Bertholdt and De Wette suppose) to his having received his education in Babylonia, but rather, in some degree, to the continuation of the Babylonian influence on the body of the exiles, though chiefly to the dependence which he everywhere manifests on earlier prophets, especially Ezekiel, who stood in immediate contact with the Babylonians.

490. Let us now consider the historical relations, under which the Prophet came forward, and upon which he was called to operate. The advantages, which had been granted to the exiles by the command of Cyrus in respect to the rebuilding of the Temple, were soon wrested from them through the machinations of their enemies, the Samaritans, in the Persian court. They were deficient in means to carry forward the erection of the Temple, and still more in theocratic zeal; this had been already greatly damped, soon after the return, by the obstacles which unexpectedly occurred, while they believed themselves justified by the former promises in expecting nothing but prosperity and happiness. Each one was selfishly intent only on the improvement of his own affairs. Under these circumstances, and in this tone of the public mind, though the prohibition to build the Temple, which had been promulgated under the usurper Smerdis, was repealed, in consequence of the accession of Darius the son of Hystaspes to the throne, yet this contributed but little to advance the work. It was still necessary that a powerful influence should be exerted on the minds of the people. For this purpose were the prophets Haggai and Zechariah called of God; of whom the former, at whose exhortation the building of the Temple was immediately

---

[1] According to chap. 1. 1.   [2] Chap. 1. 7, and chap. 7. 1.
[3] According to Nehem. 12. 4, comp. with v. 1.

re-commenced, came forward two months before the latter. Ze-chariah, as becomes a true prophet of God, has in view, through-out, not the advancement of the outer work, as such; he aims to produce among the people a thorough spiritual revolution, the fruit of which must be an increased zeal for the building of the Temple. Those on whom the Prophet was called to operate, belonged to two classes. First, the upright and true believers. These had fallen into great despondency and strong temptations, in consequence of the apparent contradiction between the Divine promises and the actual appearance of things. They doubted both the power and the will of God to help them. It would often appear to them, that their own sins and those of their fathers were so great, that God could not again show them mercy. Here, where the Prophet had to deal with troubled consciences, his office was to console. This he does, while he points from the gloomy present to the brighter future; and, while resuming the yet unfulfilled portion of the former prophecies, he represents the fulfilment as yet to be accomplished. The objects of his prediction are particularly the happy completion of the Tem-ple; the increase of the new colony by the return of the exiles remaining in Babylon; the preservation of Judea during the victories of Alexander, so destructive to the neighbouring nations; the inde-pendence of the people, to be won by the triumphs of the Maccabees; the blessings, which the believing part of them should receive through the Messiah, immediately on his first appearance; the final restoration of the ungodly part, once rejected on account of their disbelief in the Messiah; the protection and prosperity, which God will grant to Israel, when they shall have again become the centre and most important part of the kingdom of God. This aspect of the Prophet's prediction was the more weighty, the stronger were the assaults which threatened the faith of even the upright, in that future period when there would be no immediate ambassadors of God, and the more they needed a sure prophetic word to illuminate the darkness of their faith. The second class consisted of the hypo-crites. These had returned in no less numbers from Babylonia, induced, not by the true motive, the love of God and his sanctuary, but by selfishness, the hope of sharing in all the blessings of God promised to those who returned, which they expected immediately, and in which, in their foolish delusion, notwithstanding the most emphatic declarations of the older prophets, they believed they had a right to participate, because renouncing gross idolatry, they exchanged it for idolatry of that more refined kind, which consisted in the outward righteousness of works. It could not but happen that even then, in many instances, the disappointed hope would strip from unbelief the mask of hypocrisy. Still more frequently, however, must this be the case at a later period. For these also, the Prophet describes the future blessings of God, in order to excite them to true conver-sion. But at the same time that he most emphatically declares, that this conversion alone can give them a part in these blessings, he reminds them of the judgements, which had fallen upon those who derided the warnings of the former prophets, and threatens them with new and equally fearful punishments, a new destruction of Jerusalem, and a new dispersion of the people, after they shall have despised the last and greatest manifestation of Divine mercy, the sending of the Messiah [1].

491. Though Zechariah, on account of the prevalence of symbolical and figurative language, as well as the roughness and abruptness of his style, is, in a degree, more obscure than the other prophets, yet the interpretation of him is facilitated by two circumstances, almost peculiar to himself. In the first place, a careful comparison of the parallel passages in the interpretation of this Prophet, who leant upon his predecessors, gives more decisive results, than in that of any other. Then, as he lived after the exile, he does not embrace in his prophecy near so large a circle of events as those who flourished at an earlier period. The *clare obscure*, which *e. g.* in the second part of Isaiah, and in Jeremiah and Ezekiel, arose from the circumstance, that the whole series of future blessings, namely, the deliverance from captivity, and the Messianic time, were presented to them in one vision, here, where the Prophet takes his position between the two events, in a great measure disappears.

[1] With respect to the arrangement of the prophecies, the collection consists of four parts, distinguished by the time of composition. (1) The inaugural discourse of the Prophet, chap. 1. 1—7, held in the eighth month of the second year of Darius ; on what day is uncertain. (2) The emblematic portion of the collection, chap. 1. 7. 6, consisting of a series of visions, partly, as chap. 1—4, of a consoling and encouraging, partly, as chap. 5, of a threatening character, all imparted to the Prophet in one night, the 24th of the eleventh month in the second year of Darius. (3) A discourse, at the same time didactic and prophetic, chap. 7, 8, held in the fourth year of Darius, occasioned by the earnest inquiry of the people, whether they should still observe the ·day of the destruction of Jerusalem as a day of fasting and mourning, or whether so favorable a turn of their fortune was now soon to be expected, that the former adversity would thereby be forgotten. (4) A prophetic picture of the future destiny of the covenant people, essentially like the second discourse, so that no chief point of that is wanting in this, but differing from it, partly in the method of the representation,—here the ordinary prophetic discourse, there a series of visions,—partly in the omission here of the distinct reference to the building of the Temple, both in the exhortation and the prophecy. From this, taken in connexion with the position of the prophecy, at the end of the collection, we are authorized to conclude, that it was composed after the completion of the Temple, therefore at all events after the sixth year of Darius. Hence it may be explained why the prophecy is without date. This was of importance in the three preceding discourses. In the first, because thereby the *terminus a quo* of the agency of the Prophet was determined, which is noted, even by prophets who were accustomed elsewhere to subjoin no mark of time, comp. e. g. Isaiah, chap. 6. In the second, because it contained the promise, without doubt a few years afterwards fulfilled, of the happy completion of the Temple by Zerubbabel. In the third, because the inquiry of the people was occasioned by definite circumstances existing in the fourth year of Darius. In the fourth discourse, on the contrary, which, as what was predicted in the second, as the nearest future, had already become the past, related only to events of the more distant future, it was entirely sufficient to know only in general the age of the Prophet, which was already shown by the former notes of time.

Chapter 1

CHAPTER 1. 1—6

492. The first revelation, imparted to the Prophet in the second year and eighth month of the reign of Darius, the son of Hystaspes. This prophecy, in which the Prophet warns the people not to bring upon themselves the punishment of their fathers by a relapse into their sins, and exhorts them to turn to the Lord in sincerity, may be regarded as a sort of introduction, as well to the whole course of the Prophet, as also to the collection of his prophecies. New and suspicious indications of inward apostasy from the Lord already showed themselves among those who had returned. Such particularly was the negligent prosecution of the building of the Temple, which must be combated by a true prophet, not separately from its source, but in the deepest root from which it sprung. The Prophet in his later predictions had to furnish a succession of consoling views to the troubled and desponding. In order that these might not be appropriated to themselves by those to whom they did not belong, and abused to the promotion of carnal security, it was necessary that true repentance should be prominently exhibited as the condition of the coming prosperity. The threatening of new judgements for those, who would not fulfil this condition, contains already in the germ all that the Prophet in the fifth and eleventh chapters more definitely predicts concerning a new and total desolation and destruction, which should come upon the land, after ungodliness should there have regained the ascendancy, and the good Shepherd have been rejected ; with this difference only, that here the threatening is expressed conditionally, and there absolutely, since the Lord reveals to the Prophet that the condition of the Divine judgements, the development of the germ of ungodliness already existing in his time, would actually ensue, and the greatest portion of the people would not fulfil the condition of the prosperity by true repentance.

CHAP. 1. 7.   Chap. 6. 15

493. The second revelation, imparted to the Prophet in the same year, in the eleventh month and twenty-fourth day, consists of a series of visions which all belong to one night, and furnish a complete image of the future destinies of the people of God.

1. *The Vision of the Rider among the Myrtle Trees*

Chap. 1. 7—17

494. In the stillness of night, when the soul, freed from the bonds imposed by external objects, is strengthened for the contemplation

of Divine things, the Prophet, not in a dream, but an ecstasy, sees a proud horseman on a red horse, who halts among the myrtle bushes of a deep valley, surrounded by red, bay, and white horses. He recognises, in the horseman in front, the angel of the Lord; in his companions, his ministering angels. He asks an angel, who approaches him, and makes himself known as the *interpreting angel*, concerning the import of the vision. By his mediation he receives from the angel of the Lord the disclosure, that the horsemen are the servants of the Lord, who traverse the whole earth to execute His commission. For what object, he learns from the account which they render to the angel of the Lord, in his presence, and audible by him, since the *interpreting angel* has opened his ears. They have found the whole earth quiet and peaceful. From this account, which places the sad condition of the people of the Lord in a stronger light, by contrasting it with the prosperous condition of the heathen, the angel of the Lord takes occasion to offer an intercession for the former with the Most High God, in which he earnestly inquires, whether, since the seventy years of affliction destined by Him for the people according to the prediction of His prophet Jeremiah, have long since passed away, there is still no deliverance for them to be expected. He receives from the Lord a consoling answer. This is communicated by the *interpreting angel*, together with a charge to make its contents publicly known. They are as follows. The vengeance of the Lord shall in His own time overtake the nations, as they now are peaceful and prosperous, who have executed His commission to punish the covenant people, not from regard to His will, but to gratify their own desires, and at the same time with a malicious cruelty which went beyond His commands. In like manner also shall the promises made to the covenant people be fulfilled, although they seem to be delayed. They shall receive rich proofs of the enduring election of God; the building of the Temple shall be completed; Jerusalem shall arise from its ruins.

495. The following remarks may promote a nearer insight into the import and object of this vision. It is very important in order to an understanding of this, as well as the following visions, to inquire whether the *interpreting angel* is identical with ' *the angel of the Lord*,' or different from him. The former is asserted by the majority of interpreters [1]; the latter by Vitringa, with whom we decidedly agree. In favour of their identity the following arguments are urged. (1.) " In the ninth verse, where the Prophet addresses the *interpreting angel* by ' *my Lord*,' the address must necessarily be directed to ' *the angel of the Lord* ;' since no other person had been mentioned before." But in arguing thus, it is overlooked, that in the prophecies generally, and especially in the visions (agreeably to their dramatic character), persons are very often introduced as speaking, or are spoken to, without being previously mentioned. (2.) " In the ninth verse, the *interpreting angel* promises the Prophet a disclosure con-

---

[1] Mark, Ch. B. Michaelis, Rosenmüller.

cerning the import of the vision. This, however, is imparted [1] by ' the angel of the Lord,' who must therefore be identical with the *interpreting angel.*" But it is said, in the ninth verse, " I will make thee to *see* what these are." This relates to the opening of the spiritual eyes and ears of the Prophet. Until this was done by the *interpreting angel* the Prophet would not be able to understand the declaration of the angel of the Lord, and the report made to him by the ministering angels ; compare the first verse of the fourth chapter, according to which the *interpreting angel* awakens the Prophet, as a man who is awakened from sleep. (3.) " According to the twelfth verse, the angel of the Lord presents an intercession to the Most High God for the covenant people. According to the thirteenth verse, the Lord returns to the *interpreting angel,* good, consoling words ; but now it is not to be supposed that he who receives the answer is any other than he who makes the inquiry." It may, however, here be assumed, either with Vitringa, that the Prophet has only omitted the circumstance, that the answer was in the first place directed to the angel of the Lord, and afterwards conveyed by him to the *interpreting angel,* or, which is more probable, that the Lord directed the answer immediately to the *interpreting angel,* because ' the angel of the Lord ' had inquired, not indeed on his own account, but only in order to impart consolation and hope through the *interpreting angel* to the Prophet, and through him to the people.

496. On the contrary, the following arguments go to prove the *interpreting angel* to be different from the angel of the Lord.

497. (1.) Even the constant designation of the *interpreting angel* by ' *the angel who talked with me,*' serves to designate him as a different person from ' the angel of the Lord.' This would not be the case, if the designation occurred only where an address of the angel to the Prophet had preceded. But its occurrence elsewhere also [2] shows, that it relates not to a single action, but to the *office* of the angel,—*angelus collocutor,* or *interpres.* In order to make the designation known as a *name of office,* the Prophet employs it exclusively, without the smallest deviation [3].

498. (2.) The fifth and three following verses of the second chapter are entirely decisive. The Prophet there sees a form occupied in measuring the future circumference of Jerusalem. The *interpreting angel* withdraws himself from the Prophet, in order to make inquiries for him concerning the import of the vision. But he has not yet reached his goal, when another angel meets him with the command, " Run, say to this young man," &c. The identity of the *interpreting angel* with ' *the angel of the Lord*' being assumed, the latter would receive commands in an authoritative tone from an inferior angel, which is entirely irreconcilable with the high dignity in which he elsewhere constantly appears, and particularly in Zechariah. To this

---

[1] Ver. 10.   [2] Comp. e. g. ver. 9. 13.

[3] Without ever exchanging the construction of the verb דבר with ב for that with עם or את elsewhere common, which may be explained by the circumstance, that the words were carefully treasured up in the mind of the hearer.

it must be added, that he who measures Jerusalem is in all probability the angel of the Lord himself. This being assumed, his
identity with the *interpreting angel* becomes the more improbable,
since the latter is with the Prophet at first, and afterwards withdraws
from him, to make inquiries about the vision.

499. (3.) It is remarkable, that a Divine work or a Divine name
is never attributed to the *interpreting angel*, as to the angel of the
Lord, that his agency is always confined to communicating higher
commands to the Prophet, and giving him insight into the visions,
which are never through him, but always through the Lord [1], presented to the inward contemplation of the Prophet.

500. (4.) The result already obtained is confirmed by a comparison of it with what occurs in other writings of the Old Testament.
In the thirty-fourth verse of the thirty-second chapter of Exodus,
another angel is associated with the highest revealer of God, ' the
angel of the Lord,' as standing to him in the same relation which *he*
sustains to the Most High God. But what is found in Daniel on
this subject is peculiarly important in the interpretation of Zechariah.
The angel of the Lord, the great Prince, who represents his people [2],
appears there under the symbolical name of *Michael*. As a mediator
between *him* (who is present for the most part in silent majesty, and
only sometimes, as here, speaking a few words), and the Prophet,
Gabriel appears, whose office it is to interpret the visions to Daniel,
and enable him to understand them [3].

501. The angel of the Lord halts on a red horse among the
myrtle bushes, in a deep valley. The latter is a striking image of
the Theocracy,—not a proud cedar on a high mountain, but a modest
yet lovely myrtle in a deep valley [4]. While outward splendour surrounded the kingdoms of the world, the kingdom of God was always
small and obscure, and appeared, especially at that time, to be near
its extinction. That the angel of the Lord halts among the myrtle
bushes indicates the high protection which the Church of God, helpless in itself, enjoys. The import of the appearance of the angel of
the Lord as sitting on a horse, and that a red horse, we cannot better
express than in the words of Theodoret: " *He sees him sitting on a
horse with reference to the swiftness of what is done: and the redness
of the horse declares his indignation against the hostile nations.*"
Red is the colour of blood; it is in red garments [5] that the angel of
the Lord comes from Bozrah, after he has crushed the enemies of his
kingdom; it is on a red horse [6] that Satan appears, to whom it is
given to take peace from the earth, that men shall slay each other,
and who bears a great sword. By the colour of the horse, therefore,
is symbolized what the angel of the Lord [7] says of himself: ' *I am
inflamed with great wrath against the secure and quiet nations* [8].'—
The inferior angels, which surrounded the angel of the Lord, sym-

---

[1] Comp. 2. 3. 3. 1.   [2] Ch. 12. 1. comp. Zech. 1. 12.   [3] Comp. 8. 16. 9. 21.
[4] Similar is the comparison of the Theocracy with the still waters of Siloa, in
contrast with the roaring waters of the Euphrates. Isa. 8.
[5] Isa. 63.   [6] Apoc. 6. 4.   [7] Ver. 15.
[8] Comp. Isai. 47. 6.

bolize the thought, that all means for the prosperity of his people
and the destruction of his enemies are at his command. The colour
of their horses signifies the judgements impending over the latter,
about to be executed with victorious might. *White* is the colour of
victory ; compare the second verse of the sixth chapter of the
Apocrypha : ' *And I saw, and behold a white horse : and he that sat
on him had a bow ; and a crown was given unto him : and he went
forth conquering, and to conquer.*' That the angels are sent to spy
out the condition of the earth, and that they bring back the answer,
that the whole earth is at rest, is designed to symbolize the thought,
that it is now time for the accomplishment of the promises in favour
of the covenant people, and the threatenings against their enemies.
There reigned in the second year of Darius a general peace ; all the
nations of the former Chaldean kingdom enjoyed a peaceful and
uninterrupted prosperity. Even the Babylonians [1] had soon recovered from the disadvantages they had suffered from the capture of the
city by Cyrus, which was still rich and prosperous. Judea alone,
the seat of the people of God, exhibited a mournful aspect ; the
capital still lay for the most part in ruins ; no protecting walls surrounded it ; the building of the Temple, which had been some
months before re-commenced at the exhortation of Haggai, had
hitherto been obstructed by difficulties which the dispirited people
despaired of being able to overcome ; the number of inhabitants was
but small ; the greatest portion of the land still lay waste [2]. This
state of things must have been a great temptation to the pious, and
have served the wicked as an excuse for their ungodliness [3]. It
required great strength of faith, under such circumstances, not to
doubt either the truth of God or His omnipotence. His promises to
the covenant people had only begun to be fulfilled, and that in a
small degree, by their return ; his predicted judgements upon
Babylon extended much further than to a mere capture of the city,
and even this beginning of their fulfilment had apparently ceased,
since the city was continually regaining its former prosperity. To
counteract the temptations, destructive of all active zeal for the
Theocracy, which this condition of things must bring with it, is the
object of the prophecy. That ' the angel of the Lord' appeared as
protector of his people afforded them of itself a rich source of consolation. That he presented an intercession for his people showed
still more clearly that the time of compassion was at hand. For *his*
intercession cannot be in vain, nor the will of God unknown to him.
By the answer, which the Lord imparts to him, must every remnant
of fear and despondency be removed ; it showed that his promises

---

[1] That to them the words, "the whole earth is at rest," principally refer,
appears from ver. 15. Jun. and Trem. appropriately remark : " *Delitias agit
Babylonius et quisquis adversarius ecclesiæ, dum ecclesia tua maximis tempestatibus
agitatur.*"

[2] Comp. Neh. 1.

[3] Comp. Mal. 2. 17, where the latter inquire, " Every one that doeth evil is
good in the sight of the Lord, and He delighteth in them; or, Where is the God
of judgement ? " and 3 15, " Therefore we praise only the despisers, for the
ungodly increase ; they tempt God, and all goes well with them."

and threatenings would certainly be fulfilled, though gradually, and at the time determined in His holy and wise counsel.—We have now still to remark a few words concerning the fulfilment. Its commencement ensued even in the nearest future. The rebellion of the Babylonians, under Darius the son of Hystaspes, brought the city near to its predicted entire destruction. Not to insist that it may be regarded as a consequence of the capture by Cyrus, it inflicted upon the city still deeper wounds. A great slaughter was occasioned, and its walls were destroyed. The building of the Temple was happily completed in the sixth year of Darius. The arrival of Ezra, and somewhat later, that of Nehemiah, who restored the walls of the city, and greatly increased its population, were a strong proof to the people of the Divine mercy, and a sign of their enduring election. But we must not seek for the fulfilment in all its extent at this early period. The prophecies of Zechariah, like those of the earlier prophets, embrace the whole *compass* of the salvation and judgements of God, with the exclusion only of what had already taken place, as, namely, the capture of Babylon and the return of the covenant people. What, therefore, is here said in reference to the anger of the Lord upon Babylon, and the remaining enemies of the kingdom of God, has its completion only in their entire destruction; what is said of the renewed mercy of God towards His people, in the sending of the Messiah. The *beginning* of the fulfilment in the nearest future served the people for a pledge of the certainty of its completion.

2. *The Four Horns and the Four Smiths (Carpenters* in E. T.)

Chap. 1. 18

502. This vision also is of a consoling import. The Prophet sees four horns, and receives from the *interpreting angel* the disclosure, that they signify the enemies of the kingdom of God. He then sees four smiths, who break the horns in pieces. The sense is obvious. The enemies of the people of God shall be punished for their crimes; the Lord will secure His feeble Church against every assault[1]. The number of the horns (*four*) relates to the fact, that the covenant people were surrounded by enemies on *all sides*, all quarters of the heavens. This appears from the tenth verse; ' *According to all the four winds have I scattered you;*' but still more clearly from the sixth chapter, as we shall there see.

3. *The Angel with the Measuring Line*

Chapter 2

503. The symbolical apparatus is here but small. The Prophet, like Ezekiel before him[2], sees a form employed in measuring the future circumference of Jerusalem, since its present limits will not be

---

[1] The true interpretation was seen by Theodoret.
[2] Chap. 40. 3.

sufficient when the city shall be enlarged by the mercy of the Lord. This form is in all probability none other than ' the angel of the Lord ;' that the employment is entirely suited to *him*, who, as the protecting Lord of the covenant people, should accomplish this enlargement, needs no proof.   His sending an inferior angel to the *interpreting angel*, and imparting commands to him, indicates a higher dignity than that of an inferior angel.   We then have the advantage of an accurate agreement with Daniel, in the twelfth chapter, where the very same persons appear in action ; Michael (the angel of the Lord), in company with Gabriel (the *interpreting angel*) and another angel.   The *interpreting angel*, who had hitherto remained with the Prophet, who was a somewhat distant spectator of the scene, withdraws himself from him, in order to receive from ' the angel of the Lord' a disclosure concerning the import of his conduct. But scarcely has he departed, when ' the angel of the Lord ' sends him this disclosure by another angel, with the command to impart it to Zechariah.   From the designation of the latter, in the discourse of the angel, as "*this young man*," the youthful age of Zechariah at the time has been justly inferred ; but still there is certainly something else also as the ground of this designation.   This was perceived by Jerome, who remarks, "*Ad comparationem dignitatis angelicæ omnem humanam naturam pueritiam vocari, quia non angeli in nos, sed nos in angelos proficimus* [1]."   The interpreters have erred only in adopting exclusively one of the two references.   The youthful age of the Prophet is made prominent, because youth is a type of the condition of man in relation to God and His holy angels. What the other angel imparts to the *interpreting angel* for Zechariah is as follows: The city shall be extended far beyond its previous limits, and protected and · glorified by the Lord.   This should excite all the Jews remaining behind in Babylon to a speedy return to their native land, that they may participate with their brethren in the promised blessings, and escape the judgements which the Lord has determined upon Babylon, and all the other nations, who have showed themselves hostile to the covenant people.   Lastly, Jerusalem shall experience the highest exaltation from the fact, that the Lord Himself shall make her His dwelling-place ; the consequence of which will be, that many nations shall join themselves to the Theocracy when glorified by His presence. We have yet some remarks to make on this prediction.   (1.) '*Flee out of the north country, deliver thyself from Babylon* [2],' points to a great calamity coming upon Babylon.   That such a calamity actually fell upon the city under the reign of Darius the son of Hystaspes, we have already seen.   With these words, in the twelfth and thirteenth verses, are connected [3], since the general proposition, the annunciation that the angel of the Lord would punish the enemies of

---

[1] In like manner, Vitringa: " *Hominem brevis ævi multarum rerum imperitum, cœlestium maxime ignarum non tam contemtus, quam differentiæ causa appellat* נער, *et liceat dicere rudem, multa docendum, quo eodem sensu Ezechiel passim* בן אדם *appellatur.*"

[2] Ver. 10, 11.   [3] By the causative כי.

his people for their crimes, and that in such a manner that they would fall under the power of Israel, as it happened in respect to several neighbouring people in the time of the Maccabees, constitutes the ground of the special direction which had preceded. Hence it appears with what justice some have denied the genuineness of the second part of Zechariah, because several nations are threatened in it with Divine judgements, who in his time were subject to the Persians. If *their* independence could be inferred from this, so also could that of the Babylonians from this prophecy and the foregoing, and therefore *even the first part* could not belong to Zechariah. (2) The prediction of prosperity for Jerusalem here also relates in the end to the time of the Messiah. We must refer exclusively to this time what is said [1] of the dwelling of the Lord with Jerusalem, and the consequent pressing of the heathen nations to the Theocracy, as a splendid demonstration of the Divine mercy, which (according to the seventeenth verse) all flesh shall behold with astonishment and wonder. That he, who will glorify the Theocracy by his presence, is ' the angel of the Lord,' the sharer of His dignity and His name, who, according to the predictions of the Prophets, shall appear in the Messiah, is evident from the fifteenth verse, ' *And then will I dwell in the midst of thee, and thou shalt experience that the Lord of Sabaoth has sent me to thee.*' According to this, he, who will dwell in the midst of the covenant people, in like manner as he was formerly present among them in the pillar of cloud and of fire, is the same, who, being now sent from the Most High God, brings to the people, through the Prophet, this glorious message, and who, in the fourteenth verse, is called Jehovah, and is here distinguished from Him as the ambassador from Him who sends him. That he is identical with the Messiah, appears from the ninth verse of the ninth chapter, where the arrival of the latter is announced to the people in almost the same words : here, ' *Sing and rejoice, O daughter of Zion, for behold I come ;*' there, ' *Rejoice greatly, O daughter of Zion, shout, O daughter of Jerusalem, behold the king cometh unto thee.*'

504. The eleventh chapter gives a further explanation, according to which ' the angel of the Lord,' appearing in the person of the Messiah among the people, with whom he had hitherto been invisibly present, and whom he had represented before God, undertakes to exercise the office of shepherd over them. While here, in the ninth chapter, only the bright side, there, in accordance with the fifth chapter, at the same time the dark side, the unbelief of the greatest part of the people in the manifested Messiah, and his rejection, is prominently exhibited. The reference of the prophecy to the Messianic times was acknowledged by the older Jewish interpreters in Jerome, as well as by Kimchi and Abarbanel.

[1] Ver. 14, 15.

4. *The High Priest Joshua before the Angel of the Lord*

Chapter 3

505. Ver. 1. ' *And (the Lord) showed me Joshua, the High Priest, standing before the angel of the Lord, and Satan standing at his right hand to oppose him* [1].' The subject in, " *he* showed me," is without doubt *the Lord,* as the Seventy and Jerome have already perceived. It is the most natural, because he had mentioned Him immediately before, and that in a sentence which is immediately connected with this [2]. In addition to this, is the comparison of the third verse of the second chapter, ' *The Lord* showed me four smiths.' According to the common supposition, the subject is the ' *angel who talked with him;*' but uniformly only the *interpretation,* not *the presenting of the images,* belongs to him. The expression, ' *the High Priest,*' stands here [3] with peculiar emphasis. It shows, that Joshua is not here considered according to his *person,* but his *office ;* not according to his *private,* but his *public* character. The phrase, ' *standing before the angel of the Lord,*' is, for the most part, misunderstood by interpreters. They regard it as a judicial expression ; the angel of the Lord is supposed to appear as a judge, Satan as an accuser, Joshua as one accused. Considerable injury has thus been done to the interpretation of the whole vision. The expression, ' to *stand before* any one,' is never spoken of the appearance of the *accused* before the *judge,* but rather always of the appearance of the *servant* before the *lord,* to tender him his services and await his commands [4]. Accordingly the Prophet here also sees the High Priest Joshua, as such, engaged in serving ' the angel of the Lord,' who in the second verse appears under the name *Jehovah,* which belongs to God alone, and who, in the fourth verse, ascribes to Himself a work exclusively divine, *the forgiveness of sins.* Joshua implores His mercy for himself and the people, and presents to Him prayers and intercession [5]. The following also, ' *and Satan stood at* (properly *over*) *his right hand,*' is commonly misunderstood. Proceeding on the supposition

---

[1] The *fut.* with *vav convers.* closely connects this vision with the foregoing, and gives us one of a series of visions granted to the Prophet in the same night.

[2] By the *vav convers.*   [3] As ver. 8, and chap. 6. 11.

[4] Comp. e. g. Gen. 41. 46, ' Joseph was thirty years old when he *stood before* Pharaoh.' 1 Sam. 16. 21, ' And David came to Saul and *stood before him,* and he loved him greatly, and he became his armour-bearer.' 1 Kings 1. 28. 10. 8, Deut. 1. 38. But the phrase is most frequently employed in reference to the service of the Lord ; those of the prophets, 1 Kings 17. 1. ' Elias saith, As the Lord liveth, *before whom I stand,*' Jer. 18. 20. Of the whole people, 2 Chron. 20. 13, but chiefly of the priests, for whose service it became a technical term ; comp. Deut. 10. 8, ' At this time the Lord separated from the tribe of Levi,—to *stand before* the Lord, to serve him, and to bless in his name,' 2 Chron. 29. 11 : ' My sons, be not slack, for the Lord has chosen you to *stand before him,* to serve him, and present to him incense.' Ps. 135. 2, ' The servants of the Lord who *stand* in the house of the Lord.' Judges 20. 27, ' Phineas *stood before* the Lord at that time.' Deut. 17. 12.

[5] Theodoret, τὰς ὑπὲρ τοῦ λαοῦ πρεσβείας προσφέρων τῷ Θεῷ.

already shown to be false, that a judicial trial is here represented, this has been referred to an alleged custom of the ancient Hebrews (for which, however, there is no proof), in accordance with which the accuser stood on the right hand of the accused [1]. But that by *standing on the right hand* in this passage, a *violent* and *successful assault* is signified, appears especially from the two parallel passages. In the twelfth verse of the thirtieth chapter of Job, ' *Upon my right hand rise the youth;* they push away my feet, and they raise up against me the wages of their destruction;' and in the ninth verse of the hundred and sixth Psalm, ' Set an ungodly man over him, and let an adversary *stand at his right hand.*'—The scene is accordingly as follows : The High Priest is in the Sanctuary, the building of which has been commenced, employed in supplicating the mercy of ' the angel of the Lord;' who, in order to testify his good pleasure, condescends to appear in the Temple [2], attended by a host of angels. Satan, the sworn enemy of the Church of God, sees with envy the restoration of a state of reconciliation between her and the Lord. He endeavours to interrupt it by his accusations. The supposition of some of the older interpreters [3], that Sanballat and his associates, who endeavoured to hinder the building of the Temple, are here figuratively represented by Satan, needs no refutation. It is at once shown to be groundless by a comparison of the prologue to Job, which Zechariah, who always imitates those who had gone before him, had certainly in view [4]. This comparison is also important, inasmuch as it teaches us, what here belongs to the drapery and what to the subject. In both places, and in the tenth verse of the twelfth chapter of the Apocalypse, where Satan is called ' *the accuser of our brethren,—which accused them before our God day and night,*' the doctrinal import is merely, that Satan makes every effort to deprive the individual believer and the whole Church of the mercy of God. That to this end he appears before God in heaven, or in the temple at Jerusalem, as an accuser, appertains only to the poetical or prophetico-symbolical representation, whose essence requires that it should present spiritual relations in a sensible form to the contemplation.—It remains only to inquire, what means Satan employed, in order to build up a partition wall between the High Priest and ' the Angel of the Lord [5].' The correct view is as follows. The High Priest appeared here, as has been already shown, in the discharge of his office, and represented in some measure the whole people [6]. This appears, among other passages, from the twenty-seventh and twenty-eighth verses of the twentieth chapter of Judges, where the High Priest Phinehas says to the Lord, ' *Shall I yet again*

[1] The truth was seen by Werner in his valuable treatise, *De Josua Summo Sacerd. ex Zach.* 3. 8. Jena, 1741.

[2] Comp. ver. 7.   [3] Kimchi, Drusius.

[4] Comp. also there chap. 1. 10, with Zech. 6. 5.

[5] The views rejected by Hengstenberg are (1) that the charge of Satan against the High Priest was the marriage of his sons with foreign women (a supposition incautiously adopted from the Jewish interpreters by Jerome), and (2) that he had *no* well-founded charge to bring.

[6] Cyril: ὁ δέ γε ἱερεὺς νοηθείη ἂν ἀντὶ παντὸς τοῦ λαοῦ.

*go out to battle against the children of Benjamin, my brother, or shall
I cease? And the Lord said, Go up; for to-morrow I will deliver
them into thine hand.'*

506. Just as[1] the sins of the High Priest were imputed to the
people, "if the anointed priest sins to the making of the people
guilty,"—so, on the other hand, the High Priest appears before the
Lord laden with the sins of the whole people, whose representative
he was. This representative character of the High Priest is, moreover, here peculiarly evident, since the grounds whereby the Lord[2]
rebukes the assault of Satan refer, not to him *personally*, but to the
relation of the whole people to the Lord. It is only in this way that
the object and import of the whole vision are placed in their true
light. The people, after their return from exile, mindful of the
grievous sins of their fathers, conscious of their own sinfulness, and
beholding in what was visible only the first and faintest manifestations of the Divine mercy, began to despair of the same; they believed that God had for ever rejected the high priesthood, which He
had established as a mediatorial office between Him and them. This
despair of the mercy of God could not but be attended with equally
injurious consequences as false security. Among these, remissness
in the work of rebuilding the Temple, which has been unduly magnified by many interpreters, was *only one*, and that comparatively
unimportant. Experience shows, that all fear of God ceases with
despair of the forgiveness of sins, as the Psalmist of old expresses the
close connexion between them by the words, ' *For with thee there is
mercy and plenteous forgiveness, that thou mayest be feared.*' The
Prophet now represents the Lord, in a glorious manifestation of Himself, not indeed as lulling the people to repose in their sins from a
false trust in their own righteousness, but as giving them the assurance, that, notwithstanding the greatness of their sins, He would of
His free mercy continue as before the office of High Priest, and
accept his mediation, until the time should hereafter come, when the
true High Priest, he of whom Joshua was only a type, should appear
and accomplish a perfect and perpetual reconciliation.

507. Ver. 2. ' *And the Lord said to Satan; The Lord rebuke
thee, thou Satan, the Lord rebuke thee, he who chooses Jerusalem.
Is not this a brand rescued from the fire?*'

508. It is not on the *worthiness* of Joshua and the people, but on
his *own election alone*, on his compassion shown in the restoration of
the people from exile, and which he could not now deny without
contradicting himself, that the Lord grounds His rebuke of Satan's
accusation[3].

509. The *election* stands opposed to the *temporary rejection* during

---

[1] According to Lev. 4. 2.   [2] Ver. 2.

[3] Excellently Cyril: ὅμοιον γὰρ ὡς εἰ λέγοι, τυχὸν πεπλημμέληκεν ὁμολο-
γουμένως ὁ Ἰσραὴλ, καὶ ταῖς σαῖς φιλοψογίαις ἐπεσχημένος ὁρᾶται, πλὴν
ἐκτέτικε δίκας οὐ μετρίως, ἀνέτλη τὰς συμφορὰς, ἐξεσπάσθη μόλις, ὡς ἐκ πυρὸς
δαλὸς ἡμίφλεκτος· οὕτω γὰρ τὰ ἐξ αἰχμαλωσίας ἀπεικονίσατο βλάβη, ἄρτι καὶ
μόλις τῆς ἀνηκέστου ταλαιπωρίας διέδρα τὴν φλόγα, παῦσαι δὴ οὖν ἐγκαλῶν
τοῖς ἠλεημένοις· Θεὸς γὰρ ὁ δικαιῶν, τίς ὁ κατακρίνων;

the Babylonian exile [1]. It had continued even during that period, but *its manifestation* had been prevented. This had recommenced with the return from exile [2], and no machination of Satan should hinder it any more.—The expression, '*a brand rescued from the fire,*' is taken from the eleventh verse of the fourth chapter of Amos, '*Ye are as a brand rescued from the fire,*' as a designation of a great calamity, which nevertheless, through the mercy of the Lord, has not issued in a total destruction.—In the words, '*the Lord said; The Lord rebuke thee,*' the Lord and His Angel are indeed distinguished from each other, yet the latter is made equal with the former in respect to the Divine dignity and honour.

510. Ver. 3. '*And Joshua was clothed in unclean garments, and stood before the Lord* [3].' The *filthy garments* [4] signify *sins*, with reference to the ordinance which required the High Priest to appear before the Lord only in clean garments. The High Priest, engaged in the service of the Lord, appeared before Him, not in the purity required by the Law, but laden with his own sins and those of the people. Satan sought to find therein the surest handle for his attack, but he deceived himself. The Lord, who had purified His people, yet not as silver [5], and who was satisfied, though the furnace of affliction had removed only the coarsest dross of sin, and had produced in the people the beginning of true repentance, a hunger and thirst after righteousness, which must not be stifled by severity, but nourished by being met with kindness, imparted to them of His grace, what they did not possess; He granted to the High Priest, and in him to the people, the gift of justification.

511. Ver. 4. '*And he answered and spake to those who stood before him, Take away from him the unclean garments; and he said to Joshua, Behold I take away from thee thy sin, and they shall clothe thee with festal garments.*' As the *filthy garments* are a symbol of *sin*, so the putting on *clean and splendid garments* at the command of the Lord, signifies the *imparting of forgiveness and justification* [6]. '*Those who stood before the Lord,*' or before His Angel, are His *higher servants*, the Angels [7]. These are to adorn His inferior servant with the *sign* of forgiveness, which *He only can grant*.

---

[1] Comp. 1. 17.   [2] Comp. Rom. 11. 1, sqq.

[3] According to several interpreters (Eichhorn, Theiner, &c.) the unclean garments signify the condition of the accused, who, among the Romans, thus appeared before a tribunal, and were called *sordidati*. But no trace of such a custom is found among the Hebrews.

[4] According to the frequent usage of Scripture (e. g. Is. 64. 5, 'We are all as an unclean thing, and all our righteousness as a filthy garment.' Is. 4. 4. Prov. 30. 12).

[5] Is. 48. 10.

[6] A similar symbolic representation of the forgiveness of sins is found in Is. 6. 6. The Prophet, on beholding the Divine holiness, regards himself as undone, because he is unclean, and dwells among a people of unclean lips. "And then flew to me one of the seraphim, and in his hand was a red-hot stone (fire, a symbol of purification),—and he caused it to touch my mouth, and said, Behold this touches thy lips, and thine iniquity is done away, and thy sin is forgiven."—The true interpretation was seen by Vitringa, on Zechariah 1. 11.

[7] Comp. Is. chap. 6.

512. Ver. 5. '*And I said, Let them place on him, moreover, a clean turban; and they placed on him a clean turban, and put on him garments, and the angel of the Lord was still present.*'—The Prophet, hitherto only a silent spectator and narrator, emboldened by love towards his people, here suddenly comes forward as one of the actors.

513. Several interpreters suppose, that, by the bestowing of *clean garments* upon the High Priest, the forgiveness of his sin, so far as he was a representative of the people, was signified; by the putting on of the *clean head-dress*, on the contrary, the confirmation of his office. But this supposition is clearly erroneous, since the clean turban must symbolize the same as the clean garments. Moreover, it could not then be explained, why the putting on of the turban *precedes* that of the garments. The true interpretation is rather as follows. The Prophet designs to express the thought, that the Lord imparts to the High Priest, and through him to the people, entire purity before him. This thought he thus symbolizes. The Lord gives merely the command to put clean garments upon Joshua. But, before this was accomplished, the Prophet prays that the unclean part of the clothing of the High Priest, of which nothing had been said in the command, might also be removed. His prayer is heard, and Joshua is now clothed anew from head to foot: hence the putting on of the turban precedes. That the 'Angel of the Lord' remains present during the whole action, not committing the execution of his order solely to his servants, is a proof of his high esteem and tender concern for his people.

514. Ver. 7. '*And the angel of the Lord testified to Joshua and said.*'

515. Ver. 8. '*Thus saith the Lord; If thou wilt walk in my ways, and keep my commandments, thou shalt judge my house and guard my courts, and I will give thee guides among these my servants.*' The cleansing of the High Priest from sin, and of the people through him, is here followed by his confirmation in his office, including also a promise for the people; since the High Priest being the mediator between God and them, the people could not be rejected, so long as the High Priest, in his official character, remained acceptable to God. The opposite of what is here promised had taken place in the times of the Babylonian exile [1]: "*Thy first father* (the High Priest, as is evident from the parallelism, and from the twenty-eighth verse) *has sinned, and thy mediators have transgressed; therefore I profane the princes of the sanctuary, and give Jacob to the curse.*" The judging or ruling of the house of God signifies *supremam curam rerum sacrarum*. The guarding of the courts of the Lord implies the obligation resting upon the High Priest carefully to keep away every thing idolatrous and ungodly, first from the outward Temple [2], and then from the Church of God, of which the Temple was the central point. Here this appears, not as a duty, but as a reward, inasmuch as activity in promoting the kingdom of God is the highest honour and mercy which God can grant to a sinful mortal.—In the words, '*I give thee*

---

[1] Comp. Is. 43. 27, 28.   [2] Comp. 2 Chron. 19. 11. 23. 18. Jer. 29. 26.

guides among those who stand there,' the Lord promises to His inferior the aid of His higher servants[1].

516. Ver. 8. ' *Yet hear, O Joshua, High Priest, thou and thy companions, who sit before thee ; for ye are types ; for behold ! I bring my servant the Branch*[2].'

517. By the *companions of Joshua,* who, with him, are summoned to attend, are to be understood his colleagues, the priests of an inferior rank.   This appears (1) from the object of the whole prophecy. Joshua is spoken of throughout, not as a private person, but as a High Priest. He appears as occupied with the functions of his office ; he is addressed even in this verse emphatically as a High Priest. When, therefore, his companions are here spoken of, they cannot be such as were connected with him in any other relation, but only his colleagues in the priestly office.   (2) The addition, ' *who sit before thee,*' leads to the same conclusion.   This designates, not, as Michaelis erroneously supposes, the relation of the teacher to his pupils, but rather that of a president in a college to his associates, and, generally, that of a person of higher rank to his inferiors[3]. Joshua and his companions must listen to the promise of the Messiah with peculiar attention, *because,* as his types, they stand to him in a more intimate relation, because their order will be glorified through him, since he perfectly realizes the idea of it[4].—That by the *Servant of the Lord, the Branch,* was meant the *Messiah,* was

---

[1] One can scarcely conceive how this simple sentence should have been so frequently misunderstood. מהלכים is a Chaldee form of a participle in Hiph. instead of the usual מולכים. Hiph. in the sense *to guide.*

[2] The connexion with the foregoing is thus aptly given by Kimchi : " *Dicit, Quamvis adducam nunc vobis hanc salutem, adhuc adducam vobis salutem majorem, quam hanc, tempore, quo adducam servum meum Zemach.* It is commonly supposed that the original meaning of מופת is *demonstratio, ostensio ;* we, on the contrary, affirm it to be that of *astonishment* and *wonder.* מופת is used especially of a thing or a person, which attracts to itself *surprise* and *attention, because it typifies and predicts one that is future.*   Is. 8. 18, calls his sons, on account of the names prophetic of salvation, which the Lord had given to them, and thereby appointed them as types of the coming deliverance, *signs* and *wonders* (אותות and מופתים) in Israel. According to Is. 20. 3, the Prophet, as a type of the Egyptian people, goes naked three years for a *sign and wonder* upon Egypt. Ez. 12, 6, the Lord says to the Prophet, after he has commissioned him to typify by his actions the future destinies of Israel, " For I have set thee as a *wonder* for the house of Israel ;" comp. ver. 11, " Say, *I am your wonder,* as I have done, so shall ye do ; ye shall go into captivity." Ez. 24, the Prophet's wife dies ; in obedience to the command of the Lord, he durst not utter lamentations over her ; the attention of the people is thereby excited to the highest pitch, they suspect that there is a deeper reason for the conduct of the Prophet. They receive from the Lord the answer, " Ezekiel shall be to you *for a wonder ;* as all that he has done, ye shall do" (ver. 24, comp. ver. 27).   In all these passages מופת (which we have rendered *type*) corresponds to τύπος τῶν μελλόντων, with this difference only, that the latter exhibits merely the objective meaning of the thing, without regard to the subjective sensation produced by it.

[3] Comp. Ezek. 8. 1. Numb. 3. 4. 1 Sam. 3. 1. Such sessions of the priests, when the High Priest presided, were not unfrequent ; comp. Lightfoot on Matt. 26. 3. Lond. p. 517.

[4] Much difficulty has been occasioned to the interpreters by הֵמָּה, inasmuch as it appears to refer exclusively to *the companions* of Joshua, while *he himself,* as

the prevailing belief of the older Jews : in the Christian Church also this view was always predominant [1].—It now only remains to answer the question, in what sense the priests are here called types of the Messiah? It is impossible it should be any thing else than what constitutes the characteristic of their office. For that regard was had to the *office*, and not to the *person* of Joshua, is evident from the circumstance that his colleagues were associated with him. The characteristic of the priestly office consisted, however, in the mediation between God and the people, and this, in accordance with the circumstances of the latter, was exercised chiefly in procuring forgiveness of sins by sacrifice and intercession. The Messiah, therefore, can be represented as the antitype of the priesthood, only so far as he should *perfectly accomplish* the mediation and deliverance from sin, which was but *imperfectly accomplished* by it. This is further confirmed by the following arguments. (1) We have already seen that the people, troubled concerning the forgiveness of their sins, are consoled in what precedes by the assurance, that, notwithstanding their transgressions, the Lord would not reject the priesthood. When, therefore, hitherto the priesthood has been solely considered only in reference to the deliverance of the people from sin, and when Joshua has appeared as occupied in procuring it, how can it be thought otherwise, than that the antitypical High Priest here promised is contrasted with the typical, only in reference to the perfect deliverance from sin to be effected through him? (2) The Lord promises expressly, in the ninth verse, that He will remove the sins of the whole land through His servant. (3) Forgiveness of sin is a constant characteristic mark of the Messianic time. Zechariah [2] exhibits, as the chief blessing to be imparted to those who should look upon him who was pierced, that a fountain should be opened for them for all impurities and sins. But this passage derives the clearest light from the fifty-third chapter of Isaiah, where the Messiah is represented, at the same time, as the true sacrifice, and as the true High Priest. As the latter, he sprinkles many nations [3]; he presents a sin-offering [4]; he makes intercession for sinners [5]. The only difference between the two passages is, that here the method is not pointed out, as it is there, whereby the true High Priest shall effect the removal of sin. Finally, the Messiah appears as a High Priest also in the hundred and tenth Psalm.

518. Verse 9. '*For behold, the stone, which I have laid before Joshua, upon this one stone shall seven eyes be directed; behold, I*

the head, most completely typified the Messiah. This difficulty is removed by the remark, that the Prophet makes a sudden transition from the second person to the third, as if he had said, "Joshua and his companions should hear; for they are," &c. This is evident from ver. 9, where the discourse is concerning Joshua in the third person. Examples of a similar transition are very frequent : comp. e. g. Zeph. 2. 12, "Also ye Cushites, slain of my sword are *they*" (הם). Ezek. 28. 22, 'Behold, I come upon thee, Sidon, and glorify myself in thee, and they shall experience that I am the Lord, when I in her,' &c. Jer. 7. 4.

[1] Theodoret and Eusebius, who are followed by Grotius, &c. suppose *Zerubbabel* to be meant. See this notion refuted in the original work.

[2] Chap. 13. 1.   [3] Chap. 52. 15.   [4] Chap. 53. 10.   [5] Ver. 12.

will hew it out, saith the Lord of Hosts, and remove the sin of the land in one day.' The *for* shows, that this verse must be the reason of the proposition immediately before; " for I bring my servant, the Branch," in like manner as the first *for*, in the eighth verse, and the second must be respectively that of ' hear,' and ' they are types.' Appearances were altogether against the manifestation of the Messiah ; the miserable condition of the new colony seemed to cut off all prospect of the fulfilment of such splendid promises [1]. The Lord, therefore, the Almighty (Jehovah of Hosts), by pointing to His lively concern for the best good of the Theocracy, as the ground of these blessings, withdraws the attention from the outward appearance. That the seven eyes must not be regarded as *belonging to* the stone, but as *directed to it*, scarcely needs a proof, as is generally confessed by modern interpreters. It is sufficient even to refer to the tenth verse of the fourth chapter, where the seven eyes of the Lord are designated as those which look on the plummet in the hand of Zerubbabel, and are cited as having been already mentioned in what had preceded.—The eye of God is not seldom employed to designate the Divine Providence. It is, however, peculiar to Zechariah, that he designates the most special concern of God for the stone by the resting of his seven eyes upon it. It appears that he had here in view the symbolic representations of the Babylonians or Persians. That similar figurative designations were employed, particularly by the Persians, appears from the fact, that certain confidential servants of the king were called *his* EYES ; a designation probably borrowed from their theology, as the whole Persian kingdom was supposed to be a visible representation of the heavenly kingdom of Ormuz, of which the king was the representative.—It is further to be inquired, what is meant by the stone, to which the seven eyes are directed. It is almost unanimously supposed by the older interpreters to be the Messiah. But this is contradicted by ' *which I have laid before Joshua*,' whereby the stone appears as something already present only to be ornamented hereafter, as also by, ' *I will grave it.*' Others suppose it to be the foundation stone of the temple ; but we do not perceive how this was to be graved. The correct view is rather that the unhewn stone, to be polished and graven by the Lord, is an image of the Theocracy, and its seat, the Temple, signifying its present low condition, and its future glorification by the Lord. The stone is then with entire propriety described as lying before Joshua, since, as had been said in the seventh verse, the chief oversight of the Theocracy, at that time, devolved upon him. The polishing and graving of the rough, precious stone [2] consists pre-eminently in the sending of the Messiah, though without excluding the earlier mercies of God. According to the contemporary prophecy of Haggai [3], the second temple was to be filled with glory, and made more illustrious than the first, through him.—By *this* land is meant Judea, which (although the deliverance from sin to be effected by the Messiah should extend further, even over the whole

[1] Comp. chap. 4. 10.
[2] Comp. Exod. 28. 9. 11. 21. 36. 39. 30.   [3] Chap. 2. 7—10.

heathen world) is here alone mentioned, because in this whole prediction the Prophet aims only to comfort the troubled minds of his
people.—The expression, '*in one day*' (where day stands for the
shortest portion of time) implies, that the removal of sin, to be
effected by the Messiah, would not be continually repeated, like that
accomplished by the typical priesthood, but completed *in a single
action*.

519. Verse 10. '*At that time ye shall call one to another, To the
vine, and to the fig tree !*' These words contain an image of the rest,
peace, and prosperity, which would be a consequence of the forgiveness of sins procured by the Messiah.

5. *The Candlestick with the Two Olive Trees*

Chapter 4

520. Between this and the preceding vision a pause is to be supposed. The *interpreting angel* had withdrawn for a time from the
Prophet, and the latter, his ecstasy having ceased, had recovered his
ordinary condition of mind. '*And the angel who conversed with
me* (it is said in the first verse) *returned and awoke me, as a man
who is awakened from sleep.*' The condition of the Prophets while
prophesying, and their ordinary state, stand related to each other as
sleep to *being awake*. The ordinary condition, in which, given up
to sensible impressions, we are unable to raise the spiritual eye to
the contemplation of what is divine, is that of *spiritual sleep;* the
ecstasy, on the contrary, when the senses are at rest, and the whole
of our conscious agency ceases, and the images of divine things are
represented in the soul as in a pure and smooth mirror, is a state of
being *spiritually awake*. This sense, which is the only true one,
Cyril alone among all the interpreters has perceived, who remarks :
"*Our condition, in comparison with that of the angels, is to be
regarded as a state of sleep.*"

521. The new vision, which now presents itself to the Prophet, is
as follows : He sees a candlestick of pure gold, and on it an oil vessel, out of which the oil flows down into each of the seven lamps of
the candlestick through seven tubes. On both sides of the candlestick, and rising above, stand two olive trees. The *interpreting
angel*, after he has at once reminded the Prophet of his human weakness, and called his attention to the deep import of the vision by the
inquiry, '*Knowest thou not what this means*[1]*?*' gives the explanation
of it in these words : '*This vision* (so far as it was prophetical) *is
the word of the Lord to Zerubbabel; Not by might and not by power,
but by my Spirit, saith the Lord of Hosts. Who art thou, thou
great mountain before Zerubbabel? Become a plain! He brings
forth the top stone*[2] *with the shouting (of the angels), Grace, grace*

---

[1] Ver. 6, 7.

[2] So is האבן הראשה to be translated, not with most interpreters, *the foundation
stone*, as this had already been laid many years before ; comp. also ver. 9, " his

unto it !'   Accordingly this is the import of the vision ; the affairs of the Theocracy will not be promoted by human power, but by the Spirit of God alone, who animates, protects, sustains it.   The immediate object (for the accomplishment of which, this general truth, at all times valid for the Church of God, was here symbolized), was to impart consolation to the desponding people and their head, and thereby energy for a zealous prosecution of the erection of the Temple.   For of what consequence was it, if whole mountains of difficulties opposed this work, since it did not depend on human power, which indeed was not at hand, but the Lord had taken it wholly upon Himself?   In this interpretation what is general and what is special appear in their true relation to each other, which has been misunderstood by most interpreters.—Let us now see how the symbol and its signification are related to each other.   The candlestick is an image of the Theocracy ; the *point of comparison* is the light, which both possess and radiate into the surrounding darkness [1]. That the candlestick is entirely of the most precious metal, *gold*, signifies the excellency of the Church of God.   The two olive trees symbolize the Spirit of God ; the oil, which flows from them into the lamps and illuminates them, and causes them to give light, His influences on the Church of God.   The abundance of tubes, seven for each of the seven lamps, intimates the manifold ways in which the mercy of God flows to His Church, as well as its exuberance.

522. It is commonly supposed that the Prophet, in the representation of the symbol, has omitted through negligence, and afterwards introduces, in the eleventh and following verses, one circumstance, namely, that in the two olive trees were two boughs full of olives, which, lying in two *presses* [2], conducted the oil to the candlestick. But this omission was rather from design.   The mention of this special circumstance would have weakened the impression of the symbol as a whole, and have prevented the insight into its chief meaning.   The Prophet, therefore, does not direct the attention to this special circumstance, until he has learnt and explained the import of the symbol as a whole.   He first asks, in the eleventh verse, ‘ *What are these* two *olive trees?*’   This question does not relate to the import of the olive trees as such (for the Prophet has *already been informed* that they symbolize the Spirit of God), but to there being *two* of them.   Before, however, the Prophet receives the answer of the angel, he perceives that this *quality* of the olive trees is not of itself significant, that it has rather been chosen

hands have founded this house, and his hands will also *complete* it.”   Unless one chooses, which now appears to the author to be almost better, “ he *has* brought forth the ground stone.”   But if, according to the current interpretation, the *præter* is taken as the *præt. propheticum*, the explanation given in the text is indispensable.

[1] Comp. Apoc. 1. 20, “ The seven candlesticks are seven churches;” Luke 12. 5, the parable of the wise and foolish virgins, &c.

[2] So is צַנְתְּרוֹת in ver. 12, to be explained, as is evident, among other reasons, from בְּיַד, which cannot possibly be explained as it has been by many interpreters, by “ near by.”

merely on account of the significancy of the duality of the *boughs*. Accordingly he corrects himself, and in the twelfth verse puts the new question : " What do the two *ears* [that is, *loaded boughs*] of the olive trees, which are in the two golden presses, import[1] ? " And his receiving from the *interpreting angel* an answer only to *this* question, and not to the former, implies that the duality of the olive trees is not of itself significant. The answer is : " *They are the two children of oil, which stand before the Lord of the whole earth.*" The question now arises, who are the *two children of oil*, the servants of the Lord, κατ᾽ ἐξοχήν. Several interpreters suppose them to be Zerubbabel and Joshua. But that these, *considered as individuals*, could not be meant, is evident, because the supplying of the candlestick with oil (the imparting of the Divine mercy in the Theocracy) cannot be connected with the existence of two frail and dying men. Others, therefore, have rightly supposed, that by the two children of oil, the two whole orders were designated, which in the Theocracy eminently served as instruments of the Divine mercy, the sacerdotal and the regal, or, generally, that of the civil magistrates. These alone could be called *children of oil*, in order to designate the *official favour* bestowed upon them by God, which was symbolically represented by anointing. Compare, in reference to the High Priest, the important parallel passage, in the twelfth verse of the twelfth chapter of Leviticus. That this was no longer practised in the case of the *civil magistrates* after the exile, is nothing to the purpose : they were anointed in their predecessors, and the grace suited to their office, the thing expressed by the symbol, was continued to them. To assure this favour to them and the High Priests, and through this assurance to console and gladden the people, who believed themselves forsaken of God, is precisely the object of the present symbolic representation. The spiritual and the civil government shall continue, as in the former Theocracy, to be the medium through which the Lord imparts His gracious gifts to His Church. This promise in the highest and fullest sense was accomplished in the manifestation of Christ, who (according to the sixth chapter) was to combine both offices, that of a King and High Priest in his person, whom the Prophet represents in the third chapter especially as a High Priest, and in the ninth chapter as a King, and through whom the oil of the Divine favour, immeasurably richer than that imparted through all former servants of God, is poured into the candlestick of the Church.

6. *The Flying Roll*

Chapter 5 1—4

523. This vision, as well as the following, is of a mournful character. They show, like the eleventh chapter, that it was by no

---

[1] Kimchi : " *Comparat ramos olearum cum spicis, quod sicut hæ granis, sic illi olivis pleni essent.*"

means the object of the Prophet to promote at all events the building of the Temple, but that it was rather his principal purpose *to bring the people to repentance and faith*, which would necessarily be followed by zeal for the outward work, which had been commenced. Excited by the tenth verse of the second chapter of Ezekiel, the Prophet here sees a flying roll, twenty yards long and ten broad. Its dimensions coincide entirely with those of the porch of the Temple[1]. This cannot possibly be accidental, as several interpreters have supposed. The porch, the outermost part of the temple proper, was the place from which God was regarded as dealing with His people, in like manner as Solomon[2] judged the people in the *porch* of his palace. Before the porch, therefore, in the court of the priests stood the altar of burnt-offering. In a great public calamity the supplicating priests drew still nearer into the porch, to embrace as it were the feet of an offended father; compare the seventeenth verse of the second chapter of Joel, "*Let the priests, the ministers of the Lord, weep between the porch and the altar of the Lord, and say, Spare thy people, O Lord, and give not thine heritage to reproach.*" When, therefore, the Prophet gives to the flying roll the symbol of the Divine judgement upon the covenant people, the dimensions of the porch, he intimates, that this judgement is a consequence of the Theocracy. A similar symbolic representation occurs, when in the first verse of the sixth chapter the chariots, the symbols of the Divine judgements upon the nations hostile to the Theocracy, go forth from between the two mountains, the symbol of the Theocracy. The roll is inscribed on both sides[3]. On the *one side,* are the curses against those who abuse the name of the Lord by perjury; on the other, those against thieves. The one stands as an individual example of those who violate the commands of the first table; the other, of those who violate the commands of the second; so that the one side of the roll contains the Divine threatening against the transgressors of the command, "*Thou shalt love the Lord thy God with all thy heart;*" the other against the transgressors of the command, "*Thou shalt love thy neighbour as thyself*[4]." This curse was to go forth over the whole land; it was not merely to strike the transgressors slightly and superficially, but entirely consume them, with all that belonged to them.—In the expression, '*It consumes their house, and its wood, and its stone,*' is an allusion to the thirty-eighth verse of the eighteenth chapter of the first book of Kings. We have here, therefore, a prediction of a more severe judgement of God to be inflicted upon Judea, after the ungodliness, already at the time of the Prophet present in the germ, should have taken root and put forth boughs. How this ungodliness will lead the people to reject the Messiah, and thus deprive themselves of the last means of their deliverance, is further unfolded in the eleventh chapter.

---

[1] 1 Kings 6. 3.   [2] 1 Kings 7. 6.

[3] מִזֶּה וּמִזֶּה, exactly as the tables of the law, Exod. 32. 15, whence the expression is borrowed, and also as the roll, Ez. 2. 9, 10.

[4] This was seen by Theodoret.

7. *The Ephah and the Woman sitting therein*

Verses 5—11

524. The *interpreting angel*, who had withdrawn for a while into the choir of the heavenly angels, returns to the Prophet, in order to explain to him the import of a new vision. The Prophet sees a form as if rising from a mist, but is not able to recognise it. The angel instructs him, " *This is the Ephah which goes forth*," not, which is ungrammatical, "This, which goes forth, is an Ephah." It is by no means necessary to suppose, with Jonathan, that the Prophet alludes to *false* measures. Of this there is no trace in the text. The sense is rather: As the Israelites have *filled up the measure of their sins*, so also shall the *full measure of the Divine punishment* overtake them. As a symbol of this thought, the Ephah, one of the largest measures, was peculiarly suitable. That we are not, with several interpreters, to stop short at the sins, is shown by, ' This is the measure *which goes forth*,' which includes the idea of the Divine judgement, as the comparison of the second and third verse shows. The *exclusive reference* to the punishment, attempted by others, appears however to be refuted by the interpretation of the angel, ' *This is their eye in all the land*,' i. e. it is the effort of the whole people to fill up the measure of their sins, and thereby bring upon themselves a full measure of the Divine punishment. And, though one might indeed give prominency only to the *punishment*, ' *they are intent upon nothing but to draw down the Divine punishment with violence upon themselves*,' still a concurrent reference to the *sins* is manifest from what had gone before, where the Jewish nation, personified as a woman, is already sitting in the Ephah, before the Divine punishment breaks in upon them [1].—On a nearer view the Prophet perceives that a woman sits in the middle of the Ephah [2]: " *This was* (namely, what I saw ; i. e. behold there) *a woman sitting in the middle of the Ephah*." She is designated by the *interpreting angel* as *ungodliness* [3], the ungodly Jewish people, who, as they had heretofore sat in their sins, were now to be surrounded by their punishments. Thereupon the woman in the Ephah, in which she had hitherto sat upright, so that she appeared above it, is thrown down, and a great lump of lead laid upon her, symbolizing that the Lord by His judgement would arrest the people in their sinful course. Two winged women appear, and with the swiftness of wind bear the Ephah with the woman through the air into the land of Shinar. There the Ephah is let down, and the woman receives her permanent dwelling-place. The women, no doubt, designate the instruments, which God will employ for the punishment of His people, hostile nations, as formerly the Babylo-

---

[1] The word עין is not by any means *aspectus*, but *eye;* comp. chap. 9. 1, " To the Lord is the eye of men," for " The eye of the Lord is directed upon men."
[2] Ver. 7.   [3] Comp. Mal. 1. 4.

nians.—The *duality* belongs to the symbol, as such, not to the thing
signified by it; two persons being required for the carrying of so
great a measure as the Ephah.—Great difficulty has been occasioned
to the interpreters by the mention of *Shinar*, as the land into which
Israel should be carried away. It has led Rosenmüller to suppose
that the Prophet does not here *predict the future*, but *describe the
past*, the carrying away of the Jews to Babylonia. But this supposition is entirely untenable. All other visions of Zechariah relate to
the future; how should this only make an exception? Immediately
before, a future judgement is predicted; how then should this prediction refer to past times? And besides, the residence in Shinar, in
the eleventh verse, in contrast with the former, which was brief, is
represented as of long, and indeed as of perpetual duration. Ignorance of the custom of the Prophets, arising from the nature of the
prophetic vision, to represent the future under the image of the past,
and to call the former by the name of the latter, has led to these and
other unnatural assumptions. Of this custom we have here a splendid
and incontrovertible example, which serves completely to repel
several attacks (which arise from ignorance of it) against the genuineness of the second part. The future dwelling-place of the Jews
when driven out of their own land, the Prophet here designates without further explanation by the name of the country of their former
exile, just as he, in the eleventh verse of the tenth chapter, calls their
future oppressors by the names of *Ashur* and *Egypt*.

8. *The Four Chariots*

Chapter 6 ver. 1—8

525. The import of this vision stands in close connexion with the
foregoing. After (such is its simple meaning) Israel shall have been
visited by severe Divine judgements, equally fearful chastisements
shall be inflicted upon the instruments, which God had in part
employed in the punishment of His people; upon all nations, from
one end of the earth to the other. Here, therefore, the last general
judgement is described, which, according to the unanimous prediction of the prophets, will follow the partial judgement upon Israel,
and close the present course of the world. See further, on the twelfth
chapter, which is exactly parallel: as in general between the visions
of the first and the prophecies of the second part a remarkable parallelism exists, which will hereafter be more fully noticed.

526. We now take a nearer view of the imagery in which this
revelation is imparted to the Prophet.

527. He sees four chariots [1]. With respect to their import, he is
taught by the declaration of the *interpreting angel* [2], '*These are the
four winds of heaven, which go forth after they have appeared as
ministers before the Lord of the whole earth.*' The four winds of

---

[1] Ver. 1.   [2] Ver. 5.

heaven serve as a symbol of the Divine judgements. From their personification is explained the circumstance, that chariots are attributed to them, and that these are afterwards *identified* with the winds, of which they are to be considered as the *vehicles*. The figurative representation receives light from some passages of Jeremiah and Ezekiel, whom the Prophet seems here, as commonly, without prejudice to his independence, to have imitated. The Divine judgements breaking in from all sides appear also, in the thirty-sixth verse of the forty-ninth chapter of Jeremiah, under the image of the four winds : '*And I bring against Elam the four winds from the four ends of heaven, and I scatter them according to all these winds.*' In the first chapter of Ezekiel, the judgements to be extended over all regions of the earth are symbolized by the four cherubim, over whose heads the Lord is enthroned, and whose chariots are driven towards the regions for which they have been destined; by the wind, the Divine anger, or the Divine sentence of punishment [1], they come with a great storm from the *north*, to indicate that the Divine judgement breaks in upon Judah from Babylon. Similar also is the second verse of the seventh chapter of Daniel, '*I saw the four winds of heaven strive upon the great sea,*' a symbol of the whole multitude of the inhabitants of the earth, in the first verse of the seventh chapter of the Apocalypse, '*And after these things I saw four angels standing on the four corners of the earth, holding the four winds of the earth.*' The only difference is, that here, as in Ezekiel, *it is not the winds themselves* who ride on the chariots, but *angels, who are placed over the winds and driven by them.*

528. The chariots go forth from the two mountains, and these mountains are of brass. The judgement is hereby designated as a consequence of the Theocracy. The symbolic representation is to be explained from the geography of Jerusalem [2]. " A deep valley [3] runs parallel with the Jordan from north to south, but after a course of some hours turns eastward towards the Dead Sea. It is the very narrow *valley of Jehoshaphat,* and the *wadi* in it is the bed of the brook Kedron, which lies dry a great part of the year. On both sides of this valley, above where it turns towards the sea, steep hills of limestone rise to different heights ; three of their summits, on the east side of the brook, are naked on the eastern declivity, but on the western shaded with shrubbery, especially with olive trees, from which they have from the most ancient time borne the name of the Mount of Olives." That the Prophet had in view particularly the *valley of Jehoshaphat* appears from the parallel passage [4], where, in a sense to be hereafter determined, an extension of this valley, by the cleaving asunder of the Mount of Olives, is promised. '*And the Mount of Olives is divided in the midst, so that there is a great valley from west to east : and one half of the mountain falls back towards the north, and the other towards the south ; and ye flee through my valley of the mountains, for the valley of the mountains will reach to*

---

[1] Comp. ver. 12, as in ver. 4.
[3] βαθεῖα φάραγξ, *vallis profunda.*

[2] Ritter, Erdk. 2. p. 406.
[4] Chap. 14. 4.

Azal.' As, in the passage before us, the discourse relates to the valley between two definite mountains, so there the valley of Jehoshaphat is called, *by way of eminence,* '*the Lord's valley of the mountains.*'—But why does the Prophet, in order to designate the judgement as a consequence of the Theocracy, make the four chariots go forth particularly from this valley of the mountains? Because it lay under the *mountain* of the Temple, which was the dwelling-place of the Lord under the Old Covenant, and was the nearest place to it that was accessible to carriages. Here, therefore [1], the four winds of heaven stationed themselves, expecting the commands of the Lord. For a similar reason, because this place was the nearest to the Temple, which was suited to contain a great multitude of men, Joel [2] represents the Lord as *here* collecting the heathen nations for judgement. "*For behold, in those days, at the time when I shall restore Judah and Jerusalem, I will gather all nations, and will bring them down into the valley of Jehoshaphat, and will plead with them there for my people and for my heritage, Israel, whom they have scattered among the nations, and parted my land.*"—Wherefore were the two mountains called *brazen?* To indicate that the Lord surrounds His kingdom with a wall of protection, which can neither be scaled nor broken through. This truth was symbolized by the position of Jerusalem, as the Psalmist had already expressed it in the words, '*The mountains are round about Jerusalem, and the Lord surrounds his people.*' In order to make the type more conformable to the reality, the Prophet converts the mountains, which cover Jerusalem on the eastern side, into brass.—That the whole description is to be figuratively understood, and that we cannot infer from it that the Temple will be in existence at the time of the judgement upon all the nations of the earth, appears partly from this very designation of the mountains, partly from the foregoing chapter; according to which, before the coming of this judgement, Jerusalem shall be entirely destroyed and the people carried into exile.

530. The colour of the horses (as in the first chapter) indicates the destination of the chariots to execute judgement upon the enemies of God, red being the colour of blood, black that of mourning, white that of victory. Since no *significant* colour remained for the horses of the fourth chariot, the Prophet was compelled to give them an unmeaning colour, '*speckled*' ['grisled,' E. T.], and by a special epithet, '*strong,*' to signify the attribute, which, in the case of the others, was already implied in the colour [3].

531. After the Prophet, in the fourth and fifth verses, has received, in reply to his questions, information from the *interpreting angel* respecting the import of the four chariots, he describes in the sixth and seventh verses the direction which in inward contemplation he sees them take. '*The chariots with the black horses go forth towards the north country, and the white follow after them, and the speckled*

---

[1] Comp. ver. 5.   [2] Chap. 4. 1.

[3] Not perceiving this, the interpreters following Bochart (Hieroz. 1, p. 111, sqq.) have invented a meaning (*purpureus*) for אמצים

go towards the south country. And, as the strong went forth, they desired to go over the whole earth, and the Lord said, Go and pass over the earth, and they passed over the earth.' The difficulty here, which has given occasion to the interpreters for the most forced explanations, is, that the black horses of the second chariot are mentioned first, and that the red of the first appear to be entirely passed over. On a nearer inspection, however, this difficulty entirely disappears ; the red horses of the first chariot are here *the* strong (disregard of the article is the chief cause of the errours of interpreters), those *in comparison with which* the rest were to be regarded as weak, although in themselves considered they were strong, and had before in part been designated by the same epithet.—These are mentioned last, because feeling their power, and not satisfied like the rest with any particular portion of the earth, they desire permission of the Lord to go over the whole, whereby it is intended to express the thought that the judgement shall be strictly universal, no portion of the earth shall be exempted from it.

532. The chariot with the black and that with the white horses both go towards the north country. There must be a reason why this country is expressly mentioned, and two chariots depart for it. The inhabitants of the north country—according to constant usage, the Babylonians and Assyrians—had been in times past the most dangerous enemies of the covenant people. They, therefore, served the Prophet, in the fifth chapter, as a type of their future enemies. In order now to express the thought, that after the latter shall have returned again to the Lord[1], the former shall eminently experience the Divine chastisement, he makes the executioners of God's justice go forth in a peculiar manner towards the north country. That the north country is here to be understood, not properly, but typically, appears even from the foregoing chapter, where the Prophet calls the country of those whose punishment is here announced the land of Shinar, not in a literal but in a figurative sense.

533. Nearly the same is true in reference to the south country. On the south of Palestine dwelt the Egyptians, the first oppressors of Israel, who were elsewhere also combined by Zechariah with the enemies from the north, as a type of the future enemies of the covenant people[2]. That only one chariot departs for them, represents them as comparatively less guilty, since their misconduct from length of time now appeared in a less striking light.

534. The vision closes with an explanation of the Lord to the Prophet, concerning the design of the departure of the chariots. ' *Behold those which depart for the north country make mine anger to rest on the north country :*' compare the thirteenth verse of the fifth chapter of Ezekiel, ' *I make mine anger rest ;*' and the first verse of the ninth chapter of Zechariah, where the land of Hadrach and Damascus is represented as the *resting-place* of the Divine sentence of punishment, which included in itself the fulfilment. The explanation refers indeed in the first instance only to one part (which,

---

[1] Comp. chap. 12.   [2] Comp. chap. 10. 10, 11.

however, according to the above remarks, was the chief object of the
Divine judgement); but the Prophet could easily deduce from this
the destination of the rest sent forth under similar circumstances.

9. *The Crown on the Head of Joshua*
Verses 9—15

535. The future developments of the kingdom of God, which the
Prophet had described in the preceding context, the judgement upon
the former covenant people, as well as also, after their restoration,
upon the remaining people of the earth, had their cause and source in
the promised Anointed of the Lord, and presupposed his appearing.
To fix the attention of the Prophet, and through him that of the
people upon this point, it is once more presented to his inward contemplation towards the close of his ecstasy, and with this, as the
last words indicate, at once lovely and terrific image, the whole
series of visions, whose collective contents in some way refer to it, is
closed.

536. Ver. 9. ' *Then came the word of the Lord to me :* (ver. 10)
*Take from them of the captivity, from Heldai, from Tobijah, from
Jedaiah, and from Josiah the son of Zephaniah, who have come from
Babylon, when thou goest into the house of the last named ;* (ver. 11)
*take, I say, silver and gold, and make crowns, and place them on the
head of Joshua the son of Josedech, the High Priest.*' The prophecy
presupposes certain historical circumstances, the knowledge of which
is necessary in order to understand it. It appears that the Jews
(great numbers of whom remained in Babylonia), on hearing of the
rebuilding of the Temple, which had now been going on for five
months, had sent deputies with pecuniary aid to Jerusalem [1]. ' *And
then it happened* [2],' connects this vision with the foregoing; it was
delivered to the Prophet in the same night with the others, and contains a charge in respect to a symbolic action to be afterwards performed.—' *From them of the captivity,*' precedes the naming of the
particular persons, in order to indicate that these have not come
privatim, but as *representatives* and deputies of a whole corporation,
the Jews still living in the exile [3]. This *representative* character of
the individuals was important for the object of the Prophet. Only in
this respect were they suited to become a type of the heathen nations.

[1] This does not indeed appear from the expression ' *of the captives,*' or of the
exiles, in ver. 10. For הגולה in the Book of Ezra, is sometimes a designation, not
indeed of *those still in the exile*, but of *those already returned*, commonly called *the
sons of the captives*. It is manifest, however, from a comparison of ver. 15. There
the representatives of the ' *captivity* ' are described as a type of the distant
heathen nations, who will hereafter actively promote the building of the Temple
or Church of God. This type disappears, if by the captivity the exiles, who had
long since returned, are understood.

[2] וַיְהִי.

[3] Just as in chap. 7. 2, Scharezer and Regemmelech appear as deputies of the
Palestine Jews (' *The house, the church of the Lord sent Scharezer,*' &c.), and speak
in the name of the whole people, (' *Shall I weep,*' &c. ver. 3.)

—The interpreters, for the most part, suppose that only three deputies had come from Babylon, and that Josiah, the son of Zephaniah,
was the person by whom they were entertained at Jerusalem.   They
translate, ' *When thou goest into the house of Josiah, into which they
have come* ¹ *from Babylon.*' But this is contradicted by the fourteenth
and fifteenth verses, where Josiah appears as a partaker in the dedication of the crown, as a *joint type* of the distant heathen nations, who
should ' build in the temple of the Lord.'—The reason why the Prophet was to go into the house of Josiah probably was, that he was
the treasurer of the community, in whose house the presents which
had been brought were deposited.   In the view of the Prophet the
names of the deputies are as typical as their persons ; he regards
them as intimations of the attributes of those whom the persons
typified, and of the blessings destined for them.   This appears from
the comparison of the fourteenth verse.   There two of the deputies
bear a name different from that which here occurs, but of the same
import.   Heldai, ' *the robust,*' is there called Helem ' *the strong ;*'
Josiah, ' *God founds* (or) *sustains,*' is there Hen, ' *grace.*'   This va-
riation is designed to show that the names should be taken, not as
current coin, but in their original worth.   That the other names also,
besides those already explained,—Tobijah, *goodness of God*, Jedaiah,
God knows, Deus prospicit, and Zephaniah, *God protects*,—were
suited to the design of the Prophet, needs no further proof ².—*Take
silver and gold and make crowns.*   The Prophet was to obtain as
much of the silver and gold, which had been brought, as was requisite for executing the commission he had received from the Lord.
There is a difference among the interpreters with reference to the
number of the crowns to be made.   The common opinion is in favour
of two ; in support of which, it is said, that this number is required
to make the type correspond with the following prophecy, which
announces the union of the high-priestly and the regal dignity in the
person of the Messiah, and with the reality.   But against this argument Mark has already very justly objected : " *It is not here the
crown, but the person and office of Joshua, which leads us to think of
the priesthood.*"   One cannot perceive why that should be made
the subject of an additional type, which Joshua, as has been said in
the third chapter, already typified himself.   Besides, we find no trace
of two crowns, certainly not in the duality of the metals, which
might just as well be applied to one as to more.   Besides this, could
the name *crown*³ be given to the *head-dress of the High Priest*,
which, to say the least, it receives no where else ?—The choice,
therefore, can be only between two views, either that *but one*, or that
several crowns were made.   The latter cannot indeed be sustained by
the plural ⁴ : for this is sufficiently explained by the supposition of

---

¹ *Quam ingressi sunt.*

² On the phrase בַּיּוֹם הַהוּא Michaelis justly remarks : " *Die isto, quo scil. facere
debes, quæ nunc mando.   Forte Deus in visione diem aliquem certum determinaverat,
quem vero in visionis descriptione exprimere propheta minus necessarium duxit.*'

³ אֲמָרָה.   ⁴ עֲטָרוֹת.

one consisting of *several small crowns or diadems*. It occurs entirely
in this sense, in the thirty-sixth verse of the thirty-first chapter of
Job, " *I will bind it around me as crowns*," where only one *complex*
crown can be spoken of, as also in the twelfth verse of the nineteenth
chapter of the Apocalypse, " *And on his head* (were) *many crowns*,"
where not several separate diadems, but one composed of many, is
attributed to Christ, as the mark of His regal dignity. The idea of
one crown is favoured partly by the unsuitableness and insipidity of a
plurality, partly by its being placed on the head of one, Joshua, and
partly by the connexion of the singular of the verb [1] with the plural [2],
which however of itself would not be decisive of the subject.—
Let us now inquire how far the prophecy, thus expressed by a
symbolic action, could be intelligible to Joshua and his enlightened
contemporaries, even without the following verbal prophecy. The
putting on of the crown manifestly signified the conferring of the
royal dignity. Hereby, therefore, the thought was forbidden, that
the *acted* prophecy could refer to his person as such. Never could
the kingdom be taken from the house of David without a violation
of the promises which God had made to him. Joshua, therefore,
could not doubt that the crown was placed upon him only as the
type of another. Who this was, he had the less reason to doubt,
because he had just before [3] been greeted as a type of the Messiah ;
because, according to Ezekiel [4], the diadem and crown were to be
taken from the royal stock, until they should be conferred upon
the Messiah ; and because David [5] had already predicted, that the
priesthood of the Messiah should be like that of Melchisedech, that
he should unite in himself the dignity of High Priest and King. All
possible uncertainty, however, was done away by the following verbal
prophecy. This was designed to explain the foregoing symbolic
action in two respects ; first, what was intended by the placing of
the crown upon the head of Joshua, and, secondly, why the material
of this crown was taken from the deputies and representatives of
their brethren, who were dwelling in distant lands. The twelfth and
thirteenth verses relate to the former, and the fourteenth and fifteenth
to the latter.

537. Ver. 12. ' *And say to him, Thus saith the Lord : See there a
man whose name is* (the) *Sprout ; out of his ground shall he spring forth,
and build the Temple of the Lord.*' The prophecy is here placed after
the equivalent symbolic action, as if independent of it. The particle ' *see* ' points to the Messiah as present, and admonishes Joshua,
who represents him in name and office, to direct towards him his
spiritual eye. The manner in which the appellation is here employed,
as a sort of *proper name* of the Messiah (yet, as the context shows,
with a close regard to its appellative import), points back to the
earlier prophecies, especially those of Jeremiah [6], in which the Messiah had been represented as *a Sprout* of David to be raised up by

---

[1] תִּהְיֶה.   [2] עֲטָרוֹת, ver. 14.

[3] Chap. 3.   [4] Chap. 21. 31, &c.   [5] Ps. 110.
[6] Comp. on chap. 3.

the Lord. The great subject of promise will justly bear the name *shoot* or *sprout*. For he will not descend from above in full glory, but, like a plant *slowly springing up from the ground* beneath, raise himself by degrees from his original obscurity.—*He builds the temple of the Lord.*—That the building of the outward Temple cannot here be spoken of, as the Jewish interpreters dream, has been well proved by Reuss. Nowhere is a building of the outward Temple attributed to the Messiah. Our Prophet had himself declared in the name of God [1] that the building of the Temple *begun* by Zerubbabel should also be *completed* by him; and this same Temple, according to his predecessor Haggai [2], and his successor [3], was to be glorified by the presence of the Messiah. Still the building of the Temple and the High Priesthood of the Messiah must stand in a certain relation to each other. If now the purity to be effected by the latter is *not outward*, but *inward ;* if, as Zechariah, from his zealous study of his predecessors [4], must have known, and according to the twelfth and thirteenth chapters, actually did know, this purity was to be obtained, not by the blood of animals, but by the High Priest's own blood, then surely must the Prophet, when he is led by the building of the Temple in his time to attribute such a work to the Messiah, be understood figuratively ; and the more so, since, as we have already had frequent occasion to show, it is his constant custom to rise from the shadow of future blessings to the blessings themselves, and to represent the *future* under the image, and by the name of *the present*.—It is further to be observed, that it is not here asserted that the Messiah would build *a* Temple to the Lord, but *the* Temple of the Lord. The Temple is thus designated as perpetually existing, as constantly the same ; it is, however, to be exalted by the Messiah to a glory never anticipated before.—We now enquire, in what sense the building of the Temple is attributed to the Messiah. The Temple was the seat of the kingdom of God under the Old Covenant ; it is this, not the walls, or any thing else of an outward nature, which constituted the essence of the idea. Thereby, however, was it suited for an image and type of the kingdom of God itself, the Church, which by no means began with Christ, but, under the Old and New Covenant, is one and the same. This Temple Solomon and Zerubbabel had contributed to build, so far as their outward efforts proceeded from faith, and were not directed to what was external, as such ; not to the shell but to the kernel, which remained when the shell had long been broken.

538. Verse 13. ' *And he will build the Temple of the Lord, and he will bear majesty ; and he sits and reigns on his throne, and is a Priest on his throne, and the counsel of peace shall be between them both.*' The repetition of ' *And he will build the temple,*' is by no means an idle one. As these words, in the twelfth verse, in the antithesis with ' *he will spring out of the earth,*' direct the attention to the fact, that a glorification of the kingdom of God, never anticipated before, would

---

[1] Chap. 4. 10.   [2] Chap. 2. 7—9.   [3] Mal. 3. 1.   [4] Comp. 1. s 53.

proceed from the Messiah, notwithstanding his original obscurity, so
do they here closely relate to the following, ' *and he will bear majesty.*' They call the attention to the circumstance, that the building
of a far superior Temple, an infinitely greater glorification of the
Theocracy, was to be expected from the Messiah clothed with majesty
than from the poor and obscure Zerubbabel. They thus opened for
those who were mourning over the feeble and small beginning of the
new colony a rich fountain of consolation ; they raise their view from
the poor present to the splendid future.—The words, ' *he will bear
majesty,*' contain the explanation of the putting on of the crown in
the symbolic action ; and they the more naturally occurred to the
Prophet, since he had before him Joshua, *bearing* on his head
the crown, the badge of dominion.—' *He sits,*' and ' *he reigns,*'
differ from each other in this, that the former signifies the *possession* of the regal honour and dignity, the latter the *actual exercise*
of the regal power.—In the repetition, ' *reigns on his throne,*' and
' *is a priest on his throne,*' the object of the Prophet is to render prominent the thought, that the Messiah would be *both a King* and
a High Priest on one and the same throne. This truth was in the
highest degree consoling to the covenant people. It gave them a
pledge, that their future head should possess both the power and the
will to help them. As a true High Priest, the Messiah should represent his people before God, and procure for them forgiveness of their
sins, as the Prophet had already more fully predicted [1] : as a true King,
of whose glory all who had preceded were only a feeble copy, he would
protect the objects of his favour, and, in general, make them partakers of all the blessings designed for them by God.—In the last
words there is a difference in the interpretation, first, of the phrase
' *between them both.*' ' *Between both,*' that is, *between* the *two
offices* or *persons* of High Priest and King united in the Messiah.
The objection, that the king was not expressly mentioned in the
foregoing context, is of no importance, as the Messiah had been
plainly enough designated as a King. The *distinction* between him
as King and as High Priest is the less strange, since a reference to
the earlier Theocracy plainly lies at the foundation, where the *two
offices united in the Messiah* were administered *by two persons.* Mark
cites as analogous the distinction between the *inward* and *outward,*
the *old* and the *new* man [2].—By ' *the counsel of peace* [3] ' is meant
' *the counsel about obtaining, establishing, preserving peace,*' just as in
Isaiah [4], ' *the chastisement of our peace* ' means ' *the chastisement
which has our peace for its object* [5].' The Prophet, therefore, repre-

---

[1] Chap. 3.

[2] After Jerome : ("*Et consilium pacificum erit inter utrumque, ut nec regale
fastigium sacerdotalem deprimat dignitatem, nec sacerdotii dignitas regale fastigium,
sed in unius gloria domini Jesu utrumque consentiat,*") several, as Michaelis, (" *Bene
eis conveniet suavis inter utrumque concordia erit*") refer these words to the harmony of these two offices united in the Messiah.

[3] שָׁלוֹם as *gen. objecti.*

[4] Chap. 53. 5. מוּסַר שְׁלוֹמֵנוּ

[5] So ' *the judgement of peace,*' Zech. 8. 6. So Jerome. Others ' *inter germen
et Jehovam.*'

sents the Messiah as King, and the Messiah as High Priest, devising the best method and way to secure peace and prosperity to the covenant people. If at the present time the common efforts of Zerubbabel and Joshua to promote the best interests of the Theocracy had been attended with happy results, what might be expected when the true High Priest and the true King, the Messiah, should strive with anxious care for this object ; when he should employ all the means which these two dignities united in himself supplied !

539. Ver. 14. ' *And the crowns shall be to Helem, and to Tobijah, and to Jedaiah, and to Hen, the son of Zephaniah, for a memorial in the temple of the Lord.*' The Prophet here proceeds to explain the other point of the symbolic action, the circumstance that the material of the crown had been received from the deputies and representatives of the Jews, who dwelt far from their native land. The crown should be to these for a memorial, not, as is shown by what follows, on account of their *personal*, but their *typical* quality ; so far as each one at the sight of the crowns would call to mind, that those who had consecrated them, in reality and name typified the heathen, who hereafter, as *they* had done now, hastening from distant lands, would make every effort with the greatest readiness in order to adorn the Temple, to promote the kingdom of God.—Whether the action here commanded to the Prophet in vision was afterwards actually performed by him outwardly, is extremely doubtful. At all events the account of the Talmudist [1], respecting the place where the crown was hung up in the Temple can prove nothing. The opposite opinion is in some degree favoured by the eleventh verse, where the Prophet is commanded to *make* the crowns, which can indeed, if necessary, be understood of causing them to be made. A far stronger argument, however, is drawn from the prevailing fondness of Zechariah for what is internal, which in his case, as in that of Ezekiel, awakens a prejudice against the outward representation, which can be set aside only by weighty reasons ; and especially from the analogy of the other symbolic action, in the eleventh chapter, which was certainly performed only in inward contemplation, to which also all the remaining visions of this portion were confined.

540. Verse 15. ' *And they that are far off shall come and build in the temple of the Lord ; and ye shall know that the Lord of Hosts hath sent me unto you, and if ye will hearken to the voice of the Lord your God, so*' . . . . How the participation of those who were distant [2] in the building of the Temple is to be understood, needs no particular illustration after what has been said respecting the building of the Temple by the Messiah.—If we looked merely at this passage, we might be induced to take the words, ' *and ye shall know,*' &c., as words of the Prophet ; but the comparison of the ninth and eleventh verses of the second chapter, and the ninth verse of the fourth chapter, where they are spoken by the Angel of the Lord, through whom

---

[1] Middoth 3. 8.
[2] The heathen in distant lands ; comp. 2. 11. 8. 20. Is. 60. 9, 10, and other passages.

the Prophet receives his revelations, shows that here also they belong to him; and this supposition is the more natural, since the Prophet, in the twelfth verse, expressly introduces as speaking Jehovah of Hosts, as the Angel of the Lord in the former passage also is called. The result, the active participation of the heathen in building up the kingdom of God, was in the future to furnish a proof of the Divine origin of both the symbolical and the verbal prediction.—In the last words we must suppose an *aposiopesis*, which gives a peçuliarly emphatic sense [1]. ' *If ye will hearken to the voice of the Lord, so — ye shall have a part in all these blessings; so will the Messiah deliver you from sin as your High Priest, and make you happy as your King.*' With this earnest word of admonition, the Angel of the Lord closes at the same time this particular revelation, and the whole connected series of revelations, which, in this memorable night, he imparts to the people through our Prophet.

Chapter 7 and 8

541. These two chapters, which contain a distinct discourse, are simple and easy, compared with the foregoing and the following; and we need not dwell upon them long, since they contain little that immediately serves our purpose. The prophecy is separated from the foregoing by a period of about two years; it falls in the ninth month of the fourth year of Darius. This date, subjoined by the Prophet, is important, because it throws light on the event which occasioned the prophecy. This was the following: The congregation (the house of God [2]) caused enquiry to be made by certain deputies, sent to the Temple, whether they should continue to observe the fasts hitherto kept on the day of the destruction of the Temple by the Chaldeans, and which contained a penitential confession of guilt, and a prayer for forgiveness and restoration of the former prosperity. In this *question* there is at the same time included a *supplication*, that God would very soon change the days of mourning into days of rejoicing. Therefore, it is said [3], the deputies have come to supplicate the Lord. Both enquiry and supplication presuppose, that in the relations of the present, there was ground to hope for a favorable future. But this can be shown to be the case in precisely the fourth year of Darius. The building of the Temple had hitherto been unremittingly and successfully prosecuted. The new machinations of the Samaritans in the Persian court, with a design to arrest its progress, had been already completely defeated (compare Prideaux). The pusillanimity of the returned exiles was thus put

---

[1] Comp. similar examples, besides the entirely analogous one in Zechariah himself, chap. 7. 4. 2 Sam. 2. 27. 5. 8; in the New Testament, e. g. Luke 13. 9; κὰν μὲν ποιήσῃ καρπόν· εἰ δὲ μήγε, εἰς τὸ μέλλον ἐκκόψεις αὐτήν.

[2] Ver. 2.   [3] Ver. 2.

to shame, and they gave themselves up henceforth to the most joyful hopes in reference to the future.

542. The question was directed to the Priests and Prophets collected in the Temple, in the hope that God would reveal His will by one of them. This was done through Zechariah. His answer consists of two parts. In the first [1], he employs himself in rebuking the base motive from which the question, at least with a part of the enquirers, originated. That dead, hypocritical self-righteousness already existed in the germ, which, continually gaining ground, became at a later period as destructive to the new colony, as outward idolatry, resting on the same principle, had been in former times. This self-righteous spirit exerted the most prejudicial influence on the view entertained of fasts. They attributed an intrinsic value, as a mere *opus operatum*, to that which had no meaning, except as an outward manifestation of a penitent heart. They believed merit to be thereby attained, and wondered and murmured that God so long delayed to acknowledge and reward it. The Prophet shows how absurd was this notion ; and that the Lord required something entirely different, the fulfilment of the moral precepts of His law, without which all outward worship was only hypocrisy ; he reminds them that the disregard of this requisition, loudly and repeatedly expressed by the former Prophets, brought upon the people the previous inexpressible calamity, from which they had not yet recovered, and that a like cause would be attended with the like effect in future.—In the second part of the discourse [2], the Prophet then proceeds to give a direct answer to the question, which could not now serve to confirm the hypocrites in their carnal security, but might well console and strengthen the weak in faith in his own and subsequent times, until the appearing of Christ. For the covenant people —this is the sum—so great prosperity is destined—that the day of the destruction of the Temple, as well as the remaining fast-days, at that time observed in remembrance of particular melancholy events of the past ; the day of the capture of Jerusalem in the fourth, the day of the murder of Gedaliah in the seventh, and the day of the beginning of the siege in the tenth month, should be changed into days of rejoicing, because the future blessings would be far greater than those which had been lost. The Prophet here also embraces the whole of the prosperity destined for the covenant people, and his prediction was first completely fulfilled in Christ. We must refer exclusively to the glorification, conferred through him upon the kingdom of God, the conclusion, in the twentieth and three following verses ; where, as an enlargement upon the second verse of the fourth chapter of Micah, the third verse of the fourth chapter of Isaiah, and the sixth verse of the thirty-first chapter of Jeremiah, the zeal of the heathen nations for admittance into the Theocracy is described.

---

[1] Chap. 7. 5—14.   [2] Chap. 8.

Chapter 9 1—10

543. A victorious hostile army inundates the kingdom of Persia, and precipitates it from the summit of its power. The Prophet represents particularly its march through those provinces of the kingdom of Persia, which lay nearest to Judea, in order by the contrast with their mournful fate to place the better lot of the covenant people in a stronger light. While Damascus and Hamath are overtaken by the Divine judgement and captured by the conqueror, while Tyre, unprotected by all its riches, its bulwarks, and its position in the sea, is plundered and burnt, while the adjoining Philistia loses its ancient splendour, and its chief cities, Askelon, Gaza, Ekron, and Ashdod, sink into the deepest abasement, Jerusalem under the Divine protection remains unhurt[1]. There can be no doubt that we have before us a description of the march of Alexander, as plain as the difference between prophecy and history, which must always be observed, would allow. In the principal points the exact fulfilment of the prediction can be shown by express historical testimony. The capture of Damascus is described by Arrian[2], Curtius[3], and Plutarch[4]. The fate of Tyre and Gaza is so well known, that it need not more particularly be pointed out. According to Arrian[5], Alexander changed the latter, once a flourishing city, into a mere castle, after he had repeopled it with a colony from the neighbouring tribes, exactly as had been predicted in the sixth verse concerning Ashdod. That the capture of Hamath is not expressly related is not surprising, since the historians follow Alexander himself, who kept along the sea-coast, while the land of Hamath must have been in the way of Parmenio on his march to Damascus. Just as little is an express mention of the fate of the remaining cities of Philistia besides Gaza to be expected, since the historians of Alexander in describing his march through Syria and Palestine are so remarkably brief, and since in general they select from the great mass of events only the most important, particularly those which throw light upon the character of Alexander, who is every where, especially with Arrian, the chief object of attention[6].

544. In the ninth and tenth verses, the Prophet contrasts the inferior blessing of God with the higher, the sending of the Messiah, at which he had already, in the seventh verse, cast a passing look. (See on the relation of the two predictions in the Introduction to the ninth and eleventh chapters, &c.)

545. Before proceeding to the interpretation, we must determine what land is spoken of under the name of *Hadrach*. — The only true interpretation is, that *Hadrach* is not a geographical, but

---

[1] Ver. 1—8.   [2] 2. 15.   [3] 3. 25.
[4] Alex. cap. 24.   [5] 2. 27.
[6] It has been fully shown in the *Beiträgen*, 1, p. 277, how history fully confirms what is here predicted, of the preservation of the covenant people during that expedition, so destructive to the neighbouring lands.

a symbolical name[1]. It is a compound word, meaning *strong-weak*[2]: so that the land of *Hadrach* (or *strong-weak*) is a land which was *strong* and *powerful* at the time the prophecy was delivered, but should be *weakened* and *brought down*, when the threatened judgement took place; the symbolical appellation of the land comprehending at the same time the prediction of its impending fate[3].

546. It still remains for us to enquire, what kingdom Zechariah intended by this symbolic appellation. Every thing here is in favour of Persia. (1) The appellation itself shows that the kingdom must be one, which was at that time at the summit of its elevation and power. But of those connected with the covenant people this was the case only with the Persian. To this all the rest were subject; with none of them did the predicate *strong*[4] agree. (2) This explanation is the most in accordance with the whole contents of the first eight verses. If in them the expedition of Alexander is described, nothing is more suitable than that the Prophet should not proceed to describe the fates of the particular regions dependent on this kingdom, until he had mentioned, in the first place, the kingdom itself, the chief object of the expedition. (3) It is easily explained on this supposition, why Zechariah employs a symbolical name in this instance only. He lived under the dominion of the Persians; and to name them would have been the more dangerous, since the enemies of the Jews did all in their power to calumniate them as seditious; compare the twelfth and thirteenth verses of the fourth chapter of Ezra. The naming of the other regions, which were subject to the Persians, could not so easily furnish a ground of complaint, since it

---

[1] No evidence has been furnished of the existence of a city and province of Hadrach.—We have the less reluctance to regard Hadrach as a figurative designation, since the use of such designations by the prophets is so very frequent. It is known that in Isaiah, Jerusalem is designated by the symbolical names *Ariel*, "lion of God," and *valley of vision*, as a residence of the prophets; Babylon, by *the Desert of the Sea*; Idumea by *Dumah*; in Ezekiel, Jerusalem by *Aholibah*; in Jeremiah, Babylon by *Sesach*..

[2] Jarchi and Kimchi say: "*Allegorice interpretabatur R. Juda filius Elai* (a pupil of Akibah in the time of Adrian, comp. Wolf, Bibl. Hebr. 1, p. 411), *de Messia, qui sit acutus* (חד) *gentibus, et mollis* (רך) *Israeli.*" Jerome: "*Assumtio verbi Domini, acuti in peccatores, mollis in justos: Adrach quippe hoc resonat, ex duobus integris nomen compositum: Ad a c u t u m, Rach m o l l e t e n e r u m q u e significans.*" We readily relinquish to both their Messianic interpretation, and receive from them only their explanation of the words. The word, חד properly signifies indeed *sharp*, spoken of the sword, Ps. 57. 5. Is. 49. 2. Then, however, in a metaphorical sense, *acris*, "active, powerful." In reference to the word רך no further explanation is necessary, since all agree (comp. e. g. Winer s. v.), that it signifies *mollis, tener*, and secondarily, *debilis, infirmus.*

[3] These sentences give the *result* only of Professor Hengstenberg's able investigation, in which he also establishes the meaning of *Sesach*, as applied to the land of Babylon by Jeremiah, to be '*sinking down;*' it being a word formed by the Alphabet *Atbash*, which consists in taking the *last* letter of the common alphabet for the *first*, the *last but one* for the *second*, and so on. The actual use of this alphabet by Jeremiah seems to be proved by the arguments our author adduces.

[4] חד

would be perceived, that, in case of a rebellion, the Persians themselves would be the conquerors.

547. Ver. 1. ' *The word of the Lord burdens the land of Hadrach*
[*Persia*]; *Damascus is its resting-place; for the eye of the Lord
looks upon men and upon all the tribes of Israel*[1].' The *burden* of
the word of the Lord strikes or falls on Hadrach [*Persia*]; its *rest* is
Damascus. It is scarcely necessary to remark, that the Prophet by
these words indicates that a heavy calamity, and one which could
not be evaded (because it was threatened by the Lord, and would be
inflicted by Him), would come upon Hadrach and Damascus. A
parallel passage is Is. 9. 7; " *The Lord sends a word to Jacob; it
falls upon Israel.*" Precisely as Damascus is here represented as
the *rest* of the Divine word, or decree of punishment, it is said,
chap. 6. 8, of the ministers and symbols of the Divine justice, ' *They
make my anger to r e s t on the north country.*'

548. In the second part of the verse, the ground of the Divine
judgement upon Hadrach and Damascus, as well as upon the nations
afterwards mentioned, is given : the providence of God rules over
the whole earth, which lies open to His view : He cannot fail, therefore, to remove the equality which exists between the fate of the
covenant people and that of the heathen nations apparently favoured
by Him. The Prophet has in view the *true members* of the Theocracy.
He promises them that the Lord at a future period, removing the
existing inequality, will humble the proud heathen, and in the present instance protect His people during the hostile invasion, and,
finally, by the sending of the Messiah, complete their joy.

549. Ver. 2. ' *Also Hamath will border thereon, Tyre and Sidon,
because it is very wise.*' As Hamath is nearly connected with Damascus by locality, so shall it be also by a common calamity. The
phrase, ' *because she is very wise,*' is the same in substance as, ' *because she* thinks herself *very wise,*' because, as Ezekiel[2] says, ' *she
has corrupted her wisdom, tha tnoble gift of God ;*' according to the
uniform usage of Scripture, agreeably to which, since the blessings of
this life, from the natural depravity of man, are commonly abused,
and made the occasion of pride, the words which designate them
express at the same time the associated idea of their *abuse,* in like
manner as the words, which express their absence, have at the same
time the associated meaning of inward freedom from the temptation
inseparable from their possession[3].—Wherein the *wisdom* of the Ty-

---

[1] The original work contains a very able argument to prove that מַשָּׂא
in the subscription of a prophecy means *burden* (a weighty sentence, *verborum
pondera*), and not *declaration, prophecy.* Jerome, who (on Neh. 1. 1) says,
" *Massa autem nunquam præfertur in titulo, nisi cum grave et ponderis laborisque
plenum est, quod videtur.*"

[2] Chap. 28. 17.

[3] For the reasons why כִּי should be construed *because,* and not (as in English
Bible, Rosenmüller, &c.) *although,* see the original work.

rians consisted, appears partly from the following verse, where the
acquisition of immense riches, and the erection of fortifications, apparently impregnable, are cited as its effects, partly from Ezek. 28. 4, 5.
" *By thy wisdom and thy prudence, thou hast acquired for thyself
power, and filled thy treasures with gold and silver.   By thy great
wisdom in traffic thou hast gained great power, and thy heart has lifted
itself up on account of thy power.*"

550. Verse 3. '*And Tyre has built herself strong holds, and
heaped up silver as dust, and gold as dirt in the street.*'   Similar is
Ezek. 28. 2, where the king of Tyre boasts, that he sits in the heart
of the sea, and is therefore beyond the reach of every assault.   According to Diodor. Sic. [1] the Tyrians were determined to resist Alexander, '*trusting both in the strength of their island and the preparations they had made in it.*'

551. Ver. 4. '*Behold the Lord will give her into the power of her
enemies, and in the sea will strike her bulwarks ; she herself shall be
consumed by fire.*'   By the particle '*behold,*' the Prophet, who, in
inward vision, sees the threatening storm approach, admonishes his
hearer and reader to see how the proud hopes of the Tyrians are
annihilated.   Tyre, trusting to her possessions, becomes herself with
all her treasures a possession of her enemies.   That the walls should
be struck (not *into* the sea but), *in the sea*, is an important circumstance.   There were three things on which the Tyrians grounded
their invincibility, their treasures, their fortifications, their *position in
the sea*.   The last, and that the most important, and especially magnified by Ezekiel, and also by the Tyrians at the time of the fulfilment [2], is here first subjoined by Zechariah.

552. Ver. 5. '*Ascalon beholds it and fears, Gaza beholds it and
trembles greatly, also Ekron ; for her hope is put to shame ; Gaza
loses her king, Ascalon shall not reign.*'   Following the march of the
conqueror along the Mediterranean sea, the Prophet proceeds from
Phœnicia to Philistia.   Zechariah here also appears to have had in
view passages of former prophets, especially Isaiah, in the twenty-
third chapter, where the fear is repeatedly described, which the fall of
insular and fortified Tyre would spread among the neighbouring
nations and cities.   Thus, " *When the report reaches Egypt, they
will tremble at the report concerning Tyre* [3]:" "*Be ashamed, O Sidon* [4],"
but especially, " *He stretches out his hand over the sea, and shakes
the kingdom* [5]." And he says, " *Thou shalt no longer rejoice, thou disgraced daughter of Sidon* [6]."   " *Gaza will hereafter have no king.*"
Comp. Amos 1. 8 ; "*I extirpate the inhabitants from Ashdod, those
who bear the sceptre from Askelon.*" Jer. 49. 38.   These parallel
passages show that, by the disappearing of the king from the city, its
entire ruin and destruction are signified, so that this member fully
corresponds to the last : ' *Askelon will not reign*' (erroneously most

---

[1] **17.** 40.
[2] κατεγέλων τοῦ βασιλέως, εἰ τοῦ Ποσειδῶνος ἑαυτὸν δοκεῖ περιέσεσθαι.
Diod. Sic. **17.** 41.
[3] Ver. 5.   [4] Ver. 4.   [5] Ver. 11.
[6] אָבַד מֶלֶךְ מֵעַזָּה, not " *the* king," but " *a* king, ceases from Gaza."

interpreters, '*it will not be inhabited*,' compare 12. 6). It should not excite surprise here to find, under the reign of the Persians, the mention of a king of Gaza. It is known that the Philistines from the most ancient times were ruled by kings. Now the rulers of the great Asiatic empires generally suffered the regal dignity to continue where they found it, in the conquered lands; they contented themselves with making their kings tributary, and distinguishing themselves from them by the title, '*king of kings* [1].' It was not till after repeated insurrections, that the Chaldeans deprived the Jews and Tyrians of their kings; to the latter the royal dignity was restored even during *their* dominion. In the expedition of Alexander express mention is made of the king of Tyre and the king of Sidon, a sure proof that the Persians also, as well as the Chaldeans, suffered the regal dignity to remain in those regions.

553. Ver. 6. '*And a rabble dwells at Ashdod, and I extirpate the pride of the Philistines.*'—After Ch. B. Michaelis, Jahn and Rosenmüller erroneously assume, that '*I extirpate the pride of the Philistines*,' is i. q. '*I extirpate the proud Philistines.*' This the Prophet cannot wish to say, since in the following verse he predicts the future conversion of the remnant of the Philistines. The pride of the Philistines is rather, that wherein the Philistines placed their pride, their fenced cities, their military power, their wealth, and their riches. These shall be entirely taken from them, and they shall sink into degradation. These words comprehend the whole extent of the prophecy against the Philistines, since they express that of the whole people, which had been said before of the individual cities.

554. Ver. 7. '*And I remove his blood out of his mouth, and his abomination from between his teeth; also he shall be left for our God; he shall be as a prince in Judah; Ekron as the Jebusites.*' The ground of the whole verse is a personification of the Philistines; hence are explained [2] the much misunderstood words, '*He will be as a prince in Judah.*' By *blood* is not here to be understood, as several interpreters erroneously suppose, that of enemies, particularly the Israelites, shed by the Philistines, but the *blood of sacrificial animals*, which was drunk by the idolatrous nations at their sacrifices, either pure or mixed with wine. The abolition of one particular idolatrous abomination here designates, as a part of the whole, the abolition of idolatry in general. The Prophet is led, by the mention of the beastly practice of drinking blood, to represent the Philistines under the image of a wild beast, who holds fast his prey with his teeth. In this way, he points out that idolatry was deeply rooted among the Philistines. '*Also he shall be left for our God*,' is a concise expression for '*also he will not entirely perish, but a remnant of him will be preserved, in order that he may, at a future period, return to the true God.*' The reference is to the lands mentioned before, Hadrach, Syria, Phœnicia. By these few words the Prophet discloses the prospect of their future conversion. Parallel is chap. 14. 9, "*Then will the Lord be king over the whole earth.*"—In the

---

[1] Comp. Ezek. 26. 7.   [2] Also the *sing. suff.* הוא, and the pronoun.

words, ' *and he will be as a prince of a tribe in Judah,*' the thought
that the Philistines would hereafter be received among the covenant
people, and enjoy equal privileges with them, is expressed as though
their representative, their ideal head, should obtain the dignity of a
prince in Judah. A similar mode of representation prevails in Matthew [1], where Bethlehem is called the least *among the princes of
Judah*, which, in like manner, can be explained only by supposing a
personification of the city.—Much the same thought is expressed by
the last member, ' *Ekron will be as the Jebusites.*' The Jebusites,
the ancient inhabitants of Jerusalem, had, until the time of David,
dwelt at Jerusalem with the Jews, who could not expel them. They
were vanquished by David, and a remnant of them, after they had
embraced the religion of the Israelites, were incorporated into the
Theocracy. This appears from the example of Araunah the Jebusite,
who [2] dwelt among the covenant people as a respectable and wealthy
man, and whose estate was destined by David for the site of the
future Temple [3]. Similar transitions from the representations of the
judgements, which threatened the heathen nations, to the prediction
of their future reception into the kingdom of God, for which all their
humiliations are only preparatory, and which, as the termination of
all the dealings of God, first place in their true light the preceding
events, are elsewhere also not rarely found [4].

555. Ver. 8. ' *And I establish for my house an encampment against
the invading foe; no oppression shall any more overcome them; for
now I see with mine eyes.*' ' To establish a camp, *for* any one, that
is, in order to his protection. The same figurative designation of
protection is found, Ps. 34. 8, and a similar one, chap. 2. 9, where
the Lord promises that he will be *to* Jerusalem like a *wall of fire.*
' *The house of the Lord* ' is the Temple restored by Zerubbabel.
The ' *now* ' refers not so much to the time when the prophecy was
spoken, as to that of the fulfilment, when the Lord established His
camp around His house. This is explained from the nature of prophecy, in which the future appears as present; the determination of
time, therefore, relates not to the *actual*, but to the *ideal* present. The
phrase, ' *for now I see,*' &c. is spoken after the manner of men.
When a friend *sees* the misfortune of a friend, he *comes to his help.*
Hence in the Psalms, we frequently find the supplication, ' *behold
my affliction,*' for ' *deliver me from it.*'

556. Ver 9. ' *Rejoice greatly, thou daughter of Zion, shout for
joy, thou daughter of Jerusalem. Behold thy king comes to thee: he
is just and protected of God, afflicted and riding upon an ass, and*

---

[1] Chap. 2. 6.   [2] 2 Sam. 24. 1 Chron. 21.

[3] Others, as Rosenmüller, after the manner of Theodoret, prefer to understand
by the Jebusites, the later inhabitants of the city Jebus, the Israelites. The sense
would then be : The inhabitants of Ekron shall enter into the same relation to
the Lord as the inhabitants of Jerusalem ; the Philistines, at a future period,
shall belong to the covenant people as well as the Israelites. But, not only is
there no instance where the later inhabitants of Jerusalem are called Jebusites,
but this designation, as Mark has already observed, is here entirely out of place,
since it would not be honorable, as the context requires, but degrading.

[4] Comp. e. g. Is. 19. 18, seq. 23. 15. Jer. 12. 15, 16.

upon a foal the son of a she-ass.' The preliminary exhortation to exulting joy intimates the importance of the subject, and at the same time the greatness of the necessity, which was to be satisfied with this gracious benefit of God. Cocceius has already reminded us that the exhortation contains also a prophecy. The Prophet had in view only the better part of the covenant people, the true members of the Theocracy, not the whole of the natural Israelites. On this account he gives prominence only to the joy and salvation, which the Messiah's Advent will bring.—The evangelists, who were concerned only with the substance of the prophecy, have not verbally rendered this exhortation to joy. Matthew has instead, from Isaiah [1], ' *Tell the daughter of Sion;'* John, ' *Fear not, daughter of Sion.'* ' *Behold'* indicates that the Prophet sees the future king already present, and about to make his entrance into Jerusalem. ' *Thy* king,' with peculiar emphasis: ' he, who alone in the complete and highest sense is thy king, so that all others scarcely deserve this name [2].' The expression at the same time shows, that the Prophet speaks of a king generally known from the former prophecies, and eagerly expected. ' *To thee,'* that is, ' *for thy benefit,'* ' *for thy salvation;'* compare the fifth verse of the ninth chapter of Isaiah, ' *A child is born to us,* a son is given *to us.'* The Prophet here exhibits only the blessings, which the Messiah should confer upon the believing portion of the covenant people, because his prophecy was chiefly, and in the first instance, designed for them. That the heathen to be received into the kingdom of God should also participate in these blessings appears from the seventh and tenth verses. The epithet *just,* designates the first virtue of a king, and is therefore made particularly prominent in the prophecies where the Messiah appears as a king [3].—The participle which we have interpreted ' *protected'* occurs in other passages in this sense, of being ' *sustained with help,'* ' *blessed with salvation.'* Thus Deut. 33. 29, ' *Salvation to thee, O Israel; who is like unto thee* [4] *? a people which is clothed with salvation by the Lord* [5], *thy helping shield, thy proud sword* [6].' This interpretation gives a sense in the highest degree appropriate. As righteousness and salvation are ascribed to the invisible head of the Theocracy, as the sum of those attributes whereby he makes his people happy [7], so was it the highest glory of his visible representative to be clothed by him inwardly with righteousness [8], and outwardly with salvation, which flows forth from him to his subjects. In both respects the Messiah was to be *perfectly,* what the best previous kings had been only very imperfectly [9].

---

[1] Chap. 62. 11.   [2] Comp. Ps. 45. 72.

[3] Ps. 45. 72. Jer. 23. 5. Is. 11. 3—5.

[4] עַם נוֹשַׁע בַּיהוָה.

[5] ביהוה also in the passage before us is to be supplied.

[6] See Is. 45. 7. Jer. 23. 6. Ps. 33. 16.

[7] Comp. e.g. Is. 45. 21, אֵל צַדִּיק וּמוֹשִׁיעַ.   [8] Comp. Ps. 72. 1.

[9] The meanings rejected by our author are (1) ' *saving,'* or ' *saving himself;'* the partic. in *Niphal* being supposed equivalent to that of Kal (in which form the verb does not occur:) (2) ' *saved,'* ' *delivered.'*

557. While the first two predicates express that which was *common* to the great king of future times with the best of those who had reigned before, the two latter were designed to point out wherein he was characteristically *different* from them [1].—The second predicate, *riding on an ass*, is taken by many interpreters as a designation of a lowly-minded, *peaceful* king. In favour of this interpretation, it has been urged, that the ass in the East is altogether a different animal from what he is with us; that in the Scripture even the most eminent men appear as riding on asses, and that this is still the case, according to the testimony of travellers. But it is evident, from the following reasons, that this interpretation is inadmissible, and that riding on an ass signifies rather the *low condition* of the king.—It is indeed true, that the ass in the East is of a nobler nature, and therefore more esteemed than with us. But still he ever remains *an ass*, and cannot rise to the dignity of *a horse*. Since the appearance of Michaelis's History of the Horse and of the breeding of Horses in Palestine [2], it has no longer been customary to appeal to the passages of Scripture, in which distinguished persons appear as riding upon asses. During the dominion of the Judges the horse had not yet been brought into use among the Israelites, *therefore* even men of rank made use of the ass for riding. With the rise of the regal dominion, first mules and then horses came into use. From this period, particularly from the reign of Solomon, we no longer find even a single example of a royal, or of any very eminent person riding on an ass. And yet examples of this date would alone be of importance in the present instance. With respect to the accounts of recent travellers, it is to be considered, that they generally speak of the ass only *relatively*, with reference to the extreme contempt in which he is held by us. When they relate, that in the East even distinguished women are accustomed to use him, nothing can be inferred in reference to this passage; that there is another reason for this than the nobleness of the ass, is evident from the fact, that this also happens among us, notwithstanding he is the object of the greatest contempt. That even the higher officers in particular regions of the East, according to Chardin's account of the lawyers in Persia, make use of the ass for riding, can only prove that this practice is not there, as with us, *ridiculous*. It is explained by the circumstance, that the ass in the East goes tolerably fast, is better suited than the horse for riding, especially on the mountains, on account of his being more surefooted, and moreover is easily kept, and with very little expense. Of a king who generally rode upon an ass, our accounts of the Oriental ass, which are particularly full, do not afford a single example; nor an instance where a magistrate of a higher order mounted an ass on a solemn occasion, though here it is to be

---

[1] *Poor*, by which, after Jerome and Symmachus, many other interpreters translate עָנִי, is not entirely correct. עָנִי is of wider import; it signifies the whole of the low, miserable, suffering condition of the Messiah, as it is more fully described, Is. 53. 2, 3.

[2] Hinter Th. 3, von. d. Mos. R.

well observed, that riding on the ass is predicated of the King, *as King*. On the contrary, proofs are not wanting, that the ass even in the East shares in a measure the contempt in which his more unfortunate brother in the West is held [1]. A proof drawn from the most ancient time is furnished by Gen. 49. 13. When Issachar is there called ' *an ass*,' the point of comparison, as the context shows, is plainly, not merely *strength of bones*, but likewise *that laziness*, which will not suffer its repose to be disturbed at any price, and patiently endures whatever burden is imposed upon it. Still more provokingly is the honour of the ass attacked by Jesus, the son of Sirach, in the twenty-fifth verse of the twenty-third chapter, ' *To the ass belongs his fodder, whip, and burden.*' Mohammed says, " *The voice of the ass is the most abominable of all, yea it is the voice of the Devil.*" The ancient Egyptians asserted, that the evil god, Typhon, was like an ass, and that this animal was peculiarly agreeable to him [2]. That Christians and Jews in Egypt, by way of degradation, are confined to the use of the ass, while the horse is reserved only for the Mahommedans, is well known. But should any doubt remain respecting the import of riding on the ass, it must surely vanish when we look at the fulfilment. We can scarcely conceive any thing more humble than the entrance of Christ into Jerusalem. The city, into which David and Solomon had so often ridden on mules or horses splendidly adorned, attended by a multitude of proud horsemen, the Lord entered on a borrowed ass, which had never yet been ridden ; the poor garments of His disciples supplied the place of the usual covering; His train consisted of those who were regarded by the world as the people and rabble. In every feature of the symbolic action is manifested the design of the Lord to represent His kingdom as destitute of all worldly splendour, as poor and lowly, so that Heumann justly remarks: " This deed of the Lord may be regarded as an *ironia realis*, whereby the false imagination of the Jews respecting the Messiah's kingdom was derided."

558. The two members, ' *he rides on an ass*,' and ' *on a young ass, a foal of the she-asses* [3],' sustain to each other the relation of a climax.

---

[1] The very etymology of אָתוֹן, *laziness* (comp. Ges. *Thes.* s. v.), expresses this contempt.

[2] *Jablonsky, Pantheon Æg. III.* 45.

[3] The *plur.* אֲתֹנוֹת has here led to strange interpretations. That of Michaelis, Bauer, and Jahn, borders on the ridiculous, according to which, "a foal of the she-asses," signifies, " a foal of a good stock," whose mother is known for some generations back ! Of the genealogy of asses hitherto, at least, no trace has been found. The plural is not seldom placed where only one undetermined individual, out of a multitude, is meant, and where it is not important to be more definite ; comp. Ewald, page 584. Thus e. g. Gen. 21. 7, " *who would have said to Abraham, Sarah gives suck to sons,*" בָּנִים. Sarah had only *one* son, the number, however, of her children was not here important, but only the fact of her becoming fruitful ; and this was rendered the more striking by the use of the plural. Completely analogous, however, is the frequently occurring בֶּן־בָּקָר *filius boum*, for *vitulus bovinus*, also עֵגֶל בֶּן בָּקָר and פַּר בֶּן בָּקָר. For the same reason as here, viz. in order the more strongly to express the mean condition of the king by the Evangelists, also the youth of the ass is carefully

It is a great sign of poverty and abasement when a king rides on
any ass, but it is a far greater one when the animal is young and has
never yet been ridden. This interpretation is plainly grounded in
the words. Without it the last proposition has no meaning [1].—
According to the general opinion of the older and later interpreters [2],
in both members *one and the same ass* is spoken of [3]. This interpretation would never have arisen, if interpreters (proceeding on the
supposition that the passage relates *immediately* and *exclusively* to
the entrance of Christ into Jerusalem, and observing that *only one
ass* is mentioned by three of the Evangelists), had not feared that
prophecy and fulfilment might be involved in contradiction. The
former supposition, however, is plainly erroneous. The riding on
the ass is here, in the first instance, a mere individualization of the
foregoing '*poor.*' Now, even if it were a bare synonymous parallelism, the supposition, that, in both members, one and the same ass is
spoken of would be utterly untenable. When it is said [4] of Judah,
'*He binds* his ass *to the vine*, the foal of his she-ass *to the choice vine,
he washes his garment in wine, his dress in the blood of grapes ;*' who
would not regard as ridiculous the assertion, that ' the ass,' and ' the
ass's foal,' are the same individual ; ' the vine ' and ' the choice vine '
one and the same ; ' the blood of grapes ' and ' the wine ' the same
portion of wine ; ' garment ' and ' dress ' one and the same piece of
clothing? But this supposition must appear the more inadmissible
in this passage, since, as we have shown, it contains a *climax ;* as the
Prophet first designates the low condition of the Messiah, by his
riding either on an ass in general, or on a full-grown ass, and then
more strongly by his riding on a *young one, which had never been
ridden* [5]. It can scarcely be denied, that the Lord Himself has confirmed our view by the manner in which the symbolic action was
performed, which was to embody, as it were, the figurative representation of Zechariah. It cannot otherwise be explained why He commanded, according to Matthew, that not only the young ass, but also
the she ass should be brought. He could mount only one of the two
animals : for the change, as Bochart has already remarked, would
have been unbecoming in so short a distance. He chose *the young
ass*, because in Zechariah this was the symbol of the deepest humiliation. The *she-ass*, however, must accompany it, in order fully to
represent the image of Zechariah, and to make visible the climax
which he had employed. That the she-ass made a necessary part of

exhibited. John, ὀνάριον : Mark 11. 12, πῶλον, ἐφ' ὃν οὐδεὶς ἀνθρώπων
ἐκάθισε. Luke 19. 30, ἐφ' ὃν οὐδεὶς πώποτε ἀνθρώπων ἐκάθισε.

[1] *Vau* often stands in climaxes, e. g. 1 Kings 8. 27. ' Behold the heaven, *and*
the heaven of heavens' contain thee not.' Prov. 6. 16, ' Six things and seven.'
for, yea seven.

[2] *Vau*, having the sense of *namely*, ' *that is to say.*'

[3] It might indeed, *if necessary*, be justified on grammatical principles ; for,
although *vau* never occurs precisely in the sense *namely* (see Ew. l. c.), yet, in
many instances, though retaining its ordinary meaning, it can be translated by
et quidem.

[4] Gen. 49. 11.

[5] To this must be added, that the repetition of עַל does not accord with the
supposition that the *vau* is exegetical.

the symbolic action, and was not taken along for some subordinate object,—that the foal might the more readily follow, as most interpreters suppose,—is evident from the words of Matthew[1], '*And brought the ass and the colt, and put on them their clothes, and they set him thereon*[2].' The use of the plural can have no other object than to show that *both animals* were destined for the use of the Lord; so that with the one, the other also, as it were, was covered with garments and mounted. That the other Evangelists do not indeed mention the she-ass can prove nothing. John narrates, in general, with extreme brevity, and omits all subordinate circumstances. He presupposes the facts to be known, and only subjoins the remark, that the reference of the symbolic action to the Old Testament prophecy, was not made clear to the disciples till after the glorification of the Lord. Mark and Luke entirely omit the reference to the prophecy, which Matthew, in accordance with the object and uniform character of his Gospel, renders especially prominent. Under these circumstances, the mention of the she-ass would have been inappropriate; since the design of her accompanying the foal would be evident *only from the reference to the prophecy;* far more important was it to extol the wonderful circumstances with which the event was attended.

559. Ver. 10. '*And I abolish the chariots from Ephraim, and the horses from Jerusalem, and the battle-bow shall cease; and he speaks peace to the nations, and his dominion extends from sea to sea, from the Euphrates to the ends of the earth*[3].' The Prophet proceeds to give the characteristic difference of the Messianic kingdom from all worldly kingdoms, and especially from the former Theocracy; whether with special reference to the carnal conceptions of his contemporaries is uncertain. While earthly kingdoms are upheld and extended only by the power of arms, while even the Theocracy formerly employed them, it shall in the time of the Messiah be deprived of every external weapon, since it will need them no more, because its head, the Prince of Peace, by his bare word extends peace over the whole earth, which willingly and joyfully submits to him[4]. What follows, where the

---

[1] Ver. 7.

[2] Otherwise, even were we to refer the second αὐτῶν to the garments (Theophylact: οὐχὶ τῶν δύο ὑποζυγίων, ἀλλὰ τῶν ἱματίων), still the first αὐτῶν would remain inexplicable. The usual expedient that the *plur.* stands for the *sing.* is scarcely tenable. The *plur.* is indeed used where a more accurate determination of the particular subject is unimportant; and for this usage not a few examples can be cited from the New Testament also. Here, on the contrary, it was in the highest degree necessary to be *definite*, if the Evangelist wished to express that the Lord rode *only* on the foal.

[3] Our author justifies the interpretation of the last clause very ably on critical grounds. '*From sea to sea,*' occurs also, Mic. 7. 12. Amos 8. 12, in the sense of '*over the whole earth,*' as far as it is surrounded by seas.'

[4] Others, after Theodoret, find in these words a prediction of the political extinction of the covenant people by the Romans. Others, as Grotius, after the Chald.: "*Conteram facientes bella et castra populorum,*" and the Seventy (Ἐξολοθρινθήσεται τόξον πολεμικὸν καὶ πλῆθος καὶ εἰρήνη ἐξ ἐθνῶν), are reminded of hostile chariots and cavalry, and explain the phrase, "to abolish out of Ephraim," &c., by "to make harmless for," &c.

kingdom of the Messiah is designated as a kingdom of peace, shows, that, by the abolition of the war-chariots, &c., the entire uselessness of every external weapon is signified. Entirely analogous is Is. 2. 4, Mic. 4. 3, ' *Then will the Lord be a judge between the people, and rebuke many nations; they shall beat their swords into ploughshares, and their spears into pruning-hooks; no people will lift up the sword against another, they will learn war no more.*' This passage is also so far explanatory of the one before us, as that there the reason of the destruction of all warlike apparatus *precedes*, and therefore can the less be mistaken, while here it *follows*. Further, Hosea 2. 20, ' *I make for them a covenant with the wild beasts,*' &c., ' *and will abolish bow and sword and war, out of the land, and cause them to dwell securely.*' Likewise in the fourth verse of the nineteenth chapter of Isaiah. Similar for the most part, according to the words, is the ninth verse of the fifth chapter of Micah, and it was probably present to the mind of Zechariah: nevertheless, according to the sense, it so far differs, as that there the extinction of the warlike apparatus is predicted with a special regard to the sinful confidence placed upon it by the covenant people [1].—' *He* (that is, ' *the king*') *speaks therein to the nations.*' What worldly kings effect by the power of arms, he accomplishes by his bare word [2].

CHAP. 9. 11.—10. 12

560. That a new portion here commences, or rather that a new scene presents itself to the spiritual eye of the Prophet, is so clear from the contents, that it is scarcely conceivable how it could be overlooked by ancient and modern interpreters. The Prophet, in the ninth and tenth verses, had described a kingdom of peace, which, deprived of all earthly weapons and bulwarks, should be extended over the whole earth, and embrace all the heathen nations. Here on a sudden all is warlike. The covenant people appear in conflict with their mighty oppressors, and as such the Greeks are particularly mentioned. The victory obtained by the aid of the Lord is followed, in connexion with other Theocratic blessings, by that freedom, of which the covenant people under Zechariah were still painfully destitute. And, in order to make the prosperity complete, Ephraim also, who, at the time of the Prophet, appeared, according to human view, to be a branch for ever separated from the vine, is at last led back by

[1] That no argument against the genuineness of the second part can be derived from the connexion of Judah and Ephraim, has already been shown in the *Beiträge*, 1. p. 377.
[2] Comp. Ps. 148. 5. 33. 9, and especially Is. 11. 4.

the Lord from his dispersion, and again incorporated into the Theocracy.

561. It is evident from this representation, that the prophecy, with the exception of the last prediction, which reaches to the time of the Messiah, refers not merely in the first instance, but exclusively to the time of the Maccabees. What the Lord would then do to complete the work begun among the covenant people by the restoration from the Babylonian exile, the Prophet represents to his contemporaries, who are mourning over the feeble beginnings of the new colony.

562. This sudden transition from the time of the Messiah to that which preceded it, need not appear strange. The Prophet had spoken [1] of the expedition of Alexander, and of the protection of the covenant people during its progress. The transition from this point to the times of the Maccabees would have been altogether more in accordance with the actual succession of events. But in the period between the two events his spiritual eye had fallen upon the far greater blessings which should be conferred upon the covenant people by the Messiah. This we cannot explain, with Jahn, by supposing a contrast of the great Prince of Peace with the great worldly conqueror described, in the first eight verses. Had this been the design of the Prophet, the person of the latter [2] would not have been kept so much in the back ground. It was rather owing to the fact, that the Messianic hopes so entirely fill the soul of the prophets, that they pass over from every inferior blessing to this last and highest, to which all others refer, unconcerned whether in the mean time other blessings of God still await the covenant people, in the representation of which, in a manner equally easy and unobserved, they again return to the Messianic time, the images of which every where force themselves upon them with an irresistible charm, and sometimes even mingle with those of the nearer benefits.

563. Ver. 11. '*Even thou,—on account of thy covenant sealed with blood, I release thy prisoners out of the pit wherein is no water.*' '*Even thou,*' that is, although thou art in a state of total helplessness, although thou appearest to be lost beyond deliverance [3].—'*Even thou, in the blood of thy covenant I dismiss,*' &c., i. q. '*however miserable thou mayst be, nevertheless, because thou art in the blood of the covenant, thou art thereby freed from sin, and consecrated to me,*' &c. After the conclusion of the covenant on Sinai, Moses had sprinkled the people with the blood of the victims, saying, 'Behold, that is the blood of the covenant, which the Lord makes with you concerning

---

[1] Ver. 1—8.   [2] In ver. 1—8.

[3] This, so far as we are informed, is peculiar to Calvin : "*Particula* ‏גם‏ *emphatica est, quasi diceret: Video me non multum proficere apud vos, quia estis quodammodo attoniti malis ; deinde nulla spes vos recreat, quoniam putatis, vos esse quasi centum mortibus obrutos. Ergo utcunque hæc congeries malorum vos exanimet, —tamen redimam vinctos vestros,*" &c.

all these words [1].'—By this symbolical act,—the blood a sign and
means of deliverance from sin [2],—were the people solemnly declared
as purified, consecrated to the Lord, and, therefore, at the same time
also under his peculiar protection, a declaration which was constantly
repeated by the sacrificial institutions ordained by God. The blood
of the covenant was accordingly a sure pledge to the covenant people
of deliverance from every distress, so long as they did not make its
promises of none effect by a wicked violation of the conditions which
God had imposed [3].—Empty cisterns were used in the East instead
of prisons [4]. In consequence of the mud remaining in them, they were
exceedingly unwholesome and noxious. The words, ' *in which there
is no water,*' are taken by several, as Calvin, as a designation of a *second*
distress (that of *thirst*), not necessarily connected with confinement in
the cistern. But this addition, which, so far as the language is concerned, alludes to the twenty-fourth verse of the thirty-seventh chapter of Genesis, ' *And the pit was empty, there was no water in
it,*' serves rather for a more accurate description of the pit itself.
It was only into cisterns without water that prisoners were thrown.
Mark, therefore, is likewise in errour when he perceives herein an
allusion to a quality of the pit itself, which would make it insupportable, that of its bottom being deep, foul, and fetid mud [5].—
Many interpreters suppose the *abiding in the pit* to be a figurative
designation of *imprisonment;* but this supposition has no justification
in the figure itself. It occurs elsewhere also in a wider sense, as a
designation of the deepest distress and misery [6]. That this extended
meaning prevails in this passage appears from the following grounds.
(1) As the *stronghold*, in the twelfth verse, is an image of prosperity
and security, so must its contrast also, the *pit*, be an image of misfortune and helplessness. We find exactly the same antithesis in
the third verse of the fortieth Psalm : ' He brought me up also out of
a horrible *pit*, out of the miry clay, and set my feet upon a *rock*.'
(2) The way in which the covenant people, according to the thirteenth verse, were to be delivered from their distress by a brave

[1] Exod. 24. 8.   [2] Levit. 17. 11. Heb. 9. 18. sq.

[3] There is no doubt that שִׁלַּחְתִּי is the *præteritum propheticum,* and that the
Prophet speaks of a *future* deliverance of the covenant people. On the opposite
supposition the discourse is too abrupt, and requires something to be supplied.
The expression, ' *return to the stronghold,*' ver. 12, which, as will hereafter appear,
relates " *to the pit in which there is no water,*" shows, that we are not here to look
for a designation of an affliction which has long since passed ; and besides the
reference to the oppression in Egypt, or to any calamity which had already taken
place, is irreconcileable with the correct interpretation of the first words of the
verse. In what follows also, and which is generally acknowledged to relate to
the future, the *præter* is constantly interchanged with the *future*, comp. e. g. v. 13.
[4] Hence the latter, even when they were not cisterns, received the name
בּוֹר.
[5] Ps. 40. 3, Jer. 38. 6.
[6] Thus e. g. Ps. 40. 3. 88. 7. Lam. 3. 53, where the reference to a special event
in the life of Jeremiah is evidently erroneous. Also Isa. 42. 22, the image of a
prison stands for a designation of the deepest misery.

effort, favoured by the Lord, shows that it is not a carrying away into exile, connected with a deprivation of all the means of defence, which is intended. Finally, it must still be added, that the supposition of a captivity in a strange land being here the subject of discourse, presupposes one of two erroneous hypotheses, viz. either the reference of the eleventh verse to something past, or the spuriousness of the second part.—We now examine more closely *what distress* and *what misery* here presented themselves to the spiritual eye of the Prophet. The Greek and Latin fathers, likewise the later Christian interpreters, almost unanimously refer the passage to the spiritual distress and misery, from which the Messiah should deliver. But this is plainly erroneous. The distress in this verse is the same from which, in the twelfth verse, deliverance is promised; and from the more accurate description of this deliverance, in the thirteenth verse, it appears that it should consist in a victorious conflict against the Greeks. According to this close connexion of the eleventh and two following verses, which is undeniable, the distress can be no other than the oppression experienced from Alexander's successors in the kingdom of Syria. This is so very obvious, that it surely would not have been overlooked, if critics had not been led astray by the supposition, founded on ignorance of the prophetic vision, that it would be unnatural for the Prophet to make a sudden transition from the Messianic time to an earlier period, from the highest deliverance to an inferior one. The greater portion of them were so blinded by this supposition, that they explained the whole portion allegorically; others, as Theodoret and Mark, feeling how unnatural this would be, suppose that the portion from the thirteenth verse referred directly to the times of the Maccabees [1].

564. Ver. 12. ' *Return to the stronghold, ye prisoners of hope. Even to-day do I declare; The double will I return to you.*'—' *Turn back to the stronghold,*' has been the subject of many false interpretations. One of the most common is that, according to which Zion or Jerusalem is understood by the stronghold, and the Prophet exhorts those, who still remain in exile, to return to their native land. The difficulty that Jerusalem was an open place in the time of Zechariah, and was not fortified again until a later period by Nehemiah, they endeavoured to remove in various ways. Calvin supposes Jerusalem to be called a stronghold, because the protection of the Lord surrounds it as a wall of fire. Jahn finds an intimation of the future fortification of Jerusalem; others, as Mark and Grotius, an exhortation to return to God, as the true bulwark of those who flee to Him for refuge. Others finally, as Rosenmüller, after the Chaldee paraphrast, explain ' *Return, that ye may become* (that is, *become again*) *fortified cities* [2].' All these

---

[1] Certainly with less consistency than the rest, as Cyril, Cocceius, Ch. B. Michaelis; since ver. 13, sq. cannot possibly refer to any other subject than the two foregoing, with which they are most closely connected with כי.

[2] Against which Mark justly observes, that ל connected with שׁוּב could naturally point out, as it does every where else, only the *terminus motus ad quem.*

interpretations have arisen from mistaking the very obvious contrast of the *stronghold* and the *pit*, an attention to which shows at once that the *stronghold*[1], in like manner as the *rock*, the *high place*, &c., in numerous passages, is only an image of security and prosperity. The *imper.* '*return*' stands for *fut.*, to express the thought, that the return depends on nothing else but the will of the covenant people, just as in the first verse of the tenth chapter, '*Ask* of the Lord rain,' i. e. ye need only *ask* rain.—By the address, '*prisoners of hope*,' the Prophet calls the attention of his people to the covenant and the promises, which, even in the deepest misery, afforded them a pledge of their future deliverance.—The Prophet is transferred in the spirit to the time when the oppression of the covenant people has reached its summit, and thence beholds its approaching end. Without this supposition (sufficiently grounded in a correct view of the nature of prophecy), it is inconceivable how a stress so entirely peculiar can be laid upon *to-day* by the subjoined '*even*.' Moreover, this transition to the time of the oppression, some hundred years distant, is placed beyond a doubt by the preceding address: '*Return* to the stronghold, *ye prisoners of hope*.'—'*I will render back to thee double*,' viz. of the prosperity which thou formerly possessedst[2].

565. Ver. 13. '*For I bend to me Judah, fill the bow with Ephraim, and raise up thy sons, O Zion, against thy sons, O Javan, and make thee like the sword of a hero*.' The Prophet here more particularly describes the distress, and the way in which the deliverance from it, predicted in general in the preceding verse, should take place. By the help of the Lord, they were to obtain, notwithstanding their own weakness, splendid victories over their powerful oppressors, the Greeks. By a bold figure the Prophet represents Judah, as the bow bent by the Lord, Ephraim, as the arrow shot by Him, to express the thought, that Judah and Ephraim would both take a part in the glorious struggle, perhaps also intimating a certain subordination of Ephraim to Judah. A figure somewhat similar has been adduced by Jahn from Abulfeda[3]. The host appears there as the bow, the leader as the arrow shot from the same.—'*I fill the bow with Ephraim*.' Mark unjustly objects that the arrow *does not fill the bow*: for as only one arrow can be shot with the bow, it is *full* as soon as this is applied[4].—'*I awake thy sons, O Zion, against thy sons*,

---

[1] בִּצָּרוֹן, *locus inaccessus, munitus.*

[2] Parallel passages, which Zechariah had in view, are Isa. 40. 2, 'That she receives of the Lord *double*, כִּפְלַיִם, for all the punishments of her sins;" 61. 7. " Instead of your shame will I give you double, מִשְׁנֶה ; instead of reproach, they shall rejoice over their inheritance ; in their land they shall possess double; everlasting joy shall be to them."

[3] *Annal. Moslem*, t. 3, p. 474.

[4] Abundant examples are found in Syriac ; a *full* bow, for one *furnished with an arrow*, Is. 21. 15, and " *to fill the bow*," for to *supply it with an arrow*, Ps. 11. 2, as a free, though not, as J. D. Michaelis supposes, a verbal translation of the Hebrew קֶשֶׁת and דָרַךְ קֶשֶׁת דְרוּכָה.

O Javan.'—The *land of Greece* is here named only as *one* of the most distant lands, into which individual Israelites had been carried prisoners by the traffic in slaves, not through the fault of its inhabitants, but of the Tyrians, against whom alone on this account the Divine punishment is threatened. The name *Javan*, to which the Homeric forms, *Iaon* and *Iaones*, as well as the Syriac, *Jaunoje*, approach the nearest, and which, for this very reason, we must not, with J. D. Michaelis, hastily change into *Jon*, designates the Greece of the Hebrews in a wider sense, as is evident from the fact, that Alexander[1] is called *king of the land of Greece*. Numerous traces of an original wider import of the name, even among the Greeks themselves, have been pointed out by Bochart[2]. The Prophet, now raised, indeed, by Divine illumination above the horizon of his time, represents, in passing, the victory which the Jews under the Maccabees, by the aid of the Lord, should gain over the Grecian rulers of Syria, as it had already been fully predicted by Daniel. The nearer the prophetic order approached its termination, the more necessary it became that the holy seers, who still remained, should apprize, not only their contemporaries, but also their successors to the time of Christ, that the Lord had deposited for them, in the prophecies, a treasure of consolation and strength in their distresses, the exact prediction of which afforded them the proof, that they were not under the control of chance, but of their God, and at the same time the pledge that the predicted deliverance would no less surely come.

566. Ver. 14. ' *And the Lord will appear over them ; and his arrow goes forth as the lightning ; and the Lord will blow with the trumpet; he moves in the storms of the south.'* The wonderful aid which God affords His people is represented under the image of that wherein His omnipotence is most strikingly exhibited in nature, namely, a thunderstorm[3]. The Lord draws near in the thunderstorm, the lightnings are His arrows, the thunder the trumpet wherewith He gives to His host the signal for the assault. The image is strictly carried through, except only that the arrows of God are *compared* with the lightning ; not the lightnings, as in the fifteenth verse of the eighteenth Psalm (' *He sent his arrows, and scattered them, lightnings in abundance, and put them in confusion,'*) represented directly as the arrows of God.—The Lord appears in the thunderstorm *over* His people, His host, and thence hurls the lightnings, His arrows, at the enemy.—Storms of the south occur also in other passages[4] as peculiarly violent, while elsewhere those from the east commonly appear as the most vehement[5].

567. Ver. 15. ' *The Lord of Hosts will protect them ; they eat, tread under foot sling-stones, drink, make a tumult as from wine, become full as the sacrificial bowls, as the corners of the altar.'* Israel

---

[1] Dan. 8. 21.   [2] *Phaleg*, III. 3, cap. 154.
[3] As, only far more fully, in Ps. 18.
[4] Job 37. 9. Is. 21. 1, in the latter place in reference to Babylonia.
[5] Comp. Bochart, *Hieroz.* II. c. 102.

appears here, as in the fourth verse of the twenty-third chapter of Numbers, under the figure of a lion, '*which does not lie down until he devours prey, and drinks the blood of the slain ;*' they eat not, indeed, as several interpret, the good things of the enemy, but their flesh ; as plainly appears from the following word, *drink*, referring to the blood.—' *They tread sling-stones under their feet*,' so that the enemies, in order to designate their weakness and contemptibleness, are themselves represented as sling-stones. The figure of the lion is carried forward. That portion of the prey which he cannot devour he proudly treads upon with his feet. Entirely analogous is the fifth verse of the tenth chapter, ' *They are as heroes trampling on the dirt of the streets ;*' where the enemy, just as they are here represented as sling-stones, appear as dirt of the streets, while they are only *compared* therewith by Micah [1], who is less bold. In another respect those passages are parallel, where, in the figure borrowed from wild animals, the eating and trampling under foot are connected with one another. Thus in the seventh verse of the fifth chapter of Micah : ' *Israel will be among the nations as a lion among the beasts of the woods, as a young lion among the flocks of sheep, who, passing through, at once tramples under foot and tears in pieces, while no one is able to deliver.*' In the seventh verse of the seventh chapter of Daniel : ' *It devoured and brake in pieces, and stamped the residue with his feet.*'—' *They make a noise*,' signifies the drunkenness of the Israelites with victory and joy.—' *As wine*,' i. e. ' *as those who drink wine.*' This interpretation has in its favour the natural connexion with the verb immediately preceding ; the suitableness of the concise expression (indicating a whole proposition by a single word) to the character of the whole verse ; and lastly, in a very peculiar manner, the parallel passage, in the seventh verse of the tenth chapter, ' *Their heart rejoices as wine*,' for ' *as though they had drunk wine.*'—In the phrase, ' *they become full as the sacrificial bowl*,' the article shows that we are not to understand every sacred bowl, but only those in which, after all the veins of the victim had been opened, the blood was received by the priests, and in part sprinkled upon the horns of the altar of burnt sacrifice.—' *As the corners of the altar.*' The blood was properly sprinkled, not against the corners, but the horns of the altar which were upon them. The Prophet, however, here mentions the corners, because he considers the horns as belonging to them. Several, therefore, have been mistaken in concluding from this passage that the horns of the altar were only its four corners.

568. Ver. 16. ' *And the Lord grants them prosperity in this day, his people as a flock. For they shall be crown-stones raising themselves up on his land [2].*' A shepherd takes care of his flock, so the Lord takes care of His people.—The second part of the verse is very

---

[1] Chap. 7. 10.

[2] הוֹשִׁיעַ does not here stand for mere rescue and deliverance, but moreover for the imparting of prosperity in general.

variously interpreted; the correct explanation is, '*For in thy land they raise themselves up as crown-stones.*' Induced by the comparison of the enemies with *sling-stones*, the Prophet represents the Israelites under the figure of costly precious stones, which set in high crowns, that stand in the holy land of the Lord, widely diffuse their radiance. That it is the land *of the Lord*, in which the Israelites attain to this honour, constitutes at once its *cause* and the *pledge of its continuance*, and heightens their prosperity and their dignity[1].

569. Ver. 17. '*For how great is his goodness, how great his beauty! Corn makes young men spring up, and new-wine young women.*' It is very appropriate that the Prophet should praise with an exclamation of wonder the goodness of God, which He manifests to His people, and the beauty in which He appears to him. This explanation is confirmed by the parallel passage in the twelfth verse of the thirty-first chapter of Jeremiah, '*They come and exult on the height of Zion, and flow together to the goodness of Jehovah, to the corn and the must and the oil,*' which so harmonizes with the passage before us, that its use by Zechariah might almost be assumed; compare also the fourteenth verse, '*My people shall be full of my goodness.*' In the twentieth verse of the thirty-first Psalm, '*How great is thy goodness, which thou hast prepared for those who fear thee.*' In the seventh verse of the twenty-fifth Psalm, corn and wine are here first mentioned, as *a part* for *the whole* of the Divine blessings. Where there is an abundance of both, there is a rapid increase of the population. Altogether similar is the seventeenth verse of the seventy-second Psalm: '*If also there be only a handful of corn in the land, yet shall its fruit rustle on the summit of the mountains, like Lebanon, and they shall bloom forth from the city, as the grass of the earth;*' by which latter words, at the same time, the figure of *making to spring up* in this verse is illustrated. The abundance of the means of subsistence and increase of the population belongs to the Theocratic blessings, as the opposite to the Theocratic judgements. The specification of young men and maidens indicates that the children should not be prematurely taken away, as happens in the time of public calamity, but attain to full age; compare the twentieth verse of the sixty-fifth chapter of Isaiah, '*There shall no more be there children, who do not reach their days, or old persons, who do not fill up their years.*'

Chapter 10

570. Ver. 1. '*Ask the Lord for rain at the time of the latter rain; immediately the Lord causes lightnings, and gives to them an abundant*

---

[1] Some, as Mark, explain, "*Boundary stones are raised on this land.*" Many other interpreters explain after the Vulgate, "*Sacred stones are erected:*" that is, as *memorials of victory and Divine deliverance.* This interpretation has indeed more to recommend it than the former; but yet such a sense of מֵר cannot be proved, and the double כִּ can scarcely be accounted for.

rain, to each one grass on his field.' This verse stands in the closest connexion with the foregoing. The exhortation *to ask*, expresses the highest readiness of God to give what is desired, i. q. Ye need only ask, it requires but a mere request [1]. After this apostrophe, which contains indirectly the promise, the Prophet returns to the direct expression of it, as in the twelfth verse of the ninth chapter. The phrase, ' *at the time of the latter rain,*' is merely, as *a part* for the *whole*, an expression of the thought, ' *at the time when ye need rain;*' and we cannot thence conclude, that the latter rain was more necessary for the growth of vegetation than the former. Elsewhere [2] both are united. The choice of the name *Jehovah* is not without design. Rain was one of the *Theocratic* blessings, which the people enjoyed in case of true dependence on the Lord. The Prophet has in view the passage, Deut. 11. 13—15, the words of which he partly employs, ' *If thou will hearken to my commandments,*' &c. ' *so give I thee the rain of your land in its time, the former and the latter rain, and thou gatherest thy corn, thy wine, and thy must. Also give I grass [3] on thy field for thy cattle.*' The rain, among the multitude of the Theocratic blessings, is here rendered prominent only as a part for the whole. The lightnings are mentioned as its precursors, in the thirteenth verse of the tenth chapter of Jeremiah, ' *He maketh lightnings with rain.*' In the seventh verse of the hundred and thirty-fifth Psalm, the word used [4] means a peculiarly abundant rain, as is usual in a thunderstorm [5].

571. Ver. 2. ' *For the teraphim speak nothingness, and the soothsayers see lies, and the dreams speak vanity ; falsely do they console ; therefore do they wander as a flock : are harassed because they have no shepherds* [6]. ' *For'* does not refer to the first verse alone, but to the whole compass of the Divine promises contained in the preceding context. ' I will have compassion on my people and abundantly bless them : *for* now they have fallen into great distress by their apostasy from me.' The inquiry now arises, how the Prophet could place in the future manifestations of apostasy from God, which, according to the testimony of history, hardly appeared any more in the present (compare nevertheless the accounts of false prophets even in the new colony, Neh. 6. 10, &c., and the mention of conjurors, Mal. 3. 12), but on the contrary had been of frequent occurrence in the past [6]. The explanation is this. Shortly before and during the

[1] Altogether similar is chap. 9 12; comp. also 1 Kings 3. 5, " God said to Solomon; Ask what I shall give thee." 2 Kings 2. 9. Ps. 2. 8.

[2] As Joel 2. 23.

[3] עֲשֹׂב   [4] מִטַּר־נָשֶׁם

[5] The phrase, ' *every one,*' &c., indicates the extent of the blessing, which is not limited, as is usually the case with thundershowers, to one particular place.

[6] That that solution of the difficulty, which assumes that the second part was composed before the exile, is not the true one, appears, apart from every thing else, even from the verbal agreement of this passage with several of Ezekiel and Jeremiah, whom Zechariah most frequently imitates, comp. e. g. Jer. 27. 9, ' And ye shall not hearken to your prophets, and your soothsayers, and your dreamers, and your augurs, and your magicians.' 29. 8, ' Let not your prophets and your soothsayers deceive you, and ye shall not hearken to the dreams which ye dream.'

exile, in the most calamitous times of the state, false prophets in greater numbers than at any former period appeared in Jerusalem, as well as among the exiles; and the willing obedience, which the people rendered to them, was one chief cause of their misery. By foretelling nothing but prosperity, they effaced the impressions, which the threatening predictions of the true prophets had made, whom they endeavoured to represent as gloomy fanatics, thus hindering the people from that conversion, which was the only means of their deliverance. Jeremiah[1] brings against the priests and false prophets the charge, that, through their guilt, the whole land was filled with crimes and cursings. '*They strengthen*,' he says[2], '*the hands of the evil-doers, that they repent not.*' '*From the prophets of Jerusalem*,' he complains[3], '*crime has gone out over the whole land.*' Now Zechariah, who had taken for his model chiefly the prophecies of Jeremiah and Ezekiel, and to whom the fearful effects of this manifestation of the apostasy were so obvious, represents under its image that, which in future times should lead the people away from the law of God, and cause them to apostatize from Him. That this supposition is entirely natural is evident even from the analogies in this chapter alone. What is it else, e. g. when[4] *Egypt* is used to designate the land from which the covenant people shall at a *future* period be brought back ? Or when, according to the eleventh verse, God conducts Israel *anew* through the Red Sea ? Is not *the future* here also represented under the image of *the past*, which is essentially identical with it, and only differs in its individual character ?—The teraphim occur for the last time, before we meet with them in this passage, in the twenty-sixth verse of the twenty-first chapter of Ezekiel, where the king of Babylon, uncertain what resolution to form, consults them. Among the Hebrews, they were intermediate beings, by which they sought to learn the future from Jehovah; the consultation of them, therefore, did not involve total idolatry[5]. This remark makes the passage harmonize with those of Jeremiah and Ezekiel, concerning the false prophets shortly before and during the exile, in which they always appear as those who prophesied falsely in the name of Jehovah, and not in the name of a strange God. As intermediate beings, the teraphim in every religion to which they belong must have a different place and import. By *nothingness* is meant prophecies followed by no corresponding result; especially promises of a happy future, by which they deceive their votaries.—They *see lies.* Zechariah, even when speaking of the false prophets, employs the verb, which designates the peculiar form in which the true prophets received their revelations, because the false hypocritically imitated the '*ecstasy*' of the true; and of this they were sometimes perfectly aware, and at others more or less unconscious[6].—In '*dreams*

Ez. 21. 34, ' While the false prophets see for thee a nullity, and while the sooth-sayers prophesy for thee lies.' 22. 28, 'They see a nullity and prophesy to thee lies.' 34. 7, ' See ye not vain visions, and speak lying prophecies ?'

[1] 23. 9, 10.   [2] Ver. 14.   [3] Ver. 15.   [4] Ver. 10.
[5] This appears from Judges 17. 5, comp. with 18. 5, 6 ; Hos. 3, 4.
[6] In like manner, Ezekiel, in the passages cited in the note 6, p. 318.

speak vanity,' dreams are *personified,* and made to speak.—The verb [1] *to depart,* here especially of the straying of sheep from their .protecting folds, and of their dispersion, compare Jer. 50. 6, ' *My people are like perishing sheep, whose shepherds lead them astray; they make them wander on the mountains, they go from mountain to hill, and forget their folds.'*—Because they have *no* shepherd, i. e. no one who really deserves this name, who discharges the duties of his office. For it appears, from the third verse, that the people should not be without shepherds, though they rather deserved the name of wolves.

572. Ver. 3. ' *My anger is kindled against the shepherds, and I will punish the he-goats; for the Lord of hosts visits his flock, the house of Judah, ard makes them like his parade-horse in war.'* The miserable condition of the people, their destitution of shepherds, had been represented in the preceding verse as their own fault. But the Lord here promises, notwithstanding, that He will deliver them from their wicked leaders, the culpable instruments of their punishment. The interpreters hesitate whether by the shepherds to understand merely the *civil magistrates,* or, at the same time, *the spiritual leaders* of the people. It is true, that both sometimes occur combined under this appellation (compare the eighth verse of the eleventh chapter); here, however, the Prophet seems, like Ezekiel and Jeremiah [2] in most passages, to have in view only the former. This appears from the antithesis in the fourth verse, where the discourse relates only to able civil and military leaders, which the Lord would give to the people instead of their former base ones. It is also evident from the expression, ' *They are harassed, because they have no shepherd,'* where by the ' *because,'* the evil shepherds are represented as the direct, and [3] *the lying prophets,* or generally *the evil spiritual rulers* of the people, as the *indirect* cause of their misery [4]. Finally, the figurative representation of the deliverance of the flock, by freeing them from their evil shepherds, is very common in Ezekiel and Jeremiah, and probably derived from them by Zechariah [5]. We have here only still to inquire, whether we are to refer this to *native* or to *foreign* evil magistrates. That the latter were chiefly intended is at least highly probable from the emphatic contrast in the fourth verse, where a prominence entirely peculiar is given to the thought, that the new leaders provided for the people by God would be out of *the midst of them.* Accordingly prophecy and fulfilment most accurately coincide, although in the time of the latter native evil rulers of the people also were not wanting.—By the *he-goats,* according to Jahn,

---

[1] נָסַע.

[2] Comp. e. g. chap. 23, where the Prophet, ver. 1—8, threatens the wicked shepherds, the kings, and magistrates, then, ver. 9 to the end, the false prophets, and the wicked priests, as the second cause of the calamities of the people.

[3] By the עַל־כֵן.   [4] Comp. Num. 27. 17. Ezek. 34. 5.

[5] Comp. e. g. Jer. 23, where the Lord promises to punish the shepherds, to collect the flock from their dispersion in all lands, and give them good shepherds, at last the Messiah ; Ez. 34. 10, where God delivers the flock out of the hand of their evil shepherds, and now undertakes to be their shepherd Himself.

in the antithesis with the *shepherds*, are meant the inferior officers of the people ; but the *he-goats* are plainly only a different figurative designation of the same persons. The image is taken from the he-goats which march at the head of the flocks ; compare the eighth verse of the fiftieth chapter of Jeremiah, where the leaders are admonished, ' *Be as the he-goats before the flocks* [1].' In a manner entirely similar, Ezekiel [2] announces that God would judge between *the sheep* and *the he-goats*, and deliver the former from the injustice of the latter [3]. ' *For* ' gives the reason of the punishment to be inflicted on the evil rulers. It is the tender care of the Lord for His people, and His will to deliver them from their misery. They are *His* flock ; therefore He can no longer suffer them to be ruined by evil shepherds.— The last member is explained by Jonathan, Jarchi, Kimchi, Jahn, and others : ' *He makes them like a horse whose excellence is in war*, that is, ' *like an excellent war-horse.*' But the interpretation, '*He makes them* His *splendid charger* [4] *in war*,' has in its favour not only the accents, but also, what is of considerable importance in a prophecy of Zechariah, the great boldness and sublimity of the figure. Judah is here, in the war which the Lord carries on against the oppressors of His people, His stately, richly-ornamented war-horse, just as before Judah was His bow and Ephraim His arrow.—A parade-horse [5] is a select horse, such as an earthly king is accustomed to ride in war, stately by nature, and decorated with costly housings and other ornaments.

573. Ver. 4. ' *Out of the midst of him will be the corner-stone, out of him will be the peg and battle-bow, out of him will come forth every ruler.*'—' *Out of the midst of him,*' that is, of *Judah.* The sense is : Having attained to perfect freedom by the help of the Lord, who gives victory to their arms, they shall now receive rulers and magistrates *from among themselves*, and an independent power in war ; and, whereas they were formerly a prey to foreign conquerors, they shall now inspire even foreign nations with terrour.—The frequent figurative designation of princes, or rulers of the people, by *corner* or *corner-stone*, is grounded on the comparison of *the state* with *a building*, which rests on the prince as its corner-stone. This is evident from passages, like the twenty-second verse of the hundred and eighteenth Psalm, ' *The stone which the builders rejected has become the corner-stone.*' In the sixteenth verse of the twenty-eighth chapter of Isaiah, ' *I lay in Zion a precious corner-stone.*' The opposite of what Isaiah here predicts to Judah, Jeremiah (in the twenty-sixth verse of the fifty-first chapter) predicts to Babylon : ' *They will no more take from thee a stone for a corner, and a stone for a foundation,*' on which Michaelis justly remarks. The sense is, *There shall no more be taken from the race of the Chaldeans a support of the state* ;

[1] Is. 14. 9.   [2] Chap. 34. 17, 48.
[3] The verb פָּקַד with עַל " to visit for punishment," with the *acc.* ; to visit only to benefit.
[4] *Prachtross.* I inadvertently left Dr. Keith's translation, '*parade-horse,*' on the preceding page.
[5] סוּם הוׄר.

that is, a king or prince. This word *peg* has been very strikingly explained by Lowth on Isa. 22. 23, where it is said of Eliakim, ' *I drive him in as a peg in a firm place,—and they hang upon it all the splendour of his father's house.*' It is customary in the East to furnish the inside of apartments with rows of large nails, or pegs, which are fixed into the wall when it is built [1]. On these firm nails, already prepared, they hang all kinds of household stuff. They serve, therefore, as a suitable image of those men who are *the supports* and *pillars* of the whole being of the state.—The *battle-bow* stands here for the military power, or the *apparatus bellicus* in general. Thus not unfrequently, ' *to break the bow,*' or ' *strike it out of the hand,*' for ' *to deprive one of his armour and weapons* [2].' The word translated, *ruler,* means a *tyrannical ruler;* nor is there the smallest reason here to relinquish the usual sense, if we only refer the hardness and severity expressed by the word, not to the *covenant people,* but to *their enemies.* Similar is the second verse of the fourteenth chapter of Isaiah, ' *They take captive those who led them captive, and rule over their tyrants.*' It is in favour of this interpretation that what follows then becomes appropriate.

574. Ver. 5. ' *And they are heroes* [3] *trampling on the mire of the streets in war* [4], *and they fight, for the Lord is with them, and the horsemen are put to shame.*' " *They* fight ;" there is a contrast with the hitherto passive conduct of the covenant people, their passive subjugation. Now by the aid of the Lord brave warriors are formed from despised slaves. On the contrary, their oppressors, hitherto the proud hostile horsemen, are covered with shame and disgrace. The *cavalry* in Daniel [5] is also designated as the chief strength

---

[1] Comp. Chardin, in Harmer's *Observations,* iii. p. 49.

[2] 1 Sam. 2. 4. Ezek. 39. 3. Hos. 1. 5. נוֹשֵׁק.

[3] כְ stands here again as in the third verse. Thus, even in prose, in Neh. 7. 2, 'he is a true man,' i. q. he corresponds to the idea, he is the lively image of a true man.

[4] בּוֹסִים בְּטִיט חֻצוֹת, several translate, "treading (viz. their enemies) in the dirt of the streets." Our interpretation, especially as it is confirmed also by chap. 9. 15, "they trample on sling-stones," would certainly have been generally adopted, if the construction of the verb בּוּם with a following בְ, while it elsewhere always takes the *accus.,* had not made a difficulty. The explanation is the following. בּוּם stands here, not, as commonly, in a transitive, but an intransitive sense: properly, they tread down, or they tread about, on the dirt of the streets. In the same manner, Ps. 49. 15, the elsewhere transitive synonyme רָדָה is connected with בְ of the person, וַיִּרְדּוּ בָם, "they will tread about *upon* them." Here the intransitive meaning is indicated by the form itself. The participial form קוֹם is not, as is commonly supposed and even by Ewald, p. 406, an unusual contraction of the *part. trans.,* but it is a participial form of the intransitive *Kal.* This is evident from the fact that it occurs only in intransitive verbs, e. g. בּוֹשׁ, אוֹר, קוֹם. The only forms where it is supposed to occur in a transitive sense, גֹחִי, Ps. 22. 10, and גֹזִי, Ps. 71. 6, rest, as may be easily shown, on a false interpretation. The verb נוּחַ never occurs, not even in Mic. 4. 10, in a transitive sense, and therefore, even in the cited passage, גֹחַ cannot be understood as a *part.* גֹזִי is not to be derived from גַּז, but from גָּזָה.

[5] Chap. 11. 40.

of the host of the Grecian ruler of Syria, namely, Antiochus Epiphanes.

575. Ver. 6. ' *And I strengthen the house of Judah, and give prosperity to the house of Joseph, and I make them dwell; for I have compassion on them, and they shall be as though I had not cast them away, for I am the Lord their God and will hear them* [1].' The mention of the *return* does not begin till the eighth verse : here the Prophet still speaks of Judah and Israel in connexion ; the former *had already returned;* only to the latter, most of whom at least still continued in exile, is the return promised in what follows. The verb *to dwell* is especially emphatic. Hitherto the covenant people, under a foreign dominion, had been as strangers in their own land. Now, for the first time after their oppressors are vanquished and driven out, shall they become properly dwellers and possessors, as they had been in the times before the exile. Similar is Ezekiel [2], ' *I make you to dwell as in your former time, and do you good as in your past time.*'—' *And they shall be,*' ' *and I will hear them,*' is the looser Hebrew connexion for, ' *therefore* shall they be,' ' *therefore* will I hear them.' God's compassionate benevolence, and His covenant relation to the people of Israel, are the ground of their deliverance : compare the seventeenth verse of the forty-first chapter of Isaiah, ' *I, Jehovah*' (the Theocratic name of God) ' *will hear them. I, the God of Israel, will not forsake them.*'

576. Ver. 7. ' *And Ephraim is as a hero, and their heart rejoices as wine, and their sons see it and rejoice, their heart exults in the Lord.*' The Prophet, from this verse onward, occupies himself exclusively with Ephraim. At first he promises that descendants also of the citizens of the former kingdom of the ten tribes shall participate in the glorious struggle; he then gives the greater promise, that, after this struggle, the large mass of the people also, who during its continuance were still scattered in all lands, should return to their native country, and to their ancient covenant relation to the Lord. That the Prophet occupies himself so earnestly and fully with Ephraim, is explained, as Calvin rightly saw, only by the circumstances of the time in which he lived. Had the predictions of the older prophets in reference to Judah then but begun to be fulfilled, and did they therefore need, in order that the people might not believe themselves deceived, to be resumed ; much more was this the case in regard to those which related to Ephraim. The great mass of this tribe were still in exile, although a part of them had joined themselves to the returning Jews, and the hope of the great future restoration, promised by the prophets, had only a weak point of connexion with the present.—With respect to ' *as wine,*' compare what has been said on the fifteenth verse of the ninth chapter. A similar merely *suggested* comparison is, ' *as potash,*' in the twenty-fifth verse

---

[1] הוֹשֵׁבוֹתִים. Zechariah, by a permutation of the verbs עו with those פ, *peculiar* to that late period, has employed this anomalous form, instead of the regular הוֹשַׁנְתִּים (comp. Ewald, p. 489.)

[2] Chap. 36. 11.

of the first chapter of Isaiah, for ' *as potash purifies.*' That the sons of the Ephraimites should participate in their prosperity, shows that it was not to be merely of a short duration.

577. Ver. 8. The Prophet now proceeds from that portion of the Ephraimites, who should take part in the struggle of the Jews against the Greeks, to the far greater portion, who at that time were still in exile.—' *I will hiss to them and collect them, for I have redeemed them, and they become numerous, as they were before.*' The figure of hissing is taken from the bee-master, who, by means of a whistle, calls the swarm of bees out of and into their hives [1]. The meaning of the figure is (as Calvin saw) that God would *easily*—by a whistle, by a nod, as it were—collect them, though dispersed in different lands. — ' *For I have redeemed them.*' This is to be understood of the Divine *counsel*. As soon as this has once been taken, nothing can hinder the execution.—The question now arises respecting the restoration here mentioned. Grotius supposes, that the Prophet here announces that the victory of the Maccabees, and the happy condition of the land afterwards, will be to many of the Israelites, still in a strange land, an inducement to return. But the sense of the promise, which is far more comprehensive, is hereby, to say the least, not exhausted ; especially, as in the ninth verse, the return of the exiles is placed in close connexion with their conversion. The return of the ten tribes always belongs in the Prophets to the Messianic hopes. We must, therefore, with Calvin, Mark, and others, assume that the Prophet, chiefly at least, had in view here the reception of the Israelites into the Theocracy by Christ. That this was represented by a return to Palestine, the seat of the Theocracy at the time of the Prophet, is justified by the general character of the prophetic discourse, and is particularly free from difficulty in the case of one with whom this figure, in general, so much prevails [2].

578. Ver. 9. ' *And I will sow them among the nations, and in distant lands will they remember me, and with their children live again and return.*'—The exile, which seemed to be a sign of the perpetual rejection of Israel, shall be a direct means of his conversion and restoration. This Moses had already prophesied [3], ' *The Lord will scatter you among the nations.—And ye will there serve strange gods. —Finally, however, ye will seek the Lord your God, and find him, because ye will seek him with all the heart, and all the soul. In thy distress thou wilt at a future period return to the Lord* [4].' This prophecy, which, in reference to the Jews, had already in part been fulfilled by the change of mind they experienced in the exile, and by the return which resulted from it, the Prophet here resumes in reference to the Israelites. The verb *to sow* is frequently used of the *dispersion* of the covenant people *as a punishment:* but here the context and parallelism require that the words, ' *and I will sow them,*' should contain, at least, at the same time something of a joyful cha-

---

[1] Comp. Lowth on Is. 5. 26.
[2] Comp. e. g. ver. 11.
[3] Deut. 4. 27 sq.
[4] In like manner, Ezek. 6. 11.

racter. The dispersed Israelites, who are hereafter to be still more scattered, shall be a seed sown of God, which will bring forth rich fruits. An entirely similar double sense, ' *God will disperse,*' and ' *God will sow,*' is found in the name *Jezreel,* which Hosea gives to one of his sons, the type of the Israelitish people [1]. It is worthy of remark that there is here predicted (what has been confirmed by the result) a still wider dispersion of the Israelites, than that which then happened.—In the expression, ' *and they live,*' is intimated in one word the image, which Ezekiel [2] has so well carried out ; compare e. g. in the fourteenth verse, ' *And I put my spirit within you, and ye revive, and I make you rest in your land.*'—The often misinterpreted phrase, ' *with your children,*' designates here also, as in the seventh verse, the *permanency* of the benefit. This is shown by the parallel passage of the twenty-fifth verse of the thirty-seventh chapter of Ezekiel, ' *And they inhabit the land, which I have given to my servant Jacob, they and their children, and their children's children for ever.*'

579. Ver. 10. ' *And I bring them back out of the land of Egypt, and out of Ashur will I collect them, and to the land of Gilead and Lebanon will I bring them, and they shall find no room.*' This verse is an individualization of the foregoing. The interpreters here find a difficulty in the mention of *Egypt,* as a land out of which the exiles shall be brought back, while no carrying away of the citizens of the kingdom of the ten tribes to Egypt can be pointed out in history. Most assume, that, at the destruction of this kingdom by the Assyrians, many of its inhabitants fled into Egypt, to avoid being carried away. It is, however, a suspicious circumstance, that history is entirely silent on this point. Moreover, though the fact were conceded, still this passage cannot be referred to it. The comparison of the eleventh verse particularly shows that the Egyptians, as well as the Assyrians, must be regarded as *powerful oppressors* of the Israelites, while, in the case supposed, they must have given them a hospitable reception. It therefore only remains for us to assume, that Egypt is here mentioned because it was the first land in which the Israelites had suffered an oppressive captivity [3] ; that it is a *figurative designation* of the lands in which the ten tribes were in exile at the time of the Prophet, and would be at a future period. The transition to this mode of representation appears in passages like the twenty-fourth verse of the tenth chapter of Isaiah, ' *Fear not, my people, before Ashur, who smites thee with a staff and raises his rod against thee as Egypt.*' As now it was the constant practice of the prophets, and the poets generally, to place *the comparison* instead of *the thing compared,* the transition was easy to the representation which prevails in the passage before us. In favour of it, however, not only analogies (compare page 111, and above, on the tenth verse of the fifth chapter), but even passages can be produced, where Egypt itself is placed

[1] Comp. 1. 4. 2. 24.   [2] Chap. 37.

[3] Comp. Is. 52. 4, " *My people went down in the beginning to Egypt, in order to dwell there, and Ashur did them violence in the end.*"

in a manner entirely similar.   The two most remarkable are Hosea
8. 13, ' *Now will he remember their sins and punish their misdeeds;
they shall return to Egypt.*'   Chap. 9. 3, ' *They shall not dwell in
the land of the Lord, and Ephraim turns back to Egypt, and in
Ashur they shall eat what is unclean.*'   It is obvious that here, the
lands into which the Israelites should in future be carried away captive, are *figuratively designated* by *Egypt*, a land in which they had
at first been reduced to bondage, and a return to which could not
have been in the mind of the Prophet, who anticipated danger only
from the Assyrians.   It is further remarkable, that the Prophet, in
the sixth verse of the ninth chapter, extending the image even further,
names *Memphis* as a city where the Israelites would find their grave.
—If now it is established, that Zechariah in this place does not mean
Egypt proper, so neither by *Ashur*, which is connected with it, here
and in the eleventh verse, are we to understand any particular kingdom.   Ashur is rather, in like manner, a figurative designation of
those kingdoms in which the Israelites were in exile during the time
of the Prophet, and would be at a future period.   This demonstration, however, does not entirely invalidate the argument, which has
been derived from the passage before us, against the integrity of
Zechariah.   The question still arises, how a Prophet, *after the captivity*, could choose the *Egyptians and Assyrians* as the type of the
oppressors of his people, *while he omitted the Chaldeans, who had
been their most destructive enemies.*   This difficulty would be invincible, if the Prophet were here speaking of the Jews alone, or even
merely of the whole of the covenant people [1].   But in the passage
before us, the Prophet *speaks solely of the Ephraimites.*   For *them*
Egypt and Assyria had actually been *exclusively* the most dangerous
enemies of former time ; therefore they only (and *not the Chaldeans*,
who did not make their appearance *until the extinction of the kingdom
of the ten tribes*) were suited to be a type of their enemies in general.
Zechariah here occupies the same point of view as Hosea, who [2], in
reference to the Israelites, prophesies, ' *they will return out of Egypt
and Ashur.*'   Finally, the Prophet certainly had directly before his
eyes the cited passages, in which Egypt and Ashur are connected in
the same relation with each other as here.—The whole argument
serves at the same time to show how little reason there is to protest
against understanding the restoration to the promised land figura-

---

[1] When e. g. Is. 27. 13, it is said, ' *The exiles in the land of Ashur, and the
banished in the land of Egypt, come and pray before the Lord on the holy mountain of
Jerusalem,*' although Egypt and Ashur are here in like manner typical, as Gesenius very justly remarks, "instead of the different lands of the world in which
the Jews have been scattered, Assyria and Egypt are here mentioned," yet
Kleinert is in the right, when he considers this passage as an incontrovertible
proof against the composition of the whole portion, chap. 24—27, in the exile,
and in favour of its genuineness.   Or when, Isaiah 19. 23 sq., Egypt and Ashur
are mentioned as the two kingdoms heretofore most hostile to the covenant people, and to one another, which in the time of the Messiah should be closely
united with the covenant people, and with one another, by the common worship
of the Lord, and live in the most peaceful intercourse ; so is the genuineness of
this portion even thereby sufficiently established.

[2] Chap. 11. 11.

tively. If it cannot be denied that the lands, *out of which the Israelites are brought back*, are to be understood only as *types*, what objection can be urged, if the land *to which they shall be restored* is, in like manner, regarded as a *type ?*—The land of Gilead and Lebanon is here not a designation of *the whole promised land*, as most interpreters suppose, but specially of the former country of the ten tribes. This was divided into two parts, that beyond the Jordan, the land of Gilead, and that on this side, which extended to Libanus, and therefore might suitably receive its name from it.

580. Ver. 11. '*And the Lord goes through the sea, the distress, and smites in the sea the waves, and all the floods of the Nile are put to shame, and the pride of Ashur is overthrown, and the staff of Egypt shall yield.*' The former deliverances of the covenant people served them as a pledge of those that were future ; since they revealed, at the same time, the power and the will of the Lord to help them, who is at all times the same. Nothing, therefore, is more natural than that the Prophet, in the description of the *future*, should bring to memory *the past ;* thus, as it were, calling upon the Lord, not to be unlike Himself, and also strengthening the faith of the people in the promises which contradicted indeed the appearance of things. This frequently happens when the past and future are brought into comparison, compare e. g. the ninth verse of the fifty-first chapter of Isaiah, '*Awake, put on strength, thou arm of Jehovah, awake as the days of former times, as the ancient generations.*'—'*Art thou not he who driedst up the sea, the water of the great deep, who madest the depths of the sea for a way on which the redeemed went through ?*' But, in like manner also, they often employed *the past* as a type for the *future;* they frequently transferred the former in its individual character to the latter, which is explained partly from the flowing together of figure and reality, proper to poetry in general, and partly from the nature of prophecy in particular. Thus it is said, in the second verse of the thirty-first chapter of Jeremiah, '*The people find favour in the wilderness, who remain of the sword; the Lord goes to bring Israel to rest:*' as the Lord once pitied His people, when sorely plagued in the wilderness, on account of their continual apostasy, and led the remnant of them to Canaan ; so also will He pity them in their present distress, of which they are themselves the cause', and lead them back into their native land. Thus in the sixteenth and seventeenth verses of the second chapter of Hosea, '*I lead her into the wilderness, and speak to her heart, and give her her vineyards there, and the valley of Achor, for a door of hope;*' for, '*as I comforted Israel aforetime in the wilderness by promises of prosperity, and then, at the very entrance into the land of Canaan, filled them with joyful hopes by a sight of the fruitful region; so will I also in the future comfort and richly bless them.*' Especially remarkable, however, is the passage, Isa. 11. 15, 16, which Zechariah has so plainly imitated, that it must of itself be sufficient to render very suspicious the idea, that the second part was composed by an earlier writer, especially as it also serves at the same time to prove other later prophets, between whom and Zechariah a similar agreement is

found, particularly Jeremiah and Ezekiel, to have been independent
in relation to him[1].—'*He goes through the sea, the distress.*' It is
not merely a crude cleaving to the letter, regardless of all analogy
and the whole substance of the prophecy, when the Jewish interpreters, as Jerome relates, refer the word to a future wonderful passage of the Israelites through the strait between Byzantium and
Chalcedon ; it is at the same time a gross misunderstanding of the
letter itself[2].—The *article* points to a definite sea, *the Arabian gulf*,
the same through which the Israelites had already once been led ;
compare the fifteenth verse of the eleventh chapter of Isaiah, '*The
Lord lays a curse upon the tongue of the sea of Egypt.*'—In the
words, '*he smites the waves in the sea,*' a personification of the wave,
as the enemy subdued by God, lies at the foundation.—The words,
'*all the floods of the Nile are ashamed,*' contain a manifest allusion
to the passage through the Jordan. This comparatively small stream,
however, is not sufficient for the Prophet ; he mentions instead of it
the Nile, as Isa. 11. 15, the Euphrates[3]. That in the last words,
Ashur and Egypt, as the most powerful oppressors of the Israelites
formerly, stand merely as types of their tyrannical rulers in general,
has already been shown[4].

581. Ver. 12. '*And I strengthen them in the Lord, and in his name
will they walk, saith the Lord.*' The Lord is designated[5], He
on whom the strength of Israel depends. The use of the noun
instead of the pronoun is emphatic. It calls the attention to what it
means, " to receive strength from the Lord, the Almighty, and the
living one." The '*name of the Lord*' signifies the whole compass
of His perfections, as it is designated by His name, the image and
the expression of His being. A walking, which is in the name of
the Lord, is one in which His perfection reveals itself in all its

---

[1] In reference to the subject of '*shall pass through,*' interpreters are not
agreed. The people is commonly taken as the subject ; then however the change
of persons, which immediately occurs without any notice, since the following,
'*and he smites,*' must refer to the Lord, is unnatural. The truth was seen by
Mark. It *is the Lord*, who, at the head of the Israelites marches boldly through
the sea, and strikes down their proud opposers, the roaring waves. " He goes
through the field of floods, the victorious hero." A complete parallel is furnished by Ps. 114, where the sea, as it sees the Lord advance in front of the
Israelites, quickly flees, the terrified Jordan turns back. It was unnecessary
expressly to mention the Lord, Him, who was continually present to the soul of
the Prophet, who alone could accomplish such deeds, the only deliverer of His
people. צָרָה standing in apposition.

[2] The explanation of Jonathan (*fient eis miracula et virtutes, sicut factæ sunt
patribus eorum in mari*), shows that this misunderstanding was not universal, even
among the Jews.

[3] The latter, several interpreters, as Grotius and Mark, would here also understand by אוֹר; Jahn takes it for the Jordan. But both suppositions are inadmissible. It is true, that *Jeor*, Job 28. 10, occurs in the sense *stream*, in
general ; in Dan. 12. 5 sq. of the Tigris. But in the passage before us, the
omission of the article, which is found in Daniel, shows, that the word stands as
a proper name. As such, however, it can mean only the Nile.

[4] Parallel passages are Is. 10. 27. 14. 25. 9. 3.

[5] In בְּיהוָה.

strength.   Walking, according to the context and parallelism, cannot
here relate to the conduct, but must be taken literally.

Chapter 11

582.   Hitherto had the Prophet chiefly [1] copied in his prophecies
only the joyful side of the great picture of the future condition of the
covenant people ; here another scene suddenly presents itself, and, in
describing it to his hearers and readers, he completes the correct,
indeed, but partial representation of the future, which he had hitherto
given, and guards against the abuse to which it might be liable by
the carnally minded.

583.   The whole portion may be divided into three parts.   The
three first verses, which serve as it were for a prelude to the rest,
describe the desolation of the whole land by foreign foes.   The relation of a twofold symbolical action of the Prophet, which took place
in vision, gives a deeper insight into the causes of this event.   In the
first (in the fourth and ten following verses), the Prophet supplies
the place of the great angel and revealer of the Lord, and typifies
his future actions.   Israel, devoted to destruction by the Divine
decree, appears as a flock destined to the slaughter.   The Prophet
makes an attempt to rescue them ; he undertakes the office of a
shepherd over the poor flock, and labours to deliver them from the
evil shepherds, who would lead them to destruction.   But the re-
fractoriness of the shepherds and the flock compels him to give up
his office, and abandon the flock to the full misery from which they
had hitherto been preserved by himself.   He now demands his
reward ; they give him the contemptible one of thirty pieces of
silver.   In this way is the last manifestation of the Lord's mercy
towards His people by the Messiah, and the rejection of him typified.
The Prophet then represents, at the command of the Lord, in a
second symbolical action, the wicked shepherds, who will consume
and destroy the flock, after the rejection of the good shepherd.

584.   Ver. 1.   ' *Open, O Lebanon, thy gates, and let fire devour thy
cedars.*'   The representation is altogether dramatic.   Gates are attributed to Lebanon as being a natural fortress, for the Prophet, instead of
announcing to it its future desolation, commands it to open its gates.
The sense is : ' *Thou, O Lebanon, wilt be stormed and devastated by
the enemy.*'   Lebanon is mentioned as the *northern bulwark* of the
land, which being stormed, it would stand open to the invading enemies ; the oak forests of Basan on the one side, and the shrubbery of
the Jordan on the other, point out that the destroying host of enemies
spread themselves over the whole land.   We must not, however, so
adhere to the literal sense, as to refer the hostile devastation merely to
the individual objects mentioned in the three first verses ; nay, it

[1] Compare, however, chap. 5.

does not even imply that all these objects, the cedars and cypresses of Lebanon, the oaks of Basan, the shrubbery of Jordan, should be actually laid waste during the hostile invasion. In such representations, particular instances serve merely to designate the whole by an individual example ; *a total devastation of the land by an invading enemy from the north* is the theme which lies at the foundation of the Prophet's description, and, in carrying this out, he particularly mentions what is especially distinguished in the land. Lebanon, with its proud cedars, must here receive the first place, even on account of the dependence of Zechariah on the earlier prophets, with whom Lebanon is a constant designation of all that is high, invincible, strong [1]. It here designates, by way of individualization, *all that is exalted in the land of Judea ;* in the case of such an *individualization*, the object named is also *included*, while in the case of *an image*, it serves only as a designation of something else. By confounding the two, particularly in the Prophets, a multitude of false interpretations has been occasioned [2].

585. Ver. 2. ' *Howl, thou cypress; for the cedar falls, laid waste are the lofty. Howl ye oaks of Basan; for the strong forest is overthrown.*' The cedars, in relation to the cypresses, and the mountain forest of Lebanon, in contrast with the groves of Basan, stand here as an individualization of what is most distinguished and exalted in relation to what is indeed less so, but nevertheless still excellent and distinguished above the rest. Has the former not been able to withstand the conqueror, the latter sees its destruction to be the more certain ; and the low and insignificant is so inevitably given up to ruin, that it need not be particularly mentioned. The *cypresses* [3] are indeed placed below the cedars, but occupy the second place after them, on account of their hard and firm wood, suited to the building of palaces and ships ; and hence elsewhere also [4], they are joined with them. In like manner the *oak forests of Basan* were in great esteem, as the oak in general was reckoned among the noblest trees, compare Isa. 2. 13, Ezek. 27. 6. It is, in general, a custom of the prophets, when the strong has fallen, to exhort the weaker to fear and lamentation, and in this way to express the thought that there now remains no deliverance for the latter. Thus: Isa. 23. 14, ' *Howl ye ships of Tarshish; for your stronghold is destroyed.*' Jer. 49. 3, ' *Howl, Heshbon, for Ai is destroyed.*'—The words, ' *which* are magnificent,' expresses either the ground, why in general the cedars are named, and the cypresses, on account of their fall, exhorted to lamentation (the cedar is the queen of the forest; ' *Does this happen in the green wood, what will be in the dry ?* ' compare Ezek. 21. 3, ' *Behold I kindle in thee a fire, and it consumes in*

---

[1] Cf. Is. 2. 13; 40. 16: 37. 24 ; 14. 8. Jer. 22. 6.

[2] Calvin, and indeed he only, has discerned the truth in the passage before us. Others understand by *Lebanon*, (1) the temple at Jerusalem ; (2) Jerusalem; (3) all Palestine ; (4) the kingdom of the ten tribes.

[3] That these are to be understood by בְּרוֹשׁ has been proved, among others, by Gesenius in the *Thes.* s. v.

[4] As Is. 14. 8. Ezek. 31. 8.

thee every green tree and every dry tree')—or it refers to a difference
among the cedars themselves ; the cedar forest on Lebanon consists
even now of two kinds of trees, the *high and majestic ancient trees*,
(in Jeremiah l. c. called ' *the choice of his cedars*,') and those of a
more recent growth. Accordingly, the words contain a climax,
even the most splendid cedars have fallen, how then can the rest of
the forest expect to be spared ? The latter sense, on account of the
parallel passage of Jeremiah, is certainly to be preferred.

586. Verse 3. ' *The sound of the howl of the shepherds ; for laid
waste is their ornament: the sound of the roaring of the lions ; for laid
waste is the pride of the Jordan.*' The Prophet describes what he
perceives in inward vision, and hence the absence of the verb is explained, and there is no occasion to assume an ellipsis [1]. *The pride
of Jordan* is the stately shrubbery, which covers its banks, so that its
waters cannot be obtained until a path has been made through it,
and which serves as an abode for innumerable wild beasts, though
now no longer for lions. *The pride of Jordan* occurs in three passages of Jeremiah, and in him alone ; and also in all these three passages it is designated especially as an *abode of lions*, which it certainly did not become till the land by the desolating wars towards
the end of the Jewish state was more and more depopulated [2]. At
the time to which the second part of Zechariah has been recently
assigned, it had not yet become so [3].—The *ornament of the shepherds*
according to a comparison of the parallel passages of Jeremiah, are
the excellent pastures, not, as Rosenmüller supposes, the trees, which
afforded them shade. What the Prophet here expresses by way of
individualization, the thought, that each one loses that which is his
pride, his joy, the desire of his eyes, the love of his soul, Ezekiel, in
the twenty-eighth verse of the thirty-third chapter, embraces in the
general proposition, ' *I make the land a waste, its mighty pride is
extinct, the mountains of Israel are made desolate, so that no man
passes through.*' The howling shepherds and the roaring lions,
frightened from their lairs, are the representatives of all in the land,
who have any good to be lost.

587. Ver. 4. With this verse, to which the three preceding ones
are a sort of prelude, the relation of a symbolical action commences,
in which the Prophet represents another person, and typifies his
future actions and fate. That this is customary in the symbolical
actions of the prophets every one of them proves. Thus e. g. Isaiah [4]
typifies the future fate of the Egyptians and Ethiopians. So Jeremiah [5], and Ezekiel [6], typify the circumstances of the covenant

[1] An exactly parallel passage is found in Jer. 25. 34 sq. There can indeed be
no doubt that Zechariah had it in view.
[2] Comp. 2 Kings 17.
[3] Jer. 49. 19, in the prophecy against Edom: " Behold, as a lion will he go up
from the *pride of Jordan* to the fold of the strong." It occurs also *verbatim*
50. 45, in the prophecy against Babylon. Chap. 12. 5, " In the land of peace
dost thou confide, but what wilt thou do in *the pride of the Jordan*," a secure
region is contrasted with the environs of the Jordan, dangerous on account of
lions.
[4] Chap. 20.   [5] Chap. 20.   [6] Chap. 4.

people.   In the symbolical action, which is related in the three first
chapters of Hosea, the Prophet represents the Lord, and typifies in
his actions his future conduct towards the covenant people.—In
determining the person represented by the Prophet in the present
instance, the choice lies only between *the Lord* and *His Angel*, or
revealer.   In favour of the latter we cannot argue, that the Lord is
several times [1] *distinguished* from the subject of discourse; this distinction belongs, as the comparison of Hosea shows, to the nature of
symbolic action; it refers not to the subject, but to the drapery;
the person represented tells him, who makes the representation,
what he must do, in order that the representation may correspond
to the subject.   Just as little, however, can we appeal in favour
of the first to the fact, that [2] Jehovah calls the base reward which
had been given to the shepherd the splendid price which had been
paid to Himself, the Lord.   As the Angel of the Lord, united with
Him by a unity of being, is throughout the Scriptures at one time
distinguished from Him, as the person sent from Him who sends, at
another shares in His name and in His actions, so also in Zechariah.
The most remarkable example is chap. 2. 12, 13, ' *Thus saith* Jehovah of Hosts : *after the glory* [3] *he has sent me to the heathen who rob
you ; for he that touches you touches the apple of* his *eye. For behold,
I brandish my hand against them, and they become for a prey to them
whom they served.   And he shall know that Jehovah of Hosts hath
sent me.*'   The person speaking here *distinguishes himself* from Jehovah of Hosts, who has sent him, but the Prophet nevertheless *gives
him the name of Jehovah of Hosts,* and he attributes to himself a
Divine work, the destruction of the enemies of the covenant people.
—The decision depends rather on the result furnished by the collective contents of the predictions of the Prophet respecting the relation of the Lord and His Angel to the covenant people.   But here it
is soon perceived, that all relations of the Lord to His people are
conducted through the mediation of His revealer, endowed with the
entire fulness of His omnipotence, that all blessings to be imparted
to them proceed from Him, that He is the proper protecting and
covenant God of the Israelites.   It is He, who, in the eighth verse
of the first chapter, accompanied by a host of angels, is present in
the valley of myrtle-bushes, the symbol of the covenant people; who,
in the fourteenth verse of the second chapter, promises to dwell in the
midst of them ; who, in the first and following verses of the third
chapter, rebukes the complaint of Satan against the covenant people,
in the person of their representative Joshua, and out of his own full
power imparts to him the forgiveness of sins.   To whom, but to
Him, the constant shepherd of the people, could the last and greatest
attempt described in this portion, to prove His pastoral fidelity
towards them, be attributed?   This result, thus independently obtained, is still confirmed by the fact, that we meet again with the

---

[1] As ver. 4—13.   [2] Ver. 13.
[3] Rightly Jonathan : " Post gloriam, quæ promissa est, ut adducatur super
vos."

reward of thirty pieces of silver in the history of the Angel of the
Lord, manifested in the Messiah, and that he is designated in the
New Testament as the subject of the Prophet's representation.—
Whether the symbolic action here described took place *inwardly* or
outwardly, we scarcely need inquire, since the former, as Maimonides has already shown [1], is so very obvious. The guarding of the
flock of slaughter, the destruction of their three shepherds, the imparting of the reward of thirty pieces of silver,—all this cannot have
taken place outwardly ; the less so, since the subject matter often
appears behind the symbol, as e. g. in the eleventh verse, where the
miserable sheep are spoken of, who adhered to the great high shepherds, and who observed that it was the word of the Lord, and in the
twelfth verse, where the Prophet treats with the flock itself concerning the reward ; both which are inexplicable, if the Prophet fed a
literal flock of sheep. The supposition, moreover, that the symbolic
action was *internal,* is favoured by the analogy of the visions of the
first part, which differ from it only in this, that here the Prophet
himself comes forward as the chief actor in the scene, while there he
mostly co-operates only so far [2] as the disclosures respecting the
import of the symbolic representations are imparted to him. But in
general the symbolic actions in the prophets, who appeared after the
connexion with the Chaldees, viz. Ezekiel and Daniel, are almost
uniformly *internal,* which was owing to a participation in the exceedingly rich Chaldeo-Babylonian imagination.—With respect to
the import of the symbolic action, those interpreters are at once to be
rejected, who find here references to events *before the exile.* The
reference then to the time of the second Temple being established,
the choice can lie only between two interpretations, the one which
finds here typified *the whole condition of God towards the covenant
people under the second temple ;* the other, which regards the symbolic representation as a type of *one particular effort* under the
second Temple to rescue the people, who were near destruction,
namely, the pastoral office of Christ, and the rejection of the people
as the consequence of their rejection of Him. Now it is said, in the
eighth verse, ' *I destroyed the three shepherds* in one month.' We
have here a clear explanation by the Prophet, that his symbolic
action typifies *one single act* of the pastoral fidelity of the Lord, to be
completed in a comparatively short time. In addition to this, the
designation of the covenant people as ' *a flock of slaughter,*' agrees
well with the condition of the people at the time of Christ's appearance, but not during the whole second Temple, and, least of all, at
the time of the prophet.—Finally, the breaking also of the staff,
Grace [3] (signifying the withdrawal of the protection which the Lord
granted His people against the heathen nations), and the breaking of
the staff of The Covenanted (signifying the termination of harmony
among the people themselves) appear here altogether as one par-

---

[1] Mor. Neb. 2. 46. Buxt. p. 324.
[2] Compare, nevertheless, chap. 3, 512.
[3] In the Eng. Bible ' *Beauty,*' and ' *Bands :*' in margin ' *Binders.*'

ticular action of lasting consequences; compare the eleventh verse, *' and it was broken in that day.'* The Lord gives up the people, not as in their former history, to transient punishment, in order to receive them again into favour, when they shall have turned to Him, but the peremptory decree of rejection is pronounced against them. And yet we should expect the former, if the representation relates to the whole proceeding of the Lord with the covenant people during the second Temple. If, however, the rejection is an individual act, so also must the conduct of the people by which it is occasioned, be the last and highest manifestation of their refractory spirit, as it appeared in the rejection of Christ. As such, it plainly appears from the comparison of the fourth and sixth verses: *' Feed the flock of slaughter,*—FOR *I will no more spare the dwellers in the land, saith the Lord.'* Here the feeding is designated as the *last* effort for the deliverance of the unhappy people, to be *immediately* followed by their total rejection, if, as actually happened, that effort should fail. The *' flock of slaughter'* may signify a flock which *has been already slaughtered,* or one *which is to be so at a future time.* The Lord may give the covenant people this name, in order to point out, as the ground of His pastoral office, His sympathy with the miserable condition they were in, *before He undertook it,* or His sympathy with them on account of the judgements *still to be inflicted* through His righteousness. It is best however to combine them both. The miserable condition of the people at that time under evil rulers, both domestic and foreign, was an effect of the Divine justice. This was necessarily to continue for the future, and be increased, if the people did not sincerely repent; and, in order to furnish them with the means for this, the Lord Himself undertakes the office of a shepherd, and comes to deliver that which is lost.

588. Verse 5. *' Whose buyers slay them, and do not become guilty, and whose sellers say: The Lord be praised, I enrich myself; and their shepherds spare them not.'* The parallel passages show, that 'the Prophet would express the thought, that the misery of the people does not proceed from human caprice, but from the righteous judgement of God. The third verse of the second chapter of Jeremiah is especially to the point, *' Sacred was Israel to the Lord, the first-fruits of his increase. All who destroyed it were guilty, misfortune came upon them, saith the Lord.'* The Prophet here contrasts the *former time,* when no one could injure the theocratically disposed people, *without making himself guilty* and liable to punishment, with the present, when they are given up by the Lord Himself to their enemies, as His instruments, and become their *lawful* booty. In like manner, chap. 50. 6, 7, *' Perishing sheep are my people; their shepherds lead them astray; they cause them to wander about on the mountains, they go from mountain to hill, forgetful of their fold. All who find them consume them, and their enemies say, We make not ourselves guilty* [1]*, because they have sinned against the Lord, the dwelling-place of righteousness, against the Lord, the hope of their*

---

[1] לֹא נֶאְשָׁמוּ.

fathers.' Here, as the cause of the innocence of the enemies, the apostasy of the people from their God is expressly given, which brought upon them the tyranny of their enemies as a righteous Divine judgement.—' *Their sellers say,*' is, *as to the sense,* i. q., ' *they can say.*' It is very frequent to attribute that to any one as actually said by him, which, from the nature of the case, he *might* say. Still the comparison of Isa. 36. 10, where Sennacherib says, ' *Have I invaded this land in order to destroy it, without the Lord? Yea, the Lord said to me, Invade this land and destroy it,*' shows that the enemies of the Israelites sometimes actually had a presentiment of their higher destination.—That is a *lawful* gain, in respect to which one can say, *Blessed* or *praised be God,* for the imparting of which a man can thank the Lord.   By the *buyers* and *sellers* of the flock are designated here those who dealt with and ruled the covenant people according to their pleasure.   We can by no means, with Theodoret, Cyril, and others, refer this to the evil leaders of the people from among themselves, but rather to their *foreign oppressors,* as Jerome has rightly understood, by the buyers and sellers, the Romans. This plainly appears from the cited parallel passages, still more, however, from the thing itself; how could the flock, Israel, be a lawful gain to their domestic shepherds ? for these were themselves a chief *cause* of their apostasy, and were therefore chiefly subject to the punishment[1].   On the contrary, by ' *the shepherds who spare not the flock,*' it is highly probable, that the *domestic leaders* of the people, and indeed these exclusively, are to be understood, as appears from the comparison of the eighth verse, as well as of the fifteenth and two following verses.   The former passage at the same time decisively proves, that, by the *shepherds,* not merely the *civil leaders,* as Abarbanel and Grotius suppose, are to be understood, but likewise *the ecclesiastical,* and, in general, those who had in any way been called by the Lord to the guidance of the people.   There is therefore a climax ; the people sigh, and will sigh, not only under the oppression of foreign tyrants, but even their own leaders deal unsparingly with them.—The apparently feeble expression, ' *they spare not,*' when used of the native shepherds, is stronger than any other merely positive designation of their conduct, because it expresses how nature and duty required them to spare their own flock, and, therefore, how it was a severe Divine judgement when they denied them both[2].

589. Ver. 6. ' *For I will no longer spare the inhabitants of the land, saith the Lord, and I will give one into the power of the other, and into the power of his king; and they lay waste the land, and I will not deliver out of their hand.*'   The *for* refers to the expression, *Feed the flock of slaughter.*   " Make the last effort to conduct them to prosperity ; for I cannot and must not longer suffer their shocking

---

[1] Comp. ver. 17. Jer. 23. 1.

[2] The plural, *the sellers* and *the shepherds,* is joined with the singular of the verb. The Prophet would point out, that notwithstanding the apparent plurality of the actors, there is yet properly but one principal, that it is the Lord who works by the sellers and the shepherds.

apostasy to go unpunished."—*The land* is the land which had been
the subject of discourse in the preceding context, *the land of Israel.*
The explanation of this verse also depends upon the comparison of a
parallel passage of Jer. 19. 9, made use of by the Prophet, '*And I
make them eat the flesh of their sons, and the flesh of their daughters,
and they shall eat one the flesh of the other, in the anguish and distress wherewith their enemies shall oppress them, and those who endeavour to take their life.*' A twofold reason of the destruction, a
twofold punishment sent by the Lord, is here given, the discord of
the people among themselves, heightened by the distress and the
oppressions of the enemy. It is exactly the same here also; the
former is indicated by, '*I give them one to the other,*' the second by,
'*I give them a prey to their king.*' For that we are not to understand
by the king a domestic ruler, but rather a *foreign oppressor*, appears
from the fact, that neither had the covenant people, at the time of
the Prophet, a domestic king, nor has he made mention of any such,
the Messiah excepted, in his description of the future. Internal discord and external enemies are combined as the two chief instruments
of punishment, which God employs for the discipline of His people,
not only in the cited passages of Jeremiah and Isaiah 9. 7 sq. [1], but
also by Zechariah himself, chap. 8. 10, '*Before these days,—there
was no peace before the enemies, and I sent all men one against the
other.*' This miserable condition of the people, at the time of the
carrying away into exile, is then designated here as returning in
greater measure on account of their guilty ingratitude for renewed
mercies and their apostasy. If we look to the fulfilment, it easily
appears that the Roman Cæsar is here designated by the king; compare the fifteenth verse of the nineteenth chapter of John, where the
Jews say, '*We have no king but Cæsar.*' How accurately this
prophecy agrees with the fate of the Jews after the rejection of
Christ, the frightful rage of the parties against one another, until at
last the city was taken by the Romans, need not be pointed out, and
is confirmed by the well-known passages from Josephus, which Jahn
has supplied with a liberal hand.

590. Ver. 7. '*So fed I then the flock of slaughter, out of sympathy
with their misery ; and I made me two staves, the one I named Grace,
the other I named the Allied, and I fed the flock.*' We give first
the explanation which appears to us as without doubt the true one,
and then we examine those which deviate from it [2].—*The miserable*

---

[1] Compare especially ver. 18, 19, and 3, 4.

[2] The words לָכֵן עֲנִיֵּי הַצֹּאן. We translate *therefore* (or, *this reason*) *the most miserable
of the sheep.* לָכֵן we take in its usual meaning *therefore*. We find no grammatical
ellipsis, but only a concise form of expression, which occurs as a *result of passionate
emotion* in every kind of discourse, and with especial frequency in the prophets.
The sentence, when completed, would read : " *I did this because they were the
most miserable sheep.*" We cite only a few examples of a similar concise method
of expressing passion. Zechariah himself furnishes us with three in chap. 4. 6, 7.
The most striking is ver. 7. " *Zerubbabel brings forth the foundation stone ; acclamations ; grace, grace to it ;*" i. e. '*acclamations are thereupon heard or uttered.*'
We have a similar example in the same verse : " *Who art thou, O mountain, thou*

of the sheep, according to the Hebrew usage, are *the most miserable sheep.* But the question now arises, What is *the whole*, the *flock* of sheep, with which *the part* is here compared? If we assume as such a definite flock of sheep, the people of Israel, then, by *the miserable*, one particular portion, peculiarly miserable, is designated; if, on the contrary, we take for *the whole*, sheep in general, as an image of all men and nations, then *the most miserable sheep* would signify the whole of the covenant people. The *former* interpretation is the more usual; it supposes that there is here a contrast, similar to Ezek. 34. 16, '*I will seek that which is lost, bring back that which has wandered, bind up that which is wounded, and strengthen that which is sick ; but that which is fat and strong will I destroy.*' It is also held, that the most miserable here are those who, at the same time humbled by their misery, long for deliverance.—But a closer examination shows that the latter interpretation is the true one. It is no objection to this, that in the eleventh verse, by '*the most miserable sheep*,' only a *part* of the people (those who feared God) *are* designated. For this more particular description does not there lie in '*the most miserable sheep*' itself, but in '*which adhere to me;*' and this very addition shows rather that '*the most miserable sheep*,' in *itself considered*, was *general*, and belonged to no particular class, but to the whole people. What however is especially decisive for the latter, are the two parallel passages of Jeremiah [1] ; '*Of a truth they* (the Idumeans) *will worry the smallest sheep* [2].' Entirely the same is the forty-fifth verse of the fiftieth chapter, in reference to the Chaldeans. In both passages '*the smallest sheep*' is the designation of the *Israelites* in opposition *to all the neighbouring nations.* To this must be added, that the Lord, according to the sixth and ninth verses, undertakes the pastoral office, not over a *part* of the people, but over the *whole*, and for their good. Finally, this interpretation alone is reconcilable with the words themselves. These cannot be explained with Calvin : '*Quoniam erant misellæ quædam oves.*' The ellipsis must rather be thus supplied, '*because they* were the most miserable sheep;' so that '*the most miserable sheep*' are identified with '*the flock of slaughter*,' which signifies the whole people.—The shepherd's staff is the instrument with which he affords protection and safety to his flock [3]. ' *Thy rod*

great before Zerubbabel? To a plain,' for ' *Thou shalt become a plain ;*' and, v. 6, ' *Not by power and not by strength, but by my Spirit,*' viz. are the affairs of the Theocracy in general, and especially the building of the temple, accomplished. We refer also to Is. 44. 12, where, in the representation of idolatry, which is in the highest degree passionate and concise, it is said, ' *the smith the axe,*' (חָרַשׁ בַּרְזֶל מַעֲצָד), as the sense certainly, i. q. ' *the smith prepares the axe,*' though the assumption of a pure grammatical ellipsis of the verb, here and elsewhere, could by no means be justified. The mere mention of the subject and object is sufficient to awaken in the reader the conception analogous to that of the author. As there indignation at the folly of idolatry is the passion which the concise expression excites, compare the almost still more remarkable example 66. 18, ' *I, your works*,'—so here it is the tenderest love of the Lord towards His people, and grief over their misery. That grief, in particular, loves abruptness, is well known.

[1] Chap. 49. 20.   [2] צְעִירֵי הַצֹּאן.   [3] Ps. 23. 4.

and thy staff, they comfort me.' The taking of *two* staves accordingly signifies the turning away of a *twofold danger* by the faithful shepherd, from outward enemies and from internal discord, being the very same by which the people, according to the sixth verse, should in case of their stiff-necked obduracy be destroyed. Now, so long as the last effort to lead them to repentance endures, the danger is still warded off by the faithful shepherd. Afterwards it breaks in upon them with fearful power.—The name of the first staff is not *loveliness* or *beauty*[1], but *grace* or *favour*. The staff signifies, even according to the tenth verse, the mercy of the Lord, whereby He secures the people against destruction from outward enemies. The verb from which the name of the other staff is derived has always the sense of *binding*[2]. The word itself is a participle in a *passive* sense, "*the allied,*" or "*the confederated*[3]." By the second staff therefore is designated the *brotherly concord,* existing among the covenant people themselves, through the influence of the Lord during the time of mercy.—"*And so I fed the flock,*" is not a superfluous repetition, but indicates that the staff was used in feeding.

591. Ver. 8. '*And I extirpated the three shepherds in one month, and I was disgusted with them ; and also their soul rebelled against me.'* We here first inquire, who are to be understood by the three shepherds. There can be no doubt that the Prophet speaks, not of *three individual shepherds,* but of *three orders* of shepherds : this being established, the only correct course must be, to inquire whether in Zechariah himself, or in the other authors of the Old Testament, especially those who lived nearest to him, *three classes of shepherds* are mentioned as the only leaders of the Theocracy. If we proceed in this way, it appears that Zechariah cannot possibly have had in view any other than the *civil magistrates, the priests,* and *the prophets*[4]. Numerous passages of Jeremiah may be compared, e. g. 2. 8, '*The priests spake not, Where is the Lord ? the students of the law* (likewise the *priests*) *knew me not,* the *shepherds* (here *especially of the civil magistrates*) *sinned against me, and the prophet prophesied in Baal*[5].' But how, it may be asked, can the prophetic order here be mentioned as forming one of the three orders of leaders in the Theo-

---

[1] Seventy, κάλλος. *Aquila* and *Symm.* εὐπρέπεια. Jerome, *decus.*

[2] נֹעַם, however frequently this may have been asserted, never has the meaning *loveliness,* but rather always that of *kindness, favour,* which has been proved to belong to it in this passage by J. D. Michaelis. We very much wonder that the meaning *corrupit,* which has already been contested by Gousset, and so admirably by Schultens (*ad Jobum,* p. 964), should still be always given in the Lexicons as undoubted. חָבַל, *to bind,* and *to be bound,* in Pi. *to ensnare,* and then *destroy.*

[3] So De Dieu, and others.

[4] This interpretation is the most ancient of all. It is found in Theodoret : Τοὺς Ἰουδαίων λέγει βασιλέας, καὶ προφήτας καὶ ἱερέας. διὰ γὰρ τούτων τῶν τριῶν ἐποιμαίνοντο ταγμάτων. Likewise Cyril, only that he substitutes the scribes for the prophets, for a reason which may be easily conceived.

[5] Ver. 26. Chap. 18. 18. If we compare Zechariah himself, we find the *two other* classes of shepherds, together with the *prophetic* order, which he himself represents, most definitely mentioned, chap. 4. 12—14.

cracy, since it had already ceased at the time of the fulfilment ? We answer, the Prophet, in accordance with the nature of prophecy, here also designates the future by an analogy existing in his time. As the order of the civil shepherds continued, even when the kingdom had come to an end, so also the prophetic order, as to its essence, continued after the cessation of the prophetic gift. Its destination was to impart to the people the word and will of God [1]. Before the completion of the Canon, this was done by a revelation granted immediately to them, and afterwards by the investigation of former revelations under the guidance of the Spirit of God, and by the application of them to the existing relations. In the place of the *prophets* succeeded the *scribes*, to whom, according to Sirach, in the thirty-ninth chapter, the Lord richly gave the spirit of understanding, who studied the wisdom of the ancients and searched the prophets, who propounded doctrine and judgement, and by whom wise sentences were invented. They stood to the ancient prophets in the same relation as the enlightened teachers of the later Christian Church to the prophets of the New Testament.—The question now arises, what is to be understood by the extirpation of the three shepherds. It cannot be a literal extirpation which is spoken of, because immediately thereafter, the shepherds appear as still in existence. It is they who provoke the good shepherd to impatience, and manifest the utmost hostility towards him [2]. It is their obstinate resistance, rendering useless all his pastoral efforts, which moves him to break the staves, and relinquish his office. We can therefore conceive only of an extirpation of the shepherds, *as such*, i. e. *a deposition of them from their pastoral office*. To effect this was the most zealous object of the Lord during *his* pastoral office ; but the same disposition, which rendered them deserving of this, also prevented the sentence, spoken against them with full authority, from being carried into execution in its whole extent. Only the most miserable of the sheep, who have regard to the Lord (the eleventh verse), withdrew themselves from their pernicious guidance. It was not till after the rejection of the whole people, who knew not their own good, that the sentence was executed in its whole extent by *foreign foes*, while the people did not now receive good shepherds instead of bad, which would have been the case, if they had themselves carried into execution the good shepherd's degree of extirpation.—The extirpation of the shepherds happened *in one month*. This cannot, as Kimchi, Calvin, and others suppose, stand simply for ' *in a little time*.' Hitzig might then justly ask, " Why then the *month*, when probably a *day* or *hour* would be more suitably mentioned ? " That the Prophet, if he designed merely to express the shortest time, would rather have said, ' in one day,' appears especially from the parallel passage in the ninth verse of the third chapter, where it is said of the atonement to be effected by the Messiah, " I blot out the sin of this land

---

[1] Jer. 18. 18.

[2] Which likewise, on account of the use of the *fut.* with *vau convers.* (וַתִּקְצַר) is not to be regarded as preceding the extirpation, but as its consequence.

in one day [1]." The expression, ' *in one month,*' expresses rather, in
relation to the phrase, ' *in one day,*' a *longer*, and in relation to all
other periods, a *shorter* time. It shows, that the extirpation of the
three shepherds is not, like the atonement, to be considered as a
single act, but as one protracted for some time. Thus, therefore, in
a very appropriate manner, the continued efforts of Christ are designated, to deliver the poor people, the lost sheep of the house of Israel,
out of the spiritual power of their blind and corrupt leaders [2].—' *I
was disgusted in them*'—literally, ' *my soul was made narrow in them,*'
a phrase expressing *indignation* arising from a sense of *intolerable
injury*—an indignation that *chokes* and *strangles*, as it were, the
indignant person. The evil shepherds are inflamed with mean
hatred against the good shepherd, because he exposes their meanness, and will take from them their dominion. They do all in their
power, therefore, to hinder him in the execution of his commission.—
' *Their soul*' does not stand for the bare personal pronoun, just as if
one should assert, that ' he causes me grief *in the soul,*' is nothing
more than, ' he causes *me* grief ;' it rather signifies the *violence* and
depth of the abhorrence.

592. Ver. 9. ' *Thus said I then : I will not feed you; that
which dies, shall die, that which is destroyed, shall be destroyed,
and those that remain shall consume one another.*' We must understand the futures as prophetical. By *the dead* and *the destroyed*
is meant that which is devoted to so sure a destruction, that it may
be *already* considered as dead and destroyed. This destruction could
have been turned aside only by obedience to the good shepherd.
Now, since he has been compelled to relinquish his office, the matter
takes its natural course. A threefold sort of destruction is here
given, as the comparison of parallel passages shows ; contagious
diseases, as they are accustomed to arise in besieged cities (' *the dead
will die*'), a violent death by foreign enemies, and a fearful rage of
the citizens against one another, occasioned by the distress. These
passages are as follow : Jer. 15. 1, 2, ' *And the Lord said to me :
Though Moses and Samuel stood before me, my mind could not be
towards this people, cast them out of my sight, and let them go forth.
And if they say unto thee : Whither shall we go forth ? then thou shalt
tell them, Thus saith the Lord, he that is for death (is destined,* that is,
to death goes), to death, and he who is for the sword, to the sword; he

---

[1] בְּיוֹם אֶחָד.

[2] וַתִּקְצַר נַפְשִׁי בָּהֶם, properly *brevis facta est anima mea in eis.* Rightly Schultens
on Prov. 20. 21 : " *Ea phrasis non tam tædium significat, quam indignationem ex
intolerandis injuriis oriundam, sub quibus anima velut angatur ac suffocetur.—Ubique
impatientia gravissime vexati, oppressi, elisi, qui vix respirare queat amplius, elucet.*"
The verb בָּהֵל is here explained by most interpreters, according to a comparison
of the Syriac, by *to experience disgust.* But this is not entirely accurate. In
Arabic بَخِل designates, in general, a low, vile disposition, and is used especially of base avarice. In Hebrew this meaning prevails in the only passage
besides, where the *verb* occurs, Prov. 20. 21. נַחֲלָה מְבֹהֶלֶת is there, an inheritance
obtained in a base manner.

who is for hunger, to hunger ; and he who is for captivity, to captivity.'
34. 17, ' *Behold, ye have not hearkened, that ye proclaim liberty, every*
one for his brother, and every one for his neighbour ; behold, I pro-
claim then for you a liberty to the sword, to the pestilence, and to the
famine.' Ezek. 6. 12, ' *That which is afar off shall die by the pesti-*
lence, that which is near shall fall by the sword, and that which re-
mains and is preserved shall die by hunger[1].' That this threefold
sort of destruction actually effected the overthrow of the Jewish state
needs no further proof.—' *And those which are left shall eat the flesh*
one of another.' Mark : ' *Ex rabie fera, in quam præter naturam*
hæ oves degenerabunt.' In a manner entirely similar the rage of the
citizens of the kingdom of Israel against one another before its destruction, occasioned by their distress, is described in Isaiah[2]. ' *They*
spare not one another. They devour on the right hand, they devour
on the left hand, and are not satisfied ; each one devours the flesh of
his arm' (he rages against his own flesh, inasmuch as those who
devour one another are members of one community, one political
body).

593. Ver. 10. ' *And so I took my staff Grace and brake it, that I*
might abolish my covenant which I had concluded with all nations.'
That which had been predicted in the preceding verse in words, is
here, and in the fourteenth verse, indicated by a double symbolical
action ; the devastation by foreign nations by the breaking of the staff
' *Kindness'* or ' *Grace,'* the internal discord by the breaking of the
staff of ' *the Allied ;'* or more correctly, the prediction contained in
the following verse, is here followed by the account of its execution.
—The image of *the flock* is not strictly preserved ; the thing signified appears in the phrase, ' *with all nations ;'* in accordance with
the image, it must have been, ' *with all wild beasts.'* Compare
Is. 56. 9, ' *All ye beasts of the field, come to devour ; come, all ye*
beasts in the wood.' The thought, that hitherto the covenant people
had been preserved by a secret influence of the Divine omnipotence
from destruction by foreign foes, is figuratively expressed, as though
the Lord had made a covenant for the good of the Israelites, with all
nations of the earth, which is now abolished by the breaking of the
staff Grace. A similar figurative representation is found in other
passages[3]. That which Zechariah seems to have had immediately in
view, is that of Ezek. 34. 25, ' *And I conclude for them a covenant*
of peace, and make the evil beasts to cease out of the land, and they
dwell in the wilderness securely, and sleep in the woods,' which
differs from the one before us, only in more strictly preserving the
image of a flock. Zechariah announces, that this covenant, concluded after the return from the exile by the Lord, for the good of
His people, should now be abolished by the punishment of their
shocking apostasy.

594. Ver. 11. ' *And so was the covenant in that day abolished ;*

---

[1] Comp. also below, chap. 13. 8, where 'they shall die on the sick-bed,'
יִגְוָ֫עוּ, and 'they shall be extirpated;' יִכָּרֵ֫תוּ, correspond to תָמוּת and תִּפָּקֵד.

[2] Chap. 9. 18 sq.   [3] Job 5. 23. Hos. 2. 20.

*and therefore the most miserable sheep, who adhered to me, expe-
rienced that this is the word of the Lord.'* It appears from this verse
that the efforts of the good shepherd were still *not entirely in vain,*
but that a *small remnant* of true disciples joined him. These were
designated by those who *observed him,* had their eye directed continually to him, did all in accordance with his nod and will. As,
after the abolition of the covenant, the enemies invaded the land,
they perceived that what had been spoken beforehand of the destruction to be effected by the Lord, was no empty human threatening,
but really a Divine prophecy. The Prophet here also employs the
past, because that which was represented in his inward vision had
already taken place. Were the prophecy divested of the drapery of
a symbolic action, it would read, ' *Then when my covenant has been
abolished, my worshippers shall know, from the fulfilment, the divine
origin of this my sentence concerning Israel.'* That the *fulfilment*
would testify for the Divine origin of His prophecies, is a favorite
remark of Zechariah, comp. 2. 13, where the angel of the Lord says,
' *Then shall ye know that the Lord of Hosts has sent me*[1].' *In the
day,* viz. *on which I had broken my staff;* or, without a figure,
*after I had turned away my favour from the people, the hostile na-
tions, hitherto restrained by me, fell upon them.*

595. Ver. 12. ' *And I said to them; If it seems good to you, give
me my reward; if not, withhold it; and they weighed to me as my
reward thirty pieces of silver.'*—'*And I said to them :'* Jahn remarks,
that this cannot refer to the flock, but to the shepherds, because only
from them could the reward be demanded. But this is incorrect.
The shepherd, by dealing with the flock itself, respecting that which
in other cases was wont to be transacted only with the owner, shows
that this flock consists of rational creatures. With the exclusion of
the inferior and more despised portion of the people, with whom the
pastoral office of the Lord, as had been said in the foregoing verse,
had been attended with a desirable result, he here treats with the
greater and more powerful portion, who had compelled him by their
obstinacy to relinquish his office. It is true, that in this transaction
the *leaders* of the people are chiefly to be considered, not, however,
as shepherds, but *as members* of the flock, as also in the thirty-fourth
chapter of Ezekiel, they appear now *as shepherds,* now *as he-goats,*
or *as fat sheep,* in contrast with those which are *poor.* Of the shepherds as such, the Lord could not demand the reward, because He
had not devoted Himself at all to their service, but had endeavoured
to rescue the flock from them.—The sense of the words, *If it seems
good to you, give me my reward; if not, withhold it,* is well unfolded
by Calvin : " *He expresses the greatest indignation, as if a man
should reproach his neighbour with malice and ingratitude.* ' *Acknowledge the benefit, if you will : if not, let it have been thrown away : I
care not ; I see that you were a scoundrel, unworthy of being so libe-
rally treated. I therefore care nothing for your compensations : but
all the time it was your business to see what you owed me.'* " The
parallel passages are Jer. 40. 4, ' *If it is good in thine eyes to go with*

---

[1] In like manner, ver. 15. 6. 15.

me to Babylon, go ; and, if it is evil in thine eyes, refrain.'   Ezek.
3. 27, ' *Thus saith the Lord : He that hears, let him hear, and he
that refrains, let him refrain.'*—*My reward,* that which I deserve,
which I have earned by severe labour.—*They weighed ;* gold for a
long time was not counted, but weighed ; hence, long after this practice had ceased, they used the expression ' *to weigh'* for ' *to count.'*
We cannot, by the reward, understand *faith* or *piety of heart ;* for
the Lord does not demand this reward until He has already entirely
given over the people, withdrawn His favour from them, until therefore they could no longer bring forth the fruits of repentance, but
were rather devoted to destruction.   This demand was made during
the time of His pastoral office.   By the *thirty pieces of silver,* we
cannot understand the repentance and faith of *the few believers ;* for
then they would be something good, while still, according to the
thirteenth verse, they were to be thrown into an unclean place.   As
little can they mean sacrifices and ceremonies, without faith.   For
these must be more particularly specified, which is not done in any
measure except on the false supposition, that by the reward which
the Lord required faith and sincere piety were designated. – Rather,
only the thought is expressed, that after the Lord has given up His
pastoral office, and already proclaimed the woe upon Jerusalem, the
people have sinned against Him by an action of the blackest ingratitude.   That the good shepherd had *well-grounded claims* to the
gratitude of the people is expressed by his asking them for the reward of his services ; the wicked ingratitude of the people, by their
offering to weigh him thirty pieces of silver, a sum so contemptible [1],
that the offer of it for such services, performed by such a person, is
more offensive than an entire refusal, and therefore suited rather
to heighten than diminish the ingratitude, a thought which in the
following verse is embodied in a symbolic action.   That by this, the
only correct interpretation, much insight is gained into the prophecy
itself, as well as its relation to the evangelical history, is obvious.

596. Ver. 13. ' *And the Lord said to me, Throw it to the potter,
the glorious price at which I am estimated by them; and I took the
thirty pieces of silver, and cast them into the house of the Lord, that
they might be carried from there to the potter.'*   The Lord addresses
the Prophet, who represents His person.   This clearly appears from
' *at which I have been estimated.'* ' *Throw it,'* with the accessory
idea of *contempt.* ' *To the potter,'* here is the same as ' *in an unclean
place,* to *the executioner,* or *to the flayer.'*   *The potter,* who is here
meant (probably, as appears from the concurrent use of the article
here, in Jeremiah, and Matthew, *the potter who worked for the Temple,* since it cannot be supposed that there was but *one potter* for all
Jerusalem), had his workshop in the valley of Hinnom, probably
because the earth, required for his business, was found there in peculiar abundance, or of a better quality.   This appears from the following
reasons.   That the workshop was out of the valley, and that in the

[1] *Maimonides, Mor. Neb. C.* 40, Part 3, " *Ut plus minus reperies hominem libe-
rum æstimari sexaginta siclis, servum vero triginta;*" comp. Exod. 21. 32.

valley which lies beneath it, appears from the first verse of the
eighteenth chapter of Jeremiah, where the Prophet, while in the
Temple, receives the command, ' Arise, go *down* to the house of the
potter ;' compare ver. 3, ' *And I went* down *to the house of the potter.*'
But we are led especially to the valley of Hinnom by Jer. 19. 2,
' *Go down to the valley of the son of Hinnom, which is by the Brick
Gate, and proclaim there the words which I will speak to thee.*' According to this, the gate which led to the valley of Hinnom was
called the *Brick* or *Pot Gate,* from the pottery before it. Now the
valley of Hinnom, however, formerly the scene of the most frightful
idolatrous abominations, was regarded by the later Jews with disgust
and horrour, as an unclean place, after Josiah had polluted it by car-
rion, human bones, and such like [1], so that finally even the opinion
expressed in the Talmud was formed, that there was the mouth of
hell. That Zechariah caused the base reward to be *thrown into the
valley of Hinnom,* in general, and that he designates, as the particular
place, *the workshop* or *the field of the potter,* have each a distinct
reference to a prophecy of Jeremiah, and presuppose readers acquainted with his writings. The first refers to the nineteenth chapter
of Jeremiah. The Prophet there throws an empty earthen flask into
the valley of Hinnom, accompanied by several of the oldest of the
people and most distinguished priests. The meaning of this symbolic action is thus given : ' *Because they have filled this place with
the blood of the innocent,—so I* empty out *the council of Judah and
Jerusalem in this place, and I make them fall by the sword before
their enemies, and by the hand of those who seek their life, and give
their corpses for food to the fowls of heaven and the beasts of the
earth.—So will I break this people and this city, as one breaks the
vessels of a potter, which can no more be mended ; and in Tophet shall
they bury, because there is no more room.—Thus will I do to this
place and its inhabitants, and make this city like Tophet. And the
houses of Jerusalem and the houses of the kings of Judah shall be unclean as the place Tophet.*' Zechariah now causes the base reward
to be thrown into the valley of the son of Hinnom or Tophet, in
general because this was an unclean place, but especially in order to
resume the prophecy of Jeremiah, and show that a second fulfilment
of it was at hand, because the Divine penal justice which had called
forth the threatening and its first fulfilment, had been provoked
anew, and that in a still more fearful manner. The memorial of the
wicked ingratitude of the Jewish people, the *corpus delicti,* is conveyed to the same place, from which their former abominations had
cried to God, and provoked His vengeance. It was there deposited,
as it were a new pledge, which the people at the appointed time must
redeem.—That precisely the possessions of the potter in the valley
of Hinnom are chosen, is owing to Jeremiah, in the eighteenth chapter. Jeremiah, at the command of the Lord, there makes a visit to
the potter, who was just then at work. ' *And the vessel, which he
was making out of the clay, was marred under his hands ; then he*

---

[1] Comp. 2 Kings 23. 10.

made again out of the clay another vessel, as it pleased him.' The meaning of this symbol is then given. *' Can I not therefore do to you also, ye house of Israel, as this potter, saith the Lord? Behold, as the clay in the hand of the potter, so are ye in my hand.—Behold, I prepare for you misfortune, and entertain towards you thoughts of evil; therefore return each one from his evil disposition, and amend your disposition and your conduct.'* This truth, that the Lord both *could* and *would* reject His apostate people, if they did not repent in time, is here anew rendered prominent by Zechariah, when he causes the poor reward to be brought into the place in which Jeremiah had originally uttered the threatening; a place which was again, in Zechariah's days, calculated to make the truth to be conveyed *perceptible by the senses*, the potter having again set up his workshop there.— *This* prophecy of Jeremiah had again resumed its full power, because the former apostasy, which, in the first instance, occasioned it, was but slight in comparison with the present, the wicked ingratitude of the people towards the Lord, who had *Himself* taken charge of His flock.— *The excellency of the price which I have been estimated by them*, for *the excellent price*, ironically, at which my person and my work have been valued by them; compare Deut. 32. 6, *' Give ye to the Lord such a reward, ye foolish, unwise people.'* — *' And I cast it (the sum or the price) into the house of the Lord, that it might be conveyed from thence to the potter.'* It is very obvious that the gold could not be carried at the same time into the Temple and to the potter. For the potter did not work in the Temple, nor even in the city, but, as we have already seen, in the valley of Hinnom. It must, therefore, necessarily be assumed, that the Temple was the first, the potter's the second station; hence *' to the potter,'* for *' that it might be carried from thence to the potter.'* The question however now arises, why the gold, which was finally to remain with the potter, was first cast into the Temple. Plainly, because the Temple was the place where the people appeared before the face of the Lord, the council-house, as it were, where the magistrates and citizens transacted their affairs with one another. Here, therefore, must the shameful ingratitude of the people also be cast upon them by the return of the contemptible reward. From there it must then be conveyed to the potter, because unlawful gold must not remain in the Temple [1].

597. We have hitherto unfolded the sense of the thirteenth and fourteenth verses, without reference to the fulfilment. The result is as follows. The Lord has at last once more undertaken the pastoral office over the flock devoted to destruction, the unhappy people, Israel; as He again relinquishes it on account of their stiff-necked unbelief, He demands His reward; they give Him thirty pieces of silver,

---

[1] Comp. Deut. 23. 19, *Talm. Sanhedrin*, f. 112.

about the yearly wages of a common herdsman. He is not satisfied with this contemptible reward, and casts it into the Temple. From there, as unclean, it is conveyed to the possession of the potter, where it is deposited until the day of judgement upon the people, as a pledge of the Divine vengeance. We have learned, as the sense of this figurative representation, that the obduracy of the people, after the Lord should have given them up on account of it, would yet break forth in one great act of ingratitude towards Him, and thereby make them fully ripe for the judgement.

598. The agreement of prophecy and fulfilment is here so striking, that it would force itself upon us although it were indicated by no declaration of the New Testament. What else could the last and most fearful expression of ingratitude towards the good shepherd, here predicted, be, but the murderous plot by which the Jews rewarded the pastoral fidelity of Christ, and for the accomplishment of which Judas was bribed? Not merely in general, but in the particulars also we find the most accurate agreement between history and prophecy. The small reward of thirty pieces of silver, serves here in the first place only for a figurative designation of the blackest ingratitude and the highest contempt on the part of the Jews. But that, among all small sums, precisely this only was chosen, which afterwards the betrayer Judas actually received, must still surprise us, and cannot be without an object. As in the bribing of the betrayer Judas, in general, the blackest ingratitude is obvious, so are the foulest avarice, and the deepest contempt towards the Lord, manifest in the circumstance, that the priests allowed to Judas, when he left to them the determination of the reward (compare the fifteenth verse of the twenty-sixth chapter of Matthew) only the contemptible sum of thirty pieces of silver. It cannot with Paulus [1] be replied, that, according to Zechariah, the thirty pieces of silver are counted to the Shepherd, not to his betrayer. For, in the small reward which they gave to the betrayer, their contempt towards the Shepherd manifests itself. It happened by the arrangement of God, under whose secret influence even the ungodly stand, that Judas cast the gold into the Temple, and that therefore their ingratitude, as inwardly in Zechariah, so here outwardly, is charged upon the people by a symbolic action in the place where they appeared before the face of the Lord. The priests removed the gold as unclean out of the Temple, and purchased therewith a mean spot in the same valley, which already at an earlier period, polluted by innocent blood, had brought upon Jerusalem the vengeance of the Lord, predicted by Jeremiah, the same spot where Jeremiah once predicted to the people their rejection. Here now lay the *price of blood* [2], the reward for the betrayal of the *innocent blood* [3], from which the field received the name of *the field of blood* [4], as a testimony against Israel, as a pledge by which he had bound himself to suffer the Divine punishment, similar to the former, which he must now redeem ; so that the threatening, which Jeremiah had uttered in reference to this

---

[1] Comm. III. p. 683.
[2] $\tau\iota\mu\grave{\eta}$ $\alpha\ddot{\iota}\mu\alpha\tau o\varsigma$ (Matt. 27. 6).   [3] $\alpha\dot{\iota}\mu\alpha$ $\dot{\alpha}\theta\tilde{\omega}o\nu$, ver. 4.
[4] $\dot{\alpha}\gamma\rho\grave{o}\varsigma$ $\alpha\ddot{\iota}\mu\alpha\tau o\varsigma$, ver. 8, comp. Act. 1. 19.

former abomination, is now again in full force. Chap. 19. 4 seq., "They have made this place full of innocent blood,—therefore, behold, days come, saith the Lord, when they shall no more call this place Tophet, and the valley of Hinnom, but the valley of slaughter." We find the same also in the thirty-second verse of the seventh chapter. In accordance with what appears from a comparison of the account of the New Testament with Jeremiah and Zechariah, tradition also places the field of blood in the valley of Hinnom[1].

599. Still the result so clearly furnished by a comparison of the prophecy and history is confirmed by an express testimony of the apostle Matthew, in the ninth verse of the twenty-seventh chapter. This testimony presents certain difficulties, which we shall here examine. The form of citation must here first be considered, in which the prophecy is attributed not to *Zechariah*, but to *Jeremiah*, ' *Then was fulfilled that which was spoken by Jeremy the prophet, saying,*' &c. Several older interpreters[2] express the opinion, that Matthew cited a passage compounded out of Jeremiah and Zechariah, under the name of the former, only as the more distinguished. But the well-grounded reply has been made, that then the passages of Jeremiah, a reference to which they assume, must actually refer to the event related by Matthew. They were not able to answer this objection, partly because they did not see in what relation the passage of Zechariah stood to those cited from Jeremiah, partly because they did not observe what deep meaning Matthew sought, in the fact *that the potter's field was purchased with the price of blood*, which, of all the interpreters, Grotius alone perceived[3]. This objection is entirely removed by what has already been remarked. We have shown that the prophecy of Zechariah, as to its principal parts, is only *a resumption of that of Jeremiah;* that he announces a *second fulfilment of it*, which stands in a connexion with it by no means *accidental*, but *necessary*, because it rests on the idea of the Divine penal justice, which must call forth a new fulfilment of the prophecy, as soon as it shall have been again provoked.

600. Matthew might indeed have cited *both* prophets. But such prolixity in citation is entirely contrary to the custom of the authors of the New Testament, which may be explained by a twofold reason. They presuppose their readers to possess an accurate knowledge of Scripture, and the human instrument was kept far behind the Divine author, the Spirit of God and of Christ, who spake in all the prophets in the same manner. Very frequently, therefore, and indeed almost always, the human author is not mentioned at all; they content themselves with the forms of citation : ' *The Scripture saith,*' ' *as it is written,*' ' *for it is written,*' ' *as saith the Holy Ghost,*' &c. Not unfrequently two or three passages of different authors are combined

---

[1] Comp. *Lightfoot in Acta Ap., Opp.* 2. p. 690. *Pococke*, 2. 38. *Bachiene*, 2. 1. p. 342.

[2] Sanctius, Glassius, Frischmuth.

[3] " *Cum autem hoc dictum Jeremiæ per Sach. repetitum hic recitat Mat., simul ostendit tacite, eas pœnas imminere Judæis, quas iidem prophetæ olim sui temporis hominibus prædixerant.*"

in one, and yet only a single author is mentioned. The closest analogy with that before us is presented by Mark 1. 2, 3, '*As it is written in Esaias the prophet*¹; *Behold, I send my messenger, which shall prepare thy way before thee. The voice of one crying in the wilderness*,' &c. Here, under the name of Isaiah, *two prophecies of Malachi and Isaiah* are cited, of which, moreover, the former precedes. Isaiah was the more celebrated prophet; it was so usual to consider the minor prophets *combined in one collection as a whole*, that an individual of them is very rarely mentioned by name².

601. Had Matthew designed to awaken attention merely to the fulfilment of the prophecy of Zechariah, he would have contented himself with a general form of citation. This appears from the analogy of all other citations out of this prophet, in *none* of which is he mentioned by name. So John 19. 37, the passage, chap. 12. 10, is cited merely with the words, '*And again another Scripture saith*,' John 12. 14, the passage, chap. 9. 9, by '*as it is written*.' Matt. 26. 31, the passage, chap. 13. 7, with the words, '*for it is written*.' (Compare Mark 14. 27.) Matt. 21. 45, the passage, chap. 9, 9, by '*that which was said by the prophet*,' where the article shows that Matthew presupposed Zechariah to be well known to all his readers. While, however, the mention of Zechariah might appear to him as unnecessary, it was otherwise with Jeremiah. The fact, that this prophecy was realized in the event before him, and how far it was so, was not so obvious as to render superfluous a hint requiring further investigation. And yet, without this insight, the sense of the prophecy of Zechariah must remain in the highest degree obscure, and its fulfilment in essential points misapprehended.

602. The result which we have gained is not unimportant. It appears that the apostle, precisely in the passage which the new critics cite as a certain proof of the proposition that the authors of the New Testament were not free from errour, manifests a deeper insight into the sense of the Old Testament prophecy than all these critics taken together, no one of whom has perceived that we can just as little interpret the passage of Zechariah, without the aid of Jeremiah, as we can, without that of Daniel, determine what the Lord intended by the *abomination of desolation*. Indeed, the assumption of an errour is the most convenient for those who abhor labour; and at the same time affords an advantage not to be despised against the literal interpreter; but such proceedings cannot for ever hide the truth, as certainly as it is not the will of the Lord that one iota of His word should fail.

603. It now remains to show that the citation of Matthew perfectly coincides with this passage in sense, if not in words. We must here in the first place endeavour to settle the meaning of the words³. We translate them: '*They received the price of him who*

¹ The English translation has "*in the prophets*," but the authority for the other reading is considerably greater.
² Comp. e. g. Matt. 21. 5, with Isaiah 62. 11, and Zech. 9. 9, Matt. 21. 13, with Isaiah 56. 7, Jer. 7. 11, Rom. 9. 27, 1 Pet. 2. 6 sq.
³ Καὶ ἔλαβον τὰ τριάκοντα ἀργύρια, τὴν τιμὴν τοῦ τετιμημένου, ὃν ἐτιμήσαντο ἀπὸ υἱῶν Ἰσραήλ.

was valued, for which they had valued him, on the part of the sons of Israel¹.' We apply here the Hebrew and Aramæan usage, according to which the indefinite third person, which then supplies the place of the passive, is designated by the third person of the plural². The noun is used by Matthew instead of the pronoun, in order to awaken attention to the *meanness* of the valuation. This was done, not indeed by heathen, but by the covenant people themselves, who had received such numberless proofs of the love and mercy of the Lord. The apparent deviation, that in Matthew the receiving of the pieces of silver and the casting of them into the fields of the potter, are attributed to the leaders of the Jews, in Zechariah, on the contrary, to the shepherd, Matthew removes by subjoining at the close the words, *' as the Lord appointed me³.'* By these words he indicates, that he regards the leaders of the people, not as acting independently, but only as instruments, by which the Lord accomplishes His purposes, so that nothing is wanting to make the coincidence complete.

604. Ver. 14. *' Then I broke my second staff, the Allied, to abolish the brotherhood between Judah and Israel⁴.'* We have already had occasion often to remark, that in the representation of *future things* the images are borrowed from the *past*. Thus, e. g. in the eleventh verse of the tenth chapter, the *future* deliverance is described as a *passage through the Red Sea;* so likewise as a *deliverance from the yoke of the Assyrians and Egyptians,* who had long been deprived of their power at the time of Zechariah. In such cases, the usual blending of image and reality properly lies at the foundation. Instead of saying, e. g. *' I will deliver Israel as gloriously as before, when I led them through the Red Sea;'* the prophet says directly, *' The Lord will lead them anew through the Red Sea.'* Such passages would not have been so grossly misunderstood if more regard had been paid to the analogy of poetry in general, and particularly that of Christian hymns. When e. g. the poet says,

> " Deep it is not—on boldly—the Red Sea
> By God's command shall make a way for thee!"

who can really suppose that he is on the point of passing the Red Sea? or when it is said, *' Egypt, good night,'* that he has prepared himself for a journey from Egypt to Canaan? Thus also is it here. The most melancholy dissension of the past was that between Judah and Israel, which caused the separation of the two kingdoms, and,

---

¹ We do not supply before ἀπὸ τῶν ὑ. 'I. the pronoun τινές, which Fritzsche properly rejects, without however being justified in his extremely forced interpretation.

² Comp. the examples in *Ges. Lehrg.* p. 798. Instances out of the New Testament are such passages as Luke 12. 20: τὴν ψυχήν σου ἀπαιτοῦσιν ἀπὸ σοῦ, " they demand," for " one demands," and this then for " it is demanded." The expression ἀπὸ υἱῶν Ἰσραὴλ, "on the part of the sons of Israel," (comp. Winer, p. 318, James 1. 13, ἀπὸ θεοῦ πειράζομαι, " I am tempted of God,") corresponds to מֵעֲלֵיהֶם in Zechariah.

³ Corresponding to וַיֹּאמֶר יְהוָה אֵלַי in Zechariah.

⁴ Comp. ver. 7.

continuing afterwards, consumed the energies, which fitted the people
to withstand their heathen foes.   The prophet now wishes to say,
that after the Lord shall have forsaken the people, the most destructive internal discord will arise among them, even as destructive as
the former contention between Judah and Israel.   This he expresses
by saying directly, ' *The Lord will abolish the brotherhood between
Judah and Israel,*' altogether the same as his previous declaration,
' *They will eat the flesh one of another.*'   The fulfilment took place,
as has been already remarked, at the time of the Roman invasion,
when the Jews were destroyed by the rage of parties against each
other.   This is so plain, that it forced itself even upon Abarbanel.

605. Ver. 15. ' *Then said the Lord to me, Take to thee again the
vessels of a foolish shepherd.*'   *Again,* i. q. ' *while thou proceedest to
symbolize the fortunes of the people.*'   It is obvious, that by the
foolish shepherd must be understood not an individual, but the whole
body of the wicked rulers, who, after the rejection of the good shepherd, destroyed the people.   We are not, however, to refer it to
foreign but domestic leaders.   For it is only against the latter that
the Divine punishment could be threatened, as is done in the seventeenth verse, because they were at the same time *instruments* of the
punishment and *partakers of it,* as well as of the horrible apostasy ;
and indeed of this they were the chief authors, while the former,
according to the fifth verse, were not guilty.   That there, in like
manner, the domestic rulers under the name of *the shepherds,* are
contrasted with the foreign, the buyers and sellers, we have already
seen.   The designation of the shepherd, as *foolish,* instead of *ungodly,* points out how the leaders of the people, blinded by the
Divine penal justice, will not perceive that they destroy themselves
when they rage against the people.   This view of ungodliness, that
of *the foolishness connected with it,* is often exhibited, compare e. g.
Jer. 4. 22, ' *For my people is foolish, they have not known me ; they
are sottish children, and they have no understanding ; they are wise
to do evil, but to do good they have no knowledge.*'—By the implement
of the foolish shepherd, more accurately determined by the antithesis
with what precedes, may be understood simply the shepherd's staff,
or, at the same time also, his other implements.   We may suppose
that the implement of the shepherd consisted of a strong staff, armed
with iron, wherewith he wounded the sheep, while the good shepherd
kept them in order with the soft blows of a thin staff ; we can at the
same time imagine a perforated shepherd's-pouch, which contained
nothing which was useful to the sheep and the shepherd, &c.

606. Ver. 16. ' *For behold, I raise up a shepherd in the land ; he
will not visit that which is perishing, not seek that which has wandered, not heal that which is wounded, not nourish the feeble, and the
flesh of the fat ones he will eat, and divide their hoofs.*'   Here also the
prophet has several passages of Ezekiel and Jeremiah in view.
Compare Ezek. 34. 3, 4, ' *The diseased have ye not strengthened,
neither have ye healed that which was sick, neither have ye bound up
that which was broken, neither have ye brought again that which was
driven away, neither have ye sought that which was lost.*'   Jer. 23.

1, 2, ' *Woe be unto the pastors that destroy and scatter the sheep of my pasture! saith the Lord. Therefore, thus saith the Lord God of Israel against the pastors that feed my people ; Ye have scattered my flock, and driven them away, and have not visited them.*' The reference to these passages is not merely external : indeed, in general we must regard the dependence of Zechariah on the older prophets, on account of the great power and originality of his genius, as chiefly voluntary. By a righteous Divine judgement, the people had been punished before the exile by bad rulers ; Jeremiah and Ezekiel had promised them deliverance from these ; and this had actually happened after the exile, particularly at the time of Zechariah, when Zerubbabel and Joshua guided the people in a truly paternal manner. Zechariah however announces, that in future the same cause would produce the same effect, and indeed in a higher degree.—The ' *for* ' at the beginning is explained by the circumstance, that the reason why a symbolical action was performed, is the same which the action signified [1]. The expression, ' *he will divide their hoofs,*' does not indicate, as most interpreters suppose, the extreme *cruelty*, but the extreme *greediness* of the shepherd, which has indeed, for its attendant, cruelty against his sheep : it is a climax of, ' he will eat,' &c. He will even break the hoofs apart, that no fibre of the flesh may be lost.

607. Ver. 17. ' *Wo to the unworthy shepherd, who forsakes the flock, a sword comes upon his arm, and upon his right eye ; his arm shall be altogether palsied, his right eye altogether blind.*' As the object of the punishment, the arm and the right eye are mentioned by way of individualization, those being the two members of the body, which the good shepherd chiefly employs for the care and protection of his flock, but which the bad shepherd most shamefully abuses to its destruction. The arm the organ of strength, the right eye the organ of prudence. An apparent difficulty here arises, from the circumstance that two punishments, inconsistent with each other, are mentioned for each member ; first, for both, the sword ; then for the arm, palsy ; for the eye, dimness. But on a closer examination this difficulty vanishes. The particular punishments serve here only to individualize the idea of punishment in general, and the prophet combines several, in order to exhibit the greatness of the punishment, and consequently the greatness also of the crime. He could do this the more readily since the shepherd is not an individual, but a collective body.

Chapter 12

CHAP. 12. 1.—13. 6

608. The mournful prospect is here again followed by a joyful one. A totally different scene presents itself to our view. The

---

[1] The particulars of the verse are admirably illustrated by Bochart, *Hieroz.* 1. p. 445.

people of the Lord, in the conflict with all nations of the earth, feeble in themselves, but strong in the Lord, every where come off victorious [1]. The Lord has broken their hard heart, and given them grace to repent, so that, with bitter distress, they regret the wickedness which they have committed against Him [2]. In Him they have now the forgiveness of their sins [3], and this produces an upright striving after sanctification, and the avoiding of all ungodliness [4].

609. The interpreters are divided in reference to the time of the fulfilment of this prophecy, as well as its subject. With respect to the former, several, at the head of whom is Grotius, suppose a reference to the times of the Maccabees. But this supposition is for several reasons altogether untenable. It is contradicted by the relation to the foregoing chapter. The reception of the people of God here described, stands in plain contrast with the rejection of them there; and if the latter belongs to the time after the appearing of Christ, the former cannot be placed in the time before His coming. This is also confirmed by the comparison of the tenth verse of the twelfth chapter. The penitential and believing looking upon the crucified Messiah there predicted, leads us beyond the time of the Maccabees to that of the Messiah, with which also the characteristics given at the thirteenth chapter, the forgiveness of sins, and the general striving after holiness, taken by themselves, and compared with the parallel passages, can alone agree. Lastly, in the former prophecy, referring to the times of the Maccabees, one particular people, the Greeks, are mentioned as hostile to the covenant people, in the thirteenth verse of the ninth chapter; here, on the contrary, all the nations of the earth appear as their enemies; a sure proof that we must seek the fulfilment not in the past, which presents nothing of the sort, but in the future, and that the prophecy is analogous to those of earlier prophets, which, as in the fourth chapter of Joel, and in the thirty-ninth verse of the thirty-eighth chapter of Ezekiel [5], relate in like manner to the last great struggle against the kingdom of God, to the last great victory of the Lord over His enemies. Notwithstanding the untenableness of this view, it has still some foundation in truth. As in general the chief events under the Old Testament are typical of those under the New Testament—of which we have one remarkable example in Zechariah himself, chap. 6. 9 sq., where the Jews dwelling in Babylonia, cut off from the sanctuary, but still contributing to rebuild it, are represented as a type of the distant heathen nations, who, in the Messianic time, should promote the building up of the kingdom of God; as also in the second part of Isaiah, where the return from the exile is so constantly regarded as a type of the future return of the heathen nations from the captivity of sin and errour, that it is often difficult to decide what belongs to the type and what to the antitype,—so also the splendid deliverance of the people of God from their oppressors, through the Maccabees,

---

[1] Ver. 1—9.   [2] Ver. 10. 14.
[3] Chap. 13. 1.   [4] Ver. 2—6.
[5] Compare, as respects the latter, however, the introduction to chap. 14.

typified their future last and great deliverance. Consequently it was represented under images borrowed from the former, so that since we are not here aided by a comparison with the fulfilment, it is difficult, and in part impossible to distinguish what belongs to the figurative drapery, and what to the subject.

610. The other diversity relates to the subject of the prophecy. The view which considers it to be the Christian Church is very ancient. Jerome designates it as the general and peculiarly *Christian* view, in opposition to the Jewish. So also Cyril, Mark, and many others. But that this interpretation, in the sense in which it is for the most part delivered, is inadmissible, needs no detailed proof drawn from the contents of the prophecy. Only the interpreters of the prophets, not the prophets themselves, know any thing of a spiritual, in contradiction to a natural Israel. This view can obtain our concurrence only when so modified, that the covenant people here signifies that portion of Israel, which received the manifested Messiah with faith, and in whose bosom the heathen nations were embraced, instead of independently, and on equal grounds, uniting with them in one Church. The conflicting view will then be, that the subject of the prophecy is not the Church of the New Testament in general, whose original stock consisted of the first-fruits of Israel, but the Church of the New Testament in the last ages, when the *whole* people of the Old Testament, freed by the Divine mercy from the judgement of obduracy inflicted upon them, will again be received into the kingdom of God, and form its central point. This last view, adopted by Vitringa, Michaelis, Dathe, and others, has so much in its favour, that its rejection can hardly be explained, except from an aversion to the opinion of a future restoration of the whole people of Israel to their ancient gracious relation to the Lord. In appearance there is indeed much against this ; but we must not therefore be led to set aside, by a forced interpretation, the plain declarations of Scripture, which teach it, declarations not merely of the Old Testament, but also of the New Testament ; not merely of the apostles, particularly of Paul in the Epistle to the Romans, but also of the Lord Himself, Matt. 23. 39, ' *For I say unto you : Ye shall not see me henceforth, till ye shall say, Blessed is he that cometh in the name of the Lord.*' The principal proof is found in chap. 12. 10 sq. According to this passage, those who now experience the powerful help of the Lord are the same who have formerly put him to death ; with the former *national guilt*, as it had been represented in the eleventh chapter, and the consequent punishment, the *national mourning* on account of it is here contrasted, with the strongest expressions of its universality, which exclude every reference to those individual Israelites, who, immediately after the crucifixion of the Lord, smote upon their breasts.

611. We must here still direct attention to the accurate agreement between the first and second part of Zechariah, which has been already intimated. Chap. 1—4 exactly corresponds with chap. 9 and 10. Both represent the blessings which should be conferred upon the believing part of the covenant people, until the manifesta-

tion of the Messiah, chiefly however through that event. Chap. 5
corresponds with chap. 11. Both represent the Divine judgements,
which should come upon the unbelieving and ungodly part of the
covenant people, after their ungodliness had most signally manifested
itself in the rejection of the Messiah. Chap. 6. 1—8, describes
briefly what is more fully detailed in the prophecy before us, and in
chap. 14, God's protection of Israel, and the punishment of their
ungodly enemies, when they have again become the people of God.
What a decisive ground for the genuineness of Zechariah this remarkable parallelism furnishes, is obvious.

612. Ver. 1. ' *The burden of the word of the Lord upon Israel.
Saith the Lord, who stretches out the heavens, and establishes the
earth, and forms the spirit of man within him.*'—Israel is here the
object of the threatening prophecy.   Hence it follows, that Israel
cannot be a designation of the covenant people ; since for them the
prophecy is not of a *threatening*, but *consoling* character.   Of all the
interpreters, only Ribera, as far as we know, perceived the truth :
" *Israel significare puto Judæos* (?) *inimicos ecclesiæ, et ceteros ejus
persecutores.*"   The enemies of the kingdom of God are certainly
those whose overthrow is predicted in the prophecy itself, they must
therefore be those also whose overthrow is predicted in the superscription. The ground of this designation, which at first sight appears strange,
was twofold. 1. The etymology of the name. This was very significant
in reference to the object of Zechariah. *Israel* signifies *God's wrestler*, he who has wrestled, or still does wrestle with God [1].   2. The
relation of the kingdom of Judah to the kingdom of Israel was a type
of the future relation of the kingdom of God to its enemies.   The
kingdom of Israel, by the worship of images and idols, had been
guilty of an apostasy from God, which deserved to be punished, and
was constantly endeavouring, partly alone, partly in alliance with the
heathenish Syrians, to overthrow Judah, the tribe which the Lord had
chosen, and where He had built His sanctuary [2].   Their later exile
was the righteous punishment of this hostility against God and His
kingdom [3].   That the Prophet, in the choice of the name *Israel*, had
in view, besides the etymology, this allusion also, appears from his
employing *Judah* and *Jerusalem* throughout the prophecy, as a designation of the covenant people, while elsewhere he frequently couples
the mention of *Judah* with that of *Israel* or *Ephraim*.—The predicates attached to the name of God, as is very frequently the case in
the older Prophets, particularly in the second part of Isaiah, serve to
suppress the doubt of the fulfilment of the promise arising from present appearances, by pointing to the omnipotence of its author.
What is here *implied*, is, chap. 8. 6, directly expressed in the words,

[1] Comp. Gen. 32. 29. Hos. 12. 4.   [2] Ps. 78. 10. 11. 67, 68.
[3] Comp. 2 Kings 17. Is. 7. 7. 8. 6. 9. 7 sq.

" *If it shall be wonderful in the eyes of the remnant of this people in those days, will it therefore also be wonderful in my eyes? saith the Lord Almighty* [1]."—' *Which stretcheth forth,*' &c. In opposition to the cheerless view, according to which the works of God, after they have been once created, stand related to Him as a house to its builder, their preservation is in a certain respect always regarded in Scripture as a *continued creation*. God *daily* stretches out the heavens anew, *daily* lays the foundation of the earth, which, if not restrained by His power, would wander from its course and be shattered in pieces. The last predicate (' *and formeth the spirit of man within him*') also refers not merely to the original creation of the human soul, but at the same time to the *continual creating and sustaining influence* which God exerts upon it. The formation of the spirit of man is here rendered especially prominent among the many works of the Divine Omnipotence, because this is the ground of the absolute and constant influence exerted upon it by Him who turns the hearts of kings as the waterbrooks. How should not the Creator of the spirits of all men, ' the God of the spirits of all flesh [2],' be able to strike all the horsemen of the enemy with madness, as it is said in the fourth verse, or to fill the leaders of His people, according to the sixth verse, with sacred courage [3]?

613. Ver. 2. *Behold! I make Jerusalem for a threshold of shaking* [4] *to all nations round about; and also upon Judah will it be, in the siege against Jerusalem.*' We follow without hesitation the translation of the Seventy [5], and regard as certainly correct what Theodoret remarks in explanation of the words : " *I will make, he says, this city a city easy to be taken and conquered by all the nations; and I will make it like doors, that are violently shaken, and about to be flung down ; so that its enemies, seeing it deprived of my providence, shall come against it and besiege it, and bring upon it the misery to which a siege gives birth.*" There lies at the foundation the comparison of Jerusalem with a building, which totters throughout as soon as its threshold is shaken. Thus in the fourth verse of the sixth chapter of Isaiah, the bases of the thresholds tremble; in the first verse of the ninth chapter of Amos, the entire shaking of the Theocracy is signified by the *shaking of the thresholds* of the Temple.—In the designation of enemies there is a climax,—here *all the nations round about*, in the third verse, first *all nations*, afterwards *all the nations of*

---

[1] The participles נטה and יסד are not, as several interpreters suppose, to be referred exclusively to the past.

[2] Numbers 16. 22. 27. 16.

[3] In a manner precisely similar is the omnipotence of God, Ps. 33. 15, founded on His being the Former of the hearts of all men. The same three predicates, Is. 42. 5, are joined with one another. בְּקִרְבּוֹ is well explained by Calvin thus : " *Quum dicit* in medio *ejus, intelligit spiritum habitare intus : quia scimus corpus nostrum esse instar tabernaculi.*"

[4] See the original work for the objections to the usual translation, " *a bason* (or *cup*) *of intoxication.*" E. T. " *a cup of trembling,*" or (Marg.) " *of slumber,*" or " *of poison.*"

[5] Who render סַף־רַעַל by ὡς πρόθυρα σαλευόμενα.

the earth. The strongest designation is reserved until the Divine aid has been announced. In the contrast with this, it was no longer terrible to the covenant people, and the Divine omnipotence was thereby rendered the more manifest.—The second part has ever been a *crux interpretum,* plainly because the false interpretation of the first has prevented them from arriving at the truth here [1]. The correct interpretation is : ' *Also upon Judah will it come in the siege of Jerusalem.*' The sense has already been perceived by Luther, ' *It will concern Judah also when Jerusalem is besieged.*' Grammar does not require us to supply ' *each one of them*' as the *subject,* which lies rather indirectly in what precedes, that Jerusalem would be to the enemies a *threshold of shaking,* and in what follows, that they would besiege it. From this the idea of adversity, of a hostile siege, may be readily derived, and the more so since the sentence is connected with the foregoing [2].—The antithesis of *Judah* and *Jerusalem* seems here to be that between the *lower* and the *more respectable portion* of the covenant people, just as in the eighth verse, in Jerusalem itself a similar antithesis is presented by *the house of David* and *the other inhabitants.* The type of this relation was furnished by that of Jerusalem, the civil and religious capital to the rest of Judah, which looked up to it with wonder [3] in the past and present [4]. The antithesis here serves only to prepare the way for the following annunciation, that the Lord, in order that the deliverance might more clearly appear as His work, would interpose first for the most feeble and helpless portion of the covenant people.

614. Ver. 3. ' *And it shall come to pass the same day, that I will make Jerusalem a burdensome stone for all the nations ; all who lift it up shall bruise and cut themselves ; and there shall be gathered together against her all the nations of the earth.*' (Rückert.) With this verse the prediction of prosperity begins, with which the additional expression, ' *it shall come to pass in this day,*' perfectly coincides. The image of a heavy stone, which inflicts dislocations and bruises upon those, who, overrating their strength, raise it up, is in itself so plain, that there is no occasion to assume, with most interpreters, a direct reference to a gymnastic exercise practised in Palestine in the time of Jerome, according to his account, which has already been too often copied.—In the words, ' *and they assemble,*' &c., the Prophet describes once more in the strongest language the danger, in order that in contrast with it the deliverance might appear the more wonderful, and at the same time that the believers might not be discouraged.

615. Ver. 4. ' *In that day, saith the Lord, I will smite all horses with fright, and their riders with madness ; and upon the house of*

---

[1] According to one of the most prevalent interpretations the sense is : " Judah also, compelled by enemies, shall take part in the siege of Jerusalem." Thus the Chaldee, Jerome, and Grotius, &c.

[2] By וְגַם.   [3] Comp. e. g. Ps. 122.

[4] The strictly literal understanding of this antithesis, which is also found in the first part, chap. 1. 12. 2. 16, is particularly unsupported in Zechariah on account of his uniformly figurative and typical character.

*Judah will I open mine eyes, and all horses of the nations will I smite
with blindness.*' The horsemen are here mentioned as *the flower of
the hostile army* [1]. What the smiting of them with madness imports
is exemplified in the eighteenth verse of the sixth chapter of the
second book of Kings, where the Lord, in answer to the prayer of
Elisha, so blinds His enemies, that, instead of seizing Him, they
rush upon their own destruction.—The *opening of the eyes* is a designation of the Divine care; God appeared *to have closed his eyes* as
long as He gave up His people to affliction. The opening of the
eyes of God on the house of Judah stands in contrast with the
smiting of the enemies' horses with blindness, and is the more appropriate, since he upon whom God opens His eyes, now sees clearly
himself, while before he groped in darkness [2].—The *house* of Judah
(not bare Judah, as in the preceding and following context, where
Judah stands in the antithesis with Jerusalem), seems here to comprehend the whole covenant people. The house of Judah is elsewhere frequently called the kingdom of Judah, in contrast with the
house or kingdom of Israel; and that the Prophet here also has this
antithesis in view, is evident from the foregoing typical designation of
the enemies by Israel.

616. Ver. 5. '*And the princes of Judah say in their hearts:
the inhabitants of Jerusalem are strength for me in the Lord, the Almighty, their God* [3].' The passage before us receives light from the
sixth and seventh verses. It is there made prominent, that God
would first deliver the feeblest portion of the covenant people most
exposed to hostile assaults, designated by the inhabitants of the province in contrast with those of the capital, and give them the most
splendid victory over the common enemy, in order that the former
splendour of Jerusalem might not receive by the new advantage such
an accession, that Judah would be thereby entirely eclipsed. This
annunciation is prepared for in the verse before us, by its being declared how little Judah stood in expectation of such prosperity and
honour, and how in quiet lowliness and modesty he expected his
prosperity only from the capital, which was peculiarly favoured of
God, and standing under His special protection. His own confession

---

[1] As in chap. 10. 5.   [2] Comp. Is. 59. 10.

[3] Remarkable here, as in chap. 9. 7, is the use of the noun אַלֻּף, of princes and
leaders of the covenant people. This word occurs besides only as a designation
of the *Idumean princes* of tribes, comp. Gen. 36. 15 sq. Exod. 15. 15. 1 Chron. 1.
51 sqq. Several lexicographers cite indeed in favour of the more general meaning, besides the above passages, that of Jeremiah 13. 21; but Schultens, *Animadvv.
Phil.* on Jer. 13. 21, has so clearly proved that אַלֻּף here has not the meaning
prince, but, as elsewhere also in Jeremiah (3. 4), that of *friend,* that nothing
further need be said. This entirely peculiar use of אַלֻּף in Zechariah is not
unimportant. (1) It refutes the hypothesis of those who assume that chap. 9 is
the work of a different author from that before us. (2) It furnishes a testimony
for the composition of the second part in the period after the exile, and therefore
for its genuineness. Such an idiom—much the same as if we should generally
use *Margrave* for *Prince*—can be explained only from his learning the language out of the more ancient writings, which, as we have already seen, Zechariah constantly imitates.

of lowliness makes his subsequent glorification more manifestly a work of God, who gives grace to the humble. The Jehovah of Hosts[1] points to the omnipotence of God; '*their God*,' to His will to help, grounded on His covenant relation to His people.

617. Ver. 6. '*In that day will I make the princes of Judah as a fire under wood, and as a torch of fire under sheaves; and they shall devour, on the right hand and on the left, all the nations round about, and Jerusalem continues to sit on her throne at Jerusalem.*' How far this verse is to be understood figuratively, and how far literally, must be learnt from the fulfilment, which it would be rashness to attempt to anticipate. Considering the constant practice of Zechariah, to employ what belongs to the Old Testament as an image and type of the New Testament, the figurative interpretation cannot be rejected beforehand. The substance would then be only, "the victory of the covenant people over their enemies;" the special designations belonging only to the type considered in itself[2]. In the last member Jerusalem is, as usual, personified as a *matron*. She continues to sit on the throne, from which her enemies thought to cast her down. Explanatory in every respect is the passage, Is. 47. 1, where the opposite is said of Babylon : "*Descend and sit in the dust, thou virgin daughter, Babylon; sit on the earth without a throne, thou daughter of the Chaldeans.*"—'*On her throne,*' literally '*under herself,*' i. e. on that which she had hitherto had under herself, on her throne.

618. Ver. 7. '*And the Lord will help the tents of Judah first : in order that the splendour of the house of David, and the splendour of the inhabitants of Jerusalem, may not exalt itself above Judah.*' The tents of Judah here stand in plain antithesis with the capital. A similar antithesis occurs wherever the tents of Judah or Israel are mentioned[3]. The use of the term *tents* for *houses*, in these passages, is occasioned by the effort to lessen that which was dispersed and scattered, in contrast with that which was concentrated ; just as in Germany any one, who inhabits a respectable house, might say, "I am quitting the capital for my own hut;" and we need not, with J. D. Michaelis and Winer, find a relic of the old nomadic times. In this passage, however, the designation seems to have a special subordinate reference to the helplessness of Judah, and thus to make more emphatic the expression, '*And the Lord will help*[4].' Parallel is Ezek.

---

[1] κύριος ὁ παντοκράτωρ.

[2] Still a remark of Vitringa on Apoc. 19. 19, where exactly the same representation occurs, so that this cannot be regarded in any event as peculiar to the Old Testament, and belonging to its inferior character, deserves all regard : "*Deus non pugnat cum hostibus suis corporali modo; nec Christus etiam suæ ecclesiæ rex. Quando tamen suâ curat providentiâ, ut ecclesia nanciscatur vindices suæ causæ, per quos ipse hostes suos dejicit et prosternit : tum vero ipse,* spirituali *quidem modo* pugnans, vincit etiam corporaliter: *suntque effecta victoriæ Christi ejusmodi in casu per orbem manifesta.*"

[3] Comp. e. g. 2 Sam. 20. 1, '*A wicked man said: We have no part in David; every one to his tents, O Israel :*' ver. 22, '*And they dispersed themselves from the city, each one to his tent.*' So 1 Kings 8. 66. Judges 20. 8.

[4] Calvin: "*Per tabernacula meo judicio intelligit propheta tuguria, quæ non*

38. 11, ' *And thou shalt say, I will go up to the land of unwalled villages; I will go to them that are at rest, that dwell safely, all of them dwelling without walls, and having neither bars nor gates.*' The expression, ' *in order—not,*' &c., refers to *first*, and not to the Divine help, which was to be granted to Jerusalem, as well as to Judah, and that through the latter. There is a good reason why *the splendour* is not repeated before *Judah*. Burk: " *The simple mention of Judah shows that she had not otherwise any splendour, on ac-count of which she might have exalted herself*[1]." The discourse is here only of the possession of advantages, which however might easily be abused by the corruption of human nature to self-exaltation above others and above God, and the too great accumulation of which must therefore be guarded against. It appears that the Prophet here had in view such an abuse as Jerusalem at an earlier period had made of its advantages over the country. The strong shall be delivered by the weak, in order that the true equilibrium may be restored between both, in order, as Jerome remarks, that it may be manifest : " *That in the case of both the victory is the Lord's.*"

619. Ver. 8. ' *In that day the Lord will defend the inhabitants of Jerusalem ; and he that stumbleth among them in that day shall be as David, and the house of David like God, as the Angel of the Lord before them*[2].' The inhabitants of Jerusalem are divided into two parts, the weak and the strong. The latter are afterwards designated by *the house of David*. The former shall attain to the degree which the strongest among the latter, their ancestor, the brave hero and king, David, once occupied ; the latter shall rise to an elevation unknown to the former Theocracy. The Prophet thus, by way of individualization, expresses the thought, that at that time the Lord will exalt His people to a glory not imagined in the former Theocracy. Similar, Is. 60. 22, " *The few will become thousands, and the feeble a strong people*[3]."—' *Like Elohim,*' is by most interpreters translated, *as an angel*. But this import the word *never has*. The reason however that is given for this interpretation well deserves to be considered, namely, that otherwise the progress to the following, ' *as the angel of the Lord,*' will not, as we should naturally expect, be a climax. The difficulty however may be removed by the following remark. *Elohim* expresses (as even the plural form, the usual designation of the *abstract*, shows) the *abstract conception of Deity*. When it is not rendered concrete by *the article*, it often stands where merely what is *superhuman*, or *more than earthly*, is designated. Especially remarkable in this respect is Ps. 8. 5, ' *Thou hast made man a little lower than God*[4].'

---

possunt tueri suos hospites vel inquilinos.—Est hic tacita comparatio inter tuguria et urbes munitas."

[1] תִּפְאָרֶת, not *gloriatio*, but *decus, majestas*.

[2] The article in הַנִּכְשָׁל must not be overlooked.

[3] נִכְשָׁל, properly a *stumbler*, then in general one who is weak, 1 Sam. 2. 4.

[4] מִן מֵאֱלֹהִים according to usage, can indicate only the thing in which the deficiency is.

Here those who understand by *Elohim* '*the one true God,*' are in as great an errour as those, who, merely from the difficulty of escaping from this unpleasant sense, give, as here, the sense *angel* to *Elohim*, which, however, does not suit, for the simple reason, that *the angels have no dominion over nature*, while nevertheless the subject of discourse is solely that dignity which man possesses as God's vicegerent. Hence those expose themselves to ridicule, who would deduce from this Psalm a proof of the moral dignity of man since the fall. We find the true interpretation in Calvin : ' *Thou hast exalted him almost to a divinity.*' This, when applied to the passage before us, where *Elohim* stands in like manner without the article, shows at once that there is actually a progress from the *lesser* to the *greater*. ' *The house of David will be as something more than earthly,*' is not so strong as, ' *it will be as the Angel of the Lord.*' We must not with some translate as '*an* angel,' or '*an* angel of the Lord,' but ' *the* angel of the Lord,' His Revealer, to whom Zechariah constantly attributes His names and works.—The last words [1] are understood in different ways. After the Syriac, several (Michaelis, Burk, Rosenmüller) : ' *Who was before them.*' Eichhorn : '*As (once) Jehovah's Angel in the front of Israel.*' But we do not see the use of this forced interpretation ; since in the other, ' *The house of David will be as the Angel of the Lord before them,*' there is no difficulty. According to this also, there is an allusion to the march through the wilderness, where the Angel of the Lord went before Israel. Parallel as to the expression is Mic. 2. 13, ' *Their king marches before them* [2], *and the Lord in their front.*'—The ' *as* ' does not here denote *equality*, but *resemblance*, just as 2 Sam. 14. 17, ' *For as the angel of the Lord, so is my lord the king, to hear the good and the evil.*' Ver. 20. ' *My lord is wise, as the wisdom of the angel of the Lord, to know all that is on earth.*' *Equality* is surely not intended there.—The house of David forms here (as the antithesis in the verse, and also the comparison of the twelfth verse, show), only a *type* for *the noblest of the covenant people, and their future leaders ;* just as the Prophet designates the *future enemies* of the covenant people by *Egypt* and *Ashur ;* their *future deliverance*, as a *passage through the Red Sea ;* the land of their *future* exile, by *Shinar*.

620. Ver. 9. ' *It will be in that day, that I will seek to destroy all nations, who come against Jerusalem.*' Ver. 10. ' *And I pour out upon the house of David, and upon the inhabitants of Jerusalem, the spirit of grace and of gracious supplication, and they look on me whom they have pierced, and they lament for him as the lamentations for an only son, and mourn for him as the mourning for the first-born.*'—On ' *I pour out* [3],' Jerome remarks justly : " *Verbum effusionis sensum largitatis ostendit.*" It is at first view remarkable, that here, as in the first verse of the thirteenth chapter, only the house of David and the inhabitants of Jerusalem are mentioned, and not Judah. This is explained by the frequent practice of the more ancient prophets of designating the Theocracy by its capital or central point,

---

[1] לִפְנֵיהֶם.   [2] וַיַּעֲבֹר מַלְכָּם לִפְנֵיהֶם   [3] וְשָׁפַכְתִּי

Jerusalem or Zion. The Prophet could the more readily adopt this usage here, since the former contrast between Jerusalem and Judah no longer existed; and in reference to the outpouring of the Spirit there was not, as in respect to the deliverance, a difference which could induce him, as there, to make a separation. In the first part also, Jerusalem only is mentioned several times, though the Prophet had in view the whole Theocracy. Thus e. g. [1] ' The Lord rebuke thee, who chooses *Jerusalem* [2] ;' while in other passages [3] the Theo- cracy is designated by *Jerusalem and the cities of Judah.*—The ' *spirit of grace* ' is the spirit which *works grace; brings grace with it;* com- pare the entirely similar idiom, Is. 11. 1, ' *The spirit of wisdom, of power,*' &c. Grace [4] is not here to be understood as an *attribute of God,* but its *operation* as a new principle of life in man. Very sig- nificant is the combination of *grace* and *gracious supplication.* By the very choice of the expressions derived from the same root, it is intimated that this supplication has its source in grace.—' *To look on* [5],' often stands, where a *spiritual* or *corporeal* looking upon an object, with *confidence* in it, is intended [6]. Thus is it, Num. 21. 9, in reference to the brazen serpent, by *looking upon which* the Israelites were healed. It stands here in silent antithesis with the contempt and disgust with which Israel had formerly *turned away* his face from the Messiah [7].—Very remarkable is, ' *on me.*' The speaker, according to the first verse, is THE LORD, *the Creator of heaven and earth.* That we are not, however, to understand by Him, the one invisible God exalted above all suffering, is shown by what follows, where this Jehovah represents Himself as pierced by Israel, and now bewailed by him in bitter repentance. We are rather led thereby to the Angel and Revealer of the most High God, to whom the Prophet, on account of his participation in the Divine nature, attributes all, even the most exalted names of God [8], who had also (according to the eleventh chapter) undertaken the office of shepherd over the people, and been rewarded by them with the basest ingra- titude. They lament for the murdered one, not as though he were still subject to death, but in painful consciousness that he had been slain by their sins. That the Lord had turned to good what they intended for evil, cannot mitigate their distress. They behold in this only their own deed and its natural result. That their forefathers, and not they themselves, performed the deed, affords them no con- solation. They are conscious that the guilt is national; that by participating in the disposition of their fathers, which caused the crime, and by their bitter hatred against the Messiah, they have made themselves partakers in the guilt of this crime; and that it can be punished in them also, with the same right as, at the time of the invasion of the Chaldeans, the sins of former generations were pu- nished in their forefathers, with whom they stood in the closest con-

---

[1] Chap. 3. 2.   [2] Chap 8. 8.   [3] e. g. I. 12.
[4] הֵן
[5] הִבִּיט with אֶל.
[6] As θεωρεῖν, e. g. John 6. 40.   [7] Comp. Is. 53. 11.
[8] See above, 503, p. 273.

nexion through their crimes.—The lamentation for *an only son* occurs
also elsewhere as a designation of the deepest mourning[1]; '*And I
make it as the mourning of the first-born*[2].' '*Daughter of my people,
put on sackcloth, cover thyself with ashes, make for thyself a lamentation of the first-born.*' The mourning for the first-born was typified
in Egypt, comp. Exod. 11. 6, '*And there was a great cry in the
land, such as never had been and never will be.*'—The fulfilment of
the prophecy of our verse was remarkably *typified* immediately after
the crucifixion of Christ, and has been erroneously supposed by
several interpreters to have then actually taken place; compare
Luke 23. 48, '*And all the people that came together to that sight,
beholding the things that were done, smote their breasts and returned*[3].'
The multitude who shortly before had cried out, '*Crucify him,*' here,
struck by the manifestation of the superhuman dignity of Jesus,
smite upon themselves, and lament for the dead, and their own
crime; and the probably transient emotion of those individuals
served as a feeble type of the thorough repentance of the whole
people.—We have still to notice the reference to this passage in the
New Testament. The only proper citation is that of John 19. 37,
'*And again another Scripture saith : They shall look on him whom
they pierced.*' In regard to the relation of this citation to the prophecy, we offer the following remarks. (1) The only deviation from
the words of the original is the change of the first person into the
third. In Zechariah the Messiah himself speaks, John speaks of
him. That the apostle, who here, leaving the Septuagint, translates
immediately from the Hebrew, had before him another reading, is
the more improbable, since in the citation from the ninth verse of the
twenty-seventh chapter of Matthew, and from the thirteenth verse of
the eleventh chapter of Zechariah, we find exactly the same phenomenon, arising from the effort after greater clearness. (2) Although Vitringa[4] and Michaelis have taken pains to evince the
opposite, yet is it plain that the citation of John refers directly only
to *the piercing with the lance,* and not to the *whole crucifixion* of
Christ. He relates [5] how the bones of the Lord were not broken, as
in the case of the others [6]; how His side was pierced. He then [7]
adduces an Old Testament witness for the first [8], and then for the
second. But, allowing that John cites the prophecy only in reference to this particular circumstance, it by no means follows that he
extended it no further, but only that he found it fulfilled in it, and
indeed most justly, since the piercing with the spear, as well as the
whole crucifixion, according to the twenty-third verse of the second
chapter of Acts, was a work of the Jews in respect to the spiritual,
though not to the material cause. That John is very far from always
limiting the prophecies to the object to which he immediately refers

---

[1] Amos 8. 6.   [2] Jer. 6. 26.
[3] This the ground meaning of the verb סָפַד, that originally designates an
especial manifestation of mourning, comp. Is. 32. 12, '*They beat upon their
breasts,*' Winer s. v.
[4] Obss. 2. 9, p. 172.   [5] Ver. 31—33.   [6] Ver. 34.
[7] Ver. 26.   [8] Ver. 27

them, is very evident from the ninth verse of the eighteenth chapter. But the prophecy would plainly lose in importance, if the verb *to pierce* should be limited to the single fact of the *piercing with the lance,* as has been already shown among others by Lampe. It rather designates *the whole suffering* by which the death of the Messiah was effected. That this was the substance, and that the *instrument* and *kind of death* were unimportant, appears from the comparison of chap. 13. 7, where the *sword* is mentioned as the instrument, while *to pierce* rather suggests the notion of a *spear.*—Besides this direct citation, there is also in two passages, and plainly by design, an allusion to this place, Matt. 24. 30 ; ' *And then shall all the tribes of the earth mourn, and they shall see the Son of man coming in the clouds of heaven.*' Apoc. 1. 7 ; ' *Behold, he cometh with clouds ; and every eye shall see him, and they also which pierced him.*' These passages are a kind of sacred parody of that in Zechariah. They show, that, with the wholesome repentance, the godly sorrow, of which Zechariah speaks, there is another repentance, the despair of Judas ; with the voluntary looking to him who had been pierced, another involuntary, from which even the unbeliever cannot escape. The thrilling sublimity of this allusion every one must perceive. It shows, moreover, that the Lord Himself and His apostles referred the passage to Him.

621. Ver. 11. ' *At that time there shall be a great lamentation in Jerusalem, like the lamentation of Hadadrimmon in the valley of Megiddo.*' The Prophet here exerts himself to the utmost in order to make the lamentation appear as great, and as general as possible, thus refuting every reference of his prophecy to any event, which was only a prelude of its proper object. ' The lamentation of Hadadrimmon' is here not a lamentation *which happened at Hadadrimmon,* but one which so far belonged to that place, as there was the object of it, the pious King Josiah being slain there. That the lamentation over *him who was pierced,* is compared particularly with that over the death of this king, appears from the following reasons. (1) The lamentation, which the Prophet here takes for the comparison, must have been one of the most distressing that had ever occurred. This was evidently that for Josiah. According to the twenty-fifth verse of the thirty-fifth chapter of the Second Book of Chronicles, Jeremiah composed an elegy on his death ; others were composed and sung by male and female singers. These became current in Israel as popular songs, and continued so until the time of the writer of the Chronicles. They were received into a collection of songs of lamentations concerning the mournful fate of the nation, which after the death of Josiah was rapidly hurried to its ruin. Herein we have the proof, as well of *the greatness* of the lamentation, as also of a *continued lively remembrance* of it in later times, until after the exile. (2) The subject of the lamentation must have been

a *pious* king, and the comparison becomes the more suitable, when he
is one, who in a certain respect died for the sins of the people. Both
of these were fully realized in Josiah. He was [1], of all the kings of
Judah, the most pious; but still God was not therefore moved to
change the decree of destruction. He died, not so much a sacrifice
to the improvidence with which he engaged in a war with the more
powerful king of Egypt, as a sacrifice to the sins of his people. Had
these not called forth the vengeance of God, He would have preserved
him, either from this improvidence itself, or from the consequences of
it. (3) The comparison requires the person slain to be a king of
Judah, and lamented at Jerusalem. '*At Jerusalem*,' is plainly to be
supplied also in the second member: '*The lamentation will be great
at Jerusalem, as there the lamentation of Hadadrimmon was great*[2].'
Both these happened in the case of Josiah. Mortally wounded, the
king was brought back to Jerusalem, where, immediately after his
arrival, the last spark of life was extinguished, and now began the
lamentation for him, the beloved one, with whom the Theocracy
seemed to be borne to its grave;—compare the twenty-second verse of
the thirty-fifth chapter of the Second Book of Chronicles. The apparent contradiction between this passage and that in the Book of
Kings, which makes Josiah die at *Megiddo*, is to be explained merely
from the effort at brevity in the later historian, who, in harmony with
his design, is throughout less accurate than the writer of the Chronicles, in *reference to external and unimportant circumstances*. It
was not a matter of moment to him, that the king still retained a
feeble spark of life. He represented him as dying at Megiddo, because there he received his mortal wound. (4) The place accurately
coincides. Verbally the same as here, it is said in Chronicles, Josiah
was *pierced through*[3]. The difference is only that here the place is
especially designated in which Josiah received his mortal wound.
That Hadadrimmon was situated in the valley of Megiddo or Jezreel
is expressly testified by Jerome[4]. That it is not elsewhere mentioned in the Old Testament, and was entirely unknown to the
Seventy, as their understanding of the word as an appellative shows,
can be explained either from the mere insignificance of the place, or[5]
from the fact that *Hadadrimmon, decus granatorum*, was less the
proper name of the place than an *honorable epithet*.—We may remark
how decisively the verse refutes the reference of the foregoing to
Jehovah, and establishes that to the Messiah. How absurd were the
comparison of the lamentation over the Most High God offended,
with that over the King Josiah slain! How well suited, on the contrary, is the latter to be a type of the Messiah! He was slain on

---

[1] According to 2 Kings 23. 25, &c.

[2] The *gen.* precisely as in חֶרְפַּת מִצְרַיִם, " the reproach from Egypt."

[3] בִּבְקְעַת מְגִדּוֹ.

[4] " *Hadadrimmon urbs est juxta Jezreelem, hoc olim vocabulo nuncupata, et hodie
vocatur Maximianopolis in campo Mageddon, in quo Josias rex justus a Pharaone
cognomento Necho vulneratus est.*"

[5] With Wichmanshausen, *De Planctu Hadadrimmon* in the *Thes. N. Theol.
Phil.* I. p. 1007 ff.

account of the sin of his people; his reign was the last gracious
look of the Lord; henceforth inexpressible misery followed; the
lamentation for his death arose from the mingled feeling of love,
and of anguish for their own sins, which had caused him to be
sacrificed.

622. Ver. 12—14. The reason why the Prophet so fully describes
the lamentation for him who was pierced, is (1) To represent the
lamentation of Israel as *real*, and not *ceremonial;* his conversion as
inward and *genuine*. The Prophet accomplishes this object by continuing the figurative representation he had begun, and causing every
family, and again in every family, the men and women, to mourn
apart. It is thus intimated that every family, and every division of
the same, would mourn, as if they had to lament the death of one of
their own members. (2) Next, his object was to represent the
lamentation as strongly as possible, as extending through the whole
people; the conversion, not perhaps as relating to a few, as at the
coming of Christ in humiliation, and shortly after that of the most
miserable sheep, who esteem the good shepherd[1], but as a national
affair. To accomplish this object, the Prophet mentions first two
chief tribes, and connects with them, in order to show that the conversion would extend from beginning to end, two of their chief
families, and then joins with them, in order to express the idea of the
whole of the people, all the remaining families. And thus, like Paul,
in the twenty-sixth verse of the eleventh chapter of Romans, he
makes all Israel to be saved. Ver. 12. '*And the land mourns every
family apart, the family of the house of David apart, and their wives
apart, the family of the house of Nathan apart, and their wives apart.*'
Ver. 13. '*The family of the house of Levi apart, and their wives
apart, the family of the house of Shimei apart, and their wives apart.*'
Ver. 14. '*All the remaining families, every family apart, and their
wives apart.*'—To understand why these particular families are mentioned as participating in the lamentation for the Messiah, we must
determine correctly the family of Shimei. This can be done with
certainty from Num. 3. 18, sq. Levi had three sons, *Gershon,
Kohath, Merari;* Gershon two sons, *Libni* and *Shimei*. The
family of the latter is named, in the twenty first verse, exactly as
here, *the family of the Shimeite*[2]. Accordingly an individual family,
and that a subordinate one of the tribe of Levi, is here associated
with the *whole tribe*. No doubt now remains that the family of the
house of Nathan, also, cannot be the posterity of the Prophet in the
time of David, still less the prophetic order, which, as not being descended from Nathan, cannot possibly be designated as *his family*.
The family of Nathan must rather be a *branch of the family of David*,
in like manner as that of Shimei is a branch *of that of Levi*. It is therefore evident that the Prophet intended the family of Nathan, a son of
David, who is mentioned in the fourteenth verse of the fifth chapter
of the second book of Samuel, and in the thirty-first verse of the

---

[1] Chap. 11. 11.   [2] מִשְׁפַּחַת הַשִּׁמְעִי.

third chapter of Luke. That among the sons of David he mentions this particular one, happened, because Nathan, like Shimei, was the founder of only a *subordinate* family. We have, therefore, the two chief families of the earlier Theocracy, the *kingly* and *the priestly* families, and, joined with them, *two of their subdivisions*, in order to show that the conversion of every family would extend to *all* its members, without exception, from the highest to the lowest.

Chapter 13

623. Ver. 1. '*At that time a fountain shall be opened for the house of David and the inhabitants of Jerusalem, for sin and for uncleanness.*' The penitential sorrow of Israel will not be in vain, as indeed it cannot be, since it has been awakened in him by the Lord.—The fountain is the Divine grace, which imparts to the penitent people the forgiveness of sin; the water here is not, as elsewhere, represented as assuaging thirst, but as purifying. The *open* fountain, according to most interpreters, is here contrasted with one *shut up*, whose water is accessible only to the possessor. But more correctly Schultens: the fountain is *shut up* so long as it is concealed in the stones; it is opened when it breaks forth [1].

624. Ver. 2. The consequence of the forgiveness of sins is a new life of righteousness and holiness, a renunciation effected by the aid of the Lord, of all that opposes His revealed will. '*And it shall come to pass in that day, saith the Lord of Hosts, that I abolish the names of the idols out of the land, and they shall not be mentioned any more; and also the prophets, and the unclean spirit, will I remove from the land.*' The removal of every thing ungodly from Israel, now again become the covenant people, is here expressed by the abolition of the two manifestations of ungodliness, idolatry and false prophecy, which in the former Theocracy had most prevailed, and we need not hence infer their prevalence in the time of the prophet, or in the future which he describes. These particular manifestations are only accidental, the substance is ungodliness, which is always the same, whether it reveals itself as idolatry and false prophecy, as in this instance, or as Pharisaical self-righteousness. This supposition can here cause the less difficulty, since we have so many striking examples of a designation of the future by the past or present, agreeing with it in substance, though differing in form. '*And they shall no more be mentioned,*' is a frequent designation of the most complete extinction [2].—'*The prophets.*' That we are not, with

---

[1] Parallel is Is. 41. 18, 'I will open, אֶפְתַּח, on the high places streams.' 35. 6. נִבְקְעוּ מַיִם וּנְחָלִים. On נִדָּה, comp. Ezek. 36. 17. Is. 64. 5.

[2] Comp. e. g. Hos. 2. 19. 14. 9. Mic. 5. 11. 13.

Eichhorn and Rückert, to regard the Prophet here as predicting the
abolition of the prerogatives of *prophecy*, but rather only the extirpation of *the false prophets*, appears from the collocation of the prophets with the idols on the one hand, and with the unclean spirit on
the other ; from the phrase, ' *I will cause to pass out of the land*,'
which points to a violent expulsion of something bad in itself and
polluting to the land ; and from the further description, which follows, where two kinds of false prophets are spoken of ; those who
speak falsehood in the name of the Lord, and those who combine
false prophecy with idolatry.   The false prophets are called also in
other passages simply prophets (compare on the second verse of the
tenth chapter), because the use of this name, which they had usurped,
in contrast with their real character, served to make their guilt appear
in a stronger light, just as the Prophet in the foregoing chapter calls
the wolves in the shepherds' clothes, shepherds.   The article can
prove nothing in favour of the prophets in general being intended,
since it rather points to a species of prophets defined by the whole
context.—The *unclean spirit*, on the one hand, stands in antithesis
with the Holy Spirit, who [1] was to be poured out, and with the fountain for the removal of uncleanness [2], on the other.   The special
reference to idolatry and false prophecy, chiefly to the latter, appears
from the collocation with them ; that the Prophet had in view a person, or even merely a personification, does not appear from the article.
For this can be explained, either by an allusion to the former Theocracy, the unclean spirit, who is known to you by his former dominion
and ruinous effects ; or, from the antithesis with the Holy Spirit, or
from the reference to the false prophets, the unclean spirit by whom
they are moved.   So much, however, certainly appears from this
designation, that the false prophets, as well as the true, perhaps also
the worshippers of idols as well as the worshippers of the true God,
were under the dominion of a principle foreign to themselves, to
which they had surrendered themselves by their own free act.   For
' *spirit* [3] ' never stands merely for a man's own disposition.   The same
also is evident from the relation, in the twenty-second chapter of the
first book of Kings, where the spirit of prophecy, which, in accordance with the character of the vision, appears personified, offers to
deceive Ahab by putting false predictions into the mouth of the
prophets of the calves.   It is here evident that the false prophets, as
well as the true, were under an influence foreign from their nature, a
doctrine which is confirmed also by the fundamental view of the New
Testament concerning the kingdom of darkness and of light, both in
like manner having possession of the minds of those subject to them
(comp. e. g. the parable of the tares and the wheat).—In numerous
passages of the Sohar, the fulfilment of this promise is placed in the
Messianic time.   We here bring forward only a few.   ' Sin will
not cease from the world until the King Messiah will come at a
future time, as the Scripture says : I will cause the unclean spirit,'
&c.—' The left side will have the upper hand and the unclean be

---

[1] According to chap. 12. 10.   [2] Ver. 1.   [3] רוּחַ

strong, until the Holy God shall build the temple, and firmly establish the world ; then will his word gain its deserved honour, and the
unclean side will go out of the world.   And that is what the Scripture says : I will cause the unclean spirit,' &c.

625. Ver. 3. '*And it happens, if a man still prophesy, his father
and mother, who begat him, speak thus to him : Thou shalt not live,
for thou hast spoken lies in the name of the Lord ; and his father and
his mother, who begat him, pierce him through in his prophesying.*'
The fundamental thought is : At that time the command to love God
above all, to renounce all that a man has for His sake, will be obeyed.
In the expression of this thought the Prophet has in view the passages, Deut. 13. 6—10, and 18. 20, where the nearest relation of the
false prophet was commanded, regardless of all natural feelings, to
put him to death, as a violation of the majesty of God.   The fact of
false prophecy, as Ch. B. Michaelis has justly remarked, is here
stated only hypothetically ; the Prophet employs it only as a foundation for his description of the entire devotedness of the covenant
people to God.—The phrase, '*his begetters,*' is peculiarly emphatic,
and is therefore repeated in the relation of the command.   It intimates, how hard it must be for parents to deny their natural feeling
of parental love, and how great therefore must be their love for God.
That *a mortal piercing* is meant appears partly from what precedes,
'*Thou shalt not live,*' since here the execution of the sentence only
is related ; partly from the passages of the law, e. g. Deut. 18. 20 :
'*The prophet, which shall presume to speak a word in my name,
which I have not commanded him to speak, or that shall speak
in the name of other gods, even that prophet shall die.*'—Moses, in
his laws relating to false prophets, had mentioned *two classes* of
them ; those who predicted falsely in the name, that is, under the
authority, of the true God, giving themselves out as His servants
and ambassadors ; and those who prophesied in the name of strange
gods, deriving inspiration from them.   Here the Prophet brings
before us one of the former ; in the fifth and sixth verses, one of
the latter.—'*In the very act of prophesying.*'   The parents, as soon
as they see the sin, without taking long counsel with flesh and blood,
inflict the punishment.

626. Ver. 4. '*And in that day the prophets shall desist, ashamed,
from their vision in their prophesying, and they shall no longer put on
the hairy mantle to lie.*'   On the prophets themselves, the deceivers
who are least susceptible of good impressions, the great revolution of
affairs shall have such an influence, that they will give up their profession from shame. '*In their prophesying,*' again, i. q. '*in the very
act of prophesying.*'   In the very commission of sin, when it is the
sweetest and most captivates the mind, they determine to renounce
it.   The *hairy mantle* was the garment of the true prophets, which
was imitated by the false, in order to impose on the people, with
whom the garment makes the man [1].   According to the prevailing
view, defended at length particularly by Vitringa, on Is. l. c., the

[1] Comp. Is. 20. 2.   2 Kings 1. 8.

prophets wore this garment as *ascetics*. But as the hairy garment is elsewhere always peculiar to mourners, and as the prophets themselves not unfrequently exhort to put it on, as a sign of anguish for sin and the Divine judgements, either still impending or already inflicted, it is certainly more obvious to assume, that, with them also, this dress had the same meaning; that it was a symbol of the lamentation of the Prophet over the sins of the people, and over the Divine judgements which they called forth ; and the more so, since elsewhere we do not find in the prophecies of the Old Testament any trace of a properly ascetic life.—'*In order to lie,*' can either mean, in order thereby to give themselves out as true prophets, to deceive the people by this dress ; or in order thereby to procure admission for their lying prophecies. The former is to be preferred on account of the following verse, where, to the former attempts of the false prophets to pass themselves off for the true, is opposed their open confession to the contrary.

627. Ver. 5. '*And he says, I am no prophet, I am a husbandman. For a man has sold*[1] *me from the time of my youth.*' The false prophets were mostly of the lowest order. The ruling motive with them was indolence, which caused them to hate a life of labour; and ambition, which stimulated them to force themselves into the more respectable order of teachers of the people. This appears from Isaiah 9. 13, 14, among other passages, where there is a contrast between the honorable, as the head of the people, and the false prophets as the tail, as the representatives of the rabble. Now at that time the better principle will so gain the ascendency over them, that they will rather wish to appear what they are, even though they are hired husbandmen, than what they formerly aspired to. The Prophet represents a scene between a former false prophet and some one who asked him concerning his circumstances, and from whom he sought to conceal with shame that he had ever been a false prophet, until he is forced (compare the sixth verse) by a new question to this mortifying confession. The phrase, '*from my youth,*' is intended to obviate the suspicion, that perhaps the present husbandman might *formerly* have been a prophet. If he were, not an independent husbandman, but a servant in the employment of another, even with the best inclination to act the part of a prophet, he was, as it appears, restrained therefrom by outward circumstances. He had better, to be sure, if he wished entirely to set aside the suspicion, not have begun with, "I am no prophet." But the anxiety lest he should be known as a former prophet so overcomes him, that he loses his self-possession, and by the very denial puts the inquirer on the right track.

628. Ver. 6. '*The former says : What then are these wounds*

---

[1] The *selling* of servants, especially of debtors and their whole families, was so common, that the expression מִקְנַת כֶּסֶף became almost the usual appellation of servants; compare Michaelis, Mos. R. II. § 123. The general designation אָדָם is chosen because the person of the seller was here not important, but only the action, the sale.

*between thy hands; he says, They were inflicted upon me in the
house of my lovers.*' We agree without hesitation with those, who
here find a reference to the wounds commonly inflicted in idolatrous
worship [1]. We content ourselves here with showing that this custom
also existed in the idolatrous worship which prevailed among the
Hebrews. The chief proof is furnished by the passage of Kings,
where it is said of the priests and prophets of Baal: ' *They cried
louder and scratched themselves, after their manner, with knives and
awls, until the blood flowed down from them.*' In proof also is Jeremiah 16. 6. 41. 5; according to which, the heathenish practice of
wounding themselves in their lamentation over the dead or a great
public calamity, as it prevailed among the surrounding people, particularly the Philistines and Moabites [2], was introduced also among
the Hebrews. For this usage was not indeed a mere symbol of distress, but it was closely connected with idolatry and the wounds
usually inflicted in the practice of it. This appears from Deut. 14. 1,
where the infliction of wounds in mourning is interdicted to the
Israelites on the ground, that, inasmuch as they were the holy people
of God, they must not pollute themselves with *idolatrous* practices.
This connexion will be more manifest, if we more closely investigate
the origin and import of the practice of inflicting wounds in idolatrous
worship [3]. It arose from an obscure consciousness of guilt, and the
necessity of reconciliation, which manifests itself in such manifold
ways in idolatrous worship. Man raged against his own body, in
order thereby to make a sort of satisfaction, and gain for himself the
favour of the angry gods. This feeling of guilt, however, was
awakened with peculiar vividness by the death of beloved persons,
not merely because their loss was regarded as a punishment, but also
because death in general, which comes the closer to ourselves the
more dear to us its victims, awakens even in the rudest minds an
anticipation of what it really is, the wages of the sins of mankind.
In like manner also was this feeling awakened by public calamity,
so far as this was generally regarded as the punishment of an angry
God or angry idols.—We are not, however, without proofs, that this
usage stood especially in close connexion with the prophecies of the
idolatrous prophets. In this connexion it occurs immediately in the
cited passage of Kings (compare the twenty-ninth verse), as in

---

[1] The chief passages for this custom, which is still continued in modern times
in the East, are found in Le Clerc, Calmet, and Dereser, on 1 Kings 18. 28. The
two last incorrectly cite in its favour Herod. 7. 191, for the ἔντομά τε ποιεῦντες
there practised by the Magi, can be regarded as belonging to this practice only
by a false interpretation; and further in Rosenmüller, *A. u. N. Morgenl.* 3,
p. 189 ff., and Creuzer, *Symbolik,* II. p. 40.

[2] Comp. 47. 5. 48. 37.

[3] Compare Apuleius, cited by Le Clerc, l. c.: " *Infit vaticinatione clamosa,
conficto mendacio, semet ipsum incessere atque criminari, quasi contra fas sanctæ reli-
gionis designasset aliquid, et insuper justas pœnas noxii facinoris ipse suis manibus
exposcere. Arrepto denique flagro, quod semiviris illis proprium gestamen est* . . . . .
*indidem sese multimodis commulcat ictibus, mira contra plagarum dolores præsumtione
munitus. Cerneres prosectu gladiorum ictuque flagrorum solum spurcitie sanguinis
effeminati madescere.*"

general the whole of that relation bears testimony to the close connexion of idolatry and false prophecy. The priests of Baal are at
the same time his prophets. Especially remarkable, however, is the
passage of Tibullus, lib. 1. Eleg. 1. ver. 43, sq., concerning the
service of Cybele :

> " *Ipsa bipenne suos cædit violenta lacertos,*
> *Sanguineque effuso spargit inepta deum,*
> *Atque latus præfixa veru stat saucia pectus,*
> *Et canit eventus, quos dea magna movet.*"

This connexion is explained by the feeling, that a man must render
satisfaction to the Divinity for his sins, before he can be worthy to
enjoy his favour, and be employed in his service [1].—An apparent objection might yet be derived from ' *I have been smitten,*' while most
accounts of this practice speak only of a self-infliction. But it appears from the accounts of more recent travellers (compare Olearius,
p. 332), that *mutual* wounds are given, and moreover, ' *I have been
smitten,*' does by no means exclude wounding oneself.—'*My
lovers,*' stands manifestly in contrast with ' *I have been smitten.*'—
The connexion of this verse with the foregoing is as follows. The
former prophet, being asked concerning his occupation, seeks in the
first place to remove from himself all suspicion of having abandoned
his inferior calling. As however the inquirer reminds him of the
suspicious scars which were found upon him, he confesses with shame
his former folly, the consciousness of which he at the same time
betrays by his manner [2].

CHAP. 13. ver. 7—9

629. The shepherd of the Lord, closely united with Him, shall be
torn away by a violent death from his flock, the covenant people ; de-

---

[1] No consideration is due to the doubt of Rosenmüller, whether מַפּוֹת
could be used of these inflictions and the scars arising from them. Apuleius
designates them, as we have already seen, by the entirely corresponding *plagæ*.
Seneca, in Augustine, *De Civ. Dei,* 6. 10, says : " *Se ipsi in templis contrucidant,
vulneribus suis ac sanguine supplicant.*"

[2] בֵּין יָדֶיךָ, " Between thy hands," i. e. "*in* and *near* them." *Between* is then
chosen for *in,* to show that not precisely the hands alone are intended ; it determines only in general the region, in such a manner, however, that the hands are
chiefly meant, not such distant members, as the head or the shoulders. That the
hands, however, are chiefly mentioned is not indeed owing entirely to the circumstance of their being uncovered, and the wounds upon them therefore chiefly
visible. It appears from Jeremiah 48. 37, where it is said, in the description of
the lamentation of the Moabites, עַל כָּל יָדַיִם גְּדֻדֹת, " Upon all hands are cuts,"
that the hands were wont especially to be wounded. The passages of the classic
writers and the fathers speak chiefly of the *arms,* which are here certainly included, e. g. " *lacertos secat,*" Seneca ; " *sua quisque brachia dissecant,*" Apuleius.

prived of the shepherd, the flock shall then disperse, and be given up
to extreme misery. But the Lord will not withdraw His hand from
them for ever. He will rather restore His people again to favour
after He has cleansed and purified them. First, two-thirds shall be
taken away by a fearful Divine judgement; the remaining third shall
then be led by the Lord through the severest trials and purifications,
until at last it truly turns to Him.

630. This prophecy forms a brief repetition, and at the same time a
supplement, of that in chap. 11 and 12—13. 6. It is in vain to attempt
to connect it closely with what immediately precedes. It stands in
about the same relation to both prophecies as Is. 52. 13—15, to
chap. 53. It presents us in one view with what had been separated
by the length of the preceding representation.

631. Ver. 7. ' *Sword, awake against my shepherd, and against a
man, my nearest relation, saith the Lord of Hosts; smite the shepherd
and the flock is scattered, and I bring back my hand upon the small.*'
There can be no doubt that here, by the shepherd of the Lord, is to
be understood the same person, united with Him by a mysterious
unity of being, who, according to the eleventh chapter, undertook
the pastoral office over the miserable people, and made the last effort
to preserve them, but whose faithfulness was rewarded with base
ingratitude, who was even, according to the tenth verse of the twelfth
chapter, put to death by them; whose rejection, according to the
eleventh chapter, had entirely the same results for the covenant
people, as are here attributed to his death, the destruction of the
greater part of the people [1]; nay, whose death is even represented [2]
as indirectly the cause of all the sufferings experienced by the people; since repentance for his murder, appears there, as the cause of
the deliverance from all these sufferings. Hence it is sufficiently
evident, that all those interpretations are to be rejected, which understand by the shepherd any other than the Messiah [3].—All other interpretations have against them, besides the authority of Christ, the
following context: "*Against a man, my nearest relation.*" This
would not, to be sure, be the case, if the word translated '*fellow*[4]' (in
the Eng. Bible) could, as is often asserted, designate a fellow in every

[1] Comp. ver. 8 with chap. 11. 6. 9. 15—17.   [2] Chap. 12. 10.
[3] Whether, as, with most of the Jewish interpreters, the ideal pseudo-Messias,
Ben Joseph; or, with Jarchi, a hostile general, who is called by the Lord ironically his shepherd; or, with Grotius on Matt. 26. 31, "the foolish shepherd," of
whom chap 11. 15—17; or with the same critic on this passage (who, as is apt
to be the case where a man brings forward merely his sudden thoughts, is inconsistent), and Jahn, Judas Maccabæus; or, with the Rationalist interpreters, *an
ideal general*, who should be slain in battle with the enemy; or lastly, with Calvin
and Drusius, *the collective body* of all the spiritual and civil rulers of the people,
Christ being included.
[4] עֲמִית.

relation. The shepherd would be called the *fellow* of the Lord, because He also is the Shepherd of His people. But this supposition is entirely untenable. It is one of those words, which, peculiar to the Pentateuch, have entirely disappeared from the later idiom. It occurs in the Pentateuch eleven times, and nowhere else. Hence it appears that Zechariah took it [1], not from the living language, but from the Pentateuch, and that we must understand it therefore in precisely the sense in which it is there used. It occurs there only in the laws respecting the injury of *a neighbour*, and always with peculiar emphasis, intimating how grievous a crime it is to injure those connected with us by a common corporeal and spiritual origin. It is interchanged as synonymous with *brother*, which in the laws of the Pentateuch uniformly refers to the common corporeal and spiritual descent [2]. We hope every one will concede that '*fellow*' in all the places where it occurs [3], is used to designate the *closest possible relation* among men, and one which cannot indeed be arbitrarily formed, but comes by birth, and continues even against one's will, exposing a man to condemnation when he violates it. But hence it appears, that when this designation is transferred to the relation of an individual to God, he cannot possibly be a mere man, but rather he who is united with the Lord by a mysterious unity of nature, and who has already, in chap. 11. 12, as such, so plainly appeared.—The Prophet, by using this term, gives prominence to the apparent contradiction between the command of the Lord, ' *Sword, awake against my shepherd,*' and the requisitions of his own law, which *forbids* any one *to injure his neighbour*. He shows in this way, how exalted must have been the aim, for accomplishment of which the Lord disregarded that relation, whose type He had commanded to be held sacred among men. He directs their attention, to speak after the manner of men, to the greatness of the sacrifice which this must cost the Lord.— The personification of the sword, in the address to it, finds a complete analogy in the prophecy of Jeremiah against Philistia [4], where the Prophet, from human sympathy with the fate of those against whom he prophesies, exclaims : ' *Ha, sword of the Lord, how long wilt thou not rest ; return back into thy sheath ; be quiet and still ! Yet how*

---

[1] As well as אַלּוּף (comp. on chap. 12. 5.)

[2] We will here cite the eleven passages in which it occurs. Levit. 19. 11, "Ye shall not lie nor deceive אִישׁ בַּעֲמִיתוֹ," (comp. Ephes. 4. 28). Ver. 15, "Righteously shalt thou judge עֲמִיתֶךָ." Ver. 17, "Thou shalt not hate thy brother in thy heart; thou shalt reprove עֲמִיתֶךָ." Levit. 18. 20, "Thou shalt not defile עֲמִיתְךָ אֵשֶׁת." 24. 19, "When any one inflicts a corporeal injury בַּעֲמִיתוֹ, as he has done, so shall it be done to him." 25. 15, "When thou buyest any thing of thy *neighbour* or sellest any thing to thy *neighbour*, you shall not injure each one his brother." In like manner, ver. 16 and 17, "And ye shall not injure each one his neighbour, and thou shalt fear before thy God." Levit. 5. 20, "A soul, if it sins and does wickedly against the Lord, and lies against his neighbour (in that which was intrusted to him), or oppresses his neighbour."

[3] In a manner entirely different from our word *neighbour*, diluted and deprived through sin of its original worth, and for the most part suggesting only *any* other person.

[4] Chap. 47. 6.

*canst thou be quiet, since the Lord has commanded it, since against
Askalon and against the bank of the sea has he sent it.*' It is shown
by this command, that the Lord is the first cause of the death of His
shepherd, that the human authors are only His instruments ; as the
Lord, in the eleventh verse of the nineteenth chapter of John, says to
Pilate, ' *Thou wouldst have no power against me except it were given
thee from above.*'—The expression, *awake*, shows that the sword, in
accordance with the personification of it, is to be regarded as hitherto
at rest.   That the *sword* is called upon to smite the shepherd
of the Lord, expresses (like *pierced*[1], which intimates not *a cut*
but a *stab*) only his impending death without defining the manner of
it.   The sword, as the usual instrument of the judge and the warrior, often stands for *any fatal instrument*, where the instrument
itself is not important, but only the infliction of wounds and of death.
The most striking example is 2 Sam. 12. 9, ' *Thou hast slain him,
Uriah*, by the sword [2] *of the children of Ammon*,' while, according to
2 Sam. 11. 24, he was pierced by the *arrows* of the Ammonites.—
2 Sam. 11. 25, after David receives from Joab the message that
several of his people had been slain by the hostile *archers*, he makes
him say again, ' *Let not this thing displease thee ; for* the sword
*devoureth one as well as another ; only make thy battle strong against
the city.*'   A similar general use of the *sword* is found also in
Exod. 5. 21, ' *Ye have made our savour to stink before Pharaoh
and his servants, giving* the sword *into their hands to kill us ;*'
Jerem. 2. 23, ' *Your* sword *has devoured your prophets ;*' Psalm
22. 21, ' *Deliver from the* sword *my soul*' ; Matt. 26. 52, ' *He
who takes* the sword *shall perish by* the sword.'   What murderer
would avoid the application of the sentence to himself, which is a
repetition of what is expressed in altogether general terms in the
sixth verse of the ninth chapter of Genesis, on the ground that he
had killed his neighbour, not by the sword, but by another instrument?   According to the same idiom the right of the magistrates
among the Romans to inflict every kind of capital punishment, was
called the *jus gladii.*—The address, ' *Smite the shepherd*,' is still
directed to the sword.—' *Smite the shepherd, and then the herd will
disperse.*'   Is the shepherd either in the natural or spiritual sense
slain, the flock is wont to disperse.   The Prophet seems here to have
special reference to the seventeenth verse of the twenty-second chapter of the first book of Kings, where the Prophet Micah says to
Jehoshaphat and Ahab, predicting the death of the latter, ' *I saw all
Israel scattered on the hills as a* flock, which has no shepherd : *and
the Lord said, These have no shepherd, let them return each one to
his house in peace* [3].'   By a misunderstanding of the New Testament
citations of the passage, many interpreters have been led to take the
flock here in too limited a sense, and refer only to a part, what
belongs to the whole. *The* flock must embrace the sheep collectively,
which *the* shepherd had to feed.   These however were not, according

---

[1] Chap. 12. 10.   [2] בְּחֶרֶב.

[3] Comp. 1 Macc. 9. 18.

to the eleventh chapter, the believers alone, but the *whole* Jewish people; the most miserable sheep, who regarded the shepherd, appear [1] only as one part of this flock. Still more decisive however is what follows. The flock are plainly the small ones, who are represented immediately afterwards as an object of further Divine care. But, that we cannot by these understand the believers only, or indeed the apostles, without destroying the whole connexion between the seventh, eighth, and ninth verses, we shall soon see. Accordingly, under the image of sheep without a shepherd, the whole Jewish people, after the death of the Messiah, are here described. In what manner, and how long they were without a shepherd, and consequently wretched, depended on their spiritual condition, and on the corresponding dealings of the Lord. The desertion of the apostles and other believers by their shepherd, was only temporary; the Lord soon returned to them. The unbelieving portion of the people still wander about as sheep, who have no shepherd.—The phrase, ' *to bring back the hand upon any one*,' i. e. to make him again the object of an action or an operation, is of itself indefinite; and whether it stands in a good or a bad sense, must in every case be decided by the connexion. Several interpreters here assume the latter, after the Chaldee, the Seventy, and the Greek interpreters, who follow them. This supposition appears at first sight to be favoured by what follows, since in the eighth verse the discourse relates to a heavy judgement to be inflicted on the dispersed flock. But on a closer examination we find that the former interpretation is the only correct one. The judgement described in the eighth verse, according to another mode of considering the subject, was a proof of the further exercise of the special providence of God over the people; God thereby realized the condition, on which alone they could be restored to their ancient gracious relation to Him, and become again the people of God. Every judgement upon the ungodly is indeed a benefit to the Church of the Lord. That this view here prevails appears sufficiently evident from the ninth verse; it is also evident from ' *the small*.' For this designation intimates the sympathy of the Lord with the wretched condition of the poor sheep, just as, in the seventh verse of the eleventh chapter, the shepherd undertakes to feed the flock, because they are the most miserable sheep. We find the same mode of representation in Malachi. After the Prophet, in the first five verses of the third chapter, has announced a great purifying judgement upon the covenant people, he adduces the sixth verse as a reason for it, the covenant faithfulness of the Lord, who could not suffer His people to go to utter ruin, as must necessarily have been the case without this judgement. Still more exactly parallel, even in the expression, and perhaps distinctly in the view of Zechariah, is the passage in the twenty-fourth and following verses of the first chapter of Isaiah, ' *I will take vengeance on my adversaries* (the ungodly members of the Theocracy), *and I* will bring back my hand upon thee (the church of the Lord), *and purify, as alkali (purifies), all*

---

[1] Ver. 11.

thy dross, and take away all thy tin.—*Then shalt thou be called a city of righteousness, a faithful city.*' That the expression, ' *I will bring back my hand upon thee,*' stands here, in a good sense, of the gracious benefit which the Lord confers upon His people by their purification, while He seemed to have forsaken them, so long as He neglected this, has been so strikingly proved by Vitringa, that Gesenius, when without proof he takes it in a bad sense, can scarcely have read him. There is between Zion in the twenty-fifth verse, and the enemies of God in the twenty-fourth verse, a manifest antithesis, precisely as in the twenty-seventh and twenty-eighth verses.—*The small* ones are the same, who, in the seventh verse of the eleventh chapter, had been called the *most miserable* sheep. That the trope is not here to be dissolved, that after *the small* we are rather to supply *sheep*, appears from[1] *the smallest of the sheep*, as a designation of a miserable people, in Jer. 49. 20. 50. 45[2]. The ancient translators, the Greek as well as the Chaldee, have, as we have already remarked, taken, ' *I bring back my hand,*' in a *bad* sense, and then understand, by *the small*, the inferior *shepherds*, in contrast with the chief shepherd of the people. This interpretation is entirely arbitrary. The bringing back of the hand of the Lord over the *small*, here promised, was first experienced by the apostles, and all those who from among the Jews became at that time believers in Christ, or who have become such in all succeeding centuries down to the present day. In another way, by the unbelieving part of the people also ; for the judgements which the Lord inflicts upon them are, on the one side indeed, punishments of His justice, on the other side however manifestations and means of His mercy ; until at last, when all Israel is saved, the bringing back of His hand upon them is most illustriously manifested, and our prophecy receives its complete fulfilment.—We now cast a look at the New Testament citations of the passage. The chief place is Matt. 26. 31, 32 (comp. Mark 14. 27): ' *Then saith Jesus unto them, All ye shall be offended because of me this night : for it is written, I will smite the shepherd, and the sheep of the flock shall be scattered abroad. But after I am risen again, I will go before you into Galilee.*' Here the original is followed, not the Septuagint. The figurative mode of representation retained by these, the address to the sword, the Lord resolves into literal language : ' *I will smite.*' The last words[3] are of a consoling character ; an annunciation, that the Lord, after a short interruption, would resume His pastoral office over the apostles and the other believers, and therefore an individualizing of the expression in Zechariah, ' *I bring back my hand over them.*' Hence it appears that the phrase, ' *I bring back the hand,*' was taken by the Lord in a *good* sense, and that by the *small* he understood sheep, not *shepherds*, according to the misunderstanding of all the Greek interpreters and the Chaldee.

---

[1] צְעִירֵי הַצֹּאן.

[2] In Jer. 14. 3, the synonymous צָעוֹר stands opposed to אַדִּיר. " And their nobles send their little ones to the waters."

[3] As the δὲ intimates.

That the special application of what is said in Zechariah concerning the dispersion of the flock, to the apostles, does not exclude its wider import and reference, we have already seen.—But how great stress the Lord laid on the passage, appears from his having before used its words when predicting what was to happen to His disciples, without expressly citing them, as he does here, because they had not rightly understood the former reference. He says, John 16. 32, '*Behold, the hour cometh, yea, is now come, that ye shall be scattered, every man to his own, and shall leave me alone : and yet I am not alone, because the Father is with me* [1].'

632. Ver. 8. '*And it comes to pass in the whole land, saith the Lord, two parts in the same are exterminated and die, and the third part remains therein.*' The article points to the land, with which the Prophet had constantly been concerned in the preceding context, over whose inhabitants the shepherd of the Lord had undertaken the pastoral office [2]. The whole Jewish people appears here as an inheritance, left behind by the shepherd, who has been slain, which is divided into three parts ; of which death, asserting the right of the first-born, receives two, and life one, a division similar to that, which, 2 Sam. 8. 2, was made of the Moabites by David. '*And David smote the Moabites, and measured them with the measuring line, casting them down to the ground, and measured two parts for death and one part for life.*'—The double portion of the inheritance of death is then divided again among the two different kinds of death. By the words, '*are exterminated,*' and '*die,*' two kinds of deaths are indicated ; *death by the hostile sword,* and *death by pestilence* (accompanying the war, blockade), and famine. This is shown by the parallel passage, Ezek. 5. 12 : '*A third part of thee shall die with the pestilence, and with famine shall they all be consumed in the midst of thee ; and a third part shall fall by the sword round about thee ; and I will scatter a third part into all the winds ; and I will draw out a sword after them.*' This coincidence with Ezekiel is not by any means accidental, or consisting merely in the expression. The Prophet rather here *resumes the whole prediction* [3], and announces a second fulfilment of it, just as we have before shown to have been the case in reference to a similar one of Jeremiah [4]. Ezekiel had threatened the people that the Lord would make a *threefold division* of them on account of their sins ; for the sword, for pestilence and

---

[1] Besides this, allusions are found perhaps 10. 13. 11. 52, and Luke 12. 32.

[2] Comp. 7. 5. 12. 12. The expression פִּישְׁנַיִם is here, as 2 Kings 2. 9, taken from Deut. 21. 7. It signifies properly *a mouth* (i. q. *a mouthful, a mouth-portion) of two,* and originated in the custom of placing before those who were to be honoured, a double, or even a larger portion of food ; comp. Gen. 43. 34. It then serves, Deut. l. c., in a metaphorical sense, to designate the share of the first-born in the inheritance, who received a double portion. In this metaphorical sense, פ for *portion, part* in general, the word does not elsewhere occur ; and there is no doubt that Elisha, l. c., when, as the first-born of Elias in a spiritual sense, he desires a double portion of his spiritual inheritance, and our Prophet also borrowed the expression directly from Deuteronomy.

[3] Ezek. chap. 5.　　　　[4] Comp. on chap. 11. 13.

famine, and for dispersion. This threatening had now already been fulfilled, but the people still suffered the consequences of this judgement, as the Prophet here announces to them, that on account of their renewed apostasy the Lord would make a new threefold division, as He afterwards actually did by the Romans. Isaiah, some hundred years before, had already comprehended the contents of both prophecies in the remarkable picture of the fortunes of the covenant people, which was presented to his inward contemplation when he was consecrated to the prophetic office. He predicts (chap. 6. 11), in the first place, the entire desolation of the land, and the carrying away of its inhabitants into distant regions. This cannot possibly refer to any thing else than the Babylonian exile. The predictions of the Prophet in reference to the predecessors of the Chaldeans, the Syrians, and Assyrians, announced from the beginning, prosperity. This part of the prediction is accordingly, in the fifth chapter of Ezekiel, more fully carried out. It is further asserted: ' *Again there is in the land a tenth part of its former inhabitants, but it shall be destroyed anew.*' It is self-evident, that by this *tenth part* is not to be understood the few people of the lowest order, who, according to the fortieth chapter of Jeremiah, under the superintendence of Gedaliah, were left behind in the land by the Chaldeans. These were much too unimportant to be noticed in this very general sketch. We are rather obliged to refer it to the new destruction of the national independence of the people by the Romans. The phrase, ' *a tenth part,*' here accurately expresses, as the nature of the case required, the relation of the returned exiles to the former citizens of Judah. This second destruction is that of which Zechariah here speaks. What Isaiah moreover predicted of the holy seed, which should be preserved amidst the ruin of the whole people, and attain to prosperity, completely harmonizes with the ninth verse.— *The third part.* The foregoing indefinite *two parts* is defined by the article. For, if besides two parts, only *the third part* still remains, these two parts must be two thirds [1].

633. Ver. 9. ' *And I bring the third part into the fire, and purify them, as silver is purified, and prove them, as gold is proved. They will call upon my name, and I will hear them. I say, They are my people ; and they answer, Jehovah my God.*'—' *To cause to go through the fire,*' is the technical term for the purification of metals [2]. ' *I purify them,*' &c., indicates both how highly the Lord esteems those who are to be purified,—they are compared with the most precious metals,—and how difficult this purification is, how greatly the furnace of affliction must be heated for them. That the latter idea is not to be excluded is shown by the passage Is. 48. 10, ' *Behold, I have purified thee, yet* not *as silver, I have chosen thee in the furnace*

---

[1] Overlooking this, Winer asserts, s. v. רִי, erroneously, that פִּישְׁנַיִם, otherwise than in the remaining places, here designates precisely *two thirds*. It first appears by הַשְּׁלִשִׁית, that two parts of a whole divided into three parts are intended.

[2] Comp. Num. 31. 23.

of affliction.' While the Lord there declares, that He would be satisfied, if, by the Babylonian exile, only the coarsest dross of sin was separated, if among the people only the first beginnings of true repentance and a new life appeared ; that He would not purify them as silver, which, if it is to be entirely cleansed, must be melted seven times (compare the seventh verse of the twelfth Psalm), but before the purification is entirely completed, while they are still in the furnace of affliction, He will receive them again into favour;—He here declares of the second purification, directly the opposite.—The Lord will not be satisfied with this until He has removed *all* dross [1].

Chapter 14

634. A new scene presents itself to the Prophet. All the people of the earth are assembled by the Lord against His holy city ; this is taken ; the greatest part of its inhabitants are cut off by the sword, or carried away into captivity [2]. Then, however, the Lord interferes for His people, hitherto preserved uninjured by His wonderful providence, and the judgement is suddenly directed from the Church of the Lord to her enemies. The Lord appears in majesty upon the Mount of Olives, and while an earthquake announces His coming to judgement, and fills all with terrour, the mountain divides in the midst, so that henceforth the people of the Lord find a safe and easy way of flight through the lengthened valley of Jehoshaphat. Then the Lord appears, with all His saints, to establish His kingdom on the earth [3]. At first, thick darkness reigns ; then follows, for a short time, a mixture of light and darkness, a twilight ; and lastly, when least expected, breaks the full day of salvation for the elect [4]. Then a stream of living water pours itself forth from Jerusalem through the whole land, communicating life and fruitfulness [5]. The Theocracy, hitherto confined to one single land, now embraces the whole earth [6]. In order that Jerusalem alone may be exalted, all hills in the whole land are levelled, the city rises in splendour from its ruins, henceforth secure from every change, to enjoy the Divine favour [7]. After the enemies, who have besieged Jerusalem, have been chastised by a Divine judgement [8], the remnant of them will turn to the Lord, and

---

[1] Precisely as here the verbs צָרַף and בָּחַן are combined, Jer. 9. 6; see besides 6. 30. Ps. 76. 10. Ezek. 22. 18. Job 23. 10. The phrase קָרָא בְשֵׁם יְהֹוָה has the double meaning, to call *out* the name of the Lord with emotion, to praise him, comp. 1 Chron. 16. 8, with Is. 44. 5, and in the same manner to call *upon* the name of the Lord. In both cases the בּ is a designation of the object on which the emotion of him, who calls *out*, or who calls *upon*, rests ; properly *to call upon* or *to call out, since* it is the name of the Lord, with which one has to do, which is a copy and outward representation of his nature.

[2] Ver. 1, 2.   [3] Ver. 3—5.   [4] Ver. 6, 7.   [5] Ver. 8.
[6] Ver. 9.   [7] Ver. 10, 11.   [8] Ver. 12—15.

annually come to Jerusalem, there to celebrate the feast of tabernacles[1]. A heavy punishment will overtake those who neglect this
duty[2]. The distinction between the profane and sacred will then
entirely cease, and also the mingling of the pious and ungodly, as it
existed in the former Theocracy[3].

635. The interpreters mostly suppose this prophecy to be only a
resumption and further extension of that contained in chap. 12.
But, for this opinion, there is in the first place no ground whatever.
The prophecy receives an entirely new addition; of a connexion
with chap. 12, and a reference to it, there is no trace. Both prophecies give a cycle of events independent of one another, in which
what follows is always connected with what precedes, by the constantly recurring *in this day*. On the contrary, there are not wanting
grounds for the opposite assumption, that the two prophecies refer to
different events and times. In chap. 12, Jerusalem appears indeed
as closely besieged, but not as taken ; from the inhabitants of Jerusalem, the princes of Judah, according to ver. 5, expect deliverance.
From them, according to ver. 6, 7, the enemy is vanquished without
the city, and before he could take it. Here, on the contrary, the
help of the Lord does not come until the city has been taken, and
the greatest part of the inhabitants carried away into captivity.
According to chap. 14. 14, Judah fights *in* Jerusalem. According to
chap. 12. 7, he gains the victory without the city, which is thus
delivered. Of such splendid promises for the people of the Lord
after the overthrow of their enemies, as we here find, there is in
chap. 12 no trace; all continues in the usual track. The result,
thus obtained by internal evidence, is confirmed also by a comparison
of the Apocalypse. There, a twofold great oppression of the Church
of God in the last times is plainly described. The first, chap. 19.
19—21. Then follows the so-called reign of a thousand years, a
condition of the church better than the preceding, but still without a
removal of the existing earthly relations. To this period chap. 12
refers. The second, chap. 20. 8, 9. Tempted by Satan, the heathen
nations from all the four ends of the earth, once more surround the
camp of the saints and the beloved city. That this prophecy, as
well as that of Ezekiel, chap. 37 and 38, is thus parallel with the
one before us, and of course that *it*, and not that of chap. 12, must
be compared with that of Ezekiel, appears from the fact, that here
altogether the same results of the victory granted by the Lord are
mentioned as there. According to Zechariah, in like manner as
Ezekiel and the Apocalypse, Jerusalem is gloriously rebuilt, immediately after, the Lord establishes in her his dwelling-place; there
will be no more exile, a stream of living water goes forth from her,
all the ungodly are excluded, &c.

---

[1] Ver. 16.   [2] Ver. 17—19.   [3] Ver. 20, 21.

636. Ver. 1. ' *Behold a day comes to the Lord, and thy booty is divided in the midst of thee* [1]. The designated day *comes to the Lord*, not only in so far as *he introduces* it, but also and chiefly, in *so far as he is glorified in* it. All other days have come rather *to men*, this alone is proper to *the Lord*. Thus it is said, Ezek. 39. 13, of the day of the overthrow of Gog [2], " the day of my being honoured, saith the Lord." Thus, according to Is. 2. 12, the day of the Lord comes upon all that is high and exalted, and, according to ver. 17, the Lord alone is exalted in that day.—As a day of the Lord is almost always spoken of in reference to the judgements to be executed by Him, the question arises whether these judgements, which serve to glorify the Lord, here overtake merely the heathen nations, or whether the sufferings of the Church of God here described are to be considered as chastisements; whether we are therefore to assume, that after the great outpouring of the Spirit and regeneration, described chap. 12. 10. 13. 6, a predominance of the tares among the wheat, a mingling of true believers and of hypocrites in the Church of God, is again to be expected, so that here the last glorifying of the Church of God is described, the last verifying of the proverb, that judgement must begin at the house of God. This latter supposition is indisputably correct. It receives confirmation particularly from the second verse. The Prophet shows already by the expression, that those who are carried away into captivity are not to be regarded as suffering innocently, that those who are outwardly cut off are rather also spiritually cut off, and those who are outwardly retained as also inwardly quickened.— *Thy spoil*. The Prophet addresses Jerusalem, the seat of the kingdom of God at his time, under whose image this kingdom presented itself to his inward vision, exactly as in the Apocalypse. How little we are here to adhere to the letter, is evident from the figurative character of the whole description, which no one can deny ; especially the impossibility that all the nations of the whole earth should be collected against the outward Jerusalem to battle, and, after being vanquished, should annually go up there, in order to celebrate the feast of tabernacles, &c. [3]—The opinion of Mark, who, after several others, particularly the fathers [4], here finds the description of the captivity by the Romans, is already sufficiently refuted by the fact, that it requires the Prophet, in the third verse, to make a sudden transition from the literal to the spiritual Zion.

---

[1] The phrase יוֹם־בָּא לַיהוָה is not to be explained, " the day of the Lord comes," for the לְ can stand instead of *stat. constr.* only when this cannot be used, therefore only when an indefinite thing is to be designated; while the second noun, however, as here *Jehovah*, is definite, comp. Ewald, p. 582, 603; therefore, not " *a* day of the Lord," for then we cannot see why יוֹם should not be joined with לַיהוָה ; rather, " a day comes to the Lord," so that לַיהוָה belongs to בָּא.

[2] יוֹם הִכָּבְדִי.

[3] *In thy midst.* Strengthening this, Jerome says, " *Solet frequenter accidere, ut quæ subito impetu in civitate direpta sunt, foris in agro, aut in solitudine dividantur, ne forte hostes superveniant: his autem tantum malorum pondus incumbet, ut, quæ direpta sunt, in civitatis medio dividantur pro* securitate victoriæ."

[4] Theod., Cyril, Euseb. *Demonstr.* 6. 18. Jerome.

637. Ver. 2. ' *And I collect all the heathen against Jerusalem to battle, and the city is taken, and the houses plundered, and the women dishonoured, and the half of the city go forth as captives, and the remnant of the people is not cut off from the city.*' We will not here engage in doctrinal inquiries, how it can be reconciled that the same effect, the collection of the heathen against Jerusalem, which is here attributed to God, is, in the eighth verse of the twentieth chapter of the Apocalypse, attributed to Satan, a phenomenon which is known to be often met with in the Scriptures. If, however, God must employ the evil as a means of realizing His purpose concerning the world ; if Satan, who appears in Job in poetic representation among the angels of God, is, though against his own will, his servant, as Ashur is called the rod of anger in his hand, Nebuchadnezzar his servant ; if, without the will of God, he cannot hurt a single hair of the Church of God, the constant aim of his assaults (compare the third chapter) ; it easily appears that the contradiction is only apparent, and such as daily occurs, without any one thinking it necessary to deny the one or the other side of the antithesis.—The Lord collects the nations to the judgement in the first instance upon Jerusalem, and then upon themselves. Parallel is Ezek. 39. 2, ' *The Lord brings Gog out of the extreme north, and conducts him to the mountains of Israel, there to destroy him*[1].'—The phrase, " *The houses are plundered, and the women dishonoured,*" is taken from Is. 13. 16[2] —' *And the remnant of the people will not be exterminated from the city.*' There is here a plain contrast with the former judgement upon Jerusalem, executed by the Babylonians. The advantage enjoyed by those who remained behind, at the first deportation, over those who were carried away, was only apparent ; it was only a reprieve : it was here to be real and lasting. The Prophet alludes to the similar passages even in the expression (comp. Jer. 29. 16), ' *For thus saith the Lord to the king, who sits on the throne of David, and to the whole people who dwell in this city, your brethren ; behold, I send upon them the sword, and the famine, and the pestilence, and scatter them in all the kingdoms of the earth*[3].' The carrying away of the half into captivity was at the same time a cutting of them off from the city, from the Theocracy, because this carrying away over-

---

[1] אֶל does not stand, as Rosenmüller asserts, for עַל, but it designates merely the direction according to which the heathen were collected. The hostile purpose is first expressed by the following " to war."

[2] יִשַּׁסוּ בָּתֵּיהֶם וּנְשֵׁיהֶם תִּשָּׁגַלְנָה. The following member is translated by most interpreters, "And the half of the city shall go forth into captivity." It is altogether a mistake that גּוֹלָה, a word which it is remarkable never occurs in the Pentateuch, although the thing signified is there so often spoken of, and except in Amos 1. 15, only in the writings composed during the exile, ever signifies *captivity*. Even the form, the *partic. femin.*, should have made critics distrustful of this opinion. For the participial form can never constitute abstract nouns.

[3] The expression, ' *He will not be exterminated from the city,*' is chosen in reference to the forms continually occurring in the Pentateuch, וְנִכְרְתָה הַנֶּפֶשׁ הַהִוא מֵעַמֶּיהָ, or מֵעֲדַת יִשְׂרָאֵל, or מִיִּשְׂרָאֵל.

took them as a deserved Divine judgement[1]. The portion of the
people who remained true to the Lord were saved from this judgement. That, apart from this reference, the phrase, ' He is *cut off*
from the city,' is not to be explained, with Winer, by *ex urbe patriâ
ejectus, in exilium actus est*, is self-evident. As parallel in sense we
have yet to compare Isaiah 4. 3 : ' *Every one who shall be left behind
in Zion and remain in Jerusalem, he shall be called holy, every one
who is enrolled for life in Jerusalem.*' Here also, to be spared
during the judgement of God, and to be a true member of His kingdom, are interchangeable ideas.

638. Ver. 3. The purification of the Church of God is now completed, and the Lord, following the course of His love towards her,
can grant her deliverance and prosperity.—' *And the Lord goes forth,
and fights against those heathen, as in his day of conflict, in the day
of battle*[2].' ' *To go forth,*' is a military technical term, comp. Is. 42.
13 ; ' *The Lord* will go forth *as a hero, as a man of war, awaken zeal.*'
Hab. 3. 13, ' Thou goest forth *for the salvation of thy people.*' More
as a general contrast to the rest, in which the Lord seems to indulge,
so long as He delivers up His Church a prey to her oppressors, the
word occurs in the passage—very explanatory of the relation of the
verse before us to the preceding—Is. 26. 20, 21 : ' *Up, my people,
go into thy closets, shut thy doors after thee. Wait but a little, until
my anger is overpast. For behold,* the Lord goeth out *from his place
to punish the wickedness of the inhabitants of the earth against him.*'
The phrase, ' *as in the day of his combat,*' &c., is explained by most
interpreters, ' *as he is wont to combat,*' and referred to all the combats, which the Lord engaged in for His people[3]. Others, on the
contrary, assume a special reference to the combat of the Lord against
the Egyptians[4]; which is plainly to be preferred. For we are led to
one particular event by the expression, ' *as in his day of combat;*' the
suff. refers to the compound idea. The judgement of the Lord upon the
Egyptians is expressly called a *combat*, a *fight*, Exod. 14. 14, 15. 3 sq.
And the deliverance from Egypt so far surpasses all later ones, that
it is considered as *the* deliverance, κατ' ἐξοχὴν, and those of a later
period, in order to designate their greatness, are compared with it,
without distinguishing them by a more particular description from
the rest; compare especially Is. 11. 11, ' Then will the Lord stretch
out his hand a *second time,*' &c. Among the weapons with which the
Lord contends, only the earthquake and corruption inflicted upon
His enemies are here mentioned ; Ezekiel is more full in the description of them.

---

[1] The extirpation from the Theocracy, threatened against the transgressors of
the law, is by no means to be limited to the punishment of death ; compare, on
the contrary, Ezr. 7. 26. 10. 8; but, which the general expression implies, referred
to every thing, whereby God, according to the different degrees of their guilt,
either immediately, or through the instrumentality of the magistracy established
by him, expels his disobedient subjects from his kingdom. The correctness of
this remark will be confirmed by an independent examination of the subject.

[2] יֵצֵא.

[3] Comp. e. g. Jos. 10. 10. Judges 4. 15. 20. 1 Sam. 7. 10.

[4] So, after the example of the Chaldee, Jerome.

639. Ver. 4. '*And his feet stand in that day on the Mount of Olives, which lies before Jerusalem, eastward, and the Mount of Olives is split in the midst, from east to west, a very great valley, and a half of the mountain gives way towards the north, and a half towards the south.*' The question arises, why the Lord appears here as standing precisely on the Mount of Olives. The answer is furnished by the subjoined, " which lies before Jerusalem eastward." For these words, as a mere geographical notice for the contemporaries of the Prophet, who had the Mount of Olives always in view, would have been entirely superfluous ; they could designate the position of the mountain only for the purpose of intimating that this gave the Lord occasion to select it for His station. The Mount of Olives lay before and above Jerusalem ; it afforded the best position for overlooking the city ; from it therefore the Lord orders the battle against His enemies found in it, and adopts His measures for the deliverance of His people ; from there particularly, He, before whom the mountains flow down, makes for them a way of escape, that they may not be judged with the ungodly heathen. That the cleaving of the mountain is to be regarded as the effect of an earthquake, seems to be implied in the fifth verse. The earthquake is also mentioned in the sixth verse of the twenty-ninth chapter of Isaiah, among the punishments which the Lord inflicts on the enemies of Zion : '*By the Lord shalt thou be visited with thunder and* earthquake [1], *and a loud voice, with storm and wind, and with the flame of a consuming fire.*' The passage, however, which the Prophet seems to have distinctly in view, is that of Ezek. 38. 19, 20, '*In that day there will be a great earthquake over the land of Israel. And before me quaked the fish of the sea, and the fowls of heaven, and the beasts of the field, and every multitude that throngs the earth, and all men, which are on the earth ; and the mountains will be destroyed, and the hills fall, and every wall will fall to the earth.*' This earthquake, threatening destruction to the enemies, is a signal for flight to the believers. For they fear to be consumed by the Divine judgement with the heathen, in the midst of whom they are placed ; as the Prophet admonishes the exiles still in Babylon to flee in haste, that they may not be likewise smitten by the judgements which threaten her ; comp. 2. 6 : '*Ha ! ha ! escape from the north country ;*' ver. 1 : '*Ha ! Zion, deliver thyself, thou inhabitant of the city of Babel.*' And, as Jeremiah had already done before him, chap. 51. 6 : '*Flee out of Babel and deliver each one his soul, that ye be not destroyed each one for his misdeeds, for it is the time of vengeance for the Lord, he renders to her the reward.*' — While the believers therefore are desiring flight, the Lord opens for them the way by the same earthquake that brings destruction to the enemy. Whoever, as in the present instance, where there was a real danger in delay, wished to escape by speedy flight from Jerusalem, met with no inconsiderable hindrance in the Mount of Olives, bordering on the valley of Jehoshaphat, which David in his flight had to ascend [2]. This was removed when the Lord divided

---

[1] רָעַשׁ.　　　　　　　　　　[2] Comp. 2 Sam. 15. 30.

the mountain; the flying multitude of believers rushed through the lengthened valley of Jehoshaphat, and now, when they were beyond the reach of the Divine judgements, these fell with unrestrained violence upon the enemies of God, as formerly upon Sodom, when Lot had reached Zoar. That the whole representation is *figurative*, the main thought, the deliverance of the believers and the destruction of the enemies, being merely clothed in imagery taken from the local relations of Jerusalem, is so obvious, that whoever does not see it without further proof, is hardly capable of being convinced.—It is only one simple division of the mountain, which is spoken of, in which (in much the same manner as formerly, when the Jordan was divided) the one half goes towards the north, the other towards the south, and so from west to east, from Jerusalem towards the Jordan, a great valley is formed.—' *Towards the east and towards the west,*' does not point out the direction in which the two halves draw back, but the direction of the opening; the mountain was not cleft in its length, but in its breadth. Lastly, we are informed whither the two halves recede; not toward the west, for then the miracle would have been useless to the believers, but towards the north and south.

640. Ver. 5. ' *And ye flee into my mountain valley; for the mountain valley will reach to Azal, as ye fled before the earthquake in the days of Uzziah the king of Judah, and the Lord my God comes, all holy ones with thee*[1].' The lengthening of the valley gives the reason for fleeing into it; no one would think of doing so as long as it was surrounded by mountains.—The *mountain valley* of the Lord is the valley of Jehoshaphat, not merely the valley between the two halves of the Mount of Olives, which is here considered only as *a lengthening* of the valley of Jehoshaphat.—' *For the mountain valley will reach to Azal.*' *Azal* must not here be taken as a mere geographical designation, but with reference to its *appellative import*, that of *standing still*, or *ceasing*, as is manifest from the whole nature of the description[2]. The valley therefore shall reach to a place which actually affords to the fugitives what its name promises, the *cessation of the danger*, because when they have attained it, they are beyond the reach of the Divine judgements. Whether this place is the same as that mentioned by Micah, can neither be denied (since the Beth in proper names is frequently omitted, and similar variations in their form, as *Ezel* and *Azal*, elsewhere often occur); nor with certainty affirmed, because the situation of the place in both passages is left indefinite, only that, according to Zechariah, it must have been eastward of Jerusalem beyond the Mount of Olives.—' *And ye flee,*' viz. from fear of being swallowed up with the enemies of God by the

---

[1] וְנַסְתֶּם גֵּיא־הָרַי, not, with Mark, *per vallem*, but *ad vallem*.

[2] Mic. 1. 11. " *The lamentation of* Beth Haezel *will deprive you of its* standing still (will not continue to you the ceasing of the lamentation, as might be expected from the etymology of the name of the city). *For also* (the more distant) *Maroth shall experience pain. For evil comes down from the Lord upon Jerusalem.*" According to this passage, Beth Haezel must be a city not far from Jerusalem, and signify *the house of standing still*, a meaning easily derived from the usual one of the verb אָצַל, *to lay by the side.*

earth, which opens during the earthquake; compare Num. 16. 34,
'And all Israel round about them fled, for they said, lest the earth
swallow us up.'—The earthquake in the time of King Uzziah is not
mentioned in the historical books, but only in the first verse of the
first chapter of Amos. The way in which he speaks of it, *in the days,*
as well as the subjoined, *of the kings of Judah,* to prevent any one
from regarding Uzziah as a king of Israel, shows that the Prophet
lived at a time far distant from the event compared.—'*And there
comes the Lord my God, all holy ones with thee.*' The Prophet here
speaks of another coming of the Lord, than that described in the
third verse, for the judgement of His enemies. After the Lord has
delivered His people, He comes in order to dwell with them on the
glorified earth. The Prophet is so ravished with this delightful prospect, that for a time he entirely loses sight of the enemies, and afterwards resumes his description of their punishment. *My* God is
explained by the circumstance that the Prophet, while he sees the
Lord draw near in the most glorious manifestation of His grace, is
seized with lively joy, because this God is *his* God [1].

641. Ver. 6. '*And it comes to pass in that day, there will be no
light, that which is precious will become mean.*' The Prophet here
describes the transition from the deepest darkness which attends the
judgement upon the enemies of the Divine kingdom and the birth of
the new world, to the most splendid light which irradiates the new-
formed world; first, entire darkness, in the verse before us, then a
mixture of light and darkness, and, lastly, pure light, in the seventh
verse, analogous to the first creation, where at first darkness covered
the chaos, then, the matter of light having been created on the first
day, a twilight arose, until the matter of light was concentrated in the
heavenly bodies created on the third day, and the brightness became
perfect [2]. The parallel passages of the Old Testament (when they
either, like Zechariah, describe the last great judgement, or in the
description of inferior judgements borrow their images from that,)
always speak of the *darkening of the sun, moon, and stars:* this
thought is with them so uniform, so predominant, that we must have
greatly wondered if we had not found it here. Compare Joel 2. 10:
'*Before him the earth trembles, the heavens quake, the sun and the
moon mourn, the stars withdraw their splendour.*' In like manner
4. 4. 3. 4, '*The sun will be changed into darkness and the moon to
blood.*' Ezek. 32. 7: '*And I cover the heavens, and make the stars*

---

[1] By קְדֹשִׁים many interpreters understand the *angels;* others, as Mark, the
saints, the Church of God on earth; others, as Vitringa on Apoc. 15. 3, both,
sancti tam angeli, quam homines. The decision is difficult; the first interpretation
is favoured by, "*He comes with ten thousand of saints,*" the angels, Deut. 33. 2,
and still more by, "*All his saints are in thy hand,*" (ver. 3) "*they stand prepared
for thy service, serve thy prosperity, O Israel;*" and also Matt. 25. 31: ὅταν δὲ
ἔλθῃ ὁ υἱὸς τοῦ ἀνθρώπου ἐν τῇ δόξῃ αὐτοῦ, καὶ πάντες οἱ ἄγγελοι μετ'
αὐτοῦ. Mark 8. 38: ὅταν ἔλθῃ ἐν τῇ δόξῃ τοῦ πατρὸς αὐτοῦ μετὰ τῶν
ἀγγέλων τῶν ἁγίων. Apoc. 19. 14.

[2] יְקָרוֹת can signify nothing but *costly things. Pretiosa vocat cœlum, solem,
lunam, cæteras stellas, aërem, terram, aquam, quæ vere sunt pretiosissima mundi.*—
De Dieu.

to mourn; I will conceal the sun with a cloud, and the moon will not give her light.' Ver. 8: *'All the lights in heaven will I cause to mourn for thee, and I give darkness over thy land.'* Is. 13. 10: *'For the stars of heaven and their constellations will not give their light. The sun is dark in its going forth, and the moon causes its brightness not to shine.'* Amos 8. 19.—In accordance with these passages, we understand by *precious things* the *luminous bodies of heaven* (and with the more reason, since Job 31. 26. the *moon* is designated as *precious*, as walking magnificently [1]), and translate, *' costly things become vile, the heavenly bodies will lose their most beautiful ornament, the light.'*

642. Ver. 7. *' And it will be : one day, it will be known to the Lord, neither day, nor night, and at the time of even it will become light.'* The correct view was seen by Cocceius, *' One day, no long time.'* As a designation of the comparatively shortest portion of time, we meet with *one day*, chap. 3. 9, and, as a designation of a comparatively short period, *one month*, chap. 11. 8. The times, in relation to which that of the mingling of darkness and light is designated as very short, are those of the perfect darkness and perfect light. The phrase, *' it will be known,'* or *' it is known,'* does not relate, like similar expressions, Matt. 24. 36. Mark 13. 32, only to the *time* of the appearing of this day, but rather chiefly to its *nature*. Correctly Burk ; *' Solus Dominus plene planeque sciet, quæ ejus diei sit ratio.'* The phrase, *' not day and not night,'* Mark explains better than he is aware of, since he hesitates between this and several other untenable interpretations : *' So that from a certain mingling of the light of day with the darkness of night, the name neither of this nor of that is applicable to that time; but it is like some morning or evening twilight.'* The phrase, *' in the evening it will become light,'* is explained by the antithesis, Amos 8. 9 : *' And in that day, saith the Lord, I cause the sun to go down at mid-day, and bring darkness over the earth in the day of light.'* As there it becomes dark where the clearest light was possessed and expected, so here it becomes light at the time when only darkness is expected, where a day of mixed darkness and light comes to an end, and now, according to the natural course of things, the entirely dark night appears to succeed.

643. Ver. 8. *'And it happens in that day, living waters will go forth from Jerusalem, half of them to the east sea, and half of them to the west sea, in the summer and in the winter will it be.'* The east and west, or Dead and Mediterranean seas, stand here only as the *termini ad quem* of the course of the living waters ; not ~~as~~ in Ezekiel, chap. 47, where the sea is improved by these waters. By the choice of this *terminus*, the Prophet indicates that the water would pass through the whole promised land, which was bounded on the east by the Dead, and on the west by the Mediterranean sea. To what purpose, is shown by the parallel passage, Joel 3. 18, *' And it shall come to pass at that time, that the mountains will drop with must, and the hills will flow with milk, and all the brooks of Judah will flow*

---

[1] יָקָר הֹלֵךְ.

*with water, and a fountain goes forth from the house of the Lord and
waters the valley of Shittim.'* However the valley of Shittim may
be defined, so much is certain, that it is a dry, unfruitful place ; and
as the first part of the verse foretells abundance and fruitfulness for
dearth and sterility, so the water was intended at once to fertilize the
soil, before barren for lack of moisture, and to supply the thirsty
with refreshing drink [1]. Water, as well that which descends from
the clouds, as that of fountains, brooks, and streams (where the
comparison is not expressly limited to something special), is always
an image of the Divine blessings in their whole compass, and in all
their fulness, which quicken the dry and thirsty waste of man's
necessity. This will be evident from a citation of several of the
principal passages ; the departure of God, the withdrawal of His
favours and blessings, appear as a destitution of water, e. g. Is. 41. 17 :
' *The suffering and poor seek for water, and it is not there, their
tongue faileth for thirst; I, the Lord, will hear them ; I, the God of
Israel, will not forsake them.*' Still more to the purpose are such
passages as Is. 44. 3 : ' *I will pour water upon that which is thirsty,
and streams upon that which is dry ; I will pour my Spirit upon thy
seed, and my blessing upon thine offspring* [2].' 41. 18 : ' *I open upon
the hills streams, in the valleys fountains, and make the desert pools of
water, and the dry land springs of water. I will give in the wilderness cedars,*' &c. 30. 25 : ' *And there shall be upon every high mountain, and upon every high hill, streams of water in the day of the
great battle, when the towers fall.*' Ezek. 34. 26 : ' *I give them and
the environs of my hill for a blessing, and cause the rain to come down
in its time* [3].' It may be still further asked, why the Prophet causes
the water, the image of the Divine blessings, to go forth *from Jerusalem.* The answer is, that, under the image of the central point of
the militant church under the Old Testament, of the place which the
Lord glorified by His typical presence in the Temple, is here exhibited to the Prophet the central point of the triumphant Church,
the place where the Lord, when He comes with His saints, establishes
His residence ; comp. ver. 6, 2. 15 ; his *rest,* Is. 11. 10. From
Jerusalem, therefore, go forth the waters, in so far as here is the seat
of the Lord, the place from which He imparts His gracious favours
to His subjects. This appears still clearer from the comparison of
the parallel passages. According to Joel and Ezekiel, the water

---

[1] No one surely will agree with the explanation of Grotius, " *aquæ ductus fient
egregii, ut in altâ pace,*" which is entirely characteristic of the exegetical manner
of its author, which nevertheless is not surpassed by other strange things, which
he brings forward upon the chapter, when, e. g., he understands by him who
appears on the Mount of Olives the son of Bacchus, who from there orders the
siege, and concerning the cleaving of the mountain remarks, " *Multa humus
egeretur, ita ut hiet mons in magnâ sui parte,*" &c.

[2] " My blessing" is here the whole of the substance of the figure ; "my
Spirit" is a part of the same, and we must not, in order to make both expressions
entirely synonymous, either with some interpreters attribute a false meaning to
רוּחַ, or with others, limit בְּרָכָה.

[3] Comp. yet Is. 43. 20. 44. 8. 48. 21. 49. 10. 58. 11.

goes forth from *the Temple;* according to Apoc. 22. 1, from the *throne of God and the Lamb.*—If now Jerusalem stands here as a designation of its antitype, so must accordingly the whole compass of the Jewish land, over which the fountain pours itself, signify that which bears the same relation to the glorified Jerusalem, as this bears to the typical, i. e. the whole compass of the glorified kingdom of God, which indeed (according to the ninth verse, and the constant predictions of all other prophets) is to be extended over the whole earth. The whole earth therefore shall be watered with the stream of the Divine blessings, Ps. 36. 6.—The last words, '*in summer and in winter it will be,*' signify the *permanency* of the Divine blessings, in contrast, partly with the frailty of all human enjoyments, partly with the frequent interruptions of these Divine gifts themselves, during the time of the militant church, when the Lord must often conceal His face in order to cleanse the church, in which were mingled the holy and profane, by purifying judgements : whereas, when the whole Church consists of the righteous, and there is no more a Canaanite in the house of the Lord, there will be no more curse. Jerome explains, " *Ut nec gelu constringantur hyeme, nec æstatis nimio fervore siccentur ?*" But the comparison of the parallel passages shows, that the Prophet here had only the last in view ; that the winter is named as the time when even other brooks give forth abundance of water. Job[1] compares his friends with brooks, which are swollen in the winter, and have an abundance of water ; but in summer, when their water is most needed, dry up, and therefore painfully deceive the hope of the traveller. Isaiah[2] represents the Divine mercy, and those who were its objects, under the image of a fountain whose waters do *not lie.*

644. Ver. 9. '*And the Lord will be king over the whole land ; in that day the Lord will be only one, and his name only one.*' Many translate '*over the whole earth.*' There can be no doubt that the discourse *is* concerning an extension of the dominion of the Lord over *all nations of the earth in contrast with its former limitation to a single people*[3]. We must however with Rückert prefer the translation, '*over the whole land.*' For, ver. 8, the new kingdom of God had represented itself to the Prophet under the image of the former ; ver. 10, we find the same mode of representation, and it is certainly unnatural to assume that the words[4] stand here in a sense different from there, so immediately after. Mark correctly observes : '*The question here is not of a kingdom of nature and ordinary providence, but of a special kingdom of grace,—such as God formerly had in Israel.*' The Lord is the natural king of the whole human race ; but this relation was disturbed by the fall : this was the commencement of a series of rebellious efforts, which terminated in nearly all his subjects withdrawing their allegiance from Him, and choosing for themselves other lords and kings in heaven and on earth, according

---

[1] 6. 16—18.   [2] 58. 11.
[3] Compare chap. 9. 9, 10. Ps. 72. 8—11. Ps. 2. Dan. 2. 35, &c.
[4] כָּל־הָאָרֶץ.

to their hearts' desire. The Lord, for whom it would have been easy to destroy His unfaithful subjects by a word of His omnipotence, willed, in accordance with His love, instead of this, their voluntary return to obedience. Because the whole mass was not yet prepared, He commenced by restoring the natural relation among one particular people. With the first appearing of Christ commenced the extension of the plan to which the special Theocracy had served only as the means ; its completion will be introduced with His return in glory, when all opposers will either by His mercy be converted from His enemies to His servants, or be destroyed by His punishment from His kingdom, which will then embrace the whole earth. Especially remarkable in this connexion is Ps. 22. 28, 29, '*All the ends of the earth shall remember and turn to the Lord ; all nations of the heathen shall fall down before thee. For to the Lord is the dominion, he ruleth among the heathen.*' That all the heathen will hereafter be subject to the Lord is grounded on the fact, that He is their rightful and natural king, and their present relation to Him, an unnatural one, which therefore cannot be lasting. '*The Lord will be one, and his name is one,*' is well explained by a Lapide : '*Now those who are considered and called gods in the world are many,—but at that time one Being will be called God and worshipped by all nations.*' '*The Lord will be only one,*' is illustrated by the Arabic, where idolaters bear the standing name [1], '*who add companions to God.*' '*His name,*' &c. has been variously misunderstood. It is explained by the circumstance, that all names of idols may be considered in a certain sense as different appellations of the true God, because though these '*gods*[2]' are really nonentities, yet the heathen chose to designate God by them. It is entirely analogous, when, in the second part of Isaiah, the efforts of the makers of idols are constantly represented as attempts to represent God by an image, and on this ground their folly is shown. It may be supposed that the Prophet was here led by the events of his time to give prominence to the fact, that at that time the name of the Lord would be only one. The edicts of the Persian kings, as contained in the books of Ezra and Nehemiah, make it highly probable that the Persians, who were greatly addicted to religious amalgamation, were prepared to represent their God Ormuzd and the God of Israel as one and the same Deity, differing only in names and modes of revelation, without going any further, because they naturally thought that every people must preserve their own name of God, and hold fast to the mode of revelation vouchsafed to them, which cannot indeed be separated from the name.

645. Ver. 10. '*All the land will change, as the plain from Gebah to Rimmon, south of Jerusalem ; and she will be exalted, and seat herself on her throne, from the gate of Benjamin, to the place of the first gate, unto the corner gate, and from the tower of Hananeel to the wine-presses of the king.*' The object in the verse is twofold. First, the exaltation of Jerusalem, effected by all the rest of the land being

المشر كون [1]   אֱלִילִים [2]

changed into a plain; then, her restoration to her former greatness, after having been destroyed by being taken by the enemy, in the second verse, still more however perhaps by the earthquake, in the fifth verse, and the other judgements inflicted upon the enemies found in her.—We first explain that which relates to the former object. *Geba* and *Rimmon* are the two extreme boundaries of the land of Judea on the *south* and the *north*, by which the Prophet here designates its *whole compass*, as he did in the eighth verse, by its *east* and *west* boundaries. Rimmon, here designated as south of Jerusalem, to distinguish it from the rock Rimmon, lay in the extreme south of the tribe of Judah, and, like Beersheba, was a city of the Simeonites on the borders of Idumea[1]. That Gebah lay on the north border, appears from the fact that, 2 Kings 23. 8, the whole extent of the kingdom of Judah is designated by the expression, '*from* Gebah *to Beersheba*[2].'—The sense is, '*All mountains in Judea, those of Jerusalem excepted, shall be changed into plains, so that the whole land is like the great flat, which hitherto constituted only one portion of it.*' The design of the change is intimated by, '*and Jerusalem will be exalted.*' The whole land will be depressed, *in order* that Jerusalem alone may appear elevated.—We now investigate the import of this symbolical representation. Jerusalem here again designates[3] the central point of the glorified kingdom of God; Judea denotes this kingdom in its whole compass, in its extension over the whole earth. How then could the sense well be otherwise, than that '*the Lord alone will be exalted in that day, his rest glorious*[4]*, his dominion, as that of the king of the whole earth, will destroy all earthly and apparent greatness, which rises up in opposition.*' By a somewhat different image, thereby showing that the crude literal understanding found in Jewish interpreters is entirely untenable, the same thought is expressed elsewhere[5]. '*The temple mountain will be placed on the summit of all the mountains of the earth.*' A third image is found in Dan. 2. 35. '*The stone, the symbol of the Messiah's kingdom, smites the colossus which represents the kingdoms of the world in contrast with that of God, and becomes a mountain, which fills the whole earth.*'—We now proceed to explain what concerns the second object, the rebuilding of the city. "She *seats herself* on her throne, in the place of the gate of Benjamin," &c.—The whole compass of the city is the *seat* or *throne*, which she takes possession of. The point, from which this determination of the boundaries proceeds, is the gate of Benjamin. This gate is no doubt the same, which is elsewhere called '*the gate of Ephraim.*' The way to the land of Benjamin was by the gate of Benjamin[6]. It lay therefore northward. The gate of Ephraim is designated 2 Sam. 13. 23,

---

[1] Comp. Josh. 15. 21. 32.

[2] עֲרָבָה, with the article, always signifies the greatest and principal of all the plains of Judea, that of the Jordan, " the low land between the mountain ranges, which encompass the Jordan on the east and west side," in Josephus, μέγα πεδίον. Comp. Reland. I. p. 359 sq.; Bachiene, I. § 154 sq.; Ritter, II. p. 321.

[3] As in ver. 8.   [4] Is. 11. 10.

[5] In Is. 2. 2. Mic. 4. 1. Ezek. 40. 2.   [6] Comp. Jer. 37. 12, 13.

as directed towards Ephraim[1]; the way towards Ephraim however passed through Benjamin. The first *terminus ad quem* is the *place of the first gate*. This gate does not occur elsewhere under the same name; it is however no doubt the same which bears the name[2] of "the gate of the old," that is, "the *gate of the old* city." For as the cities were personified as matrons, every addition was properly unnecessary. By the name of the old city, that part of Jerusalem was probably designated, which already existed at the time of the Jebusites, in contrast with the later enlargement by David and his successors,—in like manner as, at a later period, that which was recently built was called *Bezetha*[3], in contrast with the whole of the former city. The 'first gate' was the gate of this old city. As now the *old* city was the *first*, so also was its gate, among all the gates of the later Jerusalem, the first. In favour of this we have, secondly, its position; just as here the *first* gate appears as the first *terminus ad quem* from the gate of Benjamin, in Neh. 12. 39 (where the gates are numbered according to their geographical position), the old gate follows immediately after the gate of Ephraim. We must not seek the '*first gate*' to the west of the gate of Benjamin, but east. For, as the *terminus ad quem* from the gate of Benjamin towards the west, the corner gate is immediately mentioned; and that we must by no means seek the first between this and the gate of Benjamin is evident from the very small distance, four hundred cubits, by which[4] the two gates were separated from each other. Entirely corresponding with this is the position of the gate of the old city. It was nearest to the gate of Ephraim towards the east, probably at the north-east extremity[5]. '*Unto the corner gate*' designates a new *terminus ad quem* from the gate of Benjamin westward. For that the corner gate lay not eastward, but westward, appears from Jer. 31. 38, where, by the antithesis of the *tower of Hananeel* lying on the east side, and of the *corner gate*, the whole breadth of the city is designated.—The tower of Hananeel lay on the east side of the city near to the sheep gate[6]. From this tower the Prophet begins a new line[7], which he continues to the *wine-vats of the king*, without doubt on the south side of the city, where, according to Neh. 3. 15, were the royal gardens. Thus therefore we have here a description of the compass of the city according to all the four regions of heaven.—And now a highly remarkable phenomenon presents itself, which alone is sufficient to prove the genuineness of the second part. The Prophet mentions only the edifices, which had remained uninjured in the destruction by the Chaldeans, none which were not in existence in the time of Zechariah after the destruction, and before the rebuilding of the walls by Nehemiah. In the first place, two gates, the gate of Benjamin and the corner gate, serve as *termini*: for the third, the first gate by the addition *unto the place*,

---

[1] עָם אֶפְרַיִם

[2] שַׁעַר הַיְשָׁנָה

[3] καινὴ πόλις, in Josephus.

[4] According to 2 Kings 14. 23.

[5] Comp. Faber, p. 332.

[6] Neh. 3. 1. 12. 37. 39.

[7] Before כִּידֵל, מִן is to be supplied out of the preceding.

unto its former site, is expressly designated as no longer existing.
One of these, the corner gate, appears also in the prophecy of Jer. 31.
38, composed after the destruction, as still standing. Both were
omitted in the description of the rebuilding of the gates by Nehemiah, chap. 3, which (especially when compared with 12. 39) cannot
be explained otherwise than by supposing that it did not need to be
rebuilt, but only perhaps slightly repaired. On the contrary, the
old gate, appearing here as destroyed, is mentioned among those
which were rebuilt. The tower of Hananeel appears, as well in
Jer. l. c., as also Neh. 3. 1, as still standing.—The royal wine-vats
cannot easily be supposed to have been destroyed. This was scarcely
possible, since, as is still the case in the east[1], where the ground
allows it, they are hewn out of the rocks[2]. Such being the nature
of the royal wine-vats, it is perhaps as likely as not, that they
still exist among the great mass of the excavations in the rocks,
which are found particularly in the neighbourhood of the fountain of
Siloa. For why should they not as well be preserved as the cisterns
and graves? Their destruction, properly speaking, was impossible,
though they might have been filled up. We can however abundantly
prove by a special witness, that they were still in existence. They
lay, as already remarked, without doubt in the royal gardens, and
these appear, Neh. 3. 15, to have been spared during the destruction
by the Chaldeans.—We now inquire what the Prophet intends to
express by the image of the rebuilding of Jerusalem. For that we
are not to take him literally, is evident from the whole character of
the description, particularly in the eighth and ninth verses, where,
under the image of Judea, the whole earth presents itself; and in
like manner the first half of the verse before us, where Jerusalem, in
relation to the rest of Judea, designates the central point of the
future kingdom of God, in relation to its circumference, which
embraces the whole earth. The rebuilding of Jerusalem here predicted, stands in close relation to its capture described, in the first
and second verses, and the desolations occasioned by the Divine
judgements inflicted upon the enemies found in it. The sense is;
The kingdom of God, after the Lord shall have removed all traces of
the calamity to which it had been subject, will recover its ancient
splendour. This the Prophet expresses, in accordance with the
representation of the distresses inflicted upon the same, under the
image of a capture of the city, by the image of its restoration to its
ancient limits, which are accordingly more accurately defined by a
special mention of the particular bounds.

646. Ver. 11. ' *And they dwell in her, and there shall be no more
curse, and Jerusalem sits securely on her throne.*' After ' *they dwell
therein,*' there is no occasion, with most interpreters, to supply a *scil.*
' *securely ;*' for then would the last member contain an empty tau-
tology. Rather, the bare sitting or dwelling, is here sufficient, in
the antithesis with, ' *she seated herself,*' in the preceding verse; and

---

[1] Comp. Chardin, in Harmar, Th. III. p. 117.
[2] Comp. Is. 5. 2. Matt. 21. 33. *Nonni Dionysiac.* 12. 330.

at the same time with the going forth, partly as prisoners, partly as fugitives, in the second and fifth verses. The expression, '*there shall be no more curse,*' designates the Church of God as consisting, after this catastrophe, purely of the righteous and holy, and therefore no longer, as in former times, to be purified by Theocratical judgements [1]. In the new Jerusalem the penal justice of God will no more find an object; his whole conduct towards her therefore will be an uninterrupted manifestation of His love and mercy. The same thought Jeremiah l. c. expresses by including the valley of Hinnom, a place desecrated by the most frightful abominations, within the compass of the new Jerusalem, and then subjoining, '*they shall no more be destroyed for ever.*' Compare also Apoc. 22. 3.

647. Ver. 12. '*And this will be the plague wherewith the Lord will plague all nations, which have warred against Jerusalem; his flesh will rot while he stands on his feet, and his eyes will rot in their sockets, and their tongue will rot in their mouth.*' The Prophet, having first described the judgements upon the house of God, contented himself with a mere intimation of the destruction, which the Lord would bring upon its enemies, the instruments, and no less the objects, of His penal justice, in the third and two following verses, and had proceeded directly to an object most attractive to his heart, to the blessings to be conferred by the mercy of God upon His purified church. Here he interrupts the description, in order more fully to describe the punishment of the enemies. According to the nature of the prophetico-symbolic representation, which exhibits every thing in vision, and at the same time with reference to the corporeal judgements under the former Theocracy, as e. g. that upon the Assyrians, the punishment here appears exclusively as corporeal, in like manner as the crime also is made an object of sense, by being represented under the form of a military expedition against Jerusalem. Not perceiving this, Cocceius and Mark would transfer the spiritual element of the punishment into the words themselves. They suppose that the Prophet speaks of a wasting away of the body, arising from remorse of conscience! The correct view is rather, that the *substance* of the Prophet's prediction is merely the punishment itself; that he leaves the mode of this to the fulfilment; and that what he seems to say concerning it belongs only to the dress, instead of which another might have been chosen, as appears e. g. from a comparison of Isaiah 66. 24, where the enemies of the kingdom of God appear under the image of living corpses, which lie as an everlasting prey of the worms, and the fire without the gate of the residence of the holy, i. e. of Jerusalem [2]. The expression, '*and he stands upon his feet,*' magnifies the fearfulness of the judgement. They will be living corpses. If we look at that which is corporeal alone, such a putrefaction of a living body is far more terrifying than death [3]. That besides the

---

[1] Comp. on ver. 21.

[2] On the *Infin.* הָמֵק, which gives prominence to the action alone, in order to direct attention to its fearfulness; comp. Ewald, p. 559.

[3] Cyril: ὁ μὲν γὰρ κοινὸς οὗτος καὶ ἐκ τῆς φύσεως θάνατος τήκει μὲν τὰς

flesh, the *eye* and *tongue* are especially mentioned, is not (as the comparison of the sixteenth verse of the eleventh chapter shows) without reason. The *tongue* is mentioned, because it insolently con-temned God and His people[1]; the *eye*, because it spied out the nakedness of the city of God; the *whole body*, because it invaded Jerusalem.

648. Ver. 13. '*And it happens in that day, great will be the con-fusion caused by the Lord among them, and they seize each one the hand of his neighbour, and his hand raises itself up against the hand of his neighbour.*' There is here an allusion to the example of panic terrour, sent by the Lord upon His enemies, and a confusion, which led to mutual destruction in the former history of the people of God[2]: principally however to the history of Jehoshaphat. Com-pare particularly 2 Chron. 20. 23 : '*And the children of Ammon and Moab stood up against the inhabitants of mount Seir, utterly to slay and destroy them; and when they had made an end of the inha-bitants of Seir, they helped to destroy one another.*' It is a certain sign of the curse of God when allies rage against one another[3].—By the *seizing of the hand*, we are to understand *a hostile assault*, accord-ing to the connexion and the parallel passages. Still more plainly is *hostility* implied in '*the hand raises itself,*' &c. Each one seeks to *master* the hand of his neighbour in order in this way to disarm him; and having done this, he cuts at him, and that chiefly at his hand, because whoever is deprived of that can be slain without danger.

649. Ver. 14. '*And Judah also will fight in Jerusalem, and the riches of all the heathen round about are collected, gold and silver and garments in great abundance[4].*' The explanation, '*Judah will fight against Jerusalem,*' is to be totally rejected. Of a *hostile* relation between Judah and Jerusalem, we find no trace either here or in the twelfth chapter, but rather the opposite. It is however entirely decisive, that here the fighting of Judah stands in manifest connexion with the gathering of the booty in what follows. This connexion,

---

ἀπάντων σάρκας, καὶ ἀποκείρει ὀφθαλμοὺς καὶ γλώσσας, πάνδεινον δὲ καὶ τῆς εἰς λῆξιν ἠκούσης συμφορᾶς εἴη ἂν εἰκότως τὸ ζώντων καὶ ἑστώτων ἔτι τακῆναι μὲν σάρκας καὶ ἀποῤῥεῖν ὀφθαλμοὺς, κολάζεσθαι δὲ καὶ γλώσσας.

[1] Jerome: *Lingua magniloqua, quæ Dei populum blasphemabat, solvetur in saniem, et intra vallum dentium computrescet.* Comp. Ps. 12. 4. Is. 37.

[2] Comp. Deut. 7. 23. Judges 7. 14. 1 Sam. 14. 20 ("and behold the sword of a man was against his neighbour, a very great confusion," מְהוּמָה).

[3] Comp. chap. 11. 14. Is. 19. 2.

[4] Passages, in which the local meaning of בְּ before the names of places after the verb נִלְחַם, is entirely obvious, and the common understanding of it by *against*, plainly untenable, are the following: Is. 30. 32. Judges 9. 45. 2 Sam. 11. 1. 12. 26. 2 Sam. 21. 19, "The war was again בְּגוֹב, in Gob;" comp. ver. 20. The only doubtful passage is that 1 Sam. 23 1, "And they showed to David, behold, the Philistines fight in Kegilah, and plunder the threshing-floors." That the city itself was not taken, is evident from what follows; yet we are not thereby compelled to give up the local meaning of בְּ. It is only necessary to assume, that the city here includes its nearest environs, in which were the threshing-floors; comp. Judges 6. 37. 2 Sam. 24. 16.

however, cannot exist, unless the fighting is taken, not in a hostile,
but in a friendly relation, precisely as, 2 Chron. 20. 24, &c., both
Judah and Jerusalem, as formerly they shared the danger, so now
also participate in the spoil.

650. Ver. 15. '*And so will be the plague of the horses, the mules,
the camels, and the asses, which shall be in those camps, as this
plague.*' The verse contains an amplification of the crime and the
punishment. They have so grievously sinned, that their possessions
also have become polluted, and subject to the Divine malediction.
The representation of the Prophet here proceeds from the same
feeling with the Mosaic ordinance respecting the curse of God.
When a whole city had made itself guilty of idolatry, not only were
its inhabitants, but also the cattle, to be slain; so that here, on a
small scale, the same relation of the irrational part of the creation to
the rational is repeated ; according to which the creature, on account
of the sin of man, was made subject to vanity against its will [1]. The
case is also analogous, when, for the crime of Achan, besides himself
and his children, his oxen, asses, and sheep also, were burnt [2].

651. Ver. 16. '*And it comes to pass, all the remnant of all the
heathen, which come against Jerusalem, shall go up from year to year
to supplicate the King, Jehovah of hosts, and to celebrate the feast of
tabernacles.*'—That the journeying of the nations from all the regions
of the earth to Jerusalem, is to be understood figuratively, that the
Prophet, as already, chap. 8. 22, 23 [3], employs the method, in which
the fear of God, and participation of the kingdom of God, manifested
itself under the Old Testament, as a type of its manifestation in the
Messianic time, appears partly from the nature of the case itself,
('*For how would it be possible that all the inhabitants of the whole
world, the dwellers in Japan, in China, in the neighbourhood of either
pole, should visit Jerusalem every year to celebrate the festival [4] ?*')
partly from the nature of the whole description [5]. The selection of
the particular *feast of tabernacles* is properly attributed by Dachs,
Ch. B. Michaelis, and others, to the peculiar nature of that festival.
It was, according to the thirty-third verse of the twenty-third chapter
of Leviticus, a festival of thanksgiving for the merciful protection of

---

[1] Comp. Michaelis, *Mos. R.* III. § 145. V. § 246.   [2] Josh. 7. 24.
[3] As Mic. 4. 1. Is. 2. 3.
[4] Dachs, *Dissert. ad Sach.* 14. 16. *ad calc. cod. Talmud. Succah*, Utrecht, 1726,
p. 547.
[5] Comp. especially on ver. 8—10. That he has not done this without a
definite reason, appears from the impossibility of otherwise conceiving why he
should not have retained the festivals mentioned in the passage Is. 66. 23 ; with
which that before us in all respects, even in expression, accurately coincides :
" *And it comes to pass from new moon to new moon, from sabbath to sabbath, all
flesh will come to pray before me, saith the Lord.*" Here, in order to express the
zeal of the new citizens of the kingdom of God, in the worship of the Lord, those
festivals are chosen, *which return most frequently.* Under the Old Testament
only *one people* went up to Jerusalem *to the three great annual feasts*, now *all
flesh* journey thither on *each sabbath and new moon.* This parallel passage serves
at the same time to place the absurdity of the literal interpretation in a stronger
light.

the Lord in the journey through the wilderness, to which alone it was owing that the people, instead of being overcome by the dangers which threatened their destruction, were purified by them, and attained to the possession of the land of Canaan. This wandering of the people of Israel was however a type [1], not only of the similar proceedings of God with this people in future times, particularly of the Babylonian and present exile [2], but also of His conduct towards those who were destined at a future day to become His people. This people will then celebrate the feast of tabernacles, not *outwardly* but *spiritually*, as the Sabbath [3] and the passover [4]. In the feast of tabernacles, as well as in the two remaining great festivals, the benefits of God in nature were celebrated, together with that manifested in the history of His people. It was at the same time the thanksgiving feast for the completion of the harvest. Perhaps the Prophet had this design of the festival also in view, regarding the feast of tabernacles at the same time as a feast of gratitude for the rich gifts of grace imparted to the new citizens of the kingdom of God.—'*All that remains*,' &c., reminds us of the coincidence between the type and the antitype. As not all who came up out of Egypt reached Canaan, and there celebrated the feast of tabernacles, as, on the contrary, the greatest part of them were cut off during the journey through the wilderness by the Divine judgements; so also will not *all* the heathen, who formerly went up *against* Jerusalem, now go thither in thankfulness and love, but only *the remnant* whom the mercy of God spares after the greater part, all the stiff-necked despisers of God shall have been destroyed by the judgements formerly described [5].—The Lord is here also called *king*, not in reference to his general government of the world, but in the Theocratic sense ; compare the ninth verse.

652. Ver. 17. '*And it comes to pass, that whoever of all the families of the earth will not go up to Jerusalem to pray to the King, Jehovah of hosts,—upon them there will be no rain.*' The representation of this verse, like ver. 12, is *throughout* figurative ; the Prophet represents *spiritual relations* by *external objects*. The thought that, at that time, instead of leaving the heathen to themselves as at present, the Lord would demand of them the fulfilment of their duties towards Him, the Prophet expresses, by declaring that all who do not

---

[1] Comp. 1 Cor. 10. 11.

[2] Comp. Ezek. 20. 34: " I bring you to the *wilderness of the nations*, saith the Lord, and there contend with you face to face ; as I have contended with your fathers in the wilderness of Egypt, so will I contend with you, saith the Lord. In this wilderness will the Lord purify the people, and cut off the ungodly members ; I expel from among you the sinners and the transgressors against me."

[3] Heb. 4. 9.   [4] 1 Cor. 5. 7, 8.

[5] The assertion of several Jewish interpreters is erroneous, that the circumstance, that מֶלֶךְ stands without the article, not לַמֶּלֶךְ, but לְמֶלֶךְ, indicates, that we must translate, " to the king of the Lord," and that by this king, not the Lord himself, but the Messiah is to be understood. The article, which occurs far more rarely in poetry than in prose, comp. Ewald, p. 568, is here not strictly required, because the nearer determination follows, in which case also we could omit it, and entirely the same connexion is found, Is. 6. 5.

join in the journey to Jerusalem, should be afflicted with the want of
rain ; a punishment threatened in the law against its transgressors,
and frequently inflicted, particularly in the case of Ahab.   It cannot
however be inferred from this passage, that at that time there will
actually be such refractory persons.   The passage is rather entirely
analogous to that of Is. 65. 20.   The supposed existence of such
serves the Prophet merely as a foundation for the thought, which we
have already designated as containing the substance of the representation.   The appellation, ' *the families of the earth,*' seems to be
intentionally chosen, in order to indicate the changed relation of the
heathen to the Lord, the Theocratic relation, in which they now
stand to Him, as it contains the basis of their far stronger obligation
henceforth to serve Him.

   653. Ver. 18. ' *And if the family of Egypt does not go forth, and
come up, so will there not be rain upon them, but there shall be upon
them the plague, wherewith the Lord will plague all the nations, who
will not go forth to celebrate the feast of tabernacles.*'   The Prophet,
in naming the Egyptians as an individual example of one people,
who should be visited with the punishment of withholding of rain,
probably thought but little, whether this special punishment, which
is here to be regarded only as an outward exhibition of the punishment in general, must have been peculiarly felt by this people on
account of the natural condition of their land.   The *plague* is the
withholding of rain.

   654. Ver. 19. ' *This will be the sin of Egypt, and the sin of all the
nations who will not go up to celebrate the feast of tabernacles* [1].'
Formerly nations were punished, on account of *other* sins ; now,
since the Theocratical dominion of the Lord was extended over the
whole earth, there is *only one* great sin, before which the rest entirely
disappear ; *only one* cause of the Divine judgements, the refusal of
that reverence which they owe to their king, or its root, unbelief.
This *one sin* is their refusal to go up to Jerusalem.

   655. Ver. 20. ' *In this day there will stand on the bells of the
horses, Holy to the Lord, and there will be pots in the house of the
Lord, as the sacrificial bowls before the altar.*'   It is generally acknowledged that the Prophet alludes to the holy plate on the diadem
of the high priest, whereon [2] was engraven ' *Holy to the Lord.*'
While, under the Old Testament, many things are designated as
' *holy to the Lord,*' this was the only one which bore the above
inscription, and which therefore entirely coincided with that before
us ; since it is here by no means said, that the bells of the horses
will be holy to the Lord, but upon the bells of the horses will be,
stand engraven, ' *Holy to the Lord.*'   It was an ancient custom, par-

---

[1] The interpreters mostly explain, "this will be the punishment," &c.   But
this explanation is to be rejected, even for this reason, because חַטָּאת and חַטָּאָה
never occur simply in the sense *punishment of sin,* as is evident from a more
accurate view of the passages cited for this idiom, e. g. Gen. 20. 9. Num. 32. 23.
Besides, according to it, the verse would be a mere *resumption,* contrary to the
custom of Zechariah, and would contain no new thought.

[2] According to Exod. 28. 26.

ticularly in the east, to hang bells upon horses and mules, partly for
use, for the same object for which it is done among us, partly for
ornament[1]. The sense is : ' *With the symbol of holiness, which formerly only the high priest bore, will the Lord at that time adorn the
horses.*' Herein a very deep truth is contained. With the fall of
man originated the distinction between holy and profane. To *abolish*
this, to give sole dominion to that which is holy, was the design of
all the Divine institutions ; while the prince of this world strove, on
the contrary, entirely to abolish that which is holy. In order the
more surely to gain His final purpose, the Lord for a long time
suffered the contrast to become greater and greater. He separated
to Himself one holy people, in comparison with which all others
were profane ; He gave to this people a law in which the separation
between holy and profane extended from the greatest to the least.
He contented Himself for a long time with only one certain outwardly
defined province, because otherwise, if both the opposing principles
had been mingled with one another, the evil would entirely have
swallowed up the good. With the first manifestation of Christ the
last design of God began to approach its realization ; the *external*
contrast between the profane and the holy now became less obvious,
because, by the Spirit of Christ, a far stronger support and aid was
given to the latter. Both however still continued to exist ; even in
the believer the good does not attain in this life to complete and
sole dominion. Hereafter, however, when the Lord shall be all in
all, a time will come when every contrast of the holy and the unholy,
every impure mixture of both, every distinction of degrees even in
that which is holy, will cease[2].—As the first member predicts the
conversion of all that is profane into that which is holy, so the second,
the doing away of the distinction of *degrees* between the holy things
themselves. To the *most holy* vessels, under the old covenant,
belong the bowls before the altar, the basins, into which the blood of
the victims was received, and then from them sprinkled against the
altar, and poured out at its foot. For of all vessels, these were most
immediately used for the most holy service of the Lord. To the
utensils on the contrary, which were the *least holy*, belonged the
pots, *those*, viz. *in which the flesh of the victims was cooked.* For
that these are here spoken of, appears from the twenty-first verse.
They were used in the service of man[3]. Ezekiel, chap. 43. 12. 45. 3,
expresses by another image the same thought, *the doing away of all*

[1] Thus it is said, e. g. by *Diodorus Sic.* 1. 18, ed. Wessel. II. p. 279, in the
description of Alexander's funeral procession : ὥστε τοὺς ἅπαντας ἡμιόνους
εἶναι ἑξήκοντα καὶ τέσσαρας· ἕκαστος δὲ τούτων ἐστεφάνωτο κεχρυσωμένῳ
στεφάνῳ καὶ παρ' ἑκατέραν τῶν σιαγόνων εἶχεν ἐξηρτημένον κώδωνα χρυσοῦν.
And Nicetas Choniates says of the Persians, they sat upon beautiful horses,
which besides other ornaments καὶ περιηρτημένους ἔχουσι ἠχετικοὺς κώδωνας.

[2] The case is analogous, when, according to Jer. 31. 40, the whole valley of
corpses shall be קֹ֫דֶשׁ לַיהוָֹה, and brought within the circumference of Jerusalem.

[3] The Jewish interpreters, according to their opinion of the eternal duration
of the ceremonial law, for the refutation of which this passage alone, as well as
that Mal. 1. 11, is sufficient, *must* endeavour here also by a forced explanation to
set aside the true sense, which is so unpleasant to them.

degrees of difference among holy things. The whole mountain, upon which the new Temple stands, will be the holiest of all [1].

656. Ver. 21. '*And every pot in Jerusalem and Judah will be holy to the Lord of Hosts, and all the offerers come and take therefrom, and offer therein, and there will be no more a Canaanite in the house of the Lord of Hosts in that day.*' As the *pots* in the Temple will be all *equally holy* with the *sacrificial bowls*, so *all pots* in Jerusalem and Judah, which heretofore were only *clean*, not *holy*, will be equally holy with the pots in the Temple. When the Prophet says, that at that time there shall be *no longer* a Canaanite in the house of the Lord, it necessarily follows, that at his time *Canaanites were found* in the house of the Lord. For this reason alone, Canaanites, *according to corporeal descent*, cannot be intended; since the Gibeonites, whom several interpreters here mention, were not in the Temple itself, from which all foreigners were kept at a distance with the greatest care. We have here rather an instance of the idiom, of frequent occurrence, whereby the *ungodly members of the Theocracy themselves*, in mockery of the arrogance founded on the outward participation of the same, are designated as heathen, or uncircumcised, or especially as Canaanites, or some other heathen people. Circumcision had the power of a seal of the covenant, only when the spiritual condition, typified by the outward action, actually existed; where this was not the case, the circumcision was considered void. As even the Pentateuch speaks of a *circumcision of the heart*, to which outward circumcision bound the Israelites [2], so Jeremiah [3] designates the ungodly Israelites as uncircumcised in heart. Ezekiel goes a step farther. He designates [4] the ungodly priests and Levites, not merely as *uncircumcised in heart*, but also in *flesh*, and as sons of the stranger. For that here, by the '*uncircumcised*,' and the '*sons of the stranger*,' not heathen properly, as most interpreters strangely enough assume, but the *ungodly Levites* are designated, appears, among other reasons, from the fact, that priestly actions, namely, the presenting of sacrifices, are attributed to these persons [5]. Similar also is Is. 52. 1, '*There shall no more come into thee one uncircumcised, and unclean.*'—Examples of a designation of the ungodly by the name of *one particular idolatrous people*, distinguished by peculiar depth of moral depravity, are the following. Isaiah [6] addresses the *princes of Israel* directly as princes of *Sodom;* the

---

[1] קֹדֶשׁ קֳדָשִׁים

[2] Comp. Deut. 10. 16. 30. 6.

[3] Jer. 4. 4 ('Circumcise your heart, and take away the foreskin of your heart, ye men of Judah, and ye inhabitants of Jerusalem,') and chap. 9. 25 ('for all the heathen are uncircumcised, and the whole house of Israel are uncircumcised in heart').

[4] Chap. 44. 9.

[5] Comp. ver. 7 with ver. 15. Other reasons are supplied by the כִּי אִם in ver. 10, (which, by these interpreters, e. g. B. Rosenm., is unphilologically translated, *yea also*, or *moreover*, instead of *but*); and ver. 15 and 16, where, to the threatening against the *ungodly* priests and Levites, contained in ver. 7—14, the prediction of a reward for the pious is opposed.

[6] Chap. 1. 10.

people as people of *Gomorrah*. In Zeph. 1. 11, the destruction of the covenant people is announced by the words, ' *The whole people of* Canaan *shall be extirpated.*' The Chaldee paraphrases very correctly, ' *The whole people whose works are like the works of the Canaanites* [1].' Accordingly, the sense of the passage before us can no longer be doubtful. It is altogether parallel with such as Is. 4. 3, ' *Whosoever remains in Zion, and is left in Jerusalem, he will be called holy.*' 60. 21 : ' *Thy people are all righteous.*' Apoc. 21. 27 : '*And there shall in no wise enter into it any thing that defileth, neither whatsoever worketh abomination, or maketh a lie ; but they which are written in the Lamb's book of life.*' 22. 15 : ' *For without are dogs, and sorcerers, and whoremongers, and murderers, and idolaters, and whosoever loveth and maketh a lie.*' The mixture of the pious and ungodly, as it existed in the church of the Old Testament, and as it in part still continues in that of the New (with this difference, nevertheless, that the dead members who join themselves to it have no sort of right in it, and participate in none of its blessings, all of which are received only through faith), is here contrasted with the perfect purity of the Church in the last days, to be effected by the Lord.

THE SEVENTY WEEKS OF DANIEL

General View of Chapter 9:24-27

657. In the first year of Darius the Mede, Daniel is reading the prophet Jeremiah, and his spirit is deeply moved, as he reads anew his well-known prophecy, according to which, the affliction of the covenant people, their servitude, was to endure seventy years, after which, their return, and the consequent commencement of the rebuilding of the city and Temple, was to take place. The sixty-ninth year was now already arrived ; and one of the chief objects of the prophecies of Jeremiah [2], the overthrow of Babylon, had already happened. With respect to the other, Daniel was far from doubting the Divine promise ; but the more firmly he trusted the mercy of God, and the more deeply he understood the divine justice (for even this required the fulfilment of the promise, when it had once been given), so much the

---

[1] Still there lies at the foundation, as is shown by what follows, an allusion to the import of the word, *merchant*, which is too much magnified by Cölln (*Spicil. in Zeph.* p. 32). The appeal to Ezek. 17. 4, can prove nothing, since there also נְּ certainly cannot be translated by *merchant*. Babylon was a second Canaan. Ezek. 16. 3, it is said, "Thus saith the Lord to Jerusalem ; Thine origin and thy descent are out of the land of the Canaanite ; thy father is the Amorite, and thy mother a Hittite."

[2] Chap. 25—29.

more did he feel himself impelled to intercede for the people, the Temple, and the city of the Lord :—as in the Psalms we constantly observe, that the assurance of Divine help, when embraced with living faith, is always followed by *new supplications* for the *actual bestowal* of the promised blessing. He at the same time reflected, that, though the *that* and the *when* of the *beginning* stood irrevocably firm ; yet in reference to the *how* and the *when* of the *completion*, the Lord had left himself free. Daniel therefore sends up to the Lord a prayer full of power and unction, for the forgiveness of sins, and for the restoration of the Theocracy ; a prayer, whose spirit, like that of all prayer which really deserves the name, is, "we do not present before thee our prayer, on account of our own righteousness, but of thy great mercy." The prayer is heard by Him who had given it, and Gabriel, the mediator of all revelations[1], receives a command to impart to the expectant prophet the decree determined in heaven. The speediness of his coming indicates a joyful message. The substance of it is this : As a compensation for the seventy years in which the people, the city, and Temple have been entirely prostrate, seventy weeks of years, seven times seventy years of a renewed existence, shall be secured to them by the Lord ; and the end of this period, far from bringing the mercies of God to a close, shall for the first time bestow them on the Theocracy in their complete and full measure. With it coincide the finished forgiveness of sins, the introduction of everlasting righteousness, the actual conferring of the saving blessings, which the prophets promise, the anointing of a Holy of Holies. This general view[2] is followed[3] by a more accurate detail, the date of the *terminus a quo*, the division of the whole period into several smaller ones, with a determination of the characteristic mark of each (the Divine blessing, by which it is distinguished), the determination of the person by whom the last and greatest benefit shall be obtained, and of those to whom it belongs, with the exclusion of those for whom it is *not* destined. [1.] As the *terminus a quo* of the seventy weeks is given the command of God to rebuild the city in its ancient extent and glory ; a point of time which is *not coincident* with the *terminus ad quem* of the prophecy of Jeremiah, as this relates only to the *return from captivity*, and the *first beginning* of the rebuilding of the city necessarily connected therewith. The intermediate time between this *terminus* of Jeremiah, and that of Daniel, is given to the covenant people, over and above the seventy years ; just as the *former intermediate condition*, the eighteen years from the fourth year of Jehoiachim to the destruction of the city and Temple, were mercifully *included* in the seventy years of affliction. [2.] The whole period is divided into three smaller periods ; of *seven* weeks, *sixty-two* weeks, and *one* week. The close of the first is distinguished by the completion of the rebuilding of the city ; that of the second, by the appearing of an Anointed One, a Prince ; that of the third, by the finished confirm-

---

[1] Comp. p. 269, § 500.   [2] Contained in ver. 24.
          [3] Ver. 25—27.

ation of the covenant with the many for whom the saving blessings (designated in the twenty-fourth verse, as belonging to the end of the whole period) are destined. This last period is again divided into two halves. While the confirmation of the covenant extends *through* it, from beginning to end; the cessation of the sacrifice and meat-offering, and the death of the Anointed One, on which this depends, fall in *the middle* of it. [3.] As the author of the saving blessings completed in the end of the seventy weeks, a Messiah, a Prince, appears; who, after having, in the end of the sixty-nine weeks from the *terminus a quo*, entered upon his office, and throughout the half of the seventieth week confirmed the covenant with many, dies a violent death, by which sacrifices and meat-offerings are made to cease, while the confirmation of the covenant continues even after his death. [4.] The saving blessings to be bestowed through the Anointed One, are not destined for the whole people; on the contrary, the greater part of them, being excluded, for the murder of the Anointed One, from his kingdom and blessings, will become a prey to the host of a foreign prince: which, an instrument in the hands of an avenging God, will utterly destroy the fallen city, and the polluted Temple.

658. The whole annunciation is of a consoling import, even that part of it, which relates to the destruction of the city and the Temple, and which the more necessarily belongs to the whole, the more uniformly the prophets combine with the highest manifestation of the Divine mercy the highest manifestation of the Divine justice against those who despise the former. The purifying judgements of God are for his church, a blessing; for his believers, a joy[1]. Daniel had not indeed prayed for the obdurate and ungodly, but for those, who heartily joined with him in the penitential confession of sin. These are the only objects of all promises, and of the tender concern of the prophets. Daniel mourns over the destruction of the city and the Temple by the Chaldeans. For by that, the outward Theocracy, which still existed, was in part done away. It is only in this respect, that the destruction of the city and Temple is the object of his complaint; it is only on this account that he prays for their restoration[2]. It was entirely different in respect to the destruction here described. What distress can the prediction of the exterior Temple's destruction cause, when it is accompanied by that of the anointing of a *new* Holy of Holies? What the cessation of the Anointed One's dominion over the covenant people, since it is accompanied by the confirmation of the covenant for the many, who alone were dear to the prophet? What the abolition of sacrifices, since that which it partly only prefigured, and partly outwardly procured for the outward Theocracy, the forgiveness of sin and justification, should be first

---

[1] Comp., besides the passages already cited on Zech. 13. 7. Is. 65. 13, 14; 66. 24. Mal. 3, 21. Luke 21. 28. 2 Macc. 6. 13: καὶ τὸ μὴ πολὺν χρόνον ἐᾶσθαι τοὺς δυσσεβοῦντας, ἀλλ' εὐθέως περιπίπτειν ἐπιτιμίοις, μεγάλης εὐεργεσίας σημεῖόν ἐστι. κ. τ. λ.

[2] Comp. ver. 15—19.

really and perfectly procured by that very event, whereby the sacrifice was done away? We are now lamenting over the downfall of the Evangelical Church, as Daniel lamented over the Chaldean desolations. But, which of us would continue this complaint, if the Lord had made all new, and abolished all outward churches? Who would then bewail the loss of the '*beggarly elements*,' the corpse from which the spirit had departed?

Interpretation

Verse 24

659. 'Seventy weeks are cut off upon thy people, and upon thy holy city, to shut up transgression, and to seal up sin, and to cover guilt, and to bring everlasting righteousness, and to seal up vision and prophet, and to anoint a Holy of Holies.'

'*Seventy weeks*[1].'

660. What justifies us in understanding by the *weeks*, weeks of *years*, periods of *seven years*? The chief ground is the reference to the seventy years of Jeremiah. From this we learn, that seventy ordinary weeks cannot be intended. For what sort of a consolation would it have been for Daniel, if it had been announced to him, that, as a compensation for the seventy *years* of desolation, the city should continue seventy *ordinary weeks* until a new destruction? Moreover, Daniel himself could perceive that the discourse did not refer to *ordinary weeks*, from the variety of the events which were to occur within the period. Now, if the weeks spoken of were *extraordinary*, he would be the more compelled to regard them as *weeks of years*, since these weeks occupy so important a place in the Mosaic constitution, and since the exile had brought them anew into lively remembrance, inasmuch as the *seventy years*' desolation was considered as a punishment for neglecting to celebrate the *sabbatical years*[2]. The obscurity, which perhaps still remained, was removed by the fulfilment. The more indefinite determination of time (the mere verbal expression of which was to be developed into a further meaning) was intentionally chosen, in order not to destroy the boundaries between prophecy and history, and render it unnecessary to call the latter to our assistance. The effort to avoid, on the one

[1] The original work discusses the *gender* of the word '*weeks*' (which is here masc. but elsewhere usually *fem.*), and justifies the placing the numerals *last*, of which numerous examples are found in numbers from twenty to ninety.
[2] Comp. 2 Chron. 36. 21. It is true that these *periods of seven years* in the law are not called שָׁבֻעִים or שָׁבֻעוֹת, but that they were nevertheless to be considered as weeks, appears from the frequent designation of the seventh year, as the great Sabbath, or as the Sabbath simply; comp. Lev. 25. 2, 4, 5; 26. 34; 35. 43. 2 Chron. 36. 21.

hand, such a vague indefiniteness, as might be made an objection against the Divine origin of the prophecy, and prevent its aim ; and, on the other, the destruction of its proper relation to history, appears throughout in this section, and has been in a wonderful manner attained[1]. But what induced the prophet to choose precisely *this* measure of time ? In the first place, this very effort after *concealed* definiteness. The *concealment* could not be realized, if he used the ordinary mode of reckoning, and gave the number of the years which would elapse before the given *terminus ad quem*. And just as little could the *definiteness* have been attained, if he had chosen an arbitrarily invented and before unknown measure of time. It might then have been replied, that it were very easy to give such determinations of time, which were rendered definite *solely* by the fulfilment. Another ground is furnished by its relation to the seventy years of Jeremiah. It was very important, in respect to the relation of the Divine mercy to the Divine anger, that to the seventy years (which, according to the second verse, were to be completed upon the ruins of Jerusalem) there should be placed in opposition *a seventy* of another sort—multiplying the seventy years by seven—to be enjoyed by the city after it should be rebuilt. And besides, seven and seventy were perfect and sacred numbers, and the more adapted to the Divine chronology, as the remembrance of the creation of the world was connected with them. Lastly, that in the choice of this determination of time there is a reference to the year of Jubilee, cannot well be doubted. *Seven* weeks of years formed a cycle, in the end of which fell the civil *restitutio in integrum ;* all debts were remitted ; all slaves emancipated ; the alienated lands restored to their possessors. The last week of *seventy weeks of years* is the highest of all Sabbaths, the time of the spiritual *restitutio in integrum,* the removal and the expiation of all guilt[2].

' *Are*[3] *cut off.*'

661. Several interpreters assume, that *to cut off* here stands precisely for *to resolve,* appealing to the fact, that the verbs of *abscission* in

---

[1] An entirely analogous example of a determination of time, indefinite in itself, but rendered definite by the aid of history, is found in Zechariah himself, chap. 4. ver. 20 ; comp. *Beitr.* i. p. 112 ff.

[2] There are to be found also in heathen writers traces of a similar mode of reckoning. Marcus Varro, after he had developed, in the first of his books, called *Hebdomades,* the significancy of the number seven in natural things, (in 4. 11 ; the extract in Gellius, 3. 10,) subjoins, " *se quoque jam duodecimam annorum hebdomadam ingressum esse, et ad eum diem septuaginta hebdomadas librorum conscripsisse.*" Here also, as in Daniel, the choice of this mode of reckoning rests on definite grounds ; partly on the preceding exhibition of the importance of the number seven, partly on an intentional combination of the seven years, and seven books.

[3] The apparent anomaly of the number is explained by the circumstance, that the seventy Hebdomades here come under consideration, not as particulars, but as one whole, i. q. a *period* of seventy Hebdomades is determined. The meaning of the ἅπ. λεγ. חָתַךְ is sufficiently ascertained, by a comparison of the Chaldaic and Rabbinic חֲתַךְ *to cut off.*

the Semitic languages are not unfrequently used in the sense of *determination*[1]. But the very use of the word, which does not else-where occur, while, if Daniel had wished to express the idea of *determination*, others much more frequently used were at hand, and of which he has elsewhere, and even in this portion, availed himself, seems to argue that the word stands here from regard to its original meaning, and represents the seventy weeks as a period *cut off* from subsequent duration, and accurately limited.

' *Over thy people, and over thy holy city.*'

662. Why is Jerusalem called the holy city of *Daniel*[2]? The *thy* intimates the tender love of Daniel towards his people, as expressed in the preceding prayer. It was this love that compelled Daniel to intercession, and this intercession is in the twenty-third verse repre-sented as the occasion of the decree, which is here revealed to him; so that the *thy*, at the same time, reminds him of this occasion[3].

" *To shut up transgression*[4]."

663. Sin, which hitherto *lay naked* and *open* before the eyes of the righteous God, is now, by his mercy, *shut up*, sealed, and covered, so that it can no more be regarded as existing; a figurative designation of the forgiveness of sin, analogous to those, where it is said, "to hide the face from sin[5]," &c.

' *And to seal sin*[6].'

664. There is nothing, so far as the words are concerned, against

---

[1] Thus the Seventy: ἑβδομήκοντα ἑβδομάδες ἐκρίθησαν ἐπὶ τὸν λαόν σου.

[2] After Theodor., Chrysost., Jerome, Vitringa remarks, " *Non meæ sed tuæ, quod indignationis divinæ argumentum est, peccatis populi nondum expiatis.*"

[3] Comp. 12. 1.

[4] In the word לְכַלֵּא the points do not belong to the *Kethib*, which is rather to be pointed לְכַלֵּא, but to the *Keri*. When the difference between a received reading and a supposed emendation, consisted only in the vowels, the Masorites did not write in the margin the consonants of the latter, which coincided with those of the former. They indicated a double reading by another method, which varied indeed according to circumstances. 1. Where the word itself, or the context, did not distinguish as such the vowels of the marginal reading, which were placed under the reading of the text, where, therefore, entirely against their principle, the marginal reading, if they had simply placed under its points, would have appeared as the only one, they gave to the word a mixed punctuation taken from both readings. 2. Where, from the context, or from the word itself, the vowels could be *known* as *not belonging* to the reading of the text, the Masorites simply place them under it. Thus the verb כלא *never occurs* in Piel; it was sufficient, therefore, to give to the word the vowels of Piel, in order to show that along with the usual reading, sufficiently indicated by the form itself, there was another, which pointed the form according to its derivation from כלה = כלא.

[5] See the original work for the reasons in favour of this meaning of *shutting up*, and against that of *finishing*.

[6] The explanation of *sealing*, by *bringing to an end*, is untenable. It is true,

understanding this passage in a bad sense. We might regard sin as *shut up* and *sealed*, by the *punishment* and *extirpation* of the sinners, just as well as by the *forgiveness* of sin, as in Is. 4. 4, 'By the destructive Divine punishment, the filth of the daughter of Zion is washed away, and the blood of Jerusalem is removed from the midst of her.' That this interpretation is nevertheless untenable, and that only a Divine blessing is intended, the shutting up and sealing of sin by forgiveness, appears from the following reasons. 1. In the second part of the verse, a threefold positive good is mentioned, which the Lord at the end of seventy years will impart to His Church. If we take the first two members in a good sense, the removal of a three-fold evil corresponds to this imparting of a threefold good in the first part[1]. 2. There can be no doubt, that, as the threefold designations of sin, which are elsewhere combined[2], must not be separated from one another; so neither must the threefold designation of that which is to be done in reference to sin, the *shutting up, sealing, covering;* especially, as all three expressions are grounded on the same figura-tive representation of its removal out of sight. If, therefore, it can be proved of one of these expressions, that it can stand *only in a good sense*, this proof serves also for the other two. Now this is per-fectly the case with respect to *covering* guilt[3]. This frequent expres-sion never designates any thing else than *the forgiveness* of sin, the covering of sin by the veil of mercy, so that the eye of the angry Judge cannot find it. 3. The prediction in the first three members stands in a close relation to the manifold confession of sin in the fifth verse, and the prayer for forgiveness connected therewith. On account of this relation, even if the third member were just as ambi-guous as the two first, we should prefer understanding it in a good sense, because it is not probable that the angel would have made such haste (comp. 22), in order to announce to Daniel the very

that this import of חָתַם, arising from the custom of putting a seal at the end of a letter or writing, is very frequently met with in the Arabic. In Hebrew, how-ever, it is never found. The figurative use of חתם in Hebrew, is exclusively taken from the custom of sealing, for greater security, things which a man has enclosed, or laid aside. For לַחְתֹּם we have the marginal reading, the vowels of which stand under the reading of the text, לְהָתֵם, as *infin.* in Hiph. from תָּמַם, *to be completed.* Instead of the plur. חֲטָאוֹת, the sing. חַטָּאָ֫ת is found in not a few manuscripts and editions, in Kennicott and De Rossi. But we are surely not justified with Bertholdt, in giving this reading the preference to that in the text. It probably owes its origin merely to the effort to make the word conform to פֶּ֫שַׁע and עָוֹן.

[1] This relation of the two halves, having each three members, to one another, must, however, be the more assumed, since otherwise the חתם, of which one evidently corresponds to the other, is not found in both halves in the second member. With the sins, the prophecies also are sealed, because that which is predicted as future, as the chief mark of the Messianic time, the doing away of sin, has now taken place. This accurate correspondence of the twofold חתם, serves also to protect the first against the encroachments of the marginal reading.

[2] Comp. Exod. 34. 7, above ver. 5.   [3] כִּפֶּר עָוֹן.

opposite of what he had prayed for. It was only through this prediction of prosperity, which preceded, that the announcement of the
destruction of the city and Temple lost its terrours. It now appeared
as running parallel with the greatest blessings towards the pious
members of the Theocracy, and, in so far as it put an end to their
present mingling with the ungodly, even as itself a gracious benefit.

' And to cover transgression.'

665. Several interpreters find a climax in the expressions concerning the forgiveness of sin, in the three members ; but it is far
more correct to assume, with Geier, a mere συναθροισμός, as is found
also e. g. Exod. 34. 7. Levit. 16. 21. A climax would require that
the strongest designation of sin should stand last. This, however, if
the import of words is accurately considered, is precisely the term
which stands first ;[1] which designates sin according to its worst character ; as apostasy from God, and rebellion against Him[2].

' And to bring everlasting righteousness.'

666. Righteousness, where it appears not as an *inherent quality*,
but as a *gift of God*, always designates the same thing on the
positive side, as forgiveness of sin on the negative ; the latter implies
that God, according to His free mercy, *will not* regard men any longer
as sinners ; the former, that He *will* regard them as righteous. Hence,
it necessarily follows, that He will also treat them as such, and,
consequently, *righteousness* and *prosperity* are often combined with
each other, though the former does not lay aside its proper sense[3].
—Righteousness, as a gift of God, (comp. Ps. 85. 11—14, where
' *righteousness looks down from heaven, and goes before God, who
draws near to His people,*') forms a constant characteristic mark of
the Messianic times. According to Jer. 33. 16, Jerusalem, at the
time of the Messiah, shall be called '*the Lord our righteousness ;*'
according to 23. 6, the Messiah Himself will bear this name. According to Mal. 3. 20, the *Sun of righteousness* will then arise upon
those who fear God, i. e. righteousness that beams forth like a sun,
and healing is under its wings. As '*terebinths of righteousness*'
does Isaiah (61. 3) designate the members of the kingdom of God in
his time. The procuring cause of this righteousness we learn from
Is. 53. 11, according to which, the servant of God, the righteous
one, shall make many righteous.—This righteousness is here called
everlasting, both from its origin in the eternal counsels of the

---

[1] פֶּשַׁע

[2] e. g. Job 34. 37, "he adds עַל הַפָּאתוֹ פֶּשַׁע, to sin, transgression," is contrasted
with הַפָּאָה, as the heavier with the lighter. The prediction of the forgiveness
of sin, differs, therefore, in this relation from the confession of sin, ver. 5, where
a climax is actually found.

[3] Dathe translates צֶדֶק, *prosperity*. Our author discusses and rejects the
translations of (1) Michaelis, &c., '*the ancient righteousness,*' or, '*the righteousness
of former times,*' and (2) that of Berthholdt, '*the ancient freedom.*'

everlasting God, and on account of its eternal duration, in contrast with the transient gifts of righteousness and grace under the old
covenant, and with all that is created and mutable. This contrast
is found, also, in several passages of Isaiah, where the eternity of the
righteousness and prosperity of the Messianic time, is declared in the
most emphatic manner[1]. Finally, the pardon of sin, and the gift of
the Divine righteousness are connected, just as they are in the
passage before us, in Ps. 69. 28, '*Impute to them their sins, and let
them not receive a part in thy righteousness.*'

'*And to seal up[2] vision and prophet.*'

667. With the sealing up of sin, the prophecies also in which this
was predicted are sealed up. As soon as the fulfilment takes place,
the prophecy (although in other respects it retains its great importance) reaches the end of its destination, in so far as the view of
believers, who stand in need of consolation and encouragement, is no
longer directed to it, to the future prosperity, but to that which has
appeared; as they no longer rely on the *word* of the Lord, but on
His *deeds,* and exclaim with Philip (John 1. 45): '*We have found
Him, of whom Moses in the Law, and the Prophets, did write, Jesus
of Nazareth, the son of Joseph[3].*'

668. The use of the *sing.,* and the omission of the article, serve to
designate the object in its widest universality. This universality
may be intended, either to designate the object as indefinite, or to
give, in the representation, an *indefinite extension* to that which, in
itself, was *definite.* That it is better to suppose, that the *latter* of
these two objects is that which really accounts here for the indefiniteness of the expression, is probable from the general character of the
section, in which the article is often omitted, where, if the expression corresponded to the real definiteness of the subject, it must
necessarily have stood[4].

669. There can be no doubt that we have here a reference to the
prediction which runs through all the prophetical writings, of the
forgiveness of sin to be conferred in the days of the Messiah[5].
When this, the substance of the work of Christ, has been accomplished, the prophecies may, in the sense we have explained (667),
justly be regarded as abolished.

---

[1] e. g. Chap. 51. 6—8. 45. 17.

[2] Most interpreters suppose, that *to seal up,* here, is as much as *to fulfil, confirm, ratify,* with reference to the custom of confirming the contents of a writing,
by affixing to it a seal. We have already seen that the Hebrew knows no other
metaphorical use of חָתַם, than that taken from the custom of sealing things
which are laid aside, and concealed.

[3] According to this interpretation, the passage is entirely parallel with
Matt. 11. 13, where we have combined the sense of the two interpretations, the
usual one, and our own.

[4] Comp. e. g. מָשִׁיחַ, ver. 25, 26.

[5] Comp. on Zech. 13. 1.

' And to anoint a Holy of Holies.'

670. The *anointing* cannot be understood *literally;* for we do not find the slightest evidence that the sanctuary of either the first Temple or the second was anointed, as was the case according to Exod. 30. 22, &c., with the *Tabernacle.* On the contrary, according to the uniform tradition of the Jews, (comp. Lund, 1. 29,) the holy oil was wanting under the second Temple. In the case of the first Temple, the anointing might have been omitted, because the holy vessels of the Tabernacle, which had already been anointed, were transferred to it. In respect to the second, it was probably thought, in accordance with the character of that whole period, that it would be better to wait for the restoration of the old and most sacred oil, than to prepare new.

671. The *anointing* must be regarded as a figurative expression for imparting the gifts of the Holy Spirit. Even when an actual anointing *did* take place, the oil was a symbol of the Spirit of God [1]. What now is intended by the '*Holy of Holies*,' to be consecrated and supplied with the gifts of the Spirit [2]? Plainly '*the new Temple of the Lord*,' the Church of the new Covenant. That *the Temple,* as the seat of the Theocracy under the old covenant, not unfrequently occurs as a designation of *the Church,* we have already seen on Zech. 6. 12 [3].

672. The Prophet designates the new Temple which should be anointed by the grace of the Lord, as '*a* Holy of Holies,' in contrast with the former, only one particular part of which received this name. Just as Ezekiel (43. 12.), for the same reason, described

---

[1] The "Holy of Holies" of the earthly Temple is called without any exception, קֹדֶשׁ הַקֳּדָשִׁים; on the contrary, קֹדֶשׁ קֳדָשִׁים (the term here used) serves always to designate other objects besides the "Holy of Holies," which are the most holy in their kind, as the altar of burnt-offerings, and other vessels in the sanctuary, in comparison with the outer court, &c. 1 Kings 19. 15, sq., where Elijah receives the command to anoint Hazael as king over Aram, Jehu as king over Israel, and Elisha as a prophet; a symbolic action, and a symbol, are combined with one another in a remarkable manner, as a clear proof how little, in case of the former, depended upon the material. Jehu and Hazael were actually anointed; the latter only in order to symbolize the divine power, which should be imparted to him as an instrument of the divine penal justice for the destruction of Israel. Of an *anointing of the prophets,* we find elsewhere no trace; and in reference to Elisha, therefore, the anointing must be regarded as a figurative designation of the imparting of the gifts of the Spirit.
[2] See Zech. chap. 4. Professor Hengstenberg gives in the original an able review of the passages where the image is *embodied* in an outward action, and of those in which (as in the present) the *mere* image occurs.
[3] The following passages from the Psalms will prove how general this more spiritual consideration of the Temple was; where, disregarding the shell, only the kernel, the gracious presence of the Lord, was seen. Ps. 15. 1; Ps. 5. 5; Ps. 63. 4; Ps. 73. 17, מְקִדְּשֵׁי אֵל, Ps. 27. 4. The whole of the 84th Psalm, '*How amiable are thy tabernacles,* O Lord of Hosts,' can receive an easy and natural interpretation only by supposing that the Temple is wherever God is. The absurdity of the literal understanding is especially evident in ver. 4.

the whole compass of the hill, on which the new Temple should be built, as a '*Holy of Holies.*' The passages of the Pentateuch[1] in which the anointing of the outward Temple is enjoined, lie at the foundation of the figurative representation. The outward anointing was a type of this. The anointing of a '*Holy of Holies*' stands in antithesis with the desolation of the sanctuary, and the destruction of the wing of abomination in the twenty-sixth and twenty-seventh verses. The former sanctuary is destroyed, because it has become a mere shell without a kernel; because, through the guilt of the people, that which made it the sanctuary, the presence of the Lord, has departed from it; a new sanctuary, without a covering and shell, a new dwelling-place of God on earth, is consecrated. What gives to this interpretation the advantage over that of the *person of the Messiah,* besides this double reference, is as follows:—(1.) Although it neither can, nor should be denied, that the representation of the Messiah under the image of the true Temple, is, in general, possible; still, it never occurs in the Old Testament; while the supposition, that the '*Holy of Holies*' signifies the *Church of the Lord,* has a multitude of analogies in its favour. (2.) By '*the anointing of the Messiah,*' nothing else could be understood, than the imparting of the gifts of the Spirit for the execution of his office, as it is described Is. 11. 1, and as it took place at his baptism. This, however, falls in the end of the sixty-ninth week. Its relation to the remaining blessings promised in this verse, is that of the cause to its effect, and it would, therefore, be very surprising, if it were mentioned co-ordinately with them, nay, even occupied the *last place* in the enumeration[2].

Verse 25

673. 'And thou shalt know and understand, from the going forth of the word to restore and to build Jerusalem, until an Anointed One, a Prince, are seven weeks, and two-and-sixty weeks. The street is restored and built, and it is firmly determined, and in times of distress.'

---

[1] Exod. 30. 22, sq.; 40. 9, sq.

[2] And the more so, as the ל repeated before each particular blessing, shows that they are not to be considered, in general, as being imparted *during the period* of the seventy weeks of years, but as existing in their full completion at the *close* of this period, while the anointing of the Messiah, as one particular action, not progressive, like the rest, would not reach this *terminus ad quem.* Nor is it an argument against this, that the sealing of sin also, &c., as effected by the death of the Messiah, would not reach this termination. Its *objective completion* falls, it is true, in the middle of the seventieth week of years; the *subjective,* however, (the imparting of the treasures of grace and forgiveness, procured by the Messiah) reaches its termination; as, in ver. 27, the confirmation of the covenant for many, is described as extending through the whole seventieth week. Even therewith, also, was the sealing of the vision first to be completed. For the prophets speak, throughout, not merely of the atonement as an objective transaction, but, at the same time, of the appropriation of the same by the covenant people.

' And thou shalt know and understand [1].'

674. About to impart to Daniel, by carrying on the picture which had only been sketched, a further disclosure concerning the future condition of his people, and thus to fulfil the design of his coming, announced in the twenty-seventh verse, (*'I am come to give thee insight,'*) Gabriel awakens attention by these introductory words, which *indirectly*, at the same time, contain an admonition to attend, as the promise to give insight presupposes, that this is not attainable by human power, and that things would be treated of, respecting which God only could make a disclosure. Finally, it is not to be overlooked, that *' Thou shalt know and understand'* expresses only the *design* of the teacher, and not the *capacity* of the scholar; that therefore the promise was only so far fulfilled as the latter allowed, and that, in the case of this prophecy also, there remained for Daniel no less darkness, than with respect to that, in the twelfth chapter, which the angel in the ninth verse describes, as *shut up* even for him.

' From the going forth of the word.'

675. That *' the going forth of the word'* means the *publication of the decree*, there can be no doubt [2]. The only question is, who must be regarded as the *author* of the *command?* By far the larger number of interpreters take a Persian king as such; we, however, assert, that a *going forth of the command* from God, or from the heavenly council, must be intended, and that for the following reasons :—1. It is in the highest degree unnatural, that the command of an earthly ruler should be here designated by *'word[3],'* without a single syllable being said of such a person in what precedes and follows, either directly or indirectly. Nothing is effected by an appeal to Dan. 2. 13, and Esth. 4. 3. For, in the first passage, he, from whom the command goes forth, as well as the command itself, is *mentioned* in the foregoing context, and in the second (*' in all places, where the word of the king and his command arrived'*), the meaning is rendered definite in the verse itself. He, from whom the word here goes forth, must rather be the same, through whom all the fortunes of the covenant people, predicted throughout the prophecy, are determined, who has cut off the seventy weeks over his people, from whom the

---

[1] וְתֵדַע וְתַשְׂכִּיל is not to be explained with most interpreters by, "mark well," but rather, as the Seventy (καὶ γνώσῃ καὶ διανοηθήσῃ) and Theodotion (καὶ γνώσῃ καὶ συνήσεις), the *fut.* must be taken in the sense of *fut.*; the Vulg. (*scito ergo et animadverte*) has led the way to the false interpretation, which takes it in the imperative. This mistake is refuted even by the form, which, only in exceptions which are seldom found, stands for the *imper.* and *optat* ; comp. Ewald, p. 527.

[2] מֹצָא דָבָר so (2. 13,) it is said of the *command* to slay the Magians, *' it has gone forth,'* by *word;* it occurs elsewhere also (e. g. 1 Sam. 15. 23; 17. 29; Esth. 4. 3.) in the sense of *command.*

[3] דָּבָר

decree of the ruins in the twenty-sixth verse, and the final sentence in the twenty-seventh verse, proceeds ; and the more so, since, at the end of the verse[1], he is expressly mentioned as the person, by whom the decree for the rebuilding of the city was formed. 2. The expression *'going forth of the word*[2] *'* is used in the twenty-third verse, of a *divine* decree; viz. that seventy weeks of years should be determined upon the people. Surely, no one could find it easy to suppose that here, where, because the discourse continues to relate to the transactions of Daniel with the heavenly messenger, the agent is expressed in a manner equally indefinite, another person is suddenly to be supplied as such.

676. But how can an *invisible* fact be placed as *terminus a quo,* since that must be perceptible by the senses, if the whole prophecy is not to be illusory, if it is to be possible, after the fulfilment, to be convinced of its truth by chronological calculation? We answer, with God the difference in point of time between word and deed ceases. Word and execution are one with him. He commands, and it stands there. He speaks, and it is done. The *terminus a quo,* therefore, is the time when the divine *command* began to be executed[3].

' To restore and to build Jerusalem[4].'

677. We may consider this, not merely as the *object* of the *command,* but as a first *terminus ad quem,* which serves at the same time as *terminus a quo* for the second : *'from the going forth of the word* (to restore Jerusalem), *until the restoration of Jerusalem,* (and from thence) *until an anointed One, a Prince.'* Then the first of the two following dates would designate the compass of the first period, from the command for the restoration of Jerusalem, till its execution. The second, the compass of the second, from the finishing of the restoration, until the anointed One. An entirely similar union of two *termini ad quem,* of which the first serves again as *terminus a quo* to the second, is found e. g. Jer. 31. 40[5], *' to the brook Kedron* (and from thence) *to the corner of the horse-gate.'* This interpretation is favoured even by the following twofold determination of time, which leads us to expect, that in the foregoing also, where this twofold period of time is determined as to its beginning and end, its

---

[1] וְחָרוּץ   [2] יָצָא דָבָר

[3] This coincidence of the word and deed is impressed even on the language. Thus the verb גָּעַר, which of itself can signify only the verbal rebuke, and used of men designates only that, occurs, in respect to God, also of the *real chastisement.* Thus צִוָּה, *to command,* includes in itself also the execution of the divine commands.

[4] We take both לְ in לְהָשִׁיב and עַד as a designation of the *term. ad quem.* The prepositions which of themselves designate a mere direction *whither,* are, in all languages, placed also where the motion proceeds until it *reaches* the object, without thereby losing their proper meaning. In Hebrew, such a use of לְ is so frequent, that it is scarcely worth the trouble to cite examples.

[5] עַד־נַחַל קִדְרוֹן עַד־פְּנַת שַׁעַר הַסּוּסִים

consisting of two parts would be mentioned [1]. The verb rendered 'to restore' [2] is here, as always, transitive : *to cause to return, to bring back.* ' To cause a city to return,' or ' to bring back a city,' designates its complete restoration to its former condition [3]. In this passage before us, the *restoration to the former condition* receives [4] especial limitation. ' *To bring back and to build,*' &c. 'bring back to build, or, building to bring back,' to build up the city again in its ancient circumference, the same which Jeremiah (33. 7.) expresses by the words ' to build as in the beginning [5].'

678. We gain from this the important result, that we must not seek the *terminus a quo* of the seventy weeks of years, in the time of the first *poor commencement of a rebuilding*, but rather in that, when, according to the testimony of history, a work was commenced, which promised to restore the city nearly to its ancient condition, with respect to its extent and the beauty of its edifices. This supposition, which is hereby alone fully established, receives further confirmation from the following arguments. (1.) " *Seventy weeks are determined upon thy people and thy holy city,*" seems to show, that both the city and the people will be *already in existence* at the beginning of the seventy weeks of years; and that consequently the first commencement of *any* rebuilding of the city cannot give the *terminus a quo.* (2.) In the prediction of the destruction, in the twenty-sixth as well as in the twenty-seventh verse, the Temple is mentioned together with the city. That it is not mentioned here, in the prediction of the rebuilding, that merely the building of the streets of the city is spoken of, presupposes that, at the commencement of the building here treated of, the sanctuary will have been already built; since we cannot suppose, that the angel would have omitted what was most important, and the very thing on account of which Daniel had chiefly mourned and had most earnestly prayed (comp. e. g. ver. 17—20); and, on the other hand, the existence of the Temple *necessarily implies*, that some rebuilding of the city must have already *commenced* [6].

---

[1] We need not object to this interpretation, that מִן־מֹצָא דָבָר would then stand too much apart. This is still more true of יָצָא דָבָר in ver. 23.

[2] הָשִׁיב.

[3] This is shown, among other passages, by Ezek. 16. 55.

[4] Through the subjoined לִבְנוֹת.

[5] The importance of the farther definition by הָשִׁיב, subjoined 'to build,' sufficiently appears from the fact, that before נִבְנְתָה, הָשׁוּב is afterwards repeated.

[6] Several interpreters take בָּנָה here in the sense, *to fortify*, and indeed בָּנָה עִיר often occurs in this sense, not as though the verb received a new meaning, but *ex materiâ subjectâ*, partly because the building, in the case of a city already in existence, is necessarily limited to its fortification, partly because the idea of a city, taken in its whole compass, *includes* its fortification. But that this meaning is not applicable here, sufficiently appears from what follows, '*streets are built,*' where the internal part of the city is precisely designated, as that which was to be built. This interpretation is owing merely to the wish to be able to place the *terminus a quo* in the time of Nehemiah, the gratification of which was expected from this false interpretation of לְהָשִׁיב and תָּשׁוּב.

' Until an Anointed One, a Prince[1].'

679. The prophet, in accordance with the uniform character of his prophecy, has chosen the more indefinite, instead of the more definite designation, and spoke only of *an* Anointed One, *a* Prince, instead of *the* Anointed One, *the* Prince, κατ᾽ ἐξοχήν, leaving his hearers to draw a deeper knowledge respecting him, from the prevailing expectations, grounded on earlier prophecies of a future great King, from the remaining declarations of the context, and from the fulfilment; the coincidence of which with the prophecy must here be the more obvious, since an accurate date had been given.

680. That the reference to Christ is so manifest as to force itself upon even the most prejudiced, appears from the following remarkable confession of Bertholdt: " That by these words[2] we should be led to think of the Messiah, Jesus, and at those in the twenty-sixth verse[3], of his crucifixion, though not absolutely necessary, is still very natural." We leave out of view for the present the confirmation which this reference receives from *the fulfilment*, and unfold only the grounds, which were accessible to Daniel himself, and his contemporaries, on a deeper investigation. (1.) The blessings predicted in the foregoing verse, the forgiveness of sin, the introduction of everlasting righteousness, &c., belong, as already mentioned, to the uniform characteristics of the Messianic time in the prophets. When now, in a representation which announces itself by 'thou wilt know and understand' as a further continuation of the contents of the twenty-fourth verse, the discourse relates to an exalted King, who should make his appearance after sixty-nine weeks of years, and therefore shortly before the time in which the finished conferring of these blessings upon the covenant people was placed, how could it be thought otherwise, than that this King should be the author of these blessings, the Messiah, announced as such by all the prophets[4]? (2.) As ' Prince' does not exclude the reference to the

[1] Several recent interpreters explain, 'until *an*, or, until *the* Anointed Prince.' But מָשִׁיחַ cannot be regarded as an adjective, belonging to נָגִיד, because the adjective in Hebrew is placed after the substantive. This rule is entirely without exception. That *Appellatives*, when they pass over into *proper names*, gradually lose the article, because the individual thereby designated as the only one of his kind needs not to be distinguished from others, is well known. This, at a later period, has occurred, in reference to מָשִׁיחַ; e. g. John 4. 25, where the Samaritan woman says, " I know ὅτι Μεσσίας (not ὁ Μεσσίας) ἔρχεται, ὁ λεγόμενος Χριστός." But this interpretation however just if מָשִׁיחַ stood alone, appears as untenable, if we consider the subjoined נָגִיד. For as this word cannot *also* be regarded as a *proper name*, as it occurs (ver. 26,) as a designation of the heathen prince, so, if this interpretation were correct, it must have the article, *the* Messiah, *the* Prince, as e. g. we cannot say דָוִד מֶלֶךְ, but only דָוִד הַמֶּלֶךְ.

[2] מָשִׁיחַ נָגִיד   [3] יכרת משיח ואין לו

[4] Add (3.) That this connexion between the person and the imparting of the blessings, is farther especially indicated by the relation of the designation of the person as מָשִׁיחַ to the phrase לִמְשֹׁחַ קֹדֶשׁ קָדָשִׁים. " By the Anointed One shall a holy of holies be anointed." Precisely in order, to make this reference prominent, is לִמְשֹׁחַ קֹדֶשׁ קָדָשִׁים placed at the end, and מָשִׁיחַ before נָגִיד.

Messiah, as it occurs of him Is. 55. 4. (comp. *in loco*,) so does Messiah (Anointed), which here relates to 'Prince' as the special to the general, notwithstanding its indefiniteness decidedly point to him [1]. It serves more closely to designate 'Prince' as a *Theocratic* ruler, just as 1 Sam. 10. 1, ('*And Samuel took the oil vessel, and poured it upon his (Saul's) head and kissed him, and said, Of a truth the Lord hath anointed thee, as a prince over his inheritance,*') the anointing makes Saul not a ruler in general, but a *Theocratic* ruler, who, as God's representative, is furnished by him with the gifts necessary for his office. The assertion is entirely false, that every heathen king also could bear the name (Messiah) *Anointed*. It is refuted, as well by the already established import of the symbol, and figure of anointing, as by the usage of the language. In all the books of the Old Testament, only one single heathen king (Cyrus, in Is. 45. 1,) is called Anointed, and he not *qua* a king, but on account of the remarkable relation (of which there is no other example in history), in which he stood to the theocracy, the rich gifts with which God endowed him for its benefit, the commencement of the true knowledge of God enjoyed by him, as exhibited in his edict in the book of Ezra, and the *typical relation*, which he sustained to the author of the higher deliverance, the Messiah. Cyrus might, in a measure, be regarded as a Theocratic prince, and as such he is represented in Isaiah [2]. (3.) The context furnishes us with still another proof, besides that which lies in the word itself, that not a heathen, but a *Theocratic* king is intended. This is found in the manifest antithesis between '*an Anointed One, a Prince*,' and '*the Prince that should come*' in the twenty-sixth verse. The general term Prince is common to both designations. In opposition to 'an Anointed One,' as a special characteristic of the Theocratic king, stands '*he who comes*,' *advena*, as a designation of the heathen prince. If then it is established, that by '*an Anointed One, a Prince*' only a Theocratic king can be designated, who else can he be than the Messiah, since the whole time after Daniel affords no other subject ; since he is the only Theocratic king, whom the prophets living at the time of the exile and afterwards have predicted as future ; and since, e. g., Ezekiel (21. 32) expressly says, that the insignia of the regal dignity should be taken away from Israel, until the appearance of the great object of promise ?

681. If, then, by '*an Anointed One, a Prince*,' Christ must be understood, the question still arises, whether his *birth*, or the time when he was consecrated as Messiah by *the anointing* from above, is to be regarded as the *terminus ad quem*. The latter is the usual supposition of the Messianic interpreters, and may be established by an irrefragable proof. After the course of seventy weeks shall the whole work of salvation, to be performed by the Messiah, be completed ; after sixty-nine weeks, and (as it appears from the more accurate determination in the twenty-seventh verse), in *the middle* of the seventieth, he shall be cut off. As now, according to the

---

[1] Like the corresponding שַׂר, Is. 9. 6, מֹשֵׁל, Mic. 5. 1, and נָשִׂיא, Ezek. 34. 24.

[2] Comp. the striking remarks of Vitringa on Is. l. c.

passage before us, sixty-nine weeks shall elapse before the Messiah, there remains from that event only a period of seven to the completion of salvation, and, until his violent death, one of three years and a half; a certain proof, that *until Messiah* must refer, not to his birth, but to the appearance of the Messiah *as such*, (comp. Peter, Acts 1. 21; Luke 3. 23,) who, indeed, before his baptism was not yet the Messiah,—only Jesus, not the Christ.

'*Are seven weeks and threescore and two weeks.*'

682. The prophet in what precedes, 'from the going forth of the word for the rebuilding of Jerusalem, until an Anointed One, a Prince,' had given an extreme *terminus ad quem*, the appearing of the Anointed One, and a *terminus medius*, forming a subdivision of this period, the restoration of Jerusalem. Accordingly he here designates the whole distance, '*from the going forth of the word, until the Anointed One,*' by a twofold determination of time. Sixty-nine weeks in all, shall elapse. Seven until the completed restoration of the city, sixty-two from that time until the Anointed One, the Prince.

683. No man can deny to this interpretation [1] the advantage of being easy and unforced. No one has ever been able to bring an objection against it; and this will be the more difficult hereafter, since, according to our interpretation of the words, '*from the going forth,*' &c. the twofold division of the period is already contained in these words, and, therefore, a twofold determination of the time must naturally be expected [2].

---

[1] As Theodotion has it, ἕως Χριστοῦ ἡγουμένου ἑβδομάδες ἑπτά, καὶ ἑβδομάδες ἑξήκοντα δύο, and also the Vulg., "*usque ad Christum ducem hebdomades septem et hebdomades 62 erunt*," while the text of the Seventy lies here in total confusion, and therefore cannot be used.

[2] The only plausible objection against our interpretation, is the Athnach under שִׁבְעָה, which proves (according to Marsham), that the two periods must be *separated*, and the *latter* referred to what follows: "*ab exitu verbi usque ad Messiam ducem sunt hebdom. VII. Et hebdomadis 62 ædificabitur platea et fossa.*" But the proposition, which lies at the foundation of this assertion, that the Athnach must always stand in the verse, where *we* place a full stop, is false. It not unfrequently stands (if the place of the full stop is manifest of itself) in members of a sentence, which we distinguish by a lesser stop, to prevent portions that should be separated from being taken together. Thus it stands, e. g. in ver. 2, under הַסְּפָרִים, instead of הַשָּׁנִים, according to the common usage; so, Ps. 36. 8, under אָדָם, instead of אֱלֹהִים, comp. Ps. 84. 3. Prov. 6. 26. Here, however, the separation of the two periods was of greater importance, in order to indicate that the seven and the sixty-two weeks were not a mere arbitrary division of one whole period, but that its own characteristic mark belongs to each of the two. Professor Hengstenberg proves that the words וְשָׁבֻעִים שִׁשִּׁים וּשְׁנַיִם cannot mean *within* sixty-two weeks. Ch. B. Michaelis, although faithful to the Messianic interpretation, has been led by this false view of the Athnach (which is overthrown in the note) to connect the sixty-two weeks immediately with what follows: "until the Messiah are seven weeks, and in two and sixty weeks will the city be rebuilt; and that in the time of distress." Professor Hengstenberg combats this in the original work with great ability.

' *Street is restored and built* [1].'

684. Street stands in the singular, and without the article, to designate the object according to its widest extent.

'*And firmly is it determined, and in a time of distress* [2].'

685. '*It is firmly determined,*' and the '*in a time of distress*' obviate every temptation, which could disquiet the pious Israelites. Present appearances afforded but a small prospect of a return, and much less of a restoration of the city to its ancient extent. After the return actually took place, a whole series of years elapsed in which the circumstances gave no hope of the restoration of the city, instead of which the Jews were obliged to content themselves with an open place of comparatively small compass. What more natural than the supposition, that the promise of the Lord, having been only conditional, had been rendered inoperative by the sins of the people? This opinion the prophet guards against by the consoling '*it is firmly determined.*' Another temptation must arise from the fact, that even when this promise was already fulfilled, the circumstances of the people were any thing but prosperous. Hence, doubts of the Omnipotence of God might easily arise, as we see them, e. g., so strongly exhibited in the discourses of the ungodly in Malachi. In opposition to this temptation, the '*and in a time of distress*' afforded the proof that the time of distress would not take place without the knowledge and will of God; that it was not something forced upon Him by another, but foreseen and predestinated by Himself [3].

Verse 26

686. ' And after the sixty-two weeks, shall be exterminated an Anointed One, and there is not to him——, and a people of a Prince which is to come shall lay waste the city and the sanctuary, and it will end in the flood, and until the end is war, a decree of ruins.'

---

[1] רְחוֹב

[2] וְחָרוּץ can mean nothing else than, " it is cut off," " firmly decreed," and must therefore be separated from what precedes. The sense of the root חָרַץ has been admirably developed by Schultens, on Prov. 22. 5. The ground meaning is that of *præcidere, decidere ;* from this is derived that of accurate, precise determination and decision. In the latter it occurs e. g. 1 Kings 20. 40. Job 14. 5. Is. 10. 23.

[3] Only *one* difficulty rests upon this interpretation; that it apparently makes, ' in distress of the times,' stand for, 'in *an unprosperous time will this decree be executed.*' This very harsh brevity, which we are obliged to assume, as long as we refer חָרוּץ to a decree of God *already formed*, is, however, avoided, as soon as we assume that the decree is here only *predicted*, and is not made until the beginning of its execution. This interpretation, philologically necessary, according to which the decree itself falls ' in the times of distress,' not it *is* determined, but it *becomes* determined, serves also, at the same time, to confirm our understanding of מִן מֹצָא דָבָר, which accurately corresponds to חָרוּץ

' *And after the sixty-two weeks will an Anointed One be cut off* [1].'

687. ' *An Anointed One* [2],' in accordance with the whole character of the prophecy, is intentionally left indefinite, with no article to indicate his identity with the ' *Messiah a Prince.*' It was the less necessary to point out this identity, because the careful and unprejudiced reader might easily determine this from the context. As *an Anointed One* of itself implied a king of *Israel;* as this designation was made still clearer by its being opposed to a Prince *who was to come ;* so the reader would necessarily be led at once to think of *the* Messiah, because prophecy knows no other *king of Israel* after the exile. At the end of the sixty-nine weeks should the ' *Messiah a Prince* ' appear. Who but *this Messiah* could well be thought of, when here, in the further prosecution of the subject, the violent death of *an Anointed One* is announced, to take place after the completion of the seven and the sixty-two weeks ? The death of the Anointed One is placed in the verse before us in a causal connexion with the desolation of the city and the Temple, in like manner as, in the twenty-fifth verse, is his appearance with the imparting of all the blessings which had been promised in the twenty-fourth verse. How could one fail to perceive, that cursing and blessing, as they fall in the same period, belong also to the same author, that the former was the consequence of the violent slaying, here predicted of the same Anointed one, who should bestow the fulness of the blessing, and has actually bestowed it, upon those who have received him, and allowed themselves, through him, to confirm the covenant? And indeed the more so, since the violent death of the Messiah had already, before the time of Daniel, been predicted by Isaiah, in the fifty-third chapter, where (in the eighth verse) the entirely corresponding expression occurs, ' he has been cut off from the land of the living,' and after him, by Zech. 12. 10. After the fulfilment, all uncertainty is perfectly inexcusable, since the calculation of the years might readily remove it.

' *And* [there] *is not to him.*'—

688. It is certain [3], that the words are not complete in themselves, and that something must be *supplied.* This must be taken only from what immediately precedes, and all interpretations, in which this is not done, are entirely capricious, and cannot receive our con-

---

[1] נִכְרַת, without a further addition like that in the frequent phrases נִכְרַת מֵעַמּוֹ, or מֵעֲדַת יִשְׂרָאֵל, &c. designates, without exception, a violent mode of death. Thus, Zech. 13. 8, 9, it stands opposed to גוע as a designation of death by the sword, while the latter imports that by hunger and pestilence ; comp. 1 Kings 11. 6. Thus is it the standing expression for the ruin of the ungodly, comp., e. g., Ps. 37. 9. Prov. 2. 22, which, in order to render a supernatural cause more manifest, is constantly represented as violent and sudden.

[2] מָשִׁיחַ   [3] As H. *proves* in the original.

currence. That which is wanting must be something which belongs
to the Anointed, as such. As 'he will be cut off' expresses the
extinction of his personal existence, so must 'and is not to him'
express the extinction of his possession, and that not an accidental
one, but that which constitutes his essential characteristic. What
this is, in respect to an Anointed One, a Prince, cannot in itself be
doubtful, and appears plainly enough from Ezek. 21. 32 ; 'until He
comes, to whom the judgement (the dominion) is, and I give it to
him.' That the *dominion* is to him, is here the characteristic of the
Messiah, as King. 1 Sam. 10. 1 ; Samuel says to Saul, 'The Lord
has anointed thee over his inheritance for a Prince.' The characteristic mark of an anointed one was, therefore, to be a Prince
over God's inheritance, over Israel. This mark vanished, the
dominion of the Anointed over his people was destroyed, when by
their crime he was violently put to death. As to the sense, therefore, the Vulgate is entirely correct : ' *Et non erit ejus populus, qui
eum negaturus est.*' And Jahn errs only in supplying the unnatural [1]
people. The correctness of the above interpretation is strikingly
confirmed by what follows. With the *negative* consequence of the
cutting off of the Messiah (the cessation of his dominion over the covenant people), the *positive* consequence (the desolation of the city and
sanctuary by the people of a prince who should come) is well connected ; just as in the eleventh chapter of Zechariah, after the Messiah, hindered in the execution of the pastoral office by the resistance of the people, has relinquished it and broken his shepherd's
staff, the poor flock is given up without rescue to the greatest misery,
and the whole land is overflowed with enemies, who have hitherto
been restrained only by the visible power of the good Shepherd and
King.

*'And people of a Prince, who comes, will lay waste the city
and the sanctuary.'*

689. The ' *Prince who comes,*' is not the same as the ' *Messiah
a Prince,*' but rather a *heathen*, and, as the result showed, a *Roman*
Prince, and by ' *people,*' (not as it is commonly translated, ' *the*
people,') his host is designated [2].

' And it will end in the flood.'

690. The flood is a figurative designation of the warlike expedi-

---

[1] עַם

[2] See the original for the critical proofs of the correctness of this assertion.
Several interpreters translate ' *people of a Prince, that come.*' But this interpretation is refuted by the circumstance, that הַבָּא is plainly designed to distinguish
the person of a certain prince, from that of another. In respect to the people,
such a distinction, which the article in הַבָּא shows to have been intended, would
be entirely inadmissible, since in the whole prophecy (the omission of the article
shows that עַם has the sense, *people*, according to the connexion, *warriors*,) there
is nothing said of a domestic host.

tion *inundating* the land, which had been spoken of immediately before, and the sense is, "*the desolation of city and Temple*" will not be merely partial or transient, but be completed during this same expedition, which may be compared to a great inundation. This explanation is confirmed by the usage of Daniel elsewhere, in which warlike expeditions are compared to a flood [1].

691. It now appears still more clearly, how inadmissible it is, to refer these words to the heathen prince (as if *his* end were predicted), and especially as the recent interpreters suppose, to Antiochus Epiphanes. For, did *he* meet his end in the same expedition, in which he laid waste the city and Temple? The force of this argument appears from the circumstance, that even such interpreters as Hitzig, who have made the grammatical interpretation their chief object, and who, therefore, can scarcely be supposed to have committed an oversight, have felt compelled to disregard the article. He remarks, l. c. p. 150; "He (Ant. Epiph.) found an end in *a* military expedition, for which *flood* [2] is figuratively used." There is rather here a plain *antithesis* with the oppression by Antiochus Epiphanes. Of this Daniel never prophesies, without at the same time announcing its end [3].

'*And unto the end is war, a decree of ruins.*'

692. The sense is, "the war, and the decree of ruins, will terminate only with the end of the object." It is not a *transient* hostile oppression, which is here treated of (like that, e. g., in the time of Antiochus Epiphanes), but such a one as would cause utter destruction to the city and the Temple. Remarkable is the reference in which these last words stand to the close of the twenty-fifth verse [4]. By an irrevocable decree of God, will the city, now lying in ruins, be rebuilt; by an equally irrevocable decree, will it again sink in ruins.

Verse 27

693. '*And one week will confirm a covenant with many, and the half of the week will cause sacrifice and meat-offering to cease, and over the summit of abomination comes the destroyer, and that, till what is completed and cut off shall drop-down over the desolated [one].*'

---

[1] Thus 11. 12. 26.   [2] שֶׁטֶף

[3] Chap. 11. 36, it is said of him; 'And he is prosperous, *until* the anger is completed.' This oppression, therefore, is not עַד־עֵת (11. 25); it first reaches its end with the end of its object. This is here expressly asserted, and appears also from the fact, that the prophecy closes with the threatening of the entire ruin of the city and Temple, excluding a mere partial desolation by the expression itself, and containing not the smallest allusion to a restoration.

[4] Indicated by the use of the verb חָרַץ in both passages.

'*And one week will confirm the covenant with many.*'

694. We have here an instance of the frequent idiom, according to which, a *place* or *space of time* is said to *do* what really *is done* in it. Thus Ps. 65. 4; '*The* hills *exult, the* valleys *rejoice.*' Mal. 3. 19; '*The* day that cometh *shall burn them up.*' Job 3. 3; '*The* night *which said, A man is conceived.*' Ver. 10, where the *night* is cursed, '*because* it shut not up *the doors of the womb.*' 30. 17; '*The* night *pierces my bones.*'

695. Some interpreters (lastly Scholl, l. c. p. 20, 24,) maintain, that the " one week " is not to be so connected with the preceding sixty-nine, as though it immediately belonged to them, that the discourse is only of 'some one week,' which must not indeed be very far removed from the remaining sixty-nine. This " *one week* " is (we are told) that, at the end of which the destruction of Jerusalem falls. But it is easy to see, that this supposition did not spring from an impartial investigation of the text, but from a difficulty arising from a comparison of the prophecy and fulfilment. Precisely seventy weeks in all are to elapse : how, then, without the most unrestrained caprice, can we assume a *not inconsiderable intermediate period* between the sixty-nine and the one, which, together, plainly make up these seventy ? Who that proceeds in such an arbitrary manner, can still continue to lay any stress on the chronological proof of the agreement of prophecy and fulfilment ? Whoever takes to himself this liberty must also grant it, and can make no objection if another chooses, e. g., to insert between the seven and the sixty-two, a dozen intercalary weeks. What, however, especially refutes this supposition, is, that in the week which it assumes it cannot point out the *characteristic mark* of this last week, *the confirmation of the covenant.* For in the time of the Roman invasion, where were those mighty demonstrations of mercy, which were such a confirmation of the covenant, as to render it proper to give prominence to them alone, and pass over in silence those, which belonged to the actual seventieth week, as well as the week itself ? The advocates of this interpretation would gladly free themselves from this objection, by regarding the *one week* to which the confirmation belongs, as the actual seventieth, and only the following half week as lying *without* the cycle of the seventieth, and embracing the time of the Jewish war. But here a fatal objection intervenes; the article in '*the week*[1],' which does not allow us to think of the half of *any week*, but only of the definite week before-mentioned.

696. This false view has been occasioned by the opinion, that the destruction of Jerusalem by the Romans must necessarily be drawn within the circle of the chronological determinations of the prophecy; an opinion, which led the sagacious Scaliger to the most forced assumptions, whereas Vitringa adopts the sound canon, "*that these weeks end in the three years, which immediately preceded the death*

1 הַשָּׁבוּעַ ·

of Jesus Christ ; which death of Jesus Christ was to happen in the middle of the last week, after seven weeks and sixty-two weeks had already elapsed." That this opinion is entirely destitute of support, we shall see when we come to explain " the half of the week will cause sacrifice and meat-offering to cease."

697. Nothing whatever is said, as to whether the covenant is *one already existing*, or one *entirely new*. The indefiniteness belongs, indeed, only to the *expression*. As to the *fact*, the ' *confirming the covenant*[1] ' stands contrasted with the quality of the previous covenant, which, because not confirmed by such illustrious manifestations of the divine mercy as now appear, must be considered as weaker than that now to be confirmed, which rests on the forgiveness of sins, the imparting of the everlasting righteousness, and the anointing of a Holy of Holies. Finally, throughout the whole book[2], ' *covenant*' occurs only of the covenant of God with Israel, which is of itself sufficient to refute, what is liable to so many objections, the explanation of Bertholdt, of a covenant which Antiochus Epiphanes had made with apostates from among the covenant people.

698. It is really ' *the many.*' The article shows that the discourse is not concerning many in general, but definitely concerning those, who were manifest to the reader, from the circumstances of the discourse, as definite in their kind (comp. Ewald, p. 567). Such a definiteness, however, can be derived only from the twenty-fourth verse. The imparting of all the blessings, which the prophet there promises, he here embraces in one comprehensive expression, " to confirm a covenant ;" and that he does this, he shows by representing the objects of the confirmation, as those, who do not here first come forward, but are already known from what precedes, and who were the objects of the former gracious promises.

699. That here, as in the twenty-fourth chapter, that only is spoken of, which the Messiah should vouchsafe to *the believers* from among the Jews, is evident from the occasion of the prophecy. Daniel was moved to make intercession, by their concern, lest the Lord would entirely reject Israel, on account of their sins. What, therefore, was more natural, than that the divine answer should embrace only what was suited to remove this concern ?

' *And the half of the week will abolish sacrifice and meat-offering.*'

700. That the confirmation of the covenant extends throughout the whole week, in the midst of which the sacrificial service ceases, shows that this must be, for *believers*, not a distressing, but a joyful result ; its standing in connexion with the destruction of the Temple, predicted immediately after, proves that, *in respect to the unbelieving part of the people*, it is to be considered as a judgement. If now we inquire for the cause of this cessation of the sacrificial service, we

---

[1] Far more emphatic than הֵקִים בְּרִית   [2] בְּרִית

find it to be the death of the Messiah.   That the expression, 'after the sixty-two weeks,' (that is, reckoning from the going forth of the word, after the sixty-ninth[1],) must not be understood, as though the Messiah should be cut off at the very *commencement* of the seventieth week, is evident from the fact, that otherwise his *appearance* (comp. ver. 25, 'from the going forth of the word .... until the Messiah, are sixty-nine weeks,') and his death would *coincide;* and that we must not go *beyond* the *middle* of the seventieth week, in which the abolition of the sacrificial service is placed, is plain, from the words, 'after sixty-nine weeks.'

701. But how far was the *sacrificial service abolished* by the death of Christ? This question, so far as this abolition is to be considered as a blessing, is easily answered.   The Levitical service, as weak and unprofitable, (Heb. 7. 18,) was done away, when, by the death of Christ, the true forgiveness of sin had been obtained ; the everlasting righteousness brought in ; and, instead of the ancient visible Temple, a new spiritual Holy of Holies anointed.   The shadow vanished before the substance, the type before the antitype.   The sacrificial service was an attestation by God himself, of his covenant with Israel[2].   As *this covenant was abolished* by the murder of his Son, so also at the same time was the sacrificial service abolished, *as to its substance* (which rested on its being introduced and approved by God), and it was of no importance, if the cessation of sacrifices, *as outward actions,* did not follow till some time afterwards—this *actual cessation* being only an *outward declaration* of the decree already passed at the moment of the death of Christ.   It served only to take visibly from Israel, what they no longer possessed, except in imagination. Just so the destruction of city and Temple by the Romans was only the *outward manifestation* of what, in fact, already existed. The moment the death of Christ took place, Jerusalem was no longer the holy city, the Temple no longer a house of God, but an abomination.   Hence, in reference to all the three objects in the prophecy, what is made prominent and chronologically designated, is only *that* in which all that followed was already included, and from which it was afterwards developed.   An exactly similar mode of representation occurs in Zech. 11, where the madness of internal dissension and the desolation of city and land by outward enemies, are placed in immediate connexion with the rejection of the Messiah, and the relinquishment of his pastoral office.   The supernatural agency, which had hitherto guarded both, *ceased* with this event ; and it was of little consequence *how much* or *how little* time the natural causes, which accomplished both, required for their development.

702. It is a very just remark of Theodoret, that what is here predicted as a *consequence of the death of Christ,* was *symbolised,* at the moment of its taking place, by the rending of the veil of the Temple.

---

[1] Ver. 26.   [2] Comp. on Zech. 9. 11.

' And over the summit of abomination comes the destroyer.'

703. Literally, *' over summit of abomination comes destroyer.'* We take *wing*[1], as a figurative designation of the *summit*. In respect to *abomination*[2] we do not exclude the special reference to idols, partly because this reference is the usual one (it is wanting, perhaps, only in Nah. 3. 6), partly on account of several passages hereafter to be cited from older writers, which seem to serve as the ground-work of this, and in which this reference prevails. The *' wing of abomination,'* in our view, is *the summit of the Temple*, so desecrated by abomination, as no longer to deserve the name of the *Temple of the Lord*, but that of the *temple of idols*. We find, in this desig-nation, the reason why the ruin here predicted comes upon the Temple[3].

704. That the destroyer should *be* or *come* over the summit of the Temple, we regard as a designation of its utter ruin, inasmuch as the *seizure of the highest part* presupposes the possession *of all the rest;* a stronghold, e. g., is completely taken, when the enemy has mastered its highest battlements.

705. In favour of our interpretation, the philological correctness of which no one will venture to doubt, and the characteristic mark of which is, that it makes the *destruction* of the Temple to be occa-sioned by a *profanation* of it caused by the covenant people them-selves, we offer the following positive arguments.

706. (1) This interpretation admirably coincides with the whole remaining contents of the prophecy. The ancient Temple is de-scribed as converted, by the unbelief of the people and the murder of the Messiah, from a house of God into a house of abomination, which must be destroyed; and it is contrasted with a new real Temple, a Holy of Holies, which, according to the twenty-fourth verse, should be anointed at the end of the seventy weeks. To the cessation of sacri-fices which are sacrifices no longer, corresponds the destruction of the Temple, which is no longer a temple, a dwelling-place of the true God.

707. (2) The destruction of the second Temple stands in the closest relation to that of the first. How both, to the exclusion of all accident, were solely an effect of the penal justice of God, who avenged the apostasy of his people and the desecration of his sanc-tuary, he has made known in a way which should open the eyes of the most blind, and show him that the Theocracy was not an illu-sion, but a reality. The second destruction happened on precisely

---

[1] כְּנַף, Thus the *wings* of a garment, for its *ends;* the *wings* of the earth, Is. 11. 12, for its *extremities;* in the New Testament, πτερύγιον τοῦ ἱεροῦ, Matt. 4. 5. Luke 4. 9, spoken of the *summit*, not, as some suppose, *of a wing*, but of the Temple itself; so Fritzsche.   [2] שִׁקּוּצִים

[3] We take מְשֹׁמֵם in the sense *destroyer*. Relying on the usual meaning of *Poel*, on chap. 11. 31, where the *part.* מְשֹׁמֵם undeniably occurs in this sense, on the manifest antithesis between מְשֹׁמֵם and שׁוֹמֵם, the latter of which, unless all philological investigation is to be contemned, can mean nothing else than the *destroyed.*

the same day as the first. "Now," says Josephus[1], (after relating how Titus had determined to spare the Temple, a determination, which was rendered nugatory by the previous divine decree) "the fated period of time was arrived, on the tenth day of the month Loüs, on which, as now, it was burnt down by the king of Babylon." Surely it requires a strong degree of false belief, and of genuine unbelief, to suppose that chance should have so skilfully discovered the only prize among three hundred and sixty-four blanks! If, however, it were *not* chance, what a seal has the hand of God impressed on the book of his revelations!—The connexion of the two events affords no small argument for the true interpretation of a passage, which predicts the latter, when, according to it, cause and effect appear in the same relation as in the predictions of the former destruction; and the more so, since Daniel himself was a witness of this relation, and, converting the writings of the older prophets into flesh and blood, had by his study of them been excited to the intercession, which occasioned the prophecy before us. We now proceed to a consideration of these passages[2]. ' *Manasseh did evil in the sight of the Lord, after the abominations of the heathen, whom the Lord had cast out before the children of Israel;—and built altars in the Temple of the Lord,—and he placed the image of Ascherath which he had made, in the Temple.—And the Lord spake by his servants the prophets, Because Manasseh has done these abominations,—and has made Judah also to sin with his idols,—therefore, thus saith the Lord,—Behold I bring evil upon Jerusalem and Judah, and I stretch over Jerusalem the line of Samaria,—and I destroy the remnant of mine inheritance, and deliver them into the hand of their enemies,—because they have done evil in my sight.' ' They* placed their abominations *in the house which is called by my name in order to pollute it.—Is then this house, which I called by my name, become a den of thieves in your eyes?—Therefore will I do unto the house which is called by my name, wherein ye trust, and to the place, which I have given to you and your fathers, as I have done to Shiloh[3].' ' Wherefore, as I live, saith the Lord God[4], surely because thou hast defiled my sanctuary with all thy detestable things, and with all thine abominations[5], therefore will I also take away, neither shall mine eye spare, neither will I have any pity.' ' I recompense thee[6] for all thine abominations—I will recompense thee according to thy ways, and thine abominations shall be in the midst of thee.'* Ver. 20; ' *And his beautiful ornament he hath changed into haughtiness, and the images of their abominations they made for detestable things therein, therefore do I give it to them for impurity, and I give it (their ornament) into the hand of the strangers for a prey, and to the ungodly for a spoil, and they pollute it.'* Ver. 22; ' *My face will I turn also from them and they (the enemy) pollute my secret place (the Holy of Holies), and the evil doers enter therein, and defile it.'* Ver. 20; ' *I give it them for impurity (the sanctuary, which they have polluted,*

---

[1] *De Bello Jud.* 6. 4, 5, p. 385. Haverc.   [2] 2 Kings 21. 2, &c.
[3] Jer. 7.   [4] Ezek. 5. 11.   [5] בְּכָל־שִׁקּוּצַיִךְ וּבְכָל־תוֹעֲבֹתָיִךְ
[6] Ezek. 7. 8, 9.

shall serve them for impurity instead of sanctification); the parallel passage, 24. 11, ' *Behold, I desecrate my sanctuary, my splendid orna-ment, the desire of your eyes, the food of your souls;*' comp. Jer. 7. 4. Is. 66. 3, 4. Now to these prophecies that of Daniel stands in the same relation, which we have already pointed out between Zechariah, in the eleventh chapter, and the two prophecies of Jere-miah.

708. (3) ' *Where the carcase is, there the eagles collect.*' This declaration of our Lord's discloses to us the cause of all the desola-tions which have passed, and will still pass over his church, under the old and the new covenant. This connexion between the *where* and the *there* is also found in the case of the oppression by Antiochus Epiphanes; and if an attentive consideration of the passages relating to that oppression shows us that in *that* instance Daniel not only recognized this relation of cause and effect, but brought it pro-minently forward; if we perceive that he expressly represented the desecration of the Temple by the heathen as a consequence of one which had proceeded from the covenant people themselves; we are the more inclined to assume, that here also he directs our attention to the repetition of this fundamental law. These passages are the following : Chap. 11. 31, it is said, ' *And arms (brachia) will arise out of him, and pollute the sanctuary, the strong place, and take away that which is con-stant, and give* the abomination[1] *as one that lays waste.*' This passage is the more important, since it even has characteristic expressions in common with the one before us, which implies an internal relation-ship between the two. In the expressions, ' *they take away,*' and ' *that which is constant,*' there is a manifest antithesis. They take away, that which *should not* be interrupted for a moment, every sign of the worship and dominion of the Lord. Most interpreters erroneously refer this exclusively to the daily sacrifices. The word as it stands here[2], never occurs of one particular object, but with the adjuncts, not only of the daily sacrifice, but also of the *fire of the altar*, of the *sacrificial lamps*, of the *show-bread*, &c. They *give* is opposed to they *take away*. They put it in its place. By *the abomination*, is designated *idolatry* in its whole compass and extent. They *give* this as a *destructive* thing, because their conduct brings destruction, as a righteous punishment, exactly corresponding to, ' *they desecrate the sanctuary, the strong-hold.*' *Because* they have polluted that which hitherto afforded them a sure protection, the Temple, so are they henceforth by a righteous retribution given up as a defenceless prey to their enemies. A contrast to the giving of the abomina-tion as a thing *that destroys*, as of the terminus *a quo* of the oppression, is formed by the giving of the abomination as a thing *that is destroyed*, (its destruction to be effected by God,) as the *ter-minus ad quem*. According to this interpretation, therefore, this passage entirely coincides with the one before us, according to the explanation we have given. Both make the *abomination* one "*which draws after it the train of devastation, as sin draws after it punish-*

[1] הַשִּׁקּוּץ   [2] תָּמִיד

ment. The abominations are considered as the antecedent sin, which, by means of the supervening destroyer, is avenged by the righteous judgement of God[1]*."* In favour of our interpretation of both passages, the historical fulfilment gives a remarkable testimony. In all the three sources of the history of the oppressions by Antiochus Epiphanes, they are uniformly designated as a *consequence of the abomination proceeding from the covenant people themselves;* as a righteous retribution. The *Jews,* and *not the heathen,* appear as the proper authors of the desecration of the Temple. We the more readily produce some passages, since they serve at the same time to exhibit clearly the general mode of God's proceeding in this respect, as it lies at the foundation of prophecy and its fulfilment, and therefore constitute a testimony in favour of our interpretation, entirely independent of the passages of Daniel. The apostate members of the covenant people were the cause of the suffering, not only so far as they first caused Antiochus to intermeddle with the affairs of the covenant people (comp. 1 Macc. 1. 11), but also in the higher point of view, inasmuch as they hastened the divine vengeance by their crimes; comp. 2 Macc. 4. 15, sq. '*Not setting by the honours of their fathers, but liking the glory of the Grecians best of all. By reason thereof sore calamity came upon them: for they had them to be their enemies and avengers, whose custom they followed so earnestly, and unto whom they desired to be like in all things. For it is not a light thing to do wickedly against the laws of God: but the time following shall declare these things.*' Through them the city lost its prosperity, which the Lord had formerly secured to it, while a better disposition yet prevailed; comp. 3. 1, 2. '*Now when the holy city was inhabited with all peace, and the laws were kept very well, because of the godliness of Onias the high priest, and his hatred of wickedness, it came to pass that even the kings themselves did honour the place, and magnify the temple with their best gifts.*' The apostates were, mediately, the only cause of that desecration of the sanctuary in which they actually assisted; comp. 1 Macc. 1. 34, sq.: The Syrians built a castle, and '*they put therein a sinful nation, wicked men, and fortified themselves therein.*' That here by the sinful people and the transgressors of the law, apostate members of the covenant people are designated, appears partly from the words themselves, partly from Josephus[2]; Ver. 36, 37: '*For it was a place to lie in wait against the sanctuary, and an evil adversary to Israel. Thus they shed innocent blood on every side of the sanctuary, and defiled it.*' Even the setting up of '*the abomination of desolation,*' the abomination which brought desolation after it, the heathenish altar, was effected by the aid of these apostates; comp. ver. 52, 53, 54, sq.: '*Then many of the people were gathered unto them, to wit, every one that forsook the law; and so they committed evils in the land; and drove the Israelites into secret places, even wheresoever they could flee for succour. Now the fifteenth day of the month Casleu, in the hundred forty and fifth year, they set up the abomination of desolation upon*

---

[1] Lampe. [2] *Archæol.* 12. 5. 4.

*the altar, and builded idol altars throughout the cities of Juda on
every side.'* And on account of all these crimes, the wrath of God
fell upon Israel; comp. ver. 64: '*And there was very great wrath
upon Israel.*' As the gates of Jerusalem were opened to Antiochus
by the apostates [1], so when, with impious hand, he defiled the sanctuary, he was guided by Menelaus (2 Macc. 5. 15), '*that traitor to
the laws, and to his own country, being his guide.*' The ground
why the Lord permitted this desecration is in the same place,
ver. 17, thus given: '*for the sins of them that dwelt in the city, and
therefore his eye was not upon the place.*' The connexion, in general, of the fate of the Temple with the conduct of the people is
admirably unfolded in ver. 19, sq.: '*Nevertheless God did not
choose the people for the place's sake, but the place for the people's sake. And therefore the place itself, that was partaker with
them of the adversity that happened to the nation, did afterward
communicate in the benefits sent from the Lord; and as it was forsaken in the wrath of the Almighty, so again, the great Lord being
reconciled, it was set up with all glory.*'

709. (4) This interpretation has the testimony of tradition in
its favour. This appears from Josephus [2], who tells us "*that
there was an ancient saying among men, that the city should be
taken, and the holy places burnt down by the law of war, when sedi-
tion should break out, and native hands pollute beforehand the Temple
of God.*" That the *ancient saying* was this prophecy is beyond a
doubt, and it shows that the *abominations* were believed to be those
*through which the Temple had been polluted by the corrupt members
of the covenant people themselves;* and how generally diffused was
not only the reference to the destruction by the Romans in general,
but also *this special interpretation*, appears from the express remark
of Josephus, that the Zelotes themselves adopted it [3].

710. (5) This interpretation is confirmed by the most weighty
of all authorities, that of the Lord himself. This, however, on
account of the manifold misinterpretations of his declarations concerning it, needs to be pointed out more at large. Passages are,
Matt. 24. 15, 16, '*When ye therefore shall see the abomination of
desolation, spoken of by Daniel the prophet, stand in the holy place,
(whoso readeth, let him understand): Then let them which be in
Judæa flee into the mountains;*' and Mark 13. 14, '*When ye shall
see the abomination of desolation, spoken of by Daniel the prophet, standing where it ought not, (let him that readeth understand,) then,*' &c.[4] By '*the abomination of desolation,*' we understand (with Olearius, Lampe, Reland, and Elsner,) *the abomination, which*, being set up by the covenant people themselves,
must have for its inevitable consequence, the desolation; the abomina-

[1] Comp. Jos. 12. 5. 3.   [2] *Bell. Jud.* iv. 6. 3, p. 292.
[3] Comp. also 6. 2, 3.
[4] According to the prevailing interpretation, βδελ. τ. ἐρημ. is rendered
abominatio devastationis, abominatio devastanda, which, according to Kuinöl,
stands as the *abstr.* for *concr.*, for *detestabilis desolator.* This now designates
*exercitum Romanorum Hieros. devastaturum, milites paganos idolorum cultores,
ideoque vel hac de causa abominandos.*

tion to which the desolation belongs, as effect to cause. The genitive
is exactly like that in αἱρέσεις ἀπωλείας, 2 Pet. 2. 1, and similar to
the ἀνάστασις ζωῆς. As in Daniel, so here the abomination whereby
the Temple was polluted is spoken of as idols *set up;* a figure borrowed from an earlier period, when this was the form in which the
abomination actually exhibited itself. This explains the participle
'*standing* ¹.'

711. The chief argument brought for the prevailing explanation, viz.
that, in the parallel passage of Luke ², the *encompassing of the city by
the Romans* is given as a mark of the impending destruction, and as
a sign that it is time to fly, has no validity. For why may we not
assume, that the Lord (whether at the same or at another time)
might direct attention to *various signs* of the destruction from the
prophecy of Daniel; that Luke records the *outward* sign, which he
had taken from Dan. 9. 26, because it was both the plainest in itself
and did not, like the other, presuppose, in order to be understood, a
deeper acquaintance with Daniel, which Luke could not expect from
his readers, while Matthew and Mark, on the contrary, recorded the
internal, derived from ver. 27, which coincided, as to time, with the
outward, so that the attentive observer might find satisfaction concerning both ?

712. The difference between the words of Daniel, and those of the
Lord, consists only in the circumstance, that in Daniel the language
is more general; the Temple in general, at and after the death of
Christ, is represented as one desecrated by idolatrous abominations,
and therefore devoted to destruction, while the Lord, whose chief
object was to give to his followers an outward and perceptible sign
of the immediately impending destruction (comp. the ὅταν ἴδητε),
renders prominent one particular moment of this desecration, that in
which what previously existed, but was more invisible, is made perceptible to the outward senses in so frightful a form, that even many
of those, who had been the abettors of the invisible desecration, were
seized with horrour in view of it; just as the history of the Zelotes
in Josephus is conceivable only by the fact, that crime, when it has
arrived at its highest pitch, always becomes a sort of madness.

'*And that, till what is completed and cut off shall drop-down over
the desolated*' [one] ³.

713. [Or, as in Eng. Bible '*even until the consummation and that
which is determined shall be poured upon the desolate.*' I have removed the comma after *consummation*, to join it to what follows.]

¹ That even Titus himself perceived, that the fearful abomination, whereby
the Temple had been defiled, caused the destruction, is manifest from several
passages of Josephus. Josephus is thoroughly penetrated with this thought.
He says, e. g. (*De Bell. Jud.* lib. 4. 5. 2, 287,) after he has related the death of
true friends of their country, ἀλλ' οἶμαι κατακρίνας ὁ Θεὸς ὡς μεμιασμένης
τῆς πόλεως ἀπώλειαν, καὶ πυρὶ βουλόμενος ἐκκαθαρθῆναι τὰ ἅγια, τοὺς ἀντ-
εχομένους αὐτῶν καὶ φιλοστοργοῦντας περιέκοψε.
² Luke 21. 20.
³ נֶחֱ never occurs, except as the *fem.* or *neut.* for that which is finished.

The '*completion*' is not only used for a *decree* in general, but is limited especially to the *finished determination to inflict suffering upon any one.* In a good sense, it never occurs. That it [1] is here also to be referred to a thing completed as to the *purpose*, not the *execution*, is evident, 1. from its collocation with another word, designating the firmness and irrevocable nature of the decree ; 2. from [2] '*will drop down,*' which is always used of the *cause of the destruction,* the divine anger, or the *divine penal sentence;* never of the *destruction itself;* 3. from the comparison of Is. 28. 22, where the same phrase [3] is designated as an object of *hearing :* '*A thing completed and cut off, heard I from the Lord, the Almighty.*'

714. The entirely similar connexion of both words in the passage before us, and in the two of Isaiah (in which they were rightly understood by the Apostle Paul, Rom. 9. 7, and after him by Vitringa, but erroneously by Gesenius), makes it highly probable that in this connexion, they formed a *judicial technical term,* the *firm and irrevocable final decree.* Perhaps especially in the case of life and death.

715. We do not, with nearly all the interpreters, consider the sentence as a completely independent one, '*until the completion,*' (as they translate,) '*and until the judgement will it drop,*' &c. ; but we place it in connexion with the preceding, '*over the summit of abomination comes the destroyer, and that until,*' &c. The final sentence is itself represented as *dropping down,* because with God decree and execution happen at the same moment ; exactly as it is said, in the eleventh verse, '*Since the curse and the oath are poured upon us, which is written in the law of Moses,*' and Mal. 2. 2, '*I send upon you the curse,*' and as Zech. 5. 4. '*The roll written with the curse comes to the house of the thief and the false swearer, and destroys it.*'

716. The destruction of Sodom and Gomorrah, as the type of all future annihilating judgements of God, lies at the foundation of the expression, '*it will drop down upon* [4].' The *word* is used originally of *natural* rain ; but it was by a *supernatural* rain, (comp. Gen. 19. 24, '*and God caused it to rain* upon Sodom and Gomorrah fire and brimstone,*') that the destruction of Sodom and Gomorrah was effected. This passage of Genesis in a remarkable manner forms the basis of a multitude of others, in which the destruction of the ungodly is described [5]. The reference is manifest in the following passages, which are more nearly related to the one before us : 2 Chron. 34. 21, '*great is the rage* (lit. *glowing fire) of the Lord which* has poured itself upon *us* [6]*, because our fathers have not observed the word of the Lord, to do according to all that is written in this book.*'

---

[1] כָּלָה   [2] חָתַךְ   [3] כָלָה וְנֶחֱרָצָה   [4] נָתַךְ

[5] It is most closely adhered to in Ps. 11. 6, '*God* will rain *upon the ungodly,* cords (not '*lightnings,*' which is entirely arbitrary : the image taken from a judicial proceeding ; the transgressor is *chained* before the capital sentence is passed upon him; there is a contrast with the previous independence of the ungodly), fire and brimstone,' and Ezek. 38. 22, '*Fire and brimstone* will I rain *upon him.*'

[6] נִתְּכָה בָּנוּ

12. 7 : '*And my glowing anger* will not drop down[1] *upon Jerusalem.*'
Jer. 7. 20 : ' *Behold my anger and my fury* is poured out[2] *on this
place, over* (as in the passage before us) *man and beast and trees of
the field, the fruit of the earth, and they turn and are not quenched.*'
42. 18 : '*As my anger and fury* has poured itself[3] *over the inhabitants
of Jerusalem, so will my fury* drop down[4] *over you, when ye come to
Egypt.*' 44. 6 : ' *My fury and my anger*[5] *pours itself, and burns in
the cities of Judah and in the streets of Jerusalem, and they become
a ruin and desolation*[6]. From these parallel passages it appears,
that *the violent rain of divine anger* was the constant designation of
the judgement which caused the destruction of the covenant people,
and so usual that it occurred even in the simplest historical prose.
Daniel, who had himself, as a contemporary, lived to witness such a
rain of fire[7], and had even interceded for its awful ruins, receives
here the intelligence, that when they have been rebuilt, and the
anger of God shall again be called forth against them, more fearful
than before, a new rain of fire will convert them again into ashes
and desolation. The expression always implies a total annihilation,
and for this reason alone cannot be referred to the time of the Maccabees. In order to evade this unpleasant consequence, recent interpreters[8] remove the glowing anger from the covenant people to their
enemies, ' *over the destroyer.*' In this, as might easily be supposed,
they are not without predecessors among the Jewish interpreters,
although these unanimously maintained the reference of the prophecy
to the destruction by the Romans. The choice of this unphilological explanation shows, that no other resource was left ; and its
refutation therefore is a virtual confession, on the part of the Rationalist interpreters, of the untenableness of their interpretation.
The verb[9] is without exception intransitive, never transitive, ' *to
destroy*[10].'

The Terminus A Quo of the Seventy Weeks[11]

717. We have shown in the exegetical part, that this does not
consist in the *commencement* of the building of the city in general, but
rather in that of its *finished restoration*, according to its ancient extent and ancient dignity.

[1] תִּתָּךְ   [2] נִתְּכָה   [3] נִתַּךְ   [4] תִּתַּךְ
[5] Comp. Is. 42. 25, חֵמָה אַפּוֹ as a composite noun, 'his glowing anger.'
[6] Comp. still, Nah. 1. 6. Lam. 2. 4. Is. 42. 25.
[7] Comp. ver. 11.   [8] Taking שֹׁמֵם actively.   [9] שָׁמֵם
[10] Ezek. 36. 3. Our Author examines and explains all the passages where it is
supposed to have a transitive meaning.
[11] Our Author, in the original work, takes off all the current objections to the
intended *definiteness* of the dates.

718. If merely the *commencement* of the rebuilding were meant, those would unquestionably be right, who place the *terminus a quo* in the *first year* of Cyrus.   Then would the argument have force, that the returning exiles could not dwell under the open heavens, and that to assert, that under Cyrus nothing was yet done towards the rebuilding of the city, is to make Isaiah, who praises Cyrus as its rebuilder, the author of a false prophecy [1].   But, indeed, every chapter of the sacred Scriptures which concerns the time from Cyrus to Nehemiah, clearly presupposes the existence of *a Jerusalem* during this period.

719. But we assert *that until the twentieth year of Artaxerxes, the new city of Jerusalem was an open, thinly inhabited village, exposed to aggressions of every kind from its neighbours.*

720. We will first remove the *objections*, which have been brought against this view of the condition of Jerusalem.   In Hag. 1. 4, it is said, ' *Is it a time for you to dwell in your ceiled houses, and my house is laid waste?* '   But we can no more draw a conclusion from this, as to the condition of the *whole* city, than we can infer from such statements of Isaiah [2] as, ' *Your hands are full of blood,*'—' *Righteousness dwelt in her, but now murderers,*' that Jerusalem was *entirely filled* with murderers.   If there were only *some* ceiled houses,—(and who would deny this?)—the appeal of the prophet was fully justified.   We are also referred to Ezra 4. 12, where the enemies of the Jews write to Artachschasta (Smerdis), ' *Be it known to the king, that the Jews, who have come from thee to Jerusalem, are building the rebellious and wicked city, and completing its walls, and restoring its ruins;*' comp. ver. 16, '*We make known to the king, that when this city is built and its walls completed, thou wilt have no portion on this side of the river.*'   But this only proves, that the enemies of the Jews were *gross calumniators;* for not a word is said before or after *by Ezra himself* of the building of the walls. If we infer from this statement the *attempted rebuilding of the walls,* we might with just as much reason conclude from Neh. 6. 6, 7, (' *Thou and the Jews, ye think to rebel,—and thou wilt become their king,—also thou hast set up prophets, who shall cry out concerning thee at Jerusalem: King of Judah,*') that it was the object of Nehemiah to shake off the Persian yoke, and *make himself king.*   When the prohibition of the usurper Smerdis, caused by this writing, was repealed by his death, which followed soon after, it was only the building of the Temple that was carried forward under Darius the son of Hystaspes [3]: had the allegations of the enemies been well founded, would not the *rebuilding of the walls* also have been recommenced?   Finally, an appeal is still made to Neh. 1. 3, '*And then they said to me* (those, who had come from Jerusalem to the Persian court), *Those who remain, who are left of the captivity there in the city, are in great affliction and disgrace, and the wall of Jerusalem is broken down, and her gates burnt with fire.*'   It is asserted, after the example of J. D. Michaelis, that from this it necessarily follows, that

---

[1] Isaiah 45. 13.   [2] Isaiah 1, 15, and 2, 21.   [3] Ezra 5. 6.

the walls of Jerusalem had been rebuilt by those who had returned, and then a *second time destroyed* by the surrounding nations; since the *devastation of Nebuchadnezzar* was not *unknown* to Nehemiah, and could be *no new ground* of his lamentation. But what necessity is there for supposing, that those who came to Nehemiah did announce any thing *entirely new ?* He *knew* that the walls and gates were *not* then rebuilt, but the bustle of the court had *drawn off his attention* from the subject. But *now* he had a lively sense of the contradiction between the visible appearance and the promise, and was led thereby to an earnest intercession, which laid the foundation for the removal of this contradiction. The inference is neither better nor worse than that from the impression which the reading of the law made on Josiah, to his former entire unacquaintance with it. Can we conclude, from the circumstance, that, according to Neh. 8. 9, the people wept on hearing the law read by Ezra, that they had previously not the least knowledge of it ? Besides this, the statements, ' *they are in great affliction and disgrace,*' and ' *the walls are destroyed,*' stand to each other in the relation of the *effect* to its *cause.* Nehemiah had never so deeply considered before, that the destruction of the walls would be attended with such ruinous consequences, and so entirely hinder the rebuilding of the city, by exposing its inhabitants to every species of disgrace and injury from their neighbouring enemies. It appeared to him, therefore, now, in an entirely different light, and therefore awakened his sorrow, his intercession, his resolution to render active assistance. That this destruction of the walls and the gates is that by the Chaldeans, and that it continued —until the time of Nehemiah, we prove by the following reasons : (1) In a manner entirely similar, the Chaldean devastation, in respect to walls and gates, is described, Lam. 2. 8, 9, comp. also 2 Kings 25. 10. (2) The enemies of the Jews know only of *one* long past destruction ; comp. Neh. 3. 34, where Sanballat says, ' *What are the withered* (the feeble) *Jews doing ? Will they make the stones alive out of the heaps of rubbish where they are burnt ?* ' (3) The book of Ezra says not one word of the rebuilding of the walls. And yet it is inconceivable, that an event should have been passed over in silence, the importance of which is evident, since the enemies of the Jews, when it was about to take place, sought to hinder it by cunning and force, and were at nothing more enraged. (4) From the second part of Zechariah, composed after the sixth year of Darius, (chap. 14. 10, sq., comp. with several passages of Nehemiah, there cited,) it appears that in the time of both these prophets, the walls and gates were still in precisely the same condition, in which the Chaldeans had left them ; that the very same fragments, which they had spared, and no others, were still standing. Comp. further Neh. 3. 8. ' *And as they completed* [1] *Jerusalem unto the broad wall :*' from which it appears that there was no occasion to rebuild the broad wall, westward from the gate of Ephraim (which, according to the cited passages, re-

---

[1] As we must translate on account of the *fut. c. vav conv.,* which excludes the idea of *plusquamperf.,* and on account of the thirty-fourth verse.

mained standing [1]), because this wall was still in existence, in consequence of the manner in which it had been strengthened by Uzziah. (5.) It is, in itself, highly improbable that the Jews, before Nehemiah, even made an attempt to rebuild the walls and gates. In the edict of no Persian king was there even a trace of any permission to do this. And who would venture to assert that this was implied of itself? It is one thing to suffer a defenceless people to return to their native land, and another to supply them with the means of defence, which, in case of a general rebellion, they might use even against the giver himself. The latter presupposes a confidence which we do not find among the Asiatic monarchs, who well knew that their power depended only on the weakness of their subjects; a confidence which, in this instance, was produced in a very unusual way, only by the near relation which Nehemiah sustained to Artaxerxes. If the Jews ventured, on their own responsibility, to do what was not permitted, they could the less hope for connivance, because they were surrounded by malicious enemies, who sought by every means to awaken the jealousy of the Persian king. If this had already been effected by falsehood, how much more must the Jews expect the worst, if they gave a *real ground* for complaint, by overstepping the king's command?

721. This refutation, of what has been urged against the view we have given, of the condition of Jerusalem until the time of Nehemiah, contains, at the same time, in part, the positive proof of it, which, therefore, we need now only complete.

722. In Zechariah the condition of Jerusalem appears throughout, a *provisional* one. According to chap. 1. 16, the measuring line was not to be drawn over Jerusalem till a *future* time; the present still belongs, according to the twelfth verse, to the period of the affliction, not to that of the restoration; it is still a remnant of the Chaldean servitude. According to the second chapter, it is the future that is to complete the destruction of Babylon and the building of Jerusalem; nay, what has hitherto taken place in reference to the latter, is so insignificant, that the prophet does not even take it into account at all, but speaks as if the city were still to be rebuilt from the beginning. Comp. especially vv. 1 and 2, ' *And behold a man, in his hand a measuring line; and he said, Whither goest thou? And he said, To measure Jerusalem, to see how great will be her breadth, and how great her length.*' Chap. 7. 7, the past, when Jerusalem was *sitting* and *free*, is contrasted with the present. Jerusalem is therefore now still a city, which [2] ' *sits not, but lies down* [3].' Chap. 8. 5, the prophet promises, that ' *the streets of the city will hereafter yet be full of boys and girls playing in them;*' and how little there was in the present to justify this promise, appears from the fact, (ver. 6,) that he finds it necessary to refer those to the Divine omnipotence, who regarded such a turn of affairs as strange and incredible.

723. If now, (for the book of Ezra furnishes nothing for our

---

[1] Comp. 2 Chron. 26. 9.   [2] לֹא חָשׁוּב.   [3] Comp. on Zech. 9. 5.

purpose,) we turn to Nehemiah, the same, if not a still more mournful image, presents itself to our view.   That the number of the inhabitants was very small, appears even from the expression, '*the remnant who have remained of the captivity there in the city.*' It appears to follow from this, that the small number of the inhabitants of Jerusalem had even diminished in the time between Zechariah and Nehemiah.   Weary of the constant oppression of their enemies, who had directed their attention especially to Jerusalem, the people may have scattered themselves over the rest of the land.   Especially, however, does chap. 2. 3 and 5, show the absurdity of placing the restoration of the city in the time before Nehemiah.   Nehemiah there says to Artaxerxes, ' *The city where the graves of my fathers are, lies waste* [1], *and its gates are burnt with fire.*—*Send me to Judea, to the city of the graves of my fathers, that I may build it.*' It hence appears, that the difference of the condition of Jerusalem then, from its condition during the exile, was so small as to be entirely overlooked, and the former could be described, just as the latter is, e. g., in the chapter before us.   That Nehemiah did not exaggerate before the king of Persia, appears from the seventeenth verse, where, in Jerusalem itself, he describes the condition of the city in the same manner; ' *Ye see the affliction in which we are ; Jerusalem is laid waste, and her gates burnt with fire.*'   Very significant also is Neh. 7. 4 ; ' *The city was wide and great, and only a few people in it, and there were no houses built.*'   This passage refers to the time immediately *after* the completion of the walls of the city.   In reliance on the divine promise, they had given to them their ancient circumference ; now, however, there was the most striking disproportion between the extent of the city and the amount of what it contained.   The few houses seemed in the broad space entirely to vanish.

724. We have hitherto been showing, that the beginning of the restoration of the city *cannot* be placed *before* the time of Nehemiah ; we will now show that it *was made* by him.   That at a later period he was regarded as the rebuilder, not only of the walls and gates, but also of the city itself, appears from Jes. Sir. 49. 13.   ' *Nehemiah whose renown is great, who raised up for us the walls that were fallen, and set up the gates and the bars, and raised up our ruins again.*'   Joshua and Zerubbabel, on the contrary, are extolled (ver. 12,) only as rebuilders of the *Temple*.   Still we can produce a far stronger proof from Nehemiah himself.   In close connexion with chap. 7. 4, which is interrupted only by the relation of what happened between the purpose and its execution, Nehemiah relates, chap. 11. 1, 2, what he did in order to increase the population of Jerusalem.   By his influence, all the heads of the people, in the first place, removed from the country into the city ; then a tenth part of all the rest of the people, according to lot, was compelled to do the same.   And, finally, a large number of families voluntarily removed from the country into the city.   This, which at first, from the sudden disruption of all relations which it involves, must have been a sacri-

---

[1] חָרְבָּה.

fice voluntarily made from a theocratical disposition, must afterwards have frequently happened in the case of those, who were not
led by such a motive; for Jerusalem, as the *only fortified city of the
land*, possessed such an advantage, that all who possibly could, would
choose it for their residence. The buildings of the walls of Jerusalem, and ' *there shall be no more reproach*,' are placed as connected
with each other, Neh. 2. 17. Partly for this reason, and partly
because Jerusalem was the seat of the sanctuary, none of the
Jews, who still continued to return from their dispersion, would
readily fix his dwelling-place elsewhere. And, doubtless, many would
be induced to return, precisely on account of the intelligence of the
rebuilding of Jerusalem. How prosperously and rapidly the city
henceforth advanced, while in the long period from the first year of
Cyrus to Nehemiah it had made no progress, will be apparent from
the passages of heathen writers hereafter to be cited.

725. If now we seek to determine still more accurately the *terminus a quo*, we find it to be the prayer of Nehemiah, for the restoration of the city; chap. 1. In consequence of the hearing of
this prayer, the divine decree for the rebuilding of the city went
forth; and, indeed, this is given in the twenty-fifth verse, as the
terminus a quo of the seventy weeks. To the hearing of this
prayer, Nehemiah (comp. chap. 2. 8. 18.)[1] refers all that follows,
particularly the favorable audience that Artaxerxes gave him.
This prayer falls in the month Chisleu, in the third month of the
civil year, in the twentieth year of Artaxerxes, from the time of
whose reign, therefore, in the chronological reckoning of the seventy
weeks, we have to subtract only nineteen complete years, and then
we have the *terminus a quo* of Daniel's prophecy.

726. We must still examine some objections which have been
brought against the *terminus a quo* assumed by us, after the example
in general of the most and best interpreters, as well as that of Jul.
Africanus in Jerome, who, on the whole, perceived the truth in
reference to the prophecy, only he calculated according to lunar
years[2]. 1. ' *Daniel must necessarily have been living at the time of
the edict, which is here spoken of, otherwise it could not serve to console him, and he would not have known where he should begin to
reckon ; his own prophecy, therefore, would have been to him unintelligible*[3].' But this objection proceeds on the erroneous assumption,
that all was then imparted to Daniel merely *for himself*, while,
according to the correct view, he was only an organ, by which God
made disclosures, which in part could not be understood in their
whole extent till centuries afterwards. We say according to the
correct view : for it is that which lies in the book of Daniel itself.

---

[1] Bengel, *Ordo Temp.* p. 346. " Mandata regum (ἐξελθόντα δόγματα, ut habet
phrasis Luc. 2, 1) illi verbo subserviebant."

[2] A mode of reckoning, which, as it is never found among the Hebrews, is so
entirely destitute of all ground, that we need not stop to refute it; comp. in
opposition, Vitringa, l. c. p. 260; Frank, *Syst. Chronolog.* I. 1. § 8. Ideler,
Chronologie, I. p. 490, ff.

[3] Thus Hassencamp. *Ueber die* 70 *Wochen*, p. 9, ff.

The vision, in the eighth chapter, was to be *shut up*, according to the twenty-sixth verse, until a far distant time of fulfilment. Daniel himself *wonders* at this, ver. 27, and no man understands it. According to chap. 12. ver. 4, the whole preceding prophecy is *sealed up until the time of the end;* then will many investigate it, and great will be the agreement. Chap. 12. 7, the angel gives a determination of time. Daniel hears it and understands it not, and prays the angel for clearer discoveries, ver. 8. He answers, in the ninth verse, that he cannot impart these to him, because the prophecy is shut up and sealed until the last time [1]. In especial reference to the last-cited passage, it is said, 1 Pet. 1. 10—12, ' *The prophets have inquired and searched,*' in reference to the future salvation. It was, however, revealed to them, that the prophecy, given through their instrumentality, was *not destined for them*, but for those who should be living at the time of the fulfilment. Daniel need not know where he should begin to reckon; it was sufficient if he could only infer from the prophecy itself, that he *need not* begin yet, that the *terminus a quo* had not yet arrived. The accurate reckoning belonged only to those of a later period, and even for these there remained, before the fulfilment, so much darkness (partly on account of the method of determining the *terminus a quo* itself, where, as in all the rest of the prophecy, the effort is obvious, to *avoid on the one hand objective indefiniteness*, and on the other *such* clearness, for those who lived *before* the fulfilment, as *would have converted the prophecy into a history*, and partly on account of the absence of an accurate chronological investigation of the whole period, as it is manifest even in Josephus), that they must content themselves with ascertaining from the prophecy *about* the time of the appearing of Christ; and that this has actually been accomplished, in respect to the more intelligent, can be historically proved. A *subjective* insight into the prophecy, corresponding to its *objective* definiteness, was reserved for the times after the fulfilment.—The assertion, however, is erroneous, that, this *terminus a quo* being assumed, the prophecy could have afforded to Daniel *no* consolation. Was not then the '*that*' of itself a rich source of comfort? And then Daniel was not entirely uncertain as to the '*when.*' The *when* of the return from the exile was accurately known to him. He was aware that only two years were yet to elapse. Cyrus, who was to accomplish it, was already on the stage of history. That the return, however, could not be separated from the finished restoration by a long series of years, seemed to lie in the nature of the case. The prediction might be the more consoling to Daniel, because he supposes *both* to be much nearer to each other than they really were. That he actually did this, may, perhaps, be inferred from the deep sorrow, which, according to the tenth chapter, he expresses, when, in the third year of Cyrus, the rebuilding of the Theocracy met with an unexpected hinderance [2]. A more accurate determination of the period between the *terminus ad quem* of the prophecies of Jeremiah, and the *terminus a quo* of that before us,

---

[1] Comp. on this passage, *Beitr.* I. p. 215, ff.   [2] Comp. *Beitr.*

would only have served to *dishearten* those who were returning, or even entirely to prevent them from going back ; in favour of which, without any such object, so few comparatively decided.

727. 2. " *Quanta erat calamitas, tantum beneficii exoptabatur et promittebatur. Uno tempore templum et urbem vastarant Chaldæi ; in ruinis et templum et urbs jacebant, quum Daniel oraret ; quare uti prædictio vastitatis Jerem.* 21. 10, *etc., sic descriptio vastitatis et ædificationis sub urbis mentione templum quoque innuit. Hinc omnia Daniel precibus complectebatur, urbem, montem sanctum, populum, sanctuarium. Eademque omnia complectitur responsio per angelum allata.*" Bengel[1]. But all this proves nothing more, than that in the divine disclosure, the Temple also must be considered. This appears also indirectly, since, in the beginning of the seventy weeks, or of the restoration of the city, it is presupposed as already completed. For how could the city, without the Temple, be well called the holy city ? The prediction of the destruction of the Temple also, after the end of the seventy weeks, presupposes that it had been rebuilt. But to assert, that the rebuilding of the Temple and the city must necessarily happen at the same time, is the same as to say, that the historical facts must be different from what they are. If both events *are really separated* from each other, why also in the prophecy should not *one of them* only be placed as the *terminus a quo ?* from which, if the seventy weeks of years were reckoned, they would expire at the definite *terminus ad quem.*

728. To the investigation of this *terminus a quo,* we here subjoin that respecting the historical confirmation of what is given, as *properly* belonging to the first period ; the seven weeks beginning with this *terminus a quo.* The restoration of the city was to extend entirely through it, and be completed with its termination. This falls—the twentieth year of Artaxerxes being, as will hereafter be shown, the year 455 before Christ,—in the year 406, two years before the end of the nineteenth year of the reign of Darius the Second, the successor of Artaxerxes. And here, in reference to the demonstration of the agreement of prophecy and fulfilment, we must speak with modesty, partly on account of the nature of the object, which is not one accurately defined and limited, partly on account of the extreme deficiency of our records for this period, since Josephus passes over it in total silence. These modest expectations, however, we are able, in an unexpected way, to exceed.

729. The most remarkable testimony is furnished by Herodotus, whose history cannot have been composed *before* the year 408, because he relates events which happened in this and the preceding year[2] ; *nor much later,* because otherwise quite too great an age would be attributed to him. What he says, therefore, respecting the greatness of Jerusalem, can tolerably well be applied to the time of the end of the seven weeks. We must, indeed, allow to ourselves an assumption, the proof of which must be reserved for another place, viz. that

---

[1] *Ordo Tempor.* p. 343.
[2] Comp. Clinton, *Fasti Hellenici,* p. 85, and especially Dahlmann, *Forschungen,* I. p. 98, ff.

the *Kadytis* of Herodotus is Jerusalem. But we venture to do this
more readily since the case speaks for itself, and since the former
learned vindications of this opinion, as that by Lightfoot [1], by Prideaux [2], by Cellarius [3], by Heine [4], by the acute author of the *Obser-
vatio de Cadyti, magná Syriæ urbe* [5], by Zorn [6] and by Dahlmann [7],
are any thing but refuted by the treatise of Hitzig, after the appearance of which Niebuhr [8], also, and Bähr [9], have joined these defenders.
Herodotus speaks of *Kadytis* in two places. The former (2. 159,
μετὰ δὲ τὴν μάχην Κάδυτιν, πόλιν τῆς Συρίης ἐοῦσαν μεγάλην,
εἷλε) refers, indeed, to the time before the exile, to the capture of
Jerusalem by Pharaoh Necho, after Josiah had fallen in the battle
of Megiddo. But yet Herodotus describes Jerusalem as a city which,
even in his time, was still great. But more important is the second
passage, 3, 5 : ἀπὸ γὰρ Φοινίκης μέχρι οὔρων τῶν Καδύτιος πόλιος, ἥ
ἐστι Σύρων τῶν Παλαιστινῶν καλεομένων· ἀπὸ δὲ Καδύτιος, ἐούσης
πόλιος (ὡς ἐμοὶ δοκέει) Σαρδίων οὐ πολλῷ ἐλάσσονος, κ. τ. λ.
That the predicate ' great,' in the former, is to be taken in its full
sense, is evident from the comparison with Sardis ; which very
ancient city had also retained, under the Persian dominion and later,
the greatness and population, which it had formerly possessed as a
residence of the Lydian kings. This appears, among other sources,
from Pausanias [10] : Ἦν γὰρ δὴ τῆς Ἀσίας τῆς κάτω μέγιστον μέρος
τηνικαῦτα ἡ Λυδία, καὶ αἱ Σάρδεις πλούτῳ τε καὶ παρασκευῇ προεῖ-
χον· τῷ τε σατραπεύοντι ἐπὶ θαλάσσῃ τοῦτο οἰκητήριον ἀπεδέδεικτο,
καθάπερ γε αὐτῷ βασιλεῖ τὰ Σοῦσα. Pliny designates [11] this city as
the ornament of all Lydia ; Strabo [12], as one of great antiquity and
extent ; and the epithet ' *great* ' is so constantly given to it [13], that it
seems to have been a standing epithet.

730. Another testimony, belonging indeed to a later period, but
not the less remarkable on that account, is that of Hecatæus Abde-
rita, a writer of the time of Alexander and Ptolemy Lagus [14], in a fragment in Josephus [15], and in Eusebius [16] : ἔστι γὰρ τῶν Ἰουδαίων τὰ
μὲν πολλὰ ὀχυρώματα κατὰ τὴν χώραν καὶ κῶμαι· μία δὲ πόλις ὀχυρὰ,
πεντήκοντα μάλιστα σταδίων τὴν περίμετρον· ἣν οἰκοῦσι μὲν ἀνθρώ-

---

[1] *Opp. t.* II. p. 408.
[2] Prideaux, p. 106, sq.
[3] Cellarius, 3, 13, ed. Schwarz, II. p. 456.
[4] Heine, *Observv. sacræ*, lib. I. c. 5, p. 63.
[5] In the *nova var. script. coll.* fasc. I. Halle, 1716.
[6] Zorn, on *Hecatæus Abder.* p. 94.
[7] Dahlmann, *Forschungen*, II. p. 75.
[8] In the first volume of the *hist. phil. Schriften, Abhandlung über die Armen.
Chronik des Eusebius.*
[9] *Herodoti Musæ*, I. p. 922.
[10] *Lacon*, p. 175, ed. Wech.
[11] *Hist. Nat.* 5, 29, " *Celebratur maxime Sardibus.*"
[12] Strabo, p. 625.
[13] Comp. also Ovid, *Metam.* 11. 137. " *Vade, ait, ad* MAGNIS *vicinum Sardibus
amnem.*"
[14] Comp. concerning him, *Beitr.* I. p. 281.
[15] Joseph. lib. I. c. Ap. § 22.
[16] Eusebius, *Præp. Evang.* lib. IX. c. 4.

πων περὶ δώδεκα μυριάδες, καλοῦσι δ᾽ αὐτὴν Ἱεροσόλυμα, on which Scaliger remarks, " *Vides, quanta fuerit Hieros. urbs, quam totius Orientis ornamentum vere vocare poterant tempore Hecatœi.*"

731. As a special characteristic of the restoration, to take place in the seventh week, it is mentioned in the prophecy that it would happen in a troublous time, *in angustiâ et pressurâ temporum.* This also *exactly coincides with the result.* One cannot sufficiently wonder, how in the very time of this tribulation the secret blessing of God could still be so efficacious, that in a comparatively short time, in place of a heap of rubbish, a city should arise, inferior in greatness to few in Asia. How entirely suitable to the commencement of this period was the predicate of a time of distress, is evident from Neh. 4. Harassed by surrounding enemies, the builders were obliged to carry arms in one hand, while they laboured with the other ; their strength, exhausted by the labours of the day, was again called into requisition by watching at night. And, even after the completion of the building, the affliction and toil still continued. This appears from the lively description, Neh. 9. 36, 37, ' *Behold we are still servants, and the land that thou hast given to our fathers, to eat its fruit and its good things, behold we are servants in it. And it gives its increase for the kings, whom thou hast set over us, on account of our sins, and they reign over our bodies, and over our cattle, according to their pleasure, and in great distress*[1] *are we.*' Of this also the prophecies of Malachi, which belong to this period, afford a clear proof. He has perpetually to contend with those who murmured against God, on account of the distressing condition of the new colony, and were in danger of being led thereby to total unbelief.

Chronological Determination of the Terminus Ad Quem

732. The extreme *terminus ad quem* of the prophecy, the period at which the forgiveness of sins, the imparting of the everlasting righteousness, &c. should be completed, falls in the end of the seventy weeks. It is, however, erroneous to lay this as the foundation of the chronological reckoning, because it is designated by no single accurately limited fact. We do however find such a one in the close of the sixty-ninth week ; and we adopt this *terminus ad quem*, the public appearing of Christ, his anointing with the gifts of the Spirit, the more readily as the ground of our calculation, since, which is very remarkable, in the history of the fulfilment it appears also designated with the same chronological exactness, as here in the prophecy ; more accurately, indeed, than any other point, as, for instance, the birth, or His resurrection or ascension.

733. We read, Luke 3. 1, ἐν ἔτει δὲ πεντεκαιδεκάτῳ τῆς ἡγεμονίας Τιβερίου Καίσαρος, ἡγεμονεύοντος Ποντίου Πιλάτου τῆς Ἰου-

---

[1] בְּצָרָה גְדֹלָה.

δαίας,—ἐγένετο ῥῆμα Θεοῦ ἐπὶ Ἰωάννην. According to this the public appearing of John the Baptist and of Christ falls in the year 782 v. c. An attempt has indeed been made on different grounds (partly to rescue the authority of several fathers, whose dates differ from this, partly in order to unsettle the firm historical grounds of the sacred history) to invalidate this determination. But with very little success. For when Paulus and Kuinöl, e. g., remark, that it is uncertain what mode of reckoning of the years of Tiberius is here employed, Ideler [1] has already proved, in opposition, that history in general knows no other mode than that from the beginning of his actual reign, after the death of Augustus ; and when they assert, that Luke determines only the year in which John, not that in which Christ publicly came forward, it is left out of view, that even the accurate determination of the time of John's appearing, and the immediate connexion of the appearing of Christ therewith, without a new date, shows that both fall in the same year. To the coincidence of the appearance of both in the same year,—perhaps separated by the period of six months,—we are also led by καὶ αὐτὸς ἦν ὁ Ἰησοῦς ὡσεὶ ἐτῶν τριάκοντα ἀρχόμενος, in the twenty-third verse. If we interpret, ' also Jesus himself,' it follows that John also, at his entrance on his office (ἀρχόμενος), was about thirty years old, and, of course, since John was only six months older than Christ, that he came forward only six months earlier. If we translate, " and Jesus himself," then it is presupposed, even by this reference to John, that the preceding designation of time in the history of the world is here also to be supplied, and that it only receives an addition through the mention of the age of Christ ; which again (as it was not accidental, that Christ did not enter upon his office until the completion of his thirtieth year, but in accordance with the legal appointments of the Old Testament, which were also applicable to John,) settles likewise the age of the latter. The objection against the coincidence of the year of Christ and of John, which has been deduced from the twenty-first verse compared with Matt. 3. 5, is quite unmeaning. For had the extent of Judea ten times as great, yet such was the general excitement, and such the religious intercourse carried on by means of the capital, that a period of about half a year would have been completely sufficient to awaken the attention of the whole land. Finally, the opinion of Sanclemente, cited by Ideler, that the determination of time does not refer to the public appearance of John and of Christ, but to the sufferings and death of the latter, is a fit subject for summary justice, having no claim, whatever Ideler may assert, to be previously examined before a solemn tribunal of Biblical critics.

[1] *Chronologie*, I. p. 418.

THE AGREEMENT OF PROPHECY AND FULFILMENT WITH
RESPECT TO THE
Distance of Terminus A Quo from the Terminus Ad Quem

734. According to the prophecy, the *terminus a quo*, the twentieth year of Artaxerxes, is separated from the *terminus ad quem*, the public appearance of Christ, by a period of sixty-nine weeks of years, or four hundred eighty-three years. If, now, we compare history with this, it must appear, even to the most prejudiced, in the highest degree remarkable, that among all the current chronological determinations of this period, not one differs more than ten years from the testimony of the prophecy. This wonder must rise to the highest pitch, when it appears from an accurate examination of these determinations, that the only one among them which is correct, *makes the prophecy and history correspond with each other, even to a year*.

735. Happily, to attain this end, we are not compelled to involve ourselves in a labyrinth of chronological inquiries. We find ourselves, in the main, on sure ground. All chronologists agree, that the commencement of the reign of Xerxes falls in the year 485 before Christ, the death of Artaxerxes in the year 423. The difference concerns only the year of the commencement of the reign of Artaxerxes. Our problem is completely solved, when we have shown that this falls in the year 474 before Christ. For then the twentieth year of Artaxerxes is the year 455 before Christ, according to the usual reckoning [1] :   = 299 U. C.

Add to this,   483 years.

___

782 U. C.

736. We should probably have been saved the trouble of this investigation, had not the errour of an acute man, and the want of independence in his successors, darkened what was in itself clear. According to Thucydides, Artaxerxes began to reign shortly before the flight of Themistocles to Asia. Deceived by certain specious arguments, hereafter to be examined, Dodwell, in the *Annall. Thucyd.*, placed both events in the year 465 before Christ. The thorough refutation of Vitringa, in the cited treatise, remained, strange as it may appear, unknown to the philologians and historians even, it would seem, to those of Holland, as Wesseling. The view of Dodwell, adopted also by Corsini in the *Fasti Attici*, became the prevailing one, at which we cannot wonder, when we consider how seldom, in modern times, chronological investigations in general have been fundamental and independent. Even Clinton (*Fasti Hellenici, lat. vert. Krüger*, Leip., 1830), though he clearly perceives,

___

[1] The intelligent reader will perceive that the author has intentionally made his investigation entirely independent of the difficult inquiries respecting the year of the birth of Christ, which, in his judgement, have in recent times, by the introduction of uncertain astronomical combinations, particularly by Münter and Ideler, been led far astray.

that Dodwell has confused the whole chronology of this period, has not been able to free himself from him in the most important points, though he has successfully opposed him in several; and thus the confusion only becomes still greater; since now neither the actual chronological succession of events, nor that ingeniously invented by Dodwell, any longer remains. Nevertheless, the truth is advanced by this increased confusion; for the harmony introduced by Dodwell into the fictitious history is destroyed. The honour, however, of having again discovered the true path, belongs to Krüger alone, who, after more than a hundred years, as an entirely independent inquirer, coincides with Vitringa in the same result, and in part in the employment of the same arguments[1]. He places the death of Xerxes in the year 474 or 473, and the flight of Themistocles a year later. This treatise may serve to shame those, who reject in the mass the grounds of our opinion (to the establishment of which we now proceed) with the remark, that the author has only *found what he sought*. Whoever does not feel capable of entering independently upon the investigation, should at least be prevented from condemning, by the circumstance, that a learned man, with no other design than to elucidate a chronologically confused period of Grecian history, gives, for the event which serves to determine the *terminus a quo* of our prophecy, the precise year which places prophecy and fulfilment in the most exact harmony.

737. We examine first the grounds which seem to favour the opinion, that the reign of Artaxerxes commenced in the year 465. (1) "The flight of Themistocles must precede the transfer of the dominion of Greece from Athens to Sparta by several years. For this happened during the siege of Byzantium, when the treasonable efforts of Pausanias first commenced; the flight of Themistocles, however, was a consequence of the complaint, which was raised against him out of the documents found after the death of Pausanias. But Isocrates says, in the *Panathenaikos*, that the dominion of the Lacedemonians had lasted ten years. The expedition of Xerxes taken as the *terminus a quo*, this transfer falls in the year 470." But we may spare ourselves the labour, which Vitringa takes, to invalidate this alleged testimony of Isocrates, since all recent scholars, in part independent of one another, agree that Isocrates speaks of a ten years' dominion, not *before*, but *after* that of the Athenians[2]. (2) "That Themistocles in the year 472 was still in Athens, Corsini infers (*Fasti Att.* III. p. 180) from *Æl.* lib. 9. c. 5. According to this, Themistocles sent back Hiero, who was coming to the Olympic games, asserting, that, whoever had not taken part in the greatest danger, could not be a sharer of the joy. (The fact is also related by Plutarch.) Now, as Hiero began to reign Ol. 75, 3 (478), only the Ol. 77 (472) could be intended." But who does not at once perceive, that the reference to the games of the Ol. 76

---

[1] In the acute treatise, *Ueber den Cimonischen Frieden* in the *Archiv f. Philologie und Pädagog. von Seebode*, I. 2. p. 205, ff.

[2] Comp. Coray, on *Pan.* c. 19. Dahlmann, *Forschungen*, I. p. 45. Krüger, p. 221. Clinton, p. 250, ff.

(476) was far more obvious, since the occurrence presupposed that the μέγιστος τῶν κινδύνων was still fresh in remembrance ? (3) "According to this supposition, Xerxes would reign only eleven years ; Artaxerxes, on the contrary, fifty-one. This is in opposition to the testimony of the *Can. Ptolem.* (comp. thereon Ideler, i. p. 109, ff.) which gives to Xerxes twenty-one, and to Artaxerxes forty-one years ; and to that of Ctesias, who gives to Artaxerxes forty-two years, and to those of some other writers ; compare the passages in Bähr on *Ctesias*, p. 184." *Ceteris paribus*, this argument would be wholly decisive. But when other weighty authorities are opposed to it, it is not of itself sufficient to outweigh them. The canon has high authority only where it rests on astronomical observations, which is here not the case. Otherwise it stands on the same ground as all other historical sources. The whole errour was committed, as soon as an ια′ in an ancient authority was confounded with a κα′ ; for when a reign of twenty-one years had thus been attributed to Xerxes, the shortening of the reign of Artaxerxes to forty one years necessarily followed. Wesseling (on *Diod.* 12, 64,) attributes forty-five years to Artaxerxes, thus without hesitation rejecting the authority of the canon.—To these arguments, already adduced by others, we subjoin the following :—(4) It seems to be evident from Ctesias, chap. 20, that Artaxerxes was born a considerable time after the commencement of the reign of Xerxes. Ctesias, after relating it, proceeds : γαμεῖ δὲ Ξέρξης Ὀνόφα θυγατέρα Ἄμιστριν καὶ γίνεται αὐτῷ παῖς Δαρειαῖος, καὶ ἕτερος μετὰ δύο ἔτη Ὑστάσπης, καὶ ἔτι Ἀρταξέρξης. If he relates the events in the true chronological order, Artaxerxes in the year 474 could at most have been seven years old. On the contrary, however, all accounts agree, that at the death of Xerxes, although still young [1], he was yet of a sufficient age to be capable of reigning himself. We must not be satisfied with the answer, that it is very improbable that Xerxes, who was born at the beginning of the thirty-sixth year of the reign of Darius [2], and was already 34-35 years old at his death, was not married until so late a period. Ctesias himself frees us from the embarrassment into which we were thrown by his inaccuracy. According to chap. 22, Megabyzus was already married, before the expedition against Greece, to a daughter of Xerxes, who, being already mentioned in chap. 20, could not, if Ctesias is there chronologically accurate, have been born till about that time. According to chap. 28, Megabyzus, immediately after the return of Xerxes from Greece, complained to him of the shameful conduct of this wife of his. (5) There can be no doubt that the Ahasuerus of the book of Esther, is the same as Xerxes. Now the twelfth year of this king is there expressly mentioned, chap. 3. 7, and the events related in the following context fall, in part, about the end of the same year. But this difficulty vanishes, as soon as we include the years of the co-regency of Xerxes with Darius. According to the full account in Herodotus [3], Xerxes, two years before the death of

---

[1] Comp. Justin, 3. 1.   [2] Comp. Herod. 7. 2.
[3] Herodot. 7, chap. 2—4.

Darius, was established by him as king, comp. e. g. chap. 4 : ἀπέδεξε δὲ βασιλῆα Πέρσῃσι Δαρεῖος Ξέρξεα. Of the custom of the Hebrew writers to include the years of a co-regency, where it existed, we have a remarkable example in the account concerning Nebuchadnezzar [1]. But we find even in the book of Esther itself, plain indications of this mode of reckoning. The account of the great feast, chap. 1, is placed in its true light by this supposition. The occasion of it was the *actual* commencement of the reign of Xerxes, though we need not on this account exclude what has hitherto been regarded as the exclusive object, consultations with the nobles respecting the expeditions about to be undertaken. What is related, chap. 2. 16, then falls precisely in the time of the return of Xerxes from Greece, while otherwise, and this is attended with difficulty, about two years after that event.

738. We now proceed to lay down the positive grounds for our view ; and, *in the first place*, the *direct*, and then the *indirect* proofs, which latter are far more numerous and strong, since they show, that the flight of Themistocles, which must precede the reign of Artaxerxes, cannot possibly be placed later than 473 before Christ.

739. To the first class belong the following :—(1) It must appear very strange to those who assume a twenty-one years' reign of Xerxes, that the *whole period from the eleventh year* is a complete *tabula rasa*. The biblical accounts stop short at the close of the tenth year. Ctesias relates only one inconsiderable event after the Grecian war, chap. 28, which occurred immediately after its termination. No later writer has ventured to introduce any thing into the ten years, which, according to our view, the permutation of an ι and κ adds to his age.

740. (2) We possess a twofold testimony, which places the return of Xerxes from Greece and his death in so close a connexion, that, without rejecting it, we cannot possibly assume a fifteen years' reign after this return, but are rather compelled to place his death not beyond the year 474. The first is that of Ælian, *Var. Hist.* 13. 3 : εἶτα ἐπανελθὼν, αἴσχιστα ἀνθρώπων ἀπέθανεν, ἀποσφαγεὶς νύκτωρ ἐν τῇ εὐνῇ ὑπὸ τοῦ υἱοῦ. The second, that of Justin, 3. 1. " *Xerxes rex Persarum, terror antea gentium, bello in Græciam infeliciter gesto, etiam suis contemtui esse cœpit. Quippe Artabanus præfectus ejus, deficiente quotidie regis majestate, in spem regni adductus, cum septem robustissimis filiis,*" etc.

741. (3) The testimonies of Justin, l. c., respecting the age of his sons at his death, are not reconcilable with the twenty-one years' reign of Xerxes. " *Securior de Artaxerxe, puero admodum, fingit regem a Dario, qui erat* adolescens, *quo maturius regno potiretur, occisum.*" If Xerxes reigned twenty-one years, his first-born, Darius, according to a comparison with Ctesias, chap. 22, could not at his death have been an *adolescens*, but at least thirty-one years old. On the contrary, if an eleven years' reign be assumed, these determinations are

---

[1] Comp. Beitr. I. p. 63.

entirely suitable. Darius was then towards twenty-one years old : Artaxerxes, according to Ctesias, chap. 20, nearly four years younger than Darius, about seventeen. This determination shows, also, that it cannot be objected against a fifty-one years' reign of Artaxerxes, that it would give him too great an age. The suggestion may be refuted by the simple remark, that *the length of his life* remains exactly the same, whether he reigned fifty-one or forty-one years. If he ascended the throne at seventeen, his life terminated at sixty-eight.

742. (4) According to the most numerous and weighty testimonies, the problematical peace of Cimon was concluded after the battle of the Eurymedon (before Christ 470). Now, as all agree that this peace was concluded with Artaxerxes, the commencement of his reign must, in any event, be placed before 470 [1].

743. (5) The history of Nehemiah is scarcely reconcilable with the supposition, that Artaxerxes reigned only forty-seven years. After Nehemiah had accomplished all that is related in chap. 1—12 of his book, he returned to Persia to discharge the duties of his office, at court. This happened, according to chap. 13. 6, in the thirty-second year of Artaxerxes. The time of his return is not accurately determined. It says merely, *after a considerable time* [2]. That his absence, however, must have continued *a whole series of years*, appears from the relation of what took place in the mean time. The law against marriage with foreign women, to the observance of which the people had bound themselves anew [3], was *first* violated during his absence ; *then again* by a decree of the people, executed in all severity [4], and *then again* broken, as appears from the fact, that Nehemiah, at his return [5], found a great many foreign women in the colony. That these marriages *had already existed for some time* appears from the twenty-fourth verse, where it is said, that the children of them had spoken half in the language of Ashdod, and could not speak Hebrew. A long absence is also implied in the other abuses which Nehemiah, according to chap. 13. 10, sq., found on his return. He saw the fruits of his former labours almost destroyed. The same is also evident from the prophecies of Malachi, which were delivered exactly in the time between the two periods of Nehemiah's presence at Jerusalem [6]. The condition of the people appears here, such as it could have been only after they had already been deprived, *for a considerable time*, of their two faithful leaders, Ezra (who, having arrived thirteen years earlier, had co-operated for a considerable time with Nehemiah), and Nehemiah himself. But, if we consider barely the first-mentioned fact, the marriages with foreign women, it will be evident, that a longer period than nine years would be required. For each change, there will then only three years be allowed, and as this

---

[1] Comp. Krüger, l. c. p. 218.   [2] לְקֵץ יָמִים

[3] Chap. 10. 30.   [4] Chap. 13. 1—3.

[5] According to v. 23.

[6] Comp. Vitringa's excellent *Dissert. de Ætate Mal.*, in his *Obbs. SS.* VI. 7. t. 2. p. 353, sq.

is undeniably too little for the third, according to the twenty-fourth
verse, the two first must be still more shortened, which is inadmissible. Besides, we have not even nine years for these events, if the
reign of Artaxerxes is fixed at forty-one years. For the relation of
Nehemiah presupposes, that Artaxerxes was still alive at the time of
its composition. This, however, cannot be placed in the time immediately after the return of Nehemiah, since it must have been preceded by the abolition of all these abuses. If, however, we are
conducted by the authority of Nehemiah (which is liable to no
exception, since he was contemporary, and closely connected with
Artaxerxes) a *few years over forty-one*, we have gained much. For
then the only objection to our determination, the testimony of the
canon, is completely set aside.

744. We must premise a remark, before we bring forward our
indirect proofs, in order to justify the connexion, in which we place
the commencement of the reign of Artaxerxes with the flight of
Themistocles. This connexion has not, indeed, the unanimous testimony of the ancient writers in its favour. The vouchers for it are,
Thucydides, chap. 137, where it is said of Themistocles, who had
come into Asia, ἐσπέμπει γράμματα ἐς βασιλέα ᾿Αρταξέρξην τὸν
Ξέρξον, νεωστὶ βασιλεύοντα, and Charon of Lampsacus, who, according to Plutarch, *Them.* chap. 27, makes him in like manner fly to
Artaxerxes. On the contrary, others, as Ephorus, Dinon, Klitarchus,
and Heraclides (comp. Plut. l. c.), represent him as going to *Xerxes.*
If, now, we examine these testimonies, according to the authority
of the witnesses, the decision will unquestionably be in favour of that
of Thucydides and Charon. Thucydides was contemporary with
Artaxerxes, and was born about the time of the flight of Themistocles. This prince of Greek historians gives [1], as the cause,
why he relates the events between the Median and Peloponnesian
war, that all his predecessors had passed over these events in silence,
and that the only one who touched upon them, Hellanicus, βρα-
χέως τε καὶ τοῖς χρόνοις οὐκ ἀκριβῶς ἐπεμνήσθη, from which it is
evident, first, how little certain are the accounts of this period in
later authors, because they *can have no credible contemporary voucher*
(since he could not have been unknown to Thucydides) ; and
secondly, that Thucydides himself claims to be regarded as a careful
and accurate historian of this period, and therefore must be esteemed
such, because so honest a man would assume nothing to himself,
which did not belong to him. The other witness, Charon, was the
less liable to err, since, at the very time of this event, he was a writer
of history, and even lived in Asia. On the other hand, the oldest
witnesses for the opposite supposition lived more than a century
after the event. Ephorus [2] outlived the dominion of Alexander in
Asia ; Dinon was father of Klitarchus, who accompanied Alexander.

745. In weighing these grounds, the authority of Thucydides and
Charon was unhesitatingly followed in ancient times. Plutarch, l. c.
does this, with the remark, that the testimony of Thucydides agrees

---

[1] Thucydides, chap. 97.   [2] See on his *Akrisie*, Dahlmann.

better with the chronological works. Nepos says : " *Scio plerosque ita scripsisse, Themistoclem Xerxe regnante in Asiam transiisse : sed ego potissimum Thucydidi credo, quod ætate proximus de his, qui illorum temporum historias reliquerunt, et ejusdem civitatis fuit.*" Suidas, and the Scholiast on *Aristoph. Equites*, from which the former borrowed *verbatim* his second article on Themistocles, makes him flee, πρὸς τὸν 'Αρταξέρξην, τὸν Ξέρξου τοῦ Πέρσου παῖδα, without even mentioning the other supposition. And in this respect, we have the less fear of contradiction, since, as far as we know, all modern critics, without exception, follow Thucydides and Charon. We only still remark, that the opposite view may the more easily be rejected, since *its origin can so readily be explained*, either from the fact, that this event fell on the border of the reigns of Xerxes and of Artaxerxes, or from a simple confounding of the two names, the assumption of which is the more easy, the more frequently it occurs ; we find it even in Aristotle, the contemporary of those writers, *Pol.* 5, 8, and twice in Ctesias, chap. 35, where Bähr would make a change in opposition to all the manuscripts, and chap. 44. Comp. Bähr on the passage, and Reimarus on *Dio Cass.* II. p. 1370. Finally, the errour might arise also from the circumstance, that the flight of Themistocles was placed in the right year, but twenty-one years were attributed to Xerxes, from which it necessarily follows, that he took refuge with Xerxes. This last opinion is favoured by the coincidence of several contemporary writers in the same errour, which presupposes some plausible reason for it.

746. We now proceed to lay down our *indirect* proofs. (1) We begin with the testimony which gives precisely the year of the flight of Themistocles, that of Cicero, *Lœl.* chap. 12. It is true, Corsini[1] asserts, that Cicero speaks of the year in which Themistocles was banished from Athens ; but we need only examine the passage, to be convinced of the contrary : " *Themistocles—fecit idem, quod* 20 *annis ante apud nos fecerat Coriolanus.*" The flight of Coriolanus to the Volsci falls in the year 263 u.c., b.c. 492. The flight of Themistocles is accordingly placed by Cicero in the year 472, a year later than by us, which is of no importance, since the round number twenty was the more suitable to the object of Cicero, as the more accurate nineteen, for the Chronologists. If Dodwell's view were correct, there would be the space of twenty-seven years between the two events.

747. (2) Diodorus Siculus, who, (11. 55.) places the flight of Themistocles in Ol. 77, 2 (b.c. 471), at all events, favours our determination, which ascends only two years higher, far more than the opposite one. We remark, however, that he also places in the same year the residence of Themistocles at Magnesia, and his death ; and thus it is evident, that, whether by mistake or design, he compresses the events in the life of Themistocles, which filled up some years, into the year of his death. If this took place in the year 471, his flight must be dated at least as

far back as 473. Our determination differs only by a single year from that of Eusebius, who records the flight of Themistocles in Ol. 77, 1.

748. (3) But the most convincing argument is, that the whole series of transactions, as they have been recorded in accurate order, especially by Thucydides, will not allow us to place the flight of Themistocles lower than the year 473. That the expedition of the allied Greeks under the direction of Pausanias, against Cyprus and Byzantium, the capture of the latter city, and the transfer of the supremacy from the Lacedemonians to the Athenians, occasioned by the insolence of Pausanias, fall in the year 477, we may regard as established beyond dispute by Clinton, p. 270 sq.[1] The view of O. Müller (*Dorier*, II. p. 498), who distributes these events into a period of five years, is contradicted by the expression ἐν τῇδε τῇ ἡγεμονίᾳ (Thucydides, chap. 94), whereby the capture of Byzantium is brought into the same year with the expedition against Cyprus. That these words cannot be connected with what follows, without a change of the text in opposition to all critical authority, is shown by Poppo. Moreover, the very last of these events is placed, by the unanimous testimony of antiquity, in the year 477. Clinton shows, p. 249, that, in calculating the duration of the Athenian *supremacy*, all writers set out from this year, and that their calculations differ from one another only in reference to the assumed termination. Also, in Thucyd. chap. 128, the expedition against Cyprus, and that against Byzantium, are connected as immediately succeeding each other. If, however, Dodwell were compelled by the force of the arguments to acknowledge, that these events, which he too compresses into one year, do not, as he assumes, (p. 61,) belong to the year 470, but to the year 477, he would undoubtedly be compelled, perceiving it to be impossible to lengthen out the thread of the events until the year 465, to give up the whole hypothesis. The dissatisfaction of the allies was followed by the recall of Pausanias. That this belongs still to the same year, plainly appears, partly from the nature of the case itself, since it presupposes a continuance of supremacy, partly from Thucydides, chap. 95 : ἐν τούτῳ δὲ οἱ Λακεδαιμόνιοι μετεπέμποντο Παυσανίαν, ἀνακρινοῦντες ὧν περὶ ἐπυνθάνοντο. Pausanias having come to Sparta, and been there set at liberty, now betook himself, without any command, in a galley to Byzantium. This cannot have happened long afterwards, for Thucydides, chap. 128, immediately subjoins it, and what is of the most importance, Pausanias finds the fleet still at Byzantium. That his residence there did not continue long, appears from the account of Thucydides, chap. 131, that he was forcibly expelled thence by the Athenians. He now retired to Colone in the Troad ; from thence, he was recalled to Sparta, after it had been reported that he kept up

---

[1] The grounds are thus briefly summed up by Win., p. 252. " Dodwelli rationi neutiquam favet Isocratis auctoritas. Repugnat rerum gestarum series, repugnat quod Thucyd. significat, Plutarchus et Aristides deserte tradunt, repugnat denique temporis spatium, quod Atheniensium imperio assignant Lysias, Isocrates ipse, Plato, Demosthenes, Aristides, quibus fortasse addendus est Lycurgus."

an understanding with the barbarians.   The Ephori threw him into prison, but soon after released him.   At this time, his intercourse with Themistocles took place, who, being at the time already expelled from Athens, resided at Argos, and thence made excursions into the rest of the Peloponnesus.   That Pausanias then for the first time drew Themistocles into his plan, when the latter had been driven from Athens, is asserted by Plutarch, and a personal intercourse between them is rendered certain by all accounts.   That there was no considerable period between this release of Pausanias, and his death, is clear.   Pausanias was not condemned, because there was no certain proof against him.   It is, however, psychologically improbable, that he did not soon afford one, but prudently kept himself from giving open offence for a *series of years*.   What ! Pausanias do this ? he, who by his pride, which reached the height of *insanity*, was so deprived of reason, that he himself rendered the execution of his treasonable plan impossible; the man, who, according to Thucydides[1], went about in a Median dress, caused himself to be accompanied on a journey through Thrace with Median and Egyptian satellites, had his table served in the Persian fashion, made the access to his person difficult, gave free course to his passions; the man of whom Thucydides himself very significantly remarks, καὶ κατέχειν τὴν διάνοιαν οὐκ ἠδύνατο, ἀλλ᾽ ἔργοις βραχέσι προὐδήλου, ἃ τῇ γνώμῃ μειζόνως ἐσέπειτα ἔμελλε πράξειν, and of whose senseless arrogance the same historian, in the hundred and thirty-second chapter, gives an example, even from the time immediately after the battle of Platea.   The discovery was effected by him who was to bring to Artabazus the last letters to the king.   With what haste the transactions were carried on, and that no such space as four years was consumed in them, is evident from the fact, that the king, in order to accelerate them, had expressly sent Artabazus to Asia Minor.   His death immediately followed the discovery[2].   We surely do not assume too little, when we allot to these events a period of three years.   That we need not go beyond this, is shown by Diodorus, who compresses all of them into the year 477 (Ol. 75, 4).   How could he have done this, or how could such an errour have arisen, if the beginning and end had been separated from each other by a period of 8 – 9 years ?   How impossible his authorities made it for him, to place the destruction of Pausanias much before this time, appears from his fiction, which can in no other way be explained, of a two-fold accusation of Themistocles.—If, now, we must place the death of Pausanias about the year 474, and in no event later, the flight of Themistocles cannot be placed further back than the year 473.   For, at the death of Pausanias, Themistocles had already been a considerable time in the Peloponnesus.   His accusation followed immediately after that event[3]; and the combined interests of the Lacedemonians, to whom nothing could be more desirable than to have the Athenians share their disgrace, and of the enemies

---

[1] Thucydides, chap. 130.   [2] Comp. Thucydides, 133.
[3] Comp. Thucydides, 1. 135.

of Themistocles at Athens (Plut. *Them.* chap. 23 : κατεβόων μὲν αὐτοῦ Λακεδαιμόνιοι, κατηγόρουν δ' οἱ φθονοῦντες τῶν πολιτῶν) would cause the decision to be hastened as much as possible. Themistocles, persecuted by both the Athenians and the Lacedemonians, now flees from the Peloponnesus to Corcyra. Being denied a residence there, he retires to the opposite continent. In danger of being overtaken by his persecutors [1], he sees himself compelled to flee to Admetus, the king of the Molossians. Nor can he have resided there long, for, according to Thucydides [2], he was sent away by Admetus, as soon as his persecutors arrived. And how can we suppose, that *they would have been years behind him?* How long could his place of residence have remained a secret? It is expressly said by Thucydides, that the coming of his persecutors, and the flight of Themistocles to Asia, happened very soon [3]. It is true, that if we could credit the account of Stesimbrotus [4], we must assume that the residence of Themistocles with Admetus continued some months. For this author relates that his friends brought to him there his wife and children, whom they had secretly conducted out of Athens. But that no dependence is to be placed upon this, is evident from the absurd fiction that immediately follows, which, to the surprise even of Plutarch [5], he brings forward, without observing that the one fable does away the other, viz., that Themistocles was sent by Admetus to Sicily, and had desired Hiero his daughter in marriage, with the promise to bring Greece under subjection to him. Plutarch designates Stesimbrotus as a shameless liar [6]. That the sons of Themistocles remained in Athens, is manifest from a relation in Suidas; and the testimony of Thucydides [7] and Plutarch, that the gold was sent to Themistocles by his friends, *after his arrival in Asia*, to enable him to reward the service of the captain who conveyed him to that continent, shows at once the incorrectness of Stesimbrotus's assertion, and confirms the opinion, that Themistocles remained in no one place of his flight long enough for his friends to send to him there the necessary gold. Themistocles was conducted by Admetus to Pydna, and from thence he betook himself in a boat directly to Asia. This accordingly (since between the death of Pausanias, and the coming of Themistocles into Asia, there could be only a year at most,) must at latest have happened in the year 473, perhaps in 474; and even in the former case, we are completely justified in placing the beginning of the reign of Artaxerxes, which however cannot have immediately coincided with the coming of Themistocles, in the year 474.

749. (4) On the supposition that the commencement of Artaxerxes' reign, and the flight of Themistocles, fall in 465, an extra-

[1] Thucydides, chap. 136: καὶ διωκόμενος ὑπὸ τῶν προστεταγμένων κατὰ πύστιν ᾗ χωροίη.

[2] Thucydides, chap. 137.   [3] ὕστερον οὐ πολλῷ.

[4] In Plut. chap. 24.

[5] Εἶτ' οὐκ οἶδ' ὅπως ἐπιλαθόμενος τούτων, ἢ τὸν Θεμιστοκλέα ποιῶν ἐπιλαθόμενον, πλεῦσαί φησιν κ. τ. λ.

[6] Pericles, chap. 13.   [7] Thucydides, chap. 137.

vagant old age must be attributed to Charon of Lampsacus. According to Suidas, he was still flourishing under the first Darius, Ol. 69, 504 B. C.   Since now, in his history, he mentions the flight of Themistocles to Artaxerxes, if this is placed in 465, he must have been employed in writing history at least forty years.   This is not, indeed, *absolutely impossible;* but in a doubtful case it must be rejected as the *more improbable* alternative.   That this argument is not without force, is evident even from the efforts of some advocates of the false chronology, to set it aside by cutting the knot.   Suidas, after citing the above-mentioned determination of the time of Charon, as he found it in his more ancient authorities, subjoins, μᾶλλον δὲ ἦν ἐπὶ τῶν Περσικῶν.   Creuzer [1] rejects this date without further examination, because it gives too great an age to Charon.

750.   (5) According to Thucydides [2], Themistocles, on his passage to Asia, fell in *with the Athenian* fleet, which was besieging Naxos. Now this siege of Naxos, according to the testimony of Thucydides [3], which makes all other arguments superfluous, happened before the great victory of the Athenians on the Eurymedon, which, according to Diodorus, belongs to the year 470, and cannot be placed later, because this was the first considerable undertaking of the Athenians against the Persians, the war with whom formed the only ground for the important requisitions which they made upon their allies [4].   Hitherto, since the supremacy had passed over to the Athenians, scarcely any thing had been done against the Persians, except the taking of the unimportant Ægon.   Thucydides also leads us to about the same year as that given by Diodorus, who connects the defection of Thasos (467) with χρόνῳ ὕστερον, which cannot stand where events immediately succeed each other.   Even for these reasons the siege of Naxos and the flight of Themistocles do not fall after 471.   If, however, we consider, that Naxos was the first confederate city with which the Athenians were involved in discord [5] (which, from the nature of the case, as is rendered especially clear by the remarks of Thucydides and a comparison of the later history, must surely have happened before the seventh year), and if we further consider the way in which Thucydides, chap. 98, connects the events, from the transfer of the supremacy until the capture of Naxos, with one another, we shall, without hesitation, place the latter some years earlier, in the year 474 or 473.

751.   (6) The flight of Themistocles falls at least three years earlier than the battle on the Eurymedon, because in all probability he was dead before the latter event.   His death, however, must have been some years subsequent to his coming into Asia, comp. Thucyd. chap. 138.   One year passed in learning the language, and *some* time, at all events, was required for what is implied in ταύτης ἦρχε τῆς χώρας, δόντος κ. τ. λ.   Thucydides relates, that, according to the account of some, Themistocles took poison, ἀδύνατον νομίσαντα

[1] Creuzer, on the *fragm. historr. Græc.* p. 95.
[2] Thucydides, 1. 136.   [3] Thucydides, chap. 100.
[4] Comp. Thucyd. 1. 94.   [5] Comp. Thucyd. P. 1. 98.

εἶναι ἐπιτελέσαι βασιλεῖ, ἃ ὑπέσχετο. This presupposes that Themistocles was then loudly called upon to fulfil his promises ; and this must have been the *actual state of things* at the time of his death, for otherwise Thucydides *could not* have mentioned the report without refuting it, nor, indeed, could it have ever arisen. Plutarch expressly connects the death of Themistocles with the expedition of Cimon. This is done by several writers, with the mention of the most special circumstances[1], all which may be regarded, as they are by Cicero[2] and Nepos, as fictitious, and yet the historical basis, on which alone every thing depends, *the fact* that Thucydides died before the battle on the Eurymedon, be firmly established.

752. (7) Krüger[3] has shown that the account of Plutarch, that Themistocles reached an age of sixty-five years, forbids us to place his death beyond the year 470, and therefore his flight beyond the year 473. According to an account which has internal evidence of credibility in Ælian, *Var. Hist.* III. 21, Themistocles, when a little boy coming from school, declined going out of the way for the tyrant Pisistratus. Assuming that this happened in the last year of Pisistratus, B. c. 529, and that Themistocles, was at that time six years old, he must have been born in 535, and died in 470. Nor is it a valid objection, that, according to Plutarch, Themistocles was still living at the time of Cimon's expedition to Cyprus (449 B. c.), and was still young at the battle of Marathon. For the former rests on a manifest confounding of the former event with the victory over the Persian fleet at Cyprus, which is supposed to have immediately preceded the victory on the Eurymedon[4], and the latter merely on a conclusion drawn from this errour. "Whoever," remarks Dahlmann, p. 71, "reads without prejudice the passage, Thucyd. 1. 138, will perceive that the death of Themistocles followed pretty soon after his settlement in Persia ; probably in the second year, if Thucydides is worthy of credit."

753. Until all these arguments are refuted, it remains true, that the Messianic interpretation of the prophecy is the only correct one, and that the alleged Pseudo-Daniel, as well as the real Daniel, possessed an insight into the future which could have been given only by the Spirit of God ; and hence, as this favour could have been shown to no deceiver, the genuineness of the book necessarily follows, and the futility of all objections against it is at once manifest.

The Last Week and Its Half

754. We have shown, that the last week begins with the public appearing of the anointed, and that his death falls in the middle of it, while the confirmation of the covenant extends entirely through it. There is here no occasion to show the accurately exact fulfilment

---

[1] Compare the passages in Staveren on *Nep. Them.* 10.
[2] *Brut.* chap. 11.   [3] Krüger, l. c. p. 218.
[4] Comp. Diodor. 11. 60. Dahlmann, *Forschungen,* I. p. 69.

of the prophecy, except for the single point of Christ's death. For the *terminus ad quem* of the confirmation of the covenant, being more or less indefinite, is incapable of any accurate chronological determination. It is sufficient to remark, that in the first years after the death of Christ, the ἐκλογή was collected from among the ancient covenant people,—with what success is shown, e. g., by the history of the first Pentecost,—and that then the message concerning Christ was carried also to the heathen, so that the prophet might justly represent the salvation, as both subjectively and objectively completed for the covenant people (of whom alone he is speaking) at the end of the seventy weeks.

755. The view, that the death of Christ is separated from his baptism by a period of three and a half years, is found in several fathers. Thus in Eusebius, *Hist. Eccl.* 1. 10 : οὐδ᾽ ὅλος ὁ μεταξὺ τετραέτης παρίσταται χρόνος ; and while this historian makes an erroneous calculation to sustain his result [1], in Theodoret an entirely correct basis, almost beyond his age, is adopted. See on the passage, tom. II. p. 1250, ed. Hal.: εἰ δέ τις καὶ τὸν χρόνον καταμαθεῖν ἐθέλει, ἐκ τοῦ κατὰ Ἰωάννην εὐαγγελίου μαθήσεται· ὡς περὶ τὰ τρία ἔτη καὶ ἥμισυ κηρύξας ὁ κύριος καὶ τοὺς ἁγίους αὐτοῦ μαθητὰς τῇ διδασκαλίᾳ καὶ τοῖς θαύμασι βεβαιώσας, τότε τὸ πάθος ὑπέμεινε.

756. The decision depends entirely on the Evangelist John. Three passovers during the ministry of Christ are *expressly* mentioned by him [2]. A fourth is the subject of controversy. According to what may be proved from chap. 5. 1. (μετὰ ταῦτα ἦν ἑορτὴ τῶν Ἰουδαίων, καὶ ἀνέβη ὁ Ἰησοῦς εἰς Ἱεροσόλυμα,) must the death of Christ be placed in the *fourth* or in the *third* year after his public appearance.

757. The answer of the question, *what feast is meant* in this passage, is greatly simplified by the circumstance, that in recent times it is generally confessed, that the choice can lie only between the *feast of Purim* and the *Passover*. This concession, moreover, rests on so good a ground, that we may confidently pass over the remaining opinions in silence. It appears, particularly from John 4. 35, where the Lord says, *There are yet four months to the harvest,* that at that time, *before* the feast mentioned in chap. 5. 1, and *since* the first Passover mentioned, in chap. 2. 13, *eight months* had already elapsed. For the termination of these four months coincides with the new Passover, since, according to both law and custom, the harvest in Palestine began with the Passover. The feasts of Pentecost and of Tabernacles of this year are therefore *excluded*, because both lie within the abovementioned period of eight months, and, should any one suppose the feast intended to be one of these feasts in the *following year*, it would be equally in favour of our view. The supposition would take it for granted, that John has omitted to mention one Passover.

758. The assertion, that the feast meant is the feast of Purim, the more deserves a thorough investigation, since, having in former times been kept in the background, it has lately found

---

[1] Comp. Valesius, *Ann.* on the passage.
[2] One in 2. 13, the other in 6. 4, and then the last.

many able defenders. Among these the first place is occupied by Hug[1], who is followed by Lücke and Tholuck.

759. The chief argument advanced for this opinion, and against the passover, is the following :—" As our Lord remained at home till after the passover, of which mention is made some days after His return, He did not appear in Jerusalem from the time of *the supposed passover*, until this, i. e. for a whole year, and then for six months longer, until the feast of tabernacles. Consequently he neglected the duty of the public worship of God for a year and a half. This supposition entirely contradicts the purpose of Jesus to fulfil even external righteousness; besides, by such conduct, He would have exposed Himself to public reproach."—A strange argument indeed ; for, by his going to the feast of Purim, the case of Christ would have been neither better nor worse. His presence at *this* feast could not be reckoned as a fulfilment of righteousness; for it was not prescribed in the law of God, and it was only under this law, and not under that of human ordinances, that the Son of God was placed. Just as little could prudential reasons have moved him to this course ; for *no human ordinance required the celebration of the feast of Purim at Jerusalem*. If, therefore, the difficulty were real, it would affect the defenders of this view, no less than ourselves. Let a man be at Jerusalem through the whole of the rest of the year, absenting himself only at the three feasts whose celebration in Jerusalem had been prescribed, and he was just as much guilty of the violation of the law, as the man who never set his foot in Jerusalem. Besides, the whole difficulty is only an apparent one. The reason why Jesus remained so long away from Jerusalem, is plainly enough given, chap. 7. 1: '*for he would not walk in Jewry, because the Jews sought to kill him.*' But this reason was completely decisive for our Lord, according to the position which He always took in reference to the ceremonial law. He held himself bound to the observance of it, only so far as it did not conflict with higher purposes. These were never sacrificed to it. In this respect the passage, Matt. 12. 3, is a *locus classicus*. To prove that the ceremonial law is not binding under all circumstances, our Lord there refers those who accused His disciples of violating it, to the example of David, who, without being on that account blamed in the Scripture, ate the shew-bread, contrary to the law. He next points to his absolute authority, which justifies Him in breaking the law, when this would promote his higher purposes. He calls Himself the Lord of the Sabbath. He designates Himself as a greater than the Temple. The hour of Christ was not yet come; his presence at Jerusalem must have been an occasion to His enemies to strive to hasten it before the time ; not to employ all human means to avoid this danger, would be to tempt God.—Even for one who was not like the Son of God, the Lord of the Sabbath and of the feasts, but unconditionally subject to the law, the binding force of the outward religious ordinances of the law was daily becoming weaker. Was the Temple at the time already changed into a den of robbers [2];

---

[1] *Einl.* Th. 2, p. 197, ff. ed. 2.   [2] Luke 19. 46.

was the ungodliness already in the process of full developement, which soon afterwards made it completely a house of abomination? how then could the laws be applied in their whole extent, which relate to it as the house of God? The Temple by no means consisted of lime and stone; as to its essential nature, it was at that time already as much destroyed, as during the Babylonian exile; and the neglect to visit it was therefore as little censurable now as then, if circumstances directed the attention to that view, according to which, it was no more a house of God.

760. This argument is, however, the only one which has been thought valid in recent times. The remaining " *argumenta ficulnea*," which Lamy and D'Outrein [1] have adduced, we may therefore well omit, especially as Lampe has already thoroughly refuted them. Let us then proceed to lay down the arguments for our own view.

761. (1) It can admit of no doubt, that John does not here speak of a *festum aliquod*, but designates *a definite feast*. Otherwise, he would act in direct opposition to the object which the accurate mention of the feasts by him serves every where to promote. They are the dates, according to which he orders the whole history. He mentions the passover, accordingly, even where Christ does not observe it, chap. 6. ver. 4. Every feast is always elsewhere accurately designated by him; and this is entirely natural, since an *indefinite* feast cannot serve as a measure of time. We translate, therefore, *the* feast of the Jews, without availing ourselves of the occurrence of the article in many manuscripts, except as a proof that this interpretation is very ancient. The omission of the article should not have been objected against it by Lücke and Tholuck. According to a Hebraism as widely spread through the Seventy and the New Testament, as it has been little observed [2], the definite article stands before the second instead of the first of two nouns, connected by the genitive case. We cite only a few from a number of examples. Deut. 16. 13, ἑορτὴν τῶν σκηνῶν ποιήσεις σεαυτῷ [3]. Matt. 12. 24, ἐν τῷ Βεελζεβοὺλ ἄρχοντι τῶν δαιμονίων, where Fritzsche, because this use was unknown to him, in opposition to all manuscripts, proposes to change the text: ἐν Β. τῷ ἄρχοντι τῶν δαιμονίων. In Luke 2. 11, ἐν πόλει Δαβίδ, the *Nom. propr.* [4] is equivalent to an appellative with the article. Acts 8. 5, εἰς πόλιν τῆς Σαμαρείας, to *the* city, the capital of Samaria [5]. But if it is established, that here the discourse is concerning *the feast of the Jews*, κατ᾽ ἐξ., who could think of any other feast than that of the passover? It is this which had already been mentioned in the preceding context, chap. 2. 13. No other can come in competition with it. Among all, it was by far the greatest [6]. The τῶν Ἰουδαίων is never used by John of any

---

[1] In the *Bibl. Brem.* I. p 610.   [2] Comp. Ew. p. 579.

[3] In the Hebr. חַג הַסֻּכּוֹת. [Deut. xvi. 3, cannot prove that the gen. τῶν Ἰουδαίων can make ἑορτή = ἡ ἑορτή, for there was but *one* ἑορτὴ τῶν σκηνῶν. See Lücke ad loc.]

[4] As also in Hebrew, where עִיר דָוִד can only mean *the*, not *a*, city of David.

[5] Comp. Heumann and Kuinöl on the passage.

[6] Comp. the proofs in Lund, p. 974.

other feast than the three great ones appointed in the law, twice
of the passover, otherwise of the feast of tabernacles. How can
it be proved, that the idea occurred, even at a later period, to
place the feast of Purim upon a level with these feasts, and particularly the passover? The passages cited by Hug, p. 200, do not
refer to the feast, but to the book of Esther. That feast was always
regarded more as *a feast of the people*, than *a religious ordinance*.
The knowledge of the original opposition to its introduction was
not forgotten [1]. And then how can we argue from that later period
to the former? It was entirely natural, that the feast should gain
in esteem, as the Jews became more carnally minded; that the three
chief feasts, on the contrary, should retain their distinctive dignity,
so long as the Temple stood, and the whole mass of the people went
up for their celebration to Jerusalem.

762. (2) An invincible difficulty in the way of a reference to the
feast of Purim, is presented by the ἀνέβη ὁ Ἰησοῦς εἰς Ἱεροσόλυμα,
in connexion with the fourteenth verse, from which it seems evident,
that *the city was filled with those who sought the festival*. That men
did not journey to Jerusalem to celebrate the feast of Purim, arose
from the nature of the case. The feast stood in no relation to the
Temple; even in Jerusalem it was not celebrated with any divine
service. The whole celebration was limited to reading the book of
Esther, which was brought into the synagogues, to abstaining from
labour, and to eating and drinking. The feast was kept by the
Jews of the dispersion, at an earlier period than by those of Palestine. We can abundantly show, from definite testimonies, that a
journey to Jerusalem on the feast of Purim was never thought of.
Josephus [2] says, the feast of Purim was celebrated by the Jews of
all places, and was attended by feasting. In the Talmud Cod.
Megillah, cap. 1, § 1—3, it is determined, at what time the Purim
should be celebrated in the cities, which, in the days of Joshua, were
surrounded with walls, in those which at that time were without
walls, and in the villages [3]. An appeal cannot be made in opposition
to this, that, according to the tenth chapter and twenty-second verse,
Jesus was still in Jerusalem at the *Enkænia*, which, in like manner, might be celebrated out of Jerusalem. This would at most only
be of importance, if Jesus *had journied* to Jerusalem for this purpose.
But the object of his journey was only to attend the feast of tabernacles. He still remained a considerable time afterwards in Jerusalem, and during his stay there the *Enkænia* happened. And
besides, if this were not so, still the *Enkænia*, as a feast of the dedication of the Temple, stood in so close a relation to it, that, in this
instance, many probably performed what the law did not require.

763. (3) It is in a high degree improbable, that Jesus sought the
feast of Purim, and neglected the passover, which happened a month
later. After every effort, it is impossible to adduce even a plausible

---

[1] Comp. Lightfoot on John 10. 22.   [2] *Arch.* 11. 6.
[3] Comp. on the ground of these determinations, Vitringa, *de decem otiosis*,
c. 18, in *Ugolini Thes.* t. 21, p. 421 sq.

reason for this. The cited passage, John 7. 1, in which Lücke, though with great hesitation, believes he finds such a proof, proves directly the opposite. In the feast of the passover, Christ was protected by the Galilean ὄχλοι; in the Purim his enemies had free scope (Mark 14. 2. Lücke on 10. 22). And was there any thing in the nature of the feast of Purim, which could attract Jesus? We are far from wishing to attack the authority of the book of Esther, but still, in respect to the true standard, its reference to Christ, it undoubtedly holds the lowest place among all the books of the Old Testament. Is it conceivable, that He, who never even in the slightest manner mentions this book, whose apostles no where appeal to it, should have made a point—as Hug asserts—of attending at the feast, which was consecrated to the remembrance of the event described in this book, in order to manifest esteem and regard for it? And was indeed a feast like this, where drinking was *meritorious*, where it was customary to drink until they could no longer distinguish between *Blessed be Mordecai*, and *Accursed be Haman*, suited to effect the object of the Lord in all his journeys to Jerusalem? Surely even a human teacher would not thus choose time and place.

764. (4) The healing of the sick person happened, according to the ninth verse, on the sabbath; and that this sabbath belonged to the feast, appears from the mode in which the first and second verses are connected, and also from the thirteenth verse. Here, however, the feast of Purim is entirely excluded; this feast *could not* be celebrated on the sabbath, because the two were inconsistent with one another, and because the divine institution could not give way to the human. If it happened on such a day, it was deferred [1].

765. (5) The sick man whom the Lord healed, had been sick thirty-eight years. We consider this man as a type of the Jewish people, and find in the thirty-eight years a reference to the thirty-eight years' affliction of Israel in the journey through the wilderness, which was terminated by the first passover in Canaan; which was at the same time the feast of reconciliation with the Lord, after the immediately preceding renewed circumcision had removed the reproach of Egypt from the people, and freed them from the guilt of the impurity which they had brought with them out of Egypt: comp. Josh. chap. 5. We know that this ground will appear strange to some, but perhaps they will recover from their astonishment, if they more carefully consider the many New Testament analogies in its favour, as they have been collected in part by De Wette [2]. Is it indeed any thing else, when John (19. 36) refers a passage which originally concerns the Easter lamb, directly to Christ? when, according to him, Jesus, in the sixth chapter, takes occasion from the nearness of the passover, to speak of himself as the true bread, and true flesh, that which the unleavened bread and the Paschal lamb typified? Or when, chap. 7. 37, he represents himself as the substance of a

---

[1] Comp. the proofs in Reland, *Antiqq. Sacr.* IV. 9, and in Schickard, *De Festo Purim* in the *Crit. Sacr.* VI. p. 491, sq. Fft.

[2] In the *Beiträge zur Characteristik des Hebraismus* (*Studien*, 1807, II. p. 245).

sacred usage, which prevailed during the feast of tabernacles? On this subject much might still be said. The elucidation of the doctrine of types, which are now entirely neglected, is an important problem for future theologians. Still, we hope that even for those with whom this argument has no weight, our assertion is sufficiently proved and at the same time our problem solved[1].

The Non-Messianic Interpreters[2]

[There follows in the original a refutation of the arguments of *Bertholdt* and *Bleek*. The professor adds with great truth:— 1. That the so often repeated assertion, that Josephus regarded, or at least *declared*, Vespasian to be the Messiah, (comp. z. B. Ittig. *Prolegg.* in Havercamp, II. p. 93, and Bretschneider, *Capp. Theol. Jud. Dogm. ex Josepho*, p. 36,) is entirely erroneous, although even Origen, whose testimony is abused to render suspicious that concerning Christ, seems to have held this opinion, while Suetonius, in the fifth chapter, more considerately attributes nothing to Josephus, but what actually belongs to him, the annunciation of the establishment of the power of the Cæsars, in Vespasian. The foundation of this proof is the passage chap. 10. 10, 4, where Josephus, in believing confidence, expected the future establishment of the kingdom of glory; only he expressed himself with that forethought, which his difficult position, the great hatred of his countrymen, which even led them to accuse him before the Romans of *studii rerum novarum* (comp. *De Bell. Jud.* 7. 11), required. 2. That the passage concerning Christ is neither spurious, nor interpolated; and 3. That Josephus at the time of the composition of his works was a Christian, —if we can give this name to one, who has lively impressions of the truth of Christianity, although still weak and unsettled in the faith, —perhaps had become one by the mournful catastrophe, which he lived to witness.]

766. We now look around for the arguments against the Messianic interpretation, but one only presents itself; which, even if it were something more than a theological invalid, would still scarcely come off victorious in the contest with such a host of powerful opponents. "On the supposition of the genuineness of those prophecies, we must in no wise interpret them, so that therein will be given an accurate determination of the time of the establishment or completion of the kingdom of heaven. For when the Redeemer denies to

---

[1] In reference to an important argument, arising from a comparison of the remaining Gospels, see the acute essay of Süsskind, in Bengel's *Arch.* 1. p. 185 sq.

[2] The reference to the time of the Maccabees, and the whole Non-Messianic interpretation, will remain false, as long as the word *of Christ remains true*, therefore, *to all eternity*. That the passage, Matt. 24. 15, refers to this prophecy, has been shown in *Beitr.* I. p. 263, and that the Lord cites it, as a real prophecy, which concerned the destruction of city and Temple, to be first fulfilled at a future time, in the same place, p. 266.

the angels of heaven, and even to Himself, such a knowledge of the future in reference to the time and hour, (Matt. 24. 36. Mark 13. 32,) and that even after His resurrection, (Acts 1. 6, 7,) we cannot possibly assume, that this should be revealed to another prophet, and moreover to one of a much earlier period, so that he could have communicated that time with chronological accuracy to his people, whether in the usual, or in any so called mystical measure of time, so far as this is still to be regarded as definite." Thus Bleek, l. c. p. 234. That is to say, in other words, because Christ did not consider it suitable to give to His disciples, who were eager for the reward before they had endured the conflict; who inquired about things beyond their comprehension, and not suited to their present condition, and thus forgot to strive for the one thing necessary for them, the being born from above; who were still carnal, and to whom the Lord had still much to say, which they were as yet unable to bear; because, I say, He did not give these disciples a revelation concerning the establishment of the *regnum gloriæ*, which, on account of their condition, could only be injurious, the more so the further distant the completion of the salvation, and the more necessary it was that they should now be pointed directly to its *ground*,—therefore God cannot have given to a prophet of the Old Testament a disclosure of the time of the establishment of the *regnum gratiæ*; and although a prophecy, investigated according to all the laws of a sound interpretation, accurately gives this time even to a year, and although no errour in the interpretation and chronology can be pointed out, yet it is certain, beforehand, that it is false. But what right have we to refer what was said in respect to the *regnum gloriæ*, directly to the *regnum gratiæ?* What right to understand, as universally denied, what even concerning the *regnum gloriæ* is denied only in respect to a definite time? Bengel, in the most admirable manner [1], has already refuted those, who have argued from these passages against the existence of definite dates in the Apocalypse. He says, among other things, " *Non dixit, nemo sciet, sed nemo scit. Ipse jam jamque sciturus erat, et quum scientiam diei et horæ nactus fuit, ipsius erat scientiam dare, cui vellet et quando vellet.*"—That the ground of the Saviour's refusal lay in the condition of the disciples, is evident from Acts 1. 7, οὐχ ὑμῶν ἐστι γνῶναι χρόνους ἢ καιρούς, οὓς ὁ πατὴρ ἔθετο ἐν τῇ ἰδίᾳ ἐξουσίᾳ, comp. with ver. 8, ἀλλὰ λήψεσθε δύναμιν ἐπελθόντος τοῦ ἁγίου πνεύματος ἐφ' ὑμᾶς, i. q., it is not *this* which is necessary for you, but *something else*, and while God denies the former, he will grant the latter. The only course by which this argument would have the appearance of validity, would be to say, should God have imparted chronologically definite disclosures respecting future things to a prophet, when the Lord, who, even in his state of humiliation, was greater than all prophets, designated such disclosures as beyond his condition? Then, however, the contest would be carried on at the same time against all other chronologically definite prophecies, not merely of the Old Testament, but also of Christ Himself, who

---

[1] In the *Gnomon*, and in the *Ordo Tempp.* p. 301 sq.

certainly predicted that after three days He would rise again, and even against all prophecies, in which other contingent circumstances are predicted. For how are chronological determinations different from others ? At the same time the greatest difficulties of other kinds arise. For how can we regard a whole province of divine knowledge as absolutely inaccessible, even when it would serve his purpose, to Him who knew that the Father *always* heard Him, John 11. 42, to whom the Father showed *all* things that He did, John 5. 20.   These passages, and a multitude of others, show that the correct view of the ignorance of the Lord, is rather this : Christ, in the state of humiliation, in which the divine nature was quiescent, received all that was requisite for the execution of His office, beyond the powers and gifts of His human nature, by communication from above, which He supplicated in prayer.   In Himself He possessed neither the power to do a miracle, nor to look through the future ; but never was this power denied to His prayer, since on account of the unity of His will with that of God, He could pray for nothing, which was not in accordance with God's designs.   Hence, it appears that the *ignorance* of the Son was a simple consequence of His *not willing ;* and this, again, was owing to the condition of His disciples. In like manner the Lord, *without thereby in the least encroaching upon His power of working miracles,* might have answered the demand of Satan to change stone into bread, that He *could not* do this.   If, however, the ignorance of Christ was a consequence of the unsuit-ableness of the required knowledge in reference to time and persons, how can we infer from this, that He did not at another time impart to His servants, the prophets, and through them to His people, the chronologically definite disclosures respecting the future that *were* suitable ?

THE PROPHET HOSEA

[In his general preliminary observations to this prophet, Professor Hengsten-berg shows that his mentioning *all the kings of Judah* under whom he prophesied, but only *one* of the kings of Israel, does not prove him to have been by birth a Jew ; for the pious Israelites, especially the prophets, considered the whole sepa-ration *an apostasy ;* so that they still acknowledged the princes of the house of David as their sovereigns *de jure,* though they paid civil obedience to their sovereigns *de facto.* He would probably not have mentioned *even one* of the kings of Israel, had it not been necessary to mark out that he began to prophesy in the early part of Uzziah's reign, when Jeroboam was the king of the ten tribes ; for, as Uzziah survived Jeroboam twenty-six years, the overthrow of Jeroboam's family, which Hosea predicted, would have been a *prophecy after the event,* if the prediction had not been delivered till the *latter half* of Uzziah's reign. The probability that he was an Israelite is (says our author) as a hun-dred to one.—He also shows that the long duration of the Prophet's agency (sixty years at the least) is no argument against the genuineness and authenticity of the superscription. It is his opinion, that we do not possess the whole of the prophecies of Hosea, but only the substance of their most important contents, a review given by himself towards the end of his course.]

767. The kingdom of Israel, from its very commencement, con-tained within itself a twofold germ of destruction, the institution of

the worship of the calves, and the apostasy from the dynasty of David. As to the former, the consequence of this apparently isolated violation of a Mosaic ordinance extended much further than would appear on a superficial view. It was shown here also, that a little leaven leavens the whole lump. Still more important than the low conceptions of God, which were caused by this symbolical representation of Him, was another aspect of the transaction. The prohibition of the worship of images in the Pentateuch was as definite and clear as possible. The kings of Israel were far from rejecting this prohibition; but as they allowed themselves to pervert and explain away this law against their better conscience, probably asserting that it was given only in reference to the rude and sensual conception of the first generations, so were they prepared to do this in other instances also, as often as they were incited by their corrupt heart. Every action of conscious unfaithfulness which is nevertheless cherished and both internally and outwardly excused, must draw after it a total apostasy in the case of a community, no less than in that of an individual. Moreover, this first change in the nature of religion proceeded from the civil power, which secured to itself for the future also unlimited influence in the affairs of religion, by bringing into subjection the *ecclesiastical* power, which was independent and opposed to it. The Levites, who declared against the worship of the calves, without resorting to the miserable sophistry which the king invented to excuse it, were exiled; and, in their place, creatures of the king were made ministers of the sanctuary. And this measure would subject[1] to *his* caprice the sanctuary of THE KING, and the whole substance of religion, in direct contradiction to the Mosaic constitution: the consequence of this would necessarily be the more disastrous, the more corrupt the kings were, and, from the base foundation on which the regal power rested, necessarily must be.

768. With the worship of images idolatry was soon connected. But neither are we to regard this as an open opposition to the true God. Such opposition is found only during *one* reign, that of Ahab, in which the apostasy was carried to the utmost extremity. That it has been supposed to be practised at other times, is wholly owing to the circumstance, that the Scripture, disregarding the multitude of wretched excuses, calls that a *direct* apostasy from God, which was so as to its essence, though not its outward form. Men rendered outward obedience to Jehovah; they celebrated His feasts; they brought the sacrifices prescribed in the Pentateuch; they regulated, in general, the whole of religion, according to His ordinances, as may be shown from the books of Kings, and still more from Amos and Hosea; but they contrived a way of *identifying* light with darkness, of combining (that is) the worship of idols with the worship of the true God. As the eye was not single, this was not very difficult. They had the example of heathen nations before them, who were entirely prepared to render reciprocal acknowledgement to their dei-

---

[1] Comp. the remarkable passage, Amos 7. 13.

ties, in whom they perceived only different manifestations of one and the same divine Being, and who also readily extended this acknowledgement to the God of Israel, so long as they were not led into intolerance themselves by meeting with intolerance on the part of His worshippers. Among the nations in the midst of whom the Israelites lived, this mutual acknowledgement of their religions manifested itself in the fact, that they *all* designated their highest deity by the same name, *Baal*, designating the form of revelation peculiar to each, by an added epithet. Thus the Israelites thought at once to satisfy the requirements of *their* God, and to conciliate towards themselves the idols of the surrounding and powerful nations, particularly the Phœnicians, if they removed the wall of partition between both. In their view, Jehovah and Baal were in their nature identical. The former, as the form of revelation belonging especially to *them*, was the chief object of their reverence, according to the method prescribed by Himself in His revelation ; the latter, however, was not to be neglected, because they might thereby become partakers of the blessings which this particular manifestation of the Deity brought with itself. And thus they named Jehovah *Baal* also[1]; they celebrated the days of Jehovah[2], but also the days of *Baal*[3]. And thus is explained the at first sight striking phenomenon, that we find, in Hosea and Amos, every thing full of the worship of Baal, while, at the same time, the books of Kings would lead us to believe, that, with the reign of Ahab, the prevalence of this worship had ceased. It was only their hostile opposition to the worship of Jehovah which had disappeared. A far more dangerous amalgamation of religion took its place. It is evident on which side the advantage would lie in this division. Plainly on that which *always* prevails when the heart is divided between truth and falsehood. Outwardly, the worship of Jehovah would predominate, but inwardly idolatry would be exalted to an almost sole dominion. And the danger was increased by the very circumstance, that they still continued to rely on the covenant and the promises of Jehovah, and on their outward service, and thus were strengthened in their false security.

769. The *natural* consequence of this apostasy from the Lord was a frightful corruption of manners. The first result of this spiritual adultery was that which is corporeal. Licentiousness constituted a fundamental principle, as of the Asiatic religions in general, so especially of those with whom the Israelites came into contact. But the deadly influence spread still wider over the whole region of morals. Where there is no holy God, there there are no efforts of man after holiness. All divine and human rights were trampled under foot; all the bands of love, of law, and of order were dissolved. Thus is the condition of the land, in a moral respect, uniformly described by its two prophets; comp., e. g., Hos. 4. 1, 2, ' *There is no faithfulness and no love, and no knowledge of God in the land. To curse, and lie, and murder, aud steal, and commit adultery ;—they break through, and blood touches blood.*' From this moral cor-

---

[1] Hos. 2. 16.　　　[2] Ver. 13.　　　[3] Ver. 15.

ruption, then, again followed the internal dissolution of the state, and its external weakness.

770. The *supernatural* consequence of the apostasy from the Lord, was a severe punishment which He inflicted upon the people. God will be sanctified *upon* him with whom He enters into a near and gracious relation, when, by the person's own fault, He is not sanctified *in* him. Because Israel was the people of the Lord, he could not always continue to appear outwardly, what inwardly he no longer was.

771. As the second germ of corruption, we pointed out the apostasy from the house of David. His dominion rested on a divine right. The new Israelitish kingdom was built on the sandy foundation of human caprice. Its first king had raised himself to the throne by his own power and cunning, and the favour of the people. Every one, who had the same means in his possession, believed that they gave him a right to do the like. And thus dynasty succeeded dynasty, regicide followed regicide ; in the bloody conflict thus occasioned, the people became more and more lawless ; sometimes interregnum's occurred, times of total anarchy ; by these internal struggles the power of the state to resist invaders was continually more and more weakened. No king could stop this fountain of adversity : for to do this he must have given up his existence as a king. And just as little could he apply a remedy to the other sources of evil ; for if once the religious partition-wall between the kingdoms of Israel and Judah was removed, the civil one also threatened to fall.

772. Such, in general, were the circumstances under which Hosea, like the other prophets of the kingdom of Israel, came forward. That these circumstances were far more difficult than those in the kingdom of Judah, is obvious. There, also, was the corruption great, but it was not so closely interwoven with the foundation of the whole state. Thorough reforms, such as those under Hezekiah and Josiah, were possible ; and in the *outward* preservation of the true religion the interests of a whole tribe were concerned.

773. The reign of Jeroboam II., which was outwardly highly prosperous, and in which Hosea entered upon his prophetical office, had still more increased the apostasy from the Lord and the corruption of manners, and therefore laid the foundation of the series of misfortunes, which, beginning soon after his death, conducted the people with rapid steps to their total ruin. They were still more confirmed in their security by prosperity ; for, instead of being led by the unmerited mercy of God to repentance, (comp. 2 Kings 14. 26, 27,) they regarded this prosperity as a reward of their apostasy, as a seal whereby Jehovah-Baal confirmed the correctness of their course. The false prophets did their utmost to strengthen them in their delusion ; the true preached to deaf ears.

774. Immediately after the death of Jeroboam, it began to appear, which of the two had the truth on their side. A ten years' interregnum followed. After its termination, Jeroboam's son, Zachariah, began to reign ; but in the short space of six months, he was mur-

dered by Shallum[1]. This king was slain by Menahem, after he had reigned only a month[2]. Menahem reigned ten years in Samaria. Even in his reign the catastrophe was preparing, which brought the kingdom to total ruin. He became tributary to the Assyrian king Phul[3]. He was followed by his son Pekahiah, in the fiftieth year of Uzziah. After a two years' reign, this prince was slain by Pekah, the son of Remaliah, who held the throne twenty years[4], and by his alliance with the king of Assyria against Judah[5], hastened the ruin of Israel. The Assyrians, under Tiglath-pileser, who had been summoned by Ahaz, carried away into exile, even at that time, a portion of the citizens, the tribes beyond the Jordan. Pekah was slain by Hosea, in the fourth year of Ahaz, who began to reign in the twelfth year of Ahaz[6], after an interregnum of eight years. He became tributary to Salmanassar, and the end of his nine years' reign was also the end of the kingdom of the ten tribes. By an attempted alliance with Egypt, he brought the vengeance of the king of Assyria upon himself and his people. The position which Hosea assumed under these circumstances, may now be very well understood from the portion[7] we are about to explain. This portion is to be considered as a sort of sketch, of which all the following prophecies were an enlargement, just as in Isaiah the sixth chapter, and Ezekiel the two first chapters[8].

Chap. 1, 2, 3

775. We believe that the prophet here relates *actions*, which took place *really*, but not *outwardly*, and that we shall be able to decide this question on grounds so certain, that henceforth this controversy will be considered as settled.

776. (1) The defenders of an outward proceeding rely on the sup-

---

[1] 2 Kings 15. 10.   [2] Ver. 14.   [3] Ver. 19—21.   [4] Ver. 27.
[5] Comp. Is. 7.   [6] Chap. 17. 1.   [7] Chap. 1—3.
[8] In *Commentarius in Hoseam*, by Jo. Heinr. Manger, Campen, 1782, 4to, the interpretation of Hosea has reached its highest point, i. e. relatively, for absolutely it is still very far from it. 1. A great many interpreters affirm, that all the actions here related *actually* and *outwardly* happened. Thus, among the Fathers, with great decision, Theodoret, Cyril of Alexandria, and Augustine; most interpreters of the Lutheran church; of the Reformed, e. g. Manger; in recent times, Stuck. 2. Others assume a parabolic representation. Thus Calvin, who expressly controverts the supposition not only of an *outward*, but also of an *inward* actual proceeding. So Bauer, Rosenmüller, &c. The strange opinion of Luther is, that the prophet has given to his own chaste wife only the name and works of an adulteress, and therefore performs with her before the people, a sort of play. 3. Others believe [correctly] that the prophets relate events which happened *really* indeed, but not *outwardly*. This view is, for that time, very well defended by Jerome in the *Epist. ad Pammachium*, and on chap. 1. 8. According to Rufinus, it was believed in Palestine and Egypt by all those who laid peculiar stress on the authority of Origen, that the prophet's marriage was performed only in spirit.

position, and this is almost their only argument, that their interpretation is the most obvious and natural; that they are already in possession, and can be driven from it only by forcible reasons; that the proceeding, had it been internal, would have been expressly designated as such by the prophet. But precisely the reverse is true; the most obvious view is, that the symbolic action took place in vision. If *certain* actions of the prophets, viz. seeing, hearing, speaking with the Lord, &c., when nothing is said expressly to the contrary, are to be understood as internal, why not the rest also? For surely the former presuppose, that the world in which the prophets exist is entirely peculiar; not the outward, but the spiritual world. It is surely not accidental, that *seeing*, in the case of the prophets, is to be taken inwardly; and if there is a *reason* for this, this reason must be equally applicable to the case of *going*, &c. We do not, indeed, wish to assert that *all* the symbolic actions of the prophets were performed merely in internal contemplation. An inward process always lay at the foundation, but sometimes, when it was suitable, they embodied this in an outward representation also. For this very reason, this argument cannot be conclusive: but it furnishes an important presumption. If the proceeding in such cases is *regularly and naturally internal*, we must suppose it to be so here, unless the *contrary* is *proved*.

777. (2) That a merely *internal* action would have been without an object, no one will venture to assert, since there are many instances in the Bible of symbolical actions, which undeniably and confessedly *were* merely internal. The inward proceeding was related and committed to writing. It had this advantage over the naked declaration of the same truth, that it was more an object of sense, and more impressive. Sometimes, in the case of momentary actions, this advantage may be increased by the inward proceedings being *also* represented *outwardly*. Here, however, precisely the opposite was the case. We have before us a symbolic action, which, outwardly performed, would have continued during several years. If thus extended, it could not have been taken in at a single view, and its impressiveness would of course have been lessened. What, however, is still more important, the *outward action* would here have so occupied the attention, that the *idea* would have been entirely overlooked: the domestic relations of the prophet would have become the object of a multitude of city tales, and the idea would have been called to mind only to give point to ridicule.

778. (3) The command of God, considered as relating to an outward act, can in no way be justified. This becomes most strikingly obvious, if, with several interpreters, we understand, that the prophet was to beget children upon an unchaste woman without a lawful marriage. Every one must share in the displeasure which Buddeus expresses against Thomas Aquinas, who, following this interpretation, asserts, that the law of God was, in this special instance, set aside by His command. God Himself cannot set us free from His laws. They are an expression of His being, a copy of His holiness. To ascribe caprice to God in this respect, is, at the same time, to

annihilate the idea of God and of goodness.—This view, then, is so decidedly erroneous, that no further proof need be brought against it. But the interpretation of Buddeus and others is also liable to an invincible difficulty. This supposes the prophet to have married a wife who had before been unchaste. Now the Law forbids [1] a priest to marry a whore, or an unchaste woman. What relates only to the priests, as to the *letter*, applies in its *spirit* to the *prophets*, and that even more forcibly ; as is evident, when the ordinance is referred back to the *idea*. This is easily inferred from the reason given, viz. that the priests are holy to their God. The servants of God must represent His holiness ; they must not, therefore, by so near a contact with sin, inwardly and outwardly defile and desecrate themselves. Even if the *internal* pollution might in a particular case be prevented by the special assistance of the Divine grace, still the outward defilement always remains. It is inconceivable, that God would have commanded the prophet, at the very commencement of his office, to do any thing which must hinder its successful execution. Several, particularly Manger, who felt the difficulty of this interpretation, opposed to it another, which, in their opinion, removes all doubt. The prophet, they say, married a person, who, being chaste before her marriage, fell after it. This view is, without all doubt, the true one. This appears from the relation of the figure to the reality. According to the second verse, the thing to be typified was, how the people went a whoring from Jehovah. The spiritual adultery presupposes that the spiritual marriage has already been concluded. Accordingly, it is only on account of the infidelity which she has practised after marriage, that the wife can be called an adulteress. This is also confirmed by chap. 3. 1, where the more limited expression *to commit adultery*, is substituted for the more comprehensive one *to whore*. The *previous* unchastity of the wife would be entirely without meaning ; indeed it would directly contradict the fact to be represented, for, before the marriage concluded at Sinai, Israel was given to the Lord in true love ; comp. Jer. 2. 2, '*I remembered the tenderness of thy youth, the love of thine espousals, thy walking after me in the wilderness, in the land that was not sown.*' Comp. also Ezek. chap. 16, where Israel, before her espousals, appears as a *virgo intacta*. But correct as this view is, it does not remove all doubt. It is liable to the same objection which has been urged against the preceding. The prophet might better have married one previously unchaste, in the hope that her subsequent better conduct would wipe out her former shame, than one previously chaste, who *must* become unchaste, and for a long time remain so, because otherwise the symbolic action would lose its whole import.—It can scarcely be meant in earnest, when it is said, that what is absurd as an outward action, would be also absurd as a mere internal one. Here every one knew that the prophet was a mere type. But a nuptial union outwardly entered into, is never purely typical ; it has always a separate import, and must be justifiable independently of its typical character.

[1] Lev. 21. 7.

779. (4) Were the transaction an outward one, it would be impossible to explain the transition which we here find, from the symbolic action to the mere figure and naked declaration. In the first chapter, the symbolic action is pretty well kept up. But in the promise, chap. 2. 1—3, belonging to the same portion, it almost entirely disappears. As the corporeal adultery was the type of the spiritual adultery and consequent divorcement ; so should the prophet's receiving back again his wife, rejected on account of her infidelity, but now reformed, typify the mercy of the Lord towards His people. Of this, however, there is no trace. Nor can it be said that the ground of this lies in a difference of the type from the thing signified, in the fact, that the wife of the prophet *had not reformed.* For if such a difference had existed, the type would not have been chosen. The contrary appears also from chap. 2. 9. In the whole second portion, chap. 2. 4—25, regard is indeed had to the symbolic action, but in so free a manner, that it becomes a mere figure, behind which the matter of fact continually shows itself. In the third chapter, the symbolic action becomes again more uniform. These appearances can be explained only on the supposition, that the proceeding was an internal one. In the case of an outward action, the transition from the symbolic action to the figure, and from the figure to the substance, is not so easy. The substratum of the idea is then far more material, the idea is more inseparably connected with it.

780. (5) An insurmountable difficulty in the way of understanding the transaction as an outward one, is found in the third chapter. This is, indeed, of itself, sufficient to decide the question. ' *Then the Lord said to me again, Go, love a wife, beloved of her friend, and unfaithful.*' The interpreters, who adopt this view, here find themselves in no small embarrassment. Several suppose, that the wife whom the prophet is exhorted to love, is his former spouse, Gomer : that he is again to be reconciled to her. This is altogether inadmissible. In opposition to it is the entirely indefinite designation ' *a wife ;* ' then, in the second verse, the *purchase* of the wife, which presupposes that before it she was not in the husband's possession ; then, again, the fact, that ' *beloved of her friend, and adulteress,*' according to the true interpretation can mean only, ' *who,* although *she is beloved by her true husband,* will *yet be unfaithful ;* ' so that, consequently, if the *reunion* with Gomer is referred to, it must be assumed, that she became *again* unfaithful, after being received back, to which nothing corresponding in the subject can be pointed out. Lastly, ' *love,*' cannot mean ' *love again,*' *restitue amoris signa.* For the love of the prophet to his wife must correspond to the love of God to his people Israel. Now that this cannot be limited to the love which God *will* cherish towards the Church *after her conversion,* is evident from the addition, ' *And they turn themselves to other gods, and love grape-cakes.*' Hence, it appears, that the love of God continues even during unfaithfulness, and consequently also the love of the prophet, which typifies it.—Equally erroneous also is the other opinion, that the prophet is here required a second time

to typify the relation of the Lord to the covenant people, by forming
a new marriage.   It is then assumed, either that Gomer had been
rejected because she would not return, or had died.   In either case,
she would not have been chosen by God as a type of Israel.   The
ground of this choice can be no other than the coincidence with the
antitype.   This would then fail in precisely the most important point.
It was of the highest importance, in order that all hope might not be
cut off from the ungodly, all consolation from the pious, to show that
the rejected Church would also be the object of mercy, the *Lo
Ruhamah*, the *Ruhamah*.   But, according to this supposition, exactly
the opposite would be typified, *two different wives* would very naturally lead to the idea of *two different people*.   And, moreover, the
supposition that Gomer did not return, is directly contradictory to the
prophet's own assertions.   That her relation to him lies at the foundation also of the representation, chap. 2. 4, sq., cannot be doubted,
for it is *her* three children, whose former unpropitious names[1] are
changed into those which promise salvation ; also[2], the whole relation
described in the foregoing portion is presupposed.   But now she,
who[3] says, ' *I will go and return to my first husband, for then was it
better with me than now,*' is the same who had said[4], ' *I will go after
my lovers who give my bread, and my water, my wool, and my flax.*'
We are led to the same result also by the showing of mercy to her
children, as predicted in the first portion[5], where the prophet plays
upon their names, and still more clearly in the second[6].   But the
showing of mercy to the children, implies the conversion of the
mother, and, as a consequence, her reception of mercy.   As it was on
account of the infidelity of the mother[7] that they were to be rejected,
the ground of their restoration can be nothing but the mother's fidelity.
As begotten in adultery, it is only through the mother that they stand
related to the prophet ; as soon as he had rejected *the mother*, he had
nothing more to do with *them*.   The supposition that Gomer was
dead, is plainly the result of an embarrassment, which sees itself
compelled to invent such fictions.—Finally, several, after the example of Augustine, suppose, that the subject of discourse here, is *not
a marriage*, but only a certain *friendly feeling*, that the prophet was
to show towards a wife, to encourage her return.   But this is contradicted by the circumstance, that the love of the prophet to his
wife must be of the same extent, and the same nature, as the love of
God to Israel, and also by the circumstance, that it is *only wedded
love*, that is suited to the image, and that this view, when רֵעַ is referred, as it must be, to the prophet, is evidently erroneous, and that
the purchase of the wife cannot then be satisfactorily explained, &c.
There is still, against all these suppositions, the common objection,
that, according to them, the omission of very important circumstances cannot be explained, which the prophet leaves his hearers

---

[1] Ver. 25.   [2] Vers. 4—6.   [3] Ver. 9.
[4] Ver. 7.   [5] Chap. 2. 1—3.   [6] Comp. ver. 25.
[7] Comp. chap. 2. 6, and especially the כִּי at the beginning of ver. 7.

and readers to supply out of the preceding symbolic action. Only two points are rendered prominent, the appropriation of his wife by the prophet, ver. 2, and the course which he pursues in order to her reformation, ver. 3. The intervening, criminal, long-continued infidelity of his wife is passed over in silence. If we assume an outward action, this cannot be explained. For then we cannot draw a conclusion from the first case to the second, but the second must be as fully related as the first. On the supposition of an internal proceeding, all is plain ; the question then no longer exists, whether she was Gomer or another. If Gomer was only an ideal person, what was true of her, is also true of the other ideal spouse of the prophet, since both typified the same thing, and, without having any independent existence, were considered only as types. And thus the second representation is very naturally supplied out of the first, and it was only necessary for the prophet to give prominency to those particular points, which were here especially important.

781. (6) If the whole is taken as an outward proceeding, no small difficulty arises in respect to the children mentioned in the first chapter. These were begotten in adultery. Even when the mother had reformed, they could never be regarded by the prophet as his own in the fullest sense. And here is a great want of resemblance between figure and reality. On the supposition, however, of an internal proceding, this difficulty vanishes. The physical impossibility then no longer comes into consideration. That which is possible in point of fact (that those, who were formerly not children of God, become children of God), is also transferred to the figure. In reality, the mother has no existence apart from the children. She stands related to them, as the whole to the parts. Therefore, also, in chap. 2. 25, the mother and children, though this is not pointed out by the prophet, coalesce together.

782. (7) The symbolic names of the first wife, and her father, lead to a mere inward proceeding; as, on the other hand, when such a symbolic import cannot be pointed out, this becomes a valid argument for a literal interpretation, though, indeed, but *one* argument, which must give way to the stronger proofs on the other side. For it is easy to suppose, that the prophet, in order the more to give to the inward proceeding the appearance of an outward one, has mentioned names usual at the time; in like manner as poetry is not satisfied with the Caius, &c. of Logic, but chooses names which every one does not at once see to be fictitious.—*Gomer* can mean only *completion*, in the passive sense. Now, in what sense the wife, the image of the Israelitish people, is named *completion*, as she who had proceeded to the utmost extremity in her whoredom, is so evident from the connexion, as to render nugatory the objection which Maurer deduces from the omission of an express intimation of this reference, in order thereby to recommend his utterly unphilological interpretation. A significant proper name can never give any thing more than an *intimation ;* and this is here entirely sufficient, since the mention of the *wife of whoredom* had preceded. As for the rest,

comp. Zech. 5. 5—11, where the thought, that the Israelitish people have filled up the measure of their sins, is typified by a woman sitting in an Ephah.—*Bath-diblaim* can mean only, '*a daughter of the two fig-cakes*' = *filia deliciarum* = *deliciis dedita*. ' Daughter' serves to designate the relation of one who is *dependent*, and looks to another for instruction. Fig-cakes were regarded as one of the greatest dainties [1]. Sensuality was the ground of the apostasy of the Israelites from the severe and strict religion of Jehovah to idolatry, which was soft, sensual, and licentious. The cause which gave rise to it among their neighbours, recommended it to them [2]. Our whole interpretation, however, (which, in substance, though without being sufficiently established and justified, occurs even in Jerome,) is raised above the condition of a mere hypothesis, by a comparison of chap. 3. 1; the language there, '*they betake themselves to other gods, and love grape-cakes*,' is a mere periphrasis of Gomer Bath Diblaim. That the difference between *grape-cakes* and *fig-cakes* did not here come into consideration, since both belong to the dainties that were sought after, need scarcely be remarked; and it is equally evident, that to *love* them, and *to be the daughter* of them, expresses the same idea.—Now if the symbolic import of this name is established, so also, at the same time, is the correctness of the supposition of a mere internal proceeding. The symbolic names of these children could not indeed of themselves establish this supposition; an appeal might justly be made, in opposition, to *Shear-Jashub* and *Maher-shalal-hashbaz*, who *cannot* have been mere ideal beings. The prophet *gave* them these names. But the case is entirely different with the wife, who *already had* her name when the prophet took her.—Were the name not symbolic, did it belong to the actual spouse of the prophet, it would be difficult to explain why he did not afterwards mention also the name of his second spouse, but contented himself with the general expression, '*a wife.*'

783. (8) A chief argument against the literal understanding is furnished by chap. 3. 2, according to the true interpretation, which we must here first give. The common translation is: '*And then I*

---

[1] Comp. Faber on *Harmar*, I. p. 390, sq.

[2] The *masc.* form can present no difficulty to the derivation from דְּבֵלָה *fig-cakes*, for this form of the plural occurs also, 1 Sam. 25. 18. 1 Chron. 12. 40. Just as little can the Dual. This is explained by the circumstance, that fig-cakes usually consisted of a double layer of figs, or of one double cake. (Hesych. παλάθη,—which is a corruption of דבלה, ἡ τῶν σύκων ἐπάλληλος θέσις.) The Dual, however, is used of objects, which are commonly conceived of as a whole consisting of two parts, when the discourse relates to a plurality of them. Ew. p. 329. The correctness of this explanation of the Dual is shown by its occurrence, as the name of a Moabitish city, Beth Diblathajim, Jer. 48. 22, and Diblathajim, Num. 33. 46, which was probably celebrated on account of its fig-cakes. The prophet had perhaps still a special ground for choosing the Dual, and indeed in the *masc.* form, that Diblajim was favoured by the analogy of other proper names of men, as Ephraim, &c. Such an analogy must have existed, otherwise the name would not have been, as it should be, a riddle.

purchased her to me for fifteen pieces of silver, and an homer of barley, and a letheck of barley,' Hos. 3. 2. The verse is explained from the custom prevalent in the east of purchasing wives from their parents. But this is liable to a very important philological objection [1].—We assume the fact already established by J. D. Michaelis, that the *whole price amounted to thirty shekels.* This the prophet paid, *half in gold* and *half in the value of gold.* The homer, according to Ezek. 45. 11, contained ten ephahs, and a letheck was the half of an ephah; we have, therefore, fifteen pieces of silver, and also fifteen ephahs, and it seems evident, that the ephah of barley was at that time equal to a shekel. We are as yet unable to say *why* half was in gold, half in natural productions; but there must certainly have been a reason, since no other trait is without meaning. Perhaps it was determined by the custom of paying in this manner the sum by which servants were purchased. We are necessarily led to the idea of servants or slaves, by the mention of the sum. It is precisely the same which was usually given for a man-servant, or for a maid [2]. When a servant was bound to render *perpetual* service to his lord to whom he belonged, *his ears were bored* [3]. Hence the phrase [4], ' *to bore the ears,*' for ' *to appropriate,*' Ps. 40. 7. Here (according to the custom of omitting the names of members of the body in phrases of frequent occurrence [5]) we have, merely, " *to bore.*" Therefore, i. q., ' *I made her my slave.*' It was not a free woman that the prophet desired in marriage, but a slave, whom he must first redeem from bondage, who was, therefore, doubly bound to him, over whom he had a double right. The reference to the fact represented, is self-evident. It was not a free, independent people, whom the Lord chose, but one which he was obliged to redeem from disgraceful bondage, before they could sustain a near relation to him. This redemption appears, throughout, as a ransom from the house of bondage, the wonderful manifestations of the Lord being the price which he paid, comp., e. g., Deut. 7. 8 : ' *for because the Lord loved you, and because he regarded his oath, which he sware to your fathers, he hath brought you forth with a strong hand, and ransomed you from the house of servants from the hand of Pharaoh, king of Egypt,*' 9. 26. On this redemption is grounded the exhortation to the people, that henceforth, as a servant of the Lord, they should serve Him alone; comp., e. g., the introduction to the Decalogue. Thus we have here also a trait,

---

[1] The verb used does not mean *purchased*, but *dug* or *bored*. We may as well give כָּרָה any other meaning, as that of purchasing. This is not once found in the dialects, still less in the Hebrew. In the only passage to which an appeal is still made, Deut. 2. 7, the usual meaning, *to dig*, is entirely appropriate: " And also shall ye dig water for them for gold and drink." And, moreover, the sum is entirely too small for the proposed object ; and, besides that, the circumstance would be wholly without import, while every thing else in the whole description is full of meaning.

[2] As is expressly mentioned, Exod. 21. 32, comp. on Zech. 11. 12.

[3] Comp. Deut. 15. 17.   [4] כָּרָה אָזְנָיִם.   [5] Comp. Ewald, p. 190.

which is so manifestly figurative, has so manifestly passed over from the subject to the type, that an external proceeding is no longer to be thought of.

Chap. 1. 2. 1—3

784. The portion chap. 1—3 (distinguished from the remaining prophecy, by the circumstance, that the relation of the Lord to the people of Israel is represented *throughout* under the figure and symbol of a marri·.ge, while the same representation, when it elsewhere occurs in the prophecy, is soon relinquished again,—by which close resemblance, the objections of Böckel and Stuck against the usual division of the collection into two parts, are set aside) may be divided into three parts, which, although intimately connected, as appears from the *fut.* with *vav convers.* in chap. 3. 1, and also from the fact, that this chapter must be completed out of what precedes, still, in another respect, may also be regarded as a whole, complete in itself.   They are not so distinguished as to their contents, that the first would represent the apostasy, the second the punishment, the third the return and restoration ; but each contains all the three ; and that in such a manner, that here the one, and there the other, is more fully carried out, so that the description does not receive its full completion till all are embraced together.   In the portion before us, the covenant relation into which the Lord entered with Israel, is typified by the marriage of the prophet, concluded at the command of the Lord ; the apostasy of the people, especially the ten tribes,—for only to these was the prophet sent,—by the infidelity of the wife ; the Divine punishment by the unpropitious names, which he gave to the children, which sprung from this infidelity. Then follows chap. 2. 1—3, more directly, and with a bare allusion to the symbol, the prediction of prosperity.

785. Ver. 1. ' *The word of the Lord, which was to Hosea, the son of Beeri, in the days of Uzziah, Jotham, Ahaz, and Hezekiah, and in the days of Jeroboam, the son of Joash, king of Israel.*'   Ver. 2. ' *At the first, when the Lord spake to Hosea, then said the Lord to Hosea, Go take to thee a wife of whoredoms, and children of whoredoms, for the land goes away a whoring from the Lord.*'—*A wife of whoredoms*, and *children of whoredoms*.   The wife sustains this character, as being *devoted*, in body and soul, to this vice, the children, as being the *product* of it.   It cannot be assumed of the children, that they are themselves designated as given to whoredom. This were here an entirely foreign thought.   The prophet is to *receive* with the wife those, who, without his agency, have been born

of her. That they are not children which the wife had previously
borne *to the prophet,* but rather, those whose birth is related, ver. 4.
sq., is self-evident, and has already been abundantly proved. And
that the children are not to be considered, as they are by several, as
children of the prophet, (Drus.; *accipe uxorem et suscipe ex eâ
liberos,*) appears from their designation, by *"children of whoredoms,"*
from the word *take* itself, which expresses the passive conduct of the
prophet, and from the fact, that, in the following context, the subject
of discourse is always merely the wife's *conception and bearing,* never
as Is. 8. 3, the prophet's *begetting;* and, lastly, from the relation
of the figure to the reality. This necessarily requires, that the
children and mother should be in the same state of *alienation from
the lawful husband and father.* Nor is this contradicted by '*and she
bare to him a son,*' ver. 3. Thereby are designated only the bringing
forth of the wife, who presents to the man the children begotten in
adultery as his own; and the patience and forbearance of the husband, who receives and educates them as his own, though he well
knows that they are not; just as the Lord for centuries treated the
apostate Israelites *as though* they were His children, gave them the
inheritance destined only for His children, and so many of His blessings, until at last He declared them to be bastards, by the carrying
away into exile.—In the last words, the design of the symbolic
action is given[1].—The preceding *infin. absol.* gives emphasis to the
verbal idea[2]. The prophet thereby shows, that he uses the expression, *"to whore,"* in its full sense, as accurately corresponding to the
thing, and would have it understood in its whole strength and compass. He silences beforehand every attempt at palliation by giving
to the thing its true name. In such attempts, the Israelites were
very fertile. They did not perceive that they had been wholly
unfaithful to the Lord; they considered their intercourse with idols,
as only trivial and allowable gallantries, which they manifested
towards them.—That we are not to understand by *whoredom,* (with
Manger,) not only idolatry, but also reliance on human help, is
shown by what follows, where idolatry is always the subject of discourse. If we trace this back to its idea, it is indeed true that *trust
in man* is comprehended under it, the idea is *the apostasy from God
to that which is not God.* From this dependence of that which is
more special on the general idea, it follows, that the representation
is eternally true, and does not become antiquated, where the folly of
gross idolatry has long been perceived.

786. Ver. 3. '*And he went and took Gomer, the daughter of Diblaim, and she became pregnant, and bare to him a son.*'—Many interpreters assume that by the three children, three different generations,
the perpetually increasing degeneration of the people is designated.
The correct view is rather "wife and children are *both* the people of
Israel, only considered according to different relations." According
to the first, as a unity, to the second, as a plurality, dependent upon

---

[1] The causal בְּ is explained by the circumstance, that the ground of a symbolic
action is its import.   [2] Ew. p. 560.

it. That the prophet causes children to be born at all, and that the number should be precisely *three,* has its ground in their names. The children exist only in order to receive a name. The three names must not be considered separately, but taken together. It is thus they present an image corresponding to the destinies which the people of Israel had to expect.

787. Ver. 4. '*And the Lord said to him, Call his name Jezreel; for yet a little while and I will visit the blood of Jezreel on the house of Jehu, and make an end of the kingdom of the house of Israel*[1].'— Jezreel was the place where the last great judgement of God upon the kingdom of Israel was executed. There had Jehu, the founder of the reigning dynasty, in the time of the prophet, avenged on Jezebel and the whole house of Ahab, their apostasy from the Lord, and the innocent blood of his servants, which had been shed by them[2]. Jehu, at the command of God, is anointed as king by one of the sons of the prophets sent by Elisha[3]. Through him the Lord speaks to Jehu: "And I anoint thee king over the people of the Lord, over Israel. And thou shalt smite the house of Ahab thy lord, *and I will avenge the blood of my servants, the prophets, and the blood of all the servants of the Lord, by the hand of Jezebel, and the whole house of Ahab shall cease* . . . And I will make the house of Ahab, as the house of Jeroboam, son of Nebat, and as the house of Baasha, son of Abijah." The execution corresponded to the command. As Jehu drew near to *Jezreel,* Joram, son of Ahab, came forth against him, and they met in the portion of Naboth the Jezreelite[4]. There, at the command of Jehu, his corpse was thrown, with an appeal to the declaration of the Lord[5]: "Surely I have seen *the blood* of Naboth and *the blood* of his sons, and *I will requite thee in this estate.*" It was at Jezreel, also, that Jezebel found her shameful death. It was to Jezreel as to the central point of vengeance, that the seventy king's sons, who had been slain, were sent[6]. It was there that Jehu slew all the rest of the king's house, all his nobles, and all his friends, and his priests[7].—Now the royal house, and with it all Israel, was again to become *a Jezreel,* i. e., the same divine vengeance was to be executed upon it anew, which was then manifested at Jezreel. The reason is given in the explanation. The house of Jehu, and all Israel, becomes *as to punishment* a Jezreel, because it has become a Jezreel *in guilt,* because, as once in Jezreel, the blood which has been shed cries again to the Lord for vengeance.—From this, it already appears how we understand the expression "*I will visit the blood of Jezreel,*" in the

---

[1] Most interpreters, and lastly Rückert, explain *Jezreel* here, by *God disperses.* They regard this as the proper etymology; the rest only as allusion. But this interpretation, as Manger has rightly perceived, is false. For, first, there is no example of this meaning of the verb זרע. 2. What follows is to be considered as an explanation of the name *Jezreel,* compare the corresponding explanations of the names *Lo Ruhamah,* in ver. 6, and *Lo Ammi,* in ver. 9, which accurately agree with this name. In this explanation, however, there is not a word of the dispersion of the people of Israel.

[2] 2 Kings 9.   [3] Ver. 6 – 9.   [4] Ver. 21.
[5] Ver. 26.   [6] Chap. 10. 1—10.   [7] Ver. 11.

explanation. The *new blood-guiltiness* (murder, as the climax of all
crime, presupposes the rest; the house of Jehu, and all Israel, a band
of murderers, comp. Is. 1. 21,) is called *by the name of the old*, and
so too its punishment. We must not overlook, what a deep impression this mode of representation must have made. The sins before
committed at Jezreel were acknowledged as such by the whole people, and particularly by the royal house, whose whole authority
depended on this acknowledgement. The remembrance of the fearful
punishment was still in the minds of all. But they did not reflect,
that *they* were involved in like guilt, and exposed to like punishment. *With one single word, the prophet recalled to the present, that
which was regarded as passed away for ever.* With one single word
of fearful sound, he terrified them out of the self-deception and
carnal security, in which they refused to perceive their own sins in
the image of the sins of others. The threatening of punishment contains two points. First, shall *the house of Jehu*, then shall *all Israel*,
become *a Jezreel* in respect to *punishment*, as they *were* already in
guilt; whereby the significant paronomasia between *Israel*, the
honorable name of the people, and *Jezreel*, the base, in deed and
condition, is to be observed. In the expression, ' *I will make to cease
the kingdom of the house of Israel,*' the cessation of *every domestic
regal government*, and consequently of the entire national independence
of the people, is predicted : this is so obvious as to need no further
proof. Both points, in the fulfilment, were separated by a considerable period of time, and yet they were closely connected. At the
same time with the ruin of the house of Jehu, the power also of the
kingdom of Israel was broken. It had been predicted to him [1], that
his children should sit on the throne *until the fourth generation*. As
now Jeroboam was the *great-grandson* of Jehu, the glory of this
family must come to an end with *his* son. But never did the house
of Jehu and the kingdom of Israel seem to be so far from ruin, as
under the reign of Jeroboam [the 2nd]. It was time, therefore, that
the forgotten prophecy should be again called to their remembrance,
and at the same time further carried out.

788. Ver. 5. ' *And it shall come to pass in that day, that I will break
the bow of Israel in the valley of Jezreel.*'—In the valley of Jezreel
Israel was to become, as to punishment, what he already was in
guilt, a Jezreel. The verse is a further extension of the last words
of the foregoing to which the expression, ' in that day,' referred. He,
whose bow is broken, is disarmed and helpless [2]. That the subjection of Israel by the Assyrians, the consequence of which was the
ruin of the kingdom of Israel, is here intended, is manifest.—Where
this took place, the historical books do not relate. Jerome on the
passage says, that it happened in the valley of Jezreel; this is probably nothing more than an historical conjecture. It is, however,
altogether probable, apart from the passage before us. The valley
of Jezreel, or Esdrelon, the broad, elevated plain of Galilee, formerly
very fruitful, but now entirely desolate, according to Burckhardt,
about eight stadia long, and four broad, was the natural field of

---

[1] 2 Kings 10. 30.   [2] Comp. Gen. 49. 24. Jer. 49. 35.

battle in the wars which were carried on within the limits of the ten tribes, especially when the enemies came from the north. " It was the station of a Legion (μέγα πεδίον λεγεῶνος) in the first centuries. It is the place where the armies of Nebuchadnezzar, Vespasian, Justinian, the sultan Saladin, and many conquering hosts encamped, down to the unsuccessful expedition of Bonaparte, whose success in Syria here terminated. Clarke found here the tents of the troops of the pasha of Damascus.—In later times it was the field of the skirmishes between the parties of hostile hordes of the Arabian and Turkish pachas. To this locality, in connexion with the political relations of hither Asia, must the complete desolation and depopulation of Galilee be ascribed, which was once so flourishing, full of towns and thickly inhabited [1]." We add, that in the same plain, also, the battle was fought, in which Saul and Jonathan perished, for the plain Esdrelon is bounded on the south-east by the mountains of Gilboa; also the battle between Ahab and the Syrians; to it likewise belonged the plain near the city of Megiddo, where Josiah was mortally wounded in the fight with Pharaoh Necho [2].

789. Ver. 6. '*And she again became pregnant, and bare a daughter. And he said to him, Call her name Lo Ruhamah,* [one who has not found mercy,] *for I will no longer have mercy on the house of Israel, for I will take away from them.*'—That the *female birth* designates *a more degenerate race,* cannot, with Jerome and others, be assumed. For, if so, why should the third again be a male? The reason is rather to be sought in the *name.* The verb [3] designates, not *every* kind of love, but only that of the *high* to the *low,* and of the *strong* to the *weak.* Hence the Seventy here, whom Peter follows, 1 Pet. 2. 10, (οὐκ ἠλεημένη,) render the word more accurately than Paul, Rom. 9. 25 (οὐκ ἠγαπημένη). It never occurs, therefore, of the love of man to God, but always only of the love of God to man, of his mercy. The female sex, however, as the weaker, *needs* the compassion of man more than the male. The female birth presents the *helplessness of the people* in a more striking contrast with *the denial of help* from him who alone can grant it. The phrase, '*I will no longer continue,*' refers back to *the former* great manifestations of the Divine mercy, especially to the last under Jeroboam, which the people still enjoyed [4]. '*And the Lord showed them mercy, and pitied and turned to them on account of his covenant with Abraham, Isaac, and Jacob, and would not destroy them nor cast them out of his sight.*' On this antithesis, also, rests the apparently mild expression, '*I will not pity,*' which is thus rendered more severe than any other. The denial of compassion is here not to be understood *absolutely,* but *relatively.* Not for ever is mercy withdrawn from the house of Israel, but only until the penal justice of God shall have been satisfied. She, who is here called Lo Ruhamah, is afterwards called Ruhamah. Just as *Israel* will not always remain *Jezreel,* and *Lo Ammi* at a future period will become again *Ammi.*—'*For I will take away from them.*' The *object* is not mentioned, because *even all* is

---

[1] Ritter. Erdk. II. p. 387.
[3] רָחַם.

[2] Rosenm. II. 1. p. 149.
[4] Comp. 2 Kings 13. 23.

to be understood. The prominence given to the verbal idea[1] is explained by the antithesis with the compassion, which includes also the *giving*. At the same time, there is a very striking antithesis with the standing phrase[2], '*I will take away from them*,' not, however, as heretofore, *guilt*, but '*all that they possess.*'

790. Ver. 7. '*And upon the house of Judah will I show mercy, and I will deliver them by the Lord their God, and I will deliver them not by bow, and by sword, and by war, and by horses, and by horsemen.*'—The object of the prophet, in predicting the mercy which *Judah* would experience, can only be to sharpen the goad, in order the more effectually *to disturb Israel in his false security*, and rouse his attention to the bad foundation of his civil and religious constitutions, whereby that was *legalized* there, which in *Judah* was only *abuse*.—As the showing of mercy to Judah runs parallel with the withholding of mercy from Israel, we must suppose that the prophet referred directly and chiefly to the different fate of both during the dominion of the Assyrians. Judah's wonderful deliverance on this occasion, is predicted in a manner entirely similar, in Is. 31. 8; '*And Ashur shall fall under the sword, not of a man, and the sword, not of a man, shall consume him.*'—We must not, however, look at this event alone. A preference of Judah to Israel, a residue of the Divine mercy, appears also in respect to the carrying away of Judah into exile. The Jews were not, during its continuance, so entirely bereft of signs of the continued Divine election; prophets still appeared among them, as immediate ambassadors of God. Wonderful events manifested in the mean time among the heathen the supremacy of their God, and prepared the way for their deliverance; they maintained, far more than the Israelitish nation, their national independence. And, lastly, their affliction endured only for a much shorter period. Contrary to all human expectation, their affairs soon took a favorable turn, in which only a comparatively small number of their Israelitish brethren participated, while mercy continued to be withheld from the rest. It is only by this antithesis with the lot of Judah, that the prediction of Israel's fate appears in its true light. Without this it might have been supposed, that the prediction of the prophet did not extend beyond his natural powers of foresight; that a kingdom,—so feeble in comparison with the great and ambitious kingdoms of Asia, as that of the Israelites,—it being, moreover, placed between these kingdoms and their natural enemy and rival, Egypt,—could not be lasting, was of itself highly probable. But this probability was still greater in respect to the far smaller and feebler kingdom of Judah, which had been greatly injured by Joash, the father of Jeroboam[3], under the latter of whom, the splendour and the power of the kingdom of Israel first became distinguished. That which prevented this probability from becoming truth, in respect to the kingdom of Judah, lay entirely beyond the circle of human calculation; as Hosea himself so expressly says. By *such*

---

[1] By prefixing the *infin. absol.*   [2] נָשָׂא עָוֹן לְ or barely נָשָׂא לְ.

[3] 2 Kings 14. 3.

help would the kingdom of Israel have been delivered, no less than the kingdom of Judah. True, this prophecy of Hosea is no prediction of a *contingent* event. It rests on *the idea*. The lot of Israel and Judah *could* not be otherwise than diverse, when their different position in reference to the covenant God was once assumed. It is not a prophecy which ceases in its first and proper fulfilment, but one which is continually realized anew. God's proceeding towards the different churches and states is constantly regulated according to their different relation to Him. The history of the world is the judgement of the world. But the possession of this idea is itself a supernatural gift, and it can be handled with certainty, only by those who, like the prophet, have received from God an insight into the mysteries of His government of the world. This becomes very manifest, when we observe how often the predictions of those, who were merely in possession of the idea, down to Bengel [1] and his followers, have been disappointed by the result. God's ways are not our ways. No one knows them but He, and he to whom He will reveal them. The resting of the prophecy on the idea, manifests itself, moreover, very clearly in the words '*And I will deliver* them *through Jehovah their God* [1].' We have here the *ground* of the deliverance. Jehovah is Judah's God, and therefore the source of his prosperity, which ceases not to flow, though all human fountains be dried up. The ground, that Israel finds *no* mercy, *no* pity, must therefore be, that Jehovah is *not* his God. That such an antithesis is here intended is confirmed by chap. 3. 5 ; '*Afterwards will the children of Israel return and seek the Lord their God, and David their king.*' What they shall seek at a future time, and thereby attain to prosperity, that must they now have lost, and this loss must be the source of their misfortune. In contrast with Him who alone could give help, and whom Israel did not possess, though Judah did, the prophet mentions in the following context the aids, which could not furnish any real help, in which Israel was at that time far richer than Judah, and in which they placed a false confidence ; comp. chap. 10. 13, "Thou trustest in thy way, and the *multitude of thy heroes* [2]." At the same time he has in view the great events of their former history, where, in the absence of all human aids, the Divine power had shown itself, as alone sufficient for their help. *War* here comprehends *all that belongs to war*, the skill of the commanders, the bravery of the heroes, the strength of the host, &c. The horses and *the riders* are still especially mentioned, because in them, in ancient times, lay the chief strength of the army. Mahommed even held himself authorized to declare a victory, which he had gained without cavalry, as a miracle wrought immediately by God [3].

791. Ver. 8. '*And she weaned Lo Ruhamah, and became pregnant and bare a son.* Ver. 9. '*And he said, Call his name Lo Ammi* [not

---

[1] The allusion is to this excellent, able, and holy man's *apocalyptic* prophecies, which have been falsified by the event.

[2] Ps. 20. 8. Mic. 5. 9, sq. Deut 33. 29.

[3] Comp. Abulf. *Vit. Moh.* pp. 72. 91.

my people]; *for ye are not my people, and I, I will not be yours.*'
The mention of the *weaning* can hardly be supposed a merely descriptive touch without definite meaning. "*I have no doubt* (says
Calvin, with truth) *that the prophet thus points out the long-continued mercifulness of God towards that nation.*" The infidelity of
the wife, the patience of the prophet, endures for years.—Literally,
"*and I will not be to you*," i.q. "*no more belong to you.*" As God
speaks, so is the *to you*, or *yours*, sufficiently definite[1]. It is the
highest prosperity to *possess* God Himself, with all His benefits and
blessings; the highest misfortune to *lose* Him. The fulfilment is
related, 2 Kings 17. 18, '*And the Lord was greatly enraged against
Israel,* and removed them from his sight, *and there remained only
the tribe of Judah*[2].'

792. Ver. 10. '*And the number of the children of Israel shall
be as the sand of the sea, which cannot be measured nor numbered.
And it shall come to pass in the place, where it was said to them, Ye*
[are] *not my people, it shall be said to them, Sons of the living God.*'—
The people of the ten tribes, the same who, according to the
foregoing verse, are called *Lo Ammi*, shall now be called, *Children
of the living God.* The sudden transition to the Christian Church,
which is assumed by several of the older interpreters, would be a
salto mortale. Nor can we understand by the *children of Israel, all*
the descendants of Jacob ; for the children of *Judah* are distinguished
from them in the second verse. As to the *fact*, however, they too are
comprehended, as appears even from this verse ; for both will then
constitute one fraternal people. The prophet, however, here has in
view only one portion, because it was to this alone that the threatening
was directed, to this alone that his agency referred. Hence it is explained, how the prophet can apply to *the part*, the promises of Genesis,
which there relate *to the whole*.—The reference to these promises in
the first half of the verse is not to be mistaken. Compare particularly, as most literally corresponding, the passage chap. 22. 17, '*I
will multiply thy seed as the stars of heaven, and as the sand, which is
on the sea-shore,*' and particularly chap. 32. 13, '*I will make thy seed
as the sand of the sea, which is not numbered for multitude.*' A similar
verbal allusion occurs, Jer. 33. 22, '*As the host of heaven is not
numbered, and the sand of the sea not measured, thus will I multiply
the seed of David my servant.*' Now this allusion cannot here be
accidental. It presupposes that those promises were then generally
known in the kingdom of Israel. They served to confirm the
ungodly in their false security. Relying upon these, they objected to
the prophets, that they made God Himself a liar, when they predicted
the impending overthrow of the state. For the promise had not yet
been fulfilled in its whole extent. The prophet now, while he

---

[1] Similar, Ez. 16. 8, 'And I entered into a covenant with thee, and
thou becamest mine,' לִי וָאֶתְּדְּרִי.   Ps. 118. 6, 'The Lord is mine, לִי יְהֹוָה,
I will not fear.'

[2] Compare also Is. 7. 8.

almost literally repeats the promise, shows that the threatenings are
not excluded by it.   It is an analogous case, when corrupt Christian
Churches persist in their confidence in the Lord's promise, that He
will be with His people always, and that the gates of hell shall not
prevail against His Church.   The Lord knows how to execute His
judgements in such a manner, that His promises shall not suffer
thereby ; nay, that their fulfilment shall thus be rendered possible.
—The relation of the passage to that of Is. 10. 22, is still to be observed : ' *For although thy people, Israel, shall be as the sand of the
sea, still only the remnant will return.*'   Here, also, the reference to
the promises of Genesis is not to be mistaken.   The difference, however, is, that in Isaiah, the people, considering the partial fulfilment
of the promises of God in their flourishing condition at this time, as
a pledge of the Divine mercy, grounded thereon their future security ;
to which the prophet opposes the consideration, that even the *complete* fulfilment would not justify this ; whereas in Hosea they rely
on the complete fulfilment's not having yet taken place.—Hosea
has however the pious in view, no less than the ungodly.   To the
former he shows, that the declaration, Num. 23. 19, ' *God is not a
man that he should lie, or the son of man that he should repent.
Shall he speak and not do, promise and not fulfil ?*' would here also
be verified.—Finally, it is not to be mistaken, that in the words
there is an allusion to the name of the first child, *Jezreel*, as also in
the second verse ; and as, in the second member of the verse, to *Lo
Ammi*, in the third verse to *Lo Ruhamah*.   The name *Jezreel* is
now taken in a good sense, probably the very same in which it
was given to the city by its builders.   It means *God sows*.   The
builders thereby expressed the hope, that God would give a glorious
harvest from a small sowing, a glorious end from a small beginning.
So will God now sow the small seed of Israel, and from this sowing
an immensely rich harvest shall be reaped [1].—If we inquire after the
historical reference of this declaration, we must necessarily go back to
the sense of those declarations of Genesis.   These are by many
referred merely to the *natural descendants* of the Patriarch ; by
others, at the same time, to his *spiritual seed*, his successors in the
faith.   Both interpretations are equally false.   The latter is entirely
arbitrary, and the former would then only be justified, if the theocracy
had been destined for the natural descendants of the Patriarch alone ;
if admittance into it had been denied to all the heathen.   That
this was not so, is evident from the command to circumcise
every bond-man ; for by this rite a man was received among
the people of God.   It is also evident, from the ordinance,
Exod. 12. 44, that every stranger, who would be partaker of the
passover, must be previously circumcised ; which implies that
foreigners *might* participate in the sign and feast of the covenant, if
they pleased ; also from Deut. 23. 1—8, where the Edomites and
Egyptians are expressly declared *capable* of being received into the

[1] Compare on ver. 25.

Church of God; from the grounding of the interdiction of this privilege to the Ammonites and Moabites on especial reasons, in the same place; and, lastly, from the Jewish practice at all times. The heathen, however, who had been received among the people of God, were regarded as belonging to the posterity of the patriarchs, as their adopted sons. How could it be otherwise, since, through intermarriages, every distinction must soon vanish? They were, not less than others, called '*children of Israel*,' and '*children of Jacob*.' Hence we see how far the promise to the patriarchs refers also to the heathen, viz. so far as they became believers in the God of Israel, and joined themselves to the Israelites : compare Is. 44. 5, ' *One shall say, I am Jehovah's, and another shall call upon the name of Jacob, and another shall write with his hand, To the Lord! and glory in the name of Israel.*' Such an accession of the heathen to the theocracy always took place, when either the God of Israel made Himself known by particular extraordinary manifestations of His omnipotence and glory (as, e. g., in the deliverance from the Egyptian and Babylonian captivities, where, in both instances, we find, in the train of the Israelites, a multitude of those who had been heathen), or the feeling of the nothingness of the idols of the heathen world was especially awakened, as in the times after Alexander the Great, in which Greek and Roman heathenism was becoming continually more obsolete, and rapidly hastening to its end. Both these causes most powerfully co-operated in the time of Christ. Were the now prevalent view the correct one, which makes the Church of the New Testament independent of the congregation of Israel, originating out of a free and equal union of believers from both Jews and Gentiles, the promise before us would indeed no longer refer to the New Testament times. The New Testament Church would then be an entirely new generation, who no longer acknowledged Abraham, Isaac, and Jacob, as their fathers. But this view rests entirely on caprice. According to the constant doctrine of the Old and New Testament, there is only one Church of God from Abraham to the end of time, only one House under two economies. Even John the Baptist goes on the supposition, that children of Abraham must necessarily be also members of the new covenant, otherwise God's covenant and promise would cease. But as corporeal descent from Abraham was no security against the danger of being excluded from his posterity, of which Ishmael was the first example: and as it is said even in the Pentateuch, in reference to every greater transgression, ' *This soul is cut off from its people;*' so, on the other hand, God, of His unlimited freedom, can give to Abraham, in the place of his degenerate natural sons, adopted sons without number, who shall sit down with him and with Isaac and Jacob in the kingdom of God, while the sons of the kingdom shall be cast out.—After these remarks respecting the promise to the patriarchs, it can no longer be difficult to determine the historical reference of the prophet's declaration. It cannot refer to the increase of the *natural* descendants of Abraham as such, any more than the promise of a son to Abraham was fulfilled by the birth of Ishmael, or than the Arabians stand in any relation to the promise of the countless number of his descendants, which was repeated to Isaac and Jacob in precisely the same extent, although they were not ancestors of the Arabians. *Reprobate sons* are *no blessing,* no objects of the promise, *no sons* in the complete sense. No man is a son of Abraham except so far as he is the son of God. Hence, ' *sons of Israel,*' and ' *sons of the living God,*' are here joined together. Not as though the corporeal descent were something entirely indifferent; the natural descendants of the patriarchs had the nearest claim to be their sons in the full sense. They eminently enjoyed, in the first place, *the means* of becoming such. Theirs was the covenant, and the promise, and the adoption [1]. But all these outward advantages availed them nothing, if they suffered them to lie useless. Then the promise to Abraham, then also the declaration of the prophet, had no reference to them. Both would be unfulfilled, even though the children of Israel, if unconverted, should increase to be the most numerous nation on the whole earth. Hence it appears, that this declaration was first fulfilled in the times of the Messiah, and in part is *still to be fulfilled* when the family of the patriarch shall receive an immense increase, and ever continue to receive still more, partly by the reception of an innumerable multitude of adopted sons, and partly by the exaltation of sons in an *inferior,* to sons in the *highest* relation. It was but a faint prelude, when, after the Babylonian exile, the Lord roused a company of Israelites to participate in the return to Palestine. For this multitude was too small to correspond in any measure to the vast extent of the promise; and among them there were certainly only a few who deserved the name of the children of Israel in the fullest sense. That the higher name, *Israel,* indicative of the relation to God, is here emphatic, appears especially from a comparison of the fourth verse, where it is taken away from the degenerate children, and interchanged with the name *Jezreel.*—The *place* here can only be either that where the people first received the name of Lo Ammi, *Palestine,* or *the place of the exile,* where they first experienced its full import; the affliction, a *sermo realis* of God. In favour of the latter (Jonath. *in loco, quo abducti sunt inter gentes*), the following verse is decisive, where ' *the land*' (sc. *of the exile*) answers to '*place*' in the verse before us. In both cases the second mode[2], to be understood as a *present* tense, is intentionally used. The antithesis becomes the more clear by disregarding the difference of time.—By the *people* and *children* of God, the same thing is designated, according to different relations. The Israelites were *a people* of God, in so far as He was their *King; children* of God, in so far as He was their *Father;* their Father, not as in the New Testament, in reference to the spiritual begetting of *the individuals,* but in reference to the spiritual begetting of *the whole,* and to the love and guardianship founded upon it. In this relation, all Israel is often personified as *the* son of God; thus, e. g., Ex. 4. 22, ' *Speak thus to Pharaoh: Israel is my son, my first-born.*' Sometimes also

---

[1] Rom. 9. 4.   [2] יֹאמֶר.

the Israelites are called *children* or *sons* of God (e. g. Deut. 14. 1, '*Ye are sons to the Lord your God;*' compare also Deut. 32. 19), though each individual could not on this account bear the name *son of God*, which therefore never occurs, plainly because under the Old Testament *sonship* did not rest so much as under the New, on the personal relation of the individual to God, but the individual rather participated in it only as a member of the whole. This whole, as a people of God, was, as it were, begotten, or born anew of God; compare Deut. 32. 6, '*Is he not thy father? He has made and prepared thee;*' ver. 18, '*The Rock, which bare thee, forsakest thou, forgettest thou God, who brought thee forth?*' Nevertheless, there was an easy transition from the adoption of sons in the Old Testament to that in the New Testament sense. The former cannot exist in its highest perfection without the latter. The *whole Church* can then only be considered and treated, in the full sense, *as a child of God*, can then only *realize* her *destination*, when her *individual members* have been born of God. For this is the only way to attain resemblance to God, the condition of admission to the rights of children. Hence it appears, that the υἱοθεσία, under the Old Testament, *was an acted prophecy* of the times of the New Testament; and also, that the final reference of the declaration before us is to the same times. Earlier fulfilments, particularly the return from the Babylonian exile, are not to be excluded (the *idea* comprehends every event, without exception, in which it is realized, even in the smallest degree); they are, however, to be considered only as a prelude to the proper fulfilment, to take place when the reality entirely coincides with the idea, so that we must not stop short even at *the commencement* of the Messianic time, but take this and its final completion together.— The inquiry still arises, why God is here designated as the *living God*. Plainly, to awaken attention to the antithesis between the true God and dead idols, who, because they do not live, cannot love, and thus to show the importance of being the child of such a God. Exactly the same antithesis is found, Deut. 32. 37 sq., '*Where are their gods, their rock in whom they trusted, which did eat the fat of their sacrifices, and drink the wine of their drink-offerings? Let them rise up and help you, and be your protection. See now that I, even I, am he, and there is no god with me; I kill, and I make alive; I wound, and I heal.*' This antithesis still continues; the world has only changed its idols. It still seeks life from the dead,—from the gross idols of sin up to the refined idol of an abstract god of their own creation, whether he is compounded from conceptions or from feelings. Let them, as they please, strive to breathe life into these idols; though they may give an appearance of vitality, they still remain dead. The true God, on the contrary, continues to live, however much they may seek to slay Him; He shows Himself as the living God, either by smiting and killing them, if they persevere in their impenitence, or by healing and making them alive, if they become His children.—Finally, the two citations of this passage in the New Testament are to be considered. The one, 1 Pet. 2. 10, οἱ ποτὲ οὐ λαὸς, νῦν δὲ λαὸς Θεοῦ· οἱ οὐκ ἠλεημένοι, νῦν δὲ ἐλεηθέντες, must appear remarkable, since this epistle, on conclusive grounds (compare Steiger, p. 14 sq.), must be considered as not directed exclusively to Jewish Christians. Still more striking, however, is the second, Rom. 9. 25, 26, ὡς καὶ ἐν τῷ Ὡσηὲ λέγει· καλέσω τὸν οὐ λαόν μου, λαόν μου, καὶ τὴν οὐκ ἠγαπημένην, ἠγαπημένην. Καὶ ἔσται ἐν τῷ τόπῳ οὗ ἐρρήθη αὐτοῖς· οὐ λαός μου ὑμεῖς, ἐκεῖ κληθήσονται υἱοὶ Θεοῦ ζῶντος. Here the calling of the heathen is proved in opposition to the Jews, from the passage, which is not merely alluded to, but directly cited. But how can a declaration, which, according to the whole connexion, belongs only to Israel, be referred directly to the heathen? The answer is easy, as soon as the prophecy is referred back to its idea. This is no other than that of the Divine mercy, which can be hindered by apostasy and unfaithfulness in its manifestation, but never extinguished, because it is founded in the nature of God; compare Jer. 31. 20, ' Is Ephraim a dear son to me? a child of joy? For as oft as I speak of him, must I remember him still. My bowels are moved for him, I will pity him, saith the Lord.' Now as this idea is realized in the restoration of the children of Israel to be the children of God, so is it also in the reception of the heathen. The discourse here is by no means concerning a mere application, but a proper proof. Because God has promised to restore the children of Israel, so must He also receive the heathen. Otherwise must the former Divine purpose rest on caprice, which is inconceivable in God. If the heathen are not so near as Israel, still, even because He acknowledges the nearer claim, must He satisfy the more distant. This necessity of referring back to the idea is not less manifest, in respect to the commands than to the promises. We cite only one example, which is particularly suited to serve as parallel to the case before us. It is indisputable, and only prejudice could have denied, that, in the Pentateuch, by neighbour (friend) and brother, an Israelite is throughout to be understood. In the New Testament, the command of Christian brotherly love is given. Paul, after recommending truth, subjoins, " because ye are members one of another," which can refer only to those who have Christ as their common head. Now, from this limitation, can any thing be inferred to the prejudice of universal philanthropy, of the obligation to love all without distinction? Exactly the contrary. Because the Israelite should love all Israelites, and the Christian all Christians, so also should he embrace all men with love. If the special relation to God, as the common Redeemer, is the foundation of peculiar love, so also must the general relation to God, as the Creator and Preserver, be the ground of universal love; just as, from the command, that a man should honour his father and mother, it necessarily follows, that he must honour also his uncle and aunt, and his king and superiors. This, which alone is the correct view of the law and prophecies, when applied throughout, brings water out of the rock, and makes streams in the desert. It is owing to the opposite method, that the rich treasures of the Old Testament are now used by so few. Here, alas! μετανοεῖτε is to be urged upon many Christian theologians, and the author of this work himself openly confesses, that he now perceives that in the first volume[1] his efforts were too predominantly of an externally apologetic character.

793. Ver. 11. '*And the children of Judah, and the children of Israel, shall assemble themselves together, and appoint for themselves a head, and march out of the land, for great is the day of Jezreel.*'—At first view, the expression, ' they shall appoint for themselves a head,' appears strange. It is not *any* union of Judah and Israel, which the prophet expected from the better future, but a union founded in a return of Israel to the true God, and to the royal line of David. This plainly appears from the fifth verse of the third chapter. The difficulty is removed by a comparison of the passage of the Pentateuch, to which the prophet seems to allude : ' *Thou shalt place over thee a king, whom the Lord will choose*[2].' From this it appears, that the *choice* of a king by *God* (who had promised an eternal dominion to the royal line of David), and his *election* by the *people*, do not exclude one another. The reference manifestly lying at the foundation throughout the whole verse is to the Exodus from Egypt, which was now to be *repeated*. To this does the expression, ' *they shall assemble themselves together*,' refer. The *assembling* of the whole people preceded the departure from Egypt. The mention of the head refers back to Moses. In his case, however, the choice of the people was only an acknowledgement of his divine call.—There can here be no doubt, that by ' *the land*,' *the land of their captivity* is intended. The words are borrowed from Exod. 1. 10, where Pharaoh says: ' *If war comes upon us, they will join themselves to our enemies, and fight against us, and go forth out of the land.*' And the prophet explains himself in the seventeenth verse of the second chapter, where he expressly compares this new entrance into the promised land, with the former Exodus from Egypt, ' *As in the day when he came up out of the land of Egypt,*' just as he elsewhere describes the carrying away, under the image of a carrying away to Egypt,—Assyria, a second Egypt,—compare 8. 13, ' *Now will he remember their sins, and punish their misdeeds ; they shall return to Egypt.*' Chap. 9. 3, ' *They shall not dwell in the land of the Lord, and Ephraim shall return back to Egypt.*' To this it must be added, that, in the other prophets also, the deliverance out of Egypt uniformly lies at the foundation of the descriptions of the second great restoration. And this naturally, since both events stand in the closest connexion with each other ; both proceed from the same Divine being, and the former was an acted prophecy and a pledge of the latter. The deliverance of the people of God out of Egypt sealed their election, and this was necessarily followed by the new deliverance, a connexion which is repeated also in the case of individuals. Hence we can explain how, in the Psalms, the singers so uniformly, from the former mercies of God, prove to Him, and to themselves, that now also He must afford His aid. It is, therefore, by no means a mere outward resemblance, which gives occasion to the prophets always to go

---

[1] Of the *three* volumes of the original work.   [2] Deut. 17. 15.

back to the deliverance from Egypt[1], just as little as the passover is a mere memorial, a thing which can have no place in the true religion, that has a living God, and therefore knows nothing absolutely past.— The article in *the* land is explained by the circumstance, that a carrying away into *a* foreign land had been at least indirectly spoken of before.   Were Israel no more a people of God, did he no longer enjoy His mercy, then it was implied, that he could not remain in the land, which he had received only as a people of God, and had hitherto retained only by His compassion.   The article, however, refers, in the first instance, to the '*place where it has been said to them*,' in the foregoing verse.—That the *children of Judah* also assemble and go forth with *the children of Israel*, implies what the prophet, as not relating immediately to his purpose, had not expressly said, that the Jews also should be carried away into exile, and completes therefore the seventh verse of the first chapter, since it shows that the mercy there promised to the Jews is to be only relatively understood.   Such anticipations plainly show, with what clearness the future was unveiled to the eyes of the prophets.—In respect to the historical reference, it must first be remarked, that what is here made out concerning it must likewise serve for all parallel passages, in which, as here, a future *reunion of Israel and Judah*, and their *common return to the promised land*, are predicted ; compare e. g. Jer. 13. 18, '*In that day the house of Judah shall go up with the house of Israel, and they shall come together out of the north country, to the land that I gave to their fathers.*'   Chap. 50. 4, '*In those days the children of Israel shall come, they and the children of Judah together, weeping shall they come, and seek the Lord their God.*'   Is. 11. Ezek. 37. 19, 20.   Here several interpreters, as Theodoret of old, refer to the return from Babylon.   The one head is to be Zerubbabel. And it is not to be mistaken, that there is in this event a feeble commencement of the fulfilment.   But had this been the *completion*, Hosea would be far more like a fanatic, than a true prophet of the living God.   The obvious objection that the greatest part of the ten tribes, and a very considerable portion of the Jews, remained in exile, is by no means the strongest.   Even if both Jews and Israelites had all returned, still the prophecy, and its final fulfilment, could not be sought in that event.   It is not the renewed possession of the land, as such, which the prophet promised, but rather a *certain kind* of possession, whereby the *land would become completely the land of God*, partake in the entire fulness of His blessings, and therefore become a suitable residence for the people of God and His children. A man may be *in Canaan*, and at the same time in *Babylonia* and *Assyria*.   Or, was the threatened punishment of God *not* executed upon those, who, during the Assyrian and Babylonian exiles, still perhaps wandered about in the land in affliction and distress, as well as upon those who were carried away ?   Are the Jews who still dwell in Jerusalem in the deepest wretchedness, a proof that the loss of the promised land, with which the people were threatened, has not been completely fulfilled ?   It is true, indeed,

---

[1] Micah 2. 12, 13.   Jer. 23. 7, 8.

that in the times of the Old Testament the higher possession and the
lower stood in a certain connexion. As soon as the people were no
more a people of God, along with the former, having been often
warned by its being taken from them, they finally lost also the latter ;
as soon as they recovered the inferior possession, which could happen
only in case of their conversion, they recovered also in a certain degree (in proportion to the sincerity and completeness of their conversion) the higher possession. A commencement of the fulfilment
must therefore be assumed in the return from the Babylonian exile ;
but only a feeble beginning. As their conversion was only very
superficial, so the degree of the higher possession was very small, the
manifestations of the mercy of God were very few, the condition of
the new colony, on the whole, was poor ; they did not possess the
land as their own inheritance, but only under foreign masters.
What in one respect was the end of the exile, in another was far
more truly a continuation of it. It was not the true Canaan which
they possessed, any more than any one still possesses a beloved
object, who embraces his corpse. Where the Lord is not, with
His gifts and blessings, there *Canaan* cannot be; it was as a land
in which the Lord was present, that it was so valuable and dear
to all the pious. —From what has been said, it also appears,
that, in respect to the historical reference, we ought by no means
to stop at the times of the Old Testament, and *just as little to
dream of a still future return of Israel to Canaan.* Luther's explanation, ' *They shall ascend to a heavenly country from this land of
their sojourning,*' is perfectly just, not indeed as to the letter, but
as to the reality. It is not the *form* of the Divine inheritance, but the
substance, which the prophet has in view. Under the New Testament, where the whole earth has become a Canaan, the *form* is
changed, the *substance* remains. To stick to the form here, is just
as absurd as if any one who has left all for Christ, should complain
that he has not, according to the letter of the promise, received in
return precisely *an hundred* fold, *brothers, sisters, mothers,* &c.,
Mark 10. 30. The words of God are spirit and life, and with spirit
and life must they be understood. Granting that the children of
Israel *should* hereafter return to Canaan, this would have nothing to
do with our prophecy. In a religious point of view, it would be
a matter of perfect indifference, and could not serve in the least to
confirm the covenant faithfulness of God. Under the new covenant, *Canaan must even in the north joyfully bloom for the
beloved.* The three stations, *Egypt,* the *wilderness,* and *Canaan,*
for ever remain ; but we go from one to another only with the feet of
the spirit, not as under the old covenant, at the same time with the
feet of the body.—The fulfilment of the prophecy is therefore progressive, and will not terminate until the whole of God's saving plan
is completed. It commenced at Babylon, was carried forward at the
appearance of Christ, whom many out of Judah and Israel placed as
their head, as the common leader to Canaan ; it is still daily realized
in our sight in every Israelite who follows their example ; it will
hereafter reach the final fulfilment in the last and greatest proof of

the covenant faithfulness of God towards Israel, which, happily, is just as much secured by the New Testament as by the Old.—The last words of the verse, as to the substance, have already been explained on the first verse. The name *Jezreel* stands here in reference to its appellative meaning. Israel appears here (compare the twenty-fifth verse) as a *seed*, which *sown* by the Lord in a fruitful land, will produce a rich harvest. The figure is applied somewhat differently in Jer. 31. 27. Ex. 36. 9, where the house of Israel, and the house of Judah, appear as *the field*, which is sown by God ; analogous also is Ps. 72. 16, '*If there be a handful of corn in the land on the summit of the mountains, its fruit shall rustle like Lebanon, and they shall bloom out of the city as the grass of the earth.*' The *for* is explained by the circumstance, that the sowing can take place *only in the land of the Lord* (compare the twenty-fifth verse). If then the day of the sowing is *great*, is regarded by God as high and important, then must also the *leading forth* (being the condition under which alone the *sowing in the land of the Lord* is possible) necessarily follow.

794. Ver. 3. ' *Say to your brothers, My people! and to your sisters, Ye who have found mercy.*'—The phrase, ' my people,' is concisely said, for ' Ye whom the Lord has named My people.' The mention of the brothers and sisters is explained by the reference to the male and female portion of the prophet's family. The expression ' say,' is, in substance, i. q., ' then will ye be able to say.' The prophet sees the pardoned people of the Lord before him, and calls upon his contemporaries joyfully to greet one another with the new name which had been given to them by God. This is the simple sense of the verse, which has been darkened by a multitude of forced interpretations.

Chapter 2 verses 2—23

795. "The significant pair," remarks Rückert, "vanishes into the thing signified. Israel himself appears as the ' incontinent wife.' " This is the only essential distinction between this portion and the foregoing, which is the less, because there also, towards the end of the portion, the symbolic action passes into a mere figure. Moreover, this portion, like the former, alternates between punishment and threatenings on the one hand, and promises on the other, the promises beginning with the sixteenth verse. Features of the image, which, little regarded in the preceding verses, are here particularly finished, are the rejection of the unfaithful spouse, and her gradual reception again. Calvin : "*Deus postquam ostendit hominibus peccata, adjungit aliquam consolationem et temperat asperitatem, ne scil. despondeant animos. Postea rursum revertitur ad minas, et hoc facit necessario, quia etiamsi homines territi fuerint metu pœnæ, non tamen in solidum resipiscunt.*" Manger : "*Novo veluti cum impetu ad idem argumentum uberius exponendum a tristioribus initio iterum ducto repente revertitur.*"

796. Ver. 2. '*Contend with your mother, contend, for she is not my wife, and I am not her husband, and let her put away her whoredom from her sight, and her adultery from her breasts.*'—'*Strive with* (against) *your mother,*' that is, '*It is high time to call her to account, if you would not go to destruction with her.*' We cannot infer from this, that the moral condition of the children was better than that of the mother; the prophet only designed to say, without regard to their moral character, that their *interest* would require them to do this. He might, if he did not directly desire to carry out the image of unfaithfulness, have exhorted the mother also to strive against the children, as it is said, Is. 50. 1, '*Behold, ye are sold for your misdeeds, and for your crime is your mother put away.*' In point of fact, the mother has no existence apart from the children. Just as little can it be inferred from this exhortation, that a reformation and' a turning away of the threatened punishment is still to be hoped for. This is contradicted by what follows, where the wife appears as irreclaimable, and her rejection as inevitable. The fundamental thought is only the necessity of reformation, if the threatened judgements are still to be averted. That this reformation would not actually take place, the prophet foresaw. He therefore afterwards speaks unconditionally. It does not, however, follow, that his exhortations and threatenings would then be entirely in vain. Were no reformation to be expected from the people, still individuals might be converted. At the same time, it was of great importance in reference to the future, that the true view of their misdeeds should be opened to the people, before their calamity broke in upon them. It is of much importance, that when a man is chastised, he should know why. The instruction in the doctrine of Christ, which an evil-doer received in his youth, often seems, for a long series of years, to have been entirely in vain; often, however, when punishment has softened his heart, it brings forth its fruit.—In the words, '*for she is not my wife, and I am not her husband,*' the ground of the exhortation is given. They designate not its *outward*, but rather its *moral* dissolution, the guilt of the wife; i. q. '*our marriage is de facto dissolved.*' This virtual divorce, however, in the spiritual marriage, is always, sooner or later, followed by the legal *divorce*, according to the greater or smaller measure of the long-suffering of God. Without a figure; where sin is, there also punishment always comes. God bears with much weakness in His people; but where the relation to Him is dissolved by them in its essence, there He also abolishes it. The παρεκτὸς λόγου πορνείας serves also for the spiritual marriage. The devotion of the soul to something that is not God, is here put upon a level with corporeal adultery. And thus we clearly see the connexion between *strive* and *for*.—The transgression is first designated as *whoredom*, then as *adultery*. How they are related to one another is evident from chap. 1. 2, where the idea of *adultery* is paraphrased by '*to go a whoring from Jehovah.*' Whoredom designates the *genus*, adultery the *species*, where the sacred rights of another are at the same time violated. Transferred to spiritual things, the worldliness of those to whom God has entered into no near relation, chiefly constitutes the

idea of *whoredom;* while, on the part of individuals and communities with whom God has formed a spiritual marriage, and who apostatize from it, such conduct, being more aggravated, is designated as *adultery.* Even in the case of the children of Israel, the prophet speaks in the first instance of whoredom, leaving out of view the aggravating circumstances.—The *face* and *breasts* are mentioned, because those are the parts in which impure desire is openly manifested; so that the highest degree of impudence is designated. This shows that there is no longer any struggle within, any conflict of the better principle with the evil. An impudent whore of this kind does he resemble, who openly manifests, without shame or concern, his devotedness to the world.

797. Ver. 5. ' *Lest I strip her naked, and expose her as on the day of her birth, and make her like the wilderness, and make her like a dry land, and slay her by thirst.*' Connected with the marriage here spoken of, was the special circumstance, that the husband redeemed the wife out of the most deplorable and wretched condition, before he united himself with her, and therefore he became her *benefactor* before he was her *husband*[1]. During the marriage state, the husband continues to manifest his liberality towards the wife. But now the gifts, which had all been imparted to her, only in reference to her intended or concluded marriage, were to cease, because the marriage contract had been broken by her guilt. She is now reduced to that condition of the deepest misery, in which she was involved before her union with the Lord.—There is an allusion to the clothing and nourishment, which, in the case of an actual marriage, the husband was bound to give to the wife; compare Is. 4. 1. If God withdraws His gifts, the consequence is immeasurably more terrible, because, unlike an earthly husband, he has *all* in his possession; if He does not give to drink, He kills by thirst. If this aggravation of the punishment, grounded only in the person of the husband, is considered, it easily appears, that the reference is to the *withdrawal of the nuptial gifts, in consequence of the divorce,* and we need not, with several, e. g., Manger, assume an allusion to a punishment of adultery alleged to have been common at that time, *Ut vestibus spoliatæ, ludibrioque publico expositæ, fame et siti enecarentur.*—The eternal and universal truth, which, in the verse before us, is expressed in the special reference to Israel, is, that *all the gifts of God are imparted to individuals and to nations, only to bring them to a state of communion with Him, or as a consequence of such a state already existing;* as the Lord says, that to him who seeks first the kingdom of God, all else shall be added. If this design of the gifts of God is disregarded, if they are not received and enjoyed as gifts of God, if a man declines the spiritual marriage, or breaks it when concluded, then, sooner or later, the gifts are withdrawn.—Naked ' *as the day of her birth,*' we have here one of the frequent cases where the comparison is merely intimated, and not carried out; compare, e. g., ' *As the day of Midian,*' Is. 9. 3; ' *Let your heart rejoice as*

---

[1] Compare chap. 3. 2. Ezek. 16. 4.

wine,' Zech. 10. 7, &c. The question arises, whether the mention of the *day of her birth* here belongs only to the figure, is a mere designation of entire nakedness (because man is never more naked than when he comes into the world), or whether it is so far to be taken literally, that we must understand by the *birthday* the condition of the people in Egypt, to which they were now to be reduced. This latter reference is favoured, not merely by the parallel passages of Ezekiel, but still more by the purely matter-of-fact character of the whole description.   Israel in this portion is not *compared* to the wife, so that figure and reality stand by the side of each other, but *he appears as the wife herself.*—' *I make her as the wilderness*,' &c. The wilderness and desert are here *personified*, and represented as hungry and thirsty.   This was too figurative for several prosaic interpreters.   That by '*the desert*,' the desert of Arabia, the desert κατ' ἐξοχήν, is especially intended, is evident from the article. That this, however, is regarded only as being peculiarly desolate, and not as the former residence of the Israelites, appears from what follows, '*in a dry land*,' without the article, not, as we should otherwise expect, '*in the* dry land.'   Parallel, finally, is the threatening, Deut. 28. 48, '*And thou shalt serve thine enemy, whom the Lord will send upon thee, in hunger and thirst, and in nakedness, and in great want.*'

798. Ver. 6. '*And her children will I not pity, for they are children of whoredom.*'   That these children were to be rejected on account of their *origin*, not on account of their *moral character*, appears from the seventh verse.   That the children are children of whoredom, constitutes the reason of their rejection ; and that they are such is proved by the fact, that their mother practised this crime ; compare also chap. 5. 7, ' *They have been faithless to the Lord, for strange children have they borne.*'   In point of fact, the sinful origin and sinful nature coincide.

799. Ver. 7. ' *For your mother has played the whore, she who bore you has been disgraced ; for she has said, I will go after my lovers, the givers of my bread and my water, my wool and my flax, my oil and my drink* [1].'   The *for* confirms the proposition, that the mother has played the whore and *been disgraced*, by a further exposition of the crime and its origin.   The same delusion which here appears as the cause of the spiritual adultery, we also find as such, Jer. 44. 17, 18 ; where the people (the exiles in Egypt) answer Jeremiah, who warns them not to sin by that idolatry, which was the cause of all their present misery, and of the still greater misery that threatened them, that they will continue to burn incense and bring drink-offerings to the queen of heaven, as they and their forefathers had formerly done in their native land : ' *for since we have ceased to do this, we have been destitute of all things, and destroyed by hunger and the sword.*' The antithesis between the fountain of living water and the broken

---

[1] הוֹבִישָׁה is explained in two ways. The usual interpretation is, " *She has practised what is disgraceful, acted shamefully.*"   Thus, e. g., Winer, Gesenius, Rückert.   Others, " *She has been put to shame.*"   [So the English version, " Hath done shamefully:" so too both *Ewald* and *Umbreit*.]   This latter interpretation is unquestionably to be preferred.   For the reasons of this preference see the original work.

cisterns that hold no water, refers also to the same delusion (Jer. 2. 13). That, however, which is the cause of gross whoredom, is a consequence of spiritual whoredom. The *inward* apostasy must already have taken place, when a man speaks as the wife in the verse before us. So long as he faithfully perseveres in communion with God, he beholds with the eye of faith His hand in the clouds, from which he receives all, by which he is led, on which every thing, even what is apparently most independent and powerful, depends. As soon as he has broken off communion with God by unbelief, and heaven is shut against him, he looks around upon the visible world, and seeking for whatever seems to manifest itself as an independent and superior power, makes this the object of his affection, in a word, his God. In such an effort as this, the Israelites would chiefly look to the idols : for they saw the surrounding nations rich and powerful, and they themselves attributed their power and wealth to the idols. To them, therefore, the Israelites now attributed the gifts which they had hitherto received, and the more readily, because they could more easily satisfy their requisitions than those of the true God, who requires precisely that, and nothing else, which it is most difficult to give, the heart ; because having first determined not to give this, they deeply felt that they had no good to expect from Him ; for what He still left to them could be considered only as a gift of unmerited mercy, intended to lead them to repentance, from which the natural man revolts, who always dreams of merit in his relation to God. What we here perceive in them is still daily repeated. If we only put in place of idols *the abstract god* of the Rationalists and Deists, or *human power*, either their own or that of others, &c., it will be manifest, that ' *I will go after my lovers, who give my bread,*' &c., is still the motto of the world,—*Bread* and *water*, to express the *necessaries* of life ; *oil* and (*strong*) *drink*, to express that which serves rather for *luxury*.

800. Ver. 8. ' *Therefore, behold I will stop up thy way with thorns, and build up her wall ; and her path she will not find.*' The faithless wife is first addressed ; *thy* way ; then there is a transition to the third person ; *her* wall, *her* path. The wife was to be shut up in her way, first, by a hedge of thorns, then by a stone-wall, precisely as, Is. 5. 5, the vineyard is first surrounded with a *thorn-hedge*, then with a *wall*. *Her* wall = ' *a wall, which is one for her ; which she cannot break through or scale ;*' therefore, i. q., ' I make for *her* a wall.' *Behold*, designates the *unexpectedness* of the result ; the wife thought she should be able to accomplish her purpose with security and ease. No thought of her husband, who had heretofore, from weakness, as she supposed, suffered her to go quietly her own way, had entered *her* mind, when she saw herself suddenly fast enclosed and walled in.—The chief point still remains, viz. to determine what is to be understood by the *enclosure with a wall*. The reference to the seventh verse, and the connexion with the ninth verse, plainly show that the wall was intended to *cut her off from her lovers ;* that it cannot, therefore, be an image of distress ; not the way, or way of escape in general, but the way to her lovers. It represents

therefore an impediment to further idolatry, laid by God in the way of the Israelites; and that, an *inward* impediment; for outwardly the Israelites, even in the exile, living in the midst of idolatrous nations, had still more opportunity for idolatry than in their native land. Of what sort this was, we learn from the seventh verse. The people reasoned from the *gift* to the supposed *giver*. The *bread*, &c., was a temptation which the idols presented to them, for which they felt bound to make returns, and seek for further favour. All depended, therefore, on *interrupting this communication with the idols;* the worship of them would then cease of itself. Now this was done, when God removed the gifts in which the people beheld their idols, instead of Him. It is this removal, which is here represented under the image of a *wall of enclosure.*—What God here threatened the Israelites with, He still daily executes. Whoever does not acknowledge His gifts as such, but suffers himself to be led by them to idolatry, from him He takes them away, in order that he may thus acknowledge the former giver. Thus he establishes a gulf between him and the object of his idolatrous love, and drives him to seek the living God, instead of a god of his own making, who cannot help. This is required on the one hand by His righteousness, which must punish the adultery, and change the sweetness of sin into bitterness ; on the other, by His mercy, which betimes employs the means, which, if not the only ones, are still well suited to deliver the sinner. Both attributes demand this proceeding the more strongly, the nearer the relation is to God; righteousness, in so far as the sin is greater, mercy in so far as the love. To the heathen God often leaves their ways open for a long time ; to Israel they were soon hedged up. He still proceeds in the same way with nations and individuals.

801. Ver. 9. ' *And she shall follow her lovers, and not overtake them, and shall seek, and not find them. Then will she say, I will go and return to my first husband, for it was better with me then than now.*' The separation from the object of idolatrous love at first heightens the desire for it, and the efforts to approach it. But if, by the care of God, it is impossible to enjoy the object of an impure love, those who yield to the operation of the Holy Spirit gradually come to themselves, perceive the vanity of their idols, and return to the true God [1]. The ' *not overtaking,*' and ' *not finding,*' of the idols, means the failing of all which formerly appeared as the proofs of their power and their love. ' *I will go and return to my first husband,*' forms a beautiful antithesis with, ' *I will go after my lovers,*' in the seventh verse. This shows that God's mercy is most efficacious, precisely where it seems to have entirely vanished, and where His penal justice (for this must on no account be excluded,—there is no suffering, which does not at the same time proceed from this, no punishment which is inflicted *merely* for the sake of improvement,) appears alone to act.

[1] This apostasy, and this return, are pathetically represented by our prophet also, chap. 14. 2—4. *To pursue*, and *to seek*, are expressed in the *præt.*, the *not overtaking*, and *not finding*, in the *fut.*, because the former precedes the latter.

802. Ver. 10. ' *And she, she knows not that* [*it is*] *I* [*who*] *have given her the corn, and the must, and the oil, and* [*that it is*] *I* [*who*] *have increased her silver and gold, that they have spent upon Baal.*' The blessings here recounted were a gift of God to Israel in an entirely peculiar sense. He conferred them upon the Church, as her covenant God, as her husband. Thus were they already predicted in the Pentateuch, comp. e. g. Deut. 7. 13, ' *And he loved thee, and increased thee, and blessed the fruit of thy body, and the fruit of thy land, thy corn, thy must, and thine oil.*' 11. 14, ' *And I will give the rain of the land in its time, and thou shalt gather thy corn, and thy wine, and thy oil.*' That Hosea mentioned the three objects in precisely the same succession as they occur in the two passages, is by no means accidental. The Israelites were to express the acknowledgement, that they derived these gifts of God from His special providence, from the covenant relation, by the celebrating of the feast, and by presenting the first-fruits [1]. There is a striking antithesis between what the Israelites *did*, and what they *should* have done. What *the Lord* gave to them, *that* they consecrated to *Baal,* instead of Him to whom alone this manifestation of gratitude was due. Not satisfied with depriving the true God of the honour and gratitude which were His due, they transferred both to His enemy and unworthy rival ; a proceeding, which, bearing testimony to the deep corruption of human nature, has been constantly repeated up to the present day, and must hereafter be repeated, because this corruption constantly remains the same. It is in substance just such a consecrating of their gold to Baal, when our great poets devote their rich spiritual gifts, received from God, to the world and its prince. The ' *and she knew thee not,*' is, in both cases, equally blameable, and deserving of punishment. The *giver* has not concealed Himself ; the *objects of His bounty* have shut their eyes, that they may not see Him, whom they are unwilling to thank [2].

803. Ver. 11. ' *Therefore I will return and take my corn in its time, and my must in its season, and withdraw my wool and my flax to cover her nakedness.*' The *therefore* is very emphatic. It points to the eternal law of God's government, according to which He will be sanctified *upon* those, *in* whom He has *not* been sanctified, and the more so, the nearer His relation to them, and the greater His gifts. Whoever is not moved by them to give himself, from him shall they be taken ; and nothing remains to him, who was before richly endowed, but his natural poverty and nakedness. Happy when they are taken away *in time* for him still to perceive the giver in Him who has taken away, and to betake himself to Him, as it is said (chap. 3. 5) of the Israelites, with deep repentance for his ingratitude. When this is done, it appears that he is not an object of the Divine *justice* alone, that the *mercy* of God is still extended to him. The

---

[1] Several, from the Chaldee to Rosenmüller, explain, " *which they have made for a Baal, whereof they have made images of him,*" appealing to 8. 4, " *their silver and their gold they have made into idols for themselves.*" But this is erroneous.

[2] Ezek. 16. 17, 18, is parallel to the passage before us, perhaps an imitation of it.

longer God continues His gifts to the *unthankful*, the more gloomy is their prospect in the future. What He has given in mercy He continues only in anger.—Most interpreters explain, ' I will *again* take [1],' but the interpretation, ' I will *return* and take,' is clearly to be preferred. The Scripture says, that God *appears*, when He merely makes Himself known in the operations of His omnipotence, righteousness, and love,—a mode of expression originating in a lively sense of God's presence, which, by the eye of faith, perceives the invisible author in the visible effect; compare, e. g., Gen. 18. 10, where the Lord says, ' *He will* return to *Abraham at the same time in the following year*,'—since He did not, as at that time, *appear again* in a *visible form*, but only in the fulfilment of His promise. As God, therefore, formerly appeared to Israel as a *giver*, He now, as they do not acknowledge Him as such, *returns* as one who takes away. ' She knew not that I *gave*, therefore will I return and *take* [2].' —' *My* corn,' &c. in the antithesis with the seventh verse, where Israel calls all this *his*. What God gives remains always His, because He gives it only as a *loan*, and under conditions. If any one regards himself as its absolute lord, He causes him, by taking it away, to learn his errour.—'*At its time*,' and ' *at its appointed season*,' because it was then that God usually *gave;* it was then that His *gifts* were confidently looked for : but all at once He appears at that very time for the purpose of *taking away ;* that is, of *withholding* the gifts that were so certainly expected, as to be already looked upon as *their own*. ' *To cover*,' &c., concisely, but without a grammatical ellipsis, for ' *which hitherto served to cover her nakedness* [3].' That the Lord must cover her nakedness, refers us back to the *natural poverty* of man, who, in the whole world, has not a single patch or shred, not even any thing wherewith to cover his shame, which is especially to be understood by his nakedness. We find also, Ezek. 16. 8, ' *I spread out my skirt over thee, and covered thy nakedness*.'

804. Ver. 12. ' *And now I will uncover her shame before the eyes of her lovers, no man shall deliver her out of my hand* [4].'—' *Before the eyes of her lovers*,' means, the Lord will make her an object of dislike and abhorrence, even to those who formerly sought after her.

---

[1] אָשׁוּב וְלָקַחְתִּי, two verbs frequently joined together, of which the one indicates only an accessory idea of the action. Ew. p. 631. But the mode of expression is far less frequent than is commonly supposed.

[2] It appears that the prophet would intimate, that the word should be so understood, by the very change of the tenses. It is entirely natural that a *verb* used adverbially should *conform, as nearly as possible*, to that which contains the principal idea ; and there is scarcely *one* example, certainly not many, where, in such a case, there is a diversity of tenses. Entirely analogous is Jer. 12. 15, " And it comes to pass, after I have destroyed them, אָשׁוּב וְרִחַמְתִּים, I will return, and have compassion upon them;" where, by the explanation, " I will again have compassion upon them," the sense is very much weakened. With the same design the tense appears to be changed also below, chap. 3. 5.

[3] Correctly, as to the sense, the Seventy, τοῦ μὴ καλύπτειν τὴν ἀσχημοσύνην αὐτῆς.

[4] The ἅπ. λεγ. נַבְלוּת is best explained by *decay, corpus multa stupra passum*.

The idea is this : *God will make him who leaves God for the world, disgraced even in the eyes of the world ; and the more so, the nearer the relation in which he formerly stood to himself.* Now this idea is here expressed in a manner suited to the figurative representation, which runs through the whole portion. The making naked as a crime, is followed by the same thing as a punishment ; and all the world, especially the lovers, turn away with disgust from the hateful spectacle. They now see at once her who had heretofore made a show with the apparel and gifts of her lawful husband, in her true character, as a withered object of abhorrence [1]. To make the scene more lively, the prophet imparts to the *idols* life and feeling. Had they these, they would so act, as is here said, and as their worshippers afterwards actually did.—The second member, '*and no man,*' &c., is so far parallel with the first, that both describe the fearfulness of the Divine judgements. Parallel is 5. 14, '*For I will be as one who roars to Ephraim, as a lion to the house of Judah ; I will tear in pieces, and go ; take away, and there is no deliverer.*'

805. Ver. 13. '*And I will make all her pleasures to cease, her feasts, and her new moons, and her sabbaths, and all her times of assembling.*' The feasts were designed for a twofold purpose ; they were days of sacred devotion, and days of joy [2]. Israel having abolished the former (as now, throughout a great part of Christendom, the *holy days* bear this name only by a sort of *Catachresis*)—as a deserved punishment, God makes the second to cease. *They* had *desecrated* the festival days, by *God* they are rendered joyless. In order to show that He predicts the cessation of the feasts in this respect *as days of joy*, He premises '*all her joy,*' to which the following relates, as the *species* to the *genus*. The following three nouns are rightly distinguished by Jerome. *A feast* [3] is a designation of the three principal yearly feasts. In addition to which were the feasts of the new moon, in each month ; and in every week, the sabbath. The combination is a standing one, which also occurs in the New Testament ; compare Col. 2. 16. By *Moadim* the interpreters understand *all festival* times, in the widest extent. But at any rate, only *the feasts ordained of God* can be intended, for otherwise the *jus talionis* would not be applicable ; *God* here *takes from the Israelites* only what *they have taken from Him.* The days of the Baalim are still (in the fifteenth verse) particularly mentioned. The days of God are *taken from them ;* for the days of the Baalim they *are punished.* But we are not to suppose that *all* the feast days appointed by God are intended. *Moadim* signifies only a certain class of them, as most clearly appears from Lev. 23. 3 sq., where, after the superscription, '*these are my Moadim,*' are mentioned the *Sabbath*, the *Passover*, the *Pentecost*, the *New Year*, the *Day of Atonement*, and the *Feast of Tabernacles.* That this numeration of the Moadim was intended to be complete, appears also from the

---

[1] Compare Nah. 3. 5. Lam. 1. 8. Jer. 13. 26. Ezek. 16. 41. Is. 47. 3.

[2] Comp. Num. 10. 10.   [3] חַג.

close [1]. The *New Moon* is often distinguished from the Moadim, as not belonging to them [2]. That all extraordinary festivals did not belong to this class appears from Num. 15. 3. The determination of what class of feasts the Moadim constitute must be taken from Lev. l. c. The Moadim, in the second verse, are explained by *sacred festivals, assemblies*, and, in respect to each individual feast, the *calling of the holy assembly* is expressly mentioned. Altogether correctly, therefore, the Seventy, in the passage translated καὶ πάσας τὰς πανηγύρεις αὐτῆς. But why does the prophet still particularize the feasts, in part already cited, wherewith holy assemblies were connected? Plainly, because the loss of these feasts, or rather the loss of the feasts in this respect, was the most painful for the people. It was only by the assembling of the people that the feast became such in reality. A common spirit of joy was created, which carried the individuals along with it.—Finally, it is evident from the passage, and placed by our prophet, in several other passages, and by Amos, beyond a doubt, that outwardly the service, regulated according to the prescriptions of the Pentateuch, still continued.

806. Ver. 14. '*And I will lay waste her vine and her fig-tree, of which* [3] *she said, A reward of prostitution are they to me, which my lovers gave to me : and I will make them a wood, and the beasts of the field shall devour them.*' The vine and the fig-tree, as the two noblest products of Palestine, are here, *as elsewhere*, conjoined to represent the rich gifts with which God has blessed this land. *Reward of whoredom* [4]. The sacred writers are not ashamed to employ this term. They speak throughout of common thing sin common language. The morality of a people, and of an age, may be measured by their speaking of common subjects in common language or not. Where, in the language, a *woman of pleasure* has come in the place of a *whore*, there also the like change has taken place in the *thing*. True, the people Israel designated what they believed that they received from their idols, not as the *wages of prostitution*, but of true love. The prophet, however, at once annihilates the whole of the pleasing imagination, by putting into the mouth *suitable expressions*, which (the tongue and ear are tender in proportion as the heart is gross) would doubtless to tender ears sound harsh and coarse. She who would be thought delicate sees herself at once greeted as a common whore ; the sweet proofs of inward love, which her beloved gave to her, must be called wages of prostitution : a good corrective for our language, for our

---

[1] Ver. 37. Comp. still, ver. 44.

[2] Comp. Num. 10. 10. Is. l. 14. Ez. 3. 5.

[3] אֲשֶׁר is often prefixed to a complete sentence, in order to designate it in general as relative. Ew. p. 648. It is the looser instead of the closer connexion, ' concerning which.'

[4] אֶתְנָה, *reward of whoredom;* not from the *imaginary* root תָּנָה *largiter donavit*, &c. (תָּנָה, as a root, has in Hebrew, Arabic, Syriac, the sense *to praise, extol, recount*. But another תָּנָה occurs below, 8. 9, 10, not in the general sense *to give*, but in the special one, *to give as a reward of whoredom*. This cannot be primitive. It can be derived only from אֶתְנָה = אֶתְנָה, נָתַן, in this passage, and Ezek. 16. 34.

whole method of viewing things, for our own easily befooled heart.
All love of the world, all striving for her favour, all yielding to the
spirit of the times, is whoredom; all that she gives us in return,
therefore, is the wages of prostitution, which must not be brought
into the temple of the Lord, 'for an *abomination* is it to the Lord
thy God,' Deut. 23. 19.   As wages of prostitution will it melt away,
' of wages of prostitution has she collected, and to wages of prosti-
titution will it return.'—As to the substance itself, egotism, and the
selfishness arising from it, are the ground of the love of every thing
which is not God, especially in the case of those who have already
known the true God; for where this is not the case, there may be at
the same time a better element in idolatry, which only seeks a false
gratification, because it is ignorant of the true.   Hence, it appears
that the idolatry of the Israelites (only a species of that of all who
have had opportunity to know the true God, to all of whom the
proverb applies, "The last is worst than the first,") was much
baser than that of the heathen, whose poets and philosophers in part
zealously opposed the disposition here expressed.   Egotism is here,
as always, folly.   For it betakes itself to him who has in himself
only a borrowed and stolen good, which the rightful Lord can at any
moment take from him again.   And in order that this folly might
strikingly appear as such, He actually manifests himself here, and
takes away what the idols were supposed to have given as a reward,
but which, in reality, *He* had conferred from compassion.—The vine
and fig-gardens, carefully tended, enclosed and hedged around, were
now to be deprived of their enclosure and hedge, and all culture be
converted into a wood, and given up to the ravages of wild beasts
(' *and they shall devour it,*' is not to be referred merely to the fruits[1]).

807. Ver. 15. '*And I will visit upon her the days of the Baalim,
to whom she burnt incense, and put on her ring and her ornament, and
went after her lovers, and forgot me, saith the Lord.*'   The days of
the Baalim are the days which were devoted to their worship, whether especially selected for that purpose, or originally consecrated to
the worship of the Lord, whom they sought to confound with Baal.
In the eleventh verse, the discourse is only of *a* Baal, here of
several.   This is explained by the circumstance, that one and the
same Baal was honoured according to his different modes of manifestation expressed by the *epithets.*— In the words, ' *and she put on her
ornament,*' &c., most interpreters suppose the wearing of nose-rings,
and other ornaments in honour of idols, to be here spoken of.   A
whole multitude of false explanations has arisen from disregarding
the freedom of the sacred writers, who now speak simply of the
spiritual antitype, and now transfer to *it* the peculiarities of the
corporeal type.   Had this been regarded, it would never, e. g., have
been asserted, that David, Ps. 23. 5, 6, has relinquished the image of
the good shepherd, because he does not speak of a *trough*, which the
corporeal good shepherd sets before his sheep, but only of a *table*,

[1] The same image of a totally desolated land occurs in Is. 7. 23 sq. Comp.
5. 6. Mic. 3. 12.

which the spiritual good Shepherd places before His people. Now here, by הִקְטִיר an action is designated, which only the *spiritual* adulteress performs; in the phrase, '*she put on*,' &c., her conduct is described under the figure of that of her *corporeal type*. The corresponding matter of fact is the making herself agreeable, employing every means to gain her spiritual lovers. The putting on of costly ornament in honour of her idols comes into consideration only so far as it makes one of these efforts, and that a very subordinate one. The burning of incense, the offering of sacrifice, &c., are far more important[1].—From what has been said, it appears that in substance, chap. 4. 13, is entirely parallel. ' *On the summit of the mountains they sacrifice, and upon the hills they burn incense.*'—' *She went after her lovers*,' and ' *she forgot me*,' both serve to represent the transgression as the more detestable. Sin must already have poisoned the whole heart, when the opportunity for the practice of it is involuntarily sought.

808. Ver. 16. ' *Therefore, behold, I will allure her, and lead her into the desert, and speak to her heart.*' The consolation and promise begin here at once, just as abruptly as in the former portion. It is related, how the Lord gradually brings back His apostate wife to reformation, and a reunion with Himself, her lawful husband. The ' *therefore*,' at the beginning, has given much difficulty to interpreters. It is most natural to take it here, as standing in a simply *co-ordinate* relation with the ' *therefore*' in the eighth and eleventh verses. The *because*, corresponding to the *therefore*, is, in all three places, the infidelity of the wife. Because she has forgotten God, He recalls Himself to her remembrance, first, by the punishment, then, after this has accomplished its purpose, after she has said, ' *I will go and return*,' by the manifestations of His love. The leading back to Egypt, in the desert, in the land of Canaan, all rest on her infidelity as their ground. *Without* it, the Church would have remained in quiet possession of the promised land. *Through* it, God was moved, *both* according to righteousness and mercy, to take it from her, and conduct her back to Egypt; according to His mercy *alone*, to lead her into the desert, and thence to Canaan[2].— ' *I will allure her :*' the verb signifies *to allure by tender discourse*. The conduct of God, whereby He formerly allured the people to Himself in Egypt, and moved them to follow Him out of the spiritual and corporeal bondage into the wilderness, was to be repeated. The alluring always follows the affliction. God first takes away the objects of sinful love, He then comes alluring and persuading, that we should make Him, who alone is justly worthy of it, the object of our love. He is not satisfied with the strict prosecution of His

[1] Our interpretation is also confirmed by the parallel passages, in which the same figurative mode of representation is found. That, e. g., Is. 57. 9, "Thou lookest upon the king (this is the only correct interpretation. The usual one, "thou goest to the king," is unphilological) in oil (smelling of ointment), and multipliest thy incense,"—plainly a figurative designation, borrowed from a coquettish woman, of the application of all means to gain favour. So Jer. 4. 30. Ezek. 23. 40—42.

[2] פָּתָה, in *Pi.*

rights, but seeks to make duty sweet to us, to cause by His love, that we should perform it from love. If He has thus allured us, He leads us out of Egypt into the wilderness.—The words, '*I will lead her into the wilderness*,' have been, for the most part, greatly misunderstood by interpreters.—According to Manger, the desert is here that through which the exiles passed on their return from Babylon. But that is sufficiently refuted by the objection, that on account of the foregoing verse, by *the* desert, (the article is not to be overlooked,) no other desert can be understood but that which separates Egypt from Canaan; but this can here be only a figure and type; for the march of those who returned from the *Assyrian exile* could not be through the *literal Arabian desert;* and the comparison *expressed* in the foregoing verse, '*as in the day when she came up out of the land of Egypt*,' shows, that here also there is an implied comparison. It was only of importance to determine the *substance*, the essential character of that first *leading through the wilderness*, which that here predicted must have in common with it. The principal passage which must guide us in the investigation (a passage pointed out to us as such by the fact, that the Lord appeals to it when *He* is spiritually led through the wilderness, which, for a sign, took place also outwardly in the wilderness) is Deut. 8. 2—5, '*Thou shalt remember all the way which the Lord thy God led thee these forty years in the wilderness, to humble thee, and to prove thee, to know what was in thine heart, whether thou wouldest keep his commandments or no. And he humbled thee, and suffered thee to hunger, and fed thee with manna, which thou knewest not, neither did thy fathers know, that he might make thee know that man doth not live by bread only, but by every word that proceedeth out of the mouth of the Lord doth man live. Thy raiment waxed not old upon thee, neither did thy foot swell these forty years. Thou shalt also consider in thine heart, that, as a man chasteneth his son, so the Lord thy God chasteneth thee.*' The essence of the leading through the desert is, accordingly, the *temptation*. Through the wonderful manifestations of the omnipotence of the Lord, and His mercy in their deliverance from Egypt, a hearty love was awakened towards Him in Israel; compare its expression in the ode, Ex. 15, and likewise the passage, Jer. 2. 2, '*Thus saith the Lord, I remember thee, the kindness of thy youth, the love of thine espousals, when thou wentest after me in the wilderness, in a land that was not sown;*' the reference of which, to the earliest abode in the wilderness, before the giving of the law on Sinai, is manifest, from the mention of *youth* and *espousals*, which were succeeded by the *marriage* at Sinai. This love was also manifest in the whole conduct of the people at the giving of the law, the great readiness with which they promised to do all that the Lord should command. Thus, therefore, the first station was reached. The people now hoped to be put in immediate possession of the inheritance promised to them by the Lord. But as He knew the constitution of human nature better, He pursued another course; to the state of entire alienation from God succeeded one of temptation and trial. The first love is too often, indeed always more or less, only a fire of straw; sin is not entirely destroyed, but only temporarily subdued. It waits but for a favorable opportunity to resume its former dominion. It would never be thoroughly rooted out, if God suffered this condition always to continue; if He kept this fire always burning by a constant supply of fresh fuel, by uninterrupted proofs of love. If this love of impulse and fancy is to become *heartfelt*, established, and dutiful, it must be *proved*, that it may so learn its own weakness, and how necessary it is that it should strike its roots deeper. The means of this trial are, —God's afflicting us, arraying Himself against us, leading us in a different path from that which we had expected, seeming to forsake us. But because He, who is so merciful, will not suffer us to be tempted above our power, He, who has Himself commanded us to pray to Him not to lead us into temptation (i. e. into such a one as would surpass our strength), He bestows also His gifts, together with His chastisements. He, who suffered Israel to hunger and to thirst, gave them also to eat and to drink; He, who led them over the burning sand, suffered not their shoes to wax old. This counterpoise against affliction, however, becomes, on the other hand, itself a temptation. As Satan seeks our fall by *pleasure*, as well as by *pain*, so God proves us by what He *gives*, no less than by what He *takes away*. In the latter case it appears whether we love God *without* His gifts, in the former whether we love Him *in* His gifts. Now this second station is, for many, the last. Many bodies fall in the wilderness. But while a multitude of individuals perish there, the Church of God always goes forward to the third, the passage of Canaan. The station of trial is for her also, at the same time, a station of purification. That which is a calamity to individuals, is for her a blessing.—That we have thus rightly determined the nature of the leading through the wilderness, is also confirmed by the temptation of Christ, which immediately succeeded the gift of the Spirit corresponding to the first love. That the temptation corresponds to the leading through the wilderness (so far as it *could* correspond in the case of one who was tempted in all things, *yet without sin*, whereas in respect to us, *no* temptation, even that which is victoriously resisted, takes place without sin), is evident from the two outward characteristics, the *abode* in the desert, and the *forty* days; still more, however, from the internal characteristic, the fact, that the Saviour, as a sign that He recognized how the residence in the wilderness was repeated in Himself, opposed to the tempter a passage in relation to it from the *locus classicus*, already cited.—We now proceed to cite the parallel passages, which serve to explain the one before us, and confirm the explanation of it which we have given. The most important is Ezek. 20. 34—38 : '*And I will bring you out from the people, and will gather you out of the countries wherein ye are scattered, with a mighty hand, and a stretched out arm, and with fury poured out. And I will bring you into the wilderness of the nations, and there will I plead with you face to face. Like as I pleaded with your fathers in the wilderness of the land of Egypt, so will I plead with you, saith the Lord God. And I will cause you to pass under the rod, and I will bring you into the bond of the covenant :*

and I will purge out from among you the rebels, and them that trans-
gress against me : I will bring them forth out of the country where
they sojourn " (the standing designation of Egypt in the Pentateuch),
" *and they shall not enter into the land of Israel: and ye shall know*
that I am the Lord." Here also the abode in the wilderness appears
as a state of trial between the *residence among the nations* (corresponding to the not merely corporeal, but at the same time also
spiritual, bondage in Egypt), and *the possession of Canaan,* which
resulted variously, according to the different characters of the individuals. Some were entirely cut off; even the appearance of communion with the Lord, which those who came out with them from
the land of their pilgrimage maintained, was laid aside ; others, by
the same means which brought destruction to their brethren, were
confirmed in their fellowship with the Lord, and more cordially
united to Him. Hosea, who, in accordance with the personification
of the Church of Israel, looked more to the *whole* than to individuals,
regards chiefly the latter side. A very remarkable circumstance in
Ezekiel must still be explained, because it essentially promotes an
insight into the passage before us. What is meant by ' *to the wilder-*
ness of the nations? ' Several interpreters think of the desert between Babylon and Judea. But why the desert should be called
especially *the desert of the nations,* we can by no means perceive ; it
was not more traversed by Nomades than any other. What, however, is entirely decisive, is this : ' *I will bring you to the desert of*
the nations,' stands in direct reference to, ' *I will lead you forth from*
among the nations.' Hence it appears, that the people *to whom* the
Israelites *were brought,* could be no other than those *out of the midst*
of whom they were led forth. In the first leading away of the Israelites, the two spiritual conditions were *locally distinct :* the first belonging *to Egypt,* the second *to the desert.* But it is not to be so in
the mere predicted repetition of this leading away. When the second
spiritual condition commences, it is only in a *spiritual* sense that they
are *led forth* out of the midst of the people, among whom they *cor-*
poreally still remain. The *desert* is *in* the second Egypt itself. The
residence in the desert is repeated only as to its *substance,* not as to
its accidental outward form, just as, in Zech. 10. 11, that which apparently implies a repetition of the outward form, ' *And he shall go*
through the sea,' is limited merely to the essence, by the subjoined,
' *the distress.*' Hence, we acquire for the passage before us the
important result, that the leading away here predicted is not limited
to one definite place, and just as little to one definite time. And
what is true of the *leading through the wilderness,* must of necessity
be extended also to the *introduction into Canaan.* Just as *Egypt might*
begin, and actually *did* begin, even in *Palestine* (since Israel found
himself there in a condition of sore spiritual and corporeal bondage),
and just as, though outwardly still under Ashur, he might spiritually
find himself in the wilderness, so would the residence in the wilderness relatively have still continued, *even in Canaan,* although, which
was not the case, the whole people had returned there with Ezra.
Whereby does Canaan become Canaan, the promised land, the land

of the Lord ? *By the Lord's being there present, with all His gifts and blessings.* This, however, was by no means the case in the new colony. Because the inward condition of those who had returned was more in accordance with the *second*, in part also with *the first* station, than with the last, so also was their outward condition. The Baptist symbolized the continuance of this state, by coming forward *in the wilderness* with the preaching of repentance, and the annunciation, that now the *introduction into the true Canaan* was at hand. By giving himself out, as the voice of one crying in the desert, promised by Isaiah, he sufficiently showed the erroneousness of the carnal interpretation, which, incapable of distinguishing the idea from the drapery, understood (and still understands) in our prophet, by the *desert*, a limited and definite *portion of the land*, and then murmured, because the supposed boundary did not correspond with the actual one.—As in the case of Israel, so also in our own case, these states are not *absolutely*, but only *relatively* distinguished. Even he, who in one respect has already *been led through to Canaan*, remains in another *still in the desert.* Canaan, in the full sense for individuals, as well as for the whole Church, belongs, *not to this side*, but to the other side of the Jordan. Another parallel passage is that of Jer. 31. 1, 2 : '*At this time, saith the Lord, I will be a God to all the families of Israel, and they shall be to me a people. Thus saith the Lord, The people who have escaped from the sword shall find mercy in the wilderness; I go to give rest to Israel* [1] '—properly, '*to speak over the heart;*' because the words, 'fall down upon the heart,' designates an affectionate and consolatory address ; compare Gen. 34. 3, ('and he loved the virgin, and discoursed over the heart of the virgin') 50. 21. Is. 40. 2, here that whereby the wife is comforted, who had been deeply cast down by the consciousness of her former infidelity, and by the experience of its bitter consequences. Much too limited is the interpretation of those, who understand by it, only the consoling discourses of the prophet, though they indeed are included. It chiefly expresses the *sermo realis* of the Lord, all the proofs of tender and cordial love, whereby He animates the weary and heavy-laden, and causes those who were formerly unfaithful, but now suffer themselves to be led by Him out of the spiritual bondage into the spiritual wilderness, to be able heartily to embrace Him ; as He formerly spake to Israel, '*in the desert, in the waste and desolate land, in the land of drought and shadow of death* [2], and afterwards provided for all his necessities, in order that he might know that He was the Lord *his* God [3].'

809. Ver. 17. '*And I will give to her her vineyards from there, and the valley of Achor* (of trouble) *for the door of hope ; and she will answer thither, as in the days of her youth, and as in the day she came out of Egypt.*' The same true love which led into the wilderness, now conducts into Canaan, and the entrance into the promised land is immediately followed by the possession of all its blessings

---

[1] דַּבֵּר עַל־לֵב.   [2] Jer. 2. 6.   [3] Deut. 29. 4, 5.

and gifts, which now rightly *belong* to the *faithful* spouse (*her* vineyards), but which had previously been wrested from the unfaithful by the giver, ver. 14. ' *From there,*' rightly, Manger : ' as soon as she quitted that desert.'—' *The valley of Achor'* (= *trouble*); to understand this reference, we must consider what was the nature of the event, the repetition of which is here announced. At the very entrance into Canaan, the people were deprived of the enjoyment of the Divine mercy by the crime of one individual, Achan, which, however, was only a particular fruit on the tree of sin, common to all. God himself in mercy made known the means whereby that which was lost should be recovered, and so the place which seemed to be the *door of destruction*, became the *door of hope*[1]. The remembrance of this event was rendered perpetual by the name of the place, compare ver. 25 : ' *And Joshua said, Why hast thou troubled us? may the Lord trouble thee in this day,—therefore they called the name of the place the valley of Achor until this day.*' This particular proceeding of God rests on His nature, and must, therefore, when Israel comes into like circumstances, and, in general, when like circumstances occur, be repeated. Even those *who have already entered the promised land*, who have already come to the full enjoyment of salvation (*full*, so far as this is considered as a whole, *as the last station*, which, however, has still different degrees, therefore *relatively full;* were it absolutely full, so that nothing of the wilderness remained, the case here mentioned could no more occur, for an *absolutely full salvation* presupposes *perfect righteousness,*) and to the degree of righteousness, which corresponds to this salvation, still need the mercy of God. Without this they would soon lose their salvation. This mercy, however, is vouchsafed to them in rich measure. God's whole conduct towards the objects of His mercy *is a conversion of* the *valley of trouble* into a *door of hope*. He so leads them on, that by their sins the bond of communion between Him and them, for whom all things must work together for good, instead of being broken, as it would be, if only righteousness were considered, is only more closely connected. The same thought returns in the twenty-first verse. The new marriage covenant is there grounded, not on righteousness alone, but on mercy also[2].— ' *Thither will she answer,*' is an instance of elliptical conciseness = ' *thither will she* [*go and there*] *answer.*' Thus, e. g., Jer. 18. 2, ' *Go into the house of the potter, and thither will I cause thee to hear my voice,*' concisely for, ' *I will send thee* thither, *and* there *cause thee to hear.*' 1 Chron. 4. 41, ' *who were found* thither,' for ' *were found* there, *when one went* thither '—[But to what will she answer?] We must consider, that *a question* need not always be expressed *in words*, especially for the lively orientals, for whom the dumbest

---

[1] Comp. Schultens on *Hariri*, III. p. 180.

[2] שָׁמָּה does not mean *there*, but always *thither ;* and the verb עָנָה means neither ' *to begin the discourse,*' nor ' *to sing responsively,*' but no where any thing else than ' *to answer.*' [For the proof, see the original work. Ewald translates it ' *will answer* ' = ' *respond to :*' Umbreit, ' *will sing.*']

things have language [1]. As now no *verbal* question or address had preceded, the question arises, what *real* or *acted* address calls forth the answer? The reply is furnished by the relation of '*thither*' to '*from thence.*' Whither the answer is sent, there must the address lie. Accordingly, this must consist in the *giving of the vineyards*, and, in general, of the *blessings of the promised land.* At her entrance into it, she is welcomed by this friendly address from the Lord, her husband, and *there she answers.* What the answer consists in appears from what follows; '*as in the days*,' &c. On that occasion Israel answered the Lord by a song of praise, full of gratitude for *the deliverance out of Egypt*; and so it is by a song of praise that she will now answer him on the occasion of her *being led into Canaan.* If history had mentioned any song of praise, that Israel sang *upon entering into Canaan*, the prophet would here have alluded to *that* : but as it is, he can only refer to the song which was sung upon a somewhat different occasion. Exactly the same drapery is found, arising from the same cause, Is. chap. 12 (where even the words of the thanksgiving song of Moses are employed), and chap. 26.—*Days* and *day* are nominative, not accusative, which cannot stand here, because the discourse is not *of an action extended through a whole period*, but of one happening *at a particular* point *of this period.* The comparison is here also merely intimated, because the *tert. compar.* is sufficiently evident from the foregoing : '*As the days of her youth*,' for, '*as she formerly answered in the days of her youth.*'

810. Ver. 18. '*And it shall be in this day, saith the Lord, thou wilt call, My husband, and wilt not call to me any more, My Baal.*' The full performance of her duty corresponds to the full admission to her rights. The prophet individualizes these thoughts, by predicting the abolition of both the forms, in which the apostasy of the people from the true God,—the breach of the marriage covenant, which was entirely exclusive,—manifested itself in his time,—the amalgamation of the religion of Jehovah and heathenism (according to which they gave the name and worship of *Baal* to the *true God*), and the more gross sin of proper idolatry. The former here ; the second in the foregoing verse. Both, in like manner, are joined together, Zech. 14. 9, '*at that time will the Lord be one, and his name one.*' In reference to the fundamental thought, are parallel, Deut. 30. 5 sq. '*And the Lord will bring thee into the land which thy fathers possessed,—And the Lord will circumcise thy heart, and the heart of thy seed, to love the Lord thy God with all thy heart, and all thy soul, that thou mayest live.*'—A passage which shows, that our verse also, no less than the foregoing, contains a *promise* ; that the mentioning, and the mentioning no more, is an effect of the Divine grace, which '*I will root out*,' in the nineteenth verse, also implies [2].

---

[1] We cite as examples only 1 Sam. 21. 12. 29. 5.   Ps. 147. 7.   Comp. v. 8 sq.

[2] So Jer. 24. 7. Ezek. 11. 9. Another interpretation of this verse is recommended by its apparent depth, according to which, בַּעֲלִי is understood as an appellative : Marriage-Lord, in contrast with אִישׁ *husband*. The people shall

811. Ver. 19. '*And I will remove the names of Baal out of her mouth, and they shall no more be remembered with their name.*' The people shall conceive such an abhorrence of idolatry, as to fear to be defiled even by the utterance of the name of the idols. The words are borrowed from Exod. 23. 13, '*The name of other gods ye shall not mention, and it shall not be heard in your mouth.*' That each particular manifestation of the idea must be referred to the idea itself (which is, *abhorrence of their former* sin), is self-evident; and that consequently such a *mentioning* is not here spoken of, as that in the passage before us, which has *nothing to do with the sin.*

812. Ver. 20. '*And I will conclude a covenant for them in that day with the wild beasts of the field, and the fowls of heaven, and the worm of the earth; and bow, and sword, and war will I break out of the land, and I will make them to dwell securely.*' 'I conclude,' &c. Manger: "*Fœdus pangendum, causa pro effectu, sive ipsa securitate ponitur.*" For the benefit of Israel, God concludes a covenant with the wild beasts; that is, He *commands them not to injure him* [1]. The expression, 'I break,' &c., Manger has well explained: "*Prægnans et nervosa brevitas, qua frangere quævis belli instrumenta, ipsumque adeo bellum e regione valet, fracta ex ea abolere.*" That *war* as little means '*weapons of war*' here, as any where else, is self-evident. The prophet, as it appears, had in view the passage, Lev. 26. 3 sq. '*If ye walk in my laws, and keep my commandments, then will I give your rain in its time, and the land shall yield its produce, and the tree of the field its fruit.—And I will give peace in the land, and ye shall dwell, and there shall be none to make you afraid; and I will destroy the evil beasts out of the land, and a sword shall not come into your land.*' The supposition of a reference to this passage is the more easy, since Ezek. 34. 25 sq. almost verbally imitates it. On account of the fatal *if*, the promise has hitherto been only very imperfectly fulfilled, and often exactly the contrary has taken place. Now, however, since the condition is complied with, the promise also will be fully realized. Here, however, it is to be observed, that in the present state of the world, the hope remains *always* more or less ideal, because the condition is never perfectly fulfilled. The idea is, 'as evil, as a punishment, is the inseparable companion of sin, so prosperity is the inseparable companion of righteousness.' It is realized even during the present course of things, so far as every thing must serve to promote the salvation of the righteous. The full realization belongs to the παλιγγενεσία, where, along with sin, evil also, which is here necessary for the purification of the righteous, shall be extirpated. Parallel are Is. 2. 4; 11; 35. 9; Zech. 9. 10.

813. Ver. 21. '*And I will betroth thee to me for eternity; and I will betroth thee to me in righteousness, in justice, and in grace, and in mercy.*' Ver. 22, '*And I will betroth thee to me in faithfulness, and*

henceforth be ruled entirely by love. But it is liable to a multitude of objections.

[1] Job 5. 23. Through the mediation of God, the beasts themselves entered into covenant with Job, after his restoration.

thou shalt know the Lord.' The word [1] which points to an entirely
new marriage to a wife of youth, is not employed without design.
The very receiving the unfaithful wife again was itself a great mercy ;
she might justly have been for ever rejected ; the only valid ground
for a divorce existed ; for years she had lived in adultery. But
God's grace extends still further. Old offences are not only to be
forgiven, but *forgotten;* an entirely new relation commences, in
which there is to be no suspicion and bitterness on the one side, and
no painful retrospect on the other ; as is usual under similar circumstances among men, where the consequences of sin do not entirely
disappear, but a bitter relish always remains behind them. The
same proceeding of God is still daily repeated. Each believer can
joyfully exclaim, ' *Old things are passed away, behold all things are
become new.*' The greatness of this promise is intimated by the
direct address, the Lord having hitherto spoken of the wife in the
third person. ' *She shall hear, face to face, the joyful word out of
his mouth, that she may certainly know that she is the object of it.*'
The threefold repetition of this word expresses its greatness, its
joyfulness, and the difficulty of believing it ; and it is here the more
consoling, from being each time accompanied by *the promise of a new
benefit* from the new relation. First, the *eternal duration ;* then, as a
pledge of that, the *attributes which God unfolds in bestowing it ;* and
lastly, *those blessings which He will impart to His betrothed.* For
eternity refers back to the painful dissolution of the former marriage
covenant. This new one shall not be subject to such a fate, Is. 54.
10, ' *For the mountains shall remove and the hills depart, but my love
shall not depart from thee, and my covenant of peace not remove.*'
Of the accompanying gifts we must not assume either, with some,
that *all* relates to *one* of the two parties, or with others, that *all*
applies equally *to both.* This is evident, not only from the intervening repetition of ' *and I will betroth thee to me,*' but also from
the internal nature of the gifts mentioned. *Compassion* cannot be
mentioned in the relation of the *wife* to *God*, nor *knowledge of God*
in that of *God* to the *wife.* The four relations of God here mentioned
are joined in *two pairs, righteousness* and *right; love* and *compassion.*
We frequently find both combined in the same manner, e. g. Is. 1. 27,
' *Zion shall be redeemed in* right, *and her inhabitants in* righteousness.'
The distinction between them is, that the former [2], *the being righteous,*
denotes the *subjective* attribute, the disposition and action following
from it ; the second, *right objectively.* A man can render to any
one his right, and still not be righteous. Now God's *righteousness*
and His *doing right* in relation to the Church, consists in the faithful
fulfilment of the obligations which He assumes, by entering into the
covenant with her, in His bestowing all which He promises. This,
however, is not sufficient. The assumed obligations are mutual. If
now the covenant is broken on the part of the Church, what hope
remains for her ? Therefore, God, for the fuller satisfaction of His
spouse (who well knew, from former experience, what might be ex-

[1] אָרַשׂ, *to woo.*   [2] צֶדֶק.

pected from *righteousness* alone), subjoins a second pair of attributes, *love* and *compassion*. *Love* can be exercised by *man towards God*, as well as by God towards man ; although, since God's love so immensely outweighs that of man, the word seldom occurs of *human* love ; *compassion* is exercised only by God towards man.—Still, a distressing doubt might, and must, be felt by the spouse. God's mercy and love have their limits. They extend only to the one case whereby also marriage amongst men, the type of the heavenly, the great mystery which the apostle refers to Christ and the Church, is dissolved. What, now, if this case should happen again ? True, her heart is now full of pure love, but who knows whether this love will not cool ; whether she will not again yield to temptation ? For this new necessity, a new consolation is provided. God Himself will give what human power cannot indeed supply,—faithfulness towards Himself,—and *cause her to know Him*. The knowledge of God is here to be *genuine*. Whoever knows God in *this* manner, *cannot fail to love Him*, and be true to Him. All idolatry, and all sin, are owing to ignorance of God.

814. Ver. 23. '*And it shall come to pass in that day, I will hear, saith the Lord, hear the heaven, and it will hear the earth.*' Ver. 24, '*And the earth will hear the corn, and the must, and the oil, and they will hear Jezreel [God-sows].*'—'*I will hear,*' namely, *all prayers which are presented to me by you, and for you.*—By a bold prosopopœia the prophet makes the heaven pray, that it may give to the earth that which is necessary to her fruitfulness, &c. Hitherto they have been hindered from fulfilling their *destination ;* since God has been obliged to withdraw His gifts from an unworthy people, chap. 2. 11. Now, since this hindrance is removed, they *pray for permission to resume their office.* The prophet thus renders visible the thought, that, in the whole world, there is no good independent of God ; nothing which would not be ours, as to its destination, and in reality, if we stood in the right relation to Him ; nothing which is not His, and which will not be taken from us, when we choose to have the benefit without the giver.

815. Ver. 25. '*And I will sow her to me in the land, and I will have mercy upon Lo-Ruchamah* [her that had not obtained mercy], *and will say to Lo-Ammi* [not my people], '*Thou art my people, and they shall say to me, My God*[1].' The three symbolic names of the prophet's children here occur once more.

Chapter 3

816. The prophet, at the command of the Lord, takes to himself a wife, who, notwithstanding his true love, lives in continued infidelity.

---

[1] The *fem. suff.* in וְזַעְתִּיהָ, referring to יִזְרְעֶאל, need not appear strange. For, throughout the whole portion, the sign is lost in the thing signified. In point of fact, *Jezreel = that which is now to be sowed anew* (not *to be planted anew ;* this is a totally different image, sowing always refers to increase), is *Israel*.

He does not entirely reject her, but that she may come to a better disposition and conduct, places her in a condition where she is inaccessible to her lovers. The meaning of the symbol is given in the fourth verse. Israel, forsaken by the world, will pass a long period in sad seclusion. The close consists, without a symbolic representation, of a view into the wider future. The punishment will finally produce conversion. Israel will return to the Lord his God, and to David his king.

817. Ver. 1. ' *Then said the Lord to me, Go again, love a wife beloved of her friend, and* [*yet*] *an adulteress, as the Lord loves the sons of Israel, and they go after other gods and love grape-cakes.*' The true point of view in which this verse is to be regarded, has already, in many important respects, been established. (Compare 780.) We here take for granted the result there obtained. Of greater importance, in respect to an insight into the whole portion, is the remark, that this symbolic action, just as that in the first chapter, embraces *the whole* of the Lord's relation to the people of Israel, and not, as most interpreters suppose, merely *a part of it*, the time subsequent to the commencement of the exile. This errour, which was first clearly seen by Manger, has been occasioned by the circumstance, that, in relating the execution of the Divine command, the prophet (omitting very important points, to be supplied by his readers, partly from the command itself, partly from the preceding portions where they had already been treated at large) immediately makes a transition from the *first conclusion* of the marriage to that point which was of chief importance in this portion, the *disciplinary punishment* which *he* inflicts upon his *wife*, the *Lord* upon *Israel*. His object was to give to the people the right view of the impending exile; to cause them to regard it neither as an accidental event, having no connexion with their sins, nor as a pure operation of the Divine anger, aiming at their total destruction; but rather as a work at the same time of penal justice and sanctifying love. Between the second verse, ' *and I purchased her to me*,' &c., and the third, ' *then said I to her*,' &c., must be supplied, ' *and I took her in marriage, and loved her, but she proved unfaithful.*' That this is the right view appears from the second verse. According to the only well-grounded interpretation (compare 783), this sense can be referred only to the very commencement of the relation between the Lord and the people Israel; only to that whereby at their deliverance from Egypt He gained over this people the right of possession. This is also confirmed by the second half of the verse itself, ' *as the Lord loves*,' &c. Here the discourse is of the love of the Lord to Israel, in its widest extent; any limitation of it to one particular manifestation, to a renewal of love after the apostasy, or to disciplinary affliction, sent in love, is arbitrary, and the more so, since by the addition, ' *and they turned themselves*,' &c., the love of God is represented as running parallel with the apostasy of the people. This is evident also from

the first half. How can we be justified in explaining ' *love*,' by
' *love again*,' or even by *restitue amoris signa*, as is done by the
defenders of the assertion already refuted, that the wife is Gomer?
Love accurately corresponds to ' *as the Lord loves*.' If this must be
understood of the *Lord's love in its whole extent*, and designates not
merely the *expression of love*, but *love itself*, how then can a more
limited meaning be given to *love?* How can we, with the defenders
of the reference to a new marriage, make ' *beloved of her friend, and
unfaithful*,' refer to a former marriage of the wife, i. q., ' *who* had
been beloved *by her former husband, and nevertheless broke her
nuptial vow?*' Then there would be the greatest dissimilitude between figure and reality. Who would then be the type of the Lord?
the former husband, or the prophet? If the figure is to correspond
to the reality, the first member to the second, the *friend* can be no
other than the *prophet himself.*—We now proceed to particulars.
Love is stronger than *take*, in chap. 1. 2. There it is merely *marriage*, here *marriage from love*, and *in love*. The ' *beloved of her
friend*' makes this more prominent by contrasting it with the conduct of the wife: ' *and* [*yet*] *an adulteress*.' ' *Take in love a wife,
who, although she is loved by thee, her tender friend, nevertheless
breaks her covenant ; with whom thou, I tell thee beforehand, wilt find
thyself in a perpetual contest between love and ingratitude, the grossest
violation of love.*' The participles stand here entirely in accordance
with the general rule, according to which they express the *action*
with the *idea of its continuation* [1].—*Love* designates that which *precedes* and *effects the marriage* ; *beloved*, the love which *continued
uninterrupted during the marriage*, and notwithstanding the constant
unfaithfulness ; unless, which is also admissible, we choose at the
same time to include in *love*, ' *take, from love*,' and ' *love hence-
forward*.' That ' *beloved of her friend*,' is placed instead of ' *beloved
by* thee,' which so many have misunderstood, is not without a cause.
The antithesis thereby becomes more emphatic [2]. He, whom the
wife criminally forsakes, is *not a severe husband*, but *her loving
friend*, whom she herself formerly acknowledged as such, and who
always remains the same. Completely parallel is Jer. 3. 20, ' *as a
wife is faithless toward her friend, so have ye been faithless to me ;*'
compare ver. 4, ' *Hast thou not long ago called to me, My father?
friend of my youth art thou.*' Song of Sol. 5. 16 [3].—The phrase,
grape-cakes, has, in substance, been already explained (782), It is
a total misunderstanding, when some here think of love for feasting
and banqueting, and others, as Rosenm. and Gesen., take pains to

[1] Ewald, p. 533.

[2] רֵעַ has only *one* meaning, *friend*.

[3] In the second half of the verse, we find an agreement with the passages of
the Pentateuch, so verbal, that it cannot well be accidental, compare on
כְּאַהֲבַת יְהוָֹה אֶת־בְּנֵי יִשְׂרָאֵל, Deut. 7. 8., מֵאַהֲבַת יְהֹוָה אֶתְכֶם, an agreement which the
more deserves attention, since we have already pointed out the relationship of
this passage with ver. 2. Also on פֹּנִים אֶל־אֱלֹהִים אֲחֵרִים, comp. Deut. 31. 18, " I
will conceal my face in that day, on account of all the evil which they do ; for they
betake themselves to other gods," פָּנָה אֶל־אֱלֹהִים אֲחֵרִים.

show that this kind of cakes was used in sacrifices to idols. The grape-cakes are rather idolatry itself; '*they love grape-cakes*,' adds, however, an essential idea to '*they betake themselves to other gods.*' It points to the *sinful origin* of idolatry. The earnest and strict religion of Jehovah is *substantial* and *wholesome diet.* Idolatry is luxurious food, which is sought only by the dainty and squeamish. This which is true of idolatry, is equally so of the service of sin and the world in general; which appears also in Job 20. 12, under the image of a diet, which, in the mouth, is sweet as honey from the comb, but in the stomach is changed into the gall of serpents[1].

818. Ver. 2. '*And I redeemed her to me for fifteen pieces of silver, and a homer of barley, and a letheck of barley.*' Compare the explanation of this verse, § 783. Ver. 3. '*And I said to her, Many days wilt thou sit for me, thou wilt not whore, and not belong to a man, and so also I for thee.*' The *sitting* has the accessory idea *of being forsaken and left alone*, to be explained by the circumstance, that he who is not invited to go with us *remains sitting*[2]. We cannot take the future here, and in the following member, as the imperative, '*thou* shalt *not sit, thou* shalt *not whore.*' This is contradicted by the explanation in the fourth verse, and likewise by the parallel passage, chap. 2. 8, 9. It is not a *moral probation* to which the husband will subject the wife, but he will lock her up, so that she *must* sit alone, and *cannot* whore. With reference to the '*for me*,' Manger well remarks, that it is '*a mark of gentleness in that very bitterness; for me, who have indeed been shamefully treated by you, but still am your loving husband, and, though removed from you, will not utterly forget you.*' The phrase itself (which cannot be explained by '*to sit in expectation of any one*') expresses nothing as to the *manner* in which the sitting relates to the prophet: that it is not, however, to be considered merely as *a deserved punishment inflicted by him*, a consequence of his righteous *anger*, but rather chiefly as *an effect of his compassionate love*, which avails itself of this means to render the re-union possible, is shown by the close of the verse, where the re-union is not obscurely designated as the aim of this measure, by the circumstance, that the prophet promises the wife, during its continuance, to enter into no new connexion.—The distinction between '*to whore*,' and '*to be for a man*,' is obvious.—The first imports *vagos et promiscuos amores*, the other the marriage union with an individual; comp. e. g. Ezek. 16. 8. Lev. 21. 3. The question, however, arises, who is to be understood by the man? Several suppose *the prophet* exclusively[3]. The current interpretation assumes at least a concurrent reference to the prophet = the Lord. By

---

[1] Only the derivation of אֲשִׁישִׁים, whose meaning is sufficiently established by parallel passages, still requires an investigation. We do not hesitate to derive it from אֵשׁ, *fire*, אֲשִׁישָׁה, properly, "*that which has been subjected to fire;*" comp. אֻשָּׁה, i. q. "*what has been baked cakes.*" In Is. 16. 7, the meaning, *cakes*, must also be retained.

[2] Thus, e. g. Gen. 38. 11. Is. 47. 8.

[3] Thus Jerome.

'*thou wilt not whore,*' all intercourse with her lovers is, they say, excluded ; by '*thou wilt not be for a man,*' *likewise* all intercourse with her husband ; i. q. '*thou shalt have marriage intercourse neither with me, nor with any other man.*' We, on the contrary, maintain, that *both* refer to the *intercourse with the lovers;* the first to a *promiscuous connexion,* the second to a *permanent union* with one individual ; just as, as a matter of fact, the former relation of the Israelites to their idols was one of *whoredom,*—they made, according to their pleasure, now this and now that god of the neighbouring nations, the object of their worship,—but a *marriage relation* would be established, when they should enter into a simple, permanent, and exclusive union with one of them, like that which they had heretofore formed with the Lord [1].—The question now arises, by what means was the fact, corresponding to the figure, to be effected? how was the adulterous Israel to be hindered from whoring, and from being for a man ; by what means was idolatry to be extirpated from among the people ? The answer has already been given on chap. 2. 8, 9, and its correctness is here confirmed by the fourth verse. The idols manifested themselves to Israel in their supposed gifts. Were these taken from him, were he entirely stripped and reduced to want and misery, he must perceive the vanity of all his previous efforts, as well as that of their object, and his love to it must vanish ; he must betake himself again entirely to Him, who, by now *taking away,* proves that He formerly *gave.*—The last words, '*and I also for thee,*' are mostly explained by interpreters, *ego quoque tuus ero.* But it is rather, i. q. '*and I also will conduct myself in like manner towards thee.*' The wife, having herself broken the marriage covenant, cannot demand that *he* should observe it. But what she cannot demand of him, he performs from a necessity of his nature. He promises her, that during the proceeding which has been commenced against her, he will enter into no new relation, and by this prospect of a return hereafter to her former relation to him, he makes it more easy for her to break off those sinful connexions which have destroyed it. Without a figure, '*the Lord waits with longsuffering and compassion for the reformation of those who have hitherto been his people, and does not drive them to despair by taking another in their place, and thus putting an insuperable obstacle in the way of their return to him.*' God's proceeding in this respect leads us to a right understanding of the παρεκτὸς λόγου πορνείας, in regard to earthly marriages. It releases him who divorces his wife, on the ground of adultery, only from the crime of *adultery,* which a divorce for any other cause incurs. He may still sin grievously in another way; and he does sin grievously in every instance, where he separates himself, without having employed all means to bring the offender to repentance and reformation ; a truth which lies at the foundation of the Catholic practice of divorce, which is nevertheless contrary to Scripture, and unlike the heavenly type ; for God finally withdraws all communion from the obdurate.

---

[1] For the reasons see the original work.

819. Ver. 4. ' *For many days will the children of Israel sit with-out a sacrifice, and without a pillar, without an ephod, and without teraphim.*'—*For* is used, because the ground of the choice of the symbolic action is its meaning. On *to sit*, see the third verse; comp. still, Lam. 1. 1, ' *How does the city* sit solitary, *that was full of people! she has become as a widow.*' The question arises, whether, under the religious objects here mentioned, only such are to be un-derstood as belong to the *worship of the idols*, or such also as *belong to that of Jehovah*. The answer is, that only the *pillars* can be considered as belonging exclusively to the idolatrous worship. Such pillars always occur as consecrated only to the idols, especially to Baal, and it cannot be proved, that, in the kingdom of Israel, against the express ordinance [1], they were also consecrated to the Lord [2]. On the contrary, there is also one among those mentioned, the *Ephod* (the mantle of the high priest, on which the Urim and Thummim were placed), which must be regarded as *belonging exclu-sively to the worship of Jehovah*. At least, there is not the smallest *trace* of its having been part of any idolatrous worship. It is true, that Gesen. gives to *Ephod*, under 2, the sense *statua, simulacrum idoli*, appealing to Judges 8. 27. 17. 5. 18. 14. 17, and to the passage before us. But it is only necessary to examine these passages more closely to be convinced, that the change of Jehovah into an idol, is as arbitrary and inconsiderate as the changing of the garment into a statue. At Judges 8. 27, the very character of Gideon, who was zeal-ous for the Lord against idols, *forces* us to think, not of *idolatry proper*, but only of *image-worship*. As the high priest received the Divine answer only when clothed with the ephod, it was thought that the presence of Jehovah was enveloped in the ephod in a magical manner, first, indeed, only in that of the high priests, but afterwards in others also, made after its image. It was in order the more to enjoy this presence, and prepare a worthy dwelling for the Lord, that Gideon made his ephod as splendid as possible, entirely out of gold. On chap. 17. 5, we need only observe what follows, ' *And Micah had a house of God, and he made for himself* an ephod, *and teraphim, and consecrated one of his sons, and he became his priest.*' Afterwards Micah took a *Levite* for a priest. But why was *he* better suited than any other for the purpose? The answer is given in the thirteenth verse, ' *And then Micah said, Now I know that* Jehovah *will do me good* (will be favorable to me), *for the Levite has become my priest.*' The ignorant man knew at least that the only legitimate ministers of Jehovah were the Levites. He rejoiced, therefore, that he had now remedied this former anomaly. Chap. 18. 14, needs no special illustration; for the subject of discourse is still the same ephod. We must, however, show the application of the fifth and sixth verses of that chapter. ' *Then they said* (the Danites) *to him* (the Levite), *Ask God, that we may know whether our way will prosper in which we go. And the priest said to them, Go in peace, for* Jehovah *is your way, which ye walk.*' We have here an

---

[1] Levit. 26. 1.   Deut. 16. 22.
[2] Comp. 2 Kings 3. 2. 17. 10. 10. 26—28.

alleged revelation imparted to the priest, by ephod and teraphim ; only this is referred, not *to the idols*, but to *the Lord*, whom alone the Levite wished to serve. From which it appears, that the carved and molten images also (which, in the fourteenth verse, are mentioned as being found in the house of Micah *along* with the ephod and teraphim, and must therefore have been *different* from both,) must be regarded *as representations of Jehovah*, like the calves in the kingdom of the ten tribes. In case of the two others (the sacrifice and the teraphim), at all events, the *exclusive* reference to an idolatrous object cannot possibly be maintained. If sacrifices in the most *general* sense were spoken of, without any limitation in the preceding context, how should we be justified in *excluding sacrifices which were offered to Jehovah ?* The teraphim, as has been shown (571), were intermediate deities, who aided in penetrating the future, and *might* be placed in connexion with *any* religious system, but yet *are* found but once in connexion with any other than that of *Jehovah*, and that when the discourse is not concerning an Israelite. —But how can this remarkable amalgamation of what belongs to the idols and to Jehovah, which cannot be otherwise than intended, be explained ? How can the reference to Jehovah be reconciled with the third verse, where the discourse is only of the cutting off of all connexion with the lovers, and likewise with chap. 2. 8, 9 ? The answer is, that we must distinguish between *Jehovah the true God*, and *the Jehovah of the Israelites*. This latter was only a God in appearance, in reality an idol[1]. As he was called *Baal* by way of alternation, so did he *stand on the same level with Baal*. Here we have the true solution of the problem, which, at first sight, is very difficult.—But in what respect are the Israelites to have no sacrifice, &c. any more ? All this can in no way be *outwardly* taken from them. How could the exile have hindered them from sacrifices ? how from the erecting of statues, &c. ? The true view is, that these things should *so far* be taken from them, as that *every thing should cease, which had hitherto nourished the erroneous opinion, that the self-made gods could afford them aid*. What was the cause why the Israelites had hitherto brought sacrifices to *Baal*, and *their Jehovah ?* They believed themselves indebted to *them* for all the blessings they enjoyed, and then expected others from them for the future. If these *blessings* ceased, so also would the *sacrifices*. If they supposed themselves entirely forsaken by them, they could no longer think of dedicating statues to them, and inquiring of them by ephod and teraphim. Now also we see the reason of the collocation of *king* and *prince* with the sacrifice. The preservation hitherto of the civil government, with all its blessings of political freedom and independence, had been considered by the Israelites as a seal upon their ways, as a token of favour from their lovers, *Baal* and *their Jehovah*. Therefore, this supposed sign of their power and love, with all others, must be taken from them, which would then serve to bring about the fulfilment of ' *thou wilt not whore*.' And so it appears how the

---

[1] Comp. 2 Kings 17. 8.

explanation corresponds entirely with the symbol. God's first proceeding, when He would draw any one from the world to Himself,
is a *taking away;* for those who thus learn the nothingness of the
former supposed giver, and recognize the previous giver in Him who
takes away, there follows then the conferring of blessings.—As to
the historical reference, the interpreters hesitate between the Assyrian, Babylonian, and Roman exile. The most refer exclusively to
the last. Thus the Jewish interpreters, e. g. Kimchi. The chief
defenders of the most direct reference to the Assyrian exile are
Venema and Manger. The decision depends chiefly on the question,
who are to be understood by the '*children of Israel?*' If they are
the whole people, it is arbitrary to set narrower limits to the *word* of
God than His *deed;* the prophet must then comprehend all those in
whom its idea is realized; and the more so, since the spiritual eye of
the prophet, directed only to the idea, does not generally regard the
intermediate periods, which, *in fact*, lie between the different realizations of the idea. But the fifth verse appears to us to imply, that
the prophet has in view, first, the *children of Israel, in the strictest
sense.* '*They will return and seek* David their king,' includes a
reference to the existing *apostasy of the Israelites from the tribe of
David.* In point of fact, however, there is no difference. If the
prophet announces the realization of the idea only in reference to the
Israelites, still, as being an *idea*, grounded in the *nature* of God, and
not depending on caprice and accident, it must *also* manifest itself
in the fate of the Jews; and that the prophet was himself aware of
this, and mentioned the Israelites alone, only because he had been
sent to them alone, appears from chap. 2. 2. There it plainly appears
in what a close connexion the condition of the Jews, from the destruction of Jerusalem to the present day, stands to this prophecy.
They have forsaken Jehovah their God, and David their king. *Their*
Jehovah has degenerated into an idol, no less than the Jehovah *of
the children of Israel.* That they may now know Him as He is, and
return to the true *living* God, all has been taken from them, in which
they believed they saw the manifestations of His power, His mercy,
and love. We must, however, by no means suppose that the idea is
exhausted, when its realization is acknowledged also in the fate of
the Jews. It gives also the key to the dealings of God with the
Christian Church, with Christian nations and individuals.

820. Ver. 5. '*Afterwards will the children of Israel return, and
seek the Lord their God, and David their king, and tremble to the
Lord and to his goodness in future days*[1].' What is to be regarded

---

[1] יָשֻׁבוּ must not be regarded as constituting, with בִּקְשׁוּ, only one verbal idea,
'they will again return.' This is contradicted, not only by the grounds already
cited on chap. 2. 11, but most decidedly by the parallel passage, chap. 2. 9, 'I
will go and return to my first man;' comp. also chap. 6. 1, 'Up, let us return to
the Lord;' 5. 15, where the Lord says, 'I will go and return to my place, until
they feel their guilt, and seek my face. In their distress they will seek me.'
Jer. 50. 4, 'At that time, saith the Lord, the children of Israel will *come* together
with the children of Judah, weeping will they come and seek the Lord their
God.' Is. 10. 21.

as the object of their return to the Lord their God, and David their
king, from whom they had shamefully turned away, appears so
plainly from the context and the parallel passages, that those who
think of a *return to Canaan* deserve no refutation. The expression,
' *Jehovah, their God,*' exposes the delusion of the Israelites, who
fancied, that, in the idols which they *named* Jehovah, they still possessed the true God, and at the same time rebukes their ingratitude.
The *God of the Israelites sustains* to the *God of Israel* the same
relation as the God of the Deists and Rationalists to the God of the
Christians.—The question here arises, who is to be understood by
' *David their king ?*' Some, after the example of Theodoret [1], think
of *Zerubbabel,* but by far the greater number of interpreters, after
the Chaldee (*et obedient Messiæ, filio Davidis, regi ipsorum*), refer
the prophecy to the *Messiah.* The latter interpretation is *in substance* perfectly correct, but not *in the form* in which it has, for the
most part, been delivered. That the Messiah is not here, as elsewhere [2], named *David* as an individual, is evident from ' they will
return and *seek.*' The *return* presupposes a *former departure;* the
seeking, a *former neglect.* The expression also, ' *their king,*' is to be
well observed. It shows, in the antithesis with the king in the
fourth verse (comp. chap. 8. 5, ' They have made a king, and not
by me ; a prince, and I knew it not'), that it is not *a king to be
newly chosen,* which is here spoken of, but *one whom the Israelites
were bound to obey, as already given to them of God.* The correct
view is, that, by *the king David,* the *whole royal house of David* is
designated, just as in the promise, 2 Sam. 7, and in a whole series
of Psalms which celebrate the mercies of David, those which have
been and were to be vouchsafed to him and his race. These mercies
are most completely concentrated in Christ, in whose manifestation
and eternal dominion the promises made to David first receive their
full accomplishment. That the prophet, when he calls the whole ' *the
stock of David*' (because it was only in this way that the antithesis between the apostasy and the restoration could be rendered prominent),
has *him* especially in view, that he expected a return of the children
of Israel to David in Christ, is shown by ' *in the latter days* [3],' which,
in the prophets, never occurs, except of the times of the Messiah [4].
This argument is itself sufficient to refute the reference to *Zerubbabel,* though it must be conceded, that the adherence of a part of
the citizens of the kingdom of the ten tribes to him, the sprout of
the house of David, may be considered as *a prelude* to the general
return.—The close connexion between the seeking of Jehovah their
God, and David their king, is to be well considered. David and his
race had been chosen of God as a mediator between Him and the
people ; the channel through which all His blessings should flow to
them ; the visible image of the invisible ruler, which, in the last
days, should in Christ most perfectly reflect his glory. When,

---

[1] T. II. pt. 2. p. 1326.   [2] Comp. on Jer. 30. 9.
[3] בְּאַחֲרִית הַיָּמִים.
[4] Compare, in a philological point of view, on Amos 9. 1.

therefore, the Israelites departed from David their king, they departed at the same time from Jehovah their God, as was too soon evinced by the other signs of apostasy from Him, the introduction of the worship of the calves, &c. He, who will not acknowledge God in what He Himself has declared to be His visible image (from Christ down to every relation that in any respect represents God, e. g., that of a father to his son, of a king to his subjects), knows Him not even in Himself. As, however, the Israelites apostatized from God in David, so did they exclude themselves, by their apostasy from Him, from the participation in the mercies of the people of God, which could be derived to them only through him. Not until they return to David in Christ, do they forsake the god of their own invention for the true God, and come within the sphere of His blessings. How this is repeated among us, in the case of those who have forsaken Christ their king, and still think to possess God, how they can attain to true communion with the Lord their God, and to a participation in His blessings, only by returning to the brightness of His glory, is so evident, that it need only be suggested. The expression, '*they tremble to the Lord*,' paints the state of a man's heart, when, shuddering with terrour and anxiety on account of the danger and distress with which he is threatened, he flees to Him who alone can afford him help and deliverance. Their *terrour* is not voluntary ; it is forced upon them by the Lord ; but that they tremble *to the Lord* (suffer themselves to be led *to the Lord* by their fear), is their own free act, though possible only by the assistance of grace.—How the expression, ' *and to his goodness*,' is to be understood, is most clearly shown by ' *I will return to my Lord*, for *better was it for me then than now* [1].' Along with the Lord they have also at the same time *lost* His goodness, the gifts proceeding from it ; now necessity again drives them to *seek* the Lord and His goodness, which is inseparable from Himself [2].

THE PROPHET JOEL

Preliminary Observations

821. For the determination of the age of Joel, we have an external argument in the position which has been assigned to him in the collection of the minor prophets. There can be no doubt that the collectors were governed by a regard to chronology. When, therefore, they placed the prophecies of Joel between those of two prophets, who, according to both the superscription and contents of their prophecies, belong to the age of Jeroboam and Uzziah, this is like an express testimony that he also lived and acted at that time.

[1] Chap. 2. 9.
[2] This interpretation is also confirmed by other parallel passages, as Jer. 31. 12. Ver. 14. Comp. Ps. 31. 20. Zech. 9. 17.

822. This testimony must continue valid until overthrown by other evident facts, until the collectors have been convicted of an historical errour.   In attempting to do this, we must be the more cautious, since all their other assumptions are verified by a careful examination, and not one of the other minor prophets has had a place assigned to him which was not really his.   Such facts, however, are not to be found.   On the contrary, every thing serves to confirm this testimony [1].

823. In few prophets is the resting of the prophecy on the idea so conspicuous as in Joel.   No where, therefore, can that false method, which, leaving the idea out of view, regards only isolated facts of history, a method, the evil consequences of which extend to the interpretation of the New Testament also [2], operate more injuriously than here.   The book contains a connected representation.   It commences with a lively description of the ruin which God, by means of outward enemies, will bring upon His apostate Church.   These present themselves to the inward contemplation of the prophet, as an all-devouring swarm of locusts.—The fundamental idea is, ' where the carcass is, there will the eagles gather together,'—where corruption manifests itself in the Church of the Lord, there will punishment come.   Because God has sanctified Himself *in* the Church, and graciously imparted to her His holiness, so must He sanctify Himself *upon* her, manifest His holiness in her punishment, when she has become like the profane world.   He cannot endure, that when the Spirit has departed, the dead mass should continue to appear as His kingdom.   He strips off the mask of hypocrisy from His degenerate Church, by exhibiting her outwardly as what she has inwardly become by her guilt.   This idea usually appears in a special application, with a mention of the particular people whom God would employ, in the nearest future, for its realization.   Here, on the contrary, its inherent dignity and power are sufficient.   The enemy are designated only as *north-countries*.   Now from the north (from Syria), *all* the principal invasions of Palestine proceeded.   We have, therefore, no reason *to think exclusively of any one of them*. Nor ought we to limit the prophecy to the people of the Old Covenant.   Throughout all centuries, there is but one Church of God existing in unbroken connexion.   That this Church, during the first period of its existence, was concentrated in a land into which hostile irruptions were made from the north, was purely accidental.   To make this circumstance the boundary stone of the fulfilment of the prophecy were just as absurd as if one were to assert, that the threatening of Amos, ' by the sword *shall all sinners of my people die*,' has not been fulfilled in those who perished in another manner.

824. The threat of punishment, joined with exhortations to repentance, to which the people willingly hearken, and humble themselves before the Lord, continues until chap. 2. 18.   Then succeeds,

---

[1] In the original this question is examined at length.

[2] It is owing to it, that the declarations of Christ, respecting his coming to judgement, are usually so entirely misunderstood, and that even diligently laboured writings, as those of Schott, must entirely fail of their chief object.

until chap. 3. 2, the prediction of prosperity. The showing of mercy begins with God's sending a *teacher of righteousness*. This teacher directs the attention of the people to the design of their suffering, and invites the weary and heavy laden to come to the Lord, that He may refresh them. His voice is obeyed by those who are of a broken heart, and now a rich divine blessing follows, and, as its highest degree, the outpouring of the Spirit. Here, again, we have only the everlasting way of the unchangeable God in His Church ; His proceeding through hundreds and thousands of years.

825. The prediction of prosperity to the covenant people is followed in the third and last part by its opposite, that of the *judgements upon the enemies of the Church of God*, whose hatred of it, proceeding from hatred towards God, does not cease to be an object of His penal justice, because He employs it as a means for the chastisement and purification of His Church. The ground idea of this part is given in the words, 1 Pet. 4. 17, '*For the time is come that judgement must begin at the house of God; and if it first begin at us, what shall the end be of them that obey not the Gospel of God? and if the righteous scarcely be saved, where shall the ungodly and the sinner appear?*' It might seem as though this part, unlike the two preceding, refers to one *single* event,—the last judgement ; and that every reference to an inferior one is excluded by the repeated mention of *all* nations. But still it only appears so. In order that the full force of the *idea* may be perceived, it is presented in the form of its final and most complete realization ; but for the very reason that the final judgement is only a realization of the idea, this idea must previously manifest itself in circles of smaller extent. There could be no *final* judgement, if the whole history of the world did not already consist of judgements of God. But, because it *does* consist of these, there *must* be a final judgement; ay, though the Scripture did not contain expressly *one word* upon the subject. The prophecy was verified in the destruction of the Assyrians, in the time of Hezekiah, in the ruin of Babylon, in the destruction of Jerusalem after the kingdom of God had been taken from Israel, and given to another people, who brought forth its fruit in their time (Matt. 21. 43), in the whole history of Christianity. Whoever understands this prophecy, has also the key to Matt. 24 and 25, where, moreover, this assertion is erroneous, that the representation refers, at the *same time*, to the destruction of Jerusalem, and to the judgement of the world, as though the whole intervening period were to be regarded as empty ; God being, in this respect, no God at all during its continuance. We must here only avoid confounding the substance with the form, the idea with the temporary clothing which the prophet has prepared for it, in accordance with the nature of a prophetic vision, in which every thing spiritual must necessarily be represented in outward sketches and forms. This clothing is as follows.—In the nearest place to the temple capable of containing a great multitude of men, the valley of Jehoshaphat, (which probably received this name from the passage before us, as a proper name, which the prophet here attributes to it, only to designate its destination,—'*the Lord judges*,' or '*valley of*

judgement,' compare § 528,) all the heathen are assembled. The Lord, enthroned in the temple, exercises judgement upon them. Thus the idea is revealed in outward forms, that the judgement upon the heathen is a result of the Theocracy, that they are not punished on account of their violation of the law of nature, but on account of the hostile attitude which they have assumed against the bearers of God's revealed truth, against the Lord, who dwells in His Church. Every violation of the law of nature may be forgiven to those who stand in no nearer relation to God, even though they have proceeded to the most fearful extent in depravity.   Those who were once disobedient, when the long-suffering of God waited in the days of Noah, were not yet given up to final damnation, but kept in prison (the middle condition of Sheol) until Christ came and preached to them. This was the iniquity of Sodom ; pride, fulness of bread, and abundance of idleness was in her, and in her daughters; neither did she strengthen the hand of the poor and needy, but was haughty, and committed abomination before the Lord, therefore He took them away as He saw good.   Nevertheless the Lord will hereafter turn away the captivity (the affliction) of this Sodom and her daughters, and they shall be restored as they were before,—not corporeally, for the last trace of her seed is blotted from the earth, and even her site is destroyed,—but spiritually [1].   On the contrary, far heavier punishment overtakes those who have rejected not the abstract, but the concrete God; not Him who is shut up in heaven, but Him who has powerfully manifested Himself on earth, in His Church.   True, so long as this revelation is still imperfect, as under the Old Testament, and therefore the guilt of rejecting God is the less, there is room for compassion.   The outward destruction does not involve in it the spiritual also.   Moab is destroyed, that he is no more a people, because he hath exalted himself against the Lord.   ' *But in a future time I will turn away the captivity of Moab, saith the Lord* [2] ;' but when the revelation of the mercy of God has been *completed*, so also will His righteousness be completely revealed against those who despise this revelation, and rise up in hostility against those who bear it.   Their worm shall not die, and their fire shall not be quenched, and they shall be an abomination to all flesh [3].   In these remarks lies the key to all the Lord declares in respect to the future judgement, which is only future in its completion.   Its object is not the world, as such, but the world to which the Gospel is preached, in the midst of which the Church has been established [4].

Chapter 1-2:18

[Professor Hengstenberg, in his remarks on this portion, maintains (1) that Joel is not describing a *present*, but a *future*, calamity: (2) that there is no truth in Credner's hypothesis, that a *twofold devastation* is described, proceeding from

---

[1] Comp. Ezek. 16. 49 sq.   [2] Jer. 48. 47.
[3] Is. 66. 24.   [4] Comp. Matt. 24. 14.

two different swarms: (3) that the devastation by *locusts* is *figurative* (an interpretation which has the testimony of exegetical tradition in its favour) : but that the devastating hosts were not *merely compared* by him to locusts, but really *presented* to him, in vision, under that form. This just observation explains the possibility of *their being compared* to the thing itself, which they were intended to represent. It is the very nature of an allegory that the figure *becomes*, and must be spoken of as a *reality*. Hence many traits will be introduced, that belong only to the figurative representation; and this, being raised to an *ideal reality*, may, in its turn, be *compared* to the *real object*, which it represents.]

Chapter 2:23

826. ' *And, ye sons of Sion, exult and rejoice in Jehovah your God ; for he gives you the teacher of righteousness, and then will he pour down upon you former and latter rain first.*'—' *The Teacher of righteousness ;*' so Jon., Vulg., Jarchi, Abarb., Grotius, and nearly all the early interpreters of the Lutheran church. Others translate the word not by *teacher*, but by *rain*[1]. This interpretation was not unusual, even in ancient times. Among the Rabbins, it is found in Kimchi, Abenezra, S. B. Melech, who think of a *timely* rain. [Then follows in the original a critical examination of the passage.] ' *The rain*' is found in the English [translating it ' *rain in just measure*,' but ' the teacher of righteousness,' in the *margin*] and Genevan translations, and in many reformed interpreters. Mark supposes that the rain is necessarily required by the connexion ; this, however, on account of the *righteousness*, is to be spiritually understood, the Messiah, with his wholesome doctrine and his spirit. Among the interpreters of the Lutheran church, Seb. Schmid thinks of a *pluviam tempestivam*. Among recent interpreters, the explanation by *rain* has become so entirely prevalent, that it is thought scarcely worth while to mention the others. We regard this explanation as decidedly wrong, and the other as the correct one. The words ' of *righteousness*' are translated,—by Eckermann : ' *for a proof of his good pleasure :*' by Justi, ' *for fruitfulness.*' Calvin, Rosenmüller, Holzhausen, and Credner, translate ' *in just measure :*' others, ' *at the right time ;*' ' *in the right place ;*' ' *according to his righteousness ;*' ' *to your righteousness.*'

827. A causal connexion of this kind between the *sending of the Teacher of righteousness*, and the *effusion of rain*, is found in a passage of the Pentateuch, which the prophet, it would seem, had in view. Deut. 11. 13, 14, ' *And it shall come to pass, if ye shall hearken diligently unto my commandments which I command you this day, to love the Lord your God, and to serve him with all your heart and with all your soul, that I will give you the rain of your land in his due season, the first rain and the latter rain, that thou mayest gather in thy corn, and thine wine, and thy oil*[2].' Here, as there, the righteousness of the people is the *antecedent*, the divine

---

[1] Taking מוֹרֶה in the sense *to rain*, and לִצְדָקָה as a nearer designation of its nature.
[2] יוֹרֶה וּמַלְקוֹשׁ.

benefit the *consequent*. Because the former is wanted, the Lord
commences the course of His mercy by sending him who produces
it.   At the same time, the objection falls to the ground, that the
mention of the teacher of righteousness is unsuitable in a connexion
where the prophet speaks only of *temporal* blessings, in order after-
terwards, in the third chapter, *to rise to those which are spiritual*.
There were no *purely* outward blessings for the covenant people ;
they were always, at the same time, signs and pledges of the good
pleasure of God, which depended on the righteousness of the people,
and this again on the Divine mission of a teacher of righteousness.

828. Our interpretation is clearly favoured by the word *first*,
which stands in a close relation to the ' *afterwards*,' in chap. 3. 1.
The sending of the Teacher of righteousness has a twofold consequence ; *first*, the outpouring of the *natural rain* (an individualizing
designation of every sort of outward blessing, chosen with reference
to the cited passage of the Pentateuch, but especially to the representation of the calamity under the image of the devastation by the
locusts) ; *then*, the outpouring of the *spiritual rain*, the sending of the
Holy Ghost.   It is only necessary to point out this reference, overlooked by the interpreters, in order to set aside the many different
interpretations of ' first,' which are all unphilological.

829. It still only remains to inquire, who is to be understood by
the teacher of righteousness.   The Messiah is regarded as such, not
only by nearly all Christian interpreters who follow this explanation,
with the exception of Grotius, who conjectures him to be Isaiah, or
another prophet, but also, after the example of Jonathan, by several
Jewish commentators, e. g., Abarbanel : " *Is autem est rex Messias,
qui viam monstrabit, in qua debeant ambulare, et opera, quæ facere
deceat*." We are forbidden by the article to think of any particular
human teacher, which must also be subjoined to the arguments
against the explanation of the early rain.   The choice can be only
between the Messiah as the long-promised teacher, $\kappa\alpha\tau$' $\dot{\epsilon}\xi o\chi\acute{\eta}\nu$, and
the ideal Teacher, the collective body of all divine messengers, which
presented themselves to the prophet, because their individuality was
unimportant for his object, in a personal unity.   Even with the latter
explanation the passage deserves the name of *Messianic*.   For it was
in Christ that this promise was first completely realized.   We are
induced to prefer it to the direct and exclusive reference to the Messiah [1], by the comparison of the passage, Deut. 18. 18, 19 ; by the
absence of every individual reference to the Messiah, and the bare
mention of *instruction in righteousness*, which was common to him
with all former servants of God ; finally, by the nature of the whole
remaining description of Joel, which always adheres closely to the
idea, and is never occupied with one particular historical fact considered in itself.

---

[1] What was remarked upon it concerning the נָבִיא, may be transferred to the
מוֹרֶה.

Chapter 3

830. Ver. 1. '*And it shall come to pass afterwards, I will pour out my Spirit upon all flesh; and your sons and your daughters shall prophesy, your old men shall dream dreams, and your young men have visions.*' The imparting of the Spirit of God ever constituted the prerogative of the covenant people, which, indeed, the idea of such a people necessarily requires. For the Spirit of God is the only inward bond between Him and the creature. But there can be no covenant people without such an internal union. As a constant possession of the covenant people, the Spirit of God appears in Is. 63. 11, where the people, in the deepest destitution, remembering the Divine mercy, say, "Where is he who put his Holy Spirit within him?" But it lay in the nature of the Old Testament economy, that the outpouring of the Spirit of God was less rich, its effects less powerful, and the participation in them less general. It was not till after the relation of God to the world had been changed by the death of Christ, that the Spirit of *Christ* could be imparted. The conditions under which the Spirit was imparted in the Old Testament were far less easy to be fulfilled ; the view of Christ, in his historical personality, in his life, suffering, and dying, was wanting ; God, though infinitely nearer than among the heathens, still continued, relatively, a God far removed ; since the procuring cause of the mercy of God, the merit of Christ, was not yet so clearly revealed ; it was far more difficult to apprehend it; the by-path of a merely legal righteousness lay then far nearer than it now does. And thus the *immediate* possession of the Spirit was enjoyed only by a few, especially the prophets ; the majority even of the better-minded possessed the spiritual life *mediately* only, and therefore in an inferior degree, by attaching themselves to the prophets. That a richer and more powerful effusion of the Spirit of God must take place at a future time, lay in the nature of the case. And for this reason the wish of Moses, that this might happen, that the whole people might prophesy [1], was, at the same time, a prophecy. What he wished was, that the people of God might come to *realize* the *idea* of such a people, and this must hereafter happen, because the almighty and faithful God could not leave His work incomplete. What Moses, as far as his words went, expresses only as a *wish*, Joel [2] utters directly as a *promise*. In its final reference, it belongs to the Messianic times ; but we must not, on that account, exclude all reference to the preparatory events. The prediction of the outpouring of the Spirit rests on a thorough knowledge of the nature of God's relation to His kingdom. It is entirely without reference to time. God's judgements, in which He draws near to the people, and becomes, instead of an abstract, a concrete God, awaken in the people an earnest desire for communion with Him ; a teacher sent of God gives this desire the right direction, and now an outpouring of the Spirit follows. This course is, and must be, perpetually repeated

[1] Num. 11. 29.
[2] With whom particularly Is., e.g. 11. 9. 54. 13. Jer. 31. 33. Ezek. 36. 27. Zech. 12. 10. agree.

in the history of the covenant people. The complete fulfilment of
the prophecy in the time of Christ could not have taken place, if the
imperfect fulfilment had not extended through the whole previous
history ; and that no regard was paid to this in the prophecy before
us, could not be asserted without some intimation in the text, that
the prophet *intended* to speak only of the *last realization* of the idea.
It is equally arbitrary to take only *one particular portion*,—the occurrence on the first pentecost,—of the whole fulfilment in the time
of the Messiah. That fulfilment was no further *final*, than as it
contained a pledge that this should take place, and thus *virtually*
comprehended the *whole* subsequent development till the end of the
world ; no further than as it converted the *verbal prophecy* of Joel
into an *acted prophecy* of infinitely greater power.—From the reference already proved of *afterwards* to *first*, in chap. 2. 23, it appears
that it is not so much a determination of the *succession of time* as
that of *rank*. Of the two consequences of the sending of a new
Teacher of righteousness, first the *inferior* presents itself to the
prophet, then *the higher*. The determination of time is not the
essential thing ; it serves only to make clear the relation of the facts,
the gradation of the Divine blessings.—The expression, ' *I will pour
out*,' refers back to the *rain* in ver. 23. The idea of *abundance*, in
contrast with the former *scarcity*, is indeed implied ; still this must
not be exclusively regarded ; the attributes of the rain indicated in
ver. 24 sq., the *quickening* of what was *dead* before, the *fructifying
power*, must not be overlooked.—The expression, ' *upon all flesh*,' is
explained by the following ; ' *your sons, your daughters, your old,
your young, the servants, and the handmaidens;*' therefore, the *all*
does not do away with the *limitation to one particular people*, but
only, among this people themselves, with the limitations of sex, of
age, and of rank. The participation of the heathen in the outpouring
of the Spirit did not here come immediately under consideration,
since the threatening of punishment, with which that of prosperity is
connected, had concerned only the covenant people. The *flesh* designates human nature, with reference to its *feebleness* and *helplessness ;* the *spirit* is the principle of *life* and *power*.—As ' *your sons*,'
&c., is a specification of ' *all flesh*,' so is ' *they prophesy*,' ' *they see
visions*,' ' *they dream dreams*,' that of ' *I pour out my Spirit*.' Hence,
it is evident, that the *particular* gifts are not here considered according to their individuality, but according to their common essential nature, as operations of the Spirit of God ; and also that we
need not inquire *why* the gift of prophecy, &c., should be imparted
precisely to the *sons* and *daughters*. It being the object of the
prophet to *individualize* and expand the fundamental thought, the
universality of the Spirit's operations, he chooses for this purpose his
extraordinary operations, because these are more visible than the
ordinary ones ; moreover, from among them, he selects those which
were common under the Old Testament, without thereby excluding
the rest, or in reality subjoining any thing to, ' *I will pour out my
Spirit*.' This appears also from ver. 2, where the expression, in
reference to the servants and handmaidens, again becomes general.
In the distribution of the gifts of the Spirit among the particular

classes, there is no more regard to any internal *principle* of *division*, than in the words of Zech. 9. 17, ' Corn *shall make the* young men *cheerful, and* new wine *the* maidens.' ' *Your sons and your daughters shall prophesy,*' &c., is, i. q., ' your sons and your daughters, your old men and your young men, shall prophesy, shall have *divine* dreams (for that *such only* are intended is a necessary consequence of their being caused by an outpouring of the Spirit), and see visions,' and this = ' *they will enjoy the Spirit of God, with all his gifts and blessings.*' In this way only has the passage always been understood by the Jews; how otherwise could Peter have so confidently explained the occurrences on the day of Pentecost (when there were neither dreams nor visions) to be a fulfilment of the prophecy of Joel ? Here, to cling to the letter is to misunderstand the nature, not only of the prophetic representation, but even of poetry in general, in such a manner as would, in any other case, be ridiculous. —As for the rest, it belongs to the nature of the case, that, in the principal fulfilments of the prophecy of Joel, the extraordinary gifts of the Spirit, the witnesses and means of the ordinary,—at the same time, however, the basis on which they rest, so that times, like those described 1 Sam. 3. 1, where the word of God is scarce in the land, and there is no prophecy, must necessarily be poor also in the ordinary gifts of grace,—accompany the latter, from which they differ not *in essence*, but only in *the form of their manifestation*, just as the outward miracles of Christ differed from those which were internal. As, however, Joel (in accordance with the strict adherence of his prophecy to the idea) here had the *substance* only in view, what can be historically shown to have been extraordinary (as, e. g., in the time of the Apostles, the gift of prophecy and of tongues) comes under consideration no further than that which was ordinary.

831. Ver. 2. '*And also upon the servants, and upon the handmaidens, in those days will I pour out my Spirit.*' As in the foregoing verse, the distinctions of *sex* and *age*, so here those of *rank* are done away. The extension of the gifts of the Spirit *even* to the servants and the handmaids, who appear to the carnal mind unworthy of such a distinction, is to be considered as something unexpected and extraordinary. It is not without design, that it is made so prominent in the New Testament, that the Gospel is preached to the *poor*,—that God has chosen those who, in the judgement of the world, are mean and despised. The natural man is always disposed to assume, that what is esteemed by the world must be especially important also in his relation to God. This is evident, even from the deep contempt of the Pharisees towards the *multitudes* [1].

832. Ver. 3. ' *And I will give wonders in heaven and on earth, blood, and fire, and vapour of smoke.*' Every manifestation of mercy towards the Church of God is accompanied by a judgement on her enemies. Here, and in the fourth verse, its *precursors* are described ; in the whole fourth chapter the judgement itself. There is here a manifest allusion to the plagues of Egypt, which were now to be repeated in a still higher degree. The prophet had especially in view

---

[1] Comp , e. g. John, 7. 49.

the passage in Deut. 6, 22, '*And the Lord gave signs and wonders, great and evil upon Egypt, upon Pharaoh, and his whole house, before our eyes.*'—The miracles [1] are divided into those in heaven and those on earth, then the latter are here individually designated, the former in the next verse. With respect to those on earth, by *blood, fire, and smoke,* extraordinary natural phenomena are intended, whose symbolic language a guilty conscience interprets, and perceives in them the precursors of the coming judgement. The *blood* is directly taken from Exod. 7. 17, '*Thus saith the Lord, In this thou shalt know that I am the Lord: behold, I will smite with the rod that is in mine hand upon the waters which are in the river, und they shall be turned to blood.*' In like manner also the *fire,* comp. 9. 24, '*And there came hail, and* fire *mingled with the hail.*' This supposition is the more obvious, since, in the former description of the judgement upon Israel, the *plague of locusts* lies at the foundation, and since also the contents of the following verse have their type in those events; comp. Exod. 10. 21, '*And the Lord said to Moses, Stretch out thy hand over the heavens, and there shall be* darkness *over the land of Egypt* [2].' We must call to mind appearances like those described Exod. 19. 18, '*And mount Sinai was altogether on a smoke, because the Lord descended upon it in fire: and the smoke thereof ascended as the smoke of a furnace, and the whole mount quaked greatly.*' Here, as well as there, the *fire* and the accompanying *smoke* rendered visible the truth, that God is a *consuming fire* [3]. Remarkable is the belief running through all antiquity, that the angry Deity announces by natural signs the coming of His judgements. This belief cannot be a mere illusion. It must have a deep root in the mind. Nature is the echo and reflection of the disposition of man. If there reigns in him, because he feels his own sin and that of others, a fearful expectation of things which are to come, every thing outward harmonizes with this expectation, and chiefly that which is the natural type and symbol of the Divine penal justice, but which, without this interpreter within, would not be perceived as such. Having regard to this relation of the mind to nature, God before great catastrophes often causes these precursors of them to appear more frequently and strikingly than in the ordinary course of nature [4]. Many other forerunners are mentioned, 6. 5. § 3.

---

[1] Compare on מוֹפְתִים, page 279, note [2].

[2] תִּימָרָה is a noun formed from the third *fem. fut.* of יִמר, with a *suff.* ה, in form exactly corresponding to תְּמוּרָה, derived from the third *fem. fut.* of the verb מוּר. The Hebrew מוּר and יָמַר occur only in the derived sense *to transform, to change, to exchange.* The ground meaning, however, is furnished by the Arabic. It there means, *huc illuc latus, agitatus fuit, fluctuavit;* compare the thorough demonstration by Scheid., *Ad Cant. Hisk.* p. 159 sq. According to this, הִימָרוּת can mean only *clouds* or *vortices* (in Arab. מוּר, *pulvis vento agitatus*).

[3] Heb. 12. 29.

[4] This happened in a very remarkable manner, before the destruction of Jerusalem, comp. Joseph. de Bell. Jud.4. 4, § 5. Διὰ γὰρ τῆς νυκτὸς ἀμήχανος ἐκρήγνυται χειμών, ἄνεμοί τε βίαιοι σὺν ὄμβροις λαβροτάτοις, καὶ συνεχεῖς ἀστραπαὶ, βρονταί τε φρικώδεις, καὶ μυκήματα σειομένης τῆς γῆς ἐξαίσια. Πρόδηλον δ' ἦν, ἐπ' ἀνθρώπων ὀλέθρῳ τὸ κατάστημα τῶν ὅλων συγκεχυμένον, καὶ οὐχὶ μικροῦ τις ἂν εἰκάσαι συμπτώματος τὰ τέρατα.

These will never be wanting, as surely as punishment never comes without sin, and sin is never present without consciousness, without expectation of the judgement.

833. Ver. 4. ' *The sun shall be changed into darkness, and the moon into blood, before the great and terrible day of the Lord comes.*' Of all interpreters, Calvin has most admirably explained this verse : " *The sun's being turned into darkness, and the moon into blood, are metaphorical expressions, by which he signifies that God will exhibit signs of his wrath through the whole frame of the world, to fill men with terrour, as if a horrible change were taking place throughout all nature. For as the sun and the moon, ministering light to the earth, each in its turn, are witnesses of God's parental favour towards us, so, says the Prophet, shall they contrariwise become the heralds of an angry and offended deity.—By the darkness of the sun, by the bloody eclipse of the moon, by the vapour of smoke, the prophet wished to express that, whithersoever men should turn their eyes, there would every where appear, from above and from below, many prodigies to strike terrour into their hearts. It is as if he had said, that never had things been in so wretched a plight in this world, never had there been so many and such fearful signs of the anger of the Almighty.*" We have already seen that here the prophet has the type in Egypt in view. The darkness over the whole land of Egypt, while there was light in the dwellings of the Israelites, represented in a very impressive manner the anger of God in contrast with His mercy, the symbol of which is the light of His heavenly luminaries. Its extinction is in the Scripture a standing precursor of the approaching Divine judgements. As such had it already here occurred in the description of the former judgement, comp. 2. 2, ' *a day of* darkness *and obscurity, a day of* clouds *and* mist ;' ver. 10, ' *before him the earth quakes and the hills tremble. The sun and moon mourn, and the stars withdraw their splendour.*' As such does it recur again, chap. 4. 14, ' *Near is the day of the Lord in the valley of judgement. The sun and the moon mourn, and the stars withdraw their splendour.*' Such passages are not to be limited to one particular natural phenomenon. All by which the splendour of the heavenly lights is obscured or disturbed, darknesses of the sun and moon, earthquakes, storms, &c., fill those with fear in whose hearts the sun of grace has gone down.

834. Ver. 5. ' *And it shall come to pass, that every one who calleth on the name of the Lord shall be delivered ; for on Mount Zion and at Jerusalem shall be that which is delivered, as the Lord hath spoken, and amongst the spared is whomsoever the Lord calls* [1].'—The phrase, ' *to call upon the name of the Lord,*' has already been explained [2]. It neither *does* nor *can* occur of a mere outward calling, but always of such a one as is an *outward expression* of the *faith of the heart.* The prophet therefore could not have intended a deliverance of the *promiscuous multitude* of Israel, in contrast with the heathen. For

---

[1] Our author proves that פְּלֵיטָה does not mean *deliverance,* but *that which is delivered.*

[2] Page 379, note.

the condition is one of a purely inward nature. It furnishes a hint for the right understanding of what follows. The *for* by which it is connected is inexplicable, if Mount Zion and Jerusalem are to be regarded as bringing deliverance to *all* found there. This is evident also from *that which is delivered* [= *the delivered*]. It is not all the inhabitants of Zion and Jerusalem, all the members of the outward Theocracy, who will be delivered, but there will those be, who *are* delivered, viz. *those who call on the name of the Lord,* while the rest will be consumed by the Divine judgement.—*Purely inward* also is the second condition mentioned, the calling *by* the Lord. Those who *call on* the Lord are at the same time those whom *He calls,* out of the general distress, to come under His protection; and the prophet has sought to exhibit the *close connexion of the two callings* by the choice of the words.—The expression, '*as the Lord hath spoken,*' awakens attention to the reason why believers may surely rely upon this promise, since it is the word of God and not of man.—The relation of the whole verse to the foregoing and the following is this: The prophet, in the third and fourth verses, had given the precursors of the great and terrible day of the Lord. He now points to the only means of abiding in this day. Then he describes, in the fourth chapter (connected by *for*), the judgement itself.

835. If now we inquire for the historical reference of the third, fourth, and fifth verses, we meet with a great diversity of views. The destruction of Jerusalem by the Chaldeans is assumed by Grotius, Cramer, Turretin, the Socinians, Episcopius, &c. Others (Jerome) think of the resurrection of the Lord; others (Luther), of the outpouring of the Spirit; and others (Münster, Cappell, Lightfoot, Dresde), of the destruction by the Romans. The verses are referred by Ephraim Syrus to the judgement on the enemies of the covenant people soon after the return from the Babylonian exile; by the Jewish interpreters to the impending overthrow of Gog in the time of the Messiah; to the general judgement, by Tertullian, Theodoret, Crusius; to the destruction of Jerusalem *and* the final judgement by Chrysostom and others.

836. This diversity of references has arisen solely from omitting to refer back the prophecy to its *idea*. This is the *manifestation of God's penal justice against all that is hostile to His kingdom*, running parallel with the *manifestation of His mercy towards the subjects of this kingdom*. This idea is here presented in its entire universality, without being limited to any particular realization of it in time. None of the above interpretations, therefore, can be absolutely correct. One class of them are *entirely false* (inasmuch as they assume a reference to events which do not fall under the *idea*), the others are only *contracted* and *partial* views of the truth.

837. To the former class plainly belong the references to the resurrection and the outpouring of the Spirit. This could have been occasioned only by the separation of the verse from the following chapter. These events stand in *no relation whatever* to the *idea*. The destruction by the Chaldeans *does*, indeed, sustain a certain

relation to it, in so far as that event was actually a manifestation of the Divine penal justice. It would, however, have belonged here, only in case the prophet was describing, in an entirely general way, such manifestations. That this, however, is not so, that the object of the prophecy is rather the manifestation of the Divine justice in relation to what is hostile to God's kingdom, is evident, even from a comparison of chap. 1. 2. The defenders of this view have entirely mistaken the economy of Joel's prophecy, or else they would have seen that the destruction by the Chaldeans belongs to the threatening in the first and second chapter, where the judgement upon the house of God is described ; whereas here, that upon those who are without is the subject of discourse.

838. This appears also at first view equally applicable to the destruction by the Romans. But, on a nearer examination, we perceive a difference between the two events, which brings the latter far more within the scope of the prophecy. It was, indeed, far more than the former, connected with a total rejection of the people. The former covenant people had already, at the death of Christ, become, in a great measure, numbered with the heathen. They were no longer apostate children, who were to be reformed by punishment, but they were strangers, who were to be judged on account of their hostility to the kingdom of God.

839. That such a time should come, when that which they considered as belonging only to the heathen according to the flesh, should be realized by the carnal Israelites themselves, is foretold by Malachi, chap. 3. 23, where the verbal repetition of ' *before the great and terrible day of the Lord cometh*,' in reference to the judgement upon Israel, can be explained only from the design to oppose the prevailing carnal interpretation of the prophecy before us.

840. It now also appears, how the phenomena at the death of Christ, the darkening of the sun, the quaking of the earth, the bursting of the rocks (comp. Matt. 27. 45. 51. Luke 23. 44), stand related to the passage. Like the *wonders* here, they were manifestations of the Divine anger, precursors of the approaching judgement, and were recognized as such by the guilty, whose consciences interpreted this language of signs; compare Luke 23. 48 : ' *And all the people that came together to that sight, beholding the things which were done, smote their breasts, and returned.*'

841. We have still some remarks to offer upon the citation, Acts 2. 16 sq. That Peter found in the miracle of Pentecost a *proper fulfilment* of the promise in the first and second verses, only prejudice can deny. That this citation was owing to the *fact*, that the reference of the prophecy to the Messianic time was the prevailing one among the Jews, is probable [1]; it is also favoured by the rendering of ' *after this*,' by ' *in the last days*,' which, in the New Testament, always designates the Messianic time. To this must be added the express declaration in the thirty-ninth verse, that the promise concerned the then present generation. How could Peter have made

---

[1] Compare the passages in Schöttgen, p. 413.

this declaration, had he supposed that the prophecy had long ago been fulfilled? It is, however, equally certain, that Peter was so far from regarding the whole treasure of the promise as completely exhausted by that miracle, that he rather looked upon it as only a beginning of the fulfilment, though such a *beginning* as included the completion in itself, as the germ the tree. This appears even from ver. 38, ' *Repent, and be baptized every one of you in the name of Jesus Christ for the remission of sins, and ye shall receive the gift of the Holy Ghost.*' How could Peter, relying upon the prophecy, promise the gift of the Holy Ghost to those who should repent, if the prophecy were already entirely fulfilled? Still more, however, from ver. 39, ' *For the promise is unto you, and to your children, and to all that are afar off, even as many as the Lord our God shall call.*' The inquiry here arises, who are meant by those who are *afar off.* That they are the *heathen,* no one would ever have doubted, if two entirely distinct things had not been confounded, the uncertainty of Peter concerning the *fact* of the reception of the heathen into the kingdom of God, and concerning the *mode.* The latter is easily explicable from the nature of the Old Testament prophecy. The former cannot possibly be allowed. To select only one from the mass of proofs, the way in which the promise to Abraham is cited by Peter in chap. 3. 25, clearly proves, that through his seed he supposed the nations should be blessed; and it is rendered still more incontrovertible by the fact, in ver. 26, that he regarded the heathen as partakers in the kingdom of Christ. To understand by those *afar off,* foreign Jews, is inadmissible, because such were present in large numbers, and therefore already included in the term *to you.* Peter addresses throughout *all who are present.* How should he here now, all at once, confine himself merely to *a part?* Finally, there is a manifest allusion to the close of ver. 5; in the Septuagint, οὓς Κύριος προσκέκληται. At the same time, this allusion contains a proof of the concurrent reference to the heathen, which is not found in express words in the prophecy, unless we give an arbitrary interpretation to '*flesh.*' It calls upon us to observe, how, in that passage, the deliverance, which requires as its condition a participation in the outpouring of the Spirit, is not connected with any human cause, but solely with the calling of God, with His free mercy. In a manner entirely similar, Paul proves, Rom. 10. 12, 13, from the *beginning* of ver. 5, the participation of the heathen in the kingdom of the Messiah; ' *For there is no difference between the Jew and the Greek: for the same Lord over all is rich unto all that call upon him. For whosoever shall call upon the name of the Lord shall be saved.*' If the calling upon God was the condition of salvation, it was as accessible to the heathen as to the Jews.—Now if the prophecy especially concerns the still unconverted Jews, their children, and the heathen, it is evident, that, according to the Apostle's views, it did *not terminate* in that *one* instance of the fulfilment, but rather extended as far as the *fact,* the outpouring of the Spirit itself. This appears also from the allusions to this passage in the account of later effusions of the Spirit[1]. How could Peter possibly have limited to the few, who, at that time, had already received the Spirit of God, a prophecy, in which the idea of universality is so intentionally rendered prominent? Even had this not been so, yet assuredly he would never have imagined a limitation of this kind; for such a crude and literal method of interpreting the prophecies was far from him, as well as from all the Apostles.

842. The question is still to be answered, Why does the Apostle cite also ver. 3—5, since, as it would seem, only ver. 1 and 2 properly belong to his design, and what sense does he attribute to those verses? The answer is furnished by ver. 40: '*And with many other words did he testify and exhort, saying, Save yourselves from this untoward generation.*' Even in the few words of the brief summary of what Peter said in this respect, imparted to us by Luke, a reference to the passage before us is contained. Peter employed the threatening, which was, in the first instance, to be realized against the covenant people, to terrify his hearers into a participation of the promise which alone could deliver them from the threatened judgement; and that he succeeded in this appears from the '*fear fell on every soul*,' in ver. 43.—Several interpreters have been led by ver. 22 to an entirely erroneous conception of the sense in which Peter cites ver. 3—5. The *signs and wonders* are surely not there employed without any reference to the passage of Joel. Peter awakens attention to the fact, that those who, through obduracy, do not recognize the *wonders* and *signs* with which God accompanies the manifestation of His mercy, shall be visited by those of a totally different sort, from the terrible impression of which they should not be able to escape.

843. We come now to particulars. The citation coincides essentially with the Seventy. In particulars, however, there are deviations. At the very beginning, the Seventy, adhering more closely to the Hebrew text, have '*And it shall be after these things;*' Peter, '*And it shall come to pass in the last days.*' The ground of this deviation is the design so to determine the expression, in itself indefinite, by the subject, that the point of time to which the prophecy chiefly refers, and of course its application to the case in hand, should be rendered more obvious. The '*saith God*' is wanting in the Seventy, as well as in the original text. It is borrowed from ver. 5, and in the antithesis with the '*That which was spoken by the prophet Joel,*' awakens attention to the divine source of the prophecy, and thereby to the necessity of its fulfilment. Peter reverses the two members, '*And your old men shall dream dreams, and your young men shall see visions,*'—probably in order to place the youth with the sons and daughters, and to assign to the aged a place of honour. In '*My servants,*' and '*My handmaids,*' he follows the Seventy, and that in a sense which—whether it was so intended by the translators or not—gives prominence to a point that is *really* implied in the passage itself. That the *servants of men* were at the

---

[1] Comp. e. g. Acts 10. 45. 11. 15. 15. 8.

same time *servants of God*, constituted the very ground of their participation in the promise [1]. Therefore, i. q., ' *upon* servants and handmaidens of men, *who are, at the same time*, My *servants and handmaidens, and therefore, in spiritual things, as well born as the free.*' To render prominent this perfect equality of birth, is also the design of the addition, ' *and they shall prophesy,*' after ' *I will pour out of my Spirit.*' That Peter held it necessary to make this addition, which, as we have already shown, is entirely suitable to the design of the prophet, seems to show, that, even at that time, interpretations were current which tended to deprive servants and handmaidens of their part in those blessings. In ver. 3, Peter subjoins to ' *in heaven*' the word ' *above ;*' to ' *upon earth,*' the word ' *below,*' in order to make the contrast more obvious and striking. All his deviations from the original text, as well as from the Seventy, are therefore of the same kind, designed further to unfold what lies in the passage itself. Not one of them originated in the Apostle's citing from memory.

THE PROPHET AMOS

Preliminary Observations

844. These may be the more brief, since in the chief point, with respect to the circumstances under which Amos came forward as a prophet, the introduction to the prophecies of Hosea may be considered as entirely applicable to him. They fall, according to the superscription, in the time in which the prophetic agency of Hosea also began, in the latter part of the reign of *Jeroboam II.*, after *Uzziah* has ascended the throne in Judah.

845. The relations of the prophet we learn in general from the words of chap. 1. 1, ' *who was among the herdsmen of Tekoah.*' Were this the *only* information, the remark of many interpreters might appear just, that we cannot infer poverty and an inferior condition from the office of herdsman. But another statement, chap. 7. 14, shows, that by a herdsman, is not meant one who was at the same time a possessor of herds, or such a one as the father of David, but a *poor servant herdsman*. To the command of the priest at Bethel, Amaziah, to avoid the land that did not concern him, and return to his own country, the prophet there replies, ' *I am not a prophet, nor the son of a prophet, but I am a herdsman*, and such a one as gathers sycamores. *And then the Lord took me away from the herd, and the Lord said to me, Go, prophesy to my people Israel.*' The fruit of the sycamore, called by Dioscorides ἄτροφος and κακοστόμαχος, served as food only for the poorest and lowest of the people.

846. But this passage deserves attention for another reason. In

---

[1] The same antithesis is found, e.g. 1 Cor. 7. 22, 23.

what sense does Amos here deny himself to be a prophet? Plainly in one entirely special. He cannot deny that he *possesses* both the prophetic gift and the prophetic office. Otherwise he would put weapons into the hand of his enemy, before whom he wishes to justify himself.

847. The truth will be found in the following remarks. The prevailing idea is certainly erroneous, that there was no sort of organization in the prophetic order, that each prophet sustained to all the rest no other relation, than that he, as well as they, had been called by the Lord. This is contradicted by the institution of the schools of the prophets, which were continued without interruption from the time of Samuel. We must not consider them of such a character, as that, after a training of some years, the sons or scholars of the prophets attained to complete independence. For the most part, they remained *sons* through their whole life. The schools of the prophets were a sort of cloisters: even those, who, for special reasons, ceased to remain there, and were scattered through the land, still always acknowledged their authority. Let any one attentively read the histories of Elijah and Elisha, which afford the most information upon this subject, and he will soon be convinced of the correctness of the view here presented, the establishment of which we must reserve for another time.

848. How then could Amos urge, as a proof of the divine authority of his mission, that he was neither a prophet, nor the son of a prophet, in this sense, i. e. '*neither a higher nor an inferior member of the Jewish prophetic order?*' The answer is this. It resulted from the *organization of the prophetic order*, that the relation to the Lord was more or less *mediate*. If a man wished to deny the *immediate influence* of the Deity upon them, it was the more easy for him to do so. Their education, their principles, the form of their prophecies, all admitted of an explanation founded upon *natural* causes. The *Spirit* indeed which animated them made such an explanation utterly and ridiculously untenable; but this Spirit was in them less *palpable* [than it would have been if not so fettered by outward circumstances]. Whoever, therefore, without standing in that connexion, still came forward as a prophet, and that in full possession of all prophetic gifts, in demonstration of the Spirit and of power, that man presented a case far more difficult to be explained; especially when, like Amos, he had likewise been cut off by his outward condition from all the usual human sources of education. Whether, however, Amos, on this account, was an *uneducated* man, is a question to be affirmed or denied, according to what is understood by the term *education*. So much is certain, that he was in possession of the chief part of the true Israelitish education, the knowledge of the law. The most intimate acquaintance with the Pentateuch every where appears. We have so many examples, even in our day, how vital piety breaks the ice in this respect, that we need not be surprised at this, or invent various means and ways by which Amos may have obtained this education.

849. In the case of Amos, also, much pains have been taken to

assign a time and occasion for the individual portions. But with as little success as in the case of Hosea and Micah. It is evident, even from the superscription, that we have before us a whole, composed at the same time, the substance of what had been before separately delivered. The whole is here placed in one definite point of time, two years before the earthquake; and, therefore, in a manner intelligible to the contemporaries of the prophet, who knew when the earthquake happened, the point in the more extended period given before, the days of Uzziah and Jeroboam, is fixed.

850. The book may be easily divided into two halves, naked prophecies, chap. 1. 6, and those which are connected with a symbol, which is always very simple, and briefly described, chap. 7—9.

851. In the first half the prophet begins with the prediction of the anger of the Lord, ver. 2. He then proceeds in order, through the kingdoms upon which it should be discharged, Damascus, Philistia, Tyre, Edom, Ammon, Moab, Judah, until, finally, the storm reaches Israel, and, according to Rückert's appropriate expression, remains standing over *him*. The fact that we can discover no certain beginning and no plainly marked end, sufficiently justifies us in regarding the whole first part, chap. 1—6, as one connected discourse.

852. The second part, the visions of the destruction, falls, indeed, into different portions, as the nature of the subject indispensably requires. Every new vision, with the discourse therewith connected, must form a new portion. Chaps. 7, 8, and 9, form each a whole. That we have not, however, here *disconnected* pieces, arranged in chronological order, is sufficiently evident from the fact, that the promises stand precisely at the end of the whole collection. This cannot possibly be accidental. The prophet had rather to chastise and threaten, than to console; but he cannot refrain, at least at the close, from causing the sun to break through the clouds. Without this close, a chief point of the prophetic discourse in Amos would be wanting, one which is wanting in no other prophet, and which is necessary to place the rest in their true light.

Chapter 9

853. This chapter commences with a vision. The foundations of the Temple being vehemently shaken by the angel of the Lord, it falls, and buries Judah and Israel under its ruins; without a figure, the unfaithfulness of the covenant people brings destruction upon them. The prophet endeavours to strengthen the impression of this threatening upon their minds by removing the supports of false security by which they sought to evade it. There will be no deliverance, no escape[1]. For it is the Almighty God who is their enemy and pursuer[2]. No mercy on account of the covenant, for Israel is no longer the covenant people; only they shall not be entirely destroyed; amidst the destruction of the sinful mass, a pious rem-

---

[1] Ver. 2—4.   [2] Ver. 5, 6.

nant shall be preserved [1]. This great sifting is followed by a restoration. The fallen tabernacle of David (the kingdom of God among Israel, connected with the tribe of David,) will be again erected [2], glorified by extension over the heathen [3], and blessed with the abundance of the Divine gifts [4].

854. Ver. 1. ' *I saw the Lord stand upon the altar, and he said, Strike the capital, and make the thresholds tremble, and dash them upon the head of all ; and the remnant of them will I slay by the sword : he that fleeth of them shall not flee away, and he that escapeth of them shall not be delivered.*' To whom is the commission to destroy here imparted by the Lord? As, in accordance with the dramatic character of the prophetic discourse, the person is not designated, so can he be no other than the *constant executioner* of the judgements of God upon the enemies of His kingdom ; the same who is also the preserver and protector of the true members of this kingdom, the Angel of the Lord. It was he who, as the destroying angel [5], smote the first-born of Egypt [6]; from him proceed the overthrow of the Assyrians [7]. When the anger of the Lord was kindled against Israel, after the numbering of the people, it was he who inflicted the punishment [8]. As he encamps round about those who fear the Lord, so, in reference to the ungodly, he is like the storm which scatters the chaff [9].—We have still a special reason for referring here to ' the Angel of the Lord.' This is furnished by Ezek. chap. 9, which is to be considered throughout as a further extension of the verse, and the oldest and surest commentary upon it. There, at the command of the Lord, who will avenge the apostasy of his people, six ministers of his righteousness appear, in the midst of whom is ' *a man clothed in linen ;*' the former with implements of destruction, the latter with an inkstand. They tread (the scene is in the Temple) near the brazen altar; from there the glory of the Lord appears to them out of the Holy of Holies, in the threshold of the Temple. It imparts to him who is clothed in linen the commission to preserve the pious, to the others to destroy the ungodly without mercy. Who now is the one clothed in linen? No other than ' the Angel of the Lord.' This appears from Dan. 10. 5: 12. 6, 7, where *Michael* [10] (= ' *the Angel of the Lord* ' [11]) is designated in the same way ; a remarkable agreement of two contemporary prophets, which was left unnoticed in the *Beiträge.* It is also evident from the subject itself. The clothing is that of the earthly high priest (Theod.: τοῦ ἑβδόμου τὸ σχῆμα ἱερατικόν· οὐ γὰρ ἦν τῶν κολαζόντων, ἀλλὰ τῶν λυτρουμένων τοὺς σωτηρίας ἀξίους). Now the heavenly mediator, high priest and intercessor, is ' the Angel of the Lord,' comp., e. g.,

---

[1] Ver. 7—10.   [2] Ver. 11.   [3] Ver. 12.   [4] Ver. 12—15.

[5] הַמַּשְׁחִית.   [6] Exod. 13. 23, comp. with ver. 12, 13.

[7] 2 Kings 19. 34, 35. Is. 37. 35, 36.   [8] 2 Sam. 24. 1. 15, 16.

[9] Ps. 34. 8. 35. 5, 6.

[10] [On the Archangel *Michael* see Dr. Mill's Christian Advocate's Publication for 1841, p. 93.]   [11] Comp. Beiträge, I. p. 166.

Zech. 1. 12, where he makes intercession for the covenant people, § 619, and the Lord answers him good consoling words. Concerning the earthly high priest as a type of Christ, and therefore as an image of the angel of the Lord, comp. § 506. He who was *clothed in linen*, is not, however, to be regarded as solely engaged in the work of delivering the pious; not as standing in contrast with the six ministers of righteousness. These are rather to be considered as subordinate to him, as accomplishing the work of destruction only by his command, under his authority. The punishment proceeds from him no less than the prosperity. This appears even from general grounds. Both have the same root, the same object,—the prosperity of the kingdom of God. The six cannot be regarded as evil angels. This would be in contradiction to the whole doctrine of Scripture on the subject. It uniformly attributes the punishment of the ungodly to the good angels,—the trial of the pious, under God's permission, to the evil,—see, e. g., the trial of Job, the temptation of Christ, the messenger of Satan by whom Paul was buffeted. If, now, this is established, it is equally so that the judgement here belongs to 'the angel of the Lord.' For all inferior angels are subordinate to him, the prince of the heavenly host, so that all they do is done by his command. But in addition to these general grounds, there are special reasons, which are entirely decisive. It deserves consideration, that he who was clothed in linen appears in the *midst* of the six. They surround him as his followers, his servants. Still more weighty, however, and of itself sufficient, is chap. 10. 2—7, '*And the Lord spake to the man clothed in linen, and said, Go between the wheels under the cherubs, and fill thy hand with coals of fire which are between the cherubs, and scatter them over the city, and he went before mine eyes.—And a cherub stretched out his hand between the cherubs, to the fire that was between the cherubs, and took and gave it into the hands of him who was clothed in linen. And he took it and went forth.*' The fire is an image of the Divine anger. The angel of the Lord is here, therefore, expressly designated as the one who executes the judgements of the Divine justice.—The importance of this transaction extends beyond the explanation of the passage before us. We have here the Old Testament foundation of the doctrine of the New, that all judgement has been committed to the Son, and a remarkable example of the harmony of the two Testaments, which, in recent times, has been but too much overlooked. Compare with the cited declarations of the Old Testament, only such passages as Matt. 13. 41: '*The Son of man shall send forth his angels, and they shall gather out of his kingdom all things that offend, and them which do iniquity :*'—25. 31; '*When the Son of man shall come . . . and all the . . angels with him, then shall he sit upon the throne of his glory.*' It should still be observed, if we wish to be convinced of the identity of the Angel of the Lord and of Christ, that the Angel of the Lord, who is met with throughout the whole Old Testament, suddenly disappears in the New, and that every thing is attributed to Christ, which had been before appropriated to Him.— A second important question is, what is to be understood by *the* altar[1]. Several, with Cyril, suppose it to be the altar at *Bethel*, or some other idolatrous altar in the kingdom of *Israel*. Others suppose that the article is here without force, that God is represented as appearing merely on *an* altar, thereby to show that he requires the blood of many men[2]. But the article alone is decisive against these interpretations. *The* altar can be only that of which every one would think when the subject of discourse was an altar κατ' ἐξοχήν, without a more particular designation. This was the brazen altar, or altar of burnt offering in the outer court of the Temple at Jerusalem[3]. That this, and not the altar of incense before the Holy of Holies, received in common language the name of *the altar*, is easily explained from the circumstance, that it stood in a much nearer relation to the people, than the other, which was withdrawn from their sight. Upon it were all the sacrifices of the people presented. It is every where to be understood, where the subject of discourse is *the* altar of the Lord.—But whatever doubt may remain, is removed by the parallel passage of Ezekiel. There the scene is in the Temple at Jerusalem. Near the *brazen* altar tread the ministers of the Divine justice. In the threshold of the Temple proper, the glory of the Lord moves towards them. This parallel passage leaves no doubt why the Lord here appears *upon the altar.* It is a sensible representation of the truth, ' *where the carcase is there the eagles collect.*' The altar is the place of transgression ; there lies accumulated the unexpiated guilt of the whole people, instead of the rich treasure of love and faith which should have been presented there, embodied in the sacrifices. In the place of transgression, the Lord appears in order to glorify Himself in the destruction of those who would not glorify him by their life.—Several, who, like Michaelis, have hit upon the right understanding of *the* altar, have inferred from it that the whole prophecy concerns the kingdom of Judah ; but this is contradicted even by the general reason, that a prophecy relating exclusively to *Judah* is by no means to be expected from a prophet whose *mission is especially to Israel*[4]. Further, the close of this prophecy, the prediction of prosperity, belongs, as has been already shown, to the whole collection. If this be referred merely to *Judah*, an *essential element is wanting in that which is directed to Israel;* we have then *judgement without mercy, threatening without consolation*, which is inconceivable and without analogy in any of the prophets. To this must be added the express references, or joint references to Israel through the whole chapter; comp. the mention of *Carmel* in ver. 3, the *children of Israel*, in ver. 7, the *house of Jacob*, ver. 8, the *house of Israel*, ver. 9, the *breaches thereof*, in ver. 11, *my people Israel*, in ver. 14. The supposition of an exclusive reference to Judah arises from understanding as real, what is only *symbolical.* When this errour is avoided, there remains *no reason* whatever for denying the reference to *Israel.* The *Temple* symbolizes the *kingdom of God ;* its *falling down upon the people*, the punish-

---

[1] הַמִּזְבֵּחַ.   [2] Thus, e. g., Mark.
[3] [Hävernick, Hofmann, and Umbreit, all oppose this opinion.]   [4] Comp. 7. 15.

ment, which overtakes them in consequence of this kingdom. The immediate subject of discourse is by no means a destruction of the Temple in the proper sense. The latter, to be sure, was inseparable from the former. Were the covenant people at large *outwardly desecrated*, because they had *inwardly desecrated themselves*, so also, at the same time, was the outward sanctuary taken from them, which they had converted into a den of thieves by their crimes. If, now, as was certainly the case, and is proved even by the mission of this prophet, Israel at that time still belonged to the kingdom of God, there can be no ground for its exclusion ; for Israel, as for Judah, was the Temple of Jerusalem, the seat and central point of their government, the place from which blessings and punishments proceeded,—and thus the prophet, in the very commencement, makes the Lord to roar out of Zion, and utter his voice from Jerusalem. Upon the altar of Jerusalem all the crimes of Israel, no less than of Judah, were laid down. For there was the place where the people of both kingdoms ought to present the embodied expression of their pious disposition. Hence *virtually*, though not *actually* and *locally*, it was there also that the fruits of their impiety lay.—It is, indeed, true, that the *joint reference to Judah* is necessarily required by the symbolic representation. The rejection of Israel alone, could not be symbolized by the destruction of the Temple. This reference appears also from the prediction of prosperity. This promises, not, indeed, the restoration of the dynasty of David among the people of Israel, but that of the entire government of David, which had been prostrated. The fallen Tabernacle of David refers back to the destroyed Temple. Both designate essentially the same thing ; with the destruction of the Temple, fell also the Tabernacle of David, to the ruin of which belonged also the overthrow of the kingdom of Israel. For in this also the family of David still had the dominion *de jure*, although it was *de facto* suspended.—The passage is likewise remarkable, as furnishing an irrefragable proof of the custom of designating the kingdom of God according to its existing seat and central point, and therefore justifies us in other passages in separating the kernel from the shell.—The *capital* (properly *a sort of ornament on the summit of the pillars*), and *the thresholds*, stand in antithesis, to express the thought, that the building should be shaken and destroyed from the summit to the foundation. The shaking of the *thresholds* occurs also Is. 6, to designate, that the concussion extended to the lowest foundations.—The prophet beholds, in inward contemplation, the whole people collected before the Lord in the threshold of the Temple. The Lord appears before them as a judge, in the place of transgression, upon the altar. At His command, the whole assembled multitude are buried under the ruins of the Temple. Hence, also, it appears that a destruction of the Temple, in the literal sense, is not to be thought of. How could the whole people be buried under its ruins ? The same thing is also evident from ' *I saw* ' at the beginning. This shows that we have here before us a sensible representation entirely corresponding to that in chap. 7. 1. 4. 7. 8. 1. —Hitherto the Lord, addressing Himself to another, had given to him the commission to destroy ; He now proceeds with an " *I* will slay." This shows, that the one addressed is ' *the Angel of the Lord.*' Entirely the same appearance is found in most of the passages which speak of ' the Angel of the Lord.' The action, in constant alternation, is attributed now to him, now to Jehovah [1].—In the last words, the second member seems to contradict the first. For if there is no one who escapes, how can there be *any* who is delivered [2] ? The contradiction is entirely similar to that which occurs also in what precedes, where *all* are dashed in pieces by the ruins, and yet still *a remnant* is spoken of. It vanishes as soon as we consider, that it was the design of the prophet to cut off all even barely possible ways of escape, whereby carnal security sought deliverance, and evaded the impression of his discourse ; as if he had said *all* will be buried under the ruins, and *even if* some should escape this method of destruction, still God's avenging sword shall pursue and destroy them ; flight will be possible to no man, and even if it were to some, still it would avail them nothing, for God would be their pursuer.— Not to be overlooked, however, is another apparent contradiction ; the destruction is here described with great emphasis, as one *entirely general ;* as such is it fully represented in vers. 2—4. We plainly perceive, that the prophet earnestly desires to prevent every one from thinking of the possibility of deliverance. On the other hand, in the eighth verse, it is announced, that the house of Jacob should *not* be entirely destroyed ; according to the ninth verse, all the pious should be preserved ; according to the tenth verse, the judgement should be limited to the sinners of the people, which is also presupposed throughout the whole description in the eleventh verse, &c. Already, in chap. 3. 12, the preservation of a small remnant, amidst the general destruction, had been promised. The explanation of this apparent contradiction by most of the interpreters who assume an hyperbole in vers. 1—4, is certainly erroneous. To prevent all thought of this, to show that the words are to be taken in all their strictness, is plainly the reason why the same thought is represented under such various aspects. The limitation may, however, be fairly explained in another manner. There is, in the nature of ungodliness, that levity which flatters each individual with the hope of deliverance, although a threatened general calamity is about to ensue. Then all the possibilities of deliverance are sought after, and easily converted by the imagination into probabilities and realities, because that is wanting which proves them to be improbable and unreal, the consciousness of a living Almighty God. And thus the sinner frees himself from fear, and at the same time from the burdensome obligation to escape from it in another and lawful way, by a true conversion. Now this levity the prophet here sets himself to oppose. He shows how every *possibility* of deliverance of which the sinner dreams, must fail of being realized, and, that, because he has not to

---

[1] [In the original there is an able vindication of the meaning of '*remnant*' here given to אַחֲרִית ; the real meaning of which is '*result,*' ' *end.*']   [2] נוּס.

do with human enemies, from whom, though they were never so powerful and artful, he might yet escape by human means, but with the Almighty God, who is every where present and can arm all His creatures against His despisers, so that they can retreat to no place where He who reigns without controul in heaven and on earth has not ministers of His vengeance. Every thought of the possibility of deliverance by *human means* is therefore here cut off, and at the same time, with respect to the ungodly, every thought of deliverance in general; for that God would not deliver them, they were told by their own conscience. For the pious, the same thought must be a fountain of consolation. Can no man, though he hide himself in heaven, escape from God the avenger, so also can no man, though in the midst of enemies, with the sword already suspended over him, be lost to God the deliverer.—The inquiry has still been made for the historical reference of the threatening. It extends just as far as the *idea* lying at its foundation, ' *You only have I known of all the families of the earth, therefore will I visit upon you all your transgressions.* ' Those interpreters who refer the prophecy exclusively to the Assyrian, the Chaldean, or the Roman desolation, have all, in an equal degree, truth and falsehood on their side. All this, and more, is *essentially* included in the prophecy; the difference in time and circumstances is really *unessential.* That a prophet has exclusively in view any one of these manifestations of the Divine penal justice, can be asserted only when he distinctly declares this; and even in that case it is only the *form* of the prophecy that is confined to such event; its *idea* does not vanish with that single fulfilment.

855. Ver. 2. ' *If*[1] *they break into the world below, from there will my hand take them; when they ascend to heaven, from there will I bring them down*[2]*.*' By placing the condition, in reality impossible, as possible, the denial of the result becomes the more emphatic and impressive. That this has been done here, is evident from the fourth verse, where the prophet assumes the actual possibility; so that we can by no means translate, ' *if they should even go.*' This mode of expression is, in general, very frequent. It is found, e. g., in the parallel description of the Divine omnipotence and omniscience, Ps. 139. 7, 8, ' *Whither shall I go from thy Spirit, and whither shall I fly from thy presence? If I ascend to heaven, thou art there; and if I make hell for my bed, behold thou art there.*' That we must not here translate, ' should I ascend,' ' should I make,' appears from the ninth verse, ' I *will* take the wings of the morning, and dwell in the end of the sea.' In the New Testament, e. g., Matt. 5. 29, where

---

[1] [This form does not, in English, *assume* the impossible condition, so strongly as *wenn* with the Indicative.]

[2] The 2 *mod.* is not to be taken here and in what follows as *potential*, " *if* they should conceal themselves," but as *fut.* " *if* they shall conceal themselves." That, as Winer asserts, אִם, with the 2 *mod.*, is used only *de re dubia*, is equally erroneous as that, with the *præt.*, it supposes the condition as already performed. The truth is found in Gesen. in the *Thes.*, and in Ewald, who, p. 661, remarks, the *fut.* can stand with אִם not only as *potential*, but in its other senses.

Tholuck [1] has been led astray from the only right understanding of
'*if thy right eye offend thee*' by overlooking this usage, we must
not, indeed, translate, '*if it should offend thee ;*' but whether the
condition here *supposed* as possible, is possible in reality, must be
decided from other grounds ; and these show, that here, that which
is impossible is assumed as possible, only for the sake of greater
emphasis.—Heaven and Sheol form a standing antithesis, as the
loftiest height and the lowest depth. The prophet descends from a
mere supposed probability, to one that is actual. And if the former
cannot afford protection, because God's hand reaches even where
one has escaped from every human power, how much less then the
latter [2] !

856. Ver. 3. '*And if they conceal themselses on the top of Carmel,
I will seek and take them from there; and if they hide themselves
from mine eyes in the abyss of the sea, I will there command the serpent, and he shall bite them.*' The question arises, why Carmel
especially is here mentioned? The interpreters remind us of the
great multitude of its caverns, which make it peculiarly suited for
concealment. O. F. von Richter, in the *Wallfahrten im Morgen-
lande*, p. 65, remarks, "The caves are extremely numerous in Carmel, especially on the west side ; it is said there are more than a
thousand, and in ancient times they were inhabited by monks,
who, nevertheless, do not seem to have been the makers of
them. In one region, called *the caves of the people of orders*, four
hundred are found near each other. Further below, in the hard
limestone hill, there is one distinguished for its magnitude, about
twenty paces long, and more than fifteen broad and high." Still
mere accurate details are given by Schulz. [3] According to him,
the way is of pure rock, and very smooth ; and so crooked, that
those who precede, cannot see those who follow ; "when we
were only ten paces apart, we could very well hear each others'
voices, but were invisible to one another." The mouths of these
caves are often so small, that only one man can enter at a time ; the
passage to them so serpentine, that the pursued can escape his pursuer, and hide himself in one of these small openings, of which there
are often three or four together, before he has been seen. "Consequently, when any one hides himself, it is, for human eyes at least,
very difficult, nay, almost impossible, to find him."—But the case is
not yet fully made out, although it were to be assumed, moreover,
that the mountain, as at present, was covered with shrubbery to the
summit. The expression, '*on the summit,*' must not be overlooked,
and the less so, since it stands in plain contrast with the *bottom* of the
sea, similar to the antithesis of the height and the depth in the pre-

---

[1] *Comm. zur Bergpredigt*, p. 226.

[2] חָתַר with the *accus. to break through*, Job 24. 16, with בְ *to make a hole in any
thing;* thus, Ezek. 8. 8. 12. 7, 12 (חָתַר בַּקִּיר, *to make a hole in the wall*). These
parallel passages show, that we must conceive of Sheol as surrounded with a
strong wall, whereby is designated its inaccessibleness to all the living.

[3] In the *Leitungen des Höchsten*, vol. v. pp. 186. 383.

ceding verse,—heaven and hell, the summit of Carmel and the bottom of the sea. The elevation of Carmel must, therefore, at all events, come into consideration. This is, to be sure, not very great ; it rises only some hundred feet above the level of the sea [1] ; but the prophet chose it in preference to other higher mountains, partly for the reason already mentioned, but especially on account of its position immediately on the sea, which is overhung by its summit, and can be seen to a great distance from it, comp. 1 Kings 18. 40—44. It is as true in natural, as in spiritual things, *opposita juxta se posita magis elucescunt.* An inferior elevation appears higher than one greater in reality, by the force of contrast. Besides, the position of Carmel on the extreme west of the kingdom of Israel, is to be considered. He who there hides himself, must be ignorant of any place of greater security in all the rest of the land. And if security cannot be found there, nothing further remains but the sea.—*To bid, to command* is intentionally chosen, to show, that even irrational creatures are the servants of the Almighty God, so that it only needs a word from Him to make them the instruments of His vengeance. We are not obliged by the ' *thence* ' to assume that the prophet was acquainted with a very dangerous kind of water-serpent, of which Pliny speaks, 19, 4. This was here of no importance. The serpent occurs also, chap. 5. 19, in an individualization of the thought, that God is able to arm all nature against his foes ; ' *as when a man flees before the lion, and the bear meets him, and he comes to his house, and puts his hand on the wall, and the serpent bites him,*'—the antithesis of ' all things must work together for good to those who love God.' The apostates are threatened with the poison of creeping things, Deut. 32. 24, together with the teeth of the wild beasts ; and the import of this threatening, Israel might know from their former history, comp. Num. 21. 6, '*And the Lord sent against the people serpents, and they bit the people ; and much people of Israel died,*' to which there is an allusion, Jer. 8. 17, ('*For, behold I will send against you serpents, basilisks, against which there is no conjuration, and they shall bite you, saith the Lord,*') and probably here also.

857. Ver. 4. '*And if they go into captivity before their enemies, I will there command the sword, and it shall slay them, and I will fix my eye upon them for evil and not for good.*' The carrying away into captivity presupposes that they have found mercy, he who is carried away being usually secure of his life. But from God nothing can give security.

858. Ver. 5. '*And the Lord, Jehovah, of hosts, who touches the earth, and it dissolves and all its inhabitants mourn, and it rises up wholly as the stream, and sinks down as the stream of Egypt.*' The prophet proceeds to cut off every false hope with which levity flatters itself. How dare you dream of escape, since you have the *Almighty* God for your enemy [2] ! The discourse is abrupt. We have to sup-

[1] Comp. Richter, Th. II. p. 382.
[2] Similar representations of the Divine omnipotence, in opposition to unbelief and a weak faith, are very frequent, e. g., 5. 8. 27. Is. 40. 22 45. 12.

ply either at the beginning, "*And who is your enemy?*" or at the end, "*he is your opponent.*" This abruptness of the language is entirely suitable to the subject[1]. The accumulated appellations, the *Lord, Jehovah, of hosts*, serve to exalt the omnipotence of God. The believer, in his prayer, accumulates these appellations, in order to awaken his confidence and his hope, comp. e. g., Is. 37. 16, where Hezekiah begins his prayer thus : '*Jehovah, of hosts, the God of Israel, Thou who art enthroned upon the cherubim, Thou art God alone for all the kingdoms of the earth;*' they are exhibited to the ungodly in order to cast down all his hopes. We have separated the epithet "Sabaoth," as a special appellation of God, by a comma, from what precedes. Since Gesenius asserted, cn Is. 1. 9, that *Sabaoth*, in connexion with *Jehovah*, is to be regarded as a *genitive*, dependent upon it, this view has become pretty general. It is, however, certainly false.—'*Who touches the earth and it dissolves.*' What God can do at any moment He pleases, is here attributed to Him as a continued action. Parallel is, e. g., Ps. 97. 5, '*Mountains flow down like wax before Jehovah, before the Lord of the whole earth.*' Nah. 1. 4, 5, '*Rebuking the sea, so does he make it sink away, and all streams he dries up; Basan and Carmel wither, and the flowers of Lebanon wither. Mountains tremble before him, and the hills dissolve, the earth rises up before his face, the round world and all its inhabitants.*' —We must here suppose a dissolution of the earth similar to its condition before the days of the creation, and also at the time of the flood, which the prophet, as appears from '*all its inhabitants mourn,*' and especially from '*it rises up,*' &c., had particularly in view.— '*It rises up,*' &c., is explained by the circumstance, that the earth, changed into a great stream, cannot be distinguished from the water which covers it ; the earth rises up, it is overflowed, the earth sinks down, the water subsides. The last member must not be translated, with Rosenmüller and Gesenius : '*as by the stream of Egypt is it overflowed.*' This explanation is in all respects unphilological, and, at the same time, contrary to the parallelism. The last words contain rather the antithesis to the last member but one. This would have been found entirely suitable, if it had been perceived, that here only God's omnipotence came into consideration, to which the *sinking* of the water belongs, no less than *its rising*. To be compared still is Jer. 46. 7, 8, where, as here the earth, Egypt rises up as the Nile, to be sure in another sense ; '*Who is he who rises up as the Nile, whose waters flow as the streams? Egypt rises up as the Nile, and as the streams, flow its waters, and it says, I will go up, cover the earth, destroy the city and its inhabitants.*'

859. Ver. 6. '*Who builds in the heavens his steps, and his vault, upon the earth he founds it ; he calls the waters of the sea, and pours them out over the earth, Jehovah his name.*' The steps must be supposed to lead to God's heavenly throne, as the word, 1 Kings 10. 19, 20, occurs of the steps of the earthly throne. That God has established His throne in the heaven, is given as a proof of His omnipotence also

---

[1] Altogether similar is chap. 5 7, 8.

in Ps. 103. 19, ' *The Lord has prepared His throne in the heaven, and His kingdom ruleth over all.*' Comp. Is. 66. 1. That such passages are not to be materialized, but only give, in a symbolic dress, the idea of God's power over the earth, and His glory, is evident from other passages, as 1 Kings 8. 21, ' *Behold the heaven and the heaven of heavens contain Thee not.*'—Opposed to the *steps* of the throne is the *vault*, the foundation on which they arise, the side of God's heavenly dwelling next to the earth [1]. ' *At His bare word the waters of the sea cover the surface of the earth,*' comp. Gen. 6. 17, ' *And behold, I bring the flood of waters upon the earth.*' We need not, with Rosenmüller and others, refer the words to the origin of the rain : ' *Who draws the waters of the sea as vapours on high, and then again sends them down as rain upon the earth.*' It is contradicted by the comparison of the fifth verse, which does not allow the *calling* to be thus separated from the outpouring. Besides, this proof of the Divine omnipotence is not sufficiently obvious.—The name of *God* designates here, as always, His being, so far as it is manifested and made known. The name is distinguished from the being, just as the being known from existence. Therefore, Jehovah is his name, = " He is, according to his relation to the world, wholly God." After the example of Exod. 15. 3, these words are often used to exclude all that is earthly from the conception of God.

860. Ver. 7. ' *Are ye not as the sons of the Cushites to me, O children of Israel ? saith the Lord. Have I not brought Israel out of the land of Egypt, and the Philistines out of Caphtor, and Aram out of Kir ?*'—The prophet here wrests from the people another prop of false security. They boasted of their election, by which God Himself had bound His hands ; they considered its pledge, the Exodus out of Egypt, as a charter of security against every calamity, as an obligation to further help in every distress, which God, even if He would, could not retract : there lay at the foundation of this errour, a great truth, which the interpreters have mostly overlooked, and therefore have forced upon the prophet an entirely false sense. The election of the people, and their rescue out of Egypt, really *were* what the people considered them to be. God *had* thereby really bound His hands ; He *must* deliver the people, He *could not* cast them off. The election was a work of His free grace, the preservation of it by deed, a work of His righteousness. But the errour lay in this, that the election was appropriated to themselves by those to whom it did not belong ; an errour which is constantly repeated, particularly by the believers in the doctrine of predestination, in whom it often appears in a frightful form. One need only think of Cromwell, e. g., who, in the hour of death, silenced all the accusations of his conscience by this false trust. ' *For circumcision verily profiteth,*' says the Apostle, Rom. 2. 25, ' *if thou keep the law : but if thou be a breaker of the law, thy circumcision is made uncircumcision.*' The deliverance from Egypt stands on the same ground with circum-

---

[1] It is here, indeed, to be observed, that the meaning of אֲנֻדֶּה is not perfectly certain.

cision. That also *profited;* that secured to those who showed themselves to be the children of Israel, that God would manifest Himself
as *their* God ; for those, however, who had degenerated, it became
merely an ordinary event. For them it was something that had
entirely passed away, that contained in itself no assurance of a renovation. Now the prophet here detects this errour, as he had already
done, chap. 5. 14, ' *Seek good and not evil, and so the Lord of Hosts
will be with you.*' He reminds them how, according to the covenant
relation, which was *mutual,* the party who violated the covenant had
nothing to demand, nothing to hope.—' Are ye not,' &c. The
tertium compar. is plainly their alienation from God. The sons of
Israel,—the *nom. dign.* intentionally chosen in order to render more
striking the contradiction between appearance and idea,—are so degenerate, that they no longer stand any nearer to God than the sons
of the Cushite. ' *Ye are to me,*' is, i. q., ' *ye stand to me in no other
relation.*' But why were the Cushites chosen as an example of a
people particularly estranged from God ? The colour comes still
more perhaps into consideration than the descent from Ham, the
corporeal blackness as an image of the spiritual. Thus does it appear, Jer. 13. 23, ' *Will the Cushite change his skin, and the leopard
his spots ? will ye be able to do good, who have been accustomed to do
evil ?*'—The right interpretation of these first words furnishes the
key to the following :—" Only for the covenant people is the deliverance out of Egypt a gracious pledge, but ye are no longer the
covenant people, consequently the deliverance out of Egypt stands
to you on the same ground with the leading of the Philistines out of
their former dwelling-places in Caphtor to their present, and also
with that of the Syrians out of Kir, wherein no man beholds a pledge
of the Divine favour, a preservative against every danger, especially
an assurance of the impossibility of a new exile." The geographical
inquiries respecting Caphtor and Kir, would here lead us too far
aside ; the view now current, according to which Crete is to be understood by the former, in contradiction to the old translators, who
have Cappadocia, and to Gen. 10. 14, (so lóng as by the Kasluchim,
the Colchians are understood,) demands a thorough investigation,
which is more suitably reserved for another place.

861. Ver. 8. ' *Behold the eyes of the Lord, of Jehovah, are
against the sinful kingdom, and I will exterminate it from the earth,
except that I will not destroy the house of Jacob, saith the Lord.*'
The sinful kingdom, the kingdom of the ten tribes, or the kingdom
of Judah and Israel considered as one. *This* sinful kingdom is not
less an object of penal justice than all others ; ' the holy God has by
no means, as ye imagine in your blindness, given you a license to
sin.' Only in this respect there is a difference between Israel and
other nations, that *the people* do not in the former case, as in the
latter, perish with *the kingdom.* Though not among other nations,
yet among the people of God, there always remains a holy seed, an
ἐκλογή, which the Lord must protect, and make the nursery of His
kingdom, from the same necessity of His nature, according to which
He extirpates the sinners of His people. The first part of the verse

also verbally resembles Deut. 6. 15, '*For Jehovah thy God is a jealous God in the midst of thee ; lest the anger of Jehovah thy God be kindled against thee, and he destroy thee from the earth.*' The prophet says nothing new; he only resumes the threatening of the holy lawgiver [1]. In the last words, the giving intensity to the verbal idea, by prefixing the *infin.*, is owing to a silent antithesis, '*I will not destroy* the house of Jacob like the kingdom, but only *sift* it, only root out the sinners from it;' an antithesis which is expressed in the ninth verse.

862. Ver. 9. '*For, behold, I will command, and will shake among all nations the house of Israel, as a man shakes a sieve, and nothing that is bound up shall fall to the earth.*'—Such *sieve* is here to be supposed as performed a similar service to the *winnowing shovel*, in which the grain is violently shaken and thus cleansed. A sieve of this kind, a sort of fan, is mentioned, Is. 30. 24, together with the *winnowing shovel ;* it occurs also Luke 22. 31, 32, where σινιάζειν means *to agitate with a fan.* Even the Seventy have not here understood an ordinary sieve, but an instrument answering a similar purpose as the winnowing shovel [2]. Comp., e. g., Jer. 51. 2, '*I will send winnowers against Babel, and they shall winnow it, and cleanse its land,*' 15. 7 ; Matt. 3. 12. The use of the *common sieve* for such a purpose never occurs, and an image is never taken therefrom. The many nations are the *spiritual sieve*, the means of purification. The Lord, whose instruments they are, employs them to extirpate the ungodly. By His secret judgements, for the accomplishing of which He employs the heathen, they shall be taken away [3] ; comp. ver. 10.—'*Nothing that is bound up.*' To the ungodly, as loose chaff, exposed to the play of the wind, the pious are placed in opposition, who are *bound together in a bundle* by the Lord, and therefore do not fall through the sieve [4]. The false explanation of this passage, as of so many others, arises from a want of freedom in dealing with the *images* of Scripture ; from the notion, that every one of them must be consistently and strictly carried through ; an obligation which even a modern poet does not acknowledge. Accordingly, the arbitrary meaning of *corn* [5] was adopted, because it was supposed that what was contrasted with the *chaff*, must necessarily be the *corn*.

863. Ver. 10. '*By the sword shall all the sinners of my people*

---

[1] The construction of פְּנֵי יְהֹוָה with בְ is explained by the fact, that by the face of the Lord in this connexion, only His angry face, = the anger of Jehovah, in the cited passage, can be understood, but verbs and nouns of anger are connected by בְ with the object on which the anger rests; comp. Ps. 34. 17.

[2] καὶ λικμιῶ (A. λικμήσω) ἐν πᾶσι τοῖς ἔθνεσι τὸν οἶκον τοῦ Ἰσραὴλ, ὃν τρόπον λικμᾶται ἐν τῷ λικμῷ. Hesyc. λικμῷ, πτύῳ. *The Seventy.*

[3] צְרוֹר, according to many interpreters, signifies *corn*, according to others, *a small stone.* Both senses, however, are entirely arbitrary, and assumed merely for the sake of the context. The word always means *something bound together, a bundle.*

[4] The *binding together* in a *bundle*, as an image of careful preservation, is found also 1 Sam. 25. 29.

[5] Comp. Hos. 13. 12. Job 14. 17.

die, who say, The evil will not draw near and come upon us.' In
order that the preceding mitigation of the threatening might not be
appropriated to themselves by those to whom it did not belong, the
prophet once more presents it in all its severity, before he proceeds
further to unfold the promise.

864. Ver. 11. *'In that day I will raise up the tabernacle of David,
which is fallen down, and wall up its breaches, and restore its ruins,
and build it as the days of eternity.'* 'In that day,' an expression
altogether general, then, when the Divine judgements have broken
in, and completed their work upon Israel, the μετὰ ταῦτα, by which
James, Acts 15. 15, renders it, fully expresses the sense [1]. The word
tabernacle of itself suggests a sunken condition of the house of
David. The prophet sees the *proud palace* of the house of David
changed into a mean tabernacle, every where in ruins, and perforated [2].
—It might now appear as though the prophet merely *presupposed* the
ruin of the house of David, without having expressly *mentioned it* in
what precedes. But it is not so. The whole preceding threatening
relates to the ruin of the house of David. For if the kingdom suffers,
so also does the reigning family. The close connexion of the two,
the prophet himself points out in what follows [3].—The foundation is the
promise to David, 2 Sam. chap. 7, especially ver. 16, *'And established is thy house and thy kingdom to eternity before thee; thy
throne will be firm to eternity.'* The dominion of David had already
suffered a considerable shock by the separation of the two kingdoms
existing in the time of the prophet. Still it should sink, and the
people with it, far lower in the future. But, notwithstanding, all
the promise of God remains true. God's judgements do not close,
but open the way for His mercy. That the promised salvation can
be imparted to the people only through the tribe of David, the prophet plainly declares. Otherwise, how could he identify the tabernacle of David with the two kingdoms, and with the people? The
person of the restorer he does not more particularly designate. The
chief object with him, as well as Hosea [4], is to remind the *house of
Israel* that the salvation would come to them only from *a reunion
with Judah*, from being again incorporated in the stock of David [5].
When this is once established, no doubt can remain respecting the
person. That the promise imparted to David would find its complete fulfilment in the Messiah, was at that time generally known.

[1] The *part.* נֹפֶלֶת, according to the usual sense of the *partic.* Ew. p. 533, expresses a permanent condition.

[2] So Isaiah, chap. 11. 1, the house of David is called the *stem* of Jesse, which
has been cut down, and which puts up a new shoot.

[3] Certainly the change of the *suff.* is not without reason; that in פִּרְצֵיהֶן
refers to the two kingdoms, that in הֲרִיסֹתָיו to David, that in בְּנִיתִיהָ to the tabernacle, the *subj.* of יִרְשׁוּ is the people. Thereby it is intimated, that David, his
tabernacle, the kingdom, the people, are essentially one. One stands and falls
with the other. יְמֵי is *nom.*, not *acc.* The comparison is merely intimated.
Comp. on Hos. 2. 17.

[4] Comp. on 2. 2, and 3. 5.   [5] Comp. Ezek. 37. 22.

The Messianic reference of the passage was unanimously acknowledged by the older Jews [1].

865. Ver. 12. *' That it may receive the remnant of Edom, and of all the heathen over whom my name is called, saith the Lord, who does this.'* There is here a manifest allusion to the times of David, to which the discourse had related in the last words of the foregoing verse. This appears from the mention of the Edomites. They had been subjected to the Theocracy by David. Afterwards they had regained their freedom by availing themselves of the ruins of the tabernacle of David. To the restored tabernacle of David, the glorified Theocracy, not only they, but also the remaining heathen nations, should be subject. With reference to that former event, which served as a type and prelude to the latter, resting on the same ground, the protection of God over His Church, His care for His kingdom, the verb *' they may possess* [2]*'* is here chosen. This designates only the *fact* wherein both events coincide; respecting the *mode* wherein they differ, it gives no disclosure; this is reserved for what follows.— When the prophet speaks only of the *remnant* of Edom, he refers back to the threatening in chap. 1. Those only who have been preserved during the judgement there predicted, are to come under the dominion of the kingdom of David, which is to be rich in blessings. The nature of this dominion, that it was not to debase, but exalt, is shown by the words, *' over which my name is called.'* This phrase by no means allows us to think of such a relation of the Idumeans, and the remaining nations, to the Theocracy, as that sustained by the conquered nations in the time of David. It always necessarily designates the relation of near and cordial dependence. For the name of God is never a mere empty title, its mention is not a matter of caprice; rather, the mention of it over any one is the outward manifestation of His presence *in Him* and *with Him.*—As consecrated to God, belonging to His holy people, like Israel at present, shall they be considered and treated in the future,— *non spectentur amplius in persona sua, sed in persona Dei.* One need only consider the inferior use of the phrase, Gen. 48. 5, where *' over the name of their brothers shall they be called in mine inheritance,'* is the same as *' they shall be incorporated with their brothers, no one shall have an existence separate from the rest.'* Its higher import, in respect to the people of Israel, may be seen, Deut. 28. 9, 10, *' The Lord will exalt thee to him for a holy people, as he has sworn to thee : and all people of the earth shall see that the name of the Lord is named over thee, and fear before thee.'* Here the mention of the name of God over Israel corresponds to *' to be a holy people of the Lord, separated from the profane world by the imparting of His holiness.'* It is the same which is elsewhere expressed by *' I am in the midst of thee, or in thee,'* only that this being of God in the people, and of the people in Him, is here at the same time designated according to its

---

[1] From this passage, the Messiah received the name בר נפלים, *filius cadentium,* he who springs forth from the fallen family of David.

[2] יִירָשׁוּ.

outward appearance.　Jer. 14. 9, '*And thou art in the midst of us,
O Lord, and thy name is called over us.*'　Is. 63. 19, '*We are those
over whom thou hast not reigned since eternity, and over whom thy
name has not been named.*'—Further concerning the Temple, Jer. 7.
10, 11, '*And ye come and stand before me in this house, over which
my name is called.　Is, indeed, this house, over which my name is
called, a den of robbers in your eyes?*'　It is by no means the ground
of the greatness of the crime, that the Temple, like that at Bethel,
merely *bore the name* of the house of God by the caprice of the
people, but that it truly *was* the house of God ; that God was there
really present out of gracious condescension, as a prelude to His
dwelling in Christ; comp. Deut. 12. 5, '*The place which the Lord
will choose out of all the tribes to place his name there.*'　Finally, of
particular persons, whom God, in a special sense, has made His own,
His representatives, the bearers of His word, the mediators of His
revelation.　Jer. 15. 16, '*I found thy words and ate them, and thy
words became to me for joy and delight of heart, for thy name was
called over me, Jehovah, God of hosts,*' i. q., 'for I was a messenger
and representative of thee, the Almighty God.'—'*Thus saith the
Lord, who does this,*' should strengthen faith in the promise, which
appears incredible, by calling attention to the fact, that He who promises, and He who executes, is the same ; comp. Jer. 33. 2, '*Thus
saith the Lord, who performs it, the Lord, who builds it to the completion, the Lord is his name.*'—In all probability, a false understanding of this verse has been the sole cause of an important historical event.　Hyrcanus compelled the Idumeans conquered by him
to circumcise themselves, and thus to be incorporated into the
Theocracy, so that they entirely lost their national existence and
their name.　Josh. 13. 9. 1.　Prideaux, vol. v. p. 16.　This proceeding was so extraordinary,—David never thought of doing any
thing like this towards the Idumeans, and other nations conquered
by him,—that it necessarily requires a special ground of explanation, and this is furnished by the passage before us.　Hyrcanus
wished to make the prophecy contained in it true.　But in this he
did not succeed.　He did not consider, (1) that the reception of the
Idumeans into the kingdom of God is here placed in connexion with
the restoration of the tabernacle of David, and hence could proceed
only from a king of the line of David.　(2.) That the discourse here
is not of a reception into the kingdom of God depending on human
caprice, but of an internal nature, bringing with it the full enjoyment of the Divine blessings, and one, of which God alone could be
the author.　How easily Hyrcanus might fall into such an errour, is
evident from the example of Grotius, who stopped short at this
apparent fulfilment, although he had the real one before his eyes.
By a similar misunderstanding of Old Testament prophecies, other
important events also have been brought to pass, e. g., according to
the express testimony of Josephus, the building of the Egyptian
Temple, and, as we shall afterwards see, that of the Temple of
Herod.

866.　It still remains for us to consider the New Testament citation of the passage, Acts 15. 16, 17. Olshausen has directed our attention to a difficulty here, which has been overlooked by most interpreters. One does not see how the citation refers to the question at issue. That the heathen should be received into the kingdom of God, was the doctrine of both parties ; the only question respected the manner, whether with or without circumcision, and this is not expressly determined by the prophecy, which is limited entirely to the *fact*. This difficulty, however, rests only on the view, which, although very prevalent, is yet false, that James cites two entirely independent grounds, first, in the fourteenth verse, God's declaration, by giving His Holy Spirit to the heathen without circumcision, and then, in the sixteenth and seventeenth verses, the testimony of the Old Testament. The truth is rather, that both together constitute but *one* ground. Without that testimony, which God, who knoweth the hearts, gives to the heathen, when He imparts to them the Holy Ghost, and makes no distinction between them and Israel, the prophetic declaration would have no meaning ; but, taken with it, it becomes intelligible. Now also, even His silence in reference to the condition required by those of a pharisaic temper, becomes significant. Simeon has related how God at first was pleased to take a people to His name from out of the heathen, and even the Old Testament passage, where the *fact* is so strongly declared, knows nothing of another *method*.

867. The Apostle does not content himself with the citation of the twelfth verse. He places before it the eleventh verse, because this furnished the proof that the declaration contained in the twelfth verse referred to that time. Through Christ, that had already taken place,—at least as to the germ, which included the whole substance in itself, which was afterwards developed,—wherewith the conversion of the heathen is here immediately connected. Because, however, in respect to the eleventh verse, only the leading idea was important, it is somewhat abbreviated. The translation of the Seventy plainly lies at the foundation.

868. The citation of the twelfth verse as good as verbally cor·responds with the Seventy. It follows them in their important deviation from the Hebrew text. Instead of ' *that they may possess the remnant of Edom*,' they have, ' *that the residue of men might seek after Me*' (for which Luke has *the Lord*, which is also found in the Cod. *Alex*., but probably taken from him [1]).

---

[1] How this translation arose,—whether the Seventy used another reading, למען ידרשו שארית אדם or whether they merely selected for themselves, or whether, according to Lightfoot's opinion (on Acts, l. c.), they intentionally thus distorted the words, or whether they wished merely to give *about* the sense, in which two latter cases we must suppose, that, as it so frequently happens in the Talmud, and as Jeremiah so often does in respect to the older prophets, they chose words which accurately corresponded to the Hebrew text, changed in certain characters,—to determine this is of little importance, only that the supposition of a properly different reading, one which rested on the authority of good manuscripts, must be set aside as irreconcilable with the character of the deviations of the Seventy elsewhere, and with the uniformity of our Hebrew manuscripts in the passage before us.

869. But the assertion of Olshausen, perhaps, deserves our attention, that the passages in the Hebrew form could not appear to James at all suited to his purpose; he must, therefore, on this occasion, have spoken Greek in the assembly.

870. Whether this was so, we leave undecided; it can be made probable from other grounds. But it by no means follows from that advanced by Olshausen. The passage was just as well suited for proof according to the Hebrew text, as the Alexandrine version. For as to the idea, it is perfectly true and just. The *reception*, in the sense of the *seeking* as its necessary ground. How, indeed, can a spiritual possession, a spiritual dominion by the people of the Lord exist, unless the Lord is sought by those who are to be reigned over? Comp. '*and the isles shall wait for thy law,*' Is. 42. 4.—That the mention of *Edom* by Amos, is only an individualization, that the *Idumeans* are particularly named only as a people, whose former peculiarly violent hatred against the covenant people [1], would cause their later humble subjection the more to appear as a work of the Almighty God, and of his love reigning over his people, and at the same time also, with respect to the former conquest under David, appears very evident from what follows, "and all the heathen." The Alex. have done nothing further than to substitute the general for the special, already included in it, and which is designated even by Amos as a part.

871. Whether, however, James or Luke cited the words according to the Alex. version or not, this passage is one of the many which show the extravagance of the effort to improve the vernacular version of the Scriptures, as made, e. g., by Meyer and Stier. The Saviour and his Apostles, without hesitation, adopted the version current in their times, where its deviations concerned only the words, not the idea. If we proceed upon this principle, how will the mountain of complaints melt away which has been raised against Luther's translation!

872. Ver. 13. '*Behold, days come, saith the Lord, and the ploughman shall reach to the reaper, and the treader of the wine-press to the sower. And the mountains shall drop must, and all hills flow down.*' The fundamental thought is, "*where the Lord is, there also is the fulness of his gifts.*" The drapery in the first half is taken out of Lev. 26. 3—5, '*If ye will walk in my laws, and keep my commandments, and do them, then will I give your rain in its time, and the land shall give its increase, and the tree of the field shall give its fruit. And your threshing-time shall* reach *to the vintage, and the vintage shall* reach *to the seed-time.*' When the Lord hath purified His Church by His judgements, then will come the joyful time of blessing promised by Him through His servant Moses. The second half corresponds, which is not accidental (comp. the introduction to Joel), with Joel 4. 18, '*At that time the mountains will drop must, and the hills give milk.*' According to a comparison of the passage, the *flowing down* of the hills can signify nothing but their being dis-

[1] Comp. chap. 1. 11.

solved into a stream of milk; must and honey, in allusion to the designation of the promised land in the Pentateuch (Exod. 3. 8), as one that *flows with milk and honey.*

873. Ver. 14. ' *And I will turn the captivity of my people Israel, and they shall build wasted cities, and dwell, and plant vineyards, and drink their wine, and make gardens, and eat their fruit.*' The phrase, " to turn the captivity," designates here, as always, the *restitutio in integrum.* The captivity, an image of affliction.

Ver. 15. ' *And I will plant them in their own land, and they shall no more be torn away from their land that I have given them, saith the Lord thy God.*' Comp. 793.

THE PROPHET MICAH

Preliminary Observations

874. Micah prophesied, according to the superscription, under Jotham, Ahaz, and Hezekiah. But we need not, on this account, undertake to separate his prophecies, and assign particular discourses to the reign of each of these kings. The entire collection rather forms only one whole. At the end of his prophetic course under Hezekiah, the prophet committed to writing what had been revealed to him by God, during its whole continuance, as important for all times. Combining into one collection all the separate revelations which had been granted to him at different times, he gave us the essence (nothing of which, in the case of any inspired person, has been lost); with the exclusion of what was accidental, or purely local and temporary [1].

Chapter 1, 2

875. The prophet begins with the words ' *Hear, all ye people, hearken, O earth, and all that therein is, and let the Lord God be witness against you, the Lord from his holy temple. For, behold, the Lord cometh forth out of his place, and will come down and tread upon the high places of the earth. And the mountains shall dissolve under him, and the valleys be cleft, as wax before the fire, and as the waters that are poured down a steep place. For the transgression of Jacob is all this, and for the sin of the house of Israel*' (ver. 2—5).

876. This majestic exordium has been variously misunderstood. In the first place, by those who would understand by the *nations* [2],

---

[1] So Lightfoot (*Ordo Temporum*, Opp. I. p. 99), Majus (*Œconomia Temporum* p. 898). Professor Hengstenberg defends this opinion, in the original, by both internal and external arguments.　　　[2] צַמִּים.

in the second verse, the *Israelitish tribes*. Those, on the other hand, who justly understand by ' the nations ' the *nations of the whole earth*, err in regarding these as merely witnesses, whom the Lord invokes against His ungrateful people, instead of those against whom He Himself bears witness, as they must necessarily be, according to the words, " let the Lord be a witness *against you*[1]." Then there is commonly an errour in the determination of the method of the Divine testimony, which is supposed to be found in the following admonitory, hortatory, and threatening discourse of the prophet. On the contrary, it appears from the third verse, that the testimony here, precisely as Mal. 3. 5, consists in the practical attestation of the guilt by the *punishment*, the Divine judgement described in the third and fourth verses.—To the expression, ' *out of his holy Temple*,' corresponds there ' *the Lord goes forth from his place, and comes down*,' from which it also appears, that by the *Temple*, the *heavenly Temple* is to be understood.

877. We have, therefore, in ver. 2—4, the description of a sublime theophany before us, not for the partial judgement of Judah, but for the judgement of the *whole world*, the nations of which are admonished to assemble themselves before their Judge (whom the prophet sees already approaching, coming down out of his glorious dwelling-place in heaven, accompanied by the signs of his power, the precursors of the judgement), and dumb and silent, to wait His judicial and penal sentence.

878. But how is it then to be explained, that in the words ' *for the sins of Jacob is all this*,' &c., there is a sudden transition to the judgement upon *Israel;* so much so, that the prophet proceeds, as though Israel had been the only subject of discourse? The only true solution is, that the two judgements, though distinguished by space, time, and other unessential circumstances, are in *idea* and *essence*, completely one, so that the world is already judged in every partial judgement of Israel ; every previous judgement of the Theocracy is a prediction by matter of fact of the last and most general. The limitation to one particular people is only *accidental*, and owing to the existence of the conditions, on which the Divine penal justice is to be realized only among this people ; as soon as the *carcase* is extended over the whole earth, then *the eagles* also collect over the whole. In consequence, however, of this essential unity of the Divine judgements, the prophets, in order to increase the dread of the Divine majesty, often describe a *previous* judgement ; limited to the covenant people, under the form of the last and general one. In order to express the thought, that it is the *judge of the world* who will *judge Israel*, they make him appear for the judgement of the whole world, which, indeed, was actually judged in Israel, a world in itself. A completely analogous case we have, e. g., in Is. 2—4. That in chap. 2, (after the prophet has described in a few strong lines the moral reprobation of the covenant people, ver. 6—9, and

---

[1] Comp. in reference to עֵד followed by בְּ, e. g., Mal. 3. 5.

designated their haughtiness as its last source,) the subject of discourse is the last judgement of the whole earth, can be denied only by the most forced interpretation ; a judgement whereby the vanity of all created things, and the exaltation of the Creator alone, concealed during the present course of the world, will be most clearly revealed and acknowledged by those who now close their eyes against them. The sublimity of the whole description, the express mention of the whole earth, e. g., 2. 19, the selection of the high and lofty who should be humbled, (in the individualizing description, ver. 12 sq.,) not out of Judah alone, but from the compass of the whole world, are sufficient evidence of this. In chap. 3. 1 sq., however, the prophet suddenly proceeds to the typical judgement of Judah, and that he regards this object, not as one absolutely new, but rather as substantially the same with the preceding, appears from כי at the beginning, which calls to mind the mode in which, in the prophecies of the Lord Jesus, the references to the destruction of Jerusalem and those to the judgement of the world are combined with one another. Nor is it merely in prophecy, that this close connexion of the judgement of the world with the inferior judgement of the covenant people appears. Thus, Ps. 82. 8, after the unrighteousness prevailing among the covenant people has been described, the Lord is summoned to the judgement, not of them alone, but of the whole earth.

879. The prophet, therefore, in the fifth verse, makes a transition from the general manifestation of the Divine justice to the special among the covenant people, and mentions here as the most prominent points which it would strike, Samaria and Jerusalem, the two chief cities, from which the apostasy from the Lord extended itself over the rest of the land. That he first mentions Samaria, and then ver. 6, 7, describes its judgement by the Assyrians, before that of Jerusalem, is owing to the fact, that it was there that the apostasy first took place, and consequently the punishment was hastened ; which latter, a mere consequence of the former, the interpreters, for the most part, after the example of Jerome, render exclusively prominent. At the same time, the prophet wished first to finish with Samaria, that he might then be entirely occupied with Judah and Jerusalem, the chief object of his prophetic agency.

880. The transition he makes, ver. 8, with the words, ' *Therefore I will lament and howl, go naked and bare, set up lamentations like the jackals, and mourning like the ostriches.*' It is generally supposed that the prophet here speaks in his own person. The correct view is, however, rather that the prophet, seeing in inward vision the Divine judgement, instead of stopping at Samaria, pour itself, like a desolating stream, over Judah and Jerusalem, suddenly sinks his own consciousness in that of the suffering people ; that, accordingly, we have here an incomplete symbolic action (similar to the finished one which occurs, e. g., Is. 20. 3, 4), which can be explained only from our view of the nature of prophecy, according to which, the dramatic character being inseparable from it, the transition

is easy, from the mere description of what is present in vision, to the prophet's own action [1].

881. In ver. 9 sq., the prophet returns from the symbolic action, to which he had been led by his emotions, to a quiet description. The theme of which he gives in the words, ' *It comes to Judah, to the gate of my people, to Jerusalem.*' He endeavours to give a lively view of these thoughts by individualization. After having commenced with an allusion to the elegy of David upon Saul and Jonathan [2], he designates the stations by which the hostile army advances towards Jerusalem, and then causes it to spread from thence over the whole land, and carry away the inhabitants into exile. But he always chooses those places whose names allow of some sort of connexion with that which they now suffer. So that the whole section forms a chain of paronomasia's.

882. The question still arises, in what event did the threatening contained in chap. 1, so far as it related to Judah, find its fulfilment. It is supposed to be the Assyrian invasion by Theodoret and Cyril, Tarnov, Mark, Jahn, and others; the carrying away by the Chaldeans, after Jerome, by Michaelis and others.

883. We consider that the Assyrian invasion cannot be regarded as the proper object of his threatening. This is, indeed, inadmissible, even if we view the subject in a purely human light [3]. The predictions of the prophets, in reference to the Assyrians, are, from the commencement, encouraging. The Assyrians were, indeed, to be the Lord's rod of correction for His people, but they were never to effect their total ruin. By an immediate Divine interposition, their plan of capturing Jerusalem was frustrated. So, perpetually in Isaiah, so Hos. 1. 7, where, after the annunciation of the overthrow of Israel by the Assyrians, it is said, ' *and I will have compassion on the house of Judah, and give them prosperity in Jehovah their God.*' We can even bring the proof from our prophet himself, that his spiritual eye was not chiefly, or, at least, exclusively, directed to the Assyrians. In the prophecy, chap. 3—5, where he describes the judgement upon Judah in entirely the same manner as here, he passes over the Assyrians in silence. Babylon is mentioned, chap. 4. 10, as the place whither Judah should be carried away into exile.

884. Still, however, we must here, as always in respect to the threatenings and promises of the prophets, be on our guard, lest, in referring to one particular historical event, we lose sight of the idea which lies at the foundation. If this is rightly understood, it becomes evident, that a particular historical event may indeed be chiefly regarded, but *can never exhaust the prophecy;* that in the case before us we must by no means, on account of the chief reference to the Chaldean destruction, exclude that in which before, as in the invasion of the Syrians and the Assyrians, or afterwards, in

---

[1] For the reasons see the original work.—Compare the similar lamentations of the prophets in other passages. Jer. 48. 31. Is. 15. 5. Chap. 16. 9—11. Is. 21. 3, 4.

[2] 2 Sam. 1. 20.

[3] For other reasons see the original.

the destruction by the Romans, the same law of retribution was realized. That *dead* understanding of the prophecies in former times, whereby, separated from the idea, they became like the predictions of soothsayers, has contributed much to produce the other extreme, the entire departure from historical grounds. He only who combines both can avoid the numberless caprices which each of these extremes must necessarily bring with it.

885. The prophet, having hitherto described in general terms the impending Divine judgement, proceeds, in the second chapter, to chastise particular vices, which, however, are at the same time to be considered chiefly as indexes of the depraved condition of the people, and of the punishment to ensue. What he here has especially in view, what therefore must have been, at the time of the composition, a peculiarly prominent manifestation of depravity, are the unrighteous acts and oppressions of the great; the representation of which presents a striking similarity to that of Isaiah, chap. 5. 8 sq. The prophet interrupts this description, only to refute the false prophets, who charged him with the severity of his discourses, and asserted that they were unworthy of the merciful God. This severity, replies the prophet, is true mildness, since it alone can avert the impending judgement; his God (he says) does not punish from want of long-suffering, or from unmercifulness, but the guilt lies with the transgressors, who have violently drawn upon themselves His judgements.

886. The prophecy closes with the promise in ver. 12, 13. It is introduced entirely separate, in order to place it in stronger contrast with the threatening. It is but brief, far briefer than in the following discourses, and enters far less into detail. The prophet would first terrify the sinners out of their security; he therefore causes only a feeble glimmer of hope to fall on the dark picture. ' *I will collect, yea, O Jacob, I will collect thee wholly, I will collect the remnant of Israel. Together will I bring them as the sheep of Bozrah, as a flock upon their pasture, they shall make a tumult before men. The breaker goes forth before them, they break through, pass through the gate, and go forth, and their king marches before them, and the Lord in their front.*'

887. The whole description receives much light from the remark, that its lines are nearly all borrowed from the deliverance out of Egypt. Israel there, under oppression and affliction, constantly increased in numbers by the Lord's blessing concealed under the Cross, comp. Exod. 1. 12; when the time of redemption came, the Lord, who had long remained concealed, again made Himself known as their God; in the first place, the people were *collected,*—then the Lord *marched before them* in a pillar of cloud by day, and in a pillar of fire by night. He led them out of Egypt, the house of bondmen. Just so here also. The increase and assembling are described in the twelfth verse, the deliverance in the thirteenth; here, as there, Israel's affliction is exhibited under the image of a residence in the house of bondage, a prison whose gates the Lord opens, whose walls He breaks through. In this leaning to the former deliverance,

which has its deeper ground in the typical import of the latter, an *acted* prediction of all later deliverances, and which fully contains in itself their germ, and their pledge, Micah harmonizes with his contemporaries Hosea and Isaiah; comp. Hos. 2. 1, 2 ; Is. 11. 11 sq. This reference to the typical deliverance, clearly shows that in the description, the idea and its clothing must be separated from one another.

888. Ver. 12. [1] By *Jacob* and *Israel*, the *whole nation* is designated. The promise in the passage before us stands in a close relation to the threatening in the fifth verse. All Israel is given up by their sins to destruction ; all Israel is delivered by the mercy of God. This view is confirmed by a comparison of the parallel passages of Hosea and Isaiah, where the whole is designated by its two parts, *Judah* and *Israel*. Micah leaves this division here unnoticed, because the visible separation was already overbalanced by an invisible unity, and in the future, when, as there should be one shepherd, so also would there be one flock, would entirely disappear.—The *remnant of Israel* (corresponding in the second member to ' *Jacob, thee wholly,*') shows that there alization of the promise, far from doing away the threatening, rather rests on its previous accomplishment. *Wholly* collected will be the Church of God, purified by the Divine judgements ; the Divine mercy has no limits in itself, and those at present existing in its object, will then be removed.—The words, ' *together will I bring,*' &c., show, at the same time, the faithfulness of the great Shepherd, who collects His scattered flock out of all regions, and the unexpected and wonderful increase of this flock [2]. We take Bozrah as the name of the capital of the Idumeans in Auranitis, four days' journey from Damascus. The great wealth of this city in herds appears from Is. 34. 6, and may be easily explained by its position. In its neighbourhood, particularly, begins the immeasurable Arabian plain, which extends on the one side without interruption to Dschof in the heart of Arabia, and reaches northwards under the name of El Hamad to Bagdad. Its length and breadth are reckoned at eight days' journey. It contains an abundance of flowering plants.—The *tertium comparationis* is to be sought in the *assembling*, in antithesis with the *dispersion*. The *multitude* comes under consideration here only as a necessary consequence of the *collection*. We must think of the flocks of Bozrah as being not merely *numerous*, but at the same time as *crowded together*.—The last words graphically describe the *tumult*, which a numerous and crowded flock occasions.

889. Ver. 13. The whole verse is to be explained by the figure, lying at the foundation of a prison, in which the people of God are shut up, but are now to be delivered by the powerful hand of God. By the breaker-through, we understand the *dux et antesignanus* raised up by God. Every divine deliverance begins with the raising

[1] The emphasis which lies on *collect*, in contrast with the previously announced *carrying* away and *dispersion*, which, apart from God's mercy and omnipotence, seemed to admit of no favourable turn, is expressed by the *infin. absol.*, at the head of both clauses.

[2] Comp. Jer. 23. 3. 31. 10.

up and preparing of such a leader; and what the typical leader, a Moses, a Zerubbabel, was in the *inferior* deliverances, that was *Christ* in the highest and last. The three verbs, they ' *break through,*' they ' *pass through,*' they ' *go forth,*' vividly describe the progress which can be hindered by no human power.—The last words give a view of the *highest leader* of the expedition [1]. In the Exodus from Egypt, besides Moses (the breaker-through), there went before the host a visible symbol of God's presence. On the return from Babylon, the Angel of the Lord was visible only to the eye of faith, as formerly, when Abraham's servant journeyed to Mesopotamia, Gen. 24. 7. In the last and highest deliverance, the breaker-through was at the same time the king and God of the people.

890. As the prophecy throughout contains in itself no limitation, we are fully justified in referring it to the whole compass of the prosperity destined for the covenant people, and in seeking its fulfilment in every event of the past or the future, in the same measure in which the fundamental idea, God's mercy towards His people, is therein revealed. Every limitation to any single event is clearly inadmissible. And most of all, its limitation to the deliverance from the exile, which can be regarded, particularly in reference to Israel, only as a faint prelude of the fulfilment. Those have come nearest to the truth who assume an exclusive reference to Christ, provided they acknowledge that the conversion of the first-fruits of Israel, at the time of his appearance in humiliation, was not the end of His dealings with this people.

Chapter 3, 4, 5

891. The discourse begins with a new chastisement and threatening. It is directed in the first place, ver. 1—4, against the covetous and cruel great men ; it then passes over, ver. 5—7, to the false prophets. The prophet, in passing, contrasts their hypocritical, feeble, selfish character, with that of the true prophet, represented by himself, who, with power constantly renewed by the Spirit of the Lord, serves only the cause of truth and justice, and declares the transgressions of the people, led astray by the false prophets, ver. 8. The prophet proceeds to do this, ver. 9. 12. The three orders of the divinely-called leaders of the Theocracy, the princes, the priests, and the prophets, are so degenerated, that God's glory is nothing, their own advantage every thing, and, in this inward apostasy, the promises, which God gave to His people, and which, in hypocritical self-deception, and without regard to the accompanying condition, they appropriate to themselves, serve to strengthen them in their security. But God, in a terrible manner, will punish them for their apostasy, and drive them from this security. The inwardly-profaned Theocracy shall be outwardly profaned also. Zion shall become a common ploughed field ; Jerusalem, the city of God, shall sink in

---

[1] Comp. besides Exod. 13. 21. Is. 52. 12. 40. 11. Ps. 80. 3.

rubbish and ruins; the temple-mountain shall become again what it had been before it was God's seat, a thickly-wooded hill, which then appearing in its natural inferiority, will stand entirely in the back ground in comparison with the nearer mountains.

892. Still, the infidelity of the covenant people cannot make void God's faithfulness. The prophet, therefore, makes a sudden transition from the threatening to the promise.

893. The exact relation in which the first part of the promise stands to the preceding threatening, has already (888) been pointed out. For the illustration of ver. 1—3, we refer to 266 sq. We only remark, that with respect to the words, '*for from Zion shall go forth a law, and the word of the Lord from Jerusalem,*' we now agree with Vitringa, that the notion is not that of a *stream* of doctrine *flowing forth* from Zion, but of *commands* issued by a monarch from his court [1]. Zion, the residence of the true God, from which He sends out His commands over the whole earth, forms the most suitable antithesis to ' *Zion will be ploughed as a field,*' and at the same time the most suitable foundation for the flowing of the nations to the mountain of the Lord. To this we may add the comparison of ver. 7 and 8, where Zion in like manner appears as the seat of the dominion.

894. From ver. 4—7 the blessing is described, which that great revolution of things should diffuse over the covenant people. In reference to ver. 4, compare 519. In reference to ver. 6 and 7, above, 888. Explanation is required only of the words, which, as far as we know, have been uniformly misunderstood by the interpreters, ver. 5: '*For all nations shall walk, each one in the name of his God, and we shall walk in the name of the Lord our God, for ever and ever.*' That the true interpretation was not perceived, can be explained only by a mistake of the deeper import, which the *name of God* has in the Scripture. This is more than a *mere sound;* it is the *transcript of His being;* this being itself, so far as it communicates itself outwardly, and makes itself known. ' *To walk in the name of the Lord,*' accordingly, means to enjoy a lot in which the whole excellence of this name expresses itself; and the sense of the whole verse is, ' *that the Theocracy will be exalted from the deepest debasement to the highest elevation, over all the kingdoms of the world, the people of which shall joyfully become subject to it,—this should not awaken your wonder, it is entirely natural. The lot of every people corresponds to the nature of their God. Why then should not all other nations be humbled, since their gods are idols; Israel, on the contrary, exalted, and gifted with eternal prosperity, since his God is the only true God* [2] *?* ' The last words of ver. 7, '*and the Lord shall reign over them upon Mount Zion,*' are happily illustrated by Calvin thus: " *Though it was God who ruled the people of old by the hand of David, of Josiah, of Hezekiah, yet there was, as it were,* a shadow

---

[1] תּוֹרָה never has, any more than מִשְׁפָּט the sense, *doctrine, religion,* but always that of *law.*

[2] A parallel passage, according to this interpretation, which is also confirmed by Is. 2. 5, we find, Is. 45. 16, 17. Comp. also on Zech. 10. 12.

interposed, so that he reigned obscurely.—*The prophet, therefore, intimates a difference between that shadowy kingdom and the new one, which he will publicly establish at the coming of the Messiah.—And this was truly fulfilled in the person of Christ, who, though the true seed of David, was also, at the same time, Jehovah,—God manifest in the flesh.*" Only it must be observed, in respect to this promise also, that it will not be finally fulfilled till the establishment of the kingdom of glory (comp. Matt. 19. 28).

895. The prophet had hitherto described the new kingdom to be erected only as a kingdom of God, without mentioning a channel by which His mercy should be poured upon the Church; a mediator, who should represent Him in the midst of her. This representation, therefore, was still defective. It still wanted a connexion with the promise imparted to David, and so much extolled by him and other holy singers and prophets, of an eternal dominion of his tribe, according to which every great manifestation of favour must be mediated by a sprout of this stock, which must form the constant substratum for the most complete manifestation of the Divine power and the Divine Being. This connexion is furnished by ver. 8, ' *And thou, O tower of the flock, hill of the daughter of Zion, unto thee shall there come — : and the former dominion, the dominion over the daughter of Jerusalem, shall fall to thee.*' The interpreters all agree, that by *the tower of the flock,* and by *the hill of the daughter of Zion,* the stock of David is designated; but they differ very much as to the ground of this designation.

896. We proceed to the establishment of our interpretation. Jerusalem was built on two opposite hills, Akra and Zion; the city placed upon the latter Josephus designates as very high and steep, e. g. 6. 40 : Τὴν ἄνω πόλιν περίκρημνον οὖσαν. The aspect which the towers situated upon this steep elevation presented, he compares with that of the lighthouse at Alexandria from the sea [1]. Above, upon this high and steep elevation in the *upper city,* lay the royal castle [2], called the *upper house of the king.* Its position must have insured to it extraordinary security. This is shown by the ridicule of the Jebusites, when David, who did not build, but only enlarge it, wished to capture it. They suppose that the lame and blind would be sufficient for its defence [3].

897. Far above this royal castle, which David had already chosen for his residence, (comp. 2 Sam. 5. 9, ' *And David dwelt in the castle, and called it the city of David, and enclosed it,*') rose a *tower,* presenting a majestic appearance. It is often mentioned in the Scripture; the principal passage is that of Neh. 3. 25, ' *Opposite the tower which advances from the king's upper house* (appositely the Vulg., *quæ eminet de domo regis excelsa*) *to the court of the prison ;*' comp. ver. 26, where, in like manner, the advance of the tower, elevated far above the king's castle, is spoken of. Respecting ' *to the court of the prison,*' we receive information from Jer. 32. 2, ' *Jeremiah the prophet lay imprisoned in the court of the prison, which is in*

---

[1] B. 6. c. 6.   [2] Neh. 3. 25.   [3] 2 Sam. 5. 7—9.

the house of the king of Judah,' comp. 38. 6, according to which, the
pit, into which the prophet was let down, was in the court of the
prison.   Accordingly, the *court of the prison*, agreeably to the oriental custom, formed a part of *the royal castle* upon Zion, and in this
court of the prison rose the tower.   The other chief passage is that
of Song of Sol. 4. 8, " *Thy neck*, like David's tower, *is built for an
armory, a thousand shields are hung thereon, all quivers of the heroes.*"
"*All* quivers of the heroes," shows that the armour of all those who
were enrolled in the number of *the heroes* [1], was hung up in that
tower as an outward sign and diploma, as it were, of this enrolment.
The designation of the tower, which is moreover manifestly identical
with that mentioned by Nehemiah as David's tower, refutes the supposition of Le Clerc on Nehemiah, l. c., that the subject of discourse
there is not David's castle on Zion, but another alleged to have been
built by Solomon, and its tower in the lower city; a supposition
which is disproved, even in the passage itself, by the designation of
the castle as the upper, or the high castle.

898. Now Micah considers *this tower* as the symbol of the race of
David, and how well it was suited to this purpose, and how naturally it represented the designated subject, scarcely needs a detailed
proof.   It was, indeed, the highest part, the castle, which, after the
elevation of the race of David to the regal dignity, had been for
centuries, and still ought to be, the seat of this race.   Its elevation
symbolized the *fastigium regium;* its relation to the rest of the city,
which it overlooked and commanded, and which looked up to it in
wonder, the relation of the subjects to their king.

899. Micah designates this tower as '*the tower of the flock.*' The
chief ground of this is to be sought in the immediately preceding
ver. 6 and 7.   As in chap. 2. 12, 13, so here also, Micah had represented the covenant people under the image of a flock, which should
be collected out of its dispersion and estrangement, and protected
against every hostile attack.   What now was more natural, than
that, in continuation of the image already begun, he should designate the tower which symbolized in his view the race by which, under
the guidance of the Lord, the assembling should be affected, by
'*the tower of the flock ?* '   In the East they observe, from the *towers
of the flock*, whether beasts of prey or hostile bands are approaching; into them, in regions where there are no cities and villages,
they drive together the herds, if danger appears.   Micah had the
type immediately before his eyes.   Uzziah and Jotham [2] actually
erected in the woods, and on the pastures, castles and towers for the
protection and refuge of the flocks.   Besides this chief ground of
the designation, there appears to have been another of a subordinate
character.   In Gen. 35. 21, we read of a '*tower of the flock,*' near
which Jacob took up his residence for a time [3].   If, now, we recol-

---

[1] The constant designation of David's faithful friends.
[2] 2 Chron. 26. 10, 27. 4.
[3] מִגְדַּל עֵדֶר precisely as it stands here, does not elsewhere occur, except in
the passage in Genesis.

lect, that in Micah, plain references to the Pentateuch occur in other places, and that, indeed, in comparison with the extent of his prophecies, they are peculiarly numerous[1]; and still more if we consider, that, chap. 5. 1, the appellation *Bethlehem Ephratah*, is taken out of the same 35th chap. of Genesis, ver. 19, in which, ver. 21, the mention of '*the tower of the flock*' occurs, we shall surely not be guilty of trifling when we assert, that any interpretation must be suspected of errour, which is unable to place '*the tower of the flock*' in Micah, in connexion with that in Genesis. Ours, however, is by no means liable to this charge. Why should not Jacob and the *tower* which he built for the protection of his *literal flock*, serve the prophet as a tyre and a substratum for the spiritual relation which he had in view? It must not be overlooked, that the chief and the subordinate ground which we have assumed run into each other, and stand mutually related as the general and particular. For that the prophet had especially in view *Jacob's tower of the flock*, was owing to its having the nature of *all* such towers. The *tertium comparationis* is not thereby *changed*, only the image is rendered more specific, and thereby more lively and impressive. A retrospect of the pastoral life of the patriarchs, is, in general, one ground of the frequent use of images borrowed from that mode of life. But in the passage before us, the image of '*the tower of the flock*' was the more suitable, since the founder of the royal house, before he was chosen to be a shepherd of the people, had been for a long time a *shepherd of lambs*, and therefore had himself typified his future condition[2].

900. No great difficulty can now remain in the explanation of '*hill of the daughter of Zion*.' The '*daughter of Zion*' is Zion itself, personified as a virgin; and when *her* hill is spoken of, what else could well be understood, than the mountain of Zion in a narrower sense, the mountain κατ' ἐξοχήν, before which Akra and Moriah are changed into plains? We have, then, the most suitable relation of the two designations to one another, '*the tower of the flock*' is the special, '*the hill of the daughter of Zion*' the general; we have, moreover, a friendly harmony with the last words of the verse (the hill which commands the daughter of Zion, physically and morally, is the same which obtains the dominion over the daughter of Jerusalem); and, finally, the most appropriate antithesis with chap. 3. 12.

901. *Unto*[3] *thee*, appears here to be emphatic [i. e. *quite up* to thee], indicating that the object in motion actually *reaches* its goal. It points to all the hindrances which seem to make it impossible for the dominion to reach its goal, and represents them such as would be removed by God's omnipotence. The subject of '*will come*,' is indefinite. "The[4] indefinite subject has a peculiar energy. By

---

[1] Comp. 2. 12, 13 (see above), 6. 4, 5, 7. 14, where the words שֹׁמְנִי לִבְדָד receive light only from Numbers 23. 9.

[2] Comp., e. g., 2 Sam. 5. 2, 7. 7.

[3] Whereas עַד אֶל merely expresses *direction towards* the goal.

[4] Hävernick on Daniel, p. 386.

omitting the definite idea, it is left, as it were, to the reader to supply every thing possible (there the compass of all that is glorious),
for which the writer has no adequate expression."

902. "The first," or the ancient, "dominion," refers back to the
splendid times of the Theocracy under David and Solomon, but likewise presupposes a time when the dominion had been entirely taken
away from the royal line of David. Such a time the prophet had
already predicted in the first discourse, since it was implied in the
carrying away of all Judah into exile ; still more clearly, however,
chap. 3. 12, according to which Zion, the seat of the dominion of
David, should be ploughed as a field. This prediction occurs again
in the ninth verse, with the express mention of the king, and in
contrast with it, that of the restitution of the dynasty of David,
chap. 5. 1.

903. The last words of the verse are translated by many interpreters (Calvin, Michaelis, Rosenmüller) by *regnum, inquam, erit
filiæ Hierosolym.*, so that Jerusalem is here not the object, but the
subject, of the dominion. But this explanation is to be rejected, even
for a grammatical reason [1]. To this, we add the relation to the foregoing. To the '*hill which rules the daughter of Zion,*' not to the
daughter of Zion herself, should the dominion over the daughter of
Jerusalem come. That the prophet here causes the Theocracy to be
represented by Jerusalem, arises from a regard to the relation of Zion
and the king's castle to the city, which symbolized the relation of
the stock of David to the Theocracy.

Chapter 4:9-14

904. The prophet, at the end of the foregoing chapter, had
announced heavy judgements; in the preceding, he had imparted
glorious promises. In what follows, he combines the two together;
and first, in chap. 5, makes the promise again appear by itself. The
interweaving of the judgements in the prediction of prosperity,
was designed to preserve believers from idle hopes, which, when not
confirmed by the result, sink men into greater despondency. At the
same time, it imparts *indirect* consolation; for the future must be
under the control of him who predicts it. The greatest cause of our
despondency under the cross, is, indeed, the doubt whether it actually
comes from God. But the prophet gives also *direct* consolation. To
every calamity which he announces, he immediately subjoins the
prediction of a Divine deliverance. The prediction of suffering in
this portion, is essentially distinguished from the former ; it is not
like that, threatening, but consoling. Hence, it is evident, that it
must have a different destination. While the threatening was
destined chiefly for the ungodly, this, like the preceding pure pro-

---

[1] מִמְלֶכֶת is *stat. constr.*, the ל serves, therefore, as a circumlocution for the
genitive, and it is inadmissible to supply the substantive verb.

mise, has chiefly in view the truly pious members of the Theocracy, and aims to strengthen them in the manifold temptations into which they must fall, and which would come upon them in consequence of their outward connexion with the ungodly.

905. It is a threefold affliction, joined with deliverance from it, which presents itself to the prophet in inward vision, and which he accordingly describes. This appears even from the threefold *now*, (comp. 9. 11. 14,) which every time indicates that a new scene presents itself to the prophet. This is also evident from the different character which each bears. In that announced in the ninth and tenth verses, the carrying away to Babylon, it is the hand of the Lord alone which delivers His people. In the oppression described, ver. 11—13, he supplies Israel with courage in war, and gives victory to his *arms*; the plan of the enemies to destroy Zion is frustrated, while there it succeeded. The fourteenth verse presents to us Zion sorely pressed anew by enemies, and captured by them; the deliverance is accomplished, according to chap. 5. 1, which is closely connected with the foregoing by the Messiah.

906. Ver. 9. ' *Now, wherefore dost thou raise a cry? is there no king in thee? is thy counsellor gone? for pangs have seized thee like a woman in travail.*' The prophet sees in the spirit, Zion dissolved in anguish and lamentation. In sympathy he inquires the cause of her mourning, whether haply she has suffered the loss of her king, and then answers the question himself in the affirmative, because such anguish could be produced only by such a cause. In order fully to comprehend the mourning of Zion over the loss of her king, one must realize that the visible head was a representative of the invisible, the medium of his favours; so that his removal was a sign of the Divine anger, and the extinction of every hope of prosperity. How deeply the loss of the king was felt, when what was here *present in idea* became an actual occurrence, appears from Lam. 4. 20, ' *The breath of our life, the anointed of the Lord, is imprisoned in their pits, of whom we said, In thy shadow shall we live among the heathen.*' In Zech. chap. 4, the civil magistrate, next to the *spiritual*, appears as the greatest gift of God's grace. Both shall henceforth again, as they had been before the exile, be the medium through which the Lord imparts His gracious gifts to the Church. It must still be remembered, that all promises of the future were connected with *the kingdom*. With its extinction, therefore, every prospect of a better future seemed to have vanished.

907. Ver. 10. ' *Writhe, and break forth, O daughter of Zion, like a woman in travail, for now shalt thou go forth out of the city, and thou shalt dwell in the field, and come even unto Babylon; there shalt thou be delivered, there shall the Lord redeem thee out of the hand of thine enemies.*' The *imperative* is not an *imper. consolationis*, but a declaration, that the *anguish would be extreme*, clothed in an admonition to submit to it. *Writhe and break forth*, i. q., 'thou must

not only bear the sorrows which precede the birth, but also, the severest of all pains, *those of childbirth itself.*' What these are to preceding pains, that, in the view of the prophet, is the carrying away out of the holy city, and land (as an expulsion from the face of God, like that of Cain when he was driven from Eden), in comparison with the mere capture of the city. *Break forth* designates emphatically the *pain of childbirth*, which is here alone intended. It is as it were a *dissolution* of the whole being, a *violent breaking* of it to pieces.—The *dwelling in the field*, is the middle station between the going forth and the arrival at Babylon. Under an open heaven, exposed to all injuries of the weather, were the prisoners collected, in order afterwards to be carried away. *Even unto* is emphatic, and likewise the double *there.* The Divine *judgement* unceasingly advances to *its goal;* the Divine *mercy* irresistibly wrests from the enemy the prey which seemed to be given up to him for ever.

908. Ver. 11. '*And now many nations gather themselves against thee, who say, Let her be profaned, and let our eyes look upon Zion*[1].' Israel, with his claim to be alone the people of the only true God, was to the heathen a thorn in the eye. They here burn with desire to furnish a proof, by matter of fact, that this claim was groundless, and by the destruction of the city, to take from it its imaginary and apparent holiness. Its destruction and profanation are in their view necessarily connected with one another. The antithesis with this verse is contained in chap. 7. 10. '*And mine enemies shall see it, and shame shall cover her who said to me, Where is the Lord thy God? mine eyes shall see her, now will she be to be trodden upon as dirt in the streets.*'—'*Where is the Lord thy God,*' essentially corresponds to '*let her be profaned.*' The historic reference of the prophecy has already been correctly unfolded by Calvin, thus: "*After the release of the nation from the Babylonian captivity, the promised kingdom shall nevertheless not arrive immediately; for before that, the neighbouring nations shall gather themselves together against Jerusalem under the notion that she is polluted and will be to them a sight of joy. This happened under Antiochus [Epiphanes].*" What the prophet here only intimates, yet so that the true reference can by no means be mistaken, (for when here a great hostile oppression is described, which should happen after the people had returned from Babylon, and be removed by the Theocratic courage of the people themselves, and when this second oppression is still followed by a third, described in the fourteenth verse, there remains no choice, and the times of the Maccabees can alone be thought of,) that Zechariah, in whose time the deliverance from the first calamity had already taken place, chap. 9—11 sq., has carried out, mentioning the enemies by name, precisely as the authors of the first calamity are expressly named here.

909. Ver. 12. '*And they know not the thoughts of the Lord, and understand not His counsel; for He collects them as a sheaf for the*

---

[1] Respecting the apparent anomaly of the *num.* in the last member, compare Ewald, p. 639.

thrashing-floor.' *And* is used where *we* should employ *but.* The *thoughts of the Lord* are, that the suffering, when it reaches its end on Zion, shall pass over to her enemies, that these, while they so confidently expect to destroy Zion, shall themselves be destroyed by her. *For* gives the reason, ignorance of the way of the Lord. If they knew this, they would not express such a wish, and such a hope. *For* it is they themselves whom the Lord devotes to destruction.—*Sheaf* need not be taken collectively; on the contrary, the force of the image would be thereby weakened, since it is here designed, not so much to express, (as Joel 4. 13,) *ripeness* for punishment, as the *facility* with which it may be inflicted. Calvin : " *What is a sheaf?* *it is a small portion of wheat: say three hundred, or, it may be, a thousand ears : yet at most it is but so many ears, and they are carried in the arms of a single man. And for what end is a sheaf bound together? Is it not, that it may be thrashed out in the thrashing-floor? This it is that it is hard to believe, that the enemy, while they are thus gathering together all around, are but, as it were, a sheaf.*—Whenever, therefore, our enemies shall be exceedingly numerous and powerful, let us learn to raise our minds to this secret purpose of God, of which the prophet now discourses."—Perfectly correct ; for the purpose of God here mentioned is only a result of His general relation to His Church, and must therefore always be repeated under like circumstances. He punishes her, indeed, but He does not give her up to destruction. His *judgements* are always at the same time the *forerunners of His blessings.*

910. Ver. 13. '*Arise and thrash, O daughter of Zion ; for I will make thy horns iron, and thy claws will I make brass, and thou shalt crush many nations, and I will consecrate the gain to the Lord, and their power to the ruler of the whole earth.*' The image rests on the oriental mode of thrashing. Strictly taken, only the one attribute of thrashing oxen, the *crushing power of their hoofs,* belongs here ; the prophet, however, extends the comparison to that also whereby the bullock is terrible, besides his work of thrashing, to his *horns.* In this respect, 1 Kings 22. 11, is to be compared, where the Pseudoprophet Zedekiah makes for himself iron horns, and explains the import of this symbolic action ; ' *thus saith the Lord, With these thou shalt push Aram, until it is destroyed.*' As at the beginning, where the Lord collects the sheaves on the thrashing-floor, so also at the end, does the prophet show that the victory is *God's* work. It is He Himself, the true God, the Lord of the whole earth, who reminds His rebellious subjects of their true relation to Him, by claiming for Himself, as happened once in Egypt, a portion of the good things which He had bestowed upon them. This thought, which contains the reason why the *noun* is placed instead of the *pronoun* of the first person, i. q., ' *to me, the only God, the Lord of the whole earth,*' is entirely destroyed, if, with several both ancient and modern interpreters, we change the first person into the second. We must not on any account think merely of consecrated gifts, which were offered to the temple. This interpretation would be necessary only in case the subject of discourse were the good things of the

covenant people, or this people themselves, as those who had made the dedication; then by that which was dedicated, could be understood only the special property of the Lord, that which was exclusively devoted to Him, and for ever withdrawn from the use of His subjects, for whom it was, as it were, annihilated; comp. Levit. 27. 28, '*Every thing consecrated, which any one consecrates to the Lord, of men and of cattle, and of his own field, that shall not be bought nor redeemed; every thing consecrated is sacred to the Lord.*' Here, however, where the Lord consecrates, and the good things are those of the heathen, it is only the heathen who are to be considered excluded from the possession, as those in reference to whom the consecration has been made; the people of God, on the contrary, are to be regarded as the *participants* in His inheritance. The community of goods between God and His people, is elsewhere also, where the object requires it, rendered prominent. Thus, e. g., Joel 4. 5, where it is laid to the charge of the Phœnicians and Philistines, '*My silver and gold have ye taken, and my precious things, and have used for your places.*'—The fundamental thought of the verse (which is here expressed only in reference to this particular case,) is that of the victory of the Church of the Lord over the world.

911. Chap. 5. 1. '*Now shalt thou troop together, O daughter of troops. They lay a siege against us; with the rod they shall smite the judge of Israel on the cheek.*' A new scene presents itself to the prophet; Zion, victorious on the preceding occasion, appears to him here as without strength, and confined within her walls; she is taken; shameful maltreatment overtakes the leaders of the people. The designation '*daughter of troops,*' occasioned by the intentional paronomasia, plainly alludes to *daughter of Zion,* and refers back to the preceding description of Zion, as a brave and victorious hero. That the pressing together, in antithesis with the former spirited expeditions [1], is a consequence of anxiety, feebleness, and the hostile oppression, appears from the words "a siege (not as De Wette supposes, 'a rampart') is laid or directed against us." It is appropriately paraphrased by Justi, "*But now why dost thou press so together, thou who art accustomed to press upon others.*"—In the expression, *against us,* instead of *thee,* the prophet is hurried away by his emotions, to show *himself* as one of the people whom he sees to suffer so severely. The shameful treatment of the judge of Israel presupposes the capture of the city, as already taken place in the inward vision of the prophet. This *judge of Israel* is an *ideal person,* formed by the prophet, in order to be able to place in contrast with him the ruler of Israel in 5. 1, the representative of all Theocratic leaders; comp., e. g., Isa. 3. 12, where the corrupt leaders of the Theocracy present themselves conjointly to the prophet in the person of a distinguished child. The customary name of a *collective,* is, in such a case, very badly introduced. It must also be observed, that here the discourse is not of a king of Israel, but very significantly only of a *judge,* with reference probably to the times before Saul, when Israel

---

[1] As designated by גְדוּד.

was governed by judges. The *regal dominion*, now interrupted, shall first be restored through the Messiah.—*Israel* as *nomen dignitat.* of the people, stands here by design. It magnifies the baseness of the action, the contrast of the reality with the idea in the destinies of the people, called forth by the preceding similar contrast in respect to their conduct,—since Israel has inwardly profaned himself by his own guilt, he shall now also be outwardly profaned by a righteous punishment.—With respect now to the historic reference of this prediction of calamity, the fulfilment cannot be sought, without the greatest caprice, in any other event than that of the invasion by the Romans. Among the calamities of the people here presented in a general sketch, this is the only one known to history besides those already designated; that still a second judgement, subversive of the national independence, should pass over the returned exiles, is announced also by Isaiah, the contemporary of Micah, chap. 6. With peculiar clearness, however, is this judgement described by the prophets who lived after the exile, for whom it had already appeared more in the foreground. The only plausible ground against this reference is, that the capture of the city by the Romans was later than the appearing of the Messiah, and yet the latter constitutes the object of the prediction of prosperity, chap. 5. 1, relating to the affliction in the verse before us. This ground, however, is set aside by the following remarks. (1.) The prophet, it is true, designates the affliction which came upon the covenant people through those enemies, merely according to its greatest extremity, the siege and capture of the city ; he had, however, no less in view *its whole extent* from its first beginnings. These, however, so far as the Romans are concerned, fall in the time before Christ. The Jewish people had already been subdued by Pompey. (2.) This alone, however, is not sufficient. If, with Verschuir, we stop short at the conquest by Pompey, we cannot avoid the feeling, that the fulfilment does not exhaust the prophecy. But we are completely justified in adding also the extremity of the affliction, the destruction of Jerusalem by the Romans, joined with its still enduring consequences, if we only consider, that the prediction of prosperity in chap. 5, as its contents incontrovertibly show, and as accords with the analogy of all Messianic prophecies, does not limit itself to the brief time of the first appearance of Christ ; that this is rather considered only as the seed corn, from which a tree arises, under which all the fowls of heaven should dwell ; that therefore the prosperity, no less than the punishment, is to continue, until, in the end of the days, it reaches its most glorious completion.

Chap. 5. 2

912. '*And thou, Bethlehem Ephratah, too small art thou to be among the thousands of Judah, out of thee will come forth (one) to me to be a ruler in Israel, and his goings forth are of old, the days of eternity.*'

The prophet considers Bethlehem as a type of the Jewish people in their misery, described in the foregoing verse, and its wonderful exaltation by the Divine omnipotence, as a pledge of a like result for the whole people.—Bethlehem and Ephratah, according to Bachiene [1], are so distinguished from one another, that the former alone designates *the city*, the latter, at the same time, *its whole environs*. Bethlehem Ephratah, therefore, is, i. q., *Bethlehem* lying in *Ephratah*. But if we compare Gen. 35. 19, where Ephratah is explained as perfectly identical with Bethlehem, and observe, that the prophet before alludes to the contents of this chapter (comp. 889), and considers the former events, which happened in the vicinity of Bethlehem, as a type of the future; that, in the second verse, he parallelizes the new birth, there about to happen, with a former one, which had taken place in its immediate vicinity, in the relation of which precisely the same designation occurs ; we shall find ourselves obliged here also to regard both as a designation of the city, without deciding whether the above-mentioned distinction be well grounded or not with reference to other passages.—The ground of the twofold designation of the place, is commonly sought solely in an intentional distinction from another Bethlehem in the tribe of Zebulon, comp. Josh. 19. 15. But then, instead of Bethlehem Ephratah, we should expect rather the usual Bethlehem Judah. That the writer, in the choice of his language, was guided by a regard to the passage in Genesis, is not to be doubted. But it is highly probable, that he would at the same time allude to the appellative import of those names, *bread-house* and *fruit-field*, and give to them a typical import. The place whose blessing in inferior things is expressed by its name, shall hereafter, in a higher relation, be blessed and made fruitful. That Bethlehem is addressed as *masc.*[2], is explained by the circumstance, that the prophet beholds the city under the image of its ideal representative, without, indeed, afterwards retaining this image (see on Zech. 9. 8). In such personifications, the *genus* may be disregarded [3]. Ewald, p. 640. The littleness of Bethlehem appears even from the circumstance, that it is omitted in the catalogue of the cities of the tribe of Judah, in the book of Joshua [4]. This induced the Alexx. to insert it, Josh. 15. 60, together with several other cities which had been omitted, probably not so much with regard to its outward importance, as the interest which it received from the recollection of an event of former times (comp. Gen. 35), its being the birth-place of David, and still more from the prophecy before us, which directed the eyes of the whole people to its external insignificance. The assertion of Jerome, that the Jews have omitted the name in the Hebrew text, in order that Christ might not appear as sprung from the tribe of Judah, has been refuted by Reland [5] more thoroughly than it deserved. Among the

---

[1] II. 2, p. 7, sq.   [2] Comp. צָעִיר, אַתָּה and מִמְּךָ.

[3] Comp. e. g., Gen. 4. 7, where sin, חַטָּאת, on account of the image of a ravenous beast, appears as *masc.*

[4] Comp. Bachiene, § 192.   [5] p. 643.

cities too, which, after the Babylonish exile, came into the possession of the tribe of Judah, Bethlehem is not numbered. In the New
Testament it is designated as a mere village (κώμη, John 7. 42), and
Josephus honours it, indeed, a few times with the name of a city,
but elsewhere designates it by χωρίον, *Antiq.* 5. 2. 8. *A thousand*
stands as a designation of a *gens,* because this usually consisted of
about a thousand heads. A place of few inhabitants, like Bethlehem,
did not enjoy the honour of forming an independent *gens;* but
was included among several others. We must content ourselves
with this general remark, since the effort has not succeeded to make
out, from the different passages where the *thousands of Judah* occur [1],
any thing more definite respecting the *nature* of this division, its
origin, and its *relation* to others, which elsewhere occur. To the
passage before us, however, this is not important. The sense is
obvious without: ' *Bethlehem takes a very inferior rank among the
cities of the covenant people, can scarcely be numbered among her distinguished sisters, who proudly look down upon her.*'—That [2] *to go
forth,* can be used of *being born,* of *descent,* is self-evident, comp.,
e. g., 2 Kings 20. 18, where *to go forth,* and *to be born,* occur as
interchangeable terms [3]. A definite subject for *shall go forth* is
wanting. It is best to supply one, which is indirectly implied in
what follows. The construction, which is entirely unusual, was
occasioned by the effort to call attention, even by the very words,
and their position, to the contrast of the Divine greatness of Bethlehem, with its natural inferiority.

> "Thou art small to be among the thousands of Judah,
> Out of thee will go forth to me to be a ruler in Israel.

Out of the place which is too small to constitute an independent
member of the body, goes forth the head. ' *A* ruler in Israel' stands
where we should expect to hear of *the* ruler in Israel κατ' ἐξοχήν. Had
the prophet adopted the latter, then this antithesis would have been
less prominent, as well as that, which is also intended, with the *Judge*
of Israel, who is represented in the foregoing verse as deprived of his
dignity. More depended in the first instance upon the *genus,* than
upon the individual; more upon the idea of the dominion in general,
than upon its kind and method. The individual is then so characterized, partly in this verse, and partly in that which follows, that he
cannot be mistaken. If, indeed, nothing further were contained in
the words before us, than that, in future times, a ruler over all Israel
would arise out of Bethlehem, and if they stood alone, and, in the
time after Micah, a ruler over all Israel arising out of Bethlehem,
other than the Messiah, could be pointed out, which, however, cannot be done, the choice between the two might be difficult. *To
me* is referred by several to the *prophet.* But the reference *to God*
is required by the antithesis between the human meanness, and the

---

[1] אַלְפֵי יְהוּדָה   [2] יֵצֵא.

[3] Still we must not on this account attribute to יָצָא this sense, which it receives through the connexion, as *its proper meaning,* which many older interpreters of the passage have done.

Divine greatness. Calvin : " *Egredietur* mihi. *Hac voce pronuntiat Deus sibi non ita decretum esse perdere populum, quin velit iterum restituere post aliquod tempus. Revocat igitur fideles ad se et consilium suum, acsi diceret: Sic ad tempus vos abjeci, ut tamen aliqua vestri cura me tangat.*" How forcible this *to me* is, and how God is able to exalt that which is low, was seen by believers in David the type, and there is no doubt, that the prophet indirectly alluded to this type, with a view thereby to strengthen faith in the promise, which appeared incredible. David sprung from the humble Bethlehem, he was the youngest among his brothers, without power, without reputation. In order that the *to me* might be the more evident, God so ordered the circumstances of his election, that his human inferiority should be most strikingly exhibited. It was God who raised him from a shepherd of lambs to be a shepherd of the people.

913. The last words magnify the Divine greatness of the Messiah in the antithesis with his human inferior origin, with reference to the similar antithesis in respect to Bethlehem. Here also has the prophet so clearly expressed the antithesis in the words, that it has forcibly impressed itself upon the *homines bonæ voluntatis*, among the interpreters of all centuries. Thus, e. g., Chrysostom, *Demonstratio adv. Judæos et Gentiles, quod Christus sit Deus, Opp. t. v.* p. 739: " This prophet shows both his *divinity* and his *humanity*. For by saying ' *his goings forth are from the beginning, from the days of eternity,*' he made manifest His existence before the worlds: but by saying ' *there shall come forth a ruler, who shall rule my people Israel,*' he intimates His generation according to the flesh [1]."—We translate the clause, ' *and his places of egress are from ancient times, from the days of eternity,*' = ' *the places from which he goes forth, are the ancient times, the days of eternity,*' precisely as in the two passages, Ps. 19. 7, and 1 Kings 10. 28, the insertion of *from*, which might be omitted, is here especially occasioned by the effort to make the reference to the corresponding member more obvious. This interpretation alone gives a satisfactory explanation of the plural. The words ' *from ancient times, from the days of eternity,*' contain, according to it, a climax. The existence of the Messiah in general, before His temporal birth at Bethlehem, is asserted; and then His eternity in contrast with all time is mentioned here. This could not but afford great consolation to Israel. He who should hereafter deliver them out of their misery by a visible manifestation, exists already during its continuance, before it, and through all eternity.

THE CITATION MATT. 2. 6 [2]

914. Several, particularly Paulus, have asserted, that the interpretation of Micah here given, is that of the Sanhedrim, not of the

---

[1] Professor Hengstenberg shows that מוֹצָאֹתָיו does not designate the *action* of *going forth*, but either *place* of *egress*, or *that which goes forth*. He here takes the *first meaning.*

[2] The original contained an able *history* of the interpretation, (1) by the Jews, (2) by Christians.

evangelist, who merely records what was said and done. But this assertion is refuted the moment we look at the design which Matthew pursued in his whole description of the early life of Jesus. He did not aim, like Luke, to impart to his readers historical information. *This*, he could regard as already known to *his* readers, and it was of importance to him, only so far as it served to confirm Old Testament prophecies. He therefore touched upon an historical circumstance, precisely when the mention of it would serve to promote his design. Thus the design of the genealogy is to show how Christ, according to the prophecies of the Old Testament, derived His origin from Abraham, through David. Thus, all which is related, chap. 1. 18-21, only serves to prepare the way for the citation of the prophecy of Isaiah, concerning the birth of the Messiah of a virgin, which in the twenty-second verse, is closed with the words '*Now all this was done, that it might be fulfilled,*' &c.—Even the *all* shows, that all which preceded had been cited in reference to the prophecy. The strange παρερμηνεία of Olshausen, which refers the *all* to the *totality*, in contrast with that which is *individual*, can be explained only from the embarrassment in which this distinguished commentator must have been here involved by his view of the prophecy of Isaiah, according to which, even after the greatest effort, only an appearance of agreement can be made out between it and the event in which Matthew finds its fulfilment.—But besides, all the features of the narration belong too plainly to the prophecy afterwards to be cited. In respect to it, he most sedulously renders prominent, how Christ was born of a pure and unspotted virgin, and still subjoins, in the twenty-fifth verse, emphatically, that Mary had not lived in marriage intercourse with Joseph before the birth of Jesus, because a virgin should not only conceive, but also should bear the Emmanuel. To '*thou shalt call His name* Jesus,' accurately corresponds, '*and they shall call His name Emmanuel.*' This latter name the evangelist explains, which cannot be without an object, by '*God with us.*' With him, the name *Jesus* has the same sense, '*salvation of God.*' We first pass over the portion chap. 2. 1—12. In the thirteenth verse follows the account of the flight to Egypt, with reference to the passage Hos. 11. 1. This passage refers, indeed, in the first instance, to Israel. He, however, comes under consideration here, as even His designation as *Son of God* shows, not according to His natural condition, but only according to his divine destination and election. Israel was called to preserve the divine truth in the midst of errour, to proclaim God's mighty deeds among the heathen, to be His messenger and ambassador. In this relation, Israel was a type of the Messiah; He, a concentrated and spiritualized Israel; a relation, from which alone, many appearances in the second part of Isaiah can be explained, and on account of which the Messiah, chap. 49. 3, is called directly *Israel*. If, now, between Israel and the Messiah, there existed such a relation, not accidental, but designed of God, of the type and the antitype, it must appear to us beforehand, as highly probable, that the residence of the children of Israel in Egypt, and that of Christ in the same place, stand in relation to one another. This supposition rests on

the perception of the remarkable coincidence, which, through Divine
Providence, generally exists between the fortunes of the typical
persons and the antitype, so that the former are to be regarded as a
matter-of-fact prophecy of the latter. But this coincidence here
must not be sought solely in the residence in the same land; this
circumstance rather serves only to call attention to the deeper internal resemblance, and outwardly to represent it. Not of his own
choice, but led by a series of the most remarkable providences, at
the express command of God, Israel journeyed to Egypt. He thus
escaped the ruin which threatened him in the land of his proper
destination. He was there prepared for it, and when this preparation was completed, in accordance with the Divine promise, previously given, he was conducted into the land in which it should
be realized. The same providence of God, which there took this
method for the preservation of His kingdom, at that time connected
with the existence of the typical Israel, even now employs the same
means where its hopes are concentrated in the person of its future
head. Egypt must afford him a place of refuge until the danger is
over.—Then follows, ver. 16—19, the relation of the murder of the
children of Bethlehem, with a sole reference to the passage, Jer. 31. 15,
and on its account. Here we are not to suppose a bare *simile*. In
Jeremiah, the mother of Israel laments for the destruction of her
children. The Lord appears and consoles her; her sorrow shall,
hereafter, be turned into joy; she shall behold the prosperity which
the Lord will still impart to her sons. Accordingly the essence of
the passage is the antithesis of the deserved punishment, which Israel
has drawn upon himself by his sins, and the undeserved prosperity
which the mercy of God will impart to him. Now we perceive
entirely the same antithesis also in the event before us. As was the
tyranny of the Chaldeans, so also was that of Herod, a deserved
punishment of the sins of the covenant people. He, born in a
foreign land, was, like Nebuchadnezzar, a rod of correction in the
hand of the Lord. The cruel deed which he performed under Divine
permission, precisely in the place where the Saviour was born, was
designed to bring into remembrance what the covenant people had
deserved for their sins, by means of a fact, which was, at the same
time, a prophecy of the more comprehensive impending judgement,
to make the sending of the Messiah the more to appear as a pure
work of the Divine mercy, destined only for those who acknowledge
it as such. Hence it appears, that the Old Testament event, to
which the prophet in the first instance appeals, the carrying away
into exile, and the deliverance from it, was a prophecy by matter of
fact, of those New Testament events,—in which the indicated typical
relation of the murder of the children of Bethlehem must not be
overlooked—that both were governed by the same laws, were a
necessary result of the same Divine being, a declaration, therefore,
which referred directly to the first, might, at the same time, be
regarded as a prediction of the second.—Ver. 19, 20, have, for their
central point, the passage Exod. 4. 19, where the Lord, after He
admonishes Moses to return, subjoins, '*for all the men are dead*

which sought thy life.' What the Lord there says to Moses, and here to Joseph, arises from the same ground. Moses, like all the servants of God, under the Old Testament, is a type of Christ. There is the same rule of the Divine providence, the same direction of all events for the good of the kingdom of God. Moses is withdrawn from the threatening danger only by flight into distant regions ; as soon as it is time for him to enter upon his vocation, the door of return to the scene of his agency is opened to him. Just so in relation to Christ. Ver. 21—23 have for their only central point the prophetic declaration, ὅτι Ναζωραῖος κληθήσεται. The circumstances particularly mentioned, that Joseph had purposed to settle down in Judea, but was warned of God to retire into Galilee, were designed to make it plain, that God purposely fulfilled this declaration.

915. From this representation, it sufficiently appears, that the aim of Matthew, in chap. 1 and 2, was by no means an historical, but a doctrinal one. From this it follows, when we proceed to apply our investigation, that the portion, chap. 2. 1—12, also must have an Old Testament central point. Now that this must be sought, in the first instance, in the prophecy of Micah, appears from the mention of Bethlehem as the birth-place of Christ, in ver. 1. That the evangelist does not mention this, which was known to all his readers as a mere historical circumstance, as such, appears from the fact, that he passes over in entire silence the earlier residence of the parents of Jesus at Nazareth, because it stood in no relation to the prophecy of the Old Testament ; and merely by the fact that Bethlehem is first designated in the account of the birth of Jesus as the residence of his parents, intimates, that what had previously been related happened in another place ; that, on the contrary, he mentions the abode of the Holy Family in Nazareth after the return from Egypt, only for the manifest purpose of connecting it with the prophecy. To this we must add, that the relation, ver. 1—6, particularly the imparting of the answer of the Sanhedrim to the question of Herod, according to the demonstrated aim of Matthew, would be altogether without a purpose, if he had not considered the answer of the lawyers as perfectly corresponding with the truth, and therefore omitted his usual ἵνα πληρωθῇ. In order to show how much Matthew is governed by a regard to the Old Testament, and at the same time, also, how he often contents himself with giving his reader, familiar with the Old Testament, a mere intimation, as is manifest even from ver. 20 and ver. 23, we must yet present the second Old Testament reference, which he has in view in ver. 1—12. The passages to which he refers, are Ps. 72. 10, ' *The kings of Saba and Sheba will bring offerings,*' and Is. 60. 6, ' *All they from Saba will come, bring gold and incense, and declare the praise of the Lord.*' The representation in these and other similar passages is figurative. Gifts, in the East, are signs of reverence. The thought, lying at the foundation, is this ; the farthest, richest, and mightiest nations of the earth will reverence the Messiah, and consecrate to him their all. But what is there predicted in a figurative representation began to be fulfilled by

the symbolic action of the Magi, in which the image was embodied. The gold, the incense, the myrrh, which they consecrated to the new-born child Jesus, symbolized the reverence which they offered him. As for the rest, these gifts were certainly mentioned expressly by Matthew, because they occur in the Old Testament passages. As this event constituted on the one side the beginning of the fulfil-ment, so did it on the other a prophecy by matter of fact, a type of a future, greater, and more proper fulfilment. The Apostle considers these Magi as the types and representatives of the whole mass of the heathen nations, who should afterwards reverence the Messiah. They came, as it were, the ambassadors of the heathen world, in order to greet the new-born king; as the shepherds, selected by God Himself, were the deputies of the Jewish people.

916. But if it is established, that, in general, the view of the prophecy which the Evangelist gives, as that of the Sanhedrim, is, at the same time, to be considered as his own, so must it also be assumed, that the citation, even in its particulars, is also approved by him, and that the view advanced by Jerome, ("*Arbitror Mat-thæum volentem arguere scribarum et sacerdotum negligentiam, sic etiam posuisse, uti ab iis dictum est,*") and recently by Paulus, cannot be made use of to justify deviations, if such should actually be found. In order to ascertain whether this is the case, we must more closely compare the citation with the original text of the passage. Καὶ σὺ Βηθλεέμ, γῆ ᾽Ιούδα, οὐδαμῶς ἐλαχίστη εἶ ἐν τοῖς ἡγεμόσιν ᾽Ιούδα· ἐκ σοῦ γὰρ ἐξελεύσεται ἡγούμενος, ὅστις ποιμανεῖ τὸν λαόν μου, τὸν ᾽Ισραήλ. *Land of Judah,* for the *Ephratah* of the original, first demands attention. This deviation is plainly owing to the circumstance, that the name *Ephratah* had become unknown in the days of the Evangelist; he therefore substitutes another, which occurs in other passages of the Old Testament. With respect to the grammatical interpretation of γῆ ᾽Ιούδα, it stands, by a laconic mode of expression used in geographical and other similar designa-tions, and which is found even in the Old Testament[1], for '*Beth-lehem, situated in the land of Judah.*' The Evangelist here no more follows the Hebrew text, than the Alexandrine version. This has Καὶ σὺ Βηθλεὲμ οἶκος ᾽Εφραθά. (Thus without an article, the *Cod. Vatic.*) The translator plainly regarded *Ephratah* as the *nom. propr.* of the wife of Caleb, 1 Chron. 2. 19. 50. 4. 4, from which others also, as Adrichomius, derived the name of the place, and did nothing further than more definitely to designate, by the subjoined οἶκος, the relation of dependence expressed by the supposed genitive. The apparent contradiction, that the prophet calls Bethlehem '*small,*' the evangelist '*by no means small,*' has already been so satisfactorily ex-plained by ancient and modern interpreters[2], that we need not dwell

---

[1] בֵּֽית־לֶ֥חֶם יְהוּדָ֖ה.

[2] Comp., e. g., Euthym. Zigab., l. c. p. 50: "Ὅτι εἰ καὶ τὸ φαινόμενον εὐτελὴς εἶ, ἀλλά γε τὸ νοούμενον οὐκ ἐλαχίστη τις ὑπάρχεις ἐν ὅλαις ταῖς ἡγεμονίαις τῆς τοῦ ᾽Ιούδα φυλῆς. Michaelis: "*Parvam vocat Mich. respiciens statum externum, minime parvam Mat. respiciens nativitatem Messiæ, qua mirum in modum condecoratum illud oppidum ac illustratum fuit.*"

upon it. We only remark, that the assumption of Paulus, that the members of the Sanhedrim understood the proposition interrogatively, "*Art thou perhaps too small to be*," &c., receives no confirmation from the passage cited in its favour, from the *Pirke Elieser*, c. 3, but which is found only in the Latin translation of Wetstein. For in the ground-text the verse is there cited in literal agreement with the Hebrew original (comp. Eisenmenger, I. p. 316). That the deviation has its ground solely in the effort to express the sense more clearly and definitely, is confirmed by a comparison of the Chaldee, which, with similar freedom, paraphrases, "Thou Bethlehem Ephratah wilt soon be able to be numbered." Calvin justly remarks, in reference to such deviations, "*Semper attendant lectores, quorsum adducant Evangelistæ scripturæ locos, ne scrupulose in singulis verbis insistant, sed contenti sint hoc uno, quod scriptura nunquam ab illis torquetur in alienum sensum.*"—The representation of Bethlehem by the person of its representative, which occurs in Micah, Matthew does away with, at the beginning of the verse, using, not the *masc.* adj., but the *fem.* (ἐλαχίστη). On the other hand, he renders בְּאַלְפֵי by ἐν τοῖς ἡγεμόσι, which seems again to lead to this representation.—The correct view would seem to be, that the figurative representation is not consistently carried through in either of them. Micah begins with personifying Bethlehem, and, had he been consistent, instead of אֲלָפִים, he must have placed שָׂרֵי אֲלָפִים ; Matthew introduces Bethlehem as a city, but afterwards by placing the ἡγεμόνες, instead of the tribes, he proceeds to a personification. For this he had a special reason, a regard to the following ἡγούμενος. Bethlehem, although outwardly small, yet considered from a higher point of view, is already by no means small among the *leaders* of Judah, for hereafter shall go forth from it the great *leader* of the whole nation. This so obvious reference must the more be assumed, since another antithesis, entirely similar in sense, is found in Micah (comp. 912). It serves, at the same time, as a proof against the unfortunate assumption, that Matthew's gospel was composed originally in the Aramaic dialect, which is opposed in general also by the free handling of the Old Testament text in the whole citation. The inconsistency in the use of the personification is finally the more easily explained, since this is merely an ideal one, and person and city are not in reality different from each other ; comp. on Zech. 9. 7, 8.—The last words in Micah, '*and his goings forth,*' &c., are omitted by Matthew, because they do not serve his purpose, —the demonstration, that, according to the prophecies of the Old Testament, the Messiah should be born in Bethlehem. On the other hand, the בְּיִשְׂרָאֵל of Micah is paraphrased by ὅστις ποιμανεῖ τὸν λαόν μου, τὸν Ἰσραήλ. These words have reference to 2 Sam. 5. 2, where it is said of David, ' The Lord says to thee, *Thou shalt feed my people Israel,* and thou shalt be for a prince over Israel.' They point to the typical relation of the first David, born at Bethlehem, to the second, the Messiah.

917. In reference to the relation between prophecy and fulfil-

ment, we have here still one general remark to make. That the fulfilment of the prophecies of the Old Testament was a concurrent aim of the events of the New ; that in no case, however, is this aim the only one ; that rather, each event, even apart from the prophecy, had its meaning, and that prophecy and history were equally governed by this meaning, we have already seen (on Zech. 9. 9). This is confirmed by the case before us. The birth of Christ at Bethlehem testified, on the one side, the divine origin of the prophecy of the Old Testament ; on the other, the fact, that Jesus was the Christ. But its main object, which was independent of this, was outwardly to exhibit the descent of Christ from David. This the Jews already knew at the time of Christ, as appears from the addition Κώμη, ὅπου ἦν Δαβίδ, John 7. 42. Of the two seats of the family of David, Bethlehem and Jerusalem, the former was chosen, because, in general, on account of its outward inferiority, it was well suited to represent the lowliness of the Messiah at the outset ; a circumstance, which is expressly mentioned by the prophet, partly because it was appropriated to the family of David during its obscurity, while Jerusalem, on the contrary, belonged to their regal condition : but the Messiah was to be born in the fallen tabernacle of David, to be a sprout from the stem of Jesse, after it had been cut off. That this reference also was before the prophet's mind seems to be evident from a comparison of 3. 12, and 4. 10. In any event, he considered the family of David, at the time of the appearing of the Messiah, as utterly fallen.

918. Ver. 3. ' *Therefore will he give them up until the time when she who bears has brought forth, and then will the rest of his brothers return to the sons of Israel.*' Here begins the description of what the Messiah should impart to the covenant people, and this is carried forward through the whole chapter. *Therefore* shows the close connexion of chap. 4. 14, with 5. 1. Michaelis : " *Quia hoc est consilium Dei, Sionem propter peccata prius affligere ac tum demum in Christo Bethlehemi nascituro reficere.*" With respect to the words, ' *until the time when she who bears brings forth,*' we understand, for the following reasons, *the mother of the Messiah ;* for, 1. If the reference were to the Church of Israel, we should expect the article. She was, in point of fact, mentioned in what immediately preceded, being only a personification of those who should be given up. 2. The personification is, indeed, frequently not carried consistently through ; but that here, in the same sentence, the children of Israel should be spoken of in the plural (' he will give *them* up'), and that in what follows also, there should be no trace of a personification, the sons of Israel being expressly mentioned, causes the alleged personification to appear as extremely broken, and its assumption admissible only in case of necessity. 3. If the reference is to the Church of Israel, the relation of the Messiah to that great change of things is not intimated by a single word. He is treated of in ver. 1, and in ver. 3—5. How then should ver. 2 at

once have passed over to the general Messianic representation [1]? 4. Add to this, that the prophet had in view one who was to bring forth in Bethlehem : this appears from the reference to Genesis, chap. 35, already pointed out. Bethlehem, which had already been distinguished in ancient times by a birth, shall, in future times, be honoured by one infinitely more important. 5. To this must be subjoined the comparison of Is. 7. 14, where, in like manner, mention is made of the mother of the Messiah (comp. on the passage).—By the brothers of the Messiah, only the members of the Old Covenant people, his brothers according to the flesh, can be understood. The reference to the heathen has no Old Testament analogy in its favour. As is shown by the antithesis [2], Israel is here to be taken as a name of *dignity*, the *children of Israel* are the true members of the Theocracy. To these should others, likewise brothers of the Messiah, and therefore descendants of Jacob, return, which implies a previous turning away, or alienation from the true Church of the Lord, and her head. The Messiah, accordingly, appears here as one, who, by uniting all under himself as the head, should abolish all discord and alienation among the members of the covenant people ; a thought which constantly returns in the Messianic descriptions, and is individualized, in Hos. 1. 11, and Is. 11, by the predicted removal of the enmity between Judah and Israel. We pass over other interpretations, because they refute themselves.

919. Ver. 4. ' *And he shall stand and feed in the strength of the Lord, in the glory of the name of the Lord his God, and they shall dwell, for now will he be great to the ends of the earth.*' The *standing* has here not the import of *remaining*, but merely belongs to the graphic description of the habit of the shepherd, comp. Is. 61. 5, ' *And strangers shall stand and feed your flocks.*' The shepherd stands leaning upon his staff, and overlooks his flock. The connexion of ' *he shall feed,*' with ' *in the power of the Lord,*' we cannot better explain than in the words of Calvin : " *Verbum pascendi exprimit qualis Christus sit erga suos h. e. erga gregem sibi commissum. Non dominatur in ecclesiam tanquam formidabilis tyrannus, qui suos metu opprimat, sed pastor est et tractat oves suas quâ optandum mansuetudine. Sed quoniam cingimur undique hostibus, addit propheta, pascet in virtute etc. h. e. quantum est potentiæ in Deo tantum erit præsidii in Christo, ubi necesse erit ecclesiam defendere et tueri contra hostes. Discamus ergo non minus sperandum esse salutis a Christo, quam est in Deo virtutis.*" The great king is so closely united with God, that the whole fulness of the Divine power and majesty belongs to him. Such things never occur of an earthly king. Such a king has strength in the Lord, Is. 45. 24, ' The Lord *gives* strength to his king, and exalts the horn of his anointed,' 1 Sam. 2. 10 ; but the whole strength and majesty of God are not his possession. The

---

[1] The *suff.* in אֶחָיו referring to the Messiah, requires a preceding indirect mention of him, which only then has place when the יוֹלֵדָה is, ' she who will bear the ruler,' predicted in ver. 1.

[2] יֶתֶר אֶחָיו.

name also of God is here emphatic.—The *dwelling* stands in the antithesis with the disquietude and dispersion, and we need not supply after it, *securely*. The ground of the present rest and security of the Church of the Lord is rather, that her head has now extended his dominion beyond the narrow bounds of Palestine over the whole earth. (Comp. chap. 4. 3.)

920. Ver. 5. '*And this* (man) *shall be peace. When Ashur shall come into our land, and when he shall tread our palaces, we shall oppose against him seven shepherds, and eight principal men.*' Ver. 6. '*And they shall eat up the land of Ashur with the sword, and the land of Nimrod in his gates, and he will protect against Ashur, when he comes into our land, and when he treads our palaces.*'—And this (he whose glory has just been described) is peace ; he supplies what we have so painfully felt the want of in the troublous times before his appearing. In like manner, and with reference to this passage, Ephes. 2. 14, αὐτός ἐστιν ἡ εἰρήνη ἡμῶν, comp. also Judges 6. 24, ' And Gideon built there an altar to the Lord, and called it *Jehovah peace*[1].' What follows till the end of ver. 6 is a carrying out by examples of the words, '*and he shall be peace.*' That Ashur, the most dangerous enemy of the covenant people at the time of the prophet, here stands as a type of their enemies, is agreed by all the interpreters. Even Bauer translates, "and when another Ashur," with reference to the passage of Virgil, already compared by Castalio : "*Alter erit tum Tiphys et altera quæ vehat Argo Delectos heroas.*" This, however, is not sufficient. The sense can by no means be,—"The covenant people will meet every hostile attack with the most powerful resistance, oppose to it brave leaders with their hosts, even carry the war into the enemy's land." This sense would be diametrically opposed to the perpetual description of the Messianic kingdom, as a kingdom of peace ; comp. 4. 3, according to which, at that time, all war and strife will cease ; it would stand in the grossest contradiction with ver. 9 sq., according to which, God will, at that time, deprive the covenant people of all means of self-defence, and then the more powerfully protect them by His immediate help. We must, therefore, separate the fundamental idea, the complete security of the kingdom of God through the power and the protection of the Messiah, from the drapery borrowed from the existing relations of the Theocracy. The Messiah will accomplish for his people the same as a large number of brave leaders with their hosts,—the usual means under the Old Testament whereby God delivered His people.

921. As for the rest of the chapter, we content ourselves with a bare indication of its contents. The Church of the Lord will, at that time, be richly blessed (ver. 7), and terrible to all her foes (ver. 8, 9) ; not, indeed, by her warlike energy, but solely by the immediate agency of the Lord ; who, after he has rendered her outwardly defenceless, and thus rescued her from the temptation to a sinful confidence in her own strength, to which she so often yielded in former times (comp. Is. 30. 16. 31. 1. Hos. 1. 7. 14. 4), after He

[1] יְהֹוָה שָׁלוֹם.

at the same time has removed from the midst of her every thing else which formerly presented a wall of partition between her and God, and caused her outward profanation, when she had become inwardly profaned by her guilt, will powerfully defend her, and, since every distinction between her cause and His own has disappeared, severely punish her enemies.

THE PROPHET HAGGAI

922. The circumstances under which this prophet came forward are entirely the same as those of Zechariah, and we may therefore content ourselves with a simple reference to 490. His prophecies have altogether for their object the promotion of the building of the Temple. In the first discourse, chap. 1, he comes forward to *chastise*. He zealously rebukes the prevailing indifference, the selfish forgetfulness of God, and shows how this would punish itself, since God, in righteous retribution, would now take from those who had deprived Him of His own, what belonged to them. This discourse accomplished its purpose. Four and twenty days after it was delivered, on the twenty-fourth of the sixth month of the second year of Darius, the work on the Temple was zealously recommenced, under the direction of Zerubbabel and the high priest Joshua.

923. But soon a new occasion for appearing in public was presented to the prophet. As the work had so far advanced, that the relation of the new Temple to the former could be judged of, a great lamentation seized the people. With the cry of joy at the laying of the foundation, loud weeping was mingled, especially that of the aged, who had seen the glory of the first Temple ; comp. Ezra 3. 12. Promise and appearance seemed to stand in striking contradiction. How splendid the former, how wretched the latter! The new Temple, according to Isaiah (comp. especially chap. 60), Jeremiah, and Ezekiel, ought immensely to surpass the old in glory. And what did they see it now? It was as a nonentity in their eyes (comp. 2. 3). Troubled thoughts now arose even among believers. Will this Temple, indeed, be that which God has promised? Has not He Himself, by the miserable circumstances in which we are placed, given us an intimation to desist from the fruitless undertaking? Is it becoming to build Him a hut instead of a Temple? He may have entirely rejected His people on account of their sins, and retracted His *conditional* promise, or He may, perhaps, choose to fulfil it hereafter, to another generation more worthy than we, who still sigh under His anger, who are outwardly, indeed, in Canaan, but in reality still in Babylon,—at any rate, by the circumstances in which we find ourselves, He declares us unworthy of so great and holy a work.

924. In such a state of mind, *consolation* was required, and Haggai was called of God, in order to impart it. He executed his com-

mission by the discourse, chap. 2. 1—9, held on the twenty-first of the seventh month.

925. He exhorts the people and their leaders to be of good courage, pointing to the covenant of the Lord, which, being perpetual, was a pledge of all prosperity, so that to despair was to make God a liar ; and to the Spirit of God, which for ever dwelt in His Church, as a never-ceasing fountain of strength for the feeble, of salvation for the wretched, whose existence made despondency folly ; since, though its effusions might be for a time restrained, it must, in the future, be more abundantly poured forth.

926. After the prophet has again opened the closed fountain of consolation under *every* discouragement, he directs their attention especially to that which had, in the present instance, dispirited the people, and filled them with distrust of God and His favour. The incipient meanness of the new Temple ought not to distress them. God would remove the hindrances, which, viewed with the eye of sense, rendered impossible the fulfilment of the splendid promises of the older prophets concerning the accession of the heathen with all their riches and gifts. He, the Almighty, would shake the mighty kingdoms of the earth, and deprive them of that power which caused them, in proud self-exultation, to forget His own (ver. 6, 7). The heathen, therefore, would humbly come, with their treasures, to reverence the Lord, whose Temple now rises to higher glory, ver. 7 ; which cannot, indeed, be otherwise, since God is the possessor of all earthly goods, ver. 8 ;—a glory so great, that it far surpasses that of the former Temple, accompanied also with peace for the people of the Lord, ver. 9.

927. Ver. 6. ' *For thus saith the Lord, Sabaoth, It is yet a little, and I will shake the heavens and the earth, and the sea, and the dry land.*' How does the idea of shortness of time suit here ? Every difficulty vanishes with the true interpretation, which makes the shaking refer to the great political concussions whereby the power of the heathen should be broken, their pride humbled, and they should thus become qualified to receive the salvation. This shaking began even in the nearest future. The axe already lay at the root of the Persian kingdom, whose later manifest fall was only the revelation of the far earlier, which was hidden.

928. Had the prophet *barely* announced the glorification of the Theocracy, by the flowing into it of the heathen, with all their riches and gifts, his prediction would have met with little success. The contrasts were too striking ; on the one side, the poor, miserable, despised Israel, who were even then, under a permission with difficulty obtained from their heathen masters, employed in building for their God a mean tabernacle, instead of a splendid Temple ; on the other side, heathenism, in the bloom of its power, full of pride in its own might, and the might of its idols, scarcely deigning to cast a look at Israel and their God. These contrasts could be reconciled only in a supernatural way by the God of heaven, Who delivers up

the powerful to ruin, and exalts the lowly and the miserable from the dust. The prophet points this preparatory agency out to the people. He would *shake* the might of the heathen, and humble their pride.

929. But the prophet does not speak *merely* of the *violent destruction* of *human power* by God, but also of a *moral result*, which should thereby be produced among the destroyed themselves. *Freely* do the shaken heathen come and consecrate themselves and their all to the Lord. To effect this, is the direct aim of the shaking, the highest object which God pursues in the government of the world.

930. Now, in how far was this means suited to the accomplishment of this object? This question must be answered from a comprehensive scriptural view of the economy of suffering. From this we learn, that, from the corruption of human nature, the possession of the good things of this world brings with it the danger of their abuse, of the devotion of the heart to them, of confidence in them, of proud contempt of God; and this danger can be avoided only by God's withdrawing these good things; a view which is stamped even on the *language* of Scripture. As the individual must necessarily enter the kingdom of God through tribulation, as only he can reap with joy, who has sown in tears, so is it also with whole nations. How Israel was continually *shaken*, in order that his beauty might come to the Lord, is shown by his historians and prophets on every page. '*In their distress they will seek me,*' Hos. 5. 15; this is the key-note which runs through them all. Never, until God has smitten Israel, does he turn himself to Him, and seek to be healed. The application of this fundamental view of the nature of human sufferings to the dealings of God with the heathen, we find, although notices of it every where occur, the most clearly and completely in Isaiah [1].

931. Now, in what relation does the idea, in the general form in which it is expressed in the passage before us, stand to history? It is plain, that *no shaking* here comes under consideration, except so far as the *accession of the heathen* stands in connexion with it, is a consequence of it. We must not by any means suppose that the prophecy reached its completion with the first manifestation of Christ. Its fulfilment must rather be progressive, so long as the antithesis of earthly power, in opposition to the kingdom of God on earth continues; therefore until the establishment of the kingdom of glory.

932. How then was the idea realized in the time *before the first appearing of Christ?* Here, one shaking of the heathen followed upon another. How the Persian power was undermined was manifest, even in the war which Xerxes, the successor of Darius, waged against the Greeks. That its time would now soon be fulfilled, might even then have been anticipated, and this anticipation was realized by the rapid conquests of Alexander. Even *his* power, apparently destined to be eternal, soon yielded to the lot of all that is temporal. "*Inde,*" says Livy, " *morte Alexandri distractum in*

---

[1] Of chap. 19. 1—15. ver. 16 sq. Amos 9. 1.

multa regna, dum ad se quisque opes rapiunt lacerantes viribus, a
summo culmine fortunæ ad ultimum finem centum quinquaginta annos
stetit." The two most powerful kingdoms which arose out of the
monarchy of Alexander, those of Syria and Egypt, destroyed each
other. The Romans now attained to the dominion of the world,
but, at the very time when they appeared to have reached the
summit of their greatness, their overthrow was already far advanced.

933. Let us suppose that Christ had appeared when one of these
kingdoms was in the freshness and vigour of its youth. Would he
have found admission ? Under the Persians, intoxicated with victory, just as little as under the triumphant Greeks, and in the
ancient iron Rome. But thus a feeling of the vanity and perishable
nature of all that is earthly, a longing after indestructible heavenly
blessings, a firm and unmovable heavenly kingdom, had been exten-
sively awakened among the nations, the strength of which may be
learned even from the fact, that,—a feeble commencement of the
promised coming of the heathen,—they sought this kingdom itself in
its then imperfect form, and either suffered themselves to be received
into it, or leaned upon it.

934. It only remains for us to consider the New Testament
citation of the passage, Heb. 12. 26 sq. The author, in ver. 25,
exhorts his readers not to expose themselves, by a rejection of the
far more complete revelation of God in Christ, to a far sorer punishment than those had experienced, who hardened themselves against
the revelation of God under the Old Testament. The higher dignity
of the former he demonstrates, ver. 26, from the fact, that while at
the establishment of the old covenant, only a comparatively small
shaking took place (as a sign of the sovereignty of God over created
things, of the destroying power which He exerts over them, Mount
Sinai had then been shaken), in reference to the time of the New
Testament, an immensely greater shaking is predicted, such a one
as affects, not merely the *whole* earth, but also the heavens. What
this shaking in the prophecy of Haggai, whose words he represents
as spoken by God at the beginning of the period of time to which
the prophecy refers (comp. the similar case, chap. 10. 5), may import,
he declares, ver. 27, ' *And this word, Yet once more, signifieth the*
removing of those things that are shaken, as of things that are made,
that those things which cannot be shaken may remain.' Although the
truth was seen by Calvin (" *In voce ἅπαξ non insistit apostolus.*
Tantum ex concussione cœli et terræ infert, totius mundi statum
debere Christi adventu mutari,") yet many errours have been occasioned by the circumstance, that the whole emphasis was almost universally assumed to rest on the ' *yet once more,*' while, nevertheless,
the author has no further respect to these words, after which a κ. τ. λ.
is to be supplied, but he explains only the following σείω οὐ μόνον,
&c. In like manner, the ἵνα also has been mostly erroneously taken
as *ecbatic*, ' so that *what is immovable remains,*' instead of ' *in order*
that what is immovable *may* remain.' That the immovable may
remain, is the *design* of the displacing what is movable ; whose
remaining, therefore, must stand in an unavoidable contradiction with

that of the immovable. After these remarks, it at once appears, that what the author advances as the fundamental idea of this prophecy, and what we have discovered to be such, perfectly coincide. Every thing created, so far as it stands in opposition to the kingdom of God, must be shaken and broken to pieces, in order that this may endure and remain. How great and glorious then, the author hence infers, in ver. 28, must this βασιλεία ἀσάλευτος be! How earnestly must those to whom God grants admission into it, strive, by continuing in His favour, to walk in a manner well pleasing to Him! How must they govern their conduct with fear! For their God,— as the mercy shown to them so far surpasses that which had been before vouchsafed,—infinitely more than the God of the Old Testament (Deut. 4. 24), is a consuming fire.—The author has well perceived, that what is a mere image in respect to the inferior realization of the idea, the shaking of the heaven and the earth, will be literally true in its highest and last realization. It is the same Divine agency which shakes the kingdoms of this world for the benefit of the kingdom of God, and which, in the last day, will annihilate the world itself (the fashion of which passes away [1]), so far as, pervaded by sin and evil, it is not suited for the seat of the glorious kingdom of God ; so that the prophecy and its citation are closely connected with those passages where the creation of a new heavens and new earth is predicted, Is. 65. 17. 66. 22; which passages have found, and still find, the prelude and the commencement of their fulfilment, in the shaking of the heathen and their kingdoms. For this renovation contains the germ, and the commencement of that which is to take place at the end of time. From these remarks, also, we may explain the near coincidence of the passage which rests upon Haggai, in the Epistle to the Hebrews, and that which rests upon Isaiah, 2 Pet. 3. 10 sq., the close connexion of which has not been sufficiently perceived and made use of by the interpreters of the Epistle to the Hebrews.

935. Ver. 7. ' *And I will shake all the heathen, and the beauty of all the heathen shall come, and I will fill this house with glory, saith the Lord, Sabaoth.*' We hold that the *person* of the Messiah is *not* here intended ; the old interpretation is erroneous only in respect of *form:* in substance the passage is still Messianic. By ' the *beauty* of all the heathen' [not the *desire*, for the word has never that meaning, though etymologically it *might* have it], we understand only ' *whatever is beautiful amongst them, all their costly good things* [2].'

936. With respect to the last words of the verse, ' *and I will fill this house with glory,*' they are referred by most of the older interpreters to the glorification of the Temple by the appearing of the Messiah, by Abarbanel and Hasæus, to the inhabitation of the Holy Spirit, with an appeal to Ex. 40. 34, 35. 2 Chron. 5. 13, 14. 1 Kings 8. 10, 11, and Ezek. 43. 4, where nearly the same words occur of the

---

[1] Comp. 1 Cor. 7. 31.

[2] This explanation is the oldest of all extant. It is found in the Seventy : καὶ ἥξει τὰ ἐκλεκτὰ πάντων τῶν ἐθνῶν. The Syriac also has it : *et excitaturus sum omnes gentes, ut afferant optatissimam quamque rem cunctarum gentium.*

dwelling of God in the tabernacle, in the Temple of Solomon, and in the new spiritual Temple.

937. Now we can hardly suppose that this coincidence is entirely accidental. Still, far less is to be inferred from it than has been by those interpreters. Against this is the very essential difference between those passages and the one before us, that there the discourse relates to a *definite glory*, the glory of *God*, the manifestation of His majesty, here only of *glory in general*[1]. This compels us to look, for the nearer determination of the glory, to what precedes. It consists in the coming of the beauty of all the heathen, which serves the Temple of the Lord for glory and for ornament, precisely as, Is. 60. 13, ' *The glory of Lebanon shall come to thee,*' &c., ' *to adorn the place of my sanctuary, and the place of my feet will I honour.*' The same reference requires also the ' *mine is the silver, and mine is the gold,*' of the following verse; and in like manner, ver. 9, where the predicted greater glory of the second Temple than that of the first should be referred, according to a comparison of ver. 3, only to that which according to ver. 3 was painfully missed in the present, and which the first Temple enjoyed. These remarks, however, do not preclude a very significant reference to those passages. The same God, who condescended at that time to lend to the Temple the highest ornament, the sharing of His honour, will even yet fill it with glory by the coming of the beauty of the heathen. And the conferring of this new glory presupposes the re-impartation of the former, and that in a far larger measure. For wherefore do the heathen come with their beauty? Surely for no other reason than because they perceive that God dwells in the midst of His people.

938. We must still notice an objection, which, with most older interpreters, Chladenius raises against the whole interpretation favoured by us: " *Commotio cœli, terræ, aridi, omnium gentium maximum quid spondet, et ecce quid tandem eveniet? scil. templum Hieros. auro gentium complebitur. Vehementer auri argentive splendore fascinatum esse oportet, qui cum commotione cœli etc. ornamenta aurea et argentea templi sec. conjungere cogitando queat.*' The most obvious answer is this : " Was it becoming for Isaiah, who has undeniably prophesied such things, and that in very lofty words, to do this? why not also for Haggai ? " But the full and true solution presents itself at once, when we understand only how to separate form and substance, kernel and shell, from one another. What was the deepest ground of the distress of the believers, on beholding the plan of the new Temple ? Certainly, not that the *taste* was not satisfied by a beautiful edifice. They beheld rather in the relation of the new Temple to the old one a copy of the present relation of God to themselves; a virtual declaration that His favour had departed from them, a matter-of-fact prophecy that it would not return. The distress, therefore, related to what was external, only so far as they regarded it as a copy of what was internal : and this form of the distress determined also the form of the consolation. Under the

---

[1] כָבוֹד, without the *artic.* and without a *suff.*

form of a prediction, that the Temple, to the building of which they were to be encouraged, should be glorified, God caused the assurance to be imparted to them that He *had not rejected His people ;* that all His promises were ever yea and amen, and that His now despised kingdom should hereafter, when His time arrived, surpass all the kingdoms of the world in glory. There is, undeniably, a true Divine accommodation, which affects only *the form* of the truth ; there is a *false* one, which perverts its very essence. This true accommodation runs through all God's deeds and discourses, from Paradise to Christ. What else was it, when He promised to His disciples a hundred fold more of earthly goods than they should lose on His account ? What else, when He encouraged them by the prediction, that they should sit on twelve seats judging the twelve tribes of Israel ? When He allowed their supposition, that there was such a thing as sitting on His right hand and on His left, and did not correct this form (in which the idea must necessarily be represented, in accordance with their education and spiritual state), but only their view, which related to the essence, and had its root in sin, of the conditions of this honour ? When, without meeting the erroneous physical conceptions, which might, in the minds of His disciples, be so easily connected therewith, He taught them to pray to a God *in the heavens ?* Such an accommodation is found in all that He reveals, either personally, or by His apostles, concerning the state after death, and the kingdom of glory. He gives it to us precisely as the description of the paradisiacal condition, in the form in which *we can comprehend it.* Ought he entirely to withhold from us *the idea,* because it is *inconceivable* by us in its *own proper form ?* This latter example is the more illustrative, since the pious of the Old Testament stood in the same relation to the kingdom of grace that we stand in to the kingdom of glory. The same is here true of prophecy which was true of the law. It may be said of it also, that heaven and earth shall sooner pass away, than one jot or tittle of it fail ; comp. Matt. 5. 18. 24. 35. But as in the law, so also in the prophecy, that which is *eternal,* even *in its smallest elements,* because grounded in the nature of God, is not the *letter,* but the *spirit,* which is not to be sought apart from the letter, but is involved in it. Such an accommodation is set before us also for imitation. Or ought we not, perhaps, to speak with children at all of heaven, because we can only speak with them concerning it in a childish manner ? Rather the childish form of the idea is exactly the *true one* for the child. For it is only in this form that the idea is comprehensible by him. Every other would lead him into errour in respect to the very essence.

939. It will now also easily appear, what should be held in respect to the fulfilment of this prophecy. Even in the form and drapery in which it is here presented, there was a feeble prelude of the fulfilment. To this belonged every gift, which, in the time when the Old Testament still continued, was consecrated to the Temple by proselytes out of heathenism from true love to the God of Israel, just as in every outward assistance which the Lord vouchsafes to

His people, His promise, Matt. 19. 29, is realized. But we must *not* regard as belonging to the fulfilment that which several interpreters, adhering to the letter, take as its completion, the adorning of the Temple at the time of the Maccabees, and that at the time of Herod. Not the former, for here the discourse is of a glorification of the Temple, which should proceed from the *heathen*, awakened to repentance and faith by God's outward and inward dealings. Not the latter, for although Herod was a heathen by descent, still his zeal for the Temple did not spring from faith and love. In reference to that event, the remark of Calvin is entirely just: " *Conatus est diabolus larvam ipsis objicere, ut desinerent sperare in Christum.*" Only we must go still further; not merely had Satan this conscious purpose, but his instrument, Herod, had it also. It was not accidental, that the second Temple was so very far behind the first in glory, that the literal fulfilments of the prophecy were so seldom and so small, and, in general, the whole condition of the people, from the exile until the time of Christ, was so poor and mean,—precisely, as God has His own wise and holy purposes in being so sparing in the literal fulfilment of Matt. 19. 29. " *Si æque opulentum fuisset Templum,*" remarks Calvin, " *et si regni etiam species fuisset, qualis antea fuerat, Judæi acquievissent in illis externis pompis ; ita contemtus fuisset Christus, imo pro nihilo fuisset spiritualis Dei gratia.*" The inferior realizations were withdrawn from the people, in order that they might not cleave to the accidental, "*the gold and silver,*" and, satisfied with the present, cease to long after the complete fulfilment. This longing seemed to Herod too strong ; he feared that the heavenly kingdom might infringe upon his earthly dominion. His building of the Temple proceeded on the same principle as his murder of the children in Bethlehem. He wished to hinder the coming of the kingdom of God. He wished to transfer the longed-for *last days* to the present. This purpose, even the special reference to our prophecy, clearly appears in the account of Josephus, *b.* 15, *c.* 11. It explains, e. g., the assumption in the discourse of Herod, that the second Temple must necessarily equal the first in height.—Haggai had, indeed, prophesied, that the glory of the second Temple would be greater than that of the first, comp. Joseph. 15. 11. § 1 : Τὸν γὰρ ναὸν τοῦτον ᾠκοδόμησαν μὲν τῷ μεγίστῳ Θεῷ πατέρες ἡμέτεροι μετὰ τὴν ἐκ Βαβυλῶνος ἀνάστασιν· ἐνδεῖ δὲ αὐτῷ πρὸς τὸ μέγεθος εἰς ὕψος ἑξήκοντα πήχεις· τοσοῦτον γὰρ ὑπερεῖχεν ὁ πρῶτος ἐκεῖνος, ὃν Σολομὼν ἀνῳκοδόμησε. Thence the words : Ἐπειδὴ δὲ νῦν ἐγὼ μὲν ἄρχω Θεοῦ βουλήσει, περίεστι δὲ καὶ μῆκος εἰρήνης καὶ κτῆσις χρημάτων καὶ μέγεθος προσόδων, τὸ δὲ μέγιστον, φίλοι καὶ δι' εὐνοίας οἱ πάντων, ὡς ἔπος εἰπεῖν, κρατοῦντες Ῥωμαῖοι κ. τ. λ. Here the reference to our prophecy is not to be mistaken. Herod seeks to show, that all the conditions of the glorification of the Temple contained in it were actually present. With him the πάντων κρατοῦντες Ῥωμαῖοι equal ' all the heathen,' who should promote the building of the Temple ; called by God to the dominion, he has gold and silver enough ; the words, ' I will give *peace* in this place,' are now fulfilled. How he employed every means in order to fulfil 'greater will be the glory,' &c., appears from the words in § 3, τὰς δαπάνας τῶν πρὶν ὑπερβαλλόμενος, ὡς οὐκ ἄλλος τις ἐδόκει ἐπικεκοσμηκέναι τὸν ναόν. Fictitious miracles must serve to announce the work as under the special guidance of God. And many —such, that is, who were no loss, and who *were* to yield to this trial of their faith—did actually suffer themselves to be so far befooled, as to hold the very man whose dominion was the greatest proof of God's displeasure,—a hammer by which God designed to break in pieces the hard heart of Israel,—as an instrument of the Divine mercy. The believers, however, continued to wait, as before, for the consolation of Israel. They put in the place of the apparent fulfilment the true, whose highest completion will then first take place, when the whole fulness of the heathen shall have come into the kingdom of God, and this shall have been exalted to full glory.

940. In the controversy with the Jews, great stress was laid upon our prophecy; not so much, however, in the time of the fathers, when by the 'house of God,' the *Church* was understood, as at a later period. During the existence of the second Temple [it was urged] the desire of the heathen, the Messiah, was to make his appearance. How vain, therefore, is the hope of Israel, who still expect a Messiah, since the Temple has long been destroyed. Against this argument only *one* doubt seemed to arise,—the rebuilding of the second Temple by Herod. Some sought to remove this doubt by a wrong method, by the supposition, opposed to the plain letter of Josephus, that this rebuilding was not total. On the other hand, the correct course for removing the difficulty was taken by J. A. Ernesti, when, in the treatise *de Templo Herodis M.* he undertook to prove, and actually did prove, " 1. *Herodem templum totum a fundamentis reædificasse, destructo per partes vetere.* 2. *Ex consuetudine loquendi historica, omninoque populari Templum illud nihilominus secundum et fuisse et recte appellatum esse.*" We still subjoin to the grounds brought forward by him, that the very design of Herod, already pointed out, necessarily required the identity of his Temple with that of Zerubbabel; that this was certainly a chief reason why he caused it to be pulled down and rebuilt by one part at a time; further, that the name of a *new* Temple, not in an architectural, but a religious sense, can, with right, be given only to one whose erection coincides with a new era in the history of the Theocracy, so that the new period is outwardly represented by the new Temple.

941. Now this older method of arguing seems entirely to lose its force, according to our exposition. The reference to the *person* of the Messiah vanishes. The Temple comes no further under consideration as an edifice, but as a seat of the kingdom of God, as designating this itself. On a closer examination, however, it appears, that the argument only needs a new application, in order completely to regain its power. We need only understand the destruction of the second Temple, not *outwardly*, but as *what it was*, a declaration on the part of God, that His kingdom had been removed from the Jews; and consider, moreover, that this declaration

has been continually made in the destinies of the Jews for eighteen centuries past; we shall be convinced, that if a continuation of the kingdom of God, and a fulfilment of the promises of Haggai, cannot be elsewhere pointed out, he must necessarily appear as a fanatic, and that all those who regard him as a prophet of the true God, must be compelled to seek the fulfilment elsewhere. If the glorification was to be imparted to the second Temple, (= the kingdom of God, which the Temple represented in its second period,) we cannot conceive an *interruption* of this glorification, a *cessation* of all manifestations of God, as the covenant God, during a period, in comparison with which the former, which designates the cessation of the first period, comes the less into consideration, since, during that, love and mercy, in the most manifold expressions, accompanied earnestness and severity. If the glorification was to be imparted to the second Temple, no destruction of it can consist with the credibility of the prophet, but such as, according to the idea, was a glorious *improvement;* a decay, like that of the seed corn which perishes in the earth in order to bring forth much fruit. But here [we may say to the Jews] we have, in your view of things, a destruction, which is only destruction! Should a final fulfilment of the promise of the prophet be still expected with reason, no period must intervene entirely without current fulfilments. Even he himself designates his promise as one which wanted only yet "a little" of the fulfilment. Here, however, we have eighteen centuries, in which God is not God, in order that, on occasion, he may once more *become God* again! He is a fool who rests his hopes upon what is absolutely future. He feeds upon wind and ashes. Either the Lord is with us every day, or He comes not again. He who does not taste in the present how good and gracious the Lord is, will not do it in the future. There is in the future no pure commencement; there is only completion, as certainly as God will not first *become* God in the future, but *is* God already in the present. The believers in Israel, who, before the appearing of Christ, waited for the consolation of Israel, would have been just as foolish as the modern Jews, if they had not already experienced this consolation in the present and the past. The modern unbelief of the Jews is only a manifestation of that which existed before unconsciously. A man may, perhaps, *fancy* himself to hope in the absolute future; may *fancy* himself to believe in a God, who will show himself a God, for the first time, hereafter, so firmly, as to become a martyr for this imaginary faith and hope; but for all this he does not yet *really* hope and believe. For the true hope and the true faith is an ὑπόστασις τῶν ἐλπιζομένων, Heb. 11. 1, and this has the relative present as a necessary foundation of the future. Now the longer God delays to become God, the more generally must this imagination vanish. Atheism is the goal to which modern Judaism is rapidly advancing. A renovation of the more ancient, which, with all its abhorrence of idolatry, is still, in precisely the principal point, identical with it, since it reverences a God who gives no evidence of His power and goodness in the present, is entirely inconceivable. Christianity and atheism will divide the spoil between them.

942. Ver. 8. '*Mine is the silver, mine is the gold, saith the Lord, Sabaoth.*' The phrase ' mine is,' forms the ground of '*mine will be,*' in what precedes and follows.

943. Ver. 9. '*Great will be the glory of this last house, above the first, hath spoken the Lord, Sabaoth, and in this place will I give peace, saith the Lord, Sabaoth.*' The place is Jerusalem. The promise belongs to it, so far as it is a seat and central point of the kingdom of God. To understand with most Christian interpreters, by this *peace*, spiritual peace, is equally arbitrary, as when, with Vitringa and others, for the *gold* and *silver* here, as in Isaiah, a *spiritual good* is substituted, which can be called so only figuratively. That outward peace is intended in the first instance, is evident, even from the parallel passage, Is. 60. 18, '*There is no more violence in thy land, wasting and destruction in thy borders, and thou shalt call thy walls Salvation, and thy gates Praise.*' If, however, the promise is carried back to its idea, it appears, that what the interpreters erroneously attach to the *word* (i. e. *pax spiritualis* or *quævis benedictio et prosperitas*) is virtually comprehended under its full meaning.—We may remark however that this prophecy, with all those that make *peace* the characteristic mark of the Messianic times, looks forward, for its final and *literal* accomplishment, to the kingdom of glory,—to the new earth on which dwelleth righteousness.

THE PROPHET MALACHI

Preliminary Observations

944. The grounds which Vitringa advances for his thesis (p. 360), " *Editam hanc prophetiam esse circa illud tempus, quo Nehemias altera vice ex Persia rediit in Cananæam, quod accidit post a.* 32 *Artaxerxis,*" have met with general acceptance. The only room for doubt is, whether the coming forward of Malachi is to be placed *shortly before,* or *shortly after,* or *entirely coincides with* the reformation, which marked the second coming of Nehemiah. The last supposition is the most probable[1]. The time *before* cannot so well be thought of, since the power of the abuses then existing appears as wholly unbroken, which presupposes, that God for a time had left the people more to themselves ; and, moreover, because, chap. 1. 8, a leader of the civil affairs is mentioned as being present among the people. Nor the time *afterwards,* because the reforming agency of Nehemiah, from the nature of the case, and his own official account, cannot be considered as without effect. Probably, therefore, the *contemporary activity* of Malachi stood to that of Nehemiah in the same relation as that of Haggai and Zechariah to that of Joshua and Zerubbabel. By the side of the reforming labours of Nehemiah, which were chiefly outward, proceeded those of Malachi, which were internal. Nehemiah cast all the furniture of the house of Tobias out of the chamber, ver. 8. ' *If ye do it not,*' — thus does he threaten the sabbath-breakers, ver. 21,—' *so will I lay hand on you.*' The men who have taken strange wives he smites, and plucks off their hair, ver. 25. Malachi, on the contrary, smites merely with the Divine word. He points emphatically to God's punishment already commenced among the people, and which would constantly become more manifest and severe, in proportion as the germ of corruption, already present, should the more develop itself. Such a parallel of internal and external reforming agency, runs through the whole history of Israel,—think, e. g., only of Isaiah and Hezekiah, Jeremiah and Josiah ; a merely external reformation is without example. [Dr. Hengstenberg then defends the opinion of Vitringa, that *Malachi* (= ' *my messenger,*') is the name not of *a person*[2], but of *an office :* shows that the prophecy contains but *one* discourse of like import, not consoling and promising, but warning and

---

[1] See, for the more accurate date, 735.

[2] Even in very ancient times the historical personality of Malachi was doubted. The Seventy certainly held the name as a mere name of office. They translate מַלְאָכִי בְּיַד by ἐν χειρὶ ἀγγέλου αὐτοῦ. Also the Chaldee, which, after the name of Malachi, subjoins *qui alias Ezra scriba vocatur.* Jerome also certainly followed the Jewish tradition, when he expressed this same view.

threatening : but that this is no mark of "a feeble and superannuated spirit" (as Eichhorn and De Wette have asserted), but arose necessarily from the particular manifestations of self-righteousness which the Prophet had to combat. He then reviews the general argument, and traces its connexion.]

Chapter 2:17-3:6

945. Ver. 17. '*Ye weary the Lord by your words, and ye say, Whereby do we weary him? With your saying, Every one who doeth evil is good in the eyes of the Lord, and in them hath he pleasure, or, Where is the God of justice?*' The persons represented as wearying God by their speeches, are the great mass of the people, with the exception of the truly pious ; they yet manifested, though with an unwilling heart, their reverence for the Lord by sacrifice, fasted, longed for the appearance of the covenant angel, &c. The expression, '*ye weary*,' shows the greatness of the transgression. How ungodly must discourses be, whereby the long-suffering God, who has patience with the *weakness* of his people, is, as it were, overcome, and compelled to manifest his penal justice. On the phrase, '*Whereby do we weary?*' Calvin appropriately remarks, that they asked this, not in a spirit of *doubt*, but in a spirit of hardened obstinacy, that, denying the charge, despised and mocked at the objurgations of the prophet—'*Every one who doeth evil is good in the eyes of the Lord.*' By the '*evil-doers*,' the *heathen* were understood. Agreeably to the nature of hypocrisy, the murmurers take cognizance of sin only when *not committed by themselves ;* and especially does that appear to them as such, as deserving the most fearful punishment, whereby they themselves are injured. As for the rest, the difference here is manifest between the enemies whom Malachi opposes, and the open despisers of God, whom we often find mentioned in the earlier prophets[1]. The latter deny the existence of God, or, at least, His omnipotence ; they ridicule and mock : the former, for the very reason that they fully acknowledge His omnipotence, believe that they must deny His justice. For, if nothing external can hinder Him, and they have fulfilled their duties towards Him, they *must* then be perplexed with regard to His justice. They murmur. The nature of their unsatisfied expectation we learn more clearly from the following verse, according to which, they expected the angel of the covenant. They hope, that as he had once led their fathers out of Egypt, and punished the Egyptians, so he would appear, immediately after the return from the exile, for judgement upon all the heathen, and blessing upon all Israel.—The words, '*and in them hath he pleasure*,' seemed to refer back to chap. 1. 10. '*No pleasure have I in you*,' had the Lord there declared to them. '*True, indeed*,' they answer, '*thou hast not pleasure in us, the righteous, but in the evil-doers.*'—The phrase, '*or where is the God of justice?*' i.q., "or, if it is not so, if God has no good pleasure in the ungodly, then

[1] e. g. Is. 5. 19. Jer. 17. 15.

point out to me the deeds in which the just God reveals Himself. Are not the prosperity of the heathen, and the affliction of Israel, directly opposed to such a revelation?" The errour consisted only in assuming with confidence that the question, ' *Where is the God of justice?*' could be answered only with *No where.* Although no where else,—the answer was near at hand,—still He shows Himself, even in your present affliction, which so corresponds with your moral condition ; and if this is not sufficiently obvious to you, He will hereafter manifest Himself in such a manner as will make you cease to ask, ' *Where is the God of justice?*'

946. Before the illustration of chap. 3. 1, we must necessarily consider the passage which we have merely touched before, Is. 40. 3—5, for upon it rests the answer made by Malachi to those who venture to call in question God's justice.

947. Ver. 3. ' *A voice crying in the desert, Prepare the way of the Lord! Make level in the wilderness a course for our God.* 4. *Let every valley rise up, and every mountain and hill subside, and the steep place become a plain, and the rugged place a valley.* 5. *And unveiled shall be the glory of the Lord, and all flesh shall behold it together ; for the mouth of the Lord hath spoken.*' The third and fourth verses contain the *antecedent* preparation for the coming of Jehovah, by the making a road for Him in the desert. The fifth verse describes the manifestation itself of Jehovah, with the glory and the salvation that He has to procure for man. The speech is abrupt : we must supply, *Hark! what do I hear?* a voice, &c. The reasons against joining in *the desert* with either the preceding or the following words are so strong, that it is better to consider them as standing independently with a virtual reference to both clauses. The *crying voice* proceeds from the *covenant people.*

948. The whole choir of the divine servants and heralds are those to whom, in the first verse, God's commission is given. The prophets do, indeed, take a very important position in this choir : but this the Prophet does not yet take into view. He has, in ver. 1, 3, and 6, exactly as in the ninth verse, to do only with an ideal person, the *messenger of the Lord* (comp. Mal. 3. 1), and in his declaration the actual persons have part, only so far as the ideal is realized in them. Members of the covenant people, who, endowed by God with the gifts of His Spirit, are appointed His heralds, speak to the covenant people. The expression, ' *our God,*' in a connexion where the discourse is of the God of Israel, shows this clearly.

949. ' *Preparing a way,*' designates the removal of every thing which can hinder the revelation of the Lord. But it is rendered more definite by the circumstance that the people themselves are exhorted to engage in the work. All *outward* preparations for the manifestation of the salvation, belong to the Lord ; the people can only remove its *internal* obstacles, by turning themselves, with His assistance, to the Lord in true repentance   Of this alone, not of any

thing outward, does Malachi think; *this* was found here by the Saviour, John the Baptist, the Evangelists.

950. Now also the meaning of the *desert* is evident. The people find themselves in the condition of spiritual and corporeal wretchedness, the latter of which is to be considered only as a reflex of the former. Out of this condition (which is represented under the *image of the desert,* because they formerly found themselves in a like condition in *an actual desert;* not accidentally, but so that the outward residence was chosen by God as a true emblem of the condition), will the Lord deliver them; but in order that this may happen, they must first perform their own part. The Lord *can* prepare no way through the desert, unless the people themselves have first prepared such a one; and to do this, He causes them to be exhorted by his servants.

951. Now also is the relation of ver. 3—5 to ver. 1, 2, clear. In ver. 1, 2, it is announced to the people, that the Lord has determined to show them mercy, and impart to them the fulness of his salvation. With this promise is connected the exhortation to the people, to cast away every thing which can restrain the course of the salvation. John says: Μετανοεῖτε· ἤγγικε γὰρ ἡ βασιλεία τῶν οὐρανῶν: the Prophet changes the order,—but still with entirely the same sense — ἤγγικε ἡ βασιλεία τῶν οὐρανῶν, μετανοεῖτε οὖν. Every exhortation to repentance necessarily pre-supposes God's mercy; out of every promise of salvation arises the exhortation to repentance. For there is no purely external salvation for the covenant people. Entirely analogous, e. g., is Jer. 31. 22. The apostate Israel is exhorted to return to her rightful lord. For he is now preparing a new condition of things; he chooses again to receive into his communion her who had been rejected on account of infidelity.

952. In ver. 5, a diversity of interpretation is found in reference to the last words.—The word '*to see,*' frequently occurs in his writings in the way in which the Seventy have here understood it, sometimes with a definite object expressed, as chap. 52. 10 (from which the Seventy take what they supply): '*and all the ends of the earth shall see the salvation of our God* [1];' sometimes with something to be supplied out of the preceding, as chap. 52. 14. Had we not, however, these analogies, still the '*glory of the Lord*' must be regarded as the *object* of the seeing, because '*shall see*' too plainly refers to '*shall be revealed.*' The glory of the Lord is unveiled, and now all flesh beholds this splendid sight.—The expression, '*for the mouth of the Lord hath spoken,*' is the constant one with the Prophet, to confirm a prediction which appears incredible; it will surely be fulfilled, for it has not a shortsighted, feeble man, but the allwise and almighty God for its author; comp. 1. 20. 34. 16. 58. 14. (οὐ γὰρ θελήματι ἀνθρώπου ἠνέχθη ποτὲ προφητεία, 2 Pet. 1. 21.)

953. But what is to be understood by the '*revealing of the glory*

---

[1] So 35. 2. 62. 2. 66. 18.

of the Lord ?' The expression plainly rests on Exod. 16. 10, '*And it came to pass, as Aaron spake to the whole assembly of the children of Israel, that they turned themselves toward the desert, and, behold, the glory of the Lord appeared in the cloud.*' The glory of the Lord, his excellent being, making itself known in the symbol of the fire, usually concealed by the covering of clouds, because Israel was not yet ripe for its revelation, for an immediate communion with the divine,—even their leader, Moses, not yet, to whom, on his wish to see God without a veil, it was explained, that he could not endure his countenance,—where it was important to convince the doubting and murmuring people, that God was among them, appeared more strongly than usual through the covering.   This covering, the prophet announces, will entirely disappear on the renewing of the march through the desert, when the people have first prepared the way.   A new period arrives, in which God reveals Himself far more clearly and gloriously, the people behold God far more plainly, are joined with Him far more inwardly, possess Him far more really with the fulness of His gifts and blessings, than formerly.

954. It scarcely needs to be remarked, that the prophecy, in its essential reference, is Messianic.   The bringing back out of the exile was only a prelude and preparation for the proper fulfilment. The measure of the revealing of the glory of the Lord stood in an entirely equal relation to the degree in which the way was prepared. The complete revelation took place in Christ, but the beholding was vouchsafed only to those who had prepared the way, for only those who are pure in heart can see God.   We now return to Malachi from this necessary digression.

955. Chap. 3. 1. ' *Behold, I will send my messenger and he shall prepare a way before me, and suddenly the Lord, whom ye seek, will come to his Temple, and the covenant angel, whom ye desire, behold, he shall come, saith the Lord of Hosts.*'   The reference to Isaiah is by no means to be mistaken.   It is especially evident in the ' *he shall prepare (a) way,*' compared with '*prepare ye (a) way*' in Isaiah[1]. Our attention being awakened by this coincidence in the expression, we then soon find that the coincidence in the *substance* runs through the whole verse.   Here the messenger of the Lord levels the way before him.   In Isaiah the servants of the Lord call aloud to the people to prepare the way ; but there is no real difference, for the *preparation* here spoken of is evidently a *moral* preparation.   And how can the messenger of the Lord otherwise *prepare the way*, than by exhorting those to whom he had been sent to prepare it them- selves, than by loudly and unceasingly urging upon them the '*pre-*

---

[1] It even extends to the similar omission of the *artic.* in דֶּרֶךְ to be explained by the fact, that פַּנָּה דֶרֶךְ was regarded in a measure as one word, *to prepare a way*.

pare ye the way,' the μετανοεῖτε? In Isaiah the *preparation of the way* is followed by the *revealing of the glory of the Lord,* as here by His coming to His Temple. This similarity is no *accidental reminiscence,* but a designed agreement. Of all the prophecies, those of the second part of Isaiah were those which caused the greatest dissatisfaction to the Israelites. In these the salvation was painted in the most attractive colours, and the threatening kept more in the background; the whole being mainly designed to impart consolation to the *believing* portion of Israel. These prophecies were, therefore, those on which the hope of Israel in affliction chiefly fastened; and after the exile, when these hopes were so little realized, they became those which were chiefly used in complaining of the covenant faithfulness of God and His righteousness. Malachi, therefore, proves the injustice of these complaints by showing the people that it was not to *them,* being such as they were, that the Lord had promised such glorious things. The '*preparation of the way*' was to precede the revelation of God's glory. The Prophet therefore says in effect: "Ye, who, in inconsiderate zeal, complain of the non-fulfilment of the promises of the Lord, reflect that, according to his own declarations, the *bestowing of mercy* presupposes *repentance.* To this end He is now furnishing you, and will furnish you, with the means. Then will He appear suddenly, and make Himself known as a God of justice; not barely in bestowing blessings upon the pious, but also in inflicting punishment upon you, the *ungodly* members of the covenant people."—The question arises, who is to be understood by the '*my messenger.*'—We must, in the first place, prove, in opposition to Kimchi and Jarchi, that the discourse here is not of a heavenly, but of an earthly messenger of God. This appears especially from the following reasons. (1) From Isaiah. That there the voice, which admonishes to prepare the way, proceeds from the covenant people themselves, we have already seen. (2) From the parallel passage, ver. 23. He who is here named '*my messenger,*' is there designated as '*Elias the prophet,*' while, to the '*preparation of the way*' here, the *restoration of the disposition of the pious fathers,* there corresponds. (3) From the manifest contrast of '*my messenger,*' and '*covenant messenger.*' If we were to think of a heavenly messenger, it could be none other than the '*angel of the Lord;*' for that we must not change '*my* angel' into '*an* angel,' is self-evident. But '*my messenger*' must necessarily be different from '*the angel of the Lord,*' who, after Him, comes to His temple.—Still some truth lies at the foundation of the interpretation of Kimchi. The reference to Exod. 23. 20. is manifest, and cannot be accidental; the less so, since here, as well as there, a '*journey through the desert,*' and a '*preparation of the way,*' are treated of. It serves to draw attention to the essential unity to be found in the subject, notwithstanding the diversity of the persons. The one and the other, the sending of the heavenly and the earthly Messenger, flows from the same covenant faithfulness of God, the same favour towards the chosen race; so that since God has sent His Messenger to lead the people through the natural desert, He must now also send His Messenger to prepare the way through the spiritual desert. That former proceeding of God is accordingly prophetic of the present. At the same time, however, the reference to that former analogous proceeding of God, serves to awaken attention to the responsibility which here, as well as there, the abuse of the mercy brings with it. The sending of a divine messenger is never without its consequences; it either brings a blessing, or a heavier punishment.—If, now, it is established, that the messenger of God is an *earthly* one, the question first arises concerning the correctness of the most widely diffused interpretation, that which makes him '*John the Baptist.*' This question, however, can only relate to the *form* in which this explanation is commonly delivered, and, according to which, '*my angel*' is John, in his historical personality, to the exclusion of all other individuals. In essence, this interpretation remains perfectly correct, even when we find ground to understand by '*my messenger,*' an ideal person, the whole choir of the Divine messengers, who should prepare the way for the appearing of the salvation, should open the door to the coming mercy. For as the idea of the messenger chiefly concentrates itself in John, since God must send him because he had given the prophecy, and gave the prophecy because He must send him, he is surely in the most proper sense its object. But that not the whole fulfilment, but only its highest point, is to be sought in the appearance of John, that the prophecy rather embraces all, by whom, from the coming forward of our Prophet himself, God sought to lead the people to repentance, is manifest, for the following reasons. (1) The comparison of Isaiah favours it. That there the voice crying in the desert belongs to the whole choir of the servants of God, we have already seen ; ver. 1, where the address of God is directed to them in the plural, shows this clearly. (2) The expressions '*behold,*' and '*suddenly,*' scarcely allow us to think of an entirely vacant period of about five hundred years. (3) The Prophet has indicated, by taking from this passage the *name* of *Malachi*, that he considered *his own* agency as an efflux of the idea here presented; although he was very far from the thought of regarding it as solely and completely realized in himself, as appears particularly from ver. 23. (4) We are not justified in separating the judgement upon the covenant people, predicted in this portion, from that which is threatened in all the rest of the book. The latter, however, belongs, as to its commencement, to the nearest future, nay, even to the present, This is shown, e. g., by chap. 2. 1, 2 : '*And now this command is to you, ye priests, saith the Lord ; if ye will not hear, and not lay to heart, that ye give glory to my name, saith the Lord, Sabaoth, then send I upon you the curse, and curse your blessings ; yea, already have I cursed them* (as to the beginning), *for ye do not lay it to heart.*' (Well to be observed is '*if ye do not hear ;*' the preparation by His messenger, here also, precedes the manifestation of the Lord.) Further, chap. 3. 9 : '*With the curse are ye cursed, and still ye defraud me, the whole people,*' and ver. 10, according to which the windows of heaven are already shut, the blessing already withheld. If, now, according to the view of the

prophet, elsewhere expressed, the appearing of the Lord for judgement, and therefore also for blessing, commencing in the present,
extends through all times, we certainly cannot, without definite
grounds to justify us, assert, that He has in view exclusively the
last and most complete appearing, to the exclusion of all the preceding, without which the last could, indeed, have no reality. But
if now the predicted appearing of God belongs only, as to its completion, to the Messianic time, the same also is true of the sending
of the messenger; for this, indeed, precedes the appearing. (5) Not
to be overlooked is the reference of the words to chap. 2. 7, 8 : '*For
the lips of the priest should keep knowledge, and the people should
seek the law from his mouth; for the messenger of the Lord of Hosts
is he. And ye have departed from the way; ye make many stumble in
the law; ye have destroyed the Levitical covenant.*' Because the
priestly order, the usual messenger of the Lord, have not performed
their duty, therefore the Lord sends His extraordinary messenger;
He does what they should do; He brings back many from evil
doing; comp. 2. 6. with this verse, and ver. 24; then appears the
heavenly messenger of God to bless or to punish, according to the
relation to the covenant, and according to the regard paid to the call
to repentance by the earthly messenger. If, now, the priestly order,
as a messenger of God, is an ideal person, then also the same is to
be expected from the extraordinary messenger of God, who should
discharge the duty they had neglected. In contrast with the priest,
stands the prophet, comp. ver. 23. Now the promise, thus understood, rests on the same idea as that of Joel, concerning the sending
of the teacher of righteousness, comp. 826. In the Messianic
time it found its fulfilment, not merely in the coming forward of
John, but also in the incipient action of Christ, and the apostles
themselves, so far as this was a supplement and carrying forward of
that of John, one which pointed to the *approach* of the kingdom of
God, and prepared the way for it. John, however, may with justice
be regarded as its proper goal, since in him the idea presented itself,
not relatively, but absolutely; he was the forerunner of the Lord,
and nothing further, so that whatever of the agency of Christ was of
this character, may properly be reckoned with his own, while the
peculiar work of Christ belongs to the second promise of the Lord
coming to His temple, and of the covenant angel [1]. The divine
messenger is designated as a '*covenant messenger*,' because he is a
messenger on account of the covenant, His manifestations, as well
for blessing as for punishment, a consequence of the covenant. The
two earthly messengers also might have been thus named. But the
prophet had a special reason for thus naming the heavenly one,
because his appearing had been desired by the murmurers with an
appeal to the covenant. The covenant designates not one individual
act, but the covenant relation of God to Israel, enduring through all
times. Violation of this covenant on the part of the people, espe-

---

[1] מַלְאַךְ הַבְּרִית, not '*the messenger of the covenant*,' but '*the covenant messenger.*'

cially the priests, was the chief theme of the preceding discourses, comp. 2. 10, 11. 14; violation of this covenant on the part of God, was the chief object of the complaints of the people. The appearing of the covenant angel was to demonstrate the injustice of these complaints, and show the reality of the covenant in the punishment of its despisers.—But mere punishment is not conceivable among the covenant people : the blessing must always accompany it; nay, the punishment itself, according to another mode of conception, must be a blessing, since, by excluding the ungodly, it opens again a free course for the manifestation of God's mercy towards His purified people. That the covenant Messenger was to bestow blessings, clearly appears also in ver. 4. and 6. And so, afterwards, in ver. 17, 18. 20, according to which, God's mercy and His righteousness were to be equally visible in His appearing. That *punishment appears* to be his exclusive destination, is occasioned only by the circumstance, that his mission must bring punishment to those with whom the prophet had immediately to do.—We now briefly sum up the result. To the complaint of the people, that the appearance of things annihilated the idea of a righteous God, the prophet answers, that God would soon remove this apparent contradiction of the appearance and the idea. He, who now seemed to be absent, would soon appear in the person of ' *His heavenly messenger,*' after He had before made known His covenant faithfulness by the sending of an ' *earthly messenger.*' That this prediction received its final fulfilment in the appearing of Christ, in whom the ' *angel or messenger of the Lord,*' the λόγος, became flesh, need scarcely be remarked. In like manner, it is self-evident, that this final fulfilment must be sought, neither in the state of humiliation, nor in that of exaltation alone, but that both rather belong together as an inseparable whole. The appearing of Christ in humiliation contains in itself the germ of all which He accomplished and accomplishes, either of blessing or punishment in his state of exaltation.—It is still to be remarked, that the emphatic repetition, ' *behold, he shall come, saith the Lord of Hosts,*' is to be explained by the antithesis of the doubt of his coming, and the open denial of it, as expressed in chap. 2. 17.

956. Ver. 2. ' *And who shall endure the day of his coming, and who shall stand at his appearing? For he is like the refiner's fire, and as scourers' lye.*' The answer to the question ' Who?' is not ' *only a few,*' but ' *no man,*' precisely as Is. 53. 1. The prophet speaks, indeed, to the ungodly. Appealing to their conscience, he seeks to disclose to them the gross contradiction between their moral condition, and their longing after the coming of the Lord, which must be their destruction. Parallel is Amos 5. 18. only that there the discourse is of those who, *openly* ungodly, desire the day of the Lord in mockery; ' *Woe to those who desire the day of the Lord. Wherefore then the day of the Lord for you? It is darkness and not light.*' The coincidence of ' *And who shall endure the day of his coming,*' with Joel 2. 11, ' *Great is the day of the Lord, and very terrible, and*

who shall abide it [1] *?*' can the less be regarded as accidental, since a similar verbal reference to Joel is found also in the twenty-third verse. The prophet, in entire accordance with his conduct in the first verse, supports himself by the authority of a zealous predecessor, who had already, centuries before, designated the day of the Lord as destructive for the covenant people themselves, while those hypocrites regarded only the heathen as the object of the penal justice of God.—The *standing* is an antithesis with the *sinking* down of the guilty, from anguish and fearful expectation of the things which will then come. There is an allusion to the passage in Eph. 6. 13, '*that ye may be able to withstand in the evil day, and having done all, to stand.*' Luke 21. 36, '*Watch ye therefore, and pray always, that ye may be accounted worthy to escape all these things that shall come to pass, and to stand before the Son of man* [2]*.*' Apoc. 6. 16, 17, '*And said to the mountains and rocks, Fall on us, and hide us from the face of him that sitteth on the throne, and from the wrath of the Lamb: For the great day of his wrath is come; and who shall be able to stand?*' The case is the same with these passages in reference to Malachi, as with Malachi in reference to Joel. They do not contain an involuntary reminiscence, but stand like a citation, and show how the Lord and His Apostles understood our prophecy.—In the second half of the verse [3], the image of *fire* and of *lye* has a double reference; they are, in relation to the *dross* and the *filth*, burning and destroying; in reference to the *metals* and *clothes*, purifying. The former reference, as that belonging to those addressed, is here the prevailing one, as the '*for*' shows; that the prophet, however, has the other in view, is shown from the following verse, comp. Is. 1. 25, where the *purifying* appears as *a promise*, not as a threatening, '*and I will purify as the lye thy dross, and remove all thy lead.*'

957. Ver. 3. '*And he shall sit, refining and purifying silver, and shall purify the children of Levi and refine them as gold and as silver, and they shall become the Lord's, bringing sacrificial gifts in righteousness.*' In the foregoing verse, the Lord is as the fire; here, as the refiner Himself. The covenant people had this advantage over the heathen, that amidst all the mixture of dross, they still always retained a portion of noble metal, and therefore *could* be an object of purification. Passages like those of Ezek. 22. 18, '*All Israel* has become dross,' are to be understood relatively; as even the connexion there shows, where the image of the refiner is most fully carried out, —and then that the Lord *must* purify them, even on account of the covenant. That which is true of the covenant people as a whole,— a multitude of its outward members are *mere* dross,—is also true of

---

[1] וּמִי יְכִילֶנּוּ.

[2] Before ver. 34, '*and so that day come upon you unawares,*' with reference to פִּתְאֹם יָבוֹא in ver. 1.

[3] Gesenius, after J. D. Michaelis, would change the double image of *the fire* into a single one, appealing to the fact, that potash is used also in the purification of metals.

the individual believer [1]. That the *children of Levi* are especially
mentioned, as the object of the refining, is explained by the fact that
has been already pointed out, that they are the chief mark of the
prophet throughout his whole prophecy. Those who, according to
chap. 2. 8, had caused many to stumble in the law, he had represented as the chief authors of the prevailing corruption ; they had
also certainly been the leaders of the murmurers, to whose discourse,
cited in chap. 2. 17, the prophet here answers, comp. 1. 13. וְהָיוּ לַיהֹוָה
must, according to the accents, be separated from what follows, '*they
are to,*' or '*of the Lord,*' '*they now truly belong to him again, whom
they had so shamefully forsaken, and by whom they had been rejected,*'
1. 10, 2. 8. The explanation of Jahn, " *Ut sint Jehovæ offerentes
dona in justitiâ,*" not the priests, but who he does not determine, has
arisen only out of the effort to do away the reference to the priests.
His errour, even if the times of the chief fulfilment are regarded, is
shown by passages like Acts 6. 7 (πολύς τε ὄχλος τῶν ἱερέων ὑκήκουον
τῇ πίστει), and it is refuted even by the circumstance, that the action
of the Lord, in reference to the children of Levi in what precedes, is
described as purifying and not destructive. In consequence of it,
they now come forth from the furnace as (purified) silver and gold,
or, without a figure, they become the servants of the Lord, bringing
offerings in righteousness. The latter words refer back to, '*presenting upon mine altar polluted bread,*' chap. 1. 7. To the polluted
bread of the priests of that time, the prophet had already, in the
eleventh verse, opposed the *pure* meat-offering which the heathen
should thereafter present ; here he contrasts with it the righteous
meat-offering of the purified priesthood itself. The mere *outward
sacrifices* are not pleasant to God ; they are to Him like a corpse, an
abomination. The *animating spirit,* the thing designated, must first
be present ; then also will the body, the symbol, be well pleasing to
God.—By *offerings,* here, the older interpreters, with the exception
of several Catholics, who avail themselves of the passage to prove
the necessity of the sacrifice of the mass, for the most part understand
precisely the *spiritual sacrifices* of the New Testament : concerning
which see 1 Pet. 2. 5, '*to offer up spiritual sacrifices, acceptable to
God by Jesus Christ,*' comp. Rom. 12. 1. Heb. 13. 15, 16. But it
would be more correct to say, that the prophet (wishing to represent
the unchangeable *substance* in the Old Testament form, in which the
idea is visibly embodied,) leaves it undecided,—the decision not
belonging to *his* object,—whether the substance, devotion to the
Lord, would always manifest itself in this form or not : this was to
be decided from other passages. This view seems the more to be
well founded, when we reflect, that the prophecy is not Messianic,
except in its *final reference ;* that preliminary fulfilments of it would
happen even in the times of the Old Testament, where the substance
could not appear without the form. That, finally, the prophet did
not transfer the perpetuity of the substance to the Old Testament

[1] יָשַׁב may be taken either as a designation of continuance, implying that it
is a long operation, or as serving merely for description, as עָמַד Mic. 5. 3.

form, is evident from chap. 1. 11 ; where the prediction, that '*in all places of the earth*,' a pure offering should be presented to the Lord, presupposes *a total change of the form*, the cessation of the strict ordinances concerning the unity of divine service, the cessation of the whole Levitical worship. Ver. 24. also suggests a great revolution. If the land is smitten with the curse, so also must the Temple be profaned and destroyed, and thus the possibility of the bringing of offerings done away. It is hardly accidental, that, as well here as also chap. 1. 11, in respect to the converted heathen, and converted Israel, only unbloody sacrifices are spoken of, while the chastisement refers especially to the bloody sacrifices. In the case of the *offerings* [1], the thought of an *opus operatum* is far less likely to present itself. That which is external is far more easily known as a mere form, as a covering of the idea.

958. Ver. 4. '*And pleasant to the Lord shall be the offering of Judah and Jerusalem, as in the days of the ancient time, and as in the years of the past.*' If the priestly order, and with it the people, have returned to their former rectitude, so also does the *former* mercy of the Lord return. It is not without reason that the prophet magnifies the *former* mercy. The future brings to the covenant people nothing absolutely new. The revolution is an ἀποκατάστασις, the promise has the pledge of its reality in what had already existed. If the former has proceeded from the nature of God, so *must* it, when the conditions are again present in the future, manifest itself in a like manner [2]. The prophet had, perhaps, especially the times of David, and it is probable also those of the patriarchs, and the first years of the residence in the wilderness (comp. Jer. 2. 2) in his eye. The feeling of the wretchedness of the present caused these times to appear as far more distant than they really were, as lying as it were beyond all time. That, however, which appears to them in their distress as the most absolute past, shall hereafter again become the present.

959. Ver. 5. '*And I will draw near to you for judgement, and I will be a swift witness against the sorcerers, and the adulterers, and those who swear falsely, and oppress the hireling in his wages, and the widow, and the orphan, and bow down the stranger, and fear not me, saith the Lord.*' The means in the hand of God for the introduction of that better time, is the judgement upon those who, believing that it would not fall upon them, so earnestly desired it, and murmured at its delay. The discourse cannot here be of a judgement, which belongs purely to the distant future, but only of such a one as commences even in the present, and then, keeping pace with sin, constantly advances until it reaches its highest point. How the drawing near to judgement commences already in the present, is shown especially by the words 'ye *are* cursed with the curse,' in the following section, which is closely connected with this ver. 9, comp. also ver.

---

[1] מִנְחָה.

[2] Comp. Is. 1. 26. Lam. 5. 21. The expression, 'as the days,' &c., is concisely for 'as it was in the days,' &c.

11, according to which the devourer is already present [1]. *Hasty, quick*, stands in manifest antithesis with the procrastination of which the murmurers had accused God.—The address, as the manifest reference to chap. 2. 17 shows, is directed to all murmurers, to the whole ungodly mass. The *testimony* of God against the soothsayers, &c. is not, as several erroneously suppose, *verbal*, by His messenger, but *actual*, by matter of fact. The punishment suspended over them testifies of their guilt, which they so carefully concealed, while they even proceed so far in their wickedness as to challenge God to the judgement. The crimes particularly mentioned, which, at the end, in the words '*and fear not me*,' are referred back to *one* source, are altogether such as are severely threatened in the law, and intentionally designated by the prophet almost throughout, with the words of the law.—*Magic* was forbidden in the law under penalty of death, comp. Exod. 22. 17, Deut. 18. 13. How greatly it prevailed among the Jews after the exile, is evident from passages like Acts 8. 9, 13. 6, '*At Salamis they found* τινὰ μάγον, ψευδοπροφήτην Ἰουδαῖον, ᾧ ὄνομα Βαριησοῦς[2].'—As belonging to the category of adultery, the prophet had already, chap. 2. 10—16, characterized those connexions with heathen women, to the prejudice of Jewish wives, as also the levity with which divorce was practised. Where these more refined sorts of adultery are prevalent, there also the more gross are always common.—'*And who swear*,' &c., refers to Levit. 19. 12, "And ye shall not swear in my name לַשָּׁקֶר, i. e. *to a lie*,' so that *your oath belongs to a lie, is false. To swear in the name of* God, is so to swear, that a man thereby finds himself in the name of God, incorporated with it. Whoever now breaks such an oath, as much as in him lies, makes God a liar. As it is said in the decalogue, he carries God's name to that which is nothing, does all in his power to bring together the greatest of all extremes, God, and that which is nothing. According to this mode of consideration prevailing in the Scripture, though usually mistaken because the emphatic meaning of the name of God is not regarded, perjury is the extreme of hypocrisy, the fundamental characteristic of which is the transferring of the name of God to that which is nothing, in opposition to the command to sanctify the name of God, to transfer that which is nothing to it, in order that, as it is holy in itself, it may become more and more holy also in the world. —The words '*and they oppress*,' &c. allude to Deut. 24. 14. '*And turn aside the stranger*,' refers back to Deut. 27. 19. 24. 17, '*And thou shalt not receive in pledge the garment of the widow*' (the same three also combined, ver. 19.) The law breathes the tenderest love towards the *strangers*[3] sojourning in Israel,—the expression is entirely general, comprehending as well those who had been incorporated with the covenant people by circumcision, as those who had not[4]; affording a certain proof that the charge against the religion of the Old Testament, of the *odium humani generis* is groundless, and that the special love commanded towards their own nation did not

---

[1] מְמַהֵר.   [2] Jos. *Arch.* 20. 6. *B. Jud.* 2. 12. 23.   [3] גֵּרִים.
[4] Of the former, e. g., Exod. 12. 19; of the latter, Deut. 14. 21.

exclude universal philanthropy, but laid the foundation for it.
Thus it is said, Exod. 23. 9, '*And the stranger thou shalt
not oppress, and ye know the heart of the stranger, for ye were
strangers in the land of Egypt.*' '*And ye fear not me,*' properly
stands in the front, as the source of all other transgressions ; but the
prophet places it last, because he has to do with hypocrites, to whom
the badness of the tree must first be proved from the badness of its
fruit.

960. Ver. 6. '*For I am Jehovah, I change not, and ye children of
Jacob do not come to an end.*' The attempts to give the *for* another
meaning, have originated solely from overlooking how every *judgement* upon the people of God is, at the same time, a *mercy*. '*I am
Jehovah,*' the name *Jehovah* (properly *Jahvah*, *fut.* of the verb הוה,
the older form for היה, *he is*, or *he who exists*)—designates God as the
pure existence, in antithesis with all that is created, the existence of
which is always relatively a non-existence. Out of the *purity* of the
existence, arises the *immutability* of the being ; because *God is*, so is
He also *He who is* perpetually the same. And out of the immutability of the *being*, necessarily results the immutability of the *will*
resting upon the being. If, then, God had concluded a covenant
with Israel, and sealed to him his election, so must God *cease to be
Jehovah*, and therefore the true God, if He suffered Israel to go to
ruin ; and because He *is*, and *remains Jehovah*, the existing, the immutable, so does He now exercise judgement upon the covenant
people, to preserve them from destruction. Finally, '*are not consumed*,' or '*come not to an end*,' is casually connected with '*sons of
Jacob*,' as '*I change not*' is with Jehovah, so the sense might be expressed : "*for I am Jehovah, and you the children of Jacob.*' The sons
of Jacob are at the same time sons of Irsael. *Israel*, however, imports,
according to the meaning given by God Himself, at the solemn imparting of this name to the father of the tribe, and in him to his
descendants, Gen. 32. 29, *God's wrestler*, him who, by prayer and
supplication, has overcome God, not letting Him go until he was
blessed, and forcing his way through all hindrances and temptations
to his favour [1]. In the struggle with God, the struggle with men
also is implied, who could injure and destroy only as God's instruments, comp. Gen. 1. c. ; and where once a whole church has gained
this victory, and made her election sure, there must *Israel* so surely
remain *Israel*, as *God is Jehovah*. The individuals who merely bear
the name and appearance of the sons of Israel, the faithless sons,
Deut. 32. 10, the souls which have been cut off from among their
people, because they have destroyed the covenant, not only *can*, but
must be destroyed by the judgement of God ; but the whole can
never perish [2].

[1] Comp. also Hos. 12. 4.
[2] Parallel passages which concern Jehovah's immutability in general, are
Num. 23. 19. 1 Sam. 15. 29. James 1. 17. Parallel passages in reference to
Israel's indestructibility, grounded on the unchangeableness of Jehovah, are
Jer. 30. 11. Lam. 3. 22, 23.

Chapter 3:13-4:6

961. Ver. 13. ' *Ye do violence to me with your speeches, saith the Lord, and [yet] ye say, What do we speak against thee* [1] *?* '

962. Ver. 14. ' *Ye say, Vain is it to serve God, and what gain, that we keep his guard, and walk mournfully before the Lord of Hosts* [2]*.*' ' *To walk mournfully,*' properly *atrate*, signifies the outward habit in fasts. Black is the colour of mourning, comp. Ps. 35. 14. 39. 7. 42. 10. Eccl. 9. 8, but at the same time the mourning and penitential garments were of very coarse stuff, and the wearing of them immediately upon the body was a sort of penitence. When a man treated himself harshly [3], he declared by his action that he felt himself to be a sinner, and deserving of every punishment. Here the discourse is especially of voluntary fasts, where the notion of merit was especially easy, partly of the whole people, partly of individuals [4]. To the voluntary chastisements of the latter even the law has regard, (comp. Num. 30. 14,) which *expressly* commands fasting, only in reference to the feast of atonement, (comp. Levit. 16. 29. 31,) *indirectly*, however, voluntary fasts also. For since it demands repentance for every sin, and fasting at that time was the usual embodying of repentance, so that the thing signified could scarcely be thought of without the sign, the former was properly commanded together with the latter.—The fasting is designated as proceeding from the face of the Lord, because it is undertaken for His sake, and for this very reason do the people think it so unjust, that they have no gain therefrom.—In reference to the sense of the whole verse, the expression of a reprobate mind must not be sought in the expression, *what gain*. The demand for such a resignation as is far beyond the reach of joy and suffering, may, perhaps, suit modern philosophers, for whom God is one absolutely afar off; but does not suit the Scripture, which expects the manifestation of the omnipotence, righteousness, and love of God in the future, only because they already manifest themselves in the present. ' *Godliness,*' says the Apostle, 1 Tim. 4. 8, ' *is profitable unto all things,*

---

[1] The meaning *gravis, durus, molestus fuit*, ' *have been* [*stout* ' in Engl. vers.] which the interpreters commonly here assume, is not established by the usage, and the meaning *to do violence* is to be preferred, even on account of the accurately corresponding הוֹגִיעַ, in chap. 2. 17. God bridles His anger, Is. 48. 9, but they go so far in their wickedness, as at last to exhaust His patience.

[2] מִשְׁמֶרֶת (comp. on the *fem.* in the nouns with מ, whereby the abstract is more definitely expressed, Ewald, p. 315), has the meaning *attention, observation, care*, comp. e. g. Num. 18. 8, ' *Behold, I give to thee the care of my heave-offerings ;*' other passages in Gesenius. ' The attention of any one,' or ' to attend to a thing,' is to observe him or it. This meaning is, without a single exception, applicable to all the passages where the phrase occurs.

[3] The *term. tech.* in the Pentateuch for fasting is עִנָּה נֶפֶשׁ, *to afflict the soul ;* it is remarkable, that צוּם with its derivatives, does not occur in all the Pentateuch.

[4] Comp. Josh. 2. 15. Judges 20. 26. 1 Sam. 7. 6. 31. 13.

having promise of the life that now is and of that which is to come.'
And where this promise seems to be contradicted by the appearance,
there do we frequently hear from the true believer a complaint which
is outwardly entirely similar to that here expressed, and still is not
sinful like it; comp. e. g. Ps. 73. 13, *' Only in vain have I cleansed
my heart, and washed my hands in innocency.'* The sinfulness here
lies rather in the opinion, that their merely outward service, poor as
even this must have been according to the foregoing accusations, was
a real service of God; that their fasting,—a body without a soul, a
corpse without a spirit—an *empty* form,—was a true fast.

963. Ver. 15. *' And now we call the proud happy, the workers
of iniquity are built up, yea, they tempt God and escape.'* There
is here a clear r .ference to ver. 12. Even this reference shows, that
here by the *proud* the heathen must be understood. The being
built up, is, i. q., *incrementa capere*, (comp. Jer. 12. 16, 17. Exod.
1. 21,) which latter passage, *'And it came to pass, because the mid-
wives feared God, that He* built them houses,' the murmurers perhaps had especially in view. "How, indeed, (they asked,) can God
still be God? Once, as a God of justice, He built houses for *those
who feared God,* now He builds them for the haughty despisers."
The *proud* is a direct antithesis of the *' they tempt God*[1].' The
prophet had in ver. 10 exhorted the people to prove God by true
righteousness, whether He would manifest Himself by blessings as
the God of justice. "What need of this trial on our part?" answer
the murmurers. The heathen have already made it. They have,
as it were, diligently endeavoured to call forth, by their crimes, God's
judgments. Now if God does not stand this trial, if He does not
show His justice in their punishment, how dare we hope that He
will manifest Himself to us as the God of right by the imparting
of blessings?

964. Ver. 16. *' Then those who feared God spake often to one
another; and the Lord attended and heard, and a book of remembrance
was written before him for those who feared God, and who thought
upon his name.'* To the accusations against God of the ungodly
mass (comp. the *whole* people in ver. 9), who thought themselves
pious, the discourses of the truly pious remnant who justified God,
are here opposed. The *then* shows that the latter were occasioned
by the former, and were opposed to them. And thus the contents
of their discourses are sufficiently designated, and there was less
need of a verbal citation of their Theodicæa, since it must be essentially identical with that given by the prophet himself. They held
the same language as Peter, in an entirely similar case, in the last
times of the Jewish state, when the spirit of murmuring against God,
having reached its highest point, passed over from the Jews to the
weaker portion of the Jewish Christians,—a fact, the knowledge of
which alone furnishes the key to the Second Epistle of Peter, as also
the Epistle to the Hebrews: it necessarily implies an influence of

[1] Compare respecting the intentional repetition of זֵדִים and רִשְׁעָה עֹשֵׂי in the
answer of the prophet, ver. 19.

the Jewish spirit of the times upon the converted Jews, analogous to that which, in our time, the revolutionary spirit exercises upon many Christians; we need only, as the counterpart of the seducers with whom the Apostle contends, think of such a person as the Abbé Lamennais,—comp. 2 Pet. 3. 9, '*The Lord is not slack concerning his promise, as some men count slackness; but is long-suffering to us-ward, not willing that any should perish, but that all should come to repentance.*' Ver. 15, '*And account that the long-suffering of our Lord is salvation.*' Ver. 17, '*Ye therefore, beloved, seeing ye know these things before, beware lest ye also, being led away with the error of the wicked, fall from your own stedfastness.*' As therefore the substance of the speeches of the pious is sufficiently determined, there can be no ground (with v. Til, J. D. Michaelis, Bauer, Theiner, and others,) to force upon the prophet a verbal citation by an interpretation contrary to the usage of the language. We have an admonition to the pious, in the form of history. The prophet, while he describes what they did, shows them what they *should* do, and that, more emphatically than if he had addressed them in the form of a requisition. He thereby shows, that a proper admonition was unnecessary, it being the nature of faith thus to express itself, so that whoever failed to do it, could not be a believer. Like the admonition, the promise also is clothed in an historical dress. The image of the writing down in a book of remembrance lying before the Lord, was probably borrowed from the custom of the Persians, among whom the names of those who had rendered service to the king, with the mention of what they had done, were entered in a book, in order that they might be rewarded at the proper time, comp. Esth. 6. 1.

965. Ver. 17. '*And they shall be mine, saith the Lord of Hosts, in the day when I make a possession, and I will spare them as a man spares his son who serves him.*' We have here the ground of the entry in the book of remembrance. Not *any possession* [1], but one of peculiar worth and preciousness, distinguished from every other possession, comp. Eccl. 2. 8, '*I collected for myself also silver and gold, and an* élite [2] *of kings and provinces.*' (The περιούσιος also corresponding to it in the Seventy, and often in the New Testament, does not mean, as Schleusner, Wahl, and others assert, *proprius alicui, peculiaris*, but according to *Gloss. in Oct.* περιούσιον, ἐξαίρετον.) There is here a plain reference to those passages in the Pentateuch, where the word occurs of the people of Israel in contrast with the heathen [3]. As then, at Sinai, God made Israel for a *peculiar possession* to Himself, out of all nations, so now does He make out of the *whole of carnal Israel* the *true Israel* for a *possession* to Himself, or rather He causes those alone to appear as His *possession*, who only always were so.—After the preparatory siftings, which occur throughout the whole history, a great sifting must come at last, whereby the *uncircumcised in heart* will be placed on an equal foot-

---

[1] סְגֻלָּה.   [2] A סְגֻלָּה.
[3] Exod. 19. 5. Deut. 7. 6. 26. 18. (Ps. 135. 4.)

ing with the *uncircumcised in the flesh* [1]. This great separation first took place at the appearing of Christ.—According to this explanation, the reference also to the complaint of the murmurers is obvious. That God made no " possession", was their objection ; " God *will* hereafter make a possession," answers the prophet, " but to your own injury, and the benefit of those who truly fear God, not of those who, in foolish blindness, think themselves such." Entirely analogous is the reference to the complaint in the fifth verse, " Ye ask, ' Where is the God of right ? ' He is already approaching, but to show Himself as such in your punishment."—The expression *to spare*, to manifest tender love, is explained out of the contrast with the not sparing those who were not sons.—The expression, ' *who serves Him,*' is especially emphatic. If paternal love is to manifest itself in all its strength, there must be something more on the part of the son than the mere natural descent, which forms only the first ground of the relation between father and son ; he must, by the free act of his will, have become *really* a son. So is it with Israel in relation to God ; the reception into the family of God by circumcision, is equal to the corporeal descent. The prophet reminds them, that this reception, if it remained merely an *outward one*, far from giving them a claim to God's fatherly treatment, only served to increase their responsibility, and subject them to unsparing treatment.

966. Ver. 18. ' *And ye shall see again the difference between the righteous and the wicked, between him who serves God, and him who serves him not.*' The clear reference to the complaint of the murmurers, that God made no difference between the righteous and the wicked, an objection which was common to them with the purely outward Israel and the heathen, shows that the address was here directed to the hypocrites. "Ye will experience that your complaint is groundless, but to your own injury." ' *Ye shall return,*' refers to *former* separations, e. g., that in Egypt (comp. Exod. 11. 7, ' *Thereby shall ye know that the Lord separates between Egypt and between Israel* '), to which the hypocrites appeal, and from which they sought to show, that now, when no traces of such a distinction were to be found, God could no more be God [2]. In its completion, this separation is still future (comp. the representation, which rests on the same idea, and therefore is in substance identical, Matt. 25. 31 seq.) : but as surely as God not *will* be, but *is* from eternity, and through all times, the God of right, so surely also must the cleansing of the floor, the burning of the chaff, and the gathering of the wheat into the garner, extend through all times.

967. Ver. 19. [Chap. 4. 1, Eng. Vers.] ' *For, behold, the day cometh,*

---

[1] Comp. Jer. 9. 24, 25.

[2] בֵין is taken by most interpreters, after the example of De Dieu ("*Videbitis interstitium s. discrimen justi ad improbum*"), as a noun. But this is entirely untenable, since, among the mass of passages where בֵין occurs, there is not one where it is to be taken as a noun. The meaning, *between*, is here entirely suitable. " We do not see," say the murmurers, "what we ought to see, *between* the righteous and the ungodly ; " ' The time will come,' says the prophet, ' when ye will again see the difference between the righteous and the ungodly.'

*burning as an oven; and all the proud, and all the evil doers, are chaff;
and the day that cometh shall burn them up, saith the Lord of Hosts,
which shall not leave them root or branch.'* In the foregoing verse a
great separation had been predicted between the righteous and the
ungodly. Here the destruction is represented, which this separation
should bring upon the ungodly ; and in the two following verses, the
blessings which *it* should confer upon the pious.—From the '*day that
cometh*,' we must not exclude the striking realizations of the idea
here expressed, from the time of the utterance of the prophecy, to
the destruction by the Romans (as that in the time of the Maccabees,
when the ἄνομοι, παράνομοι, ἐργαζόμενοι τὴν ἀδικίαν, ἀσεβεῖς, ἄνδρες
λοιμοὶ, as they are called in the books of the Maccabees, with reference to this and similar prophecies, learnt by experience the truth
they ridiculed, that God is the God of right), nor the invisible
realizations, to be perceived only by the eye of faith, which extend
through this whole period, including the revelation of the Divine
righteousness in the destinies of particular individuals. Nor, again,
have we any right to exclude the whole period from the destruction of
Jerusalem till the last judgement, as if in the great book of history
only the first and last leaf were written with the finger of God, and
the rest left vacant. God's judgement upon the false seed, the dead
members of His Church, is here described,—of that Church which,
through all centuries, is one and the same ; so that the prophecy
can by no means be regarded as finished with the times of the New
Testament, but its fulfilment begins precisely where its object begins, the judgement which is never far off, and runs parallel with
it through all times. Not *solely*, but only most manifestly, do they
coincide in the end of the two economies (of the latter so far as it is
a kingdom of grace). '*Behold*,' calls attention to it as to a *present
thing*. To the *consuming fire* the *reviving sun* is opposed in the
following verse. '*As the (consuming) oven*,' serves to give intensity.
In the glowing oven, the fire burns fiercer than in the open air [1].
The '*proud and evil doers*' stand in plain reference to ver. 15 ; you,
who are such above all, not those whom ye so name. The same
antithesis of root and branch occurs in Job 18. 16, '*Below his roots
dry up, and his branch above.*'

968. Ver. 2. '*And upon you who fear my name, shall the Sun of
Righteousness arise, and healing is under his wings, and ye shall go
forth, and leap as the calves of the stall.*' The phrase *Sun of
Righteousness* is a sort of compound noun. The *sun* is the
righteousness itself. It is compared with the natural sun, because,
though now obscured, it will then shine bright, but especially,
because it will afford rich consolation to the miserable. The
righteousness is not *subjective righteousness*, but that imparted by
God on the ground of it, which has prosperity for its inseparable
companion ; or rather it *is* the prosperity itself, considered as a
practical justification, and declaring as righteous. The Fathers, from

---

[1] Fire, which consumes chaff and stubble, occurs as an image of the ruin of
the ungodly, Is. 5. 24.

Justin downwards, understand by the ' *Sun of Righteousness,*' *Christ.*
This interpretation is in the main well grounded ; He through whom
righteousness should be imparted to the pious, at whose appearance
the Sun of Righteousness arises upon them, is, according to the first
verse of the third chapter, the heavenly Mediator of the covenant,
who realizes its promises, and its threatenings, the λόγος. But there
are two things in the interpretation to be set aside. (1) It finds
here a definite mention of the *person* of *Christ :* it makes Him
the Sun of Righteousness, whereas here it is the righteousness
that is designated as the Sun. This difference, however, concerns
merely the *form.* For He who causes the Sun of Righteousness to
arise, may also Himself be regarded as the Sun, just as the *author of
peace* (Mic. 3. 5,) is Himself called *peace.* (2) It understands by
righteousness, at least *chiefly,* the *forgiveness of sin.* Thus, e. g.,
Luther, on the passage, explains the Sun of Righteousness by
"which makes righteous, which gives such a splendour, that the
people are justified by it, and *delivered from sins.*" This difference
is more essential than the former one. As the murmurers had desired
that God should give to every one, the righteous and the unrighteous, according to his works ; so the prediction of the prophet
is limited to this judgement of righteousness, the reward of the
pious and the punishment of the ungodly. It was, therefore, not
to his purpose, to speak here of the forgiveness of sins ; though
this is included in the more incidental annunciation, that God
would send His messenger to prepare His way before Him.
Whoever suffers Him to exercise this His office on himself, receives the forgiveness of sins ; whoever does it not, upon him
the wrath of God abides. When the Lord Himself is already
come, there can be no further change of the relation to Him, but
only a revelation of it. The passage, therefore, is parallel to such
as Ps. 102. 4, ' *To the upright there comes a light in darkness.*'
—Wings are attributed to the morning dawn, as here to the sun,
Ps. 139. 9, to the wind, Ps. 104. 3, in both cases, as a symbol of
swiftness ; comp. Macrob. Sat. 1. 19, "*Hoc argumentum Ægyptii
lucidius absolvunt, ipsius solis simulacra pennata fingentes.*" Eurip.
Ion, ver. 122, "Αμ' ἠελίου πτέρυγι θοῇ. Virgil. *Æn.* lib. 8. 396,
" *Nox ruit et fuscis tellurem amplectitur alis.*" Upon the Antonine
pillars Jupiter himself is represented under the image of a winged
sun. Now the wings are here to be considered, either as the means
whereby the sun hastens to bring the healing, or as that which it
spreads out over its object for protection and warmth, comp. Ps. 91.
4.—In the term *healing,* regard is paid to the healing, animating, and
enlivening power of the natural sun. The winter, and the night of
affliction, had made the righteous feeble and miserable. By the
term *go forth,* their former condition is designated as one of confinement and imprisonment. Now they are led forth from their damp
prisons to the free plain, irradiated by the clear sunshine.

969. Ver. 3. ' *And ye shall trample down the ungodly ; for they
shall be ashes under the soles of your feet in the day that I shall create,
saith the Lord of Hosts.*' The image of the ashes refers back to that

of fire, ver. 19. The temptation, arising from the prosperity of the ungodly, is met by pointing to the day determined by the Lord, which will change all. Parallel is μακάριοι οἱ πραεῖς, ὅτι αὐτοὶ κληρονομήσουσι τὴν γῆν.

970. Ver. 4. '*Remember the law of Moses, my servant, which I commanded him upon Horeb for all Israel, laws and statutes.*' This declaration, to the great importance of which the Seventy would call our attention by placing it at the end of the whole book, the Massorites by the *littera majuscula* ۱, has been usually misunderstood by the older interpreters, who supply a *provisionally*. For the insertion of this *provisionally*, there is no reason whatever. For Elias brings nothing new; he only restores life to the old; the Covenant Angel appears, not as teaching and giving laws, but as judging. And just as little occasion is there for it. The Law—which has also been overlooked—comes under consideration here, according to its nature, as a copy of the holiness of God, precisely as Matt. 5. 17. In this attribute, it is equally eternal with God, not one jot or tittle of it can fail. It is only from this point of view, that we can rightly perceive the connexion of this declaration with what precedes and follows. The prophet had predicted a judgement; here he refers it back to its ground, and thus, at the same time, shows how the whole people and each individual might escape it. God's law and his people are inseparable. If the law is not fulfilled *in* the people, which amounts to the same thing as the sanctification of the name of God,—for the law has this dignity only because God's being is made known by it; but a *people of God* must necessarily *represent God*, and have His name, and *His being*, so far as it is manifested, *in* themselves, or else *upon* themselves,—then must it be fulfilled *upon* the people. But before God proceeds to execute this fulfilling it *upon*—that is *against*—the people, before He smites the land with a curse, He leaves nothing undone, to enable Himself to fulfil it *in* the people : and this, not accidentally, but according to the same necessity of the relation which requires the *in* and the *upon* : —the prayer '*hallowed be thy name*' is, at the same time, a *promise;* God requires nothing which He does not also give; not merely are the people His people, but He is also their God. He sends Elias the prophet. The expressions, '*of my servant,*' and '*which I commanded him,*' both serve to separate every thing human from the law, and thereby to enhance the obligation to observe it. Moses is only an instrument; God is the lawgiver. Hence it follows, which is still expressly urged in '*for all Israel,*' that it does not concern merely the generation to which it was at first given at Horeb, but that its requisitions extend to all generations[1]. The prophet seems to have Deut. chap. 4, especially in view. The whole chapter contains a lively inculcation of fidelity towards the law.—*Laws* and *Statutes* are joined with one another, ver. 1 and 8, Horeb is mentioned ver. 15, comp. especially ver. 5, '*Behold I will teach you a law, and statutes, as the Lord my God commanded me.*' Ver. 14, '*And*

---

[1] Comp. Deut. 29. 13, 14.

*the Lord commanded me at that time to teach you laws and statutes,
that ye should do them, in the land whither ye go to possess it*[1].'
The laws afterwards given in the plains of Moab are included
in the expression, ' *at Horeb.*' For they were only further exten-
sions and developments; the groundwork was completely given at
Sinai. The charge, ' *remember,*' refers back to the seventh verse,
' *from the days of your fathers ye have gone away back from my commandments.*' The prophet does not exhort without cause; he does
not warn them against a *future* apostasy ; the axe already lies at the
root. Let Israel of his own accord remember the Law ; before the
Lord awakens him out of the sleep of forgetfulness by the thunder of
his righteousness.

971. Ver. 5. ' *Behold, I will send to you Elias the prophet,
before the day of the Lord comes, the great and the terrible.*' Elias
the prophet is identical with the messenger whom the Lord will send
before Himself, ver. 1. If, then, we have there shown, that this
messenger is *ideal*, a *personified preacher of repentance*, this must be
equally true here. In both cases the idea is the same; God, before
he manifests Himself in punishment and blessing as the covenant
God, shows Himself as such, by supplying the children of the curse
with the means of becoming children of the blessing. It is self-
evident, that the power of the Spirit of God must not be separated
from the outward sending of His servants, and thus the gift turned
into ridicule. It was unnecessary to point to it especially, because
it *always* accompanies the outward preaching, and is always in proportion to it, so that, out of the measure of the outward mercy
imparted to any age, the measure of the inward grace may always
with certainty be inferred.—We have only here to enquire respecting
what is peculiar to the passage, the designation of the messenger by
the name of Elias. The ground of this designation must be sought
in that which the prophet himself gives as the office and the destination of the messenger, and of Elias, the preparing of the way before
the Lord, and the bringing back of the heart of the fathers to the
children, and of the children to the fathers. Therefore, as a reformer
raised up by God, the messenger is designated by the name of him
who was pre-eminent among his predecessors in πνεῦμα and δύναμις,
who lived in an exceedingly corrupt age, and whose rejection was
followed by a peculiarly terrible day of the Lord, first the judgement
by the Assyrians, then the carrying away of Israel into captivity,
then the curse wherewith the land was smitten, because it was no
longer, according to its destination, a holy land. All these relations
revived with the name of Elias. The people were roused from the
dream of their self-righteousness, when they heard this name, and saw
themselves placed on a level with the corrupt generation in the time
of Elias ; and the future coming of the Lord received a firm support
in this former coming. Why precisely Elias is mentioned, appears
the more clearly, when we follow in the historical books the proofs of
the view, that he was the head of the prophetic order in the kingdom

---

[1] Comp. also Levit. 26. 46.

of Israel, nay, in a measure, the only prophet, since his successors possessed the spirit only mediately, a view to which we are led even by the great similarity of the deeds of Elias with theirs, to be explained by this relation, analogous to that to be derived from the same principle between Isaac and Abraham, Joshua and Moses. 1 Chron. 21. 12, ' *There comes to the king a writing from Elias the prophet,*' when *Elias, as an individual,* had long since ceased to be upon earth. 1 Kings 19. 15, 16, ' *And the Lord says unto Elias, Thou shalt go and anoint Hazael king over Damascus, and Jehu the son of Nimshi thou shalt anoint king over Israel.*' Neither of which was done by Elias as an individual; the former by Elisha, comp. 2 Kings 8. 13, the latter by a pupil of Elisha, 2 Kings 9. 13.—Elisha modestly confessing, that his relation to God could not be equal originally to that of his master, desires the portion of the first-born in his spiritual inheritance [1]. He considers, therefore, the other prophets also as *spiritual sons,* and *heirs* of Elias, standing to him in the same relation that the Seventy elders, to whom was given *of his spirit,* stood in to Moses. The scholars of the prophet of Jericho said, according to the fifth verse, ' *The spirit of Elias* (the Spirit of God in the definite form, which it had assumed in the case of Elias) *upon Elisha.*' As an outward sign that his agency was a mere continuation of that of Elias, Elisha receives his mantle. It would be easy to point out this relation beyond the bounds of Scripture,—one need only think, e. g., of Luther, in relation to Jonas and Bugenhagen ; of the reformers generally, in relation to the Churches founded by them, —easy also to show that the so often abused ' *be ye not servants of men,*' is not applicable to this relation in itself, as one ordained of God, although sin cleaves to it, as to every thing human. But this does not belong to our purpose. We only call attention to the circumstance, that, if, according to these views, we must not regard the Elias of former times as an individual historical person, if to Elias must be attributed every thing by which the *idea* is realized, until the coming of the terrible day for Israel ; the less ground is there to seek the Elias of the future, in one particular individual in any other manner, than so far as the same can be regarded as the *personified idea,* as the reality coinciding with it.—That the prophet has intentionally borrowed from Joel (3. 4.) the words ' *before the day of the Lord comes, the great and the terrible,*' has already been remarked. That day of Joel, the judgement upon the enemies of the kingdom of God, was earnestly desired. The prophet shows by announcing the preacher of repentance, how unjust it would be for them to identify themselves with the kingdom of God, and then, in the following verse, expressly declares, that if the preaching should make no impression, the great day must be terrible precisely to those who long for it, and who, imagining themselves the supporters, were in reality the enemies, of the kingdom of God. Finally, in reference to the day of the Lord, what has already been remarked on the nineteenth verse, is perfectly just.

[1] בְּרוּחוֹ, 2 Kings 2. 9, comp. 377, note.

972. With respect to the interpretation of the verse, it is known, that, relying upon this passage, the Jews expected a personal reappearing of Elias before the coming of the Messiah. Among the Christians, too, the reference to the person of Elias is very ancient, and at certain times has been widely diffused. They considered that in John the Baptist, and the judgement upon Israel, the prophecy had been only improperly and imperfectly fulfilled; it looked for its proper and complete fulfilment, in the personal appearance of Elias, before the judgement upon the world. Thus the author of the *Dial. c. Tryph.* urges against Trypho the πρὶν ἐλθεῖν ἡμέραν κυρίου τὴν μεγάλην καὶ ἐπιφανῆ. This, he argues, is the δευτέρα παρουσία τοῦ Χριστοῦ: Elias would precede it. This, he maintains, Christ Himself has said, since He designates (comp. Matt. 17. 11) the coming of Elias as *future*. As a justification of the supposition of a beginning of the fulfilment in John, he declares: Ὅτι τὸ ἐν Ἠλίᾳ τοῦ θεοῦ γενόμενον προφητικὸν πνεῦμα, καὶ ἐν Ἰωάννῃ γέγονε. So Chrysostom [1], Theophylact [2], Tertullian [3], Jerome [4], Augustin [5], Origen, Cyril, Theodoret. The expectation of Elias before the last judgement, even passed over to the Mahommedans, comp. Herbelot, *s. v. Ilia*, and certainly more out of the Christian Church, than from among the Jews. That the interpreters of the Catholic Church would adhere to the view of the Fathers, might naturally have been expected. Bellarmine says, the opposite one is "*Vel hæresis vel hæresi proximus error.*" (*De Rom. Pontif.* lib. iii. c. 6.) The interpreters of the evangelical Church, on the contrary, unanimously rejected this view, and maintained the exclusive reference to John the Baptist. Nevertheless, Olshausen has recently endeavoured to vindicate the above-mentioned older interpretation.

973. Ver. 6. '*And he shall turn the heart of the fathers to the sons, and the heart of the sons to their fathers, lest I come and smite the land to a curse.*' The true interpretation is found in the New Testament; and among the Fathers, in Augustin [6], who expressly remarks, that the Seventy [7] have translated the passage incorrectly. The Fathers are the pious forefathers, the patriarchs, especially David, and the pious generation living in his time [8]. The hearts of the pious fathers and the ungodly sons are estranged from each other. The bond of union, the common love for God, is wanting. The fathers are ashamed of their children, comp. Is. 29. 22, and the children of their fathers. The great chasm between the two, is filled up by Elias the prophet; who brings back the sons to God, in

---

[1] Hom. 57 in Matt.   [2] On Matt. 17. 11, 12.   [3] Jerome *De Anima, c.* 50.
       [4] On Matt. 17. 11.   [5] *De Civ. Dei,* 20. c. 29.
[6] *De Civ.* 20, 29.
[7] Ὃς ἀποκαταστήσει καρδίαν πατρὸς πρὸς υἱὸν, καὶ καρδίαν ἀνθρώπου πρὸς τὸν πλησίον αὐτοῦ.
[8] Iken: "*Quando de integro populo Judaico sermo est, parentum nomine solent ejus majores, liberorum autem posteri intelligi.*" Ezek. 18. 2. "*Patres comederunt,*" etc. Ps. 22. 5; Mal. 3. 6, 7.

whom the fathers and the sons are united. Were there no pious fathers, had not God in times past shown Himself as a covenant God, by giving them a heart that feared Him, then would the hope of a reformation of the sons, to be effected by Him at a future period, be a mere fantasy. The hopes of the kingdom of God are grounded perpetually upon that which has been. This is a pledge, not merely of the possibility, but also of the necessity, of the repetition. Every word that the prophet directs to the corrupt priesthood would be lost, if there were not (chap. 2. 5, 6) in the former purity, the pledge, that the idea *could* and *must* again become a reality. It must be remarked, however, that the outward agency of Elias must not be separated from the inward agency of the Spirit of God, which necessarily accompanied it; and then the *he shall turn* designates, not so much the result, as the Divine appointment, which, indeed, can never be without effect. That the prophet well knew how the great mass of the people would despise the gift of God, offered to *all* (comp. Luke 7. 30), and therefore bring upon themselves the threatened judgement, appears from what precedes, where this judgement is unconditionally announced.

974. '*I strike the head to a curse,*' i. e., *make* it a *curse* by my smiting it. By a *curse* is meant a thing *accursed* or *devoted to God*, and *given* up *to destruction* as a punishment for sin. Every thing terrible, which can be conceived, is contained in this one word '*Harem*[1].' There can be no doubt that the prophet refers back to those passages of the Pentateuch which relate to the *cursing*[2] of the Canaanites. As a matter-of-fact prophecy of the future fate of Israel, is this represented even in the Pentateuch itself. As a holy people of the holy God, Israel received Canaan for a possession. He had only the choice between *holy* and *harem*, if he has become a Canaan in disposition, so is he also a Canaan in his lot; comp. Levit. 16. 24—28, Deut. 12, 29. 63, 64.

THE PROPHET JEREMIAH

Preliminary Observations

975. In Malachi, chap. 3. 1, the Lord promises He will send His messenger, that he may prepare the way before Him, who will come to His Temple to judge and punish; ver. 23. 24: He will, before the coming of His day, the great and terrible, before He smites the land with the curse, send a second Elias, that he may bring back the heart of the fathers to their children, and of the children to their

---

[1] חֵרֶם is *accus.*, the second object of הִכֵּיתִי.

[2] In the original is an able investigation of the *Harem* or *judicial* curse by which sinners, &c. were devoted to God for destruction: and a very full discussion of the relation of Malachi to the New Testament.

fathers.   Before this prophecy was spoken in words, it was *acted*
out, as it were, in the existence of Jeremiah, who, during the long
period of forty-one years before the destruction of Jerusalem,
announced the judgements of the Lord ; with glowing zeal and burning love, preached repentance to His people, and, even after the
destruction, pursued the small remnant that was left, and sought to
secure them before the new day of the Lord, which they were bringing upon themselves by their obstinate impenitence.   This typical
relation of Jeremiah to John the Baptist, and to Christ (anticipated,
though understood in a gross and crude manner, in the Jewish tradition, that Jeremiah, in the end of the days, would again appear on
earth,) gives to the consideration of his agency, the study of his prophecies, a peculiar charm ; and the more so, when we further regard
the preaching of repentance by John and Christ, not as a dead fact,
but perceive how the past lives again in the present and future.

976. Jeremiah, while still a youth, was called to his office in the
thirteenth year of Josiah, one year, therefore, after the first reformation of this king, who, in the sixteenth year of his age, and eighth of
his reign of thirty-one years, began to seek the Lord.   Such a king,
unlike any of his predecessors, who turned himself to the Lord with
his whole heart, his whole soul, and all his powers, 2 Kings 23. 25,
in the midst of an evil and adulterous generation, is a remarkable
phenomenon, as little conceivable from natural causes, as the existence of Melchizedek, without father, without descent,—apart from
all natural development,—in the midst of the Canaanites, who, with
bold and unceasing steps, hastened to the completion of their sin.
His existence has the same root as that of Jeremiah, which becomes
the more evident, when we take into view the *union* of the regal and
prophetic offices in Christ, for the salvation of the people, hastening
anew to their destruction ; God's covenant faithfulness, his long-
suffering which makes every effort to lead the apostate sons to
repentance.   The zeal of both, though sustained by manifold
assistance from other sources, as by the prophetess Huldah, and the
prophet Zephaniah, was unable to restrain the stream of the prevailing corruption, and, therefore, that of the Divine judgements.   The
corruption had become so deeply seated, that only individuals could
be rescued, as a brand out of the fire.   Under the long reign of
Manasseh, whose disposition must be regarded as a product of the
prevailing spirit of the time, and he, not as its author, but only as
its representative, it had made frightful progress (2 Kings 23. 26, 27 ;
24. 3, 4).   The few fruits of his late conversion had been entirely
consumed under the short reign of his ungodly son Ammon.   It had
so little influence that was extensive and durable, that the author of
the books of Kings passes it entirely over.   It was difficult to set
bounds, even to the outward idolatry : how imperfectly this was
done, appears from the prophecies of Jeremiah, uttered after the
reformation ; and even where it *was* effected, where an emotion, a
wish, showed itself to return to the living fountain, which had been
forsaken, there the corruption soon broke forth again, only in another
form.   With grief does Jeremiah charge this upon the people, whose

righteousness was as a morning dew, chap. 3. 4, 5, ' *Hast thou not but lately called Me, My father, friend of my youth art thou? Will He reserve (his anger) for ever, will He keep it to the end? Behold, so spakest thou, and soon didst thou evil, thou didst accomplish it.*' The foolish inclination to idolatry, the disease not being cured, but only driven out of one part of the system, was followed by an equally foolish confidence in the miserable righteousness of works, and the Divine election, the only condition of its validity being held to be the offering of sacrifices, &c. ' *Trust ye not in lying words,* —must the prophet cry out to them (chap. 7. 4), ' *saying, The Temple of the Lord, the Temple of the Lord, the Temple of the Lord,*' *are these*' (the people, in their opinion, could not be destroyed, because the Lord had established his perpetual dwelling among them).—' *Thou sayest, I am innocent, His anger has entirely departed from me; behold I will reckon with thee, because thou sayest, I have not sinned,*' 2. 35,—' *Wherefore should incense come to me out of Saba, and sweet cane, that which is good, out of a distant land? your burnt-offerings are not acceptable, and your sacrifices are not pleasant to me.*' —Towards the end of Josiah's reign the judgement of God approached nearer to Judea; the former Asiatic dominion of the Assyrians passed entirely over to the Chaldeans, whose rude and youthful strength threatened destruction to Judea, the more, because, along with the inheritance of the Assyrians, they had also received the enmity against Egypt, which must give to Judea a great importance in their eyes. To the people, involved in the conflict of these two hostile powers, the deathblow was to come from the Chaldeans, according to the prediction of the prophets in general, and especially of Jeremiah, to whom the prediction of the calamity out of the north was assigned, as his chief object immediately on his call ; the first severe wound, however, was given them by the Egyptians ; Josiah fell in the battle with Pharaoh Necho. His death filled the people, conscious of their guilt, with anxious expectation of the things that should come. They surmised, that they now stood on the limit where grace and anger separate [1], and this surmise was soon raised to more bitter certainty by their experience. Jehoiakim, who, after Jehoiachin, or Schallum, after a short reign, had been carried away by the Egyptians, ascended the throne, sustained the same relation to his father Josiah as the people to God, in reference to the mercy which he had granted to them in Josiah. A more striking contrast (see its exhibition in chap. 22) can scarcely be conceived. Jehoiakim exhibits throughout an entire want, not merely of love for God, but even of fear of God. He is a bloodthirsty tyrant, an exasperated enemy of the truth. In the commencement of his reign, some influence of that of Josiah is still seen. The priests and the false prophets, rightly perceiving the signs of the time, come forward with the manifestation of their long restrained rage against Jeremiah, in whom they hate their own conscience. They accuse him of deserving death, because he predicted the ruin of the city and the

[1] Comp. on Zech. 12. 11.

Temple; but the leaders of the people release him (comp. chap. 26). Soon, however, this reflex influence ceased. The king became the central point, around which all that was ungodly collected; which, under Josiah, had kept itself more concealed. It soon became a power, a stream, which overflowed the whole land; the more easily, the weaker were the dams which had been raised in the time of Josiah. As one of the first sacrifices to the truth, fell the prophet Urijah: the king imagined that he might destroy the truth itself in its messengers; and the thought being insupportable to him, that he lived then in distant Egypt; he caused him to be brought thence (comp. the same place). That Jeremiah, under the eleven years' reign of this king, escaped every mortal danger, although he constantly threatened anew death to the king, destruction to the people, was a perpetual miracle, an illustrious fulfilment of the Divine promise, imparted to him at his call (1. 21): ' *They will contend against thee, and not overpower thee; for I am with thee, saith* the Lord, *to help thee.*' Under Jehoiakim the Divine threatening of punishment advanced several steps towards its complete fulfilment. In his fourth year, Jerusalem, for the first time, was taken by the Chaldeans [1], after the power of the kingdom of Egypt had been for ever broken in the battle at Carchemish, on the Euphrates. Still, the victor for this time acted with tolerable mildness; the sin of the people was to appear in its true light, by the fact, that God gave them a time for repentance, and did not at once proceed to the utmost severity, but gradually inflicted his judgements. But here also it became evident, that crime in its highest degree becomes insanity; the nearer the people and king approached the abyss, with so much the greater haste did they rush towards it. They did not, indeed, continue entirely insensible, as the threatenings of the prophets began to be fulfilled, as appears from the day of fasting and repentance, which was appointed in remembrance of the first capture by the Chaldeans [2]. But transient emotions could not restrain the course of sin. They soon became more wicked than they had been before, and so also the Divine judgements soon reached a new station. Political wisdom already counselled the king, that he should quietly submit to the comparatively light dependence on the Chaldeans. That he alone could effect nothing against the Chaldean power was obvious; and to the *unprejudiced* observer it was equally clear, that the Egyptians could not help him, and had this even been possible, he would still only have changed his master. But these political grounds, although they were so obvious, were to have no influence upon him, according to the counsel of God, who takes away the understanding of the prudent, because his obdurate heart hindered him from regarding the religious motives which Jeremiah urged. Melanchthon (*Opp.* II. p. 407 sq.) considers it as remarkable, that while other prophets, as Samuel, Elijah, Isaiah, under a promise of Divine aid, exhort to powerful resistance against the foe, and even themselves co-operate as instruments of the deli-

---

[1] Comp. *Beitr.* I. p. 52 ff.   [2] Comp. *Beitr.* p. 59.

verance, Jeremiah, on the contrary, perpetually preaches unconditional submission.   That this difference was not grounded in the *persons*, but in the *thing*, is shown by the event, which is as different as the counsel.   The seventy years of Chaldee servitude had been irrevocably determined upon Judah; how firm and definite was the decree, is shown, even by the exact mention of the years, elsewhere so unusual, in reference to the fate of the covenant people.   They had given themselves up entirely, more fully than at any other period, to the inward power of heathenism; they must, therefore, according to a Divine necessity, be given up also into the outward power of the heathen for punishment and for reformation.   God Himself could not change the decree, since it rested on his nature. It would be in vain, therefore, if even the greatest intercessors, Moses and Samuel, stood before Him (Jer. 15. 1 sq.).   Intercession can be efficacious only when it is offered in the name of God.   Now such being his condition, how foolish was it for him to rebel against the Chaldeans,—to wish to prevent the effect, while the cause was suffered quietly to remain, to stop the brook, while the fountain continued to bubble!   It would have been foolish, even if the relation of the Jews and Chaldeans, as to power, had been exactly the reverse.   For, when the Lord sells a people, then one can chase a thousand, and two put ten thousand to flight (Deut. 32. 30).   But the shepherd of the people had become a fool, and asked nothing according to the Lord; therefore he could not act wisely, and the whole flock was scattered (Jer. 10. 21).   Jehoiakim rebelled against the Chaldeans, and remained some years in the delusion that he had acted prudently, since Nebuchadnezzar had to bring a more important affair to a close.   Then, however, he marched against Jerusalem, and put an end both to his reign and to his life [1].   Still God's longsuffering, and therefore also the patience of the Chaldeans, were not exhausted.   Jehoiachin was raised to the throne of his father.   The short reign of three months gave to the young king sufficient opportunity to manifest the wickedness of his heart, and his apostasy from God. His fidelity became suspected; a Chaldean host broke anew into the city, and carried away the king, and with him a multitude of people.   This was the first great deportation.   By the providence of God, it happened, that among those who were carried away, was found precisely the flower of the nation.   The apparent calamity was for them a blessing.   They were sent away from the place upon which the storm of God's anger was soon to fall, into the land of the Chaldeans, for their good, and there they constituted the nursery of the kingdom of God in the new form it was about to assume [2]. There now appeared nothing more to restrain the course of the Divine judgements upon the ungodly mass that remained, like the bad figs, which could not be eaten for badness; those whom the Lord threatened, that He would make them for an abuse, for a calamity in all the kingdoms of the earth, for a reproach, and for a by-

---

[1] Jer. 22. 12; 2 Kings 24. 2; comp. *Beitr.* p. 59.
[2] Comp. Jer. 24.

word, and for a mockery, and for a curse, in all the places whither He would drive them, Jer. 24. 9. And yet the Lord waited still before He executed this threatening, and smote the land to a curse. Mattaniah or Zedekiah, son of Josiah, uncle of Jehoiachin, who was given to them for a king, might, at least partially, have averted the evil. But he also must experience, that the fear of God is the foundation of prudence. In recent times, he has often been exculpated; his fault, it is said, was only weakness, which made him an instrument of a corrupt party. But the Scripture judges otherwise concerning him, and he who looks deeper into his character, will find its decision correct. We can only concede to him the preference over Jehoiakim, which Ch. B. Michaelis attributes to him: "*Joiakimo durius atrociusque ingenium fuit; aliquo Dei timore, quamquam servili et hypocritico afficiebatur Tsedekias, sed Joiakimus nullo penitus.*" And this preference, on a nearer examination, amounts to nothing; for it belongs to nature and not to grace. Whether corruption manifests itself as weakness, or as a carnal and strong opposition to the Divine truth, is accidental, and depends on the diversity of the physical and mental organization, especially the strength or weakness of the nervous system. That Zedekiah did not entirely put away from him the Divine truth and its messengers, is not to be attributed to himself; it was *forced upon him*, upon one, that is, who was unable to resist a powerful impression of any sort whatever. In such a character as Jehoiakim, the same amount of the fear of God would require a softening of the decision, since it could not exist without some ground within.—Trusting to the aid of the neighbouring nations, especially of the Egyptians, persuaded by the false prophets and the great men, himself seized by that spirit of giddiness and intoxication, which was hurrying forward the whole people with irresistible violence to the abyss, Zedekiah broke the sacred oath which he had sworn to the Chaldeans, and, after an obstinate resistance, Jerusalem was taken and destroyed. Still the long-suffering of God, and therefore of men also, was not *wholly* at an end. The conquerors left a comparatively small portion of the inhabitants in the land; God's mercy gave to them Gedaliah, an excellent man, for their civil, Jeremiah for their spiritual, head, who preferred to remain on the smoking ruins, than to follow the splendid promises of the Chaldeans; and who, in the fulfilment of his calling, although now at an advanced age, and oppressed by grief, chose to remain to the last. But it was as if the people had resolved to drain the cup of the Divine anger to the last drop. Gedaliah was murdered; those who had not taken part in the deed, yet fled to Egypt, regardless of the word of the Lord by the prophet, who announced to them a curse if they fled, and a blessing if they remained.

977. What the prophet would have to suffer under such circumstances, might readily be conceived, without inquiring of history. Had he even been free from all personal assaults, what a distress must it not have been to dwell with such a generation, to see their corruption constantly increasing, and themselves approaching nearer to the abyss, in spite of all his faithful warnings; his whole agency,

at least with respect to the mass of the people, in vain. ' *Oh that I
had in the wilderness a lodging-place of wayfaring men,*'—so does he
speak even under Josiah, chap. 9. 2,—' *that I might leave my people,
and go from them; for they are all adulterers, a band of faithless
men.*' But from these personal assaults, he neither was nor could
be exempted. Mockery, hatred, calumny, insult, plots, cursing,
imprisonment, bonds, were his portion. To bear such a burden,
must be hard for every temperament, but especially for such a one
as his. " The more tender the heart, the deeper the anguish." He
was no second Elias, he had a soft disposition, a lively sensibility ;
his eyes easily overflowed. And he who would so gladly have lived
in peace and love with all, when he came forth in the service of the
truth, must become a second Ishmael, his hand against all, and the
hand of all against him ; he, who so warmly loved his people, must
see this love misapprehended, and himself branded as a betrayer of
the people, by those who were themselves their betrayers. All this
produced in him a violent conflict, which he has repeatedly, particularly in chap. 12 and chap. 20, disclosed to us, because the Lord
was glorified by the victory, which He alone could give.

978. That which, together with his inward consolations, the wonderful deliverances, the remarkable fulfilments of his prophecies
which he himself lived to witness, sustained him, was, that the Lord
caused him to behold his future salvation with equal clearness as his
judgements, so that he could regard the latter only as transient, and,
even during the most striking contrast between the appearance and
the idea, did not lose the firm hope of the final triumph of the
former. This hope constituted the central point of his whole life.
For a long series of years, he is somewhat restrained from the expression of it ; for he has to do with secure and gross sinners, who
must be terrified by the preaching of the law, and the message of
wrath, but even here some beams of the sun constantly break
through the thick cloud. Finally, when the entire destruction is
already at the door, and his commission to break down and to destroy draws to an end, because now God Himself will speak by
deed, he can, in accordance with the desire of his heart, execute the
second part of his calling, to build and to plant (comp. chap. 1); and
how his whole heart is constantly full of this, appears from the language of his lips. The whole calling of a prophet, Calvin well comprehends in the following words : " *Dico simpliciter, Jeremiam fuisse
a Deo missum, ut populo ultimam cladem prædiceret ; deinde ut con-
cionaretur de futurâ redemtione : sic tamen, ut interponeret semper
exilium septuaginta annorum.*" How this redemption, in his view,
was destined, not merely for Israel, how the heathen also were
to share in it, appears, not merely incidentally in the prophecies to
his own countrymen, but is rendered prominent even in those against
foreign nations ; as in the prophecy against Egypt, 46. 26, against
Moab, 48. 47, against Ammon, 49. 6.

979. In reference to the style of Jeremiah, Cunæus well observes,
De Rep. Hebr. lib. 3, c. 7 : " *Jeremiæ omnis majestas posita in verborum neglectu est ; adeo illum decet rustica dictio.*" Jerome cer-

tainly seeks very superficially the ground of this *humilitas dictionis*
of the prophet, whom he at the same time names *in majestate sen-
suum profundissimum* in his birth at the *viculus Anathoth*. If his
style were different, it would be unnatural : the diction of Jeremiah
is to be compared with the garment of hair and leathern girdle of
Elias. He who is grieved and sad at heart, he whose *eyes do fail
with tears*, deals not in the ornaments and prettinesses either of attire
or of speech.

980. Chap. 3:14. '*Return, ye apostate sons, saith the Lord, for I
marry you to myself, and take you one out of a city, and two out of a
family, and bring you to Zion.*' The question arises, to whom is the
address here directed, whether to Israel, as most interpreters (Abarb.,
Calv., Vatabl., Schmid, &c.) suppose, or, as others, to the Jews.
The decision must be given unconditionally in favour of the former
view. A transition is not even intimated by a single word ; precisely the same, '*Return, ye apostate sons,*' occurs in ver. 22, of *Israel ;*
the *apostate* Israel is, in what precedes, the standing expression,
ver. 6. 8. 11, while Judah is designated as an *adulteress*, ver. 8 and 11.
The measure of transgression is proportioned to the measure of grace.
The relation of the Lord to Judah was closer ; the apostasy, therefore, the more deserving of punishment. Further, an extensive
prediction of prosperity for Judah here, where the threatening had
not yet preceded, would be by no means suitable, and the reference
of that in ver. 14—17, to Israel, clearly appears in ver. 18, '*In those
days the house of Judah will come near* (properly *upon*) *the house of
Israel.*' According to which, the return of Judah is there first mentioned, incidentally, as a secondary matter. To Israel the prophet
immediately returns, in ver. 19. For that by '*the house of Israel,*' in
ver. 20, and '*the sons of Israel,*' in ver. 21, *Israel* in the stricter sense
is to be understood, is evident from the antithesis of '*the house of
Judah,*' in ver. 18. and *Judah* and *Jerusalem*, in chap. 4. 3. Finally,
it is only on the supposition that the address is to Israel, that the
contents of ver. 16 and 17 are intelligible, as the interpretation will
show. In the explanation of the words כִּי אָנֹכִי בָּעַלְתִּי בָכֶם, we have for
predecessors the Vulg. (*quia ego vir vester*), Luther : " I will betroth
you to me," Calvin, Schmid, and others[1]. The context refutes

[1] Pococke, Schultens, on Prov. 30. 22, Venema, Schnurrer, Gesenius, Winer,
made every effort to prove that בָּעַל here, as well as in chap. 31. 32, where it
occurs in an entirely similar connexion, so that the decision must serve at the
same time for both passages, is used in a bad sense. They endeavour to establish this sense by two methods. The one class entirely disregard the Hebrew
usage, and appeal solely to the Arab., where בָּעַל is supposed to mean *fastidire ;* the
others deduce from the Hebrew sense of *reigning* that of a *tyrannical dominion*.
With respect to the *first* derivation, even if the Arabic usage were proved, still
we could not argue from it with certainty to that of the Hebrew. But this
Arabic usage is very poorly made out. To be sure, if the phrase بعل الرجل
بالامرأة, *fastidivit vir mulierem eamque expulit s. repudiavit*, actually occurred in

those, who, as Schultens, regard the whole verse as a *threatening*. What precedes and follows breathes *warm love* for poor Israel. They

Arabic, this would not be the case; but it is only by a strange *quid pro quo*, that the interpreters, even a Schultens, have forced this phrase upon the Arab., after the example of Kimchi.   The error rests upon a hasty view of *Abul Walid*, who has instead: بعل الرجل بامره, *any one is embarrassed in his affair*.   The meaning *fastidire, rejicere*, is, in general, entirely foreign to the Arabic.   The

بَعِلَ, signifies only *mente turbatus, attonitus fuit, possessed*, i. e. *deprived of the use of his powers, embarrassed, not knowing how to help himself*, comp. the *Camus*, in Schultens and Freytag.   As soon as the plain connexion of this sense with the usual one is perceived, it appears, at once, that it is not applicable here.   As to the *second* derivation, it is liable to the objection, that the fundamental meaning of *ruling*, in which that of *tyrannizing* is supposed to be included, is entirely unknown to the Hebrew.   Even Cocceius saw, that the primary, properly, indeed, the *only* meaning, of בָּעַל is that of *occupation, possession*.   It may, indeed, be used also of rulers, as Is. 26. 13, 1 Chron. 4. 22, but not inasmuch as they *rule*, but only inasmuch as they *possess*.   On the former passage: ' *Jehovah our God*,' בְּעָלוּנוּ אֲדֹנִים זוּלָתֶךָ, Schultens indeed remarks: " *Quivis hic facile agnoscat dominium grave et imperiosius.*"   But rather, that in general the land of the Lord is possessed by foreigners, is so entirely the proper point of the grief of those who complained, that the thought of the *method* of the possession scarcely occurs to them.—That the sense *to marry*, does not arise out of that of *ruling*, and is not to be explained by the *unconditional and slavish dependence of the wife* in the East, but rather from the sense of *possession*, is shown by passages like Is. 54. 1 *; 62. 4, comp. Joel. 1. 8, where the discourse is of a relation, founded on the most cordial love; then also in another way, by passages like Deut. 21. 10—13, 24. 4, where the *copula carnalis* is designated as that whereby the בָּעַל fully takes place; and, finally, from the Arabic, where the wife is no less called בְּעֻלָה, بعلة, than the man בַּעַל, بعل.—That, in the frequent combination of בַּעַל with other nouns, instead of the adjective, the meaning *Lord* is far less suitable than that of *possessor*, is obvious, comp., e. g., בַּעַל הַחֲלֹמוֹת, *the dreamer*, בַּעַל אַף, *the angry*, בַּעַל נֶפֶשׁ, *the covetous*, בַּעַל מְזִמּוֹת, *the artful*, בַּעֲלֵי עִיר, *oppidani*, בַּעֲלֵי בְרִית, *the members of the covenant, &c.*—If we look to the dialects, we gain the same result.   Here also the sense of *possession* appears as the original, and properly the only one.   In the Ethiopic, the verb means *multum possedit, dives fuit*.   In Arabic, the senses are numerous, but they may all be referred to one root.   Thus, e. g., בַּעַל, بعل، means, according to the *Camus*, " *Terram tumidiorem et elatam, quæ una tantum vice quotannis complui necesse habet: item palmam, arborem, sementem, quæ non rigatur, aut quam solum cœlum irrigat*," a land, a tree, a crop, which itself *possesses*, and is not obliged to *borrow* from another source.   This ground of the appellation plainly appears in Dscheuhari (comp. Schultens, l. c.): "*Adhibetur in palma, quæ suis sibi radicibus potum succumve præstat, sic ut necesse non sit eam irrigare*."   For the meaning *to rule*, in the case of the verb, only the following gloss, out of the *Camus*, could be cited: " *Utrumque* (the 1. and 10. conj.) *si cum* עָלֶיהָ, *super illum*, *construatur*, *notat: potitus est rei, in eamque, superbius se gessit*."   But this *in eamque &c.* must be struck out.   It has originated entirely out of the false reading الي in Schultens, for which (comp. Freytag) ابي, *noluit*, must be read.   בַּעַל with עַל accordingly means:

---

* Vitringa on the passage, altogether correctly " בַּעַל *proprie ὁ ἔχων*, habens quamcunque rem in sua potestate, quare ad maritum refertur per ellipsin, qui integre dicitur בַּעַל אִשָּׁה, habens mulierem, Exod. 21. 3."

are not (like Judah, who had not yet drunk of the cup of God's wrath) terrified by threatenings, but allured by the call, ' *Come unto me, ye who are weary and heavy laden, for I will refresh you.*'—But even those have a difficult task, who explain the meaning with Kimchi, ' *for I did indeed* [formerly] *reject you, but will* [now] *take or collect you* [1], &c. For what could be more unlikely than that the prophet, if he had wished to express this meaning, should have omitted the very words (the *formerly* and the *now*) on which the whole antithesis turns? The *marrying* and the *taking* plainly stand here in the same relation; both together form the ground for the return to the Lord. To this must be added, according to our interpretation, the beautiful parallelism of this verse with ver. 12: ' *Return, thou apostate Israel, saith the Lord, I will not be angry with you; for I am rich in love; I do not retain anger for ever.*' Israel's haughtiness is broken, but despair prevents his returning to the Lord. The Lord therefore constantly repeats his invitation, grounds it continually anew on the fact, that he delights to show mercy and love to those who have forsaken him. Entirely parallel also, accord- to our interpretation, is chap. 3. 1, ' *If a man put away his wife, and she go away from him, and become another man's, will he then, indeed, return to her? But thou hast whored with many lovers, yet nevertheless return again to me.*' In ver. 8, the *rejection* of Israel was represented under the image of a *bill of divorce* [' *Because apostate Israel had forsaken me, therefore I put her away, and gave her a bill of divorce*'], what therefore more natural than that the receiving again, offered out of pure compassion, should appear under the image of a new marriage, especially since the *apostasy* had been designated in the preceding verse as *adultery* and *whoredom?*—*And I will take you, &c.* The covenant having been concluded with the *whole* people, an *individual* might suppose that *his* repentance would be in vain: but God tells them that though *but one* should come to him from a whole city, but two from a whole tribe, He would receive them and conduct them back to Zion. The apparent limitation of the promise is in truth an extension of it. How great must the love and compassion of God towards Israel be; in what a wide extent must the proposition be true, Rom. 11. 29, Ἀμεταμέλητα τὰ χαρίσματα καὶ ἡ κλῆσις τοῦ Θεοῦ, if even a single righteous Lot is delivered by God out of the Sodom of Israel; if Joshua and Caleb, unhurt by the punishment of the sins of the thousands, reach the promised land; if *every* penitent heart at once finds a gracious God! Thus it appears, that this passage is by no means at variance with others, where a *general* restoration of Israel is promised. On the contrary, the here predicted ἐπιτυγχάνειν of the ἐκλογή

" to be a possessor of a thing, and, as such, not to wish to relinquish it to an-other.—And thus is cut off the root of the interpretation of בָּעַל, in a *bad sense*, grounded on the Hebrew usage.

[1] To support this meaning, we must suppose the *for* to relate more to the *I will take* than to the *I marry*. To translate כִּי *although*, with *De Wette*, is quite arbitrary.

(Rom. 11. 7), is a pledge of the more comprehensive and general mercy.—As to the *fulfilment*, the prophecy belongs in *substance* to all times. There was a commencement of its fulfilment, when, in the time of Cyrus, many out of the ten tribes, from true love to the God of Israel, joined themselves to the returning Jews, and were engrafted again by God into the olive-tree; a continuation, when this, in later times, particularly in those of the Maccabees, frequently happened; a preparation for the completion itself, when, in the time of Christ, the blessings of God were poured out upon the whole δωδεκάφυλον (Acts 26. 7). We are by no means compelled to stop short at these feeble beginnings, by, ' *I bring you to Zion,*' here, and ' *they will come out of the land of the north, to the land that I gave to their fathers,*' ver. 18. The idea appears here only in the form in which it must be realized, so far as this was to be done in the time of the Old Testament. Zion, and the Holy Land, were at that time the seat of the kingdom of God, so that the return to the latter was inseparable from the return to the former. Those, who, among the Israelites, were converted to the true God, either returned wholly to Judea, or, at least, they presented there their sacrifices. But Zion and the Holy Land come into consideration, *only* as the seat of the kingdom of God, and for this very reason, the course of the fulfilment advances without cessation, even in times, when the North also has become *a Zion,* and *a Holy Land.*—That *two* were assigned to a family, and only *one* to a city, shows that we must here think of a larger family, which was in possession of several cities; the connexion of the city with the family, implies that the discourse is here of the cities of the land of Israel, not of those which the exiles inhabited.

981. Ver. 15. ' *And I will give to you shepherds after my own heart, and they shall feed you with understanding and insight.*' Who are here to be understood by the *shepherds?* Calvin supposes that they are particularly the *prophets,* and the *priests.* In like manner Vitringa (*Obss.* lib. vi. p. 417), who thinks of Ezra and the *learned* men of that time in the lower, and of Christ in the higher sense. Among the Fathers, Jerome also: " *Atque hi sunt apostoli et apostolici viri, qui paverunt credentium multitudinem non in Judaicis ceremoniis, sed in scientiá et doctrinâ.*" Others refer to the *leaders* of every kind; thus Venema: " *Pastores sunt rectores, ductores et doctores.*" Others, finally, confine the expression to the *rulers;* thus Kimchi (" *Gubernatores Israelis cum rege Messiâ*"), Grot., Cler. The last interpretation is to be preferred unconditionally, for the following reasons. (1) The image of the *shepherd,* and of *feeding,* occurs, indeed, sometimes in the wider sense, usually, however, especially of the *rulers.* Thus, in the ground passage, 2 Sam. 5. 2, of David, comp. Micah 5. 3: thus in our prophet, in chap. 2. 8, ' *the* priests *spake not, Where is the Lord, and those who administered the law knew me not, and the* shepherds *sinned against me, and the* prophets *prophesied in the name of Baal,*' comp. ver. 26, ' *they, their kings, and princes, and their priests, and their prophets.*' (2) The words ' *after my own heart*' contain a plain allusion to 1 Sam.

13. 14, where it is said of David, ' *The Lord has sought for himself a man after his own heart, and placed him for a ruler over his people.*' (3) All doubt is removed by the parallel passage, chap. 23. 4, '*And I will raise up over them shepherds, and they shall feed them, and they shall fear no more, neither be dismayed.*' That here only *the rulers* could be understood by the shepherds, is shown by the antithesis with the *evil rulers of the present*, mentioned in chap. 22, and also by the connexion with ver. 5, where the general expression is made more definite; the concentration of the fulfilment of the preceding promise is placed in the Messiah, ' *Behold, the days come, saith the Lord, and I will raise up to David a righteous Branch, and he shall reign as king, and act wisely, and judge the land in justice and righteousness.*' —This parallel passage is also of great importance, inasmuch as it shows, that our prophecy also has its final reference to the Messiah. The kingdom of the ten tribes was punished with wicked kings, for its apostasy from the Lord, and his visible representative. In the whole long series of Israelitish kings, we find no Jehoshaphat, no Hezekiah, no Josiah. Very naturally; for the foundation of the Israelitish throne was rebellion. Now with the cessation of the sin, the punishment also was to cease. Israel betakes himself again to the family by which all divine blessings were conferred upon the Theocracy, and thus he again receives a share in them, particularly in their richest abundance in the exalted descendant of David, the Messiah [1].—The *antithesis* of ' *after my own heart*,' is formed by ' *they have made kings, and not by me, princes which I knew not*,' referring to the first history of the people of Israel, Hos. 8. 4. Formerly the rebels chose kings according to their own heart's lust, now they choose whom God chooses, and He must be an instrument of the blessing, according to the same necessity whereby the former were instruments of the curse [2]. The foundation of insight and wisdom, is the living communion with the Lord; to be according to His heart, is to walk according to His will. A consequence of apostasy from Him, in the case of the former rulers of Israel, was their foolish counsels, whereby they brought their people to ruin. The servants of God act wisely, because with a view to God; and, whoever acts wisely, finds prosperity for himself and his people. It is, therefore, a proof of the greatest mercy of God towards His people, when He gives His *servants* to them for kings.

982. Ver. 16. '*And it shall come to pass, when ye have increased and multiplied in the land in those days, saith the Lord, it shall no more be said, The ark of the covenant of the Lord! and it will not come into the heart, neither will it be remembered nor missed, and another will not be made.*' ' *When*,' &c. alludes to Gen. 1. 28. As God's general providence causes the fruitfulness of all creatures, so does

---

[1] Compare 820, an exactly parallel passage, and also Ezek. 34. 23.

[2] דֵּעָה and הַשְׂכֵּיל stand adverbially; comp., on the transition of nouns into adverbs, Ewald, p. 499, 631. הִשְׂכִּיל, *to act wisely*, is in *Hiph.* only apparently intransitive, comp. Ew. p. 189.

His special providence the increase of His Church, whose ranks had
been thinned by His judgements; and thus the promise to the patriarchs meets its fulfilment ; comp. the full investigation in 792.
God's future agency, in this respect, has an analogy in his former, in
Egypt, comp. Exod. 1. 12.—' *The ark of the covenant*' is to be understood as an *exclamation*, i. q., ' *it is the goal of all our wishes, the
object of all our longing.*' The bare mention of the object, of which
the whole heart is full, is sufficient for the lively sensibility [1].
' *Another will not be made*' presupposes *the coming of* a time when
the ark of the covenant will no longer exist, the time of the destruction of the Temple, so repeatedly and emphatically predicted by the
prophet. God will supply so rich a compensation for that which is
lost, that men will no longer desire it, nor, driven by this desire,
make an effort to produce it again by their own hands.—The principal question now arises, in what relation is the ark of the covenant
here regarded ? The answer is supplied by ver. 17. The ark of the
covenant is no more remembered, because Jerusalem has now become,
in the complete sense, *the throne of God;* the ark of the covenant,
therefore, comes into consideration as *the throne of God, in the
imperfect sense.* That it was so, may easily be shown, but respecting
the *how*, there has been a diversity of opinion. The current view
was, that God, as covenant God, had made Himself known *constantly*, above the cherubim, upon the ark of the covenant in a
visible symbol, that of a cloud. The first *considerable* opposition to
this proceeded from Vitringa, who, in the *Obss. s. t.* i. p. 169, &c.,
remarks as follows : " *Forte enim opus non fuerit statuere, in sancto
sanctorum super arcam ordinariam nubem fuisse in tabernaculo, aut
templo Salomonis, sed sufficiat dicere, arcam habitationis divinæ
σύμβολον fuisse ; et locum inter Cherubinos ideo dici præsens habuisse
numen, quia voluntatis suæ revelatione inde profectâ præsentem se
Israelitis testabatur deus.*" This view of Vitringa's, however, of the
mere invisible presence of God over the ark of the covenant, experienced warm opposition ; a note to the second edition shows, that he
himself afterwards hesitated respecting it. Far more decidedly, and
with a manifest design to carry it through, whether true or false,
Thalemann, a pupil of Ernesti, presented it at a later period in the
Dissertatio de Nube super Arcam Fœderis, Leipz. 1756. He nevertheless explains, that the *thing* is not to be denied, but only the *sign*
to be contested. He found a learned opponent in Joh. Eberh. Rau,
Prof. at Herborn, *Ravius de Nube super Arcam Fœderis*, Utrecht,
1760, a whole book, in which the treatise of Thalemann is reprinted.

---

[1] The phrase, עָלָה עַל־לֵב, is connected with זָכַר precisely as here, Is. 65. 17,
' *For behold, I create a new heaven and a new earth, and the former shall not be
remembered, and they shall not come into the heart*,' comp. also Jer. 51. 50 ; 7. 31 ;
1 Cor. 2. 9. זָכַר with בְּ, does not stand in this way, without any thing further,
instead of the usual connexion with the *accus.* It designates a remembering,
joined with passion, with earnest desire, comp. Ewald, p. 605. פָּקַד is here taken
by many in the sense *to visit*, but the meaning *to miss* (comp. Is. 34. 16 ;
1 Sam. 20. 6—18 ; 25. 15 ; 1 Kings 20. 39) is recommended by the connexion
with the following : ' *it will not again be made.*'

The matter is properly very simple ; both sides are partly right and partly wrong, and the truth lies between them. That, at the annual entrance of the high priest into the holy of holies, the invisible presence of God embodied itself in the symbol of a cloud, as it did elsewhere also on extraordinary occasions, as the journey through the wilderness, and the dedication of the Tabernacle and the Temple, is shown, beyond contradiction, by the chief passage, Levit. 16. 2. Aaron is there admonished not to enter the Holy of Holies on every occasion, which would evince want of reverence, but only once in the year, ' *For I will appear in the cloud over the lid of expiation* [1]. The place where God makes Himself known in so visible a manner when the high priest enters it, must be for him one of extraordinary holiness. On the other hand, the supposition of an *ordinary* and *constant presence of the cloud* in the Holy of Holies, in respect to which such questions might arise as whether it was also visible to the Philistines, is entirely without proof; what Rau cites in its favour, relates only to the *invisible presence* of God, which surely cannot be placed on a level with one merely imaginary, as has been done by him (p. 35) ; how otherwise would it stand with the presence of God in the hearts of believers (Isa. 66. 2), and in the Lord's Supper? Ezekiel, to be sure, *sees* the glory of the Lord over the cherubim raise itself out of the Temple before the destruction, 11. 22 ; but since what is represented in a vision *must* be represented *visibly*, even though invisible in its own nature, how can we infer from the *visibility* of any thing in a *vision*, its *actual visibility* in rerum naturâ ? — Still, as already remarked, this whole dispute concerns the *how*, not the *fact* of God's presence over the ark of the covenant, which here, in the wider sense, comprehends the cherubim, and ' *the glory of the Lord*' enthroned above them. That this glory of the Lord was always really present over the ark of the covenant, although it made itself outwardly visible only in extraordinary cases, can be shown from a multitude of passages [2]. To this purpose are all those where God is designated as sitting above the cherubim [3]. To this refers the designation of the ark of the covenant in the stricter sense, as *God's footstool*, 1 Chron. 29. 2, David : ' *I had purposed to build a house, where the ark of the covenant of the Lord might rest,—and the footstool of our God* [4].' Hence it is explained, why supplication in distress, and thanksgiving for prosperity, was always presented before the ark of the covenant, or towards it. Joshua, after the defeat before Ai (7. 5, sq.), tore his garments, and fell upon his face to the earth before the ark of the Lord until evening, together with the elders of Israel, and they cast dust upon their heads, and Joshua said, ' *Ah, Lord, Lord, wherefore hast thou brought this people over*

[1] This is the only correct explanation of בַּפֹּרֶת, which can never mean any thing but *lid*.

[2] Comp. Levit. 16. 2, and 9. 24, where, after Aaron's consecration for a solemn confirmation of his office, the glory of the Lord appears to the whole people.

[3] 1 Chron. 14. 6 ; Ps. 80. 2 ; 1 Sam. 4. 4 ; 2 Sam. 6. 2 ; Ps. 99. 1 ; 2 Kings 19. 15.

[4] Ps. 99. 5 ; Ps. 132. 7 ; Lam. 2. 1.

the Jordan ?' Solomon, after the appearance and promise at Gibeah, went before the ark of the covenant of the Lord, and offered burnt-offerings and thank-offerings, 1 Kings 3. 15 ; 2 Sam. 15. 32, it is related, that David, very sorrowful, had ascended the Mount of Olives, and when he had come to the place *where men were accustomed to worship God*, Hushai met him. It was accordingly the custom, when one had gained, on the summit of the Mount of Olives, for the first or for the last time, the view of the sanctuary, to cast himself down before the God of Israel, who dwelt there.—To the ark of the covenant all the passages refer, where it is said that God would dwell among Israel, in the temple, at Zion or Jerusalem ; from the promise, Exod. 29. 45, '*I will dwell in the midst of the children of Israel*,' onwards, comp., e. g., Ps. 9. 12 ; 132. 13, 14. 1 Kings 6. 12, 13, where God promises Solomon, that, if he would but walk in His commandments, and do according to His judgements, then would He *dwell among* the children of Israel, and afterwards fulfils this promise by a solemn entrance into His sanctuary. Inseparably connected therewith, was the high esteem in which the ark of the covenant was held in Israel ; it was the most costly jewel of the people, the central point of their whole existence. So the place where God's glory dwelt, Ps. 26. 8, where He made Himself known in His most glorious manifestations, was named the *glory of Israel*[1]. The high priest, Eli, heard all the rest of the melancholy news,—Israel's overthrow,—the death of his sons,—with patience. But when he who had escaped added, '*Besides, the ark of God is taken, he fell back from his seat by the door, and broke his neck, and died. His daughter-in-law, when she heard that the ark of the covenant had been taken, bowed herself in violent anguish, and brought forth ; for her pains came upon her ; and as she was now dying, the women, that stood by her, said, Fear not, for thou hast a young son ; but she answered nothing, and laid it not to heart, and she called the child, Ichabod, and said, The glory has departed from Israel, because the ark of God was taken, and said once more, The glory has departed from Israel, for the ark of God is taken.*'—But how can this dwelling of God upon the ark of the covenant be conceived ? should the Most High, whom all heaven and the heaven of all heavens comprehends not[2], whose throne is heaven, and whose footstool the earth[3], dwell in a Temple made by the hands of men[4] ? The correct view is as follows. The substance and central point in the whole relation of Israel to God, is, that the God of heaven and of earth became Israel's God ; the Creator of heaven and earth the covenant God ; His general providence in blessing and in cursing a special one. In order to bring this relation near to the people, and thus make it the object of their love and fear, God gave to them (as *a type*, and, at the same time, *a prelude*, of the condescension with which He, whom the universe did not enclose, dwelt in the womb of Mary), a *præsens numen* in His sanctuary, not as a mere symbolic representation, but as an embody-

---

[1] Comp. 1 Sam. 4. 21—22 ; Ps. 78. 61.   [2] 1 Kings 8. 27.
[3] Is. 66. 1.   [4] Acts 7. 48, sq.

ing of the idea, so that whoever would seek Him as the God of Israel, could find Him only in the Temple, and over the ark of the covenant. That He held His seat precisely there, showed the difference between this real presence of the Deity, and that fancied by the heathen. There was no fond partiality for Israel; no licence for sin. God's dwelling among Israel rested on His covenant, His holy law. According as His covenant was observed, and the law fulfilled or not, it manifested itself by a richer blessing or a severer punishment. If the covenant be entirely broken, God relinquishes His dwelling, and only the curse remaining behind, greater than that which overtakes those among whom He never dwells, indicates by its greatness the greatness of the former mercy.—If, now, this was the case with the ark of the covenant, if it was the main point of the whole former economy, what was there which would not fall when it fell? and how immensely great must be the compensation for it, if it were to cause the desire after it to cease, and itself to be forgotten, as belonging to the πτωχὰ στοιχεῖα, to the image and the shadow! How every thing sacred under the Old Testament depended on the ark of the covenant, is shown by the very fact, that it was made before any thing else. Without an ark of the covenant, no Temple,—it is by the *ark of the covenant* that it first becomes a sanctuary; for holy, says Solomon, is the place whither the ark of the Lord comes (2 Chron. 8. 11),—without an ark of the covenant, no priesthood; for whom are they to serve, when no Lord is present? Without a *Temple* and *priesthood*, no *sacrifice*. We have, therefore, here, the prediction of an entire annihilation of *the previous form* of the kingdom of God, but such a one as is, at the same time, *the highest completion of the substance*, a dissolution like that of the seed-corn, which dies only in order to bring forth much fruit; like that of the body, which is sown in corruption, in order to be raised in incorruption.— The question still arises, in what relation to our prophecy does the absence of the ark of the covenant under the second Temple stand, whose restitution the Jews expected in the end of the days? That it actually disappeared there can be no doubt [1]. To determine *why* this was so, we must not overlook other analogous phenomena, the loss of the Urim and Thummim, and the cessation of the prophetic order soon after the return from the exile. Every thing was to make the people sensible that their condition was *only provisional;* the Theocracy must sink *below* its former glory, that its future and infinitely greater glory may the more be desired. After this determination of the *wherefore*, it is now easy to determine the relation of the absence of the ark of the covenant to our prophecy. It was the *beginning of its fulfilment*. In the kingdom of God, there is no decay without a renewal. The extinction of the old is a pledge that the new is soon to be supplied. On the other side, the absence of the ark of the covenant was, indeed, also a matter-of-fact prophecy of a

---

[1] Josephus does not mention it in the catalogue of the *spolia Judaica* borne before in the triumph; he says expressly, that the holy of holies had become entirely empty. *De B. Jud.* v. 5. § 5.

mournful character. It announced to those who held fast to the form, without having embraced the substance, and who, therefore, were not capable of participating in its glorious development, that the time was approaching, when the form to which they had fastened themselves, with their whole existence, should be broken. Had the one great privilege of the covenant people, the δόξα (Rom. 9. 4), vanished, how should not that soon follow which existed only on its account, and without it had no significance ? In this relation, the non-renewal of the ark of the covenant showed, that the Chaldean destruction and the Roman were connected together, as *beginning* and *completion ;* just as, in the other, that, from the very return out of the exile, the realization of God's great plan of salvation began to be prepared. The emptiness in the place where formerly the glory of God dwelt, plainly predicted (since the most complete *fuga vacui* belongs to the covenant God) the future fulness.—Finally, it still remains for us to determine the especial reference of the verse to Israel. In the preceding verse there had been promised to Israel the imparting anew of the blessings which he had lost by his separation from the stock of David, and that with interest and increase. For David's line was to reach its completion in his righteous Branch. This shepherd *in the fullest sense after the heart of God,* which his ancestor had been only imperfectly, should feed them with wisdom and insight. *Here* a compensation is promised for the second, yet immensely greater loss, which has been acknowledged as such by the believers in Israel at all times. The revelation of the Lord upon the ark of the covenant was the magnet, which perpetually attracted them towards Jerusalem. Many sacrificed their whole earthly possessions, and took up their residence in Judea, others travelled out of their natural home to their spiritual, to the ' *throne of the glory exalted from the beginning* [1].' In vain was all that the kings of Israel did to stifle this inextinguishable longing. Every new event, whereby ' *the glory of Israel*' manifested itself as such, kindled its ardour anew. But here also is the great blessing which the believers were deprived of with pain, and the unbelievers regarded with indifference, restored to those who return, not in its former aspect, but in glorious completion. The whole people have now received eyes, and perceive the worth of the blessing in its previous form, and yet this previous form is now regarded by them as nothing, because its new and infinitely more glorious form occupies their attention.

983. Ver. 17. ' *At that time they will call Jerusalem the throne of the Lord, and all the heathen shall gather themselves to her, because the name of the Lord is at Jerusalem, and they will walk no more after the lust of their evil heart.*' The emphasis rests [not upon *Jerusalem,* as many interpreters suppose, but rather] upon the ' *throne of the Lord.* This receives from the antithesis the nearer determination, ' *The true throne of the Lord.*' In the same way, Isa. 66. 1, against those who boasted that over the cherubim was God's throne, and the ark of the covenant

[1] Jer. 17. 12.

His footstool, it is said, ' *The heaven is my* (true) *throne and the earth my* (true) *footstool,*' comp. the passages, according to which the ark of the covenant was designated as the footstool, and so the place over the cherubs of the ark of the covenant as the throne of the Lord ; comp. still Isa. 60. 13. Ezek. 1. 26.—The highest prerogative of the covenant people, their highest advantage over the world, is, to have God among themselves ; and this they shall now experience in the fullest manner, so that the idea and the reality shall coincide. In substance, completely parallel are such passages as Ezek. 43, where the Shechinah, which disappeared at the destruction, returns to the new Temple, to the kingdom of God in its new and more glorious form, ver. 2 : ' *And, behold, the glory of the God of Israel came from the east, and its voice was as the voice of great waters, and the earth was lighted by its glory.*' Ver. 7, ' *And he said to me, Thou, Son of man, behold there the place of* my throne, *and the place of the soles of my feet, where I will dwell among the children of Israel for ever, and the house of Israel will no more profane my holy name.*' Zech. 2. 14, ' *Exult and rejoice, O daughter of Zion. For, behold, I will come and dwell in the midst of thee,*' with allusion to Exod. 29. 45, ' *And I will dwell among the children of Israel, and will be their God.*' The full realization of this promise the prophet designates as reserved for the future. This, however, could not be, had it not been already realized throughout the whole past, in the dwelling of God over the ark of the covenant. 8. 3, ' *I will return to Zion, and dwell in the midst of Jerusalem.*'— If we inquire after the fulfilment, John 1. 14, ' *And the Word was made flesh, and dwelt among us, and we beheld his glory, the glory as of the only begotten of the Father,*' immediately occurs to us, and the more so, as the former dwelling of God in the Temple is here plainly alluded to, and the incarnation of the λόγος is regarded as its highest realization. From the personal appearing of God in Christ, in whom the fulness of the Godhead dwelt bodily (σωματικῶς), His dwelling among His people by the πνεῦμα Χριστοῦ, must not, indeed, be separated, which is related to the former, as the brook to the fountain ; it is the stream of living water, which flows out of the body of Christ. Both together constitute the *true tabernacle* of God with men, *the new and real ark of the covenant ;* for the old is ' *a shadow of things to come, but the body is of Christ,*' Col. 2. 17, comp. Apoc. 21. 22 : ' *And I saw no temple therein : for the Lord God Almighty and the Lamb are the temple of it.*' 11. 19, ' *And the temple of God was opened in heaven, and there was seen in his temple the ark of his testimony.*' The typical import of the ark of the covenant is expressly asserted, Heb. 9. 4, 5, and to what it referred is indicated, chap. 4. 16, ' *Let us come boldly unto the throne of grace,*' where Christ is designated as the true mercy-seat, as the true ark of the covenant. As it was only over the ark of the covenant that God was formerly found by those among His people who sought Him, so have we now, through Christ, joyfulness and access in all confidence to God, Eph. 3. 12 ; and it is only in His name, presented in living union with Him, that our prayers are acceptable, John 16. 23.—The consequence of this highest realization of the idea of the Theocracy, and at the same time a sign that it has been attained, a measure for the blessings which Israel has to expect from his reunion with the Church of the Lord, is the gathering of the heathen to it, as had been the case already by way of type and prelude, at the inferior manifestations of the presence of God among His people, comp., e. g., Josh. 9. 9, ' *And they* (the Gibeonites) *said to him, Thy servants come out of a distant land, on account of the name* [1] *Jehovah, thy God; for we have heard his fame, and all that he did in Egypt, and all that he did to the two kings of the Amorites,*' &c.   In an exactly similar manner also, in Zech. 2. 15, with the dwelling of the Lord in Jerusalem is joined, ' *And many heathen shall join themselves to the Lord in that day, and they shall be to me for a people, and I will dwell in the midst of them.*'   The לְשֵׁם יְהֹוָה לִירוּשָׁלַיִם is verbally to be translated, "on account of the name of the Lord to Jerusalem (belonging)," for, "because the name of the Lord belongs to Jerusalem, is native there."   The name of the Lord is the Lord Himself, so far as He makes known His invisible being, manifests Himself.   The name is the bridge between existing and being known.   A God without a name = θεὸς ἄγνωστος, Acts 17. 23.   There is an allusion to Deut. 12. 5 : ' *But the place which the Lord your God will choose out of all your tribes,* that He may place His name there, *to inhabit it, that shall ye seek, and thither shall ye come.*'   Formerly, since God placed His name only in an incomplete manner, only Israel assembled themselves, but now all the heathen.—The last words : ' *and they shall not walk any more,*' &c., are not to be referred to the heathen, but to the Israelites, or to the collective inhabitants of Jerusalem, the collective members of the Theocracy *besides,* but *including,* them [2].

[1] לְשֵׁם

[2] This appears from the comparison of the ground passage of the Pentateuch, as well as the Parallel passages of Jeremiah.   Every where, where the *Scherirut* occurs, the discourse is of the covenant people ; every where, the walking according to the *Scherirut* of the heart, stands opposed to that, *walking according to the revealed law of Jehovah,* which only Israel possessed.   We may say, in a certain sense, that the שְׁרִירוּת לֵב is ἅπαξ λεγόμενον.   It occurs *independently* only in a single passage, Deut. 29. 18 ; in the rest, eight times in Jeremiah, and besides, in Ps. 81. 13, it is plainly derived, not from the living language, from which it had disappeared, but from the written.   Its import cannot be determined with certainty.   So much seems to be certain, that it cannot be explained either with Jerome, from a comparison of the Arabic, by *wickedness,* or with others by *obduracy ;* that rather the expression שְׁרִירוּת לֵב is of itself *indifferent,* and acquires *a bad meaning,* only by the evil nature of the subject, the human heart.   Most probably שְׁרִירוּת לֵב is to be taken, as about synonymous with יֵצֶר לֵב, the imagination of the heart,—properly the *firmness,* or the *foundation* of the heart, which sense has also in its favour the analogy of the *masc.* Job 40. 11.

Chapter 23:1-8

984. These verses form only a part of a greater whole, to which, besides the whole 22nd chapter, chap. 23. 9—40, also belongs. In chap. 22, the prophet threatens and warns the kings of Judah, first in general, announcing the judgements of the Lord upon them and their people, the fulfilment of the threatenings, Deut. 29. 23, sq., should they continue in their hitherto ungodly course, 22. 1—9. He then, in order to make a stronger impression, exemplifies the general threatening, shows how God's avenging justice would manifest itself in the lot of the individual apostate kings. First, Jehoahaz, the son and immediate successor of Josiah, whom Pharaoh-Necho dethroned, and carried with him to Egypt, ver. 10—12. The declaration concerning him forms a commentary on the name *Shallum, the recompensed*, (he whom the Lord *recompenses according to his deeds*,) which the prophet gives to him instead of his proper name, *Jehoahaz*. Happy, in comparison with him, is his father Josiah, who found his death in the fight against the Egyptians. For he never more returns to his home, he lives and dies in a foreign land. Then *Jehoiakim*, ver. 13—19. He is a despot, who does all in his power to destroy the people intrusted to him. Therefore, the grossest contrast will ensue between his splendid name and his miserable lot. The Lord, far from raising him up, will cast him down into the lowest depth. Not even an honourable burial is given to him. Unwept, unlamented, like a trodden-down carcase, he lies without the gate of Jerusalem, the city of the great King, which he wished to wrest from Him, and to make his own possession. Then there is a digression, ver. 20—23. The apostate Judah is addressed. The judgement upon *her* kings is not foreign to herself, any more than their guilt belongs to them as individuals only. It is, at the same time, a judgement upon the people, who sink down from the height on which the mercy of the Lord had placed them, in consequence of His anger, which they have provoked by their wickedness. Then Jehoiachin, ver. 24—30. In his name, '*the Lord will establish*,' the *will* is too much. The Lord *will* reject, and cast him away as a worthless vessel. With his mother, he will be carried away out of his sweet native land, and there die. Irrevocable is the decree of the Lord, that no one of his sons will ascend the throne of David, so that he who has begotten sons in vain, is to be esteemed as one who is childless.

985. At the beginning of our portion (ver. 1 and 2), the substance of chap. 22 is embraced in *one* sentence : ' *Woe to the shepherds who ruin and scatter the flock of the Lord! Woe, therefore, to* these *shepherds who have done thus !*' With this is connected, in ver. 3—8, the prediction of prosperity for the poor scattered flock. For the same reason, why the Lord visits on those who have hitherto been their shepherds the wickedness of their doings, viz. because He is the Chief Shepherd, or on account of His covenant faithfulness, He will also receive them in love, collect them out of their dispersion, and instead of the evil shepherds, give them a good one, David's

long-promised and desired great descendant, who, as a *righteous* King, will diffuse justice and righteousness in the land, and therefore procure for it righteousness and prosperity from the Lord. So great will the mercy of the future be, that it will totally obscure the greatest mercy of the past, the deliverance out of Egypt.

986. That the whole prophecy belongs to the reign of Jehoiakim, cannot be doubted.—It must appear singular, that the same king, who, in the books of Kings, is named *Jehoahaz*, is here called only *Shallum*, the same who is there *Jehoiachin*, is here *Jeconias*, and briefly *Conias*. The pious Josiah had given his sons names prophetic of prosperity, with reference to the calamity with which Judah was more and more threatened. They were, according to his wish, to be so many *real* prophecies, and would have proved themselves to be such, if those who bore them had not rendered them void by their apostasy from the Lord, and occasioned the most striking contrast between the idea and the reality. This was first done by Jehoahaz. He, whom the Lord should *hold*, was carried by violence to Egypt. The prophet, therefore, names him *Shallum*, the *recompensed*[1],—he on whom the Lord visits the wickedness of his actions.—As to the names *Jehoiakim* and *Jehoiachin*, in the first place, their relation must be considered to the promise to David. It is there said, 2 Sam. 7. 12, ' *And I will set up* (וַהֲקִימֹתִי) *thy seed after thee, who shall come forth out of thy loins, and I will establish* (וַהֲכִינֹתִי) *his kingdom*.' This passage plainly contains the ground of *both* names. Even his former name, *Eliakim*, had probably been given to him by his father Josiah, in reference to the promise. When, however, Pharaoh desired him to change his name (for this motive to a step which was afterwards approved by Pharaoh, is, as the name itself shows, to be supplied, 2 Kings 23. 34),—he resolved to make such a change in it as would place it in still closer connexion with the promise, in which, not *El*, but *Jehovah*, is expressly mentioned as the promiser, as, indeed, the thing proceeded from Jehovah, the God of Israel. As, from the whole character of Jehoiakim, we cannot suppose that the twofold naming proceeded from true piety, nothing is more natural than to attribute it to opposition to the prophets. The central point of their annunciation was the impending calamity from the north, the decline of the family of David ; the promise to David, should, indeed, be fulfilled, but not till after a previous deep degradation, in the Messiah. Jehoiakim, reviling these threatenings, chose to transfer the prosperity from the future to the present. In his name, and in that of his son, he presented a standing protest against the prophetic prediction, and this could not but call forth a counter protest, which we find expressed in our prophecy. The prophet first overthrows the false interpretation, *Jehoiakim* is not *Jehoiakim*, and *Jehoiachin* is not *Jehoiachin*, chap. 22 ; and then he restores the right interpretation, the true *Jehoiakim* is, and remains, the *Messiah*, chap. 23. 5. With respect to the former, he satisfies

---

[1] Not as Hiller, p. 24, and Simonis, p. 267, *retributio,* comp. Ew. p. 240 ; the same, who, 1 Chron. 5. 38, is called *Shallum,* is called, 1 Chron. 9. 11, *Meshallum.*

himself with regard to Jehoiakim with the *actual* antithesis, and neglects to substitute a *truly significant* name for the one assumed, which may most easily be explained, by supposing that he holds it as unsuitable to exercise any kind of wit, even that which is sacred, on the then reigning king. It was otherwise, however, in respect to Jehoiachin. The first change of the name into *Jeconiah* had its aim not in itself; both names signify entirely the same. It had respect only to the second change into *Coniah*. He first places the future, in order that *he may*, by the removal of the ', cut off hope, a Jeconias without *J*, a ' *God-will-establish* ' without *will*.

987. Ver. 1. ' *Woe to the shepherds, who destroy and scatter my pasture flock, saith the Lord* [1].' None but the *Kings* can be intended by the wicked shepherds; all doubt of this vanishes, when the close connexion of our verse with chap. 22. is considered. That by the shepherds *usually* only the rulers are designated, we have seen already on chap. 3. 15 [2]. That this usage has for its foundation a typical understanding of the former relations of David, appears from Ps. 78. 70, 71 : ' *He chose David his servant, and took him from the sheep-folds; from following the ewes great with young, he brought him to feed Jacob his people, and Israel his inheritance,*' comp. Ezek. 34. 23, 24: ' *And I will raise up for them one shepherd, and he shall feed them, my servant David; he will feed them, and he will be their shepherd.*'—What is to be understood by *destroying* and *scattering*, must be determined, partly out of the foregoing chap. ver. 3. and ver. 13, sq., partly here out of ver. 3. The former passages show, that the violent acts of the kings, their oppressions and extortions, belong here [3]. The latter shows, that it is chiefly the heaviest guilt of the kings that comes under consideration; all that whereby they became the occasion of the carrying away of the people into exile, besides their foolish political plans, resting on ungodliness, comp. 10. 21; the both *negative* and *positive* promotion of impiety, and the consequent immorality, whereby the Divine judgements were powerfully called forth. The contrast between the *idea* and the *reality* contains the ground of the woe, further strengthened by the prominence given to the fact, that the flock which they destroy and scatter is *God's flock* [4].—It is remarkable, that the discourse here is

---

[1] Well to be observed is רֹעִים without the article here, with it in ver. 2. Ven.: ' *Generale væ pastoribus malis præmittitur, quod mox ad pastores Juda applicatur.—Cum væ Jehovæ in omnes pastores improbos denuntiatum sit, propterea v o s mali pastores, etc.*'

[2] Comp. still 25. 34—36, and the imitation, and first interpretation of our passage, in Ezek. 34.

[3] Comp. Ezek. 34. 2, 3.

[4] צֹאן מַרְעִיתִי cannot be explained by ' *the flock of my feeding,* i. q. ' *which I feed.*' For מַרְעִית, where it occurs alone, never had the sense usually attributed to it by the lexicographers, *pastio, pastus*, but always rather that of *pascuum*, comp. 10. 21; 25. 36; Is. 49. 9; Hos. 13. 6. צֹאן מַרְעִית is to be regarded as *nom. compos.*, *pasture flock*, = *a flock at pasture*, and the *suff.* belongs to the whole. מַרְעִית is not to be regarded as an idle addition. It is only when the flock is upon *the pasture*, that the virtues and faults of the shepherds can plainly show themselves.

only of the guilt of the *rulers*, and not of that of the *people*, while yet every deeper consideration of the subject shows the two to be inseparable, evil rulers, as arising from the condition of the people, and at the same time as a punishment, sent from God, of their ungodliness. The case, however, is easily explained, as soon as we only consider, that the prophet here had to do merely with the kings, not with the people. That their wickedness stood in a natural connexion with that of the people, was not sufficient to exculpate them. For that this *natural* connexion was not a necessary one, appears from the example of a Josiah, by whom, through the grace of God, it was broken through. Just as little were they justified by the fact, that they were rods of correction in the hand of God, to which the prophet himself refers, when he substitutes for the 'ye *have driven away*,' in ver. 2, the 'I *have driven away*,' in ver. 3. *They* had only to look to their call and their duty. The execution of God's purposes belonged to Him alone. From what has been said, it is evident that my '*pasture flock*' would be entirely misunderstood, if we should infer from it an antithesis of the *innocent* people, and the *guilty* kings. The moral condition of the people does not affect the kings; they have only to look at God's covenant with the people, which is for themselves a source of obligation, as much greater than that of heathen kings, as *Jehovah* is more glorious than *Elohim.* The moral condition of the people is, in a certain respect, not regarded even by God. However bad it may be, He looks at His covenant, and even the outward dispersion of the flock is, when more deeply considered, a collecting of it.

988. Ver. 2. ' *Therefore, thus saith the Lord the God of Israel against the shepherds who feed My people, Ye have scattered My flock, and driven them away, and ye have not visited them ; behold, I shall visit upon you the evil of your doings, saith the Lord.*' In the designation of God as ' *Jehovah God of Israel*,' that is already implied, which is afterwards expressed. *Because* God is this, the crime of the kings is at the same time sacrilege. They have profaned God. The expression ' *who feed My people*,' renders the idea more prominent and emphatic than the bare mention of the shepherds, and thus serves to render the contrast with the reality the more striking. The ' *driving away*,' is designated by the *fut.* with *vau conv.*, as a *consequence* of the dispersion. The flock without a shepherd first disperse, and then the individual sheep lose themselves in the wilderness. ' *Ye have not visited them*,' appears at first sight, as a stronger complaint had already preceded, to be feeble. But what they had done, first appears in all its odiousness, by considering what they *ought* to have done, but *have not.* This reference to their office, gives the greatest sharpness to the apparently mild reproof. The *visiting* constitutes the *general ground* of every *individual* act of the shepherds, so that *ye have not visited them* includes in itself all that which Ezekiel, chap. 34. 4, particularizes : ' *The weak ye strengthen not, and the sick ye heal not, and the wounded ye bind not up, and the dispersed ye bring not back, and the perishing ye seek not.*'—The expression,

'*the evil of your doings,*' refers to Deut. 28. 20, '*The Lord will send upon thee the curse, the terrour and the ruin, in all thy undertakings, until thou art destroyed, and perish miserably,* on account of the evil of thy doings, *that thou hast forsaken me.*' The faint allusion to a former fearful threatening in that part of the Pentateuch which was the most known of all, suffices to effect the completion of what is expressly uttered out of it [1].

989. Ver. 3. '*And I will collect the remnant of my flock out of all the lands whither I have driven them, and I will bring them back to their folds, and they shall be fruitful and increase* [2].' A spiritless adhering to the letter has here also led several interpreters to the supposition, that the prophet has in view merely the literal return from the exile, perhaps also the blessings of the times of the Maccabees. The opposite,—even apart from the fact, that then the fulfilment would little correspond with the promise ; Canaan was, for those who returned, too little Canaan, too little God's land to allow this return to be regarded as a realization of the promise of God,—can be easily shown out of the context. Closely connected with the collection and the bringing back, appears, in ver. 4, the raising up of the Good Shepherd ; and this promise, according to ver. 5, was to find, if not its sole fulfilment, still, at all events, its substance and central point, in the raising up of David's righteous shoot,—the Messiah. And that we can by no means here resort to the supposition of the *one after another*, appears from the comparison of ver. 7, 8. The '*therefore*' with which these verses begin, referring to the whole compass of the preceding promises, shows that we must by no means separate from one another, the bringing back from banishment and the raising up of the Messiah : and the contents of both verses lead to the same result. How could it well be said of the literal bringing back from the exile, that it would far surpass the former deliverance out of Egypt, and cause it to be forgotten ? The correct view was seen by Calvin : "*Non dubium est, quin propheta initium faciat a libero populi reditu, sed non est separandus Christus ab hoc redemtionis beneficio ; alioqui non constaret nobis effectus hujus prophetiæ.*" We justify this concurrent reference to Christ, by the fact, that the ground of Canaan's worth to Israel did not lie in its being His native land in the inferior sense, but in its being the land of God, the place where His honour dwelt ; hence it follows, that the literal return was one of value to the covenant people, only *so far as God showed Himself as God of the land ;* and therefore, because before Christ this happened only in a very imperfect manner in comparison with the idea, was of very inferior importance. And, in like manner,

---

[1] Such an allusion to the passage in Deuteronomy is demonstrable, wherever the combination רֹעַ מַעַלְלִים, probably become obsolete in later times, occurs, comp. 4. 4, and 21. 12, in which two passages also, the מִפְּנֵי is introduced, Is. 1. 16 ; Ps. 28. 4, Hos. 9. 15.

[2] Comp. the parallel passages 29. 14 ; 31. 8. 10 ; Ezek. 11. 17, sq., Mic. 2. 12, but especially Ezek. 34. 12, 13.

it follows, that the bringing back and the collecting by Christ were comprehended under the promise. For where God is, there also is Canaan. Whether it is the old stall or a new one is of very little consequence, if only the Good Shepherd is among the sheep. *As a general rule*, such external considerations lie without the province of prophecy, which, aiming at the *substance*, in regard to the *form* of its manifestation, points simply to history. To what ridiculous notions this false cleaving to the letter leads, appears from such remarks as those of Grotius on the second half of the following verse: *" Vivent securi sub præsidio potentissimo regum Persarum."* Worldly protection and worldly oppression were for the covenant people but little different. Their distress was that *heathen, any* heathen, reigned over them; and this distress must therefore remain (comp. Neh. 9. 36, 37,) although, by God's favour, the true value of which consisted only in its being a prophecy and pledge of a future and greater, in the place of the former severe dominion, a mild one had succeeded.— That the collection is promised only to the *remnant,* (comp. Isa. 10. 22. Rom. 9. 27,) indicates that *justification* and *mercy* go side by side. We must be very careful not to confound the Scriptural hope of a conversion of Israel in the main, in contrast with the *small ἐκλογὴ* at the time of Christ and the Apostles, with the hope of a *general* conversion in the strict sense. The latter, according to the relation of God to the freedom of man's nature, is simply impossible; it leads, by a necessary consequence, to the doctrine of *universal restoration.* For it is established, that God *wills* that all men should be aided; and if this *could* be done in the case of *all* the members of *one* people, it would necessarily follow that it could be done in the case of *all*. It has no Scripture expression in its favour, except the πᾶς in Paul, which must be explained by the antithesis with the *small ἐκλογή*; but it has many against it, viz. all the passages of the prophets, where salvation is promised only to the remnant, the escaped of Israel: and, besides the words of God, His deeds also, the great types of spiritual things, in the deliverance out of Egypt, where only the *remnant* reached Canaan, while the bodies of thousands fell in the wilderness; and in the return from Babylon, where by far the greater number preferred the temporal pleasures of sin to the enjoyment of the Lord in their own land.

990. Ver. 4. *'And I will raise up over them shepherds, and they shall feed them, and they shall no more fear, nor be terrified, neither be lost, saith the Lord.'* The reference here to 2 Sam. 7. 12, and to the name of *Jehoiakim,* which still more distinctly appears in the following verse, is manifest: comp. p. 637. This reference also shows, that the prophecy was composed under Jehoiakim. It was, at that time, easily understood by every one; even the slightest allusion was sufficient. The prophet had plainly in view, along with the antithesis of the apostasy of the people, and God's covenant faithfulness, still another, that of the apostasy of David's family, and God's faithfulness in the fulfilment of His promises made to David. The individual apostate members of this race, although, appropriating the promise to themselves, they expected prosperity in its name, were

destroyed, but God's mercy cannot depart from the stock ; out of it, because God is Jehovah, a true *Jehoiakim* and *Jehoiachin* must arise. And thus it appears, that the Maccabees are as little referred to here as Ezra and Nehemiah, who were conjectured to be so by Grotius. We might sooner think of Zerubbabel ; for his coming forward actually stood in a relation to the promise in David, although only as a feeble type and prelude of the true fulfilment, like the assembling out of the Babylonish exile, in comparison with that to be effected through Christ.   If any one would argue from the plural, still, the verse must in no case be separated from ver. 5, ' *First will I raise up to you shepherds,* then *the Messiah.*' We must rather, with C. B. Michaelis, subjoin, *imprimis unum, Messiam.*   Progressive degrees in the prosperity are found in *no* prediction of Jeremiah.   Everywhere the whole in its completion, the idea in its full compass, lies before him.   But there is no ground whatever to lay so much stress on the *plur.*   Every *plur.* can be employed for designating the generic idea [1].   And this was the more natural here, since the *bad genus,* to which the good is opposed, consisted of a *series of individuals.*   To the *evil pastoral care,* the prophet now, for the first time, opposes the *good ;* then, in ver. 5, he describes more particularly the individual who should represent the genus, who should completely realize the generic idea.   This explanation is confirmed by a comparison of the otherwise almost verbally coincident parallel passage, 33. 15, where the discourse is only of *one* descendant of David, the Messiah,—very naturally ; for there the antithesis with the bad shepherds, which here caused the genus to be rendered prominent at the beginning, was wanting.   In like manner, by a comparison of the imitation in Ezekiel, chap. 34.   In him also only *one* good shepherd occurs, in antithesis with the evil shepherds.—The expression, ' *and they shall feed themselves,*' stands in antithesis with ' *who feed my people,*' in ver. 2.   The former *should* feed the flock, instead of which they feed themselves (comp. Ezek. ver. 2), the latter *actually* feed them.   The former are shepherds in name, but in fact wolves, the latter are shepherds in name and reality [2].   ' *They shall fear not, and not be terrified,*' is explained by Ezek. 5. 8, ' *For this reason ; that my sheep are for a prey, and for a spoil to all the beasts of the field, because they have no shepherds, and because my shepherds do not concern themselves about the flock.*'

991. Ver. 5. ' *Behold, days come, saith the Lord, and I will raise up to David a righteous shoot* [*branch*]*, and he shall reign as a king, and act wisely, and cause justice and righteousness in the land.*' The expression, ' *Behold, days come,*' designates, according to the constant usage of Jeremiah, not an advance in time in relation to

---

[1] Ewald, p. 639.

[2] פָּקַד is to be taken in the sense *to miss,* comp. on chap. 3. 16.   There is an allusion to פְּקַדְתָּם לֹא in ver. 2.   Because the evil shepherd does not visit his flock, the sheep *are sought* (i. e. *have to be sought,* because they are lost); but now a grievous visitation comes even upon those who visit not: the Good Shepherd does visit, and *so* the sheep are not sought for.

what preceded, but *awakens attention* to the greatness of the act to
be announced. There is, at the same time, an allusion to the contrast between the *hope* and the *appearance*, by which the former by
no means seemed to be justified. Let the present be ever so discou-
raging, *still* the time comes [1].—In Is. 53. 11, where the servant of God
is described as a *high priest* and *sin-offering*, his righteousness occurs
as an essential condition of justification; here, where he appears
solely as a king, it is represented as the cause of the diffusion of justice and righteousness in the land. The expression, '*I will raise up
to David a righteous shoot*,' is here, as in chap. 33. 15, by no means,
= a righteous shoot of David. Rather, David is designated as
the person *to whom* the action of raising up refers, *on whose account*
it is performed. God had promised to him the eternal dominion of
his race. Although, therefore, the members of this race offend never
so much against God, although the people be never so unworthy to
be ruled by a righteous shoot of David, yet must God, as surely as
He is God, raise him up for David's sake. The word '*king*' is not
to be overlooked. It shows that '*shall reign*,' which, standing alone,
might well designate another government than a regal (e. g., that of
Zerubbabel), must be taken in its *full* sense. And this nearer determination was the more necessary, since the lowest humiliation of
the race of David, predicted by the prophet in chap. 22, (comp.
especially ver. 30,) was drawing near, which seemed to blast every
hope of its rising to *complete* prosperity. As faith in this event,
therefore, rested solely on the word, this must be as *definite as possible*, so that no one could pervert or misinterpret it.—'*He shall act
wisely*[2] [not, he shall prosper]: The *whole* verse treats of the gifts
of the king; all that follows, of the prosperity that is to be imparted
by these gifts to the people. Besides, there is a manifest antithesis
with the *folly* of the former shepherds, owing to ungodliness, as it
had been represented in the foregoing chapter as a ground of their
destruction, and that of the people, comp. 10. 21, '*The people had
become foolish, and they seek not the Lord, therefore they* act un-
wisely, *and their whole flock is scattered*.' But if the sense *to act
wisely*, is established here, so is it also in those passages where it
occurs of David, comp. on chap. 3. For that the prophet had these
passages in view, that, according to him, David's reign should revive
in a more illustrious form in his righteous shoot, is evident from the
fact, that the remainder also has for its foundation the description of
David's reign in the books of Samuel. Thus: '*And he shall reign
as a king, — and cause justice and righteousness in the land*,' refers
back to 2 Sam. 8. 15, '*And David reigned over all Israel, and
David provided justice and righteousness for his whole people*.' The
groundwork of the commencement of ver. 6, is formed by ver. 14,

---

[1] Concerning the צֶמַח comp. Zech. 6. 15. *Righteous* or *just* (צַדִּיק) stands
here in the same relation as in Zech. 9. 9: in Is. 53, 11, it occurs in a different
relation.

[2] In reference to הִשְׂכִּיל it has already been shown, on Chap. 3. 15, that it
never means *to be prosperous*, but rather always *to act wisely*.

(comp. ver. 6,) in the same place : ' *And the Lord gave prosperity* (וַיּשַׁע) *to David in all his ways* [1].' The providing of the *right* is the means whereby *righteousness* is provided. The *compulsory* dominion of *justice* is necessarily followed by the voluntary, as God's judgements, whereby He sanctifies Himself *upon* men, are at the same time the means whereby He sanctifies Himself *in* them. The high calling of the king, to *create* justice and righteousness, rests on his dignity as a bearer of God's image [2]. To be observed still is *the order :* ' *the king is righteous, his righteousness extends from him to his subjects ;*' then follow the salvation and righteousness of the Lord [3].

992. Ver. 6. ' *In his days shall Judah be provided with salvation, and Israel dwell securely, and this is the name which they shall give him, The Lord our righteousness.*' How the first words refer back to David has been already shown. What Jeremiah here says in several words, is more briefly expressed by Zechariah, when he says of the shoot [or branch] of David, that he is *just* (or *righteous*) *and protected by God* [4] (chap. 9. ver. 9 ; see the remarks there made). Israel is here to be taken in a narrower sense, or in the widest ; either the ten tribes *alone*, or these *with* Judah. The participation of the ten tribes in the prosperity of the future is a favorite thought of Jeremiah, which returns in all his Messianic prophecies. The

---

[1] If הִשְׂכִּיל, where it occurs of David, is thus to be taken, the Seventy also, Is. 52. 13, are right in their translation συνήσει, for there, as here, regard is had to David as a type of the Messiah.—The phrase עָשָׂה מִשְׁפָּט וּצְדָקָה is commonly translated by De Wette, " to *practise* justice and righteousness." But that this interpretation is false, appears from the fact, that, on Ps. 146. 7, he felt compelled to relinquish it. עָשָׂה is rather to be explained by *to create, to produce.* מִשְׁפָּט is here, as always, the objective *right*, צְדָקָה the subjective *righteousness.*

[2] Comp. Ps. 103. 6 ; Ps. 146. 7 ; chap. 22. 15 ; and chap. 22. 3.

[3] With interpretations like that of Grotius, who, by the righteous sprout, understands Zerubbabel, we need here the less delay, since we have already sufficiently examined them on the parallel passages, and since their obvious erroneousness appears from the circumstance, that he is without a predecessor and without a respectable follower. Indeed, if we could rely on the declaration of Theodoret (Ταῦτα οἱ ἐμβρόντητοι Ἰουδαῖοι εἰς τὸν Ζοροβάβελ ἕλκειν ἀναιδῶς ἐπιχειροῦσιν, then the refutation), the older Jews would have broken the way to this perversion. But we have already frequently seen, that we cannot confidently rely upon such assertions of Theodoret. And in the Jewish writings themselves, there is no trace of such an interpretation. The Chaldee is decided in favour of the reference to the Messiah. Alex. Version thus Καὶ τοῦτο τὸ ὄνομα αὐτοῦ, ὃ καλέσει αὐτὸν κύριος, Ἰωσεδέκ. That the translators themselves proceeded on this false understanding is not to be supposed. *Jehosedeck* was the father of Joshua, the high priest, and an entirely undistinguished person. Certainly they only designed, by retaining the Hebrew form, to express that here a *nom. propr.* occurred, to which they were led, especially by the circumstance, that, in their time, this name was generally current, as one of the proper names of the Messiah.

[4] צַדִּיק וְנוֹשַׁע. The correctness of the interpretation of נוֹשַׁע there given, is placed beyond all doubt by the comparison of this ground passage. That prosperity, the inseparable companion of righteousness, is there attributed to the king, its possessor, and here to the people, makes indeed no difference whatever ; for there also it is for the benefit of his subjects that prosperity is attributed to the king who comes to Zion ; as it is also *for Zion* that he is just.

liveliness of his hope for Israel is a great testimony for the liveliness
of his faith.   For, in respect to Israel, there was still less of *visible*
ground for hope than in the case of Judah.   There is an allusion to
Deut. 33. 28, ('And he *shall* drive out from before thee thy enemy,
and say, Destroy,') '*And Israel shall dwell securely* [1], *alone, Jacob
shall look upon a land of corn and must, and his heaven drop down
dew.*'   This glorious destination of the covenant people, hitherto
very incompletely realized, but principally under David (comp.
2 Sam. 8. 6. 14), should become so apparent under the reign of the
Messiah, that the *idea* and the *reality* would entirely coincide.   The
covenant people should appear in their whole dignity [2].—We come
now to the phrase *Jehovah Zidkenu*.   There is a great diversity in
the explanation of these words.   The better Jewish interpreters take
the words, indeed, as a name of the Messiah, but not so that He
would be named *Jehovah*, and then, in apposition, *our 'righteousness,'*
but rather so that *Jehovah Zidkenu* is an abbreviation of a whole sentence.   They appeal (besides 33. 16) to such passages as Exod. 17. 15,
where Moses calls the altar *Jehovah my banner;* Gen. 33. 20,
where Jacob attributes to it the name *El Elohe Israel*.   The older
Christian interpreters (the Vulgate excludes every other meaning by
its translation, *dominus justus noster*), on the contrary, earnestly contend, that the Messiah is here called *Jehovah*, and, therefore, must
be truly God.   Even a Calvin, who elsewhere often erred from an
excessive dread of doctrinal prejudice, decidedly adopts this interpretation.   By righteousness, he understands also *justification by the
merit of Christ* (1 Cor. 1. 30).—In reference to this interpretation,
we make the following remarks.   1. Its chief fault is, that it is not
considered how the prophet here expresses the nature of the Messiah and of His time in the form of a *proper name*.   If it read, '*And
this* is Jehovah, our righteousness,' it would then be perfectly correct
to take *Jehovah* as a *personal designation* of the Messiah.   In a
name, on the contrary, it is as usual as natural, that only the chief
words should be selected from a whole sentence, and that it should
be left to the hearer or reader to supply the rest.   Brevity is inseparably connected with every instance of *naming*, as it appears in the
usual abbreviation of the name, even when consisting of one word.
A whole proposition as *nom. propr.* is not to be found; as an example, the two cases already cited by Kimchi may serve.   '*Jehovah,
my banner,*' stands concisely for '*this altar is dedicated to Jehovah,*

---

[1] וַיִּשְׁכֹּן יִשְׂרָאֵל בֶּטַח,

[2] How the false reading יִקְרָאוּ (for יִקְרָאוֹ) first arose, is manifest from the
grounds which its later defenders deduce in its favour, comp. especially Schulze,
l. c.   The chief ground is the supposition, that only the 3 *plur.* can stand *impersonally;* comp. on the contrary, Ew. p. 644, "Where the more definite subject
is not mentioned, because it may be easily inferred from the sense, the *plur. commonly* stands, the *sing.* much more seldom ; this, however, is especially frequent
in the phrase קְרָא שֵׁם." To this must be added, the more seldom וֹ of the *suff.*,
instead of the more usual הוּ, comp. Ew. p. 181.   On internal grounds also, the
reading יִקְרָאוּ is unconditionally to be rejected.   The designation of the object of
the naming, can by no means be omitted.

my banner ;' El Elohe Israel, for ' *this altar belongs to the Almighty, the God of Israel.*' A multitude of other examples might easily be cited. Thus, *Jehoshua,* ' *salvation of Jehovah,*' stands concisely for ' *Jehovah will provide salvation for me ;*' Jehoram, *Jehovah altus,* for ' *I am consecrated to the high God of Israel.*' Most completely analogous, however, is the name of *Zedekiah,* ' *the righteousness of God,*' for ' *he, under whose reign the Lord will impart righteousness to his people.*' This name seems, moreover, to stand in direct reference to our prophecy. As the former *Eliakim,* by causing his name to be changed into *Jehoiakim,* would represent himself as the person in whom the prophecy, 2 Sam. 7. would be fulfilled, so the former *Mattaniah* caused his name to be changed into *Zedekiah* by Nebuchadnezzar (who had, indeed, no other interest than that, as a sign of his dominion, the new name should be different from the former, and who left it to be determined by him who was to be named), thinking at so cheap a rate to become the Jehovah Zidkenu predicted by Jeremiah, and desired by the people. 2. The preceding argument only shows, that the explanation of Jehovah Zidkenu by ' *he by whom and under whom Jehovah will be our righteousness,*' is liable to *no objection.* A positive argument in its *favour* is furnished by the parallel passage, chap. 33. 15, 16, ' *In those days, and at that time, I will cause a righteous shoot to spring forth to David, and he shall provide justice and righteousness in the land. In those days Judah shall be delivered, and Jerusalem dwell securely, and this is the name which shall be given to* her, *The Lord our righteousness.*' Here Jehovah Zidkenu appears as a name, not of the Messiah, but of Jerusalem in the Messianic time. The efforts which have been made to set aside this troublesome argument are in vain. They only show the impossibility of the task. 3. Besides, *Zidkenu* is not altogether correctly understood in the older interpretation, when it is referred to the forgiveness of sin. This is, indeed, often extolled, as the chief blessing of the Messianic time, but it is not intended here. According to the connexion, the discourse here is of personal righteousness, prosperity according to another mode of considering the subject. Comp. on Mal. 4. 2, p. 611. Forgiveness of sin presupposes, indeed, righteousness in the former sense, but also righteousness of life. Righteousness stands here in the parallel with prosperity ; the order is as follows : " righteousness of the king, righteousness of the subjects, then prosperity and righteousness as a reward from God." In addition to this is the antithesis with the former time. In connexion with the unrighteousness of the kings, stood the unrighteousness of the people, and therefore was the land deprived of its prosperity, and smitten by the judgements of God. What Jeremiah compresses in the name *Jehovah Zidkenu,* Ezekiel exhibits at large in the parallel passage, chap. 34. 25—31. The Lord concludes with them a covenant of peace ; a rich blessing is imparted to them ; He breaks their yoke ; He frees them from servitude ; they become not a prey to the heathen.—We must not, however, omit to remark, that the chief errour in the older interpretation consisted in attempting to force out of the word what it did not contain, but what lay, indeed, in the subject. Only a shoot of David, who was at the same time a shoot of the Lord [1], could realize in all its extent the promise here given. *Righteous*, in the full sense, is no one born of a woman, and if there is a defect in the personal righteousness of the king, then the procuring of justice and righteousness is equally defective, and prosperity and righteousness are not imparted from above in all their fulness. Of all the former kings, the predicate righteous was more suitable to none than to David, and yet in what an incomplete sense was it applicable to him ! What suffering this imperfection brought upon the nation, is shown, e. g., by the numbering of the people. To this imperfection of the will to provide justice and righteousness, was added the imperfection of the power, and the limitation of the knowledge. Only he who truly *reigns as a king*, and is *truly wise* [2], can satisfy the idea which David strove after in vain. All the three offices of Christ, the regal not less than the prophetic and sacerdotal, presuppose His Deity ; and that, in the way hitherto pursued, nothing had been effected, that only by the entrance of the Divine into the earthly such splendid promises could be fulfilled, must have been plain to a Jeremiah, whose deep feeling is, that '*all flesh is grass*,' and who lived in a time which was more suited than many others to remedy Pelagianism, which always seeks to gather grapes from thorns. If, now, we still consider that Jeremiah had before him the clear declarations of older prophets, in reference to the Deity of the Messiah, we can explain his not expressly mentioning it, only from the fact, that it was not suitable in this connexion, in which only the *that*, and not the *whence*, came under consideration.

993. Ver. 7. ' *Therefore, behold, days come, saith the Lord, when it shall no more be said, So truly as the Lord lives, who brought the children of Israel out of the land of Egypt ;* ver. 8. *But so truly as the Lord lives, who led and who brought the seed of the house of Israel out of the land towards the north, and out of all lands whither I have driven them, and they shall dwell in their land.*' The sense is : the prosperity of the future will far exceed the greatest prosperity of the past. Comp. (besides chap. 16. 14, 15, where the verse almost verbally occurs) chap. 3. 16, where, in the same sense, the ark of the covenant is described as to be forgotten in future times. Isa. 43. 18, 19 ; 65. 17.—The *Living Jehovah* [3] is an abrupt expression of passion, as is natural to the solemnity of an oath, for ' *so surely as Jehovah lives*.' It is entirely natural to designate God as the *living*, when one appeals to Him as a witness and judge ; and equally so to refer to the greatest *sign of life* which He has given respecting Himself. Now, under the Old Testament, this was the deliverance out of Egypt. In the future, one still greater shall succeed to its place. Accordingly, the form of the oath is altogether general ; the deliverance out of Egypt comes under consideration as a *manifestation of life*, and not as a showing of mercy.

---

[1] Comp. 4. 2, from which passage Jeremiah has derived the צֶמַח, and to which he alludes.

[2] Comp. וּמָלַךְ מֶלֶךְ וְהִשְׂכִּיל.

[3] חַי־יְהֹוָה.

Chapter 31:31-40

994. The thirtieth and thirty-first chapters might justly be
regarded as the hymn of Israel's deliverance. They are joined in
one whole, not merely by a material, but also by a formal unity ; so
that we cannot sufficiently wonder at those who, like Venema and
Rosenmüller, assume a compilation out of loose fragments, composed
at different times. The prophet begins, in chap. 30, with the promise of prosperity for *all* Israel. True, although he even now finds
himself, as to *both* parts into which he had been divided, far from the
land of the Lord, in a state of banishment, still the end of his oppression has not yet arrived ; the distress will rise still higher ; but
even this, as formerly in Egypt, is a prelude of the prosperity ; it is
the preparation for a better future, whose glory the prophet, after a
full description in ver. 22, comprehends in the brief, but immensely
rich and all-comprehensive words, ' *And ye shall be my people, and
I will be your God.*' The threatening for the apparent Israel in
ver. 23, 24, forms the majestic close of the promise for the true Israel,
analogous to the '*there is no peace to the wicked,*' in Isaiah. Let
them not, in foolish delusion, seize the promise for themselves.
That time of the highest blessing for the pious, and for those who
desire it, the Acharith Hajjamim, will be at the same time for the
wicked a time of the heaviest curse. By the side of the climax
of the manifestation of mercy, proceeds that of the manifestation
of righteousness, as its inseparable attendant. ' *Behold the tempest
of the Lord, glowing fire goes forth, a* constant *storm ; on the head
of the ungodly will it rest ; the glowing anger of the Lord will not
return until he has executed the thoughts of his heart ; in future days
ye shall consider it !*' The prophet had already, chap. 23. 19, 20,
uttered the same words in a threatening prophecy before the exile.
By its verbal repetition he points out, that the case was not finished
with the exile, that this must not be considered as the absolute and
last penitence for the sins of the whole nation, that, as surely as God
is Jehovah, so surely do his words also revive, as often as the thing
again exists to which they refer.

995. The more specific the consolation, the more impressive is
it, the more does it reach the heart. The prophet, therefore, causes
the prediction of prosperity for all Israel, to be followed by that for
the two divisions. He commences with Israel in the narrower sense,
the *ten tribes* (chap. 31. 1—22), and with these he delays the longest,
because, in appearance, they are the most irrecoverably lost, and
seem to be for ever rejected by the Lord. The thought of an
originally independent prediction of prosperity for Israel, is set aside
by the relation of ver. 1 to ver. 22 of the foregoing chapter, which
are closely connected, since ver. 23 and 24 contain only an intervening remark, for those to whom the promise did not belong. The
' *ye shall be my people, and I will be your God,*' is followed, the
order being reversed, by the ' *at that time, saith the Lord, will I
* (particularly) *be the God of all the families of Israel, and they shall*

be my people.' After Israel, ver. 23—26, follows Judah. The prediction is closed in ver. 26, with the variously misunderstood words,
' therefore, I awoke, and saw, and my sleep was sweet to me.' The
present has vanished from the prophet; he is not susceptible of its
impressions like one asleep. Then he awakes for a moment out
of his sweet dreams, which are not, as dreams usually are, entirely
groundless. He looks around; all is troubled, desolate, and cold;
nowhere is there consolation for the weary soul. *' Ah,'* he exclaims,
' I have sweetly dreamed;' and immediately the hand of the Lord
seizes him again, and removes him from the present.

996. A peculiar prosperity is by no means destined *separately* for
Israel and for Judah; it was *one prosperity*, in which both should
participate, having been reunited as one covenant and fraternal
people. The description, therefore, in ver. 27—40, returns from the
parts to the whole, with which it commenced and is completed, in
such a manner, as to close with the crown of the promises, the substance of the declaration, repeated here in ver. 33, *' And I will be
their God, and they shall be my people.'*

997. The whole description, in both chapters, is Messianic,
and a procedure like that of Venema, who divides the whole into
small sections, and assumes here an exclusive reference to a return
out of the exile, here to the Maccabees, whom he exalts to a sort of
Saviours, here to Christ and His kingdom, is utterly to be rejected,
as is sufficiently evident from what has been already often remarked.
The interpretation of the *whole* portion, therefore, would properly
belong here. Still, we are compelled by external grounds to limit
ourselves to the interpretation of the chief portion, chap. 31. 31—40.

998. Only we will first briefly explain chap. 31. 22, because this
passage, in former times, has been interpreted by very many commentators as personally Messianic. *' How long wilt thou ramble
about, thou inconstant daughter ? For the Lord creates a new thing
in the land, woman will encompass man.'* The older interpreters explain the last words, commonly, of the birth of Christ by a virgin.
But in opposition to this, not to mention other grounds, is the obvious remark, that precisely what is important, that the *woman* is a
virgin, the *man, Son of God*, is wanting. But certainly no better
than this interpretation is that which recent interpreters (Schnurrer,
Rosenmüller) have placed in its stead: "the woman will protect the
man, perform for him the *munus excubitoris circumeuntis.*" The correct view is as follows: the prophet grounds his exhortation to return
to the Lord, on the most efficacious of all motives, viz. that the Lord
would return to her, that the time of anger was now over, that she
need only hasten to His open arms of love. Without hope of mercy
there is no conversion; the perverse and desponding heart of man must
be allured by the preventing love of God to draw near to Him. The
importance of the new state of things, the prophet designates by the
choice of the expression. The *nomina sexûs* are here exactly suitable; even the omission of the article is intentional. The relation
is presented in its universality, and thereby the view is steadily
directed to its substance: "Woman will encompass man; the strong

will again take the feeble and tender into intimate fellowship, under its protection, its affectionate care. The woman art thou, O Israel, who hast hitherto sufficiently experienced what the woman is without a man, a reed, the sport of all the winds ; the man is the Lord. How foolish if thou dost still persist in thy independence and alienation, and wilt not return to the sweet relation of dependence and unconditional surrender, which, because it is alone natural, is alone the source of prosperity[1]!" That, even according to our interpretation, the Messianic character of the prophecy remains, is obvious.

999. The contents of the portion ver. 31—40 is as follows. The Lord, far from punishing the contempt of His former gifts by a total rejection, will rather renew, and render for ever indissoluble by a *twofold* mercy, the bond between Him and the people. The foundation of this is the forgiveness of sin ; a consequence of which is a richer imparting of the Spirit ; and now Israel, since the law no longer comes as an outward letter, but is written in his heart, reaches his destination ; he becomes truly a people of God, and God truly his God.—Ver. 31—34. Such a proof of the enduring election is incredible to the people, conscious of their guilt, and sighing under the judgements of God. That this election still continues, and must perpetually endure, so surely as He is God, God most emphatically assures them.—Ver. 35—37. Gloriously will the city of God arise out of its ashes. While formerly the unholy abomination forced its way into her, the holy, she will now extend her boundaries beyond the limit of the unholy. And the Lord, sanctified *in* her, will also sanctify Himself *upon* her ; there will be no more destruction.

1000. Ver. 31. '*Behold, days come, saith the Lord, and I will make with the house of Israel, and with the house of Judah, a new covenant.*' Ver. 32. '*Not as the covenant which I made with your fathers in the day when I took them by the hand to bring them forth out of the land of Egypt, which my covenant they have broken, but I marry them to me, saith the Lord.*' By the *making of the covenant* a formal transaction, like the covenant concluded on Sinai, is not to be thought of. This appears from ver. 32, according to which the old covenant was made in the day when the Lord took Israel by the hand, in order to bring him up out of the land of Egypt. But at that time there was as yet no proper covenant transaction. Most interpreters arbitrarily assume, that by the ' *In the day,*' &c., the abode at Sinai is designated. But since the expression commonly denotes the *day* of the deliverance out of Egypt (comp. Exod. 12. 51, sq.), since this day, as such, was marked by the yearly returning Pass-

---

[1] This interpretation is favoured by the manifest reference of תְּסוֹבֵב to תִּתְחַמָּקִין, and to הַשּׁוּבָה, which, in reference to the latter is outwardly expressed even by the alienation. " How foolish would it be still further to *depart*, since now the great time dawns when the Lord draws near."

over, so also must the *day* here be taken in its proper sense. (2) Also
in reference to the new covenant, there is no mention of being bound
by an *obligation.* *Gifts* are mentioned, and nothing but gifts. The
words [1], indeed, can *mean* nothing else than to *conclude a covenant.*
But the question arises, whether the concluding of a covenant may
not also be spoken of where no transaction between two parties, no
mutual agreement exists. Plainly, the *substance of the covenant*
precedes its *outward conclusion,* and forms its groundwork. This
does not first *make* the relation, but is only a solemn acknowledgement of that which already exists. Thus even in human relations,
every contract, the substance of which does not already exist before it
is concluded, is unnatural. Still more is this so in the things of God.
Every one of His benefits imposes an obligation upon him who receives it, whether this may have been expressed by God, and the
receiver may have outwardly acknowledged it, or not. This is very
manifest in the present instance. At the giving of the Law on Sinai,
the binding power of the commands of God rested on the fact, that
God had brought Israel out of Egypt, out of the house of servants ;
and thus it appears, that the covenant of Sinai existed, in substance,
simultaneously with the deliverance out of Egypt. Apostasy from
God would have been a breach of the covenant, even without the
solemn confirmation of it at Sinai, as, indeed, it actually was in the
time between the Exodus and the giving of the law ; it would have
been a breach of the covenant, if the people had answered the solemn
demand of God, whether they would conclude a covenant with Him,
with *No.* This appears the more evident, when we reflect, that the
new covenant really was not sanctioned by any such solemn and outward transaction. If this is, nevertheless, a covenant in the strictest
sense, if the relation is here independent of its acknowledgement, then
also must this acknowledgement under the Old Testament have been
a secondary matter [2].—We can now determine in what sense an antithesis of the old and new covenant is here presented. The discourse
cannot be of a new and more complete revelation of the law of God,
for this is common to both economies ; no jot or tittle of it can be
lost under the New Testament, nor can a jot or tittle be added to it ;
God's law rests on His nature, and this is eternally immutable (comp.
Mal. 3. 22) ; the revelation of the law belongs not to the Exodus out
of Egypt, to which the former concluding of the covenant is here
attributed, but to Sinai. Just as little can the discourse be of the
introduction of an entirely new relation which by no means has the
former as its groundwork. The covenant with Israel is eternal,
Jehovah would not be Jehovah, if an absolute new beginning could
take place. ' *Now I say,*' says the Apostle, Rom. 15. 8, ' *that Jesus
Christ was a minister of the circumcision* for the truth of God, *to
confirm the promises made unto the fathers : and that the Gentiles*

---

[1] כָּרַת בְּרִית.

[2] This is equally true of all other passages which are commonly cited as
proof, that כָּרַת בְּרִית can stand even for a bare gift and promise: e. g., Gen. 9. 9.
Gen. 15. 18 ; Exod. 34. 10.

might glorify God for his mercy.' The sending of Christ with His gifts and blessings, the concluding of the new covenant, is, therefore, a *consequence* of the covenant faithfulness of God. If, therefore, the subject of discourse is here the antithesis of an old and a new covenant, the former must designate, not the relation of God to Israel in itself, and in all its extent, but rather only the former manifestation of this relation, that whereby the Lord, until the time of the prophet, had made Himself known as the God of Israel. To this earlier, more imperfect form, the more complete future form is here opposed, under the name of the new *covenant*. The new, which should displace the old, so far as the form is concerned, (Comp. Heb. 8. 13, ' *In that he saith, A new covenant, he hath made the first old. Now that which decayeth and waxeth old is ready to vanish away.*') is, in respect to the substance, the highest realization of the old.—If, now, the old covenant is the former, the new covenant the future, form of the covenant with Israel, it may be further asked which, among the manifold differences between these two forms, was here in the contemplation of the prophet. The answer is supplied by what the prophet says concerning the new covenant. For, as this should *not* be as the former, so must the *advantages* of the new be just so many *deficiencies* of the old. Now all these advantages are purely internal, first, the forgiveness of sins, then the inscribing of the law on the heart. Hence it follows, that the blessings of the old covenant were *chiefly* outward (for that there was by no means a total absence of these inward blessings, that the antithesis of the old and new covenant in this respect was only relative, not absolute, we shall hereafter see), and this also is evident from the more particular designation of the old covenant, as concluded at the bringing forth out of Egypt, which comprehended in itself all similar later deliverances and blessings, the earnest of which was the Passover, founded upon it. The prophet, if any one, had experienced that, in the way hitherto pursued, the end could not be accomplished; the sinfulness of the people had exhibited itself in his time in so fearful an outbreak, that, considering the subject in a human point of view, he must already have most deeply felt, that little could be done for the people by outward blessings, by an outward deliverance from bondage. What availed the manifestation of mercy, which must, by Divine necessity, be immediately followed by so much the severer punishment. The condition of the true and lasting gift of outward prosperity is the imparting of that which is internal; without the latter the former is only a mockery. It is, therefore, the highest object of the prophet's desire ; he points to it here as the highest good of the future [1]. We have already, on

---

[1] Comp. also 32. 40. Of less importance is the false interpretation of אֲשֶׁר by *quia*, which is found in most interpreters. In this sense אֲשֶׁר never occurs. The correct view is given by Ewald, p. 649, who connects אֲשֶׁר with אֶת־בְּרִיתִי, —" I, whose covenant,"—unless we choose to take אֲשֶׁר as a mere general sign of the relation, as a mere indication, that the proposition stands related to the foregoing, without a more particular description of the nature of this relation, comp. Ewald, p. 647.

chap. 3. 14, indicated the meaning of בָּעַל with בְּ, *to marry to one-self*, and this meaning is here also perfectly suitable. Who then affirms, that the ground of the abolition of the old covenant must be given here? This has already been sufficiently expressed, as the author of the Epistle to the Hebrews has shown. In the very announcement of a new covenant the declaration of the insufficiency of the old is included : ' *For if that first covenant had been faultless, then should no place have been sought for the second* ' (ver. 7); and wherein this insufficiency,—grounded in human sinfulness and hard-ness of heart, which is not relieved by blessings which are chiefly of an outward nature, be they never so great, and to their future greatness, the expression indicating the most tender love, ' *When I took them by the hand,*' points [1],—consisted, why a better cove-nant, such an one ' *which was established upon better promises,*' ver. 6, was required, sufficiently appears from what is predicated, in ver. 33, 34, of this new covenant in opposition to the old. The reference is rather here, and this thought is surely in the connexion the most appropriate of all, to God's infinite love, and the greatness of His covenant faithfulness. *I* and *they* stand in the most emphatic anti-thesis. *They,* in wicked ingratitude, have broken the former cove-nant, have violated the obligations which the former mercies imposed upon them. *God* might now be expected, on His part, to annul the old covenant, and withdraw for ever the former favours. But, in-stead of this, He provides the new covenant, the greater favour. He marries the apostate Israel to Himself anew, and that in such a manner, that the bond of love now becomes firm and indissoluble.

1001. Ver. 33. ' *For this is the covenant which I will conclude with the house of Israel after these days, saith the Lord ; I will put my law within them, and I will write it upon their heart, and I will be their God, and they shall be my people.*' The *for* is here entirely in its place. The expression, ' *not as the covenant,*' is founded on the positive definition of the substance of the new covenant. *Because* it is so, it is not as the former. The expression, *these days,* designates *the present, after these days* [2], *the future.* The prophet points so repeatedly and emphatically to the *future,* because, to unbelief, and to weak faith, the history of the covenant people appeared to be finished with the present, and the future to be cut off from them. With respect to the following enumeration of the bless-ings, in and through the imparting of which the new covenant rela-tion should be established, Venema thus correctly remarks : " *Bona distinguuntur in radicale seu causale, et consequentia seu derivata.*" The second *for* in ver. 34 gives the ground of this imparting, ' for *I will forgive their sins.*'—Many interpreters take תּוֹרָה here in the sense *doctrine.* This interpretation is, however, to be entirely rejected, as destructive of the sense. תּוֹרָה *never* means *doctrine,*

[1] To this subject ground of the insufficiency, the μεμφόμενος γὰρ αὐτοῖς λέγει, Heb. 8. 8, refers. De Wette erroneously; " for finding fault he says to them; " the dative belongs to μεμφόμενος.
[2] בְּאַחֲרִית הַיָּמִים.

but always *law ;* and that here the discourse can be only of the law of God (the eternal expression of His eternal being, and therefore common to the Old and the New Testament), and by no means of a new constitution, is evident from the reference of the giving in the inward parts, and of the writing upon the heart (the tables of the heart), to the *outward giving,* and the *writing on the stone tables on Sinai.* The law is the same, only the relation different, in which God exhibits it to man. One might easily deduce from the passage before us a confirmation of the errour, that the law, under the Old Testament, was only an *outward,* dead letter. Against this, Buddeus contends, who decides that the discourse is here only of a *relative* difference and antithesis : " *Quod licet et fidelibus V. T. contigerit, hic tamen uberiorem copiam et gradum hujus beneficii deus promittit.*" Calvin declares the opinion, that, under the Old Testament, no regeneration took place, as absurd : " *Scimus raram et obscuram fuisse gratiam Dei sub lege, in evangelio autem* effusa *fuisse dona spir., et deum multo liberalius egisse cum ecclesiâ suâ.*" The idea of a purely outward giving of the law, is, indeed, inconceivable. God would then have done for Israel nothing further than He did for the betrayer Judas, in whose conscience He proclaimed His holy law, without giving him any power to repent. Such a proceeding is conceivable only where there is a subjective impossibility of the ἀνακαινίζειν εἰς μετάνοιαν. Besides, every outward revelation of God must be accompanied by an internal one, in accordance with the constitution of human nature, since we cannot suppose that He who knows it, would mock us with the semblance of a blessing. So soon as we know the outward fact of the deliverance out of Egypt, we know also that God, at that time, powerfully touched the heart of Israel : as soon as it is established, that the Law was written on Sinai by the finger of God on tables of stone, so also is it, that it was written on the table of Israel's heart. But what lies in the case itself is confirmed also by history. Even in the law, circumcision is designated as the pledge and seal of the imparting, not of mere outward gifts, but of the *circumcision of the heart,* the removal of the sin which cleaves to every one from his birth, so that man can love God with all his heart, all his soul, and all his powers, Deut. 30. 6. This circumcision of the heart, at the same time *required* and promised by God in the outward circumcision [1], is not different in substance from the inscribing of the law on the heart. Further, had the law of the Lord for Israel been a mere outward letter, how can the animated praise of it in the holy Scriptures be explained, e. g. Ps. 19 ? Truly, a bridge must already have been formed between the Law and him who can designate it as ' *rejoicing the heart,*' as ' *enlightening the eyes,*' as ' *bringing back the soul,*' as ' *sweeter than honey and the honey-comb.*' This is no longer the Law, in itself considered, which worketh wrath ; it is the Law in its connexion with the Spirit, whose commands are not grievous. A new heart was created also under the Old Testament (comp. Ps. 51. 12),

---

[1] Comp. Deut. *l. c.,* with 10. 16.

and not to know the nature of this creation, was, for a teacher in
Israel, the highest shame, John 3. 10. Indeed, what is here promised for the future, a pious member of the old covenant in
Ps. 40. 9, expresses, in the *same form*, as already vouchsafed to him,
as his present spiritual condition, ' *I delight to do thy will, O Lord,
and thy law is within my heart,*' with entirely the same contrast with
the law as an outward letter, as written on the stone tables ; comp.
Prov. 3. 1—3, ' *My son, forget not my law, and let thine heart keep
my commandments,—bind them upon thy neck, write them upon the
table of thy heart.*' 7. 3, ' *Bind them upon thy finger, write them
upon the table of thine heart.*' But how is it to be explained, that
the antithesis, in itself *relative*, here appears under the form of the
absolute ; the distinction of degrees, under the form of the specific
difference ? Plainly, in like manner as the same appearance must
be explained elsewhere also, the misapprehension of which has occasioned so many errours, e. g. John 1. 17, where it is said, that *the Law*
was given by Moses, *grace and truth* by Christ. The gift of the Old
Testament, highly important and valuable in itself considered, appears, in comparison with the infinitely more important and richer
blessing of the New Testament, as so small, that it vanishes entirely
out of sight. The case is entirely similar, when the prophet, in
chap. 3. 16, describes the highest sanctuary of the Old Testament,
the Ark of the Covenant, as sinking into entire forgetfulness in the
future, and in chap. 23. 7, 8, the deliverance out of Egypt, as no
longer worth mentioning.—Parallel with our passage, finally, is the
promise of Joel concerning the outpouring of the Spirit, chap. 3. 1, 2,
so that what has there been remarked is also applicable here. There
the relative nature of the promise is made more prominent than here ;
as under the New Testament in general, in relation to the Old, there
is no where an absolutely new beginning, but only completion,—precisely as under the New Testament itself, in the relation of the *regnum gloriæ* to the *regnum gratiæ,*—so also in reference to the imparting of the Spirit, Joel only causes the abundance to take the place of
the scarcity, the much of the little[1].—Once more, how strongly does
the Old Testament contradict the carnal Jewish notion concerning the
nature of the Messianic kingdom, analogous to the expectations of the
revolutionists concerning the future, arising from the same fountain of
the heart,—an opinion which is most crudely exhibited in the passage of the *Talmud, Massechet Sanhedrin f.* 191 : " *Non est inter
dies Messiæ et hunc mundum discrimen, nisi tantum servitus reg-
norum,*"—appears from the remarks of the Jewish interpreters on the
passage before us, wherein they cannot help perceiving that a purely
moral revolution is foretold in opposition to one merely external.
But that a preconceived opinion, when it has once determined upon
it, can overcome every, even the strongest contradiction in the subject, is shown here in the example of a Grotius : " *Efficiam ut omnes
legem meam memoriter teneant, nempe in sensu primo per multitudinem*

---

[1] Comp. besides, chap. 24. 7 ; 32. 39, but especially Ezek. 11. 19, 20 ; 36. 26,
27, comp. on the passage.

synagogarum, quæ structa illo tempore, ubi ter in hebdomade doce-batur!"—'*And I will be to them God,*' &c., follows, not without reason, upon '*and I will put my law in their inward parts,*' &c. The law is the copy of God's being ; it is only by the inscription of the law on his heart that man can be a partaker of the nature of God. But how could God, with His gifts and blessings, bestow Himself wholly and unconditionally upon those who are not of His family ? [whose God He is not, and who are not His people ?]—Finally, the *relative* nature of the promise is here manifest. God had already promised to Abraham that He would be to *him* a God, and to his seed after him ; and this promise He had afterwards repeated to the whole people of Israel[1]. In the consciousness that this promise was fulfilled in the present, David, Ps. 33. 12, exclaims, '*Happy the people whose God is Jehovah, the family that he chooses for an inheritance.*' Therefore, here also is nothing absolutely new. If the promise *were* an absolutely new thing, then the whole kingdom of God under the Old Testament would at once be changed into a mere appearance and delusion. But the small measure of the condition (from which even God Himself cannot grant a dispensation, though He can vouchsafe a richer measure), of the writing, that is, of the law in the heart, whereby man becomes a transcript of God, of the personal law, has for its necessary attendant the small measure of the consequence. And thus the complete fulfilment of the declara-tion of God to Abraham and Israel, to which the prophet here alludes, must be looked for from the future.

1002. Ver. 34. '*And they shall no more teach one his neighbour, and one his brother, for they shall all know me, small and great, saith the Lord, for I will forgive their iniquity, and remember their sins no more.*' The first half of the verse has created embarrassment to the interpreters even from ancient times. The proposition, that because all are to be taught of God, human instruction in Divine things should cease, has, at first sight, something fanatical. The case, how-ever, is properly by no means difficult. One need only consider, that here human instruction is excluded only so far as it stands *opposed* to the Divine instruction concerning God Himself ; that here, therefore, the discourse is of a *mere* human instruction, of a teaching and institution in religion, as in any other matter of com-mon knowledge, the result of which is a learning perpetually, and yet without ever coming to the knowledge of the truth. By *such* a reliance on human authority, the nature of religion is entirely de-stroyed. Even the true God becomes an idol, when He is not known through God ; when He does not make Himself a dwelling in the heart. He is, and remains, a mere thought, which, in the con-flict with sin, which is an actual power, can supply no strength, in affliction no consolation. Now under the Old Testament such a condition was very frequent ; the mass possessed only a knowledge of God, which, if not exclusively, was chiefly mediate. The new covenant was to bring richer gifts of the Spirit, in which, likewise, a

[1] Lev. 26. 12; comp. Exod. 29. 45.

larger number were to participate ; under it the antithesis between the *teaching of God* and *the teaching of men* was to cease. Teachers teach not on their own authority, but they teach as servants and instruments of God ; it is not they who teach, but the Holy Ghost in them ; the disciples hear the Word *through men*, not *as the Word of men*, but *as the Word of God ;* not because it satisfies their limited human reason, but because the Spirit testifies that the Spirit is truth. How this antithesis was done away in a higher unity, is shown, among other passages, by 2 Cor. 3. 3, '*Ye . . . are the epistle of Christ ministered by us, written not with ink, but with the Spirit of the living God.*' They are θεοδίδακτοι, but by the ministry of the apostle, who, so far as he executes this ministry, is not different from God, but only a conductor of His power[1]. In Divine things, the truth first becomes truth, for the individual, by its *existing in him*, and this can be effected only by his being united with God by God's Spirit. Being, life, and, therefore, also real, living knowledge, can proceed only from the Fountain of all being and life. But where knowledge has been imparted by the Spirit, and consequently exists in its elements, there it can and must be carried on to perfection by those to whom God has imparted His gifts, for its development and completion.—That, finally, this promise also is to be understood relatively, is obvious. All the pious of the Old Testament were θεοδίδακτοι, and under the New Testament the number of those is immensely great, who, through their own fault, stand in a connexion with the truth, which is entirely or chiefly mediate.—That in the last words of the verse the fundamental blessing is promised, we have already seen. But whether the *for* refers to the immediate context, or to all that precedes, amounts to the same thing, since what immediately precedes includes the rest. We have before us only designations of the same thing according to different relations ; all teaches the richer imparting of the gifts of the Spirit. This has the forgiveness of sin as its necessary groundwork. The sins which separate the people and their God must be taken away ; not till then can the inward means be vouchsafed to the people, whereby they become truly a people of God, and His name is sanctified in them. That here also the discourse can be only of a relative difference between the Old and New Testaments, is obvious. A covenant people *without forgiveness of sins*, is an absurdity. Forgiveness of sins is the essence of the passover, as the feast of the covenant ; without it, the sin-offerings appointed of God are a lie ; without it, that which God says of Himself as the covenant God, that He is gracious and merciful, is untrue[2]. The consciousness of the forgiveness of sins, is the ground of that state of the heart which we perceive in the writers of the Psalms. We have, therefore, here, only a difference in degree. The sin of the covenant people appeared at that time to believers to be too great ever to be forgiven ; driven away from the presence of the Lord, this people, they sup-

---

[1] In like manner, 1 John 2. 20.
[2] That God *has* forgiven the sins of his people, the holy psalmists often confess with praise and gratitude, comp., e. g., Ps. 85. 3; 32. 51.

posed, would terminate its sorrowful existence in the land of Nod,
never would the καιροὶ ἀναψύξεως return. In opposition to this
notion, the prophet declares, in the name of the Lord, not merely
that they *will* return, but that they will first *come* in the full and
complete sense. Where you believe that you behold the end of the
forgiveness of sin, there is its proper commencement. Where sin
has abounded, there will grace much more abound. Only do not
despair, and thus place a barrier in the way of the mercy of God!
Your God does not merely say, *thou shalt:* as surely as He is the
merciful and gracious God, so surely will He Himself *first sow* and
afterwards reap the harvest.

1003. Ver. 35. ' *Thus saith the Lord, giving the sun for light by
day, and the laws of the moon and of the stars for light by night,
who raises up the sea, and its waves roar, the Lord Sabaoth his name,*'
Ver. 36. ' *When these laws shall cease before me, saith the Lord, so also
shall the seed of Israel cease to be a people before me for ever.*"
Ver. 35, describes God's omnipotence, which establishes, that He *is*
God, and not *man,* and thus forms the basis of the proposition set
forth in ver. 36, so full of consolation for the despairing covenant
people, that while all men are liars, He lies not, that He can never
repent of His covenant and His promises. The *laws* are mentioned
even in ver. 35, because the fact, that sun and moon, according
to eternal and inviolable laws, must daily appear at an appointed
time, and this through hundreds and thousands of years, testifies
more strongly for God's omnipotence, for His universal rule, subject
to no foreign influence or interference, than if they now appeared,
and now failed to appear. God's omnipotence, as a glance at nature
testifies, results from the fact, that He is the pure *I am* (Jehovah His
name, comp. on Mal. 3. 6), and precisely because He is this, must His
counsels, unconditionally expressed, be immutable. To believe that
He has for ever rejected Israel, is to degrade Him, to make Him an
idol, a creature.—When in ver. 36 the unchangeableness of God's
dispensation of mercy is placed on a level with the unchangeableness
of His ordering of nature, this is done in respect to the weakness of
the people, before whom, that which is most settled among visible
things is placed, as a pledge of the constancy of their election, so
that every rising of the sun and the moon gave them an assurance
of it. But, considered in itself, the constancy of the reign of grace
is far greater than that of the course of nature. ' *The heavens wax
old as a garment, and as a vesture He changes them, and they are
changed.*' (Ps. 102. 27—29.) ' *Heaven and earth shall pass away,
but God's word shall not pass away.*'—Why וּ stands here, and not עַם,
appears from chap. 33. 24, ' *They despise my people* (עַמִּי) *that it
should be no more a nation* (גּוֹי) *before them.*' The covenant people
supposed, in their despair, that their national existence, annihilated
for the present, had ceased for ever; but if this was secure, so also
their existence as a covenant people. For as they had become *not a
people,* in consequence of being *not a covenant people,* so could they
become again *a people,* only as *a covenant people.*

1004. Ver. 37. ' *Thus saith the Lord, If the heavens are measured above, and the foundations of the earth searched out beneath, so will I also cast away the whole seed of Israel, on account of all that which they have done, saith the Lord.*' Not without reason does the prophet so frequently repeat ' *saith the Lord.*' His word was the *sole* ground of hope for Israel ; apart from it, despair would be as reasonable as it was now unreasonable. The measuring of the heavens and the exploring of the depths of the earth, are here considered as an impossibility. The expression, ' *The whole seed of Israel,*' takes from the hypocrites the consolation which they might otherwise draw from these promises. It is just as contrary to the nature of God, that He should suffer *the whole seed* of Israel, the believers with the unbelievers, to go to destruction, as that He should *deliver the whole seed* of Israel, the unbelieving with the believing. Both the promise and the threatening always leave a remnant. The covenant provides only that the *whole* should not go to ruin ; for individuals, it gives no security. The expression, ' *on account of all that which they have done,* is added by design, because the greatness of the sins of the people was the main point in that despair of God's mercy which believers experienced.

1005. Ver. 38. ' *Behold, days come, saith the Lord, and the city shall be built to the Lord, from the gate of Hananeel to the corner gate.*' Ver. 39. ' *And opposite to it the measuring line shall go still further over the hill Gareb* (of the leprous), *and turn towards Goah* (place of execution).' Ver. 40, ' *And the whole valley of carcases, and ashes, and all the plains, to the brook Kedron, and from thence to the horse-gate eastward,* (all this is) *a holy place to the Lord. No more shall it be destroyed, and it shall not be laid waste to eternity.*' This prophecy embraces two events ; *first,* the restoration of the kingdom of God, presented under the image of a restoration of Jerusalem, its seat and central point under the old covenant. And, *secondly,* the glorification of the kingdom of God, which is now made so powerful, that it can undertake to assail the kingdom of darkness, and make it tributary to itself, whereas heretofore it had been compelled to act on the defensive, and often could not prevent the enemy from penetrating to the very heart of its dominion. The prophet clothes these thoughts in a sensible form, by causing the *unholy places* by which Jerusalem the holy city was surrounded, to be *included in its circumference,* to become a sanctuary of the Lord. In the former times, the victory of the world over the kingdom of God had been embodied in the fact that the abominations of sin and idolatry were brought even into the Temple, comp. 7. 11, ' *Is then this house a den of robbers, over which my name is called, saith the Lord ?*' As the victory of the world over the kingdom of God had manifested itself in the *desecration* of these holy places, so now the victory of the kingdom of God appears under the image of *the sanctification* of these *formerly unholy places.* As to the means whereby this great change should be effected, the kingdom of God, which now lay so entirely helpless, should obtain energies which it had never possessed before, and from a servant become a lord, it was unnecessary that the prophet should here point them out; this had already been done in ver. 32—34. The difference consists in the fact, that the new covenant is not like the old, but brings with itself the proper weapons whereby sin and the world may be overcome, an immensely richer measure of the forgiveness of sins, of the gifts of the Spirit. —There is still one general remark to be premised concerning the determination of the boundaries of the New Jerusalem here given, because this must be our guide in the determination of the particular doubtful places. The correct view is unquestionably found in Vitringa, on Is. 30. 33: *Proph. reducibus promittit instaurationem urbis Hieros. in omni ejus ambitu, quem ita describit, ut incipiendo a muro orientali per clima septentrionale transiens ad occiduum, et inde per meridionale redeat ad eoum.* The prophet begins with the tower of Hananeel, which lay on the east side of the city, near the sheep-gate, comp. 645. From thence he proceeds to the *corner gate*, which lay in the angle where the north and west met (comp. the same place), and therefore embraces the whole north side. He finishes with the *horse-gate*, which he expressly designates as lying towards the *east*, and so informs us, that he has returned to the place from which he set out. And thus we have gained a sure foundation for determining those amongst the places mentioned, whose position is in itself doubtful[1].—In the two first points of the boundary, the *tower of Hananeel*, and *the corner gate*, the second chief thought of the passage does not yet appear. This is explained simply by the fact, that on the whole north side of the city, there lay *no* unholy places[2]. From what has been before remarked, it appears certain, that the places which are met with in no other passage, the hills *Gareb* and *Goah*, must have lain on the *west* side, *Gareb* being on the north-west, and *Goah* on the south-west side. *Gareb* means *the leprous*, and nothing else, and *the hill of the leprous*[3] can be only *the hill where the leprous abode.* These, even in the second year of the Exodus, were compelled to remain *without the camp*, (Numb. 5. 3,) and this law was so rigidly executed, that even Moses' sister was removed out of the camp. After the entrance into Canaan, the provisions of the law in reference to

---

[1] After יָמִים the *Keri* inserts בָּאִים. It is true, that this fuller expression is the usual one with the prophet, but, on this very account, the more concise one, which alone has the authority of the manuscripts in its favour (the *Keri* is mere conjecture, and perhaps not even that), is to be preferred. Because the full phrase had already occurred too often in the passage before us, the prophet, for the sake of variety, satisfies himself here at the end, with the bare intimation. The prophet says intentionally, '*the city will be built to the Lord*,' where the phrase, '*is built*,' is to be referred to the Lord, not '*the city of the Lord*.' The latter has become so entirely a proper name of Jerusalem, that the full depth of its meaning is no more thought of. This new city should no more be called '*the city of the Lord*,' it should be really built *to the Lord*, so as to belong to Him.

[2] The *suff.* in נֶגְדּוֹ refers to the corner gate; the measuring line קָוֶה according to the *Kethib*, קַו הַמִּדָּה, the usual form according to the *Keri*, goes opposite to the corner gate, further forward, &c.

[3] Umbreit makes '*the hill Gāréb* ('=*the hill of the leprous*') ὁ τέταρτος λόφος, ὃς καλεῖται βεζηθά (Jos. Bell. Jud. 5. 4, § 2).

the *camp* were transferred to the *city* (comp. Levit. 13. 46). Even
Uzziah could not evade it, he dwelt without the city in Beth
Chofschit [1]. Even in the kingdom of Israel,—a proof, among innumerable others, against the current view of the religious condition of
this kingdom, and of its relation to the Mosaic law,—they were so
rigid in the execution of this Mosaic ordinance, that, even during
the siege of Samaria, the lepers might not leave the place assigned
to them before the gate, 2 Kings 7. 3.—In order to a deeper investigation of the passage before us, it is indispensable that we should
search out the ground of this ordinance. Our view is as follows:
the leprosy is the bodily copy of sin; what, therefore, is done to the
leper, happens properly to the sinner: every leper was a warning
sermon, a loud admonition that men should keep themselves unspotted from the world. The exclusion of the lepers from the
camp and the holy city, taught in a figure what John taught
in plain words, in the Apoc. 21. 27, '*And there shall in no
wise enter into it any thing that defileth, neither whatsoever worketh
abomination, or maketh a lie;*' and Paul, Ephes. 5. 5, '*For this ye
know, that no whoremonger, nor unclean person, nor covetous man
. . . . . . hath any inheritance in the kingdom of Christ and of
God.*' Comp. Gal. 5. 19. 21. It now plainly appears what the
prophet means by *including* the hill of the lepers within *the holy
city*. The *hitherto impure* become *pure*, the kingdom of God now
does violence to the sinners, whereas, hitherto, they have done it
to the kingdom of God.—It is only from this view of the leprosy,
that we can explain how *precisely this disease* so usually occurs as a
Theocratic punishment of sin. The sinner before God is marked out
also as a sinner before the eyes of men, by being compelled to bear
the image of sin. God provided that, usually, *figure* and *reality*
should perfectly coincide : although there were certainly exceptions
where God, for wise and holy reasons, caused the relatively innocent
(with one perfectly innocent, if such a one could be found, this
could not be possible except with Christ, who bore *our* sickness) to
bear the image of sin, e. g., those who stood in danger of self-
righteousness. As a Theocratic punishment the leprosy occurs
especially in those who had sinned secretly, or cloaked their sin with
a good appearance, which prevented it from appearing as such before
the eyes of men; e. g. as in the case of Miriam, Uzziah, and Gehazi.
—*Goah* in this connexion, in the middle between impure places,
cannot possibly be any thing else than, in like manner, an unclean
place; and the supposition is very natural, that, even in the name,
this idea is expressed [2]. Goah = *the hill of expiring*, would
be a very suitable name of the place where malefactors were exe-

---

[1] 2 Kings 15. 5, which is explained in an entirely arbitrary way by '*house of
the sick*,' instead of '*house of emancipation*,' a place where those dwelt whom the
Lord had manumitted, who are no longer His servants.

[2] *Hitzig* considers *Goah* to be the hill or rock *Antonia*. The usual derivation
is from גָּעָה, *to bellow*, properly *part. fem., the bellowing* (one). Hengstenberg
derives it with Hiller from גּוַּע, as שׁוֹעַ from שָׁוַע. The word גּוַּע stands of a violent death, no less than of a natural one; thus Num. 17. 27, 28, of a dying like
that of the company of Korah, Dathan, and Abiram: comp. Zech. 13. 8.

cuted. Even Vitringa throws out, on Is. 30. 33, the conjecture,
that Goah, גֵּיא גֹּעָה, is, perhaps, identical with Golgotha, but retracts
it again, because the evangelists explain Golgotha by κρανίου τόπος.
But this ground is still not decisive; the name of the place might
well receive, as the Aramæan dialect became predominant, a new
etymology, perhaps as the Fathers derive πάσχα from πάσχειν, &c.
It has already been observed, that the appellation *place of a skull,*
sounds somewhat strange, since the skulls did not remain on
the place of execution; the expression, " the skull," for " the
place of a skull," has also appeared strange, and the omission of
the *L* remarkable; all which is easily explained, if the new meaning, coinciding in substance with the former, was only *suited* to the
word. The identity of Goah and Golgotha cannot be contested, at
least from the position. That Golgotha, as an unclean place, lay
without the holy city, is certain, even from Heb. 13. 12; that it
was, as Goah, precisely on the west side, is, indeed, testified only by
tradition: comp. Bachiene II. 1. § 134, Hamelsveld II. p. 155.—
We now come to the valley of *carcases* and of *ashes.* That this is
the *valley of Hinnom* is probable, even from its position. The north
and the west side are already finished; there remain, therefore, only
the south and the east side. The valley of Hinnom, however, lay
toward the south, or south-east of Jerusalem, comp. Hamelsveld II.
p. 172, Bachiene II. 1, p. 313. ' *The valley of carcases*' is here
immediately connected with ' *all the plain* (i. q. all the rest) *to the
brook Kedron,*' and, therefore, is designated as *a part* of the valley of
Kedron. Now the valley of Hinnom was the south, or the south-east
continuation of the valley of Kedron, extending on the east side. To
this must be added, that in this connexion we must naturally expect
the mention of the valley of Hinnom, which otherwise would be
wanting. Of all the unclean places around Jerusalem, this was the
most unclean. Therefore, the prophet, chap. 7. 32, and 19. 4, can
threaten nothing more severe to the impure, than that they should be
buried in this most impure of all places. There can be no greater
triumph of the kingdom of God over the world, than when this most
complete contrast to the holy city, this image of hell, is included
within the holy city. It is only concerning the ground of the appellation that there is room for doubt. פֶּגֶר, פְּגָרִים never designates any thing
else than *carcase.* It stands, in a proper sense, only for *carcases
of animals,* but is then transferred to the *corpses of those, who, by
their crimes, have fallen under the Divine judgement, and been destroyed by it.* They had become like the beasts by their sins,
(comp. Ps. 49. 21,) so were they also like them in their death [1]. According to this determination of the meaning of the word, views like
that of Venema, who supposes that the valley bears the name, as the
public burying-place of the city, are evidently erroneous. But still
there remains room for a diversity of interpretation. By פְּגָרִים, may

---

[1] Thus, e. g., even Levit. 26. 30; Num. 14. 29. 32, 33; 1 Sam. 17. 46 ; 2 Kings
19. 35, &c. Just so נְבֵלָה, which, in like manner, originally designates only the
carcase of a beast transferred also to the corpses of those who are accursed of
God, and therefore still, in death, pollute God's earth; comp. Deut. 21. 23;
28. 26; Jer. 16. 4; 19. 7; 34. 20.

be understood the *carcases of animals*,—by the *valley of Hinnom*,
the places *where carcases from the city were deposited.* That it received this designation after its pollution by Josiah, 2 Kings 23. 10,
is in itself probable, and the usual supposition. But there are not
wanting evident signs, that the valley, even at an earlier period,
served this purpose. Is. 30. 33, it is said, in reference to the Assyrians, '*For Tophet has long been prepared, even for the king has it
been appointed, made deep and broad; its wood-pile has fire and
wood in abundance.*' Now this passage, in a prophecy the genuineness of which no one denies, presupposes, that at that time the valley
of Hinnom, or Tophet (properly only a part, which, however, is
sometimes placed for the whole), had this destination, that piles
of wood constantly smoked in it, upon which the carcases of animals
were burnt. Such a place of carcases and ravens was already prepared for the carcases of the Assyrians, who rebelled against God.
The very existence of the name *Tophet*=(*abhorrence, abomination*)
is in favour of its impure destination. The second passage is that
of Isa. 66. 24, '*Without the holy city, in the place where formerly
lay the carcases of beasts, now lie the corpses of transgressors; as
the former, so now also are the latter, food at the same time of worms
and of fire.*' True, the objection of Vitringa is very plausible, that
it is inconceivable that the idolaters should have chosen so impure a
place. But such a probable ground is not sufficient to invalidate
positive testimony ; and, moreover, it might, though this would lead
us too far from our purpose, easily be set aside. It may, however,
be supposed, that the prophet refers back to his own declaration,
7. 31, and 19, 4, sq. ; and that by פְּגָרִים here, are to be understood
the *corpses of the transgressors* devoted to destruction, who should
be buried even in the place destined for carcases. But still, this
reference is too remote ; and it is certainly more correct to say, that
the quality of Tophet, as the place of carcases, forms the common
basis of those passages and of ours.—That, finally, the *valley of
Hinnom* is actually meant, appears, not only from the grounds
already cited, but from a grammatical reason. The article in הָעֵמֶק
forbids that we should regard it as standing with the following word
in *stat. constr.* We must translate, 'and the whole valley (viz. the
valley) of *carcases and ashes*' (comp. Ewald, p. 581). The place
is, therefore, first designated simply as '*the valley*,' and afterwards
is more particularly designated. But precisely the valley of Hinnom
in Jer. 2. 23, is called *the* valley κατ' ἐξ., and the gate leading to
the valley of Hinnom, the valley-gate, Neh. 2. 13. 15 (comp.
596)[1]. It is said, Levit. 6. 3, 4, '*And he* (the priest, after the
burnt-offering had been presented,) *shall change his garments, and*

---

[1] In reference to דֶּשֶׁן, Gousset has already remarked, p. 368: " *Observa de
solis cineribus altaris et eorum remotione usurpari vocabula* דֶּשֶׁן *et* דִּשֵּׁן " is the
derivation of the meaning, *ashes,* from the ground meaning, *fat,* which Winer and
others give, (*cinis,* = *pinguefactio agrorum*). Erroneous, rather the burnt fat
was still also considered as fat ; the ashes of the fat is the residuum, שְׁאֵרִית, of
the fat. By this determination of the word, the explanation is very much
facilitated.

bring forth the ashes without the camp into a clean place.' It appears
from this that the ashes of the sacrificial animals were relatively unclean. The priest had to take off his holy garments, and put on his
common ones, and carry the ashes without the camp, and afterwards
without the holy city. They were, therefore, considered, in contrast
with the sacrifice itself, as an *impure residuum*, such as is found in
every thing that man does in relation to God, as an image of the
sinful defilement which adheres to all, even the best works, the
noblest elevation of the heart, as the heaviness from which no *spirit*
on earth is free. When, now, the place where the ashes were thrown
should be received within the circumference of the holy city, and become as sacred as the place where the sacrifice was offered, what else
can well be intended, than an overpowering of that which is unholy
by the holy, of the earthly by the divine, effected by a richer
measure of the Spirit? It is entirely analogous, when Zechariah
makes the horses in the future to be adorned by the Lord with the
symbol of holiness, formerly borne only by the high priest; so that
the more full investigations given in 655 are equally applicable
here. Against the interpretation given, only *one* thing can be
objected; since, according to the law, the sacrificial ashes were to be
brought into a *clean* place (because even what is in itself impure, but has once stood in connexion with what is most pure
and holy, must not be mingled with that which is simply and
commonly impure), it is not to be supposed that the valley of Hinnom served this purpose. But in answer to this, it is to be remarked, that properly *this whole valley* was *not* impure, but only the
place *Tophet* in it; and that *the whole* is sometimes designated as
impure only because it included this most unclean of all unclean
places, comp. 7. 31, 32. 35; 2 Kings 23. 10.—That the *sheremoth,
unto the brook Kedron*, = *the fields of Kedron*, mentioned 2 Kings 23,
is not to be doubted[1] *Sheremoth* means probably *places cut off* and
excluded (from the holy city). And thus we have a very striking
antithesis between the present nature and the future destination.
That which is now wholly *cut off from the holy* will then become a
holy place (קֹדֶשׁ). As for the rest, it appears from 2 Kings 23, that
the fields of Kedron were impure. Thither, as unto an unclean place,
Josiah brought all the abominations of idolatry, and burnt them there
(comp. ver. 4). Josiah caused all the vessels which had been made to
Baal and the Asherah, to be brought out of the temple. '*And he
burnt them* without Jerusalem *in the fields of Kedron.*' Ver. 6, '*And
he brought forth the Asherah out of the house of the Lord without
Jerusalem, to the brook Kedron, and he burnt her in the valley
of Kedron, and threw her ashes upon the grave of the sons of the*

---

[1] The easiest supposition to explain the import of שְׁרֵמוֹת, is the following :
All the meanings of the verbs شرم, سرم and صرم in the Arabic, run
together in that of *cutting off*. Accordingly שְׁרֵמוֹת, *plur.* of the *fem.* of the *adj.*
שָׁרֵם *loca abscissa*, are places which are cut off, and excluded (from the holy city)
outwardly (*Aq.* προάστεια) and also inwardly.

people.' The last words (the people, = the high and low, who had defiled themselves by idolatry, comp. 2 Chron. 34. 4, '*And he strewed the dust upon the graves of those who offered to them*'), enable us, perhaps, to conjecture the cause of the impurity of these fields. They served the adherents of the Moloch worship as a burying place, who would gladly rest in the vicinity of their idol, dwelling in the neighbouring Tophet, which is the more easily explained, since the sacrifices presented to the idol, as may be rendered very probable, were, in a great measure, sacrifices of the dead. קֹדֶשׁ לַיהוָה refers to all mentioned in this verse taken together. In reference to the last words of this verse, we may simply refer to 645.

Chapter 33:14-26

1006. When the destruction had not yet taken place, but was full in view, there was imparted to him, the prophet being in the outer court of the prison, besides the revelation contained in chap. 32, that of which our section forms a constituent part. It may appear surprising, that, in the outset, the revelation of greater and unknown things is promised to the prophet, which he must obtain by calling upon God, whereas the following prediction contains scarcely one important point peculiar to itself. But this is easily explained, when it is observed, that the Scripture throughout considers a *dead knowledge* as *no knowledge;* that in the prophet, as well as in all believers, the hope of the restoration had an enemy in the natural man, that strove to darken and extinguish it; that, therefore, the promise of it was always new, the Word of God perpetually great and exalted. Now in the first part of the revelation, after the destruction had been represented as unavoidable, and, therefore, all human hope had been cut off, the restoration was described more in general expressions. In the second part the Lord meets particularly a twofold special distress of the believers. The time was drawing near when David's race would be most deeply humbled, when every trace of its former glory would be extinguished. With it, the hopes of the people seem to be borne to the grave. God Himself had appointed this race, as the medium of all the mercies, which He, as a King, had promised to show to His people. Where then were the mercies, when the channel had been destroyed through which they flowed to the people? The Temple, converted into a den of thieves by the guilt of the people, was to be destroyed. But with the existence of the Temple the existence of the Levitical priesthood was connected. And if this ceased, where then was the forgiveness of sins, which, in the Law, was connected with the mediation of the Levitical priesthood? Now the Lord meets these cares and anxieties by explaining that, in this respect, the extinction would be a new existence, life would arise from death.

1007. Ver. 14. '*Behold, days come, saith the Lord, and I will fulfil the good word that I have spoken to the house of Israel, and concerning the house of Judah.*' The *good word* may be understood generally of all God's manifestations of mercy towards Israel, in antithesis with the evil word, the threatenings, which, until now, had been fulfilled against Israel (comp. 1 Kings 8. 56). In Deut. 28, the *good* word, and the *evil* word, are placed together, the former from ver. 1—15, first the *blessing* then the *curse*. The central point and substance of this good word was then the promise to David, through whose righteous Branch (or *Shoot*) all the promises to Israel should receive their final fulfilment. But it may be also assumed, that the prophet would especially designate by the '*good word*,' this promise to David, as it had been repeated by him, chap. 23. 5, 6. This latter supposition is, perhaps, to be preferred, since, in ver. 15, 16, that repetition is cited, and ver. 17 points to the ground promise.

1008. Ver. 15, 16. '*In those days, and at that time, I will cause to spring forth to David a righteous shoot, and he shall provide justice and righteousness in the land. In those days Judah shall be endowed with salvation, and Jerusalem dwell securely, and this is the name which shall be given to her, The Lord our righteousness.*' The promise is here intentionally repeated in the previous form, in order to show that it still lived, retaining its power even in the face of the destruction, of the deepest humiliation, of the family of David. For הֲקִמֹתִי the more suitable אַצְמִיחַ is here substituted, because the reference there found to Jehoiakim ceases. For Israel *there*, we have *here* Jerusalem, because it was precisely the restoration of Jerusalem out of the destruction, described in ver. 4, sq., that was so hard to be credited by the believers. For the like reason, the prophet gives to Jerusalem the same name here as to the shoot of David there. The same city which now still sighs under the anger of God, shall yet, at a future period, be endowed with righteousness by the Lord.

1009. Ver. 17. '*For thus saith the Lord, David shall not want a man sitting upon the throne of the house of Israel.*' The connexion with the preceding is well given by Calvin, thus : "*Locutus est proph. de restitutione ecclesiæ ; eam doctrinam nunc confirmat, quia promittit regnum una cum sacerdotio perpetuum fore. Continebatur autem salus populi duabus istis partibus. Nam sine rege erant veluti corpus truncum aut mutilum ; sine sacerdote mera erat dissipatio. Nam sacerdos erat quasi medius inter Deum et populum, rex autem repræsentabat Dei personam.*" The expression, '*shall not be cut off,*' &c., is a simple repetition of the promise to David, in the form in which it was cited by David himself in the address to Solomon, shortly before his death, 1 Kings 2. 4, and afterwards twice by Solomon, 1 Kings 8. 25, 9. 5. That לֹא יִכָּרֵת does not designate a *complete uninterrupted succession*, that it only forms an antithesis with an entire cessation, appears in the ground promise, from the fact, that God reserves to Himself the punishment of the individual apostate members of the stock of David, and in Jeremiah from the frequently repeated prediction of its total humiliation.

1010. Ver. 18. ' *And to the Levitical priests a man shall not be cut off before me, presenting a burnt-offering, and setting on fire a meat-offering, and presenting a sacrificial victim always.*' In order to a correct understanding of these words, it is necessary to go back to their occasion. The consolation is explained only by the distress. The prophet had not here to do with members of the tribe of Levi, mourning over the loss of the prerogative of their tribe ; had this been the case, the letter must have been held fast, for it is only when this is retained that the promise can afford consolation for such a state of mind. Its consolations are rather designed for all believers, who bewailed the extinction of the relation to God that had hitherto existed through the mediation of the tribe of Levi. If only the *relation* continued, it was of little consequence to them *whether it were realized, as hitherto, through the tribe of Levi.* As the distress, so also the consolation, regarded solely the substance. That Israel should, even henceforth, enjoy free access to his reconciled God, is the fundamental thought. Now all whereby this thought is historically realized, in whatever form this may be, is to be considered as included under it. And thus we gain a threefold fulfilment. (1) In the times after the return from the exile, the consolation was enjoyed in the form in which it is here expressed. That God permitted and promoted the rebuilding of the Temple, was a matter-of-fact declaration of the reinstating of the Levitical priesthood in its mediatorial office. (2) The idea of the Levitical priesthood was most fully realized in Christ, who, as a High Priest and Mediator, bore the sins of His people, made intercession for the transgressors, in whom the Levitical priesthood ceased, as the seed-corn disappears in the plant. (3) Through Christ the believers became priests themselves, and obtained free access to the Father.—That we justly maintain this independence of the thought on the form, appears from the following grounds : (1) The prophet is so penetrated by the thought of the glory of the new covenant far surpassing that of the old, that it might have been expected beforehand, that, in respect to the priesthood, he would not anticipate an eternal duration of the mean form it had hitherto borne. It is only the substance that is, in his view, permanent. We need only compare the portion chap. 31. 31, sq. But especially in this respect is chap. 3. 16 to be considered. There, the cessation of the former dignity of the ark of the covenant is announced in the strongest and most impressive terms. We have already seen how the Temple, the Levitical priesthood, and the whole sacrificial service, stood in the closest and most inseparable connexion with the ark of the covenant, so that they must all fall with it. (2) Ver. 22 here furnishes an incontrovertible proof, which must be regarded as an explanation by the prophet himself, how he wished to be understood. Now the changing of *all the descendants of Abraham into Levites*, is here promised as a constituent part of the perpetual acceptance of the tribe of Levi, promised in the verse before us. This plainly shows that, in this verse also, the Levites could not come

under consideration as *natural descendants of Levi*, but only in reference to their calling and their destination. (3) Zechariah is to
be regarded as the oldest and most authentic interpreter of Jeremiah.
Now in him, who earnestly endeavours to obviate the same anxiety
which Jeremiah here meets, two of the three points embraced by
Jeremiah in the unity of the idea, appear separately, yet so that the
binding unity of the idea is not thereby placed in the back-ground.
Chap. 3, God assures the people, that, notwithstanding the greatness
of their sins, He would not only, as heretofore, suffer the office of
the high priest to continue, and accept his mediation, but also,
at a future period, send the true High Priest, who should make a
complete and perpetual atonement (comp. 505).   In ver. 8 the
high priest, and his colleagues in the priestly office, are designated as types of Christ, inasmuch as He, putting to shame the
despair of the people in God's mercy, should completely accomplish
the atonement and reconciliation which had been only imperfectly
effected by them.   In chap. 4, the priestly order, together with the
regal, is designated as one of the two children of oil, of the two
anointed of the Lord, whose anointing should always remain
(comp. 522); and that here also only the shadow belongs to the
Levitical high-priesthood, the body to Christ, is evident from
chap. 6. 13 (comp. 538), where the Messiah appears at the same
time as the true High Priest and King.   (4) There are not
wanting elsewhere plain examples, in which only the *idea of the
priesthood* is considered apart from the *peculiar form* of its manifestation under the Old Testament.   Among these is Isa. 61. 6,
where it is said, in reference to all Israel, '*And ye shall be called
priests of Jehovah ; ministers of our God, shall men say to you.*'
Here the conversion of all Israel into the tribe of Levi is announced ; for that it cannot be established that the discourse there
is only in general of priests, but in Jeremiah of Levitical priests, appears from the second passage, chap. 66. 21, '*And I will also take
of them for* Levitical *priests, saith the Lord.*' Whether by '*the
brethren,*' to which the expression '*from them*' refers, the *heathen*
are here to be understood, as Vitringa and Gesenius suppose, or the
Israelites in the exile, makes no difference in respect to our purpose.
For although the latter reference be assumed, it is still certain, that
those should be received as Levitical priests who had not descended
from Levi.   Otherwise there would be no *taking*, no special Divine
favour.—After we have thus determined the sense of the promise
relating to the Levitical priesthood, it will not be difficult to arrive
at the truth also in the case of the promise relating to the tribe of
David.   Here also we find a threefold fulfilment. (1) In the times
immediately after the exile, where Zerubbabel, a shoot of the stock
of David, was a mediator of the favours which God, as King, vouchsafed to His people.   In a certain sense also may be included the
favour which God, at a later period, in His relation as King, bestowed
upon the people through civil leaders, who were not of David's race.
For since the dominion had been for ever transferred to the stock of
David, these could be regarded only as ingrafted into it as substi-

tutes and vicegerents,—much in the same way as the blessing which
was imparted to the people by the priesthood of Samuel, who was
not a priest, is to be regarded as included in the promise in reference
to the tribe of Levi. What God bestowed through those leaders
was only for the sake of the tribe of David, which had been destined
as the perpetual channel of his regal blessings. Had the kingdom
of David come to an end, he would not have bestowed either these
rulers or the prosperity granted to them upon the people, as appears
from a comparison of the times after the reign of the great hero out
of David's stock ; where, because no representation of the tribe of
David, now again to reign to all eternity, can any more have place,
so also has every trace of the regal favour of God, in raising up
other rulers, now ceased. But in the passage before us, the separation of what, in the strictest sense, does not belong there, would be
the less suitable, since here the promise to David is not considered
in reference to him and to his family, but solely in reference to the
people ; and since, therefore, the manifestation of the regal mercy of
God constitutes the central point, while the tribe of David comes
under consideration only so far as it was destined to be the medium
of this regal mercy. (2) It was fulfilled in Christ, and that the
prophet had this chiefly in view, appears from ver. 15, 16. Both
were joined with one another also, by Zechariah in chap. 4. (3) It
was fulfilled in the exaltation of the whole of the genuine posterity
of Abraham to the regal dignity through Christ. This most striking
antithesis with the despondency,—the despondency, *there is no king*
in Israel ; the consolation, *all Israel kings,*—is expressly brought
forward in ver. 22.—We still remark, that we must not, as is commonly done, translate '*priests and Levites,*' but, as also Is. 66. 21,
'*Levitical priests.*' The epithet *Levitical*, is subjoined, in order to
obviate the thought, that the discourse might here perhaps be of
priests in the improper sense ; it serves, therefore, the same purpose
as '*he reigns as a king,*' in chap. 23. 5.—In reference to the sacrifices, we cannot assume, with the older interpreters, that precisely
spiritual sacrifices are here meant ; the correct view is rather, that
the prophet presents the *substance* in *the form it had hitherto borne*,
and in which it should now soon for a time be lost, without, since he
had to do only with the substance, expressing any opinion whether
this substance in the future, should arise again in the same form, and
whether it should endure for ever. History affirms the former and
denies the latter, and that the prophet also would have denied it upon
inquiry, evidently appears from chap. 3. 16. Finally, how well they
knew, even under the Old Testament, in the sacrifices, to distinguish
the substance and the form from one another, and regard the latter
as merely accidental, is shown by such passages as Hos. 14. 3,
'*Take with you words, and return to the Lord, and say to him,* Take
away all guilt, and give *good, and we will recompense to Thee bullocks,
our lips.*' Here, thanks are represented as the substance of the
thank-offering, and, indeed, so completely, that the thank offering,
the bullock, is *entirely* present, where there are only the thanks, the
lips. The outward sacrifice is only the vessel wherein the gift of

God is represented. Also Ps. 50. 14, in antithesis with the mere outward sacrifices, ' *Offer to God thanksgiving,*' Mal. 1. 11, &c.

1011. Ver. 19. ' *And the word of the Lord came to Jeremiah, and said, Thus saith the Lord, If ye shall make void my covenant the day and my covenant the night, so that there shall be no more day and night in its time,*' Ver. 21. ' *Then also shall my covenant with David my servant be made void, that he shall not have one who reigns upon his throne, and with the Levitical priests, my servants.*' The thought has been already explained in chap. 31. 35, sq. The *day* and the *night* in apposition to ' *my covenant ;* ' the day and the night, in their regular and perpetual alternation, *are* the covenant which is here the subject of discourse [1]. The *covenant* [2] stands here, not, indeed, in the sense *stabilis ordinatio,* nor is it to be regarded as *concluded* with the day and the night ; these are rather the *covenant blessings ;* God, who bestows *them,* and all connected with them, who causes the sun to shine by day, and the moon by night, *thereby concludes,* according to the investigation already made (on 31. 32), a *covenant with men ;* he binds them, by the uninterrupted preservation of the course of nature, to an uninterrupted observance of moral order. This is manifest, when, after the flood, the covenant of nature is concluded, and its inviolability established anew, comp. Gen. 9. 9, ' *Behold, I set up my covenant* with you, *and with your seed after you.*' 8. 22, ' *Summer and winter, seedtime and harvest, heat and cold, day and night, shall not fail.*' Then, with these covenant promises, covenant laws are connected, obligations which the covenant imposes. Now the covenant of grace, peculiar to Israel alone, is entirely like this natural covenant, common to all men, and not first concluded, but only renewed, in the time of Noah. To assert that the former could cease, is nothing else than to wish to tear the sun and moon from the heavens. It is, indeed, one and the same God, who is the author of both the covenants.

1012. Ver. 22. ' *As the host of heaven is not numbered, and the sand of the sea not measured, so will I increase the seed of David my servant, and the Levites, who serve me.*' The *literal* increase of the natural family of David lies beyond the bounds of possibility ; and even were this not so, still it would have, as well as the like increase of the Levites, not the nature of a *promise,* but of a *threatening.* In any event, the consolation would stand in no relation to the affliction. For this referred, not to the number of the posterity of David, and of the Levites, but to the *merciful reception of the latter* by God, and with them that of the people, and this has nothing whatever to do with numbers. But, in addition to this, there is still another ground. The verbal relation to the promises in Abraham (Gen. 15. 5 ; 22. 7), is manifest. Now if these *belong to all Israel,* and they are here, on the contrary, transferred to the *family of David, and to the Levites,* then is it thereby sufficiently indicated, that *all Israel* should be *converted into the family of David and the tribe of Levi.* This

---

[1] יוֹמָם וָלַיְלָה, *of day and night, daily and nightly,* for *tempus diurnum et nocturnum.*   [2] בְּרִית.

thought need not here surprise us. It has its foundation in the law itself. It is here only announced, that the destination of the covenant people lying already in the law, but hitherto only very imperfectly realized, should, at a future period, be realized perfectly. God says, Exod. 19. 6, of Israel, ' *Ye shall be to me a kingdom of priests* (מַמְלֶכֶת כֹּהֲנִים)," therefore, first a kingdom. The nature of a kingdom is to have no other power over itself than the divine. This was always the case with the covenant people, so long as they were not brought by their own wilful fault into a voluntary moral bondage to the world ; the outward bondage was always only a reflection of the inward, and never overtook the covenant people, as such, but always only as far as they had become like the world. And, even when this *unnatural* condition occurred, the individuals, who, conscious how dearly they had been redeemed, kept themselves inwardly free from the bondage of the world, did not lose this high dignity. Although in chains and bonds, they still, in this higher relation, remained free. The world, sin, death, and hell, could gain no advantage over them, nay, with all external appearance of victory, these enemies were in reality subdued by them, and even their outward bondage, more deeply considered, was a sign of their dominion. For the law of the Lord of hosts was in their inward parts ; it was the living principle of their being, and, according to this law, the whole world was ruled ; according to this law also, the bondage of their people ensued. They were, therefore, co-regents with God, and, as such, reigned over their rulers.—All the individual members of this kingdom, that consists purely of kings, should, at the same time, be priests. And thus it was already declared, that the Levitical priesthood, introduced at a later period, could not have the same meaning as the priesthood among other people of antiquity, where priests and people stood in an absolute and direct antithesis, where the *priests only* stood in an immediate relation to God. It was thus declared, that the priests,—according to one view ; in another they were types and shadows of Christ,—possessed only transferred rights, that they were the representatives of the people, that, therefore, their mediation at a future period might entirely disappear. And, in order that this might be perpetually held by the people in lively remembrance, that they might know that *they* were the proper bearers of the priestly dignity, even after the establishment of the Levitical priesthood, they retained that sacerdotal function, which formed the root and groundwork of all the rest, the slaying of the covenant sacrifice, of the Paschal Lamb, which formed the central point of all other sacrifices, which served only for its completion. That even under the old covenant, this import of the Paschal service was rightly perceived, is shown by Philo, *De Vitâ Mos.* p. 686, Frfr. : *"At the passover, the laity do not merely bring the sacrificial animals to the altar, and the priests offer them, but, according to the prescription of the Law, the whole people exercise priestly functions, since each one, for his own part, presents the appropriate sacrifices."*—Thus, therefore, we have here the highest completion of the consolation designed for the sorrowing covenant people. Not merely shall they receive back their king, their priests, but they shall be entirely changed into a royal and priestly race. In substance, this was already contained (which should not be overlooked) in the promise to Abraham ; that this did not refer to a great multitude of corporeal descendants, *tales quales*, but rather refers only to such sons of Abraham as were, at the same time, sons of God, and therefore a royal and priestly race, we have already pointed out, 792.—If, now, we look at the fulfilment, the passage which chiefly presents itself is 1 Pet. 2. 9, Ὑμεῖς δὲ γένος ἐκλεκτὸν, βασίλειον ἱεράτευμα, &c. Here the passage of Exodus appears as a prophecy, which is now first fulfilled in the present   Israel has now become, what, according to the destination, he always should be, a royal priesthood, priests who possess at the same time the kingly nature and being. What now perfectly exists in the germ shall hereafter be completely developed, according to Apoc. 5. 10, Καὶ ἐποίησας ἡμᾶς τῷ Θεῷ ἡμῶν βασιλεῖς καὶ ἱερεῖς, καὶ βασιλεύσουσιν ἐπὶ τῆς γῆς. Believers, when their sin has been extirpated, will have the freest access to God ; when His will has become theirs, and when, at the same time, His dominion over the whole world becomes visible, they will unconditionally reign with Him. How this, their dignity, is rooted in Christ, appears from the Apoc. 1. 5, 9, where the καὶ ἐποίησεν ἡμᾶς βασιλείαν (A. βασιλεῖς καὶ) ἱερεῖς τῷ Θεῷ καὶ Πατρὶ αὐτοῦ stands in a close connexion to the ὁ ἄρχων τῶν βασιλέων τῆς γῆς, and to the καὶ λούσαντι ἡμᾶς ἀπὸ τῶν ἁμαρτιῶν ἡμῶν ἐν τῷ αἵματι αὐτοῦ[1].

1013. Ver. 23. ' *And the word of the Lord came to Jeremiah, and said,*' Ver. 24. '*Seest thou not what this people speak and say : the two families which the Lord has chosen, those has He now rejected, and they despise my people, that it is no longer a people before them.*' It is scarcely to be conceived, how the recent interpreters could assert, that by *this people*, are to be understood, not the Israelites, but the heathen, the Egyptians, or the Chaldeans. It is left out of view, that the prophet here, as in the whole of the rest of the portion, and as throughout these chapters, refers entirely to those in Israel,—and to this class belong more or less all, even the most believing,—who, because they saw Israel prostrate, despaired of his future prosperity, and, indeed, for the most part, so as to give a good pretext, that of humility, for their despair. The people have so sinned against God, that He is free from all His obligations, and can by no means receive them again into favour. The prophet shows them, that such a thought, however good in appearance, is still a reproach to God. Every instance of despair degrades God to an idol, to a creature. Faith sustains itself on the word, on the promise ; it says, although there is much sin with us, there is much more mercy with God. So truly as God remains constantly God, so truly do His people

---

[1] אֲשֶׁר cannot mean *as;* it designates rather merely in general, the relation of this sentence to the preceding, in reference hereto ; and the thing to be compared is then subjoined, and designated as to be compared by the bare כְּ : " is not to be numbered—so."

remain constantly his people. He chastises them indeed, but He does not give them over to death. One need only consider the חָפְרוּ in ver. 20.—The expression ʻ this people ʼ is contemptuous. The prophet indicates, that those who use such language thus cease to be numbered among the people of God. The two families are Judah and Israel. Of these, in substance, the prophet had spoken also in what preceded ; for he had treated of the election or rejection of the tribe of Levi and the race of David, only so far as these stood related to the election or rejection of the people, so that here there is only a repetition of the same thing in a different form, from regard to the indocility of those who are weak in faith, and prone to despond. The expression, ʻ those has he rejected,ʼ was correct in a certain sense, but not in that of the speakers. They maintained, in anti-thesis with the election, a rejection for *ever*, which was as much as to assert, that Jehovah, the existing, the unchangeable, was no more Jehovah, but a man, that he might lie, and a son of man, that he might repent. As surely as God was Jehovah, so surely also ἀμετα-μέλητα τὰ χαρίσματα καὶ ἡ κλῆσις τοῦ Θεοῦ, Rom. 11. 29.—The expression ʻ my people ʼ directs attention to the fact, that they despised God in despising Israel. With respect to the antithesis of ʻ my people ʼ and ʻ a people,ʼ comp. on chap. 31. 36.

1014. Ver. 25. ʻ *Thus saith the Lord, If I have not established my covenant by day and by night, and the ordinances of the heaven and the earth :*ʼ comp. ver. 20. The covenant by day and by night, the cove-nant which relates to the constant and regular alternation of day and night. The ordinances of the heaven and the earth designate the whole course of nature,—especially the relation of sun, moon, and stars to the earth, comp. 31. 35,—so far as it is regulated by God's ordinance, and therefore is lasting.

1015. Ver. 26. ʻ *Then will I also reject the seed of Jacob, and David my servant, that I will no more take out of his seed rulers over the seed of Abraham, Isaac, and Jacob. For I will turn their imprisonment, and have mercy upon them.*ʼ The rejection of the seed of Jacob and of the seed of David are inseparably connected with each other. For since, by the promise to David, the kingdom had been for ever joined with his race, so when David was no more a servant of God, Israel also was no more a people of God, and, in general, no more a people. The *plur.* מֹשְׁלִים is explained by the circumstance, that the stress was here laid not upon the number, but only upon the fact, comp. on 23. 4. and at the same time also on v. 18. That the pro-phet had, chiefly at least, in view the revival of the dominion of David in the Messiah, is beyond a doubt. The mention of the three patriarchs recalls to mind the whole series of the promises imparted to them. The turning of the imprisonment designates here, as always, the *restitutio in integrum*,—the imprisonment being an image of misery,—not the bringing back out of captivity.

THE PROPHET EZEKIEL

Preliminary Observations

1016. The temporal relations under which Ezekiel came forward, have already been fully presented in the introduction to Jeremiah. Ezekiel was a younger contemporary of this prophet. He had been carried away into exile at the first great deportation under Jehoiachin, received his residence on the Chebar, and there came forward, as a prophet, in the midst of the exiles, in the seventh year before the destruction of Jerusalem. To this temporal relation to Jeremiah, his relation to him in other respects corresponds. He imitates him throughout, which seems to have given occasion to the later saying, that he was the amanuensis of Jeremiah. But this dependence can have been only a voluntary one, as is evident from the highly individual and independent character of Ezekiel.

1017. The sphere of Ezekiel's labours was one of great importance. A better soil, on the whole, was assigned to him than to Jeremiah. By Divine guidance, precisely the better part of the nation had been carried into exile, which, if we look to the human causes, may, perhaps, be thus explained : the ungodly, who despised the predictions of the prophets, made every effort to obtain permission to remain in their native land, while those who feared God, perceiving that the ruin of the city, the indispensable condition of its restoration, was unavoidable, joyfully obeyed the first admonition, and cheerfully met death, which was the only gate of life. This relation of the exiles to those who remained behind, appears especially from Jeremiah 24. Still, however, the distinction was only a *relative* one. The forehead of Ezekiel also must God make as a diamond, harder than a rock, that he might not fear before them and not tremble before their face ; for they were a disobedient people (chap. 3. 9). Many of the ungodly had been carried away against their will, and even the pious had dwelt among a people of unclean lips, and, through the predominance of unrighteousness, their love had grown cold. Many temptations surrounded the weak, and threatened to blast their hopes of the kingdom of God. They were placed at once in the midst of the heathen world, and the idolatrous spirit of the times assailed them with fearful violence. The long-predicted judgement upon Judea was delayed ; the kingdom of Zedekiah seemed to be altogether confirmed ; the alliance with the Egyptian power encouraged the hope of an entire restoration : the deceivers of the people in Jerusalem did not leave the exiles out of view, and found among them willing assistance ; on all hands, human hopes were rife ; soon they supposed a return into their native land would be open to them, and, with this thought, that of co-operating for such a purpose was immediately connected. But as long as they strove to find human ways of deliverance, they could not with earnestness pursue the Divine way, which led through *repentance.* To return to the Lord, was what they had to do; in this return, the return to their land was included, so surely as this land was the land of the Lord. Even those who kept themselves pure from such gross pollution, still vacillated, and needed to be strengthened. There was so much to favour the notion, that God had entirely forgotten them; they were cut off from the sanctuary, and dwelt in a strange land; their brothers, in possession of the holy land and the Temple, treated them with proud contempt, since they considered the possession as an actual proof of their right. And thus they were near despair.— Then the Lord began to fulfil His good word given to the exiles through Jeremiah, by causing Ezekiel to appear in the midst of them, who raised his voice like a trumpet, and showed to Israel his misdeeds; whose word, like a threshing-machine, passed over all these sweet hopes and purposes, and ground them to dust; whose whole manifestation furnished the strongest proof, that the Lord was still among His people, who was himself a Temple of the Lord, before whom the apparent Temple, which still stood at Jerusalem for a short time, sunk back into its own nothingness; a spiritual Samson, who, with a strong arm, seized the pillars of the temple of idols and dashed it to the ground; an energetic, gigantic nature, who was thereby suited effectually to counteract the Babylonish spirit of the times, which loved to manifest itself in violent, gigantic, grotesque forms; one who stood alone, but was yet equal to a hundred of the scholars of the prophets. The extent of his influence appears from the fact, that the oldest of the people were accustomed to assemble in his house, in order to hear the word of the Lord through him,—a sign of the public and formal acknowledgement of his spiritual dignity in the colony [1].

Chapter 11:14-21

1018. It belongs to the greater whole, chap. 8—11. In the sixth year after the carrying away of Jehoiachin, which was also the sixth year before the destruction, the elders of the colony are collected before the prophet, expecting that the Lord would send them a message through him. The occasion of this their wish, and the subject on which they desired information, we learn from the prophecy itself, especially from chap. 11. That God's righteousness did not manifest itself so swiftly as they expected in the destruction of Jerusalem, led them to doubt respecting their own conduct, and the more so, since the inhabitants of Jerusalem, elated by the possession of the sanctuary, triumphed over them. The prophet is now transferred in spirit to Jerusalem. There, in the first place, he is favoured with a survey of the greatness and aggravation of their sins. These appear as concentrated in and before the Temple (comp. on Amos 9. 1), and as the chief bearers of them, the leaders of the people *in corpore*,

[1] The Commentary of Rosenmüller on Ezekiel is favorably distinguished above those on other books.

the seventy elders, and the twenty-five princes, the former standing in the northern, the latter in the eastern gate of the Temple, and there supplicating, not, indeed, the Lord, but their idols, in striking antithesis with the leaders of the exiles, who seek the Lord in His servant. The contrast of the idea and the reality is expressed in the relation of the name of one among the Seventy, probably the most distinguished among them, Joazaniah (= *God-hears*), to his conduct. This '*God-hears*' speaks with his associates (ver. 12), '*Jehovah sees us not, Jehovah has forsaken the land.*'—The representation of the sin is followed by that of the punishment, from chap. 9. 1, sq., the certainty and greatness of which is already established by the former. It follows exactly the order of the sin. The prophet beholds how the avenging angels, with *the* angel of the Lord at their head, sent by Jehovah, enthroned over the ark of the covenant, as a sign that the judgement was a Theocratic one, begin their work on the elders who are before the north gate, the Seventy; how they then go forth and slay in the city; how, finally, the glory of the Lord removes from the Holy of Holies into the gate towards the east, the chief toward the Mount of Olives, in order there to judge the twenty-five, and then entirely to depart from the desecrated Jerusalem. Already the axe lies at the root of the heads of the people, and yet the prophet hears them utter their rash speeches. It is not near; let us build houses, say they (11. 2), *it* is the cauldron, and we the flesh. They mock, therefore, the discourses of the prophets, according to which the way to build lay through the destruction,—'*What is once destroyed, that is not so easily rebuilt; instead of suffering ourselves to be deceived by such fanatical hopes, we will rather hold what we have; nothing, neither man nor God, shall drive us out of the possession of Jerusalem. It and we are inseparable.*' The prophet receives the command to chastise this impudence with words; and scarcely has he ended his discourse, when the deed (naturally in the vision, in the ideal reality) follows the word. The Divine judgement begins, and Pelatiah the son of Benaiah first sinks beneath the stroke of the Lord. As in respect to the sin, so also of the punishment, the prophet causes its nature to appear in the name. '*God-hears*,' says *God hears not*, a contrast of the idea and the reality, in reference to the behaviour; '*God-delivers*,' son of '*God-builds*,' perishes without deliverance, and falls into ruin; the contrast of the idea and reality in reference to the event, necessarily resulting from the first contrast. The prophet recognizes this antithesis, sees that in Pelatiah the son of Benaiah this person perishes not as an individual, but as a type of the whole people. Seized with compassion, he throws himself upon his face, and cries aloud: '*Ah, Lord, wilt thou destroy the remnant of Israel* (11. 13)? *shall the name of Pelatiah henceforth be a lie?*'

1019. Now herewith is our portion connected. The Lord answers, He will not receive into favour those bold sinners who now play the master in Jerusalem; these, although of Israel, are yet not Israel; the souls which have already long been extirpated from

Israel, must now also become outwardly so. The object of his intercession, of his mediatorial office, must be the exiles, because they only are children of God; they only are his brethren, the only true Israel, over whom the apparent Israel in Jerusalem exalts himself with arrogant disdain. The Lord would, with true love, receive His own to Himself; already, during their short abode in the land of the heathen, He would be their sanctuary, and truly supply them with that which the others, for whom merely the shell without a kernel remained, thought to possess. He would then bring them back into their native land, impart to them the gifts of His Spirit, and make them, in the fullest sense, His people. But woe to the hypocrites and apostates among them!

1020. The prophet now sees the glory of the Lord entirely depart from Jerusalem; for the Lord has completed His only work, which, as a covenant God, He had still to perform there, the judgement. The vision is at an end, and the prophet communicates it to the heads of the colony.

1021. Ver. 14. ' *And the word of the Lord came to me and said,*' ver. 15, ' *Thou son of man, thy brethren, thy brethren, are the men of thy redemption, and the whole house of Israel, the whole, they to whom the inhabitants of Jerusalem say, Be ye far from the Lord! To us is given the land for a possession.*' The repetition of *thy brethren* gives force to the idea of the brotherhood, and expresses the contrast with the *apparent* brethren, in whom the prophet had interested himself as if they were his *real* brethren; the brethren merely according to the flesh, who had not one Father with Him, God, nor had they Abraham as a common father with him in the true sense, any more than the seed of Abraham was called in Ishmael and the sons of Keturah. He alludes to the Mosaic right of *redemption*, which found place only among *natural brothers*, or *nearest relations*. Only the brother was the natural ally, deliverer, avenger of the brother; no one was a *Goël* of a *stranger*, comp., e. g., Levit. 25. 25. The prophet, by undertaking the cause of those who were *not his real brethren*, would have engaged in something as unheard of as if any one should take upon himself to be *Goël* of a stranger. The *Goël* has not merely *duties*, but also *rights;* as an avenger of his brother, he has the right *hæreditatem ejus sibi vindicandi.* Finally, the *suff.* belongs to the compound idea, *thy redemption men, the men whom thou hast a right, and art bound, to redeem.*—That the brethren are the *whole house of Israel*, the Lord affirms in antithesis with ver. 13, where the prophet had spoken of *the inhabitants of Jerusalem* as of *Israel* [1]. The *imper.* ' *be far* ' is to be taken in its full sense. The removal out of the land of the Lord was regarded by the hypocrites as an actual declaration of *distance from the Lord*, just as a *residence in that land* was supposed to be a proof of *nearness to Him.*

[1] כלּה *tota ipsa* serves the same object as the repeated אַחֶיךָ. It shows that the preceding כל is to be taken in the *strictest* sense.

From this point of view they exclaim to their brethren, '*Away with you from the Lord, to us is the land given as a possession.*' They fell into a sort of holy zeal at the thought, that such profane people could still lay claim to a part and an inheritance in the Lord, and hereafter even in His land. In this attitude, which they assumed against their brethren, against the house of Israel, they bore testimony against themselves, that they were not, in the true sense, brethren belonging to the house of Israel.

1022. Ver. 16. ' *Therefore say, Thus saith the Lord God, I have, indeed, removed them among the heathen, and scattered them in the lands, but I will be to them for a short time a sanctuary in the lands whither they come.*' *Therefore* refers to the contemptuous language of the inhabitants of Jerusalem. The *therefore* in ver. 17 corresponds with it. Here the antithesis with their assertion is expressed, so far as it related to the distance from the Lord ; there, so far as it related to *exclusion from the land of the Lord.* The opposite of the former already exists, that of the latter will soon appear. The כִּי presupposes *an intervening thought to be supplied ;* ' [*they are, in a certain respect, right ; they do not speak so entirely without cause ;*] for, *indeed,*' &c. As to the substance, our *yea* would fully correspond. While the fact is conceded, the conclusion grounded thereon is contested. They infer, '*And, therefore, is the Lord far from them.*' The Lord, '*And, therefore, am I,* or *I became to them a sanctuary.*' The outward distance, viewed as to its essence, is precisely the means of approach. True, they have lost the Temple of the Lord, but the Lord Himself has become their Temple. The prophet by these words does away the triumph of the inhabitants of Jerusalem, who thought to possess God in the Temple, and the distress of the exiles, who supposed in losing the Temple they had lost Him. What makes the Temple a sanctuary is the presence of God; where this is, there is the sanctuary ; where this is not, there is no temple, but only a mass of wood and stone. The annunciation is completed by the circumstance, that the prophet sees the glory of the Lord depart out of the Temple of Jerusalem. We have here the germ out of which is developed (in chap. 40—48) the tree, with all its twigs and branches, its leaves and its flowers,—the representation of God's kingdom in the glorious completion of its new form.—As the true sanctuary of Israel, the Lord Himself is designated also Isa. 8. 14, and the passages of the Psalms, which show how general was that spiritual consideration of the Temple, in which the shell being disregarded, only the kernel, the merciful presence of the Lord, was kept in view, have been already cited, § 671, note 3 [1]. Was the Lord in the exile actually the sanctuary of the people, it must then be evident that the abode in the exile would endure but a *short time.* For Canaan was at that time still the land of the covenant ; the presence of the Lord with His people, beyond the limits of this land, could be only a *temporary* one. The phrase ' *in the lands,*'

---

[1] מְעַט is to be taken as a designation of time, *paulisper.* Thus, e. g., Exod. 17. 4; Ps. 2. 12 ; 37. 10 ; Job 10. 20 ; Is. 10. 25 ; 29. 17 ; Hos. 1. 4.

&c., intimates, that the Lord will, at a future period, again become the sanctuary of the people on its natural site, *in the land of promise,* and thus prepares the way for the contents of ver. 17, sq.— But whereby does the Lord show Himself as the sanctuary of the people in the exile? In the first instance by the sending of the prophet himself. That He gave them a preacher of repentance and salvation, and that one furnished with such rich gifts, was of itself a sign that His mercy had not departed from the people. The prophet was, in the inferior sense, what the Redeemer was in the highest, a *Temple of God.* For there was in him that which made the Temple the Temple, *the presence of the Lord.* Then, however, in other manifold ways; by the *outward helps,* which He vouchsafed to them; by the alleviation of their affliction,—they had not entirely lost even their national independence; even in the exile they had their elders, —*by inward consolations;* by the spirit of grace and of prayer, which He poured out upon those who were fitted to receive it, and thereby changed the hearts of stone into those of flesh; by *the arrangements which He, even at that time, made for their future return:* during the whole exile, His providence was occupied in bringing about the circumstances necessary to insure it: all events were directed to this purpose; Daniel's elevation, the decline of the Babylonian, and the rise of the Persian power. How different was the Babylonian exile from the present exile [of the Jews]! Now there is *no* proof of the presence of God; the people can only celebrate festivals in memory of the past, and dream of the future; between the distant past and the distant future, a vast and empty space, a whole Zahara: but in that there were, for the more deeply reflecting, in the deepest degradation, everywhere traces of the loving care of God, pledges of the enduring election, of the future glorification.

1023. Ver. 17. ' *Therefore say, Thus saith the Lord God, And I will collect you out of the nations, and bring you out of the lands wherein ye are dispersed, and give you the land of Israel.*' The expression, ' *the Lord Jehovah,*' shows, that the promiser is the Almighty, and the faithful. ' And *I will collect*' designates this blessing as connected with the former, as its continuation and consequence. That the promise of the return was not completely fulfilled under Zerubbabel, because the Canaan which they at that time trod was not the land of the Lord in the full sense; that the promise rather contains a Messianic element, scarcely needs to be remarked, after the full investigations, which have already, on several occasions, been given. When the prophet seems here to promise the return only to those who were at that time already in the exile, while he threatens those still in Judea with destruction, this antithesis is naturally understood not to relate to the particular individuals, but to the mass. Otherwise must we conclude from ver. 15, where the exiles are designated as the whole of Israel, that even Jeremiah himself was no ἀληθῶς Ἰσραηλίτης.

1024. Ver. 18. ' *And they shall come thither, and remove therefrom all their detestable things and all their abominations.*' Venema remarks : " *Inceperunt mox post reditum, sed non perfecerunt nisi diu post, temporibus Maccabaicis, quando quaquaversum per totam terram idololatriam destruxerunt, et veram religionem propagarunt, etiam inter Samaritanos et Idumæos."* But only one particular thing belongs to the *perfecerunt.* The *outward removal* of the things whereby the land of the Lord had been defiled, was regarded by the prophet, only so far as it was the result of the unconditional *surrender of the heart* to the Lord. This appears even from the connexion in which the doing of the people stands, in what follows, with the gift of the Lord on which it depended. Whether Satan drives out Satan, whether the subtler form of idolatry—even Jehovah *may* be an idol—makes war upon the grosser, is perfectly indifferent in a religious point of view, and therefore lies beyond the scope of the prophecy, just as much as the change in the modes of dress. And thus it also appears, that the outward removal of the idols in the time after the return, and in that of the Maccabees, is referred to here, only so far as God Himself was thereby the moving principle, and therefore only as a very small beginning, and that the prophecy, in its essential reference, is Messianic. How little ground there is for the *perfecerunt,* is evident even from the *outward condition* of the people, from the return until the time of Christ. If the idols had vanished out of the land with their images, the people would have been justified, when they charged God with unfaithfulness in the performance of His promises.

1025. Ver. 19. '*And I will give to them one heart, and a new spirit will I give in their inward parts; and I will take away the heart of stone out of their flesh, and give them a heart of flesh.*' Deut. 30. 1, sq. is the foundation of the whole promise of the prophet; it is a simple renewal; the circumstances foreseen by Moses had now occurred; the people of the Lord are in exile; and therefore the consoling words of His servant are revived: comp. especially ver. 5, 6, where the *circumcision of the heart* is the *removal of its impurities,* prefigured by the outward circumcision, which is at the same time its pledge; it is equivalent, therefore, to the gift of the fleshly heart, instead of the stony heart.—'*I will give to them one heart,*' shows that the people will *unanimously* seek the Lord, in antithesis with their previous condition, where only individuals were converted [1]. The *fleshly* heart, in contrast with the *stony* one, here designates one that is *soft, susceptible* of the impressions of Divine grace. That man's heart should first become so by God's grace, points to its natural condition. It is by nature, in reference to that which is Divine, as hard as stone, insensible, and unsusceptible; God's Word, and His outward dispensations, pass over it and leave no trace; the latter may, perhaps, break it in pieces, but cannot subdue it; the fragments still remain hard, nay, the hardness increases. God's Spirit alone can create a broken and soft heart: comp., as substantially parallel, Jer. 31. 33, as verbally, chap. 36. 26.

---

[1] Parallel is Jer. 32. 39; Zeph. 3. 9; Acts 4. 32, Τοῦ δὲ πλήθους τῶν πιστευσάντων ἦν ἡ καρδία καὶ ἡ ψυχὴ μία.

1026. Ver. 20. ' *That they may walk in my commandments, and keep my statutes, and do them ; and they shall become my people, and I will become their God.*' The groundwork is Levit. 26. 3, ' *If ye will walk in my laws, and keep my commandments, and do them* (ver. 4), *then will I give you your rain at its time,*' &c. Then, after a long narration in ver. 12, the comprehensive ' *and I will be to you for God, and ye shall be to me for a people,*' comp. on Jer. 31. 33. It is God's work alone, that the covenant people become, in their conduct, the covenant people ; that God's name is sanctified, His will realized in them ; and where this has first taken place, where, in this respect, the destination of the covenant people is realized, there the other also necessarily follows, there the people also become His people in their lot, there is God sanctified upon them, there does He impart to them all the fulness of His gifts and blessings.

1027. Ver. 21. ' *But to those whose heart goes after the heart of their detestable things and abominations, I will give their way upon their head, saith the Lord Jehovah.*' In conclusion, those are emphatically excluded from the favour of God, who, through their own fault, do not receive the new heart, the foundation of it ; and therefore walk not in God's commandments. Even among the new covenant people there is an impure residuum ; even with them does God's righteousness find a new object. The walking after the heart of the idols stands opposed to the walking after the heart of God. Whether the idols formally exist or not, is nothing to the purpose. Enough that their essence, the sin, is actually present. They are, indeed, only personifications of it.

Chapter 17:22-24

1028. In the collection, which is chronologically arranged, this portion stands in the middle, between the portion chap. 8—11, (which belongs to the sixth month of the sixth year,) and chap. 20, (the fifth month of the seventh year,) since the carrying away of Jehoiachin. It was, therefore, spoken about *five* years before the destruction. The representation of powerful monarchs and their kingdoms, as lofty trees, full of bows and twigs, was properly a Babylonian image, as appears from Dan. 4. 8, 9. This also appears in remarkable coincidence with Daniel from Ezek. 31. 3, sq., where Ashur appears as a cedar of Lebanon, already clothed with foliage, its summit reaching to the clouds. Here also the prophet avails himself of this image. The tribe of David is a lofty cedar upon Lebanon. Nebuchadnezzar breaks off its top, and brings it to Babylon,—the carrying away of Jehoiachin, and the rest of the royal family. He plants in Jerusalem an inferior growth, a shoot of a vine,—the setting up of Zedekiah,—but scarcely has it put forth, when it is again rooted up. The Lord now takes from the top of that great cedar a thin twig, and plants it on the top of

His holy hill, Zion. It grows up to a stately cedar, under whose shadow all fowls dwell. The remaining trees see its wonderful growth, and learn therefrom that it is the Lord who exalts and brings down all trees. Matt. 13. 32 is to be considered as an interpretation, although the Lord somewhat modifies the image, and puts the mustard seed in the place of the thin twig of the high cedar, ' *Which indeed is the least of all seeds : but when it is grown, it is the greatest among herbs, and becometh a tree, so that the birds of the air come and lodge in the branches thereof.*' The ground of this modification is to be sought in the fact, that the Lord, according to His purpose, designs to exhibit only the progress of the new kingdom of God, commenced with His appearing in the flesh, from small beginnings to a glorious completion, while the prophet aims to console for the loss of the former glory ; and must, therefore, symbolize, not merely the lowliness, but the process of humiliation, and present this as a mere transition point from the former elevation to one immensely greater.

1029. Ver. 22. ' *Thus saith the Lord Jehovah, And I will take from the summit of the high cedar, and will set* [it] ; *will break off from its crown a thin twig, and plant* [it] *upon a mountain high and elevated.*' *I* stands in emphatic antithesis with Nebuchadnezzar, who likewise has been broken off, and placed, in ver. 3, 4. He for evil, the Lord for good. He, as a feeble mortal, could work only a transient humiliation, under the Lord's permission ; the Lord, the Almighty God, makes a permanent elevation [1]. Since the *thin shoot* is taken from the (designated in what precedes) *high cedar,* the emblem of the house of David, it cannot designate the *kingdom of God in its lowliness at the beginning,* but must rather mean a *shoot* of the stock of David, and the more so, since the prophet plainly had in view the similar representations of older prophets, especially of Jeremiah ; comp. on chap. 23. 5. The cedar, therefore, here imports, precisely as in Daniel, not the *kingdom,* but the *king,* which appears also from the antithesis with the deed of Nebuchadnezzar, in v. 3, and from the whole remaining contents of the chapter, which is occupied throughout only with the *royal family.* Now, who is to be understood by the *thin* twig from the high cedar, that afterwards becomes itself such a cedar ? That it can be no other than the Messiah, proceeding from the *deeply fallen family of David,* is placed beyond a doubt by the parallel passages of Ezekiel and the other prophets. Only it might, perhaps, be assumed, that he had not in view the Messiah here, as *an individual* [2], but as Him in whom *the idea of the tribe of David* is completed ; so that also the very small commencement of its renewed exaltation,

---

[1] צַמֶּרֶת only in Ezekiel. Probably the wool of the tree, the *curly summit.* The meaning *summit* is also required by the remaining passages (31. 3. 10. 14).

[2] [*Hävernich* (Ezek. p. 278) remarks that the context requires it to be understood of the Messiah as a *definite historical person,* the whole passage having reference to *persons, Jehoiachin, Zedekiah, Nebuchadnezzar.*]

such as took place in accordance with the promise to David in
Zerubbabel, must be considered as comprehended under the prophecy, and, in a measure also, all that God did in general for the new
establishment and upholding of the civil government in Israel : comp.
on Jer. 33. As to the substance, the difference is of small importance : for although the prophet has the whole race of David in
view, and describes its progress from a small beginning to a glorious
completion, still is the Messiah not merely in fact, but also according
to his own conception, the person in whom, and through whom, this
promise is properly and completely fulfilled for the tribe of David,
and in him for the people. The lowliness of the kingdom is, moreover, closely connected with that of the head, so that ךֵ must be
referred to both.—Here it is merely said in general that the place where
the twig was planted was a high mountain, and thus its designation
hereafter, when it should have grown up to a tree, to reign over all
the trees of the plain, הֶדָשַּׁה יֵצֲע in ver. 24. was already indicated.
Then in ver. 23 this high mountain is more particularly described.

1030. Ver. 23. ' Upon the high mountain of Israel will I plant it,
and it shall put forth branches, bear fruit, and become a glorious
cedar, and all fowls shall dwell beneath it, and every winged thing shall
dwell in the shade of its branches.' That the high mountain of Israel
is Mount Zion, and that, in the wider sense, so as to comprehend
the hill Moriah, appears from chap. 20. 40, ' For upon my holy mountain, upon the high mountain of Israel, there shall the whole house of
Israel serve me, the whole of it in the land.' In this passage, the Temple
mountain is plainly spoken of, for it treats of the offering of sacrifices. The parallel holy, in the parallel passage, shows how high is to
be taken in both place. It is an elevation concealed from the fleshly
eye; elsewhere (chap. 34. 26) the prophet himself speaks only of
a hill of the Lord. But the spiritual eye sees it, the invisible
mountain far surpassing all mountains of the earth, and rising to
heaven. Even this designation (comp. on Is. 2. 2) shows, that the
holy mountain does not here come under consideration as a mountain,
but rather as the seat and central point of the kingdom of God, and
designates this kingdom itself. Altogether similar is Ps. 2. 6, ' I
have anointed my king upon Zion, my holy mountain.' High is the
place where the sprout is planted ; it grows up itself to a high cedar.
The glory of the future King has for its groundwork the glory of
the kingdom which He is placed over ; raising itself up upon it, it
serves in turn to glorify the kingdom. The fruits, the shadow, designate the blessing which all His subjects receive from this King.
That by the expression, ' all fowls and every winged thing,'—all the
nations of the whole earth are designated, appears from the comparison of chap. 31. 6. 10.—The prophet has here only the one
object, to remove the stumbling-block which must arise out of the
partly present, and partly still impending humiliation of the tribe of
David, and of the kingdom of God through it ; he therefore gives
prominence only to the one point, the exaltation, and therefore
affords us also consolation when a similar condition of the kingdom
of God and of Christ fills us with pain. We have here the germ of

the prophecy of Daniel concerning the kingdoms of the world. To describe more accurately the nature of the kingdom, to show that it was a spiritual kingdom,—in contrast not indeed with a *real*, but with a *fleshly* one,—did not lie within the scope of the prophet. Still it may be *gathered from* the representation.—A kingdom that is not ἐκ τοῦ κόσμου, which, without earthly might, or earthly weapons, by the wonderful power of God alone, is advanced with its head, from a feeble beginning to a glorious completion, can be no worldly, no fleshly kingdom; its type and pattern is not the government of earthly kings, but God's government of the world.

1031. Ver. 24. '*And all the trees of the field shall experience, that I the Lord bring down the high tree, and exalt the low tree, dry up the green tree and make green the dry tree: I the Lord speak and do.*' The trees of the field, in antithesis with the cedar upon the high mountain, are the kingdoms of the world with their kings, who will be brought down at the same time with the exaltation of the kingdom of God. This great revolution will give them a matter-of-fact proof, that the Lord, whom they had hitherto been accustomed to despise in the proud conceit of the independence of their apparent greatness, is the King over the whole earth, from whom all exaltation and degradation proceed. The preterites are to be understood as aorists; the proposition is entirely general. Still the ground of the knowledge of the general truth as appears from '*the trees of the field*,' is not barely the exaltation, so that they *concluded* from this, that the degradation also was the work of the Lord, but they likewise *have it here before their eyes*, in a great, in their own example. Indeed, the exaltation of the kingdom of God to universal dominion cannot be conceived without a humiliation of the kingdoms of the world. Their kings would thereby lose that wherein they placed their highest dignity, their fancied independence. They become vassals of God and *His* King, which, however, is, in truth, the highest honour that can be imparted to them.—The last words indicate, that what, to all appearance, was a mere dream, and the vainest that was ever entertained, becomes the greatest reality through the person who promises. It is *God* who gives the promise; *God* also fulfils it.

Chapter 21:25-27

1032. The twenty-first chapter, part of a discourse which was held by the prophet in the seventh year, in the fifth month after the carrying away, therefore about five years before the destruction, may be aptly designated as the prophecy of the sword of the Lord. Delivered to the king of Babylon for vengeance on the evil-doers, it first aims at Jerusalem, and then proceeds to the Ammonites, the most bitter enemies of the Lord and His people, who must experience in their own destruction, that the ruin of Jerusalem is not, as they supposed, a proof of the weakness, but rather of the omnipotence, of her God.

1033. Ver. 25. '*And thou, pierced through, godless one, prince of Israel, whose day comes at the time of the final-crime!*' Zedekiah, at that time the king, is addressed; and from this it appears, that the declaration which follows in ver. 26, chiefly concerns him, so that we must supply a '*hear the word of the Lord,*' omitted from emotion. The current explanation of חָלָל by *unholy, abandoned*, instead of *pierced through* [1], owes its origin solely to the circumstance, that Zedekiah had *not actually been pierced through*, though his sons were slain before his eyes, which were then put out. But this difficulty is of no importance. God's anger is represented, throughout the whole chapter, *under the image of a sword drawn* by Him. Concerning the outward mode of the punishment, nothing whatever is declared by חָלָל, any more than it is implied, that *God carries an actual sword.*—Another objection, that Zedekiah at that time had *not yet been pierced through*, has just as little force. The two years of delay, which are still allowed him, do not come under consideration. The eye of faith *sees* the punishment *as the inseparable attendant of the sin.* Before it the still prosperous sinner lies already in his blood. The generic *prince*, instead of the specific *king*, is a favorite usage of Ezekiel, which is certainly not without a reason. The day of the prince, is according to the connexion, the day of the judgement upon him, of his destruction. The עֲוֹן קֵץ occurs not only in ver. 34, but also in chap. 35. 5, in the prophecy against Edom, '*Because thou dost cherish eternal enmity, and hast given over the children of Israel into the power of the sword, at a time of their calamity, at a time of the final sin.*' That עָוֹן must not be translated, as it has been by De Wette, by *punishment*, is obvious; it never means any thing else than *guilt, crime*. The only question is, how קֵץ is to be understood. The *final* guilt may be either the *completed guilt*, its *climax*, where the vengeance of God can no longer be delayed (and then we may compare '*not yet completed is the guilt of the Amorites,*' Gen. 15. 16), or '*the guilt which draws after it the end,*' the destruction of the people, precisely as βδέλυγμα ἐρημώσεως (comp. 710) is the *abomination which has desolation for its result.* And this latter interpretation is recommended by the use of קֵץ elsewhere: comp. especially chap. 7. 2, 3. And according to this interpretation also, the ground-thought is, that there is a *fulness of the measure of sin*, its climax, where it violently calls down the penal justice of God.

1034. Ver. 26. '*Thus saith the Lord Jehovah, The headband is removed, the crown is taken off; this is not this; the low is exalted, and the high is brought down.*' By the *headband* is meant, not (according to the usual explanation) the *royal diadem*, but rather that of the *high priest:* though the meaning of the word itself is *general*, yet, after the introduction of the high priesthood, it was restricted to

---

[1] The supposed meaning *profane* is subjected, in the original, to a full critical examination.

the head ornament of the *high priest*[1]. If the diadem is referred to the king, we then give him a twofold head ornament, the diadem and the crown. And if we followed Jahn, this would occasion no difficulty. He considers it as established, that kings wore a *crown besides the diadem.* The truth, however, is rather, that the diadem and the crown were identical. How suitably here the removal of the headband, along with that of the crown, the cessation of the high-priestly dignity along with that of the regal, and, consequently, of all the prerogatives of the covenant people, would be announced, appears from the antithesis of the prophecies, where the restitution of *both* dignities is at the same time announced to the sorrowing people: comp. Zech. chap. 4 and 6, and Jer. 33.—The sole ground which can be brought *for* the reference to the regal head ornament is, that the address to the king in ver. 30 requires, that what follows should relate exclusively to him. But this proves nothing. If the king is considered as a *representative of the people*, the removal of the headband appertains to him no less than that of the crown ; both are most intimately connected. The crown without the headband is an empty show. The forgiveness of sins, procured through the mediation of the high priest, forms the groundwork of all regal blessings of God.—The *infin.* alone, without being accompanied by another verb, stands with emphatic brevity, when only the action itself as the chief thing, is to be pointed out. It is not here said, *who* should take away ; the prophet has in view the bare *fact* of the taking away. The often erroneously interpreted ' *this is not this*' is explained by what follows : *the low is made high, and the high low*, i. e. all is changed, from the lowest to the highest. This, therefore, stands for the *neuter*, and the words designate a change of the whole present condition, in which *nothing* remains *what it is ;* a total revolution. The correctness of this interpretation is confirmed by the parallel passage, Is. 24. 1, sq., which the prophet, as appears from ver. 32, had distinctly in view. There, ver. 2, the same thought, the inversion of all relations, is thus individualized : and it shall be, as the people so the priest, as the servant so the lord, as the maid so the mistress, as the buyer so the seller, as the borrower so the lender, as the debtor so the creditor[2].

1035. Ver. 27. ' *I will overturn, overturn, overturn the land; even this remains not, until he comes, to whom is the right, to whom I will give it*[3].' The reference to עָוֹן in ver. 29, 30, is obvious. They have first

---

[1] Comp. Exod. 28. 4. 37. 39 ; 29. 6 ; 39. 31 ; Levit. 8. 9 ; 16. 4. It is true, an appeal has been made to the צְנִיף מְלוּכָה, *the royal diadem*, Is. 62. 3, but thereby nothing further is proved than that the king also wore a diadem, which no one doubts.

[2] שָׁפְלָה is *masc.* with ה unaccented, which serves to make the form more full.

[3] עִוָּה is a *nom.* derived from *Pi.*, as קַלָּסָה, *mockery*, chap. 22. 4, from קָלַס ; נְאָצָה, *contempt*, chap. 35. 12, from נָאַץ. The prophet, as the comparison of those analogies shows, has chosen precisely this word, formed by himself, in order to point to the connexion of the overturning as a punishment, with the overturning as guilt.

overturned, now it is God's turn. The threefold repetition serves
only for intensity. *Even this* or *this also :* the *also* is well to be observed. It shows, that the *'this'* here designates *the* condition which
had been produced by the overturn mentioned immediately before.
This also is not permanent; overthrow follows overthrow ; no where
is there rest, no where security, all things are in a state of fluctua-
tion, until the appearing of the great restorer and prince of peace. *To
whom is the right :* the right to *what?* this is not here more particularly defined ; it is supposed to be known from what precedes. It
can only be referred to the right to the headband and the crown,
the former possessors of which have lost their right to them by
their ungodliness. Thus, therefore, the prediction is completely
parallel to that of Zechariah in chap. 6, concerning the union of the
high-priestly and regal dignity in the Messiah (comp. on Jeremiah
33. 18); and there can be the less room for doubt, that Zechariah
only resumes the oracle of Ezekiel, since he coincides with him even
in the form, and designates the regal and high-priestly dignity in
like manner by their outward sign, the diadem and the headband [1].

Chapter 34:23-31

1036. The prophecy against the evil shepherds in chap. 34 belongs
to the whole series of revelations, which the prophet, according to
chap. 33. 22, received between the evening of the day before the
arrival of the one who had escaped and brought the news of the capture of Jerusalem by the Chaldeans, and the morning of the day of his
coming. This Ezekiel knew beforehand, by the spirit of prophecy,
and sought by the word of the Lord, explanatory of the deed of the
Lord, to render certain its intended effect upon the exiles; the elders
of whom, and even a great number of others, were collected before
the prophet (comp. 33. 31), as was usual when the hand of the Lord
came upon him. The Word of the Lord by the prophet is chiefly
consoling, pointing to his favour and mercy towards Israel, and his
covenant faithfulness ; for his righteousness had been so loudly declared by matter of fact, that a mere allusion to it was sufficient. We
have in Ezekiel, in this respect, entirely the same phenomenon as in
Jeremiah. Before the destruction, the threatening is predominant
with both ; after the destruction, the promise. Both adversity and
prosperity, before they came, were equally beyond the limits of
mere human knowledge. From the same want of lively knowledge
of God arose their confidence before the destruction and their
despair afterwards, both equally destructive, both, each in its time,
equally an object of the efforts of the prophets, whose aim everywhere is to make the idea certain, in opposition to appearances. —

---

[1] There is not the smallest ground for understanding the *suff.* in נְחָתִיו as *dat.*
The *person,* as sufficiently known from what precedes, needs no further designation.

How the prophecy in chap. 34 rests on that of Jeremiah chap. 23, we have already shown on the latter passage. It is the prophecy concerning the shepherds of Israel. To the evil shepherds destruction is predicted; to the lost sheep of Israel, deliverance through the Lord, who takes upon Himself the office of shepherd over them, and executes it through His servant David. The account immediately following, of the fulfilment of the first part, relating to the punishment of the evil shepherds, must serve as a pledge for the fulfilment of the second part, the source of which is the same, the covenant faithfulness of the Lo:d.

1037. Ver. 23. '*And I will raise up over them one shepherd, and he shall feed them, my servant David; he will feed them, and he will be their shepherd.*' The *one* refers to the *former separation* of Israel and Judah ; and in vain does Jahn endeavour to vindicate for אחד the meaning *unicus, singularis,* which it never has. As to the substance, he is, indeed, right. He must be a highly distinguished descendant of David, in the fullest sense a man after God's own heart, who should receive again the kingdom of his father in its whole extent. For the kingdom was diminished, as a punishment upon the race of David, *because it was no longer after God's own heart;* and even the most pious among the successors of David, hitherto, had not been after the heart of God, in such a degree, that the promise, expressed even at the separation, of the future reunion (comp. 1 Kings 11. 39), could have been fulfilled in them. In the prediction of the *oneness* of the shepherd, therefore, that of the highest excellency was implied, and also through him the most complete mercy of the Lord should be imparted to his people [1]. The antithesis which formerly existed between the *office of a shepherd* and the *non-performance of its duties,* and brought such unutterable misery upon the people, should now be done away ; comp., finally, beside the passages already cited, Jer. 33. 15, 16 ; Hos. 3. 5.

1038. Ver. 24. '*And I, the Lord, will be to them God, and my servant David a prince in the midst of them; I, the Lord, have spoken.*' The promise *to* David shall revive again ; his descendant shall be the servant of God in so full a sense, that the former painful distinction between the mediate and immediate government of God entirely ceases [2].

1039. Ver. 25. '*And I will conclude with them a covenant of peace, and destroy the evil beasts out of the land; and they shall dwell in the wilderness securely, and sleep in the woods.*' The import of the concluding of a covenant has already been investigated, on Jer. 31. 32. The peace with God, procured by the mediation of his servant, is followed by peace with the creatures which he has hitherto armed against his apostate people. The representation of the pro-

---

[1] רֹעֶה shows the destination, רָעָה the realization of it,

[2] נָשִׂיא was probably chosen with respect to 1 Kings 11. 34.

phet here, and in what follows, rests throughout on Levit. chap. 26, comp. ver. 5, '*And I will give peace in the land, and ye shall lie down, and none shall make you afraid : and I will rid evil beasts out of the land, neither shall the sword go through your land.*' The prophet announces nothing new ; he only repeats that which the divine law-giver had already exhibited, as necessary to the idea of the covenant people. As certain as it is that this prophecy has only been imper-fectly fulfilled in Israel, so certain is it also, that its complete fulfil-ment is hereafter to take place ; comp. still, Hos. 2. 20.

1040. Ver. 26. '*And I will give them and the places round about my hill for a blessing, and will cause the rain to come down in its time ; they shall be blessed rains.*' The hill is *Zion*, the holy moun-tain. That this here designates Israel as the people of God, whose spiritual dwelling-place it was, appears from its position with *them*. Accordingly the *environs* of the hill can be only the *heathen who join themselves to Israel*. A blessing (comp. Gen. 12. 2) is stronger than *blessed*. Israel shall be a *real* blessing. The individualiza-tion of the blessing *as rain*, in respect to the natural condition of Canaan, where all other natural blessings of Providence depended on the rain, is, in like manner, taken from Levit. 26 ; Comp. Deut. 11. 13, 14 ; Joel 2. 23.

1041. Ver. 27. '*And the tree of the field shall give its fruit, and the land shall give her increase, and they shall dwell in their land securely, and they shall know that I am the Lord, since I break their yoke, and deliver them out of the hand of those who make them slaves.*' The expression ' *and ... increase*' is taken from Levit. 26. 3 ; '*and ... securely*,' from Levit. ver. 5 ; ' *and ... yoke*,' alludes to ver. 13, ' *I the Lord your God, who brought you forth out of the land of Egypt, out of bondage, and I brake your yoke.*' As at that time Israel knew by his deeds that God was Jehovah, so should he know and experience this anew, in the great repetition of this event in his redemption from the dominion of the world, in order to his sole subjection to God and his Anointed. It is pointed out by this allusion, how God, in order to redeem Israel, had no need to become another than He is, Jehovah, the sole and perfect existence.

1042. Ver. 28. ' *And they shall no more be for a prey to the heathen, and the wild beasts of the earth shall not devour them, and they shall dwell in safety, and there is none that makes them afraid.*' The *heathen* could gain the advantage over the people of the Lord, only when these had ceased to be such by their own guilt. Now, therefore, their power over Israel ceases ; comp. p. 671.

1043. Ver. 29. '*And I will raise up to them a plantation for a name, and no more shall they be taken away by hunger in the land, and no more shall they bear the reproach of the heathen.*' In a *plantation*, there is an allusion to Gen. 2. 8, 9, '*And God planted* (וַיִּטַּע) *a garden in Eden eastward, and placed therein the man whom he had formed, and God caused to spring forth out of the earth all trees pleasant to the sight, and good for food.*' With which is to be compared the declaration of God after the commission of sin, 3. 18, 19, ' *Thorns also and thistles shall it bear to thee, and thou shalt eat the grass of the field. In the sweat of thy face shalt thou eat thy bread.'* The history of the Fall is one which is constantly repeated ; the first sin shows the origin and progress of all sins, and precisely for this reason is the author so full in its relation. He himself draws attention to this its import, when he remarks, before the judgement upon the cities of the plain, that they were watered like the *garden of God, Paradise* (Gen. 13. 10). But especially is the prophecy contained in the history of the Fall realized in Israel. Even for him also had God planted a garden in Eden, full of trees, pleasant to the sight, and good for food. He had given him the land where milk and honey flowed, with all blessings connected with its possession. But Israel had hearkened to the voice of the tempter, his paradise had vanished, yet not for ever. God, at a future period, will again plant for him a garden in Eden, with pleasant trees. The new paradisiacal planting, which the Lord will prepare for his people, designates the divine blessings in their whole extent, and the blessing of the fruit-trees, which formed a part of these, was itself again symbolical. The *literal planting* was a copy or adumbration of the *spiritual*, whose water went forth out of the sanctuary, as, before, hunger had been the symbol of the general poverty and deprivation.

1044. Ver. 30. *'And they shall experience that I the Lord their God am with them, and they my people, the house of Israel, saith the Lord Jehovah.'* The *house of Israel* is emphatic, *Israel*, the *people of God*, and of the covenant, in the true and proper sense ; comp. on chap. 11. 15.

1045. Ver. 31. *'And ye are my flock, my pasture flock are ye men. I am your God, saith the Lord, Jehovah* [1]*.'* The expression *' ye men'* calls attention to the depth and greatness of the Divine condescension, and meets the objection of weak faith, that man, who has been taken from the earth (אֲדָמָה), and returns to it again, is incapable of so intimate a union with God.

Chapter 36:22-32

1046. To the discourse held on the day before the account of the destruction, belongs also the portion chap. 36. 16—38, the contents of which Venema has briefly and well determined thus : *' Causam et rationem pandit cum excidii et exitii in corruptione populi quærendam, tum liberationis et instaurationis, unice a nominis Dei sanctificatione repetendam.'* The former takes place in the introduction, ver. 17—21, the second in the principal part, ver. 22—38, of which we omit ver. 33—38, because they form a mere recapitulation.

1047. Ver. 22. *' Therefore, say to the house of Israel, thus saith the Lord, Jehovah, not on your account do I it, ye of the house of Israel, but for the sake of my holy name which ye have profaned among the heathen, whither ye went.'* In order to a right under-

---

[1] Comp. respecting צֹאן מַרְעִיתִי, on Jer. 23. 1.

standing of the whole portion, an insight into the idea of holiness in the writings of the Old Testament is necessary. In determining this, the greatest caprice reigns among the modern interpreters and theologians: those mostly restrain themserves within limits, who would subjoin to moral holiness, majesty and exaltation; while those wander the furthest, who entirely *exclude* moral holiness, and put in its place *condescension and love*. The correct view is established in opposition to all these errours, in an article in the *Ev. K. Z.* vol. 7. p. 573 ff. The holiness of God never designates any thing else than the entire freedom of His nature from sin, which at the same time includes in itself His highest abhorrence of it, the effort to sanctify Himself through His Holy Spirit *in* His sinful creatures, and, when they will not permit this, *upon* them, and the absolute necessity that one of the two should take place. Holiness must be a purely moral attribute; for otherwise, '*be ye holy, for I am holy,*' would have no meaning.—But how can the holiness of God here be represented as that attribute of the Divine Being, which necessarily requires the redemption of Israel, which at first sight appears to be only a work of grace and mercy? To these, indeed, the election of Israel alone belonged, though not the establishment of the kingdom of God in general, in which the Divine holiness had the most essential part. But after the election had once taken place, the Divine holiness stood in so essential a relation to Israel, that the name *the Holy One of Israel* became one of the standing designations of God. The decree of election had been pronounced as an unconditional one. In the moment, therefore, when God cast off the people for ever, he ceased to be Jehovah, from whom every change is excluded, the Holy One, with whom there is no variableness nor shadow of turning, James 1. 17. That the Divine holiness demands the fulfilment of every promise granted from grace through grace, because God is not a man that He should lie, nor a son of man, that He should repent, very clearly appears in the passage, Ps. 89. 36, '*God has sworn by His holiness, I will not lie to David, his seed shall be eternal.*" It also appears in the declaration, '*To whom I am gracious, to him I am gracious, and whom I pity, him I pity.*' With God is no dissembling, no caprice, He must cease to be Himself, should He will otherwise than He has once willed. Even Israel's sin, however great it may have been, did not cancel the claim for his redemption on the holiness of God. For God, the omniscient, saw these sins before He gave the unconditional promise; to Him, the God of the spirits of all flesh, they did not come unexpected. He might destroy the sinners, He must do it, precisely because He was holy, but never could He give up all Israel. He must also cause a שְׁאֵרִית to remain. The greatness of the sin was only a requisition upon Him to employ the most efficacious means to purify and sanctify; He would be unholy if He did not make holy; for then He would not have done his own part towards the fulfilling of his promise, which, on account of the condition of human nature, would be but poorly satisfied by *outward* benefits. And if He did this, He could never want an object of His mercy. Sodom was destroyed, because

there was no ἐκλογή in it, but in Israel, because Jehovah is infinitely.
richer than Elohim, this could never be the case.—Now, that the
redemption of Israel is here in opposition to all merit (comp. in
reference to the מַעֲנְכֶם, Deut. 9. 6, '*And thou knowest, that not for
thy righteousness' sake does God give thee the good land*'), grounded
solely upon God's nature, His holiness, was, on the one hand, very
humiliating, it silenced all human claims; on the other hand, however, very consoling. The anxious and broken hearts thereby perceived that their salvation by no means rested on any human ground,
and could not be disturbed by the sins of their people.—At first
sight, the ground which God here brings forward for the redemption
of Israel appears to be a very *external* one; it appears as though
he had been induced to relinquish His former decree for the destruction of Israel by something lying without himself, the reproachful
discourses of the heathen, who, because they did not perceive
the deeper reason of the procedure, drew such a conclusion from it.
But we must well distinguish the thought from its form; which is a
popular one, that wherein the thought was accessible even to those
whose perceptions had been little exercised. The *conclusion* of the
heathen was fully justified by the fact. That Israel was the people
of Jehovah, they doubted not; they knew the facts of the past,
which testified this; even to them had come the knowledge of the
splendid promises, the firm oaths which He imparted to them.
When, now, He at once entirely rejects this people, how should
not the thought arise in their minds, that the celebrated holiness of
this God was not a matter of much moment, who either had promised what He could not perform, or would not perform what He
had promised; that He was completely like their idols, in whom
only their own sinful nature was exhibited. And thus the conclusion of the heathen was entirely unobjectionable, if their premises
were correct, that God had *for ever* (this is to be supplied, ' *the people
of Jehovah are they, and out of their land have they gone,*' ver. 20)
rejected His people; and the matter-of-fact refutation of the *for ever*,
is the only possible mode of justifying God.—This view, that the
discourse of the heathen comes under consideration only so far as it
was grounded in the thing itself; that the latter, the nature of God,
contains the proper ground, is confirmed by a comparison of the
passages of the Pentateuch, which the prophet had in view,
Exod. 32, Num. 14, and Deut. 9. At first sight, it appears, indeed,
as though in them also, Israel's redemption is represented as a work
of caprice, and independent of the Divine nature. God speaks as
though He had formed the firm determination to destroy the people,
and appears afterwards to have been induced only by the intercession of Moses, and by the consideration of an outward ground, that
of guarding against the reproaches of the heathen, to limit His
judgement to the sinners, and to confirm to the people the perpetuity
of their election. But, on a nearer consideration, it appears that
God, for a definite purpose, at first caused only the one side of the
case to appear; that which He would do according to the necessity
of His nature, if the covenant and promise were not in existence.

This purpose, in all the three passages, clearly appears, comp. Exod. 32. 10, '*And now let me alone, and mine anger shall burn against them, and I will consume them, and make of* thee *a great people.*' In like manner, Num. 14. 12, Deut. 9. 14. The temptation of Israel, as the servant of God, is accompanied by the temptation of Moses, the servant of God, as we see even in the outward sign, that he fasts forty days,—the standing period of temptation in the Scripture: comp. Deut. 9. 9. This temptation reaches its climax, precisely in the circumstance that Israel is overcome by it; Moses is thus furnished with a very plausible reason to sacrifice the people to his selfish interest, and put himself in their place. The leader of the people was to be tempted in all things like them. On this account, God causes one view of His being to appear; He represents Himself (without dissembling) as though He were on the side of the selfishness of His servant. He leaves it with him to bring forward the other view of His being; and that he actually did this, was his victory over the temptation, the outward manifestation of which, the seal which God impressed upon it, was the shining of his face. Now in the method in which Moses does this, it clearly appears that he allows the validity of the charge of the heathen, only so far as it rests on the fact. For along with it he causes the naked fact itself to appear, thus, e. g., Exod. 32. 13, '*Remember still Abraham, and Isaac, and Israel, thy servants, to whom thou hast sworn by thyself, and said to them, I will multiply your seed,*' &c. Deut. 9. 27, (comp. Num. 14, 17,) &c.—That the *name* of God here also designates his *being*, so far as it is manifested, scarcely needs to be remarked. The profanation refers not to the deed, but to its result. This is shown by what precedes; intentionally, however, does the prophet attribute to Israel as an action, that which had been occasioned by what had happened to him, his fate contrary to the idea of the covenant people. For they bore the guilt of these reproaches; their fate was the necessary and natural consequence of their conduct, and so must these reproaches serve for their deep humiliation. Not the heathen, but they, had brought down the holy God within the province of sin.

1048. Ver. 23. '*And I will sanctify my name, the great, the profaned, among the heathen, which ye have profaned in the midst of you, and the heathen shall experience that I am Jehovah, saith the Lord Jehovah, when I sanctify myself in you before your eyes.*' God, holy in Himself, becomes holy in His people, when He imparts to them His holiness. Passages like this lay the foundation for interpreting the so usually misunderstood '*hallowed be thy name*' in the Lord's Prayer, the sense of which is no other than, '*may God be holy in the world, as he is in himself.*' Wherein the sanctification of God in Israel consists, is shown by the following relation. Holiness, because it designates freedom from sin, also designates freedom from its consequent evil. Thus Israel is first freed from sin by forgiveness, and by the operation of the Spirit; and then follows, as a completion of their sanctification, the imparting of prosperity. Thus is God's name hallowed. What God is in His people, loudly testi-

fies of that which He is in Himself; and as the heathen now perceive
that God is holy, so do they also perceive that He is Jehovah; for
His being a holy God, is only a particular result of His being
Jehovah [1].

1049. Ver. 24. ' *And I will take you out of the nations, and collect
you out of the countries, and bring you into your own land.*' Ver. 25.
' *And I will sprinkle upon you pure water, and ye shall be clean from
all your impurities, and from all your pollutions* (the idols) *will I
cleanse you.*' Here, in the first place, is the foundation of all sanctification of God in His people, the *forgiveness of sins*, the *taking
away*, which must precede all *giving* (comp. on Jer. 31. 3, 4). It is
obvious that there is an allusion to the *Mosaic purifications*, and
especially to the *consecrated water*, wherein were put the ashes of the
red heifer, the remedy for the greatest of all impurities, that by a
corpse (comp. Num. 19. 17—19, and Ps. 51. 9). The usual explanation of such references is this: '*the person who makes an allusion
of this kind changes what was corporeal into what is spiritual:*' but
the true view is, that '*he employs as a figure what in the law is a
symbol.*' Those who would determine the ground and aim of the
laws of purification upon different principles, involve themselves in
the grossest absurdities. One need only read, for example, the portion in reference to them in Michaelis, *M. R.* (Pt. 4. § 207 ff.); and
the symbolic import of the impurities and the purifications is fully
confirmed by a closer investigation. Throughout do we find the *outward impurities* placed on a level with the *spiritual*, the means of
outward purification with those of the internal, comp., e. g., Num.
19. 20, '*A man who pollutes himself, and does not purify himself from
sin*, that soul shall be cut off *from the congregation; for he has polluted the sanctuary of the Lord.*' The *unclean* person and the *sinner*
are treated precisely alike: the sacrifices which are offered for him
are *sin-offerings;* the priest makes atonement for him before the
Lord (comp., e. g., Levit. 15. 15). Those who assume *political purposes*, have here no other resort, than the supposition that Moses
used religion as a means to accomplish his purposes. Michaelis
asserts this (in § 212) without reserve. ' *God, who condescended to
be a civil ruler of the Israelites, availed Himself of the most powerful
of all aids, religion.*' Now, if this assertion were correct, it would
follow from it alone, that *Moses was not sent by God;* a view which
the work of Michaelis has done more to propagate than those who
openly declare it.—This assertion, however, is entirely destitute of
proof; of a political purpose, there is no where even the slightest
trace. On the contrary, the symbolical meaning has in its. favour
the analogy of the whole symbolic character of the law. To awaken
a living consciousness of sin and holiness, and of the consequent

---

[1] A remarkable example of superficial criticism is the assertion, that instead
of לְעֵינֵיכֶם we must read לְעֵינֵיהֶם. That this reading is found in many critical
authorities, proves nothing further, than that superficial critics existed before.
If it is established, that the charge of the heathen rested on the fact, so is it also
that God must vindicate His honour before Israel, no less than before them;
the reference to *both* is combined precisely as here, chap. 20. 41, 42.

necessity of substitution and atonement, was the object which Moses every where pursued, and which the laws of purification also serve to promote; what was done to outward impurity was done to sin, which the people of the Old Testament, familiar with the language of symbols, the more easily beheld in its image, since, without that, what was done would have been absurd. In reference to one of the most prominent kinds of Levitical impurity, the leprosy, we have already, p. 661, pointed this out. In reference to another sort, precisely that to which there is here an allusion, pollution by corpses, Deyling, (*Obbs.* III. p. 70,) justly remarks: "*Inde judicare licet, quanta irregenitorum et peccatorum sit fœditas coram Deo.*" The corporeally dead are the most suitable symbol of the *dead in trespasses and sins*, (Eph. 2. 1. 5 ; Col. 2. 13,) comp. the designations of sins as νεκρὰ ἔργα, Heb. 9. 14.—By these remarks, the references to the legal impurities and purifications appear in their full import. We have no arbitrary transition from the corporeal to the spiritual, but rather an *interpretation* of what *originally* related to the spiritual. Ezekiel here by no means promises any thing new, but only resumes the promise already lying in the law, and announces its complete realization. גִּלּוּלִים, properly *filth*, then of the idols, yet only so far as they are considered as filth, unclean and polluting.

1050. Ver. 26. '*And I will give you a new heart, and a new spirit will I give in your inward parts, and I will take away the heart of stone from within you, and give you a heart of flesh.*' Comp. on chap. 11. 19.

1051. Ver. 27. '*And I will give my Spirit in your inward parts, and cause that ye walk in my commandments, and observe and do my statutes.*' Comp. chap. 11. 20.

1052. Ver. 28. '*And ye shall dwell in the land which I gave to your fathers, and shall be to me a people, and I will be to you a God.*' Comp. chap. 11. 20. ' *Ye shall be,*' &c., refers here also solely to the result, they shall be treated as a people of God.

1053. Ver. 29. '*And I will redeem you from all your impurities, and will call to the corn and increase it, and no more will I inflict upon you hunger.*' Ver. 30. '*And I will increase the fruit of the tree, and the produce of the field, that the reproach of hunger may no more fall upon you among the heathen.*' Comp. chap. 34. 27, 29.

1054. Ver. 31. '*And ye shall remember your ways, the evil, and your deeds, which are not good, and abhor yourselves on account of your sins and your abominations.*' Ver. 32. ' *Not for your sakes do I it, saith the Lord, Jehovah, be that known unto you : be ashamed and blush on account of your ways, O house of Israel.*'

Chapter 37:22-28

1055. The thirty-seventh chapter also belongs to the great whole of the revelations which were imparted to the prophet the night before the arrival of a messenger, with an account of the destruction of Jerusalem, and which all tend to the promotion of one object, the counteraction of the pusillanimity and despair of the people. The chapter contains a twofold, but closely connected, *word of God;* in the first part, ver. 1—14, Israel's restoration, as a covenant people, and in the second, as a fraternal people, is predicted. On the first portion, the question arises concerning its relation to the doctrine of the resurrection from the dead. That the prophet borrows his image from this doctrine, and that it was, therefore, *not merely known to him,* but also *regarded as certain by the people,* may be regarded as a universal acknowledgement. But we must not stop short at this; we must also assume that the idea which is expressed by the image, is first fully realized in the occurrence of the thing from which the image is taken; that the image, therefore, does not merely proceed from the thing, but also reverts back to it. The idea is, so surely as God is God, so surely must every decay be at the same time an origin, every death a transition to life; and this idea it is, on which the certainty of a *blessed* resurrection alone rests, which would be sure even on account of this idea, though it had no express word of Scripture in its favour [1]. In the interpretation of the vision, ver. 12 — 14, a twofold action in reference to the restoration is distinguished. (1) The *bringing back to Canaan,* symbolized by the opening of the graves, the coming together of the dry bones, and their investure with flesh and blood, so that the former bones are changed again into corpses, in which there is as yet no living spirit. (2) The *quickening of these corpses by the Spirit of God,* of which the former served only as a preparation; in itself considered it was worthless, and no object of prophetic annunciation. This second action is symbolized by the imparting of the inferior life as the medium, which, in the vision, (which according to its nature must make every thing an object of sense,) appears as the breathing upon them by the wind, the natural symbol of the inferior and higher principle of life, and perceived as such by all nations, and in all languages of the ancient world,—the Saviour breathed upon the disciples, as a sign of the imparting of the Spirit; on the day of Pentecost ἐγένετο ἄφνω ἐκ τοῦ οὐρανοῦ ἦχος ὥσπερ φερομένης πνοῆς βιαίας, Acts 2. 2, with an allusion to the passage before us, which stands in an essential connexion with this event (comp. also John 3. 8). This revivification by the Spirit of God is then followed by the true and secure possession of the land of the Lord,—' *I will make you to rest upon your land,*' in ver. 14, must be distinguished from ' *I will bring you to the land of Israel,*' in ver. 12,—the full enjoyment of all the blessings and gifts of the Lord, which could be imparted only to His people animated by His Spirit. From the meaning of the *life,* thus made out with certainty, we can infer the import of the *death.* The carrying away of the people into exile, the destruction of Jerusalem and the Temple, is not the death, it is only its sign, the change of the corpse to corruption. The corpse was already there. The vital principle of Israel as the people of God, was the Spirit of God.

---

[1] Grotius, after his superficial manner, supposes that the prophet here speaks of a *mors civilis* and *vita civilis.*

This was still present in some persons, but the prophet here has not individuals in view; his eye is directed to the whole of the Church of the Lord; here spiritual death every where meets him, and those who mourn with him; and how the transition from it to life, how the spiritual new birth of the people lay entirely beyond the bounds of human probability (because human means had no power to effect it, because it is impossible that a heart of stone should change itself by its own power into a heart of flesh), is shown by the question of the Lord in ver. 3, ' *Thou Son of Man, will those bones live again?*' and the answer of the prophet, ' *O Lord, thou knowest.*' Before God promises life by the prophet, the latter must declare, that he knows nothing of himself of this life, that it lies above the natural course of things.—From these remarks, it appears that the whole portion is Messianic, that only in Christ, and the imparting of the Spirit through His mediation, is the complete fulfilment of the promise contained in it to be sought; and that this fulfilment is ever progressive, and takes place wherever in His Church life arises out of death, until the final completion, when death shall be entirely swallowed up in victory.

1056. The second part begins with a symbolic action. It is immaterial whether it were *internal* or *external*, though it was probably the former, according to the general analogy of Ezekiel's prophecies, in which the internal so predominates. The prophet, representing the Lord, takes two pieces of wood,—*staves*, and not *tables*, as appears from Num. 17. 17, 18, from which passage the form of the symbolic action has been derived. Upon the one he writes the names of Judah and his companions, the portion of Israel which have joined themselves to him, *Benjamin, Levi, Simeon*, and the pious, who at different times had passed over from the kingdom of the ten tribes to the kingdom of Judah; on the other, the name of *Ephraim*, with the rest, who were combined with this predominant tribe in one kingdom. These two staves he then with a firm hand presses together, symbolizing the union of the kingdom separated in the past by the sin of the people, to be effected in the future by the mercy of God. The interpretation in ver. 22—28, extends in a measure beyond the symbol. It does not limit itself to the *fact* of the union, but at the same time gives its attendant circumstances and blessed results, and points to the person of the great King, who should be the Mediator of union, the dispenser of the blessing for both. Very naturally, for it is in this connexion that the fact first appears in its true import. The union, so as to form one fraternal people, can come under consideration only as a consequence and part of a renewal of their whole condition.

1057. Ver. 22. '*And I will make thee to be one people on the mountains of Israel, and one king shall be a king to them all, and no more shall they be two people, and shall not still be divided into two kingdoms.*' Comp. chap. 34. 23.

1058. Ver. 23. '*And they will no more pollute themselves with*

*their detestable things, and their abominations, and with all their sins,
and I will redeem them from all their dwelling-places, where they
have sinned, and purify them, and they shall become my people, and I
will become their God.*' The redemption from the dwelling-places is
not local, but spiritual, and is effected by removing all traces of sin,
first from the heart, and then from the surrounding region. And
thus is the land, by the power of the Lord, converted into another
land, from a sinful to a holy one, as formerly, by the guilt of the
people, from a holy to a sinful one.

1059. Ver. 24. '*And my servant David shall be king over them,
and one shepherd shall be to them all, and they shall walk in my
ordinances, and observe and do my statutes.*' The promise of the *one*
king in ver. 22, is here more nearly determined. It is the great king
out of David's race, and thus all the glorious promises which had
been given to David, and in him to the kingdom of God, are revived.

1060. Ver. 25. '*And they shall dwell in the land which I gave to
my servant Jacob, wherein their fathers have dwelt, and they shall
dwell therein, they and their sons, and their sons' sons for ever, and
David my servant shall be the prince for ever.*' That the first עוֹלָם
is to be taken in all its strictness, appears from the second לְעוֹלָם,
comp. p. 640.

1061. Ver. 26. '*And I will conclude with them a covenant of
peace, an everlasting covenant shall subsist with them, and I will give
them and increase them, and I will give my sanctuary in the midst
of them for ever.*' '*I will give them and increase them,*' Venema
rightly explains by *dabo eos multiplicatos.* There is an allusion to
the promise to Abraham, '*And I will give thee for nations, and
kings shall come out of thee.*' That the prophet by מִקְדָּשׁ had not in
view an outward edifice, as such, but that with him the presence of
the Lord among His people is the essential thing in the idea of the
sanctuary, appears out of chap. 11. 16.

1062. Ver. 27. '*And my dwelling is over them, and I will be their
God, and they shall be my people.*' We are not permitted to regard
מִשְׁכָּן as an outward dwelling, on account of the expression ' *over
them.*' There is an allusion to Exod. 25. 8, '*And they shall make
for me a sanctuary* (מִקְדָּשׁ), *and I will dwell among them.*' (Comp.
Levit. 26. 11.) That promise—the prophet explains—looks to
the future for its complete fulfilment. Then will God for the first
time be truly among His people, and the distinction between heaven
and earth be done away. The destruction of the outward temple,
therefore, is no cause of distress. The fulfilment Vitringa justly
finds in the "*Inhabitatio Dei in medio populi per Filium et Spir. S.;*"
comp. John 1. 14, where, in the ἐσκήνωσεν ἐν ἡμῖν, the Word become
flesh is represented as the true מִשְׁכָּן of God with reference to the
same passage of Exodus, which the prophet has in view (Apoc. 21. 3;
1 Cor. 3. 16. 6. 19), where believers, on account of the indwelling of
the Spirit of Christ, are designated as the temple of God.

1063. Ver. 28. '*And the heathen shall perceive that I, Jehovah, sanctify Israel, since my sanctuary is among them to eternity.'* ' *To sanctify*,' means to deliver both from sin and its consequences, evil. Here regard is had to the latter, because this only was apparent to the heathen ; but the former is at the same time presupposed as the necessary groundwork. The antithesis between God and His Church is done away ; He is most really present in the midst of her; therefore no evil can any more reach her ; for just because the difference between her and God has ceased, would God be profaned in her. As He is holy in Himself, so is He now holy in Israel. (Comp. 39. 7.) Here is an allusion to the promise of the sanctification of Israel in the Pentateuch, comp. Levit. 20. 8; 21. 23; 22. 31—33. These had hitherto been only very imperfectly fulfilled, because Israel, through his own fault, had not sanctified God, and therefore could not be treated as a holy people. And how closely the two are connected, appears, e. g., from Levit. 22. 32. Now, in the future, God Himself, by the richer imparting of forgiveness, and the more abundant effusion of the Spirit, will cause the condition to be completely fulfilled, and consequently the result to be fully attained. It is, therefore, a promise, whose final fulfilment lies beyond the bounds of this sinful world, even because it comprehends the idea in its whole extent, and in all its depth, yet in such a manner that the germs of the fulfilment, whose complete developement is certain because the promise rests upon the idea, are already completely present.